More praise for Tim Hilton's biography of John Ruskin

"A work of astoundingly vigorous biographical assimilation and fine critical wisdom."
—Valentine Cunningham, *New York Times Book Review*

"Magisterial."—William Packer, *Financial Times*

"Superb . . . beautifully written . . . Ruskin was one of the towering figures of his age. He has received one of the towering biographies of ours."
—Geoffrey Wheatcroft, *Daily Mail*

"Simply magnificent: one of the great modern literary biographies."
—Clive Wilmer, *Times Literary Supplement*

"The model biography of a cultural figure . . . a triumphant telling of one of the saddest stories ever told."
—Dave Hickey, *Art Forum*

"Every serious scholar will have to acquire this volume, but even those who know practically nothing about Ruskin will find it enormously enjoyable."
—Quentin Bell, *American Historical Review*

JOHN RUSKIN

JOHN RUSKIN

TIM HILTON

NB

YALE UNIVERSITY PRESS
NEW HAVEN AND LONDON

First published as a Yale Nota Bene book in 2002

This Nota Bene edition comprises *John Ruskin: The Early Years*, first published 1985, first paperback edition 2000; and *John Ruskin: The Later Years*, first published 2000.

For information about this and other Yale University Press publications, please contact:
U.S. office sales.press@yale.edu
Europe office *sales@yaleup.co.uk*

Printed in the United States of America

ISBN 0-300-09099-4

Library of Congress Control Number: 2002108493

A catalogue record for this book is available from the British Library.

2 4 6 8 10 9 7 5 3 1

TO

JEANNE CLEGG

CONTENTS

List of Plates		ix
Foreword to Combined Volume		xi
Foreword to The Early Years		xxvi
Foreword to The Later Years		xxxiv

THE EARLY YEARS

CHAPTER ONE	1785–1837	1
CHAPTER TWO	1837–1840	41
CHAPTER THREE	1840–1841	55
CHAPTER FOUR	1841–1844	62
CHAPTER FIVE	1845–1846	82
CHAPTER SIX	1846–1847	104
CHAPTER SEVEN	1847–1849	115
CHAPTER EIGHT	1849–1850	128
CHAPTER NINE	1850–1852	147
CHAPTER TEN	1852–1854	173
CHAPTER ELEVEN	1854–1857	199
CHAPTER TWELVE	1855–1857	226
CHAPTER THIRTEEN	1855–1858	239
CHAPTER FOURTEEN	1857–1858	258
CHAPTER FIFTEEN	1858–1859	272

THE LATER YEARS

CHAPTER SIXTEEN	1859–1860	283
CHAPTER SEVENTEEN	1860–1861	292
CHAPTER EIGHTEEN	1861–1862	306
CHAPTER NINETEEN	1862–1863	324
CHAPTER TWENTY	1864	342
CHAPTER TWENTY-ONE	1864–1865	362

CHAPTER TWENTY-TWO	1865–1866	377
CHAPTER TWENTY-THREE	1867–1868	394
CHAPTER TWENTY-FOUR	1868–1869(i)	410
CHAPTER TWENTY-FIVE	1868–1869(ii)	425
CHAPTER TWENTY-SIX	1869–1870	449
CHAPTER TWENTY-SEVEN	1871(i)	466
CHAPTER TWENTY-EIGHT	1871(ii)	490
CHAPTER TWENTY-NINE	1871–1872	504
CHAPTER THIRTY	1872	513
CHAPTER THIRTY-ONE	1873–1874	534
CHAPTER THIRTY-TWO	1874	550
CHAPTER THIRTY-THREE	1874–1875	569
CHAPTER THIRTY-FOUR	1875–1876	587
CHAPTER THIRTY-FIVE	1875–1876	607
CHAPTER THIRTY-SIX	1876–1877	622
CHAPTER THIRTY-SEVEN	1877–1878	634
CHAPTER THIRTY-EIGHT	1878	655
CHAPTER THIRTY-NINE	1878–1880	677
CHAPTER FORTY	1880–1881	699
CHAPTER FORTY-ONE	1881–1882	712
CHAPTER FORTY-TWO	1883	735
CHAPTER FORTY-THREE	1883–1884	755
CHAPTER FORTY-FOUR	1884	771
CHAPTER FORTY-FIVE	1885	783
CHAPTER FORTY-SIX	1885–1887	796
CHAPTER FORTY-SEVEN	1887–1888	823
CHAPTER FORTY-EIGHT	1888	837
CHAPTER FORTY-NINE	1888–1900	851
Postscript		875
Notes		879
Index		913

PLATES

THE EARLY YEARS

1. John James Ruskin, father of John Ruskin, by George Watson, 1802 (*Ruskin Foundation, Ruskin Library, University of Lancaster*) 3
2. Margaret Ruskin, mother of John Ruskin, by James Northcote, RA, 1825 (*Ruskin Foundation, Ruskin Library, University of Lancaster*) 5
3. 54 Hunter Street, Brunswick Square (*Greater London Council, Photographic Collection*) 9
4. 28 Herne Hill, by John Ruskin, his home in south London, 1823–42 (*Ruskin Foundation, Ruskin Library, University of Lancaster*) 11
5. Ruskin's Rooms at Christ Church, Oxford, by John Ruskin, 1839 (*Ruskin Museum, Coniston*) 45
6. *Turner on Varnishing Day*, by S. W. Parrott, 1848 (*Graves Gallery, Sheffield*) 66
7. 163 Denmark Hill, Ruskin's home from 1842 to 1871, by Arthur Severn (*Ruskin Foundation, Ruskin Library, University of Lancaster*) 71
8. *Stone Pine at Sestri*, by John Ruskin, 1845 (*Ashmolean Museum, Oxford*) 86
9. *Tomb of Ilaria di Caretto at Lucca*, by John Ruskin, sketched in 1874 (*Ashmolean Museum, Oxford*) 87
10. Part of the façade of S. Michele ın Lucca, by John Ruskin, 1845 (*Ashmolean Museum, Oxford*) 89
11. Copy after the central portion of Tintoretto's *Crucifixion*, by John Ruskin, 1845 (*Ruskin Foundation, Ruskin Library, University of Lancaster*) 95
12. *Corner of St Mark's after Rain*, by John Ruskin, 1846 (*Ashmolean Museum*) 97
13. Euphemia Ruskin, by John Ruskin, 1848, or 1850 (*Ashmolean Museum, Oxford*) 111
14. John James Ruskin, by George Richmond, 1848 (*Ruskin Foundation, Ruskin Library, University of Lancaster*) 126
15. *La Cascade de la Folie, Chamouni*, by John Ruskin, 1849 (*City of Birmingham Museum and Art Gallery*) 135
16. Worksheet no. 99. In preparation for *The Stones of Venice*: notes on the Ducal Palace, December 1849, by John Ruskin (*Ruskin Foundation, Ruskin Library, University of Lancaster*) 142
17. Effie Ruskin, daguerrotype, taken in 1851 (*Sir Ralph Millais, Bt.*) 177
18. John Everett Millais, by C. R. Leslie, 1852 (*National Portrait Gallery, London*) 185
19. John Ruskin, by Sir John Everett Millais, 1853 (*Ruskin Foundation, Ruskin Library, University of Lancaster*) 187
20. Dr Henry Acland, by Sir John Everett Millais, 1853 (*Ruskin Foundation, Ruskin Library, University of Lancaster*) 191
21. *South Transept, Rouen*, by John Ruskin, 1854 (*Fitzwilliam Museum, Cambridge*) 201
22. Coventry Patmore, from a drawing by J. Brett, RA, 1855 212
23. Rose La Touche, by John Ruskin, *c.* 1860 (*Ruskin Foundation, Ruskin Library, University of Lancaster*) 265

THE LATER YEARS

Between pages 606 and 607

1. John Ruskin, *Self-Portrait*, 1861. (*Pierpont Morgan Library/Art Resource, N.Y.*)
2. The croquet lawn, facing the Wyatt wing of Winnington Hall, *c.* 1861. (*T. C. T., Northwich*)
3. Undated photograph of Rose La Touche. (*The La Touche Family Collection*)
4. Julia Margaret Cameron, *Carlyle like a Rough Block of Michelangelo's Sculpture*, 1867. (*NMPFT/Science and Society Picture Library*)
5. Rose La Touche and her dog, Bruno, *c.* 1866. (*The La Touche Family Collection*)
6. John Ruskin, *Abbeville, Saint Wulfran, South Door of Western Porch*, 1868. (*Ruskin Gallery, Collection of the Guild of St George, Sheffield Galleries and Museums Trust*)
7. Photograph of the Ruskin party in Venice, June or July, 1872. (*Brantwood Trust*)
8. John Ruskin, *Rose La Touche*, 1872. (*Ruskin Gallery, Collection of the Guild of St George, Sheffield Galleries and Museums Trust*)
9. Photograph of Ruskin seated on a bank near Brantwood, by Frank Meadow Sutcliffe, 1873. (*Ruskin Gallery, Collection of the Guild of St George, Sheffield Galleries and Museums Trust*)
10. Photograph of undergraduates building a road at Hinksey, Oxford-shire, 1874. (*Bodleian Library, Oxford*)
11. John Ruskin, *Self-Portrait*, 1874. (*Ruskin Foundation, Ruskin Library, University of Lancaster*)
12. Mrs Cowper-Temple, under the beech trees at a Broadlands conference, from a painting by Edward Clifford, *c.* 1876. (*From W. G. Collingwood,* Ruskin Relics, *1903*)
13. John Ruskin, *Study of Carpaccio's* Dream of St Ursula, 1876–77. (*Ashmolean Museum, Oxford*)
14. Ruskin's study at Brantwood, photograph by Miss Brickhill. (*From W. G. Collingwood,* Ruskin Relics, *1903*)
15. John Ruskin, corrected proof of *Notes by Mr Ruskin on his Drawings of the late J. M. W. Turner*, 1878. (*Ruskin Foundation, Ruskin Library, University of Lancaster*)
16. W. G. Collingwood, *John Ruskin in his study at Brantwood*, water-colour. (*Trustees of the Ruskin Museum, Coniston*)
17. Professor Charles Eliot Norton, probably in the 1880s. (*Harvard University Archives*)
18. John Ruskin and Henry Acland, 1893, photograph by Sara Acland. (*Ruskin Gallery, Collection of the Guild of St George, Sheffield Galleries and Museums Trust*)
19. Fred Hollyer, *Portrait of John Ruskin, c.* 1894. (*Ruskin Gallery, Collection of the Guild of St George, Sheffield Galleries and Museums Trust*)
20. Arthur and Joan Severn walking at Brantwood, *c.* 1920. (*Miss Janet Gnosspelius*)

While every attempt has been made to trace the copyright holders of the photographs reproduced, the publishers hope that any errors or omissions will be referred to them for correction in future editions of this book.

FOREWORD TO COMBINED VOLUME

This book contains the two volumes of my biography of John Ruskin, *Ruskin: the Early Years*, published in 1985, and its successor *Ruskin: the Later Years*, which appeared in 2000, the centenary year of its subject's death. The present volume amalgamates the two previous books for the convenience of the reader — who will, none the less, be incommoded by a sizeable publication. I therefore plead that I have always tried to be brief and that abbreviation, at least in the field of Ruskin studies, is not a straightforward task. Ruskin set many problems for those who wish to write about him. He also gave us such a wealth of precious and suggestive material that Ruskinians have never known quite how long or how short their books should be. Ruskin himself was undecided, and in a magnificent way unconcerned, about the proper length of any of his works. Ruskin scholars have been influenced by this attitude, occasionally with a tragic curtailment of their projects, as in the case of the late Helen Gill Viljoen, whom I should now commemorate.

I have already described (in the introductions to both volumes of this biography) how Professor Viljoen — then a young woman in her twenties — visited Ruskin's home at Brantwood in 1929 and there, within the ruins of the previous culture of the house, decided to convert her postgraduate research project into a biography. In that summer of 1929 she also met W. G. Collingwood, who had been Ruskin's secretary and in 1893 had published a fine but partial biography of the man whom he had first encountered in 1872. Collingwood became Viljoen's guide, perhaps in effect (to use a modern university word) her supervisor. He encouraged Viljoen to adopt a suspicious attitude to E. T. Cook's and Alexander Wedderburn's 'Library Edition' of Ruskin's complete writings (1903–12) and probably told her that future Ruskin studies would depend on a completely new retelling of Ruskin's life.

In this way, Helen Gill Viljoen became the first of twentieth-century Ruskin biographers. Her projected book was to be of immense length and was said to be forthcoming until at least 1967, nearly forty years after her visit to Brantwood. Thereafter, nothing more was heard of her book. We knew its first volume, which was published in 1956: *Ruskin's Scottish Heritage* described his family background. This book, which is 284 pages long, was, as Viljoen subtitled it, 'a prelude', for by its close she had not reached the date of her subject's birth.

Although no further installment of Viljoen's biography was ever to appear, we have had the benefit of her edition of Ruskin's correspondence with J. A. Froude (New York, 1966; and so privately published that I know of only one copy of the book in a British collection, that in the University of Lancaster, which received the volume from Bembridge School) and her transcription of Ruskin's diary of 1876–84, with a commentary that has been of most touching value to the present writer. Viljoen could have given more to the world, or at least to the handful of other Ruskinians, but held back. Perhaps she thought that her research might never end and, since it was endless, could never be superceded. In any case, none of her fellow workers could understand why she declined to make herself familiar with the Ruskin archives at Oxford and at Bembridge School. It could be that a part of her intellectual character, which was inclined to secrecy, wished to keep these archives mysterious even to herself.

Viljoen's researches are now within the public domain, for she willed her notes and the unfinished manuscripts of her biography to the Pierpont Morgan Library. It is proper to acknowledge this bequest in my own book. I have not yet studied the material in the Morgan, so am all the more indebted to James L. Spates' article '"John Ruskin's Dark Star": new lights on his life based on the unpublished biographical materials and research of Helen Gill Viljoen' in the *Bulletin of the John Rylands University Library of Manchester*, Spring 2000.

Mr Spates' article provides a preliminary (I trust) report on his thoughts about the state and the nature of Viljoen's Ruskin biography. I cannot see how much of its writing was completed. It is important to learn that Viljoen was much more affected by psychological studies than we had imagined. She believed that Ruskin's life was dominated by emotional struggles with his father. Furthermore, she saw all Ruskin's writings, even the apparently improvised *Fors Clavigera*, as a carefully constructed web or network of symbols. Spates gives one example of this symbolism. All Ruskinians agree that the description of a near-naked girl, seen in Turin in 1858 and remembered in *The Cestus of Aglaia* of 1866 and again in an Oxford lecture of 1884, must have significance. I have twice, I think reservedly, referred to this passage in the *Cestus*, and have given a quotation. We now gather from Mr Spates' article that Viljoen considered that 'the southern suburb of Turin' in Ruskin's description of that city, really represented Herne Hill and Denmark Hill. The 'Sun-God' in the same paragraph was John James Ruskin. Not only 'Dame Pacience' in this passage — Ruskin was referring to the 35th stanza of Chaucer's *The Parlement of Foules* — but also the unclothed Italian child, and in addition Monte Viso (which is seen from Turin) are, according to Viljoen, representations of Ruskin's mother, Margaret Ruskin.

Viljoen's interpretation is not fantastic, though it remains merely an interpretation. There is a kind of reality in her speculations about the 'Sun-God' and Monte Viso. Ruskin certainly had a set of private myths and symbols. Different biographers will have their own views about the importance of these symbols and will dispute their meanings. We are all agreed, however, that Rose La Touche — real or imagined Rose — was foremost in the mythologies, if not the specific remarks, of Ruskin's later books. I now think that I have underestimated the violence and horror in some of Ruskin's writings about Rose; and, more and more, *Proserpina* makes me think of the grave. We still do not grasp the mortal nature of her physical and mental disorders. I have recently heard the suggestion that Rose may have been abused by her father. This is a hateful thought that must be considered. If Ruskin was aware of such ill-treatment, or had guessed at it, then that might help to explain the peculiar nature of some passages in *The Queen of the Air* and other books. I note that in almost all of his writings Ruskin avoids the question, which he must often have had in his mind, of the relations of fathers to their daughters. There is one exception. It will be found in the *Fors Clavigera* of May 1883, carefully entitled 'Lost Jewels' (this was the first number of *Fors* to be given a title), which bursts with symbolism and is on the edge of insanity.

I had doubted whether any fresh information about Rose La Touche could be found, since I know how thoroughly Van Akin Burd researched his *John Ruskin and Rose La Touche* (1979). I am therefore much indebted to the Revd Dr John Pridmore, who is the Rector of Hackney, for sending me copies of a handful of letters that describe or mention Rose. The originals are in the Beinecke Library at Yale University and come from the correspondence of the family of George MacDonald. I now mention two of these letters. In the first of them Maria La Touche addresses George MacDonald's wife Louisa. She wrote in August or September of 1865 and describes a La Touche holiday in Scotland. 'The Hidden Life' is a literary ballad to be found in George MacDonald's *Poems* (1857). I extract Maria Ta Touche's letter as follows:

> The Wild Rose is very well but wilder than ever. Sometimes I wonder if she will ever be a civilized being — She is out in the dew like Nebuchadnezzar at break of day — & all day long she is

> in & out, let the weather be what it may, & not one single thing that girls do, does she do — except a *little* music when she pleases — She has the run of all the cottages & cabins about, & gets fed from the labourer's dinners, & is an exception to every rule & custom of society. If your husband could see her life, he would photograph her in a book — A thing happened in Scotland which reminded me so of the 'Hidden Life'. Rose being the heroine & a little shepherd boy of 15 the hero. He got lost on the moors, alone, & with her accustomed intrepidity she captured a boy to show her the way — & for miles she walked over the heather with her captive — & told me of her talk with him afterwards, & how *very* kind he was to her, helping her in rough places: & how he told her he couldn't be out of dark for the world & was surprised that she didn't mind — & how when they came to a house he said 'I hope there's no gentry here, to see *you* walking with a dirty lad like me!' Was not that nice? Nice of the Scottish boy, I mean — And at last she found us, & with her hand on her small knight's shoulder said 'you can't think what care this boy has taken of me — & he has so far to go home — & I had only my knife to give him!' The Knight & the Lady would have made a pretty picture . . .

This letter was known both to Derrick Leon, who quoted much of it in his *Ruskin: the Great Victorian* (1949) and to Van Akin Burd, who included a shorter extract in his description of Rose's character in *John Ruskin and Rose La Touche*. Thanks to the Rector of Hackney I am able to offer a longer quotation from Maria La Touche's story about her daughter. We see more clearly how she connected Rose's adventure both to literature and art. A commonplace sentiment in the Victorian mind, many will say: yet surely this Victorian attitude had some value. We are reminded of a strange and potent aspect of Rose's nature. She had a way of attracting her family and friends to make almost mythical tales from her artless ventures into the adult world. Ruskin would certainly have heard about Rose's walk with the Scottish shepherd boy, and he would have known other stories about the lovely young woman who seemed to be 'like a younger sister of Christ'. I surmise that these stories about Rose were always in Ruskin's mind and were repeated, with manic theological emphasis, in the fantasies that were a part of his illnesses after 1878.

A different biographical problem is found in another of the MacDonald letters. This one is from Lilia Scott MacDonald to her mother. I date it to 17 November 1873. Within its narrative, we discover Rose, living in a hotel in Hastings. She 'looks thinner in the [illeg] possible & I think prettier — her complexion more white & pink & wild-rose like than ever but she seemed to have lost some of the shine of those eyes . . .' The letter gives no reason why Rose should have chosen to make her temporary home in this hotel. It was probably for medical reasons. Rose had consulted no fewer than four doctors when she had recently been in London. We learn of a proposal that Rose might winter in the south of France and in Italy. She would need a companion as well as her nurse. In the Hastings hotel Rose's father had interviewed a possible companion (a former medical student) but had disapproved of her manners at the luncheon table. So the mediterranean journey was in doubt, at least for a little while. Rose was wearing a silk and black velvet jacket. Beside her on the sofa was a guitar.

I think that Rose's circumstances in Hastings may have prompted the beautiful December 1873 number of *Fors Clavigera*, 'Traveller's Rest' — for Ruskin's beloved was a traveller who could never find rest — and I interpret its reading of the Psalms as a message to the erratic young woman who was so obdurate in her faith. Ruskin's sudden departure for Margate in January of 1874, which I could not quite explain in this biography, might have been the result of a wish to be in some seaside place, as Rose was, yet in a more old-fashioned little town. A passage in *Fors* records his disappointment with Margate. Its wording recalls an older, far happier seaside life. This was at Boulogne in 1861, when Ruskin spent nearly two months at the Hotel des Bains, painted in watercolour, reread Rose's childish letters and, one night, went with the men of the Huret fishing family and caught mackerel quite near to Hastings. Such were the watery ways of Ruskin's memory.

* * * *

Ruskin was a marvellous topographer, perhaps the best in English literature. He had learnt the meditative science of topography from Turner. Ruskinians should also linger on the nature of places. To speak a little further of Margate, and the adjacent Thanet resorts of Broadstairs and Ramsgate: their social differences and unequal development in the nineteenth century (pleasantly described for the contemporary reader in Frank Muir, *A Kentish Lad*, 1997) led Ruskin to think, while he was in Margate, not only of Turner — as this biography has mentioned — but of Dickens, that lover of Broadstairs, and also of W. P. Frith's Dickensian painting *Ramsgate Sands*. As a Ruskinian, I of course turn to *The Harbours of England* to find its opinions on these marine places. This book, published in 1856, is the last account of our coastal life before the advent of railways and popular holidays. I give my thanks to Michael Gordon, who in his young days was able to explore, by bicycle, an antique England of which there is now little trace. Mr Gordon generously gave me his early edition of *The Harbours of England*, which he had bought in the Charing Cross Road in January of 1927.

Mr Gordon tells me that in extreme old age one can read whatever one likes and that, with other books awaiting attention 'in the rather short time remaining to me' he does not feel obliged to accept the gift of the present biography. This introduction therefore thanks a person who does not wish to lose the valuable hours that would be lost in reading my book. In other ways, Mr Gordon's terminal reading programme resembled that of this book's editor, whom I must now call the late David Britt. My previous introduction mentioned Coleridge's haughty remark 'ignorant as a bookseller'. In one of his murmurs of guidance, Mr Britt told me that Coleridge was probably thinking not of booksellers but of publishers. I now thank my own publishers, who are not ignorant at all, for preparing the present book. Writers such as myself are much indebted to those who toil in university presses. I wish them more spacious offices and longer lunches.

* * * *

Almost from childhood, I have found that Ruskin liberates one from the more enclosed corridors of study. As he often said, we are affected by the buildings in which we live and work, or were raised. I am sure that I owe a debt to a Ruskinian architect, John Henry Chamberlain (1831–83). He practiced in Birmingham but was not related to the well-known political Birmingham Chamberlains. J. H. Chamberlain was none the less a fellow worker in their plans for city improvement. His particular gift (though this is to ignore his domestic architecture) was in building for education. Chamberlain's practice developed with the proliferation of 'Board Schools' after the Elementary Education Act of 1870. He designed more than thirty of these schools, all in Birmingham, before his early death.

During his professional life Chamberlain made a true contribution to the Gothic Revival. Ruskin was his guide, in specific architectural matters and probably other ways, for (as George Baker tells us in the 'St George's Guild Trustee's Report for 1883', printed in *The Master's Report*, 1884) he 'had taken a warm interest in the Guild of St George from its commencement'. Chamberlain's style was indebted to Pugin and *The Stones of Venice*. Most of his buildings have now disappeared. However, some of them have been recorded, and it would be possible to match various of their features with the diagrams in Ruskin's Venetian history. Many writers have noted this derivation. I add that

Chamberlain probably appreciated the designs of some Oxford colleges, with their quadrangles, cloisters and enclosed gardens.

It happened that I was a boy in a Chamberlain Board School. In the years after 1948 I joined other ragged but quite happy children at Bristol Street Primary School, and can remember some elements of its location and design. Our school stood at the corner of Irving Street, where Bristol Street became Horse Fair. The city centre of Birmingham was little more than half a mile distant. The markets were nearby. In Horse Fair there were second-hand bookshops side by side with metal-working factories. Everything was busy, dirty and dilapidated. On the way to school children played on bomb sites.

One entered Bristol Street Primary School through a massive (or so it seemed to me) gothic archway and turned left into a cloister. Beyond its arcaded corridor were primitive lavatories and two adjoining playgrounds. Near the front entrance a curving staircase led to the upper floor. Here one began to feel a characteristic of all Chamberlain's public architecture: a sense of release or relaxation in the upper stories of a building. At the top of the stairs were classrooms. These rooms had high, vaulted walls beneath the school's roof. Their windows were enormous. The effect was surprisingly buoyant, as though the darkness of the gothic style could easily and suddenly be transformed into light and space. In many ways Chamberlain is a link between the Gothic Revival of the mid-nineteenth century and the more transparent architecture of the 1880s and 1890s; or, let us say, a link between the Ruskin of *The Stones of Venice* and the Ruskinism of his more liberal and optimistic followers.

Bristol Street Primary School was cheaply built with limited public funds and stood in a slum. Yet this was not merely a functional building. Its very fabric suggested a municipal idealism that was connected to art. Mr Brooking, the headmaster at Bristol Street in my day, was an artist. He had trained before Hitler's war at Birmingham School of Art in Margaret Street, a building also designed by Chamberlain. Perhaps it is odd that Mr Brooking was a headmaster, since his only qualification was a certificate attesting to skill in drawing. Maybe his high position was in accord with the spirit of Birmingham education in the late nineteenth century; for at that time there was a view in Mr Brooking's home city that the study of art was essential to a forward-looking understanding of the world.

The Birmingham School of Art (opened in 1885, sensitively restored in 1995) is Chamberlain's masterpiece. His work on the Birmingham Board Schools had prepared him for the far more complex college. Its exterior patterning and decoration is a thoughtful, vigorous interpretation of Ruskin's architectural thought of the 1850s. Today's visitors to central Birmingham are often startled by such a bold reinvention of Venetian gothic. They should try to make a tour of the art school's interior. Within Margaret Street, there is the same pattern that once existed at Bristol Street Primary School. Quite dark and turning staircases lead to an upper floor of wide rooms, high windows and lovely light, for here are the principal painting studios.

I was never a student at Margaret Street (though that was a teenage ambition) but know the building well because I taught there in the 1970s. We were encouraging modern art in an abode of Victorian culture. In niches and corridors of the lower part of the college — sculpture departments are usually on the ground floor of any art school — were many casts. Nearly all of them were of antique and classical busts and torsos. All except one of these relics were well known to my colleagues and indeed would be recognised by anyone with an elementary knowledge of classical statuary. I was able to identify the puzzling cast. It was of Jacopo della Quercia's funerary monument of Ilaria di Caretta, which dates from around 1413, and was first seen by Ruskin in Lucca in 1845. I recognised it because I had studied Ruskin, and I knew why it had been placed in the sculpture department. A century before I began work in Margaret Street J. H. Chamberlain, loyal follower of Ruskin that he was, must have ensured that della Quercia's sculpture should be part of the education of the youth of modern Birmingham.

Was the cast in fact ever used for didactic purposes? I think it more likely that, even in the nineteenth century, this replica of della Quercia's monument had only a symbolic role. It is possible to pursue the question, for Birmingham's art school has been much loved and its records are more complete than those of similar establishments. The old records are summarised in John Swift's *Changing Fortunes: the Birmingham School of Art Building 1880–1995* (Birmingham, 1996) and in Alan Crawford's *By Hammer and Hand* (Birmingham, 1984), which surveys the Arts and Crafts movement in the city. From Swift's history we learn of the industrious practicality of art education in Margaret Street in the late nineteenth century. The general ethos may not have been as high-flown as Chamberlain had hoped, or that some later historians (including myself) have imagined. The banausic classes described by Mr Swift could never have allowed a place for Ilaria de Caretta and Ruskin's thoughts of her iconic role in the depiction of death and immortality.

Alan Crawford's informative book draws attention to the contrast between Ruskin's views and those of the Birmingham city fathers. As

I recount in the present biography, Ruskin himself lamented that his toryism was so far removed from the 'civic gospel' that he encountered at the home of George Baker, the Mayor of Birmingham, in the summer of 1877. These differences could not be reconciled by Ruskin's followers, unless they imagined that there was more kindness than tragedy in his writing and that his view of 'social discipline' might be overlooked. After the visit of 1877 we are aware that Ruskin was appreciated, even revered, in Birmingham: but I have never found evidence that anyone in the city made an intelligent analysis of his writings of the sort undertaken by his small group of Oxford disciples, though the materials were available.

Birmingham, with its libraries and colleges, its art school, its social conscience and desire for improvement, provides us with a testing ground when we try to assess Ruskin's influence on later attitudes. In this industrial city were such prominent followers of Ruskin as George Baker, Samuel Timmins and John Henry Chamberlain, all members of the Guild of St George. The city's art school was a Ruskinian foundation. Birmingham had the largest Ruskin Society in the country. Its secretary, John Howard Whitehouse, built an unparalleled collection of Ruskin books, manuscripts and drawings. He bought Brantwood and founded Bembridge School. Yet Whitehouse's politics were not Ruskin's; the art classes in Margaret Street had no connection with Ruskin's example; and Baker, Timmins and Chamberlain held liberal views of a sort that Ruskin had always denounced.

★ ★ ★ ★

I dwell on the question of Ruskin's intellectual legacy, taking the city of Birmingham as a test case, because so much recent comment (and reviews of the second volume of this book) have stressed Ruskin's influence, almost as though he were of importance only because other people once admired him. I think that Ruskin should be studied for his own sake. He is admirable to this day. His achievements were unique and self-contained. Ruskinians are divided between those who believe he had a vast influence and those who think that his influence was limited. I am of the latter party (as was Ruskin himself). The preface to the first volume of this biography mentioned the Clarion Club cyclist and retired bookseller who introduced me to Ruskin studies in, I think, 1958. He was the late representative of a socialist tradition. We associate that tradition with self-education, free thought, lecturing societies and the desire for benevolent social change. I have mentioned these attitudes in paragraphs about Ruskinian work at Sheffield and the creation of 'Ruskin Societies'.

I have also given space to E. T. Cook's notion of a 'new Oxford movement'. Cook thought that work in Toynbee Hall, and his own journalism on behalf of the Liberal Party, were the natural outcome of Ruskin's teaching.

However, all these tendencies in British life would have been present had Ruskin never written. I think he had most effect on people who knew him personally and treasured the nature of his character. Such people — not necessarily grand, for I am interested in Ruskin's servants and 'girl friends' as well as in Carlyle and Turner — can be inspiring to a biographer. This surely is a lesson of his vast correspondence.

As to the inspiration that Ruskin gave to creative artists, I remain in doubt. His mark was on architecture rather than the more delicate practices of painting and drawing. Work on paper by his most direct pupils, some of which is preserved in the Ashmolean Museum in Oxford and was shown to me by Christopher Lloyd, to whom I give thanks, is never distinguished and often wretched. It must be significant that there is no Ruskin legacy in literature, even within the aesthetic movement. I am grateful to the late Kate Lee, a lover of Pater, for her remarks to me on this subject. We agreed that other writers did not respond to the learning and music of Ruskin's prose. This is not merely because he was a singular craftsman. 'Inimitable' writers are often imitated. Ruskin's writing was not suited to the temper of late Victorian times. After the 1870s English didactic writing became more straightforward. It served the expansion and purposes of higher education. Prose became more ordered with the growth of separate academic disciplines.

But Ruskin's creative thought, in prose that was nourished by poetry and was written at a poetic rather than a functional level, did not separate one branch of study from any other. The Igdrasil, 'this fair tree Igdrasil of Human Art' is always in growth. Learning leads to further wonderment. Ruskin knew that the first wonder of the world made by mankind is visual art. I regret that the present biography does not give sufficient attention to Ruskin's delight in painting and sculpture. It was always necessary to pass to the events of the next year. Ruskin's love of art is in any case an elusive subject. Forty years ago, I thought it sensible to make a list of works that Ruskin appreciated, and then to match that list with his comments. It was the wrong approach. I abandoned the exercise because, however much information I collected, I still could not grasp the nature of Ruskin's understanding of Turner.

I am grateful to numerous scholars who have added to knowledge of Turner in the years when I and other colleagues were thinking about Ruskin. The modern Turner connoisseurs were often led by my contemporary at the Courtauld Institute, John Gage, whose *Colour in Turner* (1969) and *J. M. W. Turner: 'A Wonderful Range of Mind'* (1987) outlined a new approach to the artist. I lament that Turnerian and Ruskinian researches have not been complementary. To our surprise, we found that we have little common ground. I am of course indebted to the series of specialised Turner exhibitions organised by the Tate Gallery since the 1980s. They have given us more than a dozen detailed accounts of, for instance, Turner's feelings for Scott, or Byron, or the Alps, or the *coteaux* of Seine. Yet we know that no similar exhibition could describe Ruskin's relationship to Turner. The subject is not only large. It is intangible.

All recent Turner studies, following Dr Gage, have stressed the quality of Turner's 'mind'. (The subtitle of Dr Gage's second book is taken from a comment by Constable, who had dined with Turner in 1813, and also, on that occasion, had found him 'uncouth'.) Turnerians say that their landscapist had an understanding of poetry, science, mythology, European history and other subjects. Such claims are often exaggerated. It is reasonable to match this 'mind' against other artists and writers. Turner's intelligence can scarcely be compared with that of, say, Rubens, who was a finer painter and a nobler man. Ruskin recognised Rubens' power (I should have said this in my biography) but could not come to terms with the *superbia* of the Flemish painter's taste. One must be moved by the contrast between the two artists' social positions. We imagine Rubens at court in three countries and acknowledge him as an uncrowned prince of European culture. Turner we see in the corner of some foreign inn, perhaps in Piedmont or Savoy, with a peasant meal of soup and black bread. He has no companions and in any case cannot make conversation. In his pocket is a precious notebook of the colours and scenes that he had witnessed in the course of his day's sketching — a notebook that, many years later, Ruskin would discover when in 1858 he opened the boxes of Turner's possessions in basement rooms of the National Gallery.

Much of Ruskin's humanitarianism came from his study of Turner's travels, whose itineraries he often followed or could reconstruct. As he learnt about Turner, he learnt also about his own abilities. Ruskin was no doubt Turner's follower, but was not far advanced in life before his intellect exceeded the 'mind' of his crabbed and mainly unlettered master. He soon attributed thoughts to Turner which in truth were his own. Ruskin was not writing art criticism so much as his own form of literature. It is possible that Turner looked on Ruskin as an unfathomable rival rather than an eager admirer, a person who had appropriated his work for his own purposes, whatever they might be. This might help to explain the tense relations between the artist and the writer. More and more, I read Ruskin's interpretations of Turner as a scattered and unstable self-portrait.

Some of the most disturbing of Ruskin's Turnerian speculations are found in the fifth and final volume of *Modern Painters*, written in 1859–60. He was on the brink of his first major crisis as a writer, and thought of the grave. Not for the first time, he associated books with the eternal life that comes after death. When still in his teens, Ruskin had declared (to his father) that 'books are the souls of the dead in calf-skin'. Now, toward the end of *Modern Painters*, he suggested that some human beings are not exactly human, but are books. A good man is a 'flesh-bound volume'. Thus Ruskin foretold his own fate. For a decade of his life this writer of so many good books was 'flesh-bound' and might as well have been dead.

This biography has not been able to say more than a few words about that final decade, when Ruskin did not write, probably did not read but turned over the pages of a familiar illustrated volume — the Findens' *Illustrations of the Bible*, for instance, with its engravings after Turner — and sometimes recognised the sound of favourite books when they were read to him by such intimates as his cousin Joan Severn or his servant Peter Baxter. In the years of Ruskin's silence an idea of the personality of his writings merged with the social hopes of a new generation. But for those close to Ruskin, in the dark valley of Coniston Water or the lakeland fells, it was a period of enclosed sadness. One important book gives us a clue to the emotions of that time and place, W. G. Collingwood's *The Life and Work of John Ruskin* (1893). It is probable that Collingwood (like another 'disciple', Jamie Anderson in nearby Windermere) devised his modest, rural and scholarly *modus vivendi* as a tribute to Ruskin. All through the 1890s, in his cottage home not more than a few hundred yards from Brantwood, Collingwood was the guardian of the books of Ruskin's mind while that mind lay in exhausted ruins and Ruskin himself 'waited for the sunset', in the phrase much favoured by his obituarists. Collingwood had no money. Music was his delight and fishing his recreation.

Collingwood's pain affected Ruskin studies until at least the 1970s. I have described how he bequeathed some of his attitudes to Helen Gill Viljoen. Like Collingwood, she was a devoted follower of Ruskin who thought that the world was not ready to understand his tragedy. We may call Collingwood Ruskin's most intimate follower, but he was not a disciple who marched toward a confident future. The decade of Ruskin's silence — when Collingwood was in his 40s — embittered him. He could not bring himself to applaud the enterprise of two other Ruskin disciples, E. T. Cook's and Alexander Wedderburn's Library Edition' of 1903–12. Collingwood suspected their motives and thought that they were remote from the awful circumstances at Brantwood and the decline of the Brantwood ideal. It is true that Wedderburn had seen little or nothing of Ruskin for twenty years and more, by the time that his old teacher died. Cook had met Ruskin only briefly, never knew Brantwood during Ruskin's lifetime and did not visit Coniston before the funeral on that rainy day of January in 1900. But neither Cook nor Wedderburn were negligent.

After the funeral Alexander Wedderburn undertook the task (among similar labours) of an index to every reference to the Bible in all of Ruskin's writings. The results will be found in the thirty-ninth volume of the 'Library Edition'. Sometimes, Ruskin's response to the Bible did not quite provide a catchword that obliged Wedderburn to make an entry in his index. An example is Ruskin's description of 'true taste' in the second volume of *Modern Painters*, which I have quoted in the present book. I surmise that Ruskin adapted his idea of taste from the verses about charity in Corinthians 13.1. In 1846 he already thought that a proper love of art was inseparable from the principles of good government. Today, not many people share this view, or would agree with Ruskin's judgements about either art or politics. None the less, Ruskin's imaginative confusion of taste with charity should be treated with respect.

For guidance in matters of Victorian belief I am indebted to at least two people who were themselves young in the Victorian age. In the 1960s one could still learn from elderly people whose minds had been formed by the previous century. Dorothy Palmer (my grandmother) was a freethinker who collected books about working-class education and owned a set of the 'Library Edition'. I inherited many volumes from her shelves. The late Canon Adam Fox made much impression on me, only faintly reproduced in this biography. In his house behind Westminster Abbey we talked about many nineteenth-century matters. He was a devoted historian of the Victorian church and a student of Plato. His study also contained a large poetry collection. Canon Fox may have been one of the last intelligent clergymen to have been brought up (during the early 1880s) to respect his father's belief that there was 'a theology of the poets'; a belief that of course could not be maintained once the son had read beyond Wordsworth and had become enchanted by Housman.

Margaret Evershed has kindly sent me information about a portrait by Lawrence, now lost but once in her family. It is recorded by a photograph, on whose back is written 'Great Aunt Gray — Grandfather Munro's sister and godmother to John Ruskin. Ruskin's father and mother's father were at Lisbon together in the British Embassy'. John James Ruskin, we learn from *Præterita*, was indeed at Lisbon with his friend Richard Gray in his earlier days as a wine merchant. 'Mr Gray', Ruskin's autobiography recounts, 'married an extremely good and beautiful Scottish girl, Mary Monro'. I had not previously known that Ruskin had a godmother, so this is useful information. No mention of a godfather is known to me.

The index of the 'Library Edition' missed *Præterita*'s mention of Lisbon, a slip that is certainly pardonable in a work of more than 150,000 references. Looking through a shorter index, that to Mary Lutyens' *The Ruskins and the Grays* (1972), I chance on a dog apparently owned by Ruskin in the earlier years of his marriage. Mungo can now be added to the list of dogs I have already given, since dogs were a part of Ruskin's daily life and sometimes of his imagination. Mungo is a good name for a Scottish dog. The Hibernian saint is not mentioned in any part of Ruskin's writing, though we do find an intemperate condemnation of the explorer who bore his name, Mungo Park. Ruskin may have expelled the saint from his imaginative world because Mungo the dog belonged to his wife rather than to himself. The contrast would be with Bruno, Rose La Touche's dog, who for Ruskin had a heavenly existence, or indeed the 'hound' who lies for ever at the feet of Ilaria di Caretta.

The publication of *Ruskin: the Later Years* brought kind correspondence which I can only partially acknowledge. I thank Alan Cole for a description of his collection of letters and other materials from the estate of Sara Anderson. Michael McGinley points out that the person who sent reports of Ruskin's Oxford lectures to Rose La Touche was J. G. Swift MacNeill, as is recounted in his autobiography *What I Have Seen and Heard* (1925). I have been able to exchange letters with John Lucas about W. H. Mallock; and with Paul Hetherington about the sale of antiquities, either to the British Museum, or to other museums or private collectors from dealers in and around Bloomsbury, in the mid nineteenth century. This (I believe) is part of the rich background of *The Ethics of the Dust* and other of Ruskin's writings. Thinking of *The Ethics of the Dust* (1865), I wonder whether one of the vivisectionists of academic literary criticism might write a comparison of Ruskin's book with Lewis Carroll's *Alice's Adventures in Wonderland*, published in the same year. Both of these works of the imagination are about girls, or a girl, who seek wisdom, or is bemused, in underground places. Carroll, I suspect, loathed all of Ruskin's writings.

There is much to be written about Ruskin's Oxford years, a subject that a biography can touch but lightly. Gail S. Weinberg sent me her observations about the Italian paintings at Christ Church that Ruskin studied when an undergraduate Richard Symons and Michael Stansfield, who is the college's archivist, have given me valuable information about Corpus Christi College and its *alumnus* Alfred Hunt — a minor painter but a true artist, and Ruskin's sincere friend. George Mackie (an artist and formerly an academic publisher) made helpful comments about the nature of Ruskin's handwriting and the difficulty of reproducing his hand in print. I mention all these correspondents for personal reasons. They have been generous to me. Thoughtful letters make me wish that I could rewrite this book and maybe correct more of its mistakes and misunderstandings. It cannot be done. I have gone fishing on the Waveney. My little boat is called the *Jumping Jenny* (see page 685).

T. H. Uggeshall, March 2002

FOREWORD TO THE EARLY YEARS

Of great English writers, there is none so prolific as Ruskin: nor, for those who love to study him, is there any writer so valued for every sentence, every touch of the pen — right down to that individual, flickering, hurrying punctuation that, as one reads his manuscripts, seems to drive his thoughts from one page to the next. His literary production was enormous, yet nothing is redundant. In a writing career of fifty-nine years, he published some 250 titles, to which we must add his lectures, contributions to periodicals, more than thirty volumes of diary, around forty volumes of published correspondence, and dozens of thousands of letters which remain unpublished, and will not see print for many a year yet. It is not easy to come to a moderately informed view of Ruskin, and not only because of his fecundity. There are no useful modern editions of his famous early works, *Modern Painters* (1843-60) and *The Stones of Venice* (1851-3). *Unto this Last* (1860) has been given an importance it does not really possess. *Fors Clavigera* (1871-84), Ruskin's best and most extensive work, was ignored in his lifetime and has scarcely been studied from that day to this. *Præterita* (1885-9), his autobiography, is an extended rumination on his childhood rather than a statement of Ruskin's purposes in adult life; and of his mature works, what does this century really know of those gnomically-entitled volumes, so often seen in second-hand bookshops, never reprinted, *The Harbours of England, The Two Paths, Munera Pulveris, Time and Tide by Weare and Tyne, The Ethics of the Dust, The Queen of the Air, Mornings in Florence, St Mark's Rest, Love's Meinie* and *The Storm-Cloud of the Nineteenth Century*?

Ruskin's books, even *The Elements of Perspective,* are without exception personal. They were formed by the events of his life, his reading, his friendships and loves, dreams, travels and memories. No doubt this is so of many imaginative writers: but Ruskin believed his life's work to be factual and analytical. This is the first problem of understanding Ruskin's writing, and one reason for a biography. A knowledge of his life, rewarding in itself, is also the best way to approach his books. They are neither straightforward nor self-explanatory, and they have an especial unlikeness to anyone else's writing. Few of them are in an obvious sense works of literature. They rarely conform to the classic *genres* of writing. Moreover, from some point in the 1850s it is impossible to prefer Ruskin's 'major' to his 'minor' works, and unfinished or unfinishable books may be more rewarding than his more crafted productions. In later years he tried to give his readers all he thought they should know about him in order to understand his writings. But his audience, such as it was, then became further confused and sometimes alienated. This was the fate of *Fors Clavigera*, which the present biographer believes to be Ruskin's masterpiece. *Fors* was the monthly letter written (nominally) to instruct and inspire a class that certainly did not read it, 'the workmen and labourers of Great Britain'. Its six hundred thousand words, a commentary on Ruskin's thoughts and experiences between 1870 and 1884, tell us more about its author than does *Præterita*, his autobiography. But much of it is obscure, however Ruskin strives to make himself understood: and perhaps *Fors* was fully comprehensible only to those who had an intimate knowledge of his life.

Præterita, whose composition began with extracts from *Fors Clavigera*, did not reach the point in its narrative at which *Fors* itself was begun; and it is not likely that the exhausted, despondent autobiography could have explained the dramas of Ruskin's life in the years that the pamphlet was issued. I hope to have written a biography that does so for him. *Præterita* does not tell us much about Ruskin's maturity. Nor does it describe his position as a great Victorian. Its bitter modesty conceals how extensive was his public career. Ruskin was twenty-four years old when he published the first volume of *Modern Painters*. He was immediately recognized as a significant didactic writer. For the next forty years and more he was a force against the basilisk of the age. His principled critique of the values of nineteenth-century society, an opposition nobly sustained and richly elaborated, is one of the most valuable expressions of that society. But his contribution did not become clearer as he published more books, and the nature of his writing precluded the composition of single, classic works. Ruskin's criticism of his times might have had more impact if it had been concentrated in ten years' work rather than forty. His extended crusade was both familiar and ignored. To be thus, for a writer of his temper, was to be truly solitary. Ruskin's complaints that he was alone in the world often appear exaggerated. His books were famous and he was a professor in the University of Oxford: what could be more social than that? He was gregarious and people sought his company; he had wide circles of friends; he had 'disciples'; many people loved him; in his own way he was a family man. Yet it is true that he stood alone and that his work was not appreciated. This was the more so the longer he lived and wrote. *Fors Clavigera* echoes a voice that found no response in those it most urgently addressed.

I have not found that Ruskin's purposes — let alone the emotions of his brave, unhappy life — have become much clearer as the result of twentieth-century interest. To some extent, he was the victim of the dismissive prejudices of a period. The scorn of Victorian gravity was of course one reason why he was neglected; another was the rise of the modern movement: a third was the triumph of liberal and democratic values. But the study of Ruskin's life was also impeded by the very instrument that seemed to be designed to promote it. The Library Edition of Ruskin's works was published in thirty-nine volumes between 1903 and 1912. It was, at that date, the most elaborate editorial homage accorded to any English writer, even including Shakespeare. But it appeared at the nadir of Ruskin's reputation. It is perhaps not surprising that its assumptions were not examined at that period. Unfortunately, all subsequent biographies of Ruskin have been deficient because they rely on the Library Edition's editorial apparatus and introductions. Its two editors were E. T. Cook, a Ruskinian since his schooldays, and Alexander Wedderburn, a lawyer who had been one of Ruskin's Balliol 'disciples' at the time of his road-building project in 1874, and who remained a friend ever afterwards. We will meet both Cook and Wedderburn in this book, and learn of their attitudes to Ruskin. For the moment it is enough to say that it was Cook's scholarship that formed the Library Edition; and that it was the firm hand of Joan Severn, Ruskin's cousin, that determined its biographical material.

The present biography differs from its predecessors in placing its emphasis on the later rather than the earlier years of Ruskin's life. I believe that Ruskin was a finer writer and, if I dare say so, a better man, in the years after 1860 and especially in the years after 1870. The Library Edition presents many difficulties of scholarship and interpretation to the historian of these later years. Its editors had to be reticent about a number of matters. Just as they had not wished to say much about Ruskin's marriage, they gave only the barest information about Rose La Touche, even though Ruskin's love for her was a major influence on all his writing after 1860. They could not discuss his repeated mental breakdowns, although these could hardly be ignored; and they could not examine the tortured relationship between Ruskin and Joan Severn, for to do so would have revealed the true nature of *Præterita,* a book which was controlled by Joan and was designed, therefore, to relate only those aspects of Ruskin's life that were uncontentious. These omissions are understandable. Some of them have been repaired by later scholarship. But I would add that Cook (and the biographers who have depended on him) misrepresented Ruskin in other ways. Cook was an excellent Ruskinian, except that he was not an art historian, nor a churchman, nor an imaginative political thinker. He could not understand Ruskin's passions and he was embarrassed by his subject's religious life. He regretted Ruskin's quarrels and shied away from the implications of *Fors Clavigera*. Above all, he deliberately softened Ruskin's political views to make them conformable with his own liberalism. In this biography I have attempted to restore to Ruskin those aspects of his career and his personality.

Modern Ruskin scholarship may be said to have begun in 1929, when the late Helen Gill Viljoen, then a graduate student, visited Ruskin's old home at Brantwood. The house had long since fallen into disrepair and many of its treasures had been sold. But Viljoen discovered Ruskin's diaries, many packets of family letters and one manuscript that meant much to her, the autobiography and diary of Rose La Touche. Helen Viljoen also met W. G. Collingwood, another disciple of Ruskin who had known him since the 1870s. Collingwood had subsequently become Ruskin's secretary, and his views on the honour due to Ruskin's memory significantly differed from Wedderburn's, or Cook's, or Joan Severn's. Viljoen's discovery of original manuscript, with Collingwood's conversation, turned her away from the account of Ruskin presented in the Library Edition. She determined to study him afresh. The first fruit of her lifetime of Ruskin scholarship appeared in 1956, when she published *Ruskin's Scottish Heritage*, an account of her subject's forebears. This was announced as the first volume of a biography. My own belief is that its purpose was to analyse the inaccuracy and bias of the Library Edition: in this way it was propædeutic. Viljoen (who was never to write more than three or four fragmentary chapters of her biography) thus laid down a principle of Ruskin scholarship. She insisted that students of his work should at all times return to the manuscript sources. I have attended to this advice, and in my own researches have been guided by Helen Viljoen's friend Professor Van Akin Burd, whose exemplary editions of *The Winnington Letters* and *The Ruskin Family Letters* have been an inspiration to all modern Ruskinians. I have also benefited from the example of James S. Dearden, Curator of the Ruskin Galleries at Bembridge School. In the many months I spent with Mr Dearden reading through the Bembridge archive I learnt (as he, Professor Viljoen and Professor Burd had learnt before me) that knowledge of Ruskin has been handed down by personal help and generosity.

Helen Viljoen believed that Ruskin scholars should approach their subject as though the Library Edition did not exist. This was an extreme position, which she perhaps held because she never worked in Oxford and did not know of the documents that had aided Cook and Wedderburn in their labours. In the Bodleian Library is an archive almost as considerable as that at Bembridge. Its main sequence is in the volumes known to Ruskinians as the 'transcripts'. These are typewritten copies of all Ruskin's correspondence which was gathered for the Library Edition but not published in it. These thousands of letters are accompanied by complete transcriptions of all Ruskin's diaries. Surprisingly, this material was not known to the editor of Ruskin's diaries, Joan Evans, with the result that her edition of these journals (1956-9), which prints less than half of the complete text, is incomplete and only randomly annotated. The full treasures of the transcripts did not begin to enter Ruskin scholarship until 1969, when Van Akin Burd published *The Winnington Letters*. I hope that this biography's use of them will repay the trust with which Alexander Wedderburn bequeathed the documents to his old university.

* * * *

Such, in brief, is the history of the main stream of Ruskin scholarship, as it has appeared to me. I have of course benefited from many other scholars and Ruskinians. They are fully acknowledged in the bibliographical notes in the second volume of this biography. I must now thank Messrs George Allen and Unwin, the Ruskin Literary Trustees, for their courtesy in allowing me to publish letters and other manuscripts of John Ruskin. For permission to publish material in their possession I thank The Education Trust Ltd, The Ruskin Galleries, Bembridge School, and its Chairman, R. G. Lloyd, CBE, QC. I am grateful to the Bodleian Library and Ashmolean Museum in Oxford for allowing me to quote from documents preserved in their collections. Permission to quote from published and unpublished letters has been kindly granted by Sir Ralph Millais, Bt., the Beinecke Library at Yale University, the Master and Fellows of Trinity College, Cambridge and the Directors of the John Rylands Library, Manchester. The Syndics of the Fitzwilliam Museum, Cambridge, have given me permission to quote material in their archives. I am grateful to the Trustees of the National Library of Scotland for allowing me to quote from manuscripts in their possession and the Trustees of the Trevelyan Estate have generously given me permission to use letters now deposited in the library of the University of Newcastle upon Tyne. Permission to reproduce illustrative material has been kindly granted by: Sir Ralph Millais, Bt., the Education Trust, Ruskin Galleries,

Bembridge; The Brantwood Trust, Coniston; the Ruskin Museum, Coniston; the Ashmolean Museum, Oxford; the City of Birmingham Museum and Art Gallery; the Fitzwilliam Museum, Cambridge; the Greater London Council Photographic Collection; the Graves Gallery, Sheffield; and the National Portrait Gallery, London.

* * * *

A biographer may be allowed some personal comment in acknowledging help and inspiration. I was introduced to the study of Ruskin in the late 1950s, by a fellow cyclist who was then in retirement from his trade as a second-hand bookseller. I grieve that I have forgotten the name of this self-educated man, Clarion Club member and socialist. I no longer believe that Ruskin had any real connection with the Labour movement: but the questions I was then told to put to myself are still the right ones. What do you think about art? What do you think about the poor? I was not a successful student of Ruskin, however. I found his books puzzling and often incomprehensible. My friend did not give me much assistance. He implied that I might grow up to them. This was true: but young men are vexed by such demands on their patience.

When I was an undergraduate in the early 1960s, I was asked to understand that an interest in Ruskin was as foolish as an enthusiasm for modern art. I wish therefore to record my gratitude to the Courtauld Institute of Art, its then director, Anthony Blunt, and my friends Michael Kitson and Anita Brookner for their kind welcome and interest while I studied there as a postgraduate. Richard and Margaret Cobb helped me in many ways when I began my research. Arthur Crook, John Wain, Nuala O'Faolain, Peter Lowbridge, Anna Davin, Luke Hodgkin, Alexander Cockburn, Peter Carter and Martin and Fiona Green all encouraged me when I decided that I would one day write about Ruskin. The late Tony Godwin gave me excellent advice on writing biography, and Marghanita Laski's generosity allowed me to explore his recommendations. I have always been able to submit my writing to the wise scrutiny of David Britt, while Andrew Best of Curtis Brown has lifted many a care. I have long valued the sympathetic interest of Catherine Lampert and Elizabeth Wrightson.

Most of this book was written in Oxford. I am especially beholden to the Warden and Fellows of St Antony's College for their hospitality during the time I held an Alistair Horne Fellowship there: I am grateful for the friendly interest of Teddy Jackson, Tom Laqueur, Harry Willetts and Theodore Zeldin, Fellows of St Antony's with a wide sympathy for the humanities. The late Frank McCarthy Willis-Bund told me much about the Irish Church in which he was raised, and I had the privilege of conversation with John Sparrow about Victorian Oxford. It has always been a pleasure to exchange views and information with Richard Ellmann. John Owen, 'Senex' of the *Oxford Times*, helped me with matters of Oxford lore and tradition. Godfrey and Peter Lienhardt asked me the sort of questions about my interests that helped me to define my views on those interests. All Oxford men are indebted to the university's librarians. My heartfelt thanks go first to Margaret Miller of the Ashmolean Museum, who enabled me to work with the museum's collection of books by and about Ruskin that were the gift of E. T. Cook: I therefore used the same editions, pamphlets, press cuttings and the like from which Cook fashioned his editorial apparatus. Jane Jakeman, now of the Ashmolean, was at that date the most helpful of all the librarians at the Bodleian — where all the librarians, I hasten to add, are efficient and sympathetic beyond the calls of duty. Fanny Stein, Ann Nimmo-Smith and Andrew and Peggoty Graham (all of Balliol families) were my friends and hosts while I lived in Oxford, and my research would not have been possible without their kindnesses to me. David Soskice, Christopher Hill, Tony Kemp-Welch, Frank and Ceci Whitford, Christopher Butler, Andrew Sugden, the late Lesley Smith, Islie Cowan, Joe Masheck, Juliet Aykroyd, Malcolm Warner, Meriel Darby, Deborah Thompson, Raphael Samuel, Mary-Rose Beaumont, John Ryle, Peter Ferriday, W. L. Webb, Eric Hobsbawm, Sheila Rowbotham and Peter Townsend all assisted with the writing of this book, whether they knew it or not.

I was fortunate that, in Oxford in the mid-1970s, there was a group of young scholars working on various aspects of Ruskin. Since there were no older specialists in British universities they were in effect (or so it appeared to me) the avant-garde of the new Ruskin studies. Nobody hoarded their discoveries, and I feel that I must have gained more than anyone else from our discussions. Robert Hewison's thesis on *The Queen of the Air* was a pioneering piece of research: so also was Dinah Birch's dissertation on Ruskin and the Greeks. Tanya Harrod and Nicholas Shrimpton wrote doctorates that stressed Ruskin's public and literary life, while Michael Simmons's examination of *Fors Clavigera* was a truly understanding approach to Ruskin's later years. The most detailed and sensitive work on Ruskin and Italy was Jeanne Clegg's: some of it was published in her *Ruskin and Venice* (1981). She is the Ruskinian to whom I am most deeply indebted, and this biography is dedicated to her. I (and other members of this group) would wish to record our indebtedness to Van Akin Burd, both for his scholarship and his interest in our own work. Of other Ruskinians, I extend my thanks especially to Naomi Lightman, Brian Maidment and Harold Shapiro.

The late Claude Rogers, Professor of Fine Art at the University of Reading, first invited me to examine the collections of the Guild of St George, which at that time (the mid-1960s) were stored in great confusion in the cellars beneath his department. All Ruskinians, and not least myself, are indebted to Catherine Williams for her work in cataloguing this material and for her suggestive comments on the early organization of the Guild of St George. I am also grateful to Peter Fitzgerald and Andrea Finn for inviting me to Reading, and thank the University of Reading Library for giving me access to the book and manuscript collections of the Guild of St George. I thank the Master and Directors of the Guild for a grant that assisted in the research for this book. I acknowledge the financial assistance of the Arts Council of Great Britain, and would add that the Council's Ruskin exhibitions of 1964 and 1983 both helped my work: the first, by its demonstration of the variety of Ruskin's interests, and the second (cogently devised by Dr Clegg) by showing the thematic unity of these interests, and their best expression in Ruskin's 'Guild period', the years of his Slade professorship and *Fors Clavigera*.

During my stays on the Isle of Wight I was made welcome by a number of Bembridge people. I must first of all thank Mr and Mrs Hastings and Ray and Sheila Rowsell for making holiday accommodation available to me in the winter months; and during Bembridge winters I was especially glad to have the company of John and Barbara Arthure, Rosalind Jenkinson and the late General Sir Michael West and Lady West. The best help in the writing of a long book is often of an indirect kind. To be blunt, one needs to be cheered up. My wife, Alexandra Pringle, has sustained me in all ways. So have some 'modern painters'. I owe a personal and intellectual debt to Clement Greenberg: I do not know whether it is apparent in these pages. Lastly, it is a pleasure to me to thank friends who are artists: they must have thought, over the years, that my Ruskinian interests were far removed from their own concerns. My gratitude for their support and patience goes especially to Terry Atkinson, Gillian Ayres, Michael Bennett, Anthony Caro, Barrie Cook, Barry Flanagan, John McLean, Ronnie Rees and John Walker.

* * * *

The spelling and punctuation from original manuscripts has been retained but normalized in quotation from secondary sources.

FOREWORD TO THE LATER YEARS

In the Foreword to the first volume of this biography I stated my opinion that Ruskin was a better writer and a more considerate person in his later rather than his earlier years. The present volume offers some explanation for this view of his life and character after 1860. As before, I have attempted to give a plain chronological account of Ruskin's life while also describing, or at least mentioning, each of his many books. I have written at greater length than I did in the first volume for the following reasons. First, the materials for a biography are more abundant and complex, and the records of many of Ruskin's intimate concerns have not previously been assessed. Secondly, Ruskin published much more writing after 1859–60, the point at which I concluded my survey of his earlier life. The circumstances in which he wrote his later books invite careful examination, for these writings not only explain his personal culture but also respond to his day-to-day experiences of the world. Thirdly, Ruskin in later life knew more people, had a more active public role and promoted his views on a wider range of topics. Fourthly, I have been in a position to explain Ruskin's love for Rose La Touche; his repeated attacks of madness; and the difficulties and confusions of his autobiography *Præterita*.

Ruskin's publications, from the poem 'On Skiddaw and Derwent Water', which appeared in the *Spiritual Times* in 1830, to the last chapter of *Præterita*, which was issued in 1889, are so numerous that no editor has been confident of having caught and described every one of his appearances in print. I do not believe that Ruskin wrote too much and in the following pages I occasionally lament, as he did himself, the absence of books that he projected but never issued. They had such subjects as agates and basalts, Apolline myths, and Carlyle's descriptions of people. Then there were to be books on clouds, on seagulls and on the proper education of working girls. Ruskin also thought about biographies of Scott, and of Pope, and he wished to tell us about his study of the life and teaching of David. I would love to be able to read the unwritten *Stones of Verona*, and to pore over his examinations of French and Swiss landscape, which he would have illustrated, perhaps with his own drawings; while Ruskin's interpretation of the Homeric poems would no doubt have been a book of peculiar value: a stern delight, no doubt, but still a volume that one could read for a lifetime, and then give to one's children to help them astonish their schoolteachers.

These 'unwritten books in my brain', as Ruskin called them, may be quite vividly glimpsed in books that he did indeed write. I hope that they may be discerned, though of course with vaguer outlines, in my descriptions of Ruskin's interests. It may be thought perverse to thus praise unwritten writing. So be it. I find that the absence of the 'books in my brain' makes one think more adventurously of the ways that Ruskin's actual and published books lack rounded and definite form. Most of them are incomplete. My feeling (after reading them for many years) is that such books may be better for their lack of termination. I do not think that they could be aesthetically completed by the addition of further chapters, or by some editor's contraction of their wandering length. Ruskin's books appear to me to be unfinished because they always point elsewhere, leading their readers to consider further facts about, say, quartz, or waves, or Titian, or to brood over the mysteries of the classical and Christian traditions. Here is another reason for the length of the present book, which at one point, perhaps a decade ago, was much longer, and its author quite lost in study. My first acknowledgement is therefore to my publisher, John Nicoll of Yale University Press. He has borne with my delays, however vexatious they have been, and he makes swift, interesting decisions when at last he sees pages of copy.

This book was edited by David Britt, who for thirty years has taken a generous interest in my writing. We have discussed every paragraph (with the exception of the present one) and at all times I have benefited from his remarkable knowledge of literature and delicate counsel. Many of his friends and colleagues hope that Mr Britt will one day give us a book of his own. I fear that we may be disappointed. Translation is probably his first love. He has the selflessness that we sometimes find in the best translators. The very exercise of their taste and judgment tends to make them invisible. So it is also with editors. I know that David Britt dislikes the word 'Ruskinian' as the cognomen of a person who studies Ruskin. I none the less cling to the word and point out that he is himself a Ruskinian, and has been since he attended a Ruskin conference organised by the Victorian Studies Centre at the University of Leicester in 1977. We often have differing attitudes to Ruskin problems. Mr Britt is a Cambridge man and therefore has less interest than I have in the nature of Oxford society and education. As a matter of literary taste, he thinks more highly of *Unto this Last* and the lectures of *Sesame and Lilies* than I do.

⋆ ⋆ ⋆ ⋆

Stirring though they are, I find less to enjoy in Ruskin's lectures, unless they are very long, or on the brink of madness, than in his other work. For me, the lectures are in general too short and formal. They might be contrasted with the letters of *Fors Clavigera*. Any Ruskin biographer must make frequent references to *Fors*, which tells us so much about Ruskin's life between 1871 and 1884 and is the basis of his autobiography *Præterita*. As I wrote in the preface to *Ruskin: the Early Years*, I believe *Fors Clavigera* to be Ruskin's masterpiece, despite the claims of the more familiar *Modern Painters*, *The Stones of Venice*, compilations of lectures such as *The Crown of Wild Olive* and *Præterita* itself. This preference is not easy to justify or explain. Few people agree with me (not that the matter is often discussed) because so few people are acquainted with this enormous series of ninety-six pamphlets. I have always known bookish people, yet I have never met anyone in my life, apart from a handful of professional Ruskin scholars, who has read more than a dozen pages of *Fors Clavigera*. So I merely mention my love of *Fors* as a personal matter. My hope is that the present biography will help to give Ruskin's longest book a role within English literature, by which I mean a place on the shelves of those who like reading books and talking about them.

Fors Clavigera was original, and still has the ring of an innovative work. The idea of a letter written to the public was of course not new in 1871. We know of such things from the pens of Addison, Cobbett, Coleridge and others. However, these writers were not of much interest to Ruskin (though he had a fondness for Addison) and had no effect on his work. In this book I point out that the immediate example for *Fors* was in Carlyle's *Latter-Day Pamphlets*. Ruskin quite quickly dispensed with this model. One difference is that each of Carlyle's letters had a particular or leading subject, and their author could see that his work would be finite. The right things would be said: then his labour, or at least his darg, would be done. Ruskin's letters do not address one topic: quite the opposite. Nor do we expect his series to come to an end once its point had been made or its arguments concluded. For although *Fors Clavigera* makes many points it cannot come to a conclusion. Nothing else in our literature so diversely and eloquently displays the continuing life of the mind. *Fors* seeks authority and continually discusses authority, yet we feel that nothing is final, that there is always more to be thought and said.

As academic historians of literature often say of books that unsettle them, *Fors Clavigera* lacks 'form'. It is true that we are pleased to read great works of literature and find that their structure is inseparable from their greatness, whether that structure is overt, as in a sonnet or a five-act play, or subdued, latent, underlying, as in books or poems that have some repeated rhythm or pattern of symbols. *Fors* is evidently not of this sort. Exegesis might reveal that it has themes. E. T. Cook, its first and only editor, found repeated concerns within its 650,000 words. But the return to any of Ruskin's favourite subjects does not thereby give form to *Fors Clavigera*. If, for instance, we were to extract all that Ruskin's letters tell us about Walter Scott, or heraldry, or public transport, then we would no doubt be wiser, yet still possessed by the feeling of troubled curiosity that *Fors* (or so I find) arouses in a person who seeks to understand the meanings that art and learning give to life, and who then finds that such meanings are ungraspable. In other words, we should regard *Fors* as art, not merely as comment and instruction.

★ ★ ★ ★

I am of course indebted to many learned writers. The first of them is Ruskin himself. The traditions of Ruskin scholarship were established within his lifetime by his followers W. G. Collingwood, E. T. Cook and Alexander Wedderburn, whose tasks were made easier by his frankness and generosity; and therefore my own puzzlements have been clarified by their accurate and detailed knowledge, which often had been gained at first hand. Obviously I do not owe a personal debt to men who died before I was born. None the less I feel 'fellowship', to use Helen Viljoen's word, with the first Ruskinians. They do not appear (to me at any rate) to be impossibly remote, and I gladly recognise their hands when I find their letters in archives. One or two people who had known Ruskin were still alive when I began to study his books. Kathleen Olander corresponded with James S. Dearden in 1961, telling him that 'Mr Ruskin' would not have liked to 'see the world as it is today'. That was no doubt true and may be true of many dead people. Personally, I think that the social progress achieved by the twentieth century was enormous, and am grateful to have lived at a time when liberal education encouraged and sometimes exemplified that progress. At the Courtauld Institute in the mid 1960s I learnt that the history of art was not necessarily a narrow discipline, and I owe much to the Courtauld atmosphere of those days, when in graduate seminars I was given the opportunity to advance the unorthodox view that Ruskin's later writing might be just as rewarding as his earlier work.

I should continue these acknowledgements with an apology. In the introduction to the first volume of this biography I wrote harshly of E. T. Cook. There is still no doubt in my mind that he tamed Ruskin's social views and wished to present him as a founder of his own political Liberalism. He was shy of Ruskin's religious life and did not fully appreciate *Fors Clavigera*. This said, I write deliberately to confess that I am more and more humbled by Cook's scholarship and dedication. I own a book from his library, William Bell Scott's *History and Practice of the Fine and Ornamental Arts* (1874) and am interested in its bookplate. In earlier days than Cook's such plates had often displayed a coat of arms, or represented a gentleman in his study, and perhaps gave a view of the bibliophile's house and parkland. Cook's design is of a more modern type. He used the late Pre-Raphaelite motif of the Igdrasil, the great tree whose branches support and nourish the universe. No doubt Cook was impressed by Ruskin's invocation of 'this fair tree Igdrasil of Human Art' in *The Laws of Fésole* (1877–8) and knew that the Norse image is discussed in Carlyle's *Heroes and Hero-Worship* (1841). I add that *Igdrasil* is also the title of the magazine of the Ruskin Reading Guild, a body founded in 1890.

The bookplate contains information and symbolism. The owner of the volume announces himself as Eduardus T. Cook, and we see that his address is 2, Tavistock Square. At the centre of the drawing is the 'River of Life'. Above this river are the arms of New College, Oxford. Two sketches at the top of the sheet are marked 'Brantwood' and 'Venice'. There are two mottos, 'Drink Deep or Taste Not the Pierian Spring' and 'Ars Longa Vita Brevis'. The Igdrasil is labelled 'Arbor Vitae'. On its various branches are inscribed the words 'Education', 'Art', 'Journalism', 'Poetry' and 'Politics'.

These we already knew to have been the main concerns of Cook's public life. The account of his career (by J. Saxon Mills, in *Sir Edward Cook, KBE*, 1921), does not suggest the idealism that we find in Cook's bookplate. Another branch of his personal 'arbor vitae' might have been blazoned with the word 'Learning'. Neither his journalism nor his occasional literary essays fully display the extent of Cook's knowledge. Only his work on the Library Edition of Ruskin's writings, unnoticed by the world at large, reveals that he was a man dedicated to study. The late Stephen Koss's *The Rise and Fall of the Political Press in England* (1981) describes the context of Cook's distinguished journalism and helped me to understand his ambitions. I owe thanks to Alan Lee of the University of Hull for writing to me about Cook. Some members of his family, in particular Islie Cowan, have encouraged me to think more sensitively about 'Uncle Teddy'.

I had a direct link with the second generation of Ruskin scholarship through James S. Dearden, to whom I am indebted in more ways than I can easily enumerate. Mr Dearden, a native of Barrow-in-Furness, only a few miles from Brantwood, was educated at Bembridge School and therefore knew John Howard Whitehouse. He became curator of the Ruskin collection at Bembridge in 1957. Mr Dearden arranged and catalogued the books, manuscripts and drawings that Whitehouse had bought but often had not troubled to unpack. This was the work of many years. Mr Dearden, as curator, solicited and welcomed gifts to the collection and, when Bembridge funds allowed, bought further materials. The vast Ruskin collection occupied an especially charming wing of the school, which is itself built on a breezy site on the southern coast of the Isle of Wight. This wing comprised two rooms that were used by visiting Ruskinians, Mr Dearden's study, and two large galleries, in which were housed many hundreds of drawings, a library and literally thousands of manuscripts. One especially revered bookcase, always locked, contained twenty-seven volumes of Ruskin's diary. These original volumes are also workbooks: Ruskin's notes, translations from Plato and so on are omitted from the published version of the diaries (ed. Joan Evans and John Howard Whitehouse, 3 vols., 1956–9). The Ruskin galleries at Bembridge had been built in 1930. Their architecture and fittings perfectly express the social ideals of progressive education at that date. Many Ruskinians wish that they had spent more time at Bembridge, which is in a slightly awkward situation for people who combine their research with university teaching. In the 1970s I was unmarried and had the good fortune to be unemployed. I lived in a succession of holiday chalets on the cliffs above Whitecliff Bay and walked to my work on sandy paths through fields. In all, I spent about a year in reading and taking notes on the manuscripts preserved at Bembridge. Mr Dearden was my guide, and has corrected many of my errors. The present book bids farewell to the unique atmosphere at Bembridge, for the Ruskin collection has now been transferred to the modern facilities of the University of Lancaster. My notes and references retain the Bembridge catalogue numbers.

Mr Dearden's *Ruskin, Bembridge and Brantwood: the Growth of the Whitehouse Collection* (Keele, Staffordshire, 1994) contains tantalising references to Ruskin material he managed to acquire from antiquarian book dealers in the Lake District in the late 1950s. All students of Ruskin make their own book collections, and I am grateful to friends who are booksellers as well as to the owners of bookshops all over the country who have preserved recondite material for many years. I give especial thanks to such dealers because, unlike Mr Dearden, I am not a disciplined collector, do not attend auctions and have only one rule: never go past a bookshop. One day I beat him. I went into a shop in Ryde on the Isle of Wight while Mr Dearden preferred to speed back to his school. My prize was Edward E. Cleal's *The Story of Congregationalism in Surrey* (1908), the book which tells us so much about the vainglorious activities of the Reverend Edward Andrews, one of Ruskin's first tutors. I remember the glee with which, in Lowestoft in 1988, I chanced upon a book with a similarly undramatic title, the Reverend S. A. Tipple's *Sunday Mornings at Norwood* (1895), which I knew would provide a telling self-portrait of the preacher who annoyed both John James Ruskin and his son.

Such books are not collected by many people. We are lucky to be able to collect them at all. Second-hand bookshops are a quiet, unsung glory of our national life. 'Ignorant as a bookseller', says Coleridge somewhere. He would not have possessed so much learning without assistance from the owners of bookshops. Among many other booksellers, I especially thank Deborah Clark of Messrs Francis Edwards, David Tobin of Walden Books, Jerry Umansco of the Flask Walk Bookshop and Paul Grinke of Messrs Quaritch. The late Harold Landry, a specialist in periodicals, kindly supplied me with many original numbers of *Fors Clavigera*, lent me his run of *St George* and gave me a copy of the list of subscribers to the *Ruskin Reading Guild Journal*, a periodical established precisely because it was so difficult for Ruskin's followers to find his publications.

Their problem was solved by the enterprise of Cook and Wedderburn's Library Edition, the *Complete Works of John Ruskin* (1903–12). Alas, it was expensive and only 2002 copies were printed. I am grateful to Barry McKay of Messrs Blackwells' antiquarian books department for his help when I acquired my set and to Dinah Birch for driving the thirty-nine large volumes in her small car from Oxford to the Isle of Wight; and then, in the following year, driving them back again. My library has been augmented by gifts of books from other Ruskinians, in particular Robert Hewison, and from publishers and literary editors, including Arthur Crook, John Willett, Holly Eley and Peter Townsend. Mikio Sumiya of the Ruskin Library of Tokyo sent me his facsimile edition of *Ruskin's Letters in the Mikimoto Collection* (1994). I treasure books given to me by Peter Carter, Jonathan Howard, Alister Warman and Malcolm Warner. The late Sir James Richards gave me his collection of pamphlets by Ruskin on architectural subjects, all of them extremely rare. As J. M. Richards, he is known for that classic work *An Introduction to Modern Architecture*

(1940), but he also had an especial interest in Ruskin's writings, however much he disagreed with them. On my shelves are many books that either belong to the dedicatee of this biography, Jeanne Clegg, or were given by her to me in the years when we worked on Ruskin side by side. One most precious book, Ruskin's own index to *Fors Clavigera*, is surely hers, but I shall keep it for a little while.

A pleasure of advanced years is to thank friends with whom I once shared a university education. Both Roger Tarr and Lynda Fairbairn were my contemporaries at the Courtauld Institute of Art. In the last three decades they have answered many of my questions about renaissance art. Lynda Fairbairn has made a singular contribution to Ruskin studies by identifying the mysterious woodcut of roses on a tomb that appears at the end of the July 1875 number of *Fors Clavigera*, and marks the death of Rose La Touche. The motif is copied, Ms Fairbairn points out, from a detail in an engraving after a painting by Fra Filippo Lippi, 'The Virgin gives her Girdle to St Thomas', which Ruskin would have found in the print room of the British Museum. Juliet Aykroyd, a friend since our Oxford undergraduate days, was my guide in Venice and Verona in the spring of 1976. I see from her notes of the time that one of the churches we visited was the Chiesa Evangelica Valdese, where I heard the authentic tones of a Waldensian sermon. Visits to other Venetian shrines were delightful. In this biography I observe that Ruskin's love for Verona is often overlooked. I thank Terence Mullaly for sending me the catalogue of his fine exhibition *Ruskin a Verona*, held at the Museo di Castelvecchio in 1966.

I owe particular debts to two senior scholars, the late John Sparrow and the late Richard Ellmann, with whom I talked about our shared interest in late nineteenth-century Oxford. Mr Sparrow told me a great deal about Walter Pater and Mark Pattison. In return, I fear, I introduced him to the especial horrors of the work of the Reverend R. St John Tyrwhitt. Neither of us could ever identify Alice Owen, the author of *The Art Schools of Medieval Christendom* (1876), though she was clearly an Oxford woman and to some extent Ruskin's protegée. My indebtedness to Richard Ellmann is of a wider nature. We discussed not only our overlapping biographical interests but also the nature of modern biography. I cannot say how much I gained from these talks. I recall only that they were both entertaining and moving. Dick Ellmann was the most serious biographer I have ever known. His seriousness was to some extent disguised. He liked a dash of wit and felt that a biographer should be tempted — though should not necessarily fall — into speculation. After his death in 1987 I inherited (helped by the kind hand of his daughter Lucy Ellmann) his filing cabinet and his typewriter. As a respectful gesture to a warm friend, a few sentences about Ruskin and Wilde in the present book were composed on the same machine that produced Ellmann's posthumously published *Oscar Wilde* (1988).

Biographers, no less than other historians, are bound by their sources. If I speculate, as I do when suggesting that Rose La Touche may have suffered from anorexia nervosa, then I hope to have stated that guesswork entered my thoughts. A difficulty in relating Ruskin's life is that we are able to discover a great deal about his character and activities, yet know very little about Rose La Touche, who influenced his life and writing in so many ways. They knew each other for seventeen years before Rose's death in 1875, and many of Ruskin's books after that date, in particular *Proserpina*, commemorate her spirit. It is none the less impossible to give a full portrait of Rose. Instead, we respond to the vivid feelings that she still arouses. A century and more after her early death, Rose seems as pathetic, elusive and exasperating as she was in life. We try to come close to her by guessing at the nature of her correspondence. Rose's habits as a writer of letters evidently reflect her character. She could write boldly to strangers, and entrance them; or sternly to people who had done no wrong. Her letters were often charming, not seldom annoying, and were always memorable. It is worth remarking that most of her letters were addressed to people who were older than she was. They wanted to help her, or to teach her, but Rose would not be taught and often was beyond help. In her letters were banal calls to piety, or sweet, baffling messages in the 'language of flowers'. Ruskin, when he saw her writing among the envelopes that were brought to his desk every morning, knew that he might be joyful for days afterwards, or filled with misery for weeks and months. In this way Rose directed — yet without true direction — the moods of her lover's books.

Of the correspondence between Ruskin and Rose, very little remains. E. T. Cook tells us that, after Rose's death, Ruskin was in possession of the letters he had written to her. The elder La Touches must have returned them, and we may interpret their gesture as a significant part of their reconciliation with Ruskin. All the letters Rose and Ruskin exchanged, hers to him and his to her, were preserved by Ruskin in a rosewood box that also held Rose *memorabilia* of various sorts. It was his most precious possession. The contents of the box would never be seen by biographers. As early as 1878, Ruskin's executor Charles Eliot Norton was suggesting that Ruskin's friends should 'make a holocaust of his correspondence'. Immediately after Ruskin's death in 1900 Norton wrote to Sir Leslie Stephen (who as it happened was then the Editor of the *Dictionary of National Biography*) that 'If it depended on me, there would be no further word of Ruskin or about him given to the public'. In June of that year Norton visited Brantwood and, with Joan Severn, made a bonfire in the garden above the house. On this fire they burnt the rosewood box. Norton had a liking for this sort of destruction, a propensity I believe to have been unnatural. We are fortunate that he was never given Ruskin's diaries, as at one time was a possibility.

Rose La Touche's diaries of 1861 and 1867 escaped Norton's bonfire. Although they are now lost, the diaries were still in existence in 1929, when Helen Gill Viljoen found these affecting autobiographical notes hidden behind some books on the top shelf of Ruskin's library. Viljoen transcribed the diaries but made no attempt to publish them. She bequeathed them to Van Akin Burd in 1974. In 1979 Professor Burd edited the diaries in his *John Ruskin and Rose La Touche*. Like all other Ruskinians, I am grateful to Professor Burd for his scrupulous attention to the scant evidence that tells us about Rose's life, and I have been encouraged by his conversation and correspondence. Both Professor Burd and I have drawn on the local (and theological) knowledge of the Reverend Robert Dunlop, pastor of the Baptist Church, Brannockstown, Co. Kildare. Pastor Dunlop's *Waters under the Bridge* (1988), a valuable account of Harristown and the La Touche family in the nineteenth century, was a gift to me from my friend Mary-Rose Beaumont, whose family are the present owners of Harristown.

Ruskin often said, in print as well as in letters and talk, that Rose La Touche had 'gone mad' or had been 'driven mad', and he used the same expressions about himself. I do not like the words 'mad' and 'madness'. They seem too abrupt and colloquial. Furthermore, when we say of a person who can walk, converse, read and write, that he or she is 'mad' — as we so often do — then perhaps we are lacking sensitivity. The word none the less serves, and at least it saves us from circumlocution. The present book is often concerned with madness. It is obvious that Ruskin's later life and writings give us ample and detailed information about a man who is losing control of his mind. Ruskin may indeed be called 'mad' as he writes beautiful, thoughtful sentences that were published in his books, are to be regarded as serious literary composition, and yet are so bizarre that we do not recognise them as part of rational discourse.

The evidence of Ruskin's approach to delirious madness has no parallel in English writing nor, probably, in the writing of any other culture. In this biography I present a great deal of such evidence and also describe Ruskin's behaviour when he was delirious; that is, when he talked wildly and disjointedly, apparently without any kind of sense, and while his ravings were often accompanied by physical violence. Previous biographies have assumed that Ruskin first went mad in 1878, at Brantwood. I believe that he was mad in Venice in 1876–7 and at Matlock in 1871. I have a rough and ready rule for saying that he was mad at these times: we know that he was subject to hallucinations while he lay in bed in the New Bath Hotel, or ruminated in his rooms in the Grand Hotel overlooking Santa Maria della Salute. What attitude should a biographer take to the records of actual or impending madness, and how do our reactions to Ruskin's madness affect our thoughts about his writing? And, in the first place, what drove him mad? I had the benefit of conversation with the late Quentin Bell about such matters. Professor Bell was of the opinion that I should give all my records of Ruskin's mental illnesses to a psychiatrist. He himself could recommend a psychiatrist, a man with literary interests. I thought about this offer, but not for long, and rejected it more by instinct than from reflection.

I give my thanks to Max Harper, of the Department of Psychological Medicine in the University of Wales, Cardiff, who has made an (unpublished) psychiatric study of Ruskin. The core of his diagnosis is as follows:

> In view of his family history of melancholia and suicide, the evidence of cyclothymic traits in his personality and the episodic nature of his psychosis, a diagnosis of manic depressive illness or schizo-affective psychosis seems more likely than the paranoid schizophrenia referred to in some texts, though the psychotic states were associated with paranoid delusions of considerable complexity and marked incoherence. The history also contains evidence of excessive activity with, in later years, massive and sustained retardation — contrasting starkly with the years of productivity and fluency.

Dr Harper notes that 'pathobiography' dates from 1860, when Henry Maudsley (1835–1918) first assembled notes on the subject of insanity in men of literary achievement. Pathobiography therefore has a relatively long history, but the genre has yet to produce its masterpieces or triumphs. I think that psychiatric studies can on occasion assist the literary biographer. James L. Halliday's *Mr Carlyle My Patient* (1949), for instance, is not highly regarded by Carlyle scholars but makes some acute remarks; and Halliday's book should be of interest to Ruskinians, for (without intending to do so) it suggests reasons why there was an especial emotional bond between Ruskin and Carlyle, whom his follower liked to address as 'Papa'. There is no doubt that most modern biographers have been affected in one way or another by 'developments in twentieth century psychology', to use Helen Gill Viljoen's words in the introduction to her first book, *Ruskin's Scottish Heritage* (1956). In this introduction she made it plain that she had been influenced by psychological studies. I in turn have been influenced by Viljoen's attitude to the central document of Ruskin's mental illness, the entries from the winter of 1878 that she edited in her *The Brantwood Diary of John Ruskin* (1971). In this work, however, she took a literary approach. Knowledge of literature, I am sure, tells us more about Ruskin than knowledge of psychiatry, and especially when we pay attention to the books that Ruskin himself produced.

All Ruskin's writings, including letters to lawyers or treatises on geology, are within the sphere and fall beneath the aegis of literature. His books were never written solely to instruct, nor simply to entertain. Although he never thought that he was contributing to literature, Ruskin could hardly take up his pen without shaping his thoughts in literary form. Once his youthful years had passed, purely creative writing in the form of poetry or fiction was beyond his capacity, as he well knew (and did not for an instant regret). In other ways he strove to give the form of art to his writing, as we may see in the nature, and the preliminary drafts, of such works as *Modern Painters* and *The Stones of Venice*. Then, in his later years, Ruskin made a strange art, as though he were unconscious of any literary model. Here is one reason why *Fors Clavigera*, which is the work of his final maturity as a writer, is so unusual, indeed without affinity: to a high degree *sui generis*.

Many 'wise, and prettily mannered, people', to use Ruskin's description of those who counselled him about his writing, find that he is to be valued most of all for his autobiography *Præterita*. This was not necessarily Ruskin's own view, especially since he had little interest in autobiography as such. Perhaps he was not partial to autobiographies because, in his day, the great majority of confessional books were written by adherents of the dissenting churches. Ruskin had no sympathy with their accounts of conversion experiences — which he caricatured in his description of 'unconversion' in a Waldensian chapel in 1858 — and disliked all recollections that were pious or self-regarding. Even St Augustine's *Confessions* were condemned: 'Religious people nearly always think too much about themselves'. The only autobiography that seems to have moved him was Carlyle's *Reminiscences*, which appeared in 1881 and led Ruskin to exclaim to George Richmond, in May of that year, that 'I think I shall have to write *my* reminiscences!'. *Præterita*, however, was not begun at that time and does not resemble Carlyle's memoir of his own life. (Nor, to our regret, do we find any extended description of Carlyle within *Præterita*'s pages).

Such omissions in *Præterita* are, I hope, partly repaired in the present biography. I have also attempted, for the most part silently, to correct *Præterita*'s numerous factual mistakes. Helen Gill Viljoen, in the introduction to her *Ruskin's Scottish Heritage*, was the first scholar to point to these errors. She believed that they vitiated the editorial apparatus of the Library Edition because *Præterita*'s authority had been held sacrosanct by Charles Eliot Norton and Joan Severn. Most subsequent writers have been content to allow for *Præterita*'s inaccuracies while praising the book's felicitous good temper. I do not believe the autobiography to be serene, however much Ruskin and his cousin Joan wished its narrative to be 'done prettily'. In my view it is best to consider each chapter of *Præterita* — sometimes, each paragraph — within the context in which it was written. The Ruskin who wrote the book's opening declarations in his father's Denmark Hill mansion in September of 1871 was not the same man who feebly tried to explain himself while living in a Sandgate lodging house in 1887–8. Very roughly, I distinguish three movements in the story presented by *Præterita*. First, we are given the earlier chapters containing material that had already appeared in *Fors Clavigera*. Secondly, we then read a touching series of somewhat disjointed reminiscences. Thirdly, there are seven chapters, after and including 'The Feasts of the Vandals', when *Præterita* is in decline. I explain the reasons for this decline in my discussion of Ruskin's circumstances during his months at Sandgate.

Most of *Præterita* concerns Ruskin's life before the death of his father: the love between John James Ruskin and his son is a constant theme of the autobiography. In a wider sense, much of Ruskin's general writing, especially in his later years, is about fatherhood. He continually thought of the ways that men learn their duties by considering parental wisdom. Ruskin believed (quite rightly) that the 'filial relation' is as beautifully explored by Walter Scott as by Virgil, and with more sympathy and invention. The topic may seem old-fashioned at the end of the twentieth century but surely has a permanent importance. I thank Mogador Empson for his thoughts on biography and many observations about fathers and sons; and I am indebted to John McLean for relating the local lore of the hinterland of Arbroath, the country of Scott's *The Antiquary* — 'Jonathan Oldbuck', the fictional character who provided John James Ruskin's *nom de plume* for his letters to the *Morning Post*, addressed from the Queen's Hotel in Norwood in 1861.

My thanks are extended to another Ruskinian with a Liverpool-Scottish connection, Peter Wardle, whose great-aunt was Edith Hope Scott, the author of the thoughtful *Ruskin's Guild of St George* (1931). She was a Guild member for half a century. Her name appears as a Companion of St George in a list drawn up by Ruskin in 1883. In 1932 she was in correspondence with Mahatma Gandhi and ensured that he received copies of *Fors Clavigera* while he was in prison. Mr Wardle, himself a member of the Guild of St George, continues Ruskin's work on the Guild land at Bewdley. I have been privileged to have the support of another Guild member, Olive Wilson, the granddaughter of Dora Livesey, the Winnington schoolgirl who could claim to be the Guild's very first member. The letters Ruskin exchanged with Dora, preserved by her granddaughter, have been an important source for this book. Anthony Harris, a former Master of the Guild of St George, is an artist who talks with equal enthusiasm about both Ruskin and Seurat. I thank him for the invitation to give a lecture to the Guild, on the subject of Carlyle and Ruskin, in 1986. I gratefully acknowledge the help of the Guild in allowing me to consult material at the University of Reading (papers now removed to the Ruskin Museum at Sheffield) and for permission to publish extracts from this material.

Yale University has always been a good friend to Ruskin studies. I have affectionate memories of the Yale students who read Ruskin with me at the Paul Mellon Centre for the Study of British Art in 1987–8. They were probably the first university students to consider *Fors Clavigera* since Ruskin's class at Oxford in 1873–4. (It is fair to add that Ruskin's group did so voluntarily.) I have been heartened by American interest in Ruskin and would be grieved if any members of Harvard University were to consider that I have not given fair treatment to Charles Eliot Norton. I benefited from the stimulating Ruskin conference and exhibition held in the Phoenix Art Museum in conjunction with the University of Arizona and especially thank Susan Gordon for her curatorial hospitality. Clair Cabot Constable helped me to complete the writing of this book and has told me of her childhood among American lovers of European art. Hilton Kramer, Roger Kimball and other friends at the *New Criterion* in New York have politely listened to my opinions on Ruskin studies in British and American universities.

I thank the Leverhulme Trust for a generous and timely grant, which

I hope soon to repay with a book about *Fors Clavigera*. I am grateful to other institutions and to many people for their long patience and continued help with my work. This foreword reiterates some acknowledgements already made in the preface to *John Ruskin: the Early Years* in ampler and (I hope) more interesting terms. I am indebted to Douglas Matthews for his compilation of the index, which covers both volumes. I am glad that the first volume brought friendly comments and corrections from John Hutchinson, Patricia Jenkyns, Georgina Sage, Charles Swann, Margaret Trumper and Alditha Wellington. My thanks also go to the late Trevor Aston, Candida Brazil, Miles Burnyeat, the late Catherine Carver, Bernard Cawley, the Revd R. G. Clarke, Morton Cohen, Esther Godfrey, Michael Henshaw, Molly Mahood, the late Colin Matthew, Geoffrey Milburn, Laura Mulvey, Sheila Rowbotham and Bryan Wilson. I am indebted to the Education Trust, Bembridge School and to the University of Lancaster for permission to publish letters and other material in their possession; and to the Bodleian Library, Oxford; the Houghton Library, Harvard University; the John Rylands Library; Trinity College, Cambridge; the Beinecke Rare Book and Manuscript Library, Yale University for allowing me to print letters that they have preserved. The Ruskin Literary Trustee, The Guild of St George has kindly given permission to publish many sections of Ruskin's published and unpublished writing.

T. H.
December 1999

JOHN RUSKIN: THE EARLY YEARS

CHAPTER ONE

1785–1837

John James Ruskin, the beloved father of the subject of this book, was born in Edinburgh in 1785. He was the son of John Thomas Ruskin, whose financial misfortunes, madness and suicide were to darken the lives of both his son and the grandson he never knew. John Thomas had gone to Scotland from London, where he had been born in 1761, the son of the parish clerk of St Bartholomew the Great. As a young man he had been apprenticed to a vintner, but gave up his indentures when, after his father's death, he removed to Edinburgh. There he became a grocer: in later years he described himself as a 'merchant'.[1] Writing *Præterita* a century afterwards, Ruskin claimed that his grandfather had married suddenly and romantically. That was perhaps because his wife came from a more genteel background. Catherine Tweddale was a daughter of the manse, and her forebears had owned land. Her father was the minister of the Old Luce church at Glenluce in Galloway. Catherine was sixteen when she married. With its usual wistfulness about family legends, *Præterita* recounts that when her daughter Jessie was born in the next year, 1783, the young mother danced 'a threesome reel, with two chairs for her partners'.[2]

John Thomas's grocery business was established in only a small way when John James, Jessie's brother, was born. Their situation improved when Catherine Ruskin inherited some money in 1794. The family then moved to a house in a better part of Edinburgh, St James Square in the New Town. Little is known of John James's childhood there. But it is clear that when he entered the Royal High School in 1795 he was an intelligent and serious boy. The school's headmaster was Dr Alexander Adam, a famous figure in Edinburgh society, the author of a Latin grammar and a book on Roman antiquities. John James quickly took to the classical authors and therefore benefited from Adam's stern regime and difficult Latin exercises. He had artistic talent as well: he studied a little under the landscapist Alexander Nasmyth. His ambition in life was to be a lawyer, a common way to advancement for an able Scottish boy without a background. Had he continued at school, in the democratic and competitive Scottish education that the Royal High School typified, John James surely would have risen in his chosen profession. However, when he was sixteen John Thomas insisted that he should go to London to begin a career in trade. John James obeyed, but he never forgot his disappointment: it is one reason why his own son's talents were so fostered. John Thomas probably had financial motives for dissuading his son from a legal career. He was expanding his business but was not doing so prudently. Acting as an agent for other merchants, he may even have speculated on his own account with remittances that were not his. At all events, we know that he did not wish to bear the cost of John James's further education, and that he wished his daughter Jessie to be settled with a practical tradesman. In 1804 he seems to have arranged that she should marry Patrick Richardson, a prosperous tanner from Perth. He was eleven years older than Jessie, and she did not marry him for love. 'Very submissive to Fates mostly unkind', was John Ruskin's view of his aunt's sad life.[3] She bore many children, lost six of them in childhood, was widowed, and died herself in 1828.

John Thomas was often away from Edinburgh. When both her children had left home Catherine Ruskin felt the need of family company. She wanted somebody to talk to, who would not be a servant but would help to run the house in New Town. Her choice fell on her niece by marriage, Margaret Cock. Margaret was the daughter of John Thomas's elder sister Mary, who had remained in the south of England when her brother had gone to Edinburgh. She had married a publican, William Cock, the landlord of the King's Head in Croydon, a small public house at the side of the market place, with two little bars and three rooms upstairs. Margaret Cock was born there in 1781. The tavern was not too large for her mother to run by herself when William Cock died. She was probably quite determined. Certainly she saw to it that her daughter got a dainty education, for a publican's daughter. Margaret attended Mrs Rice's Academy for Ladies, the best girls' school in Croydon. This might have led to a position suitable for a young lady, and the invitation from Scotland was almost such a thing. Margaret now changed her surname to Cox. In Edinburgh she probably concealed the lowliness of her background. Her modesty and carefulness became the tenets of her new life. *Præterita* describes her at this period as 'a girl of great power, with not a little pride' who 'grew more and more exemplary in her entirely conscientious career'.[4] She was by nature pious: seriously believing, that is, in the unchanging laws of her God. Her embroidery was excellent. She read a great deal in her spare time. She administered the Edinburgh household with firmness and efficiency, and was to do so for thirteen years. All her youth and young womanhood was given to this home. In these years she developed an unswerving love for her cousin, John James. In time he came to love her too. He was four years younger than Margaret, dark-eyed, romantic, a poetry lover, living by himself in London.

1. John James Ruskin, father of John Ruskin, by George Watson, 1802.

There was also much that was exemplary in his character, as Margaret knew with pride. Although he was not often in Edinburgh, their love did not suffer on that account, except in parting. Years later, Margaret recalled 'a night of passionate grief and tears spent upon the floor of her bedroom' after he had gone back to England to return to his counting house in a wine merchant's.[5]

John James Ruskin had discovered that he had the temperament of a businessman. This was what his father lacked. John Thomas was moody and extravagant. Always hot-tempered, he sometimes fell into black rages. It is recorded — from a hostile source, to be sure — that once 'coming home from one of his rounds a day earlier than he was expected, and finding his wife having a tea party, he in a fit of anger swept off the array of china into the fireplace'.[6] No evidence suggests that he was particularly mindful of his family: many letters indicate how tolerant they were of him. He was not always able to meet his financial commitments. Worse, he was not always inclined to do so. His business floundered and then collapsed. In February of 1808 Catherine Ruskin had to write to John James in London to tell him of its failure. The younger Ruskin immediately became the strength of the family. He undertook to pay off his father's debts. It was fortunate that a large part of them was owed to a Mr Moore of London for whom John Thomas had acted in Scotland and the north of England. Moore knew John James and admired him. Proceedings for bankruptcy were avoided.

In 1809, in the midst of this family trouble, John James and Margaret became engaged to be married. The engagement was to last for eight years. They had no prospects beyond those marked by John James's determination, and limited by John Thomas's insolvency. The young people's love for each other was to grow as they themselves grew older. Initially there was not a great deal of joy in it. Theirs was not a splendid match. It was as if John James were getting married to his duties. Cousin marriages were not regarded without unease. Margaret had no money and was the daughter of an innkeeper. Since John James felt that he could not marry until he had paid off his father's debts, the affianced couple had to resign themselves to separation and long labours. John James's industry was remarkable. He went for years without a holiday. Occasional visits to the theatre and to lectures were not enough of a recreation: he worked until his health was threatened. He wrote regularly to his family and, separately, to Margaret. She supervised an enforced move from New Town to a cheaper house at Dysart, on the Fife coast near Kirkcaldy. Later the Ruskins rented Bowerswell, a house on the east bank of the Tay, not far from

2. Margaret Ruskin, mother of John Ruskin, by James Northcote, R.A., 1825.

Patrick and Jessie Richardson in Perth. Margaret also applied herself to her own improvement. Dr Thomas Brown, later Professor of Moral Philosophy at the University of Edinburgh, was a family friend. He had been a mentor of John James's in his younger days and now was glad to advise Margaret on her reading. She taught herself Latin and even a little Hebrew. But in her loneliness she found her greatest comfort in the Bible.

In London, John James had risen to be head clerk of the wine importing firm of Gordon, Murphy and Co. By his exacting standards, it was not an efficient house. He complained to Margaret of 'their ridiculous stile which has resembled that of princes more than Merchants'.[7] He had a trusted but not powerful position and was conscious that the firm was not good enough for him. One other person thought the same. Pedro Domecq was a young Spaniard with French nationality. His family owned extensive vineyards in Spain and he was working in London to extend his knowledge of the wine business. Placed among the foreign clerks in Gordon, Murphy, 'he had not exchanged ten words in as many months' with John James when he decided to approach him with the proposition of a partnership.[8] But he had seen the thrifty young Scotsman at work, and discerned his qualities. The two men discussed the wine trade outside the office and found that they got on well. They determined to look for another partner with some capital. By happy chance they were both acquainted with Henry Telford. He was a Kentish country gentleman. His interest in life was horses. He hunted and went to every race meeting he could. But he never betted; and now he realized that he would not be risking his money by becoming a sleeping partner in Domecq's enterprise. Telford owned premises in Billiter Street, in the old City of London between Leadenhall Street and Fenchurch Street. Here the firm of Ruskin, Telford and Domecq was established. The amiable Telford gave advice when he was asked for it, sat in the office for only one month in the year, while John James was on holiday, and left matters to his younger partners.

John James had worked hard for his salary at Gordon, Murphy. He worked even harder now and in the years to come, as his intention was to build a fortune from his commission. He was helped by the boom in the wine trade after the Napoleonic wars. But his own industry, particularly in travelling, brought great rewards. He was entitled to boast, when he came to look back on the early history of the firm, that 'I went to every Town in England most in Scotland & some in Ireland, till I raised their exports of 20 Butts wine to 3000'.[9] His finances improved steadily after the foundation of the new business; prospects were excellent: but in Scotland there were more troubles with his father. John Thomas began to object to his son's engagement to Margaret. He perhaps thought that his son could now make a better match: but it is possible that his insensitive behaviour was part of the more general misanthropy that was overtaking him. We have hints of these difficulties in a letter home from John James in 1815:

> Oh my own Mother as you have always loved me will you and my dear Father assure Margt that you have both become reconciled to our Union & be happy — or will you see her & me both fall sacrifices to this anxiety. Neither her constitution nor mine are fit for a long struggle. I have already said that if it leads to eternal Ruin I will fulfill my engagement with Margt. I hope my Dr. Father will therefore no longer cause us any uneasiness . . . Oh if you expect me to make some efforts to keep the family united — do not let her on whom my life depends sink under my Father and your displeasure. The state of our worldly matters requires that we should not oppose each other in things to add to that distress . . .[10]

John Thomas was of course in no position to prevent the marriage. His son's letter, pleading yet firm enough, shows what great strains there were on his filial piety. It also shows his forbearance. What Margaret thought is not recorded. In later years she never mentioned John Thomas.

Only a couple of months after this letter, John Thomas broke down. Reports of his melancholia now indicate that he had fallen into madness. Six hundred miles to the south, John James wrote anxiously to his mother, to enquire how much money his father had been spending and how much the neighbours knew of what had happened. He asked her to forbid drink to him and to take over the family purse. It seems that John Thomas was raving and did not recognize his surroundings. His family did not know what to do with him. John James wanted him to be at home. He could not bear the thought of his father being committed to an asylum: 'If there be any possibility of the disease subsiding or if his intervals of reason are frequent I cannot endure the thought of his being altogether among strangers . . .'.[11] It was a tenderness that other members of the Ruskin family, sixty years later, would extend to his own son. Yet it was of a necessity compassion at a distance, and it was given to Margaret to nurse the man who had opposed her marriage. John Thomas did not fully recover, and was never able to carry on business again.

Two years after this breakdown, the whole family was broken by a series of deaths. In September 1817 old Mrs Cock of the King's Head died in Croydon. Margaret travelled south for the funeral. She had not been there long when the news came that Catherine Ruskin had died of apoplexy. John James went up to Edinburgh with Margaret to attend his mother's funeral, then returned to London. He left his fiancée, stunned by the deaths of her mother and her aunt, with a horror to face. Ten days later John Thomas Ruskin committed suicide. Margaret Cox was alone in the house with him: most accounts agree that he cut his throat.

* * * *

Three months later, as soon as was decently possible after such bereavements, John James and Margaret were married in Perth. There were no celebrations. Margaret had come to loathe the house at Bowerswell, as well she might. She wanted to leave Scotland as quickly and as quietly as possible. She never would re-enter Bowerswell, the house in which she had known so much unhappiness, not even when her own son was married there thirty years later. Margaret Ruskin was not a young wife. She was thirty-seven when she wed: she had waited long and suffered much. Nor were John James's financial troubles now over. John Thomas left debts of £5,000 behind him, money that would not be finally paid off for another ten years. But John James had bought and furnished a comfortable house for his bride. No. 54 Hunter Street, Brunswick Square, was a solid bourgeois building. It was part of a fairly recently built terrace. Each house had three storeys as well as an attic and a basement. There were areas in front and small gardens behind. In this house, quite near to Gray's Inn and the British Museum, near the open spaces in front of the Foundling Hospital, their only son was born on 8 February 1819.

John Ruskin remembered little of the Hunter Street house, and never revisited it in adult life. *Præterita* recalls the excitement of a very small boy watching the dustmen and coalmen. One London view stayed with him always, 'of a marvellous iron post, out of which the water carts were filled through beautiful little trap-doors, by pipes like boa-constrictors'.[12] He was less than five years old when the Ruskins moved from Hunter Street to a house outside London. This move accompanied not so much a change in status as a desire for a different domestic life. No. 26 Herne Hill, the Ruskins's home for the next nineteen years, was bought on a 63-year lease for £2,192. Four miles from 'the Standard in Cornhill',[13] the old coaching station from which distances from the capital were measured, it was a semi-detached

3. 54 Hunter Street, Brunswick Square, where John Ruskin was born in 1819. Photograph c.1950.

54
53

house of three storeys and a garret. Herne Hill is in fact part of the Norwood Hills, a ridge of the North Surrey Downs. This wooded country was watered by two streams forever dear to Ruskin, the Wandle and the Effra. From John James's new house, one of a group of four right at the top of the hill, one could see to St Paul's, to sailing boats on the Thames at Greenwich, to Harrow in the north and to Windsor Castle in the west. Below the hill were the rural villages of Walworth and Dulwich. The house itself was comfortable. Margaret Ruskin took most delight in the gardens. Ruskin recalled how she tended the lilac and laburnum at the front gate. At the back of the house she had the best pear and apple trees in the neighbourhood. The orchard was seventy yards long, a whole world to the small child who followed his mother while she planted and pruned, plucked the peaches and nectarines, and in the spring gathered almond blossoms, the first flowers after the snowdrops.

In this house Margaret Ruskin had the happiness of youth when she was forty. The long years of loneliness and waiting, the madness and the deaths, could all be forgotten. All her life Margaret was silent about those years. She had earned her happiness and there was no reason why she should dwell on the way in which she had earned it. She delighted in her child and in running her own home: she delighted in her love for her husband. The family letters from Herne Hill, written while John James was away collecting orders, seem often to be the messages of lovers twenty years younger than themselves: 'at night I go to bed saying tomorrow I shall hear from my beloved I rise in the morning rejoicing that I shall soon have your letter the rest of the day I delight myself with reading it and the thoughts of it . . .', writes Margaret to her husband.[14] Their intimate affection grew within the years of their marriage. Ten years after their wedding, twenty years after their engagement, John James is writing,

> My Dear my Lovely Margaret how do you contrive to inspire me with unfading Love to light up flames of passion that neither age nor familiarity can extinguish. I see you forever as young as sweet & oh I think each year still sweeter, decked anew in some fresh Beauty, in some new graces to hold me to charm me to stir my very soul with fiercer and warmer Emotions to make me think I am come into possession of some newly discovered Treasure. Such is the power of Innocence of pure womanly love & affection as they exist and adorn the sweetest the gentlest the most feminine of her Sex. If I began to love coldly I have come to love warmly & to feel every year something added to the force of my love & my admiration . . .[15]

4. 28 Herne Hill, by John Ruskin, his home in south London, 1823–42.

There are thousands of Ruskin family letters, since it was the Ruskins's habit to write every day when separated from any member of the family. John James was often away from home selling sherry, his firm's speciality, and other wines. He acted as his own salesman and as the only traveller for the firm. He would have no business with agents, but took all responsibilities on his own shoulders. This he continued long after he could have deputed work. John James had not come to the firm with capital, as Telford had with his bonds and Domecq with his Macharnudo vineyard. He contributed unwearying drive. Every night, from the commercial room of the best inn or coaching house in the town, he wrote home to his wife. This correspondence consists mainly of love letters, with talk about their son. There is little about the wine trade, and the part of the business John James must have hated: the deference to customers, the bonhomous negotiations with hoteliers and landlords, the long coach trips and the company he did not wish to keep.

John James was usually on the road for a fortnight to three weeks. Some of his itineraries can be reconstructed from the letters. In 1822, for instance, staying for one night in most places but for two or three in the cities, he went from Stamford to Newark, Leeds, Bradford, Kendal, Liverpool, Chester, Manchester, Warwick, Coventry, Leicester, Huntingdon, and thence back to London. This kind of tour did not change as the firm prospered. Fourteen years later his schedule was just as demanding. On 15 December 1836, he wrote to Margaret from Ipswich. In the next few days he was in Norwich and Yarmouth, returned to Norwich, then went on to King's Lynn. On Christmas Day he was in Lincoln — the Ruskins, being Scottish, did not celebrate Christmas — and on Boxing Day in Leeds. After that he visited Rochdale, Liverpool — staying at a hotel he detested, the Adelphi — Manchester and Birmingham. Again, the last of the sequence of letters is from Huntingdon, before reaching London and the 'head of all my possessions and heart of all my joys'.[16]

This hard-working, loving, rather proud man, stern but romantic, returned to Herne Hill from these exhausting trips, or from the long routine of the counting house, as one returns to peace, to order and love. Dinner was at half-past four, always. In summer the Ruskins took tea in the evening under the cherry tree, or in the parlour in winter, and John James would read aloud from Shakespeare, or Pope's *Iliad*, or his favourite Dr Johnson, or *Don Quixote*; classical books that were supplemented by the romantic poets of the day, in particular Byron and Scott.

A pillar of the household was Anne Strachan, young John's nurse, who had come from Bowerswell with the newly married couple and remained in their service all her life. She was a sharp-tongued, difficult person whom John Ruskin adored. Her endless disputes with Margaret Ruskin, about anything, were an accepted part of Herne Hill life, sometimes to the surprise of visitors. Perhaps she and Margaret quarrelled a little over John. Anne was a spinster; Margaret Ruskin, deeply attached to the son she had been lucky to bear at her age, spent more time with her child than was common in a similar 1820s household. Margaret would do anything for him, but she was totally unyielding in matters of right and wrong. She wrote to his father,

> Were he Son to a King, more care could not be taken of him and he every day gives proof of possessing quickness memory and observation not quite common at his age with this however I fear he will be very self willed and passionate — he has twice alarmed me a good deal by getting into such a passion that I feared he would have

> thrown himself into a fit this will I trust be cured by a good whipping when he can understand what it is for properly.[17]

Such disciplines were probably exaggerated in *Præterita*. Certainly Ruskin's claim in his autobiography that he lacked toys is incorrect. *Præterita*, or rather *Fors*, called the Herne Hill garden an Eden where '*all* the fruit was forbidden'.[18] This was not so. John Ruskin had toys, a rocking-horse, dogs, a pony, all the books and drawing materials he could wish for. *Præterita* is correct, however, to insist on the importance of the Bible in Ruskin's young life. Herne Hill was a paradise where Scripture was read every day. The Bible, Margaret's great solace in the years of her unhappiness, became the first principle of her son's serene childhood. Through it, he was taught to read and to remember. When John was three, his mother wrote, 'we get on very well with our reading he knows all the commandments but the second perfectly and the Lords prayer his memory astonishes me and his understanding too'.[19] This biblical teaching informs all Ruskin's later writing. The volumes themselves are familiar to the student of Ruskin. First of all was the old family Bible of the English Ruskin family, inscribed with the dates and hours of all their births, from John's great-grandfather's 'John Ruskin, Baptised Aprill 9th 1732 O.S.', to all his children and grandchildren; then the Baskett Bible of 1741 in which John James wrote his own birth and baptismal dates; and the Edinburgh Bible of 1816, which Ruskin opened when writing *Præterita* — noting then how the eighth chapter of first Kings and the thirty-second of Deuteronomy were worn dark, for they were his mother's favourite reading.[20] He learnt from this volume every morning, when his mother took out her own Bible from its silk bag with purple strings to begin the day and the day's learning.[21] Every single day of every week, from the time he began to read until he left home to go up to Oxford, Ruskin read two or three chapters a day with his mother and learnt some verses by heart. He wrote,

> She began with the first verse of Genesis, and went straight through, to the last verse of the Apocalypse; hard names, numbers, Levitical law, and all; and began again at Genesis the next day. If a name was hard, the better the exercise in pronunciation, — if a chapter was tiresome, the better lesson in patience, — if loathsome, the better lesson in faith that there was some use in its being so outspoken.[22]

In these morning sessions Ruskin also learnt by heart the Scottish paraphrases, the psalms rendered into eighteenth-century verse that were the hymns of the Church of Scotland. He learnt to speak them resonantly and rhythmically, giving as much attention to meaning as he would when reading from Scripture. Some literature seemed also sacred to the childish Ruskin. In *Præterita*, recalling that Walter Scott's Waverley novels were 'a chief source of delight' and that he could 'no more recollect the time when I did not know them than when I did not know the Bible', Ruskin nonetheless felt it right 'with deeper gratitude to chronicle what I owe to my mother for the resolutely consistent lessons which so exercised me in the Scriptures as to have made every word of them familiar to my ear in habitual music'.[23]

Contemporary romance and the Bible could co-exist. So could assiduous attendance at church and a cheerful home life. Letter after letter speaks of the high spirits and the happiness of Ruskin's childhood. An early one came about because John was full of things to say to his father and pretended to write them on his slate. Margaret invited him to dictate what he could hardly write: only the signature is in his hand:

> My Dear Papa I love you — I have got new things Waterloo Bridge — Aunt brought me it — John and Aunt helped to put it up but the pillars they did not put right upside down instead of a book bring me a whip coloured red and black which my fingers used to stick to and which I pulled off and pulled down — tomorrow is sabbath tuesday I go to Croydon on Monday I go to Chelsea papa loves me as well as Mama does and Mama loves me as well as papa does — I am going to take my boats and my ship to Croydon I'll sail them in the Pond near the Burn which the Bridge is over I will be very glad to see my cousins I was very happy when I saw Aunt come from Croydon — I love Mrs Gray and I love Mr Gray — I would like you to come home and my kiss and my love JOHN RUSKIN.[24]

This Richard Gray and his wife Mary were a Scottish couple who lived not far away in Camberwell Grove. Richard Gray was also a wine merchant. Without children of their own, the Grays enjoyed spoiling young John Ruskin. The cousins in Croydon mentioned in the letter were of another Richardson family, for Margaret's sister Bridget had married a baker of that name. They all lived over the shop in Croydon High Street. For the four boys and two girls who were the Richardson children Ruskin had 'a kind of brotherly, rather than cousinly, affection'.[25] In his early years they were much together. On at least one occasion Margaret expressed a fear that their rougher ways might be bad for John, but this does not seem to have become an issue. The Ruskins were not over-troubled by questions of social class.

Præterita gives a quite misleading picture of people living 'magnificently' on Herne Hill, giving splendid receptions, attended by coachmen in wigs. His parents, Ruskin claimed, could not enter such society because of their plainness and thrift: his father would not 'join entertainments for which he could give no like return, and my mother did not like to leave her card on foot at the doors of ladies who dashed up to hers in their barouche . . .'.[26] This is nonsense: there was no such society on Herne Hill. The visitors who did come to Herne Hill were numerous, and they were more interesting. John James's diaries show that he entertained practically every night, including Sundays. His friends and social circle we shall shortly examine. For the moment we can think of the Croydon Richardsons, who might come up to borrow the pony; friends of Margaret's who would have tea and play with her precocious, talkative son; a number of Scottish people; and friends who shared John James's literary and artistic tastes and belonged to the fringes of the literary world. They were the ones who would take up John Ruskin when he was fourteen or fifteen and introduce him to the excitement of meeting literary men and writing for publication.

Ruskin did not go to school until he was fourteen, and to this extent his childhood was sheltered. But there was no want of instruction. He had his mother's lessons, his father's reading and his own curiosity. From the age of ten he had tutors. He learnt to read and write early on. He copied maps and read the standard children's authors. He began Latin, at first with Margaret and then with John James, who often corrected his exercises by letter. There was much respect for learning in this Scottish household. John James was concerned for his own self-improvement. He had been denied the opportunity for study in his youth, and he wished to make up for it in his independence. In only a few years' time, his own reading and his son's would often coincide as they discovered books together. In the early '30s (as we may discover from his accounts) John James was buying such books for family use as Lindley Murray's *English Grammar,* a Hebrew grammar and a Greek grammar (the Ruskins used Dr Adam's Latin one, kept from Royal High School days). John Burke's *General and Heraldic Dictionary of the Peerage* was bought, along with works by Tacitus, Homer, Cicero, Cæsar and Livy. There was a Homer done into French, Chateaubriand (that was rather daring), and *Anecdotes of the Court of France*. John James bought a set of Scott's novels, Dr Johnson's *Dictionary*, and his *Lives of the Poets*. He subscribed to *Blackwood's Edinburgh Magazine* and every year bought a number of annuals. Maria Edgeworth's novels were there, and Bulwer Lytton's *Last Days of Pompeii.* The radical Hazlitt (whose lectures John James might have heard) was in this library, and so was Byron.[27]

Such books were the staple of Ruskin's childhood reading. We shall hear of many others, lesser known today, such as Bernardin de Saint-Pierre's *Paul et Virginie,* which had a minor effect on his later writing. The literary atmosphere of the Herne Hill parlour was felt through all Ruskin's life, for he felt that books given to him by his parents were peculiarly authoritative. John James was determined that his son would not enter trade and Margaret mentally dedicated her child to God, and wished that he might have an ecclesiastical career. They absorbed themselves in literature because they enjoyed it. Nonetheless, the cultivation of John's evident intellect and talents was somewhat forced. John James occasionally recognized that there was absurdity in the way he encouraged his son to great things, but that did not deter him from letters such as this:

> . . . the Latin being somewhat difficult I am astonished at your understanding it so well & writing so like a Classic Author. You are blessed with a fine Capacity & even Genius & you owe it as a Duty to the author of your Being & the giver of your Talents to cultivate your powers & to use them in his Service & for the benefit of your fellow Creatures. You may be doomed to enlighten a People by your Wisdom & to adorn an age by your learning. It would be sinful in you to let the powers of your mind lie dormant through idleness or want of perseverance when they may at your maturity aid the cause of Truth and Religion & enable you to become in some ways a Benefactor of the Human Race. I am forced to smile when I figure to myself the very little Gentleman to whom I am addressing such language . . .[28]

In fact, the 'little gentleman', ten years old when he received this communication (and there were others like it), was scarcely in need of encouragement. In this same year he wrote to John James,

> I do believe that the last year of my life was the happiest: and shall I tell you why? Because I had more to do than I could do without cramming and cramming, and wishing days were longer and sheets of paper broader . . . I do think, indeed I am sure, that in common things it is having too much to do which constitutes happiness, and too little, unhappiness.[29]

This now reads as a prophetic remark. All his life Ruskin felt that time was wasted, and worse than wasted, if any day had not been used for study. At the unhappiest times of his life he worked the harder, often then returning to those subjects which had brought him joy in childhood. Foremost among these was geology. Ruskin's lifelong dedication to the analysis of the materials of the earth began at about this time. John James was fond of saying that his son had been an artist from childhood but a geologist from his infancy.[30] He encouraged and perhaps initiated John's hobby when he brought home a collection of fifty minerals bought for five shillings from a local geologist in the Lake District. 'No subsequent passion had had so much influence on my life', Ruskin wrote in *Deucalion,* his collection of geological studies.[31] These golden pieces of copper ore from Coniston and garnets from Borrowdale were the more exciting in that they came from the romantic Lakes. But, like the cheap Bristol diamonds (transparent rock-crystal found in Clifton limestone) which John James brought from that centre of the wine trade, Ruskin valued his stones first of all for their visual particularity, for the way that they needed to be closely examined, pored over. They appealed to that love of detail which was so marked a feature of his visual sense. He liked to see how small, bright things stood against a background. On a family holiday in Matlock he was struck by the New Bath Hotel and

> . . . the glittering white broken spar, speckled with galena, by which the walks of the hotel were made bright, and in the shops of the pretty village, and in many a happy walk along its cliffs, I pursued my mineralogical studies of fluor, calcite and the ores of lead, with indescribable rapture . . .[32]

Ruskin began a mineralogical dictionary at the age of twelve. His first boyhood ambition was to become, as the famous Charles Lyell then was, the President of the Geological Society. In four or five years' time Ruskin progressed from making collections and classifications: he began to study the broader aspects of geology, its feeling for the great sweep and variety of the earth and its questioning of universal history. It led him early to intellectual life. He was attending meetings of the Geological Society, in those days a most animated institution, before he went to university.

★ ★ ★ ★

In 1828 there was an addition to the small Ruskin family. For some time Margaret and John James had been thinking of having John's cousin Mary Richardson, of the Perth Richardsons, to come to live with them after the death of her mother Jessie. It was a sad time. Jessie had been a comfort to Margaret in her years of exile. John had loved the visits he made as a little boy to the Richardsons' house by the Tay where the river ran just outside the back door, swift and sparkling, 'an infinite thing for a child to look into'.[33] John James wept bitterly at the thought of his sister's wasted life. But he now acted swiftly and generously to help the family. He settled one of the sons in business, gave money to the other two and brought Mary into his own home. She lived with the Ruskins until 1848 when, like John, she married. Mary was fourteen when she came to Herne Hill; from that time on John Ruskin had in effect an elder sister. They did not grow closer together as the years passed, but that was not through any lack of affection. In childhood they shared everything, from the Bible reading and drawing instruction to shared projects, expeditions and holidays. If John was the cleverer by far, Mary had four years' advantage of him. All in all, they made a contented pair. John James could not be as proud of Mary as he was of John, but he wrote to a friend, 'Mary Richardson is another treasure . . . she has an excellent understanding, & is really pious and withall possesses a Spirit & a naivete a Joyousness combined with the most perfect Innocence that makes her all we could desire.'[34] On Mary the Ruskins lavished the tuition that Perth had been unable to provide. With private tutors and at a day school in the neighbourhood she studied music, drawing, French, geography, dancing, writing, arithmetic and Italian.

A great event in the Ruskin family was the annual summer tour, wonderful holidays that opened vistas of exploration and romance. In a carriage lent them by Henry Telford, and later in one that they hired, the Ruskins toured all the parts of the British Isles that were picturesque or had literary associations. They went to Scotland, where they stayed at the Richardsons', in 1824, 1826 and 1827; to Wales in 1831; to the west of England in 1828; to Derbyshire in 1829, and to the Lake District in 1824, 1826 and 1830. Usually they set off after a ritual family feast, John James's birthday on 10 May, and were often touring for a matter of months rather than weeks, especially when their tours were extended to the Continent. 'I saw all of the high-roads, and most of the cross ones, of England and Wales,' Ruskin claimed.[35]

The Lake District, where he was to live after his parents' deaths, was from the first particularly dear to Ruskin. His earliest real memory was of being lifted up by his nurse Anne Strachan on Friar's Crag above Derwentwater. That was in 1824. In 1830 the Ruskins decided to make an extended stay in the Lakes. In the party were the three Ruskins, Mary Richardson and Anne. It took them five weeks to reach Kendal from Herne Hill, since they stayed in Oxford for a little while, lingered in the Midlands and made a detour to Manchester so that John James could do some business. Once among the Lakes they made excursions from the Low Wood Inn at Windermere and the Royal Oak at Keswick. John and Mary collaborated on a journal of the tour. One entry is of especial interest. It is one of the very few times that Wordsworth is mentioned in the early years of Ruskin's life.

> We went to Rydal Chapel in preference to Ambleside as we had heard that Mr Wordsworth went to Rydal . . . We were in luck in procuring a seat very near to that of Mr Wordsworth, there being only one between it, & the one that we were in. We were rather disappointed in this gentleman's appearance especially as he seemed to be asleep the greater part of the time. He seemed about 60. This gentleman possesses a long face and a large nose with a moderate assortment of grey hairs and 2 small grey eyes . . .[36]

From this journal, in the months after the tour, the un-Wordsworthian John wrote a poem entitled *Iteriad, or Three Weeks among the Lakes*. It contains 2,310 lines in rapid rhymed couplets and is a remarkable production for a boy of eleven. It is doggerel, of course; but a doggerel that nicely recaptures the excitement of Ruskin's picturesque explorations.

It was in 1829 that the Ruskins decided to find their son a tutor. John Rowbotham, who ran a little school near the Elephant and Castle and wrote simple textbooks, came to Herne Hill twice a week to teach him mathematics. A more important teacher was the Reverend Edward Andrews. The Ruskins worshipped in his church, the Beresford Chapel, Walworth. We must now consider the Ruskins's religious background. They gave their religious (though not necessarily their political) allegiance to the Evangelical party of the day. They appreciated Evangelicalism's fervour, its insistence on the authority of the Scriptures, its stress on salvation in the atoning death of Christ, its belief in the importance of preaching and its lack of interest in liturgical worship. Since the Ruskins believed in the inspiration of Scripture they tended to be suspicious of authority within the Church. They were openly hostile to Roman Catholicism and high church practices and doctrines. To some extent, their religion was formed by their Scottishness. John James's mother, we recall, was a daughter of the manse. Her minister father and other relatives were from Galloway, where there was a strong covenanting tradition: the National Covenant of the Scottish Presbyterians of 1638 was still real to the Tweddales. The Ruskins (and Anne Strachan) had respect for this heritage but were not bound to it. They were not rigid in religious matters, though Margaret was more conservative than was John James. Between their removal from Scotland to London and John Ruskin's matriculation at Oxford we may observe a number of shifts of allegiance. To place their son at the centre of the Anglican establishment, Christ Church, and to hope that he might become a bishop, was hardly to adhere to the Church of Scotland. No doubt the Ruskins changed their churches and their views in accordance with their own elevation in the English social scale. But this is to over-simplify, and ignores the effect of the peculiar ministers to whom they were attached.

Some of these matters became obscure in later years. The matter of the Ruskins's first London church is a case in point. Where did they worship when they lived in Hunter Street? We know that John was baptized in the Caledonian Chapel, Hatton Garden, by a bilingual minister who preached in both Gaelic and English. Only a little afterwards this chapel became famous and fashionable, for it was here that Edward Irving, Carlyle's friend, arrived from Scotland in 1821 and immediately became the most celebrated preacher in London. But the Ruskins did not attend his services.[37] *Præterita* speaks of 'The Rev. Mr Howell', whose preaching was imitated by the infant Ruskin. This mystified Ruskin's editors. They were unable to identify him because Ruskin had forgotten his real name. The Reverend William Howels, minister of the Episcopal Chapel, Long Acre (which was not very far from Hunter Street) was a Welshman. A contemporary description of Howels as a man 'of extraordinary inability & not a little eccentricity' is typical of much that was said of him at the time.[38] His preaching style was apparently ludicrous: perhaps this is why Ruskin's infant sermon in imitation of him, 'People, be good', was 'a performance being always called for by my mother's dearest friends'.[39] It is less surprising that the Ruskins should have been attending a chapel within the Church of England than that they should be sitting under a laughing stock. Be that as it may, it is worth considering that they preferred not to go to the Scottish revivalist sermons, with their emphasis on conversion, that Irving was currently giving at the Caledonian Chapel.

Edward Andrews, John Ruskin's first tutor, was an Evangelical Congregationalist. He may also have been a fabulator. He was famous for his ornate sermons, his energy, and his ambition.[40] He was described, not very flatteringly, as 'a sort of Pope' among his co-religionists. His position was apparently symbolized by his chapel in Beresford Street. Ruskin's recollection was this:

> Dr Andrews' was the Londinian chapel in its perfect type, definable as accurately as a Roman basilica, — an oblong, flat-ceilinged barn, lighted by windows with semi-circular heads, brick-arched, filled

> by small-paned glass held by iron bars, like fine threaded halves of cobwebs; galleries propped up on iron pipes, up both sides; pews, well shut in, each of them, by partitions of plain deal, and neatly brass-latched deal doors, filling the barn floor, all but its two lateral straw-matted passages; pulpit, sublimely isolated, central from sides and clear of altar rails at end; a stout, four-legged box of grained wainscot, high as the level of front galleries, and decorated with a cushion of crimson velvet, padded six inches thick, with gold tassels at the corners . . .[41]

This is accurate but satirical, and Ruskin does not mention that this memorial to suburban Congregationalism was more expensive than most of its type. Its cost led to Andrews's embarrassment, and nearly his downfall. He himself had put up some of the money to pay for it, but much more had been borrowed on a mortgage. This meant debts which could not be paid. Andrews finally had the humiliating experience of having his church doors shut against him by the mortgagee. He had to welcome his flock in the assembly room of a nearby public house, the Montpelier Tavern. This disaster occurred after the Ruskins had left the Beresford Chapel for a more established church. But they had known for some time that Andrews was no grave and steady pedagogue. One of Margaret's letters reports how the minister arrived at the house, uninvited, at eight o'clock in the morning:

> He came he said to ask me about Mrs Andrews state she had another child about three weeks ago and has continued getting weaker ever since . . . he gave me a long acct. of her complaints in the hope I am certain that I should say there was no chance of her living long the Drs say there is no hope of her he also enlarged much on the torment she had been to him for the last ten years . . . I think the Dr has wonderful talents the way he ran on while giving John a little insight into the Hebrews on monday . . . but he is certainly flighty not to say more and in many respects his habits manner of conducting his secular affairs tho' with the best and kindest intentions must to any woman with so numerous a family have caused much serious and distressing apprehension . . .[42]

Although the elder Ruskins spoke of Andrews's 'unwise indulgence of every caprice' they evidently did not consider him too little sedate to be their son's tutor.[43] They thought he had brilliance in him, and liked his popularity and energy. Crowds came to his sermons, and he toured his parish at a run. He had advanced views about women's education: he favoured the sort of liberal instruction that Mary was now receiving. The children of both families were friends. One of Andrews's daughters, Emily, was to marry Coventry Patmore and become the model for *The Angel in the House*: this was the family connection through which Ruskin was first to be introduced, by Patmore, to the Pre-Raphaelite Brotherhood. Emily and John went blackberrying in the summer when the latter was first taught by Andrews. He evidently was delighted with her, his tutor, and his tutor's sermons. He wrote to John James:

> Dr Andrews delivered such a beautiful sermon yesterday I never heard him preach one like it we were putting it down as well as we can for you to look at when we come home We that is Mary and I were so delighted with the sermon that we went out on a hunt for Dr Andrews . . .[44]

The summaries of the sermons that John and Mary made are preserved in some nine notebooks. Although they were often the work of Sunday afternoons in Herne Hill, they were not imposed on the children, and Ruskin says that he was eager to 'show how well' he could record the addresses.[45]

The Ruskins's Sunday indicates that they had abandoned the strict Sabbatarianism of Scotland. They went to church only once on the sabbath and there was no family worship at home. As so often, *Præterita* is slightly contradictory and tends to exaggeration. Ruskin wrote that 'the horror of Sunday used to cast its prescient gloom as far back in the week as Friday'.[46] But elsewhere in the autobiography he was eager to point out that his mother was not like Esther's religious aunt in *Bleak House,* who 'went to church three times every Sunday, and to morning prayers on Wednesdays and Fridays, and to lectures whenever there were lectures; and . . . she never smiled'.[47] John James invited friends to supper on Sunday evenings. The reading was devotional — Bunyan's *Pilgrim's Progress* and *Holy War,* Quarles's *Emblems,* Foxe's *Book of Martyrs,* and Mrs Sherwood's *Lady of the Manor* (borrowed no doubt from Mary), 'a very awful book to me, because of the stories in it of wicked girls who had gone to balls, dying immediately after of fever' — but that was hardly exceptional in a middle-class household of the day.[48]

* * * *

When John Ruskin reached the age of twelve his parents decided that he should be introduced to some more adult interests. A child of the early nineteenth century, in a house like the Ruskins's, would not normally dine with its parents; but on special days young John would now be allowed out of the nursery — his own room at the top of the house, which was kept for him until 1889 — to sit with John James and Margaret. At these meals, John James would read aloud from 'any otherwise suspected delight', literature that was not really for children.[49] A favourite was Christopher North's *Noctes Ambrosianæ*, then appearing in *Blackwood's Magazine*. This robustly tory column, full of coarse wit and savagery, John James read 'without the least missing of the naughty words'. More important than the *Noctes* was the enthusiasm for Byron. John James was passionately fond of his poetry. It is a mark of the independence of his taste that it did not notice any religious prohibitions. In many a home like the Ruskins's, this radical and libertine would have been prohibited. But John Ruskin soon came to know most of Byron. Margaret Ruskin made no objection. *Præterita* goes so far as to associate a shocking feature of Byron's life with Margaret Ruskin's literary tastes. Ruskin is discussing La Fornarina, Byron's mistress, the illiterate wife of a baker. Margaret Ruskin, he said 'had sympathy with every passion, as well as every virtue, of true womanhood; and, in her heart of hearts, perhaps liked the real Margherita Gogni quite as well as the ideal wife of Faliero'.[50] Twenty years later, in her sixties, Margaret would be an enthusiastic reader of Elizabeth Browning's 'Aurora Leigh'. She was not a prude, and in some respects she was a liberal mother.

At this time John Ruskin was first allowed to take wine and to accompany his father to the theatre. John James, a boy actor when at school, loved any kind of dramatic spectacle. His letters often reminisce about theatrical experiences: such things as

> . . . my first play — the *Fashionable Lover* & first afterpiece the *Maid of the Oaks* — I have never seen real Oaks with the pleasure I had in the painted Oaks in that piece. Then for greater excitement we had Lewis's *Castle Spectre* for which I waited an hour before the doors opened . . . Kemble was heroic in voice & person — but a few words of Mrs Siddons Lady Macbeth & Keans Othello dwell in my memory for ever . . .[51]

Margaret Ruskin would not go to the theatre herself, but although she thought that he ought not to contribute to theatrical charities, her husband's reactions were not a matter of contention. Nor did she object to her son being introduced to such pleasures. Ruskin was ever afterwards a lover of the popular theatre.

The freedom to enjoy the romance and excitement of contemporary literature was willingly granted to Ruskin in his boyhood. John James also indulged his son's taste in art, such as it then was. The elder Ruskin had kept up the artistic interest he once had when at school. He now, in 1831, readily agreed that John should follow Mary Richardson in taking drawing lessons. Ruskin's first instruction in art came from Charles Runciman. He was not a particularly good artist but was competent to show young people the elements of formulaic watercolour landscape. John Ruskin enjoyed these lessons and was good at them. With or without Runciman's encouragement, he soon felt the eagerness to make art as a splendid construct out of his paint box.

> I must say I was delighted when [Runciman] inquired for my colour box, and that not merely for the purpose of splashing colours over paper, but because I think that there is a power in painting, whether oil or water that drawing is not possessed of, drawing does well for near scenes, analyses of foliage, or large trees, but not for distance, or bare & wild scenery, how much superior painting would be, if I wanted to carry off Derwent Water, & Skiddaw in my pocket, or Ulles Water, & Helvellyn, or Windermere, & Low Wood, Oh if I could paint well before we went to Dover I should have such sea pieces, taken from our windows, such castles & cliffs — hanging over the ocean, And ships on those waters, in heaving commotion. There would be a night scene, with the waters in all the richness, of Prussian blue & bright green, having their mighty billows created, with Reeves best white, & the sky above, a very heaven of indigo, with the moon, & attendant stars pouring their bright rays upon the golden waters, in all the glory of Gamboge, with the moon shining out over the waters of Dover.[52]

* * * *

In 1832 John James's partner Henry Telford gave John a copy of Samuel Rogers's *Italy* for his thirteenth-birthday present. Rogers's poem is not now much read, but became greatly popular in its day. John James already had a copy in the house: the significance of this new book, the edition of 1830, was that it contained illustrations. They were vignette engravings after Prout, Stothard and, most of all, Turner. Rogers's first works had been published in the 1780s: his best-known poem, *The Pleasures of Memory*, is of 1792. *Italy*, whose first part was issued in 1822, its second in 1828, is in some ways a Byronic poem, though evidently the production of an older man. The 1830 edition, by virtue of its illustrations, has a place in the enlargement of the picturesque tradition that developed after the Napoleonic wars. The picturesque mode became less provincial, less conventional. Turner's imagination and new standards of naturalism were important in this change. In literature, the picturesque tourist who visited familiar sites was replaced by a traveller in search of personal fulfilment. This image was most potent in the third and fourth cantos of Byron's *Childe Harold.* Ruskin was slightly too young in 1832 to appreciate a connection between Byron and Turner; he had never yet been to the Royal Academy, and so did not see Turner's *Childe Harold's Pilgrimage*, exhibited with a quotation from the fourth canto, when it was shown there three months after he had received Telford's present. But Turner's steel engravings in *Italy* fascinated him: and soon he would set out to find the actual sites from which the drawings had been made. Now, in the spring of 1833, he went with his father to a printseller's in the City to look at the specimen plates for Samuel Prout's *Sketches in Flanders and Germany*. John James subscribed, the book was brought to Herne Hill, the family looked at it together. It was Margaret Ruskin who suddenly suggested that their summer tour this year should follow Prout's route: why should they not go to see all these wonderful places themselves?

John James had taken them on a short trip abroad in 1825, to Paris and Brussels, with a visit to the field of Waterloo. This was to be a longer tour. Their route was from Dover to Calais, and thence to Strasbourg by following the Rhine. The detailed itinerary, the choice of hotels, payment for horses and the like along the road were made by a courier named Salvador. The Ruskins's routine was that they would breakfast early and start early, travelling forty or fifty miles a day. They would reach their destination in time for dinner at four o'clock. After dinner John and Mary would go exploring, sometimes with Anne Strachan, sometimes by themselves. They had tea at seven in the evening. John then spent two hours writing and drawing before bed. When they drove up to Schaffhausen, however, on the eve of one of the great visual experiences of Ruskin's life, this routine had been upset. They had arrived after dark, the next day went to church, and were occupied in the town until late afternoon. Ruskin wrote:

> It was drawing towards sunset, when we got up to some sort of garden promenade — west of the town, I believe; and high above the Rhine, so as to command the open country across it to the south and west. At which open country, far into blue, gazing as at one of our distances from Malvern of Worcestershire, or Dorking of Kent, — suddenly — behold — beyond!
>
> There was no thought in any of us for a moment of their being clouds. They were clear as crystal, sharp on the pure horizon sky,

> and already tinged with rose by the sinking sun. Infinitely beyond all that we had ever thought or dreamed, — the seen walls of lost Eden could not have been more beautiful to us; nor more awful, round heaven, the walls of sacred Death . . . Thus, in perfect health of life and fire of heart, not wanting to be anything but the boy I was, not wanting to have anything more than I had; knowing of sorrow only just so much as to make life serious to me, not enough to slacken in the least its sinews; and with so much of science mixed with feeling as to make the sight of the Alps not only the revelation of the beauty of the Earth, but the opening of the first page of its volume, — I went down that evening from the garden-terrace at Schaffhausen with my destiny fixed in all of it that was to be sacred and useful . . .[53]

And this was so: Ruskin to the end of his days never ceased to study the Alps and to associate them with the broad principles of his teaching, even his political economy. The experience at Schaffhausen was as immediate as a revelation, and as subsequently haunting. As the family tour went on through Switzerland and to Italy, more and more of Ruskin's future work seems to be adumbrated. At the castle of Chillon, where Byron and Shelley had been before them, the Ruskins found Byron's name cut out by himself on a pillar. Salvador scratched out John's on the opposite side of the same pillar; and John James wrote in his diary that night, 'May he be the opposite of his lordship in everything but his genius and generosity.'[54] The Ruskins entered Italy by the most dramatic of passes, the Via Mala, and saw at Lake Como the very scene that Turner had illustrated in Rogers's *Italy*. They went on to Milan, then to Genoa and Turin; turned round, and entered the Alps again by the St Bernard Pass, thence driving to Vevey, Interlaken and Chamonix, the home of so much of Ruskin's mature work.

This rather odd party — how unlike the aristocratic youths who made the Grand Tour before them — travelled back to England through Paris. Here John first met the young woman to whom, soon enough, he would lose his heart. Pedro Domecq, John James's partner, was splendidly prosperous. He had inherited fine vineyards, his English business was successful, and so was his trade on the Continent. He proudly wore a royal crown over his arms, for in 1823 he had been appointed wine merchant to the king of Spain. The eldest of his five daughters, Diana, was engaged to be married to the Comte Maison, one of Napoleon's marshals. Domecq's other daughters, all much younger, were at home on holiday from their convent school. John Ruskin, at fourteen, was out of his depth. The adults were too sophisticated for him: at dinner the talk was of the recent death of

Bellini, whose *I Puritani* was then playing at the Italian Opera. His French was not as good as Mary's. He was a failure at the games the girls played: in *'la toilette de madame'* he had to impersonate parts of a woman's clothing. Dancing lessons that he had occasionally attended in Herne Hill disappeared from his mind when he was taken to the floor. The girls concluded that he was of no interest. All this was embarrassing enough. In two years' time, when he fell in love with Adèle-Clotilde, the second of the sisters, it would be torment.

* * * *

The Ruskins had left London in May and did not return to Herne Hill until late September. During the months they were abroad Ruskin had written constantly. He now began to write an account of the tour, illustrated by himself, in both prose and verse. Mary, previously his collaborator, was relegated to a copyist. Ruskin envisaged a finished work of 150 pieces of poetry and prose. He did not write as much as that, but his labours were prolonged. His prose, which relied on over-ornate models, was less successful than his verse.

> A low, hollow, melancholy echoing was heard issuing from the recesses of the mountains, the last sighing of the passing-away tempest, the last murmurs of the storm spirit as he yielded up his reign; it past away, and the blue rigidness of the transparent cavern of the glacier woke rosily to the departing sun.[55]

The poems are better. Often they imitate Walter Scott:

Bosomed deep among the hills,
Here old Rhine his current stills,
Loitering the banks between,
As if, enamoured of the scene,
He had forgot his onward way,
For a live-long summer day . . .
— No marvel that the spell-bound Rhine,
Like giant overcome with wine,
Should *here* relax his angry frown,
And, soothed to slumber, lay him down,
Amid the vine-clad banks, that lave
Their tresses in his placid wave.[56]

Ruskin was attempting to convert his experiences in Switzerland and Italy into the conventions established by the literature he knew. This was also the case with his art. His drawings are rather accomplished. They imitate not so much Turner as steel engravings after Turner. Perhaps more important than these artistic experiments was a piece of scientific work. The tour produced his first published prose. It is entitled 'On the causes of the colour of the Rhine' and was to appear in September 1834 in *Loudon's Magazine of Natural History*.[57]

In the autumn after his first continental tour the ebullient Dr Andrews was replaced. John Ruskin started to go to school, walking down the hill to Dr Dale's small establishment in Grove Lane, Camberwell. Thomas Dale is sourly recalled in both *Fiction Fair and Foul* and *Præterita*, but these memories ignore Ruskin's debt to him. Dale had a hard mind and liked argument. While Andrews had been easy to please, Dale was a continual challenge to Ruskin. He disliked polite learning and believed in the moral force of literature. Dale was older than Andrews and further on in his career. In 1833 he was the incumbent of St Matthew's Chapel, Denmark Hill: he had been successively a curate at St Michael's, Cornhill, and St Bride's, Fleet Street, where he was to return as vicar in 1835. Dale had made a verse translation of Sophocles and had issued his own poems as well as more purely devotional books. He was a Cambridge man and was involved with the new foundation of the University of London. The wonder is that he bothered with such a school as the one in Grove Lane. Ruskin was not prepared for his reception on his first day there. He had taken Alexander Adam's Latin grammar with him

> . . . in a modest pride, expecting some encouragement and honour for the accuracy with which I could repeat, on demand, some hundred and sixty close-printed pages of it. But Mr Dale threw it back to me with a fierce bang upon his desk, saying (with accent and look of seven-times-heated scorn) 'That's a *Scotch* thing!'[58]

Ruskin attended, in the mornings only, the school run by 'my severest and chiefly antagonist master' from September 1833 to the spring of 1835, when he broke down with a severe attack of pleurisy. For the first time in his life he mixed with a number of other boys. He seems to have ignored his schoolfellows, or at any rate to have stood apart from them.[59]

> Finding me in all respects what boys could only look upon as an innocent, they treated me as I supposed they would have treated a girl; they neither thrashed nor chaffed me, — finding, indeed, from the first that chaff had no effect on me. Generally I did not understand it, nor in the least mind it if I did, the fountain of pure conceit in my own heart sustaining me serenely against all deprecation.[60]

However, some boys at Dale's school remained friends for years. There was Edward Matson, son of a Woolwich colonel who took them to see army exercises; Edmund Oldfield, interested in Gothic architecture, of which Ruskin knew nothing; and Henry Dart, a clever and literary young man whom Ruskin was to meet again at Oxford. His closest boyhood friend, however, was not at Dale's but at Shrewsbury. Richard Fall was the son of a Herne Hill neighbour. In the holidays he often spent the mornings in John's room at the top of the house, now known as his study rather than his nursery. In the afternoons the two boys would go out with their dogs, animals for which Ruskin had great fondness, now and thereafter. Richard was practical and good-humoured, some kind of capitalist in later life. He seems to have had a robust attitude to Ruskin's poetry. He 'laughed me inexorably out of writing bad English for rhyme's sake, or demonstrable nonsense either in prose or rhyme.'[61]

However, Ruskin's feelings that he had a poetic vocation was encouraged by many around him. John James carried his son's poetry with him as he went about his business. Richard Fall's mockery was a kind of encouragement. Thomas Dale, a poet himself, was more interested in English literature than in the classics. Now, in Ruskin's teens, the possibility of publication arose. Charles Richardson, the eldest of the Croydon cousins, was apprenticed in the publishing company of Smith, Elder. Charles used to come to lunch every Sunday, often bringing with him new books that his firm had published. Smith, Elder would have seemed an estimable firm to John James. He knew their offices in Fenchurch Street, just around the corner from his own premises. He knew that the successful business had been built up by ambitious, hard-working, cultivated young Scotsmen. George Smith came from Elgin, Alexander Elder from Banff. Smith, John James's near contemporary, had begun in publishing by working for John Murray: on one occasion he had delivered proofs to Byron himself. Smith, Elder had been founded in 1816. By the time that Charles Richardson came to them in the early '30s they had developed an interesting list and were vigorously promoting their books. They were especially proud of the quality of the steel engraving in expensive art books, views by Clarkson Stanfield, or 'the Byron Gallery'. Another speciality was the keepsake annual. These books appeared every autumn and contained verse, some short pieces of prose and a large number of engravings. They were popular Christmas presents, especially for women, and the phrase that was often used in advertising them, that they presented 'sentiment refined by taste', is a good indication of their style.

Smith, Elder's annual, *Friendship's Offering,* was edited by Thomas Pringle. A superannuated poet, he had once mixed in the great Edinburgh circles of Scott and Lockhart but had been put out to grass after the failure, for which he was responsible, of the first issues of *Blackwood's Edinburgh Magazine*. Pringle it was who now in 1835 printed Ruskin's verse. The young man was proud enough to have his poetry in such a place as *Friendship's Offering*. Between 1835 and 1844 he published some twenty-seven pieces in the annual, as well as contributing to similar productions such as the *Amaranth*, the *Keepsake*, and the *Book of Beauty*.

Pringle took Ruskin to visit Samuel Rogers at his home in St James's Place, a signal honour. Ruskin was sufficiently inattentive to his manners to warmly congratulate the poet on the quality of the illustration of *Italy*. This was a rudeness, for the accurate jibe against Rogers was that the success of his poem, unnoticed when it appeared, was solely due to the format in which its second edition was published. As they left the breakfast party, Pringle warned Ruskin that he must be more deferential to great men. Another acquaintance of Pringle (and of Alexander Elder) was James Hogg, the 'Ettrick Shepherd', the contributor to *Blackwood's* and friend of Scott. When Hogg made his last visit to England he drove out to Herne Hill and was struck with Ruskin's talents. A little later on, while writing to John James, he enquired about the young poet's progress. The elder Ruskin replied in a proud but guarded manner:

> I will venture to say that the youth you were kind enough to notice, gives promise of very considerable talent. His faculty of composition is unbounded, without, however, any very strong indication of originality . . . I have seen productions of youth far superior, and of earlier date, but the rapidity of composition is to us (unlearned in the ways of the learned) quite wonderful. He is now between 14 and 15, and has indited thousands of lines. That I may not select, I send his last 80 or 100 lines, produced in one hour, while he waited for me in the city . . .[62]

Correspondence ensued, more verses were sent. Hogg wrote to Ruskin with advice, told him that he was leaning heavily on Scott and Byron, and invited him to come to stay in Scotland. The invitation produced a peculiar response, one that says much for the self-sufficiency of the Ruskin family:

> I cannot sufficiently thank you for your kind, your delightful invitation, one which it would have been such a pleasure, such an

honour for me to have accepted. Yet I cannot at this period make up my mind to leave my parents even for a short time. Hitherto I have scarcely left them for a day, and I wished to be with them as much as possible, till it is necessary for me to go to the university . . . I love Scotland, I love the sight and the thought of the blue hills, for among them I have passed some of the happiest days of my short life; and although those days have passed away like a summer-cloud, and the beings which gave them their sweetness are in Heaven, yet the very name of Scotland is sweet to me . . . But it is best not to think of it, for as I before said, I do not wish to leave my parents, and they are equally tenacious of me, and so I can do little but thank you again, again, and thrice again . . .[63]

To refuse such an invitation from a famous poet was perhaps over-reticent. But the literary ambitions of the young Ruskin were well served by a kind of society that existed between Herne Hill and the City of London. Its members were enthusiastically bookish, though often connected with commerce. They were Scottish or Irish, liberal in their interests but tory in every matter of principle. They inclined towards the Evangelical party in the Church but they distrusted enthusiasm. They opposed reform. They were bluff, hearty and convivial. These are the people we find at John James's dinner table, at parties which he might give three or four times a week. Here a minor literary world mingled with friends in the wine business. These backgrounds often overlapped. The Ruskins were good friends with Mr and Mrs Robert Cockburn, the first of whom *Præterita* describes as 'primarily an old Edinburgh gentleman, and only by condescension a wine-merchant'.[64] His wife was the Mary Duff of Lachin-y-Gair, a distant cousin of Byron's and reputedly the first of his loves. Another favourite guest was the Reverend George Croly. This Orange Irishman was renowned for his wit. John James thought him the most amusing man he had ever known, and wrote of his contribution to one party — at which the Cockburns were also present — 'Our table holds only Ten else there was fun for thirty if we could have had them.'[65] Croly was the rector of St Stephen's, Walbrook, in the City of London. He was not known for his piety, but rather for the zeal with which he held the ultra-Tory position that the constitution of 1688 was perfect and that England was the 'fortress of Christianity'.[66] He also had literary standing. He was a contributor to *Blackwood's Edinburgh Magazine* and was the author of poetry, fiction and expensively illustrated travel books: these last were published by Smith, Elder. Croly was of John James's age, and his poetry was now dated. In truth it had never been very fresh, and its derivation from Byron had earned him a derisive assault in *Don Juan*.[67] About this matter Croly cared not one fig.

Although he never wished to admit it, Ruskin owed much to Croly's belligerent opinions: they appear, for instance, in *The Stones of Venice*. As he grew up, the clergyman's acquaintances were to expand John Ruskin's knowledge of men of the world. This happened at an earlier age than *Præterita* would lead us to believe. Through Croly Ruskin met, for instance, Sir Robert Harry Inglis, an amateur of the arts and steadfast Tory Member of Parliament for the University of Oxford. Again through Croly, he touched the outside circle of those raffish Orangemen who organized the Tory press of the 1830s. They were people like William Maginn and Stanley Giffard, who had a background in *Blackwood's* and whose political views were identical with those of the Ruskins. Maginn had been a founder of *Fraser's Magazine,* which was read with appreciation in Herne Hill. But he was known for his intemperance and for his debts. Such a person could never be acceptable at the Ruskins's table.

A tory *littérateur* who was acceptable, and admirably so, now entered the family circle. After Thomas Pringle's death, Croly had a hand in the succession of the editorship of *Friendship's Offering*. It went to W. H. Harrison, who lived near to the Ruskins at Camberwell Green. This conservative-minded man spent his time between commerce and letters. He worked for the Crown Life Office and was registrar of the Royal Literary Fund. Now began a long-standing literary relationship, for Harrison not only went through Ruskin's poems with him, word for word, but looked after every detail of his manuscripts and saw them into press until 1870. In 1878, after his death, Ruskin wrote in 'My First Editor' an account of *Friendship's Offering,* Harrison's 'Christmas bouquet', in which he would assemble

> . . . a little pastoral story, suppose, by Miss Mitford, a dramatic sketch by the Rev. George Croly, a few sonnets or impromptu stanzas to music by the gentlest lovers and maidens of his acquaintance, and a legend of the Apennines or romance of the Pyrenees by some adventurous traveller who had penetrated into the recesses of these mountains, and would modify the traditions of the country to introduce a plate by Clarkson Stanfield or J. D. Harding . . .[68]

This was a slightly mocking description of the publication, for it was written at a time when Ruskin was inclined to deride his own early pretensions. He had forgotten, or chose to forget, how exciting those pretensions once had been.

* * * *

The first poems that Pringle printed in *Friendship's Offering* were inspired by the tour the Ruskins made in the summer of 1835. In the next year their route was through France to Geneva and Chamonix. From Innsbruck they crossed the Stelvio to Venice, which Ruskin now saw for the first time. They were in Venice in October, then came home through Salzburg, Strasbourg and Paris, reaching London on 10 December. Since they had left England on 1 June this was more than a holiday. For Ruskin it was an extended period of pure delight, perhaps the most important of the early family tours and a model for those long sojourns on the Continent which produced so much of his writing.

Ruskin now began to keep a diary. It was a practice he continued for the next fifty-four years, until he could write no longer. One or two of these diaries were lost, and occasionally pages were cut out of them. But they exist almost in their entirety and in many ways are an invaluable record of Ruskin's personal and intellectual life.[69] They say less about his private feelings than do his letters: nor do they tell us more about his mind than do his published writings. But in them we can often trace the origins and progress of his books, or sense the various moods of determination, or boredom, or sometimes exhilaration, that belong to the solitary work of a writer. This first volume of the diaries was clearly bought to make a serious record of the travels of 1835. In its 172 pages (nicely bound in red leather) there is no mention of any other member of the family party. Ruskin's aims were scientific. They were mostly inspired by his fifteenth-birthday present. This had been Horace-Bénédict de Saussure's *Voyages dans les Alpes* (1779-96). The Swiss geologist had expanded Ruskin's interests into landscape. Before, he had collected stones. Now he was interested in the orographic, the study of whole mountain ranges. Ruskin was always to feel that de Saussure was a kindred spirit. He 'had gone to the Alps, as I desired to go myself, only to *look* at them, and describe them as they were, loving them heartily — loving them, the positive Alps, more than himself, or than science, or than any theories of science.'[70] The diary is nonetheless dry. It begins with the 'stiff white clay containing nodules of radiating pyrites' he found at the bottom of the cliffs of Dover;[71] notes the sandstone tract in which lies Fontainebleau and the limestone, quartz and ironstone at Bar-le-Duc. At Poligny he began to study how the Jura mountains rise from the plain; and in the Alps he makes notes on glaciers and snow. By the time the Ruskins reached Chamonix there are diary entries three thousand words long describing mountain formations. These entries are accompanied by drawings and geological maps.

Another book carried on this tour contained a different form of expression. Ruskin was writing poems about what he saw. But he found his verse to be inadequate, too much bound to his stylistic models.

> I determined that the events and sentiments of this journey should be described in a poetic diary in the style of Don Juan, artfully combined with that of Childe Harold. Two cantos of this task were indeed finished — carrying me across France to Chamonix — where I broke down, finding that I had exhausted on the Jura all the descriptive terms at my disposal, and that none were left for the Alps.[72]

And so only 'Salzburg' and 'Fragments from a Metrical Journal' found their way into *Friendship's Offering*. The geological diary was sent whole to John James's friend J. C. Loudon to see if there was anything in it that might be extracted for his *Magazine of Natural History*. Loudon had already published Ruskin's short piece on the colour of the Rhine but seems not to have been attracted by the diary. He was nonetheless encouraging to his would-be contributor: he would print two long letters from Ruskin in 1836 and was soon to publish his first adult work, *The Poetry of Architecture*.

Ruskin's drawing became more interesting during this six-month stay on the Continent. Some sheets are scientific *aides-memoire*, or were meant to accompany putative geological articles; but others, especially of Unterseen, Fribourg and the Jungfrau are of artistic competence. A view of the Ducal Palace, though out of perspective, shows a talent for architectural drawing. He had probably benefited from a change of drawing master. In June 1834 he had left Runciman to study under Copley Fielding, the President of the Society of Painters in Water-colours, often called the Old Water-colour Society. This was a trade association and exhibiting society of minor artists who, by reason of their medium, were excluded from the Royal Academy. They were very largely landscapists, and had no interest in the large historical and mythological *machines* demanded by Academy taste. Their patrons were to a great extent middle class. They gave drawing lessons and supplemented their income by illustrating keepsake annuals and travel books. John James and his son were exactly of their time and class in their appreciation of Fielding, of Prout's picturesque views of the Rhine, of David Roberts (whom Ruskin was to copy), of James Duffield Harding (who was to be the last of his drawing masters).

Ruskin remembered them, in 1879, with the same affectionate and slightly satirical tone that he had used the year before in his memorial of W. H. Harrison and *Friendship's Offering:*

> What a simple company of connoisseurs we were, who crowded into happy meeting, on the first Mondays in May long ago, in the bright large room of the Old Water-Colour Society; and discussed, with holiday gaiety, the unimposing merits of the favourites, from whose pencils we knew precisely what to expect, and by whom we were never either disappointed or surprised. Copley Fielding used to paint fishing boats for us, in a fresh breeze, 'Off Dover', 'Off Ramsgate', 'Off the Needles' — off everywhere on the South Coast where anyone had been last Autumn; but we were always pleasantly within sight of land, and never saw so much as a gun fired in distress. Mr Robson would occasionally paint a Bard, on a heathery crag in Wales; or, it might be, a Lady of the Lake on a similar piece of Scottish foreground — 'Benvenue in the distance'. A little fighting, in the time of Charles the First, was permitted to Mr Cattermole; and Mr Cristall would sometimes invite virtuous sympathy to attend the meeting of two lovers at a Wishing-gate or a Holy Well. But the farthest flights even of these poetical members of the Society were seldom beyond the confines of the British Islands . . . It became, however, by common and tacit consent, Mr Prout's privilege, and it remained his privilege exclusively, to introduce foreign elements of romance and amazement into this — perhaps slightly fenny — atmosphere of English common sense. In contrast with our Midland locks and barges, his 'On the Grand Canal, Venice' was an Arabian enchantment; among the mildly elegiac country churchyards of Llangollen or Stoke Poges, his 'Sepulchral Monuments at Verona' were Shakespearian tragedy; and to those of us who had just come into the room out of Finsbury or Mincing Lane, his 'Street in Nuremburg' was a German fairy tale . . .[73]

★ ★ ★ ★

At the beginning of 1836 Pedro Domecq came to England with his four younger daughters, Adèle-Clotilde, Cécile, Elise and Caroline. John James invited him to leave the girls at his home while he travelled to call on some of his English customers. John Ruskin was now sixteen, and approaching his seventeenth birthday on 8 February. When he had met the Domecq daughters in Paris two years before, he had been socially at a loss. Now he was old enough to fall in love. The four extraordinary girls took possession of the house in Herne Hill.

John Ruskin thought all the sisters beautiful, but Adèle-Clotilde the most beautiful of them all. She was fifteen, fair-haired, graceful. She had been born in Cadiz but educated in France. She spoke French, Spanish and a peculiar broken English. She was accustomed to society in Paris; and her clothes, all Parisian cuttings and fittings, were from another world. Many years later, and in guarded terms, Ruskin confessed what had happened to him. He had never been 'the least interested or anxious about girls — never caring to stay in the promenades at Cheltenham or Bath, or on the parade at Dover; on the contrary, growling or mewing if I was ever kept there, and off to the sea or the fields the moment I got leave'.[74] Romantic love he knew only as a literary convention. That illusion was now shattered. He had never felt a great desire that was unfulfillable. But now the certainty, the safety and happiness of his young life all suddenly vanished. Adèle reduced him 'to a mere heap of white ashes in four days. Four days, at the most, it took to reduce me to ashes, but the *Mercredi des cendres* lasted four years.'[75]

Most youths desire girls before they first fall in love. John Ruskin, sheltered and innocent, experienced his sexual awakening like a blow. Ruskin said that it took him four years to recover, but it may have been very much longer than that. His first love was hopeless, as was to be the great love of his life. Adèle was physically near and in every other way remote. He could hardly converse with her, and she — through sophistication, or embarrassment — would have nothing to do with him. 'I endeavoured', wrote Ruskin, 'to entertain my Spanish-born, Paris-bred, and Catholic-hearted mistress with my own views upon the subjects of the Spanish Armada, the Battle of Waterloo, and the doctrine of Transubstantiation.'[76] It was a mistake to try to impress Adèle with his writing. He read aloud from his prose romance *Leoni: a Legend of Italy* and she laughed at it. All his attempts to please brought only 'rippling ecstasies of derision'.[77] She was not old enough, or perhaps nice enough, to have handled the business with whatever tact or kindness was demanded. Ruskin was made to feel that he was despised. The whole household was in chaos. John was besotted, Mary discomfited. The girls' French maid was in dispute with Scottish Anne Strachan. There had to be special arrangements for meals, there were difficulties about church services, and the girls were amazed at the morning Bible readings. All this incompatibility increased the bewilderment with which Ruskin met his humiliation. To make matters worse, his parents failed him. For they too had been living in a kind of innocence of his adolescence. One would have expected more from John James, especially when the obtuse Pedro Domecq raised the idea of a marriage, blithely going to his partner and 'offering to make his daughter a protestant'.[78] Such discussions were not precisely cut off; and John James and Margaret Ruskin merely waited for Adèle to go away and for it all to pass over.

Præterita tells us how, fifty years later, Ruskin could remember nothing more of what happened after Adèle's departure from Herne Hill. Benumbed by love at seventeen, he did not like to recall his suffering at the age of sixty-seven. In fact he had turned to literature. Under a mulberry tree in the Herne Hill back garden he set up a desk and wrote some of a Venetian tragedy, *Marcolino,* in which Adèle appears as the heroine Bianca. Several poems addressed to her, like 'The Mirror', 'Nature Untenanted', and 'Remembrance' went to *Friendship's Offering*. But love, though it prompts adolescents to write, does not teach them how to do it. Fortunately Ruskin now found a new kind of literary instruction. He now began to attend lectures and tutorials at King's College in the Strand. He was following an old schoolmaster. Thomas Dale was rising in the Church and had become the first Professor of English Literature and History in the new university foundation. His new incumbency was of St Bride's, Fleet Street. This was regarded as a significant position in the hierarchy of the Church of England. The professorship was also an important post. It had been offered to Southey, then Poet Laureate, before Dale was approached.

In this way, the lovesick Ruskin became one of the very first university students of English Literature, for Dale in King's College was the originator of English as an academic discipline. A letter to John James describes the beginning of the course.

> Four lectures on this subject have spoken of four celebrated authors of old time — Sir John Mandeville, Sir John Gower, Chaucer, and Wickliffe. We are made acquainted with their birth, parentage, education, etc; the character of their writings is spoken of, and extracts are read as examples of their style . . .[79]

After the lectures Ruskin, with two other students, went for tutorial discussions with Dale in his rooms in Lincoln's Inn Fields. Ruskin felt some antagonism towards his wholesome pedagogy. For he and Dale were in fact literary rivals. Dale too had a hand in keepsake annuals. He was the editor (and his wife's father was the publisher) of an annual called the *Iris*. This publication was in competition with *Friendship's Offering*, which Dale attacked in one of his prefaces, scorning such a 'Gorgeous Gallery of Gallant Inventions, or a Paradise of Dainty Devices, or a Phoenix Nest, or even a Garden of the Muses'.[80] Dale's own version of the keepsake format was dreary. The poems and tales were all religious, and were mostly by himself. His illustrations came not from the contemporary romantics of the Water-Colour Society but were engraved after Poussin, Correggio and Benjamin West.

After Dale's death one of Ruskin's essays was found among his papers. It was a heated defence of some contemporary authors. One of Dale's publications was an edition of the Reverend John Todd's classic *Student's Guide,* to which, in 1836, he contributed a foreword. Todd's manual contains a section entitled 'Beware of Bad Books' which condemns, among others, Byron, Scott and Bulwer. The essay Dale had set Ruskin was 'Does the perusal of works of fiction act favourably or unfavourably upon the moral character?', a title which gave the young author his first opportunity to write polemic. Ruskin began by attacking the censors of literature, first 'the old maid of jaundiced eye and acidulated lip, whose malice-inwoven mind looks on all feelings of affection and joy as the blight looks on the blossom . . . and makes amends for the follies of her youth by making her parrot say "Amen" to her prayers', and then the 'haughty and uncharitable sectarian' as well as 'home-bred misses who had set up for being pious because they have been set down as being ugly'. Most of the rest of this spirited essay is devoted to the proposition that Scott's fiction humanizes and polishes the mind, and that its effect is moral. Straying from fiction, Ruskin then attacked those who are 'filled with such a horror of Byron's occasional immorality, as to be unable to separate his wheat from his chaff' and concluded, 'We do not hesitate to affirm that, with the single exception of Shakespeare, Byron was the greatest poet that ever lived . . . His mind was from its very mightiness capable of experiencing greater agony than lower intellects, and his poetry was wrung out of his spirit by that agony.'[81]

Thus was dismissed Ruskin's English Literature tutor. His first writing on art dates from these months: it is rather like the essay he wrote for — against — Dale. This was an equally vigorous defence of Turner. Ruskin's admiration for the engravings after Turner in Rogers's *Italy* had not at first encouraged him to find out more about the artist. He copied them, but he did not seek out more examples. He had seen original Turners from 1833, when he first went to the Royal Academy exhibitions, but he had received mixed impressions from them. In 1835, before going on the continental tour, he was even nonplussed. *Keelmen Hauling in Coals,* for instance, which is a night piece, contrasted too oddly with Turner's version of Virgilian romance in *The Golden Bough.* The extravagant *Burning of the Houses of Parliament* Ruskin simply could not grasp: he was silent about the painting for the rest of his life. In 1836, however, Turner exhibited *Juliet and her Nurse, Rome from Mount Aventine* and *Mercury and Argus.* At seventeen, full of love and poetry, intellectually provoked by his new studies with Dale, he now had a new kind of æsthetic encounter. It was not passive: it was critical. It was the knowledge of being convinced by excellent painting. As he later explained, it was 'not merely judgement, but sincere *experience*' of Turner that he had now found.[82] When, therefore, in October of 1836, he read the review of the pictures in *Blackwood's Edinburgh Magazine* he was aroused not only by its wrongness but by its insincerity. The notice of the Royal Academy exhibition was by the Reverend John Eagles, an amateur artist and regular reviewer for the paper. He wrote of 'confusion worse confounded' in *Juliet and her Nurse*; in the Roman picture he found 'a most unpleasant mixture, wherein white gamboge and raw sienna are, with childish execution, daubed together'; while of *Mercury and Argus*, he pronounced,

> It is perfectly childish. All blood and chalk. There was not the least occasion for a Mercury to put out Argus's eyes; the horrid glare would have made Mercury stone blind . . . It is grievous to see genius, that it might outstrip all others, fly off into mere eccentricities . . .[83]

Ruskin's angry reply was in championship of the wronged. It was also elevated. He immediately made the highest claims for Turner. His imagination was 'Shakespearian in its mightiness'. For the first time we hear the voice of that extravagance in prose that would subsequently be an effortless attribute of his writing. He could now describe a painting like this:

> Many coloured mists are floating above the distant city, but such mists as you might imagine to be ætherial spirits, souls of the mighty dead breathed out of the tombs of Italy into the blue of her bright heaven, and wandering in vague and infinite glory around the heaven that they have loved. Instinct with the beauty of uncertain light, they move and mingle among the pale stars, and rise up into the brightness of the illimitable heaven, whose soft, and blue eye gazes down into the deep waters of the sea for ever . . .[84]

In such a way Ruskin's defence went beyond the inadequacies of Eagles's article. In its assertions of mightiness and attempts to write exalted descriptions of paintings we find the beginning of Ruskin's lifelong endeavour to celebrate Turner above all other artists.

John James thought that the reply ought to be shown to Turner before it was sent to *Blackwood's.* His son's writing was accordingly forwarded to the painter through Smith, Elder. This meant that there was a kind of contact between Turner and his champion. Soon Ruskin received a letter from him. It read:

> My dear Sir,
> I beg to thank you for your zeal, kindness, and the trouble you have taken on my behalf, in regard to the criticism of *Blackwood's Magazine* for October, respecting my works; but I never move in these matters, they are of no import save mischief and the meal tub, which Maga fears for by my having invaded the flour tub.
>
> P.S. If you wish to have the manuscript returned, have the goodness to let me know. If not, with your sanction, I will send it on to the possessor of the picture of Juliet.[85]

This characteristic letter closed the episode. The manuscript, the germ of *Modern Painters,* was not returned, and was not discovered for another sixty years. This was no great disappointment to Ruskin. He had not really thought that he would appear in *Blackwood's.* And he now had other things to think about, for a week after receiving Turner's letter he went up to Oxford to matriculate.

CHAPTER TWO

1837–1840

At the beginning of 1837, when John Ruskin left his family home to go into residence at Christ Church, he was just eighteen years old. A rather tall — five feet eleven — and slight young man, he had blue eyes, a thin face, a prominent nose and reddish hair. His hands were long and nervous. There was a scar on his lower lip where a dog had bitten him in childhood. His courteous manner was a combination of formality and attentiveness. There was something deliberate in his speech, however casual the conversation. The manner of rounding off his sentences was the legacy of the Bible readings and his mother's insistence on correct and meaningful pronunciation. From his father's Scottish accent perhaps came his burring way of pronouncing his 'r's. He was slightly dandyish. He enjoyed dressing up for special occasions. His clothes were not fashionable, usually, but they were distinctive. Two items of his dress were not to be altered throughout his life. He always wore a slim greatcoat with a brown velvet collar and never appeared without a large, bright blue neckcloth. Interested in other people, young Ruskin nonetheless had a certain conceit in himself. He was quite ambitious: he had started to think of winning the Newdigate prize for poetry before he matriculated. He was eager to learn but already preferred to go about learning in his own way. He was sufficiently sure of himself not to be put out by differences of social class, though he was certainly aware of such differences. He was kind, but self-willed. People noticed him, and he quickly made friends: nonetheless there was something about Ruskin which discouraged the hearty friendships of youth. In some ways he was simple and innocent, compared to his public school-educated contemporaries. But he was more advanced than they in other of the world's sophistications. He was an accomplished draughtsman, a published geologist and a published poet. He knew people in the London literary world: he was much travelled, and he was in love with a *Parisienne*. All in all, it is little wonder that few people understood this talented, complicated young man as he began his university career.

* * * *

Readers of *Præterita* will recall how 'Christ Church Choir', the chapter of autobiography devoted to Ruskin's Oxford education, invokes the regular morning worship of that collegiate body,

> . . .representing the best of what England had become — orderly, as the crew of a man-of-war, in the goodly ship of their temple. Every man in his place, according to his rank, age and learning; every man of sense or heart there recognising that he was either fulfilling, or being prepared to fulfil, the gravest duties required of Englishmen.[1]

The whole passage is more a vision than a memory, for these were the sentiments of a much older Ruskin. The Christ Church Ruskin knew at the end of the 1830s was not orderly, and duties were not much thought of. The buildings were dirty and dilapidated. Learning was perfunctory, undergraduates idle and riotous as often as not. The very choir of which Ruskin speaks was used to store beer, and dogs had to be chased from the chapel before services could begin. As elsewhere in Oxford, the customs of the eighteenth century lingered in Christ Church. An antique learning prevailed, and a sedentary Anglicanism hardly touched by the fresher piety of Evangelicalism. Wines, gambling and hunting were the undergraduate amusements. There were good men and conscientious students, of course: Christ Church was even then, as much as Oriel or Balliol, nurturing the first generation of great Victorian dons: but it was not an inspiring environment for such an eager young man as Ruskin.

Writing *Præterita*, the distinguished honorary student of Christ Church felt that he ought to say something positive about his undergraduate days in the college. Ruskin found this extremely difficult. He had not greatly enjoyed his Oxford career and he knew that his formal higher education had not been a significant part of his life. Ruskin had already had experience of a more liberal university course, one more suited to the future author of *Modern Painters*, at King's College. The routines of the classical curriculum at Christ Church were by comparison dull. Ruskin exaggerated when he said that he could only just grasp Greek verbs and that his Latin was 'the worst in the University'.[2] But the Christ Church Collections Book indicates that his attainments were little more than average. Perhaps he was too independent: he instinctively approached the ancient authors as he would read modern literature, liking some books and dismissing others. A cancelled passage of *Præterita* reveals that

> Both Virgil and Milton were too rhetorical and parasitical for me; Sophocles I found dismal, and in subject disgusting, Tacitus too

> hard, Terence dull and stupid beyond patience; — but I loved my Plato from the first line I read — knew by *Ethics* for what they were worth (which is not much) and detested with all my heart and wit the accursed and rascally *Rhetoric*, — which my being compelled to work at gave me a mortal contempt for the whole University system.[3]

Learning by rote was unwelcome to the young poet. The classical authors did not fit a sensibility that had already been formed by more modern literature. Even Ruskin's genuine love of Plato did not emerge for another twenty years. The learning that filled and inspired his earlier books came from the Herne Hill library, from architecture and painting and from a half-scientific observation of nature. At Oxford, therefore, his emergent powers are most to be seen in his letters to friends; in his poetry and drawing; and in the beginning of such independent prose writings as *The Poetry of Architecture*.

Of all Oxford colleges Christ Church is nearest to the Anglican establishment of Church and State. So numerous are its ties with government and the throne that the college, especially to its members, seems almost a part of the British constitution. Its undergraduate body is aristocratic: on occasion it is royal. The Visitor of Christ Church is the reigning monarch: the college's chapel is Oxford Cathedral. Its own constitution, with a dean, eight canons and subordinate officers, dates from its foundation by Cardinal Wolsey and Henry VIII. To enter this society was to renounce the nonconformist heritage of the Ruskin family. Moreover, John Ruskin entered Christ Church at the summit of its own hierarchies. He was a gentleman-commoner. This was a rank, which John James purchased, and was generally the province of sons of the nobility. Gentlemen-commoners had special privileges, the best rooms, sat together at separate tables, and were given distinctive gowns and mortar-boards (Ruskin preserved his, and wore it when he was Slade Professor). The social incongruity of a merchant's son among this aristocratic class was obvious. Yet Ruskin took his place without embarrassment. His contemporaries were tolerant young men. He was derided when he unwisely mentioned Adèle's aristocratic French connections: but there is otherwise no record at all that he was treated as a parvenu. Such friendliness was remarkable: G. W. Kitchin, later Dean of Durham, who was at Christ Church only five years later than Ruskin, had to become ingenious to explain it. He wrote in his *Ruskin at Oxford* that Christ Church was 'very like the House of Commons in temper; a man, however plain of origin, however humble in position, is tolerated and listened to with respect, if he is sincere, honest and "knows his subject" '.[4] This was not true of Christ Church, and did not cover Ruskin's case. The fact is that he maintained himself socially — as he would do all his life — by being exceptional.

John Ruskin cared next to nothing about what appeared to others as his peculiarities. To wish for his mother's company might seem unusual in a young man in a male society. Yet when Ruskin went into residence in Christ Church, his family came to Oxford with him. Margaret Ruskin and Mary Richardson moved into lodgings in the High Street, where John James joined them at weekends. Every evening, as his student life allowed, Ruskin went after hall to sit with his mother and cousin until Great Tom, the bell of the college, called out that its gates were closing. This arrangement continued throughout his three years as an undergraduate. What could more demonstrate the unity of the Ruskin family, and their disregard of other social forms? The naturalness of the Ruskins's dependence on each other was soon accepted by other students. Often enough, young men of the nobility came to the lodgings to meet Margaret Ruskin. There was something so frank and powerful in her, this innkeeper's daughter, that snobbishness was beside the point. The same was true of John James. For their part, the elder Ruskins took a lively interest in their son's friends, whether they met them or not. They were especially gratified that he got on well with such aristocrats as Lord Kildare, Lord March or Lord Somers — this last, Charles Somers Cocks, a friend with whom Ruskin was to have a lasting acquaintance. John Ruskin's social success was the triumph of the whole family: it represented the culmination of all that Margaret and John James had done together since the dark days, never mentioned, in Scotland.

Ruskin knew few people from other colleges, but within Christ Church the range of his acquaintance was wide. He belonged to none of those 'sets' which for G. W. Kitchin define college life. He would certainly not have allied himself to an 'idle or vicious set'; yet he was on terms with the gamblers, 'men who had their drawers filled with pictures of naked bawds — who walked openly with their harlots in the sweet country lanes — men who swore, who diced, who drank, who knew *nothing* . . .';[5] on terms too with the sportsmen, for we find him one day in an alehouse over Magdalen Bridge with Bob Grimston (later famous on the turf),

> . . . to hear him elucidate from the landlord some points of the horses entered for the Derby, an object only to be properly accomplished by sitting with indifference on a corner of the kitchen table,

5. Ruskin's Rooms at Christ Church, Oxford, by John Ruskin, 1839.

and carrying on the dialogue with careful pauses, and more by winks than words.[6]

These people were not really his friends, and those who were closer to Ruskin were still unlike him in temperament. Thus it was at Christ Church, so it would be all through his life. Ruskin became friendly with two of his tutors. The Reverend Osborne Gordon would remain a mentor to Ruskin until his death in 1883. He was the Censor of Christ Church and University Reader in Greek. His classical knowledge was more up-to-date, if less magisterial, than that of Thomas Gainsford, the Dean of Christ Church. The Dean was famed for his Greek scholarship yet knew no German, the language of all modern contributions to the knowledge of Greece. But it was not Gordon's more alert attitude to the study of the ancient world (it was not that much more alert) that made him important to Ruskin, but rather his deft, conscientious way of bringing a spirit of enquiry to his students. Gordon was a dry, rather amusing man, not too likely to be impressed; not so much argumentative as disinclined to be taken by other people's certainties. He was very sharp, almost cynical. But his personal kindness was not disguised by his quizzical ways. Ruskin learnt much from Gordon, and John James was delighted with him.[7]

Osborne Gordon was first among the people who knew the Ruskins socially in Oxford and also became visitors at Herne Hill. His earlier visits to south London were made to give Ruskin extra tutorials in the vacations. He was not paid for this help, but John James's account books show that in 1862 he gave the college the almost extravagant sum of £5,000 in Gordon's honour: it was to be used for the augmentation of poor college livings. The extra tuition indicates both that Gordon felt Ruskin's talent and that he feared that he would fall at the hurdles of the examination system. Side by side, in the Herne Hill parlour as in the rooms of the Peckwater quadrangle, they worked through the texts in which the older man found so much more pleasure than did Ruskin. Afterwards, as they walked in the familiar paths to Dulwich and Norwood, or from Oxford to Shotover and Forest Hill, Ruskin would expatiate on his religious beliefs: he was young enough to think that fervour would impress his tutor. Gordon, though, addressed himself on these walks 'mainly to mollifying my Protestant animosities, enlarge my small acquaintance with ecclesiastical history, and recall my attention to the immediate business in hand, of enjoying our walk, and recollecting what we had read in the morning'.[8] Ruskin found a similar attitude in another of his tutors. The Reverend Walter Lucas Brown was stimulating to Ruskin because he had an interest in æsthetic discussion. Like Gordon, he taught

Ruskin Greek (possibly a more wearisome task because of his charge's belief — reiterated in early volumes of *Modern Painters* — that a pagan civilization could produce nothing to compare with Christian art), and tried to win him from an inclination towards extreme Protestantism. He made Ruskin read Isaac Taylor's *Natural History of Enthusiasm* (1829), a now forgotten classic of Anglican moderation and caution against millenialism and suchlike notions: ideas which were greatly unwelcome in Christ Church but common enough in south London chapels which Ruskin knew well.

It is possible that Brown and even Gordon might have felt themselves a little under scrutiny when in the company of John James Ruskin. The wine merchant commanded any social gathering. His complete self-assurance, candid manner and outspoken opinions gave the impression of a man with whom one contends; but what made people yield to him was his good nature, however rough, and his desire of that fellowship which exists between people who love books. Evidently a man of the world, he still retained, even in his fifties, some of the ardours of his youth. John James was good company for younger men, and his enormous pride in his son was so unadorned as to be infectious: people thought more of Ruskin himself through knowing his father. His weekends in Oxford gave John James new opportunities to test his views on men and manners. He did not feel amiably towards eccentrics and he disliked lazy people in privileged positions. For these reasons he was likely to be taken with undergraduates. A contemporary of his son whom he especially liked was Henry Acland. This well-meaning medical student breathed outdoor virtues. He was not a sportsman but was brave at sailing and riding. Acland came from the Devon baronetage but had decided to stay in Oxford, where he also had family connections, to promote the study of the medical sciences. These plans had come to him early in life: he was the sort of man who plans his life. His association with Ruskin, who by comparison was quicksilver, was in many ways unlikely. It probably began because the slightly older Acland took Ruskin under his wing. But the friendship was permanent: more than forty years later *Præterita* recorded that it 'has never changed, except by deepening, to this day'.[9] While they were undergraduates, Acland guided Ruskin in the ways of Christ Church, discussed science with him, but most of all listened to him. Thereafter, Acland's more pedestrian mind was often exercised in keeping up with Ruskin. This had far-reaching consequences for them both, and for Oxford: it was Acland who first realized that Ruskin had the makings of a great teacher.

What Acland saw in Ruskin, Henry Liddell saw too, but his interest was to turn to suspicion. Liddell, whose name was once known to every schoolboy for his Greek lexicon, was to become the Dean of Christ Church. At this time he was a young tutor there, about to be ordained, and was already discussing with Henry Acland the changes they expected to make in the university. From a letter he wrote in 1837 we have a glimpse of Ruskin as he appeared to Liddell:

> I am going to . . . see the drawings of a very wonderful gentleman-commoner here who draws wonderfully. He is a very strange fellow, always dressing in a greatcoat with a brown velvet collar, and a large neckcloth tied over his mouth, and living quite in his own way among the odd set of hunting and sporting men that gentlemen-commoners usually are . . . [He] tells them that they like their own way of living and he likes his; and so they go on, and I am glad to say they do not bully him, as I should have been afraid they would.[10]

Liddell's appreciation of Ruskin's drawing was genuine, and he made sure that Dean Gainsford saw the numerous architectural and topographical studies with which Ruskin was engaged. He probably introduced Ruskin to the great collections of old master drawings which belonged to Christ Church and were then stored, in no particular order and with inexact attributions, in the college library. Liddell knew rather a lot about classical art, as Ruskin had to recognize. But his cool and Olympian manner did not encourage Ruskin to seek him out: he merely provided Ruskin with a minor lesson in growing up, his first experience of disliking someone without having good grounds for doing so.

It is clear that Ruskin lacked a friend who would be a comrade to him in the romantic discovery of literature and art. There could have been such a person — many of them, perhaps — in London, but they were not to be found in Christ Church. Here is one of those cases in which an 'advanced' taste belongs not so much to a younger generation as to a different class. Ruskin's outlook on art had more in common with his father, who was now in his late fifties, than with his peers at Oxford. In this connection the Ruskins's long and friendly acquaintance with Charles Newton is of interest. Newton, most famous today for his excavation of the Mausoleum at Halicarnassus, one of the wonders of the ancient world, was three years Ruskin's senior at Christ Church. He left the university to take a post in the rapidly expanding British Museum at the end of Ruskin's first year. They scarcely had the opportunity to become intimate, therefore, but they maintained a friendship for many years. The great difference between the classicist Liddell and the archæologist Newton was in temperament. Newton was entirely jovial. His opposition to Ruskin's picturesque, romantic and naturalist views was always cast in the form of a joke. This was often exasperating to Ruskin, though it was good for him to be laughed at; and so they concealed their differences in jests until, in the late 1860s, they simply drifted apart. At Oxford, Newton gave a shock to what Ruskin called his 'artistic conceit' when he asked him to draw a Norman arch to illustrate a talk at the local architectural society. The result, full of Proutian mannerism, was not adequate as illustration. It was salutary, Ruskin later reflected, to realize that his drawings had shortcomings. They might be admired elsewhere in Oxford, but that was not good enough. His progress as an artist had of course been halted during the time he attended the university.

Another person who found a use for Ruskin's ability with pen and brush was Dr William Buckland, the geologist and mineralogist who was a canon of the cathedral and the college. For Buckland Ruskin made diagrams. He was probably the only don at Christ Church that Ruskin had heard of before matriculating at the university, for he was a geologist of considerable repute. Ruskin had almost certainly studied his work at about the time that he was going to Dale's classes in English Literature. Buckland was perhaps as eccentric as any don in the annals of Oxford: at any rate, his eccentricities are amply recorded in those annals. In his house at the corner of the great quadrangle of the college he kept a bear, jackals, snakes and many other beasts and birds. These he ate. He claimed to have 'eaten his way through the animal kingdom'.[11] He also served his pets to his guests. It is not surprising that there are many stories about Buckland and his menagerie. They became Christ Church legends; and some of them were later transformed by Charles Dodgson into scenes in *Alice's Adventures in Wonderland* and *Through the Looking-Glass,* stories first told in the 1850s to the Alice Liddell and Angie Acland who were the daughters of Ruskin's contemporaries. Henry Liddell despised 'poor Buckland' and considered that he had not the intellectual calibre to occupy a chair in the university.[12] That is as may be. What is certain is that Ruskin's acquaintance with Buckland expanded his geological knowledge, and that this was an intellectual inspiration at a time when such inspiration was not easily found. At his table (where Ruskin managed to miss 'a delicate toast of mice') the undergraduate met 'the leading scientific men of the day, from Herschel downwards',[13] and was introduced to Darwin, thereby initiating a respectful debate between the two men that would last for decades.

We should remember that geology in the 1830s was a new and exciting science. The Geological Society, whose meetings Ruskin eagerly attended, was in the intellectual vanguard of early Victorian London. The science's dependence on field-work, its interest in natural phenomena and demand for close observation were suited to one part of Ruskin's temperament. His ambition to become President of the Geological Society was perhaps not unrealizable. For in this company the contributions of amateurs could be as valid as those of professionals, and a young man would be heard alongside seasoned practitioners. Ruskin's experience in geology later on gave him confidence to approach another new science in which he was an amateur, economics. The difference was that he did not expect to enjoy the study of political economy. Geology was pleasure, a wonderful combination of discovery and recreation. For this reason we should be wary of the theory that geological work now made progressive attenuations of his Christian faith. The bearing of geological research on the literal interpretation of Genesis did not trouble Ruskin at this stage. It might well have distressed his Calvinist mother, but both Ruskin and his father were skilled at avoiding the issue when they spoke with her about such matters. In any case, she could see nearer enemies. Her son's days as an undergraduate coincided with the headiest time of the Oxford Movement. Romanism was claiming many a young man. Margaret Ruskin greatly feared that her son might be touched by the scarlet attractions of this foreign religion. And yet we find that Ruskin, who already had a relish for theological controversy, had no interest whatsoever in the Tractarian debate. While Newman was preaching his famous sermons in the university church opposite Margaret Ruskin's lodgings, her son scarcely knew who he was. It was not that Ruskin considered the position taken by the Tractarians and then rejected it. He ignored them completely. A great religious current simply passed him by.

There was a Ruskin family tradition that Margaret, like the biblical Hannah, had dedicated her new-born son to the service of God. While he was at Oxford it was still her hope that he would enter the ministry. John James was non-committal on the subject, and kept quiet about his heart's desire, that his son should become a poet. Ruskin thought about the Church, but not as much as he thought about Adèle and poetry. He wanted to win the Newdigate. If Ruskin were to take a university prize it would not be in the classics. The prize for English verse therefore had to be his aim. When he looked at the previous winners he could see fair hope of success. The problems were that the subject was not of his own choosing and that the required length was greater than the lyric to which he was accustomed. But fluency and 'correctness' were highly regarded, and here Ruskin's experience of polishing verses with W. H. Harrison would no doubt help. Nonetheless, he failed to win the prize in the first two years that he entered the competition. He was beaten in the first year by another pupil of Dale's, J. H. Dart (in later life a translator of the *Iliad*), and in the second by Arthur Penrhyn Stanley, later Dean of Westminster. It is interesting to note that the second place in the year that Ruskin won the Newdigate was taken by Arthur Hugh Clough. The two men were never to become friends despite some shared interests. Their common task in 1840 was to write about 'Salsette and Elephanta'. These are Indian islands which were converted to Christianity. The obscure subject required research, some of which was undertaken by John James. Of the completed and victorious poem there is not much to say, except that the translation of recondite material to literary form was doubtless a useful exercise for the future author of *Modern Painters* and *The Stones of Venice*.

Ruskin's Newdigate poems are not interesting. Nor, in truth, are the verses from Oxford which are to be associated with Adèle. But we should not confuse their conventional sentiments with the real feelings of their author. Ruskin's love for Adèle was genuinely painful. It was also long-lasting. The new environment of Oxford did not help him to forget her. And if he lived a more adult life there, it did not equip him to control his despondent and yearning emotions. When Ruskin wrote his autobiography he looked back on those days with horror. Some passages which refer to Adèle were cancelled because of their bitterness. It is significant that they associate her with his ambition to carry off the Newdigate. Both were desired and both desires were vain. 'To be a poet like Byron was no base aim, at twelve years old,' Ruskin wrote, 'but to get the Newdigate at nineteen, base altogether.' So it was with his love: 'The storm of stupid passion in which I had sulked during 1836 and 1837 had passed into a grey blight of all wholesome thought and faculty, in which a vulgar conceit remained almost my only motive to exertion.'[14] Unfortunately, during Ruskin's second Oxford year Pedro Domecq sent his daughters to England for their further education. They were placed in a convent school at Chelmsford. John James had been asked by his partner to assume their guardianship and the girls were therefore brought into the Ruskin family. They came again to Herne Hill and stayed for weeks over the Christmas of 1838. Once again Ruskin was put on the rack. *Præterita* cannot conceal the feelings of waste evoked by the memory of that Christmas.

> Every feeling and folly, that had been subdued or forgotten, returned in double force . . . and day followed on day, and month

> to month, of complex absurdity, pain, error, wasted affection, and rewardless semi-virtue, which I am content to sweep out of the way of what better things I can recollect at this time, into the smallest possible size of dust heap, and wish the Dustman Oblivion good clearance of them.[15]

Relations with the Domecqs were further complicated when Pedro Domecq died in an accident at the beginning of the next year. We do not know how John James's guardianship then stood. But it is unlikely that he was involved in the negotiations which now took place for the betrothal of Adèle to a Baron Duquesne. She had never met the man, but appears to have readily acquiesced in her arranged marriage. Perhaps she was spiritless: one cannot tell. John James's concern for his son's sufferings appears in a letter to Margaret Ruskin:

> I wish John could have seen enough of Adèle to cure of the romance & fever of the passion. I trust my Dear Child will not suffer an Injury from the violence of feeling. I am deeply affected for him because I cannot bear that he should by anything have his feelings wounded. Please not to say anything until we know more.[16]

Thus John's parents adopted the policy of telling him nothing of what was happening. He did not know of the marriage plans for many more months. During this time he imagined that there was still hope that he might, some day, win some affection from her. When at last he discovered the truth the shock was brutal. There is only the bleak note in his diary, 'I have lost her'.[17] Two years later, on the anniversary, the diary records 'that evening in Christ Church when I first knew of it, and went staggering along down to dark passage through the howling wind to Childs' room, and sat there with him working through innumerable problems'.[18]

These 'problems' were from Euclid: as he would do all his life, Ruskin sought solace from love in work. He used study to drive out thoughts of Adèle. The official routines of a Christ Church education now seemed even more divorced from the real concerns of his life. His parents' hope that he would excel at the things that are highly regarded in Oxford meant that neither he nor they thought highly enough of the best achievement of his undergraduate years. This was the collection of papers known as *The Poetry of Architecture*.

Although it was not published within two covers until many years later (in an American pirated edition in 1873, and in England in 1893, when it was issued under W. G. Collingwood's supervision), we will say that Ruskin wrote a book when an undergraduate. It is a bold rumination on the picturesque. The origins of the book are in the first summer tour Ruskin made with his parents after matriculating. Between June and August of 1837 they drove together through Yorkshire, the Lake District and the Derbyshire Dales. The cottage scenery suggested a piece of writing to him: so also did the domestic architecture he noted when on a tour through Scotland and England the following year. The papers were written up in Oxford and were immediately printed in J. C. Loudon's *Architectural Magazine*. Ruskin signed them with the pen-name 'Kata Phusin', or 'According to Nature'. They attracted some attention, and the notice taken of them ought to have been gratifying. *The Times* wrote that the author 'has the mind of a poet as well as the eye and hand of an artist, and has produced a series of highly poetical essays'.[19] That was indeed so: *The Poetry of Architecture* is distinctively a poet's book, even though much of its prose style derives from Johnson's essays in the *Idler* and the *Rambler*, the Ruskins's favourite reading while on tour.

The Poetry of Architecture appears significant today because of its place in the picturesque tradition and because it announces the themes of such later writings of Ruskin's as, most notably, *The Seven Lamps of Architecture*. At the time of its composition, however, only the Newdigate seemed important, and Ruskin had little interest in his prose publication. When Ruskin took the Newdigate, in the summer of 1839, the prize was handed to him after a public recitation by none other than Wordsworth. Margaret Ruskin did not dare attend this ceremony, so splendid was it. John James wrote to Harrison, 'There were 2000 ladies and gentlemen to hear it: he was not at all nervous, and it went all very well off. The notice taken of him is quite extraordinary.'[20] Ruskin did not enjoy his triumph, for he was inconsolable about Adèle. Back at Herne Hill in the vacation his parents made uncharacteristically worldly attempts to put other girls in his path. Ruskin was polite to them. He seemed to be progressing in the world's honours, but his spirits were very low. On a family tour in Cornwall he spent hours looking at the sea. He was made a Fellow of the Geological Society: this was no comfort. In February 1830 he came of age, was given an income of £200 a year by his father and also received from him Turner's *Winchelsea*. The gift contained a dark augury, Ruskin later thought: 'The thundrous sky and broken white light of storm round the distant gate and scarcely visible church, were but too true symbols of the time that was coming upon us; but neither he nor I were given to reading omens, or dreading them.'[21]

Ruskin was referring to his first experience of breaking down after a prolonged spell of work: and he writes thus sombrely because he was reminded of more recent failures of his health and mind. In Ruskin, as in other literary people, overwork was usually self-imposed, almost self-willed. He seems almost to have courted its outcome. The breakdowns followed a rising pattern in which long hours of concentration were accompanied by nervous tension which in the end, straining and tightening, could not sustain the labour. Since Ruskin always filled his waking hours with mental activity, only those most sensitive to him could tell when danger was approaching. Nobody around him now realized how close he was to collapse. They were interested in the possibility that he might take a first. Soon after his twenty-first birthday, after consultations with Walter Brown, all parties agreed that Ruskin should not spend a further year at Oxford but should try to graduate with a splendid degree at the end of the next academic term. Ruskin, now living in rooms in St Aldate's, returned to his classical texts, his work coming 'by that time to high pressure, until twelve at night from six in the morning, with little exercise, no cheerfulness, and no sense of any use in what I read, to myself or anybody else: things progressing also smoothly in Paris, to the abyss'. By this Ruskin means Adèle's marriage. Three weeks after she was wed to another man, Ruskin was troubled late one evening by 'a short tickling cough . . . followed by a curious taste in the mouth, which I presently perceived to be that of blood'.[22] He immediately walked round to his parents' lodgings in the High Street; and the next day he was in London, with doctors.

CHAPTER THREE

1840—1841

Although he returned there eighteen months later to complete his residence and take his degree, this was the abrupt and slightly inglorious end of Ruskin's first career in Oxford. The doctors did not agree about his condition. He might seem tubercular: but there was no more blood. Certainly he was in a state of nervous exhaustion. Everyone thought that he should rest, and that he should winter abroad. At Herne Hill, feeling the empty relief that comes after prolonged intellectual exertion, Ruskin quietly obeyed medical advice. Occasionally he went into town. Then, at the dealer Thomas Griffith's home, on 22 June 1840, there was a momentous meeting. Ruskin's diary records:

> Introduced to-day to the man who beyond all doubt is the greatest of the age; greatest in every faculty of the imagination, in every branch of scenic knowledge; at once *the* painter and poet of the day, J. M. W. Turner. Everybody had described him to me as coarse, boorish, unintellectual, vulgar. This I knew to be impossible. I found in him a somewhat eccentric, keen-mannered, matter-of-fact, English-minded — gentleman: good-natured evidently, bad-tempered evidently, hating humbug of all sorts, shrewd, perhaps a little selfish, highly intellectual, the powers of the mind not brought out with any delight in their manifestation, or intention of display, but flashing out occasionally in a word or a look.[1]

'Pretty close, that, and full, to be seen at a first glimpse, and set down the same evening', Ruskin later added when he copied out the entry.[2] So it was: but of course he had thought many times about the probable character of the artist. He had also been studying Turner at the home of one of his connoisseurs, B. Godfrey Windus. In the light and airy library of his villa on Tottenham Green this retired coach-builder had collected some fifty Turners, as well as work by such artists as J. D. Harding, Clarkson Stanfield, J. B. Pyne and Augustus Calcott. Ruskin had obtained from the benevolent Windus *carte blanche* to visit the collection at any time he liked. From Windus he learnt not only about the pictures, their dates and subjects, but also about Turner himself. He heard many stories about the labyrinthine ways of selling work that were habitual both to the painter and his dealer. As the Herne Hill collection of paintings expanded, this was useful knowledge to the Ruskins. *'Be on your guard'*, said Windus of Griffith, Turner's agent, to John James at a private view, 'He is the cleverest & the deepest man I ever met with.'[3] This kind of talk seemed to make it the more difficult to approach Turner. Windus was not the sort of man to talk about the deep significance of Turner's art: Ruskin was left with the feeling that there were many great mysteries behind the evident beauties of his work. When he met Turner he did not suddenly realize anything about the man. The meeting told him what he had already suspected (and was well placed to know, with a father like John James) that rough and half-educated men can be as full as anyone of tenderness and imagination. So he observed Turner without venturing much conversation: certainly he did not tell him that it was he who had written the defence of his pictures three years before.

Ruskin had written the reply to the *Blackwood's* article just before he went up to Oxford: now he had met Turner immediately after leaving the university. These coincidences might have helped to persuade him that he had been wasting his time there, but since 'many people, including myself, thought I was dying, and should never write about anything', he was too preoccupied with his own health to think of Turner in connection with his literary career.[4] The annual continental tours had also been interrupted by Oxford: for three years the Ruskins had driven only through England and Scotland. As a winter in a Mediterranean climate had been prescribed, John James decided that the family should tour through France, rest in December on the Italian coast, and then tour home again the next spring. When autumn approached the Ruskins prepared to leave the Herne Hill house to the servants and the Billiter Street business to the clerks. They crossed the Channel in September of 1840 and did not return to England for ten months.

* * * *

In 1883, when Ruskin wrote down that rather dramatic reminiscence, that 'many people, including myself, thought I was dying', he happened to be travelling through France with his young friend, W. G. Collingwood. Their discussions often concerned universities, and his companion caught a sense of the bitterness Ruskin could still feel about his departure from Oxford. His biography of Ruskin used a poem of 1838–40, 'The Broken Chain', as 'a fit emblem of the broken life which it records'.[5] The poem, which appears to be derived from Coleridge's 'Christabel', was indeed begun in Oxford and finished on the Italian journey. But it is not especially autobiographical, whatever its deathly themes, and no public or private writings indicate that Ruskin was now afraid of dying. His diaries of that date are of some interest. Ruskin did not keep a journal in Oxford, but in his last days there began a new notebook on whose first page we find the declaration:

> I have determined to keep one part of diary for intellect and another for feeling. I shall put down here whatever is worth remembering of the casual knowledge that we gain so much of every day, in conversation, and generally lose every to-morrow. Much is thus lost that can never be recovered from books.[6]

This proposal has led some commentators to believe that somewhere there must be another diary with 'feeling' in it. But the existence of such a manuscript is unlikely. Ruskin closed his notebook of conversations after he had written the entry recording his first meeting with Turner. He then bought a new, red leather volume in which to write up notes on his foreign tour. The first thirty-four pages of this book have at some stage been cut out, and it begins now at Pontgibaud on 7 October 1840, as the party made their way through France to the Riviera. It describes weather, landscape and antiquities: the writing is almost entirely dry and factual.

The journey through France took six weeks. In Italy their route lay through Pisa, Florence and Siena. References to works of art in the diary now become more frequent. But there is little sense of engagement. At Florence,

> I still cannot make up my mind about this place, though my present feelings are of grievous disappointment. The galleries, which I walked through yesterday, are impressive enough; but I had as soon be in the British Museum, as far as enjoyment goes, except for the Raphaels. I can understand nothing else, and not much of them. At English chapel, and mass in the palace; fine music as far as execution went, but of German school . . . English sermon very good, a little slow. Walked after dinner, but weather very cold for Italy, and windy, and streets strangely uninteresting.[7]

From such entries, which are quite free of pretended appreciation, we would not expect a display of 'feeling' written down in another book. Ruskin's more formal writing at this date consists of letters to Edward Clayton, a Christ Church contemporary, and to Thomas Dale. The letters to Clayton were published with Ruskin's acquiescence in 1894, as *Letters of a College Friend,* when their sharper comments on theological subjects were omitted. Those addressed to Dale were found with the essay on Byron Ruskin had written at King's

College. They were edited and published by Dale's granddaughter in 1893. The letters are carefully composed and express conventional Protestant views. On architecture, however, Ruskin becomes more vehement. Writing from Rome, he comments,

> St Peter's I expected to be *disappointed* in. I was *disgusted*. The Italians think Gothic architecture barbarous. I think Greek heathenish. Greek, by-the-bye, it is not, but has all its weight and clumsiness, without its dignity or simplicity. As a whole, St Peter's is fit for nothing but a ballroom, and it is a little too gaudy even for that . . .[8]

Neither Rome nor Naples, at this date or any later date, were to win one word of approval from Ruskin. It was not merely that they contained so little painting or architecture that he liked: he felt an exaggerated revulsion from what he imagined to be the spirit of their civilization. To Dale he wrote of Rome:

> There is a strange horror lying over the whole city, which I can neither describe nor account for; it is a shadow of death, possessing and penetrating all things . . . you feel like an artist in a fever, haunted by every dream of beauty that his imagination ever dwelt upon, but all mixed with the fever fear. I am sure this is not imagination, for I am not given to such nonsense . . .[9]

Given such attitudes, it is not surprising how closely the Ruskins held to the English colony in Rome and Naples. They seem to have made no attempt to meet any Italians. In their letters, and in the diary of Mary Richardson, there is one repetitive theme: foreign disease and morbidity is contrasted with English health, Protestant honesty compared to Catholic superstition. Mary's diligent diary provides many reports of the sermons in English churches. In Turin she gives an account of a sect who were to be rather important to Ruskin's religious attitudes. There the family went to

> . . . a French Protestant service at the Prussian ambassador's . . . there were many of the poor Waldenses present, nearly all the women of the poorer class (who wore caps only) were of that interesting race who have suffered so much from Popish persecution . . . their church is said to be the purest of all Christian churches, but they are miserably poor . . .[10]

In Rome, 'I have today witnessed one of the grandest Church Ceremonies to be seen in the world — with the Pope in St Peters,' John James wrote home to W. H. Harrison. 'How infinitely I would prefer a sermon from Dr Croly.'[11] His son was in correspondence with

Croly (who, like Harrison, had never been in Italy) during this sojourn in Rome, and was exchanging views with him on these patriotic and anti-Catholic matters. The seeds of *The Stones of Venice* were being sown.

The English colony encouraged (as is the way in such communities) expatriate sentiments to harden into prejudice. Mary Richardson often reports on social evenings with such leading figures of the colony as

> Mr Rugg, quite a character, been in Naples for 11 years, was a martyr to rheumatism until he came here . . . a great admirer of Pitt whom he used to go and hear debate almost every night. Quite a man of the old times, a great Tory . . . does not approve of the High Church principles prevalent at Oxford . . .[12]

There were many like Mr Rugg, snobbish, curious to meet visitors, patriotic though an emigré, clinging to the politics of a previous generation. The colony was just large enough to have its own social stratifications. The Ruskins did not quite enter the height of English society in Italy. They took apartments in the same building as the aristocratic Tollemache family but were not on visiting terms. One of the Tollemache daughters, the beautiful Georgina, was greatly admired by Ruskin. He looked at her in church and later confessed that he followed her through the streets: but he could not meet her. The Ruskins inclined towards the artists. Mary tells us of studio visits they made, mostly to painters and sculptors now forgotten, but also to 'another English artist's, a Mr Lear, also young and promising . . .'.[13] One of these meetings was to be so significant as to reverberate through the rest of Ruskin's life. He had a letter of introduction to Joseph Severn (given to him by Acland), the painter friend of Keats, who twenty years before had brought the poet to Italy, and who himself had remained there ever since:

> I forget exactly where Mr Severn lived at that time, but his door was at the right of the landing at the top of a long flight of squarely reverting stair . . . Up this I was advancing slowly, — it being forbidden me ever to strain breath, — and was within eighteen or twenty steps of Mr Severn's door, when it opened, and two gentlemen came out, closed it behind them with an expression of excluding the world for ever from that side of the house, and began to descend the steps to meet me . . . One was a rather short, rubicund, serenely beaming person; the other, not much taller, but paler, with a beautifully modelled forehead, and extremely vivid, though kind, dark eyes. They looked hard at me as they passed, but

> in my usual shyness . . . I made no sign, and leaving them to descend the reverting stair in peace, climbed, at still slackening pace, the remaining steps to Mr Severn's door, and left my card and letter of introduction with the servant, who told me he had just gone out. His dark-eyed companion was George Richmond . . .[14]

As they passed him on the stairs, Ruskin had heard Severn say to his companion of him 'What a poetical countenance!'[15] The remark recalls us to Ruskin's artistic life, and his precarious health. Severn's friend was George Richmond, also a painter and one who many years before had known a great poet. With Samuel Palmer and others, Richmond had been a disciple of Blake: he had attended his deathbed and closed his eyes.[16] Two new acquaintances such as Richmond and Severn — they all met a day or two later — could not but prompt thoughts of the lives and deaths of poets. John James went with his son to the Protestant cemetery to visit Keats's grave. He afterwards reflected that young John Ruskin was made of 'sterner stuff' than the poet.[17] But when his symptoms returned and Ruskin coughed blood for three successive days the comparison with Keats was inescapable. The Ruskins's new friends were entirely sympathetic: Richmond especially showed a tenderness for the young and worried man. Thus, in grave circumstances, was born a friendship that would bind the Ruskins, the Severns and the Richmonds for years and decades to come. Joseph Severn's son Arthur would marry Ruskin's cousin Joan Agnew: his daughter Mary would be the bride of Ruskin's college friend Charles Newton. Generations of the Richmonds, neighbours of the Ruskins in Clapham and the Lake District, were always to be family friends: and when Ruskin was old and insane, Joan Severn would look to them for understanding and comfort.

It was the strain of writing the Oxford chapter of *Præterita* that brought about Ruskin's attack of madness in 1885. The autobiography alternates sour memories of the university with pleasing portraits of friends from these Roman days. Its composition was confused by Ruskin's mental breakdown, and this perhaps is why it does not dwell on the change that came over his spirits, and his health, when the Ruskin party left the south of Italy in the spring of 1841 and drove to Venice. Here he found a glad excitement such as he had not experienced before in a city. He was old enough now to feel connections between the buildings of Venice and a world of imaginative literature, romantic history and Turnerian art. What before had been only a foreign place, however picturesque, now sparkled with cultural implication. *Præterita* could not quite recapture the feeling. But an almost contemporary letter to Ruskin's Venetian friend Count Zorzi is eloquent of his rapture:

> Of all the happy and ardent days which , in my earlier life, it was granted me to spend in this Holy Land of Italy, none were so precious as those which I used to pass in the bright recess of your Piazzetta, by the pillars of Acre; looking sometimes to the glimmering mosaics in the vaults of the Church; sometimes to the Square, thinking of its immortal memories; sometimes to the Palace and the Sea. No such scene existed elsewhere in Europe, — in the world; so bright, so magically visionary, — a temple radiant as the flowers of nature, venerable and enduring as her rocks, arched above the rugged pillars which then stood simply on the marble pavement, where the triumphant Venetian conquerer had set them . . .[18]

Many long hours were spent in exploration of Venice, in drawing and note-taking. The diaries take on a different tone. Ruskin was on the mend: he had been rescued by his feelings for Venice's beauty. His convalescence seemed to be over. He became more active, even energetic, and the family set off for England. Their route on this return journey was through the Alps. The first day that they spent among the hills was a turning point in his life:

> I woke from a sound tired sleep in a little one-windowed room at Lans-le-bourg, at six of the summer morning, June 2nd 1841; the red aiguilles on the north relieved against pure blue — the great pyramid of snow down the valley in one sheet of eastern light. I dressed in three minutes, ran down the village street, across the stream, and climbed the grassy slope on the south side of the valley, up to the first pines. I had found my life again; — all the best of it. What good of religion, love, admiration or hope, has ever been taught me, or felt by my best nature, rekindled at once; and my line of work, both by my own will and the aid granted to it by fate in the future, determined for me. I went down thankfully to my father and mother and told them I was sure I should get well.[19]

CHAPTER FOUR

1841–1844

After this tour, Ruskin writes in *Præterita*, 'a month was spent at home, considering what was to be done next'.[1] He felt that to be 'free in mountain air' would restore him, and sought leave from his parents for an independent expedition. He planned to tour Wales with Richard Fall. They would be attended by a new family servant, the resourceful John Hobbs (known always as George to distinguish him from his master). Ruskin's parents asked him to call on the renowned Leamington physician, Dr Jephson, on his way to Wales. This he did: but his report of the interview persuaded his father that he should immediately return from his rendezvous with Fall in the Welsh Marches to place himself, until further notice, under Jephson's care. Thus began an odd six weeks in Ruskin's life, most of it spent in a lodging house near the Leamington medicinal wells. Jephson's regimen stipulated many glasses of these spa waters, a slender diet and regular hours. Ruskin observed these routines without interest. He took walks to Stratford and to Warwick Castle. His father came to visit him, as did Osborne Gordon. Ruskin scarcely considered preparations for the Oxford schools, which he now thought to sit the following Easter, but read Walter Scott, drew, and studied Louis Agassiz's *Recherches sur les poissons fossiles.* Out of boredom, he now wrote what was subsequently the most popular of his books, the short tale for children called *The King of the Golden River.* This story, 'a fairly good imitation of Grimm and Dickens, mixed with a little true Alpine feeling of my own', was written in fulfilment of a promise to a little girl, Euphemia or 'Effie' or 'Phemy' Gray, who had visited Herne Hill earlier in the year.[2] She was the daughter of George Gray, a Perth lawyer who administered the trust which controlled the affairs of Jessie Richardson's children. In seven years' time she would become John Ruskin's wife, and *The King of the Golden River* was published in 1850, in the second year of their marriage.

One detects an irresolution in Ruskin in Leamington. But he left Dr Jephson's care with a serious purpose in mind. He went to visit his tutor of two years before, the Reverend W. L. Brown. Now in his mid-thirties, Walter Brown had recently married. He had therefore been obliged to leave Christ Church for a college living at Wendlebury, a grey, distressed village, often flooded, nearer Bicester than

Oxford. His position there was no advertisement for a career in the Church, as Ruskin must have noted. For he had come to talk to Brown about his religious vocation. As he approached the end of his Christ Church career, the question of whether he should take orders was pressing. Certain of his contemporaries had entered the Church. His admired Osborne Gordon was just about to do so. His college friend Edward Clayton, to whom he was now writing long and serious letters, was ordained in this year: and Clayton, like many others, expected that Ruskin would follow him into the ministry. Margaret Ruskin would have been delighted to see her son in orders. But John James had reservations. He could not feel that his son's ardent temperament was fitted for the Church, for ardour in religion he mistrusted. He had written to Ruskin at Leamington, 'It sounds paradoxical but these Heavenly subjects require to be approached in the most worldly way. We must hold to the anchor of Rationality, stick to our Humanities.' Again — prophetically — he warned that 'too much enthusiasm in Religion ends in Selfishness or Madness'.[3] Ruskin's own views were not dissimilar. And Brown himself was a man of some caution in religious matters: he was the tutor who had made Ruskin read that dampening book, *The Natural History of Enthusiasm*. We know less than we might wish about the movements of Ruskin's mind in thinking of a religious vocation. No doubt he discussed the matter in prayer, and perhaps he was affected by a pleasure he took in disputing with Brown: however that may be, their subsequent correspondence shows that he left Wendlebury much doubting his suitability for a life in the Church.

His commitment to poetry also weakened in these few months. He began to realize that for him it had been an adolescent preoccupation. John James, tactfully, allowed his son time to sense that his real ambitions lay elsewhere. At no time did his father urge Ruskin towards any particular career. To say, as he now sometimes did, that he longed for his son to be a poet was scarcely to guide him towards professional opportunities. Nobody imagined that Ruskin's aspirations would lead to art criticism. But the notion of a principled attachment to art was growing in him. He would never be a professional artist, but at the same time he was determined to be more than a gentleman amateur. After his return to London in the autumn of 1841, Ruskin began drawing lessons with a new master. This was James Duffield Harding. To seek his tuition represented an æsthetic and almost a political decision. First, Harding brought Ruskin nearer to Turner. His current practice was to some extent based on Turner's art. Harding knew Turner: Ruskin had met his idol only once since their introduction more than a year before. Decades later, considering this, the writer of *Præterita* lamented that he had not known even a hint of instruction from Turner himself after their first meeting: 'If he had but asked me to come and see him the next day! He would have saved me ten years of life, and would not have been less happy in the close of his own . . .'[4] The older Ruskin knew how mechanical Harding's interpretation of Turner was. In 1841, however, his instruction seemed apposite. It also had a didactic element which, for a time, commended him to the Ruskins. Harding held an ideological view of post-Renaissance painting. His taste had a nationalist and Protestant bias. His beliefs may be crudely stated since they were themselves crude. He believed that nature and 'truth' were available only to contemporary Englishmen. He associated falsity in art with Catholicism, falsity in religion. He despised Claude's classical landscape and thought the Dutch schools ignoble. Such opinions, belligerently stated, had an effect on the young Ruskin.[5] Amplified and expanded, they would soon reappear in the first volume of *Modern Painters*.

★ ★ ★ ★

Today, it seems an absurdity to speak of Turner and Harding in the same breath. One we know to have the grandeur of a major artist: the other is a drawing master, who draws like a drawing master. But the first volume of *Modern Painters* is full of such juxtapositions. Ruskin's book rises to heights of appropriate eloquence in describing Turner and the old masters; then, immediately, we are in the company of Clarkson Stanfield, David Roberts, Copley Fielding, Samuel Prout, the minor domestic artists Ruskin saw on the walls of the Old Water-Colour Society. From his knowledge of art one would not anticipate a poetic or a magisterial book. *Modern Painters* was not written from great galleries, print-rooms and libraries: it was written from suburban south London. It is remarkable how *Modern Painters* can soar away from Ruskin's personal experience of art. It strikes great chords; but in it one finds still that boyish greed for painting and talk about painting that now began to overtake Ruskin, that made him haunt those places where he could see pictures, that directed him more and more to the Richmonds's in Clapham, where the talk was of nothing but art, that made him listen with more respect to Samuel Prout (often a visitor at Herne Hill), that sent him to Tottenham and Camberwell to call on Mr Windus and Mr Bicknell, collectors who liked to show off their treasures to this eager young man.[6]

Of course, it was Turner's acquaintance that Ruskin most desired.

The old painter was not easily approached. But he seems to have shown kindness on the earlier occasions when he met his admirer. The diary entry which records their second meeting is of 6 July 1841, just before Ruskin left town for Wales and Leamington. He writes, 'Dined with Turner, Jones and Nesfield at Griffith's yesterday. Turner there is no mistaking for a moment — his keen eye and dry sentences can be the signs only of a high intellect. Jones a fine, grey, quiet, Spectator-like "gentleman".'[7] Thomas Griffith, who that evening entertained not only Ruskin and Turner but also the water-colourist William Nesfield and the Royal Academician George Jones, attracted many an artist and connoisseur to his home at Norwood.

John James Ruskin was never among them, however: nor did he ever invite Griffith to Herne Hill. Probably the sherry merchant disliked the commercial style of the picture dealer. 'My father could not bear him,' Ruskin simply records.[8] As Ruskin's appetite for Turner grew John James's hostility to Griffith caused many difficulties. Griffith was Turner's sole agent, and John James was for that reason the less inclined to spend his money on Turner's paintings. This soured as nothing else could the tender relations Ruskin enjoyed with his father. One incident in particular remained with him all his life. It somehow grew in his imagination, filling him with resentment, a feeling that he had been thwarted in more than material possessions; a feeling that was replaced in later years by the sadness with which, in 1886, he set down the story:

> In the early Spring of [1842], a change came over Turner's mind. He wanted to make some drawings to please himself; but also to be paid for making them. He gave Mr Griffith fifteen sketches for choice of subject by any one who would give him a commission. He got commissions for nine, of which my father let me choose at first one, then was coaxed and tricked into letting me have two. Turner got orders, out of all the round world besides, for seven more. With the sketches, four finished drawings were shown for samples of the sort of thing Turner meant to make of them, and for immediate purchase by anybody.
>
> Among them was the 'Splügen', which I had some hope of obtaining by supplication, when my father, who was travelling, came home. I waited dutifully till he should come. In the meantime it was bought, with the loveliest Lake Lucerne, by Mr Munro of Novar.
>
> The thing became to me grave matter for meditation. In a story by Miss Edgeworth, the father would have come home in the nick

6. *Turner on Varnishing Day*, by S. W. Parrott, 1848.

of time, effaced Mr Munro as he hesitated with the 'Splügen' in his hand, and given the dutiful son that, and another. I found, after meditation, that Miss Edgeworth's way was not the world's, nor Providence's. I perceived then, and conclusively, that if you do a foolish thing, you suffer for it exactly the same, whether you do it piously or not. I knew perfectly well that this drawing was the best Swiss landscape yet painted by man; and that it was entirely proper for *me* to have it, and inexpedient that anyone else should. I ought to have secured it instantly, and begged my father's pardon, tenderly.

> He would have been angry, and surprised, and grieved; but loved me none the less, found in the end I was right, and been entirely pleased. I should have been very uncomfortable and penitent for a while, but loved my father all the more for having hurt him, and, in the good of the thing itself, finally satisfied and triumphant. As it was, the 'Splügen' was a thorn in both our sides, all our lives. My father was always trying to get it; Mr Munro, aided by dealers, always raising the price on him, till it got up from 80 to 400 guineas. Then we gave it up, — with unspeakable wear and tear of best feelings on both sides.[9]

Ruskin exaggerated the loss of the 'Splügen'. However, like all his many exaggerations, this one has the truth of being heartfelt. The 'Splügen' meant more than it ought to have done. All his life Ruskin was liable to confuse his personal history with the history of art. He was able to take certain works — like this Turner drawing, or della Quercia's Ilaria di Caretto tomb at Lucca, or Carpaccio's painting of St Ursula — and give them a private value that over-emphasized their cultural importance. This was usually in looking back over his life. In years to come, Turner's late Swiss drawings were to signify everything that he owed to his father. But in the spring of 1842 they were revelatory. Elegiac though they are, Ruskin could not now feel that they were the sunset of Turner's career, for he was gripped by the realization that they belonged to the dawning of his own. So strong was this feeling that it persisted long after Turner's own death in 1851, when Ruskin was still inclined, against all the evidence, to interpret the drawings as the beginning of a new stage in Turner's career, his 'third period', and would even force them on painters younger than himself, the Pre-Raphaelites, as a progressive example for their own art.

In Pre-Raphaelitism, again, Ruskin found the significance of an experience which *Præterita* recalls as of this time, the spring before he began to write *Modern Painters*.

> One day on the road to Norwood, I noticed a piece of ivy around a thorn stem, which seemed, even to my critical judgement, not ill 'composed'; and proceeded to make a light and shade pencil study of it in my grey paper pocket book . . . When it was done, I saw that I had virtually lost all my time since I was twelve years old, because no-one had ever told me to draw what was really there! All my time, I mean, given to drawing as an art; of course I had the records of places, but had never seen the beauty of anything, not even of a stone — how much less of a leaf![10]

Two pages further on in *Præterita*, Ruskin writes of how he came to draw an aspen tree in the forest of Fontainebleau a month or two later:

> Languidly, but not idly, I began to draw it; and as I drew, the languor passed away: the beautiful lines insisted on being traced, — without weariness. More and more beautiful they became, as each rose out of the rest, and took its place in the air. With wonder increasing every instant, I saw that they 'composed' themselves, by finer laws than any known of men. At last, the tree was there, and everything that I had thought before about trees, nowhere . . .[11]

Præterita attaches great importance to these experiences. But this section of the autobiography was written in 1886, after Ruskin's fourth mental breakdown, and without the *aide-memoire* of his diary. 'To my sorrow and extreme surprise,' he then noted, 'I find no diary whatever of the feelings or discoveries for this year. They were too many and bewildering, to be written.' Ruskin had forgotten that in 1872 he had given the diary in question to Charles Eliot Norton.[12] Had he been able to consult it, he would have found no reference to this moment in Fontainebleau. Nor can we now trace any drawing of an aspen, or of ivy, that would correspond with these reminiscences. Ruskin in old age was describing (as is not uncommon in *Præterita*) a gradual change of mind as a sudden conversion. The development of Ruskin's drawing from the picturesque towards naturalism was steady rather than dramatic. Certainly it cannot have been effected by a revelation while actually drawing. But it is clear that he was developing a theory of naturalism. Perhaps this contributed to a dissatisfaction with his rather artificial verses, though he nowhere says as much. He usually discussed naturalism in terms of his drawing. He wrote to Edward Clayton this year, 1841,

> Time was (when I began drawing) that I used to think a picturesque or beautiful tree was hardly to be met with once a month; I cared for nothing but oaks a thousand years old, split by lightning or shattered by wind . . . *Now,* there is not a twig in the closest-clipt hedge that grows, that I cannot admire, and wonder at, and take pleasure in, and learn from . . . Now this power of enjoyment is worth working for, not merely for enjoyment, but because it renders you less imperfect as one of God's creatures — more what He would have you . . .[13]

That is distinctly the voice of *Modern Painters,* the book that Ruskin could now have been considering, were he not distracted by his final Oxford examinations.

Ruskin returned to Oxford to take schools in the spring of 1842. He was far past his undergraduate life. Not even the proud John James cared much about the examination results. Ruskin took a peculiar degree. It was an honorary double fourth, which indicated success and failure in about equal measure.[14] John James brought the Dean of Christ Church a hamper of wine and took his son back to Herne Hill. Ruskin this spring seems pointedly the 'Graduate of Oxford', the pseudonym with which *Modern Painters* was to be signed. There were many things that he wanted to do in London. His examinations interfered with the Water-Colour Society opening, the Royal Academy opening, a Wilkie private view. His interests more and more inclined him towards such events and the kind of company he would find there. Although it is tricked out with Oxford learning, the first volume of *Modern Painters* has the flavour of Ruskin's return to early Victorian London; and its hero, the barber's son from Covent Garden, is lauded for wisdom and imagination quite beyond the cramped instruction of the university.

★ ★ ★ ★

The Ruskin family, now reunited, were looking forward to their annual summer tour. Their destination in 1842 was Switzerland. The diary Ruskin kept as they travelled from Calais through Rouen, Fontainebleau, Sens and Auxerre to Geneva, reveals a conscientious tourist. It is not an artist's diary. It is the notebook of a natural scientist, a geologist, a student of the Bible. But Ruskin had not forgotten English art. He left England with Turner's Swiss drawings in his mind, and had seen Turner's work at this year's Royal Academy exhibition, two Venetian subjects together with *Snow Storm, Steamboat making Signals, Peace – Burial at Sea* and *War: The Exile and the Rock Limpet*. A parcel of English newspapers sent on to Switzerland now inflamed his memories of the paintings. In one of them was a review which attacked Turner's contributions. The same morning that he read the review, in the Protestant church in Geneva, Ruskin knelt to pray. There he resolved to write a reply. This was to have been a pamphlet. Hot for battle, Ruskin thought to write it at Chamonix the next day. But an immensity of theme came between him and his task. It was nature. Among the rocks and the pines and the great mountains, Mont Blanc above and the green valleys below, Ruskin found that he could not confine what he had to say to a few pages. That *Modern Painters* was begun among the Alps has its significance. As from a vantage point, there spread out before him the whole length of Europe, its cities and long rivers, its seas and the island kingdom in the

North. Such vistas, which reappear ever afterwards in his writing, were early on imagined by the 'cockney cock-sparrow', as Ruskin later described himself at this age. Perhaps feeling a little shy of his resolution, he said nothing about his new writing to Osborne Gordon, who had now joined the Ruskins. Not until *Modern Painters* was actually published did he confess to his tutor how his holiday work had developed as they turned for home through Germany.

> I meditated all the way down the Rhine, found that *demonstration* in matters of art was no such easy matter, and the pamphlet turned into a volume. Before the volume was half way dealt with it hydrized into three heads, and each head became a volume. Finding that nothing could be done except on such enormous scale, I determined to take the hydra by the horns, and produce a complete treatise on landscape art.[15]

* * * *

Modern Painters was written in a new home. John James Ruskin had for some time been looking for another house. He wanted one more appropriate to his social standing, a home in which he could entertain the friends his son had made at Christ Church. At the same time there was a lack of pretension in his choice. After inspecting properties in Tooting, Penge and Fulham, he bought the lease of a house less than a mile from Herne Hill. It was No. 163 Denmark Hill, situated on the crest of this northern outcrop of the Surrey Downs, looking down to Dulwich in one direction and Camberwell in the other. John James had never aspired to own land, as one might have expected in a self-made tory of his temper. Nor had he ever wished for a town house. But he was well suited in Denmark Hill, the 'Belgravia of the South'. The Ruskins's new home was three storeys tall. There was a lodge, and the house itself was set among seven acres of land, half of it meadow, the rest divided into flower gardens, kitchen gardens, orchard. There were cows in the meadow, pigs and hens in the out-houses. Margaret Ruskin delighted in her farm management. She was also pleased to increase the number of servants. We will come to know them well, for these servants' lives became more and more interwoven with the Ruskins's, ever afterwards. David Downs, for instance, a Scotsman who came to Denmark Hill as head gardener and in later years was a factotum for all Ruskin's outdoor schemes — crossing-sweeping, road-building, moor-draining — died in Ruskin's service, as did the Tovey sisters, who were to manage Ruskin's teashop; while some, such as George Allen, married other Denmark

7. 163 Denmark Hill, Ruskin's home from 1842 to 1871, by Arthur Severn.

Hill servants, in his case George Hobbs's sister Hannah, and thus became part of the extended family network. No-one was ever cast off. At Denmark Hill they now settled into the routine of life that was to last, with disturbances, for thirty years, while in his study above the breakfast-room, looking over a view 'inestimable for its help in all healthy thought', Ruskin began the series of books that would take him from his writing apprenticeship to the Slade chair in Oxford.[16]

Ruskin said nothing to people outside his immediate family about his resolve to write on Turner. Only his parents and Mary Richardson knew what he was doing. The first volume of *Modern Painters* was composed privately, in effect secretly. Osborne Gordon, one of the first guests at Denmark Hill, was still kept in ignorance. Acland, Newton, Liddell, intellectual Christ Church men Ruskin occasionally met in the months when he was writing the book, had no idea that what was passing through his mind was being committed to paper. W. H. Harrison and all mutual acquaintances of the Ruskins and Turner were equally unaware of his labours. A consequence was that *Modern Painters* was written without any kind of professional advice.

This perhaps helped Ruskin to find his own originality: certainly it meant that nobody counselled him to be cautious. Reticent about his own large ambitions, Ruskin now listened to people but did not seek instruction from them. We have a fair idea of his life at the time when he was preparing his book. He had much talk with Richmond about art, for he was now sitting for a portrait which John James had commissioned. Richmond's son Willie recalled Ruskin at this period as a 'gaunt, delicate-looking young man, with a profusion of reddish hair, shaggy eyebrows like to a Scotch terrier, under them the gleaming eyes which bore within them a strange light, the like of which I have never seen except in his',[17] a description not very like his father's water-colour portrait, later entitled 'The Author of *Modern Painters*', which shows a rather stiff, formally-dressed person, pen in hand, sitting at a desk in the middle of a field. Ruskin was occasionally with Harding, but the lessons were more like conversations. He read Coleridge. He often called on Windus and Griffith. He took many a walk over the fields to Dulwich College picture gallery, whose collection of baroque and Dutch art is therefore much discussed in *Modern Painters*. He listened attentively to the Reverend Henry Melvill's sermons: he was the incumbent of Camden Chapel in Walworth Road, Camberwell. In Richard Fall's company he was often at the Geological Society. As his twenty-fourth birthday approached in February of 1843 he ventured to invite Turner to the celebratory dinner. His diary records, 'Turner happy and kind; all else fitting and delightful — but too late to sit writing.'[18] A few days later he 'called at Turner's . . . Insisted on my taking a glass of wine, but I wouldn't. Excessively good-natured today. Heaven grant he may not be mortally offended with the work!'[19]

This is one of the few references to *Modern Painters* in the diary. By March of 1843 the journal peters out, and we understand that Ruskin is in the final stages of his book. It resumes on 1 May. 'Couldn't write while I had this work for Turner to do; had not the slightest notion what labour it was. I was at it all April from 6 morning to 10 night, and late to-night too — but shall keep on, I hope.'[20] The completed manuscript now required a publisher. John James, who until his death in 1864 was to act as his son's literary agent, first of all approached John Murray. Without looking at the book, Murray gave as his opinion that a volume on the Nazarenes would be more popular. 'He said the public cared little about Turner,' John James wrote to W. H. Harrison, 'but strongly urged my son's writing on the German School, which the public were calling for works on.'[21] John James, not a man to be thus slighted, took the book immediately to Smith, Elder and Co. A bargain was quickly struck; George Smith changed the title from Ruskin's *Turner and the Ancients* to *Modern Painters: Their Superiority in the Art of Landscape Painting to the Ancient Masters*; edited it, as far as one may judge, hardly at all; sent it to press: and in the first week of May of 1843 the book itself was in the shops.

The reaction to *Modern Painters,* by 'a Graduate of Oxford', was not immediate, nor did the book at first sell widely. But in the first year of its life it won a distinguished audience. Wordsworth (from whose *Prelude* its epigraph was taken) thought it the work of 'a brilliant writer', and recommended it to visitors to Rydal Mount.[22] In other literary circles, we find Tennyson writing to the publisher Moxon:

> Another book I very much long to see is that on the superiority of the modern painters to the old ones, and the greatness of Turner as an artist, by an Oxford undergraduate, I think. I do not wish to buy it, it may be dear; perhaps you could borrow it for me out of the London Library, or from Rogers. I saw it lying on his table.[23]

Samuel Rogers may have pressed the book on readers other than the thrifty Tennyson. It was perhaps he who had sent a copy to Robert and Elizabeth Browning in Italy. To Mary Russell Mitford, who had also told them of it, Elizabeth Browning wrote,

> The letter in which you mentioned your Oxford student caught us in the middle of his work on art. Very vivid, very graphic, full of sensibility, but inconsequent in some of the reasoning, it seemed to me, and rather flashy than full in the metaphysics. Robert, who knows a great deal about art, to which knowledge I have of course no pretence, could agree with him only by snatches, and we, both of us, standing before a very impressive picture of Domenichino's (the 'David' — at Fano), wondered how he could blaspheme so against a great artist. Still, he is no ordinary man, and for a critic to be so much of a poet is a great thing. Also, we have by no means, I should imagine, seen the utmost of his stature.[24]

This was a more independent view than that of other literary women. Mrs Gaskell and Charlotte Brontë read Ruskin together, and Charlotte Brontë (also a Smith, Elder author) could write to W. S. Williams at the firm,

> Hitherto I have only had instinct to guide me in judging of art; I feel now as if I had been walking blindfold — this book seems to give me eyes. I *do* wish I had pictures within reach by which to test the new sense. Who can read these glowing descriptions of Turner's works without longing to see them? . . . I like this author's style

> much; there is both energy and beauty in it. I like himself, too, because he is such a hearty admirer. He does not give himself half-measure of praise or vituperation. He eulogizes, he reverences with his whole soul.[25]

And from George Eliot we have the first occasion on which Ruskin is referred to as a prophet. 'I venerate him', she wrote, 'as one of the great teachers of the day. The grand doctrines of truth and sincerity in art, and the nobleness and solemnity of our human life, which he teaches with the enthusiasm of a Hebrew prophet, must be stirring up young minds in a promising way.'[26]

These opinions were all privately expressed. Ruskin himself had no notion of them. The public reaction to the book, when it came, was not from such notable pens. John James, now pasting his son's reviews into a large ledger, was satisfied. They were unanimously flattering. They were not however of much intellectual weight.[27] The Ruskins were gratified by the *Britannia*'s notice, which they rightly guessed to be by Dr Croly, but the major journals gave no space to the book. Neither the *Athenæum* nor *Blackwood's* seemed to be aware of its publication. Turner was once again maligned for his contributions to the Royal Academy exhibition that May. And the painter himself said not one word to Ruskin about what he had written, about his 'labour for Turner'. Ruskin was not comforted to reflect that it was quite in Turner's character to say nothing on such an occasion, for the rest of his artistic acquaintance were slow to speak well of the book, whether or not they knew that it was his. *Præterita*, exaggerating somewhat, says,

> The sympathy of the art-circles, in praise of whose leading members the first volume of *Modern Painters* had been expressly written, was withheld from me much longer than that of the general reader . . . Taken as a body, the total group of Modern Painters were, therefore, more startled than flattered by my schismatic praise; the modest ones, such as Fielding, Prout, and Stanfield, felt that it was more than they deserved, — and, moreover, a little beside the mark and out of their way; the conceited ones, such as Harding and De Wint, were angry at the position given to Turner; and I am not sure that any of them were ready to endorse George Richmond's consoling assurance to my father, that I should know better in time.[28]

A personal effect of the appearance of *Modern Painters* was that it revealed to Ruskin his power as a writer. He now knew, as he had not quite known before, that writing was to be his instrument, his sword.

His desire to be valiant had found its expression. That so many people thought of his book as literature was welcome indeed to a young man who was now abandoning his poetic ambitions: he knew that there would have been no reaction to a book of his verses. To some extent this compensated for the moderate admiration of the artists he knew. Ruskin now began to find that to be known as an author gave him a special position. For a time, as it became an open secret that *Modern Painters* was his, he was a literary celebrity. He entered the world where fashion and culture were one. Under chandeliers, we find him in the company of Sir Robert Inglis, Richard Monckton Milnes, Samuel Rogers — it now was ten years since Henry Telford had given him Rogers's *Italy* — dining here, breakfasting there, leaving cards, accepting and returning invitations. This phase did not last long. As was to be the pattern throughout his life, a spell of party-going was followed by a return to his study, where he felt most at home. In any case, he was not perfectly suited to this company. He was not at ease with the women he met at such gatherings. Rogers was jealous and quarrelsome, Milnes a dilettante. There were tories 'of the old school' and Evangelicals around the dinner table at Sir Robert Inglis's. But the sentiments Ruskin heard there were somehow too worldly, too close to Parliament. Partly in reaction, he developed a hostility towards the book that had given him the *entrée* to such a world. In it, he told Liddell, 'there is a nasty, snappish, impatient, half-familiar, half-claptrap web of young mannishness'.[29] More publicly (and perhaps *Modern Painters*'s anonymity helped him here) he defended his book. Ruskin replied to the criticism which was published in the October number of *Blackwood's*. He also prepared a preface to the second edition of *Modern Painters*. But he had already realized that what was needed was a second book. With commendable self-discipline he now ignored his success and began to think again about his real, lonely, career as a writer.

* * * *

A book as various as *Modern Painters* could give its author a variety of suggestions for a sequel. Ruskin's first book is in a grand sense miscellaneous. It is philosophy and æsthetics, and much more than that. It is poetry. It is prose. It is a treatise. It is a great pamphlet. It is a defence, or rather a vindication. It is a sermon. It is art criticism, art history, a commentary on recent exhibitions, or an introduction to certain collections. It is a meditation on landscape, or an exercise in how the eye may examine nature. Ruskin did not think to choose between his various interests: hardly any book of his belongs to a *genre*. The second volume of *Modern Painters* was to be a more compact book than the first, but he prepared for it by a wide range of studies. To his irritation, the 'Graduate of Oxford' had to return to the university after the publication of his book. This was to keep the term he had lost through illness. Ruskin stayed in rooms and, he improbably claimed, 'learnt a great deal of Raffaele at Blenheim'.[30] There was more stimulus in London than in Oxfordshire. Now began Ruskin's lifelong association with the British Museum, its collections and their keepers, for he went there to talk to Charles Newton, now a member of its expanding staff. Newton's passion for classical archæology, so little in accord with Ruskin's developing tastes, gave them plenty to argue about. His knowledge of painting was growing in these quiet months after the appearance of *Modern Painters* I, yet there was something that was not quite fresh about his studies. He took notes from two books which he felt would give him a firmer knowledge of the schools of European art and, perhaps, their relevance to English painting of the day. Both were by foreigners. The first had not yet been translated. Alexis Francis Rio's *De La Poésie Chrétienne* (1836) became well known after 1854, when it appeared in England as *The Poetry of Christian Art:* it was probably the widely read Liddell who introduced it to Ruskin at this early date. Ruskin also studied G. F. Waagen's *Works of Art and Artists in England* (1838). Waagen was Director of the Berlin Gallery, and his book was written with authority. It was not sufficiently appreciative of Turner, however, and Ruskin's diary noted, 'I have had the satisfaction of finding Dr Waagen —of such mighty name as a connoisseur —a most double-dyed ass.'[31]

With Turner himself Ruskin's relations were increasingly cordial, although the old man's moods and crotchets often baffled his admirer. The relationship between the Ruskins and their favourite painter was in large part commercial, the more markedly so since Turner had still not acknowledged Ruskin's writing. John James's account book reveals that the new house on Denmark Hill was being filled with Turner water-colours of the larger and more finished sort. In that year he bought the *Llanthony Abbey, Dudley Castle, Land's End, Constance* and *Derwent Water,* for prices ranging from fifty to one hundred guineas. They were not enough for his son. Towards Christmas of 1843, when the Grays from Perth were once more staying with the Ruskins, John took the fifteen-year-old Phemy (as she was generally called) to see Windus's much larger collection. There, as usual, he was struck with an acquisitive jealousy. Two days earlier, his diary had recorded a meeting with Turner:

Very gracious: wanted me excessively to have some wine, but ambiguous as to whether he would or would not part with any of the works in his gallery. Couldn't make him out, and came away in despair. Says he fears there will be no sketches this spring; I shall be sadly disappointed. Phemy is a nice creature; played all the evening for me . . .[32]

Ruskin was perhaps attempting to buy directly from Turner without going through Griffith and without consulting his father. John Ruskin and John James Ruskin could not be in accord when thinking of buying Turners. If they talked together about possible purchases, it seemed always as if the father were making half-promises to the son. Neither of them, ever, dealt in half-promises. The discussions were painful to them both, and each feared the possibility of the other's resentment. Thus it was that John James now kept his own counsel in meditating a major acquisition. It was to be a congratulatory present. *The Slave Ship*, shown at the Royal Academy in 1840, was available through Griffith. Since he had the authority of his own son's book John James could not doubt that this was the right choice. *Modern Painters* said of the picture that it was 'the noblest sea that Turner has ever painted, and, if so, the noblest certainly ever painted by man'; and, further, that 'if I were reduced to rest Turner's immortality upon any single work, I should choose this'.[33] The price was only 250 guineas. Negotiations with Griffith went smoothly enough. The painting was brought out to Denmark Hill and, in Scottish fashion, was presented to Ruskin on New Year's Day.

The painting's full title was 'Slavers throwing overboard the dead and dying — typhon [*sic*] coming on', a theme probably suggested by an incident recounted in Thomas Clarkson's *History of the Abolition of the Slave Trade* (1808). One would look far to find a less domestic subject, and the painting appeared strangely in the entrance hall at Denmark Hill. Ruskin came down to it every morning on his way to the breakfast-room, then went upstairs past it on his way to his study. Perhaps its presence was a constant reminder to him that he should pitch high his writing. The passage in *Modern Painters* that described the picture had a kind of fame. Samuel Prout, who had seen the painting when it was still with Griffith, stood before it for some time and then exclaimed, 'by heaven all that Mr R[uskin] said of it is true!'[34] What Ruskin had in fact said (while relegating the overt subject of the picture to a footnote) was this:

It is a sunset on the Atlantic, after prolonged storm; but the storm is

> partially lulled, and the torn and streaming rain-clouds are moving in scarlet lines to lose themselves in the hollow of the night. The whole surface of sea included in the picture is divided into two ridges of enormous swell, not high, nor local, but a low broad heaving of the whole ocean, like the lifting of its bosom by deep-drawn breath after the torture of the storm. Between these two ridges the fire of the sunset falls along the trough of the sea, dyeing it with an awful but glorious light, the intense and lurid splendour which burns like gold, and bathes like blood. Along this fiery path and valley, the tossing waves by which the swell of the sea is restlessly divided, lift themselves in dark, indefinite, fantastic forms, each casting a faint and ghastly shadow behind it along the illumined foam. They do not rise everywhere, but three or four together in wild groups, fitfully and furiously, as the under strength of the swell compels or permits them; leaving between them treacherous spaces of level and whirling water, now lighted with green and lamp-like fire, now flashing back the gold of the declining sun, now fearfully dyed from above with the undistinguishable images of the burning clouds, which fall upon them in flakes of crimson and scarlet, and give to the reckless waves the added motion of their own fiery flying. Purple and blue, the lurid shadows of the hollow breakers are cast upon the mist of night, which gathers cold and low, advancing like the shadow of death upon the guilty ship as it labours amidst the lightning of the sea, its thin masts written upon the sky in lines of blood, girded with condemnation in that fearful hue which signs the sky with horror, and mixes its flaming flood with the sunlight, and, cast far along the desolate heave of the sepulchral waves, incarnadines the multitudinous sea.[35]

The passage prompts declamation: and like many another set piece in *Modern Painters* had been written aloud, as Ruskin paced the fields and gardens of his neighbourhood. Its literary background is not only dramatic — from, of course, Macbeth's

> This my hand will rather
> The multitudinous seas incarnadine,
> Making the green one red[36]

— but is also to be found in an amount of English poetry from Thomson to Coleridge, a type of verse that includes Turner's own epic 'The Fallacies of Hope'. Self-conscious about the passage, worrying over the connections between poetry, 'truth', and the factuality of painting, Ruskin was to defend his description to Walter Brown. 'If I had been writing to an artist in order to give him a clear conception of the picture, I should have said':

> Line of eye, two-fifths up the canvass; centre of light, a little above it; orange chrome, No 2 floated in with varnish, pallet-knifed with flake white, glazed afterwards with lake, passing into a purple shadow, scumbled with a dry brush on the left, etc. Once leave this and treat the picture as a reality, and you are obliged to use words implying what is indeed only seen in imagination, but yet what without doubt the artist intended to be so seen; just as he intended you to see and feel the heaving of the sea, being yet unable to give motion to his colours. And then, the question is, not whether all that you see is indeed there, but whether your imagination has worked as it was intended to do, and whether you have indeed felt as the artist did himself and wished to make you . . .[37]

The letter reflects a more practical interest in oil painting. Ruskin's own few experiments with the medium belong to the period after the publication of *Modern Painters* I. They came to nothing, or next to nothing, for he did not fully enjoy the medium. Like many other excellent critics and teachers, Ruskin was only half a creative artist. He responded to art, he could urge art on, but he did not like to fashion things. With Edmund Oldfield, he had a scheme to design stained glass windows for Camberwell Church. But this gave him no more real pleasure than did oil painting. He liked to draw; and a pen or fine pencil line, supplemented by body-colour or water-colour, was always to be his true medium. Drawing was closer to his instincts for recording, measuring and classifying. It was drawing that linked his love of geology with his love of art. Geology had the feeling, for Ruskin, of a science in its youth, a science in which all might be discovered. The foreign tour of 1844 was in essence an expedition to Chamonix and the Simplon. Ruskin's diaries witness his studies in the Alps, and an autobiographical chapter in *Deucalion,* his book devoted to geological matters, records a memorable meeting that summer. The Ruskins were staying at an Alpine inn:

> . . . my father and mother and I were sitting at one end of the long table in the evening; and at the other end of it, a quiet, somewhat severe-looking, and pale, English (as we supposed) traveller, with his wife; she, and my mother, working; her husband carefully completing some mountain outlines in his sketch-book. Whether some harmony of Scottish accent struck my father's ear, or the pride he took in his son's accomplishments prevailed over his own shyness, I think we first ventured word across the table, with view

> of informing the grave draughtsman that *we* also could draw. Whereupon my own sketch-book was brought out, the pale traveller politely permissive. My good father and mother had stopped at the Simplon inn for me because I wanted to climb to the high point immediately west of the Col, thinking thence to get a perspective of the chain joining the Fletschorn to the Monte Rosa. I had brought down with me careful studies . . . of great value to myself, as having won for me that evening the sympathy and help of James Forbes. For his eye grew keen, and his face attentive, as he examined the drawings; and he turned to me instantly as to a recognized fellow-workman, — though yet young, no less faithful than himself . . . He told me as much as I was able to learn, at that time, of the structures of the chain, and some pleasant general talk followed; but I knew nothing of glaciers then, and he had his evening's work to finish. And I never saw him again.[38]

To James Forbes's position in Alpine exploration and geology we will return, as did Ruskin. He knew his fellow guest in the Simplon inn as the author of *Travels through the Alps of Savoy and other parts of the Pennine Chain* (1843), which had extended the studies of the Louis Agassiz Ruskin had read in Leamington. Forbes was to be a controversial figure for thirty years yet, and Ruskin his distant ally, for indeed their paths were not to cross again. Now, the Ruskins hired an Alpine guide who became much more than a servant to them, and who remained a family friend until his death in 1874. Joseph Couttet, whom Ruskin called 'the captain of Monc Blanc', was of the race of guides who were becoming famous in these early years of the English conquest of the high peaks. His father had been de Saussure's guide. Joseph himself, a veteran of the Napoleonic armies, was fifty-two in 1844. Reliable, thrifty, avuncular, he soon had all the Ruskins's confidence. 'For thirty years he remained my tutor and companion', says *Præterita*. 'Had he been my drawing master also, it would have been better for me . . .'[39] Osborne Gordon joined them at Zermatt, and under Couttet's guidance the party became even a little adventurous, supping on black bread and sour milk under the Riffenberg, and then 'my mother, sixty-three on next 2nd September, walking with me the ten miles from St Nicholas to Visp as lightly as a girl. And the old people went back to Brieg with me, that I might climb the Bel Alp (then unknown), whence I drew the panorama of the Simplon and Bernese range . . .'[40]

It is in *Deucalion,* Ruskin's compendious geological volume, that one quarries further reminiscences of this summer in the Alps and its steady, joyful work; for instance, above the gorge of the Aletsch torrent — making some notes on it afterwards used in *Modern Painters*, 'many and many such a day of foot and hand labour having been needed to build that book'.[41] He kept Cary's Dante by him as he worked: he was using it to elevate his thoughts. He was full of love for the mountains and after long weeks among them was depressed by the thought of dustier work that lay before him in the Louvre on the way home. From Paris he told George Richmond, 'I have been on the hills some ten hours a day at the very least' and 'in this garret at Meurice's, the memory of snow and granite makes me testy'.[42] He was writing to Richmond to ask which pictures he should study in the Louvre. There are some notes on Venetian art in the travel diary that Ruskin had begun in Geneva on 1 June and was to close on his return to London on 20 October. One senses how perfunctory were his visits to French galleries and palaces. But the last entry in the journal is a happy one:

> Have not written a word since returning from Chamouni, for my days pass monotonously now. Only I ought to note my being at Windus's on Thursday to dine with Turner and Griffith alone and Turner's thanking me for my book for the first time. We drove home together, reached his house about one in the morning. Boylike, he said he would give sixpence to find the Harley St. gates shut, but on our reaching his door, vowed he'd be damned if we shouldn't come in and have some sherry. We were compelled to obey, and so drank healths again, exactly as the clock struck one, by the light of a single tallow candle in the under room — the wine, by the bye, first rate.[43]

CHAPTER FIVE

1845–1846

Just as some events in life, however unexpected, seem to confirm or explain what had preceded them, so Ruskin's tour to Italy in 1845 gave a shape to what had only been stirring in his mind. The first purpose of the tour, a reaction from his disappointing visit to the Louvre in the previous year, was to study Italian painting *in situ*. But he learnt more, and more about himself, than he imagined he might. He was to be away from home, and from his parents, for seven months. It changed him. Interests became convictions. His taste became active, and with added historical understanding. But some experiences of art this summer touched him so vividly that they had the effect of precluding further modulation of his taste. It was one of the ways in which his opinions on art became frozen. Inflexibility was already a danger to his sensibility. He half realized this, but explained it away by saying that he had to learn more. George Richmond attempted to make him look for good qualities in painting he instinctively disliked. But Ruskin was too impatient. He would listen to Turner, of course, but the painter was scarcely concerned to train young art critics. He often told his eloquent champion that 'all criticism was useless'.[1] He told Ruskin of his disapproval of the strictures in *Modern Painters* on his lesser contemporaries: 'You don't know how difficult it is.'[2] It was true that Ruskin knew little about working in oil. But he had a fair idea about drawing and water-colour. In the winter of 1844-5 he was working from Turner's own *Liber Studiorum*. Although the diaries are sparse, one has the impression that he saw Turner quite often. The conversations between the two men are unimaginable. What Ruskin records of them hints that they were approaching the mysterious slight on Ruskin's integrity for which, he later told Carlyle, 'I never forgave him'.[3] On the other hand, there is such a quantity of Turnerian lore in Ruskin's later writing, and of such a type, that one feels that it must derive from conversations in the studio. Ruskin later said that these were intimate. Certainly Turner was enough of a friend of the Ruskin family to give family advice. He knew how alarmed Ruskin's parents would be at the thought of their son travelling abroad without them. He constantly attempted, Ruskin later recalled, to dissuade him; and so, 'When at last I went to say good-bye, he came down with me into the hall in Queen Anne Street, and opening the door just enough for me to pass, laid hold of my arm, gripping it strongly. "Why will you go to Switzerland — there'll be such a fidge about you, when you're gone." '[4]

This of course was the first time that Ruskin had travelled abroad — or scarcely anywhere — without the company of John James or Margaret. He was twenty-six. Perhaps with reason, his parents were concerned about his safety, for which they made arrangements. He was to travel with George Hobbs and with Couttet. They would meet the Swiss guide at Geneva, and he would act as courier and watch over Ruskin's health. To travel apart from his family did not trouble Ruskin: geographical separation from those he loved never meant much to him. For his parents, however, it was painful. His eager and vital presence in Denmark Hill brightened their lives. It did more than that. For the son's constant activity had an invigorating effect on the father. When Ruskin was away from home John James was a lesser man. Margaret Ruskin felt this in her turn, for she was far more responsive to her husband's moods than to her son's. John James was hypersensitive to the movements of Ruskin's opinions. The old lady usually ignored what he was thinking. She now packed Bunyan's *Grace Abounding to the Chief of Sinners* in his bag, though he had told her often enough of his dislike for the book. Mildly and subserviently he remonstrated with her. It made no difference. This was often how theological matters were left to rest. Had she known them, she would have been alarmed at Ruskin's religious opinions this winter. Just before Christmas of 1844 he had spent a couple of days in his parish with the recently ordained Edward Clayton. His Christ Church friend's rather grim religious views prompted Ruskin to write to Henry Acland as follows, for Acland had many friends and relatives in the high church party:

> I have been in the country — for a day or two — with Edward Clayton . . .
>
> . . . Now you know — Acland, that I wish as far as may be in my power — to keep with the highest Church supporters — but I hope to heaven this is not their general doctrine . . . For — I am no ultra Protestant — on the contrary — I am far too much inclined the other way — I dispute not transubstantiation — I refuse neither to fast nor to confess myself — I would not check at praying to the Virgin — I abhor not the invocation of saints — I deny not the authority of the Church — But there are two things that I *do* deny — yea, I will deny — so long as I have sense — the first — that man can forgive sins — the second — that God can behold iniquity — i.e. — the doctrines of

> a purchased absolution — and a *merited* redemption. In these two — & in them only — it seems to me the power & poison of the Papacy rests — and as soon as the priest becomes the arbiter instead of the Performer of our righteousness — then and there I think the axe is laid to the root of our religion — and the way opened for all manner of blasphemy & sin.[5]

These remarks are so startling that the letter was suppressed by Ruskin's first editors. Those who best understood him, like Acland, knew that he would say something quite different to the next friend. To Ruskin, religious belief was often a matter for argument. Many men in holy orders were to rue his delight in being contentious. If he felt falseness in another man's God, he was capable of arguing a different view with a strange, pitiless gusto. But he had a sense of divinity in others. His feeling for George Herbert — not all that common in the earlier part of the nineteenth century — is one example. He had discussed his poetry with Clayton at Christ Church. He now used Herbert to try to show his mother how *Grace Abounding* suffered from the narrowness and inflexibility of its conviction. She took no notice, but George Hobbs probably did. Their life abroad had one constant feature. Every morning young Ruskin would read with his young servant a chapter or two of the Bible, and the English service. They would then talk about the meaning of the Scripture. We must imagine them in a Paris hotel room, taking the purity of English religion with them, in chapters and verses. As they drove south, Ruskin approached the papist Continent as though he bore St George's own banner. That did not prevent him from travelling luxuriously. His coach was a marvel, a *calèche* drawn by two horses, shining black and gilt. There were good coach-builders in Camberwell, before the railways ruined everything. The roof opened to the sun, the springs were buoyant, here was the buggy and here was the rumble-seat. Inside were any number of pockets and drawers and little bookcases; a place for his writing-case (the only part of his luggage Ruskin ever packed for himself) and clever leather frames to hold the selection of Turner water-colours he took with him wherever he went. Who could not be happy as the day is long, to travel in a vehicle such as this? At Champagnole Ruskin had two trout from the river, a woodcock, then soufflé, with a bottle of Sillery *mousseux*.

> Meanwhile the sun was sinking gradually, and I was warned of something equally perfect in *that* direction & way, by seeing my champagne suddenly become *rose*. And a beautiful sunset it was — glowing over the pinewoods, and far up into sky, long after the sun

went down. And as I came back to my souffle & sillery, I felt sad at thinking how few were capable of having such enjoyment, and very doubtful whether it were at all proper in me to have it all to myself.[6]

* * * *

The changing urgencies of the tour were only half understood by Couttet and George, compelled by their young master to linger in some places and flee from others. Sometimes there was a relaxed halt, but not often. One such produced the interesting drawing of the Italian maritime pine, done at Sestri as they passed from the French and Italian rivieras and approached the Carrara hills (Plate 8). Thence they sought Lucca, 'where I settled myself', *Præterita* says, 'for ten days, as I supposed. It turned out forty years.'[7] Ruskin meant that he found his life's interests there. His stay at Lucca was for little more than a week. But it gave a vivid prelude and direction to his studies of mediæval painting and architecture. Lucca also gave him the contrast between the old Italy and the new, between mediæval order and restive modern conditions. In 1845 the city was governed as a duchy. Soldiers lounged outside the ducal palace: a military band played. Beggars were everywhere. And in the church of San Frediano,

> Such a church — so old — 680 probably — Lombard — all glorious dark arches & columns — covered with holy frescoes — and gemmed gold pictures on blue grounds. I don't know when I shall get away, and all the church fronts charged with heavenly sculpture and inlaid with whole histories in marble — only half of them have been destroyed by the Godless, soulless, devil hearted and brutebrained barbarians of French — and the people here seem bad enough for anything too, talking all church time & idling all day — one sees nothing but subjects for lamentation, wrecks of lovely things destroyed, remains of them unrespected, *all* going to decay, nothing rising but ugliness and meanness, nothing done or conceived by man but evil, irremediable, self multiplying, all swallowing evil, vice and folly everywhere, idleness and infidelity, & filth, and misery, and desecration, dissipated youth & wicked manhood & withered, sickly, hopeless age . . .[8]

In San Frediano Ruskin first thought to trace and copy frescoes before they rotted or fell to pieces, or were simply destroyed to make way for new tombs, new monuments. At the same time he worried that this might waste his time, that paintings in the next church might be desecrated even at that moment. In search of a general knowledge of Italian art, he now found two works that kept a symbolic meaning

8. *Stone Pine at Sestri*, by John Ruskin, 1845.

for him all through his life. One was a painting, the other a recumbent statue. In the Dominican church of San Romano he stood before the Fra Bartolommeo *God the Father with Mary Magdalene and St Catherine of Siena*. This is not a picture of the first quality, and was not in fact what he called it: 'the first example of accomplished sacred art I had seen'.[9] But it gave him a serene, lofty ideal: it was a token that there had been a whole realm of art, centuries of it, that had belonged to God. A similar realization, only a day or two later, came from a piece of sculpture. This was Jacopo della Quercia's tomb of Ilaria di Caretto (Plate 9). It dates from the early fifteenth century and is perhaps more Gothic than early Renaissance in feeling. Ruskin was enraptured. It seemed to him that he had never experienced sculpture before. Nor, it seems to us, was he ever to have any feeling for sculpture that surpassed this early delight. It became a touchstone, and perhaps too much of a touchstone. The young wife lying in death had a haunting impression on Ruskin. In years to come her image would be confounded with that of Rose La Touche; and as one reads the description of the monument that Ruskin now sent to his father, one senses not only the tone but also part of the inspiration of later, desolate, marmorial writing.

> This, his second wife, died young, and her monument is by Jacopo della Querce, erected soon after her death. She is lying on a simple pillow, with a hound at her feet. Her dress is of the simplest middle age character, folding closely over the bosom, and tight to the arms, clasped about the neck. Round her head is a circular fillet, with three

9. *Tomb of Ilaria di Caretto*, by Jacopo della Quercia, at Lucca, by John Ruskin, sketched in 1874.

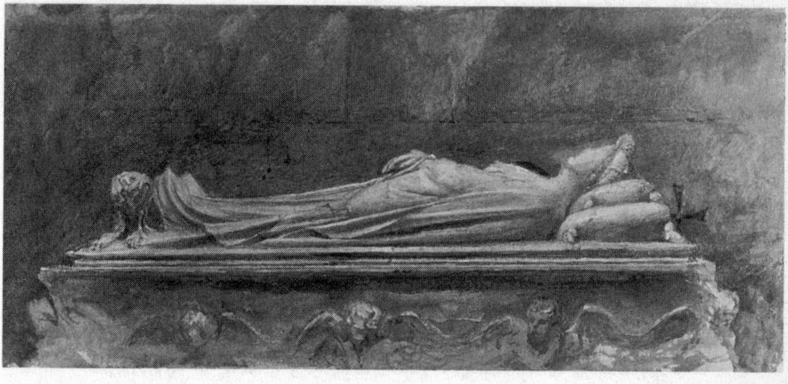

> star shaped flowers. From under this the hair falls like that of the Magdalene, its undulation *just* felt as it touches the cheek, & no more. The arms are not folded, nor the hands clasped nor raised. Her arms are laid softly at length upon her body, and the hands cross as they fall. The drapery flows over the feet and half hides the hound. It is impossible to tell you the perfect sweetness of the lips & the closed eyes, nor the solemnity of the seal of death which is set upon the whole figure. The sculpture, as art, is in every way perfect — *truth* itself, but truth selected with inconceivable refinement of feeling. The cast of the drapery, for *severe natural* simplicity & perfect grace, I never saw equalled, nor the fall of the hands — you expect every instant, or rather you seem to see every instant, the last sinking into death. There is no decoration or work about it, not even enough for protection — you may stand beside it leaning on the pillow, and watching the twilight fade over the sweet, dead lips and arched eyes in their sealed close. With this I end my day, & return home as the lamps begin to burn in the Madonna shrines; to read Dante, and write to you.[10]

In Ruskin's response to the Fra Bartolommeo and the della Quercia there was a feeling for their location, their placing in quiet holy places of the town. Lucca itself, Ruskin noted, had within its rampart walls 'upwards of twenty churches . . . dating between the sixth and twelfth centuries'.[11] His short stay included some drawing of these churches. He afterwards believed that this marked the beginning of his architectural studies. *The Poetry of Architecture,* since its stance was both English and picturesque, had to be forgotten. The change is marked by a different kind of drawing, especially of façades. Ruskin's graphic style became more notational as he looked at the church of San Michele (Plate 10). The drawings were scarcely composed and there was no attempt to finish them once the detail had been caught. In this respect they closely correspond to the visual experience of looking at a Gothic church with a will to consider it in part rather than in whole. In Pisa, where the party travelled next, he used his notebooks more fully and the study of such churches is accordingly more complete. He was teaching himself how to grasp architecture, preparing for those wonderful notebooks from which he was to write *The Stones of Venice.*

Ruskin was surprised to find how much his reactions had changed since he was last in this part of North Italy in 1840. Lucca then he had reckoned 'an ugly little town'. Pisa 'as *town* is very uninteresting'.[12] The Campo Santo in Pisa he had been 'thoroughly disappointed in: it is very narrow, not elegant, and totally wanting in melancholy or in

10. Part of the façade of S Michele in Lucca, by John Ruskin, 1845.

peace, the more so for being turned into a gallery of antiquities'.[13] In 1845 it was the Campo Santo above all that moved him: 'My mind is marvellously altered . . . everything comes on me like music.'[14] The simile had to do with the way that *quattrocento* art had displayed itself to him. It was grave sometimes, sweet sometimes, seraphic always. Ruskin gave himself up to the frescoes. Yet he was almost equally stirred by his conviction that they were all threatened. His letters are alternately filled with ecstatic descriptions of the paintings and expressions of rage at their probable fate. In his more meditative moments he found that he could make an alliance between his Protestant mind, his searching in antiquity, fresh enthusiasm, and a kind of realism he found in the pictures. The Campo Santo was a graphic Bible. In it there was an ancient truthfulness. He wrote to his father,

> I never believed the patriarchal history before, but I do now, for I have seen it. You cannot conceive the vividness & fullness of conception of these great old men . . . Abraham & Adam, & Cain, Rachel & Rebekah, all are there, the very people, real, visible, created, substantial, such as they *were,* as they must have been — one cannot look at them without being certain that they have lived — and the angels, great, & real, and powerful, that you feel the very wind from their wings upon your face, and yet expect to see them depart every instant into heaven . . .[15]

Most of these impressions are taken from paintings by Benozzo Gozzoli, but he passed swiftly to others. On 18 May he could report of his progress, 'Benozzo I have done, & Giotto I am doing, then I have Simon Memmi, Antonio Veneziano, & Andrea Orgagna [*sic*].'[16] Some of Ruskin's attributions were wrong, and remained wrong. This scarcely mattered. He had found a new way of looking at the world.

Art historians of Ruskin's and later generations knew what tact, guile, patience and willpower are needed to have a scaffolding erected in an Italian church. Ruskin, with his money, charm, and servants, somehow managed it immediately. He soared above difficulties. Couttet and George sorted things out at ground level. He drew and traced from the frescoes, aware as he did so that the whole shape and the whole subject of the next volume of *Modern Painters* was now quite changed. What the book would contain he could not foretell: but in some way he changed his plans and his itinerary in accordance with his feelings for it. A few more days, he imagined, and he might get to the end of 'my *resumé*' of Pisa: it was as though (as writers and lecturers sometimes can) he was able to feel already the further end of his peroration. The relationship between this tour and *Modern Painters* II is obvious and can be demonstrated in one hundred details. Behind that, there is a similarity in the pace and the vision of the book and the tour. There were high points and more high points, and scarcely more than breathing spaces between them. In Lucca and in Pisa, as everywhere else in Italy, he found that there was more to be done, more to be understood, than ever he had imagined. Probably it was now that he realized that *Modern Painters* would have more than two volumes. He also realized that he had thrown away parts of his past life. The first volume of his book was effaced from his mind. So was his poetry: he had no time for it. Oxford he had no thought for: he was learning more in a few months than he had in years at the university. He wrote to Osborne Gordon to say that he did not wish to meet him. Suddenly, Rogers and his *Italy* seemed beside the point. He quoted Rogers to his father, but he no longer believed in him. John James, reading his daily letters (that took the place of Ruskin's diary entries) in Billiter Street, could not keep pace with his son's discoveries. This disturbed him so much that he redoubled his warnings about health. Ruskin told his father that he would eat no figs, that he drank clean water, that his scaffold was safe. He sent him accounts of what he spent, and scarcely ever failed to be dutiful, entertaining and reassuring.

In Florence, where he arrived at the end of May, he had most need to tell his parents of his safety. There were signs of strain which could not be kept out of the letters home. Neither of his servants had any control over his mental activity. He was often at work in the churches at five o'clock in the morning and did not cease until mid-evening. Nor was this merely a tourist's long day. Only by taking the notebooks and drawings in one's own hand, and then by attempting to cover the same ground, can one appreciate the ferocity of his study. But this is to simplify. He had a different pace for different uses of the pen. Script, one can tell, is extraordinarily rapid. One gathers this not so much from the handwriting as by taking any lengthy sentence and then by discovering how its subordinate clauses, as one transcribes it, take one beyond the point where one can recall its initial impetus. Meanwhile, we note of his drawing in 1845 that it tends to be more cursive in landscape subjects such as the Sestri pine, while the study of architectural detail and outlines of paintings are of necessity drawn more slowly. They are not, however, laborious; and many personal recollections of Ruskin when drawing indicate that his pen and brush were more fluent than most people's.

In Florence, much of his time was spent in drawing. He wrote his last poem, 'Mont Blanc Revisited', feeling that his time was being wasted. 'I haven't time if I draw to see half the things — and I must draw too, for my book,' he wrote to his father,[17] adding next day that 'there is so much to be read and worked out that it is quite impossible to draw, except the little studies for my book. I regret this the more because unless I draw a bit of a thing, I never arrive at conclusions to which I can altogether trust.'[18] Thus it went on, Ruskin now adding to his labours by borrowing books from the library of Santa Croce. For relaxation he sometimes helped the monks at their haymaking, on the hill of Fiesole. But for two months, almost without remission, he was absorbed in Giotto studies, in the Ghirlandaio chapel of Santa Maria Novella, finding Masaccio and Fra Filippo Lippi in the Brancacci Chapel and Fra Angelico in the Convent of San Marco.

* * * *

Ruskin was tired by this effort. Advised by Couttet, he decided not to remain in Italy in midsummer. 'I begin to feel the effects of the violent excitement of the great art at Florence — nothing gives me any pleasure at present, and I shall not recover spring of mind until I get on a glacier.'[19] The party went up through Milan to Como and finally to Macugnaga in the Val Anzasca. Here, high in the mountains, Ruskin rented a chalet, little more than a hut. It was next to a torrent, approached by a stony path and a pine bridge, rocks and waterfalls to one side, pines and 'stunted acacias' on the other. In Switzerland they again found haymaking. Ruskin walked on the mountains from dawn and gave his hand to the peasants in the evening. The valley was his. He conceived the idea of asking Turner to stay with him there. Affecting the casual, he enclosed the invitation in a letter to John James, saying 'is the gentleman doing anything — if he isn't, tell him he may as well come here & catch fish and climb hills with me . . .'.[20] In truth, he wanted to stand at Turner's shoulder to see how he drew mountains. But the artist would not come; and Ruskin buried himself in Shakespeare.

In all Ruskin's books there are more references to Shakespeare than to any other writer, excepting only Dante. Like other great Englishmen, Ruskin learnt Shakespeare early and knew ever afterwards that he was part of his own mind: one does not often find occasions when Ruskin deliberately sat down to study him. Nor did he often write directly about the plays. The dispersion of his comments has the effect of obscuring how complete a Shakespearian he was. In 1886, looking back on his days in Macugnaga, and writing in sadness and defeat, Ruskin observed:

> . . . the writer himself is not only unknowable, but inconceivable; and his wisdom so useless, that at this time of being and speaking, among active and purposeful Englishmen, I know not one who shows a trace of ever having felt a passion of Shakespeare's, or learnt a lesson from him.[21]

Thus the despairing *Præterita* recalls but slightly perverts what indeed was Ruskin's experience of the weeks in Macugnaga in 1845: that there were no *lessons* to be drawn from reading Shakespeare that summer. And while he knew that he needed to relax, Ruskin had still a desire for books that would cut a path for him. 'Formerly I hated history, now I am always at Sismondi,' he now told his father. 'I had not the slightest interest in political science, now I am studying the constitutions of Italy with great interest . . .'[22] Jean-Charles-Leonard Simonde de Sismondi's *Histoire des républiques italiennes au moyen age* (1838), whose three volumes Ruskin carried with him, can be added to Rio's *Poésie Chrétienne* as a book which shaped Ruskin's growing mediævalism. He had an instinct and a desire for such writing. Shakespeare was put away, and study resumed.

Before he left the Alps Ruskin spent much time in that kind of work, half scientific and half artistic, which he had invented for himself, pursuing observations of sky or granite, glacier or woodland. One day 'I stopped 5 hours, watching the various effects of cloud over the plains of Lombardy, after getting the forms of the mountains that I wanted above the valley of Saas.'[23] A day or two later, from Faido, St Gothard, he writes of his location of a Turner site: 'I have found his subject, or the materials of it, here; and shall devote tomorrow to examining them and seeing how he has put them together.'[24] Ruskin was on his way to Baveno, where he had a rendezvous with J. D. Harding. They met: and sketching as they went, attended still by Couttet and the exhausted George, the two water-colourists went by Como, Bergamo and Verona to Venice. Ruskin was drawing now in genuine rivalry with his former master. But the interest they took in each other's work was brought to a halt by the experience of Venice. Ruskin's first reaction was negative: it was one of horror at modern improvements. Approaching the city, deliberately, from the picturesque angle that he recalled from 1835, he suddenly found the new railway bridge from Mestre 'entirely cutting off the whole open sea & half the city, which now looks as nearly as possible like Liverpool at the end of the dockyard wall . . .'.[25] Everywhere he seemed to find neglect of the Venetian treasures, and signs that it would shortly become even like an English manufacturing town. It wrung from him the cry that would be repeated in the first sentence of *The Stones of Venice* a few years later: 'Tyre itself was nothing to this.'[26]

For a few days, Ruskin could not settle to the study of painting, beyond noting how he could find 'among the wrecks of Venice, authority for all that Turner has done of her'. He told his father, 'I have been in such a state of torment since I came here that I have not even thought of Titian's existence.'[27] He would not much do so. Nor would he much consider the Bellinis, nor look as he had intended for Giorgione. He was to have the revelation of a quite different artist.

> I have had a draught of pictures today enough to drown me. I never was so utterly crushed to the earth before any human intellect as I was today, before Tintoret. Just be so good as to take my list of painters, & put him in the school of Art at the top, top, top of everything, with a great big black line underneath him to stop him off from everybody — and put him in the school of Intellect, next after Michael Angelo. He took it so entirely out of me today that I could do nothing at last but lie on a bench & laugh. Harding said that if he had been a figure painter, he never could have touched a brush again, and that he felt more like a flogged schoolboy than a man — and no wonder. Tintoret don't seem to be able to stretch himself till you give him a canvas forty feet square — & then, he lashes out like a leviathan, and heaven and earth come together. M Angelo himself cannot hurl figures into space as he does, nor did M Angelo ever paint space itself which would not look like a nutshell beside Tintoret's. Just imagine the audacity of the fellow — in his massacre of the innocents one of the mothers has hurled herself off a terrace to avoid the executioner & is falling headforemost & backwards, holding up the child still. And such a resurrection as there is the rocks of the sepulchre crashed all to pieces & roaring down upon you, while the Christ soars forth into a torrent of angels, whirled up into heaven till you are lost ten times over. And then to see his touch of quiet thought in his awful crucifixion — there is an *ass* in the distance, feeding on the remains of strewed palm leaves. If that isn't a master's stroke, I don't know what is. As for *painting,* I think I didn't know what it meant till today — the fellow outlines you your figure with ten strokes, and colours it with as many more. I don't believe it took him ten minutes to invent & paint a whole length. Away he goes, heaping host on host, multitudes that no man can number — never pausing, never repeating himself — clouds & whirlwinds & fire & infinity of earth & sea, all alike to him — and then the noble fellow has put in Titian, on horseback at one side of

11. Copy after the central portion of Tintoretto's *Crucifixion*, by John Ruskin, 1845.

one of his great pictures, and himself at the other, but he has made Titian principal. This is the way great men are with each other — no jealousy there . . .[28]

Experiencing the physicality and great size of the paintings in the Scuola di San Rocco, Ruskin was so overwhelmed that he could not make the correct comparisons with Titian. In truth there is not much that is essential to Tintoretto's art that had not been more beautifully expressed by Titian. But Ruskin was not able to think in such terms. All life long he overrated Tintoretto, as if in honour of this experience. Now as ever afterwards his response was personal and partial, and in expression overstated. His judgements on painting were scarcely ever tempered by the local and comparative methods of the art historian. And he now began to pit himself — as always he would — against the founders of this new intellectual discipline. The tour of 1845 produced some writing that was never collected, Ruskin's additional notes to Murray's *Handbook for Travellers in North Italy*. This material appeared in the 1847 edition signed only as '(R)'. Sir Francis Palgrave, the compiler of the original work, is bitingly criticized in his own book.

Ruskin now met another classifier and recorder, Mrs Anna Jameson, who was working on the Venetian sources of her *Sacred and*

Legendary Art. He also made the acquaintance of the English connoisseur, William Boxall, who was later to be Director of the National Gallery. The three made expeditions together. Boxall knew Wordsworth, and Ruskin rather admired him. Mrs Jameson, however, 'knows as much of art as the cat'.[29] She was older than Ruskin and had much determination. But he found that his understanding of the Italian schools was way beyond hers. Boxall was to remain a friend, though a distant one, for many years. *Præterita* remembers Mrs Jameson kindly. *Sacred and Legendary Art,* however, is a poor thing in comparison with the truly spiritual second volume of *Modern Painters,* just as her book on Shakespeare's heroines falls limply beside only two pages of comment on Shakespeare which Ruskin incorporated in the Alpine passages of the fourth volume of his earliest great work.

There is a touch of arrogance in Ruskin's dealings with Mrs Jameson. This is only to be expected. The revelations of the past few months had demanded something from Ruskin's sensibility and from his personality: he had responded with the kind of effort that a man can perhaps only make in his twenties. He had matched his own potential against his discoveries. A young man can learn, and become more learned. He can find things in life of which he was unaware. Ruskin had done these things, and had done more than that. He had enlarged himself. This could not protect him from the consequences of his overwork. Couttet, with a gentle care that Ruskin could often inspire in other men, had warned him of the reaction that might come. Harding left, Boxall left, but Ruskin stayed on to make further studies in the city. For the first time he used daguerrotypes to record buildings, but most of his labour was in drawing and making voluminous notes. Almost feverishly, he sought to capture as much of Tintoretto and Venice as he could. On the way home, after seven months abroad, he succumbed. He was ill at Padua and again, after bidding farewell to Couttet, on the journey to Paris. He did not visit the Louvre but hurried straight home, arriving at Dover on 5 November.

* * * *

Much of the tension that Ruskin felt during his tour concerned his obligations to his parents. His dutiful letters to Denmark Hill give almost daily reassurances about his health and safety. Towards the end of his long stay the messages from his parents often asked him to come home. One letter in particular made him think of his mother and her grief: it told him of two deaths, of his cousins Mary and John, of the Croydon Richardsons. When he opened his next year's diary, half-

12. *Corner of St Mark's after Rain*, by John Ruskin, 1846.

way through the composition of *Modern Painters* II, Ruskin wrote an honest analysis of his feelings at the time:

> I ought to note one circumstance — a series of circumstances — connected with the past year which ought to be as important, as any that ever happened to me. From about the close of September at Venice, to the 26th of October, or thereabouts, at Vevay, I had been kept almost without letters, except one or two at Brieg full of complaints of my stay at Venice. I was much vexed at Vevay by finding no letter of credit there and the next day I received the news of my cousins' deaths (Mary and John) — Sufficiently uncomfortable in these several respects and not very well. I received in passing through Lausanne (and that by chance, having doubted whether I should send George to post a letter half way down the town, and only let him go because I was busy drawing some figures at a fountain and couldn't interrupt myself) a short letter from my Father, full of most unkind expressions of impatience at my stay in Venice. I had been much vexed by his apparent want of sympathy throughout the journey, and on receiving this letter my first impulse was to write a complaining and perhaps a bitter one in return. But as I drove down the hill from Lausanne there was something in the sweet sunshine between the tree trunks that made me think better of it. I considered that I should give my father dreadful pain if I did so, and that all this impatience was not unkindly meant, but only the ungoverned expression of extreme though selfish affection. At last I resolved, though with a little effort, to throw the letter into the fire, and say nothing of having received it, so that it might be thought to have been lost at Brieg, whence it had been forwarded. I had no sooner made this resolution than I felt a degree of happiness and elation totally different from all my ordinary states of mind, and this continued so vivid and steady all the way towards Nyon that I could not but feel there was some strange spiritual government of the conscience; and I began to wonder how God should give me so much reward for so little self-denial, and to make all sorts of resolves relating to future conduct. While in the middle of them we stopped to change horses at Rolle, and I got out and sauntered down, hardly knowing where I went, to the lake shore. I had not seen Mont Blanc all the journey before, and was not thinking of it, but when I got to the quay there it was, a great and glorious pyramid of purple in the evening light, seen between two slopes of dark mountain as in the opposite page [where there is a drawing] — the lake lying below as calm as glass. In

the state of mind in which I then was it seemed a lesson given by my own favourite mountain — a revelation of nature intended for me only.[30]

Further notes in this diary reveal how Ruskin then devoted himself to spiritual exercises, 'continuing in earnest prayer and endeavour, or determination to do right',[31] while fighting the physical effects of what was surely a nervous illness. His sense that he was called to do great work was never in perfect concord with what his parents expected of him. There is for this reason a slight element of expiation in *Modern Painters* II, which was written in London in the winter of 1845-6 and published the following spring. If the whole of *Modern Painters* is Ruskin's great gift to his father, then its second volume is a subsidiary gift to his mother. More formally religious than the first volume, and much more like her religion than like John James's, it reads as though its intention was to gladden her. At the same time, the book could not quite present an explanation to John James of how his son had stepped away from him. Both of them knew that this had happened, and neither could do anything about it. Ruskin promised his father that the next year they would all travel together and he would show them the wonderful things that he was now writing about. But there was still a gap between them. *Modern Painters* II is in some respects a solitary book, for it is the record of one young man's pilgrimage and the formation, by revelation, of a most personal taste. What the book has to say about this is of importance. 'True taste is for ever growing, learning, reading, worshipping, laying its hand upon its mouth because it is astonished, lamenting over itself, and testing itself by the way it fits things.'[32] It is a bold image, the more so for being active and physical, a youthful thought that belongs (as Ruskin himself belongs) to the period between Romanticism and the beginnings of a modern apprehension of art. Ruskin cultivated the self-awareness of such taste. Of necessity, it was his alone.

But the reading that contributed to *Modern Painters* II was a different matter. This was shared and discussed. Osborne Gordon had recommended Hooker to him, Ruskin later recalled. He ascribed to Hooker an ornateness of language in the book. Perhaps this was to exaggerate the influence. A nearer and more potent example would be in the sermons of Henry Melvill. These were read, listened to, and discussed in Denmark Hill. They had so much effect on Ruskin that he could dream about them forty years later, and their combination of artificial language and religious fervour was surely present in the young art critic. In the early 1880s, when he looked back on *Modern Painters* II,

Ruskin thought that the book might be of interest to 'the literary student' as well as to an art lover.[33] W. G. Collingwood, whom Ruskin probably had in mind, was inclined to think that the book was 'really a philosophical work' and wished to place it 'as a reflex of the great movement of German philosophy and as the completion of the English school of æsthetics begun by Coleridge'.[34] However that may be, it is certain that much of Ruskin's university reading, which he discussed with Acland and Newton as well as with Gordon during the composition of *Modern Painters* II, finds a place in his æsthetic system. His formal æsthetic was always to be of more interest to Ruskin than anyone else, however; the popularity of *Modern Painters* II was mostly in 'passages' that were known, for a time, as glories of English prose. Such extracts rather annoyed the later Ruskin, who did not like to be famous for mellifluous sentences. He believed, rightly, that the importance of the book was in its introduction of a taste for early Italian art and for Tintoretto. Ruskin was neither the first nor the sole discoverer of early Italian art. But he was by far the most persuasive, as the respectful reviews of his book (excepting still the *Athenæum*'s notice) indicate. At the age of twenty-five he had established an artistic authority that was crusader-like. This could excite his contemporaries. Acland, writing to Liddell as another young don who hoped to change Oxford, now for the first time suggested that Ruskin be brought back to the university. Ruskin himself had no such desire. He was eager for other things. As soon as he had finished the second volume of *Modern Painters* he began the studies of architecture that were to absorb him until the end of his marriage in 1854. Not waiting to see the publication of his book but entrusting all to W. H. Harrison, Ruskin left with his parents for the Continent. This was in April of 1846: they would not return to England until six months later.

* * * *

When looking back on those days in *Præterita* Ruskin quite accurately stated:

> I had two distinct instincts to be satisfied, rather than ends in view, as I wrote day by day with higher-kindled feeling the second volume of *Modern Painters*. The first, to explain to myself, and then demonstrate to others, the nature of that quality of beauty which I now saw to exist through all the happy conditions of living organism; and down to the minutest detail and finished material structure naturally produced. The second, to explain and illustrate the power of the two schools of art unknown to the British public, that of Angelico in Florence, and Tintoret in Venice.[35]

Only by forcing arguments could Turner be introduced to such a scheme, and he makes only a minor appearance in this second volume of *Modern Painters*. Ruskin did not write again publicly about Turner until 1851, when the painter was dying. In some other ways Turner seems now to have lost his place in Ruskin's life. We hear next to nothing about the relations between the artist and the critic. Ruskin made no record of any of his conversations with Turner, nor any record of their meetings. So distant do the painter and critic seem that one cannot imagine how they corresponded; and in fact it is likely that many of their exchanges by letter were conducted through the medium of John James Ruskin. Evidence of Turner's visits to Denmark Hill is in John James's correspondence and diary rather than in his son's diary. It seems that the painter was at the Ruskins's on New Year's Day of 1846, when according to Finberg's biography of Turner he might have discussed his will with John James;[36] and was there again on 8 February, 'Mr John's' birthday. John James's diary reveals that he dined at Denmark Hill on 19 March of 1846, just before the publication of *Modern Painters* II, with Mrs Colquhoun, a Mr Young, William Boxall, George Richmond and Joseph Severn. He next visited (it appears) at Ruskin's birthday party the following 8 February, when the other guests were Charles Newton, W. H. Harrison and Mrs Cockburn; then again on 3 June of 1847, when he met William Macdonald, the son of an old Scottish friend of John James's, the water-colourist Joshua Cristall, George Richmond, C. R. Leslie, Samuel Palmer and Effie Gray; and just before Ruskin's marriage to this last, at his 1848 birthday dinner, Turner sat down with Richmond, Boxall, Sir Charles Eastlake and the Reverend Daniel Moore who had succeeded Henry Melvill as incumbent of the Camden Chapel. It will be seen that these were hardly intimate meetings. Of Ruskin's more personal relations with Turner in these years, we have little idea. He would have seen something of him at Griffith's, and we know that he had — at times — access to Queen Anne Street. But when the snatches of evidence for such meetings are accumulated, it is noticeable that Ruskin had far less to do with the artist he most admired than would have been expected.[37]

The reasons for this lack of contact might be the obvious ones: the difference in age and temperament between the two men. But one other piece of evidence suggests that their relationship had been damaged. Twenty years after this time Ruskin found himself estranged from an older man whom he revered. This was Carlyle. A dispute between them lasted for some weeks. At the height of their quarrel, Ruskin wrote to Carlyle in the hottest anger: wildly, almost, but with the anger of a man whose personal honour has been damaged. In this letter Ruskin tells Carlyle that Turner had once called his honour into question, and that he had never forgiven him. Ruskin gave no further explanation and we cannot know what had happened. But it is significant that the matter should have come to the surface at this emotional point. As long as he lived Ruskin never again mentioned that something had come between himself and Turner. One can only guess at what it was. It could have been something to do with purchasing: here was an area of Turner's life where goodwill could often fail. It could have been to do with Ruskin's writing. Turner's extraordinarily reserved attitude to Ruskin's heartfelt books cannot but have been a psychological difficulty to the writer who claimed to understand his art. Ruskin never had much to say about Turner's interest in him and his writing. But for five years of his life this must have mattered to him far more than any kind of public success. Later, Ruskin was to make an unusual and rather sinister claim about Turner's health in these years. He felt that the painter had then been not merely in physical decline but suffered from 'mental disease', whose onset he could date: 'The time of fatal change may be brought within a limit of three or four months, towards the close of the year 1845.'[38] This was the period when Ruskin was back in London and writing the text of the second volume of *Modern Painters*. Something may have passed between them then. At any rate, Ruskin felt that he could not hope for the painter's affection during his declining years. After Turner's death, Ruskin was in correspondence with Griffith. Turner's agent had gone out of his way to let Ruskin know that the painter did have some regard for the writer. Ruskin wrote back that he was 'deeply gratified . . . by what you say of Turner's having cared something for me. My life has not been the same to me as you may well imagine since he has gone to his place — nor will it ever be to me again what it was — while he was living . . .'[39]

From 1845 onwards, or after he had finished writing *Modern Painters* II, Ruskin might have thought of putting his knowledge of Turner into manageable form, with the aid of notebooks, drawings, reproductions and the like. But this approach was never congenial. The classical methods of the art historian (such as they were, at this date) found no adherent in the young art critic. He disliked systems and when he made catalogues they tended to the eccentric. Furthermore, he believed that to understand Turner it was more important to study nature than old oil paintings. At the same time, Ruskin was liable to find new enthusiasms outside art, or to return to his old pursuits in the geological sciences. When *Modern Painters* II was published in April of 1846, he was already on a different intellectual tack. The notices were almost overwhelmingly flattering. One of them brought a new friend, a doctor and writer who for the rest of his life would attempt to keep up with Ruskin's imagination. This was John Brown of Edinburgh,[40] who had reviewed the book for the *North British Review* and had written privately to its author. Ruskin received Brown's letter on the Continent, for he had taken his mother and father away from England before publication day. One part of him wanted to show his parents what he had been writing about. But he was also in search of knowledge that as yet was undefined to him: historical, religious, sculptural, architectural, or some combination of these things. Landscape art became less interesting. No further volume of *Modern Painters* would appear for ten years.

CHAPTER SIX

1846–1847

Between 1846 and 1856 Ruskin was mostly concerned with architectural studies. These are the years which saw *The Seven Lamps of Architecture* (1849), the three volumes of *The Stones of Venice* (1851-3), various lectures and occasional writings on building, and the collaborative venture of the construction of the Oxford Museum. Ruskin's interest in architecture was lifelong, of course: it extends from *The Poetry of Architecture,* written when he was an undergraduate, to the last of his Oxford lectures in the 1880s. But this decade gave him his central position in the Gothic Revival. He was led to architecture by his reading of mediæval history, by his increasing concern with the history of the Christian Church, and by a study of architecture in Turner's water-colours. His own increased ability to draw buildings also played a part in his new interest. Ruskin was now confident enough of his own drawing to show some water-colours this year, 1846, in a mixed exhibition at the Graphic Society. It is recorded that 'a member of the Royal Academy, after examining the subjects with much attention, exclaimed in our hearing — "The man who can draw like that may write anything he pleases upon art"'.[1] Ruskin might not have taken this as a compliment. His drawing had direct connections with his writing. The ability to grasp architectural subjects by the process of recording them in drawing now began to give a new kind of authority to his connoisseurship of building. His studies of architectural details, mouldings, doorways, arches, pinnacles, far outnumber the drawings he made from paintings, or sculpture; and they gave him an apprehension of building that seems to have a unique combination of the optical with the tactile.

Ruskin benefited from the scholarly attention to mediæval architecture that, in England, had preceded the analysis of earlier schools of painting. His serious introduction to Gothic building was made with the help of a book that had been published as long before as 1835, Robert Willis's *Remarks on the Architecture of the Middle Ages, Especially of Italy.* When he bought this book is not known: but many notes and drawings in his current diary testify to a careful interest in Willis. As the Ruskins travelled down the Continent towards the goal of their tour, which was Venice, we may see how he attempted to apply the method of Willis's *Remarks* to French and German buildings. In 1880, in a supplementary footnote to a new edition of *The Seven Lamps of Architecture,* Ruskin acknowledged that Willis 'taught me all my grammar of central Gothic' and that in his book on the flamboyant style he had anticipated Ruskin in the 'grammar of the flamboyant I worked out for myself'.[2] As usual, Ruskin's reading had been extensive but piecemeal. If this was to his disadvantage as an architectural historian, the lack was more than balanced by his industry before the *motif* of the buildings he studied. Nor should we underestimate the value of his distance from the architectural profession, for this allowed him to ignore all the practical problems of architecture. Ruskin made the literature of the Gothic Revival inseparable from the general revival of the arts in mid-nineteenth-century England, and gave it a spiritual inspiration that in many other writers and architects was sectarian or merely perfunctory.

John James Ruskin had not anticipated this new involvement with architecture and the effective abandoning of Turner studies. He had trouble in following his son's enthusiasms. One purpose of the tour of 1846 was for Ruskin to be able to show his father all that had excited him in his great expedition the previous year. There is no doubt that Ruskin felt guilty that his long absence abroad had distressed his parents. This loving and dutiful son could not feel content with himself until he had once again made a sort of comrade of his father. To this end he wished to show him the main subjects of his newly published book, the 'angel choirs' of *quattrocento* painting and the turbulent visions of Tintoretto. Many English travellers would go to Italy with Ruskin's famous book as their guide. John James, in Venice and Pisa, was the first but not the most appreciative of them. There is some humour in the way that Ruskin later described his reactions:

> We had been entirely of one mind about the carved porches of Abbeville, and living pictures of Vandyck; but when my father now found himself required to admire also flat walls, striped like the striped calico of an American flag, and oval-eyed saints like the figures on a Chinese teacup, he grew restive . . .[3]

In fact John James was distressed. It was becoming apparent to both father and son that Ruskin's first tour without his parents had erected a greater barrier between them than either had realized. John James now swung back to his old longing for his son to be a poet. W. H. Harrison, still editing *Friendship's Offering,* had written to Venice to ask if there were any lines — a song, perhaps, or a picturesque description — that he could publish in his annual next Christmas. Ruskin was far beyond such things. John James had to reply:

> I regret to say there is no chance of this; my son has not written a line of poetry and he says he cannot produce any by setting himself to it as a work — he does not I am sorry to say regret this — he only regrets ever having written any. He thinks all his own poetry very worthless and considers it unfortunate that he prematurely worked any small mine of poetry he might possess. He seems to think the mine is exhausted and neither gold nor silver given to the world. He is cultivating Art at present searching for real knowledge but to you and me this knowledge is at present a Sealed Book. It will neither take the shape of picture or poetry. It is gathered in scraps hardly wrought for he is drawing perpetually but no drawing such as in former days you or I might compliment in the usual way by saying it deserved a frame — but fragments of everything from a Cupola to a Cartwheel but in such bits that it is to the common eye a mass of Hieroglyphics — all true — truth itself but Truth in mosaic . . .[4]

This 'mass of Hieroglyphics' was the notebook in which Ruskin was making his architectural studies. As his father lamented, he had no interest in making frameable and finished drawings of whole buildings or scenes: he wanted to avoid settings and the picturesque. Instead, he concentrated on the details of individual forms. Here was born the knowledge of Venetian architecture that was the strong foundation of *The Stones of Venice.* However, the epic history of her building was not yet in Ruskin's mind. He was thinking of making his new studies into a chapter or section of the next volume of *Modern Painters.* The integrity of his sequence was a problem at Venice in the summer of 1846. Ruskin was now revising his text for the third edition of the first volume, and found it awkward to accommodate Titian and Tintoretto. Writing from Lucerne on the way home, he confessed to George Richmond that 'I have got some useful bits of detail . . . especially in architecture — though in Italy I lost the greater part of my time because I had to look over the first volume of *Modern Painters,* which I wanted to bring up to something like the standard of knowledge in the other . . .'.[5]

The party returned to England at the end of September 1846. The elder Ruskins would never go to Italy again. Their son had garnered much information in the summer months, but it felt miscellaneous. It took another year and more for his architectural feeling to gell into the extended essay which is *The Seven Lamps of Architecture.* Ruskin had not yet realized a simple truth about himself: how easy it was to write a book on anything that interested him at the time. For this reason, his literary production in the next two years was comparatively meagre.

The autumn of 1846 was taken up with studies in the British Museum. We might note here that this great institution was Ruskin's best-loved museum. He always enjoyed his visits to Bloomsbury more than those he made to the National Gallery. He did not neglect the country's foremost painting collection, and was often there for professional reasons. But it was too much associated with the Royal Academy and with the traditions of baroque painting. For this reason he often urged the National Gallery to buy examples of earlier Italian art. He did so with a novel and urgent authority, and often by speaking directly to the gallery's trustees and other interested parties. The identity of the 'Graduate of Oxford' had still not been revealed on Ruskin's title-pages, but there can have been few people in art circles who did not know that he was the author of *Modern Painters*. He had renown, and for that reason was invited to many a drawing-room. Ruskin's regular complaints about evenings in society no doubt tell us of his dislike of fashionable salons: they also show that he kept accepting the invitations. This pleased his parents. It also gave relief from another kind of social life which he undertook and of which he never complained. His parents entertained a great deal but never themselves dined away from home: Ruskin went to other people's houses on their behalf. Thus, many a night and for many a year, he spent hours with family friends who were a generation older than himself. They were Scottish, or in the wine trade, or were clergymen. This circle included Dale and Croly, whose conversation — if not their sermons, for Ruskin went to hear Dale preach every Tuesday until 1848 — he might well have found repetitive. Society in great London houses off Hyde Park was in comparison tinsel. That was why it was sometimes welcome.

A house Ruskin sometimes frequented was Lady Davy's, in Park Street. She was Sir Humphrey's widow: garrulous, well-connected on the Continent as well as in London, quite near to the court. But her receptions, Ruskin tells us, also 'gathered usually, with others, the literary and scientific men who had once known Abbotsford'.[6] There Ruskin met a young woman who attracted him. She was Charlotte Lockhart, Sir Walter Scott's granddaughter and the daughter of James Lockhart, the novelist's biographer. Ruskin had met the father and daughter before, in 1839, when he had dined at the Cockburns's.[7] Charlotte had been scarcely more than a child then, and Ruskin an undergraduate. Now the 'little dark-eyed, high-foreheaded' Charlotte was of age, and Ruskin looked at her with interest. His later recollections of their meetings at Lady Davy's are confused, and it is not now possible to estimate the relations between them. They were, in an empty kind of way, romantic. But they had nothing to say to each other. 'I could never contrive to come to any serious speech with her,' says *Præterita*.[8] He wrote to Charlotte instead, in letters which have not survived. Some of them were probably sent from Ambleside, where Ruskin went with George Hobbs in March of 1847. At the Salutation Inn he sat down to write a book review that had been commissioned by Charlotte's father. Lockhart was eminent in what Ruskin called 'the old Scott and John Murray circle' not only by virtue of his biography but also by his editorship of the *Quarterly Review*.[9] He had asked Ruskin to write about Lord Lindsay's *Sketches of the History of Christian Art*. The invitation was somehow confused with the young critic's feelings for his daughter; and so, as *Præterita* sardonically records, Ruskin 'with my usual wisdom in such matters, went away into Cumberland to recommend myself to her by writing a *Quarterly* review'.[10]

Lord Lindsay's book had been on Ruskin's mind. He had heard of it long before its publication. In 1845 he had written to his father from Florence asking him to enquire of George Richmond what it would contain, 'for the artists here talk very much about what he is going to do & write about old art . . .'.[11] Ruskin had thought that Lindsay's plans 'may in some degree influence me in the direction I give to parts of my book'.[12] Richmond had replied to John James that he liked Lord Lindsay, admired his scholarship and that his book was to be 'a history of Christian art from the revival of paintings up to the time of Raphael'.[13] But *Modern Painters* II was not affected by Lindsay's plans. We should not think of the two authors as being in competition. Ruskin had already become so individual a writer that the question of rivalry simply did not arise. He and Lindsay had similar interests. Lindsay is referred to in Ruskin's books, always favourably, for years to come. They met occasionally at meetings of the Arundel Society and the like, but struck no sparks from each other. Ruskin's review is rather prophetic of their relationship. It is flat, measured, and anonymous. It strikes the manner of the current reviewers only too successfully. Were it not that the sentiments were so accordant with *Modern Painters* II one would hardly know that it was by Ruskin. It is significant that Lockhart asked him to 'cut out all my best bits'.[14] The editor also excised a hostile reference to the architectural writer Gally Knight, who was a John Murray author. Ruskin tells us that 'this first clear insight into the arts of bookselling and reviewing made me permanently distrustful of both trades': and though he was to notice Sir Charles Eastlake's writing for the *Quarterly* he never thereafter reviewed a book in his life.[15]

Ruskin chose the romantic setting of Ambleside for the mundane task of his book review to separate himself from distractions in London. He also, consciously or half-consciously, went there to test his feelings for Charlotte Lockhart. As things turned out, any burgeoning love or distant contemplation of her 'harebell-like' beauty was swept away by a deadening depression of his spirits.[16] *Præterita* records: 'I fell into a state of despondency till then unknown to me, and of which I knew not the like again till fourteen years afterwards.'[17] Ruskin's autobiography, pledged to avoid painful memories, says no more. But the cause of his depression in the Lake District, where he balanced sentences in the mornings and rowed every afternoon amidst 'black water — as still as death; — lonely, rocky islets — leafless woods — or worse than leafless — the brown oak-foliage lying dead upon them; gray sky; — far-off, wild, dark, dismal moorlands', was the thought of Adèle Domecq.[18] His parents knew of his interest in Charlotte. But they simply feared the effect Adèle still had on him. Ruskin could only speak of her to his parents in broad hints. 'It makes me melancholy with thinking of 1838,' he told his mother.[19] That was when he had last been at Ambleside, when he had most suffered from love nearly ten years before. Just as he had decided to recommend himself to Adèle by his writing, so he had recently sought to impress Charlotte. But the memory of the waste and futility of his love for the French girl now made Charlotte appear trivial. When he returned to Denmark Hill from the Lakes John James realized what was wrong with his son and saw how long-lasting had been the effects of Adèle's disastrous intrusion into their lives. He wrote frankly to a friend that 'the passion however was powerful and almost threatened my son's life — various journies abroad have scarcely dissipated his chagrin nor repaired his health . . .'.[20]

The recipient of this letter was George Gray, John James's old business friend from Perth; and the subject of his son's affections was particularly in his mind because a guest at Denmark Hill was Gray's daughter Euphemia, 'Effie', the girl Ruskin would eventually marry. John James had immediately sensed that the presence of the most attractive Effie might add a further complication to Ruskin's desolation over Adèle and uncertain attitudes towards Charlotte. His early suspicions turned out to be correct, as in the three or four weeks to come the two young people came to know each other. It is important that the three affections of Ruskin's young days — Adèle, Charlotte, Effie — were present in his mind concurrently during these weeks. For her part, Effie did not at first think that John's affairs of the heart had anything to do with her. The letters she sent to Perth afford amused glimpses of the (to her) bizarre household at Denmark Hill together with overawed accounts of Ruskin's visits to town:

> I am enjoying myself exceedingly although in a quiet way, Mr Ruskin is as kind as ever and as droll — Mrs Ruskin is the same but I think she is beginning to feel old age a good deal, she sleeps so badly during the night that she falls asleep in the evenings. She is always saying that she is afraid I will weary with her but we get on admirably and she is always giving me good *advices* which I would repeat had I not so much news to tell you. John I see very little of excepting in the evening as he is so much engaged but he seems I think to be getting very celebrated in the literary world and to be much taken notice of. On Saturday he was at a grand reunion of Sir R. Peel's where everyone was, the Duke of Cambridge was there boring everybody with his noise. Sir Robert Peel and Lady Peel were there the whole time and extremely affable. On Friday John is going to a private view of the Royal Academy, the ticket is sent to him by 'Turner' who is one of the 30 Academicians who have a ticket at their disposal so that it is the highest compliment paid to any man in London. They have got home a very fine Picture by the above artist yesterday of Venice which is the largest they have and must have cost *something* . . . The Cuisine here is conducted admirably . . . Mrs Ruskin approves most graciously of my toilette, she says I am well dressed without being at all fine or extravagant . . .[21]

Since her London holiday in 1841, when little 'Phemy' had challenged Ruskin to write the fairy story that became *The King of the Golden River,* he had met her only twice, and then briefly. The first occasion was in 1843, when Effie was fifteen, and stayed at Denmark Hill with her brother George. The second was a visit she had made in the previous year, just before the publication of *Modern Painters* II, and probably before the time when Ruskin had met Charlotte at Lady Davy's. Now, in this spring of 1847, she presented a more adult charm and confidence. She had left her school, Avonbank, near Stratford-on-Avon, quite well-read and with musical accomplishments; she had helped her mother to manage a large house and family; she knew she was attractive and she knew what it was to have admirers. From Effie's lively letters to Perth we see that she was inclined to laugh a little at John's evident lack of interest in Charlotte:

> Mrs Ruskin told me of John's affaire the first night I came but I did not tell you as I thought she perhaps did not wish it to be known but she did not tell me who the Lady is and John never hints of her. He is

13. Euphemia Ruskin, by John Ruskin, 1848 or 1850.

> the strangest being I ever saw, for a lover, he never goes out without grumbling and I fancy the young lady cannot be in London . . .[22]

This was written on 4 May, shortly after Effie arrived at Denmark Hill. She could not at first decide about Ruskin. On the one hand she thought of him as 'such a queer being, he hates going out and likes painting all day';[23] on the other, she was impressed by his fame and brilliance. It took her only a little time to become relaxed in his company. She then saw his charm and came to welcome his attentions. For Ruskin also relaxed. Pleasing Effie was a pleasure to him. He put aside his objections to poetry in order to present the stanzas *For a Birthday in May* on her nineteenth anniversary. He drew her portrait.

Together they went to the opera to hear Jenny Lind. Charlotte Lockhart did not exist. John and Effie's fate was being cast. They slipped into romance because they enjoyed each other but also because there was an atmosphere of betrothal all around them. Mary Richardson had just left her adopted home in Denmark Hill to marry the lawyer Parker Bolding, a connection of the Scottish Richardson family. Ruskin's near contemporary at Christ Church, Henry Liddell, came out to dine. He brought with him his bride Lorina: she, like Effie, was nineteen years of age. Suddenly the atmosphere at Denmark Hill was youthful. Charles Newton came for the night and delighted Effie: 'He amuses us beyond expression and went on with John this morning, he is a great genius.'[24] Another guest was young William Macdonald, who is tantalizingly described in *Præterita* as 'the son of an old friend, perhaps flame, of my father's, Mrs Farquharson'.[25] Ruskin hardly knew Macdonald, but he now arranged to go to stay with him at his hunting lodge in the Highlands later that summer. Ruskin was no sportsman, but his journey to the Highlands would inevitably take him past Effie's home in Perth. It was almost a rendezvous, almost a declaration. Macdonald was later the best man at their wedding.

Effie was due to return to Scotland. John would go there later in the summer, but he first had an engagement at a meeting of the British Association in Oxford: he was to attend the geological section of this learned conference. We do not know how the two young people parted, but it seems that Ruskin was agitated by something that was not love. One querulous and unhappy letter survives from this date. Writing to his friend Mary Russell Mitford, the gentle author of *Our Village,* he announced that

> I have most foolishly accepted evening invitations, and made morning calls, these last four months, until I am fevered by the friction. I have done no good, incurred many obligations, and suffered an incalculable harm. I know not what is the matter with me, but the people seem to have put a chill on me, and taken my life out of me. I feel alike uncertain and incapable of purpose, and look to the cottage on Loch Tay not as an enjoyment, but a *burrow*.[26]

This does not seem the mood of a man who is optimistically in love: more the opposite; and when Ruskin arrived in Oxford the pall of his Ambleside depression once again settled on him. His pleasures with Effie were forgotten, replaced with the sense of failure and frustration, the twin memory of his disappointment with his university career and his love of Adèle. He now wrote to his parents:

I am not able to write a full account of all I see, to amuse you, for I find it necessary to keep as quiet as I can, and I fear it would only annoy you to be told of all the invitations I refuse, and all the interesting matters in which I take no part. There is nothing for it but throwing one's self into the stream, and going down with one's arms under water, ready to be carried anywhere, or do anything. My friends are all busy, and tired to death. All the members of my section, but especially Forbes, Sedgwick, Murchison and Lord Northampton — and of course Buckland, are as kind to me as men can be; but I am tormented by the perpetual feeling of being in everybody's way. The recollections of the place, too, and the being in my old rooms, make me very miserable. I have not one moment of profitably spent time to look back to while I was here, and much useless labour and disappointed hope; and I can neither bear the excitement of being in the society where the play of mind is constant, and rolls *over* me like heavy wheels, nor the pain of being alone. I get away in the evenings into the hayfields about Cumnor, and rest; but then my failing sight plagues me. I cannot look at anything as I used to do, and the evening sky is covered with swimming strings and eels . . .[27]

Practically all the period of Ruskin's courtship was one of neurasthenic depression, of great worry about his health and his future. This return to Oxford threw him into an illness that seems as much nervous as physical. He felt no better when he returned to London. Quiet pursuits at Denmark Hill failed to restore his spirits. Eventually it was decided that he should return to Dr Jephson's establishment at Leamington Spa. Once again Ruskin submitted himself to the regime that had seemed helpful after his breakdown in 1841. At that time he had written *The King of the Golden River* for Effie; during this stay he found no comparable amusement. The diary reveals that he drew, botanized, and worked on his second commission from the *Quarterly Review,* an account of Charles Eastlake's *Materials for a History of Oil Painting*. But the diary now gives the impression of boredom rather than of agitation, and only once among its flat descriptions do Effie's initials indicate that Ruskin was, perhaps, a lover.

I have spent a somewhat profitless day; owing, as I think, to coldness and wandering of thought at morning prayers. I must watch if this be always the case. After drawing at Warwick Castle, I went over there again in the afternoon, and walked some distance on the road beyond, past the sixth milestone from Stratford (thinking much more of ECG than of Shakespeare, by the bye). There was much most beautiful in the fresh meadows on each side of the road; and a little divergence from it, once, brought me to the side of the Avon, a noiseless, yet not lazy stream, lying like the inlet of a lake between shadowy groups and lines of elm and aspen, quiet and something sad.[28]

At some point in the months that Ruskin spent at Jephson's he was joined by William Macdonald. His later recollection was that the young Scotsman had also come to take a cure. It is more likely that he had called on his way from London, and was encouraging Ruskin to come up to his shooting lodge at Crossmount. From this point Macdonald began to have a kind of presiding influence over Ruskin's courtship. Without him, Ruskin probably would not have gone to Scotland to woo Effie in her own home. Eventually Jephson discharged him and he travelled north. At Dunbar, where he arrived on 18 August, he made a remarkable drawing of seashore rocks that (together with his review of Eastlake's book) is a significant part of the early history of Pre-Raphaelitism. But art was not on his mind. After finishing the drawing he felt 'dispirited and ready to seek for any excitement this evening'.[29] A day or two later he was in Perth, where he called on Effie's father at his office but made no attempt to see her. That night his journal records,

I have had the saddest walk this afternoon I ever had in my life. Partly from my own pain in not seeing E.G. and in far greater degree, as I found by examining it thoroughly, from thinking that my own pain was perhaps much less than hers, not knowing what I know. And all this with a strange deadly shadow over everything, such as I hardly could comprehend; I expected to be touched by it, which I was not, but then came a horror of great darkness — not distress, but cold, fear and gloom. I am a little better now. After all, when the feelings have been so deadened by long time, I do not see how the effect on them can be anything else than this.[30]

In the days to come many letters were exchanged between Ruskin, his father, his mother, and Mr Gray. The letters between Ruskin and his parents discuss Effie's character and suitability: they also dispel some lingering doubts about Charlotte Lockhart. At the Crossmount shooting lodge, high in the hills above Lochs Rannoch and Tunnel, Ruskin made one or two dispirited efforts to join in the sport. Soon he gave up following the guns in favour of drawing thistles. Thus he occupied himself for more than a fortnight before he wrote to the Grays proposing to visit them at Bowerswell. They replied immediately; and at the beginning of October, three and a half months after he had parted from Effie, Ruskin presented himself to her at the house which once had belonged to his grandfather.

CHAPTER SEVEN

1847–1849

'A man should choose his wife as he does his destiny,' Ruskin later wrote, at the time when he was begging to marry Rose La Touche.[1] His marriage to Effie was to cast a shadow over all his later life, and indeed over all his biographers' attempts to explain that life. In October of 1847 that destiny was unimaginable. He had no conception of himself at the age of fifty, or sixty, no thought of himself as a man in the prime of life or in old age. No doubt he did not differ, in this, from any other young man who is about to wed. But there was nonetheless an element of calculation in his approach to a proposal. This he owed to his parents. He could not imagine his own marriage without thinking of the most perfect marriage known to him, that of his father and mother. Nor could John James and Margaret believe that the mould of his marriage might differ from their own. For this reason the atmosphere became charged with the difficulties of a union between two families. It was as if the young people were being asked to take more responsibility than they had thought of. When John arrived at Bowerswell Effie did not quite know what was going on. Her reaction was to be cool to the man who had not declared himself as her suitor. It was a difficult few days, in which everything was left unsaid. When Ruskin left to go back to London nothing had been clarified, for of course he wished to talk to his father. Back at Denmark Hill, with John James's blessing, he must have decided to be firm, to take his destiny in his own hands. Characteristically, he did so by writing. About a week after returning home he sent a letter to Effie that contained an offer of marriage. He was immediately accepted.

> It would be doing dishonour to my own love — to think that — when I had leave to express it — it was not intense enough to deserve — to compel — a return — No — I cannot doubt you any more — I feel that God has given you to me — and he gives no imperfect gifts — He will give me also the power to keep your heart — to fill it — to make it joyful — Oh my treasure — how shall I thank *Him*?

wrote Ruskin shortly afterwards.[2] Such letters that have survived from the engagement maintain, when they can, a religious tone and a pure, literary passion. It was in the nature of John and Effie's union, unconsummated as it was, that the engagement should be as important as the marriage itself; and in their searching for higher things at this time there was a happy seriousness they were not to know again. However, there were times when Ruskin became worried and querulous. Unconsciously or not, he wished Effie to feel the same anxieties for him that his parents felt. He may have been right to believe that his intellectual labours had an effect on his second book review, a long and thoughtful account of Charles Eastlake's *Materials for the History of Oil Painting*. The effort he put into the research and writing was considerable, and when it was finished he felt the need to recuperate by the sea. At Folkestone, slightly depressed, he wondered whether he had lost the feeling for nature that had so possessed him in past years, when he was writing *Modern Painters*. As the date of their wedding approached more problems arose. The political revolutions on the Continent greatly disturbed Ruskin. Effie's father's finances suddenly took a sharper turn for the worse. He had speculated in railways, which in the Ruskins's view was the height of imprudence. But Ruskin's real fear was about himself: the belief that he was not well, and that in his marriage he had to hold himself away from any kind of excitement. Only a month before the wedding he addressed his fiancée in these terms:

> There are moments when I think you have been a foolish girl to marry me — I am so nervous, and weak, and — dreamy — and really ill & broken down — compared to most men of my age, that you will have much to bear with and to dispense with — my father was for many years in the same state, and it ended in his secluding himself from all society but that which he sees in his own house I inherit his disposition — his infirmities, but not his power — while the morbid part of the feeling has been increased in me by the very solitude necessary to my father. At this moment, the dread I have of the bustle of Edinburgh is almost neutralizing the pleasure I have in the hope of being with you — it amounts to absolute *panic*. And — above all — in speaking of me to your friends, remember that I am really not well. Do not speak of me as able (though unwilling) to do this or that — but remember the real frets — that late hours — & excitement of all kinds are just as direct and certain *poison* to me as so much arsenic or hemlock and that the *least* thing excites me. From a child, if I turned from one side to another as I slept, the pulse was quickened instantly and this condition has of late years been aggravated by over work — and vexation. I have been four years doing the mischief — and it will be two or three at any rate, before, even

with the strictest care, it can be remedied.— Take care that you make people understand this as clearly as possible.[3]

★ ★ ★ ★

Neither of Ruskin's parents wished to attend his wedding. Margaret Ruskin's horror of Bowerswell had not been dispelled by her son's engagement to the daughter of the house.[4] Nor did John James wish to return there. He wrote to Mr Gray,

> You expect that Mrs Ruskin and I should come to Perth and nothing can be more reasonable — I at once acknowledge we ought to come; but with Mrs Ruskin's feelings and prejudices I scarcely dare contend — for my own part, I am sincerely desirous of coming, but on the best consideration I can give the subject — I have decided to keep away . . . I can only exist in the absence of all excitement — that is by leading a quiet life — it is just 30 years this 1848 since I slept in a friend's house. I take mine ease at an inn continually and I go on with my business pretty well — I have thought I might come to Perth but if I were unwell — I should only be in the way — a marplot and a nuisance . . .[5]

There was some lameness in these excuses; and John James's attempts to be tactful to the Grays would always be at odds with his native bluntness. But as the wedding approached the elder Ruskins and Grays were content with their children's obvious contentment with each other. The celebrations in Perth were not spoilt by the absence of John James and Margaret Ruskin. To Effie, it made the occasion seem more like a family party for the Grays. None of John's old friends went to the wedding. One would have expected him to have asked Henry Acland or Richard Fall to be best man. Instead, William Macdonald performed this duty. Ruskin never saw him again after the wedding day. The ceremony itself was Scottish, and not elaborate. John and Effie were married in the drawing-room at Bowerswell on the morning of 10 April. The guests sat down to the wedding dinner after the couple left in the late afternoon. A letter from Mrs Gray to Margaret Ruskin describes how happy they looked as they drove off to Blair Atholl, where they were to spend the first night of their honeymoon.

The marriage was not consummated that night, nor ever afterwards. Both John and Effie wrote down why this was so at the end of the marriage six years later. Effie said in a letter to her father of 7 March 1854,

> I had never been told the duties of married persons to each other and knew little or nothing about their relations in the closest union on

earth. For days John talked about this relation to me but avowed no intention of making me his Wife. He alleged various reasons, Hatred to children, religious motives, a desire to preserve my beauty, and finally this last year told me his true reason (and this to me is as villainous as all the rest), that he had imagined women were quite different to what he saw I was, and that the reason he did not make me his Wife was because he was disgusted with my person the first evening April 10th.[6]

Ruskin's statement was written out for his lawyers at the time of the annulment. He states, no doubt correctly, that Effie had been upset by her father's financial problems, and that the fortnight before the wedding had been particularly harrowing for her.

Miss Gray appeared in a most weak and nervous state in consequence of this distress — and I was at first afraid of subjecting her system to any new trials — My own passion was also much subdued by anxiety; and I had no difficulty in refraining from consummation on the first night. On speaking to her on the subject the second night we agreed that it would be better to defer consummation for a little time. For my part I married in order to have a companion — not for passion's sake; and I was particularly anxious that my wife should be well and strong in order that she might be able to climb Swiss hills with me that year. I had seen much grief arise from the double excitement of possession and marriage travelling and was delighted to find that my wife seemed quite relieved at the suggestion. We tried thus living separate for some little time, and then agreed that we would continue to do so till my wife should be five and twenty, as we wished to travel a great deal — and thought that in five years time we should be settled for good.[7]

Thus, early in the honeymoon, something was decided between them. Effie's letter to her father further relates, 'After I began to see things better I argued with him and took the Bible but he soon silenced me and I was not sufficiently awake to what position I was in. Then he said after six years he would marry me, when I was 25.'[8] John's deposition says:

It may be thought strange that I *could* abstain from a woman who to most people was so attractive. But though her face was beautiful, her person was not formed to excite passion. On the contrary, there were certain circumstances in her person which completely checked it. I did not think either, that there could be anything in my own person particularly attractive to *her*: but believed that she loved me, as I loved her, with little mingling of desire.[9]

It is not clear from these accounts when it was that Ruskin said he would consummate the marriage when Effie was twenty-five: her phrase 'after I began to see things better' surely refers to some time later than the honeymoon. She probably began to argue with Ruskin about their sexual life after she and her husband visited France that summer: only then did she realize the extent to which he was bound to his parents rather than to her. The matter of Ruskin's 'disgust' with Effie's body is mysterious. There is no evidence, apart from his, to suggest that Effie was in any way malformed. The doctors who examined her at the time of the annulment reported, 'We found that the usual signs of virginity are perfect and that she is naturally and properly formed and there are no impediments on her part to a proper consummation of the marriage.'[10] Later in life, she bore Millais eight children. One must enquire what deficiencies there might have been in Ruskin himself, or whether he held ignorant or even fantastic notions of femininity. He might have been impotent. Or he might have been rendered impotent by something which he, in his ignorance of women, found shocking. It is possible that Effie was menstruating on their wedding night. But is it possible that Ruskin could still believe menstruation to be abnormal after six years of marriage? He and Effie shared a bed during all this time. We cannot now expect to know what Ruskin's sexual feelings were. But it is fair to say that on his wedding night his sexual impulses were in some part limited, or directed, by his ignorance of sexual matters. One wonders what John James had ever told him. Ruskin's father was a direct man, and there is ample evidence that he was no prude. Ruskin must have heard discussion of sex at university, if not at school. And would he not have gathered something of what girls are like from Mary Richardson, who came to Herne Hill when she was fourteen, and he ten?

Ignorance and shyness affected John and Effie's honeymoon. This was no exceptional thing in many young married couples. But in the Ruskins's marriage the things that were misunderstood, or never said, hardened into the unpleasant principles of the union. We know of one thing that was vehemently stated. When Effie's letter to her father mentions 'hatred to children' she was speaking of her husband's aversion to babies. After middle age Ruskin liked babies as much as people normally do: but in his earlier years he found them repulsive. Sometimes he describes his dislike with a humorous note that makes one suspect that there was pretence in his hatred of the newly-born. More often one is struck by the weirdness of his attitude. He refused to go to see his cousin Mary's child. Effie then wrote: 'I tried to enforce on John that we ought to call on her, but he won't as he says he can't bear lumps of *putty* as he terms babies . . .'[11] Effie later reported when she finally prevailed,

> John allows it to be passable for a baby because it has eyes like rat's fur and he likes it a little because it is not like a baby at all, but has a black face like a mouldy walnut, which is a great deal for him as it is quite against his principles to admire any of them at all . . .[12]

Ruskin claimed that it made him sick to be in the same room as Henry Acland's baby. It is possible that the revulsion he felt was connected in his mind with sexual intercourse. And other interpretations are possible. But Effie was unable to help Ruskin out of his psychological difficulties. She was baffled: and as the marriage went on, her bafflement was transformed to a bitter sense of the injustice and unnaturalness of her own sexual unhappiness.

* * * *

John and Effie toured in the Highlands for a few days. It was early in the season and the inns were empty. From Scotland they went to Keswick, whose vicar's sermons Ruskin admired.[13] As his father was in Liverpool on business, Ruskin invited him to come to the Lakes. This John James declined. The young couple returned to London three weeks after their wedding day. A splendid reception awaited them at Denmark Hill. The head gardener was at the gate with a bouquet of orange blossom for Effie: he, Margaret Ruskin and all the other servants welcomed the bride to her new home. A German band (John James's favourite music) played in the garden. There was a celebration dinner. Effie, John James wrote to Mr Gray, was

> . . . very well and in her usual spirits or way which we never wish to see changed — my son is stouter and better than we have ever seen him in the whole course of his Life — They are in appearance and I doubt not in reality extremely happy and I trust the union will prove not only a source of happiness to them but of satisfaction and comfort to us all . . .[14]

Effie was able to write to her mother that Mrs Ruskin 'bids me say how happy she is to have me here and she hopes I will feel quite a daughter to her'.[15] In the next few days old Mrs Ruskin gave Effie so many presents, mainly household treasures, that the girl became embarrassed. Their purpose was functional. Mrs Ruskin said that she might as well have them now since they would in any case be left to her. The young Ruskins were now using the top floor of Denmark Hill while John James was looking for somewhere they could live. This was not to be in the Denmark Hill area. John James was conscious that his son was famous, would become more famous, and that he would now need to entertain in some style. He accordingly searched for properties in the most fashionable parts of London.

Effie was a social success. She first appeared in public at the private views in May of the Royal Academy summer exhibition and the exhibition of the Old Water-Colour Society. The first people she met as a married woman were artists: Copley Fielding, Clarkson Stanfield, David Roberts, Landseer and Prout. One day she and John went to breakfast at Samuel Rogers's, where the old poet introduced her to those knowing, witty and well-known *littérateurs* whose company he most enjoyed. Ruskin took her away from the party quite early. On an impulse he decided to call on Turner. From Rogers's elegant rooms in St James's Place they went to the painter's dirty, shuttered house in Queen Anne Street. The door was at length opened by Turner himself. Effie was taken aback by his bare and miserly accommodation: but warmed to him as he produced wine, drank her health, then took her to see his painting of *The Fighting Temeraire*. A few days later Lady Davy, in whose house Ruskin had met Charlotte Lockhart, gave a dinner in honour of the newly married couple. Lockhart himself was there, and the rest of the company was no less distinguished. Around the table were Lord Lansdowne, a member of the Cabinet and a trustee of the National Gallery; Walter Hook, the famous vicar of Leeds, now half-way through the eight volumes of his *Dictionary of Ecclesiastical Biography*; and Henry Hallam, the mediæval historian for whose son Tennyson had written *In Memoriam*. Effie was not in the least overwhelmed by such men, and they found her charming. Invitations multiplied. John James Ruskin was pleased with the way that John and Effie had begun to spend their evenings. He told Mr Gray, 'I am glad to see Phemy gets John to go out a little. He has met with some of the first men for some years back but he is very indifferent to general Society and reluctantly acknowledges great attentions shown to him and refuses one half . . .'[16]

* * * *

Months before the wedding, it had been decided that John and Effie, together with Mr and Mrs Ruskin, would go on a continental tour in the summer. The plan was abandoned as the news came to England of the 1848 revolutions in Europe. Republican movements were so widespread that it seemed as if the whole of Europe would soon be at war. At the beginning of March, Ruskin had thought that he should marry as quickly as possible and set off for Switzerland immediately. Since Savoy, with other parts of Charles Albert's kingdom, Piedmont and Sardinia, was at war with Austria, it was now dangerous to travel to Chamonix, the place Ruskin most wished to show Effie. The earlier part of their marriage was overshadowed by political uncertainties. On their wedding day, the Chartists had marched to Westminster in demand of reform. The Bourbon monarchy had collapsed. The streets of Paris were barricaded by revolutionaries: Louis-Philippe and his queen had fled to England. By the summer, Hungary and all of the Lombardo-Veneto had revolted against Austrian rule. Manin's republic had been declared in Venice. All this was greatly disturbing to the Ruskins. It was republicanism, therefore evil. And what would be the consequences for the wine trade? Ruskin feared that it might be ten years before they could travel freely in Europe again. He was aware, of course, that the Napoleonic wars had kept Turner at home for just as long. And so, with much political foreboding, the Ruskins decided to take their summer tour in a calmer atmosphere, visiting the cathedrals of southern England.

Now began the period when Ruskin was most absorbed in architecture, the years of *The Seven Lamps* and *The Stones of Venice*. It was a time of deepening religious and political consciousness, but it coincided with his marriage, a time of human and personal failure. During his marriage Ruskin was thoughtless and insensitive to others as at no other period of his life. It was as though he had entered some strange second adolescence, learning rapidly but failing to be adult. Effie Ruskin now had to follow her husband as he pursued what to her were eccentric interests. Before going on the family tour round the English cathedrals, John and Effie spent a fortnight in Dover. Thence they proceeded to Oxford, calling on Miss Mitford on the way. They had been invited to stay at the Aclands's house in Broad Street. There, Ruskin took the liberties allowed to an old friend. He ignored the Aclands's baby, argued vehemently against Henry Acland's high church leanings, and read a book while they were at a concert. From Oxford John and Effie went on to a rendezvous with the elder Ruskins in Salisbury. The weather was bad. Salisbury Cathedral was damp. John began coughing badly and was annoyed at his drawings. A family expedition to see a new church at Wilton was not a success. John grumbled, his mother scolded and his father fussed and interfered. Effie was astonished to see how all three Ruskins behaved. Finally John took to his bed, where he remained for a week while Effie slept in a different room. Mrs Ruskin also had a cold and John James was suffering from stomach upsets. Effie became irritated and lost her temper with her mother-in-law. For this outburst Ruskin gravely rebuked her. The holiday became grimmer and it seemed best to go home. Very soon the whole party returned to Denmark Hill.

In such circumstances Ruskin had been meditating his work on building. He had not been engaged on a book since the spring of 1846, when he finished the second volume of *Modern Painters*. That summer's continental tour had produced many architectural notes, probably as a relaxation from his labours on the Italian primitives and Tintoretto. From that time until his wedding the thought of an architectural book had remained with him. His notes were of a practical and visual type, but in a current diary we find an undated passage that indicates the themes that also occupied him:

> Expression of emotion in Architecture as Monastic — peaceful — threatening — mysterious — proud — enthusiastic.
> Expression of ambition — Difficulty cutting, vaulting, King's College, etc., raising of spires, etc.
> Consider luscious architecture: How far beautiful.
> General style. What constitutes its greatness. First, mere labour; patience, skill and devotion (Sacrifice). Then labour of *thinking* men; if nothing be lost, nothing valueless; consider if under this head one might not have a 'Spirit of Husbandry' (consider also, awe and mystery and their spirit under head of Power). Yet it is fine to see work for work's sake, or rather for completion of a system sometimes.[17]

Readers of *The Seven Lamps of Architecture* will recognize that in these jottings lie the first thoughts of that famous book, and may reflect on the ability of Ruskin's architectural writings to make numinous notions rather specific. Perhaps this was because much of what he now wrote on architecture was derived from urgent personal experience. While preparing the second volume of *Modern Painters*, he had been appalled by the destruction of ancient buildings. A long note to the second volume's chapter on the 'Theoretical Faculty' — which Ruskin later, in 1883, cancelled in despair that his warnings had not been heeded — lists some of the recent losses. All had personal associations for him. The old houses at Beauvais, the wooden loggias at Geneva, mediæval houses at Tours and the church of St Nicholas at Rouen had all gone. Ruskin recounts how the 'restoration' of the old Baptistery at Pisa had been done so clumsily and cheaply that the building was ruined.[18] His discovery of ancient art brought with it a furious realization that the modern world had no regard for its safety. In Pisa, he saw bricklayers knocking down a wall in the Campo Santo on which frescoes had been painted. In Florence, he found that the old street running towards the cathedral had been torn down: in its place was a row of kiosks selling knick-knacks and souvenirs. The old refectory of Santa Croce was being used as a carpet factory. Ruskin saw rain beating through the windows of the Arena Chapel in Padua and dripping into buckets in the Scuola di San Rocco. It filled him with a literally religious horror. In a letter to his father in 1845 he broke into a quotation from Revelation:

> I think verily the Devil is come down upon earth, having great wrath, because he knoweth that he hath but a short time. And a short time he will have if he goes on at this rate, for in ten years more there will be nothing in the world but eating-houses and gambling houses and worse . . . the French condemned the Convent of San Marco where I am just going, and all the pictures of Fra Angelico were only saved by their being driven out . . .[19]

A part of Ruskin's hatred of republicanism was that he felt that it would bring with it the destruction of art and of ancient buildings. In such a frame of mind *The Seven Lamps of Architecture* was written, and painting for the moment abandoned. The preface to its first edition explains that *Modern Painters* could not yet be concluded

> . . . owing to the necessity under which the writer felt himself, of obtaining as many memoranda as possible of mediæval buildings in Italy and Normandy, now in the process of destruction, before that destruction should be consummated by the Restorer, or Revolutionist.[20]

Ruskin was so anxious to get on with *The Seven Lamps* that he decided that he and Effie should go to France. This they did, attended by George Hobbs, almost as soon as they came home from the dismal holiday in Salisbury. John James Ruskin accompanied them to Boulogne, then crossed the Channel back to England. The French port was full of rumours of war. An Englishman, going home, told them that Paris was full of soldiers. It was said that France had declared war on Austria, and that an army had marched over the Alps. John and Effie went by rail from Boulogne to Abbeville. Here Ruskin began work. 'I was dancing round the table this forenoon', he wrote to John James,

. . . in rapture with the porch here — far beyond all my memories or anticipation — perfectly superb, and all the houses more fantastic, more exquisite than ever; alas! not all, for there is not a street without fatal marks of restoration, and in twenty years it is plain that not a vestige of Abbeville, or indeed of any old French town will be left . . . I got into a cafe and have been doing my best to draw the cathedral porch; but alas, it is not so easily done. I seem born to conceive what I cannot execute, recommend what I cannot obtain, and mourn over what I cannot save.[21]

Effie was delighted with her first visit to France. Like Ruskin, she enjoyed being abroad: unlike him, she took pleasure in practising foreign languages. She was a little upset to attend her first mass, but enjoyed the attentions given to them at the best hotel, where they were the only guests. Most of her time was spent idly. Ruskin worked assiduously on Norman architecture. She sat on a camp stool while he drew, measured, and took notes of buildings. In the evenings she was entrusted with making a fair copy of these notes. The political situation and the threat of war seemed real, yet distant. Ruskin began to think that he might venture further into Europe, and even take his parents to Italy. As he now wrote to John James, 'I trust the negotiations which France and England have together undertaken will pacify all and that we may have another look at Venice yet before the Doge's palace is bombarded.'[22]

From Abbeville John and Effie went on to Rouen. Here was one of those cities, 'tutresses of all I know', that Ruskin believed governed his life's work, and should always be approached with reverence. To a student such as himself, Abbeville was therefore 'the preface and interpretation of Rouen'.[23] Ruskin had been to the Norman capital in 1835, 1840, 1842 and 1844, on the summer tours with his parents that had formed his taste. All through his life Ruskin would reminisce about his walks through the city in 1842 in search of the Turnerian site for a plate in *The Rivers of France*, and how in 1857 he had been able to buy the original drawing. Rouen Cathedral he loved more than any other northern church: there and in the churches of St Nicholas, St Maclou, St Ouen, St Patrice and St Vincent, he nourished the non-Italian part of his architectural sensibility. This belonged to his youth as much as to his maturity, and he associated Rouen as much with Prout as with Turner. It was with Prout in mind that he wrote of it as

. . . a city altogether inestimable for its retention of a mediæval character in the infinitely varied streets in which one half of the existing and inhabited houses date from the fifteenth or early six-

14. John James Ruskin, by George Richmond, 1848.

> teenth century, and the only town left in France in which the effect of old French domestic architecture can yet be seen in its collective groups.[24]

The greater, therefore, was his rage when he and his wife arrived there in 1848. Effie reported to her parents:

> John is perfectly frantic with the spirit of restoration here, and at other places the men actually before our eyes knocking down the time worn black with age pinnacles and sticking up in their place new stone ones to be carved at some future time . . . John is going to have some daguerrotypes taken of the churches as long as they are standing . . . he says he is quite happy in seeing I enjoy myself and if it were not for my gentle mediation he would certainly do something desperate and get put in prison for knocking some of the workmen off the scaffolding.[25]

In these trying conditions, in Rouen, at Falaise, Avranches, at Mont St Michel, Bayeux, Caen and Honfleur, sometimes patiently but more often urgently, Ruskin filled the eight notebooks and hundreds of sheets of drawing paper that were the basis of *The Seven Lamps of Architecture*. Absorbed in his work, he took little notice of Effie. It was some time before he noticed that she had become bored with sitting in churches. He was not sufficiently interested in her family problems. While they were in France, John James had been unhelpful with the problem of finding her brother a commercial position. Her father's affairs had not improved, and now she learnt that her Aunt Jessie was seriously ill. Of all this, Ruskin wrote to his father with the honesty of the totally self-engrossed:

> Even when poor Effie was crying last night I felt it by no means as a husband should — but rather a bore — however I comforted her in a very dutiful way — but it may be as well — perhaps on the other hand, that I am not easily worked on by these things.[26]

Effie was tired of France. She wanted to go back to England and then go to Scotland to see her family. Ruskin said that his own health would not permit a winter journey to Scotland, but that she ought to go there with a companion. There the matter rested, for Ruskin now made an impulsive decision to visit Paris. It might be dangerous, and he had no love for the city, but he felt that he should compare Notre Dame with the northern churches. The Ruskins arrived in Paris in the aftermath of fighting. Their trunks were opened and searched for weapons. Few shops were open, the Tuileries deserted. There were marks of fighting in the street. The republican government had reorganized the Louvre in a manner which infuriated Ruskin. Paris was, he found, as a result of the recent 'slaughterous and dishonest contest', a society plunged in 'gloom without the meanest effort at the forced gaiety which once disguised it'.[27] A week later the Ruskins were back in Denmark Hill.

CHAPTER EIGHT

1849–1850

The house which John James Ruskin had found for John and Effie, and which he had taken on a three-year lease, was in Mayfair. No. 31 Park Street was three doors away from Lady Davy's and looked out over the gardens of the Marquess of Westminster's Grosvenor House. Effie was excited by her new home and the smart brougham that her father-in-law had provided for her. Ruskin was less interested in these fashionable surroundings. He organized a study for himself in Park Street, but did not move all his books and effects from Denmark Hill. Nor was he ever to do so. He could not think of Park Street as his home, and often used to drive out to Denmark Hill to dine and stay the night. However, a good number of the Ruskins's evenings were spent at London social occasions of one kind or another. This could often be a point of contention. But there was not a simple contrast between a bookish husband and a gay young wife. There was an intellectual élite among these Mayfair gatherings which welcomed the Ruskins. It consisted of statesmen, writers, public personages connected with the fine arts and senior members of the Church of England. The Ruskins met, for instance, Henry Milman, now a canon of Westminster but shortly to become Dean of St Paul's, previously Professor of Poetry at Oxford and author of the scholarly *History of the Jews*. Milman was friendly with the historian Henry Hallam, whom Effie and John had met at Lady Davy's; and another friend of Milman's was Thomas Macaulay, the first two volumes of whose history of England had just appeared. The Ruskins met Macaulay at a party given by Sir Robert Inglis at his house in Bedford Square, where literary and political figures, both liberal and tory, met on friendly and slightly competitive terms.

In such houses Ruskin's acquaintance among the 'leading men', as his father termed them, might have been greatly increased. But he made little attempt to win friends in this society. He was rude to Milman, scorned Hallam and took no notice of Macaulay. He thought they were worldly, that they loved neither nature nor art. At Park Street he entertained old friends from Christ Church days like Lord Eastnor and Osborne Gordon. One night the Richmonds came to dinner to eat snipe from Mr Telford's estate. It was the sort of evening

Ruskin would have enjoyed, if only it had been at Denmark Hill. Towards the end of 1848 he began to press Effie to spend more time in his old family home. While they were staying there for Christmas and the New Year of 1849 Effie's relations with her parents-in-law suddenly worsened. She fell foul of Mrs Ruskin. She became ill, lost her appetite, and felt miserable. One day Mrs Ruskin found her in tears when she should have been getting ready for dinner, and scolded her. Soon she developed a feverish cold and began coughing badly. The elder Ruskins treated her illnesses as self-indulgences. They held it against her that she did not come downstairs to attend their New Year's dinner party, when Joseph Severn, Tom Richmond (George's brother), and Turner were among the guests. Try as she might, Effie could not get better. Her own doctor and the Ruskins's family doctor gave her contradictory advice. Then her mother came to stay. Effie suddenly saw a way to recover her spirits. She decided to return to Scotland with her mother, leaving her husband behind in London. Ruskin, hard at work on *The Seven Lamps of Architecture*, was not at all displeased to be left in peace. He immediately moved out of Park Street and returned to Denmark Hill. As things turned out, he was not to see his wife for another nine months.

★ ★ ★ ★

While Ruskin was living in Park Street he was invited to join the council of the newly founded Arundel Society. Its originators were C. H. Bellenden Kerr, Sir Charles Eastlake, Edmund Oldfield and Aubrey Bezzi. We may think of them as the kind of men with whom Ruskin had sporadic professional rather than social relations. Kerr was a deaf and eccentric lawyer with artistic tastes. Edmund Oldfield was Ruskin's schoolfriend at Dr Dale's who knew so much about Gothic architecture: he now worked in the British Museum. Bezzi was the Society's secretary. He had republican sympathies and had fled from Italy with Panizzi, the future librarian of the British Museum: later on he would become a member of the government of the kingdom of Sardinia. Eastlake, a busy man, made little appearance at Arundel Society meetings. The wary respect he and Ruskin felt for each other had not yet been transmuted into open hostility.

The Society was begun with a didactic and æsthetic purpose. Its founders had a partial model for their enterprise in the Society for the Diffusion of Useful Knowledge, but their intention (so their prospectus announced) was to serve a revived interest in art by copying and publishing reproductions of Italian paintings. Connoisseur-collectors who had assembled engravings after old masters in previous years had not had such an educational purpose. Nor had such connoisseurs commissioned engravings. The Arundel Society was to do this because it was their intention to concentrate on early painting rather than on the classical masters. The prospectus points out that

> . . . the materials for such instruction are abundant, but scattered, little accessible, and, in some instances, passing away. Of the frescoes of Giotto, Orcagna, Ghirlandajo, much of which has never been delineated, nor even properly described, is rapidly perishing.[1]

Other knowledgeable people who were asked to join the council of the Society at the same time as Ruskin were Samuel Rogers, Charles Newton, Lord Lansdowne and Lord Lindsay. They were Ruskin's natural colleagues. But he was in some measure the inspiration of the Society. A good number of its projected publications were taken from works described by Ruskin in the second volume of *Modern Painters*, such as Benozzo Gozzoli's frescoes of the *Journey of the Magi*, the Tintorettos in the Scuola di San Rocco, Fra Angelico's frescoes in San Marco and Ghirlandaio's in Santa Maria Novella. The Arundel Society was variously active until 1897. Ruskin was to write two monographs for it, *Giotto and his Works in Padua* (1853-60) and *Monuments of the Cavalli Family in the Church of Santa Anastasia, Verona* (1872); while its occasional publications in pamphlet form were to give him many ideas for the stream of pamphlets, illustrations and part-publications that he issued via Smith, Elder and, later, through his own publishing company.

★ ★ ★ ★

When Effie Ruskin went back to Bowerswell with her mother at the beginning of February 1849 she was still suffering from the illness that had come on her at Denmark Hill. She was tired, she suffered from feverish colds, her stomach was upset and she had blisters on her throat. We may believe that some of her complaints were generated by the strain of living with such a husband: but Margaret Ruskin knew that the girl had brought the illness on herself. Margaret was now beginning to think of the contrast between her own marriage, so immensely satisfying to her, and her son's. In one letter to John James she openly mentioned her disappointment, though to Ruskin himself she as yet said nothing. At Bowerswell, the Gray family were suffering from bereavement. Effie's Aunt Jessie had died: now Effie lost her seven-year-old brother Robert. She was still unwell herself. In these circumstances she decided to stay with her family at Bowerswell and not return to accompany the Ruskins on the continental tour they planned to take that spring. This seemed sensible, if in some ways unsatisfactory. Ruskin wanted to work in Switzerland. Effie needed rest. And, as John James wrote to Mr Gray, it was not necessarily relaxing to be with Ruskin when he was working.

> It may be his pleasure but to be with him is other people's toil — out of doors at any rate. They must however arrange their comings and goings with each other. They will no doubt settle down very delightfully at last pleased with some house at home and I hope allow you and me to come to hear them in chorus singing dulce dulce domum.[2]

Ruskin was finishing the last pages of *The Seven Lamps of Architecture* as he and his parents set off for the Continent in the middle of April. He posted them to W. H. Harrison from Folkestone. Two of the etchings for the book were bitten in his hotel bedroom at Dijon. This year, the Ruskins were to be away for five months. The tour provided material for the next volume of *Modern Painters*, though the book would not appear for another five years. Ruskin dutifully wrote to his wife during their separation. One is struck by the artificial adoption of a romantic tone. The first letters emphasize how unreal his marriage was, not based on any physical or emotional fact.

> Do you know, pet, it seems almost a dream to me that we have been married: I look forward to meeting you: and to your *next* bridal night: and to the time when I shall again draw your dress from your snowy shoulders: and lean my cheek upon them, as if you were still my betrothed only: and I had never held you in my arms. God bless you my dearest.[3]

It is hard to imagine what Effie might have made of such a declaration. Was it a letter that announced physical intentions, or merely a flourish by someone who had been reading poetry? The assurance that 'I look forward to meeting you' was clearly untrue, since Ruskin was about to spend some months in his favourite places with his parents, his favourite people. The more Effie thought about her situation the less it seemed to her that she was truly married, in any way. She had strong feelings for her own family yet the Ruskins tugged her away from them. She was too much put upon by the Ruskin parents and yet John Ruskin, her husband, in all ways eluded her. Ruskin himself could not understand this, nor begin to imagine what it might be like to be in Effie's position. Only a few days later he was writing to her in these terms:

> I often hear my father and mother saying — 'poor child — if she could but have thrown herself openly upon us, and trusted us, and would have made her ours, how happy she might have been: and how happy she might have made us all'. And indeed I long for you my pet: but I have much here to occupy me and keep me interested — and so I am able to bear the longing better perhaps than you, who have only the routine of home: I hope next summer I shall be able to make you happy in some way of your own.[4]

One explanation for Ruskin's behaviour toward Effie at this time is that like many artists he became withdrawn and egotistical when nurturing his responses to nature, or to art, in preparation for some creative effort. A curious piece of self-examination is recorded in his diary the day after he sent this letter to Effie.

> It is deserving of record that at this time, just on the point of coming in sight of the Alps, and that for the first time in three years — a moment which I had looked forward to, thinking I should be almost fainting with joy, and should want to lie down on the earth and take it in my arms — at this time, I say, I was irrevocably sulky and cross, because *George had not got me butter to my bread at Les Rousses*.[5]

Whatever else we may feel about this confession, it is important to realize that Ruskin was in pursuit of his previous Alpine experiences. He believed that he was at a nexus of his imaginative life. 'The sunset of today', he recorded on 3 June, 'sank upon me like the departure of youth.'[6] This was not merely a grandiose remark. Not for the first time, Ruskin was thinking of Wordsworth's *Immortality* ode.[7] Following the poem, he also considered whether the intensity of his earlier feelings for nature could not be recaptured. Ruskin's diary this spring and summer tells us time and again how he went back to places where he had been deeply moved in previous years. He sought out the same paths, the same resting places that he had last visited three years before and, more significantly, had known as a boy in 1835. The exercise was not only to observe the landscape and weather. It was also to observe his own responses, to try to stand outside himself as an æsthetic being.

Sometimes he used personal inducements to bring his mind to an artistic state. At Blonay, amid 'lovely scenes', he

> . . . required an effort to maintain the feeling — it was poetry while it lasted — and I felt that it was only while under it that one could draw or invent or give glory to any part of such a landscape. I repeated 'I am in *Switzerland*' over and over again, till the name brought back the true group of associations — and I felt I had a soul, like my boy's soul, once again. I have not insisted enough on this source of all great contemplative art.[8]

Such self-explorations are the source for the discussion of the æsthetic emotion found in the tenth chapter of part four of the third volume of *Modern Painters*. In that volume, as also in the fourth, there are many passages which derive from Ruskin's studies in 1849 at Vevey, Chamonix, the Rhone Valley and Zermatt. The books were not published until 1856, seven years later, and were written in 1855: but they take the experiences of 1849 as their starting point. A passage on grass in *Modern Painters*, quite famous in the nineteenth century, may be taken as an example. The 1849 diary entry at Vevey reads:

> I looked at the slope of different grass on the hill; and then at the waving heads near me. What a gift of God that is, I thought. Who could have dreamed of such a soft, green, continual tender clothing for the dark earth — the food of cattle, and of man. Think what poetry has come of its pastoral influence, what happiness from its everyday ministering, what life from its sustenance. Bread that strengtheneth man's heart — ah, well may the Psalmist number among God's excellencies, 'He maketh grass to grow upon the mountains'.[9]

Five years later, in the course of a discussion of mediæval landscape, and just after some suggestive remarks about grass in Dante, Ruskin's diary note becomes a set-piece:

> Go out, in the spring-time, among the meadows that slope from the shores of the Swiss lakes to the roots of their lower mountains. There, mingled with the taller gentians and the white narcissus, the grass grows deep and free; and as you follow the winding mountain paths, beneath arching boughs all veiled and dim with blossom, — paths that for ever droop and rise over the green banks and mounds sweeping down inscented undulation, steep to the blue water, studded here and there with new-mown heaps, filling all the air with fainter sweetness, — look up towards the higher hills, where the waves of everlasting green roll silently into their long inlets

> among the shadows of the pines; and we may, perhaps, at last know the meaning of those quiet words of the 147th Psalm, 'He maketh grass to grow upon the mountains'.[10]

In such ways, this fruitful tour of 1849 was the first stimulus of writing that would occupy Ruskin for the next decade. If he could strike his mood in these months he was beautifully alert to all he saw: mountains, wood anemones, the darkness of pine forests, or the flight of the grey wagtail. To return once again to the diary:

> Friday 4th May. — Half breakfasted at Chambery; started about seven for St Laurent du Pont, thence up to the Chartreuse, and walked down (all of us); which, however, being done in a hurry, I little enjoyed. But a walk after dinner up to a small chapel, placed on a waving group of mounds, covered with the most smooth and soft sward, over whose sunny gold came the dark piny precipices of the Chartreuse hills, gave me infinite pleasure. I had seen also for the third time, by the Chartreuse torrent, the most wonderful of all Alpine birds — a grey, fluttering stealthy creature, about the size of a sparrow, but of colder grey, and more graceful, which haunts the side of the fiercest torrents. There is something more strange in it than in the seagull — *that* seems a powerful creature; and the power of the sea, not of a kind so adverse, so hopelessly destructive; but this small creature, silent, tender and light, almost like a moth in its low and irregular flight, — almost touching with its wings the crests of waves that would overthrow a granite wall, and haunting the hollows of the black, cold, herbless rocks that are continually shaken by their spray, has perhaps the nearest approach to the look of a spiritual existence that I know in animal life.[11]

On many occasions during the summer of 1849 Ruskin chose to be solitary among the Alps. But he was enlivened by the arrival in Switzerland of his boyhood friend Richard Fall. Together with Couttet and George Hobbs, he and Fall went out on climbing expeditions. At other times Ruskin left his parents for a few days and went with George to draw and take daguerrotypes. He made notes on the angles of various peaks, examined the flora, analysed the geology, ascertained the movements of glaciers, watched the streams and clouds. Some of this material was gathered into the diary, but many other notebooks were used. Apart from sketched memoranda Ruskin made forty-seven drawings which were highly enough finished for him to catalogue, a rare procedure with his own work. This was the last time that he was to draw landscape consistently for a number of years. The

15. *La Cascade de la Folie, Chamouni*, by John Ruskin, 1849.

best known of the drawings is *La Cascade de la Folie, Chamouni* (Plate 15). It is highly detailed, dramatically unfolding a vista of mountain scenery beyond and high above the plunging waterfall. These drawings were used a few years later to write the chapter on aiguilles in the fourth volume of *Modern Painters*. A number were executed during a memorable few days, full of difficult climbing, when Couttet took Ruskin on *le tour de Mont Blanc*. The young Englishman and his guide went by St Gervais and Contamines over the Col du Bonhomme to Chapui: thence ascended to the Col de la Seigne, 8,000 feet high, where Ruskin drew, before proceeding to Courmayeur. They then went over the Col Ferret to Martigny, and from Martigny to Zermatt, where Ruskin made the study of the cliffs of the Matterhorn that enabled him to write the chapter 'On Precipices' in the fourth volume of *Modern Painters*. He then spent three days in Montanvert, where after a day's Alpine note-taking he wondered if he had ever enjoyed an evening so much in his life, sitting 'at the window quietly today watching the sunset and the vast flow of ice, welling down the gorge — a dark and billowy river — yet with the mountainous swell and lifted crests that the iron rocks have round it'.[12]

This summer among the Alps also set Ruskin to consider peasant economy and culture. In a diary entry at St Martin's we find the origin of the great chapter in *Modern Painters* IV, 'The Mountain Gloom'. Ruskin was thinking then

> . . . what a strange contrast there is between these lower valleys, with their ever-wrought richness mixed with signs of waste and disease, their wild noon-winds shaking their leaves into palsy, and the dark storms folding themselves about their steep mural precipices — between these and the pastoral green, pure aiguilles, and fleecy rain-clouds of Chamouni . . .[13]

Natural life both intermingled and contrasted with the social order in the Alps. The peasants were poor, wretchedly so. There was much goitre and cretinism. How could there be such human misery in such divinely fashioned surroundings? It was this 'melancholy knowledge', Ruskin confessed in *Præterita*, 'of the agricultural condition of the great Alpine chain which was the origin of the design of St George's Guild'.[14] But that was far in the future, and in 1849 Ruskin could not quite bring himself to think independently about social problems. He was so absorbed by nature that even the evidence of war left him only a cool observer. Chamonix is in Savoy. At this date Savoy, with Piedmont, was part of the kingdom of Sardinia. In the 1848 revolutions Charles Albert, the King of Sardinia, had fought against the Austrians. He had been defeated, had abdicated, and had given up his throne to his son Victor Emmanuel. The Ruskins saw the remains of Charles Albert's defeated army at Chambéry. John reported to Effie:

> This place is full of soldiers, returned from the last battle: shabby fellows the Savoyard troops were always and look none the better for their campaign: and as the government cannot afford them new clothes, though it is getting them into some order again as fast as it can, they look slovenly and melancholy: more beggars on the road than ever, and the people seeming hard put to it — but a quiet and gentle people, and one that with a good religion, might be anything . . .[15]

In June, when John James Ruskin thought that he had never seen his son in better health, trouble started between the Ruskins and the Grays. Effie's illnesses were still troubling her. She decided to consult Dr James Simpson, Professor of Midwifery at the University of Edinburgh. It is possible that Simpson advised her to have children: he certainly did so later on. But when Effie wrote to Ruskin to tell him about the consultation she did not report to him what Simpson had thought. Ruskin was annoyed by this, and so were his parents. John James's letters to Perth changed from concern to condemnation: 'About your daughter Mrs Ruskin and myself must continue to be anxious and as I use no reserve I will confess to you that the feeling is mixed with sorrow and disappointment.'[16] Grievances were aired about Effie's clothes, housekeeping, and the like. For a little while, as this unpleasant correspondence continued, Ruskin was markedly kinder to his wife than his parents were. But it is plain that practically all his attention was given to the mountains, not to Effie's well-being. In the circumstances, Mr Gray showed great patience. He wrote to John James Ruskin,

> If I may be permitted to hint a word by way of advice it would simply be that Mrs Ruskin and you should leave John and Phemy as much as possible to themselves — married people are rather restive under the control and supervision of parents tho' proceeding from the kindest and most affectionate motives.[17]

If this was generally so of married people, it was not so of John Ruskin. While he exchanged quite pleasant letters with his wife he made no attempt to calm the increasingly angry tone adopted by his father. Behind the whole quarrel was a simple question. Why was Effie not happier? Ruskin kept silent. One of John James's pleas was for complete frankness. Mr Gray wrote of how his daughter hated hypocrisy. But the sexual position of the young couple was unsuspected by the parents. Had Ruskin ordered Effie not to tell her mother that he refused to make love to her? A great deal was not discussed. As far as one can gather from the many letters now exchanged, neither family mentioned children. But they said many other things to each other, and on the Ruskins's side said them harshly. Towards the end of his stay in Switzerland Ruskin was writing to Effie's father with an extraordinary interpretation of her unhappiness:

> The state of her feelings I ascribe now, simply to bodily weakness: that is to say — and this is a serious and distressing admission — to a nervous disease affecting the brain. I do not know when the complaint first showed itself — but the first I saw of it was at Oxford after our journey to Dover: it showed itself then, as it does now, in tears and depression: being probably a more acute manifestation, in consequence of fatigue and excitement — of disease under which she has long been labouring . . . an illness bordering in many of its features on incipient insanity.[18]

Ruskin had not seen his wife since February. When, in late August, the Ruskins started to make plans to go home, the Grays were anxious that John should go to Perth to collect Effie. There was a simple reason for this. There was much gossip in Perth, as well there might be, about Effie's marriage. The Grays wanted John to be seen there with his wife. The elder Ruskins objected to this proposal and Effie, once more, received a most un-uxorious letter.

> As for your wish that I should come to Scotland — that is also perfectly natural — nor have I the slightest objection to come for you: only do not mistake womanly pride for womanly affection: You say that 'you should have thought the first thing I should have done after six months' absence, would have been to come for you'. Why, you foolish little puss, do you not see that part of my reason for wishing you to come to London was that I might get you a couple of days sooner: and do you not see also, that if love, instead of pride, had prompted your reply, you would never have thought of what I *ought* to do, or your *right* to ask, you would only have thought of being with me as soon as you could . . .[19]

In the event, however, Ruskin did go to Perth. He arrived there towards the end of September, thin, sunburnt, slightly distracted. Relations were bound to be difficult. There was embarrassment in the air, though Ruskin did not feel it. Now Effie made a suggestion that was both bold and sensible. She asked Ruskin to take her to Venice. It was perfectly possible. Nothing stood in their way. The bombardment of the city was over, Manin's republican government had fallen, and Venice was once more in Austrian hands. For Effie, the great advantage of going to Venice was that she could have John on her own. For Ruskin, too, there were good reasons for going there. He could continue his architectural studies at a time of relative political stability. He might never have another such opportunity. Dr Simpson was in favour of the plan. John James Ruskin wrote a sensible and generous letter giving them his blessing: he would, of course, be paying all their expenses. In this way the Ruskins's marriage was rescued for a time.

★ ★ ★ ★

Ruskin had scarcely been back in England for three weeks before setting off with Effie en route for Venice. Effie took a companion with her. This was Charlotte Ker, a Perth neighbour. In London, Effie got on perfectly well with the elder Ruskins. She busied herself with the exciting task of getting their two carriages ready, while Ruskin and George Hobbs packed books and daguerrotype equipment. From Boulogne, sometimes posting and sometimes travelling by rail, they travelled quickly towards Switzerland. Ruskin was at his most kind and charming. Effie wrote home with the news of her

> . . . first view of the Alps, the Plain of Geneva and the Lake seen from an elevation of 3,000 feet the most striking Panorama I ever beheld but curious to say I was not in the least surprised by the magnificence of the view as it was exactly like what I had always supposed it would be . . . John was excessively delighted to see how happy we were and went jumping about and executing *pas* that George and I agreed Taglioni would have stared her widest at.[20]

In the Alps, Effie and Charlotte were shocked by the condition of the peasantry. To have observed poverty in rural Scotland was no preparation for this. They saw children with no arms, women with huge goitres that had necklaces and crosses draped over them. The men were filthy and toothless. Chamonix was a cleaner village than most: it was one reason why the Ruskins stayed there so often. An arrangement had been made with Couttet to meet them there. He was delighted to see Ruskin again so soon, and even more delighted to meet Effie. Ruskin, alone, climbed up the Breven to a favourite site and took notes on the aiguilles across the valley. But he was conscious that his *Modern Painters* work would have to be put aside for architectural research in Venice. Abandoning his aiguilles, he took up a local ghost story instead. Some Chamonix children had been frightened by the apparition of a woman dressed all in black. Ruskin, who derived from Anne Strachan an interest in ghosts that would remain with him all his life, sought out these children. He talked to them, interrogated the local priest, and even organized the digging of a large hole at the place where the spectre had been seen.

The party had paused in Switzerland to allow time for Venice to recover from the cholera epidemic that had spread through the city during the siege. As they moved on to Milan the effects of war became apparent. Roads were closed, churches had been commandeered, provisions were scarce. Austrian and Croatian troops were everywhere. Ruskin's diary now becomes filled with architectural notes, while Effie's letters home are packed with social detail. In Milan she and Charlotte were hoping to set eyes on Field-Marshal Radetzky 'as he is a *decided* lion'.[21] Radetzky was the Civil and Military Governor of the Lombardo-Veneto, an elderly soldier who had commanded the Austrian army which suppressed the Italian nationalist revolts. In Milan, Effie was not sure of her political feelings. She declared, 'I am a thorough Italian here and hate oppression.'[22] Very soon, however, she took the Austrian side, as did her husband. Ruskin was only slightly less vehement than his father in expressing dislike of republicanism. As English tories, they were without sympathy for nationalist aspirations. Ruskin's view was that the Italians, unhappy as they no doubt were, had brought the occupation on themselves by their past sins and follies, and that the Austrian government was probably as wise as one could hope for from a Romanist administration. He saw the suffering, but it did not engage him. He had, he confessed, 'no heart nor eyes for anything but stone'.[23]

The railway to Venice had been destroyed, so the party had to leave their carriages outside the city. George arranged the transfer of their luggage to the Hotel Danieli on the Riva degli Schiavoni. The hotel was only a hundred yards from St Mark's Square: from the windows of their suite they could see the Campanile and could hear the Austrian band that played in front of St Mark's every night. Ruskin immediately toured the major Venetian buildings to make sure they were still standing. To his relief, the damage was not as extensive as he had feared. Quite soon he left Effie and Charlotte, with their Murray's guide, to go exploring on their own. Effie searched for the Venice of Titian and Veronese. She was pleased with the *festa* of the Madonna della Salute, held every year since 1662 as a thanksgiving after the plague. She was never to see the many festivals and holidays that commemorated Venice's proud past: the Austrians had suppressed them. The English party, since they sided with the Austrians, necessarily had a foreigner's view of the city's life, and hardly a sympathetic one. They were cut off from the proud Venetian nobility, except the collaborators, and also from most intellectuals. Effie now learnt the differences between the *italianissimi*, the patriots, and the *austriacanti*, Italians with Austrian politics. She saw how they never mixed, never went to the same social occasions, frequented different cafés. She learnt that the Austrian band in St Mark's Square was a symbol of Austrian supremacy: that was why all patriots left the square as soon as it started to play. One day she witnessed the burning of all the paper money, the *moneta patriottica*, that had been issued by Manin's government. It was an action designed to humiliate the Venetians. The city's economy was at a standstill. Thousands had no employment and nowhere to live. On the way back to the hotel at night Effie passed the homeless lying packed together at the end of bridges. 'The lower population here are exactly like animals in the way they live,' she wrote, 'and the fishermen's families live in rooms without an article of furniture and feed in the streets.'[24]

Ruskin was eager that Effie and Charlotte should go into Austrian society so that they would be safely occupied while he worked. He wrote to Lady Davy asking her to arrange some introductions. He had one contact of his own. John Murray had given him an introduction to a man who would be able to help him among Venetian archives. This was Rawdon Brown, who became a lifelong friend. Brown, ten years older than Ruskin, had lived in Venice since 1833. He was eccentric, quarrelsome, quite out of sympathy with his homeland and full of a detailed love of his adopted city. He had bought and restored a palace on the Grand Canal which he filled with Venetian art, documents and curiosities. When the Ruskins arrived in Venice he was practically the only English person there: the others, like most of the Venetian aristocracy, had left the city before the siege began. Brown's curiosity and eclectic mind had some effect on Ruskin, perhaps even beyond the writing of *The Stones of Venice*. For that book he was a guiding influence. Ruskin's researches were continually helped by him, both intellectually and practically. Brown had access to state papers and to the library of St Mark's and could show Ruskin how to use them. He also, shortly, introduced Ruskin to another English antiquary, Edward Cheney. This Shropshire landowner had a house in Venice which he visited every year. Cheney rather distrusted Ruskin's tastes — he was himself an admirer of the baroque — but opened his library

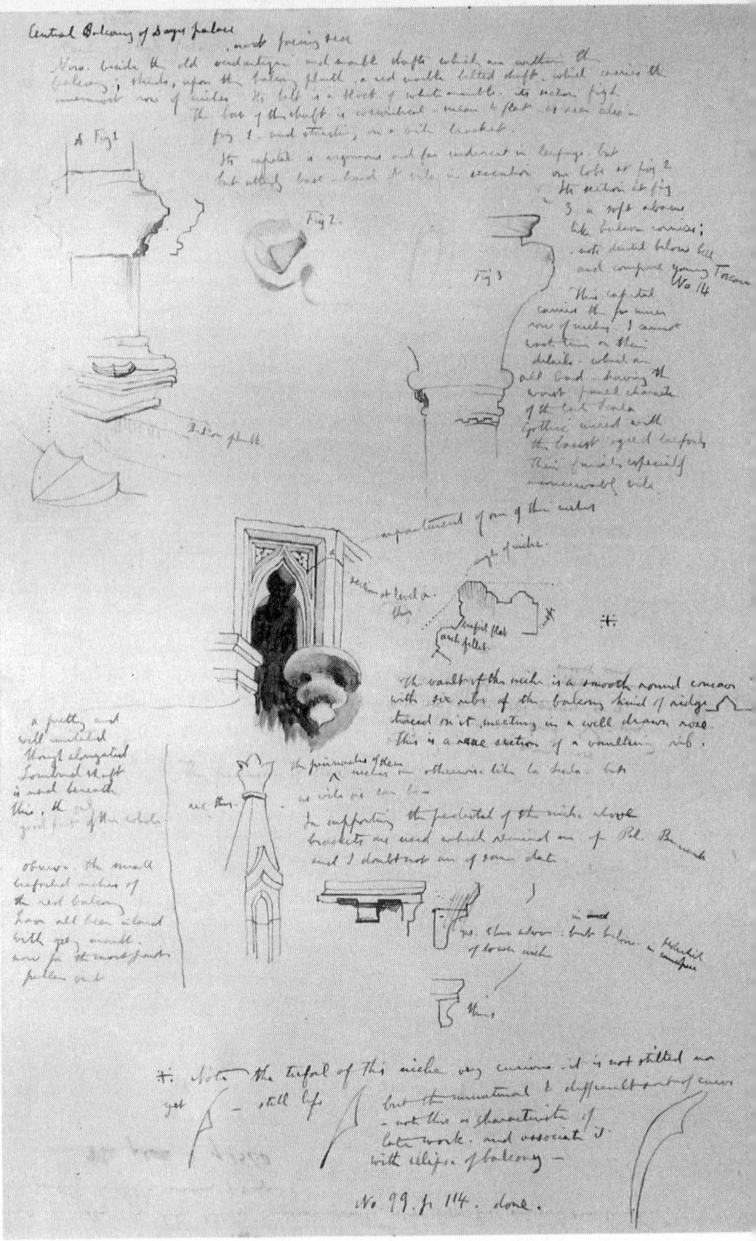

16. Worksheet no. 99. In preparation for *The Stones of Venice*: notes on the Duc
Palace, December 1849, by John Ruskin.

to him and sometimes sent a servant round to the Danieli with suggestions that he thought might be useful.

As Effie and Charlotte began to meet people in Venetian society, Ruskin became more deeply absorbed in his researches. They had some shared diversions: a picnic, improvised games of shuttlecock, trips to the islands, dinner with Brown. But they usually spent their days separately. 'I could hardly see less of him than I do at present with his work,' Effie wrote, 'and think it is much better if we follow our different occupations and never interfere with one another and are always happy . . .'[25] Effie was the centre of attention. She had beauty and high spirits. Eager to meet people, unabashed in foreign languages (she had to speak French, German and Italian), she made many friends, and certainly some admirers too. It seems that she attended parties and balls practically every night. Charlotte was a good chaperone, but Effie was not thereby the less noticeable as a woman who appeared everywhere without her husband. In the society in which she moved — enclosed, rich, cosmopolitan, full of intrigue — this could have been misunderstood. But Effie had cool feelings for propriety. She knew how to be charming without being flirtatious. Other women liked her. Mrs Gray was a little concerned, but Effie rejected her worries.

> I hope I have inherited a little of my father's sense and your discretion to some purpose. In fact John would require a wife who could take [care] of her own character, for you know he is intensely occupied and never with us but at meal times, so that we can do anything we like and he does not care how much people are with us or what attention they pay us. I understand him perfectly and he is so kind and good when he is in the house that his gentle manners are quite refreshing after the indolent Italian and the calculating German, but we ladies like to see and know everything and I find I am much happier following my own plans and pursuits and never troubling John, or he me.[26]

Effie loved Venetian society. She mixed with the officers of the occupying forces and their ladies, with the *austriacanti* nobility and with the visitors to Venice who moved in such circles. The very names that we find in her letters home are eloquent. There was the Madame Taglioni who once owned the palace in which Rawdon Brown now lived, Count Wimpffen, the Count and Countess Minischalchi, Baroness Hessler, the Countess Mocenigo and the Duc de Bordeaux. At a private musical performance attended only by Italians she met Prince Joseph Giovanelli. At balls she talked to the Baroness Wetzler, danced with the young officers Holzammer and Montzig, but mostly with Prince Troubetzkoi, whom she later decided not to see in London. She chatted to the Saxon consul Herr Becker, to the Baron Urmenyi, 'my handsome old friend who lives here in the hotel',[27] and to the Marquis Selvatico, the President of the Venetian Academy. One might not think that a twenty-year-old girl from Perth would mix naturally in this society. Yet Effie did so with great success. Her vivid personality carried her over her lack of sophistication. She had much Scottish feeling for morals. She criticized the Baroness Gras du Barry, 'a Scotch woman married to a Frenchman, just from Paris, a dashing woman attended by a handsome young French count, the kind of person I particularly dislike to see any countrywoman of mine become'.[28] Effie would not call on Marie Taglioni, the ex-dancer, because her mother felt it would be an impropriety (though she saw much of her in other people's houses); she went to German Protestant services, read her Bible in St Mark's, and refused invitations for Sundays.

Effie reported to Perth that Venetian society could not decide whether her husband was mad or very wise. Ruskin took no notice of anyone and would let nothing disturb him from his work. His activities called forth comment. In crowded squares he could be seen bent over his daguerrotype equipment, with a black cloth over his head. He climbed up ladders and scrambled over capitals. He lay full length on the floor to draw some awkwardly positioned detail. His tape measure (which he kept until he died) was constantly in play. On descending from climbs over buildings he would stand musing, or attending to his notebook, while his gondolier dusted him down. He became a figure of fun for 'the blackguard children who hinder me by their noise and filth and impudence' as he paced around their favourite playgrounds, the bombed and ruined churches.[29] Beggars followed him everywhere. Much of his work was so laborious and irritating that he was liable to fall out of love with the city. 'I went through so much hard, dry, mechanical toil there', he wrote a few years later,

> . . . that I quite lost, before I left it, the charm of the place . . . I had few associations with any building but those of more or less pain and puzzle and provocation: — pain of frost-bitten finger and chilled throat as I examined and drew the window-sills which didn't agree with the doorsteps, or back of house which wouldn't agree with the front; and provocation from every sort of soul or thing in Venice . . .[30]

One person who did not provoke him was his wife. He was indifferent to Effie's social occupations. After supper he went into his room to write while Charlotte and Effie practised waltzes and polkas with friends. If he was obliged to go out in the evening he took a book with him, or wrote. The description of champfered edges that appears in the first volume of *The Stones* was written at the opera. Ruskin, normally a theatre-lover, now wrote to his father that

> . . . operas, drawing rooms and living creatures have become alike nuisances to me. I go out to them as if I was to pass the time in the stocks and when I am in the rooms, I say and do just what I must and no more: if people talk to me I answer them, looking all the while whether there is any body else coming to take them away. As soon as they are gone I forget their names and their faces and what they said and when I meet them the next day I don't see them. When I walk with Effie she is always touching me and saying that is so and so — now don't cut him or her as you did yesterday . . .[31]

When Effie was practising polka steps her partner was an Austrian officer, a first lieutenant of artillery named Charles Paulizza whose expertise had directed the final bombardment of the city. Paulizza seems to have been a romantic type of officer. He was fair, with long moustaches. He swirled his grey military coat lined with scarlet. He was a poet, he could play the piano, and he drew. Ruskin quite liked him, but as he could not speak English and his Italian was weaker than Ruskin's, the two men found conversation difficult. Ruskin must have summoned all his politeness when invited to admire Paulizza's drawings, which appear to have been plans and diagrams for his attacks on the city: but he was glad to use his influence to gain entrance to buildings under military occupation. Effie and Paulizza conversed in German. Soon he came to escort her everywhere. Her letters home are full of him. Descriptions of his charm and his accomplishments alternate with assurances that she is in no moral danger. A great friendliness had sprung up between them. There may have been more than that on Paulizza's side, but he behaved always with courtesy. Effie's letters, so frank are they, bespeak that if she were not so content with Ruskin — as, at this period, she was — she might have loved this man. She wrote to her mother,

> He is very fond of me, and, as you say, were John unkind to me and not so perfectly amiable and good as he is, such excessive devotion might be somewhat dangerous from so handsome and so gifted a man, but I am a strange person and Charlotte thinks I have a perfect heart of ice, for she sees him speaking to me until the tears come into his eyes and I looking and answering without the slightest discom-

> posure, but I really feel none. I never could love anyone else in the world but John and the way these Italians go on is perfectly disgusting to me that it even removes from me any desire to coquetry, which John declares I possess very highly, but he thinks it charming, so do not I . . .[32]

Effie's position was plain. But she knew what gossip was like, and she knew more about Perth gossip than Venetian gossip. She asked Charlotte not to mention her friendship with Paulizza in her letters home.[33]

Ruskin's work preparatory to the first volume of *The Stones of Venice* was coming to an end by March of 1850. Effie was not happy at the idea of returning to London. She could not imagine any life that could be as pleasant as was hers in Venice. The end of their stay came quickly, and Effie felt that they must soon come back to the city she had grown to love. While Ruskin finished off some work in St Mark's she looked forward to seeing Radetzky, and perhaps even meeting him. The military governor was due to make a short visit to Venice from his headquarters in Milan, and Effie knew that she would be invited to the same functions as the famous old soldier. The Ruskins had a farewell lunch with Paulizza. An embarrassment was that Ruskin's Italian bankers came to say goodbye at the same time. Patriots, they would not speak to an Austrian. Rawdon Brown gave Effie a brooch as they went by gondola to the railway. The next night the Ruskins were in Padua, and in Vicenza the night after that before staying for a few days in Verona. By 9 April they had reached Paris, where Effie made a visit that gave her much to think about. Ruskin took her to call on the Domecqs. Adèle was now twenty-nine, and married to Baron Duquesne. Effie thought her the least attractive of all five sisters. But she looked with a special interest at Adèle's young daughter, who spoke excellent English and was playing with a doll that Mrs Ruskin had sent her. A few days later John and Effie Ruskin were back in Denmark Hill.

CHAPTER NINE

1850–1852

When the Ruskins once more moved back to Park Street in the early summer of 1850 their life fell into a predictable pattern. Effie busied herself with her friends and her entertaining. Ruskin worked on his book and occasionally, grudgingly, accompanied her to parties. Most of his writing was done at Denmark Hill. He left Park Street after breakfast and did not return there until the evening. If he did not see his parents for a day or two, he wrote to them, and these letters often express his dislike of the society in which he moved:

> My dearest mother — horrible party last night — stiff — dull — large — fidgety — strange — run-against-everybody — know-nobody sort of party. Naval people. Young lady claims acquaintance with me. I know as much of her as of Queen Pomare. Talk. Get away as soon as I can — ask who she is — Lady Charlotte Elliott — as wise as I was before. Introduced to a black man with chin in collar. Black man condescending. I abuse several things to black man, chiefly the House of Lords. Black man says he lives in it — asks where I live — I don't want to tell him — obliged. Black man asks — go away and ask who he is. Mr Shaw Lefevre — as wise as I was before. Introduced to a young lady — young lady asks if I like drawing — go away and ask who she is — Lady Something Conyngham. Keep away with back to wall and look at watch. Get away at last — very sulky this morning — Hope my Father's better — dearest love to you both. Ever, my dearest mother, your most affec. son.[1]

There were many aspects of politics and public life of which Ruskin was simply ignorant. His 'black man' was Charles Shaw-Lefevre, the rather famous Speaker of the House of Commons. Effie, on the other hand, did not make mistakes of this sort. While she knew little of politics she was interested to know who was important. She had much talent as the mistress of a fashionable house. All the same, she longed to go back to Venice. One day in May she burst into tears as she and Ruskin were looking over some of Prout's sketches of the palaces and lagoons. Ruskin then promised her that they would return as soon as he had finished the first volume of his history of the city.

It was at this time that John and Effie met Sir Charles and Lady

Eastlake. Sir Charles had recently become the President of the Royal Academy. He had also married the formidable Elizabeth Rigby. Forty years old, six feet tall, she was the only woman contributor to the *Quarterly Review*, in whose pages she wrote pugnacious articles on art and other topics. She took to Effie at once, found Ruskin 'improving on acquaintance', but was soon to come to hate him.[2] Her husband and Ruskin knew that they were opposed on all æsthetic matters but managed to be polite to each other. Lady Eastlake sensed the hollowness of the Ruskins's marriage. She went out of her way to be kind to Effie, aware that kindness to one partner in a marriage can sometimes express malice towards the other. Effie could not always see why Ruskin distrusted people like the Eastlakes, for she had little understanding of his intellectual loyalty to his tastes. But she was sure that his artistic obsessions disturbed her social arrangements. They had an invitation to the country seat of Edward Cheney, whom they had met in Venice. Ruskin did not want to go: he knew the house would be filled with the wrong sort of art. Effie could not see that this mattered at all. And when Ruskin took her out of town to visit people with whom he wished to talk she was not properly entertained.

In April of 1851, they went together to Cambridge to stay with Dr Whewell, the Master of Trinity. The two men ignored her while they discussed architecture and theology. For many reasons Effie wanted to see her family in Scotland. She took the opportunity presented by another of her mother's pregnancies to leave London for Bowerswell. While she was there she went once more to see Dr Simpson, and it was after this consultation that she began to state publicly that she wished to have children but that her husband was opposed to her desire. She might have told Lady Eastlake: certainly she wrote to Rawdon Brown about it. She declared to him,

> I quite think with you that if I had children my health might be quite restored. Simpson and several of the best medical men have said so to me and your gracious permission to me against your prejudices amuses me not a little, but you would require to win over John too, for he hates children and does not wish any children to interfere with his plans of studies. I often think I would be a much happier, better person if I was more like the rest of my sex in this respect.[3]

This was speaking quite openly: it was close to confessing to the shrewd old man the real circumstances of her marriage.

★ ★ ★ ★

The first volume of *The Stones of Venice* was published in March of 1851. While there were some objections to it in the architectural press, several accusations of bigotry and an attack in the *Athenæum*, the book was on the whole well reviewed. That is perhaps because it was treated as literature. It is indeed literature: but, as Ruskin was to discover and lament, many people were so beguiled by his prose that they took little notice of what he was saying. In the book's mixture of history, politics, æsthetics and theological polemic, two things stood out most clearly to the average reader. They were Ruskin's style and his elevated conception of the importance of art. Charlotte Brontë was typical in her response. She wrote to a friend that

> *The Stones of Venice* seems nobly laid and chiselled. How grandly the quarry of vast marbles is disclosed! Ruskin seems to me one of the few genuine writers, as distinguished from bookmakers, of the age. His earnestness even amuses me in certain passages; for I cannot help laughing to think how utilitarians will fume and fret over his deep, serious, and (*they* will think) fanatical reverence for art.[4]

Ruskin had to resort to the less literary form of the pamphlet to convey the reality of his political views. Three days after the publication of *The Stones* he issued *Notes on the Construction of Sheepfolds*. This is an expansion of 'Romanist Modern Art', the twelfth appendix to the first volume of the parent book, which attacks the Roman Catholic A. W. N. Pugin. The latter was the architect who had done most to associate the English Gothic Revival with the Catholic revival and the Oxford Movement. Ruskin wished to dissociate his own work from any taint of Catholicism. But he went further than this: he wished to claim that his own establishment Protestantism was an active spiritual force, and could be the inspiration of true modern art.

Conservative Protestant politics after the 1848 revolutions give the background to both *The Stones of Venice* and *Notes on the Construction of Sheepfolds*. An immediate stimulus was the 'Papal Aggression' and the Anglican response. In 1850 Pope Pius IX appointed Cardinal Wiseman to be Archbishop of Westminster, placing twelve English bishops beneath his authority. This restoration of the Catholic hierarchy led to an outcry quite beyond its political importance. All Ruskin's associates, and he himself, believed that it was not only the constitution that was therefore threatened: the spiritual life of the island nation had been put at risk. George Croly thought that he saw the work of Antichrist:

> England, the Archiepiscopal Province of Rome! Does not the blood of every man in England boil at the idea? England cut up into

> quarters like a sheep, for the provision of twelve Papists! England, mapped out like a wilderness at the Antipodes, for the settlement of the paupers of Rome! England, the farm-yard of the 'lean kine' of Rome![5]

Osborne Gordon was part of a deputation from Oxford which went to Windsor to protest to the Queen. While Ruskin and Effie had been at Cambridge the question had been discussed, Whewell assuring them that his undergraduates were even 'violent about the Papal aggressions'.[6] Ruskin's own views were much the same as Croly's. But they were given a far more cultured expression in the form of parallels with the history and art of Venice. *The Stones of Venice*, its appendices, and the *Sheepfolds* pamphlet all show how entangled were his political views with his literary ambitions. *The Stones* is an admonitory epic and a romantic spiritual journey. We can say with justice that it is inspired by Milton and Byron. At the same time it expresses the last vestiges of the toryism that had been defeated in 1829 and 1832 by Catholic emancipation and the Reform Bill.

Many of Ruskin's political views were inherited from his father and his father's friends. However fiery, they could have seemed quaint to men of his own age. But Ruskin was never interested in learning about politics from his own generation. He looked to older men. To John James Ruskin, Croly, and the like, we must now add the influence of Thomas Carlyle. In later years Ruskin could not remember how his knowledge of Carlyle had grown, so interwoven was his own thought with that of the man whom he liked to call his 'master'. He believed that it was George Richmond who first put a copy of *Past and Present* in his hands. In 1850 and 1851 it is probable that he was most affected by Carlyle's *Latter-Day Pamphlets* and especially the chapter on 'Parliaments'.[7] There he would have found an extremism which much of his own writing was concerned to refine and elaborate. Ruskin would never abandon such views as these. He reissued *Notes on the Construction of Sheepfolds* as lately as 1875. He had then long since thrown off his anti-Catholicism, but he still believed in many other aspects of his pamphlet. Its notions of wise monarchical government and Church discipline are a constant preoccupation of *Fors Clavigera* and would be a principle of the constitution of the Guild of St George.

Notes on the Construction of Sheepfolds resembles much of Ruskin's later writing in that it seems designed to force its readers into principled positions. There were a number of replies to *Sheepfolds*, among them another pamphlet by the painter William Dyce. It was also the occasion of some correspondence between Ruskin and F. D. Maurice.

The two men did not know each other. Maurice was at this date the Professor of Theology at King's College in the Strand, and was active in the Christian Socialist movement. Christian Socialism was so antipathetic to Ruskin's temperament that an intermediary was needed. This was F. J. Furnivall, the first of the many conciliatory messengers that Ruskin would require in his later career. Furnivall was a serious young man. He was in the chambers of Bellenden Kerr, the lawyer who had been among the founders of the Arundel Society. Furnivall one evening had met Effie, and she had invited him to Park Street. His description of Ruskin at this first meeting is interesting:

> Ruskin was a tall slight young fellow whose piercing frank blue eyes lookt through you and drew you to him. A fair man, with rough light hair and reddish whiskers, in a dark blue frock coat with velvet collar, bright Oxford blue stock, black trousers and velvet slippers — how vivid he is to me still . . ! I never met any man whose charm of manner at all approacht Ruskin's. Partly feminine it was, no doubt; but the delicacy, the sympathy, the gentleness and affectionateness of his way, the fresh and penetrating things he said, the boyish fun, the earnestness, the interest he showed in all deep matters, combined to make a whole which I have never seen equalled.[8]

Furnivall was always abjectly devoted to Ruskin. He became a regular visitor not only to Park Street but also to Denmark Hill: there, he was given hearty treatment by John James, who liked him despite thinking him a fool. He was one of the few people who took Ruskin's side at the time of the annulment of his marriage, when Effie described him, accurately enough, as 'an amiable weak young man, a vegetarian, Christian Socialist and worshipper of men of genius . . .'.[9] The letters which Furnivall carried between Ruskin and Maurice came to nothing, theologically. But they had a social effect. Quite soon, Furnivall was to bring to Denmark Hill the invitation to join the Working Men's College.

* * * *

Ruskin's protestations that he disliked going into society were exaggerated. While he disliked the glittering occasions which so excited Effie, he was no hermit. He was often at the Carlyles's in Chelsea and he kept up with his many acquaintances from the circle around Samuel Rogers. He made such new acquaintances as Dickens, Thackeray, and the painter G. F. Watts, from whom he commissioned a portrait of

Effie. Although he did not often go there he was a member of the Athenæum. Ruskin maintained his father's practice of inviting literary and artistic acquaintances to dinner three or four times a week. He preferred to do this at Denmark Hill rather than Park Street, for the atmosphere was less formal and he could show off his Turners. A frequent guest was Coventry Patmore. He was a family friend, for he had married the daughter of Ruskin's old Camberwell tutor Dr Andrews. At this time — between the Ruskins's first and second stays in Venice — Patmore held a lowly position in the British Museum. He mixed with artists as much as with his fellow writers. He was admired by the painters who formed the Pre-Raphaelite Brotherhood. William Michael Rossetti recorded that he and his brother bought Patmore's first book of poems soon after it appeared in 1844, and urged it on William Holman Hunt, Thomas Woolner and John Everett Millais, other members of the Brotherhood. In 1849 Millais had begun *The Woodman's Daughter*, a painting which illustrates a poem from this volume; and soon he would paint Emily Patmore. As he was on easy terms both with these artists and with Ruskin, Patmore was the ideal person to introduce them to each other.

Ruskin's contact with the Pre-Raphaelites was not inspired by pure camaraderie, although his influence on their fortunes made it appear that he was almost one of their number. He was to be intimate with Millais and Rossetti and, later on, with Holman Hunt. He knew William Michael Rossetti slightly in later years. Since Ruskin was older than the members of the Brotherhood by a decade and more, it was difficult for him to mix with them on equal terms. Furthermore, he mixed with them separately, and consecutively. He saw much of Rossetti in the 1850s when he was no longer on terms with Millais, and he had no real contact with Hunt until his friendship with Rossetti ended. At the time when the Brotherhood was most cohesive Ruskin was abroad, or absorbed in other matters. He may even have contributed to the break-up of the Brotherhood by championing Millais to the exclusion of his comrades. However, Ruskin's writing had certainly given some inspiration to the PRB in its early days. In the summer of 1847 William Holman Hunt had read *Modern Painters*. He later claimed that 'of all its readers none could have felt more strongly than myself that it was written expressly for him . . . the echo of its words stayed with me, and they gained a further value and meaning whenever my more solemn feelings were touched'.[10] On the basis of what he had read in *Modern Painters* Hunt urged Millais towards a high sense of purpose and naturalistic principles. This crucial resolution had an effect on the first Pre-Raphaelite pictures, Hunt's *Rienzi* and Millais's *Lorenzo and Isabella*. However, when they were exhibited in the Academy exhibition in 1849, Ruskin was in Venice. He first saw Pre-Raphaelite painting in the Academy exhibition of 1850, where there were hung Millais's *Christ in the House of his Parents, Ferdinand lured by Ariel* and a portrait of James Wyatt, together with Holman Hunt's *Claudio and Isabella*. At the private view he did not at first notice Millais's picture. 'My real introduction to the whole school', he wrote many years afterwards, 'was by Mr Dyce, R.A., who dragged me, literally, up to the Millais picture of the *Carpenter's Shop*, which I had passed disdainfully, and forced me to look for its merits.'[11]

Whatever Dyce made Ruskin see in Millais's paintings, the critic then showed no particular interest in Pre-Raphaelitism. He did not particularly like *Christ in the House of his Parents*: it is never mentioned in his writings without great reservations as to, for instance, its dwelling on 'painful conditions of expression, both in human feature and in natural objects'.[12] No writing of Ruskin's ever mentions Millais's other work of that year, the Shakespearian illustration *Ferdinand lured by Ariel*. It was not until 1851 that he looked at Pre-Raphaelite painting carefully, three years after the formation of the Brotherhood. At the Royal Academy that May Millais showed *Mariana*, *The Return of the Dove to the Ark*, and *The Woodman's Daughter*. The newspaper critics were hostile, as they had been the previous year when the meaning of the initials 'PRB' had slipped out. The subject of *The Woodman's Daughter* was from Patmore's poem 'The Tale of Poor Maud'. Millais knew that Patmore was acquainted with Ruskin, and boldly asked the poet to ask him if he would write something about Pre-Raphaelite painting. Ruskin went back to the Royal Academy to look again at the paintings, then sat down to write the first of two letters to *The Times*. The journals were already full of comment on the first volume of *The Stones of Venice* and *Notes on the Construction of Sheepfolds*. Ruskin, the controversialist of the moment, now entered another fray.

He did so with caution. Signing himself 'The Author of *Modern Painters*', Ruskin put the case for Pre-Raphaelitism. His first letter, though it ends with a large claim for the movement, is not at all vehement and is careful not to be laudatory. He began by saying,

> I believe these artists to be at a most critical period of their career — at a turning point, from which they may either sink into nothingness or rise to very real greatness; and I believe also, that whether they choose the upward or downward path may in no small degree depend upon the character of the criticism which their works have to sustain.[13]

This might seem an ordinary remark, but it has its significance. The Pre-Raphaelites, in appealing to Ruskin, were conscious that public rejection was close to professional failure. They looked to Ruskin for promotional reasons. They were all of them eloquent young men, and they all wrote: two of them, William Michael Rossetti and F. G. Stephens, already had access to the press as writers on art. They were quite able to speak for themselves, but wished to exploit Ruskin's authority. But Ruskin's view of his authority was of a different sort. It was also original. For it had not been said before that new artists, in relating their work and their ambitions to the circumstances of the time, should be directed by art criticism rather than by their professional teachers. Nor had it previously been assumed, as Ruskin now did, that the critic's function was to inspire good art by unrelenting public didacticism. And this is the first time that one meets the modern notion of a young artist, or group of young artists, at a turning point: a point that could be a 'breakthrough' in a career. On all these matters, Ruskin was convinced of his own rightness. Now, in the year when the aged Turner no longer had the strength to exhibit, he suddenly became the arbiter of a new generation.

The Pre-Raphaelites were known to be a coterie bound by a common programme. Ruskin's defence therefore insisted that he was not their friend and did not share their tastes.

> Let me state, in the first place, that I have no acquaintance with any of these artists, and very imperfect sympathy with them. No one who has met with any of my writings will suspect me of desiring to encourage them in their Romanist and Tractarian tendencies . . .[14]

But he approved of their evident desire to avoid academic history painting and their naturalistic techniques:

> These Pre-Raphaelites (I cannot compliment them on common sense in choice of a *nom de guerre*) do *not* desire nor pretend in any way to imitate antique painting, as such. They know little of ancient paintings who suppose the work of these young artists to resemble them . . . They intend to return to early days in this one point only — that, in so far as in them lies, they will draw either what they see, or what they suppose might have been the actual facts of the scene they desire to represent, irrespective of any conventional rules of picture-making; and they have chosen their unfortunate though not inaccurate name because all artists did this before Raphael's time, and after Raphael's time did *not* this, but sought to paint fair pictures rather than represent stern facts, of which the consequence has been

> that from Raphael's time to this day historical art has been in acknowledged decadence.[15]

Ruskin defended the Pre-Raphaelites against the charge that they made 'errors' in perspective drawing and closed by offering to find a larger number of errors in work by recognized academicians. A week later he wrote a further letter to *The Times*. It was to some extent modified by John James, but ended, as the first had not, with a ringing declaration of the Pre-Raphaelites' importance:

> I wish them all heartily good speed, believing in sincerity that if they temper the courage and energy which they have shown in the adoption of their system with patience and discretion in pursuing it, and if they do not suffer themselves to be driven by harsh and careless criticism into rejection of the ordinary means of obtaining influence over the minds of others, they may, as they gain experience, lay in our England the foundations of a school of art nobler than the world has seen for three hundred years.[16]

The Times was not convinced by Ruskin's two letters. Under the second they published an editorial rejoinder. It raised what would subsequently be the most common criticism of Ruskin's appreciation of Pre-Raphaelite painting: 'Mr Millais and his friends have taken refuge in the opposite extreme of exaggeration from Mr Turner; but, as extremes meet, they both find an apologist in the same critic.'[17]

Holman Hunt and Millais composed a letter to Ruskin in which they thanked him for his interest. The address given was Millais's; probably because he lived in Gower Street at his parents' house, while the other Pre-Raphaelites were in cheap lodgings. Very soon John and Effie Ruskin drove round from Park Street to call on Millais. The painter was twenty-two years old, a year younger than Effie and ten years younger than Ruskin: and he seemed younger than his age. With his curly fair hair, handsome profile and intense manner, Millais made an immediate impression. He always had. He had been a child prodigy, and his abilities had been recognized by the then President of the Royal Academy, Sir Martin Archer Shee. Thus Millais had become the youngest student ever to have been admitted to the Royal Academy Schools, at the age of eleven. Since then he had won every prize and distinction. A person as clever and as personable as Millais had found it quite easy to be a rebel: it was as easy as being a prodigy. He was proverbially lucky. In the next few weeks, he became good friends with the Ruskins. He visited them both at Park Street and at Denmark Hill. And there was a further invitation, although he may not have seen its significance. Millais reported to his earlier patron Thomas Combe that

> I have dined and taken breakfast with Ruskin, and we are such good friends that he wished me to accompany him to Switzerland this summer . . . We are as yet singularly at variance in our opinions of Art. One of our differences is about Turner. He believes that I shall be converted on further acquaintance with his works, and I that he will gradually slacken in his admiration . . .[18]

It was this connection between Turner and Pre-Raphaelitism that Ruskin now attempted to elucidate, or rather to claim, in a further pamphlet. It was entitled *Pre-Raphaelitism*, and was published in mid-August, before the Royal Academy exhibition closed. It occasioned more argument than had his letters to *The Times*. They had been judicious. The pamphlet was eccentric, and its title was misleading. It was not about Pre-Raphaelite painting: Ruskin had scarcely seen more than half a dozen examples of the school. It was largely about Turner, and was the result of Ruskin's meditations on a visit he had made to Farnley Hall that spring. This Yorkshire country seat had been the home of Turner's friend and patron Walter Fawkes: it contained around two hundred water-colours by Turner, including the fifty-one drawings of the Rhine, and a number of oils. The house now belonged to Walter's son Francis Hawkesworth Fawkes, to whom Ruskin's pamphlet was dedicated. The treatise is prefaced by a quotation from *Modern Painters*, the famous injunction to young artists to 'go to nature in all singleness of heart, and walk with her laboriously and trustingly, having no other thought but how best to penetrate her meaning; rejecting nothing, selecting nothing, and scorning nothing'.[19] It seemed to Ruskin that Pre-Raphaelite painting was inclined to follow this path: if it did not, then it should do so.

The pamphlet must have seemed beside the point to the Pre-Raphaelites themselves. No painting by any member of the Brotherhood is mentioned in it. And while fidelity to nature was a Pre-Raphaelite principle, they were not landscape painters and had no interest in Turner. Years later, Holman Hunt claimed that their neglect of Turner was simply because they did not know much about him: 'Turner was rapidly sinking like a glorious sun in clouds of night that could not yet obscure his brightness, but rather increased his magnificence. The works of his meridian days were then shut up in their possessors' galleries, unknown to us younger men.'[20] But in fact Turner had seemed irrelevant to the making of the new art. Millais and Hunt wanted paintings of social action and emotion: they wanted great detail, meticulous drawing, high-keyed colour, a minimum of modelling and a minimum of ærial perspective. Little in Turner could help this kind of painting. A desire to convert Millais into a Turnerian landscapist lay behind Ruskin's *Pre-Raphaelitism* pamphlet, as it lay behind the invitation to a holiday in Switzerland. But the plan rested on many kinds of misconception.

Ruskin would have been more attentive to Pre-Raphaelite art had his mind not been occupied with his Venetian history. There is a prayerful resolution in his diary on 1 May, the morning after he had been to the Royal Academy and had first seen the paintings he would write to *The Times* to defend: 'Morning. All London is astir, and some part of all the world. I am sitting in my quiet room, hearing the birds sing, and about to enter on the true beginning of the second part of my Venetian work. May God help me to finish it to His glory, and man's good.'[21] London was busy that morning because it was also the opening day of the 1851 Great Exhibition. Effie went to the celebrations, alone, with a ticket that had been procured for her by John James. She was not discontented with her life in Park Street, and at the moment she was on quite cordial terms with her parents-in-law. But she still longed for the day when she would leave for Venice. As controversy gathered over Ruskin's recent writings she was supervising household preparations for a six-month stay in Italy. They set off for the Continent at the beginning of August, leaving behind them the Park Street household (to which they never returned), leaving the Pre-Raphaelites busy about their own business, and all England marvelling, in Paxton's glass and iron sheds, at the exhibition of industrial and material progress.

* * * *

Millais had declined the invitation to accompany the Ruskins as far as Switzerland because he had planned to spend the summer painting with Holman Hunt. The holiday party might or might not have suited him. Charles Newton travelled with the Ruskins, for he had been appointed vice-consul at Mitylene and was on his way to take up his post. Also of the party were the Reverend Daniel Moore, of the Camden Chapel, and his wife. In Switzerland other friends joined them, a Mr and Mrs Pritchard. He was the Member of Parliament for Bridgnorth: she was Osborne Gordon's sister. An art critic, an intelligent Anglican, an archæologist rising in the consular service, an MP, all together with their ladies; here was a group of people thoughtful and cultivated beyond the ordinary. That is why they seem so out of place when we see them in Switzerland. For here was no culture, here was no society, no religion: poverty had made the people themselves into monsters. At Aosta, one in five of the population were goitred. Effie saw two funerals of children, their small coffins 'covered over with wedding-cake finery and little boys as bearers. A fat priest led the way with the Cross and was followed by a quantity of cretins and horrid looking men and women, all looking as happy and good-natured as could be and laughing like anything . . .'[22] At the Hospice of St Bernard the beds were flea-ridden and the food disgusting: it was what the peasants ate. As if to complete their contempt for the Catholicism of the valley, all the party listened while Effie played an old piano and made the monks sing merry, secular tunes. The experience disturbed people in different ways. Ruskin pretended at the time that in Aosta he soon forgot cretinism and everything else in the fields outside the walls where he and Newton walked through vineyards to the chestnut groves and looked up at the Matterhorn and Mont Velan. But in fact he did not forget; and years later the origin of the Guild of St George would be in his 'great plan' to bring health and revive agriculture in these benighted Swiss valleys.

★ ★ ★ ★

An important aspect of the *Pre-Raphaelitism* pamphlet is its interest in human happiness: a theme that always afterwards would haunt Ruskin's writing. In Switzerland and Venice he now began to think seriously about the ways in which society — whether Venetian, Swiss or English — ought to be concerned with human felicity. His thoughts were prompted by the miseries he saw around him. But he also began to consider something that he now knew about himself: that he was happy only when he was working, and working towards some noble end. The question also troubled Ruskin because he had to wonder whether the happiness his wife craved was not ignoble. When they arrived in Venice they heard of the death of Effie's admirer Paulizza. Ruskin perhaps was more distressed than she. During this visit to Venice one senses — almost daily, on reading the letters home — that there was a part of Ruskin's mind that was both darker and kinder than heretofore. Of his wife, one notices her invitations. Effie had decided that they would be more a part of Venetian society if they were not lodged in a hotel. Their new home was to be in the Casa Wetzler, at the side of the Grand Canal. They had a drawing-room and a double bedroom, a dressing-room, a dining-room and a study. Underneath were three servants' rooms and the kitchen. In this accommodation

John and Effie could entertain in a manner grand enough for most social ambitions. Once again Effie's letters home are full of the names of the aristocracy. She was thrilled and proud to meet the Infanta of Spain and, at last, Radetzky: he found her charming. Ruskin had little to do with these people. He was more interested in English visitors to the city. This year they were arriving in greater numbers, and practically all of them were in Venice for what might be called cultural purposes. Ruskin used them to test the arguments of the book he was writing, shifting his ground between English politics and art to his Venetian surroundings. With Sir Gilbert Scott, newly appointed surveyor to Westminster Abbey, he could have professional architectural conversations. With Thomas Gambier Parry, now just beginning to collect *quattrocento* paintings, he could talk about fresco techniques. David Roberts came to drink sherry. He and Ruskin understood each other rather well, and Ruskin was pleased to hear how this minor master of architectural painting had turned down Queen Victoria's request that he should paint the Crystal Palace for her. Some people fared badly in these discussions. One became an enemy. This was Henry Milman, the Dean of St Paul's, quite unable to defend Wren's building while Ruskin made comparisons with the Venetian Gothic around them.

Ruskin's letters give only bald accounts of these conversations, but provide a daily guide to his feelings as he plunged into the writing of the second volume of his Venetian cultural history. As always, he pointed out to his parents that he was not overtaxing himself. But sometimes he fails to reassure: and in Denmark Hill there were worries about his health. John James especially was pained to find how much he missed his son. He also worried that Ruskin's views of the world might be diverging from his own. Ruskin himself was no less worried that this might be so. For this reason some of his letters are full of the strident tones of the *Britannia*, John James's favoured political reading. Of the scene in St Mark's Square where the band proclaimed the Austrian supremacy he wrote,

> Round the whole square in front of the church there is almost a continuous line of cafés, where the idle Venetians of the middle classes lounge, and read empty journals: in the centre the Austrian bands play during the time of vespers, their martial music jarring with the organ notes, — the march drowning the miserere, and the sullen crowd thickening round them, — a crowd, which, if it had its will, would stiletto every soldier that pipes to it. And in the recesses of the porches, all day long, knots of men of the lowest classes, unemployed and listless, lie basking in the sun like lizards; and

> unregarded children, — every heavy glance of their young eyes full of desperation and stony depravity, and their throats hoarse with cursing, — gamble, and fight, and snarl, and sleep, hour after hour, clashing their centesemi upon the marble ledges of the church porch . . .[23]

Readers of *The Stones of Venice* will recognize how Ruskin could transform such observations into more stately political sentiments. Especially when writing in retrospect, he would always idealize politics. In 1859, thinking about the Habsburg imperial rule, he wrote of Paulizza:

> One of my best friends in Venice in the winter of 1849-50 was the artillery officer who directed the fire on the side of Mestre in 1848. I have never known a nobler person. Brave, kind and gay — as playful as a kitten — knightly in courtesy and in all tones of thought — ready at any instant to lay down his life for his country and his emperor. He was by no means a rare instance either of gentleness or of virtue among the men whom the Liberal portion of our daily press represent only as tyrants and barbarians. Radetzky himself was one of the kindest of men — his habitual expression was one of overflowing *bonhommie* . . . For a long time I regarded the Austrians as the only protection of Italy from utter dissolution . . .[24]

Effie's politics, on the other hand, tended towards the personal. She found that British foreign policy had an effect on her position in Austrian society. In February of 1852 she wrote,

> The Austrians are crowing over us finely just now at the brilliant figure England is making of herself after her paltry, mean foreign policy these last three or four years, and now she is without a foreign friend with the Caffir War, the French panic, the impertinence of the Roumanians, and last, not least, a Cabinet full of old women to trouble her, and she will find out perhaps at some cost what Lord Palmerston has in store for her. The feeling is so strong against the English and their position on the continent. It is a very different thing to what it was. Before, the English were all My Lords and their word was law and every respect was paid to them before any other nation. Now we are all considered traders and if politeness is shown it is only to individual merit.[25]

Thus Effie on individual merit. It is now of interest to know how she interpreted her husband's views. Ruskin told his father,

> Effie says, with some justice, — that I am a great conservative in France, because there everybody is radical — and a great radical in Austria, because there everybody is conservative. I suppose that one reason why I am so fond of fish — (as creatures, I mean, not as eating) is that they always swim with their head against the stream. I find it for me, the healthiest position.[26]

The first public occasion when Ruskin decided to swim against the tide came towards the end of this second stay in Venice. It gave his father much alarm. In March 1852 Ruskin wrote to Denmark Hill, 'I am going for three days to give the usual time I set aside for your letter to writing one for the Times — on Corn Laws, Election and Education . . . If you like to send it, you can; if not, you can consider it all as written to you, but you must have short letters for a day or two.'[27] These letters were written, but John James did not send them on to *The Times*. Some parts of them are preserved. The third letter, which is missing altogether, was probably the foundation of the 'Notes on Education' which is the seventh appendix to the third volume of *The Stones of Venice*. From the first letter and a portion of the second we may see that Ruskin criticized Disraeli, at this date Chancellor of the Exchequer, supported free trade, advocated direct taxes, taxes on luxuries and a property tax. He felt that income tax ought to be '10 per cent on all fortunes exceeding £1000 a year, and let the weight of it die away gradually on the poorer classes'. His electoral schemes were complicated, giving more votes to the property-owning and educated classes than to others. Ruskin thought of a radical coachman who might have fifty votes, which he would then swamp with his own 'four or five hundred'.[28] The letter on education is coloured by Ruskin's experiences at Oxford. In the appendix to *The Stones of Venice* which derives from this letter — it is one of the appendices that have no relevance to Venetian history — Ruskin advocates the study at university of natural history, of religion and of politics. By religion Ruskin had in mind 'the "binding" or training to God's service' rather than the study of theology. Politics is understood as 'the science of the relations and duties of men to each other'.[29]

All this was distressing to John James Ruskin. He did not forward the letters and he wrote back in strong terms about their contents. But in fact — except in the matter of income tax — Ruskin's views did not differ very widely from his father's, and they must often have talked together about just the same problems that he wished to raise in the newspapers. Ruskin's proposals on the franchise, for instance, might seem eccentric today: but such schemes were not uncommon among tories of the Ruskins's type in the years after the Reform Bill. It was not exactly a matter of political principle that most stirred John James's apprehensions. It was his suspicion that there was a dangerous connection between his son's thinking about the national exchequer and his inability to keep down his personal expenses. The Guild of St George, in later years, would most amply prove the justice of these fears. But in 1852 the immediate problem was his son's reputation:

> My feelings of attacks on your books and on your newspaper writing differ from yours in this way. I think all attacks on your books are only as the waves beating on Eddystone lighthouse, whereas your politics are Slum Buildings liable to be knocked down; and no man to whom authority is a useful engine should expose himself to frequent defeat by slender forces.[30]

There was already quite enough trouble in England about Ruskin's artistic writings. *Pre-Raphaelitism* had been unfavourably reviewed. The effect of the pamphlet had been to divert public debate away from Pre-Raphaelite painting and towards the peculiarity of Ruskin's opinions. The Pre-Raphaelites were now at the end of the short period when they were most criticized and least able to sell their work; and the abuse formerly directed towards them now fell on Ruskin. Many publications apart from *The Times* accused him of inconsistency. The *Daily News* and the *Builder* both spoke of contradictions. The *Art Journal* attacked the pamphlet as a 'maundering medley', and the *Athenæum* wrote of its preface that 'Rarely has any oracle's *ego* been stretched further in the demand for blind faith and acquiescence than in this pamphlet; — rarely has *ego* been more vain-glorious . . .'.[31] Ruskin wrote from Venice, considerably upset: 'When I read those reviews of *Pre-Raphaelitism* I was so disgusted by their sheer broad-faced, sheepish, swinish stupidity, that I began to feel, as I wrote in the morning, that I was really rather an ass myself to string pearls for them.'[32] John James had a vague idea that adverse reviews of his pamphleteering would be good for his son and would make him concentrate on his book. He may have been right. At all events, the matter of the letters to *The Times* was allowed to rest.

Since the publication of the second volume of *Modern Painters* Ruskin had occasionally been caught up in public arguments about the national collections. One of these had been an attack on the National Gallery conducted in 1846 and 1847 by William Morris Moore. Signing himself 'Verax', he had issued pamphlets criticizing the gallery's director, Sir Charles Eastlake, on the grounds that his cleaning policy was mistaken. Ruskin had entered this controversy. He did not do so as an opponent of Eastlake on restoration, but with a plea that paintings of the earlier Italian schools should be purchased. He wanted the paintings by *trecento* and *quattrocento* masters to come to England. Now, in Venice, Ruskin was anxious that the National Gallery should acquire more paintings by the great Venetians. He had already approached Eastlake suggesting that he should buy pictures for the nation, and when he saw a firm opportunity of buying two Tintorettos he wrote to him again. He also wrote to Lord Lansdowne, a trustee of the National Gallery whom he knew slightly from the council of the Arundel Society, and used Edward Cowper-Temple as an intermediary in approaching Lord Palmerston, the Prime Minister. Here, one might think, was the way to get things done: but in obscure circumstances Ruskin's recommendations were rejected, and the paintings were not bought.

Ruskin's belief that the governing classes were not fit to be entrusted with the artistic soul of the nation was now strengthened. He was to be even more disillusioned by the affair of the Turner bequest. Turner died in London on 19 December 1851. The news reached Venice as Ruskin worked among the tombs of Murano, in the cemetery whose long purple walls Turner once had painted. 'Every thing in the sunshine and the sky so talks of him,' Ruskin wrote to his father, 'their great witness lost.'[33] He immediately began to think what might be preserved from Turner's vast production. His thoughts were of something he had long dreaded, that the painter might have destroyed his own work. Ruskin knew that the condition of the paintings would in any case be perilous. He worried what mildewed canvases might be in the cellars in Queen Anne Street, or locked away in rooms that he had never seen opened. At the same time, he feared that many treasures would immediately come onto the art market. He therefore wrote to his father with instructions about possible purchases. But when Turner's will was published these apprehensions were largely banished. England's greatest artist had left everything to the nation. At the same time Ruskin heard that he was to be one of the executors. Turner's will was characteristic of the man. It was eccentric, blunt, generous, miserly, and whole-hearted. For such a one as Lady Eastlake, 'It is a very stupid will — that of a man who lived out of the world of sense and public opinion.'[34] She was wrong that it was stupid, but the rest of her sentence is worth pondering. All the contents of the Queen Anne Street house now became the nation's property. Turner stipulated that the paintings were to be kept together and were to be seen without charge. *Dido building Carthage* and *Sun rising through Mist* were left to the National Gallery on condition that they were to be hung next to two paintings by Claude. Ignoring his next-of-kin, who subsequently disputed the will, Turner left money to build almshouses for painters, for the establishment of a professorship of landscape in the Royal Academy schools, and for a dinner to be held annually in his memory.

Ruskin was left nothing except nineteen guineas to buy a mourning ring. This provoked John James to the sardonic comment 'nobody can say you were paid to praise'.[35] Ruskin's father had given considerable sums for the purchase of Turners over the last fifteen years, and he knew that his son's writings had helped to raise the artist's prices. But this kind of resentment was rather swept away when he found what was in the house. John James was one of the first people to go through Queen Anne Street, which he did with Turner's dealer:

> I have just been through Turner's house with Griffith. His labour is more astonishing than his genius. There are £80,000 of oil pictures, done and undone. Boxes, half as big as your study table, filled with drawings and sketches. There are copies of Liber Studiorum to fill all your drawers and more, and house walls of proof plates in reams . . . Nothing since Pompeii so impressed me as the interior of Turner's house; the accumulated dust of forty years partially cleared off; daylight for the first time admitted by opening a window on the finest productions of art for forty years. The drawing room has, it is reckoned, £25,000 worth of proofs, and sketches, and drawings, and prints . . . I saw in Turner's rooms, *Geo Morlands* and *Wilsons*, and *Claudes* and *portraits* in various styles, *all by* Turner. He copied every man first, and took up his own style, casting all others away. It seems to me you may keep your money, and revel for ever and for nothing among Turner's works . . .[36]

It is interesting that John James was so struck to find there the early works that reminded him of Morland and Wilson. Conceivably, Ruskin had talked so much of the 'truth to nature' and the imagination of his hero's work that John James scarcely realized that Turner had long painted in borrowed styles. Ruskin's letters home are slightly reserved at this point: and we do not know much about the way that he reviewed his responsibilities as executor. He started to make plans for a Turner gallery. His ideas were progressive. He wanted it to be top-lit, with all paintings hung on the line and given their proper immediate environment by using flats to subdivide the rooms. He also thought, for a short time, of a biography of Turner. This would have been a deeply interesting book, no doubt. But Ruskin thought that *Modern Painters*, in the course of time, would fulfil the proper part of such a biography's function. There were things about Turner's life and his household that could not be told. As Lady Eastlake gleefully recorded, 'His life is proved to have been sordid in the extreme, and far from respectable.'[37] Effie Ruskin was opposed to a biography because 'what is known of Turner would not be profitable to any lady . . . the sooner they make a myth of him the better'.[38] It is not likely that Effie's views on books had much effect on her husband. But this remark about making a myth of Turner is relevant. Ruskin thought that he would best serve Turner's memory by a critical assertion of his genius. The quotidian drudgery of the biographer was not for him, and

> . . . there might be much which would be painful to tell and dishonest to conceal — and on the other hand — apart from all criticism of his works, probably little to interest — and all criticism I shall keep for *Modern Painters* . . . if I were not going to write *Modern Painters* I should undertake it at once, but I will make *that* so complete a monument of him, D.V., that there will be nothing left for the life but when he was born and where he lived — and whom he dined with on this or that occasion. All of which might be stated by anybody.[39]

Ruskin's position as executor seemed at first to offer him the means to make a full study of the work of the artist he admired above all others. But his commitment to Venice had grown so intense that he did not even make a quick trip to England to see what extraordinary treasures might be in Queen Anne Street. Soon, matters became even more confused. Turner's will was disputed by his next-of-kin. The legal complications indicated that there would be a long suit in Chancery. Ruskin felt that he could not become involved in legal matters.[40] As also did Samuel Rogers, he set about resigning his executorship. His immediate work was in Venice. He genuinely believed that the Ducal Palace would not stand for many more years. He could see no guarantee that the relative political stability of the Austrian occupation would hold. The revolutions of 1848 could be repeated, and with far more terrible results. But while it was necessary for him to save Venice, as far as he could, by writing of her architecture, he could also feel that to write of Gothic was to prepare for his praise of Turner's genius. So he explained *The Stones of Venice* as follows:

> I see a very interesting connection between it and *Modern Painters*. The first part of the book will give an account of the effects of Christianity in colouring and spiritualising Roman or Heathen

> architecture. The second and third parts will give an account of the transition to Gothic, with a definition of the nature and essence of the Gothic style. The fourth part of the decline of all this back into Heathenism: and of the reactionary symptoms attending the course of the relapse, of which the strongest has been the development of landscape painting. For as long as the Gothic and other fine architectures existed, the love of Nature, which was an essential and peculiar feature of Christianity, found expression and food enough in them . . . when the Heathen architecture came back, their love of nature, still happily existing in some minds, could find no more food there — it turned to landscape painting and has worked gradually up into Turner.[41]

This was a grand design, and perhaps it is one that is not fully spelt out in Ruskin's more formal writings. For such a connection was in the first place emotional. *The Stones of Venice* is written out of knowledge, out of archæological research and some acquaintance with the city's archives. But it is bound together by passions. Ruskin did not write it with a historian's deliberation, but let himself be carried by his emotions. He knew that he had to guard himself against the nervous excitement that accompanied such efforts: at the same time his book was fashioned by such excitement. 'The thing I have to watch', he told John James, 'is the tendency to excitement and sleeplessness — the aggravation of that excitability of pulse which my mother so often used to notice when I was a boy: the least overwork any day causing a restless feeling all over — and exhaustion afterwards.'[42] Ruskin's letters from Venice pay so much attention to his own health that they have sometimes been described as hypochondriacal. We may also believe that they record the urgent ministrations of his creative self.

> I found first — that every hour of thought or work of any kind, but especially writing, was just so much acceleration of pulse — with slight flushing of cheeks and restless feeling all over — That I never was healthily sleepy at nights — and often could not sleep more than four or five hours, even if I went to sleep at a proper time. That any violent exercise would make me restless and excited for hours afterwards, instead of wholesomely fatigued — and that the slightest plague or disagreeable feeling in society would do the same — I got into a little dispute with Mr Cheney about some mosaics one day — and was quite nervous the whole day after — merely a question of whether the colours were faded or not . . .[43]

Day after day, while often he trembled with the strain, Ruskin went on writing. Every evening George Hobbs made a fair copy of his text to send home to Denmark Hill. All this was done as though in a race against time. A strange bond of tension existed between Ruskin and his father as they both sought for the book's expression. Effie knew nothing or little about this, and probably did not wish to understand what was happening between the two men. But she was now being even further excluded from the union of the Ruskin family.

Years later, writing in his diary on 3 March 1874, and thinking over past books, Ruskin wrote, 'And yet the Venice work was good. Let me make the best fruit of it I can, since he so suffered for it.'[44] That was on the tenth anniversary of his father's death. Ruskin still then felt guilt that *The Stones of Venice* had been fashioned out of his father's pain. They needed many kinds of companionship. It was important to them that they could talk freely together about religion, especially since Margaret Ruskin's faith was so inflexible. John James knew that Ruskin had not believed absolutely in the authority of the Bible since he was at Oxford. He also knew that even when he was writing the second volume of *Modern Painters*, whose religious bias seems very close to Margaret Ruskin's, his faith had been confused by 'the continual discovery, day by day, of error or limitation in the doctrines I had been taught, and follies or inconsistencies in their teachers'.[45] Ever since 1845 there had been a difference between the theological confidence of Ruskin's writings and his private misgivings. One would not think that the author of *Notes on the Construction of Sheepfolds* had any difficulties of belief. But just after its publication Ruskin had written to Henry Acland,

> You speak of the flimsiness of your own faith. Mine, which was never strong, is being beaten into mere gold leaf, and flutters in weak rags from the letter of its old forms; but the only letters it can hold by at all are the old Evangelical formulæ. If only the geologists would let me alone, I could do very well, but those dreadful hammers! I hear the clink of them at the end of every cadence of the Bible verse . . .[46]

It was as well that Ruskin could feel like this. For it enabled him to understand how John James Ruskin, now in his old age, could fall into religious despondency as he contemplated his death and his life after death.

Ruskin's religious thinking changed during this second extended stay in Venice, as did his own character. To use crude terms, he became less 'Evangelical' and more considerate of other people's religious feelings: but this is not necessarily to say that his faith became attenuated, nor that (as his mother was to fear) he became closer to the

Roman Catholic Church. Rather, he began the true development of his own faith, which in the years to come would range widely between such positions, yet at no time give the impression of compromise. The spirit of the *eirenikon* was not natural to Ruskin, but he would always wish to assist another person's piety. There is little justice, at this point in the two men's lives, in the notion of John James's 'domination' of his son, for Ruskin was now enabled to act as a spiritual pastor to his own father. He offered John James an especial comfort when his father wrote to him about his doubts of the after life. We do not know much about the nature of Ruskin's own doubts because we do not have much direct evidence of his prayers. We know that in prayer he made resolutions: that is how he began *Modern Painters*. In *Modern Painters* we find his capacity for adoration, which is another component of prayer, and we assume that his petitions would not greatly differ from those of other thoughtful men. But of his contemplative prayer we are in ignorance, except that we may say that in his understanding of God, Ruskin's doubting was akin to a spiritual exercise, that it led to a deepening of feeling and a realization that the boundaries of faith are distinct from the nature of faith.

Ruskin's notes on his Bible reading help us to understand him at this time. During his second stay in Venice his devotional thoughts were dominated by study of the Book of Job, which he began in September of 1851. By the beginning of December he had completed a commentary on Job which occupied ninety pages of manuscript. This has disappeared, but we should consider what was in his mind. Job is about innocent suffering, wisdom and the acceptance of God's ways. It is wise not to strain for a knowledge of God beyond that available to human speculation. But we also wish to know about revelation, which is both what God shows of Himself and the manner in which His nature is disclosed. Thinking of Venice, but much more of the Alps and of Turner, Ruskin enquired:

> . . . it seems to me that from a God of Light and Truth, His creatures have a right to expect plain and clear revelation touching all that concerns their immortal interests. And this is the great question with me — whether indeed the Revelation *be* clear, and men are blind . . . or whether there be not also some strange darkness in the manner of Revelation itself.[47]

He was beginning to think of those things that in the fifth volume of *Modern Painters* he would write about in the mysterious chapter entitled 'The Dark Mirror'.

Ruskin now felt himself prepared to look at Roman Catholicism with some sympathy. Before, he had scarcely considered the matter. The appendix to the third volume of *The Stones of Venice* which deals with education mentions that four out of the twelve young men who had been his close friends at Oxford had converted to Catholicism. He himself had been quite untouched by the Oxford Movement as an undergraduate. But another Christ Church man, William Russell, now arrived in Venice. They had not been intimates at the university, and Ruskin was surprised to find that both Russell and his wife had become Catholics. Russell's wife died while they were in Venice. Ruskin saw something of him after his bereavement and they talked about religion. John and Effie had other acquaintances in Venice who were in a rather similar situation. They met Viscount Feilding and his wife. She was dying of consumption; he had been estranged from his family since becoming a Roman Catholic. Feilding was not much older than Ruskin and his wife was the same age as Effie. Ruskin felt sympathy for them, and discussed matters of doctrine with Feilding with more interest than he had with Russell. His curiosity was such that it led Feilding to believe that Ruskin might himself convert. It was in part due to conversations such as these that a change of tone occurs in the second volume of *The Stones of Venice*. The passage on the Madonna of Murano, for instance, with its enquiry into the spirit of Mariolatry, would not have been written a year earlier: nor would the appendix entitled 'The Proper Sense of the Word Idolatry'. The details of Ruskin's interest in Catholicism at this time are obscure. Who wrote, in Ruskin's private diary, Hail Marys in English and Latin? The writing is in pencil, not in Ruskin's hand, nor in Effie's. All this is not to say that *The Stones of Venice* is anything but a vehemently Protestant book. The trajectory of its argument could only have come from a background such as Ruskin's. Yet a broadness of spirit characterizes its well-known chapter 'On the Nature of Gothic'. As he began to think about that chapter, in February of 1852, Ruskin told his father, 'I shall show that the greatest distinctive character of Gothic is in the workman's heart and mind.'[48] The author of *Notes on the Construction of Sheepfolds* could not have said this. For the pamphlet's intolerance implied a denial of spiritual grace in others. It was this grace that Ruskin was now anxious to discover in the workmen who had built Venice, or in those who might build Gothic architecture in England.

* * * *

As the time approached when the Ruskins were to return to England, the many problems of their marriage came into sharper focus. On

Ruskin's birthday his father, fretting for his homecoming, gave a dinner party in his honour. From Venice on that same day, Ruskin wrote a long account of his health to Denmark Hill, and Effie wrote to her mother complaining about the elder Ruskins. She claimed that 'both he and Mrs R. send the most affectionate messages to me and all the time write *at* or *against* me and speak of the hollowness of worldly society and the extravagance of living in large houses and seeing great people . . .'.[49] This was true, and Effie probably felt that she would need some allies when she left Venice for London. She remembered a slightly indiscreet conversation she had had with Charles Newton during the holiday in Switzerland the previous year. Newton and Effie were genuinely fond of each other: and the clever, iconoclastic archæologist had not concealed from Effie that he found the old Ruskins rather absurd. He also warned Effie against their influence. Recalling this conversation, Effie wrote to her mother:

> They are so peculiar that, as Newton said to me when we were travelling together, he could not understand how I got on so well — he thought two days at Denmark Hill with Mrs Ruskin without prospects of release would really kill him and yet he thought her a very good woman but very queer — but he advised me never to let John away again so long with them without me. He said it did us both a great deal of harm and he knew the effects it had on all our acquaintances . . .[50]

Newton was of course right. For Ruskin to be truly married meant that he had to be separated from his parents. But neither Newton nor Effie fully realized that such a separation, for Ruskin, would be a separation from his own self.

Ruskin was determined not to go back to Park Street. It was too near to London society, which he had now decided made him physically ill. John James was perfectly happy to give up the Mayfair house. He was less pleased now than once he had been to see his son in the company of the great. Besides, the house was expensive. It had not been much used, and three servants were paid all the time that John and Effie were abroad. Ruskin wanted to live somewhere near his parents: not necessarily in the same house, but in a house within a short walking distance of them. Letters between all three Ruskins now became even more full of devotion for each other, while John James's letters to Perth relentlessly attacked Effie for extravagance. Effie was amazed to find a poem from Mrs Ruskin to her son, 'in a style almost of amatory tenderness, calling John her beloved and Heart's Treasure and a variety of other terms which only, I believe, a lover would do in addressing a Sonnet to his Mistress . . .'.[51] At the same time, Effie was spoken of in Ruskin's letters to his father as if she were a difficult child. Perhaps this was because he was personally incapable of helping her make the transition from a fashionable hostess in Venice to a housewife in Camberwell:

> I do not speak of Effie in this arrangement — as it is a necessary one — and therefore I can give her no choice. She will be unhappy — that is her fault — not mine — the only real regret I have, however is on her account — as I have pride in seeing her shining as she does in society — and pain in seeing her deprived, in her youth and beauty, of that which ten years hence she cannot have — the Alps will not wrinkle — so *my* pleasure is always in store — but her cheeks will: and the loss of life from 24 to 27 in a cottage in Norwood is not a pleasant thing for a woman of her temper — But this cannot be helped.[52]

The prospect of her future London life made Effie all the more loath to leave Venice. She was so filled with foreboding that she became frankly hostile to her parents-in-law. She felt that the Ruskins would all be much more happy and comfortable if they could simply exclude her from any of their plans. The conclusion was inescapable. She now wrote frankly to her father, 'I wish that I had been the boy and never left you — which I believe in the end might have been better for all parties.'[53]

The Ruskins's last weeks in Venice were filled with work and with a peculiar kind of social unreality. John and Effie went twice to Verona to attend Radetzky's balls. These were enjoyable occasions, in contrast to the Venetian carnival which Ruskin must have decided to attend because of its antiquity. But this pre-Lenten feast had long since fallen into corruption. The Ruskins put on 'dominoes', black and white masks, and wandered around Venice late in the evening. The squares were full. People were throwing things, men approached Effie and said things she could not understand. Ruskin went before her to the masked ball which once had been attended by all the great people of Venice. They were not there now, and he saw that the dancing was lewd. They walked further through the streets looking for entertainment that did not exist, until Effie became frightened that 'the canaille, not the masks' had surrounded them.[54] Shortly after this slightly disturbing evening came the news that two Austrian officers had fought a duel over Effie after her appearance at the ball in Verona. The Ruskins took no notice. But the dangerous side of Austrian military honour was now to touch them very closely. Just as they were packing to leave Venice, Effie found that some of her jewels had been stolen. Suspicion fell on an English acquaintance of theirs, a Mr Foster. He was not precisely a soldier but had a position as an aide-de-camp to Radetzky. He was sufficiently close to the military establishment, therefore, for honour to be at issue. Foster's closest friend, a Count Thun, was under the impression that Ruskin had personally accused his comrade. He challenged the art critic to a duel. Ruskin mildly declined. Scandal grew. There was trouble in the Austrian garrison. The police were inefficient: Effie was hysterical. They found that they could not leave Venice. Edward Cheney came to their aid and smoothed the matter over. But it made an unpleasant end to their stay. Ruskin did not tell his father about it until they were back in England. John James Ruskin was horrified: all the more so when the story, wildly exaggerated, began to appear in the English newspapers. On 2 August 1852, Ruskin was obliged to write to *The Times* explaining as best he could the facts of the case. It is the only one of his public letters that was not subsequently collected and published. For Effie, the ludicrous aspects of the affair — augmented as they were by much gossip — made all the more bewildering her new life: a housewife, four years married and still a virgin, in a suburban villa to the south of London.

CHAPTER TEN

1852–1854

The new house that John James had found for his son and daughter-in-law was very close to his own. It was No. 30 Herne Hill. The property was next door to the house that the Ruskins had moved to when John was four, and was its duplicate. Although John James did not expect John and Effie to remain there for long he had spent much money on fittings. In doing so he acted with a thoughtlessness which often overcame him in matters concerning his son's marriage. He gave an interior decorator £2,000 and *carte blanche* to furnish the house as he thought best. The result was modern and vulgar. Ruskin, horrified, said that the house was only fit for a clerk to live in and that he would be ashamed to invite his friends there. Effie was also upset, and not comforted by the thought that it was in any case unlikely that London society would come out to Herne Hill. She made only one or two attempts to entertain in this new home. The guests there were usually Ruskin family friends like the Richmonds. To them, soon cheerfully reconciled to the suburbs in which he had grown up, Ruskin wrote in invitation:

> Ours is a most difficult house to direct anybody to, being a numberless commonplace of a house, with a gate like everybody's gate on Herne Hill — and a garden like everybody's garden on Herne Hill, consisting of a dab of chrysanthemums in the middle of a round O of yellow gravel — and chimnies and windows like everyone's chimnies and windows . . . all I can do is to advise you that some half mile beyond my father's there is a turn to the left, which you must *not* take, and after passing it we are some ten or twelve gates further on . . .[1]

More formal entertainment was carried on at Denmark Hill, as it always had been. But life there was not calm in the weeks after the long stay in Venice. There was trouble about the new house. John James was angry about the challenge to duel. He was not concerned with thoughts of physical danger: what upset him was that anyone might call his son's honour into question. Old Mrs Ruskin had taken fright after hearing about John's conversations with Catholics. As had the Feildings, she had somehow gained the impression that he was on the point of conversion. Her fears were greater because Ruskin was now seeing Henry Manning, the most recent and spectacular of prominent Anglicans who had turned to Catholicism. Manning and Ruskin (who were to remain lifelong friends) had much to talk about. Manning was a friend of Gladstone's: his book, *The Unity of the Church* (1842), resumed many of the topics of Gladstone's *State in its Relations with the Church* (1838). These matters had been the underlying concern of *Notes on the Construction of Sheepfolds*. It was natural that Ruskin should now wish to discuss them in the light of his recent study of the history of Venice. John James could see the point of such discussions: Margaret Ruskin and Effie could not. Effie's religious views, such as they were, seem now to have become more pronounced. She too believed her husband to be in some danger, but not from Catholicism. She believed that it lay in pride. Effie disapproved of his

> . . . wish to understand the Bible throughout — which nobody in this world will ever do — and unless they receive it as a little child it will not be made profitable to them. He wishes to satisfy his intellect and his vanity in reading the Scriptures and does not pray that his heart and mind will be improved by them. He chuses to study Hebrew and read the *Fathers* instead of asking God to give him Light. His whole desire for knowledge appears to me to originate in Pride and as long as this remains and his great feeling of *Security* and doing everything to please himself he is ready for any temptation and will be permitted to fall into it.[2]

For a short period Effie found herself in the unaccustomed role of an ally of her mother-in-law. Lady Eastlake, who now began to look at the Ruskins with much curiosity, was able to report to John Murray after dining at Denmark Hill that 'the old people are much kinder to their pretty daughter-in-law than they were and look to her to keep their son from going through some Ruskin labyrinth to Rome'.[3]

Margaret Ruskin's continual derogation of Catholicism eventually began to irritate her son. To Mrs Gray, who also had expressed her disquiet, he wrote a sharp, sensible letter:

> I simply set it down as something to the discredit of Protestantism that my mother is afraid after having bred me up in its purest principles for thirty four years, to let me talk for half an hour with a clever Catholic: but I shall certainly not permit this fact to tell for more than its simple worth — and that worth is really not much — for my mother's anxiety about my religion is much like that which she shows with respect to my health or safety — rather a nervous sensation than a definite and deliberately entertained suspicion of

danger in this or the other circumstance. Only I see that I must not blame Catholics for illiberality in refusing to argue with, or listen to Protestants.

The beginning of these perilous speculations of mine was only this — that one evening in St Mark's Place — getting into an argument with Lady Feilding — I was completely silenced by her — had not a word to say for myself — and out of pure shame, I determined at once to know all that could be said on the subject — and fit myself better for battle another day: as well as to look into some statements made by Protestant writers, which I had hitherto accepted undoubtingly, but which I found the Catholics denied just as indignantly as the Protestants affirmed them positively. And this I must do before I write any more against the Catholics — for as I have received all my impression of them from Protestant writers, I have no right to act upon these impressions until I have at least *heard* the other side. But I do not see why this should make either you — or any of my Protestant friends anxious. I can most strongly and faithfully assure you that I have no hidden leanings or bias towards Popery: that on the contrary I hate it for abusing and destroying my favourite works of art: my name and what little reputation I have, are entirely engaged on the Evangelical side, my best friends are all Puritans — including my wife — and all my life has been regulated by Protestant principles and habits of independent thought — I am as cool headed as most men in religion — rather too much so: by no means inclined either to fasting or flagellation: — past the age of Romance — and tolerably well read in my Bible: And if under these circumstances — you are afraid when you hear that I am going to enquire further into points of the Romanist doctrines of which I am ignorant — it seems to me that this is equivalent to a confession that Protestantism is neither rational nor defensible — if fairly put to the proof — but a pasteboard religion . . .[4]

No doubt it annoyed Ruskin to have to explain to his family that he needed his intellectual peers. But he had found a fruitful new regime for his writing. Every morning after breakfast he left his new home to walk the few hundred yards to Denmark Hill. There, in his old study, he worked all day on the second and third volumes of *The Stones of Venice*. It was to be a book that scarcely resembles anything else in Victorian literature. Yet it has a literary context. Ruskin was now expanding his acquaintance among contemporary writers. Manning's themes have a bearing on Ruskin's epic history. So have books by Carlyle. So also have a number of poems by Robert and Elizabeth

Browning. Ruskin first made Browning's acquaintance at Coventry Patmore's house at The Grove in Highbury. Effie was curious to know what the Brownings were like. She had no great interest in poetry. But she had noticed how Samuel Rogers, always jealous of other poets, had abused Ruskin when he saw that he was reading Elizabeth Browning's 'Casa Guido Windows'. Mrs Browning did not appear at Highbury that night, but Ruskin got on rather well with her husband. The talk was mostly of Italy. Ruskin had to acknowledge that, despite his liberal views, the poet knew much about the country that he did not. A few days afterwards John and Effie went to call on the Brownings at their lodgings in Welbeck Street. No record of the conversation remains. But it seems that Elizabeth Browning was not inclined to be appreciative of Effie. She wrote to a friend, 'Pretty she is and exquisitely dressed — *that* struck me — but extraordinary beauty she has none at all, neither of feature or expression.'[5]

Effie was beginning to realize that in London literary circles there was a competitive element she had not foreseen. She now came under the scrutiny of another intelligent woman who had formed an exceptional partnership with her husband. Jane Welsh Carlyle was no more impressed with her than Elizabeth Browning had been. Ruskin and Carlyle probably first met in 1850. On 6 July of that year, Mrs Carlyle's cousin John Welsh recorded in his diary that he had seen the Ruskins at the Carlyle home in Cheyne Walk, and that Ruskin had endeavoured to draw Carlyle out on the subject of religion. In December of 1850 Carlyle wrote that he had entertained 'Ruskin and wife, of the *Seven Lamps of Architecture*, a small but rather dainty dilettante soul, of the Scotch-Cockney breed'.[6] Carlyle was probably more appreciative of John James and Margaret Ruskin than he was of John and Effie. 'He used to take pleasure in the quiet of the Denmark Hill garden, and use all his influence with me to make me contented in my duty to my mother,' says *Præterita*.[7] In a few years' time Margaret Ruskin became convinced — and with justice — that Carlyle was responsible for some of her son's errant religious beliefs. But there was no feeling of distrust in the early 1850s. And Ruskin went out of his way to please the Carlyles. Cigars were produced after dinner: for no-one else but the author of *Past and Present* would such an infringement of the Denmark Hill rules be countenanced. In 1854, after Effie had run away, Jane Carlyle recalled how well they (and their dog) were entertained, when Ruskin

> . . . twice last summer . . . drove Mr C. and me and *Nero* out to his place at Denmark Hill, and gave us a dinner like what one reads of in

> the *Arabian Nights*, and strawberries and cream on the lawn; and was indulgent and considerate even for Nero! I returned each time more satisfied that Mrs Ruskin must have been hard to please . . .[8]

That was of course a misreading of Effie's situation. It was quite a common one. Perhaps only Lady Eastlake among Effie's London acquaintances was inquisitive enough about her to guess at the truth. Effie kept her problems to herself. In Venice it had been easier not to think about them. But in the new Herne Hill home she had the apprehension that her life would be irremediably unhappy. There were some questions to which she could give no answer, and which she could not discuss with Ruskin. If she could imagine herself happy as a mother, could she imagine her husband as a father? If sexual relations began, would he come to love her more, and be less bound to his parents? Did he love her at all? Did she love him? Would sex be enjoyable, or not? While she thought about these matters she came to admit to herself not only that she disliked living where she was but also that she did not like Mr and Mrs Ruskin. There was a kind of comfort in realizing this. At the end of September of 1852 she went to Bowerswell for seven weeks while Ruskin stayed in London to work at *The Stones of Venice*. She then told her parents in detail about the difficulties of living with the Ruskins. As she did not dare to tell them of her sexual problems she emphasized the niggling disputes over accounts. Here was almost daily evidence of the Ruskins's unreasonableness, for she was pursued by letters from Herne Hill accusing her of extravagance. These complaints were almost certainly unjust: in any case they were insensitive. Ruskin himself had been spending freely on his own pleasures. He had brought back many works of art from Venice. He was forming a collection of missals. In six weeks he had spent £160 on plates from Turner's *Liber Studiorum* while Effie was attempting to economize in the house that had been so lavishly over-furnished. 'How is one to please them?' she wrote despairingly.[9]

* * * *

Effie's personal history now became intertwined with the public triumph of Pre-Raphaelitism. In the New Year of 1853 (as usual, changing his mind on this topic) Ruskin announced that he had decided to 'go into society' that coming season: he thought that he would have finished *The Stones of Venice* by then. This was in part for Effie's sake, but also because he wished to meet people who might possess either missals or paintings by Turner. Effie was pleased, the more so when Ruskin rented a house in Charles Street, Mayfair. She did not know it, but this was to be her last appearance as a worldly success. The fashionable London season lasted from May until July, and its traditional opening was the private view of the Royal Academy exhibition. Here Effie shone both in person and portrayal, for she was seen to be the model in the painting of the year, Millais's *The Order of Release*.

Millais had become a most popular artist. In the previous year's exhibition there had been crowds all day long in front of his *Ophelia* and *The Huguenot*. Afterwards he wrote to the wife of his patron Thomas Combe that 'the immense success I have met with this year has given me a new sensation of pleasure in painting'.[10] His next picture, *The Proscribed Royalist*, was designed to be equally pleasing. Millais had begun to discuss his subjects with an agent before embarking on them: this painting of a hiding cavalier visited by a Puritan girl was not entirely his own invention. It was near completion when John and Effie returned from Venice in the autumn of 1852. Millais was then casting around for another subject. Finally he devised *The Order of Release*, in which a proud young wife meets her Highlander husband as he is released from jail. The painting is subtitled with the date 1746, the year of Culloden. Millais must have told the Ruskins about the painting: Effie described it as 'quite jacobite and after my own heart'.[11] Around Christmas or the New Year of 1853, probably when Effie returned from Bowerswell, Millais asked her to sit for the Highlander's wife. Etiquette demanded that he ask Ruskin first, and it is likely that Millais thought that the Ruskins might buy his picture. Determined to make a better portrait of Effie than those by Watts and George Richmond hanging in Denmark Hill, Millais began to paint her face in competitive mood. He took the picture from his own studio in Gower Street and worked on it in Herne Hill. He may sometimes have stayed the night, for Ruskin mentions in a contemporary letter that his house was crowded, had only one spare room and two attic rooms, and that he had 'promised one of these garrets to Millais, the painter, at all times when he chooses to occupy it'.[12]

One must imagine, then, that Millais moved his canvas, easel, brushes, paints, varnishes and so on into the best-lit room in Herne Hill. Effie sat to him from immediately after breakfast until dusk. Ruskin was meanwhile writing *The Stones of Venice* in his study in his parents' house. The question of chaperonage was not raised (in fact Effie was never chaperoned except when travelling) and the question of whether she should appear in a picture at all was smoothed over. It was not strictly decorous. The only acceptable way to appear in painting was as the subject of a commissioned portrait. Effie was not quite in this position. She took her place in the Academy rooms beside professional models such as the Miss Ryan — Irish — who had posed for *The Proscribed Royalist* and the half-professional Westall, who sat for both the Highlander and the jailer in her picture, and who recently had been arrested for desertion from the army. Models were regarded as loose women: so they often were. The Ruskins did not mention the belief that 'the woman who was made an Academy model could not be a virtuous woman' until Effie had run away.[13] This shows their independence from the conventions of society. But there was nonetheless some strain. Effie thought that some of John James's remarks went beyond banter. After the painting was finished she wrote to her family that

> . . . he said he had taken pen in hand to John to expatiate on my perfections of appearance and manner, that in his life he had never seen anything so perfect as my *attitude* as I lay on the sofa the night before and that no wonder Millais etc etc, but it sickens me to write such nonsense as I could spare such writing and excuse it from a fool but from Mr R it sounded, to say the least, I thought, unnatural and rather suspicious.[14]

She had begun to wonder whether the Ruskins thought that her husband's protégé was not a dangerous young man for her to know.

If these were real social difficulties, they were quite swept away by the success of the painting. A Millais family tradition relates that a policeman had to be posted in front of *The Order of Release* to keep the crowds at a distance. Effie found herself and her portrait the centre of all attention. She wrote home to Perth that 'Millais's picture is talked of in a way to make every other Academician frantic. It is hardly possible to approach it for the rows of bonnets.'[15] Effie was everywhere complimented on her part in the picture, as though she had given Millais some active assistance. She had not: but she looked forward to being painted once again, and she liked to further Millais's social career. She talked of him to her friend Lord Lansdowne, who said that he would invite the painter to dine. A few days later, when she looked in at a party given by the Monkton Milnes at their home in Upper Brook Street, she was able to introduce both Millais and Holman Hunt to this aristocratic patron of the arts. In such gatherings Pre-Raphaelitism now flourished. What Ruskin thought of this social life, apart from the fact that it bored him, is not known. But at just the time that Millais was being lionized in Mayfair, he was finishing the third volume of *The Stones of Venice*, in which we may read his opinion that an artist 'should be fit for the best society, *and should keep out of it*',[16] explaining in a footnote:

> Society always has a destructive influence on an artist: first, by its sympathy with his meanest powers; secondly, by its chilling want of understanding of his greatest; and thirdly, by its vain occupation of his time and thoughts. Of course a painter of men must be *among* men; but it ought to be as a watcher, not as a companion.[17]

★ ★ ★ ★

The Order of Release is nowhere mentioned in Ruskin's published works. We do not know what he thought of it, but we do know that he hardly discussed it during the time that it was painted. He was absorbed in *The Stones of Venice* and Millais had said that he did not wish to show his picture to anyone until it was completed. But Ruskin had some thought of improving Millais's art when, once again, he invited the artist to go on holiday with him. Ruskin wanted to journey north, to see Farnley Hall once more, and to stay with some new friends, Sir Walter Trevelyan and his wife Pauline. He thought that he and Effie, and perhaps Millais too, would tour in the Highlands and visit Perth. The Edinburgh Philosophical Institution had invited Ruskin to give some lectures there that November. It occurred to Effie that she might be able to keep Ruskin in Scotland all summer and autumn. That would separate him, and her, from the maddening life between Herne Hill and Denmark Hill. The Ruskins decided to extend their invitation to Millais's brother William and to William Holman Hunt, whom they hardly knew. Effie's father was asked to find a house in the Highlands that they could rent. She wrote:

> John and the two Millais and Holman Hunt will be very busy sketching and walking over the mountains, and I shall accompany myself in trying to make them all as comfortable as I can, for we shall not have a very extensive establishment and there seems no certainty of anything to eat but trout out of the Tummel or the Garry, but it would amuse you to hear the Pre-Raphaelites and John talk. They seem to think they will have everything just for the asking and laugh at me for preparing a great hamper of sherry and tea and sugar which I expect they will be greatly glad to partake of in case of returning home any day wet through with Scotch mist . . .[18]

Effie liked the idea of looking after a household of artists as much as she liked the prospect of going to balls. Her husband prepared for the journey by idealizing his relationship with Millais and Hunt. He told his old tutor W. L. Brown:

> We shall stay for a couple of months with the young painters of whom perhaps you may have heard something under the name of

> 'Pre-Raphaelites'. I fought for them as hard as I could when most people were abusing them — and we have a kind of brotherly feeling in consequence, and shall be very happy, I believe, painting heather together. We are going to study economy. Effie is to cook, and we are to catch trout for Cook — and we are to count for dinner and breakfast on porridge and milk.[19]

However, Holman Hunt, who admired Ruskin without feeling 'brotherly' emotion, now decided that the course of his art should lead him to Syria rather than to Scotland. He had long wished to paint in the Holy Land. Nobody else thought this a good plan. Ruskin tried to dissuade him, but to no avail. Millais was particularly upset to bid farewell to his comrade. Hunt hesitated, then left hurriedly. The rest of the party lingered in London and cancelled the house that Mr Gray had rented. Now their plans were even more fluid. Finally, on 21 June 1853, they left for Wallington by train. In the party were John and Effie Ruskin, the two Millais brothers and Crawley, the Ruskins' new servant.

* * * *

So familiar were they that Ruskin was unable to recall, in later years, when he had first met the Trevelyans of Wallington. This strange couple were perhaps the dearest friends of the first half of his life. He now visited their home for the first time. It is a very large house. Much of it was at that date empty. Suites of uncarpeted rooms presented cheerless vistas. There was a Wallington ghost. It was said that if one found a corner and brought furniture to it one could be comfortable enough at Wallington. Otherwise, the best room in the house was Sir Walter's study. Here he kept his natural history collections, his fossils and stuffed animals, books and topographical pamphlets. He was tall, with drooping moustaches and fair hair that fell to his shoulders. He was reputedly a miser: in fact he gave large sums to charities and concerned himself with the condition of his tenantry. Sir Walter was a teetotaller, and some said that he had never been known to laugh. Yet not all of the many artists and literary people who visited Wallington preferred the company of his talented wife. There were those who found him fascinating. Staying at the house, Augustus Hare, the anecdotalist, wrote:

> He knows every book and ballad that ever was written, every story of local interest that ever was told, and every flower and fossil that ever was found . . . His conversation is so curious that I follow him about everywhere, and take notes under his nose, which he does not

> seem to mind in the least, but only says something more quaint and astonishing the next minute . . .[20]

Scientific and antiquarian interests, social concern, a liking for story and romance: these of course were common components of the Pre-Raphaelite æsthetic. Sir Walter had no particular views about the future of contemporary painting. But he shows how easily and naturally one might join Pre-Raphaelitism. Ruskin's advocacy was powerful. His writings and personal interest were inspiring. But it took no great change of sensibility to like the new painting, for that sensibility was already in existence. As Pauline Trevelyan's house guests assembled at Wallington one observes how different from each other — in age, interests and background — were the champions of Pre-Raphaelitism. We may also see that it was not accepted that Ruskin was its sole arbiter. The Edinburgh physician and man of letters John Brown, with whom Ruskin had corresponded for years, greatly admired the critic. But he disliked his tone and rejected his historical arguments. When Ruskin had published *Pre-Raphaelitism*, Brown wrote to Pauline Trevelyan:

> I am glad John Ruskin is coming back to his first and best love. I read the *Stones* carefully last week; it is a great work — in some respects his greatest — but his arrogance is more offensive than ever, and his savage jokes more savage than ever, and than is seemly or edifying, and his nonsense (and his father's) about Catholic Emancipation most abundantly ridiculous and tiresome. I once thought him very nearly a God; I find we must cross the river before we get to our Gods . . .[21]

Brown passed on to Pauline Trevelyan the *Pre-Raphaelitism* pamphlet: he did not feel like reviewing it himself. Pauline had Tractarian sympathies and was quite happy to take issue with Ruskin over his religious bias. Her notice was generally enthusiastic: she nonetheless pointed out:

> Mr Collins may not paint lilies in a convent garden, but the serpent is supposed to be hid under the leaves: and Mr Millais cannot decorate Mariana's room in the Moated Grange, with some indications of the faith of her country, but the author of *Modern Painters* finds the Pope behind the curtain.

Ruskin probably accepted these criticisms: Pauline Trevelyan was able to scold him, often in jest but sometimes in earnest. She had met Millais in London the previous year and was eager to talk to him again, for her writings had supported the fortunes of Pre-Raphaelitism north of the border. When *Christ in the House of his Parents* and *Mariana* had appeared at the Royal Scottish Academy she had declared most positively for the religious subject, of which she wrote, 'It is about the most wonderful and daring picture that ever appeared on the walls of an exhibition room.'[22]

Millais, the painter of romantic Scottish history, had never been in Scotland. Here, in the Cheviot border country, he heard much of Scottish lore and legend. He felt welcome, and stirred. Ruskin was content. He wrote to his father,

> This is the most beautiful place possible — a large old seventeenth century stone house in an old English terraced garden, beautifully kept, all the hawthorns still in full blossom: terrace opening on a sloping, wild park, down to the brook, about the half a mile fair slope; and woods on the other side, and undulating country with a particular *Northumberlandishness* about it — a far-away look which Millais enjoys intensely. We are all very happy, and going this afternoon to a little tarn where the seagulls come to breed.[23]

On another day the party drove over to Capheaton, the home of Sir Charles Swinburne: his nephew Algernon, a boy at school at this date, was a devoted friend of Pauline Trevelyan. Everybody sketched. Millais drew both Trevelyans, then started on some portraits of Effie. He wrote to Holman Hunt, 'Today I have been drawing Mrs Ruskin who is the sweetest creature that ever lived; she is the most pleasant companion one could wish. Ruskin is benign and kind. I wish you were here with us, you would like it . . .'[24] Millais, Ruskin and Sir Walter walked the hills and discussed the world. One afternoon Effie borrowed a pony and rode by herself over the moors back to the tarn. Hundreds of gulls were just learning to fly.

From Wallington the Ruskins and the two Millais brothers moved on to Edinburgh. Both Millais — Everett, as they now called him, to distinguish him from Ruskin — and Effie were suffering from colds and a painful inflammation of the throat. They went together to see Effie's doctor, the distinguished Sir James Simpson. The party then set off for the Highlands. At the beginning of July they arrived at Glenfinlas, Brig o' Turk, some miles above Stirling. In this remote, beautiful, rather inhospitable spot Millais was obliged to make crucial decisions about his art. These concerned his relations with the Ruskins. John James Ruskin, back in London, would no doubt have been satisfied to hear that

> Millais . . . has been more struck by the castle of Doune than anything and is determined to paint Effie at one of its windows —

18. John Everett Millais, by C. R. Leslie, 1852.

> inside — showing beyond the window the windings of the river and Stirling castle. He is going to paint *me* among some rocks — in a companion picture. I thought you would be glad to know he is doing something for you, though he does not seem up to a *composition* . . .[25]

The nature of companion pictures is now relevant. They are usually made in celebration of marriage, and in betrothal or wedding portraits are commissioned by the bridegroom's father. They are domestic: they are made to go on either side of a fireplace or door and their composition is therefore complementary, the figure in the left-hand picture inclining towards the right, and vice versa. Millais thought this would be simple. But when he sketched Effie in the castle of Doune he saw that the complementary picture would be awkward to invent. The particularity of the naturalistic Pre-Raphaelite style tended to preclude such designs. He abandoned the idea and ordered only one canvas to be sent from London. On it he was to paint Ruskin rather than Effie. Suddenly the project had become quite different. Ruskin wrote triumphantly to his father:

> Millais has fixed on his place — a lovely piece of worn rock, with foaming water, and weeds, and moss, and a noble overhanging bank of dark crag — and I am to be standing looking quietly down the stream — just the sort of thing I used to do for hours together — he is very happy at the idea of doing it and I think you will be proud of the picture — and we shall have the two most wonderful torrents in the world, Turner's St Gothard — and Millais's Glenfinlas. He is going to take the utmost possible pains with it — and says he can paint rocks and water better than anything else — I am sure the foam of the torrent will be something quite new in art.[26]

The difference of ambition is clear. The painting would need to involve the 'utmost pains', as it would extend the range of Millais's art. He was not a landscapist, and never before had painted rocks or flowing water. This aspect of the picture would bring him into direct competition with Turner. Nobody had more to say about such matters than the critic whose portrait Millais now had to accommodate within a landscape setting. Ruskin's mention of the St Gothard drawing is significant. It was the water-colour that Turner had painted for him in 1843. In 1845, preparing for the second volume of *Modern Painters*, Ruskin had visited the site 'that I may know what is composition and what is verity'.[27] He had then taken stones, gneiss coloured by iron ochre, out of the torrent. For years he had meditated on what Turner, in conversation with him, had called 'that litter of stones which I *endeavoured* to represent'.[28] He had been back to the site the previous year, on his way home from Venice, to study the light there at different times of day. He sketched the same scene, drew, traced, and etched from the Turner original. At Glenfinlas Ruskin made drawings of the gneiss rocks in the stream. They are very like the background in the Millais picture. But they also resemble Ruskin's studies from Turner. This was the point of his increasing interest in his portrait. It was his opportunity to enforce, rather than merely assert, his old view that Pre-Raphaelitism was Turnerian.

Millais took some time to start the painting. He spent days on a smaller, more relaxed picture of Effie sitting on some rocks further down the stream. Amid the general *camaraderie* of the party an especial friendship was developing between the painter and the critic's wife. At first it was disguised by standing jokes. Millais adopted a chaffingly chivalric attitude towards Effie, referring to her always as 'the Countess': she fussed over him as though he were a great boy. On walks together they could be more straightforward. When not in the open air it became difficult. Millais, Effie and Ruskin, as they passed their evenings and as they slept, were very close to each other. For in their pursuit of economy they had moved out of the inn where they had at first lodged and had rented a small cottage. There was very little room in it. Millais and Effie slept in two boxed-in beds at either end of the parlour in which Ruskin made up his own bed. Effie described their arrangements:

> Crawley thinks Mrs Ruskin would be awfully horrified if she saw our dwelling. John Millais and I have each two little dens where we have room to sleep and turn in but no place whatever to put anything in, there being no drawers, but I have established a file of nails from which my clothes hang and John sleeps on the sofa in the parlour.[29]

In the daytime Millais and Effie were always together outside the house, while William Millais (who had remained at the inn) was happy with his fishing. Ruskin sat alone, making an index of *The Stones of Venice* and preparing the lectures he was to give in Edinburgh. One day Millais crushed his thumb when bathing in the stream: Effie bound it up for him. A little later, greatly daring, she sat him down and cut his hair. Millais began to find their physical proximity quite disturbing. Soon it would render him hysterical with longing.

* * * *

Millais was on the brink of a quite novel, utterly illicit experience. At the same time he was longing to express himself. His painting was in abeyance, for his canvas had still not arrived. In any case he was bursting with creative desires quite unconnected with the projected portrait. Ruskin was puzzled by his protégé's thwarted hyperactivity. He wrote to his father:

> Millais is a very interesting study. I don't know how to manage him, his mind is so *terribly* active — so full of invention that he can hardly stay quiet a moment without sketching, either ideas or

19. John Ruskin, by Sir John Everett Millais, 1853.

> reminiscences — and keeps himself awake all night planning pictures. He cannot go on this way. I must get Acland to lecture him.[30]

Henry Acland was on holiday in Edinburgh at the time and was to spend a few days in the Glenfinlas hotel. He did not find that Millais needed medical advice but he was fascinated by his activity. What he found at Glenfinlas he wrote in daily letters to his wife. We should pay particular attention to these reports. For while it seems clear to us that the relationships at Glenfinlas were speeding towards a ruinous conclusion, Acland saw there one beautifully unifying bond. It was art. The doctor first of all explained to his rather strict, Evangelical wife that in this highly irregular household there was yet an especial propriety. This he could not quite define, but he felt that it had to do with the way that Millais appeared

> . . . a very child of nature — and oh! how blessed a thing is this. And that is just what Mrs Ruskin is — nothing could be more wholly unintelligible to my mother (and perhaps even to you) than her way of going on here with the boys as she calls the two Millais — but it is just like a clever country girl. Thoroughly artless, witty, unsophisticated to the last degree and tho' I cannot say I should like brought up as I have been to have you so! yet there is a certain charm in it in her which will presently delight me. It unites the company. Millais is a grown up Baby — and does and says in mere exuberant childishness now just what a very [illegible] and boisterous child would do & say . . .[31]

Rather pleased with his discovery that they were 'children of nature', a formulation which he repeats, Acland could make many a parallel with Pre-Raphaelite art as Ruskin taught it. He himself had given his hand to the diligent naturalism so much enjoined that summer.

> Ruskin I understand more than I have before: truth and earnestness of purpose are his great guide, and no labour of thought, or work is wearisome to him. He has knocked up my sketching for ever. I was quite convinced that the hasty drawings I have been in the habit of, are most injurious to the doer, in his moral nature. What I can try to do is to draw *correctly* really well. I hope to be well enough to try tomorrow a bit of rock & water . . .[32]

Such sentiments are pure Ruskinism. Acland felt that he too could become a Pre-Raphaelite.. It was an effect that Ruskin had on many amateur artists. But it was not possible for Millais to think in these terms. He knew in his heart that such talk simply did not apply to him. In truth, he did not care much about either God or Turner. And the more he felt attracted to Effie the less inclined he was to feel virtuous when painting her husband's portrait to his satisfaction. At the end of July, Acland held the canvas while Millais, 'on his highest mettle' according to Ruskin, put down the first marks of the painting.[33] Ruskin's diary records his progress over the next seven weeks.[34] It went on inch by inch: technically, realist Pre-Raphaelitism was a very slow way of making a picture. In the first fortnight Millais was often painting for six hours a day with nothing much to show for his labour. Soon he decided to move to the hotel. The tension of sleeping in the tiny cottage was too much for him. He wanted to paint for Effie, but could not. The time he could spend alone with her became more and more precious, and the hours he spent at his easel more like toil.

Henry Acland was not the only visitor to Glenfinlas that summer. The Millais brothers had lunch one day with the picture dealer Ernest Gambart and the French painter Rosa Bonheur, whose work Gambart promoted in England. Millais was soon to form a profitable relationship with Gambart, and it may have been now that it was spelt out to him that his Pre-Raphaelite painting was being sold for the third or fourth time without commanding the price Gambart would give immediately for a slightly different kind of work. Millais was innocent about the rewards that painting might bring, but he did not wish to be innocent. He suspected that there was little worldly profit in the struggle to please Ruskin. But when he could interest the critic without making an effort he was delighted. On 17 August Millais wrote to his friend Charles Collins,

> You will shortly hear of me in another art besides painting. Ruskin has discovered I can design architectural ornament more perfectly than any living or dead party. So delighted is he that in the evenings I have promised to design doors, arches and windows for Churches etc etc. It is the most amusing occupation and it comes quite easily and naturally to my hand . . . Ruskin is beside himself with pleasure as he has been groaning for years about the lost feeling for Architecture. When I make a design he slaps his hands together in pleasure.[35]

There is some record of these activities in Ruskin's Edinburgh lectures. More heartfelt drawings are those in which Millais depicted Effie with natural ornament. He adorned her not with jewellery but with corn-ears, acorns and flowers. They went on long walks together over the hills, often not returning until after dark. Ruskin and William Millais stayed behind at the cottage. According to William, writing

20. Dr Henry Acland, by Sir John Everett Millais, 1853.

years later, Ruskin should now have been more firm about the proprieties of the situation:

> I may say that I think that Ruskin did not act wisely in putting JEM and ECG continually together — Every afternoon by way of exercise Ruskin and I spent our time with pickaxe and barrow and spade to try to cut a canal across a bend in the river — whilst he preferred that ECG should roam the hills with JEM & presently they did not return until quite late — Ruskin's remark to me was, 'how well your brother and my wife gets on together'! — a very dangerous experiment & had it not been *for their integrity* evil consequences must have ensued. I may add that JEM returned home helplessly in love with ECG . . .[36]

This is confused, perhaps because the Millais family liked to believe that Ruskin was so wicked that he deliberately put his wife in the way of temptation. The truth was that he was oblivious of the fact that Effie and Millais were falling in love. When William left Glenfinlas in the middle of August Ruskin took even less notice of them. They occupied themselves and he got on with his work. All through September the three were alone together and yet were strangely separated. The weather was bad. Progress on the painting was ever more slow. Millais was coming to hate it. He continued his long walks alone with Effie. We do not know what declarations they made to each other, but we do know that she told him the truth about her marriage. This was a new intimacy between them which filled Millais with a confused sense of outrage: there was a sense in which he was glad that she had never had a physical relationship with her husband. In these weeks Effie seems to have remained calm enough, but Millais was shaking with tension. Ruskin was still blind to the situation. He wrote to his mother,

> I wish the country agreed with Millais as well as it does with me, but I don't know how to manage him and he does not know how to manage himself. He paints till his limbs are numb, and his back has as many aches as joins in it. He won't take exercise in the regular way, but sometimes starts and takes races of seven or eight miles if he is in the humour: sometimes won't, or can't, eat any breakfast or dinner, sometimes eats enormously without seeming to enjoy anything. Sometimes he is all excitement, sometimes depressed, sick and faint as a woman, always restless and unhappy. I think I never saw such a miserable person on the whole. He is really very ill tonight, has gone early to bed and complains of a feeling of complete faintness and lethargy, with headache. I don't know what to

do with him. The faintness seems so excessive, sometimes appearing almost hysterical.[37]

Three days later Millais's condition was worse. Ruskin thought that he should do something drastic to restore his spirits. Characteristically, perhaps, he assumed that the cause of the trouble lay in the dissolution of the Pre-Raphaelite Brotherhood. He believed that Millais was suffering because he could not bear the idea of Holman Hunt going abroad. He therefore decided to write to the other Pre-Raphaelite. One cannot read this letter without feeling that Ruskin's concern was genuine.

My dear Hunt,
I can't help writing to you tonight; for here is Everett lying crying on his bed like a child — or rather with that bitterness which is only in a man's grief — and I don't know what will become of him when you are gone — I always intended to write to you to try and dissuade you from this Syrian expedition — I suppose it is much too late now — but I think it quite wrong of you to go. I had no idea how much Everett depended on you, till lately — for your own sake I wanted you not to go, but had no hope of making you abandon the thought — if I had known sooner how much Everett wanted you I should have tried. *I* can be no use to him — he has no sympathy with me or my ways, his family do not suffice him — he has nobody to take your place — his health is wretched — he is always miserable about something or other . . . I never saw so strange a person, I could not answer for his reason if you leave him. Instead of going to Syria, I think you ought to come down here instantly: he is quite overworked — very ill — has yet a quarter of his picture to do in his distress — and we must go to Edinburgh — and leave him *quite alone* — next Wednesday. Think over all this.[38]

Hunt did not go to Scotland but delayed his departure for the Holy Land. Millais did not know what to do or where to go. He was tortured by the thought of Effie going to Edinburgh with her husband and leaving him in Glenfinlas alone. Every thought of her increased his confusion. What could he do? What could he say to her if she left? In the event, he announced that he would leave the painting until better weather the following March, when he would return to his place by the stream and the rocks. The artistic household was dismantled. Millais left with the Ruskins and accompanied them to Edinburgh. It was while they were there that, blunderingly and almost inadvertently, he broke up the Ruskins's marriage.

★ ★ ★ ★

Ruskin's forthcoming Edinburgh lectures had been almost as much a part of the background of the Glenfinlas holiday as Millais's portrait. The four lectures had been written in the cottage, or in the open air outside the cottage, and their themes had been explored in conversation with Millais and Acland. Their delivery in the Philosophical Institution was to be the culmination of Ruskin's summer's work. That they were to be given in his father's home town was calculated to feed John James's pride, and thus allay his misgivings about appearances on public platforms. By contrast, Millais's picture was unfinished, and pretty clearly would not be finished in time to hang in the next year's Royal Academy exhibition. There was also the possibility that he might have to abandon it. The distraught Pre-Raphaelite seemed hardly in charge of his own destiny. Perhaps, if he had gone straight back to London, had gone abroad with Holman Hunt, he might have been more decisive about his life. He reflected that his best plan would be to forget about Effie and have nothing further to do with the Ruskins. This might also have been the honourable course to take. But he could not bear to distance himself from the woman he loved, and remained in the Scottish capital all the time that Ruskin was lecturing. The four addresses were on Architecture, Decoration, Turner and his Works, and Pre-Raphaelitism. They were afterwards collected into a book, *Lectures on Architecture and Painting*, which is a clear and balanced introduction to Ruskin's thinking at this time. Their success was gratifying. Over a thousand people filled the hall each time that Ruskin spoke and the press comment, comparing his message to that of a preacher, was exactly what the older Ruskins would have desired. But Ruskin himself was a little uninterested in the stir he was making. He was more concerned to take stock of his relations with Effie and with Millais. He wrote to his father, hearkening back to childhood reading:

> It is curious how like your melancholy letter — received some time ago, about our staying so long away, is to the 176th letter in Sir Charles Grandison. I wish Effie could write such a one as the 177th in answer. But I have had much to think about — in studying Everett, and myself, and Effie, on this journey, and reading Sir Charles Grandison afterwards — and then reading the world a little bit — and then Thackeray — for in 'The Newcomes' — though more disgusting in the illustrations than usual — there are some pieces of wonderful truth. The grievous thing that forces itself upon my mind — from all this — is the utter *unchangeableness* of people. All the morality of Richardson and Miss Edgeworth (and the longer

I live — the more wisdom I think is concentrated in their writings) seems to have no effect on persons who are not *born* Sir Charles's or Belindas. Looking back upon myself — I find no change in myself from a boy — from a child except the natural changes wrought by age. I am exactly the same creature — in temper — in likings — in weaknesses: much wiser — knowing more and thinking more: but in character precisely the same — so is Effie. When we married, I expected to change *her* — she expected to change *me*. Neither have succeeded, and both are displeased. When I came down to Scotland with Millais, I expected to do great things for him. I saw he was uneducated, little able to follow out a train of thought — proud and impatient. I thought to make him read Euclid and bring him back a meek and methodical man. I might as well have tried to make a Highland stream read Euclid, or be methodical. He, on the other hand, thought he could make me like PreRaphaelitism and Mendelssohn better than Turner and Bellini. But he has given it up, now . . .[39]

Such things Ruskin might say to himself, or to his father: but they were rationalizations of an emotional deadlock that could not be discussed. Effie and Millais could not speak together of their love. Ruskin now suspected that Effie had beguiled Millais, but he did not say this to his parents; and the etiquette did not exist which would allow him to warn his protégé of his wife's charms. Those charms were in any case no longer apparent to Ruskin. Effie sulked in his company. Ruskin could not resolve this situation: that is why he wished only that people were other than they were, and preferably like characters in Miss Edgeworth's improving novels. He rather badly wanted to be left alone. He was relieved when Effie went to Bowerswell and Millais left for London. With the lectures over and these troublesome young people departed he could begin to think once again about *Modern Painters* and the Ruskin family tour in the summer. The 'habits of steady thought' and the like, so often enjoined by Ruskin, had not been easy to maintain while the shallow-minded Effie and the headstrong young painter had been behaving so peculiarly. Millais, back in London, now heard that he had been elected an Associate of the Royal Academy. What Ruskin thought of this distinction is not recorded: he probably scorned it far more than did Millais's Pre-Raphaelite brethren. John James Ruskin, who entertained Millais at Denmark Hill while John and Effie were still in Scotland, was full of praise for him. 'What a Beauty of a Man he is and high in intellect but he is very thin,' he wrote to Ruskin.[40]

Millais had gone out to Denmark Hill because, once invited, he could not see how to refuse the invitation. In many ways he was still much indebted to the Ruskin family. He could think of many reasons for disliking and resenting Ruskin, and now had those feelings about him without looking for reasons. But the bluff, generous, honest John James could not be hated. There was talk of a portrait drawing of him, and no doubt Millais and the elder Ruskin discussed 'The Deluge', the proposed major painting that John had spoken of in his letters home from Scotland. However, these genial exchanges soon ended. For Millais took the bold step of writing to Mrs Gray, Effie's mother. He had met her only once, in Edinburgh, but now felt free to express his views on the marriage and on 'such a brooding selfish lot as these Ruskins'. About Effie, he wrote,

> The *worst of all is the wretchedness* of her position. Whenever they go to visit she will be left to herself in the company of any stranger present, for Ruskin appears to delight in selfish solitude. Why he ever had the audacity of marrying with no better intentions is a mystery to me. I must confess that it appears to me that he cares for nothing beyond his Mother and Father, which makes the insolence of his finding fault with his wife (to whom he has acted from the beginning most disgustingly) more apparent . . . If I have meddled more than my place would justify it was from the flagrant nature of the affair — I am only anxious to do the best for your daughter . . . I cannot conceal the truth from you, that she has more to put up with than any living woman . . . She has all the right on her side and believe me the Father would see that also if he knew all.[41]

Millais 'knew all' about the circumstances of Effie's marriage, but could not mention sexual matters to her mother. Nonetheless, in his correspondence with Mrs Gray he made it clear that there was a youthful, healthy intimacy between himself and Effie that contrasted with an unnaturalness in Ruskin. He hinted that Ruskin was a homosexual: this he may have believed. It cannot be said that Millais in this correspondence wrote naïvely or impetuously. If a break was to come, it had to be of Effie's own doing. But Millais carefully made it plain that he was not a neutral observer of the Ruskins's marriage. Effie knew this in her heart, and knew it the more surely because her mother told her what was in Millais's letters. When she and John returned to London she had another family link with Millais, for little Sophie, her ten-year-old sister, came south with them. Millais drew this sensitive, clever child in his studio in Gower Street. From her he gathered how tense the atmosphere was in Denmark Hill; and Effie gathered from Sophie something of her lover's movements. When

Ruskin came to Gower Street for work on the portrait he talked, as usual. But in truth he and his portraitist were scarcely on speaking terms, for Effie's behaviour at Herne Hill had at last made it plain to Ruskin that she had come to loathe her husband and that she had fallen in love with the artist.[42]

John James Ruskin now wrote what turned out to be his last letter to Mr Gray, complaining of Effie's 'continual pursuit of pleasure', while the unhappy girl found a *confidante* in Lady Eastlake. On 7 March, surely not before time, after weeks of agonized life between Herne Hill and Denmark Hill, she sat down to write to her father to tell him the truth about her marriage:

> I have therefore simply to tell you that I do not think I am John Ruskin's Wife at all — and I entreat you to assist me to get released from the unnatural position in which I stand to Him. To go back to the day of my marriage the 10th of April 1848. I went as you know away to the Highlands. I had never been told the duties of married persons to each other and knew little or nothing about their relations in the closest union on earth. For days John talked about this relation to me but avowed no intention of making me his Wife. He alleged various reasons, Hatred to children, religious motives, a desire to preserve my beauty, and finally this last year told me his true reason (and this to me is as villainous as all the rest), that he had imagined women were quite different to what he saw I was, and that the reason he did not make me his Wife was because he was disgusted with my person the first evening 10th April. After I began to see things better I argued with him and took the Bible but he soon silenced me and I was not sufficiently awake to what position I was in. Then he said after 6 years he would marry me, when I was 25. This last year we spoke about it. I did say what I thought in May. He then said, as I professed quite a dislike to him, that it would be *sinful* to enter into such a connexion, as if I was not very *wicked* I was at least insane and the responsibility that I might have children was too great, as I was quite unfit to bring them up. These are some of the facts. You may imagine what I have gone through — and besides all this the temptations his neglect threw me in the way of . . .[43]

After this revelation it became clear that Effie would have to escape. Her parents' first thoughts were that Mr Gray should go to London to confront John James. But what would be the profit in that? In the event both Mr and Mrs Gray came to London to consult lawyers. They then made clandestine plans with Effie, Lady Eastlake and Rawdon Brown, who was in England to arrange publication of a book with Smith, Elder. The flight was neatly arranged. Ruskin imagined, to his satisfaction, that Effie was to take Sophie back to Scotland and stay there while he and his parents took their summer tour of the Continent. He accompanied her to King's Cross and put her on the train to Edinburgh. At Hitchin, the first stop, Effie's parents joined the train. At six o'clock that evening court officials arrived at Denmark Hill to serve a citation on Ruskin, alleging the nullity of the marriage. Effie's wedding ring, keys and account book were delivered in a packet to John James. There was a fortnight before the Ruskins were due to go abroad. John James managed the legal side as best he could. There was not much to do. The Ruskins intended no defence. They wanted to end the matter as quickly and privately as possible. They determined to behave in public as they normally would. Both John James and his son attended the annual exhibitions of the Water-Colour Society and the Royal Academy, after which Ruskin wrote two letters to *The Times* outlining and praising the symbolism of two paintings by Holman Hunt, *The Light of the World* and *The Awakening Conscience*. These rather eloquent letters were widely regarded, especially among the Eastlake circle, as proof of Ruskin's hypocrisy. Thus the marriage ended, in bitterness and enmity, but with both partners glad to be free once more. Millais managed to finish his portrait, but rejected Ruskin's offers of continued friendship and artistic collaboration. The annulment was granted in the summer, while the Ruskins were abroad; and in July of 1855, a little more than a year later, Millais and Effie were pronounced man and wife.

CHAPTER ELEVEN

1854–1857

Long before Effie's departure, Ruskin had proposed to spend the summer in Switzerland. What reason had he now for changing his plans? A fortnight after his wife's flight he set out for the Continent in the company of his parents. As they left Dover, Ruskin opened a new vellum-covered notebook and diary for the year's fresh work.[1] Its first date is at Calais, on 10 May, John James Ruskin's birthday and the traditional family feast. The opposite right-hand page has been cut out. On it was the drawing of the jib of 'the old Dover packet to Calais'. Since this was reproduced in *Præterita* it is probable that Ruskin extracted it when looking up old diaries to write his autobiography. The illustration is puzzlingly undistinguished, and in *Præterita* is placed next to Ruskin's description of the tours of 1845 and 1846. But its personal meaning is clear. Departure from England in that spring of 1854 meant liberation. Still confusing the dates, *Præterita* confesses

> The immeasurable delight to me of being able to loiter and swing about just over the bowsprit and watch the plunge of the bows, if there was the least swell or broken sea to lift them, with the hope of Calais at breakfast, and the horses' heads set straight for Mont Blanc to-morrow, is one of the few pleasures I look back to as quite unmixed . . .[2]

This summer on the Continent was happy and productive because of the absence of Ruskin's 'commonplace Scotch wife', as he now called her: it was as though, with Effie gone, he could joyously return to *Modern Painters*, the book he owed his father but had abandoned during the years of his marriage.

'I never knew what it was to possess a father and mother — till I knew what it was to be neglected and forsaken of a wife,' Ruskin now wrote to Charles Woodd, an old family friend.[3] With different emphases, he also sent letters that were specifically about his marriage to Henry Acland (asking him to send the letter on to the Trevelyans), to Furnivall, to John Brown, and no doubt to others. Later this year, after his return to England, we find an especially revealing confession to Walter Fawkes.[4] None of this correspondence concerns us at the moment: how was Ruskin to know what issues it would raise when, a decade later, he was a suitor for the hand of Rose La Touche? On 15 July his legal tie with Effie seemed to be cut. On that day she received her decree. It read that the marriage 'or rather show or effigy of marriage . . . solemnized or rather profaned between the said John Ruskin and Euphemia Chalmers Gray falsely called Ruskin' was annulled because 'the said John Ruskin was incapable of consummating the same by reason of incurable impotency'.[5] When Ruskin heard of this annulment — a decision later to be of such emotional and legal significance — he probably was only glad that the business seemed to be over. We do not know what he and John James thought about the legal aspects of his case, nor how they were advised by the family solicitors. But it must always have been obvious to them that to dispute such a decision would not only be unpleasant. For to vindicate one's own honour in such a situation might mean that Effie would remain bound to the Ruskins: or, worse, would come back.

The Ruskins's itinerary was from Calais through Amiens and Chartres to Geneva; they then spent three months in Switzerland before returning to England via Paris at the end of September. If this seems by now a familiar route, we should note that to follow old paths had a purpose. Ruskin was enabled to restart *Modern Painters* by revisiting the country in which he had first found its inspiration. In the years in which Effie and Venice had occupied him he had been lost to his mountain places. He had not studied nature in his old way since 1849, the year when he had travelled abroad with his parents and without his wife. These intervening years were now swept aside. Ruskin's work in this summer of 1854 was glorious, as we may find in every chapter of the third and fourth volumes of *Modern Painters* that issue from his meditations in the Alps. In those chapters there is a Christian spirit that is not at all like the darker, programmatic religious undertow of *The Stones of Venice*. Happiness and prayer enabled his love for natural creation to take precedence over his interpretations of European culture. One would wish to know more about the manner in which Ruskin generated this revival of an old mood of worship. Perhaps it is significant that (as his diary reveals) his main devotional reading was in the Beatitudes and in Revelation. The diary tells us that at Lucerne, on 2 July, 'I . . . received my third call from God, in answer to much distressful prayer. May He give me grace to walk hereafter with Him in newness of life, to whom be glory for ever. Amen.'[6] This 'call' means a joyous resolution about his writing. We will remember that Ruskin had known such an answer to prayer on two previous occasions. The first had been in the church in Geneva in

21. *South Transept, Rouen*, by John Ruskin, 1854.

1842, before he embarked on the writing of the first volume of *Modern Painters*. The second was in 1845, coming home from the Italian tour with the second volume in his mind. Now, in July and August of 1854, at Chamonix, Sallenches, Sion, Martigny and Champagnole, Ruskin took the notes that gave us the noblest passages in the continuation of his great work.

To say this is to admit that few of the most achieved parts of *Modern Painters* are directly concerned with painting. Ruskin's reaction to the Louvre is interesting. As so often, the party stopped in Paris on the way home: as so often, Ruskin gave the great picture collection only a cursory visit. His diary records,

> The grand impression on me, in walking through Louvre after Switzerland, is the utter *coarseness* of painting, especially as regards mountains. The universal principle of blue mass behind and green or brown banks or bushes in front. No real sense of height or distance, no care, no detail, no affection . . .[7]

During the next eighteen months, while he wrote the third and fourth volumes of *Modern Painters* and prepared their fifty plates, he returned time and again to the major intellectual difficulty of his earlier life: the fact that nature is one thing and art another. But there was much else to occupy him. Nature alone could not take up all his attention. Even in the Alps he had written a pamphlet on the preservation of ancient buildings, *The Opening of the Crystal Palace*, and had contemplated an illustrated book on Swiss towns and their history. In Paris, feeling that his work in England was only a week away, he quite suddenly became full of ideas. A letter to Pauline Trevelyan lists them:

> I am going to set myself up to tell people anything *in any way* that they want to know, as soon as I get home. I am rolling projects over and over in my head: I want to give short lectures to about 200 at once in turn, of the Sign painters — and shop decorators — and writing masters — and upholsterers — and masons — and brick-makers, and glassblowers, and pottery people — and young artists — and young men in general, and school-masters — and young ladies in general — and schoolmistresses — and I want to teach Illumination to the sign painters and the young ladies; and to have the prayer books all *written* again; (only the Liturgy altered first, as I told you) — and I want to explode printing; and gunpowder — the two great curses of the age — I begin to think that abominable art of printing is the root of all the mischief — it makes people used to have everything the same shape. And I mean to lend out Liber Studiorum & Albert Durers to everybody who wants them; and to

make copies of all fine 13th century manuscripts, and lend *them* out — all for nothing, of course, — and have a room where anybody can go in all day and always see *nothing* in it but what is *good*: and I want to have a black hole, where they shall see nothing but what is bad: filled with Claudes, & Sir Charles Barry's architecture — and so on — and I want to have a little Academy of my own in all the manufacturing towns — and to get the young artists — preRaphaelite always, to help me — and I want to have an Academy exhibition — an opposition shop — where all the pictures shall be hung on the line; in nice little rooms, decorated in a Giottesque manner; and no bad pictures let in — and none good turned out and very few altogether — and only a certain number of people let in each day — by ticket — so as to have no elbowing. And as all this is merely by the way, while I go on with my usual work about Turner and collect materials for a great work I mean to write on politics — founded on the Thirteenth Century — I shall have plenty to do when I get home . . .[8]

Romantic and utopian as these ambitions might seem, there yet were ways in which Ruskin's schemes could be tested. One was presented to him almost as soon as he came home from Paris. F. J. Furnivall, loyal to Ruskin throughout the time of the public furore over his marriage, now approached him with the news of a proposed Working Men's College. At a meeting to discuss its foundation Furnivall had distributed a pamphlet which reprinted the 'Nature of Gothic' chapter from *The Stones of Venice*. He was especially eager that the experiment should have Ruskin's blessing. The other founders of the college had probably not anticipated the critic's response to Furnivall: he immediately offered to take a regular drawing class. Ruskin's outlook differed sharply from that of the college's establishment. He was distant from its principal, F. D. Maurice, and from other founders like Charles Kingsley and Thomas Hughes. He had nothing to do with their Christian Socialism. However imaginative Ruskin's view of politics, he was a tory of his father's type, opposed to democracy and liberal reform. His Christianity was certainly not of the 'sane, masculine Cambridge school' favoured by Christian Socialism and by such guiding spirits of the college as Llewelyn Davies.[9] Ruskin might therefore have brought contention into the new foundation. But this did not happen, especially since nobody of Maurice's or Kingsley's type was likely to think that art lessons were important. Ruskin conducted his drawing class on his own terms, avoided his colleagues and took little part in the management of the college. Thus he was able to participate in the educational experiment quite contentedly, teaching regularly from the autumn of 1854 until May of 1858, in the spring of 1860, then sporadically for one or two years after that.

Ruskin's absorption in the classes in a house in Red Lion Square might have had a rather personal motive. It is possible that he felt — as he often would in years to come — that it was time to cease from vanity and to work quietly at an elementary level, far from public renown. In this way, the drawing class was a reaction from the fame of his books and the glittering social life he had led with Effie.[10] A slower pace and a less excited notion of what he might achieve were also forced on him by the nature of his students. Before he began teaching workmen he told Sarah Acland that he was considering 'whether I shall make Peruginos, or Turners, or Tintorets, or Albert Durers of them'.[11] Wiser and more limited ambitions soon prevailed, and Ruskin began to think in other terms. He now looked only for a skill in drawing which might simply allow his pupils to enjoy looking at natural objects. This became the official policy of his class. He expressed it often, and in varying ways. A succinct summary of his programme was given to a Royal Commission in 1857: 'My efforts are directed not to making a carpenter an artist, but to making him happier as a carpenter.'[12] But the contemporary existence of a drawing class and much theoretical writing about drawing should not lead us to believe that the former was an expression of the latter. For what really happens in a class is that individual students manage different things differently, and the master encourages or corrects them as best he may. Ruskin was obviously good at it. Here are the recollections of Thomas Sulman, a wood engraver, who attended the Working Men's College from its earliest days:

> How generous he was! He taught each of us separately, studying the capacities of each student. For one pupil he would put a cairngorm pebble or fluor-spar into a tumbler of water, and set him to trace their tangled veins of crimson and amethyst. For another he would bring lichen and fungi from Anerley Woods. Once, to fill us with despair of colour, he bought a case of West Indian birds unstuffed, as the collector had stored them, all rubies and emeralds. Sometimes it was a Gothic missal, when he set us counting the order of the coloured leaves in each spray of the MS. At other times it was a splendid Albert Durer woodcut . . . One by one, he brought for us to examine his marvels of water-colour art from Denmark Hill. He would point out the subtleties and felicities in their composition, analysing on a blackboard their line schemes . . . He had reams of the best stout drawing-paper made specially for us, supplying every

convenience the little rooms would hold. He commissioned William Hunt of the Old Water-Colour Society to paint two subjects for the class, and both were masterpieces . . .[13]

All this is genial; and Ruskin's appointment of the unskilled Rossetti to conduct a life class makes one further suspect that art education at the Working Men's College was as much light-hearted as it was theoretical. Of course, Ruskin's deep instinct for taking matters seriously could not be long suspended. Thus there was a variable relationship in the college between grave purposes and what Rossetti called 'fun'. Rossetti's presence helped to create a contradictory and exciting atmosphere. So did the students. Some were solemn, while others were simply happy to be dabbling with water-colours. All of them seem to have responded to Ruskin, especially at his improvised lectures. Ford Madox Brown, an occasional visitor at the college, reported that 'Ruskin was as eloquent as ever, and wildly popular with the men'.[14] That popularity accounts for numerous reports of the speeches in students' reminiscences. 'We used to look forward to these talks with great interest,' writes 'One who was often present'. 'Formless and planless as they were, the effect on the hearers was immense. It was a wonderful bubbling up of all manner of glowing thoughts; for mere eloquence I never heard aught like it.'[15]

These were some of the first occasions when Ruskin spoke spontaneously in public. As such, the lectures have an important place both in his life and also in his writing. John James had been hostile to the invitations to lecture Ruskin often received. He considered lectures vulgar. 'I don't care to see you allied with the platform', he wrote, '—though the pulpit would be our delight—Jeremy Taylor occupied the last & Bacon never stood on the former . . .'[16] The 'notion of a *platform* & an *Itinerant Lecturer*' offended John James's notions of the dignity of his son's books. Recently, Ruskin had dutifully declined to contribute to a series of lectures in Camberwell: the lectern was also to be occupied by a self-educated workman to whom the Ruskins charitably gave old clothes. In Red Lion Square, there were no similar problems. There, Ruskin found a way of lecturing that depended on a difference in social class. He also expressed himself more extravagantly than his father would have thought wise. This anticipates the pamphleteering of the later Ruskin. His manner to his students was improvised and freely expository; his thoughts were paradoxical and returned upon themselves in apparent contradiction; he employed anecdote, aphorism, and dramatic questions; the tone was both rhetorical and intimate. It was a style that Ruskin would explore in print in years to come, in works that were nominally addressed to working-class audiences: to Thomas Dixon, the cork-cutter of *Time and Tide*, and then to all the 'workmen and labourers of Great Britain' in *Fors Clavigera*.

* * * *

The cold autumn of 1854 was followed by months of bitter weather, long afterwards remembered as 'the Crimean winter'. In the new year, for weeks on end, London was covered by ice and snow. That spring the hawthorn blossoms in the Herne Hill garden were perished by frosts as late as June. Ruskin was unwell. He was tired, feverish, and continually coughing. A short trip to Deal to look at ships and shipping — a visit which later produced *The Harbours of England* — failed to restore him. In late May of 1855 he went to his doctor cousin William Richardson at Tunbridge Wells. Richardson put him to bed, cured him in three days and told him not to be a fool. Perhaps Ruskin simply needed a change. Since the tour abroad the previous summer he had been trying to develop a fresh impulse for the next volume of *Modern Painters*. It was now nearly ten years since the last instalment had been published. Ruskin wanted to find a continuity with what he had then written: he also wished to clarify his experience of architecture and contemporary art during the past decade. But his plans for the book, always liable to modification and expansion, now became merely disparate. The third volume of *Modern Painters*, written at intervals between the summer of 1854 and January of 1856, is entitled 'Of Many Things'.

Ruskin lacked a direction in his life. It was now that he should have left the family home. But he did not: he could not see the point of such a personal emancipation. His writing had something to do with it. *Modern Painters* represented his continuing obligation to his father. Even if Ruskin had thought of independence, the fact that he was writing this book for John James would have discouraged a departure. The way in which he remained his parents' child now became all the more marked. Anne Strachan, his childhood nurse, still treated him as an infant. Little Sarah Angelina Acland, who came to visit Denmark Hill with her brother Harry, Ruskin's godson, tells us how 'Mrs Ruskin made us boats with walnut shells with which we had races in his bath. Anne the old maid who kept Mr Ruskin in great order, came in and said that he had no business to have water in his bath, and that as he had he must see to emptying it!'[17] Many other visitors remarked how close the Ruskin family was. The painter James Smetham, writing to a friend after an evening at Denmark Hill in February 1855, recounted that Ruskin 'has a large house with a lodge, and a valet and a footman and a coachman, and grand rooms glistening with pictures, mainly Turner's . . . his mother and father live with him, or he with them'. Smetham noticed how Ruskin deferred to parental authority, how 'Mrs Ruskin puts "John" down and holds her own opinions, and flatly contradicts him; and he receives all her opinions with a soft reverence and gentleness that is pleasant to witness'.[18]

Ruskin's dependence on his parents had a particular use after Effie's departure. Their protectiveness and pride upheld him. He had no need to consult his conscience and no reason to consider his self-respect. He now faced London and the world of what men were saying about him with equanimity. Mr and Mrs Ruskin had given their son a self-assurance in which there was a mixture of innocence and arrogance. But Ruskin's arrogance was seldom foremost. People were most struck by his openness. All through his life, in whatever circumstances, he very seldom showed signs of embarrassment. On only one occasion does he claim to be shy. This is in a letter of December 1853, written after he had inadvertently said something rude to the solicitor Bellenden Kerr at a council meeting of the Arundel Society. Asking Frederick Furnivall to help patch the matter up, Ruskin remarked, 'People don't know how shy I am, from not ever having gone into Society until I was seventeen. I forget who it is says that the mixture of hesitation and forced impudence which shy people fall into is the worst of all possible manners. So I find it.'[19] But usually Ruskin was without social inhibitions. It made him a more friendly man. His sensitivity to other people was interested and honest. This was not merely a charm of manner, though he had that. It was an appealing ability — in a man so egotistical — to deal with people on their own terms.

* * * *

A moving aspect of the personal history of Pre-Raphaelitism, so full of desperate and disappointed love, is the record of its friendships. 'True friendship is romantic, to the men of the world', Ruskin had declared in his Edinburgh lectures in 1853.[20] It was an idealistic view, given his current relations with Millais. But there are such friendships, and one may not consider Ruskin's life without regretting, as later he did himself, that in his youth and early manhood he had never known a fellow spirit of his own age and with his own enthusiasms. He had experienced nothing like the young *camaraderie* of the Pre-Raphaelite

Brotherhood. He was separated from the Brotherhood by his age and background. He knew its members only at the time when they were beginning to disperse. But he was able to sense the importance of their fellowship, and he tried to enter it. His attempts to maintain some cordiality with Millais had been rebuffed. Now, in the year after his alienation from Millais, he first became acquainted with Dante Gabriel Rossetti.

Two years after he had defended Pre-Raphaelitism in his letters to *The Times*, Ruskin had still not seen the work of one of the Brotherhood's foremost members. He became aware of Rossetti's art only in the new year and spring of 1853, just before he left for the fateful holiday at Glenfinlas. Ruskin soon found himself recommending Rossetti's drawings to Thomas McCracken, the Belfast shipping agent who was an early patron of Pre-Raphaelitism. In a letter written to Thomas Woolner in Australia, sent with the parcel of Pre-Raphaelite portraits that had been made at the very last meeting of the Brotherhood in 1853, Rossetti explains:

> M'C sent me a passage from a letter of Ruskin's about my Dantesque sketches exhibited this year at the Winter Gallery, of which I spoke to you in my last. R. goes into raptures about the colour and grouping which he says are superior to anything in modern art — which I believe is as absurd as certain objections which he makes to them. However, as he is only half informed about art, anything he says in favour of one's work is of course sure to prove invaluable in a professional way, and I only hope, for the sake of my rubbish, that he may have the honesty to say publicly in his new book what he has said privately — but I doubt this. Oh! Woolner — if one could only find the 'supreme' Carlylean ignoramus, — him who knows positively the least about art of any living creature — and get *him* to write a pamphlet about one — what a fortune one might make. It seems that Ruskin had never seen any work of mine before, though he never thought it necessary to say this in writing about the PRB . . .[21]

The evident desire for success is quite understandable. Woolner had left England because he could not make a living from his art. Rossetti, in the five years since the formation of the Brotherhood, had sold next to nothing. His painting *Ecce Ancilla Domini* had waited for three years before attracting wary interest from McCracken, who was offering only £50 for it. Millais, on the other hand, at this moment painting *The Order of Release* in Ruskin's own home, had been guaranteed eight times that amount before he even began his picture. Rossetti knew well by now that the fortunes of Pre-Raphaelitism, in the more material sense, would not be his; that the triumphs would be in the Royal Academy, where he had never shown; that success would belong to Millais first, and then to Hunt, but not to him. He might well have been piqued that neither Millais or Hunt had never brought Ruskin to his studio; and in the earliest days of their acquaintance he had to call on the generosity of his nature to avoid such pique.

Rossetti was surprised that Ruskin was favourably disposed towards his art. It could not have seemed likely that the author of *Modern Painters* would appreciate either his vision or his means. Rossetti's drawings are awkwardly managed, out of perspective, and contain no landscape. They have not the technical command that Ruskin believed essential: nor do they have the appearance of seeking such a command. Rossetti's work was not that of an artist willing to 'go to nature, selecting nothing and rejecting nothing'; and his style could never be construed as that of a natural successor to Turner. In short, he was a living refutation of Ruskin's programmatic theories about Pre-Raphaelitism. Here was a contradiction. But Ruskin now gave his blessing not only to Rossetti's art but that of his associates and followers; the mystic unrealism of his wife Elizabeth Siddall; his friend Smetham (whose work Ruskin first saw in November 1854); and his disciple Edward Burne-Jones, whom Ruskin met two years later and who was to be his lifelong friend. Ruskin's support of these artists was largely private. He did not write about them until late in life. When he did so, his impulse was less critical than autobiographical. His memory of their painting was then wound into strange relations with his own youth. For the strain of English symbolist art was not new to Ruskin when he met Rossetti. His early acquaintance with the Richmonds had introduced him to those few people, like Samuel Palmer, who in the 1830s had kept alive the Blake tradition. George Richmond, he who had attended Blake's deathbed, had acted as intermediary when, in 1843, Ruskin had tried to buy a very bold selection of Blake's, 'the Horse, the owls, the Newton, and the Nebuchadnezzar . . . the Satan and Eve, and the Goblin Huntsman, and Search for the Body of Harold'.[22]

Forty years later, when sometimes he thought of himself as Nebuchadnezzar, Ruskin would associate his own madness with Blake. Now, in 1854, when he first went to Rossetti's rooms in Blackfriars, he was surely shown Rossetti's great treasure, the manuscript notebook containing writings and drawings by Blake that the Pre-Raphaelite had bought in 1847 from Samuel Palmer's brother. The similarities between the art of Blake and Rossetti are clear. It is passionate, unnaturalistic, illustrational, made by a poet; it is religious, private, amateur, small in scale and avowedly symbolic. Ruskin quite understood its impulses, and was therefore well prepared for the second, non-naturalistic phase of Pre-Raphaelitism. He could talk to Rossetti in a way that left the young man stimulated as he had not been stimulated by certain of his Pre-Raphaelite brethren. Rossetti pretended at first that he was only interested in getting money out of Ruskin. This was not so: he was excited by him. This had nothing to do with what Ruskin wrote. When a large parcel came from Smith, Elder containing the eight volumes, three pamphlets and book of large folio plates that then constituted Ruskin's *œuvre* he did not really want to read them. But he was glad to make Ruskin a water-colour drawing in return. So began an unlikely partnership (in which Lizzie Siddall was included). Each man found the other exasperating beyond endurance, and yet the relationship was of great value to both. By May of 1855, Rossetti was writing of Ruskin, 'He is the best friend I ever had *out of my own family*.'[23] Although he did not say so, and perhaps would not have liked to admit it, Ruskin's friendship had given him a confidence in his art that he had not experienced in his years in the Pre-Raphaelite Brotherhood.

* * * *

The four or five years between the end of Ruskin's marriage and his first meeting with Rose La Touche seem to be dominated by public and social interests. He taught at the Working Men's College, collaborated with architects, scientists and reformers, encouraged the building of the new Oxford Museum; he periodically issued *Academy Notes*, his commentary on new painting, and he worked at the National Gallery in cataloguing the Turner bequest. However, this was also the time — between 1854 and 1858 — when he was closest to poets. His literary acquaintances were many: they always had been. But the likes of Miss Mitford and W. H. Harrison were the minor writers of a previous generation. So were the two poets Ruskin had previously known best, George Croly and Samuel Rogers. They were behind him now, as he began to associate with those writers in the first major wave of Victorian poetry. The Rossettis, Coventry Patmore, Tennyson, William Allingham and the Brownings were all his acquaintances: so were less distinguished poets than these. Ruskin worked hard to keep up with their production. There was a special shelf in his bookcase for verse he was currently considering. He lost no opportunities to discuss their work with the poets themselves: for he could admire them more easily than he could admire artists, and he believed that there were bright truths to be found in their company. Perhaps there were: in any case Ruskin learnt more in these years from poets than he did from reformers.

His attitude to his own verse was diffident. He was thinking of himself when he wrote,

> There are few men, ordinarily educated, who in moments of strong feeling could not strike out a poetical thought, and afterwards polish it so as to be presentable. But men of sense know better than so to waste their time; and those who sincerely love poetry, know the touch of the Master's hands on the chords too well to fumble among them after him . . .[24]

He was silent about his own early attempts as a poet. Probably only Coventry Patmore, as a family friend, would have seen the collection of Ruskin's own poems. This privately printed edition had been projected by John James Ruskin when, in 1847, he finally became reconciled to the idea that his son would write no more verse. It appeared in 1850. The book was not circulated, and Ruskin is said to have destroyed some of the edition of fifty copies.[25] Nonetheless, Ruskin felt able to criticize such a one as Patmore as a fellow practitioner. This was reasonable, given the prose he could write and the years he had spent in polishing diction and versification. Such matters he discussed with Patmore, telling him confidently, 'You have neither the lusciousness nor the sublimity of Tennyson, but you have clearer and finer habitual expressions and more accurate thought. For finish and neatness I know nothing to equal bits of the Angel.'[26] Ruskin was talking about 'The Betrothals', the first part of *The Angel in the House*, which had been published in 1854. He had an interest in this poem-sequence that was more than technical. He had known the person to whom it was addressed, Emily Patmore, since his boyhood. Patmore's poem concerns emotional and spiritual satisfaction in marriage. Ruskin's congratulatory letter regretted that 'the circumstances of my own life unhappily render it impossible for me to write a critique on it'.[27] Privately, he found the poem's attitudes rather consolatory. The more Ruskin sympathized with the ideal of *The Angel in the House* the less his own marriage seemed real to him. Patmore's Angel is an abstract of feminine docility, and could be easily fitted into Ruskin's idealized view of the marriage bond. Ruskin did not write about Patmore's poem until 1860. In that year a further instalment was published, 'Faithful for Ever'. A negative review in the *Critic* drew a response from him. He wrote to the editor to defend Patmore as 'one

22. Coventry Patmore, from a drawing by J. Brett, R.A., 1855.

of the truest and tenderest thinkers who have ever illustrated one of the most important, because, commonest states of human life'.[28] Five years later, *The Angel in the House* would reappear in *Sesame and Lilies*, the book written expressly for Rose La Touche at the height of Ruskin's love for her. It is a poem that contributed to his disastrous assumptions about the girl he wished to wed.

It was through the Patmores that Ruskin had first met Robert and Elizabeth Browning; and we hear of memorable evenings at the Patmore home in Highbury. The poetaster Sydney Dobell stumbled into one of them. Patmore wrote:

> We once had a small party consisting of Ruskin, Tennyson and Browning only. Sydney Dobell came in late in the evening, and sat down by my wife, and began talking cleverly and very predominantly, laying down the law about many things. Hearing my wife address Mr Ruskin by name, he asked in a whisper, 'Is that *the* Mr Ruskin?' and became a little less authoritative. After making similar enquiries when he heard the other names, he became quite shy . . .[29]

The question of authority was indeed an issue in this Olympian company. Ruskin's place there, and in the wider circles of Victorian literary life, was mostly as an art critic who had written wonderful books. Not everybody believed that he was always as wise about literature as he was reputed to be about art. These questions worried the Brownings a little. In the summer of 1855 they were often at Denmark Hill. On one occasion they brought Frederick Leighton with them, a young artist they had met in Italy: a month or two earlier Ruskin had given high praise to his *Cimabue's Madonna carried in procession through the Streets of Florence*. But was he as good a painter as they were poets? The Brownings could see that there was much that was immoderate in Ruskin's enthusiasms, and they were to find him unpredictable. His appreciations were evidently the judgements of a noble contemporary mind, but they lacked measure. 'I am going to bind your poems in a golden binding,' Ruskin wrote to Mrs Browning, 'and give them to my class of working men as the purest poetry in our language.' Not long afterwards, he was complaining about her 'designs on the English language'. The Brownings sensibly decided to enjoy his praise and to remain equable in the occasional storms of his criticism. When, in 1855, Browning sent a complimentary copy of *Men and Women*, Ruskin worried at the poems. He decided that he found them intellectually awkward. He made Rossetti, Browning's great champion among the younger poets, sit down with him and read them line by line. Still he could not feel their rightness. They were, he told Browning, 'absolutely and literally a set of the most amazing conundrums that ever were proposed to me'.[30] Browning took no offence, but explained his verse to Ruskin at great length. The critic was not convinced, but the episode gave him a valuable lesson in coming to terms with a sensibility unlike his own.

Ruskin knew Tennyson less well then he knew the Brownings, although their acquaintance extended over many years. Tennyson had been an admirer of Ruskin since 1843, when he first picked up *Modern Painters* from Samuel Rogers's library table. In 1855, the year in which he succeeded Rogers as laureate, he expressed a desire to see Ruskin's famous collection of Turners. Thomas Woolner arranged an invitation to Denmark Hill. There was subsequently some correspondence between Ruskin and Tennyson. It consists mostly of polite notes, but Ruskin made occasional comments about Tennyson's poetry. He was interested in the reception that year of 'Maud' and 'The Charge of the Light Brigade'. Both poems were in Ruskin's mind as he brought the third volume of *Modern Painters* to its conclusion. This volume ends with some eloquent pages on the subject of the Crimean War. The Ruskinian prose is not unlike Tennyson's contemporary verse. Ruskin's thoughts about the war, which occur in a section entitled 'On the teachers of Turner', seemed to have little relevance to a book that was nominally about art. But Ruskin was extending his writing to include anything that currently concerned him. Much of this third volume is in fact about poetry. It can be regarded as his major contribution to that community of interest which existed between the artistic and the poetic worlds during the 1850s. And its thoughts about the politics of the Crimean War indicate that Ruskin — like Tennyson — was seeking a larger and more public stage for his writing.

* * * *

It was common in all these poets (and this is an unremarked aspect of Victorian literary life) to take an interest in American literature. Ruskin too was welcoming to transatlantic writing. At one point in 1855 he had on his poetry bookshelf Dante, Spenser, Keats, Wordsworth, the two Brownings, Hood, George Herbert, Young, Shenstone ('By the bye, if Mr Browning would be a little more Shenstonian in *flow*, it would be all I want,' he wrote to Elizabeth Browning[31]), and beside them Longfellow and Emerson. He was also prepared to consider the possibility of American art. In 1851 he had been approached by the American artist and journalist W. J. Stillman, who had been impressed by Pre-Raphaelite painting on his first visit to Europe the previous year, had met Turner and had studied the first two volumes of *Modern Painters*. These were impressive credentials, and after some initial hesitation Ruskin encouraged Stillman's ambition to found a native school of art in America. If its inspiration was Turnerian and Pre-Raphaelite, and if it was true and thoughtful, then perhaps art might flourish wonderfully in a new country. Ruskin assured Stillman in 1855 that 'nothing gives me greater pleasure than the thought of being useful to an American',[32] and helped such travellers as J. J. Jarves, a Bostonian friend of the Brownings, and the collector Daniel Magoon, though he was alarmed that Magoon was buying Turners to take to the New World. Stillman had founded an art magazine, the *Crayon*, of which eight volumes were published before it disappeared in the Civil War. Ruskinian æsthetics were its main inspiration. Ruskin did not contribute to the magazine , but he looked on the publication with benevolence. He recommended William Michael Rossetti to Stillman: Rossetti wrote for the magazine and introduced his fellow Pre-Raphaelite writer F. G. Stephens to its pages; and thus two contributors to the *Germ* found themselves proselytizing for the new art in a different continent that neither of them would ever see.[33]

It was at this time that Ruskin became acquainted with an American who was to be greatly important in his later life. Charles Eliot Norton was not an influence on Ruskin, but he was his confessor; and it was in that capacity, or his conception of it, that he came to act as Ruskin's literary executor. In *Præterita* Ruskin recounts that he met Norton in Switzerland in 1856. His memory was slightly at fault: Norton first went to Denmark Hill, with a letter of introduction from J. J. Jarves, in October of 1855. Here was a contrast with Stillman. The editor of the *Crayon* was the son of a redneck tradesman. One senses in him the vigour of an American without background who wished to make art his own. Norton was nothing but background. His family had been in New England since the seventeenth century. His father was the biblical scholar Andrews Norton, the 'unitarian Pope'. The family home was at Shady Hill, Cambridge, Massachusetts, only one mile from Harvard Yard. The young Norton, after his Harvard education and a period as a businessman, first approached the artistic and literary world of London in 1850. In Florence that year he met the Brownings. Arthur Hugh Clough became a friend, and lived at Shady Hill during his American years: Norton was staying with the Cloughs in London when he first went out to Denmark Hill. Such acquaintances confirmed Norton's literary interests. In further visits he met artists. Ruskin introduced him to Rossetti; and from Rossetti, and from friends of Ruskin's like William Allingham, he solicited contributions to a new American magazine. This was the *Atlantic Monthly*, founded by James Russell Lowell and others. Through Norton, Ruskin became acquainted with the work of Lowell, and later with the poet himself. In the last volume of *Modern Painters* he is referred to as 'my dear friend and teacher',[34] rather in the same way that Norton, in *Præterita*, was to become 'my first real tutor'.[35]

* * * *

Matthew Arnold was a mid-nineteenth-century poet and critic who lived at some remove from Ruskin and the circle of Pre-Raphaelite poets. Neither his tastes nor his aspirations were at all like Ruskin's. Their mutual interest in Oxford underlines both their temperamental and cultural differences. In the autumn of 1854 the poet of 'The Scholar-Gipsy,' was staying in Balliol, where he had been an undergraduate thirteen years before. He wrote to his mother of his reactions to the contemporary university:

> I am much struck with the apathy and poorness of the people here, as they now strike me, and their petty pottering habits compared with the students of Paris, or Germany, or even of London. Animation and interest and the power of work seem so sadly wanting in them . . . the place, in losing Newman and his followers, has lost its religious movement, which after all kept it from stagnating, and has not yet, as far as I see, got anything better. However, we must hope that the coming changes, and perhaps the infusions of Dissenters' sons of that muscular, hard-working, *unblasé* middle class — for it is this, in spite of its intolerable disagreeableness — may brace the flaccid sinews of Oxford a little.[36]

Ruskin had found no particular excitement in the Oxford Movement, nor would he have believed that the '*unblasé* middle class' were potential reformers. But while Oxford, as a symbol of culture and educational purpose, seemed inert to Arnold, for Ruskin it began to appear as a city in which many of his hopes might be realized. This was not a matter of the university reforms of the 1850s, Arnold's 'coming changes'. In Oxford, Ruskin now came to believe, masters and workmen, students and artists, might have a common purpose; art and nature might be brought together, wonderful architecture built, God served and glorified.

Such ambitions were stimulated by his old friend Henry Acland. As a doctor and a scientist, Acland had campaigned for some years for the extension of the study of natural history at Oxford. As an amateur artist and, after the Glenfinlas holiday, an aspirant Pre-Raphaelite, he also wished to introduce the study of art to the university. Since 1847 he had been asking for a new University Museum that would house the materials necessary for an honours school in the natural sciences. There were principled Tractarian objections in the way. Dr Pusey told Acland that he, Keble and others felt that the study of natural science was liable to engender 'a temper of irreverence and often of arrogance inconsistent with a truly Christian character'. Acland replied with Ruskinian arguments. In 1848 he used the second volume of *Modern*

Painters in his *Remarks on the Extension of Education at the University of Oxford*: he cleared his proposed academic discipline of any supposed impiety by advancing the Ruskinian notion that 'if the teacher of Natural Knowledge fulfil his mission as he ought, he is striving to lift up the veil from the Works of the Creator, no less than the Christian preacher from His Word'.[37] Acland's idea of a Gothic university museum that would serve both scientific and artistic purposes was created by his reading of *The Stones of Venice* and the Edinburgh *Lectures on Architecture and Painting*. Although he had left Glenfinlas by the time that Ruskin and Millais had started to design architecture, it is likely that he knew something of their collaboration. Ruskin, naturally, had been sympathetic to Acland's campaign. The appendix on 'Modern Education' at the end of the third volume of *The Stones of Venice* was a clear declaration of support. But he was slow to propose a specific type of building, even when the University Commissioners, in 1852, had finally agreed that a museum should be erected. In July of 1854 he sent Acland some copies of his pamphlet *On the Opening of the Crystal Palace*, adding, 'You don't want your museum of *glass* — do you? If you do — I will have nothing to do with it.'[38] Ruskin felt that the time had not yet come for the battle of the styles to be won. On 19 October 1854 he wrote to Acland's wife Sarah,

> . . . as for the plans, it is no use my troubling myself about them, because they certainly won't build a gothic Museum and if they would — I haven't the workmen yet to do it, and I mean to give my whole strength, which is not more than I want, to teaching the workmen: and when I have got people who *can* build, I will ask for employment for them.[39]

He did not become enthusiastic until the end of Acland's labours was in sight, when the entries to the competition to design the building had been reduced to two. One of these designs was Gothic, the other Palladian. The Gothic design, submitted under the motto *Nisi Dominus Aedificaverit Domum*, was championed by Acland in a pamphlet and by personal canvass among the members of Convocation; and when the verdict was given for Gothic, by only two votes in a poll of 132, he telegraphed the result to Ruskin, who wrote back that night

> I am going to thank God for it and lie down to sleep. It means much, I think, both to you and me. I trust you will have no anxiety, such as you have borne, to bear again in this cause. The Museum in your hands, as it must eventually be, will be the root of as much good to others as I suppose it is natural for any living soul to hope to do in its earth-time.[40]

* * * *

The architects who had won the competition to build the new museum were Irish: they were the Dublin firm of Deane, Woodward and Deane. The artistic spirit among the partners was supplied by Benjamin Woodward, a civil engineer from Cork whose mediævalism had led him to take up architecture. Ruskin may have heard of him, for Woodward had already begun to design on Ruskinian principles. The library of Trinity College, Dublin, which Woodward began in 1853, was directly based on *The Stones of Venice*. William Allingham wrote to Rossetti that it was

> . . . after Ruskin's heart. Style, early Venetian (I suppose), with numberless capitals delicately carved over holly leaves, shamrocks, various flowers, birds, and so on. There are also circular frames here and there in the wall, at present empty, to be filled no doubt with eyes of coloured stone . . .[41]

Ruskin thought that *Nisi Dominus* was 'though by no means a first-rate design, yet quite as good as is likely to be got these days, and on the whole good'. The great advantage to it was that Woodward, already a Ruskinian, was malleable. 'Mr Woodward', Ruskin remarked to Acland, 'is evidently a person who will allow of suggestion.'[42] His enthusiasm was growing. Woodward's plans could be modified; more money could be raised, and Pre-Raphaelite artists could be attracted to the project.

> I hope to be able to get Millais and Rossetti to design flower and beast borders — crocodiles and various vermin — such as you are particularly fond of — Mrs Buckland's 'dabby things' — and we will carve them and inlay them with Cornish serpentine all about your windows. I will pay for a good deal myself, and I doubt not to have funds. *Such* capitals as we will have![43]

* * * *

Ruskin's pamphlet *On the Opening of the Crystal Palace* has one or two passages that are not so much concerned with architecture as with public health. In the latter part of 1854, at the time when he was beginning his drawing classes at the Working Men's College and corresponding with Acland about the Oxford Museum, Ruskin attended a committee of eminent men organized by Arthur Helps, the author of *Friends in Council* (1847), a book in dialogue form on the nature of wise government. Their purpose was to organize relief from the cholera epidemic that had broken out that summer. Ruskin's pamphlet has an interpolated question that was surely derived from the misery in the East End:

> If, suddenly, in the midst of the enjoyments of the palate and lightnesses of heart of a London dinner-party, the walls of the chamber were parted, and through their gap, the nearest human beings who were famishing, and in misery, were borne into the midst of the company — feasting and fancy-free — if, pale with sickness, horrible in destitution, broken by despair, body by body, they were laid upon the soft carpet, one beside the chair of every guest, would only the crumbs of the dainties be passed to them — would only a passing glance, a passing thought, be vouchsafed to them?[44]

The arrival of cholera could be predicted: one of Helps's pamphlets on the subject is entitled *Some Thoughts for next Summer*. The epidemic would strike slum districts with inadequate drainage in hot weather. Another member of Helps's committee, whom Ruskin now met for the first time, was John Simon. This intelligent, liberal-radical doctor, Medical Officer of Health for the City of London since 1848, had stated with horrible accuracy in which streets and courts people were likely to die.[45] Simon would soon begin to work with another man who also became a friend of Ruskin's, William Cowper. This future trustee of the Guild of St George was now beginning his political career at the Board of Health. Henry Acland, too, had been much concerned with cholera that summer, for the epidemic had visited Oxford. Like Ruskin's dinner guests, the Oxford slums had forced themselves upon the attention of the university. One might live in London and never visit the East End: the slums of Oxford are only at the other side of the garden walls of the colleges. St Ebbe's began immediately behind Pembroke and the Christ Church house in which the undergraduate Ruskin had lodged. Jericho is built against the walls of Worcester College. These districts were not served by the same water system as the university, and cholera raged in their undrained streets. Acland worked unceasingly to limit the number of deaths. But he lacked assistance and facilities. Families were lodged in compounds on Port Meadow: corpses were placed in hastily erected sheds: clothing was burnt or fumigated. Acland's experience that summer, with his analysis of the causes of the epidemic, appear in a short work he entitled *Memoir on the Cholera at Oxford in the Year 1854, with Considerations Suggested by the Epidemic.*

A remarkable feature of Acland's book, which is largely concerned with provisions for sanitation, is that it ends with a plea for art. 'The Physician and the Philanthropist must desire the success of Schools of Design, and Schools of Art,' he argued, adding that Oxford needed a Professor of Art and that 'a new page of nature and of art has been opened to us through the works of Ruskin'.[46] Acland had been taught to feel that naturalism in art had something to do with the fight against disease. The study of natural science must lead to an ameliorated public health, and natural science should be studied in the same spirit that a Ruskinian artist looks at the world. Ruskin's and Acland's joint publication, *The Oxford Museum* (1859), indicates that for them both Pre-Raphaelitism and Gothic architecture were signs of spiritual health; that this was the root of good government; and that the university could

> . . . become complete in her function as a teacher of the youth of the nation to which every hour gives wider authority over distant lands; and from which every rood of extended dominion demands new, various, and variously applicable knowledge of the laws which govern the constitution of the globe . . .[47]

Now, in the summer of 1855, Rossetti came to Oxford to look at work on the museum. He complained that he was bored by Acland's constant topic of conversation, drainage, and perhaps was dissatisfied with other matters. For Ruskin had brought Lizzie Siddall to Oxford to be under Acland's care. After his second meeting with Lizzie (whom he then rechristened Ida, after the heroine of Tennyson's 'The Princess') Ruskin had decided that something had to be done about her health. His mother's home-made medicines, prepared to complicated recipes, had been urged on the listless beauty. But they had not been effective: and so Ruskin had turned to Acland. In May of 1855 he announced to him that 'I am going to burden you still with other cares on the subject of Pre-Raphaelitism, of which you have already had painful thoughts enough', and explained the relation between her and Rossetti as best he could. 'She has a perfectly gentle expression', he wrote, 'and I don't think Rossetti would have given his soul to her unless she had been both gentle and good. She has more the look of a Florentine 13th Century lady than anything I ever saw out of a fresco.'[48] Ruskin's plan was that Acland would examine her, and then perhaps send her to some cottage on the Acland family's Devon estates. Instead, Acland invited Lizzie to come to stay in Oxford.

The visit was not a complete success. Lizzie felt social apprehensions. The girl from the Elephant and Castle had coped with being taken up by the Pre-Raphaelites: to cope with people who had taken up the Pre-Raphaelites was more difficult. Rossetti's letters from Oxford to his mother are at pains to emphasize Lizzie's social success. He reports that Acland

> . . . said he would introduce her into all the best society. All the women there are tremendously fond of her — a sister of Dr Pusey (or daughter) seems to have been the one she liked best. A great swell, who is Warden of New College, an old cock, showed her all the finest MSS in the Bodleian Library, and paid her all manner of attentions . . .[49]

Acland examined the mysterious and silent Miss Siddall, but could find little wrong with her. His vague diagnosis was that she was feeling the effects of 'mental power long pent up and lately overtaxed'.[50] She met many people, in the normal rounds of Oxford hospitality. But she was not able to feel at home at the Aclands's. Her ways were not theirs. Mrs Acland complained of the untidiness of her room, and perhaps of other things. She may have been asked to leave: for one letter from Ruskin offers to recompense the Aclands for their expenses on her behalf, and continues 'it is provoking that she can't be reasonable and take proper lodgings when she is bid'. In another letter Ruskin apologizes and makes excuses for her. The excuse is that she is a genius. 'I don't know how exactly that wilful Ida has behaved to you,' he wrote to Mrs Acland.

> As far as I can make out she is not ungrateful but sick, and sickly headstrong — much better, however, for what Henry has done for her. But I find trying to be of use to people is the most wearying thing possible. The true secret of happiness would be to bolt one's gates, lie on the grass all day, take care not to eat too much dinner, and buy as many Turners as one could afford. These geniuses are all alike, little and big. I have known five of them — Turner, Watts, Millais, Rossetti, and this girl — and I don't know which was, or is, wrongheadedest.[50]

There is little sign of genius in the drawing which Lizzie left behind her as a gift, and which the Aclands regarded as a curiosity. It is an incompetent illustration to Wordsworth's poem 'We Are Seven'. Ruskin wrote loyally that 'It is quite childish in comparison to what she *can* do. She will show you one day — if she gets better.'[51]

It is possible that a strained atmosphere between Rossetti and Lizzie and the Aclands explains why Rossetti made no contribution to the Oxford Museum, although some of his art was left in Oxford: for he now became friendly with Woodward and was to work with him on his other Oxford building, the Union, two years later. On Ruskin's, Woodward's and Acland's behalf, Rossetti delivered an invitation to Millais, but his Pre-Raphaelite brother would have nothing to do with such a scheme. Ruskin himself took the Pre-Raphaelites' place in making plans for the museum's ornamentation. He produced many drawings and was in constant communication with Woodward. The architect often went to Denmark Hill, where he met Rossetti and other artists. He also had serious talks with F. J. Furnivall, the most favoured of Ruskin's colleagues at the Working Men's College. Illustrative material from Ruskin's own collection was urged on Woodward: a direct link exists between Ruskin's Venetian sketchbooks and the new building in the meadows north of Wadham. Neither Woodward's ground-plan nor his elevations were changed, but he was flooded with ideas for detail. One of Ruskin's gifts to the Gothic Revival was the lesson that ordinary designs might be wonderfully enlivened by decoration. This decoration could be carved, painted, or introduced by differently coloured brickwork and masonry. All these expedients were important, and Ruskin's help all the more necessary, because the university would pay for only the shell of the building. The problem of funds, and perhaps of wages, was raised in other ways. Acland, Woodward and Ruskin were all eager that workmen should be able to express themselves as artists while they were engaged on the building. But they knew nothing of problems on site. Woodward had brought a number of workmen with him from Ireland. Two of them, the O'Shea brothers, were talented. One brother carved a complicated window from a drawing by Ruskin. They also invented their own designs from nature. Tuckwell's *Reminiscences of Oxford* tells us how 'Every morning came the handsome red-bearded brothers Shea, bearing plants from the Botanic Garden, to reappear under their chisels in the rough-hewn capitals of the pillars.'[52] The O'Sheas were not in all respects obedient to Acland's authority, and they provide a number of amusing stories which have found their way into a type of Oxford lore. One of them seems to have been dismissed by Acland, then reinstated. This was James O'Shea; and in his case the line that separated the professional artist from the labourer was not distinct. This may have caused the friction. Or O'Shea (who significantly is not granted a Christian name in Acland's account) may simply have rebelled against the man who could write of 'the humour, the force, the woes, the troubles, in the character and art of our Irish brethren'.[53]

Ruskin, who liked O'Shea, preserved a scrap of one of his letters. It indicates that the Irishman was scarcely literate. What culture could be shared by the different classes? The museum began to teach Ruskin how difficult this question was: the Working Men's College, on the other hand, seemed to have only facile answers to the question. A note from Ruskin's new valet Crawley (for George Hobbs had emigrated to Australia) to the Christian Socialist Furnivall has also been preserved. In this year, 1855, when Furnivall was most often a Denmark Hill guest, he gave presents of books to the servants. Crawley wrote to his benefactor:

> I am asshamed [*sic*] of miself for not writing by return of post to thank you for your kind present — which I feel deeply grateful for — I am reading Ruth to my fellow servants we are all delighted with it. The language is beautiful and deeply interesting and the morals it sets forth are very good and i trust that all who reads it will view it as a lesson and profit by so doing . . .[54]

Not all men of the working classes would be as acquiescent as Crawley. John James Ruskin was not opposed to his servants having books, but he wanted to know where it would all end. He had even heard mad talk of a Working Women's College. John James's approval of his son's ventures was in any case tempered by the large sums of money he was expected to contribute to them. But it was the sheer giddiness of the idea of a further Working Men's College at Oxford that now prompted him to write to Henry Acland:

> . . . the subject of a Working Mans College at Oxford . . . I trust no such absurdity will obtain a footing at Oxford. Mr Furnivall, a most amiable Radical & Philanthropist seems to have nothing to do but to start projects for others to work & he may have an Eye to Oxford — but I sincerely hope neither you nor my son will take any trouble about it. I think both your father and Mrs Acland must have been saddened to see the weight of work thrown on you by the Museum. That must be at least quite enough . . . My Son has enough to do with his writings and his London college. I became reconciled to the latter because he seems to do good service to some good and true men but neither kindness or charity require all plans to be made the scene of these amiable exploits — I should like these experimentalists to feel their way to go along gently and discreetly. It may be lack of enthusiasm in me makes me feel a lack of discretion in them. I hope in trying to drag up the low they will not end in pulling down the high . . .[55]

The 'absurdity' of such a college at Oxford was avoided for another half a century. When it was founded, three years after Ruskin's death in 1900, it would bear his name. Ruskin would not have approved of that college; and it is an irony of his reputation that as his political and educational beliefs became more distinct from the ordinary they also were less understood. In the late 1850s, the condescending good will one associates with F. D. Maurice has an echo in the classes given to workmen on the museum site. Ruskin's personal difficulties may be found in an unpublished address he gave there in April of 1856. It is fluent, but his unease is nonetheless discernible. The political problems raised by the museum may have guided Ruskin towards a firmer expression of views that were increasingly isolated from those held at the Working Men's College. *The Political Economy of Art*, a book which alarmed the Christian Socialists, was written while Ruskin was helping at the museum in the summer of 1857. It is probably significant that in that long vacation there was a further decline in Ruskin's belief in the social power of Pre-Raphaelite art. He had always been reserved about the Pre-Raphaelite ambition to paint frescoes. He now distanced himself from an independent Pre-Raphaelite venture, the decoration of the interior walls of the Oxford Union. This was another new Woodward building. When Ruskin visited it he found Rossetti and many another young artist heartily at work. He thought of paying for another painting in the spandrels above the debating hall. But he did not: neither did he give advice about fresco technique.

In that summer of 1857 the young Pre-Raphaelite spree in the Union was evidently a more successful collaboration than had been achieved in the museum. Both Acland and Ruskin had to note that the artists had joined forces to adorn a monument to adolescent self-importance. These same artists had not been inclined to help with Acland's under-financed cathedral of the natural sciences. The doctor gave beds to some of them, in his rabbit-warren of a Tudor house in Broad Street. But Ruskin may have recognized apostasy. He never in his life, neither in writing nor, apparently, in conversation, mentioned Woodward's Union building. He also developed his aversion to staying in Oxford. In 1857 he lived in a rented cottage in Cowley, three miles outside the city; in 1861 he stayed at Beckley, six miles away; and when he was elected Slade Professor in 1871 he took up lodgings in a public house in Abingdon, six miles away in the other direction. He also distanced himself, in this summer of 1857, from Dean Liddell's plan to have Woodward design model cottages for workers living on land owned by Christ Church. He was learning that since one must expect disappointments in Oxford it is better to maintain one's own position than to compromise with a powerful person you distrust. At some point in the 1850s Ruskin gave away his drawings for the unfulfilled museum windows to Acland's small daughter Angie. He had already hinted to the museum workmen that the only satisfaction they might find in their labour might be the vague one that they were 'laying the foundation of a structure which was calculated to exercise a very beneficial influence on succeeding generations'.[56] For his part, he might as well give his contribution to a child. Only one piece of writing came out of the museum project. The pamphlet, *The Oxford Museum*, was issued jointly by Ruskin and Acland in 1859. Its purpose was to raise more money. By this time Ruskin felt even further from the museum. But some of its lessons settled in his mind. In fifteen years' time, when he took hints from Acland for his road-mending project with undergraduates, it would be recalled. Then, he would attempt to give the experience a symbolic value: one that had no practical application, as it turned out, and which was executed by the amateur workmen who became (as no real workmen ever did) his 'disciples'.

CHAPTER TWELVE

1855–1857

During the 1850s Ruskin was often confronted by the kind of questions raised by O'Shea's artistic ability, or what there was of Lizzie Siddall's artistic ability. At the Working Men's College they could scarcely be avoided, except by saying (as Ruskin did) that he was not training professional artists. The real difficulty was in the definition of an amateur. But there were also problems concerning the status of fine art and its relation to those who might wish to own it, who would be wealthy, and those who ought to study it, who would often be poor. Ruskin, especially when addressing such an amateur artist as Lady Waterford, was inclined to hint that he did not believe that there should be a distinction between 'high' and 'low' art.[1] But he was wise not to enter this territory. It was enough that he recognized that such problems existed. His interest in the wide distribution of art came from his study of the social forms of architecture, its openness for all to see and use. At the beginning of his first letter in *The Oxford Museum*, Ruskin made some criticisms of private ownership of art. Many purchases, he argued, came about through 'acquisitive selfishness, rejoicing somewhat in what can NOT be seen by others', while he and the Gothic Revivalists hoped 'to make art large and publicly beneficial, instead of small and privately engrossed or secluded'.[2] But this was to compare painting (in this instance, two small Meissoniers) with an architectural project. The argument was hardly viable, and was not much pursued. Nonetheless Ruskin's mind was edging around the idea of a democratic art, and in *Academy Notes*, his series of criticisms on the Royal Academy summer exhibitions, it appeared that he looked to Pre-Raphaelitism for an art that would be for all men. 'The old art of trick and tradition', he argued, 'had no language but for the connoisseur; this natural art speaks to all men: around it daily the circles of sympathy will enlarge; pictures will become gradually as necessary to daily life as books . . .'[3]

Direct, immediate appreciation of 'this natural art' was not always possible for Ruskin, since he was not a contributor to magazines. But his letters to *The Times* on Pre-Raphaelitism had been successful enough for him to wish to repeat them. In the summer of 1854, while artistic London was full of the scandal of Effie's departure, Ruskin had written again to the newspaper. His two letters concerned another member of the Pre-Raphaelite Brotherhood, William Holman Hunt, who was on distant but mutually appreciative terms with Ruskin. Hunt had sent *The Light of the World* and *The Awakening Conscience* to the Academy. Of the first, Ruskin wrote,

> Standing by it yesterday for upwards of an hour, I watched the effect it produced upon the passers-by. Few stopped to look at it, and those who did almost invariably with some contemptuous expression, founded on what appeared to them the absurdity of representing the Saviour with a lantern in his hand. Now, it ought to be remembered that, whatever may be the faults of a Pre-Raphaelite picture, it must at least have taken much time; and therefore it may not unwarrantably be presumed that conceptions which are to be laboriously realised are not adopted in the first instance without some reflection . . .[4]

Evidently enough, the picture required elucidation, which Ruskin then proceeded to give, concentrating on the symbolic iconography. Of Hunt's second picture he did much the same. 'I am at a loss to know how its meaning could be rendered more distinctly, but assuredly it is not understood. People gaze at it in a blank wonder, and leave it hopelessly . . .'[5] Ruskin was discovering that even the 'natural art' of Pre-Raphaelitism was often obscure to its audience; and for this reason his *Academy Notes* is often simply exegetical as well as critical.

Ruskin published *Academy Notes* annually between 1855 and 1859, and once more in 1875. The origin of the pamphlet, within Ruskin's own work, is in the *addenda* to the second edition of the second volume of *Modern Painters*, which was written in 1848. In this section of his book Ruskin commented on some works in the Royal Academy exhibition of that year which 'either illustrate, or present exceptions to, any of the preceding statements'.[6] Works by Linnell, Mulready, Stanfield and others are then examined within the context of the main theories of the book. The rise of Pre-Raphaelitism demanded publicity for paintings more important than these; and the effect of his letters on Hunt gave Ruskin the idea of a pamphlet published at the beginning of May every year that would pick out the best paintings and make claims for the art that he supported. No doubt this form of criticism appealed to the campaigner and reformer in Ruskin: that side of his which made a contemporary, in the *Saturday Review*, describe him as 'a Luther in the world of art, protesting against the errors of its teachers, and claiming for all the right of individual reading and understanding of its scripture — the book of Nature — unshackled by the arbitrary interpretation of others . . .'.[7] But it also appealed — and this is not the same thing — to Ruskin's satisfaction in wielding his personal authority. Convinced that his own abilities were superior to those of other reviewers, he found a way of stating that his judgements were above debate. 'Twenty years of severe labour, devoted exclusively to the study of the principles of Art, have given me the right to speak on the subject with a measure of confidence,' he claimed.[8] But the growing number of his enemies suspected that he considered himself infallible.

In comparison with other art criticism of the day, Ruskin's pamphlet is splendid. In no way 'impartial', it carried the banner for the new realist painting of the Pre-Raphaelite school. It divides artists into those who belong to the movement, those who by greater effort might join it, and those who are irremediably benighted. The first *Academy Notes*, of 1855, opens with a hostile notice of a Pre-Raphaelite enemy, Maclise, who had submitted *The Wrestling*, an illustration of *As You Like It*. Ruskin commented, 'Very bad pictures may be divided into two principal classes — those which are weakly and passively bad, and which are to be pitied and passed by; and those which are energetically or actively bad, and which demand severe reprobation . . .'[9] Maclise's picture fell into the second class. It was nothing new for art reviewing to be so completely dismissive of paintings, by Academicians or not. But Ruskin's moralism was new: so was his professionalism, for he assumed an understanding of art far above that of its actual practitioners. Confidently, Ruskin's pamphlet prefers a marine scene by J. F. Lewis to the Maclise picture, then passes to Sir Charles Eastlake. Ruskin had learnt much since the time, just before his engagement, when he had reviewed Eastlake's *Materials for a History of Oil Painting*, and had respectfully applied himself to understanding Renaissance ways with pigment. Now, looking at Eastlake's Titianesque *Beatrice*, Ruskin remarked cuttingly, 'An imitation of the Venetians, on the supposition that the essence of Venetian painting consisted in method: issuing, as trusts in Method instead of Fact always must issue, — in mere negation'. Ruskin found that Eastlake 'ends, as all imitators must end, in a rich inheritance of the errors of his original, without its virtues'.[10] There was much justice in these remarks. But Sir Charles Eastlake — and Lady Eastlake, who soon would seek revenge — had no doubt that this was a personal attack: especially since Ruskin blandly commended another portrait, scarcely a better painting, by a Ruskin family friend, George Richmond, of a man much admired by the Ruskin family, Sir Robert Inglis.

Academy Notes is much dependent on concepts, not of failure and success, but of good and bad. A minor painting with minor intentions might be good: the Lewis is better than the Maclise. Painters who have good in them can be corrected and put on the right path. J. R. Herbert and William Dyce, both artists of the high church, are now examined. Ruskin places Herbert's *Lear recovering his Reason at the Sight of Cordelia* in the category of 'passively bad' paintings and recommends that he 'limit his work to subjects of the more symbolic and quietly religious class, which truly move him'.[11] For Dyce (who, one recalls, had made Ruskin look again at his first Pre-Raphaelite painting, Millais's *Christ in the House of his Parents*), Ruskin had a dismissive comment. His *Christabel* was 'an example of one of the false branches of Pre-Raphaelitism, consisting in imitation of the old religious masters. This head is founded chiefly on reminiscence of Sandro Botticelli . . .'[12] Ruskin had always preferred contemporary realism in Pre-Raphaelitism. For that reason, probably, he gave surprising praise to Millais's *The Rescue*. This painting of a fireman taking a child from a blazing house was Millais's first appearance since he showed *The Order of Release* in 1853. It was also the first time that he had showed since Effie had left Ruskin. Perhaps Ruskin was, by praising this work, attempting to show his impartiality. For one cannot imagine that in a previous year he would have said, as he now did, that 'the execution of the picture is remarkably bold — in some respects imperfect' while defending this with the argument that 'there is a true sympathy between impetuousness of execution and the haste of the action'. His final judgement was that *The Rescue* was 'the only *great* picture exhibited this year; but this is *very* great. The immortal element is in it to the full'.[13]

In Ruskin's criticism of Millais, the 'greatness' of the picture is not elucidated. Neither here nor elsewhere did Ruskin give to contemporary artists the full power of his writing. There is no comparison between the sweeping rhetoric of *Modern Painters* and the clipped remarks in *Academy Notes*. In truth, Pre-Raphaelitism did not mean to Ruskin what Turner meant to him. In 1855 it was already beginning to fail his hopes for the movement. One picture this year was an indication that the future of English art might not lie with Pre-Raphaelitism. It was Frederick Leighton's *Cimabue*, the picture of the year to most people. William Richmond, George's son (who, then a schoolboy, had an ambition to become a Pre-Raphaelite) thought it 'so complete, so noble in design, so serious in sentiment and of such achievement, that perforce it took me by the throat'.[14] Rossetti wrote to William Allingham about the art politics of this hugely successful painting: 'The R.A.s have been gasping for years for someone to back against Hunt and Millais, and here they have him.'[15] Millais must have looked nervously at this painting. He had already heard of Leighton: Thackeray had told him that there was a young artist in Rome who would be President of the Royal Academy before him. And we can imagine that Millais had felt some trepidation when opening *Academy Notes*. But Ruskin still awarded him his best praise, and was in comparison tepid about Leighton's picture. It had not

> . . . care enough. I am aware of no instance of a young painter, who was to be really great, who did not in his youth paint with intense effort and delicacy of finish. The handling here is much too broad . . . It seems to me probable that Mr Leighton has greatness in him, but there is no absolute proof of it in this picture . . .[16]

The first number of *Academy Notes* must have sold more copies than Smith, Elder had expected: for there was a second edition and then a third. To this third edition Ruskin added a supplement, in which he discussed or mentioned other paintings in the exhibition (none of them distinguished) which had been pointed out to him by friends — Rossetti was one — or which he had noticed on subsequent visits to the galleries of Burlington House. However, most of this supplement is taken up by a reply to the *Globe* newspaper, which had criticized some of Ruskin's remarks about local colour in a painting by David Roberts. Ruskin now stated, ominously, that in writing against a painting he never said 'half of what I could say in its disfavour; and it will hereafter be found that when once I have felt it my duty to attack a picture, the worst policy which the friends of the artist can possibly adopt will be to defend it'.[17] In the face of such arrogance, what would any artist's friend do? People now began to openly dislike Ruskin. Ford Madox Brown, to whom Ruskin talked in Rossetti's studio, and who answered, 'Because it lay out of a back window' when the critic asked him why he had chosen to paint Hampstead Heath,[18] now began his lifelong hostility, as did some others, especially if they had been noticed in *Academy Notes*. For Lady Eastlake, Effie's confidante and the wife of the painter whose work had been so denigrated, the time seemed right for an attack on the man she had come to loathe. She began to consider the whole of Ruskin's output, in preparation for a refutation. In the winter of 1855 she laboured over this extremely lengthy article. It was finished at the end of January 1856, after the third volume of *Modern Painters* had been published, and appeared anonymously in the *Quarterly Review* in March of that year.

Lady Eastlake's hate-filled article was the most complete and damning account yet given of Ruskin's writings and his position within the world of art and letters. Unfortunately, it is not illuminating. 'Mr

Ruskin's intellectual powers are of the most brilliant description; but there is, we deliberately aver, not one single great moral quality in their application.' And again, 'Mr Ruskin's writings have all the qualities of premature old age — its coldness, callousness and contradiction.' And again, 'his contradictions and false conclusions are from the beginning those of a cold and hardened habit, in which no enthusiasm involuntarily leads astray, and no generosity instinctively leads aright . . .'. And again, of *Academy Notes*, 'Nothing can be more degradingly low, both as regards art and manners, than the whole tone of this pamphlet, calculated only to mislead those who are as conceited as they are ignorant.'[19] Ruskin was not much troubled by this attack: he only observed, in the preface to his next year's pamphlet, that he, unlike Lady Eastlake, signed his name to his criticisms.

* * * *

Early in 1855 the dealer Ernest Gambart had approached Ruskin with a commercial proposition. Gambart was in possession of twelve Turner plates. His plan was to publish them in an expensive limited edition with an explanatory text by the author of *Modern Painters*. This was the origin of the book we now know as *The Harbours of England*. Ruskin might not have agreed to lend his pen to such a scheme. But it offered him a rare and possibly unique opportunity to complete a part of Turner's own work with one of the artist's own collaborators. For the plates were in the charge of the engraver Thomas Lupton, and the project was a revival of a plan he had made with Turner, as long ago as 1825, to issue a series entitled *The Ports of England*. Ruskin was further tempted by Gambart's offer of two fine Turner drawings in way of payment. The bargain was made: and he wrote the descriptions of plates of Sandwich, Sheerness, Falmouth and other seafaring towns while recuperating from illness at Deal in the spring of 1855.

The Harbours of England was not published until the next year, a month or so after the third and fourth volumes of *Modern Painters* had appeared. Not surprisingly, it has a number of affinities with them. It also harks back to the sections on sea painting in the first volume, while its remarks on the 'Dover' and 'Scarborough' bear on much that is said of Turnerian topography and composition in the fifth and final volume of Ruskin's great exposition of landscape art. *Harbours*, the only book that Ruskin wrote to fulfil a commission, is both serious and an occasional piece whose intention is to captivate the reader. It contains magnificent things, thoughts that could only be Ruskin's, and sentences that he alone could write. However, some of the commentary is almost light-hearted. In such a text one might overlook references to Ruskin's most personal experiences of Turner. Yet they are there. At one point, for instance, he mentions the studies of shipping that he had found in one of Turner's drawers. Ruskin had come upon these sheets after the artist's death, on one of the occasions when he had been to Queen Anne Street to look through the quantities of art that had been left there. Of these expeditions he was mysteriously silent: not until old age, and then in the delirium of his madness, did he speak of what he had found. Nor did he ever write directly of how he had searched the house. Only occasionally, in the privacy of his diary, do we stumble on the memory of his thoughts when he uncovered *The Fighting Teméraire*, lurid amid the dust and darkness of the abandoned studios. In *The Harbours of England*, the *Teméraire* is clearly and confidently judged as the last of Turner's paintings 'executed with perfect power'.[20] Ruskin thought more about the picture than that: *The Harbours of England* reminds us — as *Modern Painters* does not — how Ruskin was reluctant to relate all he knew about the painter he most admired.

When *The Harbours of England* was published Ruskin might have been gratified to read in the *Athenæum* that

> Since Byron's 'Address to the Ocean' a more beautiful poem on the sea has not been written than Mr Ruskin's preliminary chapter. It is a prose poem worthy of a nation at whose throne the seas, like captive monsters, are chained and bound. It is worthy of the nation of Blake and Nelson, of Drake and Howe, and true island hearts will beat quicker as they read . . .[21]

Ruskin's patriotism was not as simple as this, however, and much else in this favourable review would have annoyed him. From about the time of *Harbours* Ruskin (unlike his father, who still kept a book of press cuttings) paid less and less attention to his reviews. The history of his relationship with the press becomes increasingly an account of misunderstanding. But Ruskin probably felt benevolently towards one review which appeared in 1856. It was by two young men whom we may count not only as admirers but as followers of Ruskin. William Morris and Edward Burne-Jones, recent graduates of Exeter College, Oxford, had written enthusiastically in the *Oxford and Cambridge Magazine* about the third volume of *Modern Painters* in reply to Lady Eastlake's hostilities in the *Quarterly Review*. Out of a slough of conventional criticism, the authors wrote, 'this man John Ruskin rose, seeming to us like a Luther of the arts'.[22] This is the second time we have encountered the phrase; and it is to be found elsewhere in the late 1850s. It is as though those who valued the temper of Ruskin's criticism were hard put to find a parallel, though they wanted to make a mighty and valiant comparison. Those without an extravagant admiration for Ruskin, a class which would include most regular reviewers, did not know what to make of him. But they did not lack reports of his current opinions. In 1856 much of Ruskin's thinking was expressed in lectures rather than in books; in addresses to the Working Men's College; to workmen employed in the building of the Oxford Museum; and in a lecture at the Society of Arts on 'The Recent Progress of Design as Applied to Manufacture'. These were fully reported in newspapers.

* * * *

From May until October of 1856 the Ruskins were on the Continent. This was the last time but one that they travelled abroad together. The tour itself was not particularly memorable. It is most marked by the cementing of the unusual friendship with Charles Eliot Norton, who for many years afterwards received some of Ruskin's most intimate letters. The Ruskins's outward route from Calais was familiar: they were met there by Couttet, who escorted them along the old road from Amiens to Senlis, to Rheims, and thence to Basle. They then spent nearly two months in the lakes of northern Switzerland and the Bernese Oberland. There Ruskin's parents rested, while he began work on a project that had been in his mind, vaguely, for some years. This was to be a Swiss book. Ruskin had much feeling for the subject, but he could not decide how to express himself. The most obvious course was to write a history of Switzerland. He had recently been rereading Sismondi: and one can imagine a romantic Swiss version of his *Histoire des républiques italiennes*. But Ruskin was more attracted by the idea of a portfolio publication. This would consist of engraved drawings of Swiss towns with a commentary. The inspiration for such a work was clearly Turnerian. The format would no doubt have been based on that of *The Harbours of England*. Perhaps the thought of matching his own drawings against Turner's example dissuaded Ruskin from his project. In any case, nothing came of it.

Evidence of Ruskin's work on the history and topography of Switzerland is to be found in some annotated books, in a handful of drawings — sketchy, not at all suitable for engraving — and in a new diary. This vellum-covered volume was opened when Ruskin left England in May: he used it for journal and notes for the next two years and more. It gives the impression of desultory and sporadic labour. Ruskin later told Lady Trevelyan that he had done little more than ten days' work all summer. He was no doubt tired after completing the middle volumes of *Modern Painters*. It was wearisome to have to look after both his parents and Anne Strachan, who had travelled with them. As usual, Ruskin indulged his father. John James showed little interest in the Swiss illustrations. Once more he asked his son when *Modern Painters* would be completed. This is probably why the party now moved on to Geneva and Chamonix, the original homes of the book. Here Ruskin resumed geological and cloud studies. But he also had to conduct family outings. It was on a steamer in Lake Geneva, at a cabin table 'covered with the usual Swiss news about nothing, and an old caricature book or two' that Charles Eliot Norton reintroduced himself to the party.[23] In his present, rather bored mood he found Norton interesting. He was both eager and polite; an American certainly, but a gentlemanly American. Norton talked of literature and art, as he imagined he was obliged to do, and the Ruskins listened to him. Slightly puzzled that he had not been engaged in debate, Norton wrote of his new acquaintance: 'He was apt to attribute only too much value to a judgement that did not coincide with his own.' Ruskin had let him talk on, feeling himself an older and wearier man. For his part, Norton had decided that Ruskin was 'one of the pleasantest, gentlest, kindest, and most interesting of men', adding, however, 'He seemed to me cheerful rather than happy. The deepest currents of his life ran out of sight.'[24]

We will come upon these 'deeper currents' in the vellum diary. Norton was right to realize that they existed. But he would never give them enough credit. He always afterwards relied too much on his first impressions of Ruskin. He believed him directionless, a man he could himself direct. Norton had attached himself to Ruskin at a watershed in the critic's life. Ruskin was thirty-seven now, just at the beginning of the crisis of his middle age. In Switzerland he was affected with indolence and something near to depression. He was slightly indecisive, in a state of not knowing, of waiting to be persuaded. Neither people nor literature greatly affected him: and in Switzerland there was no art to be seen. He met Harriet Beecher Stowe this summer: he did not admire *Uncle Tom's Cabin*, and was not impressed by its author. He read George Sand novels, one after the other, then read them aloud to his mother for entertainment. He realized they were bad, but what of that? Ruskin raised himself from his lethargic mood, or at any rate attempted to combat it, by considering his father's age and energy. John James was now seventy-one. Ruskin, considering how his father had passed the three-score years and ten of the biblical life span, decided to calculate how the 'perfect term of human life' applied to himself.[25] This was in Geneva, on the Sunday morning of 7 September, in the same town — and perhaps on the way to the same chapel — where he had knelt to pray and vowed to write the vindication that became *Modern Painters*. The sums in the diary revealed that Ruskin could expect to live for 11,795 days. Thenceforward he wrote the diminishing figures in his daily entry, not abandoning the practice until (day 11,192) 8 July 1858: significantly, perhaps, at a time of religious uncertainty.

Quietly, (he did not announce his 'signal-word or watchword' until 1876[26]) Ruskin now replaced the *Age quod agis* on his father's coat-of-arms with a new personal motto. It was the single word 'Today'. He thought of it always with a corollary, the verse from the gospel of St John, 'The night cometh, when no man can work'. On the way home from Switzerland Ruskin gathered his forces, made sure to take notes in the Louvre, began to make new plans. Back in England, the diary suddenly indicates how full was his social and professional life. On 21 October (day 11,753) is the entry 'visit Morris and Jones'.[27] Guided no doubt by Rossetti, Ruskin had visited his young Pre-Raphaelite admirers at their lodgings in Red Lion Square. Edward Burne-Jones was simply overjoyed, especially since Ruskin proposed to call there regularly on his Thursday visits to the Working Men's College: 'Tomorrow night he comes again', wrote Burne-Jones, 'and every Thursday night the same — isn't that like a dream? think of knowing Ruskin like an equal and being called his dear boys. Oh! he is so good and kind — better than his books, which are the best books in the world.'[28] Ruskin made many other visits that autumn. We find him at the Prinseps's, where he 'heard sad report of poor Watts',[29] with Furnivall, with John Lewis; and dining at Gambart's with the celebrated French *animalier* Rosa Bonheur. In such company Ruskin was relaxed and garrulous. One might imagine him at ease with the world, were it not that the shadow of the Turner bequest had once again been cast over his mind. The National Gallery had organized a small exhibition of Turner's oil paintings. This was the first public appearance of any of the work that had been left in Queen Anne Street. The exhibition had a dramatic effect on Ruskin, with consequent damage to his health. By 28 November (day 11,716), he was ill. The diary notes 'curious illness attacking me in the afternoon of Saturday, before dinner, with shivering, weakness, loss of appetite, as if the commencement of a serious illness; feverish night with heat and quick pulse, but perspiration. Heavy headache and disgusted, incapable feeling all Sunday, going gradually off towards evening'.[30]

* * * *

The involved story of Ruskin's dealings with the Turner bequest is examined below. For the moment we should look at a book that was written in this winter of 1856-7, *The Elements of Drawing*. The book issues in part from Ruskin's Turner studies, in part from the activities at the Working Men's College; but its procedures come from Ruskin's correspondence with his admirers. Since the mid-1840s he had taught drawing by letter. The first of his pupils by correspondence were Henry Acland and the daughter of his Christ Church tutor Walter Brown: the most recent was Harriet Beecher Stowe's daughter. Whole sequences of these letters relating to drawing have survived, and such collections (lovingly mounted in albums, often enough) throw some light on *The Elements*. For of course they show how impractical and laborious such a method of instruction must be. They also indicate that the teaching was not progressive: it always returned to first principles. *The Elements of Drawing* reflects the way in which these lessons often ended in discouragement. The book was designed to relieve Ruskin from the many demands that were made on him, now that he had a class. It also had a remedial purpose. It opposed the numerous drawing manuals that demonstrated quick ways of composing picturesque landscape. In one way, the book is as near as we know to a Pre-Raphaelite manual. But its insistence on painstaking drawing from nature still meant only exercises. That they were of stones, flowers and leaves was refreshing. But they would not have taken a pupil very far. Certainly there is no intention of helping a reader of the book to become an artist. Ruskin was a better teacher (as all drawing masters must be) when he sat down side by side with someone. Then his instruction could be both efficient and inspiring. But he could not project teaching into independence and individual style. Here was one aspect of his confused and contradictory relations with Rossetti — and also with Burne-Jones, for the younger artist was now also brought into the Working Men's College. They were at one and the same time Ruskin's comrades, his colleagues and his pupils. But neither of them had anything to do with *The Elements*, and it is doubtful whether either of them could have performed its exercises. Ruskin still badgered Rossetti to correct his drawing. But he never criticized Burne-Jones, whose art was dependent on Rossetti's: not now, when Burne-Jones was in his novitiate, nor ever afterwards.

Given the principles of *The Elements of Drawing*, it is strange that Ruskin brought Rossetti and Burne-Jones to teach at the Working Men's College. He must have given them the duller or the quirkier students. He could not have let them plant bad habits or bohemian ways in the aspirant artist-workmen who were destined for duty in Denmark Hill. This is only one of many ways in which his notion of a democratic art fell down. After their dinner at Gambart's, Rosa Bonheur spoke of Ruskin from the point of view of a French professional artist. 'He is a gentleman,' she said, 'an educated gentleman; but he is a theorist. He sees nature with a little eye — *tout a fait comme un oiseau*.'[31] She had seen that, being a gentleman, he was an amateur; and that his social position had made him insensitive to the ambitions of easel painting. This combination infuriated a critic nearer home. Ruskin's theories were bitterly scorned by an art educationalist who was near to Pre-Raphaelitism. William Bell Scott was a painter who was Principal of the School of Design at Newcastle. Despite their common friends at Wallington he and Ruskin could scarcely be polite to each other, let alone agree about art. Bell Scott visited the Working Men's College drawing classes and was appalled.[32] He too taught working men. He knew how to encourage artists to make paintings. Ruskin, he was convinced, did not. And it is true that Ruskin was of most use when talking to women amateur water-colourists. Many technical matters confirm this judgement. One is the problem of perspective. In 1859 Ruskin added *The Elements of Perspective* to *The Elements of Drawing*. This was supposed to explain and demonstrate eternal rules. But the problem for a realist painter in 1859 was that the more 'correct' his perspective, the more his pictorial space looked like Renaissance space, perhaps even like that of the despised Raphael. This is the kind of painterly problem Ruskin did not enter. *The Elements of Perspective* was not a help to contemporary painters. Significantly, it is based on the exercises in Euclidean geometry that had pleased Ruskin when he was a Christ Church gentleman-commoner.

In these earliest days of avant-garde culture, it is not surprising to find great optimism for the future of art combined with the collapse, or confusion, of traditional teaching practices. We would also expect to find the most variable assessments of the worth of new art. Ruskin's comments in *Academy Notes* show how alert he was to the merits of contemporary painting. But these detached paragraphs, the most direct art criticism he ever wrote, are scarcely important when we think of the great flood of experience that formed his sensibility. That experience was not modern: it was 'of the old school'.[33] It was also provincial. As *Academy Notes*'s additional observations on the 'French Exhibition' remind us, there is little profit in reading Ruskin on modern foreign painting. He rather disliked German art, the first nineteenth-century continental school he was aware of. He would not come to dislike the Nazarenes until he looked at them in 1859, but he knew before that there must be something wrong with the school: had not John Murray asked him to write a book on them rather than on Turner? His attitude to French painting was negligent. He never in his life visited the *Salons*, the Parisian equivalent of the Royal Academy exhibitions. In Pall Mall, Gambart showed French paintings every year from 1854. Ruskin occasionally noticed them. In these years he most admired Edouard Frère, for his sentiment and his invaluable record of peasant life. French peasants were important to Ruskin, and his distrust of new French art was usually mixed with his attitude to vicious republican Paris. He loved France for its provinces and their architecture. In 1857, giving an address at the Working Men's College, he spoke of French 'manners' and cathedrals: these indeed were his real interests. But he also knew a surprising amount of modern French literature. In a few years' time, with help from Swinburne, he would acknowledge that there was talent in Baudelaire. He could not be so tolerant about art. Paintings always made him angrier than books: they as it were blinded him; and no help from Swinburne in the next few years could make him understand the French background of the most challenging artist he encountered in the years after Pre-Raphaelitism, who was of course Whistler.

CHAPTER THIRTEEN

1855–1858

Not far from the Royal Academy of Arts lay the Olympic, a public house with some music hall entertainment. Here, in June of 1855, George Butterworth had spent the evening after a visit to the annual exhibition. In his pocket was a copy of *Academy Notes*. Butterworth was a young carpenter. He had come to London from Lancashire and was living in lodgings in south London. He had enrolled at the Working Men's College art classes the previous year. His diary tells us much about the life of an artistically inclined young workman who had come under Ruskin's influence. One of its entries records the birth of the idea of the *Notes*:

> Went up to see Mr Ruskin who I heard had been to the Academy once more to look at Millais's picture, and had come back too unwell to go to college — he however would see me but for a few minutes as he said he had something on his mind which he intended to have [illegible] some criticisms of the pictures at the Academy which he intended to have [illegible] and sold at the doors along with the catalogues — the idea so tickled his fancy that he laughed aloud, he was in such good spirits that I not only got him to have two of the Turners home to work upon but his permission to take out of the frame the Carisbrooke . . .[1]

Butterworth framed for Ruskin and therefore had a good personal experience of the Denmark Hill collection. He also gave Ruskin woodworking lessons: the critic 'wanted it for exercise to keep him from thinking'.[2] Thus Butterworth came to carry away wine, money and pictures from Denmark Hill. Perhaps it is true, as Ruskin believed, that he was feckless. *Præterita* speaks darkly of him, or rather of 'the deadly influence of London itself, and of working men's clubs as well as colleges'.[3] When Butterworth's diary notes how he and a friend, another carpenter, had spent a Sunday afternoon discussing designs for an altar-piece and then reading aloud from the Working Men's College pamphlet of *The Nature of Gothic*, we might recognize a workman-artist cast in the perfect mould of the Ruskinian labourer. But the instinctive and relentless high tone of Ruskin's contact with the world prevented him from understanding the relaxations of working-class youths, particularly if they were artists. To one such,

J. J. Laing, he wrote at this time, 'The great lesson we have to learn in this world is to *give it all up*.'[4] Butterworth was too eager to experience the world to command Ruskin's good opinion. He felt it presumptuous in the young man to go on a painting holiday in Wales, or indeed to visit in his native Middleton the Turner patron John Hammersley. Butterworth thought to go up to Denmark Hill and please Ruskin with Hammersley's tales of the painter. But he was in error. He had mistaken his place.

At the Working Men's College, Butterworth had a slight acquaintance with George Allen, another northerner. Allen, a native of Newark, was already a highly qualified joiner, good enough to attract the best employment that his trade offered. Butterworth wrote in his diary that he had seen how Ruskin had an especial interest in him. 'I think he intends to make Allen into something.'[5] This indeed was so. George Allen's new career as Ruskin's *factotum* and, eventually, his publisher, began at the Working Men's College. In old age he looked back on his other opportunities with particular nostalgia. 'In the early days of the renaissance of industrial art,' he told J. W. Mackail, 'when the movement was first projected, Dante Rossetti asked me to join him and William Morris in the practical carrying out of their plans . . . I was obliged to forgo all thought of doing so having just then accepted Mr Ruskin's offer . . .'[6] In fact, Allen had himself made an offer which bound him to Denmark Hill. On Christmas Day of 1856 he married Hannah, Margaret Ruskin's maid and George Hobbs's sister. Ruskin now set Allen to learn new skills. He paid Thomas Lupton and J. H. Le Keux to teach him mezzotint techniques and line engraving. Le Keux was from an old family of engravers. Lupton had worked for Turner. Ruskin's intentions were obvious. In this way he established a direct artisanal link between Turner's work for engravers and the superb plates that illustrated his own books.

Thus, as Ruskin sensed his disillusionment with the Working Men's College, he more and more used it to recruit his personal labour force. Partly to mock the Christian Socialists, he now occasionally talked of a 'protestant convent', whose inmates would be engaged in art work and supervised by himself.[7] In practice, this meant that artists became Denmark Hill servants of a special sort. To Allen and Butterworth (who was sporadically employed until the '80s) we must now add the names of William Ward, Arthur Burgess and John Bunney. All three came from the Working Men's College and remained in Ruskin's employment until they died. Burgess was a wood-engraver who had been, according to the obituary notice Ruskin wrote, 'variously bound, embittered and wounded in the ugly prison-house of London labour'.[8] Ward had been a clerk in the City. Ruskin turned him into a

Turner copyist and drawing master, using him to teach pupils he had no time for. Bunney also was a clerk. He was employed by Smith, Elder. His contact with Ruskin therefore took him out of the commercial side of the firm and into the direct artistic employ of its most celebrated author. It was a foreshadowing of Ruskin's eventual decision to take all his publishing into his own hands.

* * * *

Letters of instruction and encouragement to these men are numerous. Ruskin had been teaching people to draw by letter since the time of the composition of the first volume of *Modern Painters*. It was a practice he maintained all his life. Recipients of such letters must be numbered in dozens, and some of these pupils must have received up to a hundred separate missives. A feature of these letters is their relative uniformity. Little or no account is taken of an individual's artistic predilections, nor much of his or her relative advancement. It was all the same to Ruskin: one and the same will was impressed on all. Of course, it was only rarely that an independent professional artist would seek instruction from him. This helped Ruskin to maintain the illusion that the same art should be made by everybody. Early in his acquaintance with Louisa, Marchioness of Waterford, he declared 'I am not surer of anything I know, than of this, that there is no real occasion for the gulph of separation between amateur and artist.'[9] It was a radical, mistaken view, one of a number of misconceptions that lay behind *The Elements of Drawing*.

What purported to be a timeless book turned out to be utterly and inescapably of its day. How could one expect any book of Ruskin's to be anything but individual, or to belong to any time other than the months in which it was written? *The Elements of Drawing* comes from such concerns as his classes in Red Lion Square, his love of detail in engravings after Turner, and his correspondence with such eager amateurs as the Marchioness of Waterford. Embedded though it is in this tiny corner of the history of drawing, the book still has a significant position in the history of that sub-branch of art education which is carried by drawing manuals. Such manuals belong to the post-Renaissance period. *The Elements* is the last one to have relevance to living fine art, and its terminal position is what confers on it a poignant importance. For there is no such thing as a drawing manual within the avant-garde tradition. Nor is such a thing quite conceivable. All manuals after *The Elements* have been either academic or vulgar in nature. Ruskin's book is in fact a witness of how fragile a period style his realism was. It also reminds us of the problems of realism, how it was troubled by compositional design and had difficulty in continuing the landscape tradition. To another young lady artist Ruskin explained, 'In general, persons who have drawn landscapes have merely blotted — and not drawn anything. And to them the book must imply the entire overturn of all previous thought or practice.'[10] In fact, anyone with serious pictorial ambitions would find in *The Elements* all the problems of becoming a modern painter, and few of the solutions. For schoolgirls and copyists, however, it had its uses. It provided them with exercises.

In the new year of 1857 there was demand for Ruskin the public man. We find him addressing the Architectural Association, then giving a lecture at St Martin's School of Art; making speeches to the committee for a memorial to the painter Thomas Seddon; and discussing plans with the council of the Arundel Society. More important than these activities was the matter of Turner's gift of his work to the nation, for the executors and lawyers had now completed their deliberations over Turner's simple and generous wishes. The question of Ruskin's resignation from his executorship was once more raised. But only a mind as narrow as Lady Eastlake's could still entertain the view that such mechanical duties should have been more Ruskin's concern than the vast spiritual exercise of which *Modern Painters* is the record. Four volumes of that book, and numerous miscellaneous writings besides, were by now the evidence of that endeavour. For those few who read him attentively, it must have seemed that Ruskin's effort to understand Turner was not distinct from his wish to understand everything about the world; its light and knowledge, its destiny. At the same time, however elevated Ruskin's conceptions, he moved in the circles of politics and administration. His bitter remark in the preface to the third volume of *Modern Painters*, that Turner's countrymen had buried 'with threefold honour, his body in St Paul's, his pictures at Charing Cross, and his purposes in Chancery' — a comment quite evidently directed at those who had charge over Turner's *œuvre* — announced that he would turn his attention to public artistic policy.[11]

Disregarding the niceties of an approach to the National Gallery's trustees, within whose purview Turner's legacy now belonged, Ruskin wrote to *The Times*. His letter offered to sort and arrange the whole of Turner's drawings and sketches: all his work, that is, not done in oil on canvas. Neither the trustees nor Sir Charles Eastlake, the National Gallery's director, responded to this letter. Ruskin then repeated his offer by approaching the newly elected Prime Minister, Palmerston. This proved effective. However, more than three months were to elapse before Ruskin received an official invitation to arrange the drawings. During this time (and repeating the strategy of *Academy Notes*) Ruskin issued a rival catalogue to the brief official publication that accompanied the first exhibition selected from the Turner bequest. This is known as *Notes on the Turner Gallery at Marlborough House*. Like *Academy Notes*, it comments on certain paintings in an exhibition not chosen by Ruskin himself. These were all oils, for the drawings were still unsorted and, indeed, not yet unpacked. This catalogue is the shortest single work by Ruskin on Turner, yet contains a wonderful amount of his understanding of the artist. One notices, first, how much better this pamphlet is than *Academy Notes*. Its judgements are surer, less wayward, more considered: they are also loving. One is astonished by the set-piece with which it ends, on the *Teméraire* of 1842. And everywhere, as the trustees of the National Gallery must have seen, there is a complete assurance in Ruskin's personal knowledge of the artist and in his ability to discriminate between his works.[12]

This was in early January 1857. Ruskin was soon worrying that he had made the wrong moves in his negotiations with the National Gallery. He had perhaps sought too high a level, through overconfidence and through disdain for Eastlake. An appendix to the Marlborough House *Notes* had made challenging remarks to the effect that 'the national interest is only beginning to be awakened in works of art': this could have irritated the trustees.[13] When, therefore, they invited him to make a trial selection, the framing to be done at his own expense, he was pleased to agree. The small private exhibition he now prepared was cleverly devised. Ruskin took one hundred drawings to illustrate an imaginary tour (but to places he and Turner knew well) from England up the Rhine, through Switzerland to Venice and back. The catalogue he wrote to accompany the show is a curiosity. It is marked 'for private circulation only' and was directed towards the trustees, whom Ruskin now addresses as though they were children.[14] One point of his selection was to demonstrate how much of his *expertise* was topographical. The ability to identify Turner's sites would be crucial to the cataloguing of the collection. But his proposals for framing, preservation and presentation were also exemplary. He had his own private work-force, in the persons of George Allen and William Ward. In short, the trustees could hardly refuse him. There was no possibility of Ruskin being a happy colleague of Sir Charles Eastlake. But one can work in a museum without speaking to its director, and Ruskin struck some kind of relationship with the keeper of the collections, Ralph Wornum. This was not easily managed:

Wornum had attempted to persuade Ruskin that Lady Eastlake was not the author of the attack on himself and Turner in the *Quarterly Review*. But they got on well enough, for Wornum knew that he could not have done the work himself.

Ruskin had been right: the legacy required his special knowledge and commitment. Turner was not the first artist to have had an obscure and private career. But he was the first whose art had to be brought into the national heritage by a critic working in consort with a national museum. Ruskin was more aware of the implications of this situation than were his temporary colleagues. And thus, as the work he now began gave him a yet deeper feeling for Turner, it also alienated him from the routines of committees and administration, meetings and deliberations, that were part of the growing professionalism of museums and exhibitions.

Ruskin's involvement with the Turner bequest was much interrupted. *The Elements of Drawing* was concluded in the spring: some of it was written concurrently with the Turner catalogues. In *The Elements* there are traces of Ruskin's current work on Turner, just as in the Turner catalogue we will find addresses to students. The 1857 number of *Academy Notes* now had to be written. It is a little shorter than its usual length and is dominated by Ruskin's criticism of Millais's *Sir Isumbras at the Ford*. The critic objected to the new fluidity of Millais's application: 'The change in his manner, from the years of "Ophelia" and "Mariana" to 1857 is not merely Fall — it is Catastrophe; not merely a loss of power, but a reversal of principle.'[15] Ruskin added some kinder remarks. His beautiful iconographical explanation of the picture is a little akin in tone to what he had said of Turner in the Marlborough House *Notes*. Millais was of course unappeased by Ruskin's suggestive remarks about his themes. The brevity of the rest of *Academy Notes* almost made it appear that the pamphlet had been issued with the sole purpose of condemning his painting. Ruskin's relations with the Pre-Raphaelite movement as a whole were, as usual, difficult. A further cause of friction and misunderstanding was now provided by the increased number of independent exhibitions. This year an exhibition was held in Fitzroy Square. It was in effect the only Pre-Raphaelite group show. Ruskin might have made the exhibition more successful: but since the organizing force behind the show was Ford Madox Brown, he had to keep his distance. When he helped with the memorial exhibition for Thomas Seddon he was good at raising money for the widow. But he was more prominent personally than other friends of the artist had wished. At a *conversazione* held in May of 1857 he delivered an address on the dead artist, whom in fact he had not known very well. Ruskin's speech is known from a newspaper report. It was rather long, and only a part of it was about Seddon himself. The artists' death (from dysentery, in Cairo, while on a painting expedition) set Ruskin off on a disquisition that introduces the themes of his later political writing. The *Journal of the Society of Arts* reports it thus:

> The simple sacrifice of life had in it nothing unusual — it was, on the contrary, a melancholy thing to reflect how continually we all of us lived upon the lives of others, and that in two ways, viz., upon lives which we take, and upon lives which are given. It was a terrible expression to use — this taking of life, but it was a true one. We took life in all cases in which, either for higher wages, or by the compulsion of commercial pressure, men were occupied without sufficient protection or guardianship in dangerous employments, involving an average loss of life, for which life we paid thoughtlessly in the price of the commodity, which, so far, was the price of blood. Nay, more than this, it was a well-recognised fact that there was scarcely an art or science in the present day, in which there was not some concomitant circumstance of danger or disease, which science had not striven to abate proportionably with the endeavours to advance the skill of the workmen. And thus, though we had abolished slavery, we literally bargained daily for the lives of our fellowmen, although we should shrink with horror at the idea of purchasing their bodies; and if these evils, arising partly from pressure of population, but more from carelessness in masters and consumers, from desire of cheapness, or blind faith in commercial necessities — if these evils went on increasing at the rate it seemed but too probable they would, England would soon have to add another supporter to her shield. She had good right still to her lion, never more than now. But she needed, in justice, another, to show that if she could pour forth life blood nobly, she could also drink it cruelly; she should have not only the lion, but the vampire . . . .[16]

Perhaps John James's fear of his son's lectures came from a realization that Ruskin was always likely to say something inapposite. The Seddon address was a case in point. One might agree with these sentiments, or not: one would still doubt that this were the right occasion to express them. Ruskin had also agreed to give two lectures in July at the Art Treasures exhibition in Manchester. He was unconcerned that what he said might not relate to the art that was exhibited. He did not attend the opening of the exhibition. Instead he took lodgings in a farmhouse in Cowley, then a village three miles outside Oxford. There, 'in the middle of a field, with a garden of gooseberries and orange lilies; and a loose stone wall round it, all over stone-crop', he began to write the lectures which became *The Political Economy of Art*.[17] Charles Eliot Norton was in Oxford at the time, and later claimed that Ruskin discussed his writing with him. If so, this was the first occasion on which the young Bostonian had ventured to tell Ruskin what he ought to be thinking and saying. It is more likely that Ruskin had helpful conversations with Henry Acland, whom he saw almost daily, for they still had much work to do on the University Museum. Ruskin tried his hand at building Acland's study: 'I built a great bit yesterday, which the bricklayer my tutor in a most provoking manner pulled all down again. But this bit I have done today is to stand.'[18] Ruskin felt the more protective of the museum because it was just now that Liddell, who had recently become Dean of Christ Church, was restoring and erecting new buildings there. Pointedly, he had not asked for Ruskin's advice. The circumstances would be bitterly recalled in an unpublished draft of *Præterita*. Ruskin now parted company with the college in which he had been educated. In this year he was elected an honorary student of Christ Church in company with Gladstone and Acland. He valued the honour in an abstract fashion: he would not go there. When at last he spent an evening in hall in 1883 he remarked that he had not dined in his own college for thirty years.

This was the Pre-Raphaelite summer in Oxford. Ruskin was calling himself a 'PRB' as though he were a member of the defunct Brotherhood, and addressing Jane Simon, the wife of John Simon, as a 'PRS', a sister in art.[19] He had a little contact with many of the artists, William Morris among them, who were working in the Union. He may also have met Swinburne for the first time. But Ruskin was not close to them and left Oxford in early July to give his Manchester lectures.[20] He travelled afterwards to Wallington and thence to Edinburgh, where he had rendezvous with his parents for a tour of Scotland. In Manchester he left behind him an amount of consternation. In 1880, when he reissued *The Political Economy of Art*, Ruskin changed its title to *A Joy for Ever (and its Price in the Market)*. Keats's phrase and the sardonic addition were employed to reassert a radicalism that had been somewhat forgotten in the previous two decades. Much that Ruskin declared in Manchester became common currency not much later on. But to reread the 1857 lectures is still to be struck by their vigour and attack. To assert that one can talk of art and political economy in the same breath, to open an art lecture with comments on poverty, was to announce, all suddenly, a political position.

John James Ruskin, so jealous of his son's public reputation, was not dismayed by the Manchester lectures. Nor, when at length it came, was he put out by the generally negative reaction in the press. After publication, when *The Times* criticized Ruskin for speaking on matters that were not the province of an æsthete, his father was still cheerfully of the opinion that there was value in the address. *The Times* had associated Ruskin with Dr Thomas Guthrie, a famous Scottish preacher of the day, a philanthropist and pioneer of the ragged schools, whose *City: its Sins and Sorrows* had recently been published. John James wrote about the matter to Jane Simon:

> Mrs R. named to me your having heard that my Son's meddling with Political Economy might weaken his Influence in matters of Art. I feared this myself, but by his own confession his studies of Political Economy have not encroached much on his time — and on this weary subject a few new ideas will do no harm. The Times couples him with Dr Guthrie and says they are both in a state of helpless ignorance of the first principles of Political Philosophy. I might, perhaps, prefer the Simplicity of Dr Guthrie to the Philosophy of the Times; but, if my Son has so greatly committed himself in his last little book, I trust to the talk of Mr Simon, Mr Helps and Mr Carlyle bringing us an amended Second Edition . . .[21]

And to E. S. Dallas, who was a journalist on the newspaper, he repeated, 'As a City man I am half with *The Times* in believing my Son and Dr Guthrie innocent of Political Economy; but these Geniuses sometimes in their very simplicity hit upon the right thing, whilst your ponderous Economy discusser twaddles on in endless mazes lost.'[22] John James was not quite near the mark in believing that a combination of Simon, Helps and Carlyle would make Ruskin a sounder critic of society. Simon the administrator, Helps the experimental liberal reformer, were both people with whom Ruskin enjoyed an exchange of views. But he took little notice of what they said. It was towards Carlyle's message that his mind tended, towards a visionary conservatism that John James could not understand. For Ruskin as the Master of the Guild of St George, Dr Guthrie's philanthropy made 'all things smooth and smiling for the Devil's work'.[23]

This will plainly appear in *Munera Pulveris* of 1862, the best of Ruskin's middle-period political writings. The book is dedicated to Carlyle. In 1857, however, the relationship between the two men might have seemed rather distant. Carlyle had no interest in art: he even seemed to dislike it. Ruskin was too busy with art work to think of Carlyle. After the holiday in Scotland with his parents (and a brief visit to Oxford to see the Pre-Raphaelite frescoes) Ruskin had to settle down to the long task of the arrangement of the Turner drawings. In some basement rooms in the National Gallery, which Ruskin scornfully called its 'cellar', he began to unpack the tin boxes in which the treasures had been crammed away. Because he had known the house in Queen Anne Street Ruskin was not surprised at the state of the drawings. But the description of their condition which he gave in the fifth and final volume of *Modern Painters* is filled with a sort of retrospective horror at what he now found:

> . . . some in chalk, which the touch of the finger would sweep away; others in ink, rotted into holes; others (some splendid coloured drawings among them) long eaten away by damp and mildew, and falling into dust at the edges, in capes and bays of fragile decay; others worm-eaten, some mouse-eaten, many torn, halfway through; numbers doubled (quadrupled, I should say,) up into four, being Turner's favourite mode of packing for travelling; nearly all rudely flattened out from the bundles in which Turner had finally rolled them up and squeezed them into his drawers in Queen Anne Street. Dust of thirty years' accumulation, black, dense, and sooty, lay in the rents of the crushed and crumpled edges of these flattened bundles, looking like a jagged black frame, and producing altogether unexpected effects in brilliant portions of skies, whence an accidental or experimental finger-mark of the first bundle-unfolder had swept it away.[24]

The first task was to ensure the safety of the drawings. In his cramped conditions, without enough natural light, sending up clouds of chalk and dust, and without the aid of any professional restoration techniques, Ruskin began his protection. He had to work with his sleeves rolled up, washing his hands every few minutes, spreading the drawings out on whatever surfaces were available, measuring and numbering them. Every evening, as George Allen recalled, 'after our day's work at the Gallery Mr Ruskin and I used to take the measurements of drawings to Denmark Hill, where I cut with my own hands about 800 thick passe-partout mounts — they were taken to the Gallery and the drawings inserted there'.[25] Many of them could not have been mounted before they were pressed. Since there were 19,000 separate drawings to deal with the variety of cleaning and cataloguing problems was enormous. At first, Ruskin seemed to be optimistic. Stacy Marks, the genial painter of birds who was to be a friend for many years, found him quite confident when he introduced himself in the 'cellar'. Marks wrote:

> I found the eloquent exponent of Turner in rooms in the basement of the building, surrounded by piles of sketch-books and loose drawings by the master, which he was arranging, mounting and framing, — a congenial employment, a labour of love, to which he devoted months of time, with no recompense beyond the pleasure which the occupations afforded him. I can remember little of our conversation except that it was chiefly about Turner and his work. I had gone to the Gallery with an ill-defined feeling of awe of the great man I was about to see, but this was dissipated directly I had shaken hands with him. There was none of the posing of the genius; I found him perfectly simple, unaffected, kindly, and human.[26]

'Every day, and often far into the night,' Ruskin claimed, he worked on. By the end of December 1857 it seemed to him that there were 10,000 drawings which were 'far enough carried forward to give some question as to whether they should be exhibited or not'.[27] In effect, Ruskin was now re-learning Turner's entire career, and more intimately than he ever before had thought possible. He wrote to Ellen Heaton, a water-colourist and collector, of the 'excitement of discovering something precious or learning something new every half minute'.[28] This was almost painful. For as more and more was unfolded of Turner's art Ruskin had the gathering impression that what he had thought of him was only what a young man might think. The drawings recalled to him what he had known of the man. In truth Ruskin had revered him, until their quarrel: and in some measure had still revered him after he had decided that he could not forgive him. But he had never loved the man as he had loved the work, and he now looked sorrowfully on all that had been hidden in the artist's character. Perhaps he had only known Turner personally in his utter decline? Ruskin found that he could not talk of these troubles to his father. He did not even formulate his thoughts until the next summer. Then, far away in Bellinzona, he wrote to his father as follows:

> You are quite right in your feeling about the later drawings in this respect, that the power of sight is in a considerable degree diminished, and that a certain impatience, leading sometimes to magnificence, sometimes to mistake, indicates the approach of disease; but at the same time, all the experience of the whole life's practice of art is brought to bear occasionally on them, with results for wonderment and instructiveness quite unapproached in the earlier drawings. There is, however, one fault about them which I have only ascertained since my examination of the Turner sketches. There is evidence in those sketches of a gradual moral decline in the

> painter's mind from the beginning of life to its end — at first patient, tender, self-controlling, exquisitely perceptive, hopeful, and calm, he becomes gradually stern, wilful, more and more impetuous, then gradually more sensual, capricious — sometimes in mode of work even indolent and slovenly — the powers of art and knowledge on nature increasing all the while, but not now employed with the same calm or great purpose — his kindness of heart never deserting him, but encumbered with sensuality, suspicion, pride, vain regrets, hopelessness, languor, and all kinds of darkness and oppression of heart. What I call the 'sunset drawings' — such as our Coblentz, Constance, Red Rigi, etc., — marks the effort of the soul to recover itself, a peculiar calm and return of the repose or youthful spirit, preceding the approach of death . . .[29]

One small group of drawings might have epitomized, for Ruskin, Turner's moral decline. Somewhere in the boxes he found work which he was later to describe as 'grossly obscene'. Ruskin had remarked in the Marlborough House catalogue, 'I never know whether most to venerate or lament the strange impartiality of Turner's mind, and the vast cadence of subjects in which he was able to take interest.'[30] At this point, Ruskin was remarking how great mythological subjects might alternate with views of the Isle of Dogs. Such a Thames-side scene might not be fully worthy of its painter, but it was still within the realm of art. These obscene drawings were not. This was also Wornum's view. For the good of Turner's reputation, and in the interests of the high view of the national culture that the bequest was intended to serve, it seemed best that these drawings should not form part of the collection. Ruskin already believed that there was no point in preserving 'valueless' scribbles or scraps. Wornum was of the opinion that even to possess these drawings was illegal. The National Gallery authorities were in favour of burning them. Ruskin agreed, and watched as Wornum lit the fire. He hardly ever made explicit mention of this episode and it is not easy to estimate what effect it had on him. It was probably only a part of the experience of working with the Turner bequest. But it was around this time that he came to believe not merely that Turner's 'mind and sight partially gave way',[31] as the Marlborough House catalogue states, but that the painter went mad and 'died mad'. Such views were always privately expressed. Just as he never spoke of his quarrel with Turner, so he would not write publicly of his feeling that the artist's mind was diseased. Many years later, when Ruskin's own mind was in pitiful disarray, we occasionally find renewed warnings about a 'passionately sensual character' that would lead to 'a kind of delirium tremens. Turner had it fatally in his last years';[32] and Ruskin's work with Wornum, otherwise forgotten, is suddenly mentioned in his diary's passages of insane free association that were written in the days before his own delirium.[33]

* * * *

> The manual labour would not have hurt me [wrote Ruskin of his work on the Turner catalogue] but the excitement involved in seeing unfolded the whole career of Turner's mind during his life, joined with much sorrow at the state in which nearly all his most precious work had been left, and with great anxiety, and heavy sense of responsibility besides, were very trying: and I have never in my life felt so much exhausted as when I locked the last box, and gave the keys to Mr Wornum, in May, 1858.[34]

The experience would be reflected in the graver tone of the fifth volume of *Modern Painters*: this spring, tired though he was, Ruskin proselytized for the future of art. In the first week of May he wrote *Academy Notes*, and published the pamphlet immediately. He noted with satisfaction that Pre-Raphaelitism had triumphed 'as I stated five years ago it would'.[35] If some of the initial impetus had left the movement, a social gain had become important. Art now had a democratic function. But this was not to be confused with mere popularity. *Academy Notes* dismissed Frith's *Derby Day* — 'It is a kind of a cross between John Leech and Wilkie, with a touch of daguerrotype here and there, and some pretty seasoning with Dickens's sentiment' — and reserved its most hopeful praise for John Brett's *Stonebreaker*.[36] With *Academy Notes* done, Ruskin felt ready for travel. After the traditional family feast on 10 May he set out, alone, for Italy: it is probable that he had arranged to meet Brett there.

In Paris Ruskin visited (a family obligation) the Comte and Comtesse Maison: the Comtesse was the eldest of the Domecq daughters. A week later he was in Basle, where he was joined by Couttet. There and at Rheinfelden he identified the sites of some of the Turner drawings he had recently catalogued. In the letters to Denmark Hill which now replace his diary we often find the themes of the last volume of *Modern Painters*. From Brunnen, in William Tell country, he wrote:

> I am surprised to find what a complete centre of the history of Europe, in politics and religion, this lake of Lucerne is, as Venice is a

> centre of the history of art. First, the whole Swiss nation taking its name from the little town of Schwytz, just above this, because the Schwytzers were to the Austrian Emperors the first representatives of republican power, in their stand at Morgarten; then, the league of the three cantons to defend each other against all enemies, first signed and sealed in this little village of Brunnen; followed by the victories of Laupen, Sempach, Granson, Morat, and gradually gained power on the other side of the Alps in Italy until the Swiss literally gave away the Duchy of Milan, the competitors for it pleading their causes before the Swiss Council at Baden; and meantime, the great Reformation disputes in religion making these hills the place of their eternal struggle, till Zwingli was killed in the battle with these same three Catholic cantons, just beyond Zug on the road down from the Albis; whilst, on the other hand, the Republican party at Geneva was Protestant, and binding itself by oath in imitation of the oath of these three cantons, and calling itself Eidgenossen — 'bound by oath' — gets this word corrupted by the French into 'Huguenots', and so to stand generally for the Protestant party in France also.[37]

Some of Ruskin's admiration for the only modern republic he could approve of was worked up from, for instance, André Vieusseux's *History of Switzerland*, translated into English in 1840, but such prosaic sources were imaginatively paraphrased. Ruskin's views of the schisms of European history were romantic and partial, and he felt that art and legend are the heart of a nation's life. Thus, since history, art and nature are intertwined, the history of Switzerland was to be treated in the chapter of the fifth volume of *Modern Painters* entitled 'The Leaf Shadows'. Ruskin was in fact returning to an ambition he had felt since completing *The Stones of Venice*, a book on the culture of Swiss towns. It was never written, partly because it stirred in him disturbing social reflections. The peoples of Switzerland, he explained to his father, 'have sunk and remain sunk, merely by idleness and wantonness in the midst of all blessings and advantages . . . every man always acts for himself: they will never act together and do anything at common expense'.[38]

Ruskin's feelings for Switzerland were to reappear years later in his plans for the Guild of St George. Now, in 1858, they have a relevance to his collaboration with two English painters. This year he met at Fluelen J. W. Inchbold, a painter much commended in *Academy Notes*, and spent some time with John Brett. His praise of Brett's *Stonebreaker* in *Academy Notes* had concluded, 'If he can paint so lovely a distance from the Surrey downs and railway-traversed vales, what would he not make of the chestnut groves of the Val d'Aosta!'[39] Another letter to his father tells us more of his attitude to these two members of the Pre-Raphaelite school:

> I sent for [Brett] at Villeneuve, Val d'Aosta because I didn't like what he said in his letter about his present work, and thought he wanted some more lecturing like Inchbold: besides that, he could give me some useful hints. He is much tougher and stronger than Inchbold, and takes more hammering; but I think he looks more miserable every day, and have good hopes of making him completely wretched in a day or two . . .[40]

There is in existence a notebook of Brett's which dates from this summer. It indicates that he and Ruskin were at one point working side by side, attended by Couttet. It contains portrait sketches of the old guide. Some pages are by Ruskin. They are marked 'JMWT': Turner's initials, for Ruskin, as before, was attempting to force his personal knowledge of Turner into the practice of a younger artist.[41]

* * * *

Towards the end of this summer, in Switzerland and Turin, we find signs that the forty-year-old Ruskin was developing a different interest in the opposite sex. Ruskin's sexual maladjustment is not an uncommon one. He was a pædophile. He is typical of the condition in a number of ways, for pædophilia generally emerges in his age-group, often follows a period of marital breakdown, and in old age is accompanied by (or is a palliative to) a sense of loneliness and isolation. An attraction to young girls was in Ruskin's sexual nature to the end of his life. In a letter to Denmark Hill from Italy, he now wrote, 'One of the finest things I saw in Turin was a group of neglected children at play on a heap of sand — one girl of about ten, with her black hair over her eyes and half-naked, bare-limbed to above the knees, and beautifully limbed, lying on the sand like a snake . . .'.[42] The image remained with him for a quarter of a century and more. The dark Italian girl appears in his diary in later years: she was even mentioned in the disastrous last lectures in Oxford in 1884. In 1865, in *The Cestus of Aglaia*, Ruskin describes her in a manner which is as close as he ever approaches to the sensual:

> She was lying with her arms thrown back over her head, all languid and lax, on an earth-heap by the river side (the softness of dust being

> the only softness she had ever known), in the southern suburb of Turin, one golden afternoon in August, years ago. She had been at play, after her fashion, with other patient children, and had thrown herself down to rest, full in the sun, like a lizard. The sand was mixed with the draggled locks of her black hair, and some of it sprinkled over her face and body, in an 'ashes to ashes' kind of way; a few black rags about her loins, but her limbs nearly bare, and her little breasts, scarce dimpled yet, — white, — marble-like . . .[43]

The sight of this girl was like a landmark for Ruskin, as he afterwards looked over his life. But pædophilia became a part of his character only gradually. The turning-points Ruskin identified were often over-precise. So it was with the history of his religious convictions, which at just this period underwent a change that Ruskin was later to exaggerate. The account in *Fors Clavigera* of April 1877 tells us:

> I was still in the bonds of my old Evangelical faith; and, in 1858, it was with me, Protestantism or nothing: the crisis of the whole turn of my thoughts being one Sunday morning, at Turin, when, from before Veronese's Queen of Sheba, and under quite overwhelmed sense of his God-given power, I went away to a Waldensian chapel, where a little squeaking idiot was preaching to an audience of seventeen old women and three louts, that they were the only children of God in Turin; and that all the people in the world out of sight of Monte Viso, would be damned. I came out of the chapel, in sum of twenty years of thought, a conclusively *un*-converted man.[44]

We must not believe that Ruskin changed his mind about religion as abruptly as this. In *Fors*, and in another account of the experience in *Præterita*, Ruskin abbreviated the way that he came to reject his mother's Evangelical beliefs. 'That day,' he claimed, they 'were put away, to be debated of no more.'[45] That was not true: he spent the next thirty years debating them. Perhaps it was his hostility to conversion that made Ruskin write in this way, as if his experience had been directly opposed to that of so many other Christians. Conversion experiences are common in Christian, and especially Protestant, cultures: but an opposite experience of shedding a faith as though by revelation is not known. Nonetheless, something happened to Ruskin's Christianity in these months. It had to do with a solitary life in an unfamiliar, enlivening place. *Præterita* notes, 'I have registered the year 1858 as the next, after 1845, in which I had complete guidance of myself.'[46] In 1845, Ruskin had worked hard. This summer he was determined to be lazy. He was glad that his father was not with him to urge the completion of *Modern Painters*. He relaxed in the social pleasures of Turin. Looking back at the Alps, and for once rather pleased to have left them, Ruskin diverted himself in what was still the capital of the old Sardinian kingdom, a town of colonnades, orange trees, soldiers, bands, theatres. He rose late, lingered over coffee and *Galignani* (the European English-language newspaper, as full of gossip as of information), sauntered to the picture gallery for an hour until 'I think it time to be idle' and 'see what is going on on the shady side of the piazzas'.[47] He dined well, drank half-pints of champagne and spent every evening at the Opéra Comique. On Sundays, the actors' *riposo*, he read French novels.

A few weeks earlier, on the second Sunday after parting from his parents, Ruskin had made a sketch of some orchises. It was the first time in his life that he had drawn on the sabbath day. There in his diary were the pen outlines of the flowers.[48] Could this be wrong? How could art and nature be ruled by Sabbatarianism? And once he had left Inchbold and Brett behind Ruskin's didacticism vanished. His appetite for art became fixed on one painting. In Turin's indifferent municipal gallery he took to copying a small detail from Veronese's *Solomon and the Queen of Sheba*, the painting mentioned in the account of the 'unconversion'. This he studied with a strange mixture of indolence and fanaticism. Augustus Hare, who passed through Turin that summer, reported of Ruskin's work:

> He was sitting all day upon a scaffold in the gallery, copying bits of the great painting by Paul Veronese . . . One day in the gallery I asked him to give me some advice. He said 'watch me'. He then looked at the flounce in the dress of a maid of honour of the Queen of Sheba for five minutes, and then he painted one thread: he looked for another five minutes, and then he painted another thread. At the rate at which he was working he might hope to paint the whole dress in ten years . . .[49]

It seems that this account was hardly exaggerated. The exercise occupied Ruskin for more than a month, and all that came of it were a few tiny scraps of overworked detail.

Ruskin's insistence that he was disillusioned with Evangelicalism in a Waldensian chapel has significance. It was his practice to read over the English service with his valet if in a foreign town without Protestant churches. In Turin, however, there were chapels of the Waldensian faith. They were newly and cheaply built: religious liberty had been granted to the sect in Turin only in 1848. The Waldensians, or

Vaudois, held a special place in the Protestant mythology of the Ruskin family, as in English Protestantism as a whole. Milton's sonnet 'On the late massacre in Piedmont', with its prayer 'Avenge, O Lord, thy slaughtered saints . . .', was inspired by the Waldensians' earlier persecution. Confined to the Swiss, Piedmontese and northern Italian valleys, they had there, some believed, preserved an uncorrupted form of primitive Christianity. Appeals to the Vaudois character may be found in the most entrenched of Ruskin's writings, in the *Pre-Raphaelitism* pamphlet and in *Notes on the Construction of Sheepfolds*. Now, however, he was exasperated by the narrowness of the faith. How could one love Veronese and believe this preacher? A long letter to his father now marks this turning point in Ruskin's views. Having put the view that 'A good, stout, self-commanding, magnificent Animality is the make for poets and artists, it seems to me', Ruskin further explained,

> One day when I was working from the beautiful maid of honour in Veronese's picture, I was struck by the gorgeousness of life which the world seems to be constituted to develop, when it is made the best of. The band was playing some passages of brilliant music at the time, and this music blended so thoroughly with Veronese's splendour; the beautiful notes seeming to form one whole with the lovely forms and colours, and powerful human creatures. Can it be possible that all this power and beauty is adverse to the honour of the Maker of it? Has God made faces beautiful and limbs strong, and created these strange, fiery, fantastic energies, and created the splendour of substance and the love of it; created gold, and pearls, and crystal, and the sun that makes them gorgeous; and filled human fancy with all splendid thoughts; and given to the human touch its power of placing and brightening and perfecting, only that all these things may lead His creatures away from Him? And is this mighty Paul Veronese, in whose soul there is a strength as of the snowy mountains, and within whose brain all the pomp and majesty of humanity floats in a marshalled glory, capacious and serene like clouds at sunset — this man whose finger is as fire, and whose eye is like the morning — is he a servant of the devil; and is the poor little wretch in a tidy black tie, to whom I have been listening this Sunday morning expounding Nothing with a twang — is he a servant of God?[50]

John James could well have anticipated these sentiments, but Ruskin's mother was in high alarm. She sent him long instructions and five pounds to donate to the Vaudois church. This Ruskin passed on, dutifully, reflecting that he had given as much recently to a ballerina at the Opéra Comique. Deference to his mother sent him on an expedition to the Vaudois villages in the hills above Turin. 'I have seldom slept in a dirtier inn, seldom see peasants' cottages so ill built, and never yet in my life saw anywhere paths so full of nettles,' he complained.[51] He sought out an unidentified 'theological Professor' to talk with. But this person could convince him of nothing. Ruskin was conscious of the gap that was opening between him and his parents and found that he did not wish to make an effort to repair it. In one respect this was damaging to his work. He was only laxly engaged with the end of *Modern Painters*, the book that John James so wanted to be a great memorial to a father's belief in his son. There are, to be sure, certain passages in the fifth volume that derive from his summer in Turin. The conjunction of Wouverman and Fra Angelico in one chapter is due to the fact that both were represented in the Turin gallery. But *Modern Painters* would have been better served if Ruskin had spent more time in Venice, as his preface to the last volume admits. On his way back to England he had some intention of working in the Louvre. But he paused there only briefly. He arrived home in London with little done, and a mind greatly changed.

CHAPTER FOURTEEN

1857–1858

Ruskin was increasingly in demand as a lecturer. The success of *The Political Economy of Art* had persuaded him that the lecture was a natural form for his writing. Unofficial addresses at the Working Men's College (which were improvised) gave him a sense of the closeness of the lecturer's audience. From 1857 until his mental collapse in 1878 there was not a year when he did not speak publicly three or four times. Such addresses were usually published soon afterwards. The assumptions of the Working Men's College drawing class were repeated at the opening of the new Cambridge School of Art in 1858. Here again is the realist, democratic argument that 'We must set ourselves to teaching the operative, however employed — be he farmer's labourer, or manufacturer's; be he mechanic, artificer, sailor, or ploughman — teaching, I say, one and the same thing to all; namely, Sight.'[1] Other lectures given in 1858 were published the next year with the title *The Two Paths*. The first of them was organized by Ruskin for his own purposes. He had instituted a competition among the students of the Architectural Museum for the best piece of 'historical sculpture'. At the prize-giving this year the chairman was C. R. Cockerell. He was an opponent, since he was a classicist and Professor of Architecture at the Royal Academy. Ruskin was graceful to Cockerell in his introductory remarks but the rest of his address on 'The deteriorative power of conventional art over nations' was a call to arms. The 'two paths' of the book's title were the clear alternatives before art students, 'whether you will turn to the right or the left in this matter, whether you will be naturalists or formalists; whether you will pass your days in representing God's truth, or in repeating men's errors'.[2] Less tendentious, wider-ranging and more deliberately entertaining was another lecture collected in *The Two Paths*, that on 'The work of iron, in nature, art and policy', given in Tunbridge Wells in February of 1858, probably at the request of his cousin George Richardson.

At the beginning of the next year Ruskin went north to lecture at Manchester and Bradford. His appearances were organized by Gambart, whom he met for breakfast at the home of a local industrialist, Sir Elkanah Armitage. There they discussed the picture market, with enthusiastic schemes 'for buying all Venice from the Austrians —

pictures, palaces, and everything', and 'asked Sir Elkanah to set the project on foot, in Manchester'.[3] 'The Unity of Art', the lecture Ruskin now gave, was milder than his previous address in Manchester at the time of the International Exhibition. It seems to have been designed to point to controversial issues without itself arousing controversy. The whole expedition was friendly. Ruskin called on the novelist Elizabeth Gaskell, his admirer since the publication of *Modern Painters* III, when they had been introduced by Furnivall, and then set off towards Bradford. He told his father that he was studying Turnerian sites at Bolton Bridge and Knaresborough. But he seems to have been excited by a landscape that is Mrs Gaskell's rather than Turner's:

> The drive from Rochdale to Burnley is one of the grandest and most interesting things I ever did in my life . . . the cottages so old and various in form and position on the hills — the rocks so wild and dark — and the furnaces so wild and multitudinous, and foaming forth their black smoke like thunderclouds, mixed with the hill mist . . .[4]

Ruskin's dislike of the industrial north was not at the pitch it would reach a decade later. He could even propose a sensible co-operation between the demands of manufacture and the demands of art. His lecture at Bradford, 'Modern Manufacture and Design', was designed to be useful rather than hortatory. It does, however, contain the first of Ruskin's many direct questions to industrialists:

> If you will tell me what you ultimately intend Bradford to be, perhaps I can tell you what Bradford can ultimately produce. But you must have your minds clearly made up, and be distinct in telling me what you do want. At present I don't know what you are aiming at, and possibly on consideration you may feel some doubt whether you know yourselves. As matters stand, all over England, as soon as one mill is at work, occupying two hundred hands, we try, by means of it, to set another mill at work, occupying four hundred. That is all simple and comprehensible enough — but what is it to come to? How many mills do we want? or do we indeed want no end of mills? Let us entirely understand each other on this point before we go any farther. Last week, I drove from Rochdale to Bolton Abbey; quietly, in order to see the country, and certainly it was well worth while. I never went over a more interesting twenty miles than those between Rochdale and Burnley. Naturally, the valley has been one of the most beautiful in the Lancashire hills; one

> of the far-away solitudes, full of old shepherd ways of life. At this time there are not, — I speak deliberately, and I believe quite literally, — there are not, I think, more than a thousand yards of road to be traversed anywhere, without passing furnace or mill.[5]

Ruskin's lecture ended with a direct comparison between Bradford and (in a magnificent description, a *tour de force* for lecture purposes) mediæval Pisa. He admitted, 'I do not bring this contrast before you as a ground of hopelessness in our task; neither do I look for any possible renovation of the Republic of Pisa, at Bradford, in the nineteenth century.'[6] And yet, although he did not realize it, all his instincts would soon lead him to propose just such a renovation. In five years' time he would address the burghers of Bradford with contempt: and in a decade he would come to the conclusion that the only way to save England was indeed to recreate there the conditions of the Gothic cities of the past.

* * * *

Ruskin's description of the 'wretch' who had talked of the election of the Waldensian faithful was followed, that summer of 1858, by further attacks on Protestant services he attended on the Continent. To John James he wrote from Paris of a 'disgraceful' English evensong, the sermon 'utterly abominable and sickening in its badness'.[7] Such outbursts were not unusual. The Ruskins's church-going habits meant that they listened to a great number of sermons, a form of literature they rarely read, and both father and son were given to a violent connoisseurship of the preaching class.[8] As we might expect from these intelligent, curious and prejudiced men, they had some unusual preferences. For about five years, from 1857, their favourite preacher was an uncouth Evangelical Baptist for whom neither felt much doctrinal sympathy. This was Charles Haddon Spurgeon. When the Ruskins first went to listen to him and sought his acquaintance he was scarcely twenty-four years old, yet had become the most popular preacher in London. At the age of sixteen he had been converted by a Primitive Methodist. 'Baptism loosed my tongue,' he said, 'and from that day it has never been quiet.'[9] It was an uneducated tongue. Spurgeon was still an Essex country boy. His early practice in his vocation had been in extempore gatherings in Hackney Fields. He had progressed to the Exeter Hall and the Surrey Gardens Music Hall, working-class venues that could accommodate his audience of thousands. His oratory was interspersed with humorous anecdote and doggerel verse. It made the fastidious wince. Spurgeon was a preacher to whom one sent the servants. 'He is likely to do really good service among the class to which he belongs,' one contemporary remarked, 'though he would be a scandal and a nuisance at St George's, Hanover Square, or in Westminster Abbey.'[10] Many intellectuals could not abide him. Matthew Arnold, for instance, was repelled. Yet Spurgeon's spirit shone beyond his vulgarity, as Lord Houghton — a fair reporter of nineteenth-century devotion — rightly saw: 'When he mounted the pulpit you might have thought of him as a hairdresser's assistant: when he left it, he was an inspired apostle.'[11]

Like Houghton, Ruskin defended Spurgeon to the sophisticated. 'His doctrine is simply Bunyan's, Baxter's, Calvin's, and John Knox's,' he wrote to the Brownings, '— in many respects not pleasant to *me*, but I dare not say that the offence is the doctrine's and not mine. It is the doctrine of Romish saints and of the Church of England. Why should we find fault with it especially in Spurgeon and not in St Francis or Jeremy Taylor?'[12] Between Ruskin and Spurgeon there developed an unlikely, warm friendship. They had next to nothing in common apart from their knowledge of the Bible and a love of its exegesis. Ruskin simply ignored all aspects of Spurgeon's views that would annoy him. The Baptist's fiery hatred of Carlyle he overlooked. He was not drawn by Spurgeon's insistence that all churches should be Greek rather than Gothic. Instead, nightly, at Spurgeon's tiny south London house, tasting wines from John James's own cellar, Spurgeon with a cigar, they would spar over their intimacy with Scripture and their utterly different natures, Ruskin provocative, Spurgeon laughing at him, each capping the other. Spurgeon recalled with amusement how 'Mr Ruskin came to see me one day, many years ago, and amongst other things he said that the Apostle Paul was a liar, and that I was a fool!'[13] But Ruskin had a real attachment to Spurgeon. The preacher's wife records:

> Towards the end of 1858 Spurgeon had a serious illness, and Ruskin called to see him during his convalescence. How well I remember the intense love and devotion displayed by Mr Ruskin, as he threw himself on his knees by the dear patient's side, and embraced him with tender affection and tears. 'My brother, my dear brother,' he said, 'how grieved I am to see you thus!' His sorrow and sympathy were most touching and comforting. He had brought with him two charming engravings . . . and some bottles of wine of a rare vintage . . . My husband was greatly moved by the love and consideration so graciously expressed, and he very often referred to it afterwards in grateful appreciation; especially when, in later years, there came a change of feeling on Mr Ruskin's part, and he strongly repudiated

some of the theological opinions to which Mr Spurgeon closely clung to the end of his life.[14]

As one or two of their contemporaries recognized, there is something of Spurgeon's fundamentalism in Ruskin's *Unto This Last*. That influence points to another difference, temperamental as well as intellectual, between Ruskin and the Working Men's College. While his politics alarmed all the Christian Socialists who gathered there, the college's principal, F. D. Maurice, on the rare occasions when he met his drawing master, was taken aback by the restless vehemence with which Ruskin expressed views on religion. There was that about Maurice which goaded Ruskin. He preferred to spend time with Spurgeon, whom Maurice greatly distrusted. Ruskin's ties with the Working Men's College were slackening. He saw Furnivall still but was bored by others of the lecturers. The students who most interested him he had taken away from the college and made his assistants. Butterworth was still receiving money from Ruskin. George Allen was taking lessons in line engraving from John Le Keux and in mezzotint from Thomas Lupton, in preparation for the illustration of the fifth volume of *Modern Painters*. This was a more advanced and significant teaching than was available at the college, for the skilled Lupton had worked for Turner himself in years gone by. Ruskin was pleased by this direct artisanal connection between Turner and his own book: it had a deeper meaning in it than the elementary drawing classes he used to give in Red Lion Square. Some of those classes were now entrusted to Allen, but most of Ruskin's instructional drawing was carried out for him by William Ward, whom Ruskin now referred to as both the college's and his own 'under drawing-master'.[15]

When Ruskin was first asked by an Irish gentlewoman, a Mrs La Touche, to give advice on her daughters' art education he sent William Ward to see her, being too busy to call himself. Maria La Touche he probably met through Lady Waterford, for she too was an artistically minded woman not quite at home among the Irish aristocracy. She was the daughter of Catherine, Countess of Desart. This countess had been twice married, first to the Earl of Desart. Their son was young Otway, Earl of Desart, whom Ruskin had known at Christ Church. Catherine was widowed in 1820, when in her early thirties. Four years later she married again. Her new husband was Rose Lambert Price. He came of a baronetcy family in Cornwall which owned large estates in Jamaica. Rose Lambert Price was much younger than the still young dowager countess: he was still in his early twenties on their wedding day. Maria Price, later Maria La Touche, was their daughter and only child, and thus the half-sister of Ruskin's Christ Church friend. She was not to remember her father, for he died two years after his marriage. Catherine, once more widowed, returned with her child to the Desart estates in County Kilkenny. There Maria spent her childhood.

With no memory of her Cornish father, with a background that was a trifle *déclassé*, Maria Price grew up to emphasize her Irishness. Intermittently educated near Brighton, in later life a traveller and the owner of a house in London, she yet had no wish to leave her native land. She was wed into another section of the Irish ascendancy. In 1843 she married John La Touche. The La Touche family had been in Ireland since the revocation of the Edict of Nantes. Huguenot supporters of William of Orange, one had fought for him at the Battle of the Boyne. They had established a silk-weaving factory in the north and a bank in Dublin that later became the Royal Bank of Ireland. In the eighteenth century they purchased a country house at Harristown, County Kildare. Their fortunes became intermingled with the Anglo-Irish aristocracy. John La Touche's mother, for instance, was a daughter of the Earl of Clancarty. John La Touche was sent to England to be educated at Christ Church. He matriculated in 1833 and would have left Oxford just before the young Ruskin arrived there. He succeeded his father as head of the family in 1844, a year after his marriage to Maria Price. They then settled at Harristown, where their three children were born.

Maria La Touche, not in sympathy with the Anglo-Irish society she knew as the mistress of Harristown and the wife of the Sheriff of County Leitrim (as John La Touche became), disliked the hunting and horse racing, the gambling, drinking and crudity of manners of her acred neighbours. She was self-consciously devoted to the life of the soul. With a few other Irish ladies like Louisa, Marchioness of Waterford, Lady Drogheda and Lady Cloncurry, both married to County Kildare landowners, she formed a little society they called the Aletheme: they rechristened themselves with Greek names and discussed art. Lady Waterford was the most cultured of this group but Maria La Touche had more energy, more of a will to be artistic. She was more than merely amateur. She published two novels, *The Clintons* and *The Double Marriage*, both of them set in Ireland, both treating of romance across the divide that separated Catholic from Protestant. She wrote verse and was noted for the vivacity of her letters. She was quick to make friends, eager to travel, a little gushing. She thought a little wildness not a bad thing. She liked to visit London. John La

Touche had banking and government business there and so they kept a house in Mayfair, at first in Great Cumberland Street and later in Norfolk Street.[16]

Maria La Touche was in London in the new year of 1858, with her daughters Emily and Rose, when she first approached Ruskin. The momentous first meeting with Rose is described in the final pages of *Præterita*, an account which is practically the last thing Ruskin ever wrote: He called at Great Cumberland Street,

> . . . and found the mother — the sort of person I expected, but a good deal more than I expected, and in sorts of ways. Extremely pretty, still, herself, nor at all too old to learn many things; but mainly anxious for her children. Emily, the eldest daughter, wasn't in; but Rosie was, should she be sent for to the nursery? Yes, I said, if it wouldn't tease the child, she might be sent for. So presently the drawing room door opened, and Rosie came in, quietly taking stock of me with her blue eyes as she walked across the room; gave me her hand, as a good dog gives its paw, and then stood a little back. Nine years old, on 3rd January, 1858, thus now rising towards ten; neither tall nor short for her age; a little stiff in her way of standing. The eyes rather deep blue at that time, and fuller and softer than afterwards. Lips perfectly lovely in profile; — a little too wide, and hard in edge, seen in front; the rest of the features what a fair, well-bred Irish girl's usually are; the hair, perhaps, more graceful in short curl round the forehead, and softer than one sees often, in the close-bound tresses above the neck.[17]

Ruskin, now in his fortieth year, was taken with the La Touches. He liked the mother and felt that there was something exceptional about Rose. He had never taught a little girl before except by correspondence. There was no reason why he should do so now, except that he wanted to. He corresponded with Mrs La Touche while in Switzerland during the summer and on his return invited her, with Rose, to visit Denmark Hill. They were shown all the treasures: the Turners, the minerals, John Brett's painting of the Val d'Aosta, which Ruskin had just bought. Old Mrs Ruskin provided apples, peaches, a copy of *The King of the Golden River* for Rose. They visited the stables, where Ruskin chaffed Rose about Irish pigs. Soon they were on pet-name terms. Ruskin charmed the child, and she charmed him. Mrs La Touche evidently felt that an extraordinary privilege had been granted her: her letter of thanks was overwritten:

> My Dear Mr Ruskin,
> I have too long delayed thanking you, in my name and in Rose's, for

23. Rose La Touche, by John Ruskin, c.1860.

> the pleasant hour we spent last Thursday — You, who live with and for Art, will not easily guess how much enjoyment you afforded to me, who am wholly unaccustomed to such an atmosphere out of dreamland. The 'Val d'Aosta' and the Rossettis and some of the Turners have been before me ever since — and Rose was very eloquent about them on the way home, she will not forget them, and will refer to them in memory hereafter, with better understanding of their meaning. Altogether we owe 'the immortal memory of one happy day' to Mrs Ruskin's kindness and yours: and more beautiful than all past sunsets was that which we saw on our way home — it was the interpretation, or rather it seemed to me the Apotheosis, of one or two of the Turners you had shown me — one of those skies no-one else ever attempted to paint — and under it, this evil London glorified into a shadowy semblance of the New Jerusalem, a city of sapphire and gold — It is a real consolation to me here, that my windows look towards the sunset: at home there would be a purple tracery of winter trees between me and the sky, and only a glow on the river's face to reveal what *it* saw. I have been wishing ever since, that you could see and tell the world about the Atlantic — I have never seen the Mediterranean — nor the subdued sea that sleeps around the 'Stones of Venice' except as you have shown them . . .[18]

There is much more of this letter, in the same manner. It closed with an invitation. Mrs La Touche wanted Ruskin and his mother to come to her new house in Norfolk Street, off Park Lane. When Ruskin went there he met other members of the family. Emily was grave and sensible, not very like the clever, inventive Rose. 'One never laughed at what she said,' *Præterita* records, 'but the room was brighter for it.'[19] But if the daughters were dissimilar it was their father who seemed almost out of place in the family. He was not the swaggering Irish sportsman that one would expect. He had been, but in a life that he had put behind him. Nor was he interested in the world of affairs and politics that, Ruskin presumed, had brought him to London. For, by fateful coincidence, he had been converted and baptized by Spurgeon. Ruskin knew of, but had not witnessed, Spurgeon's mass baptisms. Had he done so, he would no doubt have found them grotesque. He could not but find something peculiar, unnatural even, in John La Touche, who now professed a strict Calvinism far removed from the commonplace Church of Ireland Anglicanism of his wife. It was a Calvinism not only out of place in Mayfair but also extremist within its Irish context. One might compare (Ruskin was soon obliged to) the Evangelicalism of another branch of the La Touche family planted at Delgany, fifteen miles from Harristown, visited a few years before by the historian J. A. Froude. Of these La Touches, Froude recorded:

> There was a quiet good sense, an intellectual breadth of feeling in this household, which to me, who had been bred up to despise Evangelicals as unreal and affected, was a startling surprise. I had looked down on dissenters especially, as being vulgar among their other enormities; here were persons whose creed differed little from that of the Calvinistic Methodists, yet they were easy, natural, and dignified.[20]

But this could not be said of John La Touche. His religion had not this naturalness. It seems that it could be satisfied only by the severities of the beleaguered Presbyterian church in Southern Ireland and its counterparts among Ulster Orangemen. The man himself was extraordinary. As is common in such converted sectarians, John La Touche believed himself to be — from the moment of his conversion, an experience to which he constantly returned — saved, redeemed, touched by God. He was at once dourly reserved and highly emotional. This was not a man with whom Ruskin could make light conversation about Christ Church. Ruskin's own association with Spurgeon was, for La Touche, no more than frivolous. His guest's standing as an art critic meant nothing to him, for he had no culture. Ruskin's own loss of conviction in the Evangelical faith further separated them. Neither now, nor at any later time, could the two men find anything in common.

Rose and Emily La Touche came out to Denmark Hill on further occasions, sometimes with their mother, never with their father, sometimes with a nurse or maid. Some attempt was made to start the girls drawing. Leaves and flowers were brought in from the garden. Ruskin was surprised at how much Maria La Touche knew of botany. Soon it was decided to transfer the classes to Norfolk Street, where there was a proper schoolroom. Ruskin went there more and more often. Maria La Touche was delighted: she could show him off to her friends. But Ruskin preferred to arrive an hour or two before the children's bedtime and then to take his leave, pleading that he had to work on his book. It was a friendship with the children. And soon enough there came an understanding that there was an especial love between Rose and Ruskin that was not shared by Emily. He was as kind to Emily as anyone, but the sisters were not equal in his affection. In this peculiar way Ruskin became established in the La Touche household, and Rose became established in his life. It was irreversible, not to be ended until Rose died and Ruskin died: 'Rose, in heart, was with me always, and all I did was for her sake.'[21]

This was true, but for the five years after 1858 much of Ruskin's work was desultory. It was almost as though he were waiting for something to happen to him, something that would give a new direction to his life. By 1862 or 1863 he would have to identify his feelings for Rose as love. That did not occur to him now. And in these years he was lionized, even pursued, by a number of women. Ruskin was eligible. Both he and his father had the occasional idea that he might marry again. The pain of his marriage was behind him: so was the scandal. He was handsome, rich, distinguished. At forty, he was in the prime of life. All the same, his close friendships with the opposite sex were all with comfortably, happily married women. They were with people like Lady Trevelyan, with Mrs Simon, now with Mrs La Touche and soon with Mrs Cowper. These are women to whom he writes long, intimate, affectionate letters. He never writes as much to the husbands, sending a greeting only, although he is friendly with them. Within such settled relationships Ruskin could adopt a romantic attitude in which flirtation was not absent. With Jane Simon he had some secrets; to her he dropped heavy hints about women, especially Mrs La Touche, 'a lady who will perhaps be a friend in the course of time, and who is in the stage of friendship which would have been offended for ever unless it had received two notes . . .',[22] and of whom, a little later, he wrote, again to Mrs Simon, 'Yes, I think you are really very jealous. I wonder whether the "other" fault would be brought out if I were to show you what nice long letters I get now — every week or so — without being much troubled to answer them — from the other lady friend who I was fishing for . . .'[23]

Such ponderous flirting, which Ruskin too much enjoyed, had to be set aside on two occasions when women declared themselves in love with him. The first was an American, a Miss Blackwell, who knew the Simons and was a painter. We learn of her through letters to John James Ruskin, to whom Ruskin later revealed this admirer.

> The whole affair was so ludicrous and pitiable that I did not want you to be troubled with it — and still more — did not want to be troubled with it myself more than was needful. It appears this young person came from America expressly to see if I should suit her for a husband — and had been trying to get more intimate with me by all sorts of low cunning, until at last in a fit of passion she betrayed herself to Mrs Simon — who had suspected her long: — then the question was how to cut her most decisively — with least offence . . .[24]

Of Miss Blackwell we hear no more. Anna Blunden was for longer Ruskin's suitor. An artist, she began by sending him poetry, which he advised her not to publish. His first letters to her were written under the impression that he was addressing a man: not for some time did Anna reveal her sex, and not before she had assured Ruskin of her high regard for his conduct at the time of his marriage. Her importunate tactlessness Ruskin suffered for years; his patience broke down when she declared her love, and the letter he wrote then is revealing:

> My dear Anna,
> Upon my word I believe you are the profoundest and entirest little goose that ever wore petticoats. You write to me four pink pages full of nonsense about daisies and violets and 'being nothing but a poor flower' and then you fly into a passion at the first bit of advice I give you — declare that you do not want any — but that *I* do — and set yourself up for my adviser — controller — and judge. You fancy yourself in love with me — and send me the least excusable insult I ever received from a human being — it was lucky for you I only glanced at the end and a bit or two of your long angry letter and then threw it into the fire — else if I had come upon the piece which you refer to today — about my being false — I might have burnt this one as well, without even opening it. You little idiot! fancying you understand my books — and then accusing me of lying at the first word that puzzles you about yourself — fancying you love me, and writing me letters full of the most ridiculous egotisms and conceits — and disobeying the very first order I give you — namely to keep yourself quiet for a few days — and talking about suffering because you have set your fancy on helping a man whom you can't help but by being rational. Suffering! — indeed — suppose you had loved somebody whom you had seen —, not for an hour and a half, — but for six or seven years — who *could* have loved you — and who was married at the end of those years to someone who didn't love them, and was not worthy of them. Fancy *that*, — and then venture to talk of suffering again. You modern girls are not worth your bread and salt — one might bray a dozen of you in a mortar and not make a stout right-hearted woman out of the whole set. I suppose you have been reading some of the stuff of those American wretches — about rights of women. One of them came over from America the other day determined to marry me whether I would or no — and amused herself by writing letter after letter to me to slander my best friends. By the way, in the end of that long letter of yours — there was something about 'silencing the *only* tongue that pleaded for me' — or some such phrase (I wish I could silence it — by the bye, if you

write any more letters, let them be on white paper — or depend upon it the servants will open them — by mistake!) but are you really goose enough to think I have no friends? what do you think of Mrs Browning by way of a beginning — whom I have not written to for nine months — though she loves me truly — while you force me to waste my time writing to you. There again — you are so simply ridiculous in every point that I can't find words for you.

Write to a London Banker in large business and see if you can get *him* to answer love letters — and do you suppose that because my business concerns human souls, and not bags of money — that I am the more willing to interrupt it?

However, here is one more serious word for you — and try to make some proper use of it. There was some nonsense in your long letter about Britomart and Una. Both of them were in love with the man they were to marry, and who loved them. *Every* young women who loves a man who has not asked for her love, or at least if she may not naturally look forward to his marrying her — has lost proper control over her feelings: — praying to God to know whether you are to do it — is the same thing as praying to Him to know whether you are to jump down a precipice. God will not answer such a prayer — and the Devil will.[25]

There was as much pain as anger in this letter. The extremity of Ruskin's exasperation laid bare a longing of his adolescence. The reference to Adèle shows us something that normally was hidden in Ruskin, the memory of an emotion keener than any he had felt for his wife. Anna had uncovered what Ruskin wished to forget: the view that women fall in love at the devil's command refers to the buried subject of the end of his marriage. In conventional social circles, one has the impression in these years of Ruskin as a man with a winning urbanity, even when taken aback. That is the picture given by the account in *Præterita* of a new friendship with a woman he had first seen many years before. It was the beautiful Georgiana Tollemache, whom he admired from afar as a youth in Rome. They were at a party, sitting on a sofa, when he burst out with what must have been a pleasing declaration:

Having ascertained in one moment that she was too pretty to be looked at, and yet keep one's wits about one, I followed, in what talk she led me to, with my eyes on the ground. The conversation led to Rome and, somehow, to the Christmas of 1840. I looked up with a start; and saw that the face was oval, — fair, — the hair, light-brown. After a pause, I was rude enough to repeat her words,

'Christmas in 1840! — were you in Rome *then*?' 'Yes,' she said, a little surprised, and now meeting my eyes with hers, enquiringly. Another tenth of a minute passed before I spoke again. 'Why, I lost all that winter in Rome hunting you!'[26]

Georgiana Tollemache was now Mrs William Cowper. She and her husband were to play an important part in Ruskin's future life. Their names were to change twice in the coming years. They became the Cowper-Temples in 1869 and Lord and Lady Mount-Temple in 1880. That was because of William Cowper's noble birth and, it was said at the time, because of its irregularity. The gossip was so generally accepted that we can use the account of a friend of the family, Logan Pearsall Smith. 'Cowper Temple', he explains,

. . . was in law the son of Earl Cowper, but said to be the son of Lord Palmerston, who had long been Lady Cowper's friend, and who married her when Lord Cowper died. Their son had inherited Lord Palmerston's estates and great house at Broadlands; and the problem of this double paternity, if I may put it so . . . had been successfully regulated by the young William Cowper's adding Lord Palmerston's family name of Temple to that of Cowper in a double appelation. After acting as secretary to his unavowed father, he served in several posts in the governments of the time and was raised to the peerage as Lord Mount-Temple . . .[27]

Those 'several posts', no doubt easily available in the many Whig governments of the mid-century, were as Junior Lord of the Treasury, Junior Lord of the Admiralty, Under-Secretary for the Home Department, President of the Board of Health, First Commissioner of Works, and the like: not the appointments that would be given, one after the other, to an exceptionally ambitious or talented man. People remembered his wife more than him. Georgiana was now in her late thirties. She was vague, sweet-natured, hospitable; a trifle theatrical in her manner, yet not a seeker for attention; she was comforting, rather, a helpful woman who found herself in sympathizing with other people's problems. Later, Ruskin was to find her too bland, a person without an edge. This was when he took many troubles to her about his marriage and about Rose, the girl he wished to marry. Now, in the late 1850s, he was simply pleased to know her and quite interested to know her husband, and enjoyed the first of many visits to the family home at Broadlands.

CHAPTER FIFTEEN

1858–1859

A proud entry in John James Ruskin's 1858 diary reads: 'March 10th Wednesday John began 5th Volume Modern Painters.'[1] Neither father nor son had much idea what the volume would contain, although they had realized that it ought to end the book. As soon became apparent, at least to its author, to approach a conclusion was to magnify the difficulties in making a new start with each volume while also relating new matter to old. To finish *Modern Painters*, now, was not merely to terminate a body of work, nor to finalize a scheme of art. The book represented twenty years of growth, revelation, reconsideration, and to conclude it was to conclude a part of Ruskin's life. It was that portion of his life that he owed to his father. John James was now seventy-five. Ruskin knew as his father knew that this fifth and last instalment would probably be the last thing he wrote for him. These matters were not spoken of.

It is possible to find many an intellectual influence in *Modern Painters* V, and more than one stylistic influence. Despite its grave tone and elevated subject-matter it is also one of Ruskin's books in which we find traces of his daily life in London. They are perhaps the more evident because there was so much in his life that was half decided. He was caught between new experiences and the doubting of old experiences. There was no certainty to drive forward the preparation of the fifth volume, and for this reason Ruskin felt little affection for his book. He looked widely for stimulus, even to James Russell Lowell in America. To Lowell he admitted being able

> . . . only to write a little now & then of old thoughts — to finish Modern Painters, which *must* be finished. Whenever I can write at all this winter I must take up that for it is tormenting me, always about my neck. — If no accident hinders it will be done this spring and then I will see if there is anything I can say clearly enough to be useful in my present state of mystification . . .[2]

Part of Ruskin's problem was that there was no one person with whom he might discuss the contents of his book. This was to be a volume that wandered far from John James's conception of the world. The last gift was the one in which the companionship between the two men was least evident. Instead, we have a book in which we hear the echoes of conversations with schoolgirls, or with the painter John Brett; that recapitulates talk with G. F. Watts, Tennyson, and the Brownings; that at some points seems to bring Ruskin closer to the Richmond family than he had been for years; and in the aftermath of the Crimea is thoughtful of war. *Modern Painters* V is in this sense a contemporary book. But in fact it retreats from the art of the day, from modern painting. It closes Ruskin's writing on Turner as it bids farewell to his committed response to the art of his contemporaries.

The first number of *Academy Notes* had taken up some observations made in the second volume of *Modern Painters*. The last of the series Ruskin published in 1859: the pamphlet is rather unlike his current major work. Some sections of this *Academy Notes* are ordinary. One or two entries have a private background: there is praise of a (probably) unremarkable picture by 'A. Blunden'. As so many people did, every year, one turns first to the verdict on Millais's contributions. In this exhibition they were *The Vale of Rest* and *Apple Blossoms*. But those few who followed Ruskin's thinking with care would have wished to see what he made of the painting he had encouraged, in part supervised, and had now purchased, John Brett's *Val d'Aosta*. Evidently, Ruskin now felt that there was more to Brett than to Millais, if only in potential. The *Val d'Aosta*, he argued, was 'landscape painting with a meaning and a use . . . for the first time in history we have, by help of art, the power of visiting a place, reasoning about it, and knowing it, just as if we were there . . .'. Ruskin then uses the picture to describe the agronomy of the valley. But it is clear that art should have a higher function. Although he does not use the word, Ruskin returned to his theories of the imagination in finally criticizing the painting: 'It has a strange fault, considering the school to which it belongs — it seems to me wholly emotionless. I cannot find from it that the painter loved, or feared, anything in all that wonderful piece of the world . . . I never saw the mirror so held up to nature; but it is Mirror's work, not Man's.'[3]

Thus was dismissed Brett's painting. Soon afterwards his friendship with Ruskin, such as it was, came to an end. *Modern Painters* V, which at one point acknowledges him, is full of longing for a kind of painting that Brett could not provide. His Swiss landscape was the second high point, as Millais's Glenfinlas portrait had been the first, of that naturalism in English painting which Ruskin had done so much to foster. But Ruskin wanted more from naturalistic art. He wanted passion and he increasingly wanted some kind of symbolism. It was not quite in Pre-Raphaelitism, not even in Rossetti's, to provide the satisfaction that comes from such art. But it was there in Turner. Ruskin now found that he could gather more and more from the painter he had first admired, especially if he allowed Turner's thematic implications to settle and grow in his own imagination. Unconsciously or not, Ruskin looked into Turner for themes that were mythological rather than literary. This pleased a cast of his mind which sought a veracity grander and more mysterious than simple fidelity to nature. How thin and contrived, therefore, appeared Millais's invented symbolist painting, *The Vale of Rest*: what depth of meaning that picture feigned to possess already existed, ten times over, in Turner.[4]

Much of this cloudy conviction was found in Turner's Greek painting. The young Ruskin had felt it his Christian duty to attack Greek culture. But for years past he had been thinking more of the spirituality of the pagan world. His thoughts were occasionally expressed in public, in such places as the chapter 'Of Classical Landscape' in *Modern Painters* III, but more often they were kept to conversations with friends. Such friends were usually artists: they were not churchmen. Ruskin's sense of Greece did not move in strict measure with the fluctuations of his Christianity. But he allowed his instincts to find a relationship between the world of the ancient gods and the world that belonged to Christ. His study of myth was not scientific, nor archæological. He had no real feeling for the classical tradition. His Greek preoccupations — so marked in *Modern Painters* V — were more individual than they were akin to Turner's. His dark, emblematic books on Greek themes in the 1860s have no parallel in other literature of the day, though many Victorian intellectuals wrote on Greek culture. The great exponent of this kind of painting was G. F. Watts, and for him Ruskin now felt a sympathy that heretofore had been rather distant. However, Ruskin's appreciation of Watts's art hardly entered his public writings. The most telling comments are in private letters, from which we gather that Ruskin had benefited from discussions with an artist who knew as much about Titian as did the Richmonds and whose themes evoke, if they do not describe, the ancient world.

Ruskin's commendations of Titian are found at all stages of his career, but his feeling for the artist is not easily grasped. In the late 1850s there were people who heard Ruskin talk of Titian and believed his talk to be empty. One of these was probably the visually uneducated Tennyson, with whom Ruskin had a slight, wary friendship. There exists a vignette of Ruskin, by himself, in the company of this other great Victorian. In the spring of 1859 he wrote to a correspondent in the provincial north of England, a schoolmistress:

Any person interested in the art and literature of Young England would have been glad if they could have had a good sketch of one or two bits of scene yesterday.

You must have heard people speak of Watts — He's named with Rossetti sometimes in my things — the fresco painter — a man of great imagination & pathetic power: — he is painting Tennyson's portrait — both staying at the pleasant house of a lady to whose kind watching over him in his failing health, Watts certainly owes his life: — Mrs Prinsep — an old — (as far as a very beautiful lady of about eight-and-thirty can be so injuriously styled —) friend of mine also.

One of the scenes that perhaps you and one or two other people would have liked to have sketched, was this — Watts lying back in his arm chair — a little faint — (he is still unwell) with Tennyson's P.R.B. illustrated poems on his knee. Tennyson standing above him — explaining over his shoulder why said illustrations did not fit the poems, with a serious quiver on his face — alternating between indignation at not having been better understood, and dislike of self-enunciation: — I sitting on the other side of Watts — looking up deprecatingly to Tennyson — & feeling very cowardly in the good cause — yet maintaining it in a low voice — Behind me as backer Jones, the most wonderful of all the PreRaphaelites in redundance of delicate & pathetic fancy — inferior to Rossetti in depth — but beyond him in grace & sweetness — he, laughing sweetly at the faults of his own school as Tennyson declared them and glancing at me with half wet half sparkling eyes, as he saw me shrink — A little in front of us — standing in the light of the window Mrs Prinsep and her sister — two, certainly, of the most beautiful women in a grand sense — (Elgin marbles with dark eyes) — that you would find in modern life — and round the room — Watts' Greek-history frescoes. Tennyson's face is more agitated by the intenseness of sensibility than is almost bearable by the looker on — he seems to be almost in a state of nervous trembling like a jarred string of a harp. He was maintaining that painters ought to attend to at least what the writer *said* — if they couldn't, to what he meant — while Watts and I both maintained that no good painter could be subservient at all: but must conceive everything in his own way, — that no poems ought to be illustrated at all — but if they were — the poet *must* be content to have his painter in partnership — not a slave.[5]

The 'Jones' of this letter had not yet changed his name to Burne-Jones. Still now in his twenties, Jones already had a reputation in just the sort of company Ruskin's letter describes. Indeed, he was hardly known elsewhere. He owed his convenient insulation from the difficulties of an early career to Rossetti and Ruskin. From Rossetti he derived his art, and it was Rossetti who had first introduced him, with his comrade William Morris, to the critic. As undergraduates, not many years before, Jones and Morris had read *The Stones of Venice* aloud to each other. To be taken up by Ruskin himself was wonderful good fortune. William Morris did not greatly interest Ruskin. But for 'Ned' he felt immediate and unshakeable affection. This was partly because they avoided the issues raised by Burne-Jones's art. Ruskin had a feeling that it might represent the next phase of Pre-Raphaelitism. Yet he made no attempt to mould Jones to the form of his own beliefs. He gave him no instruction whatever, only gifts. Nor did he mention him in print. It was to be fully eleven years before he gave public approval to his painting. This was in a lecture at the Royal Institution in 1867. The address he gave was quite important, and fully written out, but Ruskin never published it. Nearly another two decades passed before, in his last Oxford lectures, Ruskin again praised Burne-Jones before an audience. This was in 1883. The man had meant more to Ruskin than his art: and by then the art meant more to him in memory than in reality.

In 1859 Ruskin was not sure what new art he wanted. An appendix to that year's *Academy Notes*, the last of the sequence, gives a couple of pages to two exhibitions of water-colour societies. It is one of the first of the occasions, numerous later on, where we find an important statement in a comparatively minor or sequestered part of his works. He wrote here that English water-colour was 'in steady decline', that it was characterized by falseness and vulgarity, and that art itself, not merely water-colour, now suffered from 'the loss of belief in the spiritual world'. This sentiment was not totally new. But the prescription was startling. Ruskin argued, 'Art has never shown, in any corner of the earth, a condition of advancing strength but under this influence. I do not say, observe, influence of "religion" but merely of a belief in some invisible power — god or goddess, fury or fate, saint or demon.'[6] He was calling for an art of spiritual power which did not exist and could hardly be produced on demand. The difference was in his appeal to invisible powers which might not be Christian. In the context of his previous writings this was little less than impious. When he came to write out similar thoughts in the last volume of *Modern Painters* he rather clothed and obscured them. He wrote in such a fashion as, conceivably, to hide from his mother the loss of the Evangelical thrust with which the work began.

As *Academy Notes* went to press, Ruskin's parents were uppermost in his mind. The old people were as vigorous as ever in the way that they read and argued. Travelling, however, was difficult for them: Margaret Ruskin had scarcely been into London in the last few years. They wanted to spend one more summer on the Continent. It was to be a German expedition. Ruskin felt that he ought to study the Titians in German collections before writing any more about Venetian Renaissance art. Furthermore, at the National Gallery Site Commission in 1857 he had been embarrassed by questions put to him by two enemies, Effie's friend Dean Milman and the academic architect Charles Cockerell.[7] They had made him admit ignorance of German art galleries. And so the last family tour went from Brussels to Cologne, Berlin, Dresden and Munich. Ruskin found that contemporary art was no better in Protestant Germany than in France or Italy. To Clarkson Stanfield, whose abilities had been kindly surveyed in previous volumes of *Modern Painters*, he wrote condemnations of the Nazarene school. None of the party really felt at ease in Germany. Ruskin liked Nuremberg: but he was glad to find his old routes from Schaffhausen to Geneva. Leaving his parents there, he climbed to Chamonix in search of the original inspiration and the original material of *Modern Painters*. When the family reunited they travelled quickly to Paris and thence returned to London. It had not been a particularly exciting tour, and much sadness was mixed with the pleasures the Ruskins could always find for themselves. Nor was the expedition helpful to Ruskin's book. In the end his father had to insist on its completion. Ruskin did not confess how this came about until many years later, in an Oxford lecture. His address to undergraduates on *Modern Painters* was largely unscripted, but among the notes Ruskin wrote is this reminiscence:

> Now the thing which I have especially to thank my father for is that he made me finish my book . . . He made me finish it with a very pathetic appeal. For fifteen years he had seen me collecting materials, and collecting and learning new truths, and still learning — every volume of the four pitched in a new key — and he was provoked enough, naturally, and weary of waiting. And in 1859 he took his last journey with me abroad; and when he came home, and found signs of infirmity creeping on him, and that it were too probable he might never travel far more, until very far, he said to me one day, 'John, if you don't finish that book now, I shall never see it.' So I said I would do it for him forthwith; and did it, as I could.[8]

* * * *

Immediately after this German tour Ruskin left his parents at Denmark Hill while he went to stay for three weeks at a girls' school in Cheshire. This was Winnington Hall, near Northwich. He had been there once before, briefly, in the spring before leaving for Germany. Ruskin had then found, to his surprise, that he enjoyed the company of schoolchildren. He wanted to go there again. He was indulged at Winnington; and after the strain of conducting his parents through Europe it was a relaxation to talk to young girls. The school was a retreat, and in some ways it became a second home. For the next ten years it provided a background for some of the happiest moments of his adult life.

Winnington Hall lay just outside the growing industrial area of Manchester. The school had taken over an old manor house, set among lawns and gardens. Its headmistress was Margaret Alexis Bell. She had first met Ruskin when he gave his lectures in Manchester in 1857. Their friendship had developed slowly. Neither had met anyone quite like the other. Ruskin felt that he had to explain himself to Miss Bell: it was to her that he had addressed the long letter describing his conversation with Watts and Tennyson. The world of metropolitan Victorian culture was important to the determined Margaret Bell. In some ways she wished to join it. She had been born into an unyielding type of northern Methodism but she now held liberal religious opinions, mostly derived from broad church Anglicanism. She followed recent literature. She wished to appreciate art. Like many a headmistress who owned her own school, she had a slightly uncertain social status. But she was not much concerned with the usual appearances of gentility. Her educational views were progressive, as Ruskin now came to understand. He had some distant acquaintance with school education, for he was in a position to give places at Christ's Hospital (a privilege inherited from his father's City connections). But of girls' schools he knew nothing. When he found that there were Turners on the walls at Winnington, that drawing and water-colour were central parts of the curriculum, that study was mingled with play and that nothing was learnt by rote, Ruskin was made curious. To see his own portrait hanging side by side with F. D. Maurice's only emphasized the differences between this happy place and the Working Men's College;[9] and Ruskin began to wonder what his influence in it might be.

* * * *

A life half lived, with so much left to do; a growing sense of being wiser; a feeling that he was witnessing the approach of his father's death; a hardly sentient understanding of what Rose La Touche meant to him: all these things and more were in Ruskin's mind as Christmas of 1859 and the new year of 1860 approached. In February he would be forty-one. He had found much success in the world but had also learnt that public opinion is valueless. His troubles with the Royal Academy, the National Gallery, and indeed the Working Men's College, had all shown him that such institutions were too worldly for the spirit of Turner he had tried to communicate. He had lost hope for architecture when the Oxford Museum was built. He no longer felt that he wanted to make comrades of artists. To one, J. J. Laing, who had written enthusiastically of the spreading influence of Pre-Raphaelitism, he replied bleakly, 'I entirely disclaim all parties, and all causes of a sectarian or special character.'[10] One notices how drawn he was at this time to people whose own concerns were inapposite, nothing to do with his own: Spurgeon, whose vision of heaven was so clear, or little Rose La Touche, or the girls at Winnington, or Americans. Ruskin looked often to Carlyle. But he did not feel the need of him that would come later on, and was not yet writing for Carlyle's approval. He had to finish *Modern Painters* for his father: but he did not know whether John James would like his last volume and he did not know what he would write next, or who it would be for. He had no obligation ever to write a book again. He told the Brownings that he wanted 'to be able to take a few years of quiet copying, either nature or Turner — or Titian or Veronese or Tintoret — engraving as I copy. It seems to me the most useful thing I can do. I am tired of talking.'[11] Ruskin's diaries are empty in these months, and his correspondence is not vigorous. It would take a couple of years, and the realization that he was in love, before he once again found a confident voice in which to address the world.

JOHN RUSKIN: THE LATER YEARS

CHAPTER SIXTEEN

1859–1860

Years later, at the time in the mid 1880s when he was preparing to write his autobiography *Præterita*, Ruskin looked in the diary he had kept at the end of the 1850s. There, amid some memoranda written in Germany for the last volume of *Modern Painters*, he discovered the place where he had first written the Mayfair address of the La Touche family. On other pages were early sketches of his analysis of political economy; and here were brief entries chronicling the route of the 1859 family holiday, when at Königstein he had taken 'my last happy walk with my father'.[1] Dismayed by the reminiscences that the diary stirred in him, Ruskin took his pen and wrote, in block letters, 'The Beginning of Sorrows' at the end of the vellum-bound book.[2] The darker days of his life had indeed begun at that time. But Ruskin in 1859, in his fortieth year, was a confident man. He had no notion that his relations with Rose La Touche would end in tragedy. He could not imagine that he would soon lead a life without John James Ruskin's companionship. He had no idea that the writing of his later years would be quite unlike the work that had made his reputation, and could not foretell how his mind would break in terrible spells of madness. At the end of the 1850s Ruskin had too much vigorous curiosity about the world to think of his own fate. But he was dissatisfied and restless. He now seemed to cast around him for different loyalties and friendships.

John James Ruskin had much experience of his son's sudden enthusiasms. But he had never encountered anything so outlandish as his sudden devotion to the girls' school at Winnington. Shortly after his return from Switzerland in early October of 1859, Ruskin left London for Cheshire. He remained at Winnington until 10 November. Ruskin took part in all the school's activities. He taught art, divinity and many other subjects. When lessons ended he joined the girls in games of cricket, croquet or hide and seek. There were only about thirty-five girls in the school, and Winnington was an unregimented home of learning. The atmosphere was friendly and informal. On the higher floors of the old manor house a warren of small rooms had been turned into dormitories. Eighteenth-century additions gave Winnington its library, an orangery and other quite spacious rooms in which the girls could draw, hold concerts or, seated on the floor, listen to Margaret Bell as she read aloud from a novel. 'The Lady of Winnington',[3] as Ruskin liked to call his new friend, was not one of those who disapproved of fiction. Nor was she bound to learning by exercise and catechism, methods standard in boys' schools of the day. Her teaching was based on thoughtful discovery and discussion. The school library contained books by liberal thinkers of the Broad Church movement. A number of such churchmen were known to Margaret Bell, and they entrusted their children to her care. Winnington was a sanctuary, but it was not cloistered: in fact it was rather modern. Ruskin went there to rest, to escape from his parents and to be surrounded by girls. But the school also helped him to define his future role as a critic of Victorian society. Although *The Ethics of the Dust* (1865) would be the only direct expression of Ruskin's Winnington life, the enthusiasm of Miss Bell and her teaching staff (Mary Anne Leadbetter, Lucy and Emily Pignatel and Mary Frances Bradford) prompted him to look freshly at the religious and political controversies of the day; and this had a more general influence on his thought.[4]

Ruskin was a wonderful acquisition for Margaret Bell's school: he seemed to have made a gift of himself. His presence was inspiring, and there is no doubt that Winnington became a better school as a result of Ruskin's interest. Furthermore, Margaret Bell's friendship with Ruskin helped her standing with the progressive middle-class Northerners who provided her with pupils. Ruskin's fame was as one of the great writers of the age. He was not yet regarded as eccentric or controversial; and the scandalous but vague rumours that attached to his marriage were heard in London, not in Cheshire and Lancashire. Winnington gave Ruskin a commitment to the North of England he would never lose. Meanwhile, he was simply delighted to be there. 'I wonder if you knew', he wrote to Margaret Bell, '— when you asked me to Winnington — that you could do me good — and just the good I wanted?'[5] Ruskin now began to mix in northern intellectual society. He resumed his acquaintance with Sir Elkanah Armitage, the cultivated manufacturer who was a former mayor of Manchester. He met the Mancunian Pre-Raphaelite painter Frederic Shields and encouraged his work.[6] Soon he came to know Charles Hallé and his family, though Ruskin and the musician could never understand each other. He made firm friends with Samuel Hay Cooke, whom he had known slightly at Christ Church. Cooke was the rector of the neighbouring village of Great Budworth: he still had many Oxford connections, however, because his family home was at Beckley Park, a house just six miles from the university city. Margaret Bell's acquaintance with the intellectual clergy was passed on to Ruskin. She had known Bishop Colenso's family, for instance, since at least 1854. John William Colenso was both a linguist and a pioneer of the critical examination of scripture. His daughter Fanny would become a Winnington pupil and a lifelong friend of Ruskin's. Susan Scott, the Winnington girl who in a few years would receive one of the first letters outlining the Guild of St George, had a similar background. Her father, Alexander John Scott, was the Principal of Owens College, Manchester. He had once, in his early days as a clergyman, been Edward Irving's assistant. Before removing to Manchester from London, Scott was the first Professor of English at University College and was still a friend of F. D. Maurice and Carlyle. Ruskin liked him, though he liked his daughter more.

Winnington was a religious school. So were all Victorian schools, but Winnington was not religious merely by observance. This little community of girls and young women reflected the state of mid-nineteenth-century Christian thought and especially the views of Anglican liberals. Ruskin was not as interested in Mauricean liberal theology as were Margaret Bell and Alexander Scott. He was interested to test his own views by helping girls with their knowledge of the Bible. The status and interpretation of the scriptures was a contentious area. Ruskin had known for many years that the Bible could not be treated literally. In this period of uncertainty about his own life he began more mature Biblical studies. He found this maturity in the company of schoolgirls rather than with scholars and divines of his own generation. Their innocence and burgeoning intelligence demanded especial delicacy and care in Biblical instruction. Several of Ruskin's letters to parents of the girls show how conscientious he was in discussion of scripture. A more intimate record of his instruction is also available to us, though for many years it lay buried in the private papers of Margaret Bell, Mary Bradford and their executors and descendents. This record consists of numerous long, semi-formal letters written by Ruskin to his 'birds', as he called the Winnington girls. These are his 'Sunday letters', composed every Sabbath during the school terms. They began in the spring of 1859, after his first visit to Winnington, and continued until some point in 1864, with occasional revivals of the mode thereafter. The letters were read aboud at the school and were also copied. Their first purpose was to expound the scriptures. They follow no set pattern, however, and are not exclusively concerned with the Bible. The earlier letters concentrate on the precise meanings of words, with much etymological demonstration. As the letters proceed, exegesis of Biblical verses is mixed with other matter. Then, their tone can change. When the letters are at their most miscellaneous Ruskin is alternately teasing and stern. He addresses individual girls as well as his whole class. He writes about his own thoughts and feelings, replies to questions and calls attention to current affairs, books and art. In such ways the 'Sunday letters' were a preparation for the great series of public letters that Ruskin would begin to issue a decade later, *Fors Clavigera*.

Naturally enough, much of Ruskin's teaching at Winnington was in art classes. *The Elements of Drawing* seems already to have been in use there before his arrival. In any case, there was no essential difference between the instruction he gave to girls and his classes at the Working Men's College. He brought a number of his workmen's drawings to the school as examples and supplemented them with choicer works. Thus Winnington became the home of drawings and watercolours by Turner, Rossetti, William Henry Hunt and other artists, while prints after Dürer were also left there for copying.

We may imagine that Mary Leadbetter, the drawing mistress, was made nervous by the famous art critic. Yet Ruskin was always careful to put both the children and their teachers at their ease. Many stories attest to his charm and generosity. Phoebe France, also a drawing mistress, recounted how she had broken the glass on one of Ruskin's Turners and how

> it was asserted that in fracturing the glass I had scratched the drawing. Of course I was very much distressed, although I contended that the particular scratch had been done by Turner himself. As soon as Mr Ruskin saw it he proved my assertion was right, and seeing my distressed and tearful countenance, he took my hand, and said 'Rather than have been the cause of so much grief, my dear Miss France, I would sooner have seen the picture destroyed'.[7]

At Winnington, in October of 1859, Ruskin wrote a short sequel to *The Elements of Drawing*. Although it contains some interesting remarks, one doubts whether *The Elements of Perspective* was ever of much use to a student. The book's exercises are too advanced, are difficult to follow and do not translate into painting practice. They may have been intended for Winnington girls, but their origin is in Ruskin's old fascination with the problems of geometry: one of his earliest published papers had been 'Remarks on the Convergence of Perpendiculars' in the *Architectural Magazine* in 1838.[8] His new manual announced that a thorough knowledge of the first three and the sixth books of Euclid would allow any draughtsman to follow his reasoning. The exercises are reminiscent of the geometry Ruskin studied at Oxford. It seems that the only person at Winnington who was able to appreciate the book was Mr Le Vengeur, the mathematics master.

This Mr Le Vengeur appears in a dramatic letter sent to her parents by Dora Livesey, another of the girls from Winnington whom Ruskin would know and love for the rest of his life — and who would become the first of the Companions of St George. We discover how, in November 1860, she and other girls

> . . . were in the Library, while Miss Bell packed the lease for London when the door opened with a crash & a dark figure with a watchman's lantern appeared at the other end of the room. Mr Le Vengeur stood among us in a cool fury 'I ask no leave to enter this room, I come in Miss Bedborough's name and in the name of her lawyer to say that Miss Bedborough is an equal partner with that woman' pointing at Miss Bell. I was too confused to enter all. He met Miss Bradford's eye 'Miss Bradford you are of age and responsible, remember you are of age' No one spoke, then Miss Pignatel started 'Miss Pignatel, be silent' he dashed out of the room, banging the door. We locked the door and wrote to Mr Leslie to ask for help . . .[9]

The idyllic aspects of Winnington did not always conceal Margaret Bell's financial problems and stormy relations with partners and local tradesmen. This particular dispute had arisen because of her attempt to raise money by selling a partnership in the school to Mrs Bedborough. After the exciting events described by Dora, there followed a lawsuit. Mrs Bedborough was bought out of the partnership for £450. The money was provided by Ruskin, who asked his father for it. This was not the only occasion when John James Ruskin had been asked to support Miss Bell. In April of 1859, after Ruskin's first visit to the school, we find from the wine merchant's accounts that he had sent £300 to Winnington.[10] The sum is entered under 'Charities', and John James seems not to have hoped to see his money returned. His diary contains sardonic remarks about the schoolmistress. He found her visits to Denmark Hill irritating. He also worried that her advanced religious views would upset his wife. Soon, despite his son's requests, he refused to give or lend her more money. 'He will have Miss Bell begging as before but I was not to demur,' his diary tells us.[11] Ruskin continued to give her money from his own funds. By March 1867 he had lent her a total of £1,130 15s. 4d.[12] For personal, intellectual and also financial reasons, therefore, he was tied to the school. It gave him a retreat, many happy hours, and treasured friendships among the girls. But this was at the expense of some alienation from his father, who considered his interest in Winnington to be merely foolish.

* * * *

The girls who pondered over the 'Sunday letters', copied them out and pursued their Bible references, were, as far as one can tell, intelligent. They were certainly diligent, for Ruskin's Sabbath day missives were demanding. He may have aimed rather high when he devised his perspective exercises. But there were girls at Winnington (they may have been eighteen or nineteen before they left, so we can imagine them as university students) who could respond to his difficult cultural questions. In the spring of 1859 he wanted to know how they would discuss 'the meaning of the word vulgar',[13] an enquiry he also presented to his doctor friend John Simon and to the painter John Brett. He was looking for help with the chapter of *Modern Painters V* which is entitled 'On Vulgarity'. The chapter is suggestive in many ways, but lacks a conclusive formulation of the problem itself. Vulgarity belongs to modernity, yet the book entitled *Modern Painters* could not quite deal with the issue. Ruskin knew that the problem of vulgar art had been raised by Pre-Raphaelitism. Ten years before, he had expected that the movement would bring about a democratic art — and yet a high art — that would speak to all men. Pre-Raphaelitism had done no such thing. Its realism had all too easily been united with popular academicism. The result had been a flood of painting of a vulgarity that had not previously been seen in art. Therefore, it appeared, the movement had failed. Ruskin had no intention of issuing another *Academy Notes* and, though he did not realise it, his career as an arbiter of contemporary art was now at its end.

As he worked on *Modern Painters V* in the New Year of 1860 his thoughts were all on natural beauty, Turner and Greek mythology. His ruminations were original and beautiful. They could have come from no other mind than his own. Yet they have not much connection with the artistic life of his own time. It is as though Ruskin wrote in disregard of the world around him. None the less he was interested to know how his new young friends would react to his thoughts. Successive chapters of *Modern Painters V* were sent to Winnington as he completed them, and the girls were entrusted with the compilation of the book's index. They had to consider such passages as the following, found in the chapter 'The Hesperid Ægle':

> Colour is therefore, in brief terms, the type of love. Hence it is especially connected with the blossoming of the earth; and again,

with its fruits; also, with the spring and fall of the leaf, and with the morning and evening of the day, in order to show the waiting of love about the birth and death of man.

And now, I think, we may understand, even far away in the Greek mind, the meaning of that Contest of Apollo with the Python. It was a far greater contest than that of Hercules with Ladon. Fraud and avarice might be overcome by frankness and force; but his Python was a darker enemy, and could not be subdued but by a greater god. Nor was the conquest slightly esteemed by the victor deity. He took his name from it thenceforth — his prophetic and sacred name — the Pythian.

It could, therefore, be no merely devouring dragon — no mere wild beast with scales and claws. It must possess some more terrible character to make conquest over it so glorious. Consider the meaning of its name, 'THE CORRUPTER'. That Hesperid dragon was a treasure-guardian. This is the treasure-destroyer. — where moth and rust doth corrupt — the worm of eternal decay.

Apollo's contest with him is the strife of purity with pollution; of life with forgetfulness; of love, with the grave.

I believe this great battle stood, in the Greek mind, for the type of the struggle of youth and manhood with deadly sin — venomous, infectious, irrecoverable sin. In virtue of his victory over this corruption, Apollo becomes thenceforward the guide; the witness; the purifying and helpful God. The other gods help waywardly, whom they choose. But Apollo helps always: he is by name, not only Pythian, the conqueror of death; but Paean — the healer of the people.

Well did Turner know the meaning of that battle . . .[14]

Ruskin often talked about Rose La Touche to Margaret Bell and her pupils and he began to hope that the girl might one day, perhaps quite shortly, be sent to Winnington for her education. The La Touches were in residence at their London house in Norfolk Street for the winter months. Ruskin was a not infrequent guest. The La Touches also visited Denmark Hill, where Rose, now eleven years old, was petted and indulged. John James, who grumbled in his diary about the visits from Winnington girls ('Miss Bell, 5 virgins to strawberries') felt differently about 'innocent and loving Rose', as the diary describes her,[15] while Margaret Ruskin took delight in an infant piety that was already a marked part of her character. The Irish girl was a puzzle, for she was precocious in some ways and not in others. Sometimes she had a surprising understanding of adult attitudes: at the next moment she was once more completely a child. She had pretty ways of making herself engaging, even coquettish, but could also be rather solemn. 'I don't know what to make of her', Ruskin confessed. '. . . She wears her round hat in the sauciest way possible — and is a firm — fiery little thing'.[16]

Rose was not so playful that she did not like her books. She had decided that she was a poet, and Ruskin received many of her guileless verses. These he carefully preserved, and sometimes sent on to other people. It is important that Rose loved Ruskin's company. He told her so many things about books, about nature, about the world. Certainly she heard more about wonders and poetry from Ruskin than from her father, who, in comparison, was taciturn and withdrawn. This winter, to his growing dismay, Ruskin realised that John La Touche was a man of inflexible beliefs. Like many a convert, he had no interest in opinions and no sympathy with enquiring minds. He regarded intellectuals with suspicion. La Touche had no cultural pleasures. His social concerns were in temperance and the reformation of prostitutes. The La Touches never became part of the Ruskin circle and seldom met friends of the Ruskin family. John James Ruskin's dinner table was far too lively for the dour John La Touche. Inevitably, La Touche and Ruskin were to disagree about religion. A message to the Winnington girls shows that Ruskin's 'Sunday letters' fell within an area of discussion that was prohibited to Rose:

> My dearest Birds,
>
> I am so much obliged to you for finding the letter for me and copying the end of it, though after all I can't show it to Rosie — for her father — staunch evangelical of the old school — does not believe in Greek, and might not like some expressions in this letter speaking mercifully of Error. Rosie, believing at once in him, & her mother and me, is growing up quite a little Cerberus, only her mother and I make two heads bark one way; but the third barks loudest — Indeed I should not say she believed in me — but would like to do so if I did not every now and then say much out of the way things — she pets me as she would a panther that kept its claws in — always looking under the claws to see that the velvet is all right & orthodox. She petted me yesterday, up, or down — (I don't know which) — to such a point that when I began drawing in the evening I found I didn't like the Venetians — but could only look at Angelico — But I can't write you a Sunday's letter to-day; it is all dark and rainy and I can't think now, unless in the sunshine.

> I kept this letter to try and put some more in it — being reduced to a state of frantic despair by Rosie's going away to Italy next week . . .[17]

This 'Italy' is probably a child copyist's error for Ireland, for the La Touches left London to return to their estate in County Kildare in the latter part of February 1860. It is difficult to know if Ruskin's 'frantic despair' was real. Certainly he did not suffer the crazed longings that would possess him in years to come. But his remark is not in the vein of humorous exaggeration he sometimes employed. At all events, as if in reaction to Rose's departure, Ruskin now turned to a quite different part of his acquaintance. He kept no diary during these spring months, but we gather that he was often in town. John La Touche would not have approved of Ruskin's London pursuits, for they had a bohemian aspect. His appearances at the Working Men's College were now irregular and were less serious than of old. George Butterworth, his errant assistant, managed to persuade Ruskin — who, like nearly all the world, was excited by the forthcoming and sensational Sayers–Heenan prize fight — that he could bring Tom Sayers to the College to meet its students and lecturers. Ruskin thought this a better idea than some of his colleagues might have done and provided his father's choicest wines to toast the English champion. Sayers, however, failed to appear. The wine was sent on to Turner's old housekeeper, Mrs Booth, with whom Ruskin maintained cordial relations.

It was at this period that, unknown to his over-protective parents, Ruskin took moonlight boating expeditions on the Thames, accompanied by George Allen.[18] One night we find him at the Canterbury Music Hall with the dealer Ernest Gambart; and Ruskin was certainly often in the company of Rossetti and other artist friends. In Bloomsbury, Blackfriars and Chelsea, among people who knew how to be carefree, the author of the unfinished *Modern Painters* could escape some of the worries of his study. Rossetti cheerfully twitted Ruskin about the long gestation of his book, saying that the modern painters would be old masters before Ruskin had finished. Perhaps he did not realise that Ruskin was not writing about contemporary art. But he must have wondered why it was that Ruskin, in private his friend and patron, never wrote publicly about his work.

CHAPTER SEVENTEEN

1860–1861

In this year, 1860, Ruskin gave Rossetti money to help him marry Lizzie Siddall and continued to advise him about his painting and poetry. He also, by means of a financial guarantee, enabled Rossetti to publish his translations, *Early Italian Poets*, with Smith, Elder. At the same time Ruskin was encountering difficulties and upsets in his own writing career. He had begun *Modern Painters* when he was full of conviction. Now he seemed to be describing mysteries rather than certainties. Some of the fifth volume, according to a letter he wrote to Pauline Trevelyan, was to be jettisoned. He told her: 'I'm cutting out all the wisest parts, which are too good for this generation'.[1] However, additional passages that belong to the manuscripts of *Modern Painters V* do not seem to be such 'wisest parts'.[2] Ruskin's remark probably reflects an indecision over such chapters as 'The Dark Mirror' and 'The Nereid's Guard', which are full of unlucid speculation. Today we can see that these sections of the book stand at the beginning of nineteenth-century symbolist literature. The difficulties of the end of *Modern Painters* were resolved, after a fashion, by the grave splendours of Ruskin's prose and the book was published to acclaim in June 1860.

Shortly afterwards he had the first real failure of his writing career. He was surprised and hurt by the reception of *Unto This Last*. This short book, later so famous, was originally a series of papers. Ruskin had begun to explore their themes, in correspondence and in his diary, in the winter of 1859–60. He wished to say something precisely and incontrovertibly relevant about social matters. But Ruskin's propositions found no universal assent, not even among people he knew and trusted. To his vexation, his essays on political topics were discontinued by the journal that had commissioned them. It is now obvious that this rejection was part of a publishing difficulty. None the less it was an emotional blow for Ruskin. In later years, exaggerating somewhat, he would declare that the episode was a turning-point in his life.

The four essays that make up *Unto This Last* originally appeared in Smith, Elder's *Cornhill Magazine*. This was a new, deliberately popular journal, in whose pages Ruskin's serious thoughts seem out of place.

The *Cornhill* had originally been planned in more intellectual terms. In August of 1859 Alexander Scott, Ruskin's Manchester friend who was the father of the Winnington schoolgirl Susan Scott, wrote excitedly to Carlyle about his prospects for leaving Owens College:

> You are aware that, as I have said, I wished to be otherwise occupied than in offering Comparative Grammar and Moral Philosophy to devout young believers of the Manchester School.
>
> I am led to write to you now from a prospect of deliverance unexpectedly opening up . . . Smith and Elder are about to start a magazine. Nothing can less concern you, you say. But hear me out. Their design is rather to make it the organ of individual writers of high standing than merely an amusing miscellany, or the organ of a party or school. They obviate one objection to periodical writing by publishing the name of the author with his paper, as the rule at least, and leaving the responsibility for opinion with him, and not with the journal; and another by giving a preference to papers forming parts of such a whole as may afterwards constitute a continuous volume. Their pay will be unusually high . . . My concern in the matter I mention *in confidence*. I have been requested to accept the Editorship. I have given no decisive answer until I could make some enquiries, one of the most important of which relates to probable or possible contributors. Today the offer was made to me, and you are the first person to whom I write with this view . . . They wish to begin in January. Ruskin, Thackeray, Mrs Gaskell will write for them: Tennyson probably . . .[3]

This letter reveals the original scheme for Smith, Elder's magazine. It is likely enough that Ruskin was consulted about the future journal, for he was Smith, Elder's most intellectually adventurous author. George Smith and W. Smith Williams, the firm's active partners, were family friends who often visited Denmark Hill. Both Ruskin and John James Ruskin had always had a fascination with the periodical press; and their interest was the keener because Ruskin had never found a journal, or an editor, that suited him. Perhaps, since he often praised him at this period, it was Ruskin who recommended Scott for the editorial chair. But at some point in the autumn of 1859 there was a change of policy. Scott remained at Owens College, the nature of the projected magazine was altered and Smith, Elder appointed Thackeray as its editor.

Neither Ruskin nor Carlyle (whose writing never appeared in the *Cornhill*) had any particular objection to Thackeray, just as they had no particular admiration for him. They merely felt that the work of a novelist was among the lesser of the world's tasks. One of these tasks was to make the *Cornhill* popular. Here Thackeray was triumphant. He sold 120,000 copies of its first number: when the circulation settled to its natural level a few months later the sale was still above 80,000. Perhaps no other publication was so well attuned to the middle-class household of the 1860s. Amid Tennyson's *Idylls of the King*, Trollope's *Framley Parsonage* (illustrated by Millais) and work by Thackeray himself, Ruskin's contributions on political economy seem to belong to the magazine envisaged by Alexander Scott rather than the one edited by the successful novelist. It should not be assumed that the *Cornhill* was completely unintellectual (nor that Victorian homes were); and the chapter 'On Sir Joshua and Holbein', excluded from *Modern Painters V*, was almost at home in its first issue. But a first principle of the *Cornhill* was to be uncontroversial. Thackeray explained some of his standards when he wrote to Elizabeth Barrett Browning to reject her poem 'Lord Walter's Wife'. 'He says that plain words permitted on Sundays must not be spoken on Mondays in England', Mrs Browning reported, 'and also that his "Magazine is for babes and sucklings"'.[4]

'Lord Walter's Wife' belongs to a small but significant group of mid-Victorian poems — led by *Aurora Leigh* — whose purpose was to explain the passions in modern terms. Such poems were especially inclined to deal with sexual relations. Rossetti's 'Jenny' is of this sort. He too was attracted by the *Cornhill*, partly no doubt by its generous fees, and he asked Ruskin to help him place the poem in its pages. Ruskin declined, pointing out its unsuitability for the magazine. Yet his own writing hardly suited Thackeray's style of publication. Elizabeth Browning's lesson about 'plain words permitted on Sundays' that were 'not to be spoken on Mondays' applies very well to *Unto This Last*, whose title is taken from the verse in St Matthew 20, 'Take that thine is, and go thy way: I will give unto this last, even as unto thee'.

Ruskin had in fact prepared for his writing in *Unto This Last* by turning to men of the cloth. One of them was Charles Haddon Spurgeon. The Baptist preacher was no social theorist, for his conviction of the kingdom of heaven was so intense as to make him heedless of the world's government. In 1864 he recalled Ruskin saying to him, 'Why, how foolish you are, and all the company of preachers. You tell people to think about the next world, when the best thing they could do would be to behave themselves as well as they can in this!'[5]

Many things separated Ruskin and Spurgeon, and by 1860 their friendship was fading. But something of Spurgeon's bluntness and expository manner enters *Unto This Last*.[6] Ruskin also used a clergyman of a vastly different type to build a foundation for his political essays. The Reverend Walter Lucas Brown, his Christ Church tutor, was still at Wendlebury, a quiet country parish that had scarcely changed in the twenty years that he had been its incumbent. Brown had therefore seen no need to alter the Toryism natural to his background and position. However, in the year before *Unto This Last* he found himself the recipient of a number of letters, perhaps the longest that Ruskin ever wrote, that attacked his social assumptions. 'I get so wild with contempt and anger when I think of these things that I can't write,' Ruskin admitted, for his pen had splattered ink over the pages as it hastily punctuated his thoughts:

> . . . You next say that the Parish provision for the labourer is a step against nature.
>
> It was also a considerable step against Nature when Christ provided the large Parish maintenance in Heaven for persons naturally going to the Devil. The Poor-law act on a large scale produced precisely the same phenomena which your earthly poor-law does. People got lazy. Thought of the Heavenly Parish instead of their business. Despised the life of this world — Became rascally idle saints instead of good men of business — Unfitted themselves sometimes for the poor house altogether. Not — I think — by the fault of the Overseer — but by their own. You say — people don't save — because you know they will be maintained — and you immediately conclude that it is the fault of the law of maintenance. Whereas I, finding the law of maintenance to be in literal and unmistakeable terms, declared by God — and finding myself ordered by Him to feed the hungry and clothe the naked — without the smallest reference anywhere to the *Character* of the persons to be clothed and fed — (it's a pity our modern economists don't print a new Bible with 'deserving poor' in all places instead of poor. The foot shall tread it down — even the feet of the deserving poor — and the steps of the respectable Needy etc etc) — so finding this commanded I presume if it seems to have ill consequences, they come from some other cause — and that if we leave our poor ill taught — ill disciplined — without sense of honour — without hopes of bettering themselves — without desire of independence — or understanding of their duty to God or man — they will of course make use of Parish maintenance, which you describe — But that is not because you have interfered with the laws of Nature — but because you have fallen short of the Mercy and meaning of God . . .[7]

The full sequence of these letters to Walter Brown and the 'Sunday letters' to Winnington suggest a new direction in Ruskin's manner of writing. In the end, Ruskin's purposes as a writer were to be best served by *Fors Clavigera*, which has the nature of a continuous pamphlet. At the beginning of the 1860s he did not know whether he should write long and stately books or short, concentrated tracts. Large parts of the original scheme for *Modern Painters V* were not written at all. *Unto This Last* is also unfinished; or abandoned, for Ruskin chose not to write any more of it than was published in the four *Cornhill* papers.

Little is known about the embarrassing negotiations that brought an end to *Unto This Last*. Ruskin was in the Alps at the time. He had found a final shape for *Modern Painters V* by May of 1860. Tired, he left the book for his father to see through press and left England for Chamonix. *Unto This Last* was largely composed in the Alps. High in the mountains, Ruskin attempted to reform his writing style. He reacted against the discursive and 'literary' prose of *Modern Painters*. He revised, rewrote and polished, attempting to make his manuscript (some of which survives) as precise and clear as possible. The effort to remake his writing involved a psychological strain which we often detect in later recollections of the *Cornhill* episode. Like many writers, Ruskin had an especial memory for the circumstances in which he once had written. Certain books or passages from books sent his mind back to the days and places in which he had laboured over their manuscripts. *Unto This Last*, a work he cherished, always recalled to him the Alpine summer of snow, gentians, wild roses and St Bruno's lilies when, as *Præterita* states, 'a new epoch of life and death' began.[8] That epoch was not initiated by the reaction to *Unto This Last*. It concerned Rose. Now, in the summer of 1860, Ruskin found that the more he thought about her the more he was in opposition to her father. The *Cornhill* papers are the first of Ruskin's writings in which he confronted not only the orthodox economists but also John La Touche — Spurgeon's convert, an inflexible Bible Christian, a landlord and a banker from a family of bankers.

'THERE IS NO WEALTH BUT LIFE', says *Unto This Last*, aphoristically and in block capitals. Ruskin's papers continually employ vitalist imagery, and in dismissing political economy as 'the science of darkness: probably a bastard science'[9] they insist on the true heredity of their own political notions. Moral and symbolic language discusses justice and honour, darkness and light, honesty and chivalry, life and death. Ruskin shared hardly any terminology with professional economists. This is one reason why it is difficult to know how carefully he had studied Adam Smith, Ricardo or John Stuart Mill, Carlyle's former friend, who now became, for Ruskin, the embodiment and epitome of mechanical, soulless thought.[10] As he sent his papers from Switzerland to Thackeray at the *Cornhill*, Ruskin found that he was writing not about social order but life itself. For his part, Thackeray could not foresee any end to Ruskin's eloquence. After he had published three of the essays he decided it was time to call a halt. He and George Smith asked Ruskin to contribute only one more paper to the magazine, at the same time inviting him to make it longer than its predecessors. It would not be sensible to call this censorship. The problem of the *Unto This Last* essays, especially to Thackeray, was that (as any reader may discover) they are not diverting. Ruskin did not hope to entertain his readers. He sought truths.

Relations between Ruskin, Thackeray and Smith, Elder remained friendly. Yet Ruskin's pride had been wounded. In years to come he brooded about the *Cornhill*, and then his rejection took on new dimensions. After Thackeray's death, when in 1872 Ruskin wrote the preface to *Munera Pulveris*, he maintained that 'the outcry' against his papers 'became too strong for any editor to endure'.[11] This was self-deception. There had certainly been criticism of his economics and the manner of his writing. The *Saturday Review* (in a phrase that must have stung the philosopher of Winnington) declared that the world was not to be 'preached to death by a mad governess'.[12] But much other comment was favourable, or neutral. Ruskin was hurt and angered by the attitude of such friends as Walter Brown and Dr John Brown, both of whom wrote to express disquiet. Now it was important that Ruskin had his father's support. 'I am glad to see such P. Economy', John James wrote to Jane Simon after the publication of the first paper. 'The Tone is high & our Tone in the City is much too low . . .'[13] In late October he told her how 'John sent me from abroad his first Paper kindly saying I might suppress it if the publishing would annoy me I sent it to Smith & Co saying I thought them 12 of the most important pages I had ever read . . .'[14]

* * * *

Ruskin had not been alone in the Alps that summer, but his companion, the American painter W. J. Stillman, was only a distant friend. Stillman's memoirs show how little he understood of Ruskin's background and beliefs. The two men discussed Sabbatarianism. Stillman wrote that he told Ruskin that there was no reason to believe that the weekly day of rest should be on a Sunday. 'To this demonstration', Stillman averred, 'Ruskin, always deferent to the literal interpretation of the Gospel, could not make a defence; the creed had so bound him to the letter . . . He said "If they *have* deceived me in this, they have probably deceived me in all", and he came to the conclusion of rejecting all.'[15] But in truth it is not possible to believe that Ruskin was ignorant of the vast literature, much of it recent, on the nature of the Sabbath; and Stillman's confidence in his own power of argument was probably exaggerated.

This was one of the periods when Ruskin was thinking about the problems of America and its culture, for the *Cornhill* papers were being published in New York in *Harper's New Monthly Magazine*, thanks to an astute syndication by Smith, Elder. He was in correspondence with Harriet Beecher Stowe, to whom he suggested that Roman Catholicism 'will last pretty nearly as long as Protestantism, which keeps it up: but I wonder what is to come next. That is the main question just now for everybody'.[16] This startling observation was perhaps made to provoke a person whom Ruskin found dull. He also wrote to Charles Eliot Norton and James Russell Lowell from the Alps, telling Norton that Stillman 'is a very noble fellow — if only he could see a crow without wanting to shoot it to pieces'.[17] He perhaps meant that Stillman was not noble at all. His travelling companion, who had found himself 'disappointed in the high Alps', shared little of Ruskin's sensibility. Ruskin felt it wrong that Stillman should be drawing badly in places that, for him, were sacred to the memory of Turner. His attempts to teach Stillman as he had taught Inchbold and Brett in earlier years came to nothing.

On his return to England in September of 1860 Ruskin made a number of drawings from the figure. This was an unusual and not a fruitful exercise, soon abandoned in gloom and self-criticism. There were other troubles. Just as he came home Margaret Ruskin fell and broke her thigh bone. John James still went to the City every day; and so Ruskin stayed at Denmark Hill with his mother, reading to her from works of evangelical piety while she took this opportunity to warn him against the free-thinking Carlyle. Ruskin had some lectures to prepare but was listless when he turned to their composition. In fact he was now entering the leanest period of his literary career. Dyspeptic, dissatisfied, unhappy with himself and all the world, he turned to profitless introspection. Thinking of a photograph of himself by a Working Men's College pupil, and of a slightly earlier chalk portrait by George Richmond, he wrote to Pauline Trevelyan:

> It was very naughty of you carrying off that frightful photograph with the hanging lip. I won't scold Jeffreys however. I cannot think

> what it is that has made me so very ugly; I suppose that the kind of instincts which enjoy colour & form are wholly sensual, and have the same effect on the features as mere love of eating or any other passion: —
>
> — then I never have had any of my kindly feelings developed — (my best friends taking delight in Tormenting me — like some people I could name.) — and so they — the pretty feelings — have got all crushed into a shapeless — wide, comfortless, useless philanthropy which will not show in the face; — but the Savagery which you rightly say Richmond has left out — though it is savagely against evil, is just as ugly as if it were savagery against good. The total want of wit and imagination lowers the forehead: there must however somewhere be evidence of some mathematical power; (for no one of my standing in my college knew his geometry as I did) but I don't know where it is; finally the irregular work of my life & its impulsive character have taken away what firmness there might have been in the mouth; and disappointment of all kinds — & dyspepsia — have destroyed any gleam of cheerfulness or colour that might have redeemed the shapelessness.
>
> After all it is no wonder the photograph tells such a story. Am I better: No; I'm not better I'm in the profoundest sense of the words 'don't know what to do with myself'. I hate the sight of everything I have done; and don't know what to do next. The only things I perceive any use in, are little sketches of towers that are fallen — & pictures that are soon to fade. I *think* I shall settle into a quite silent, slow, resolute copyist of Turner and Veronese; etching and engraving as well as I can, but my work is so immeasurably feeble compared to what I want it to be, that, as yet, it makes me very miserable . . .[18]

Such moods as this were common for the next three years and did not quite disappear until, in 1871, Ruskin began the valiant pamphleteering of *Fors Clavigera*. In 1861, frustrated and unable to change his life, he took a step he may afterwards have regretted. Ruskin made the decision, never explained and never subsequently mentioned, to give away his collection of Turners. These watercolours were not only his most treasured possessions. They were the most significant art he had ever known, for they had shaped both his life and his writing. Ruskin's motives for giving away the Turners were not so much philanthropic as self-destructive. Furthermore, to part with these pictures could only be done with a crazed, blinded disregard for his father's feelings. The Denmark Hill Turners represented twenty years of John

James's loving generosity toward his son. But, in March of 1861, forty-eight of the old merchant's gifts were transferred to the University of Oxford. In May a further twenty-five went to Cambridge. Ruskin's seeming largesse had no specific educational purpose. Nor was he motivated by affection for the universities. He scarcely ever thought of Cambridge, a town he had visited only twice, and he was as distant from Oxford in 1861 as at any time in his life. John James Ruskin, so sorely tried by his son, appears to have been stoical about the disappearance of the paintings he had bought. 'He began emptying his cases of Turners', he told Pauline Trevelyan, '& slightly pillaging the walls carrying off my property without scruple or remorse to present to his College & he has an equally felonious design on some Turners just bought, in favour of Cambridge. Seriously however I am not sorry for this — I had indeed told him that his costly decorated Walls & large accumulation of undivided Luxury did not accord with his Doctrines. I am now paying for my speech . . .'[19]

We know the contemporary extent of the Denmark Hill collection from a catalogue printed in Walter Thornbury's *Life of Turner* (1862), which, probably with inaccuracies and omissions, records two oil paintings (*The Slaver* and *Shylock. The Rialto at Venice*) and eighty-three drawings and watercolours. After the gifts to the universities, therefore, not many Turners were left on Ruskin's walls. Ruskin's indulgent attitude to Thornbury, a journalist who had written a poor book, is puzzling. There was no doubt that a full and accurate account of the painter's times and works would be valuable. This was one reason why Ruskin collected material about Turner. On the other hand his experience of the painter was so interwoven with his own emotional life that he cared little about other people's attempts to explain Turner's character. So he did not criticise Thornbury. He thought of himself.

One of Ruskin's lectures this spring of 1861, on 'Tree Twigs' at the Royal Institution, caused him to break down. The failure was caused by conflicting feelings about Turner, myth, and his own future. The lecture was unscripted because it consisted of material Ruskin knew well and had already half written. His spoken text came from the mass of notes he had made for the conclusion of *Modern Painters*. However, Ruskin's delivery suddenly came to a halt. He could not speak. It was as though the larger crisis in his writing had been concentrated into this single minute of dumbness and confusion. He attempted to explain what had happened in a letter to Winnington: 'I found I had no command of my subject & my brains, and was obliged to give in, half way: and talk about general results of it. I had not *altogether* to give in and walk out of the room, but I broke fairly down in the middle — and I have no doubt caused much pain to all my friends there . . .'[20] Among these friends was Carlyle, now taking more interest in his admirer; and he wrote to his brother John saying that the lecture had in truth been a success, giving him 'much more satisfaction than any of the neatest of the neat discourses I have heard . . .'[21]

Three days after his lecture Ruskin went to hear Spurgeon preach and had to contrast the Baptist's attitudes, 'so earnest & so strong in voice & thought' with his own indecision.[22] Nagging ailments, headaches especially, with colds and nervous 'agues', prevented him from reading or enjoying social occasions. He was ill even when George Richmond and Carlyle came to dine. A stay at Winnington in late March of 1861 failed to restore him and led to a dispute with his father. John James was anxious that Ruskin should accept an invitation from William and Georgiana Cowper to stay for the weekend at Broadlands in Hampshire, the great house which was both their country home and the seat of William's father, Lord Palmerston. Ruskin, who was at Winnington, at first refused his proud father's desire that he should be a guest at the Prime Minister's mansion. He gave in only after demanding that John James should buy him four Turner drawings 'for the four days I lose'.[23]

One is reminded of Ruskin's behaviour, so like that of an adolescent, during the earlier period of his marriage. Certainly Ruskin's father interfered with his son's affairs. Yet there was an admirable patience in his love. John James's strong personality knew a fair amount about the passions: fools annoyed him; yet he was not an irascible man. The younger Ruskin, always mildly acquiescent to his mother's demands, was none the less unable to keep his temper with his father. John James's diary now, in 1861, becomes a letter-book in which he summarises the restrained letters he sent to his son. Elsewhere in this diary we find brief but worried comments about Ruskin's artist friends, about Margaret Bell, and about the La Touches.[24]

It did not occur to John James, of course, nor to anyone else, that a part of Ruskin's troubles was that he was falling in love. The La Touches — and Rose had brought her cat — had been in London for the winter months of 1860–61. On many occasions Ruskin had visited the Irish family in Norfolk Street or had entertained them at Denmark Hill. In some sense, Ruskin was still regarded as a tutor to Rose. Their conversations ranged far beyond art and literature. When Ruskin taught Rose some geology he approached a dispute with John La Touche, who believed in the literal truth of the Book of Genesis. Ruskin took his pupil to the British Museum, where his friend Sir Richard Owen was giving lectures on fossils and early forms of life.[25]

The Museum, henceforward, was a place that Ruskin and Rose felt they shared. Ruskin's geological knowledge led Rose to call him 'Archigosaurus', the beginning of an exchange of pet-names that had much significance for them both. Because Rose's governess, Miss Bunnett, was known as 'Bun', Ruskin became first 'Crumpet', then 'St Crumpet', then 'St C.' (this last sometimes expanded in later years by Georgiana Cowper to 'St Chrisostom', the 'golden-mouthed', in reference to St John and Ruskin's famed eloquence). Rose became 'Rosie-posie' or 'Irish roses', Emily La Touche was called 'Wisie' and her mother Maria La Touche 'Lacerta' (i.e., Lizard), a nickname signifying, so Ruskin later said, that she had 'the grace and wisdom of the serpent, without its poison'.[26] John La Touche, usually known both on his estate and in London as 'The Master', was not a man to whom pet-names were given. He took no part in the half-childish exchanges between Ruskin and the rest of his family. These were in any case terminated after 7 March, when the La Touches left London for Dover and the continent. Their further destination was Florence, but they planned to spend some time on the French Riviera before proceeding to Italy.

After Rose's departure Ruskin's domestic behaviour became more wilful and his health further declined. One thing consoled him. He and Rose had agreed to exchange diary-letters while she was abroad. These were later burnt by Ruskin's executors. A single letter from Rose is preserved, for Ruskin quoted from it in *Præterita*. It was the first she had ever written to him. In its eager and affectionate expression we may see the charm of the girl, now just thirteen years old, who was taking Ruskin's heart:

> . . . At Toulon it was like July — I don't like such heat — Transplantation and scorching are too much for an Irish rose — but I sate with Mama and Emily on a rock & sketched Toulon Harbour (or rather tried to) for you St Crumpet. Then the next we posted, the country was so beautiful some of it & towards evening we saw snowy peaks, they were the mountains of Savoy. I was pretty tired that night & we had to sleep at Frejus such a disagreeable place. The next day we had six horses to our carriage for it was a hilly road. We walked about two hours of the way over the hills You know what sort of a view there was at the top, St Crumpet & how one stands & stares & says nothing because the words of Grand Glorious, Beautiful etc cannot in one quarter express what one thinks. *You* the author of M-Ps cd. describe it Irish roses can't. But I can tell you how my cousins the moorland roses nodded at me

> as I passed and how they couldn't understand why Irish hedge roses bloomed in July instead of March . . . Oh St Crumpet I think of you so much & of all your dearnesses to me I wish so very much that you were happy — God can make you so — We will try not to forget all you taught us . . . I hope Mr and Mrs Ruskin are well now. Will you give them our love please & take for yourself as much as ever you please. It will be a great deal if you deign to take all we send you. I like Nice but I don't much like being transplanted except going home. I am ever your rose. Yes, write packets — trunks, & we shall like them so much. Indeed I couldn't write before, I'll try to write again. You *must* see how we think of you & talk of you — rose posie.[27]

Rose also kept a diary during this holiday, but it peters out when the La Touches reached Genoa. In Florence the little girl was taken ill with a fever, 'frightening me out of my wits', as Ruskin confessed.[28] He thought of walking out of his father's house, going down the hill to Camberwell Green, taking a cab to London Bridge station, then a train to Italy to be at her side. Instead, which was just as well, he waited for her return. In early May, when the Irish party paused in London on their way back to the La Touche home at Harristown, Ruskin was able to see his young friend for one quiet afternoon. The effects of the illness had lingered. Rose had recovered but she was not strong. None the less Ruskin thought she had grown by an inch. She had a Parisian frock and a hat with a saucy feather '& she's awful', Ruskin wrote to Winnington. 'I shan't see her again for ever so long . . . and then she'll be somebody else — Children are as bad as clouds at sunrise — golden change — but change always — I was horribly sad this morning'.[29]

Ruskin had not been energetic in these last months but was so tired that his doctor friend John Simon ordered him to rest. Simon shrewdly realised that his patient's best relaxation would be in leaving the family home for a period. So that he would not be too far from his parents Ruskin simply crossed the Channel to Boulogne and went to the Hôtel des Bains (where, in 1848, he had stayed with Effie), subsequently taking lodgings, 'a little bedroom and parlour under the sand-hills north of the pier'.[30] Here he remained for seven weeks while John and Jane Simon made regular visits to the old people at Denmark Hill. Ruskin wrote to Simon with bulletins about his health, which gradually improved, but the letters to his doctor have not much other matter in them. He had little to report, for the days were spent idly. An additional manuscript belonging to the final chapters of *Præterita* —

and Ruskin's autobiography scarcely proceeds beyond this point in his life — recalls the Boulogne days as an untroubled, innocent existence, somehow out of time, away from the passing and changing world. 'If only I were back again in the bright little room at Boulogne — with a Rosie letter on the table — and for all other companionship, a shrimp or a limpet in a bucket . . .'[31] As often in the years to come, Ruskin was happiest when by himself but in correspondence with Rose. He did not need her presence. This summer she wrote regularly to him, and he to her, with messages that are now lost, except for one letter in which he describes a strawberry tea and very carefully reintroduces some of the thoughts about the kingdom of heaven that had been a theme of *Unto This Last*.[32]

In Boulogne Ruskin taught himself a little more Greek, drew shellfish he had found in the rock pools, drank Normandy cider and made his over-bookish French more natural. Here he was helped by the Huret family, fisherfolk who became his friends. One night, greatly daring, he went out in their boat, almost to England. At five o'clock in the morning they caught mackerel off Hastings, and on the way home to the French coast Ruskin took the tiller. The Hurets asked him to be godfather to their child Paul.[33] Gifts to the family, whom Ruskin always met when he subsequently travelled via Boulogne, are recorded in his accounts and correspondence for many years. His life with them in 1861 was to have been the subject of a chapter of *Præterita*, but this was never written.

Ruskin's stay in Boulogne was brought to its end by an invitation. A letter came asking Ruskin to stay at Harristown. It explained that the La Touches would be busy for the next few weeks, since their position in County Kildare meant that they had to entertain visitors from court. Young Prince Edward was receiving military training at the Curragh camp, not far from Harristown, and the Queen herself would soon be arriving to review the troops. But the La Touches trusted that Ruskin would spend a few days with them when they had done with these official obligations. Both Ruskin and his father, one collecting shrimps on a French beach and the other looking after an invalid wife in south London, suddenly saw the La Touches as much grander people than they had previously appeared. This in different ways disconcerted them. But there was no doubt that Ruskin would go to Ireland. He returned to London and in late August set off for Holyhead and Dublin.

Harristown was thirty miles from the Irish capital. The house was filled with marble and eighteenth-century paintings. Ruskin arrived there, bearing presents of scarves from his mother, late in the evening.

Rose was allowed downstairs to greet him. She, Emily and their brother Percy showed Ruskin round some of the park the next morning. They could not see all, for La Touche's estate covered 11,000 acres. In the days to come they went for rides and picnic outings. Rose taught Ruskin how to catch crayfish in the Liffey. This was all pleasant, but Ruskin was less at ease with the adults. As he strove to get on terms with 'The Master' he was shocked by contrasts of wealth and poverty in rural Ireland. He found that John La Touche was 'less worldly and with more heart than evangelicals usually have. But a park with no apparent limit, and half the country round paying rent, are curious Paraphernalia of Christianity'. He told his father that 'Mr L. certainly likes me better than he did', but still he could not speak openly to him.[34]

It was while talking to Maria La Touche that he confessed how little he now believed of the Protestant doctrines to which her husband subscribed. Maria already knew or suspected how far Ruskin had travelled from orthodoxy. She was none the less troubled by what he said, and exacted a promise from him that he would not publish his views for ten years. This was a curious compact, and Ruskin did not adhere to it. Perhaps he gave his word at Harristown because the atmosphere there became slightly frightening when questions of religious truth arose. On his last night a stately dinner had been arranged, at some other great house. Ruskin begged leave to be absent and to have a supper with the children. On the next day, 6 September 1861, he travelled back to England.

CHAPTER EIGHTEEN

1861–1862

After this inconclusive visit Ruskin stayed with the Cookes at Beckley, just outside Oxford, then went back to Denmark Hill. He had not been in London for more than a week before he set off for the continent. As though in flight, Ruskin crossed the Channel on 18 September 1861, to Boulogne; was in Paris a day later; and on the 22nd arrived at Bonneville in the Swiss Alps. There he remained until mid-October. He subsequently moved to Lucerne and was not to return to England — despite entreaties both from Rose and his parents — until the Ruskins' traditional Scottish celebrations of the New Year of 1862. Unhappy, writing nothing, by turns stubborn or irresolute, Ruskin worried his parents and vexed his friends. He could not understand how disturbed he had been by his Irish expedition. But he let his father know that his religious convictions were not clear, that he could never recover the certainties of his old faith, that he must reconsider his knowledge of the world. Ruskin's brooding had already led him to the mysterious invocations of the last chapters of *Modern Painters*. John James could not follow his son into these realms. Nor could anyone else. In this period Ruskin's mind begins to prefer symbolism to interpretative explanation, and his emotions about the real world are muffled or withheld.

Ruskin's parents were now obliged to abandon a plan to join their difficult son in the Alps, for his mother had again hurt herself in a fall. Their annual absence from Denmark Hill was used for cleaning the house, so they had to live elsewhere. As if to give themselves further annoyance, the aged couple now began to spend their time in an expanding suburb only two miles from Denmark Hill. 'Norwood is perforce our Switzerland of 1861', John James wrote to his friend Jane Simon.[1] Mr and Mrs Ruskin were staying at the Queen's Hotel, an establishment which now enters the private mythology of the Ruskin family. The hotel had been built in the late 1850s to cater for visitors to the Crystal Palace, and it was expensive. For many years thereafter it was known as the only London hotel south of the Thames in which gentlefolk would wish to stay.

John James Ruskin was not impressed. He took to writing a series of letters to the *Morning Post* to complain about modern hospitality. Signing himself 'Jonathan Oldbuck', he recalled that

> The perfection of inns of former days were those on the North-road, Barnby Moor, Ferrybridge, York etc, where the respectable landlords knew something of their visitor . . . had good waiters, and cheerful chambermaids serving the traveller with alacrity . . . the house furnished with quiet simplicity, and kept remarkably clean, for the landlords came generally out of noblemen's families. Now we have a vast and dreary house, with ponderous vulgar furniture, without landlord or landlady, but with agents working you through your meals and out of the house at the smallest possible outlay to them for your second quality of meat and drink — Knowing you only as No 23 or 150; sending a miserable underpaid German waiter to stare at you and misunderstand you . . .[2]

The unfortunate John James, longing for 'the luxury of a roadside inn, of moderate dimensions, with a smiling damsel to wait and a landlady to enquire what fare you prefer', took cross-tempered and solitary walks from the hotel, often to sample the devotions in local churches. He liked the services at Shirley Church, a Gothic revival building set below the Addington hills near Croydon (and for that reason his son and widow would bury him there), but sampled other places of worship. On Sunday evenings he went 'To hear a little creature in a little chapel of the name of *Tipple* — an extempore Baptist preacher — I like their hymns too — sung very sweetly without organ — . . .'[3] The Reverend S. A. Tipple was no intellectual, to judge from his book *Sunday Mornings at Norwood* (1895), and his theology would be harshly treated in *Fors Clavigera*. But to the seventy-five year-old John James, more inclined to quarrel with new hotels than with other people's eschatology, Tipple's simple hymns and prayers were a pleasure, and perhaps a comfort.

So was the thought of another person of Baptist persuasion. John James felt much fondness for Rose. In his letter-book we find the main heads of his daily letters to his son in Switzerland. We read, for instance, 'Fathers and sons better open. I am harrasd. with people wanting help. Miss Bell too soft . . . Miss Bell should sell school and not meddle with cash.'[4] Here was a frequent theme of the correspondence. But most of his letters seem to have discussed Rose, especially when, in early October 1861, she fell alarmingly ill.

* * * *

Because so much material relating to Rose was burnt by Ruskin's executors, we know little about her illnesses and the cause of her early death. It is probable that her health was afflicted in a number of ways. One of the servants of the La Touche family relates that she was tubercular. That is not unlikely. Another possibility is that Rose suffered from anorexia nervosa, a condition found in adolescents but quite unknown as a disease during Rose's lifetime, for it was not described in medical literature until 1879. Anorexic girls refuse to eat and can kill themselves through starvation. They do not develop breasts and they do not menstruate. Rose's unnatural thinness and some chance remarks of Ruskin's about her lack of appetite give only a little evidence to support the anorexic hypothesis. But a more general characteristic of anorexia nervosa is relevant to Rose's case. It is a neurotic condition which concerns a child's relations with her elders, and specifically with her parents. The fasting is a sign of obsessive concentration on the self. In its physical results there is a refusal of pubescence, for the sufferer does not wish to come to terms with maturity and adult life. Rose's later battle of wills with John and Maria La Touche — and with Ruskin, in so many ways a father to her — is characteristic of the anorexic personality. But the malady with which she was now struck down, in the autumn of 1861, appears to have begun in another kind of mental strain. While he was at Harristown Ruskin had told Rose that girls as well as boys should learn Greek: he may also have said that it was a Christian duty to do so. 'Rose didn't say anything at the time', Ruskin told his father, 'but as soon as I was gone — to work she sets'.[5] Rose apparently mastered the Greek alphabet in three hours. At Bonneville, on 8 October, Ruskin had a letter from her with a Greek salutation at its end: 'Peace be to thee'. His letters to her analysed Greek verbs and also contained some Christian instruction. They doubtless resembled the letters he was sending to Winnington. But Rose was not in the position of the happy girls at Miss Bell's school. Intense, lonely, already trying to make herself a child of Christ, she seems to have worked at her Greek until she broke down.

In letters exchanged between the La Touches, Ruskin and the elder Ruskins we may gather some clues about Rose's illness. Ruskin writes to his father 'What makes mama and you anxious about Rose's *brain* particularly — Did you hear or notice anything making you fear head-disease?'[6] and he defends his recommendation that she should study Greek. 'She should'nt overwork at anything — but if she learns any language at all, it should be that . . . If she is to be a Christian, she can only read her Bible with complete understanding in the Septuagint and GK text . . . To have learned *one* Greek verb accurately will make a difference in her habits of thought for ever after.'[7]

Perhaps Ruskin hesitated to write to the La Touche parents in such terms. In any case, the doctors who visited Harristown forbade Rose to study. As she gradually recovered, we hear a little more about her affliction. Maria La Touche reported that 'she seems perfectly well every day till about 5 o'clock, at that hour her countenance changes and she seems unable to occupy herself in any way, and very often at bedtime she has a slight return of the attack during which her consciousness is slightly impaired . . .'[8] These lingering symptoms at length disappeared. But a question remained in everyone's minds. Had Ruskin been a cause of this illness?

While Rose's precocious intelligence had been absorbed in her Greek tasks, Ruskin had been inventing children's rhymes for her, or perhaps about her. As he was preparing to leave Bonneville he wrote

Rosie, Posie — Rosie rare,
Rocks, & woods, & clouds, and air
Are all the colour of my pet:
And yet, & yet, & yet, & yet
She is not here — but, where?[9]

and on arriving at Lucerne he thought of Rose as he looked over the moonlit river and listened to the town clocks:

Rosie, pet, and Rosie, puss,
See, the moonlight's on the Reuss:
O'er the Alps the clouds lie loose,
Tossed about in silver tangles
. . .
Tower and steeple, chiming sadly
Say (unless I hear them badly)
'Good night, Liffey — bad night, Reuss —
Good night — Rosie — Posie — Puss'.[10]

These verses are inadequate by the standards of either an adult or a child. But they were not written to satisfy anyone. They are a baffled attempt at self-expression. Ruskin's relationship with Rose could not be defined or described, even to himself. He calls her his 'pet', as he would for some time to come. The serious child accepted this and perhaps was glad or relieved that this strange, lively, famous man had so much time for her. The contrast with her unbending father was extreme. Thus a playfulness, with much opportunity for loving teasing, was established between Ruskin and Rose. But the induction to Greek went beyond such playfulness, for it meant that they would be serious together. John La Touche distrusted these explorations. The stubborn simplicity of his position was that he 'does not believe in Greek'. The La Touches asked Ruskin not to send Rose a letter which was 'a long examination of the words *Life* and *Death*, from Greek downwards: & chiefly . . . dwelling on the last words'.[11] "Perhaps this was sensible. But when Maria La Touche asked Ruskin to write more 'in play' than in such grave terms, so as not to agitate her daughter's thoughts, something of Ruskin's emergent love began to be declared. He told his father that he kept 'as much to the childish tone as I can, because I can use terms of endearment which I could not in more serious letters'.[12]

We may recall at this point that Rose was thirteen years old. When we seek to gather information about her we find a child. One or two of her letters to Ruskin are preserved because he transcribed them in his own letters to Denmark Hill. Recovered from her illness, Rose tells Ruskin about her cats, her elder sister Emily's piano playing, her maid and the doings of the schoolroom. Then we hear something slightly different, about her mother:

> I got your letter, St C. on Saturday morning, after I had written the first part of this, just as I was going out riding. So I cd only give it one peep, and then tucked it into my riding-habit pocket and pinned it down, so that it could be talking to me while I was riding. I had to shut up my mouth — so tight, when I met Mamma, for she would have taken it and read it if I'd told her, and it wd'nt have gone on riding with me. As it was, we ran rather a chance of me, and pocket, and letter, and all, for Swallow (that's Emily's animal, that I always ride now) was in such tremendous spirits about having yr handwriting on his back, that she took to kicking and jumping in such a way, till I felt like a Stormy Petrel riding a great wave — so you may imagine I could not spare a hand to unpin my dear pocket, and had to wait in patience, till Swallow had done 'flying — flying South' (Tennyson — J. R.) and we were safe at home again.[13]

This was in early December of 1861, as the La Touches were preparing to leave Harristown for Norfolk Street. Soon, two further letters emphasise that there was a special bond between Ruskin and Rose from which her mother was excluded. One of Maria La Touche's letters to Switzerland had added that Rose sent her 'best love'. Ruskin wrote back to Rose saying that she might as well have sent her compliments, for there was neither 'best' nor 'worst' in love. This little stratagem elicited, for Ruskin, the following satisfying declaration:

> It was Mamma's invention, that, about my best love: I never sent a bit of it. I hardly ever send a message, if I can help it; I like to say it myself, and did I *ever* send my best love? as you say, one's love isn't best or worst — and, St C, if you please, if you've got my love already, how am I to send it? — No, I only write this to remind you of it, — and to wish you a merry Christmas; if it does nothing more, my wishing it won't make it unhappier — please have it, as much as you can.[14]

Next, on their arrival in London, Mrs La Touche sent Ruskin what he described to his father as 'a funny little dialogue' between herself and Rose:

> MRS L. Rosie, don't you wish St C would come home?
> ROSIE. Yes indeed I do. How tiresome of him.
> MRS L. Do you think he wants us at all?
> ROSIE. Well — perhaps he does. I think he wants to see me, Mamma.
> MRS L. And does'nt want to see me?
> ROSIE. Well — you know — well — Mamma, I think he likes your letters quite as much as yourself, and you write so very often — and I can't write often. So he *must* want to see *me*.[15]

Such exchanges allowed Ruskin to make disastrous assumptions about Rose. He thought that she was writing him love letters. Maria La Touche may not have been wise in the way that she oversaw her daughter's charms. Yet Ruskin's passion was such an unlikely one that it is hard to blame her for failing to realise what was about to happen. He was a difficult man to fathom, especially at this uncertain point of his middle life. In Switzerland in late December of 1861, waiting for the posts, Ruskin was idle and gloomy. On Christmas Eve, like a mindless youth, he spent an hour throwing stones at icicles in a ravine. He was approaching the nadir of the strange depression that had come on him a year before, and would persist for some months yet. Soon, when he took himself back to London, he would be able to see Rose, take her on expeditions, talk to her all day long if he wished. Yet the prospect did not enliven him. Nor, it seems, did their actual reunion. For the peculiar nature of Ruskin's devotion had become settled during his months in the Alps. His love for Rose was not in the nature of an active relationship with another person. It was, rather, a part of Ruskin's personality. This love, which would survive long separations and would not cease with Rose's death, was never dependent on their occasional meetings. Ruskin was always happier in his love if he had 'a word' from her, some 'message' or later a 'sign' of her sweet, distant existence.

While Ruskin was in Switzerland Rose sent him letters to which he attributed, ever afterwards, an exaggerated significance. Their messages expanded in his mind, growing from simple symbolism to a demonstration of the mystic coincidences of heavenly fates. In return for a sprig of oxalis, the trefoil flower known to the local peasantry as *pain du bon dieu*, Rose enclosed in a letter some shamrock, an emblem of the Trinity and the flower that St Patrick had used to rid Ireland of serpents.

From this time on, Ruskin would search Rose's frequent gifts of flowers for arcane and loving meanings. He believed that they indicated more than she could express by writing; and, in later years, he would often prefer to receive a flower from her than a letter, for her correspondence tended increasingly to be pious more than intimate. By 1866 Ruskin had acquired a silk wallet that would fit into his breast pocket. In this he carried his favourite letters from Rose, held flat between two plates of pure gold.[16] These letters probably dated from the earlier days of their acquaintance and would have included the star-letter, as Ruskin called it, that Rose wrote to him on the day after Christmas of 1861. Ruskin was then beginning his homeward journey and was at Basle. Rose was in London. They both, as subsequently transpired, noticed how brightly Venus shone that night; and Ruskin was to feel that there was something seraphic in Rose's clear, earnest and childish letter. She told 'Dearest St C' how 'our thoughts are crossing I suppose St C. & I thought particularly the day before Christmas, and Christmas day evening'; and then she told him how she had dreamed of him, and how 'we have a strange Peace on earth, because earth and its inhabitants do not all like the Peace that our Prince can bring . . .'[17]

Now Ruskin began to believe that Rose's character was saintly. When he came home, he told his father, he would need to find out 'if possible — whether Rosie was what her mother and you think her, an entirely simple child — or whether she was what *I* think her, — that is to say in an exquisitely beautiful and tender way, and *mixed* with much childishness, more subtle even than Catherine of Bologna'.[18]

When Ruskin first lost his reason, in 1876, he imagined that the dead Rose La Touche had sent him a flower from heaven. When he again went mad in 1878, St Catherine of Bologna, associated in Ruskin's mind with Rose and the martyred girl St Ursula, appears in the scrawled entries of his diary that were his last writings before the delirium began.[19] The notion of Rose's saintliness grew in Ruskin's imagination as he returned to England for the New Year of 1862. Her fourteenth birthday was on 3 January. Ruskin's present was an illuminated fourteenth-century psalter, the first of a number of similar gifts, precious ancient volumes that — one might easily imagine — had been written, painted and bound by angelic hands. Years later, to his exasperation and chagrin, Ruskin found that Rose had marked her place in one of these missals with a strip of torn newspaper. The real Rose was not a saint, as Ruskin continually discovered in her company. At this period, the happy time before her Christianity became obsessional, she was much like any other girl of her age and class, except that she was more intelligent than most and took her Christian duties seriously.

In the spring of 1862 Ruskin always called on the La Touches when he was in town. Official work often took him into London, for he was obliged to deal with mildew that had appeared on some sheets in the Turner bequest. He took Rose and her mother to hear a lecture given by Sir Richard Owen at the British Museum; and on occasion they came to tea at Denmark Hill. None of these meetings gave Ruskin any great pleasure, though in later years he would recall them with much lamentation, as though they had taken place in a time that knew nothing of catastrophe. In his home, Ruskin was withdrawn, even surly. 'I don't speak to anyone about anything', he wrote to Norton; 'if anyone talks to me, I go into the next room'.[20] This year he insisted on abandoning the usual family feast of his birthday on 8 February. A frank letter to John Brown speaks of his confusions and the realisation that he was in a crisis of his lifetime:

> Am I not in some curiously *unnatural* state of mind in this way — that at forty-three, instead of being able to settle to my middle-aged life like a middle-aged creature, I have more instincts of youth about me than when I was young, and am miserable because I cannot climb, or run, or wrestle, sing, or flirt — as I was when a youngster because I couldn't sit writing metaphysics all day long. Wrong at both ends of life . . .[21]

⋆ ⋆ ⋆ ⋆

Between the summer of 1860, the date of *Unto This Last*, and the latter part of 1864, when he wrote *Sesame and Lilies* for Rose La Touche, the flow of Ruskin's literary production was interrupted. He had left behind his role as a contemporary art critic; the support and encouragement of his father's pride had lost its force; and he had surrendered himself to depression and uncertainty. This bleak period contains one important work. The political papers known as *Munera Pulveris* are strikingly assured, as though Ruskin had found a confident direction. They show how much he was aligning his thought with Carlyle's. We should now consider the relations between the two men as they stood at this time.

Carlyle's was not a new inspiration. *The Stones of Venice* had been much affected by both *Heroes and Hero-Worship* (1841) and *Past and Present* (1843). Ruskin had acknowledged that Carlyle was the person 'to whom he owed more than any other English writer' in a lecture[22] given in December of 1854, and again declared his allegiance in print a few months later, in the third volume of *Modern Painters.* However, there was not a straightforward influence, and temperamental differences between the two men made their relations uneasy. In the 1850s Carlyle suspected that Ruskin was not totally serious. This was not because he had a fashionable wife, nor yet because his conversation seemed to scatter his thoughts rather than develop them. It was because of his devotion to art. Carlyle's disciple and biographer James Anthony Froude remarks of this period that 'he had long been acquainted with Ruskin, but hitherto there had been no close intimacy between them, *art* not being a subject especially interesting to him . . .'[23]

This is an understatement. In fact Carlyle had no eye for art and was irritated by artistic discussion. Here was a great obstacle to easy intercourse with Ruskin, and one reason why Carlyle's *Latter-Day Pamphlets* of 1850 had such a mixed effect on the younger writer. The deeper influence of *Latter-Day Pamphlets* was long delayed. Twenty years later, this idiosyncratic series of attacks on 'progress', democracy and modern government would be the first model for Ruskin's *Fors Clavigera.* In 1850, Ruskin had found himself both an admirer and then a victim of Carlyle's invective. Amid enraged criticisms, Carlyle issued eight of a projected series of twelve pamphlets. Then he seemed to have abandoned the project. The violence of *Latter-Day Pamphlets* broke many friendships, primarily that between Carlyle and Mill. However, not long after Ruskin had paid an official call — almost a call of homage — on Carlyle at Chelsea, one last denunciation had been published in August. 'Jesuitism' contains long passages directed against the fine arts. Though he was not mentioned by name, Ruskin realised with horror that he was Carlyle's target. All the separate *Latter-Day Pamphlets* are quoted and discussed in Ruskin's writing, but never this one. Nor was it ever mentioned in his conversation. Its sentences lay below his active mind and surfaced, in fragments, only when

Ruskin wrote the last, despairing chapter of *Praeterita*, his adieu to intellectual life. Carlyle had helped to bury the matter by never reissuing 'Jesuitism'. His first extant letter to Ruskin, of March 1851, gives warm praise both to the first volume of *The Stones of Venice* and *Notes on the Construction of Sheepfolds*. But Ruskin must have been disquieted that Carlyle did not even acknowledge receipt of the second and third volumes of his Venetian history. In January of 1855 Ruskin wrote to Carlyle to say 'how much your general influence has told on me, I know not — but I always confess it — or rather boast of it . . .'[24] However, we also gather from this letter that the two men had not met for three years.

Since that time, Ruskin's relations with Carlyle had improved: Carlyle had even given some encouragement to the later stages of *Modern Painters*. In December of 1859 Ruskin had presented him with a fine copy of Dürer's *Melancholia*. This was surely a symbolic gift; and we may well believe that the discussions in *Modern Painters V* of this engraving and the allied *The Knight and Death*, which speak of the 'dark anger' of the northern nations and of 'a mind contending with evil, and nobly prevailing over it; yet retaining the marks of the conquest, and never so entirely victorious as to conquer sadness', reveal Ruskin's view of Carlyle's character.[25] For his part, Carlyle became increasingly curious about Ruskin's worth. Uncharacteristically, he had gone so far as to attend the 'Tree Twigs' lecture in April of 1861.[26] It is possible that Ruskin's delivery of his address broke down because he saw Carlyle in the audience. Not long afterwards, Carlyle decided to use his protégé J. A. Froude, the recently appointed editor of *Fraser's Magazine*, to elicit some political papers from Ruskin. He wanted a development of *Unto This Last*. Ruskin received Froude's invitation as he was leaving England for his stay at Harristown and took some time to give a reply. He had no desire to follow Carlyle's advice that he should learn German and felt that he should study Plato and Xenophon's *Economist* before writing further about politics.

Another aspect of Carlyle's encouragement required much meditation. Writing to Ruskin about the first number of the *Unto This Last* essays, Carlyle had remarked: 'on yr. last page, and never till then, I pause slightly, not too sorrowfully, and appeal to a time coming. Noble is the spirit then too, my friend: but alas it is not Philanthropisms that will do then — it is Rhadamanthisms . . .'[27] Ruskin would have known what Carlyle meant by this last remark, which is grim in its reverberations. Carlyle was referring to a passage in his own 'Model Prisons' in which Rhadamanthus, in Greek mythology the stern judge of the dead, is invoked. When, at length, in the spring of 1862, Ruskin began to write *Munera Pulveris* he first of all reread *Latter-Day Pamphlets*. He wished to respond to Carlyle rather than to Spurgeon. And so *Munera Pulveris* is darker than *Unto This Last*; it is not philanthropic; it is learned and prophetic rather than parable-like. It is also, to a much greater degree than *Unto This Last*, unfinishable.

The papers that make up *Munera Pulveris* appeared in *Fraser's* in the months before April 1863, when they were terminated. They were irregularly issued and increasingly give the impression of having been improvised. There was no publication in book form until 1872. The essays then received their title[28] (from Horace: 'Rewards of the Dust'), and a dedication to Carlyle, and were given to the world at large, after much revision, as the first book from Ruskin's personal publishing company. The opening essay attempts to state basic definitions and incontrovertible political truths. It employs subheadings and numbered sections. Soon enough, however, Ruskin declares: 'Such being the general plan of the inquiry before us, I shall not limit myself to any consecutive following of it, having hardly any good hope of being able to complete so laborious a work . . . but from time to time, as I have leisure, shall endeavour to carry forward this part of that, as may be immediately possible . . .'[29]

By the third paper, Ruskin's schema breaks down completely, and we find a footnote that is almost half the length of the text. It concerns 'Homer, the Greek tragedians, Plato, Dante, Chaucer, Shakespeare and Goethe' and the way they knew that 'the highest truths and usefullest laws must be hunted for through whole picture-galleries of dreams, which to the vulgar seem dreams only'.[30] This long footnote (which was given a place in the main text in the book publication) is in some ways akin to the last chapters of *Modern Painters V*, though it finds its way through even more complex allusions. It is a difficult and remarkable piece of writing. Froude was impressed, and sent a letter to Ruskin to say how much he liked it. He also urged Ruskin toward social criticism of the highly placed, proposing an attack on Charles Longley, the recently enthroned Archbishop of Canterbury. Froude's enthusiasm was not shared by the publishers of his journal, Messrs Parker, Son and Brown. For Ruskin's writing had now become strangely experimental, while his views, when not opaque, had the dangerous and hostile vehemence of Carlyle. As the series of essays went on, the main text was haunted by further arcane footnotes. Its political proposals were scarcely of this world. They appeared to be dependent on notions of 'Kingship' quite at odds with democracy and modern life, while Ruskin's interest in charity — that mundane preoccupation of the Victorian middle class — would, the fourth essay warned *Fraser's* readers,

> lead us into the principles of government in general, and especially of that of the poor by the rich, discovering how the Graciousness joined with the Greatness, or Love with Majestas, is the true Dei Gratia, or Divine Right, of every form and manner of King; i.e. specifically, of the thrones, dominions, princedoms, virtues and powers of the earth: — of the thrones, stable, or 'ruling', literally right-doing powers ('rex eris, recte si facies'): — of the dominions — lordly, edifying, dominant and harmonious powers; chiefly domestic, over the 'built thing', domus, or house; and inherently twofold, Dominus and Domina; Lord and Lady — of the Princedoms, pre-eminent, incipient, creative and demonstrative powers; thus poetic and mercantile, in the 'princeps carmen deduxisse' and the merchant-prince: — of the Virtues or Courages; militant, guiding, or Ducal powers: — and finally of the Strengths, or Forces pure; magistral powers, of the More over the less, and the forceful and free over the weak and servile elements of life.[31]

'Subject enough for the next paper . . .', Ruskin went on, as he promised more to his readers. Messrs Parker, Son and Brown cannot have been eager to publish further ruminations of this sort. When, at the end of the sixth long essay, Ruskin announced that 'the present paper completes the definitions necessary for future service. The next in order will be the first chapter of the body of the work', they realised that is was opportune to finish.[32] Ruskin evidently proposed to write a bizarre book in their pages, a treatise of which the conclusion was both remote and unimaginable. Apologies were made, thanks given, and the series stopped.

At the time, Ruskin was innocently astonished and hurt that there were publishers who did not want his contributions to their periodicals. In his later years he sometimes said or implied that his papers in *Fraser's* and the *Cornhill* had ended because of their challenging contents. He was perhaps half-consciously associating his own career with the troubles that had led Carlyle to abandon his *Latter-Day Pamphlets*. But the difficulty lay only partly in Ruskin's unconventional approach to social problems. Neither the manner, the subjects, nor the implications of his writing were suited to magazines, and he made no attempt to adjust his essays to the requirements of journalism. A third abandoned series, the work we now know as *The Cestus of Aglaia* (1865: but not published in book form until it appeared in the Library

Edition in 1905) was to sit even more uneasily in the pages of the *Art Journal*. Although he could not have known it, Ruskin's *Munera Pulveris* was helping him to find a way toward the unique expression (and, necessarily, the self-publication) of *Fors Clavigera*, a series of letters that exists quite outside the norms of Victorian periodical literature. After *Munera Pulveris*, we should note, Ruskin was unable to contribute to the more measured discussions of the contemporary press. Rational and liberal values increasingly held sway in widely read magazines, as was proper. Ruskin's books belong to a quite different type of literature.

★ ★ ★ ★

This was a puzzling time for those who followed Ruskin's writings. Some readers lamented his eccentricities, others were amused and not a few were disturbed. A new friend, Frederic Harrison, was the author of much interesting commentary on Ruskin. He was the last of those associates whom Ruskin had met at the Working Men's College, was a welcome guest at Denmark Hill and understood some aspects of Ruskin's writing rather well. But his view of *Munera Pulveris* was that 'looking back over the long succession of efforts to construct a systematic sociology, which as a complete scheme has only in recent times been planned out by Spencer and Comte, it is difficult to abstain from censuring Ruskin for toying with a subject of which he was profoundly ignorant, for he knew as little of the literature of philosophy as of the practical life of our age'.[33] Harrison was himself a Comtian positivist, and could see no merit in a cultural approach to modern political problems. Ruskin knew of no other approach, and it would be some time before he studied — to the extent he felt they deserved study — the sociologists and political economists Harrison respected. Harrison brought fresh ideas to Denmark Hill, and was surprised that they were not gratefully received. The Ruskins regarded him rather as they had responded to F. J. Furnivall. They thought of him as a pleasant young radical: amiable, well-meaning but foolish. There was wisdom in contemporary England, but it was not to be found in the Working Men's College. Ruskin found himself more and more drawn to the circle around Carlyle. In Cheyne Row he entered an atmosphere that, although somewhat forbidding, was fiery. It was worth coming to terms with the pain and anger of Carlyle's personality. For then one could appreciate his talk of ultimate things, nobler far than consideration of parliaments and newspapers.

At Cheyne Row Ruskin formed a sort of companionship with Froude. It would not be a warm friendship for twenty years. The two men were brought closer, after Carlyle's death in 1881, by their bereavement. But in the 1860s and 1870s they were allied only because each knew that they stood in a filial relation to Carlyle. Ruskin felt a little the same way toward Arthur Helps, 'a true thinker', the author of *Friends in Council* (1847–59) and, in 1871, of *Conversations on War and General Culture*, of which Ruskin was the dedicatee. Such serious intellectuals as these followed Carlyle in wishing to know how men should govern, in this universe that is not ruled by men's laws. Helps liked to give weekend parties at which these matters were discussed. Ruskin did not attend them but preferred to go to Chelsea to put himself under Carlyle's personal tutelage.

It was as well that other friends of Ruskin's had a more pragmatic approach to political questions. First among them was John Simon, at this period Medical Officer of the Privy Council. His interests in housing and public health had a useful effect on Ruskin, for he persuaded him that abstract ideas seldom help the poor. John Simon, his wife Jane and their adopted daughter 'Boo' were friends of Ruskin's all their lives. Since the friendship was undemanding and uncomplicated it does not often appear in the dramas of Ruskin's later life. It was none the less real, and was not unsung. For instance because the Simons loved to take their holidays in Switzerland Ruskin wrote some of the Alpine sections of *Præterita* especially for their pleasure.

The kind, forthright and sympathetic Simons were also close to the elder Ruskins, and they often heard complaints, this spring of 1862, about Ruskin's unconcealed depression. 'I trust that John is in a better mood when he comes to you', John James wrote to Jane Simon, 'than he appeared to be in the other Evening. There is too much of a Don't Careishness about him — a sort of nought is everything and everything is nought way hanging about him . . . I hope change of air & Switzerland will give him tone again . . .'[34] Feeling hopeless and desolate in London, Ruskin had decided to return to the Alps. When he was not excited by Carlyle's urging, he was listless and could find neither purpose nor amusement. He asked Simon for medical advice. The doctor could only recommend a change of scene when Ruskin described symptoms as vague as these: 'I don't know, quite — now — *when* I am worried, and only find it out by not sleeping — or dreaming sad dreams — perhaps you know better than I do, when I am, by my face — But these *little* worries don't matter if I can only find my way out of them — some day or other — the great one is not knowing well what is — or is likely — to become of me.'[35] Although he could not say so, Ruskin's unhappiness and indecision were caused by two people more truly 'at both ends of life' (to repeat the phrase he had used to John Brown) than he was himself. He could not strike the right relationship either with young Rose or with his aged father. Rose, 'Bouton' as he now called her, using the French for 'bud', he could not possibly regard as an adult. John James still treated him as though he were not quite grown up. For all the love between them, father and son irritated each other, especially now that John James had been made short-tempered by the pains of gravel, the condition that in two years would cause his death. In July, Ruskin told Lady Trevelyan:

> I know my father is ill — but I cannot stay at home just now, or should fall indubitably ill myself also, which would make him worse. He has more pleasure if I am able to write him a cheerful letter than generally when I'm there — for we disagree about all the Universe, and it vexes him — and more than vexes me. If he loved me less — and believed in me more — we should get on — but his whole life is bound up in me — and yet he thinks me a fool — that is to say — he is mightily pleased if I write anything that has big words and no sense in it — and would give half his fortune to make me a member of parliament if he thought I would talk — provided only the talk hurt nobody & was in all the papers.
>
> This form of affection galls me like hot iron — and I am in a state of subdued fury whenever I am at home which dries all the marrow out of every bone in me.[36]

Ruskin took his complaints to Rose, at her parents' house in Mayfair. He told Simon, 'I had a walk in the East wind on Friday — R. maintaining it would do me good. Such a headache (and worse ache) as I had after it!'[37] Ruskin's headaches, neuralgic twitches and pains were always reported to Rose, for she would 'pet' him if he lamented some minor ailment. At the same time he wailed to all and sundry, as if this were all in jest, that Rose cared no more for him than for her cat. People Ruskin scarcely knew, like Lady Naesmith, whom he had met in Switzerland the previous year, received strange letters in which he declared that 'Yes — I shall be at Lucerne this year early . . . That is to say, if I survive Rosie's going back to Ireland which I don't think likely'; and to Lady Naesmith he sent many of Rose's verses, which he carefully copied out:

> And the crocuses were sleeping
> Dreaming — in their earthly rest,
> And the little birds were wishing
> It was time to make their nest . . .[38]

Rose's naïve rhymes were distributed by Ruskin to a number of adult friends who indulged his enthusiasm for them. He might have been able to take a more distant and more qualified view of Rose's attainments when he went to stay at Winnington School for a fortnight after 12 March; but the girls there, lively and pensive though they were, meant little to him in comparison with 'Bouton', of whom he continually talked. Back in London, as he struggled to record her features in watercolour, his obsession must have been apparent. But still nobody realised that his interest in Rose was about to become an uncontrollable passion. The elder La Touches even encouraged him, for at the end of their stay in England they suggested that Ruskin should become their neighbour, and take 'A little cottage dwelling-house, and garden, and field, just beside their own river, and outside their park wall'.[39]

In fact, as things turned out, Ruskin would not see Rose for more than three years after the La Touches left London on 22 April 1862. 'They took the child away from me —', Ruskin later told Mrs Cowper as he accused Rose's parents of ruining his life, '. . . and since that day of April 1862, I have never had one happy hour, — all my work has been wrecked — all my usefulness taken from me . . .' At the time in question, however, there was amity between the Ruskin and La Touche families. Once Rose had departed Ruskin hastened to finish the first of his papers for *Fraser's Magazine* and wrote a preface to the book publication of *Unto This Last*. Asking John Simon to see this introduction through the press, he then left for the continent, taking with him Edward and Georgiana Burne-Jones. 'Ned' and 'Georgie' had left their infant son Philip with his grandmother so that Ruskin could give them a holiday. This Philip was his godson, but Ruskin — who never troubled to show especial affection for his godchildren — was far more interested in Edward and Georgiana, whom he called his "children" and treated as such. He 'did everything *en prince*', Georgiana Burne-Jones was to recall: 'and had invited us as guests for the whole time, but again in his courtesy agreed to ease our mind by promising to accept the studies that Edward should make while in Italy, and all was arranged and done by him as kindly and thoughtfully as if we had indeed been really his "children".'[40] As so often, Ruskin could be wonderfully kind to people he wished to make happy, and the Burne-Joneses were quite unaware of the tensions that had recently made him so irritable. His desire to be generous now led Ruskin to be angry with his father. John James had seen his money wasted by his son in various ways, 'what with his wife & his pictures & other things' for a number of years. He had recently been asked yet again to give money to Margaret Bell's school, and to Rossetti; while in February he had been shocked by the suicide of Lizzie Siddall, Rossetti's wife. He suspected that to be interested in Pre-Raphaelitism was an expensive way to mix with people of dubious morals. Some of this unease was communicated to his son, who then wrote:

> I sent you what you would feel an unkind letter about pride &c. but I wanted to prevent your writing things to me just now which would have done me harm, all the more if I did not answer them. And I wrote that letter under the immediate sorrow caused to me by your being deprived of the pleasure and the real good which a man such as Jones is would be to both you & my mother — could you understand him. In nothing is that same 'pride' more beautiful than in the way it has destroyed through life your power of judging noble character. You and my mother used to be delighted when I associated with men like Lords March and Ward — men who had their drawers filled with pictures of naked bawds — who walked openly with their harlots in the sweet country lanes — men who swore, who diced, who drank, who knew *nothing* except the names of racehorses — who had no feelings but those of brutes — whose conversation at the very hall dinner table would have made prostitutes blush for them — and villains rebuke them — men who if they could, would have robbed me of my money at the gaming table — and laughed at me if I had fallen into their vices — & died of them; And you are grieved, and you try all you can to withdraw me from the company of a man like Jones, whose life is as pure as an archangels, whose genius is as strange & high as that of Albert Dürer or Hans Memling — who loves me with a love as of a brother — and far more — of a devoted friend — whose knowledge of history and of poetry is as rich and varied, nay — far more rich and varied, and incomparably more *scholarly*, than Walter Scott's was at his age . . .
>
> I am forced to speak openly at last in this matter, because I cannot possibly bear the injustice you do my noble friends in thinking they do me harm — and it is also very bad both for my mother and you to have the gnawing feeling of continual disagreement with me in such matters. Try and correct yourself at least in this one mistake — ask Jones out to any quiet dinner — ask him about me — ask him anything you want to know about medieval history — and try to forget that he is poor. I wish you to do this, observe, entirely for your own sake — that you may have the

> pleasure of knowing one of your son's real friends, and one of the most richly gifted, naturally, of modern painters . . .[41]

This is an emotional letter: but it was carefully written, and Ruskin was at pains to ensure that his father would be enlightened, not hurt. Its anger had been aroused not only by John James's prejudices. Ruskin hated the thought that the world might contain such different men as the aristocrats he had known in his youth and the gentle, eager Burne-Jones. His faith in his protégé was almost devout and furthermore was private. Although Ruskin had occasionally announced — to a correspondent like Lady Naesmith — that Burne-Jones 'will, I believe, if he is spared, take lead of the PRBs', he never wrote of this conviction. Nor did he wish to encourage him in the way he had 'hammered' Brett and Inchbold four summers previously. They were realists, landscapists and professional artists. Jones was a self-taught figure painter who had already approached the limits of his technical ability. Realising this, Ruskin changed the nature of his teaching. He talked to Jones about the poetic, romantic and medieval side of his inspiration; he also pointed him toward models in early Italian art. The little party travelled to Lucerne and then went over the St Gothard pass, staying in the Swiss inns Ruskin knew so well. 'I have a vision', Georgiana would later recall, 'of us all three sitting together, in a room with an exquisitely clean bare-boarded floor, and Mr Ruskin reading Keats to us'.[42] At Milan they copied frescoes together before Ruskin sent his young friends on to Verona and Venice. He himself remained in Milan to work on Bernardino Luini. Here was one of the secondary Italian masters for whom he felt an admiration partly born of the fact that he had 'discovered' their work before other connoisseurs. Ruskin sent a report on Luini to the Arundel Society, tinkered with his *Fraser's* essays and spent weeks in copying Luini's *St Catherine* in San Maurizio (Monastero Maggiore). This is a life-size copy, patched together from pieces of paper of different sizes and shapes. Despite its improvised construction it is a beautiful piece of work. Ruskin was proud of it and in later years saw that it was prominently hung in his drawing schools at Oxford. There was another reason why he liked the copy. While he was painting it he was receiving letters from Rose every few days; and it would always remind him of a time when he was on his own, without responsibilities for others, and happily in love.

CHAPTER NINETEEN

1862–1863

Rose was trying to write her most charming and loving letters to Ruskin because the plan for him to have a house on the Harristown estate had been abandoned. The elder La Touches had decided that 'their Irish neighbours would never understand it', and had withdrawn their offer. In truth Ruskin had not greatly desired the house; no one who could live wherever they wished would set up home in County Kildare: but he used the opportunity to have 'a fine old quarrel with Rosie . . . for not helping me enough' and thus received sweet letters from her, designed to smooth his temper by teasing him.[1] Rose had found a good place for writing letters, in a tree. From this eyrie, as the summer wore on, she addressed the author of *Modern Painters*, the friend of Froude and Carlyle, in more serious vein. These letters concerned religion. Ruskin probably replied with the sort of biblical exegesis he wrote on Sundays to the girls at Winnington. But Rose did not have the attitudes of her contemporaries at Miss Bell's school. She did not enquire about Christianity, but asserted it, for she had inherited certainties from her father. In a few months, for the first time, she would venture to criticise Ruskin for his wavering faith.

Ruskin left Milan at the beginning of August 1862, anxious to escape the heat, and travelled into the Alps. Walking up the Salève, feeling curiously at home now that he was in the hills above Geneva, he decided not to return to England for his mother's birthday on 2 September, as he had promised to do. There is a sparse diary for this period. Ruskin looked out the volume in 1884, when he was making plans for *Præterita*, and wrote some further comments in it. Later expressions of sorrow that he could ever have been cruel to his parents therefore appear beside his thoughts of the time. 'Desolate now in due punishment', he considered the entry for 7 August 1862 and wrote 'The fatal walk up Salève when I decided to stay in Savoy'.[2] The actual entry for that day reads: 'Resolve to have some more Turners and if I live, some of my own way at last. Stay here accordingly.'[3] As often before, the mere thought of buying watercolours by Turner seemed to represent a revolt against his father's authority. The phrase 'if I live' — which is paralleled in his correspondence of these weeks — suggests that Ruskin, whose health allowed him to stride over mountains, was trying to persuade himself that he was dying. He knew, of course, that it was his father and mother who were near the end of life. But he concentrated on his own wishes in order to break his dependence on his parents. Now he began to tell his father of different plans to find a new home. He wrote to John James to tell him that he might share a house with the bereaved Rossetti. This unlikely plan was soon dropped and it became apparent to Ruskin that the peace and freedom he sought were likely to be found in Switzerland. With Couttet, who had now joined him (and with Crawley, as always) he drove from Geneva into the surrounding country, looking for what he called 'lodgings'. By the middle of August he had found them, and had taken up residence in two houses in Mornex. The larger of them was a splendid example of the *chalet orné*, of whose minor English imitations in the form of 'Swiss cottages' he had written so scornfully, years before, in *The Poetry of Architecture*. A previous tenant had been the Empress of Russia. Ruskin needed plenty of space, for he was adding to his establishment. He invited the Simons to come to stay. He also summoned, from his home in the lodge at Denmark Hill, George Allen. The dutiful retainer then struggled across Europe with his wife Hannah, their two infant children, books, tools, Turner drawings and a printing press.

> I have slept in my new house two nights [Ruskin now wrote to his father] and passed the days in the garden, and am much pleased. The bedroom window opens on a wooden gallery about six or seven feet above the garden; beneath, there is a bed of white convolvulus rising in three spires, as high as the cottage, on hop-poles; then the garden slopes south-east, steeply; having an ever-running spring about four yards from the door, falling out of upright wooden pipes into a stone basin, forming a lovely clear pool. Beds of crimson and blue convolvulus, marigold, nasturtium, and chrysanthemum, with intermediate cabbage and artichoke, occupy the most of the little space, all afire; surrounded by a rough mossy low stone wall, about a foot and a half high at the bottom of the garden; whence the ground slopes precipitously, part grass, part vines, to a ravine about four hundred feet deep; the torrent at the bottom seen for about two miles up — among its granite blocks (something like view from Lynton in Devonshire); but on the other side of the ravine extends the lovely plain of La Roche, to the foot of the Brezon, above which I have the Mont du Reposoir, and then the Aiguille de Varens; then Mont Blanc and the Grandes Jurasses and the Aiguille Verte; and lastly the Mole on the left, where my own pear-trees come into the panorama and guide back to the

> marigolds. I keep, however, my old rooms here, for the rooms in my new house — delicious in the morning and evening — have too much sun in the middle of the day; here I have shade and larger space. The two houses are just about a hundred or a hundred and fifty yards apart. I sleep at the Empress's — (Crawley and Allen above me, Couttet here); dress chiefly outside in my balcony, the air being as soft as in Italy; then walk over here, after a turn round the garden; find breakfast laid by Franceline, and my little table beside it with Horace and Xenophon. Read till eleven; walk or garden till half-past one. Dine here, where I have a nice little dining-room; back into garden, tea among my convolvuluses there — with sunset on the Alps opposite; bed at nine or half-past.[4]

In this agreeable situation, and with such materials as his Horace and Xenophon, Ruskin continued his examination of political principles for *Fraser's Magazine*. His essays were scarcely noticed by the rest of the press but there were some family friends who sought to give him advice. One of them, again, was Dr John Brown of Edinburgh. He wrote both to Ruskin and to his father with criticisms. Ruskin replied to Brown to assure him that 'you will change your mind about these political economy papers as they go on. I do not give three years thought deliberately, and ten years thought at intervals, to a subject which I have at heart without knowing what I am about in it . . .'[5] Brown must have persisted in his reservations, and done so to Ruskin's annoyance, for we next find two letters in which he shows a characteristic of his later years: how prepared he was to take the battle to those well-meaning men who dealt only in demurrals. In the first of these letters Ruskin wrote that

> The Science of Political Economy *is* a Lie, wholly and to the very root (as hitherto taught). It is also the Damnedest, That is to say the most utterly and to the Lowest Pit condemned of God and His Angels, that the Devil, or Betrayer of Man, has yet invented except his (the Devil's) theory of Sanctification. To this 'Science' and to this alone (the Professed and organised pursuit of Money) is owing *All* the evil of modern days. I say All. The Monastic Theory is at an end. It is now the Money theory which corrupts the Church, corrupts the household life, destroys honour, beauty and life throughout the universe . . . They don't know what they are talking about. They don't even know what Money is, but tacitly assume that money is desirable as a sign of wealth, without defining Wealth itself. Try to define Wealth yourself, and you will soon begin to see where the bottom fails . . .[6]

In his next letter, presumably in response to a request from Brown that he should not be so agitated, Ruskin declared that

> there is no 'state of mind' indicated in my saying this. I write it as the cool, resolute result of ten years thought and sight. — I write it as coolly as I should a statement respecting the square of the hypoteneuse. If my hand shakes, it is from more general nervousness, vexation about my mother . . . The matter of the letter is as deliberate as if I were stating an equation to you or a chemical analysis. You say I should 'go and be cheerful'. I don't know what your Edinburgh streets afford of recreative sight. Our London ones afford not much. My only way of being cheerful is precisely the way I said, to shut myself up and look at weeds and stones, for as soon as I see or hear what human creatures are suffering of pain, & saying of absurdity, I get about as cheerful as I should be in a sheepfold strewed hurdle-deep with bloody carcases, with a herd of wolves and monkeys howling and gibbering on the top of them . . .[7]

Although the two men would always remain on amicable terms — the description of the dog Spitz, in *Præterita*, was a final gift for the author of the once famous *Rab and his Friends* — Ruskin now thought less of Brown's character. Ruskin's political economy had its antecedents; some of its aspects were shared with others: but his views were none the less so personal and so hotly defended that they separated him from 'common-sensical' friends. Far away from the life of British cities, appalled that cholera and misery should reign in them, Ruskin's political emotions were both involved and distant. At Mornex, he wandered through the meadows, read Dante, drew the wonderful views from his mountain home, tried to print tracings from Turner on his press, conducted Allen on geological rambles, collected wild flowers and paved his courtyard with stones from the ravine: flat shards of gneiss transported by the ancient donkey belonging to a widow to whom he wished to give charity. Allen would always recall how Ruskin knelt to pray with a peasant woman at a wayside chapel, in a sudden fit of sympathy with the religious life of the poor. It is probable that he now abandoned the custom of reading through the English service with his household.

Ruskin was leading his own life, as he had chosen to do. But although he often announced that he would 'seldom' leave his new home, there were many matters that tied him to England, and to Ireland. The La Touches' reaction to his *Fraser's* papers is not known. Perhaps they had none. They were not particularly alert to current intellectual affairs, unless they concerned religion. Maria La Touche was liberal in her opinions of other people's faiths, and often was curious to know how far that liberalism might be extended. Her husband, on the other hand, was vigilant against error. As Rose now began to define her own religion she discovered that it probably differed from Ruskin's. Was not the famous writer therefore wrong? John La Touche left her in no doubt that this was the case.

* * * *

After Rose's and Ruskin's deaths, and after their correspondence had been destroyed, there remained one touching personal document. Hidden behind a bookshelf at Ruskin's home at Brantwood was the manuscript diary and autobiography that Rose wrote in 1861 and 1867.[8] The earlier part of this notebook records the La Touches' travels through France and Italy in 1861. Its latter pages were written at the period of Rose's nineteenth birthday, when she decided to review her mental and spiritual life. From this source we learn of the torments of her adolescent years, of her relations with her parents and of the illnesses which — though Rose scarcely realised this — were a consequence of her striving for a flawless religious identity. In 1867, looking back to her childhood, Rose dwelt on her days in the Harristown schoolroom and thought about the various governesses who had taught her. She reflected that she 'had some impertinence . . . and a certain amount of wilfulness' and recounts that although she was eager for learning she had not taken to grammar or mental arithmetic.[9] This was surely not unusual in any young girl, but Rose was inclined to be censorious with her younger self: for at that age, she wrote, she had not developed 'the child's ambition of doing right'. From the internal evidence of this diary it appears that it was in 1862, and probably at the time when Ruskin was at Mornex, that the aim of leading a consciously religious life took hold of her. The person responsible was John La Touche. 'I took in all my father's doctrines', Rose stated. 'He taught me that there was but the one thing needful, one subject worthy of thought, one aim worth living for, one rule for conduct, namely God's Holy Word.' After many discussions alone with her father she had 'the one aim of being perfect'.[10] This, alas, led Rose not only to prayer but to fasting; and, if she was indeed anorexic, it is possible that, in trying to emulate Christ's fasting for forty days and nights, she now began the cycle of physical and psychological disorders that eventually would kill her.

In Rose's account of her early life one senses a wish that she herself could have experienced conversion, as her father had. 'The Master' had never been a warm-hearted man but, as Rose's religious education continued, John La Touche and his daughter found for the first time that they had something in common. They prayed together, read the Bible together and came to regard each other as belonging to the elect, separated from those who did not believe as they believed. John La Touche's strong will was transferred to Rose in a way that isolated father and daughter from other members of their family. Rose's mother was not serious, her sister Emily was not serious. Percy was an unsatisfactory boy. He would shortly be expelled from Harrow School. This showed Rose and her father how easy it had been for Satan to enter their own home. Inevitably, Rose was affected by tensions at Harristown that had been partly created by her fervent beliefs. She was often in pain with migraines. When she wrote her short autobiography she had been ill many times and had consulted many doctors. Still she could not consider that there was any connection between her religious exercises and her health. She thought that her afflictions had come upon her because she had encountered difficulties on the way to a true faith. The 'constant thought' she gave to such problems 'I am sure made me irritable and unchildlike too. So I got ill and things used to make my head ache constantly. I was not often happy'.[11]

Not much in Rose's sad, intense and bewildered notebook refers directly to 'Mr Ruskin', as she calls him. Two passages, however, discuss his influence. Rose writes that 'I think it was Mr Ruskin's teaching when I was about twelve years old that made me first take to looking after the poor — at least that made me first see it as a thing Right, and a part of Christ's love . . .'[12] In her pony and trap, Rose had carried puddings and tracts to the local peasantry for some years. She was a welcomed visitor to the cabins and hovels of her father's part of the county. She was no real philanthropist. Like her father and like Spurgeon who had converted her father, she thought more of salvation and heaven than of the improvement of life on this earth. In practice this meant that she thought about belief. Here she encountered the problem of Ruskin's faith. 'Mr Ruskin did not only teach me that which is good . . .', the autobiography asserts. 'I do not believe he ever taught me evil, but I used to hear conversations in London . . . of which I understood more than anyone thought, doubts about Truth said earnestly, unbelief of Christ's faith spoken of lightly (this was not by him) and indeed more pains taken by them how all might be false, than how the whole thing I lived by might be true . . .'[13]

This passage must refer to the spring of 1862, when Rose was in Norfolk Street and Ruskin had returned from his first extended sojourn in Switzerland. Now, in the late autumn and winter of that year, the question of faith became an issue. Ruskin had continued to discuss religion in his letters to Maria La Touche, and she now showed Rose parts of them that may not have been intended for her eyes. Rose wrote to Ruskin at Mornex, 'highly vexed', as Ruskin reported matters to his father, by his 'heathenism'. She told him that 'for the sake of all Truth, and Love, you must not give the one true Good — containing all others, God — up'.[14] And finally she asked him, 'How could one love you, if you were a pagan?'[15]

Many other people who were interested in Ruskin believed that he was abandoning his faith. Some of his devotional thought remains obscure, for while his mother was alive he took care to conceal his most errant sentiments. He brooded on heavenly mysteries in occultation, alone in the mountains. Perhaps Mornex encouraged unorthodoxy. Certainly it was while he remained in the Alps that he wrote to Maria La Touche with the opinions that distressed Rose. When he was in London his religious identity was rather different. To an old family friend like C. H. Woodd, an evangelical Hampstead wine merchant, Ruskin might not have seemed much changed from the young man who had appreciated the sermons of Dale and Melvill. Others found him heretical. This was because Ruskin could seldom resist arguing with clergymen. In London, he did not lack opportunities to do so, either at the Working Men's College or in his own home. Peter Bayne, for instance, was occasionally a visitor to Denmark Hill at this period. He was the editor of the *Weekly Review*, the organ of English Presbyterianism, and in 1860 had published *Terrorism for Christ's Sake*, a foolish pamphlet in which he had attempted to adjudicate between Carlyle and Spurgeon.[16] Bayne was a tiresome man, and in 1861 Carlyle had fled from a dinner with John James Ruskin when his critic suddenly arrived at the house. Bayne had more sense, though, than other religious people known to the Ruskins. Spurgeon, immersing dozens of converts in a huge pool beneath his pulpit at the Metropolitan Tabernacle (among them John La Touche, probably in early 1863), was not an extreme case of south London religious zeal. Henry Ritchie, John James's trusted clerk in the Billiter Street office, was an Irvingite. The Ruskins occasionally went to services conducted by the Reverend John Cumming, a millenarian within the Anglican Church who published, in 1861, *The End of the World in 1862*. Another visitor to Denmark Hill, to whom Ruskin gave money and introductions to publishers, was Henry Wentworth Monk, a Canadian who had been divinely appointed to found a Jewish state in the Holy Land as a prelude to the Millennium. Enormously bearded, with hair that fell below his shoulders (for he had sworn not to cut his locks until the kingdom of heaven was established on earth), Monk rather puzzled Ruskin's old mother. But it is not clear that she distrusted him, while we know that she feared free-thinkers such as Carlyle.

Beliefs such as were held by Monk, Ritchie and Cumming were the result of a conviction that the Bible contained inerrant prophecies. Ruskin had known for many years that the things claimed by such men could not be true, and that one kind of study of the Bible led to bigotry and fanaticism. Ruskin's own religion was Biblical above all else, and his study of the Book allowed him to have flexible beliefs. The Bible, as it were, belonged to him: dogma and theology were the artificial creations of other men. Ruskin read the Bible daily, not mechanically but with alert and sensitive attention, and he knew much of it by heart. He never needed recourse to a concordance. The Bible is the first influence on Ruskin's prose because it so fully occupied his mind, and the texture of his thought — grave, lyrical, admonitory, close to worship — is also biblical. His love of the Book was not uncritical. He knew from his geological studies, from enlightened friends, and from common sense, that many of its most crucial passages had to be treated as metaphor or legend. In such matters Ruskin is typical of advanced attitudes to religious study in the middle years of the nineteenth century. He knew the 'Broad Church' movement at first hand, since he had worked with Maurice, Kingsley and others. It is possible that he met Benjamin Jowett in the early 1860s. He was, in any case, aware of the furore aroused by *Essays and Reviews* (1861) in which a number of liberal thinkers, Jowett among them, had argued that the Bible must be examined critically, as we would study any other ancient text. Furthermore, Ruskin's admiration for Carlyle had helped convince him of the need for a living personal religion free from the 'dull-droning drowsing inanity' of modern Protestantism; and his acquaintance with Froude had confirmed that men of intellect must not be meek when churchmen wish to instruct them.

None the less, Ruskin was not a member of the 'Broad Church' movement. He often thought that Dean Stanley, Maurice and Kingsley were just as complacent as the conservative churchmen of the older party. The evidence that he actually read their books, even including *Essays and Reviews*, is elusive or non-existent. Ruskin's own contribution to intelligent and liberal discussion of the Bible is not in that sort of publication. It is found, of course, in private letters to a group of Cheshire schoolchildren. Through Winnington Ruskin now, from his distant abode in Switzerland, took sides in a religious controversy and at the same time finally lost his respect for Maurice. Though he witnessed the Colenso dispute from afar, it affected him deeply. Margaret Bell had long been a friend of John Colenso, the Cornishman and Cambridge evangelical who in 1853 had become the first Bishop of Natal. Colenso had begun his work in this ministry by learning Zulu, whose grammar he published in 1855. He had then translated Holy Scripture, including the whole of the New Testament, into the language. The enterprise led him to question the scriptures themselves. Asked by those to whom he taught Genesis '"Is all that true?"' 'My heart', he wrote, 'answered in the words of the Prophet, Shall a man speak lies in the name of the Lord? I dared not do so.'[17]

Ruskin, who inherited from his father a spirited dislike of missionaries, might not normally have been impressed by Colenso's work in South Africa. But when the Bishop returned to England in 1862 to publish *The Pentateuch and the Book of Joshua Critically Examined*, in which he demonstrated, or confessed, that the first five books of the Old Testament could not be treated except with intellectual reservations, Ruskin was struck by Colenso's integrity.[18] He was also distressed that Maurice, hitherto Colenso's friend, then abandoned him. Colenso, amid the fierce resentment caused by his book, sought refuge at Winnington, where his daughter Frances became a pupil. 'I will stand by your Bishop', Ruskin wrote from Mornex to Margaret Bell.[19] There was, however, little he could do to help Colenso against his prosecution by the ecclesiastical courts. The effect of the controversy was to strengthen his feeling that kindness and truthfulness were to be found at Winnington School, and not much elsewhere in England.

It is not clear that Ruskin ever met the Bishop. Frances Colenso, however, knew Ruskin well and was to become, in 1876, the second of the Companions of the Guild of St George. Late in life, the attempt at Mornex to define the irrefutable basics of his faith was associated with thoughts of Colenso. In 1887 Ruskin presented a large diamond to the Natural History Museum, desiring that it should be known as 'the Colenso diamond' in honour of 'the loyal and patiently adamantine first Bishop of Natal'. This 130-carat stone had cost Ruskin £1,000. It was given in an extravagant gesture at just the time when Ruskin found himself unable to write, in *Præterita*, about his religious thoughts during his long sojourn in Switzerland. Now, in the autumn of 1862, while Colenso was reviled in England and John La Touche in Ireland was giving his daughter her induction to Calvinism, Ruskin was writing to Margaret Bell in such terms as these:

> In short — this, which you now know, I have known ever since that winter of 1858 when I set myself to make out the mind of

Titian — I found we were all wrong. — It is only within the last two years that I have quite known *how* wrong.

And I am too weak & ill from the shock and darkness to find out much of the new right. How are we to live? — you ask? — wisely enough. Well — Early & rightly taught, it is perfectly possible to live happy — and more than possible, — *natural*, to live nobly & righteously — with no hope of another world. Nay — more — all the noblest things have, as it is, been done with no reference to any such hope. (I am myself at this moment — a better man — though a far less happy one — than I was four years ago. I have gained in self-command — in patience — in courage —)

But for those of us who have been long deceived, and who have all to forget & forsake, and desecrate — and darken it is dreadful — The world is an awful mystery to me now — but I see that is because I have been misled, not because it need be so. To those like you — who have lost those whom they loved — it is terrific — I cannot comfort you — I am *all but* crushed to pieces myself — the more because I can't talk to anyone about it — You are the first person who could understand it, who has found out for themselves, and to whom therefore I dare to say the truth.

You will find that all the men who have been the world's hated — Voltaire — Shelley — Rousseau — Keats — Byron — all the real men — that all the good steady clergymen are either fools or machines or madmen — or — worse than any — hypocrites of the uttermost kind which does not even know its own hypocrisy. With these are mingled multitudes of real liars and cheats.

. . . Just as I was getting to the worst and last of this, and broken down with it, this winter — the only little healing pleasure I had gave way to — Rosie's got too old to be made a pet of any more . . . and I've been utterly broken & good for nothing . . . & Rosie has some strange complaint of the brain — which has brought on a kind of torpor — She never works at anything without fatigue and her letters — instead of those nice long ones, are quite short and dull — though her mother says she takes twice as long in the writing as she used to do — her feet and hands as cold as marble — the doctor says she must not work at *any*thing for three or four years . . .[20]

In this distraught letter, and others like it, Ruskin was approaching — as though with some violent effort — the position from which he could state, again thinking of Colenso, that 'If you believe the Resurrection (and God forbid but that you still may —) hold to that —

and teach whatever arises out of that . . . Christianity *truly* believed — makes all its believers good and happy . . . But false, formal Christianity is, I believe of all religions ever invented on this earth, the most abominable — foolish — and in the literal sense of the word — "diabolical" — betraying . . .'[2]

In such moods he wrote hotly from Mornex to anyone in England who appeared to him to share any of the 'falsity' of the contemporary clergy. One such was the Reverend J. Llewelyn Davies, Maurice's close associate and one of the founders of the Working Men's College. Davies had criticised Colenso's book to Ruskin, who replied:

> might I ask you to tell me what you mean by 'the backbone of the Mosaic story may be received as true'. Do you mean that the waters of the Red Sea ever stood upright? that the Nile was ever turned to blood? Or Korah swallowed up alive? — or the Commandments written by God on stone tablets? If you don't mean or believe this, but only mean that there was a man called Moses — who brought some shepherds out of Egypt — all I have to say is that you and Moses may go to — Canaan — or Jericho — or wherever else you please — together, for me, and God forgive you for bothering me about him till I was forty years old. But if you do believe this — answer Colenso's book quietly and don't abuse it . . .[22]

Davies had no answer. Neither had Maurice, who agreed with Davies that Colenso's book was 'the most purely negative criticism I have ever read'. Here is one reason why Ruskin, writing *Præterita* many years later, scornfully remembered Maurice as 'securing his audiences' religious comfort, by turning their too thorny convictions the other side up, like railroad cushions'.[23]

At Mornex, Ruskin was subject to powerful, confused emotions and became worried that there was no direction to his life. Much of his anger and distress must have been caused by dilemmas in writing to Rose. In the autumn and winter of 1862, following the mysterious illness Ruskin describes in his letter to Margaret Bell, Rose's letters remained short, flat, and filled with her father's dogmas. Ruskin replied with homely descriptions of Mornex affairs and often sent her flowers. He probably did not mention his religious views, and since her mother had shown his private thoughts to Rose he may also have stopped writing about religion to Maria La Touche. His letters to Ireland were diplomatic. Perhaps this explains the vehemence with which he addressed other people. To some of them, he now came close to admitting that he was in love and could see no future for his love. An old family friend was Miss Corlass of Hull. She was a spinster whose background was in that peculiar mixture of evangelicalism and the wine trade so well known to the Ruskins. In the New Year of 1863 she received this letter:

> I won't talk with you about religion. This is not want of confidence — It is strictly because I might do you harm — and you can do me no good. Be assured of that. You could as soon 'convert' Whitby Cliffs — As for my health — I could give you a technical account of it — It is what — sentimentally — is called 'broken heart' — but — practically and effectually — it is cramp of the division of heart which sends the blood to the brain — the French *coeur serré* — is the literal truth — the result being — oppression of brain — languor — dyspepsia — & many other such bitter matters — What my heart is cramped about — it would be much too long to tell you — and you would not understand it if I did — you couldn't think that no-one could care for a picture, for instance — or for a pet lamb — so as to be hurt when one was washed out — or the other lost — I lost a pet lamb the other day — (among myriads of other variously troublesome matters) — Four years ago it was a little child of eleven — three years ago she was twelve — and was so nice you can't think — then two years ago she got to be thirteen — & was nicer still, and one year ago she got to be fourteen — & would have been nicer still — only I had to perjure myself if I wanted a kiss — and vow that I had headache or toothache or something that wouldn't go away on any other terms — And now she's got to be fifteen there's no making a pet of her any longer — and I don't know what to do . . .[24]

This was Ruskin's situation after Rose passed her birthday on 3 January 1863.

Ruskin now found, as he would for the rest of his life, that in times of stress he could relax in his geological pursuits. Many a day was passed in wandering through the footpaths of the Salève mountain, where he examined the moraines of glacial deposit. Next he traced fresh streams, their banks filled with star-gentian, to springs above the tumbling meadows. Then his expeditions reached from grassland to the boulders of the height of the Brezon. Behind Ruskin toiled Allen and the donkey, its panniers filled with watercolour materials, geological hammers and samples of the Alpine rocks. A number of precise yet eloquent drawings record both the great vistas of the mountain ranges and the minute particulars of stones and flowers. In order to extend these studies Ruskin left Mornex for a short while in the spring of 1863. He set up temporary headquarters at Talloires on the

Lake of Annecy and began to compose his lecture 'On the Forms of the Stratified Alps of Savoy'.[25] This address, with the latter parts of *Munera Pulveris*, is the only literary product of his Mornex period.

None the less, his mind was fully engaged. As his otherwise empty diary reveals, Ruskin was making the study of Plato's *Republic* that ever afterwards would direct his political thought. He did this through the medium of the Greek text. Ruskin had not been much of a classicist at Oxford. In the years he had devoted to *Modern Painters* and Gothic architecture, Greek culture had scarcely been his concern. Indeed, classicism had often seemed the enemy of true religion and naturalist art. But in these months Plato sank deeply into Ruskin's troubled mind. Here is another source of his complicated radicalism. Isolated, high in the Alps, far distant from the social troubles of his native land, he submitted his intellect to the first of all books of political philosophy, written three centuries before the birth of Christ. Nobody really knew about this study, despite the references to Plato in *Munera Pulveris*. His friends thought that Ruskin was indulging his geological and botanical hobbies. Perhaps Ruskin had always been a Platonist by temperament. Certainly he now became a committed follower of the ancient philosopher. This engagement further enriched Ruskin's mind and now, as ever afterwards, separated him from his contemporaries. His village neigbours, as we find from a reminiscent article in *Le Gaulois*, regarded this 'thin-faced, reddish whiskered Englishman' who was 'neither young nor old' as an eccentric, for they did not know that he was a writer. He was, to their minds, wasteful, pottering about his estate, beginning jobs that had to be completed by his servants or the villagers: a man who was never exactly idle, but who clearly produced nothing.[26] Ruskin, who was thinking Platonically of government by philosophers in the ideal state, observed his neighbours as they observed him. As the weather changed in the early months of 1863 he brooded on 'the contrast of spring and its blossoming with the torpor and misery of the people; nothing can be more dreadful than their suffering, from mere ignorance and lethargy, no one caring for them'.[27]

* * * *

Ruskin's first residence in Mornex, from the summer of 1862 to late May of 1863, had been broken by a short visit to England in late November, to visit his parents and to give an address on 'Reform' (which was improvised) at the Working Men's College. When he arrived in London for a longer stay at the beginning of June 1863 he had been summoned not only by his parents' anxiety but by two public obligations. The first was to give his lecture on the Savoy Alps: this was delivered before a large audience at the Royal Institution. The second was to present evidence to the Commission on the Royal Academy. Not long before, Ruskin had been the champion of art considered revolutionary within that body. He had been a critic of the way that the Academy was art's governing institution, its training school and its arbiter of commercial success. Ruskin could not feel (his evidence shows) that the Academicians should be self-elected and self-perpetuating. But he could not present any alternative method of election to the Commissioners. Democratic voting procedures meant nothing to him. When the Commissioners' questions turned to the Royal Academy Schools, Ruskin seems to have invoked Plato's firm observation that under democracy 'the master fears and flatters his scholars, and the scholars despise their masters and tutors . . .' Ruskin's evidence on practical matters of management was always beside the point. It was his Pre-Raphaelitism, now some years behind him, that informed his most telling remarks. He wished to see the Royal Academy as a university, but one not at all like those at Oxford or Cambridge, nor based on current Academy training, for

> the teaching of the Academy separates, as the whole idea of the country separates, the notion of art-education from other education, and when you have made that one fundamental mistake, all others follow. You teach a young man to manage his chalk and his brush — not always that — but having done that, you suppose you have made a painter of him; whereas to educate a painter is the same thing as to educate a clergyman or a physician — you must give him a liberal education primarily, and that must be connected with the kind of learning peculiarly fit for his profession. That error is partly owing to our excessively vulgar and excessively shallow liberal idea that the artist's profession is not, and cannot be, a liberal one. We respect a physician, and call him a gentleman, because he can give us a purge and clean out our stomachs: but we do not call an artist a gentleman, whom we expect to invent for us the face of Christ. When we have made that primary mistake, all other mistakes in education are trivial in comparison. The very notion of an art academy should be, a body of teachers of the youth who are to be the guides of the nation through its senses; and that is a very important means of guiding it. We have done a great deal through dinners, but we may some day do a good deal more through pictures . . .[28]

Dante Gabriel Rossetti, an artist far removed from the Royal Academy (and a man one cannot imagine at a Victorian university) seems to have particularly appreciated these remarks. He wrote that 'the only evidence of the lot which is worth reading as original thought and insight, is Ruskin's'.[29] The painter and the critic still had much affection for each other and could be frank about each other's work. Rossetti considered the prose of *Modern Painters* to be the best in English, but *Unto This Last*, now circulating in book form, had always annoyed him. 'Who *could* read it?' he asked, 'or anything about such bosh?'[30] Rossetti's attempts at Ruskin's portrait led, according to Ruskin, to 'the horriblest face I ever saw of a human being'.[31] The first sitting for the portrait probably took place this summer, when we often find Ruskin in the company of people he had known best in the 1850s. He saw Browning, corresponded with Leighton about his contribution to the Royal Academy summer exhibition, and told George Richmond how much he liked the picture by his son 'Willie' — William Blake Richmond, christened after his father's hero — who was now himself an independent professional artist.

On 29 June Ruskin called at Rossetti's new home in Cheyne Walk. The photographer William Downey was there, and so was Ruskin's enemy William Bell Scott. Downey took the opportunity to photograph the distinguished company.[32] Ruskin was uncomfortable, as the photograph shows. He looks thin, bad-tempered, and as if he wished to be elsewhere. Later that day he went to a party given by the Simons at their home in Great Cumberland Street. Mary Bradford, Margaret Bell's Winnington colleague, had also been invited, and a letter of hers reports that she saw Holman Hunt and Mrs Colenso among the other guests. At the Simons' party, Mary Bradford noted, Ruskin 'spoke very seriously about England's iniquity and the state of the people'.[33] He now, on his way to Winnington School, made a tour through the northern counties. This short excursion prompted some political reflections, significantly mingled with a longing for the England that Turner had known.

The least satisfactory of his social engagements was with Louisa, Marchioness of Waterford, whom he visited on her estate at Ford, Northumberland, near the Scottish border. Lady Waterford had been a widow since 1859. This rather suited her. The deceased Marquis, an energetic sportsman (our language owes him the phrase 'paint the town red', which commemorates his activities at Melton Mowbray), had not appreciated his earnest wife. She was now in her middle age, still beautiful, kind and sad, devoting her life to good works and artistic improvements. She preached teetotalism in the nearby colliery villages. At Ford she built a village school and decorated it with her own frescos, which depict stories of children from the Bible. Ruskin found that he could not bear her. This visit marked the end of a friendship that had never been very close. He had driven to Ford from the Collingwood Arms, near Coldstream, one of the old coaching inns he and his father so appreciated. This border country was especially associated in Ruskin's mind with Turner. 'It is so intensely Turner's in his youth', he wrote to John James, '— it makes me very sad'.

He could find little to praise in Lady Waterford's frescos, and she irritated him. England needed transformation, not upper-class women with amiable hobbies. 'The habit of politeness has gradually effaced the reality of her, so that I suppose only her peasantry see her as she is. They say she is very good to them, and knows them all personally, but I find in her only a graceful rose-coloured glacier'.[34] He was happy to leave Ford to call on the Reverend William Kingsley at South Kilvington, near Thirsk. Kingsley, once of Sidney Sussex College, Cambridge, had known Turner personally and had collected his work. He was one of the few Turner *cognoscenti* with whom Ruskin liked to talk, and to whom he listened with respect; and Kingsley's anecdotes, as related by Ruskin, have given us some dramatic and moving glimpses of the painter's mysterious personality.

It was Kingsley who told Ruskin how Turner had been tied to the mast of the *Ariel* after it had set off for a winter voyage from Harwich, and how 'the painter, lashed to the mast for four hours, had then suffered the tempest that he recorded in *Snowstorm at Sea*. Ruskin had written about this, quoting from a letter from Kingsley, both in his *Notes on the Turner Gallery* and in the fifth volume of *Modern Painters*. In 1863 it did not seem likely that Ruskin would write about Turner again. He had ambitions for some enormous social undertaking in literature, though he did not know what form it might take. On his way to the Trevelyans' home at Wallington, where he intended to mend his recent differences with John Brown, Ruskin forewarned Pauline Trevelyan that *Munera Pulveris* 'points to a radical change in the aims of human life — and in every custom of it thereafter . . .'[35] But if this was to be Ruskin's programme the thought of Turner none the less lingered in Ruskin's mind and heart. Thus, although Ruskin did not write about Turner he gave a fair number of extemporised lectures about the painter. These lectures must have contained much of the Turner lore and knowledge he shared with Kingsley. Alas, we have only broken records of this sort of talk, primarily in Ruskin's 1878 catalogue of his own Turner collection, to which Kingsley added some notes. Now, at Wallington, 'in the old Percy country, the broad descent of main valley leading down by Otterburn from the Cheviots', Ruskin gave a disquisition on Turner. It was witnessed by William Bell Scott, who once again had found himself in the same house as the critic he so disliked. 'The morning I left', Scott wrote, 'I overheard something concocted for after breakfast, so I went up to Lady T's room by and bye, and there came upon a sweet scene. Lady T. and Dr. Brown sitting in a rapt almost devotional attention opposite a row of Turner drawings Ruskin carried about with him, displayed on chairs, the thin figure of the critic moving fitfully about seeing that they were properly exhibited and pointing out the "wondrous loveliness" of each. Of course I joined in and cried "oh, what a glorious treat!"'[36]

In the chapter of *Præterita* entitled 'Otterburn' Ruskin has a confused memory of this visit. But he is correct to say that this was when he first met Constance Hilliard, Pauline Trevelyan's niece, who was his friend ever afterwards. 'Connie' was then eleven years old. She was the daughter of the Reverend J. C. Hilliard, of Cowley, near Uxbridge, and of Pauline's sister Mary. This important friendship was initiated by Connie's hospitality. She issued invitations to her tea party on the Wallington lawn, rebuked her guests for being late, led their conversation and in general behaved as queens do, although, as Ruskin noticed, 'it was all she could do to hold the teapot'.[37]

Unlike many Victorians of his generation, Ruskin saw that children have their own distinct personalities, and he easily made friends with some of them. Often, this led to unlikely friendships, and the parents of the child concerned could be surprised or annoyed that Ruskin did not prefer their own adult company. Connie Hilliard's father, for instance, meant little to Ruskin, who in the 1870s slept at Cowley Rectory often enough, yet took no notice of his host. This caused a little resentment. Ruskin would also ignore children to whom he was not attracted. The sons of friends like George Croly and Henry Acland grew up to know that Ruskin was their godfather, but they hardly ever saw him or heard from him, even on their birthdays. It is possible that they would not have been thus neglected had they been girls. At Winnington School, which Ruskin now visited for the fifth time, he was making girl friends who would be close to him until his death. Susan Scott, Constance Oldham (Ruskin's god-daughter: the niece of his schoolfriend Edmund Oldfield and the daughter of Sir Henry Oldham, a neighbour at Denmark Hill), Lily Armstrong, Dora Livesey and others were in their very early teens in this summer of 1863. In the years to come they would grow with Ruskin, and there is no doubt that he brought an especial joy to their lives, as they did to his. It is not surprising that, in 1876, a number of the first members of the Guild of St George were young women who had been educated at Winnington: they had already been Ruskin's followers for years.

It is worth repeating that Winnington was an individual school. There was a serious belief in the value of the arts. Music and drawing were not taught merely as 'accomplishments'. Not much attention was paid to social status. That could be because Winnington so much belonged to the industrial North. The more genteel establishments for girls were usually set in the resort and spa towns of the southern counties. In such places, a schoolmistress could not quite be regarded as a lady, even if she owned her school. She would therefore try the harder to be ladylike. This could be a satisfactory fiction for all concerned. But Margaret Bell's position was different. Her chronic indebtedness and Manchester Wesleyan background were visible to the parents of her charges. There was no pretence about her position, just as there was no pretence about her unusual ambition to attract the attention of leading intellectuals. Parents knew that the character of the school lay in its advanced attitudes to religion and social responsibility. They also knew that the school was near bankruptcy. In these obvious ways Winnington differed from other academies for girls. But its ethos resembled theirs in one fundamental way. By the 1860s, the social example for boys' schools — as we see from Thomas Arnold's influential work at Rugby — was the state. For girls' schools, however, including Winnington, the model was the large, happy family. This suited Ruskin, whose views on the state were not Arnold's, and who was so clearly seeking a family that was not his own: a family that would treat him as an adult, a master, rather than as a gifted child. For reasons deeply rooted in his psychology, Ruskin now took Edward and Georgiana Burne-Jones, the friends he called his 'children', to Winnington. They were delighted with their visit and joined in all the usual classes and activities. Burne-Jones found himself, to his pleasure, festooned with girlhood. 'I can look six in the face at one time, I can play at cricket, and read aloud, and even paint with three or four looking on, and I am deeply in love with several at a time'. Georgiana, though, may have sensed that there was something empty and tragic about Ruskin's presence at Winnington. She retained a ghostly memory of him 'taking his place occasionally in a quadrille or a country dance. He looked very thin, scarcely more than a black line, as he moved about amongst the white girls in his evening dress'.[38]

CHAPTER TWENTY

1864

Winnington's catchment area was primarily in Lancashire and the adjoining counties. A number of pupils came from Ireland, travelling to their school from Dublin and Belfast via Liverpool or Holyhead. This was not a difficult journey, and Ruskin could easily have crossed the Irish Sea from Winnington to see Rose this summer of 1863. He did not do so, for reasons which remain unclear, and in early September he left once more for Switzerland. Had he visited Harristown he would have found an unpleasant battle of wills between three members of the La Touche family. This was the dispute that occasioned Rose's first major illness, the breakdown that effectively made her an invalid for two years to come. It was caused by the question of her taking holy communion.

No information now exists on the question of Rose's baptism. And the probability is that she was not baptised as an adult. However, she fully shared the Baptists' insistence that this rite meant initiation, cleansing, dedication, fellowship with Christ; and she therefore felt, as Baptists do, that she might take holy communion without being confirmed. Rose's autobiography, which is largely concerned with her breakdown, states that she 'agreed with my Father's objections to confirmation'. She relates that, while she and her father were determined that she should take communion, her mother 'was dead against it', and attempted to forbid her to take communion without first being confirmed: 'Should I be altered from my purpose by Mama's opposition, thereby putting off the sacrament for an indefinite period . . . or should I follow Papa's wishes and remain firm in my purpose?'[1] Both parents gave Rose 'all kinds of books' that bore on the question; but she took little notice of their arguments and simply accompanied her father to see the local rector, in whose church she had determined to take communion the next day. 'Coming home I found Mama very angry', the autobiography calmly states. Maria La Touche refused to go to church the next morning to see her daughter take the sacrament. It was raining heavily that Sunday. Rose's mother said that this was 'a sign'. Perhaps it was. Rose, her father and her governess went alone to the church. Rose took communion; and the next day she collapsed.

This was on Monday, 12 October 1863. Ruskin was at Mornex, where he was negotiating to buy land on which to build a house. He heard about Rose's illness through letters from Maria La Touche, who seems to have been careful not to explain to friends that she had been at odds with her husband. Rose lay in a darkened room, to which only her mother was admitted. At first, she could not bear light, or any sound above a whisper. 'It is one of her mysterious brain attacks', her mother wrote, '. . . her brain is so terribly sensitive that all impressions give pain'. Writing four years later, Rose seems to have recalled pain above all else.

> It was a strange illness — I can't tell about it gradually but look back upon it — I know I suffered terribly. (I was in bed about four weeks.) *Everything* hurt me. People coming in and talking however kindly, used to give me tortures of pain — I seemed to *think through my head*, and every thought hurt me. I was only comfortable when I was not thinking — (really). To talk I had to think and think in words and it was dreadful to me. Light hurt me. Food hurt me (not my head). Sometimes I was hungry but had such terrible pain after eating. Everything hurt me. I can only say again — I seemed to hurt myself . . .[2]

On 1 November Ruskin wrote to his father 'I think she's dying.'[3] But at length the danger passed and Rose, drained and shrunken, was allowed out of bed. It was at this time that her mother began to give an account of Rose's illness that suggested that there had been an unearthly and spiritual quality to her affliction. This initiated the mythical notion that Rose was gifted with heavenly knowledge. On 19 November Maria La Touche was able to write that

> The child is getting quite well by degrees, but she has had a really dreadful illness, so long and full of strange changes, the only thing that never changed was her vivid and happy faith, in God and her mother. It was wonderful . . . for there were what the doctors call 'psychical phonomena' . . . Being with her was like a Revelation to me. There was a sort of clairvoyance, both of spiritual and earthly things, which was startling. For the first fortnight of her illness she was able to tell beforehand every little thing that would befall her thro' the day, and always said that she was 'guided' in everything. The doctors were perfectly amazed and actually yielded against their judgement in allowing her to follow this 'guidance' which never once erred. I do believe It — whatever It was — spared her much suffering and saved her much 'treatment' but she became frightfully

> emaciated and weak at the end of four weeks in bed. Then came the most wonderful change. From a state of weakness so great that she could not sit up in bed, she suddenly after one night's sleep awoke perfectly strong in body, but with an infant's mind, an infant's playfulness, and an entire oblivion of all acquired knowledge, and of every person and thing not known to her eleven years ago. By degrees she grew out of this state and it was quite lovely to watch her growth, a beautiful ideal infancy and childhood lived thro' in a fortnight. She told me, in the prescience that was given her before, exactly how all this would be, and named the day and hour in which her strength would return and her mind fail. Thus I was *quite* untroubled, for she had spoken with authority, and had all thro' said, that she would recover perfectly from this illness, body, mind and all, but that the mind would be the last to recover. I was both pitied and laughed at for believing her, but everything came true. She is well now, except for a weakness in her brain which makes it painful for her to have any thought or idea suggested to her in words, unless she asks for it — so she is not able to see people at all, and cannot either read or be read to . . .[4]

Ruskin would not see Rose for nearly two years, and for a year he believed that she was dying. All through 1864 Rose remained at Harristown, incapacitated. In this year Ruskin received 'only a short note or two' from her. At the end of January 1865, fifteen months after her fatal first communion, she still 'can't write or think — consecutively — so that it's just as if she's dead'.[5] At about this time Maria La Touche sent Ruskin a photograph of her daughter. He was astonished. 'Her poor little face is so thin and sad — she looks nearer 60 than sixteen.'[6]

There was a period of about eighteen months between Rose's first communion and the time when she was able to resume some ordinary activities around the house. Her autobiography does not describe this interregnum between childhood and the disturbed, sometimes deranged, half-adulthood of her few independent years. This had been a wasted, useless time for her. So it was for Ruskin, whose private motto of 'Today' was not forgotten as he suffered each *dies non* of his exiled life.[7] At the beginning of this time of anxiety, when it seemed most likely that Rose would die, Ruskin saw no reason why he should not lead the rest of his own life, however long that might be, in the Alps. In the late autumn and winter of 1863 he proceeded with his plans to build a chalet. He had already chosen, at the top of a mountain, the ideal site for his house. This was the Brezon, above

Bonneville. But Ruskin's attempts to buy this land were resisted. The local community realised that he had found gold: why else had he and his servant confederates been loading those stones on to the donkey? His financial offers were refused, and were the more suspect as they became more generous. Ruskin also found concerted opposition from his friends. While he spent fruitless days at the *mairie*, he received letters from the Simons, the Burne-Joneses, Margaret Bell and others, all begging him not to proceed with his scheme. There was no water supply at the top of the Brezon, nor a road that led there; it would take a whole year even to transport the materials to build his new home; Rossetti's and Burne-Jones's decorations (which were Ruskin's pipe-dreams) might be delayed long beyond the time when the house was erected; there would in any case have to be another house for Ruskin's servants and their dependents; George Allen would not come anyway, because his children would contract the local goitre; there would be no posts; Ruskin might fall in the dark and roll into a ravine; nobody would hear his cries because nobody would have wished to come to stay with him. Finally, the canny John James put an end to his son's fantasies by persuading Osborne Gordon, Ruskin's old Christ Church tutor, to visit the gloomy recluse. Gordon walked up Ruskin's mountain, and down again, and told him not to be a fool. Ruskin's pretensions came to an end. He briefly put up one more unlikely idea, for 'a well furnished room in Paris' with 'a good cook . . . and housemaids', then went home.[8]

This abandonment of his plans was in mid-November 1863, only two months after he had left England. Ruskin spent a week at Denmark Hill, then removed to Winnington, where he remained until the school dispersed for the Christmas holidays. Towards the end of this visit his daily letters to John James begin to contain much criticism, sorrowfully expressed, not free of self-pity. After a failing with a drawing, he wrote,

> the vital energy fails (after an hour or two) which used to last one all day, & then for the rest of the day one is apt to think of dying, and of 'the days that are no more'. It is vain to fight against this — a man may as well fight with a prison wall. The remedy is only in time, and gradual work with proper rest. Life properly understood and regulated would never be subject to trials of the kind. Men ought to be severely disciplined and exercised in the sternest way in daily life. They should learn to lie on stone beds and eat black soup, but they should never have their hearts broken — a noble heart, once broken, never mends: the best you can do is rivet it with

> iron and plaster the cracks over — the blood never flows rightly again. The two terrific mistakes which mama & you involuntarily fell into were the exact reverse of this, in both ways. You fed me effeminately and luxuriously to the extent that I actually now *could* not travel in rough countries without taking a cook with me! — but you thwarted me in all the earnest fire of passion and life. About Turner you indeed never knew how much you thwarted me — for I thought it my duty to be thwarted — it was the religion that led me all wrong there — for if I had courage & knowledge enough to insist on having my own way resolutely, you would now have had me in happy health, loving you twice as much . . . and full of energy for the future — and of power of self-denial. Now, my power of *duty* has been exhausted in vain, and I am forced for life's sake to indulge myself in all sorts of selfish ways, just when a man ought to be knit for the duties of middle life by the good success of his youthful life. *No* life ought to have *phantoms* to lay . . .[9]

John James Ruskin was not overly disturbed by such letters, but he was still worried that his son might gain himself a reputation as an eccentric rather than as a leader of contemporary thought. Ruskin was now developing some theories about the proper tuition of young girls. His reading of new verse, which at this date included Longfellow and Fitzgerald's *Rubáiyát of Omar Khayyám*, perhaps had an effect on the rather peculiar music and verses he began to compose for the Winnington pupils. These first essays in musical and dramatic education 'were not mere play', as W. G. Collingwood explains. 'They were taught as lessons and practised as recreation.'[10] Collingwood realised, of course, that Ruskin had graver thoughts than of arranging a delightful spectacle. This attention to music and dance derives from Ruskin's study of Plato, as he would explain, years later, in the eighty-second and eighty-third letters of *Fors Clavigera*.[11]

Back at Denmark Hill in the New Year of 1864, Ruskin had conversations both with Carlyle and with Spurgeon. He briefly visited Cowley Rectory and was delighted to find Laurence Hilliard as bright and attractive as his sister Connie. But most of his days were spent with his father. They both had some dealings with E. S. Dallas. As his *The Gay Science* (1866) shows, Dallas was an intelligent amateur aesthetician. He was, by profession, a journalist on *The Times*. At this time he was thinking of founding a new weekly paper, and hoped that Ruskin would contribute to it. Ruskin, however, had no particular wish to contribute to anything. He discussed *Fraser's Magazine* with Froude, but was more interested in commissioning Burne-Jones to illustrate a book version of his *Munera Pulveris* papers. This scheme was abandoned. Had the book appeared, Ruskin's thoughts on political economy would have been illustrated by the figures of Ceres, Proserpine, Plutus and Circe.

On 1 March 1864 Ruskin came home late from a dinner party. John James had waited up for him, and proudly read out two difficult business letters he had written that evening. The next morning the old merchant was shivering, and had cut himself in several places while shaving. Ruskin brought his own books from his study to sit with his father, so that he might fetch anything he needed. Soon, however, John James Ruskin got up, went to his bedroom and locked the door. There was no answer to Ruskin's knocks. The whole household was alerted. It was old Anne Strachan 'who pushed her way to the foot of the ladder placed against his window: Anne, grown white-haired in his service, who insisted on mounting it so that she might be the first at his side'.[12] John James had collapsed. He was put to bed, and his son held him in his arms all that day, all night, and until he died at half-past eleven the following morning, 3 March.

★ ★ ★ ★

Although his letters are now written on black-edged paper until May 1865 (he probably changed back to his normal stock on the 10th of that month, John James's birthday), Ruskin resisted the Victorian conventions that surrounded bereavement. He so disliked the dark trappings of public woe that he would dispute the validity of mourning, and sometimes therefore gave the impression of a hard heart. He persuaded his mother, who now bore her loss 'with unspeakable sweetness and strength of heart', not to wear a widow's cap.[13] He asked her to adopt one of a different shape, trimmed with lace and satin, fastened by a diamond and emerald brooch. Slightly to Ruskin's surprise, she did his bidding. She now regarded her son as the head of the family. A very late passage in *Præterita*, claiming that Ruskin's own life 'suddenly' became 'another ideal' to Margaret, reflects this new authority.[14] The suddenness of John James's death had an important effect on Ruskin. He snapped out of his self-indulgence, his complaints about his health and all the world. Not long before, he had been lamenting his upbringing and claiming that he had been 'thwarted' in his desires. On the night before John James's collapse, he had not concealed his boredom as his father read out business letters. Now, after a death he had not anticipated, he was both contrite and slightly masterful. He wrote brusquely to a number of friends who had offered their condolences. If they were inclined to pieties, as

Henry Acland and Charles Woodd were, he replied in terms that almost suggested that he had ceased to be a Christian. Ruskin rather wanted to be alone, or to share his sorrow only with his mother. But a death in the family confers a kind of licence on tiresome and unwelcome visitors. Denmark Hill was hushed, yet busy. The house was filled with undertakers, clergymen, relatives, lawyers, and the staff of Ruskin, Telford and Domecq — clerks to whom John James Ruskin had too seldom deputed responsibility, and who were now lost without him.

John James was buried in the churchyard he was fond of, at Shirley, near Croydon. The epitaph on his tomb reads in part:

He was an entirely honest merchant,
and his memory is, to all who keep it, dear and helpful.
His son, whom he loved to the uttermost
and taught to speak truth, says this of him.[15]

Ruskin now inherited a large sum of money. John James's will left his wife £37,000 and the house at Denmark Hill. He bequeathed his son £120,000, various houses and other properties (including a pottery at Greenwich) and his pictures, which were valued at £10,000. Margaret Ruskin made a will of her own, in which she bequeathed everything she owned to her son. Ruskin had never shown aptitude for accounts, and did not understand the investments. W. H. Harrison, a family friend since the days of *Friendship's Offering*, came to help go through the relevant papers. But he was himself a poor man, and would not have known much of finance beyond the trusts he administered for the Royal Literary Fund. It is doubtful whether Ruskin ever received sound advice about his fortune. He spent it far more quickly than it had been accumulated. In ten years' time he would be rid of much of his father's money. In twenty years he would be in financial difficulty.

Ruskin's first decision was to give £17,000 to various relatives, for he now felt that he should be generous not only to the Croydon Richardsons but also to the more removed connections of his father's Scottish family. One of them, Joan Agnew, now entered Ruskin's life. She was his second cousin, the daughter of George Agnew, hereditary Sheriff-Clerk of Wigtown, Galloway, who had died when she was five years old. This was not a prosperous branch of the family. Joan was now seventeen, and happened to be staying in London at the home of her uncle, John Ruskin Tweddale, just after John James's funeral.[16] She was invited to Denmark Hill for a few days, and was not at all overawed by the eighty-three-year-old Margaret Ruskin, who immediately became fond of her. In the chapter of *Præterita* entitled 'Joanna's

Care' there is an account of the way that this young girl became part of the household. The paragraph was written by Joan herself and is slightly romanticised. The position was that Joan had no prospects in Wigtown, and that Margaret Ruskin needed a companion. If Joan came to Denmark Hill she would have some domestic duties but would not be a servant, could visit Wigtown whenever she wished yet would not be a burden on her widowed mother. Joan was to call Mrs Ruskin 'Auntie' and was to address Ruskin as 'Cousin John'. Thus she came to live at Denmark Hill, to the great happiness of all concerned.

* * * *

In the months after his father's death Ruskin became a closer friend of the Cowper family. He especially liked Mrs Cowper. She was the Georgiana Tollemache he had admired from afar in Rome in 1840, and whom he had met at a party in 1858. We will encounter Georgiana with a number of different names. She had married the Hon. William Cowper in 1848: he became William Cowper-Temple in 1869, and Lord Mount-Temple in 1880. Ruskin called him 'Mr Cowper', then 'William'. He called Georgiana 'φίλη', or 'Phile', then 'Isola', then finally 'Mama' or 'Grannie'. In *Præterita* she is 'Egeria'. Ruskin's rechristenings, his use of nicknames and fondling names, was a new practice that would reach a height in the late 1870s, when his letters and diaries are filled with arcane cognomens. It began because he wished to avoid formal salutations. The names also dramatised and personalised his relations with people he found interesting. In the end, they would be a part of his private mythology.

The Cowpers' names went through all three of these stages. They would be forced into agonised situations with Ruskin, for they served as intermediaries in the most desperate days of his love for Rose. This is when the name *Phile*, 'beloved one', is most used. They first encountered Ruskin's troubled emotions, however, because they involved him ('Mr Ruskin', soon to be replaced by Rose's 'St C.') in their rather formal experiments with spiritualism. The Cowpers' general beliefs lay in a kind of social Christianity, a faith in the common bonds of all those who loved Christ. But liberal theology and the welfare of the poor did not excite them as much as did the idea that they might be able to communicate with ghosts.[17] Ruskin both knew about spiritualism and — like many another Victorian — knew intelligent people who believed in it. Elizabeth Browning, for instance, had told him of her mesmeric experiences. But he had no particular interest in spiritualism itself until the Cowpers described their enthusiasm and lent him a book about the subject. Shortly afterwards, in late February of 1864, the Cowpers persuaded Ruskin to participate in his first seance. Their hostess was Mrs Gregory, the widow of William Gregory, of the University of Edinburgh, who in 1851 had published *Letters to a Candid Enquirer on Animal Magnetism*. Mrs Gregory's *entrée* to the further world was made from the most fashionable quarter of this one. She lived in Grafton Street, Mayfair. She employed only the most famous mediums: Daniel Home himself often led her seances. On the occasion when Ruskin first went to her home, the proceedings were conducted by Mrs Mary Marshall, known as a 'high priest' of the spiritualist movement. She was assisted by Captain Alfred Drayson of the Royal Military Academy at Woolwich and by Miss Annie Elizabeth Andrews, two mediums who held high status, social or otherwise, in the confraternity of Victorian mesmerism.[18]

This Miss Andrews, later Mrs Ackworth, was the medium who, eleven years later, would persuade Ruskin that she had seen the ghost of Rose La Touche at his side. At this first seance, after some inconclusive attempts to receive messages from the other world, she called on spirits to make themselves known by rocking the table. In the darkened Mayfair room it 'danced in time to a country dance'. Miss Andrews was a fraud. The amounts of deception and self-deception which made Victorian spiritualism so successful are hard to calculate. But it is possible to say something about the background of Miss Andrews's appeal and popularity. The interest that attaches to a charlatan is not in the degree of his or her plausibility so much as in the origin of his or her pretensions. In Andrews's case, the claims that she could reach the spirit world and speak to the dead belong to nineteenth-century Christianity: spiritualists' messages from the dead are always Christian in character. Victorian spiritualism thrived on the erosion of orthodox faiths: it also depended on a longing for the comforts those faiths once gave. In these respects it was a hybrid offspring of traditional beliefs. But it also had some of the character of revivalism, and occasionally of the new sectarian faiths of nineteenth-century England. The Cowpers relished these confusions. Here they found their own Broad Church. Ruskin was not so easily satisfied. He no longer believed in many of the things that Christianity taught. But he believed in the immortality of the soul. Since the theology of spiritualism does not extend beyond a reassurance that this belief is valid, spiritualism itself was of little use to him. He was disturbed rather than impressed by the evening's activities.

None the less, something unsettling had entered Ruskin's imagination, already filled with the ghost stories he remembered so vividly from his childhood days with Anne Strachan. After his father's death he returned to Mrs Gregory's, and at some point he met Home. Ruskin was too enquiring to be a guest at a successful seance. He did not want to hear from his grandmother: he wished to summon the spirit of Paolo Veronese.[19] It appears that at one meeting he quoted from George Herbert, his favourite English religious poet, 'a standard of the purest unsectarian Christianity', but to bring Herbert into such a gathering was of course to disrupt it.[20] The people Ruskin met at the few seances he attended did not want to know about his personal Christianity. Had they enquired about his beliefs, the meeting would immediately have ceased to be spiritualist. But there were other people who were extremely eager to know what Ruskin believed. Two of them were George MacDonald and Maria La Touche.

MacDonald, a Scotsman who had been ordained in the Congregational Church, had left his ministry and was supporting his large and growing family by literary work.[21] Like Georgiana Cowper, he too would have some part in Ruskin's relations with Rose, whom he met, with her mother, in the winter of 1862 or the spring of 1863. In February of 1863 Rose was attending his lectures on Shakespeare. Rose liked him because he was kind, and the author of the mystical *Phantastes*, already popular among adolescents with a taste for the supernatural. Maria La Touche liked him partly because, as a result of his rejection of Calvinism, his views seemed like an entirely softer version of her husband's. She felt at home with MacDonald, to the extent that she could write this to him about Ruskin: 'Nothing will ever get *me* right, save getting *him* right — for somehow if he were holding on to a straw & I to a plank — I must leave my plank to catch at *his* straw. Still I don't care what becomes of me as long as anyway he can [be] brought to some sort of happiness and life.'[22]

Maria La Touche, who would have done better to worry about her daughter, could never have got Ruskin 'right'. She had not the wit to do so. Ruskin quite often observed that intelligence and culture had more to do with religion than faith, blind belief. For this reason we should not exaggerate the importance of his encounters with spiritualism, but instead examine his contribution to a Bible class given by an intellectual, F. D. Maurice. In the spring of 1864 George MacDonald asked Ruskin to stand as godfather to his son Maurice. Ruskin refused, on the grounds that 'first, I'm a pagan', adding that he already had too many godchildren he did not care about. A third reason, unstated, was that the child was named after the founder of the Working Men's College. At about this time Ruskin had an altercation with Maurice which put an end to his uneasy collaboration with

Christian Socialism. The account in *Præterita* begins by saying 'I loved Frederick Maurice, as every one did who came near him', but continues that

> . . . his clear conscience and keen affections made him egotistic, and in his Bible-reading, as insolent as any infidel of them all. I only went once to a Bible-lesson of his; and the meeting was significant, and conclusive.
>
> The subject of the lesson, Jael's slaying of Sisera. Concerning which, Maurice, taking an enlightened modern view of what was fit and not, discoursed in passionate indignation; and warned his class, in the most positive and solemn manner, that such dreadful deeds could only have been done in cold blood in the Dark Biblical ages; and that no religious or patriotic Englishwoman ought ever to think of imitating Jael by nailing a Russian's or Prussian's skull to the ground, — especially after giving him butter in a lordly dish. At the close of the instruction, through which I sate silent, I ventured to enquire, why then had Deborah the prophetess declared of Jael, 'Blessed above women shall the wife of Heber the Kenite be'? On which Maurice, with startled and flashing eyes, burst into partly scornful, partly alarmed, denunciation of Deborah the prophetess, as a mere blazing Amazon; and of her Song as a merely rhythmic storm of battle-rage, no more to be listened to with edification of faith than the Norman's sword-song at the battle of Hastings.
>
> Whereupon there remained nothing for *me*, — to whom the Song of Deborah was as sacred as the Magnificat, — but total collapse in sorrow and astonishment; the eyes of all the class also bent on me in amazed reprobation of my benighted views, and unchristian sentiments. And I got away how I could, but never went back . . .
>
> It followed, of course, logically and necessarily, that every one of Maurice's disciples also took what views *he* chose of the songs of the prophets, — or wrote songs of his own, more adapted to the principles of the College, and the ethics of London. Maurice, in all his addresses to us, dwelt mainly on the simple function of a college as a collection or collation of friendly persons, — not in the least as a place in which such and such things were to be taught, and others denied; such and such conduct vowed, and other such and such abjured . . .[23]

This reminiscence was published in May 1888, not long before *Præterita* was abandoned. It was immediately challenged by the Christian

Socialists John Ludlow and Thomas Hughes. Ludlow's autobiography explains that 'I had long ceased, out of pity to one who had written some noble things in his day, to read Mr Ruskin's later publications. But the above passage was brought to my attention by T. Hughes. We wrote the following letter to Mr Ruskin:

> . . . Your own part in the discussion, we also distinctly recollect, was not confined to a mere question, but was a vehement and somewhat lengthy outpouting in praise of Jael. The 'startled and flashing eyes' were not those of Mr Maurice, whose self-possessed demeanour on the occasion is still before our eyes, but your own, and struck forcibly another of our number, now with God.[24]

That third person was another Christian Socialist, Charles Mansfield, who had said to Ludlow, 'Did you notice Ruskin's face whilst Mr Maurice was speaking? It was that of a man possessed.'[25] Mansfield had been shocked by Ruskin's outburst. It was evident that some of his extremist, prophetic, socially belligerent manner had been caught from Carlyle: this was why Ludlow considered that Ruskin, 'with a woman's soul in a man's body', was so affected by 'that essentially male genius'.[26] But Ruskin's contempt of the middle way had been growing in him since his first maturity, and would remain with him until his final collapse. The prophetic denunciations only occasionally come to the surface of his deliberately pacific autobiography. There can be little doubt that Ludlow's and Hughes's recollections of the Bible class are substantially correct. None the less the autobiography was right to fix on the Song of Deborah, and in this passage we can see how the author of *Præterita* had also been the author of *Fors Clavigera*, 'Fortune with the Nail'. In *Fors* we find the significance, for Ruskin, of the story of Jael. Deborah's Song is in Judges 5. It celebrates the victory of the Israelite tribes over Sisera, accomplished by Jael's driving of a nail into the head of the rival leader: he had sheltered in her tent and believed himself safe because of the 'lordly dish' of butter she had served him before he fell asleep. Here was a barbaric story that gave difficulty to all commentators, including Maurice. But it had a firm place in Ruskin's imagination. It was not quite a symbol, nor even a theme in what he wrote. It was a warning, which he accepted, that there were implacable laws and fates beyond Maurice's 'amiable feelings'. This strain of violent fatalism brings Jael into the argument of a *Fors* letter of 1876, when the Hebrew murderess is combined with a Greek myth. The letter is entitled 'The Message of Jael-Atropos', since Atropos is the Fate that cannot be turned aside; and the message is one for 'the desperate, leathern-skinned, death helmeted skull of this wretched England', a message which will not be accepted 'till Jael-Atropos drive it down, through skull and all, into the ground . . .'[27]

Ruskin had begun to think in this dark, forceful, mythical manner during his months at Mornex. He finally realised, in his Alpine isolation, that the English Christianity he had known since he was a child could not tell him all that was in the world. It might have explained the history of Venice; about the mountains and the spirits above the mountains it told him very little. He looked increasingly to the mythology of the Greeks to content his spirit. In his notes on Horace, whom he studied at Mornex, he described 'the figure of the death-goddess Atropos, who is on the point of driving a nail [*clavus*] fast home with a hammer, the symbol of unalterably determined, or fixed, fate'.[28] Ruskin's quotidian life at Mornex seems often to have been aimless. Yet he had developed there a strange, unchristian apprehension of rectitude and ironclad doom, and tempted himself with the thought of many other gods.

Characteristically, he tested an orthodox English clergyman with his dangerously unorthodox thoughts. The Reverend Richard St John Tyrwhitt, whom Ruskin probably had not met, and who was certainly no intimate, received many difficult letters from Mornex. Tyrwhitt was much younger than Ruskin, but was a classicist from Ruskin's own college, Christ Church. His wife had recently died. Ruskin's commiserations only observe that

> if one's eyes were opened — ever so dimly — the terror and grief of this world round us would make us act — in almost one and the same temper, whether we ourselves were happy or not. — If indeed any of us ought to be happy . . .

Writing of *Modern Painters V*, Ruskin says that

> The obscurity in the end of that last volume does not come of puzzlement but of my not choosing to tell people what I know . . . Of course in some matters the mystery is not of *my* making. I assure you — the Sphinx is as alive as ever she was; and makes short work — ultimately with all demons. You will have to face her, some day — in spite of Church Catechism . . .

He tells the young clergyman that

> My personal experience of spiritual treatment has been chiefly from sun, moon, wind, and water — when the sun's bright — I'm always pious: and always wicked in a windy day. And I've the greatest possible desire to 'believe' in Apollo and Diana — and in Neseus [*sic*],

> and in water-symbols — and I do, very nearly; so that just a little touch of strong will will do it . . .

and frankly records his 'carrion nightmares':

> I was ashamed of myself for having such — thinking they indicated some carrion in one's soul . . . I saw a dead dog running about as if it were alive, once: and another time was wading up to my knees in a charnel house. I believe it is simply a warning which the stomach is appointed to give the brain of having been half killed, but I rarely have beautiful dreams, and never dream about angels or fairies or nice creatures, — so that I thought the dead dog was'nt fair. Have you looked lately at Plato's wise and beautiful direction for going to sleep — in the beginning of the ninth book of the Polity — . . . Only he says one's dreams are to tell one true, so; and mine at the best, never do that, except indeed, that they are always sad — and full of partings, and shadows, and vain hope. I am glad to see that there is some idea in you of taking art seriously . . .[29]

Tyrwhitt, on receiving these unexpected confessions, was much in the position of the future readers of *Fors Clavigera*. He was disconcerted both by Ruskin's ideas and by the sudden intimacy of his address. Ruskin questioned and challenged him as though he were desperate to try his correspondent's sincerity. Tyrwhitt was a simple man, rather fond of country pursuits. He also liked sketching (as he called it), which is why he had first written to Ruskin. He had not anticipated that he would be drawn into uncomfortable and bewildering arguments. Nor had he dreamt that he would have to deal with Ruskin's politics. But the author of *Modern Painters* asked him this: 'Please explain the meaning of "social discipline" in this sentence. There is no mercy in the world, that I see — except as social discipline between man and man.'[30]

Tyrwhitt might have given the right answer to this question if he had studied *The Stones of Venice*, *Unto This Last* and *Munera Pulveris*, together with the many sources of those books. But he was only in an official sense an educated man. Tyrwhitt's Christ Church position meant little; his writings are not exactly boorish, but books like *Our Sketching Club* (1875) and *Hugh Heron Ch. Ch.* (1880) should not have come from a university. Encountering Tyrwhitt, Ruskin had to realise that his social ideas, whatever their classical forebears, might find little recognition in the contemporary world. He now made some attempts to give immediate and dramatic form to his political thinking. He began the series of lectures which were published in 1866 as *The*

Crown of Wild Olive. The first in date of these 'brilliant lay sermons run wild', as the *Contemporary Review* called them, was given in Bradford in late April of 1864.[31] It was Ruskin's first public appearance since his father's death, and the occasion when Joan was first given charge of the house at Denmark Hill. The lecture is entitled 'Traffic', a word that occurs nowhere in the text. In an obvious way, it returns to Ruskin's public architectural concerns of the previous decade. He had been invited by a group of civic elders of Bradford to talk to them about architecture, for they were about to build a new Exchange.

Ruskin could not have failed to have an interest in the new building of the time. The previous December he had been pleased to find that the new Assize Courts in Manchester, by Alfred Waterhouse, were 'beyond everything yet done in England on my principles'.[32] When he visited the site he found a clerk of works who, when a youth, had copied out the whole three volumes of *The Stones of Venice* and had traced its every illustration. Waterhouse was a young architect who had not been heard of before he won the competition for the Manchester building. In days past, Ruskin might have seized the opportunity to direct a new architect who evidently owed much to him. But he did not attempt to meet Waterhouse; and apart from recommending him to his Bradford hosts (who in the event preferred to engage another architect) thought little more about him. The real purport of his lecture was elsewhere.

Ruskin's lectures had a unique way of being both combative and inspiring. He could be less than polite to the people who had come to hear him speak, yet also convince them that they were partners in future noble works. In 'Traffic' Ruskin satirised his audience. He also led them to a plane beyond his mockery. 'Your ideal of human life is, I think, that it should be passed in a pleasant undulating world', he told the concerned citizens of Bradford,

> with iron and coal everywhere underneath it. On each pleasant bank of this world is to be a beautiful mansion, with two wings; and stables, and coach-houses; and pleasant carriage drives through the shrubberies. In this mansion are to live the favoured votaries of the Goddess; the English gentleman, with his gracious wife, and his beautiful family; he always able to have the boudoir and the jewels for the wife, and the beautiful ball dresses for the daughters, and hunters for the sons, and a shooting in the Highlands for himself. At the bottom of the bank, is to be the mill; not less than a quarter of a mile long, with one steam engine at each end, and two in the

> middle, and a chimney three hundred feet high. In this mill are to be in constant employment from eight hundred to a thousand workers, who never drink, never strike, always go to church on Sunday, and always express themselves in respectful language . . .[33]

The 'Goddess' who has her votaries in this privileged family is the 'Goddess of Getting-on', Ruskin claimed; a deity who is worshipped by those who have no faith in true values. His peroration then gathered in his audience:

> Continue to make that forbidden deity your principal one, and soon no more art, no more science, no more pleasure will be possible . . . But if you can fix some conception of a true human state of life to be striven for — life, good for all men, as for yourselves; if you can determine some honest and simple order of existence; following those trodden ways of wisdom, which are pleasantness, and seeking her quiet and withdrawn paths, which are peace; — then, and so sanctifying wealth into 'commonwealth', all your art, your literature, your daily labours, your domestic affection, and citizen's duty, will join and increase into one magnificent harmony. You will know then how to build, well enough; you will build with stone well, but with flesh better; temples not made with hands, but riveted of hearts; and that kind of marble, crimson-veined, is indeed eternal.[34]

Such a concluding passage demanded the skills of an actor as well as those of a writer. In years to come Ruskin's perorations became famous, and sometimes they were mocked. Reports of his lectures, however, convince us that such passages were spoken with a theatrical skill that carried Ruskin's listeners into a happy communion with his meditations. Like Gladstone and Dickens, neither of whom he resembled in other ways, Ruskin was a master of the public occasion. Gladstone's political oratories, Dickens's reading from his works and Ruskin's lectures are all triumphs of the Victorian art of dramatic speech-making. Ruskin, on a stage or at a lectern, could occupy and command his audience with intense magic of personality. Furthermore — though this reflects the generally lengthy span of high Victorian utterances from both platform and pulpit — he could do so for the large part of any afternoon or evening. Very few of his lectures could have been delivered in an hour or less. Many may have occupied two hours. Ruskin would talk informally at the end of these occasions with anyone who approached him. He never 'took questions'.

Ruskin's power over those to whom he spoke is found in the other two lectures that made up the first edition of *The Crown of Wild Olive*. 'Work' was addressed in January of 1865 to an audience at the new Working Men's Institute in Camberwell, where, inevitably, he talked both as a leader of thought and as a neighbour. No doubt some Denmark Hill servants were in attendance. In 'War' he immediately gripped his audience at the Royal Military Academy in Woolwich with the words 'Young soldiers, I do not doubt but that many of you came unwillingly to-night, and many in merely contemptuous curiosity, to hear what a writer on painting could possibly say, or would venture to say, respecting your great art of war . . .'[35] There was in fact much for Ruskin to say, for he always had a curiosity about soldiers, their work and their motives. References to war in Ruskin's writings are extremely numerous, and he often wished to write a book on the subject.[36]

* * * *

Ruskin did not travel abroad for two years after his father's death. During this period his desire for knowledge of art took him to the British Museum. Rather as John James Ruskin had left Denmark Hill every morning (often by public transport) to go into the City, his son travelled to Bloomsbury (now most often in the family coach) for a day among the Museum's antiquities. The Museum's arrangements in the 1860s had begun to exhibit the triumphs of British archaeology and classical scholarship as well as palaeontology and geology. Remarkably, the collections did not generate much nineteenth-century writing: this is an absence in Victorian literature. But Ruskin's books in the twenty years after 1864 often return to the treasures of Bloomsbury, and occasionally are marked by his conversations with such museum officials as the natural historian Sir Richard Owen and the mineralogist Nevil Story-Maskelyne.[37] At the British Museum, no doubt Ruskin now often talked to a Christ Church friend. While in the consular service Charles Newton had identified the site of the Mausoleum at Halicarnassus, and had brought the remains of this wonder of the ancient world back to London. He had now become the Keeper of Greek and Roman Art (and was closer to the Ruskin family background because of his recent marriage to Joseph Severn's daughter Mary).[38]

Ruskin's approach to the collections was not that of a scholar like Newton. In some ways he resembled more casual visitors to the Museum. He would wander through the rooms until he was taken with some particular exhibit; and would then alight on an antiquity from another century, and another culture, that happened to be in the next gallery. He became more attached to certain pieces because he drew them; and he felt that these were important because, for one reason or another, they were good to draw. His habits in the Museum were those of an artist as well as an intellectual. Landscape now loses its pre-eminent place in Ruskin's art. Instead of outdoor scenes of mountains and valleys we begin to find strangely lit, morbidly concentrated versions of classical and Egyptian figures. Some of these came to have great meaning for Ruskin: but such significance was by no means identical with the meaning they had had in their parent culture.

A letter of 1864 to Henry Acland (who was suffering from scarlet fever) tells us much about Ruskin's work in the Museum, and his dissatisfactions with such previous authorities as C. C. J. Bunsen's *Egypt's Place in Universal History* (1848). Ruskin was looking for religious knowledge: but the reference to Harry Acland, Ruskin's godson, reminds us that Christian baptism was — because of Rose — never far from his thoughts about the world and the mystery of its arts.

I am trying to understand what religions hitherto have been worth understanding, in some *impartial* manner — however little of each — and as I have strength and time, am endeavouring to make out how far Greeks and Egyptians knew God; or how far anybody ever may hope to know Him.

If you know — and I think you know — much of Bunsen, you may guess how pleasant it is to me to have to wade and work through his masses of misarranged material; and if you know the state of Egyptian science in general — and contemplate a little that the only two works of value on Rome and Greece are by a polished infidel, Gibbon, and a vulgar materialist, Grote — you may wonder that I have not had fever of the very scarletest, long ago. However, one thing I *know*, that nothing can ever be done unquietly. So I do what I can — of course *my* hold on all these races is through their art, and so I am cast perforce into figure work, and quite independent research. It was within an ace of being too late for me ever to get any grasp of figures — but I shall have enough yet for my purpose. I did a life-size fresco — single figure — from Luini, at Milan, which did me much good, and when I have time to master the main laws of bone perspective, I believe I shall make memoranda truly enough for the understanding of things. I send you — as you are more interested in figures, three rough studies —

> one from the Caryatid of the Dew-temple (Brit.Mus.) . . . two, enlarged from coins, the black one, Terina, the one on the board, Syracuse — both of fine central time. They are drawn merely for disposition of hair, dolphins, etc.; when one goes for expression, one must keep to marble. But you cannot distinguish invidiously, or otherwise, between figures and landscape. The great error of modern figure work in sculpture no less than painting has been the want of understanding that chiaroscuro, and mystery, as elements of visible expression, have inseparable functions and dignity in an eyelash as much as in a pine forest — and half the force and dignity of all Greek and Egyptian conception arise out of lower organisms, and physical phenomena. The rising and setting of the sun — the Nile inundation and harvest — the sweep of sea in the Greek and Sicilian bays, are necessary swaddling clothes of all noble human conception and religion; that church font by which I held Harry had Nile water in it, if we could have seen clearly . . .[39]

Ruskin's Egyptianism is an obscure part of his sensibility, and does not become much clearer in the book in which it is most fully conveyed, *The Ethics of the Dust* (1865). Although this interest in ancient Egypt can be traced to books and exhibitions that Ruskin studied, it is an enthusiasm that fits strangely into the rest of his life and work. No doubt that is because it satisfied his instincts for mystery and longing for the unknowable, matters difficult to explain except through allusion, or in his difficult Winnington dialogues. In one simple respect, however, the Victorian response to ancient Egypt was near home. At the Crystal Palace, now removed to the Norwood hills, Ruskin would have seen the Egyptian courts, devoted to the reconstruction of the cities denounced in the Bible for their luxurious sins. He would have escorted his Winnington girls through the enormous old Assyrian rooms, past palace façades, ceremonial halls filled with winged, human-headed lions, and walls of Babylonian brick adorned with hunting scenes of the great King Assurnasipal. The Crystal Palace represented vulgarity to Ruskin, just as the British Museum represented culture; and we may believe that his Egyptianism wished to save that culture from the Palace's cardboard effigies, and hoped to use it to help schoolgirls think deeply, and 'rightly', of the awfulness of life's tasks. For Ruskin himself, Egyptianism was an alternative to his mountain culture, the love of air and landscape. It had to do with kings, gold, and ceremonial. Ruskin occasionally thought that Egypt might provide a future for Pre-Raphaelitism. He loved Rossetti's 'Burden of Nineveh', a poem which describes the installation of a marble taurine god in the British Museum; and he told Georgiana Burne-Jones in the autumn of 1864 that

> When Ned begins again to paint he must do some Egyptian things. Fancy the corselet of the King fastened by two Golden Hawks across his breast, stretching each a wing up to his shoulder, and his quiver of gold inlaid with enamel; and his bow-gauntlet of gold, and his helmet twined round with a golden asp, and all his chariot of divers colours, and his sash of 'divers colours of needlework on both sides', and a leopard running beside him, and the Vulture of Victory over his head.[40]

CHAPTER TWENTY-ONE

1864–1865

In the two years after his father's death, Ruskin devoted himself to his mother and thus to the Denmark Hill household. Though he grieved for John James, his depression lifted. He put aside the listlessness and self-indulgence of his Mornex days and became especially attentive to those around him in his own home. His first kindnesses were of course given to Margaret Ruskin, who was now in her eighties. He also showed delicate concern for the young Joan Agnew. In the spring of 1865 she returned to her native Wigtown for a month's visit. There it was finally decided that her future was to be in Denmark Hill. Joan now became Ruskin's ward. He would act as her guardian until she married Arthur Severn in 1871. A busy and cheerful girl, Joan was not in awe of Margaret Ruskin. Nor indeed was she shy of anyone, even including Carlyle. He was one of many visitors to Denmark Hill who immediately took to her. Some of the conversation between Joan and Carlyle at this time is recorded in the 'Joanna's Care' chapter of *Præterita*.[1] Joan had a more immediate effect on Ruskin's writing. He thought of her as an exalted housewife, somehow disembodied from her tasks. Together with the Winnington girls (who are often described as 'housewives', though they had no houses to keep) Joan helped Ruskin to make his contribution to the large, and growing, Victorian literature of domesticity.

Soon after John James died, Ruskin extended his domestic empire by buying property in Marylebone. His working-class houses were used to accommodate superannuated Denmark Hill servants. Ruskin initially acquired this property to test some personal theories about fair rents. These ideas he explained in September of 1865, in a series of letters to the *Daily Telegraph* on the subject of 'Servants and Houses'. He wrote in answer to the newspaper's opinion that 'the hardest thing in the world is to find a good servant'. Ruskin's demurrals ranged over many matters, including Greek slavery, but his central contention was that 'there is only one way to have good servants; that is, to be worthy of being well served'.[2] One is reminded of the length of service and general harmony within Ruskin's domestic staff. This is not to claim that such harmony was complete. The oldest servants, chief among them Ruskin's nurse Anne Strachan, had imperious or eccentric ways. Outdoor servants such as David Downs the gardener (who had come to Denmark Hill from Scotland on the recommendation of Dr John Brown) and the coachman David Fudge had their own territories and interests. George Allen and his family had now left Denmark Hill for a home of their own and considered themselves superior dependants, servants no longer. Ruskin's personal valet, Frederick Crawley, justifiably felt himself closer to his master than anyone else in Ruskin's service. He sometimes troubled other servants, guests too, by his saturnine and knowing ways. Among Joan Agnew's talents as a manager of the Denmark Hill household was the ability to direct such staff. Since they had their own fiefdoms they might have been disinclined to obey the instructions of an eighteen-year-old. Yet, as would become apparent, Joan knew how to impose her will. Gradually, she became absolute mistress first of Denmark Hill and then of the old Ruskin house at Herne Hill. In two decades' time she would effectively expel Ruskin from his home at Brantwood to make it her own.

The domestic disasters of the mid-1880s were unimaginable in the mid-1860s. As they later realised, but never quite said, Ruskin and Joan were happiest in this period. She was not an intellectual person, and Ruskin soon realised that there was no point in teaching her how to draw or how to arrange his mineral cabinets. Ruskin now ceased to give instruction within the Denmark Hill household. He still helped servants with gifts of books. Some of them received his manuscripts. Crawley owned the holograph of the rare work 'Gold: a Dialogue', written in 1863 but unknown before it was issued as a privately printed pamphlet in 1891. At that time Crawley intimated to H. Buxton Forman, the pamphlet's editor, that *Gold* had remained unpublished because of objections from John James.[3] This may have been so. In any case, we know that Ruskin wrote more freely to the press after John James's death. Taken together with the letters on 'Servants and Houses', a volume could be compiled of Ruskin's writings on social subjects addressed to newspapers and magazines in 1864–68 but not gathered together before E. T. Cook's labours on Volume XVII of the Library Edition, issued in 1905. During his first year as master of Denmark Hill Ruskin established a desk drawer that was used for press clippings. He could reply to their comments or use newspaper stories in other ways. Some newspaper editors looked at Ruskin with a reciprocal interest. They sensed his appetite for controversy. One new journal, established in 1865, was to be especially concerned with Ruskinian debates. This was the *Pall Mall Gazette*, founded and published by George Smith of Smith, Elder and edited by Frederick Greenwood. Ruskin kept his distance from Greenwood but he was a disputatious friend of the *PMG* for many years to come.[4]

Ruskin was too peculiar a journalist to be called one of the tribe of Fleet Street; yet when he walked in Fleet Street and the Strand, as he occasionally did at this period, he would meet people he knew who worked for the press. Ruskin's public letters of 1864–66 were a natural expression of his interest in newspaper debate. They are articles as much as they are letters. Those collected by Cook for Volume XVII of the Library Edition are: first, 'Gold: a Dialogue' (intended as a public letter); then the papers on 'Servants and Houses', on 'Work and Wages', and finally on 'Railways and the State', written until 1868. These last are especially spirited. It is fitting to notice here Ruskin's comments on the railway system, for they belong not only to his general sensibility but also to journalism. People who are known for their printed opinions sometimes enjoy the cultivation of a *bête noire*. Ruskin's attacks on railways are of this type. They are repeated, provocative and humorous. The denunciations were inherited from his father's 'Jonathan Oldbuck' style. John James Ruskin was a commercial traveller who had been brought up in the age of coaches and had an antipathy toward the modern progress of the 1840s. His son shared such attitudes. They both objected to the noise, the dirt, the new lines across old countryside. They also had suspicions of the 'railway interest' and its growing influence within Parliament. None the less they both used railways and had an informed interest in their facilities. The younger Ruskin, like everyone else of his generation, relished the minor adventure of an expedition by train. He accepted that the railway system would be a permanent part of modern life. Ruskin had already suggested, in *Munera Pulveris*, that conditions demanded 'quadruple rails, two for passengers and two for traffic, on every great line', an argument he repeated in the *Daily Telegraph*, while also stating in that newspaper that 'Neither the roads nor the railroads of any nation should belong to any private persons. All means of public transit should be provided at public expense, by public determination where such means are needed, and the public should be its own "shareholder".'[5]

While issuing his opinions on public matters in newspapers Ruskin was also writing on art, though with his customary divagations. The strange book we now know as *The Cestus of Aglaia* is embedded in his journalism. Ruskin contributed its nine chapters to the *Art Journal* between January 1865 and April 1866. In 1905 they were collected and reprinted by E. T. Cook for Vol. XVII of his Library Edition. Apart from a pirated American edition of 1907 the *Cestus* has never been separately issued. No doubt Ruskin's inclination toward journalism has deprived a later public of a part of English literature. The history of the appearance of the *Cestus* in print is typical of Ruskin's earlier periodical publication. A magazine might solicit his opinion on a topic. He would then reply with a series of papers containing unusual speculation about the world in general.

The *Cestus* comes from the pages of the *Art Journal* because this magazine was edited by Ruskin's friend Samuel Carter Hall. Older than Ruskin by two decades, Hall was a veteran journalist and literary man. He had begun his career by writing and editing keepsake annuals of the sort that had published Ruskin's verses in the late 1830s. Under his direction the *Art Journal* was the most prominent magazine primarily concerned with the visual arts. Hall and his wife were committed spiritualists. In the mid-1860s Ruskin often met them at London social occasions where spiritualism was discussed. He did not think that Hall was a good journalist, but Ruskin may have had him in mind as the 'friend' who encouraged the speculations of the prefatory chapter of *The Cestus of Aglaia*. At all events Hall persevered with Ruskin's contributions. This helped the difficult art critic to a new kind of expression. Some of Ruskin's paragraphs in the *Cestus* might almost be called experimental writing, so free are they from any precedent. We can call other passages 'set pieces', for they are composed with the confident bravura of a master of English prose, are self-contained and are designed to impress by their virtuosity. Here, for instance, is Ruskin's description of a railway engine as seen by a mere watercolourist:

> I cannot express the amazed awe, the crushed humility, with which I sometimes watch a locomotive take its breath at a railway station, and think what work there is in its bars and wheels, and what manner of men they must be who dig brown iron-stone out of the ground, and forge it into THAT! What assemblage of accurate and mighty faculties in them; more than fleshly power over melting crag and coiling fire, fettered, and finessed at last into the precision of watchmaking; Titanian hammer-strokes beating, out of lava, those glittering cylinders and timely-respondent valves, and fine ribbed rods, which touch each other as a serpent writhes, in noiseless gliding, and omnipotence of grasp; infinitely complex anatomy of active steel, compared with which the skeleton of a living creature would seem, to a careless observer, clumsy and vile — a mere morbid secretion and phosphatous prop of flesh! What would the men who thought of this — who beat it out, who touched it into its polished calm of power, who set it to its appointed task, and triumphantly saw it fulfil this task to the utmost of their will — feel

> or think about this weak hand of mine, timidly leading a little stain of water-colour, which I cannot manage, into an imperfect shadow of something else — mere failure in every motion, and endless disappointment; what, I repeat, would those Iron-dominant Genii think of me? And what ought I to think of them?[6]

Thus the locomotive was given its mystery: godlike, but surely made by men who were less than gods. Most of Ruskin's speculations in the *Cestus* approach the divine and then retreat in bafflement. We notice that *The Cestus of Aglaia*, with *Munera Pulveris*, begins the sequence of Ruskin's books whose contents were summarised in deliberately gnomic titles. Ruskin expected Biblical references — in a title such as *Unto This Last*, for instance — to be recognised, but his Latin and Greek titles were devised to tease or haunt the reader and to suggest a book's themes by means of allusion. The 'Cestus of Aglaia' means 'the Girdle of the Grace'. We are referred to the fourteenth book of the *Iliad*, where Aphrodite, who is not distinct from Aglaia, lends her cestus to Hera.[7] In Ruskin's interpretation this gift summarises the spiritual power of art. His book is about that power, which a locomotive cannot possess. But much of the book's manner is as obscure as its title. Today, we read *The Cestus of Aglaia* with E. T. Cook as our guide. He was its editor, thought deeply about its contents and found them troubling. Cook could never bring himself to believe that Ruskin's madnesses of the 1880s were adumbrated in his writing of the 1860s. Yet in the *Cestus* we find the first examples of the 'uncontrolled' literary composition that is found in *Fors Clavigera*. Cook gave especial attention to one of these passages. It is in the third chapter of the book, entitled 'Patience'.

> I cannot get to my work in this paper, somehow; the web of these old enigmas entangles me again and again. That rough syllable which begins the name of Griselda, 'Gries', 'the stone'; the roar of the long fall of the Toccia seems to mix with the sound of it, bringing thoughts of the great Alpine patience; mute snow wreathed by grey rock, till avalanche time comes — patience of mute tormented races till the time of the Grey league came; at last impatient. (Not that, hitherto, it has hewn its way to much: the Rhine-foam of the Via Mala seeming to have done its work better.) But it is a noble colour that Grison Grey; — dawn colour — graceful for a faded silk to ride in, and wonderful, in paper, for getting a glow upon, if you begin wisely, as you may some day perhaps see by those Turner sketches at Kensington, if ever anybody can see them . . .[8]

Cook's gloss on this passage is as follows:

> *Gris*elda brings into his head memories of the Tosa (or Toccia) falls beneath the Gries glacier (he may have visited the falls from Domo d'Ossola in 1845); then he pauses to think of the long oppression of Raetia under petty tyrants (of which a record remains in the many ruined feudal castles which stud that part of Switzerland). Their rule was at last shaken off by the formation of the Grison Confederation, in which one of the constituents was the Grey League (Graue Bund): hence the name of the present canton, Graubünden (*Fr.* Grisons). The name (though possibly referring to the several counts, Grafen, whom the League comprised) is popularly derived from the grey home-spun coats of those by whom it was formed: see the passage quoted by Ruskin in Vol. XIII, p. 516. The thought of the Grison country brings to his mind its central defile, the Via Mala, the grandeur of which had impressed him so many years ago (see *Præterita*, i.§136; ii., §131), and he doubts incidentally whether the men of Graubünden have hewn their way in the world so decisively as the foaming river. Then the colour of Grison Grey recalls to him at one moment Tennyson's Enid ('Earl, entreat her by my love, Albeit I give no reason but my wish, That she ride with me in her faded silk' — The Marriage of *Geraint*); and, at the next, Turner's brilliant water-colour sketches on grey paper (see Vol. XIII, p. 385), which allusion, lastly, leads him to a lament at the little interest taken in the sketches (see below, §104 *n*, p. 148), then shown at the South Kensington Museum (see Vol. XIII, p. xxxvi).[9]

These admirable comments should be read with Cook's career in mind. As noted above, he first published the entire text of *The Cestus of Aglaia* as part of the Library Edition in 1905. His interest in the *Cestus* was then of long standing. Two decades earlier he had been a young journalist on the *Pall Mall Gazette*. One of his tasks was to report Ruskin's Oxford lectures. In November of 1884 he attended one of the most emotional addresses of the series that Ruskin would soon abandon. Ruskin told his audience that he could not lecture that day on 'The Pleasures of England', the title of his course. Instead he read from the 'Patience' chapter of *The Cestus of Aglaia*. The subsequent discourse was quite unexpected. Cook was twenty-seven years of age in 1884 and had studied Ruskin since his teens. Yet it is not likely that he had sought out the original publication of the *Cestus* in the pages of the *Art Journal*, so would not have been prepared for the strange reminiscence that opens the chapter on 'Patience'. In keeping with the text that had appeared in the *Art Journal* in April of 1865, Ruskin's lecture began with a quotation from the 35th stanza of Chaucer's *The Parlement of Foules*:

> Dame Pacience sitting there I fonde
> With face pale, upon a hill of sonde

— and then he read, continuing to follow his 1865 paper:

> As I try to summon this vision of Chaucer's into definiteness, and as it fades before me, and reappears, like the image of Piccarda in the moon, there mingles with it another; — the image of an Italian child, lying, she also, upon a hill of sand, by Eradnus' side; a vision which has never quite left me since I saw it. A girl of ten or twelve, it might be; one of the children to whom there has never been any other lesson taught than that of patience; — patience of famine and thirst; patience of heat and cold; patience of fierce word and sullen blow; patience of changeless fate and giftless time. She was lying with her arms thrown back over her head, all languid and lax, on an earth-heap by the river side (the softness of the dust being the only softness she had ever known), in the southern suburb of Turin, one golden afternoon in August, years ago. She had been at her play, after her fashion, with other patient children, and had thrown herself down to rest, full in the sun, like a lizard. The sand was mixed with the draggled locks of her black hair, and some of it sprinkled over her face and body, in an 'ashes to ashes' sort of way; a few black rags about her loins, but her limbs nearly bare, and her little breasts, scarce dimpled yet, — white, — marble-like — but, as wasted marble, thin with the scorching and the reins of time. So she lay, motionless: black and white by the shore in the sun; the yellow light flickering back on her from the passing eddies of the river, and burning down on her from the west. So she lay, like a dead Niobid: it seemed as if the Sun-God, as he sank towards grey Viso (who stood pale in the south-west, and pyramidal as a tomb), had been wroth with Italy for numbering her children too carefully, and slain this little one. Black and white she lay, all breathless, in a sufficiently pictorial manner: the gardens of the Villa Regina gleamed beyond, grateful with laurel-grove and labyrinthine terrace; and folds of purple mountain were drawn afar, for curtains round her little dusty bed.
>
> Pictorial enough, I repeat; and yet I might not now have remembered her, so as to find her figure mingling, against my will, with other images, but for her manner of 'revival'. For one of her

> playmates coming near, cast some word at her which angered her; and she rose — 'en ego, victa situ' — she rose with a single spring, like a snake; one hardly saw the motion; and with a shriek so shrill that I put my hands upon my ears; and so uttered herself, indignant and vengeful, with words of justice, — Alecto standing by, satisfied, teaching her acute, articulate syllables, and adding her own voice to carry them thrilling through the blue laurel shadows . . .[10]

Part of this passage was quoted in the present book at the relevant chronological point in Ruskin's life. He had seen the 'sand-girl' in Turin in August of 1853.[11] There is no doubt that the vision of the girl aroused something in Ruskin's nature. It is in Turin that we first observe his attraction to pre-pubescent girls. Now, in March of 1865, when 'Patience' was written, Ruskin felt a rush of bewilderment about womanhood and his sexual feelings. Joan Agnew had come to live in his house, and it was as though he had suddenly become the father of a girl who was ready to fall in love and marry. Then he had strangely agitating news from Harristown. Rose's elder sister Emily was about to be married. Maria La Touche was delighted that her younger daughter was now so much stronger. She made a mock lamentation of the way that Rose 'is perfectly wild & how she is ever to be made a modern "young lady" of, I can't imagine. She is out from dawn till dark, & it is utterly useless to put on her any raiment that would not suit a peasant, or to expect from her any observance of any of the restraints of civilisation.'[12]

This description of Rose's wild Hibernian ways could easily have prompted the 'sand-girl' passage. For its theme is not so much erotic as a summoning of the 'restraints of civilisation'. That is why Ruskin muses on Dante and Virgil as he watches the girl. The evocation of the girl in Turin is evidently written by an art critic. Ruskin sees her as sculpture. Furthermore he writes that she is in a 'pictorial' setting. She is a figure in a landscape. Ruskin might be describing a Veronese or one of the Dionysiac details of scarcely clad maidens who lie, dance or posture in the corners of the Italian paintings that Turner produced in the 1830s.

Both the description of the locomotive and the paragraphs devoted to the 'sand-girl' recall the splendours of prose in *Modern Painters*. That perhaps is why Ruskin, in autobiographical mood, read from the *Cestus* at Oxford in 1884. In 1865 the fame of some of Ruskin's works contrasts with the occultation of other projects. While he was writing the unnoticed *Cestus* Ruskin was also preparing for press the most widely read of all his books (excepting always *The King of the Golden*

River, a children's classic at least until the First World War). This was *Sesame and Lilies*. Before discussing *Sesame and Lilies* as a separate publication it is helpful to note its place in a sequence of lectures given by Ruskin between his father's death in March 1864 and his visit to Italy in April 1866, the first since his bereavement. In order, these lectures are as follows. Ruskin spoke on 'Traffic' at Bradford on 21 April 1864. 'Kings' Treasuries' (later the first section of *Sesame and Lilies*) was at Manchester on 6 December of that year. The next day there was a talk to the boys of Manchester Grammar School. On 14 December, also at Manchester, Ruskin's audience heard 'Queens' Gardens'. There was a lecture at Camberwell on 'Work', on 21 January 1865, followed by an untitled address at the Working Men's College on 18 February. A paper was read to the Royal Society of British Architects on 15 May. Ruskin returned to the Working Men's College to talk on 'Mechanical Art' on 18 November. On 16 February of 1866 he lectured on 'War' at the Royal Military Academy, Woolwich. A number of minor or less formal addresses are recorded. They were delivered extempore at Winnington School or to groups of visitors to Denmark Hill, where Ruskin welcomed more visitors to the house than had been allowed in John James Ruskin's latest days.

It is often observed that Ruskin's writings were freer and perhaps more radical after his father's death. His expression certainly became more vocal. In Ruskin's books after 1864 we are more likely to hear the individual voice of their author. They use shorter paragraphs and more varied punctuation. Their tone is intimate, or at any rate closer to the reader. Sometimes we have the impression of soliloquy, sometimes of a personal letter. One book of 1865 is written in dialogue form. *The Ethics of the Dust*, however, is rather stiff and formal. It lacks the changefulness, the varied tone and humour of Ruskin's new writing. Of course its purpose was not to amuse. Through a series of ten dialogues Ruskin, who describes himself in a dramatis personae as 'Old Lecturer (of incalculable age)', conducts twelve girls through the strange lands of Egyptian mythology, crystallography and other subjects. The book's topics were all in Ruskin's mind in the mid-1860s, and the lectures are not simply didactic for the good reason that he found Egyptian and crystallographic matters so mysterious. *The Ethics of the Dust* is a children's book that could only be understood by adults. Yet it is not precisely a children's book; for, as we have seen, the girls whom it portrays — who were pupils at Winnington — were often thoughtful young women in their late teens. Half of the girls represented in *The Ethics of the Dust* were sixteen years of age or more. The eldest, Mary Leadbetter, was twenty and not a Winnington pupil but one of the school's teachers.

At some point before 1905, Ruskin's friend Dora Lees, née Livesey, supplied E. T. Cook with identifications of the girls whose questions and comments elicit the Lecturer's eloquence. This list was useful to Cook, who knew little about Ruskin's commitment to Winnington.[13] Yet Dora's contemporaries scarcely have individual characters in *The Ethics of the Dust*. As Ruskin says, he had not wished to indicate personalities but to 'represent, as far as I could, the general tone of comment and enquiry among young people'.[14] Readers will suspect that Ruskin idealised or otherwise misconstrued the seriousness and attention span of his teenage audience. Then, the more one ponders over *The Ethics of the Dust*, the more it becomes apparent that the ages of the characters are beside the point. For Ruskin had attempted a book that concerned aeons rather than centuries. It is absorbed in matters so utterly ancient as to be without history. There is no parallel within Victorian literature. No writer other than Ruskin, and furthermore Ruskin at this time in his life, could have imagined such a school conversation as the following. 'L' stands for 'Lecturer', 'Sibyl' was Sibyl Evelyn Herbert Noyes, 'Egypt' was Asenath Stevenson, 'Isabel' was Isabel Marshall, and 'Lily' was Lily Armstrong.

LILY. No, we are not wise, and we will believe anything, where you say we ought.

L. Well, it came about this way. Sibyl, do you recollect that evening when we had been looking at your old cave by Cumae, and wondering why you didn't live there still: and then we wondered how old you were; and Egypt said you wouldn't tell, and nobody else could tell but she; and you laughed — I thought very gaily for a Sibyl — and said you would harness a flock of cranes for us, and we might fly over to Egypt if we liked, and see?

SIBYL. Yes, and you went, and couldn't find out after all!

L. Why, you know, Egypt had been just doubling that third pyramid of hers; and making a new entrance into it; and a fine entrance it was! First, we had to go through an ante-room, which had both its doors blocked up with stones; and then we had three granite portcullises to pull up, one after another; and the moment we had got under them, Egypt signed to somebody above; and down they came again behind us, with a roar like thunder, only louder; then we got into a passage fit for nobody but rats . . .

EGYPT. You would not have had me take my crown off, and stoop all the way down a passage fit only for rats?

L. It was not the crown, Egypt — you know that very well. It was the flounces that would not let you go any farther. I suppose, however, you wear them as typical of the inundation of the Nile, so it is all right.

ISABEL. Why didn't you take me with you? Where rats can go, mice can. I wouldn't have come back.

L. No, mousie; you would have gone on by yourself, and you might have waked one of Pasht's cats, and it would have eaten you. I was very glad you were not there. But after all this, I suppose the imagination of the heavy granite blocks and the underground ways had troubled me, and dreams are often shaped in a strange opposition to the impressions that have caused them; and from all that we have been reading in Bunsen about stones that couldn't be lifted with levers, I began to dream about stones that lifted themselves with wings.

SIBYL. Now you must tell us all about it.

L. I dreamed that I was standing beside the lake, out of whose clay the bricks were made for the great pyramid of Asychis. They had just been all finished, and were lying by the lake margin, in long ridges, like waves. It was near evening; and as I looked toward the sunset, I saw a thing like a dark pillar standing where the rock of the desert stoops to the Nile valley . . .[15]

The Ethics of the Dust is (partly) about Ruskin's awed reaction to the British Museum's Egyptian galleries. It was too peculiar a book to have much popularity, and immediately went out of print until Ruskin revived it in 1877. The *Saturday Review* called it 'whimsical, incongruous, and silly beyond all measure'.[16] Significantly, though, Carlyle realised that it was not a book for schoolgirls and wrote to Ruskin that

> *The Ethics of the Dust*, which I devoured without pause, and intend to look at again, is a most shining Performance! Not for a long while have I read anything a tenth-part so radiant with talent, ingenuity, lambent fire (sheet and *other* lightnings!) of all commendable kinds! Never was such a Lecture on Crystallography before had there been nothing else in it, and there are all manner of things. In power of *expression*, I pronounce it to be supreme; never did anybody who had *such* things to explain, explain them better. And the bits of Egyptian Mythology, the cunning *Dreams* about Pthah, Neither, etc., apart from their *elucidative* quality, which is exquisite, have in them a poetry that might fill any Tennyson with

> despair. You are very dramatic, too; nothing wanting in the stage-directions, in the pretty little indications — a very pretty stage and *dramatis personae* altogether. Such is my first feeling about your book, dear R. Come soon, and I will tell you all the *faults* of it, if I gradually discover a great many. In fact, *come* at any rate![17]

This letter is perfectly Carlylean. It is full of praise yet with more than a hint of future admonitions, generous and difficult. Ruskin must have been invigorated. Carlyle's response would also have compensated for the comparatively tepid reception of *Sesame and Lilies* in Cheyne Walk. In July of 1865 Ruskin had sent this short book to Jane Carlyle as her birthday present. She had enthused about its title, writing that 'the names lift me already into the sphere of Arabian Nights!'[18] but otherwise made no comment. Her husband remained totally silent. Ruskin knew that this indicated some form of disapproval. In the world at large, however, *Sesame and Lilies* was overwhelmingly a success. When he edited the book in 1905 E. T. Cook remarked that, to that date, 160,000 copies had been printed. The lessons of the contemporary *Cestus of Aglaia* and *The Ethics of the Dust* were resisted by the wider public. *Sesame and Lilies* was less difficult to understand and its main theme was incontrovertible. 'I want to speak to you about the treasures hidden in books', Ruskin had said in Rusholme, where his first Manchester audience had gathered to support a fund for a new public library.[19] When he spoke of 'Queens' Gardens' in the second lecture of *Sesame and Lilies*, delivered at Manchester Town Hall in connection with proposed new schools in the Ancoats district, he demonstrated that he meant something simple by this title. Good women exercise a power that is more spiritual and widespread than is their quotidian effect on domestic life.

'Kings' Treasuries' stands at about the half-way point in the chronological sequence of Ruskin's lectures — of which around 180 are recorded — and is often interpreted as a central expression of his concern for the Victorian common weal.[20] Yet Ruskin's address was not as straightforward or benevolent as might have been expected. A man who was known as a great writer and teacher proposed to speak about the good that we may find in books. Ruskin still managed to be contentious, in part because this was the 'male' half of his two Manchester lectures. Nobody in his audience can have felt that the lecturer flattered their good civic will, for Ruskin soon explained that he did not believe that a wide reading of books would help to form a better country. Indeed, 'It is simply and sternly impossible', he declared, 'for the British public, at this moment, to understand any thoughtful writing, — so incapable of thought has it become in its insanity of avarice . . .'[21]

Ruskin went on with a series of denunciatory paragraphs with the beginnings 'I say first we have despised literature', then 'I say we have despised science', then 'I say you have despised Art!', continuing, 'You have despised Nature' and concluding with 'Lastly. You despise compassion.'[22] In proof of this last accusation Ruskin printed, in red ink, a recent newspaper story of a working man who had died in destitution. At the end of the lecture Ruskin returned to the subject of books. His concluding paragraphs remind us of his love of fine illustrated books (which at this time he often discussed with Edward Burne-Jones), and look forward to his own library of precious volumes, the *Bibliotheca Pastorum* of his later years:

> I hope it will not be long before royal or national libraries will be founded in every considerable city, with a royal series of books in them; the same series in every one of them, chosen books, the best in every kind, prepared for that national series in the most perfect way possible; their text printed all on leaves of equal size, broad of margin, and divided into pleasant volumes, light in the hand, beautiful, and strong, and thorough as examples of binders' work . . .
>
> I could shape for you other plans, for art-galleries, and for natural history galleries and for many precious — many, it seems to me, needful — things; but this book plan is the easiest and needfullest, and would prove a considerable tonic to what we call our British constitution, which has fallen dropsical of late, and has an evil thirst, and evil hunger, and wants healthier feeding. You have got its corn laws repealed for it; try if you cannot get corn laws established for it, dealing in a better bread; — bread made of that old enchanted Arabian grain, the Sesame, which opens doors; — doors not of robbers', but of Kings', Treasuries.[23]

'Of Queens' Gardens', the second lecture that made up *Sesame and Lilies* (before 'The Mystery of Life and its Arts' was added to the volume in the 1871 edition) is more engaging. 'Of Kings' Treasuries' had included a combative analysis of lines from Milton's *Lycidas*. 'Of Queens' Gardens' opens with a beautiful description of Shakespeare's heroes and heroines. 'The catastrophe of every play', Ruskin said, 'is caused always by the folly or fault of a man; the redemption, if there be any, is by the wisdom and virtue of a woman . . .'[24] Perhaps for the first time in the history of Shakespearian criticism, Ruskin asserted that his most admirable characters are not men but women. It follows that heroes need heroines, and that men cannot be fully heroic without the presence and inspiration of a woman of radiant character.

This opinion may have irritated Jane Welsh Carlyle, the wife of the author of *Heroes and Hero-Worship*. She had written enthustiastically about the title of the book that Ruskin gave her but sent no word at all to Denmark Hill about the messages of *Sesame and Lilies*. Jane Carlyle could have sensed a criticism of her own record as a helpmeet by the study's fireside. We know that when presiding at social occasions she seemed fierce, drained. It is striking that Froude's account of her character in the early 1860s speaks of an emptiness and fatigued want of belief. He wrote about the Chelsea household at that period:

> She was very little alone with him. She presided at the tea-table at the small evening gatherings of his admirers in her own charming fashion. But Carlyle on these occasions did not converse. He would not allow himself to be contradicted, but poured out whole Niagaras of scorn and vituperation sometimes for hours together, and she was wearied, as she confessed, of a tale which she had heard so often . . . He had taken from her, as she mournfully said, the creed in which she had been bred, but he had been unable to put anything in the place of it. She believed nothing. On the spiritual side of things her mind was a perfect blank; she looked into her own heart and into the world beyond her, and it was all void and desert; there was no word of consolation, no word of hope. She was so true that it was impossible for her to satisfy herself with fine phrases about the infinite . . .[25]

'Of Queens' Gardens' could not have inspired a new spring in the Carlyles' long, dry marriage. Both husband and wife, in their separate ways, would have been unmoved by the analysis of admirable womanhood that Ruskin found in Walter Scott, Dante, Aeschylus and Homer. Neither of them was an enthusiast for Pre-Raphaelite medievalism, so they would also have found objections to the following passage:

> In all Christian ages which have been remarkable for their purity or progress, there has been absolute yielding of obedient devotion, by the lover, to his mistress. I say *obedient*; — not merely enthusiastic and worshipping in imagination, but entirely subject, receiving from the beloved woman, however young, not only the encouragement, the praise, and the reward of all toil, but, so far as any choice is open, or any question difficult of decision, the *direction* of such toil . . . that chivalry, I say, in its first conception of

> honourable life, assumes the subjection of the young knight to the command — should it even be the command in caprice — of his lady . . .[26]

This extravagant image of devotion was often repeated in the years to come, when Ruskin declared his suitability as Rose La Touche's husband. 'Of Queens' Gardens' contains many statements that are elevated beyond the practicalities of life. The lecture none the less reflects Ruskin's actual relationships with real people; in particular, young women who were his friends and were not yet married. Joan Agnew was one of them. Numerous Winnington schoolgirls must also have been in Ruskin's mind. First of all, however, as he confessed in the preface to the 1871 edition of his book, 'I wrote the *Lilies* to please one girl'.[27]

She was Rose La Touche. The wayward Irish girl, sometimes flirtatious, often insanely pious, roaming the countryside, as her mother said, 'from dawn till dark', in 'raiment that would not suit a peasant', was the unacknowledged dedicatee of *Sesame and Lilies*. Rose never went to school in her life. It is ironic that *Sesame and Lilies* owed part of its huge circulation to its role as a school prize. Rose's own copy, presented to her by Ruskin and studiously underlined, has been preserved. The inscription reads 'Rosie, with St C's love'.[28] Rose could not have imagined that Ruskin would quite shortly ask her to become his bride. Reading 'Of Queens' Gardens' today, one has the impression that Ruskin's courtship had begun. *Sesame and Lilies* was written for Rose because Ruskin wished her to be the ideal young woman who would inspire both his home life and his valiant future writings. Such feelings were secret, though partly expressed in writing that many people found of a ludicrously high order, 'simply rodomontade', as Anthony Trollope wrote in the *Fortnightly Review*.[29] A more appreciative comment came from John de Capel Wise in the *Westminster Review*. 'Utopianism is sometimes good for us', he wrote,

> if it be only to lift us out of our usual atmosphere of prudence and pence. And we can sympathise with, though we feel how purely utopian for the present they are, his visions of a kingdom where only the great and the good shall be kings, and where the sword shall be beaten into the ploughshare, and men shall cease to stab one another, and revel in a scientific murder, which is now dignified by the name of war . . .[30]

CHAPTER TWENTY-TWO

1865–1866

Ruskin's literary friends were more likely than the professional artists of the 1860s to share a common stock of culture and education with the critic. In Ruskin Victorian poetry found a difficult, expert comrade. He had just as keen an eye for contemporary verse as any poet; and his poet friends, including Rossetti and Browning, could be taken aback by his detailed knowledge of Shakespeare and Dante — or of Pope, whom Ruskin much appreciated, though his reputation was now pretty close to its nadir. Some of these friends found that they were a little bruised after discussing poetry with Ruskin. This is probably why the only Pre-Raphaelite poet he never met was Christina Rossetti. She was sheltered from him by her brother, who had more than an inkling of his severe attitude toward her versification.

Ruskin's emphasis on flowing rhythm and diction (which did not prevent him from enjoying the Brownings, but spoilt his talks with them) may have helped him to recognise Swinburne as one of the highest poets of the day. Ruskin already knew some of the Northumberland Swinburnes, for their estates adjoined those of the Trevelyans. It is not clear when he met Algernon Swinburne, but the likelihood is that their brief friendship began in Rossetti's company in the earlier part of 1865. A letter from Swinburne to Ruskin, dated 11 August of that year, enclosed a copy (which Ruskin preserved) of a poem 'Before the Mirror: Verses Written under a Picture. Inscribed to J. A. Whistler'. The letter read

> My dear Ruskin,
>
> I send you the song you asked for, finding that I can remember it after dinner. Nevertheless it has given me far more labour to recollect and transcribe than it did originally to compose. But your selection of it as a piece of work more satisfactory than usual gave me so much pleasure that I was determined to send it when I could. Since writing the verses (which were literally improvised and taken down on paper one Sunday morning after breakfast) I have been told more than once, and especially by Gabriel Rossetti, that they were better than the subject. Three or four days ago I had the good fortune to be able to look well over the picture which alone put

> them into my head, and came to the conclusion which I had drawn at first, that whatever merit my song may have, it is not so complete in beauty, in tenderness and significance, in exquisite execution and delicate strength as Whistler's picture . . .
>
> I am going to take Jones (unless I hear from Whistler to the contrary) on Sunday next in the afternoon to W.'s studio. I wish you could accompany us. Whistler (as any artist of his rank must be) is of course desirous to meet you, and to let you see his immediate work. As (I think) he has never met you, you will see that his desire to have it out with you face to face to face must spring simply from knowledge and appreciation of your own works. If this meeting cannot be managed, I must look forward to the chance of entrapping you into my chambers on my return to London. If I could get Whistler, Jones and Howell to meet you, I think we might so far cozen the Supreme Powers as for once to realise a few not unpleasant hours. Yours very sincerely A. C. Swinburne.[1]

This 'Howell' was Charles Augustus Howell, now in his mid-twenties, who had attached himself to Pre-Raphaelite circles and would soon perform various secretarial works at Denmark Hill and elsewhere. He was the son of an English-born wine dealer who lived in Portugal. Ruskin warmed to Howell because of this background, and had first employed him to help with business matters after John James's death. Howell was friendly both with Burne-Jones and with Rossetti, who was amused by his blatantly unscrupulous character and sharp practices. He charmed Ruskin until about 1870. Howell's main use was in running errands. He also kept open some contacts between Ruskin and Rossetti, so that the master of Denmark Hill, now mostly engaged in looking after his mother, still knew something of bohemian Pre-Raphaelitism. Ruskin did not meet Whistler, nor ever would, and his acquaintance with Swinburne probably did not extend beyond the summer of 1866. But in this period, during which the poet (still himself in his twenties) published both *Atalanta in Calydon* and the notorious *Poems and Ballads*, Ruskin was his supporter. 'Have you read Swinburne's *Atalanta*?' he asked Charles Eliot Norton. 'The grandest thing ever yet done by a youth — though he is a Demoniac youth. Whether ever he will be clothed and in his right mind, heaven only knows. His foam at the mouth is fine, meantime.'[2] This was after the appearance of *Poems and Ballads*. Ruskin had not at first been in favour of their publication, so shocked had he been when he encountered their spirit. On 7 December 1865 he had called at Swinburne's lodgings in Dorset Street, off Portman Square. Drinking bottles of porter, declaiming and gesticulating, Swinburne exposed Ruskin to 'some of the wickedest and splendidest verses ever written by a human creature'. He could not but wish, he afterwards wrote to Swinburne, that he would 'some day see a change in the method and spirit of what you do'.[3] But Ruskin would never forget the experience of Swinburne's recitation. Perhaps, he conjectured, Swinburne might be akin not only to Baudelaire but also to Turner and Byron, mighty artists whose moral flaws were an essential part of their majesty.

* * * *

Only three days after Ruskin listened to Swinburne's astonishingly immoral verse he was reunited with Rose La Touche. On 10 December 1865, his diary records, they met for the first time in three years.[4] Rose was now almost well. Her parents thought it time that she should resume the life of a young woman of her class and brought her to London for the social season. There was talk of how she should be made a débutante, 'brought out' and presented to the Queen. Rose's period as a wild Irish girl seemed to be at its end. But she had no interest in balls, etiquette or introductions. Ruskin was both excited and bemused. He was not sure how she should meet his own friends. Rose was still a poet, but it did not seem wise to bring her into contact with Pre-Raphaelitism. Ruskin was prepared to introduce her to the Burne-Joneses, for he thought of the couple as innocents, and Georgiana was a minister's daughter. Social events in the more bohemian Rossetti circle could not be countenanced. Ruskin did not really want Rose to go anywhere in London other than Denmark Hill; and to his delight she thought the old house on the hill above Camberwell much more pleasant than the La Touche home in Mayfair. Rose resumed her former friendship with Margaret Ruskin, who appreciated her serious religious views. She also made best friends with Joan Agnew. This was not surprising, especially since neither young woman had close relations with other people of her own age. Rose had no other girl to talk to. Joan was fascinated by Rose and awestruck that there should be so many complications in her character. Rose's conversation and demeanour still oscillated between merry childishness and gravity. She had also inherited from her father an unyielding sense of right and wrong. In this confusing winter of 1865–66, Ruskin began to think that he should be obedient to Rose, that he should be her servant and do her bidding. Such sentiments lie behind the poem he now wrote, which he presented to Rose on 3 January 1866, her eighteenth birthday.

Ah, sweet lady, child no more,
Take thy crown, and take thy pride
Golden, from the great sea shore
Now the sands of measuring glide.

Thrice they count the noted hour.
Thrice — to changing spirits given —
Once to life — and once to power
Last, to judgement — light of heaven.

The shells that haunt the eternal sea,
And in God's garden, trees of God,
For thee have dyed, and borne for thee
The purple robe and almond rod.

And what thou wilt shall be, in deed
And what thou sayest shall be sooth
And wisdom of the old give heed
To counsel of the holy youth.

Ah, put away thy childish things
And take thy sceptre, dovelike, mild —
They must, on earth, be more than Kings
Who would, in heaven, be as a child.[5]

The only good line in this awkward poem is the first, and the whole would have been better if it had been part of the prose of the lecture 'Of Queens' Gardens'. At the heart of Ruskin's rhymed reflection is a Biblical quotation, from Jeremiah 1.11. The prophet there describes a vision of the rod of an almond tree. The point is that the almond flowers early and is used for God's purposes. The general sense of Ruskin's poem may be that his older wisdom must now submit to Rose's younger but clearer view of holy life. In her pious moods Rose would have found such a declaration satisfactory. In fact, however, she and Ruskin laughed and flirted during much of their time together. Surely they were not discussing Jeremiah on the evening of 3 January. 'I took her down to dinner on her birthday', Ruskin later recalled, 'and she was very happy, and talked to me and nobody else, and I talked to her, and nobody else (— and her mother put up her eyebrows every now and then — and looked at us out of the side of her eyes)'.[6]

The 'paradisiacal walks with Rosie'[7] referred to in *Præterita* manuscripts, were taken at this time when, in Ruskin's memory and imagination, glints of gold and bright silver in Rose's hair mingled with the flowers of his garden, by the side of the clear stream that ran between the Denmark Hill lawns. All spring was early that year. 'Did you see a gleam of sunshine yesterday afternoon?' runs a note to Burne-Jones. 'If you had only seen her in it, bareheaded, between *my* laurels and *my* primrose banks!'[8] In such an exalted mood as this, mixing reverence for her with a sort of rejoicing childish love, Ruskin suddenly asked Rose to marry him.

* * * *

Once the words were uttered the spell was broken. The playful relationship was ended. Perhaps Ruskin had spoken without thinking. In later years he would find significance in the date of his declaration, for it was on 2 February, Candlemas, the Feast of the Purification of the Virgin and also his parents' wedding day.[9] But Ruskin seems not to have planned his proposal and certainly had not approached Rose's father for permission to address her. Rose herself shied away from Ruskin's fantastic request. The most direct evidence of her response is in a letter from Ruskin to Henry Acland. We gather that Rose talked to Joan, did not refuse Ruskin but deferred any decision until she was twenty-one.

> . . . she turned to me and asked if I would stay yet three years, and then ask her — for 'she could not answer yet'.
>
> Do you know how old I shall be in three years? I said. Yes — she answered — fifty.
>
> I could hardly find any words at the time nor did I care to find them, but I wrote to her, saying (I think) what was just and right to her, — both of my utter obedience to her slightest wish, for ever; and of what she owed both to her parents & herself . . .[10]

The elder La Touches were so shocked that it took them some weeks to formulate their own official attitude to their putative son-in-law. Rose had come to London to be brought out, but they had not expected this. It was too adult. Not only had Ruskin been married and scandalously divorced, but Rose was mentally and physically unprepared for marriage. Her illnesses had left her with the body of a girl. All contemporary descriptions, and the one surviving photograph, record that she was attenuated. The reason she seemed ethereal may have been that she never became fully adolescent. There were many other reasons, temperamental, legal, social and religious, why marriage was unthinkable. Poor Rose understood less of them than anyone else. She was confused and miserable. Ruskin, full of love, was unable to help Rose deal with the crisis he had created.

He seems not to have asked himself why, on the next two occasions they were to meet, she fell ill. At a Mayfair dinner party given by her parents, her head ached so much she had to leave the table. Rose failed to arrive at a performance of Mendelssohn's *Elijah* she was to have heard with Ruskin. Amidst the jubilant music, with an empty seat beside him, he was trapped until the interval. On another occasion he managed to go shopping with her, for he had 'the reluctant permission of the father & mother to continue in any shadow of our old ways'.[11] But Rose was frightened, and we hear that she snapped at him. She refused his arm, though 'I've ordinary etiquette right to give it'.[12] He did not know how to continue their friendship, or courtship. When Ruskin had lunch alone with John La Touche, hoping to determine 'what were his real and final wishes as to my conduct to her', La Touche 'only answered "my dear friend" — and went on to other matters'.[13]

★ ★ ★ ★

In such circumstances Ruskin became agitated, while the La Touches were increasingly cool toward him. Relations were further complicated by the friendship between Rose and Joan Agnew. Towards the end of the La Touches' stay in London Ruskin was discouraged from seeing Rose alone. But when the family returned to Ireland in the first week of April 1866 they took Joan with them for a holiday at Harristown. As soon as they were back on their home territory John and Maria La Touche forbade their daughter to write to Ruskin. Rose still communicated with him, her letters replaced by messages or little tokens that were carried by Joan. Rose would let Ruskin know that she was happy; more often that she was praying for him; or she might send hymns of her own composition, with flowers and leaves. On one occasion he received a copy of Elizabeth Sheppard's *Charles Auchester* (1855), a novel in which teenaged, musical heroines are wooed by much older men.[14] Such messages were often ambiguous. But they would be the staple of his love life for years to come, sending him into elation or despair.

Now, in the spring of 1866, with Rose departed, Ruskin returned briefly to literature. In May he published *The Crown of Wild Olive*, a short volume made up of three of his recent lectures, 'Work', 'Traffic' and 'War'. He was proud of the introduction he then added. From its stately final paragraphs we gather the meaning of the book's title. Ruskin accepts the agnostic attitude that there might not be a life after death and that 'human probity and virtue are indeed entirely independent of any hope in futurity'. The crown for which men should strive is that of honour, not riches: it is not of gold but of wild olive. The sentiment is adapted from the speech by Poverty in the *Plutus* of Aristophanes. It would not have pleased the Calvinist banker John La Touche. But the book had much popularity elsewhere, and its preface was especially commended by the Public Orator at Cambridge when, a few months later, Ruskin was awarded an honorary degree.

Just as, years before, he had counted in his diary the days he might expect to live, Ruskin now numbered the days to the third anniversary of his marriage proposal. Beyond that date life was unimaginable. His immediate plans were also blank, wiped out by the frustration of his love. He considered not publishing anything at all while he waited for Rose to give him her answer. *The Cestus of Aglaia* came to its premature end. Does one gain the crown of wild olive by writing art criticism? Ruskin and Carlyle walked together over Clapham Common, talking, while Ruskin's coach waited to take them on to Denmark Hill. On another day, sitting on the Denmark Hill lawn, Carlyle suggested that he and Ruskin might find a way to write something together. But the younger man could not respond to the honour of the invitation. In these dreary and bewildered weeks, Ruskin took much notice of Joan. That was because she was his link with Rose. As summer approached, he thought he would like to take Joan on holiday. She had never been abroad, but had recently heard many stories of continental adventures from Rose and from Rose's dashing brother Percy, who had returned from a grand tour while she was at Harristown. Ruskin could not go abroad alone with Joan, so he overcame the difficulties of etiquette and chaperonage by devising a party of travellers.

In this way another girl joined the company of Ruskin's especial and favourite female friends. Constance Hilliard was the child he had first encountered when she organised a tea party at Wallington in 1863. She was eleven then, and just fifteen when she stayed briefly at Denmark Hill in the spring of 1866. Connie was Pauline Trevelyan's niece, the daughter of Pauline's sister Mary ('Mamie' to Ruskin) and the Reverend J. C. Hilliard. She had a sister, Ethel, and two brothers, Laurence and Frederick. The gifted 'Laurie' or 'Lolly' was to be Ruskin's secretary at Brantwood from the late 1870s. The Hilliard family lived at Cowley Rectory, near Uxbridge in Middlesex. In years to come, the entry 'Cowley' in Ruskin's diaries usually meant that he had sought a refuge there from life in London and, latterly, Oxford. The Hilliards would be friends of the Ruskin and Severn families for forty years and more. In this spring of 1866 Ruskin scarcely knew them, though he had been a friend of their Trevelyan connections since 1848. In her few days at Denmark Hill, Connie had got on well with Joan. So Ruskin realised that he had his party. It would consist of two Denmark Hill servants, Crawley and Emma (otherwise unidentified, so she may have come from Wallington), Joan and Connie, Ruskin himself and Sir Walter and Lady Trevelyan. The plan was that they would go to Venice and back, taking in all about six weeks for the journey.

This holiday, so generously and carefully planned, turned out to be the most unhappy of all Ruskin's continental tours. Notes exist for a projected chapter of *Præterita* that was to have described the journey to Switzerland and the Italian lakes, and the failure to reach Venice. Had this chapter been written, Ruskin's autobiography would have been an even sadder book. The holiday had partly been arranged to help Pauline Trevelyan's declining health. This hope was vain, for there was a tumour in her stomach. She died on the journey. Ruskin's role while abroad was therefore to give comfort rather than pleasure to his friends. He did so in a way that Connie, for one, would never forget. Ever afterwards their friendship was bonded by the way that it had begun in grief. The tour began in the shadow of another death. Just as they were leaving London Ruskin took a bouquet of flowers to Jane Welsh Carlyle, only to learn that she had died after running from her carriage to save a pet dog. It happened that this dog had been a gift from Pauline Trevelyan. Ruskin said nothing to his companions, who noticed his subdued spirits, until they read the news in Paris. 'Yes', he confessed, 'I knew. But there was no reason why I should spoil your pleasure by telling you'.[15] Pauline Trevelyan was ill in Paris, and for some days could not be moved from her bed. French doctors gave contradictory advice. Sir Walter looked after his wife while Ruskin took the 'children', Connie and Joan, on a day trip to Chartres. Then we find him in the Louvre, alone, drawing from Greek vases.

We trace the events of this tour through Ruskin's daily letters to his mother; and so his darker thoughts remain, for the most part, veiled. Some letters from this sequence are missing. They may have been lost at Denmark Hill, or Joan may have destroyed them after Ruskin's death. Probably they concerned Rose. In the extant correspondence Ruskin often laments that recent events had undermined the confidence with which he had previously faced the world. 'I am now quite helpless', he complained, '— and don't care to think about anything — it is all so fathomless — and so distorted & ludicrous in its gloom.'[16]

As the party travelled slowly from Paris to Switzerland Ruskin brooded over previous holidays with his parents. He especially remembered the family expedition of 1854, when they had gone to the Alps and he had been free at last from his wife:

> . . . it is very melancholy being in the old places now. We dined at Fribourg to day, in our old corner room, where my father read 'Ulrich the Farmer' to us, and where I drew in the inner little closet: the landlord is the same. We went and heard the organ. I sat in the same seat and heard the same tunes which I used to hear with my father, and it was very sad . . .[17]

Ruskin here refers to Jeremias Gotthelf's *Uli, der Knecht* (1841) and *Uli, der Pächter* (1849). These tales of the Swiss peasantry (which John James must have read in their French translation) are early examples of the sentimentalised novels of rural life common in European literature later in the century. Gotthelf was from the Emmenthal. In his village he was simultaneously a pastor, schoolteacher and farmer. Gotthelf was much loved by Ruskin. He forced him on Carlyle, and his novels were to contribute to the ideal society of the Guild of St George.[18] *Modern Painters* had already stated that in 'the sweet, quiet, half-wild, kindly and calmly inhabited Bernese lowlands' described by Gotthelf, the reader might find 'the degree of nobleness and refinement which may be attained in servile or in rural life'.[19] Now, as Paullne Trevelyan lay dying in these very lowlands, Ruskin's idea of peasant culture was struck through with sorrowful thoughts of death. She died at Neuchâtel, Ruskin and Sir Walter both at her bedside. On 16 May they read the English service as she was buried. Ruskin began an elaborate drawing of her grave and the cemetery at Neuchâtel, which he subsequently gave to Sir Walter. The bereaved husband was persuaded to continue a little while with the holiday, so the two men did some botany together; but they were never to meet again after Sir Walter returned to England. This was not exactly the end of their relationship, for one or two letters were exchanged. And Sir Walter's somewhat prosaic love of flowers affected one of Ruskin's future books. At Neuchâtel in 1866 we find the seeds of Ruskin's work of the seventies and eighties on flowers, *Proserpina*, whose themes are full of death and the hope of a future heavenly life.

The conventions of chaperonage now seemed quite pointless. Ruskin determined to continue the girls' holiday, and for more than a month he conducted them through Swiss towns and mountains, not omitting theatres and shops, before they reached Paris on 7 July and

Boulogne on the 12th. In the Hotel of the Giessbach, on the lake of Brienz, they made friends with the landlord's two daughters. The elder of them is the 'Marie of the Giessbach' who is commemorated in *Fors Clavigera* because she had been 'bred in the rural districts of happy olden days' and therefore 'taught me that it was still possible for a Swiss girl to be refined, imaginative and pure-hearted, though she waited on her father's guests, and though these guests were often vulgar and insolent English travellers'.[20]

It may be relevant to Ruskin's future memories that Marie was consumptive and, at the age of eighteen, a widow. Ruskin gave her a copy of *In Memoriam* from the travelling library he had brought for Connie's and Joan's use on wet days. Marie taught Ruskin the local folklore that attached to Alpine flowers. Sometimes she sang him songs. In her company he was almost content. He wrote to his mother that 'there is more of the sense I need, and long for, of fellowship with human creatures, than in any place I have been at for years. I believe they don't so much as lock the house-doors at night; and the faces of the older peasantry are really very beautiful . . .'[21]

Then a letter came for him. It was from Georgiana Cowper, and it enclosed one she had received from Rose. Alas, Rose's letter was of the sort that Ruskin would learn to dread. It consisted only of prayer and exhortations to prayer, descriptions of the valley of the shadow of death, yearning for the next world, all in the language of Low Church pious exaltation. Ruskin realised that the feverish outburst was 'connected I think closely with her past illness'.[22] He feared, with good reason, that her mind might have flown back to the collapse that followed her first communion.

* * * *

Joan Agnew had been invited to stay at Harristown in August of 1866. Ruskin felt conflicting emotions about the visit. Longing for Rose, he thought that the La Touches' hospitality to his ward was a further injustice to him. On the other hand, Joan would be able to tell him about Rose and her state of mind. Meanwhile, his first obligation was to stay with his mother. Ruskin now once more settled into a routine of life at Denmark Hill. He was not to go far from his south London home until his visit to Keswick a year hence, in the summer of 1867. He did not go to Winnington, partly out of exasperation at Margaret Bell's financial incompetence, and his drives took him no further than to Cowley Rectory. He maintained a lively correspondence with some Winnington or, by now, ex-Winnington girls, especially Dora Livesey, Lily Armstrong and his god-daughter Constance Oldham, who all occasionally visited Denmark Hill or came to stay. Ruskin's diary continues to count the days until Rose's coming of age. It is otherwise rather empty, expect for mention of dinner guests. Here is a familiar pattern of entertainment. W. H. Harrison, members of the Richmond family, Osborne Gordon and others had been visitors for a quarter of a century. In this summer of 1866 the old connection with Turner was maintained by the visits of the Reverend William Kingsley, one of the painter's most discerning collectors, and of Thomas Griffith, who had been his agent.

Various members of the Richardson and Tweddale families came regularly to call on Margaret Ruskin. So did her friends John and Jane Simon. Ruskin's mother now seldom left the house except to sit in the garden. But her mind was sharp and she knew that it was wise to be vigilant, especially when her son's Pre-Raphaelite friends came to visit him. The later edition of W. G. Collingwood's biography of Ruskin tells a story about those days that he probably heard from Joan:

> When Mr Secretary Howell, in the days when he was still the oracle of the Ruskin–Rossetti circle, had been regaling them with his wonderful tales, after dinner, she would throw her netting down and say, 'How *can* you two sit there and listen to such a pack of lies?' She objected strongly, these later years, to the theatre; and when sometimes her son would wish to take a party into town to see the last new piece, her permission had to be asked, and was not readily granted, unless to Miss Agnew, who was the ambassadress in such affairs of diplomacy. But while disapproving of some of his worldly ways, and convinced that she had too much indulged his childhood, the old lady loved him with all the intensity of the strange fierce lioness nature, which only one or two had ever had a glimpse of . . .[23]

In Collingwood's references to Howell we detect the animus Ruskin's most conscientious secretary felt toward his predecessor. Howell was a heartless as well as a dishonest man. He knew of Ruskin's suffering over Rose but had no sympathy for him. Indeed he made Ruskin's courtship the subject of some of his tall stories. These subsequently, through William Michael Rossetti, found their way into print. Ruskin was much in need of a more trustworthy factotum at this period. Not only was he dispensing much charity but he was busy with political controversy and was canvassing support for a poor cause. In the summer of 1865 there had been an insurrection in Jamaica. The Governor of the island, Edward Eyre, had put down the rising in a ferocious manner. He had flogged and hanged 'rebels' and executed

George Gordon, a black Baptist minister who had agitated for civil rights. Public opinion in England divided between those who supported Eyre's action and the more considerable party that wished to prosecute him. These latter formed the Jamaica Committee. They were opposed by members of the Eyre Defence and Aid Fund. It is significant that the main movers of these groups were largely outside Parliament. On the one side were the liberal and progressive intellectuals. On the other were those whose cultural commitment made them doubt the benefit of progress, democracy and modern thought. John Stuart Mill was the chairman of the Jamaica Committee. He enlisted Thomas Huxley, Charles Lyell, Charles Darwin, Herbert Spencer, Thomas Hughes, Frederic Harrison, John Bright and Leslie Stephen. The Defence and Aid Fund's chairman was Carlyle, who left most of the work to Ruskin. They were supported in various ways by Tennyson, Dickens, Charles Kingsley, John Tyndall and James Anthony Froude.[24]

Ruskin's loyalty was not to Eyre, about whom he knew next to nothing, but to Carlyle. The elder sage had the odd effect of making Ruskin oblivious to reality. In his devotion to the bereaved and grieving older man Ruskin forgot his own distress about Rose La Touche. Not long before, he had introduced her to Carlyle. It had not been a meeting of minds. Ruskin never fully unburdened himself to Carlyle about his love for the Irish girl. Instead he once more declared himself to be Carlyle's disciple, looking for his good opinion and hoping to continue his work. Here is the unlikely background of his organisation of the Defence Fund. Ruskin was one of the few people that Carlyle cared to see in the aftermath of Jane's death. He now transmitted to Ruskin even more of his prophetic and tragic political vision.

Ruskin's own social thought was now very distant from the provincial ultra-Toryism he had learnt in the 1830s. But still he had little contact with political experience or knowledge. He failed to understand the terrible events in Jamaica. Dimly aware that there was a type of peasant society on the island, he wished to impose on that island his own ideals of peasant life. When thinking of the problems of government in the wake of any kind of emancipation, his mind immediately turned to the slave society of ancient Greece. Such were the futile and inhumane deliberations in Cheyne Walk. The talks did no good in the world but produced some remarkable literature. Carlyle thought that he, Ruskin and Froude should begin a new magazine. Ruskin had an idea for a book he wished Carlyle to write: '. . . a magnificent *closing* work for you to do would be to set your finger on the turning points and barriers in European history — to gather them into trains of light — to give, without troubling yourself about details of proof, your own *final* impression of the courses and causes of things — and your thoughts of the leading men, *who* they were, and *what* they were . . .'[25]

Carlyle was not to write any such work, but the Eyre controversy spurred him to the composition, in the next year, of 'Shooting Niagara: And After?', though its nearer subject is the 1867 Reform Bill. Carlyle's essay may well be the most extreme utterance of personal and political disaffection in our language. Ruskin could produce nothing comparable. His *Time and Tide*, however (also of 1867), is related to 'Shooting Niagara', and so are many passages of *Fors Clavigera.*

In the latter part of 1866 Ruskin was helpless to write when he wondered what might be happening in Ireland. Sometimes his mind was unhinged by love. The death-filled days in Switzerland and thoughts of the poetic lives of Bernese peasants drove him to deeper and wilder gloom. When she went to Harristown in August, Joan would have reported the circumstances of Pauline Trevelyan's death. Then she would have described the subsequent wanderings of Ruskin and his two young friends through the Swiss mountains and valleys, the flowers, the songs of Marie of the Giessbach. But what could Rose understand of what had happened in the Alps, she with her mad religion, silly mother and grim father, in their pasteboard Georgian house, surrounded by the most degraded peasantry in Europe? Suddenly Ruskin had an eruption of emotion. He imagined himself as a peasant:

> . . . let Mr La Touche take me for a herdsman — *at Harristown* — give me a shed to sleep in — and the husks that the swine did eat, for food — and see if I should tire! But, as it is — I am so sick already for the sight of her, that — if it were not that it would plague herself, I would go to Ireland now, and lie down at their gate — and let them do what they chose with me, but I would see her . . . How could they help themselves, if I chose to do it? — They might have me carried away — if they chose to have talk over the whole county — but I should simply come back again, & back. What could they do — but let me see her. I would make terms for an hour's look, and no talk . . .[26]

These pleas and avowals were addressed to Georgiana Cowper. In London, in the weeks after his proposal, Ruskin had encouraged the development of a friendship between Rose and the benign Georgiana Cowper. He sensed that this might help his suit. Mrs Cowper would receive many dozens of letters like the one above in the next six years. During this period she acted both as Ruskin's confessor and as an intermediary with Rose. Thus the woman whom the adolescent Ruskin had admired from afar now became an intimate diplomat in the love that filled his adult life. Mrs Cowper not only carried messages to Rose. She received violent letters of a sort that Ruskin could not write to Rose's parents. She learnt her new role in other people's lives in the autumn of 1866. First Ruskin showed her his collection of letters from Rose. Then he explained his love and his ill-treatment by the elder La Touches. It was now that he began to call Georgiana by an intimate, spiritual nickname, 'Phile', and signed himself by the name Rose had given him years before, 'St C.' The well-meaning Georgiana was overwhelmed by the urgency of Ruskin's desire for her intervention. In late summer of 1866 he demanded that she and her husband should go to Ireland, stay with the La Touches and present his case to them. This was because Joan had returned from Harristown with little to tell Ruskin. Out of embarrassment and resignation to the wishes of Rose's parents, the two girls had simply not talked about him. Ruskin realised that he could not proceed without overcoming or indeed precipitating embarrassment, so he cast the Cowpers into County Kildare and awaited results. Two or three days later they were back in London with a judgement from the La Touches that the marriage 'could *never* be'.[27] However, a letter from Rose to Mrs Cowper gave Ruskin a slight opening. It said that, although she could not say what her decision on marriage might be in three years' time, yet 'I *could* tell him that I care for him very much now . . . and that *whatever* the end is I shall always care for him'.[28] In the same letters she recommended Biblical texts for Ruskin to consider and copied out some of her own devotional verses.

Ruskin's response to Mrs Cowper (extracted here from a much longer letter) indicates some of his emotional turmoil. And how, one wonders, could Rose respond to a letter such as this without becoming embroiled in profitless mutual biography and frightening speculation?

> One *word* of *common sense*, as to the kind of life which she believes we might live together — counting justly the difference of age — circumstance — temper and the like — and the way in which supposing herself to love me, she could bear with the difference in our faiths — one word, I say of simple forethought and advice, whether such advice related to the contingency of her accepting or refusing me, would be worth a thousand verses to me, just now. I know you

cannot get this — it is not in her power — and would not consist with her present ideas of her duty, to say anything of the kind, — & for such thought & tenderness as she expresses — do not think me ungrateful — but — forgive me — it is just because I have such perfect confidence in her truth and love that I don't much care for these pretty sayings — If I could write to her, I should say, My pettie, do you think after, through six years of my unbelieving, petulant, querulous love for you, you have never failed for a moment in your steady tenderness of care for me, that I doubt you *now*, when you know how intense the love was, and is; — (unbelieving and petulant *because* so great). Do you think I cannot trust you for three years — when I have tried you since you were a child? I know perfectly that you think of me — pray for me — and would and will — save me from all evil in your power. You need not send me any words to tell me this. But that which I *do* distrust in you, is knowledge of yourself — of me — of the world — and one word showing that you knew the real pain I was suffering, and that you had any clear conception of what my life was likely to be in *either* alternative, (your acceptance or refusal of me) — would give me more peace than a thousand texts . . .[29]

Ruskin was not to be vouchsafed such peace. His letters to Georgiana Cowper continued such tormented begging for years. In the winter of 1866–67, crippled both as lover and writer, Ruskin's main work was in botany and mineralogy. These studies could either be intellectual, or, if he chose, merely private and absorbing hobbies that took his mind away from sorrow and agitation. Ruskin's charities in this period are notable. Alas, we often trace them through Howell's function as an almoner. John James Ruskin's regular gifts were maintained by his son. But the younger Ruskin, not saying more than was necessary to either his mother of the family lawyers, began to expand his philanthropy. Howell was sent to Boulogne at the time of his father's death to give assistance to the Huret family. Years later, Paul Huret would recognise this generosity by gifts to the Guild of St George. Howell was in charge of a scheme to help George Cruikshank, fallen on hard times in his old age. Then he was entrusted with money for a shop-boy who wished to become an artist.

A more significant involvement in Ruskin's benevolence was effected by Octavia Hill. This determined and tiresome young woman had known Ruskin since 1855. She was then seventeen, equally ambitious to become an artist and to do good in the world. Octavia slept with Christian Socialist pamphlets beneath her pillow and laboured at the copying work that Ruskin had recommended, or required. For ten years he had paid her a salary to do occasional artistic tasks. The origin of her housing scheme, which Ruskin financed, was later described by a friend as follows:

> The 'grain of mustard seed' from which the sturdy plant of housing reform sprang, was first planted in Ruskin's house at Denmark Hill. One day he and Miss Octavia Hill were having a friendly chat, and he lamented the dreariness of life without an object other than the usual daily round. 'I paint, take my mother for a drive, dine with friends or answer these correspondents', said Mr Ruskin, drawing a heap of letters from his pocket with a rueful face, 'but one longs to do something more satisfying'. 'Most of us feel like that at time,' said his visitor. 'Well, what would you like to be doing?', asked Ruskin. 'Something to provide better homes for the poor', was Miss Octavia Hill's quick reply. The idea seemed to strike Ruskin, and, turning sharp round in his seat, he asked: 'How could it be done? Have you a business plan?'[30]

Octavia did have a business plan. So, at a stroke, the impoverished young woman became a person who dispensed rather than received charity. Art was forgotten. The more determined side of her character bloomed and then hardened as she pursued a new career as a manageress of philanthropy. Octavia's attentions were given first to Ruskin's property in Marylebone. She had the houses repaired, organised joyful communal festivals among the tenants and collected the rents. Ruskin himself took no part in these activities but observed Octavia's steady rise through the London Association for the Prevention of Pauperisation and Crime (to whose funds he contributed) and then the Charity Organisation Society. He also read the articles she contributed to such magazines as the *Fortnightly Review*. The title of one of her papers, 'The Importance of Aiding the Poor without Almsgiving', indicates her general approach. Octavia's attitudes recommended her to her fellow administrators yet were not happily viewed by the poor. As her biographer explains, 'her practice of offering work instead of relief and withholding relief if the work was not done, aroused bitter resentment, and . . . she found herself faced with the persistent hostility instead of the friendship of those she wished to help'.[31]

Reports of these difficulties were brought regularly to Denmark Hill. Joan Agnew was invited to Marylebone on rent-collecting day, so that she might see how bravely Octavia faced the tenants. Ruskin was not in sympathy with his little bailiff. He was more tolerant and forgiving than she. He had in large part created her but he had not formed her mind. Quite soon he would dismiss and denounce Octavia. He did not do so in a kindly fashion; but at the end of Ruskin's life, when he was himself impoverished and living in one room in a small house, she had her revenge by a further humiliation of the man who had helped her early career.

CHAPTER TWENTY-THREE

1867–1868

Rose La Touche decided to write her autobiography on New Year's Day of 1867. On 3 January she would be nineteen years old, and therefore she had not a great deal of retrospective material for her book. Most of its quite short manuscript describes her breakdown after her first communion in 1863, which Rose quite correctly and understandably regarded as the main event of her childhood. At its entry for 8 January this manuscript becomes a diary. It records the illness, and then the death on 10 January, of William La Touche, her father's younger brother. He had been a partner in the family banking business.

Rose's diary closes in February, with one or two entries written in London. The La Touches had travelled from Ireland after William's funeral and had arrived at their Mayfair house on 5 February. Ruskin was happily anticipating a meeting, for he had heard regularly from Rose during William's illness. She had sent him a 'lovely letter', then a 'beautiful letter', a letter 'with flowers on the envelope' and finally a 'divine letter'.[1] He hoped for a loving reunion. But as soon as the La Touches were installed in London Rose's parents wrote to Ruskin to say that she was not to see him or communicate with him. In his diary we find three scrawled crosses, with the annotation, written many years later, 'the awful day when I learnt what Lacerta was'. It was noted above that this nickname 'Lacerta' (i.e., 'Lizard'), as Ruskin explained in *Præterita*, was meant to indicate that Maria La Touche had 'the grace and wisdom of the serpent, without its poison'.[2] At times such as this, however, Ruskin fully believed that 'Lacerta' was an evil serpent, and a study of snake imagery in his contemporary writing reveals that Maria La Touche was connected in his mind with some deep horror, only partly inherited from Genesis.

As Ruskin knew, when he consulted his rational mind, Maria La Touche was not at all an evil or an unkind woman. But his love for Rose was not completely rational, and indeed would contribute to the spells of madness of his later life. Although he could not have expressed such a desire in the words of a reasonable adult, it is possible that Ruskin wished that Rose had not been born of womankind, as all people are. Not only was she virginal: her nature was such that her mother had failed her by not being herself a virgin. Only a little evidence supports this speculation. We know of Ruskin's strange dislike of babies. He usually avoided the subject of birth, including his own. In all his life he never approached his own birthplace, 54 Hunter Street, though he paid many dozens of visits to the British Museum and other places in Bloomsbury within a few hundred yards of the place of his mother's parturition. After Margaret Ruskin's death in 1871 she was commemorated by her son as though she had lived and died a virgin. Perhaps Ruskin could not bear the thought that his beloved Rose had come into the world as the result of a sexual act.

Maria La Touche, in the real world of February 1867, might have managed relations with the distraught Ruskin more graciously, if only for her daughter's sake. She did not know what to do about Ruskin, while Rose was now more miserable and confused than ever. Obedience to her parents meant that Rose found it difficult to talk to her only close friend in London, Joan Agnew. Since Joan was so clearly Ruskin's representative, Rose did not know what she was allowed to say about him in any conversation. She now developed the habit, never quite lost in the eight years of life that remained to her, of referring to her suitor impersonally, or by some formal locution. We do not know, so scant is the surviving information about Rose, how she addressed Ruskin when they were later alone together. It was probably by the childish nickname 'St C.' By the early months of 1867, however, she had ceased calling Ruskin 'St C.' when speaking to mutual friends. Henceforward she used the vague 'some people' whenever she referred to him in conversation or correspondence with either Joan or William and Georgiana Cowper.

It was through the Cowpers that Rose found a London milieu that encouraged her religious beliefs and was socially suitable for a girl from Mayfair. She moved among the fashionable evangelicals of the upper classes. Here was a bizarre movement, unexplained to this day by the modern study of the sociology of religion. A triumph of mid-nineteenth-century revivalism was its attraction to the rich and titled.[3] Soon after the great revival year of 1859, evangelical prayer meetings had begun in a society rendezvous, Willis's Rooms in St James's. Henceforward, in a number of West End drawing rooms during the London season one might find gatherings that had the flavour of revival meetings.[4] Ruskin had brushed against this kind of society and had greatly disliked 'a fashionable seance of Evangelical doctrine' at the home of the Earl of Ducie, conducted to 'the entire content of his Belgravian audience'.[5] He was no doubt an awkward guest in such company, but these evangelical occasions suited Rose very well. Many people she met at drawing-room prayer meetings in London also visited the Cowpers' house at Broadlands in Hampshire. Logan Pearsall Smith, the son of the famous American evangelist Robert Smith (who preached at Broadlands), has left us revealing memories of 'the beauty of Broadlands, with its park and shining river and the great house, full of history and portraits, and crowded with eminent people earnestly seeking salvation for their souls'. He recalled the curious mixture of the world with the spirit and the religious fervour among the beau monde. It was, he wrote, 'the strange world of evangelicals which was once so important, but which has now almost disappeared. It was a world, as I remember it, of large, opulent, ruddy aristocrats, living in great London mansions or country houses, and much given to immense collations and extempore prayers . . .'[6]

Rose herself now found cause to believe in the efficacy of public prayer. One recent incident had much contributed to her reputation for piety. For some, its outcome confirmed the unusual saintliness of her character. Ruskin described the circumstances to Froude:

> That subject of prayer — connected with all the sandy mirage of religious ground and hope — is a very terrible one to me in its close darkness — close, I say, for it has so often been brought to me, as it happens, by the singular character of that girl who dined with you here: — the strange purity of her life and thoughts, & the still more strange way in which apparent direct answers come to her prayers — even granting them a deception of herself and others, yet so beautiful and mysterious as to give me more pause, on the idea of their *being* deceptive, than any miracle would. The other day only, she heard, suddenly, of one of her friends being left by her physicians, as not having 12 hours to live. She was out at a party at the time, but among people who knew her. She had a hard struggle with herself for shame, but freed herself at last — and made them all sit down and pray with her. The sick girl, at that very hour, underwent a sudden change, steadily gained strength during the night, and in the morning the father came to thank Rose for his daughter's life, just as directly as if she had pulled her drowning out of the sea — and the girl is *perfectly* well . . .[7]

Rose was sometimes shy, demure, at other times startlingly bold. There was the girl who liked parties and clothes; and then the girl who made pointed enquiry of her acquaintances how things stood between them and God. To Ruskin, Rose at prayer was not as tantalising as the Rose who, two years before, had pranced along Piccadilly in a new hat, leaning on his shoulder 'like a prentice girl out for a holiday'. Not now allowed to see her, Ruskin felt wild that she might be involved in some gaiety. Joan gave him nearly daily reports of her doings. Ruskin complained that Rose should not be enjoying herself while he was 'in bitter pain'.[8] But Rose could give only one reply. 'He need not want to know so often how I feel towards him, for it is not likely I shall stop caring for him — I mean, it is not possible — and nothing will make me change and give my answer sooner.'[9] This was all Ruskin had for his comfort. His mother, though, had many devoted little messages. Margaret Ruskin's appreciation of the Irish girl's piety was as strong as ever, and in scolding her wayward son (as she often did) she told him how much she regretted that Sunday, for him, should not be 'as it is for Rose'.[10]

Perhaps Margaret Ruskin did not realise that her son was scarcely in control of his feelings. Both Joan and the Simons had to dissuade him from posting hotly written letters to Curzon Street. Much of his language, perhaps in response to Rose's own, carries images of religious torment. 'If she could understand the suffering and deadliness of it & how it kills the body and does *not* purge the soul, she might help me — not thus — Not by grave words one day — & going to the Crystal Palace within two miles of me to amuse herself the next . . .'[11] Finally Ruskin wrote to Rose's father. He begged him 'for Christ's sake — that I might see her face once more'. The reply unsettled him. 'He answered in such terms as — a Banker uses to his clerk I suppose'.[12] Ruskin in his life had never been so addressed. Henceforward there could be no dignity in his applications to his beloved's family. For they would not admit the possibility of negotiation. They forbade him to see their daughter, forbade him to write to her and declined to discuss her with him. That was all.

* * * *

In this spring of 1867, while his life was thus troubled by Rose and her family, Ruskin's mind turned from the Eyre controversy toward domestic politics. This was the year of the Reform Bill and the most intense agitation for an extension of the franchise. It was also, some thought, a time when the leaders of both great parties failed to make an intellectual case for their policies. Here is one way of stating the issue. If one fixed, say, a £10 qualification for the vote, did one do so because this was the low-water mark? Above this point, might we hope for a government of the wise and the good? Below it, must we fear the rule of the unwise and the wicked? As Ruskin noted, both Gladstone and Disraeli evaded interrogation on this question; for the wise and the good might be differently defined, by a pound or two, when either statesman next wished to win an election. For Ruskin, a

Platonist and an English 'Tory of the old school', brought up before the Reform Bill of 1832, such pragmatic indecision was dishonest. Thus, in 1867, the Reform Bill provoked his final disillusionment with parliamentary democracy. Many of his contemporaries, however, still believed that he held progressive views. They had been deceived by the obscurity of his political writing, by his charities, by his evident compassion and social idealism. But Ruskin was not interested in working men's fitness for the vote. He was interested in their fitness to be governed. Ruskin himself had never voted in his life, nor ever would. He had complicated thoughts about government but a simple attitude to the franchise. He saw no prospect that further democracy would improve society as a whole, nor any section of society. Ruskin's views were now more intransigent than they had been when he discussed the franchise with his father in March 1852. He was soon to announce that a working man's vote for Parliament would not be 'worth a rat's squeak'.[13]

This judgement was made in a series of letters to a working man, Thomas Dixon, that were published later in the year as the book *Time and Tide, by Weare and Tyne*. Ruskin had asked Dixon to send the twenty-five letters he had sent him to newspapers. Thus they had an initial publication before they formed a book. Most appeared in the *Manchester Daily Examiner and Times* and the *Leeds Mercury*, journals which served the towns in which reform leagues and reform unions were most active. Dixon was from Sunderland. By trade he was a cork-cutter who specialised in lifebuoys and bottle corks: these last to his chagrin, for he was a convinced teetotaller. Proud of his self-education, Dixon was also interested in his status. He wished to know his rights and he believed that men of other classes had duties toward him. Dixon liked to press his opinions on the great and famous. Often to their annoyance, he requested their philanthropy and involved them in protracted correspondence. He formed a library for the local co-operative society by writing to dozens of contemporary authors asking them to donate their works. The foundation of Sunderland Art School came about because Dixon had enlisted the sympathy of William Bell Scott.

Most of Dixon's correspondents took care to be courteous in their replies to his questions. But the stintless letters he received from Ruskin must often have puzzled or surprised him. They show little interest in Dixon himself. They make no concessions to working-class views. Their account of the writer's political position is not at all sequential or logical. Furthermore, Ruskin's argument is often cut by fantastic interpolations. These paragraphs seem like mad dreams or evil visions. Why, for instance, an innocent reader of *Time and Tide* might enquire, does Ruskin's treatise repeatedly describe his horrified reactions to a pantomime of *Ali Baba and the Forty Thieves*, and why does he describe a performance of Japanese juggling as an exhibition of the diabolism of modern life?

Ruskin wrote so extravagantly and irrelevantly because of his pursuit of Rose. She, her mother and Joan Agnew were regularly going to the theatre together. The Japanese jugglers described in *Time and Tide* were performing at the Crystal Palace. Joan and the La Touches saw them on 9 February. In Ruskin's diary are another three crosses and the note 'Bright morning. Deadly day'.[14] Joan saw much of Rose in the first weeks of the composition of *Time and Tide*. Ruskin, 'faint and ill all day long', quarrelled with his cousin for the first time, found it hard to remain in his study yet knew not what to do outside it. He now began to go to the theatres that Rose had visited, hating the performances but hoping that she might return to them and that, as if by chance, they might meet. He often thought of waiting outside Rose's Mayfair door, 'among the night beggars', to see her pass. He restrained himself from accosting his beloved but still wandered the streets of London in case she might suddenly appear before him. One day, on Westminster Bridge, he was taken with some fit of physical madness. He saw, thirty yards away, an open carriage with three women in it, 'going to Xl Palace I suppose'. One of them was a girl with fair hair. Ruskin ran after the carriage for a quarter of a mile as it crossed the river, then caught up when it was slowed by carts. Panting, he looked inside. 'The young lady began to look uncomfortable.'[15] She was not Rose. The sudden outbursts of longing and frustration in *Time and Tide* are purportedly concerned with public affairs. But they are evidently affected by the upheavals of Ruskin's own life. So are some of the more measured passages of this unforgettable yet largely unread book. These are often on religious topics; and in one fine exposition of the difficulties of belief in the Bible we may be sure that Ruskin is addressing the La Touches rather than the cork-cutter of Sunderland. It is the most firm and precise summary of Victorian views of scripture that we possess:

> All the theories possible to theological disputants respecting the Bible are resolvable into four, and four only.
>
> (1.) The first is that of the illiterate modern religious world, that every word of the book known to them as 'The Bible' was dictated by the Supreme Being, and is in every syllable of it His 'Word'.

This theory is of course tenable by no ordinarily well-educated person.

(2.) The second theory is, that, although admitting verbal error, the substance of the whole collection of books called the Bible is absolutely true, and furnished to man by Divine inspiration of the speakers and writers of it; and that every one who honestly and prayerfully seeks for such truth in it as is necessary for his salvation, will infallibly find it there.

This theory is that held by most of our good and upright clergymen, and the better class of the professedly religious laity.

(3.) The third theory is that the group of books which we call the Bible were neither written nor collected under any Divine guidance, securing them from substantial error; and that they contain, like all other human writings, false statements mixed with true, and erring thoughts mixed with just thoughts; but that they nevertheless relate, on the whole, faithfully, the dealings of the one God with the first races of man, and His dealings with them in aftertime through Christ: that they record true miracles, and bear true witness to the resurrection of the dead, and the life of the world to come.

This is a theory held by many of the active leaders of modern thought.

(4.) The fourth, and last possible, theory is that the mass of religious Scripture contains merely the best efforts which we hitherto know to have been made by any of the races of men towards the discovery of some relations with the spiritual world; that they are only trustworthy as expressions of the enthusiastic visions or beliefs of earnest men oppressed by the world's darkness, and have no more authoritative claim on our faith than the religious speculations and histories of the Egyptians, Greeks, Persians and Indians; but are, in common with all these, to be reverently studied, as containing a portion, divinely appointed, of the best wisdom which human intellect, earnestly seeking for help from God, has hitherto been able to gather between birth and death.

This has been, for the last half-century, the theory of the soundest scholars and thinkers of Europe . . .[16]

It was obvious that Ruskin's personal beliefs lay more within the fourth of these categories than elsewhere. *Time and Tide* reflects a further complication with the La Touches. It was as though Ruskin had been dragged into the plot of some grotesque comedy. Two days before Joan and Rose had gone to see the Japanese jugglers he had received a letter from Percy La Touche. It was a formal request to be allowed to address Joan with an offer of marriage. The letter came from Bologna, for Percy was travelling in Italy. Rose's 'botheringest of brothers' had probably not told his parents of his intention to propose. In all his pain over Rose, Ruskin saw some humour in the situation. He and young Percy were, in a way, parallel suitors. There was no other similarity. Ruskin had recently been offered the Professorship of Poetry at his old university; Percy had lasted five terms before being expelled from Harrow School.[17] Ruskin's early sojourns in Italy had brought home to England *Modern Painters*, *The Stones of Venice* and much else. Percy had returned to Ireland from his first continental expedition with a pet monkey, for a week or two the plague of Harristown. Ruskin, who at one point had helped in the resolution of the Harrow imbroglio, knew Percy to be an Anglo-Irish fool. At the same time his proposal of marriage had to be taken seriously. Joan was Ruskin's ward. His guardianship was to him a solemn undertaking. He thought about her happiness daily, as he was to do for the rest of his life. Could Percy make her happy? Everything that Ruskin knew of his character and past record indicated that he would not. And yet, as Rose had often said to Ruskin, there was good in the boy. What that was could not be easily defined, but he had great energy and bravado. Perhaps it was better to jump horses over Kildare ditches than to flute modern hymns while kneeling on Mayfair carpets. Now that Percy was approaching his majority a spirit of responsibility might be awakening in him. To choose Joan as his wife was perhaps its first expression. And she thought seriously and admiringly of Percy: she saw good in him. All in all, Ruskin decided that Percy might be very cautiously encouraged. It is likely that there was an agreement that no decisions would be made before Percy's twenty-first birthday in the early autumn.

In all these tangles there was doubtless a right path for Ruskin to follow. But the ways of duty and honour were not always clear. Ruskin was aware that his dealings with Percy might become worldly: an element of bargaining and exchange could be involved. That could not be right. Ruskin therefore turned to the one code that might give dignity to the situation. It was found in the literature of chivalry. One chapter of *Time and Tide* is entitled 'Rose Gardens'. It is a letter subtitled 'Of Improvidence of Marriage in the Middle Classes; and of the Advisable Restrictions of it'. The letter imagines May and harvest festivals in which 'permissions to marry should be given publicly to the maidens and youths who had won them in that half-year', to be followed by 'feastings of the poor'. Afterwards, Ruskin argued, 'every bachelor and rosière should be entitled to claim, if they needed it, . . . a fixed income from the State, for seven years from the day of their marriage, for the setting up of their homes; and, however rich they might be by inheritance, their income should not be permitted to exceed a given sum, proportioned to their rank . . .'[18]

Ruskin of course did not believe what he wrote. Nobody could. He simply took pleasure in chivalric fantasy and perhaps found comfort in its ideals, derived in the first place from his reading of Scott but also from Chaucer, whose 'minor' poems, especially *The Romaunt of the Rose* he preferred to *The Canterbury Tales*, from Tennyson ('Aylmer's Field' especially interested him now), and from any number of his Pre-Raphaelite contemporaries. In art, the dream of a world ruled by chivalry was conveniently illustrated by Burne-Jones, whom Ruskin extravagantly praised this summer in a lecture 'On the Present State of Modern Art'.[19] At the same time he began to think of a knightly company, an association of good men. There had always been something of this sentiment in his relations with Burne-Jones. 'All we true people', Ruskin had written to him, 'must make up our minds — if we don't see — to feel each other — & never let go. Else the wicked ones will have it all their own way.'[20] Stirring in Ruskin's mind was the thought of another Pre-Raphaelite fellowship, but one with a wider purpose. He wrote to Charles Woodd — one of his father's old friends — that those who 'have yet hearts sound enough must verily and indeed draw together and initiate a true and wholesome way of life, in defiance of the world, and with laws which we will vow to obey, and endeavour to make others, by our example, accept'.[21] In this, together with Ruskin's memories of Marie of the Giessbach and of life in the Bernese lowlands, are thoughts that led to the Guild of St George. The disarray of Ruskin's urban charities perhaps helped to direct his thoughts toward a return to the land. And, when the Guild of St George was formulated, Ruskin had Rose in mind. In 1867, despondent about Rose and Percy, Ruskin told Burne-Jones that

> Joan and I, in case everything goes wrong for us, are laying plans for getting a poor little house in the country with a garden, & doing all we can for the poor — I never giving big useless masses of money any more as I do now — but sixpencesses and shillingesses — innumerable — where one *knows* they'll do direct good — And we're to have a great bed of roses in the garden and a great bed of shamrocks, and a great bed of thistles, and a great bed of gentians . . . I don't even know whether I won't even put it to Rosie, when

> the time comes, as the only possible plan for both of us — For she couldn't live here, nor I with her sort of people. But I think she would be happy that way . . .[22]

* * * *

Apart from the 'Rose Gardens' chapter, *Time and Tide* is a Carlylean book. Its references to conversations in Cheyne Row are proud, certain of a shared purpose, devoted to the older man and defensive of his honour. But a report of such a conversation nearly cost him the friendship he most valued. In one of his letters to Dixon, Ruskin had complained — apparently as the result of a remark Carlyle had made in one of their talks — that the sage could hardly leave his house without being roughly shouldered by the disrespectful mob. The passage entered the newspapers and Carlyle (who had no quarrel with his neighbours) thereupon issued a denial, calling the paragraph 'altogether erroneous, superfluous, and even absurd'. Ruskin was astonished and not a little hurt. Had he not heard the story from Carlyle's own lips? He requested Carlyle to 'furnish me with a succinct statement of what you remember yourself to have said on the occasion in question, and to permit me to substitute that statement, in the editing of collected letters, for the one which has offended you'.[23] Not all the ensuing correspondence is preserved, but relations between the two men became almost hostile. Each felt that the other had impugned his honesty. As we know, both of them were by nature given to exaggeration. *The Times* made a leading article of the dispute. There was speculation in intellectual circles about the real cause of the estrangement. Carlyle wrote a pacific letter to *The Times*. It was reasonable, even humorous, and it publicly allied his political views with Ruskin's. But Ruskin was not appeased. His reason for a refusal of this *eirenikon* partly appears in a letter that was never to see publication. Carlyle has imperturbably marked the envelope '*ultimate* last words!'

> I more and more wonder at your not being able to distinguish between your lava-current of a mind — tumbling hither & thither and *cooling* in the odd corners of it at necessary periods — and my poor little leguminous — climbing — tendril of a vegetable mind — subduable and flexible by a touch — but utterly unchangeable and *implacable* in its poor wounded way — and changeless of temperature. One of the things that has struck deepest into me, in this, is the heartlessness with which, when I told you that I was fighting a battle of bitterest pain, now at the very crisis when of all things it was desirable that all possible should be done me by

all who loved me, for my love's sake — that you should have forgotten and trampled all this under foot — just because you could not bear some newspaper gabble — and written the most dishonouring words that could be set down in public sight —

I know you did not mean them — and that you did the whole thing frantically. But see what a deadly *fact* — this phrenzy is to me, in the new reading it gives me of *all* your doings — Your books have from this one thing — become at once a tinkling cymbal to me — and whatever the commonest wretches now assert against them — I am powerless *now* to deny! What you have said of me — I know now, when the humour is on you — you would say of any one — It is the saddest thing. —

And I always suffer this kind of thing from those I have most love for — and then I *cannot* forgive, just because I know I was the last person on earth they ought to have treated so — *Turner* did something of the same kind to me — I never forgave him — to his death.

Well — some day soon I will write the next necessary letter — you don't seem yet to understand that I intend the correspondence to be published, if necessary — Your two present letters are irrelevant — and shall not be held part of the series — unless you choose, but *after this* — remember — answer, or refusal of answer — must be for possible publicity.[24]

This was extreme. However, a reconciliation was somehow effected, perhaps with the help of such a mutual friend as Froude. Soon enough Ruskin was once more at Cheyne Walk, Carlyle at Denmark Hill. But the dispute had not been as trivial as its cause. For Ruskin had been prepared to break with Carlyle and to do so as publicly as possible. He felt misery at the prospect, but he had intended to drive on. The clash was not forgotten thereafter. It gave Ruskin a useful lesson in the public self-destruction that was to follow in his greatest years. One feels the wild, solitary Ruskin of the 1870s. The reckless certainty, the tendency to inflate a quarrel, the disposition to pursue it, the desire for publication, are all characteristic of the future author of *Fors Clavigera*.

⋆ ⋆ ⋆ ⋆

Besides his lecture 'On the Present State of Modern Art, with Reference to the Advisable Arrangement of the National Gallery', which he gave at the Royal Institution, Ruskin also delivered an address on 'The Relation of National Ethics to National Art' at Cambridge.[25] It was the Rede Lecture, given on the day after the University had awarded him an honorary LLD degree. Ruskin did not feel at home in Cambridge, and his greatest satisfaction in receiving the degree was in reporting the ceremony to his mother. Although at times he was irked by her fixed opinions, Ruskin was always tender and dutiful to Margaret Ruskin, and it was a pleasure to her to hear of his public honours. But Ruskin was disinclined to take official positions, even at Oxford. He had recently refused to stand for the Professorship of Poetry at his old university, not particularly wishing to follow Matthew Arnold, nor to be a candidate at an election; and he also declined an offer to become the Curator of the University Galleries. As yet, Ruskin had no strong feeling about university life. His feelings for Oxford were stirred not by the place and its institutions but by a visit to his old tutor, Osborne Gordon, at Easthampstead Rectory. This was Ruskin's only pleasant social occasion in the earlier part of 1867, though he enjoyed making a new friend, the poet Jean Ingelow. As soon as he was reconciled with Carlyle he left London for the North of England, brooding on the differences between his intellectual concerns and Rose La Touche's little sermons. He wrote to Georgiana Cowper that 'it seems to me quite as reasonable to expect that an Irish girl of 19, who cannot spell — reads nothing but hymn books and novels — and enjoys nothing so much as playing with her dog, should be brought finally into the faith of a man whom Carlyle & Froude call their friend, and whom very many noble persons call their teacher, as that he should be brought into hers'.[26]

★ ★ ★ ★

For most of the summer of 1867 Ruskin made his home in a coaching inn at Keswick. As usual he was accompanied by Crawley. He also took his gardener, David Downs, on this holiday. Ruskin walked, geologised, rested and wrote nothing but private letters. In his correspondence with Joan Agnew and his mother, to whom he wrote daily, we read of expeditions over the fells, of his good appetite (for salmon, lamb, muffins, claret, Irish whiskey) and of vague plans to buy a house. On the other hand, his diary does not seem lively. Then, on 7 July, it records a wonderful event. A letter came from Harristown. Though not more than a pencilled scrawl the letter enclosed a flower for him. It was only a dog-rose, but for Ruskin it was gloriously full of meaning. On his mountain expeditions Ruskin's mood even became exultant. Years later, he told Benjamin Jowett that a religious revelation had come to him among the Keswick hills, sunshine piercing rolling clouds with a vision of his beloved.[27] He now began to attend church once more. 'I go, chiefly, to please Rosie *some* day: for she does not hear of my going, now', he told his mother, 'and I am sure whatever pleases her, it must be right for me to do, if it is not right absolutely, which it most likely is'.[28] Ruskin's far longer letters to Joan tell us more about his religious feelings:

> Not much inclined to go to church [he wrote one Sunday morning] — but I shall — and see what is said to me — For you and Auntie have, I doubt not, been triumphing over me in a way which you hav'nt the least business to do. For, first, — I suppose you read the things which happened to me last Sunday as if they meant that I was always to go to church — But *I* read them, at present — quite differently — I read them 'If you *intend* to go to church, you are not to fail in that purposed duty — because you are anxious about your letter; but you are quite right in questioning whether it is good for you to go to church at all'. As this *is* at present a very principal question with me.
>
> Also — I notice in one of your late letters some notion that I am coming to think the Bible the 'word of God' — because I use it — out of Rosie's book — for daily teaching (N.B. verse for to day Ps 47.7).
>
> — But I was never farther from thinking — and never can be nearer to, anything of the sort. Nothing could ever persuade me that God writes vulgar Greek. If an angel all over peacock's feathers were to appear in the bit of blue sky now over Castle crag — and to write on it in star letters — 'God writes vulgar Greek' — I should say — 'You are the Devil, peacock's feathers and all'.
>
> If there is any divine truth at all in the mixed collection of books which we call a Bible, that truth is, that the Word of God comes *directly* to different people in different ways; and may do so to you or to me today, and has nothing whatever to do with printed books, and that on the contrary, people may read that same collection of printed books all day long all their lives, and never, through all their lives hear or receive one syllable of 'God's word'. That cross in the sky was the word of God to you — as far as I can at present suppose anything, in such matters — at all events it may have been — And in the clouds of 19th July — and in the calm sky of last Sunday morning — there may have been the word of God to me. And continually, by and through the words of *any* book in which we reverently expect divine teaching, the word of God may come to us: and because I love Rosie so, I *think* God does teach me, every morning, by her lips, through her book — at all events, I know I

get good by believing this. But one must above all things be cautious of allowing one's vanity to meddle in the matter — or of expecting a continual Divine help and interference. Most people's religion is so inwoven with their vanity that their religion becomes the worst thing about them . . .

Well — I've been to church — and have made up my mind that I shall continue to go — First, you see, the psalms for the day seemed to go straight at what was troubling me in numbering the days. (90, 12th, and 15th.) and the 91st had many things in it and the 92nd, 4th was always an old standard verse of mine — Well — then came the Obadiah & Elijah chapter — which fell in with much that I had been thinking about the fight I should have with the clergymen — showing how priests of Baal really *believe their own* mission, and have to be exposed and killed out of it — *can't* be put to shame in their own hearts . . .

Well — there wasn't much more until the sermon — which was upon the Bible's being a Revelation — and it (the sermon) was so abominably bad that it came to me as a distinct further assertion of the Bible's being no such thing, — and the more I looked at the man, the more his face seemed to me like one of the ugly faces under the cathedral gutters, spouting out dirty water, — pure once, but defiled by *them* and the dirt inside the leaden gutters they stick on — and I felt how completely here was a priest of Baal — who wanted extinction as soon as might be. And yet the man quite believed in himself — and in all he was saying — or trying to say. And then I came away — on the whole much helped and taught and satisfied that from that Rose's rose day I was meant to go to church again . . .[29]

If he was 'meant to go to church again' Ruskin was clearly inclined to do so on his own terms. While Joan (quite a puritan Galloway girl), Rose and Margaret Ruskin all feared that Ruskin was losing his faith, it would be better to say that his religious life was becoming solitary. He had never really had the temperament for communal worship, and was an especially irritable judge of sermons. Ruskin was now finding that his private devotions were of more use to him than church-going. These secluded religious exercises were of an uncommon sort. They often now concerned Rose. There were ways, entirely private to him, in which Ruskin could take the image of Rose, disregard her actual religion — which he knew to be arid — and convert her into some intercessionary being, star-like, remote and heavenly. Ruskin used her Bible, her missal, psalms that she had copied out and enclosed in her letters, to find the meaning of his day's work. He often resorted to *sortes Biblicae* and could find that certain passages in the Bible had been 'appointed' for him. On solemnly recorded occasions these verses, found by chance, might lead him to Rose. One verse he speaks of in his letter to Joan, for instance, which is 'So teach us to number our days, that we may apply our hearts unto wisdom' (Ps. 90.12), was easily connected to the numbering of days in his diary until her coming of age. Another letter to Joan gives the sense of his spiritual feelings this Keswick summer:

> I thought I should like a long, quiet day on Skiddaw by myself, so I gave Crawley some work at home, in packing stones, and took my hammer and compass, and sauntered up leisurely. It was threatening rain, in its very beauty of stillness, — no sunshine — only dead calm under grey sky. I sate down for a while on the highest shoulder of the hill under the summit — in perfect calm of air — as if in a room! Then, suddenly, — in a space of not more than ten minutes — vast volumes of white cloud formed in the west. When I first sate down, all the Cumberland mountains, from Scawfell to the Penrith hills, lay round me like a clear model, cut in wood — I never saw anything so *ridiculously* clear — great masses 2,000 feet high looking like little green bosses under one's hand. Then as I said, in ten minutes, the white cloud formed, and came foaming from the west towards Skiddaw; then answering white fleeces started into being on Scawfell and Helvellyn — and the moment they were formed, the unnatural clearness passed away, and the mountains, where still visible, resumed their proper distances. I rose and went on along the stately ridge towards the summit, hammering and poking about for fibrous quartz . . . It was very beautiful, with the white cloud filling all the western valley — and the air still calm — and the desolate peak and moors, motionless for many a league, but for the spots of white — which were sheep, one knew — and were sometimes to be seen to move.
>
> I always — even in my naughtiest times — had a way of praying on hill summits, when I could get quiet on them; so I knelt on a bit of rock to pray [here is a heavy erasure] and there suddenly came into my mind the clause of the Litany 'for all that travel by land or water' etc. So I prayed it, and you can't think what a strange, intense meaning it had up there — one felt so much more the feebleness of the feeble there, where all was wild and strong, and there 'Show thy pity on all prisoners and captives' came so wonderfully where I had the feeling of boundless liberty. I could rise

> from kneeling and dash away to any quarter of heaven — east or west or south or north — with leagues of moorland tossed one after another like sea waves.
>
> Then I got up, and set to my hammering in earnest: hiding the bits I wanted to carry down in various nest-holes and heaps, and putting signal stones by them, for I'm going to take a pony up with panniers to-morrow, to bring all down. Presently the clouds came down to purpose — as dark as some of our London fogs — and it began to rain too; but the air still so mild that I went on with my work for about two hours; and then sauntered down as leisurely as I had come up. I did not get back to the inn till seven.[30]

These letters are quoted at length (though they are still abbreviated) to give an impression of Ruskin's correspondence with Joan Agnew. From about this period he was to write to her daily whenever they were apart, and his letters are increasingly frank and intimate. Some 3,000 letters to Joan are in existence. Very few of them have been published. Certain letters were destroyed by Joan after Ruskin's death because they concerned distressing matters. Others were censored. The thick black bars that obscure what Ruskin wrote in the letter quoted above may conceal that he prayed on top of the mountain not only for Rose but also for his cousin's engagement to Percy. For Joan was then at Harristown, where she was staying under the awkward condition 'of giving her word of honour not to help me with Rosie in any way'.[31] Ruskin had left Keswick for a few days to visit Joan's family at Wigtown and discuss the proposed marriage with them. All seemed well. But when he returned to London at the end of August he found Joan in distress. Her visit to Ireland had not been a happy one. So badly had Percy behaved at his twenty-first birthday celebrations that it appeared that he had no real wish to marry her. Nor, given his 'faultful ways', could Joan any longer feel happy about marrying him. In the next sad month the half-engagement was broken. Ruskin totally lost the luminous, optimistic mood of his weeks in Keswick. Joan was sunk in her own unhappiness. Ruskin's mother wanted a change from Denmark Hill, probably because of house decoration or repairs. She could not be moved far, and so the three of them took up residence for a few weeks at the Queen's Hotel in Norwood. Ruskin saw no friends. For three weeks his diary records desolate walks and drives to Beckenham, Croydon, Addington, Carshalton, Gipsy Hill, Bromley, Hayes, Sydenham and Penge.

CHAPTER TWENTY-FOUR

1868–1869(i)

Ruskin's predicament over Rose was so unlikely that it could not have been foretold by anyone, certainly not by Ruskin himself. And yet he now knew that it was the centre of his life. The only explanation could be that he was gripped by some implacable fate. Ruskin's attitude to his own destiny is an important but obscure aspect of the writing of his middle and later years. His books discuss fate largely through a series of symbols, the most important of which is contained in the title *Fors Clavigera*. These symbols and images are also to be found in his dreams. Ruskin was one of the first men to make a record of his dreams in order to understand his own life and personality. Notes on dreams are henceforward a disturbing part of his diaries. On 12th October 1866 we find the first, 'black dreams'; and a few weeks later a dream about Rose is mentioned. We might overlook these unremarkable entries, but in August of 1867 there is the striking lament that 'I cannot understand why my dreams are not nobler'.[1]

Ruskin's concern is explained by the circumstances in which he wrote. He was at Keswick, had just received the letter from Rose that gave him so much joy, had resumed church-going, was walking the hills and believed that his mind was composed and relaxed. Perhaps mindful of suggestions in Plato, Ruskin expected some correspondence between his waking and his dreaming mind. But his dreams would not follow the earnestness and grandeur of his deliberate thoughts. Nor were they necessarily instructive. What was to be made of the dreams that followed? They concerned a wolf and a river; a haunted castle; a cathedral and music; Verona; picking damsons at a Cumberland house; a child, half-monkey, bringing keys; the court of Louis XV; a bandit exploded by pistol shots; white sloths and bitter spring water; Lake Constance; Stirling Castle; the Ruskin family's piano; and Carlyle. Ruskin also had recurring dreams. The most common are of the Alps, of swimming and wading, and of serpents. In February of 1868 the diary records the first of Ruskin's serpent dreams:

> Peasoup for dinner, no dessert. Dream of being with some embassy to Russia, and getting into a scrape about their church service. Then of four serpents in a tub, supplied as an article of luxury in one's

> bedroom with Russian chambermaid, with warning that they must be fed with fish pulled off the bones and put into their mouths, for if they ate the bones they would choke themselves. (Remembered, with remorse, having killed a serpent by that carelessness some time before). Lastly, took Joan for a walk somewhere out of a large inn, on a long stage before the horses came . . .[2]

Some days later, the diary reads

> Newton and Thos. Richmond at dinner. I took too much wine. Dreamed of walk with Joan and Connie, in which I took all the short cuts over the fields, and sent them round by the road, and then came back with them jumping up and down banks of earth, which I saw at last were washed away below by a stream. Then of showing Joanna a beautiful snake, which I told her was an innocent one; it had a slender neck and a green ring round it, and I made her feel its scales. Then she made me feel it, and it became a fat thing, like a leech, and adhered to my hand, so that I could hardly pull it off — and so I woke.[3]

Time and again, while he slept, the serpent would enter Ruskin's mind. On waking he sought for its meaning. His first thoughts were Christian. Then he considered the Greek Python, the opponent of Apollo, who is the god of light and art. He also thought of Maria La Touche. From about the time that Ruskin began to record his dreams the diary refers to her as 'L', short for 'Lacerta'. Ruskin seized on the name as though, by associating her with the serpent of his dreams, and of myth, he might begin to understand what universal forces had led him to his love of Lacerta's pure daughter. Some of these thoughts lie behind Ruskin's next book, *The Queen of the Air*, and the lecture he was soon to deliver in Dublin, 'The Mystery of Life and its Arts'.

* * * *

In the months after Percy La Touche made it plain that he had no intention of marrying Joan, her friendship with Constance Hilliard often took her to Cowley Rectory. Ruskin, who might have preferred to be at Winnington, stayed at Denmark Hill to look after his mother. Margaret Ruskin did not lack for friends who would come to hear her talk. Jane Simon, Georgiana Burne-Jones and others listened to her favourite stories of Ruskin's childhood and upbringing. Joan also heard these tales, many times; and it was in this manner that she began her training in the Ruskin family mythologies. Although she could not know it, she was already preparing for her future role as the editor and censor of *Præterita*.

A happier personal fortune was now to come her way. Arthur Severn was a young artist who had some contact with Denmark Hill. Arthur was often at the Richmonds', for he was the son of Joseph Severn, Keats's friend, whom Ruskin had met in Rome in 1840, when the Ruskin family had first become friendly with George Richmond. Arthur had a further connection with Ruskin because his twin sister Mary had married Ruskin's college friend Charles Newton. One evening in the late spring of 1868 Arthur, according to his own recollections, was at a party at the Richmonds' where there was to be a rehearsal of a play:

> I looked about me, and a few chairs off saw a pretty good-natured-looking girl with frizzy hair and a complexion like a rose, with no one to talk to. I sidled up and with no introduction began to talk. She was most agreeable, not shy, and looked amused I thought at my boldness. Soon however our talk was cut short by her being asked to go and sing or play until the curtain went up. This she did with great gusto, singing *Nelly Blythe*, *Old Folks at Home*, and other negro songs. When the party was over this young lady's carriage was announced and she kindly offered to drop my sister and me at Charles Newton's where we were staying. I was only too glad, being already rather bowled over. I knew she was a Miss Agnew, but nothing more, so when saying good night, asked her if she had a long way to go and where she lived. 'I live on Denmark Hill' was the answer. 'Oh indeed!' said I; 'Do you know Mr Ruskin? He lives there.' 'I live with Mr Ruskin and his mother.' How splendid, thought I to myself; now I shall have a good cue and can easily find an excuse to go out there . . .[4]

Soon enough Arthur found that he needed to ask Ruskin for advice on the correct way to paint clouds. He was invited to Denmark Hill and stayed for lunch. It appears that he was soon accepted as a suitor for Joan's hand. But Ruskin was also determined that Arthur should spend a long term in fealty to Joan. He felt some satisfaction that she might be married to a family connection. Yet he knew that Joseph Severn had been a failure in life and there was no good reason, looking at Arthur's mediocre landscapes and considering his lackadaisical ways, to believe that he was a young man of much promise. Ruskin was probably also aware that Arthur Severn spent time with Swinburne and the American artist Whistler.[5] At the age of twenty he was already a clubman. Here he resembled Percy La Touche. Arthur was therefore put on trial. He was to wait for three years, and during this time he was not to write to Joan. No doubt Ruskin insisted on this period of steady devotion because of his own sufferings.

There remained nine months before he himself was to be permitted to approach Rose for a second time. But Ruskin could not be patient, for she seemed to have violent alterations in her feelings. He could not know whether her fits and starts were the result of ill health or her parents' changeable prohibitions. Perhaps she simply scorned him? Rose had promised to write to him on Christmas Day of 1867, but had not. Distraught, Ruskin declared to Georgiana Cowper that she had 'cursed the day for ever to me into darkness with her broken faith — I went roaming about all Xmas day & the day after — so giddy & wild that in looking back to it I can understand the worst things that men ever do . . .'[6] Arthur Severn might have been surprised to know how Ruskin was affected by his courtship. In 'the strangest depression — unconquerable' he sought odd, physical remedies. 'At last I went out and ran for an hour round the garden and am better',[7] he told Joan on 3 January 1868.

In this winter and spring of 1868 Ruskin's published writing consisted of little more than his papers on 'Banded and Brecciated Concretions'. These studies of agates, accompanied by highly finished engravings that Ruskin made with George Allen, appeared in the *Geological Magazine*.[8] Then came an invitation to lecture in Dublin. Ruskin was asked to contribute to a series of addresses organised by a committee of prominent Irishmen. Their guests were welcome to speak on whatever topic they chose, except that discussion of religion was forbidden. Ruskin took this invitation as the opportunity to make a final statement. For he had been considering a close to his writing career, and in his chagrin at not hearing from Rose had sent a printed notice to all his friends saying that they should expect no more letters from him. Nobody took much notice of this, since letters continued to arrive. None the less, there was one sign of a change in Ruskin's writing habits. He wished his words to become more active and not to be confined to volumes in libraries. He now confessed to his cousin George Richardson

> things remain for me in a doubtful twilight — even as to my future (if I have a future) life-occupation. I am more and more driven to think that it will come to my taking a small suite of chambers in London, and devoting myself wholly to direct contest with its evil. This would not be a sacrifice for I have no peace in my present occupations. I have no pride in my writings or my knowledge (of art) — the first I know to be third rate: and the second I cannot

show. Science is a mechanical weariness to me — and every day seems lost.[9]

The Dublin lecture Ruskin therefore conceived as valedictory. It was to be 'on the Integrity of Life and its Arts — making it a farewell — and a very grave one — to all such work'.[10] In fact, however, as Ruskin once exclaimed, 'If I had been Robinson Crusoe, I should have written books for Friday!'

* * * *

We now have to resume the sad and wasteful story of his relations with the girl to whom so much of his writing is addressed. After her failure to communicate with Ruskin at Christmas, Rose had written to Mrs Cowper to say that she had judged it best if he did not hear from her, and perhaps especially not on that holy day. This threw Ruskin into fits of bitter rage. Georgiana Cowper received the first force of his passions. Since she was the intermediary between Ruskin and Rose, her task was to sweeten and transmit such accusations as these: 'She has nothing whatever to do with God's dealings with my mind. She ought to know — or to be told — and convinced that she has done (through false teaching and her own constant dwelling on her own sensations instead of other people's) an ineffably false and cruel deed . . .' Again, 'her sin is tenfold greater than Percy's, because she has betrayed a tenfold greater love . . .' Again, 'I laid my life in her hands, and she threw it to the dogs . . .'[11]

It is hard to judge Mrs Cowper's performance in mollifying such feelings. Most of the correspondence is lost. In any case, it is not clear what end she thought she would achieve. Perhaps she genuinely believed in the reality of a marriage between Ruskin and Rose. Certainly she devoted much time to her representations, occasionally with good results for Ruskin's cause. On 30 April 1868 a letter from Rose arrived at Denmark Hill, with another one a day or two later. On 4 May the one word 'Peace' is written in Ruskin's diary and on the same date he announced to Mrs Cowper that 'She is mine, and nothing can come between us any more.'[12]

As so often, Ruskin exaggerated. He also overestimated Rose's maturity. He found that her pious little notes were 'in one light, so exquisitely presumptuous and foolish — in another, so royally calm and divine' but preferred not to consider her as a confused adolescent.[13] He wanted to think that she was queenly. He also persuaded himself that she had returned to him through God's will. 'He has given her to me, and except by His word of Love, or Death, we cannot be separated more'.[14] This was only ten days before Ruskin was due to give his Dublin lecture. Its composition was quite advanced, yet might be adjusted, finished in a different manner. Taking Joan with him, he set off for Winnington. The school was on the route to Ireland. There, he thought, he would complete and polish his utterance. Soon, he imagined, he would read a magisterial lecture to an audience that would include his beloved. At Winnington the girls did not see as much of Ruskin as they had hoped, for he spent much time in this private writing. But he went on some memorable walks with them, examining hyacinths and primroses in the pale sunshine of early May. Dora Livesey, on a visit to her old school, took Joan and Ruskin for a drive around the neighbouring estates. One afternoon there was a cricket match. In the evenings Joan read aloud from Charlotte Yonge's *Heartsease*, made good friends with Dora and watched while the girls played and danced. She was able to write to Ruskin's mother that she had noticed 'the deep reverence for every word he utters — last night I went into a room and to my amusement and delight I found about seven nice intelligent girls busy writing out all they could remember of a little talk he had been giving them'.[15]

Margaret Bell could justifiably be proud of such scenes, and it is worth repeating that they reflect some of the best of Victorian middle-class education. None the less, Winnington's excellence was precariously maintained. Ruskin was of course well aware of its financial difficulties. He also now suspected that the school might have lost a part of its innocence and idealism. Margaret Bell's career would shortly founder in circumstances near to disgrace, and Ruskin's connection with Winnington would not survive the next few months. Here is a minor aspect of 'The Mystery of Life and its Arts', with its many buried themes.

This long, forlorn lecture, rewritten and concluded at Winnington, seems to bid adieu to the happy accord he had maintained with his girl friends. A number of his favourite 'pets' had now left the school. Perhaps they were to be lost to him for ever. In 1868 Ruskin could not have realised that Lily Armstrong, Dora Livesey and Susan Scott, to name just three of them, would be his friends until the end of his life and would often strengthen or console him in times of distress. It now fell to Lily Armstrong to perform such services for her old teacher. Lily was Irish. She was the daughter of Richard Armstrong, a Serjeant-at-Law in Dublin and Member of Parliament for Sligo Borough. The Armstrong family home was on St Stephen's Green in Dublin. Ruskin was to stay just around the corner in Merrion Square. Therefore he was not the Armstrongs' direct guest, but Lily had excitedly put together a programme of expeditions that would take him to the Irish countryside. While at Winnington Ruskin had received a letter from Rose at Harristown. All of Ireland seemed to be welcoming. Confident in his writing, tremulous in his love, Ruskin crossed the Irish Sea on 12 May.

The lecture was delivered in the Concert Hall of the Dublin Exhibition Palace the next afternoon. According to one newspaper report, there were 2,000 people in the audience. They heard an address filled with grave Biblical reference. But the first texts Ruskin introduced were not of the sort from which moral lessons were usually derived. They were James's question 'What is your life? It is even as a vapour that appeareth for a little time, and then vanisheth away' and the lament in the 39th Psalm that 'man walketh in a vain shew: surely they are disquieted in vain'. As the lecture proceeded it became more clear that Ruskin's thought had journeyed beyond the bounds of optimistic Christianity. The pagan Homer, he suggested, was as serious a witness of life as the Christian Dante. The tone is of general spiritual meditation. Then, towards the conclusion, came remarks unmistakably directed toward the La Touche family, and especially Rose and Percy. Ruskin criticised 'morbid corruption and waste of vital power in religious sentiment' and condemned youths who had no interests outside sport.[16] 'Can they plough?' he asked at the end of his lecture, 'Can they sow, can they plant at the right time, or build with a steady hand?'[17]

But there were no La Touches in the hall to hear Ruskin speak: and he himself, in agonised emotion, was not sure that he could manage to read his script without breaking down. His voice 'failed me a little for heaviness of heart', for the morning had brought a note from Harristown. It said only, 'I am forbidden by my father and mother to write to you, or to receive a letter. Rose.'[18] But if Rose could not write to Ruskin she could still send him messages. Her note enclosed two rose petals. Just as he had finished speaking in the Concert Hall a messenger brought a parcel. Opening it later, Ruskin found 'a large cluster of Erba della Madonna, in bloom, which was always considered as *my* plant, at Harristown, — enclosed in two vine leaves and in the midst of it, two bouquets, one a rose half open, with lilies of the valley, and a sweet scented geranium leaf, — the other a pink, with lilies of the valley, and a green and white geranium leaf'.[19] This gift consoled Ruskin somewhat. Surely the language of flowers had spelt out that Rose had sent him her love.

After Rose's death in 1875, these flowers would appear in Ruskin's botanical book, *Proserpina*. During this fortnight in Ireland he wrote nothing. He met dignitaries, was shown sights; he spent as much time with Lily Armstrong as he could; and one day he climbed to a spur of the Wicklow Hills to look down on the plain where Harristown lay. On 26 May he said his farewells to Lily, crossed the Irish Sea to Winnington — it was to be his last visit to the school — then returned to London to find, to his horror, that he had to face the most acute crisis of his courtship.[20] Maria La Touche had written to Effie and had shown her reply to Rose. Ruskin's former wife had now been married to Millais for thirteen years. Shortly she would give birth to their eighth child. The Millais family lived much of the year in Scotland, and when they were in London their paths did not cross Ruskin's. His love for Rose had obliterated Effie from his memory, where perhaps she had never been firmly lodged. But Ruskin now found that his past was being searched. Maria La Touche had gone to the one person whose testimony would certainly be hostile to Ruskin's character. He gathered from Georgiana Cowper that Effie had revealed some secret of their married life. We do not know what she wrote, and Rose's reaction to the letter is unimaginable. But it is clear that one must now approach the intimate and mysterious nature of the failure of Ruskin's marriage. We have the assistance of Ruskin's reply to Mrs Cowper, quoted below. It contains a reference to Rousseau. One theory is that Effie had written to Mrs La Touche about Ruskin and masturbation. However, it does not seem likely that Ruskin would 'often', as he puts it in his letter, have talked about masturbation to the gentle lady of Broadlands. He may have been asserting that he believed himself to be as transparent, and without artifice or dissimulation, as Rousseau in the *Confessions* had hoped to be. This observation does not solve the problem. A better hypothesis is that Ruskin may have masturbated while he shared a bed with Effie. This would account both for her accusations that he was 'impure' and 'unnatural' and for his claims that his virility could easily be proved.

Ruskin wrote to Mrs Cowper:

> Her words are fearful — I can only imagine one meaning to them — which I will meet at once — come of it what may. Have I not often told you that I was another Rousseau? — except in this — that the end of my life will be the best — has been — already — not best only — but redeemed from the evil that was its death. But, long before I knew her, I was, what she and you always have believed me to be: & I am — and shall be — worthy of her. No man, living, could more purely love — more intensely honour. She will find me — if she comes to me — all that she has thought.

> She will save me *only* from sorrow — from Sin I am saved already — though every day that I love her, I deserve her more, in all that she conceives of me — or has conceived. But it was not so always. There was that in my early life which is indeed past as the night. — I care not what she has seen — the worst of me she shall utterly know — but — let her also hear and know the best — There is more depending on her knowing me — than her fate — or mine.
>
> Therefore, now, insist upon knowing what has been shown her. Or perhaps at once — even from what I have said — you will tell her to forget me . . .[21]

At this low point in his romantic fortunes, it is fair to say that Ruskin was a brave man.

Rose, too, had to call on her own kind of courage. For some time she had been under medical care in Dublin. This attention probably involved periods in a nursing home. We also know, however, that in early 1868 she was living in the Shelbourne Hotel, the best in Ireland. This was not a complete contradiction. At later stages in her illness, Rose would often prefer to live in an expensive hotel rather than a sanatorium. In the spring of 1868 she had a slightly shrunken and nervous look. Her complexion was pallid but often shot with high colour, as though in her sadness she were prey to strange excitements. Lily Armstrong, just a few months younger than Rose, knew her only by sight and reputation. The Armstrong home was just a few hundred yards from the Shelbourne, and Lily had asked Ruskin whether the girl she had often seen in her carriage could be the Rose of whom Ruskin had talked at Winnington. 'Yes, Miss La Touche is my old Rose', Ruskin told Lily. 'I saw her often — this time two years ago. She was as tall then as she is now.'[22] Rose's illnesses had both aged her and wasted her natural growth. At the same time she clung to a conception of herself as a childlike, spiritual witness in the adult world. This was no preparation for the shocks that life now brought. Only a day or two after her mother had shown her Effie Millais's letter, Rose's elder sister Emily died, far away at sea, on a voyage from Mauritius. Percy La Touche was not a person who could give comfort to a sister. Rose's parents seemed increasingly remote; and since they had expelled Ruskin from her life, she realised that she would have to grow up alone.

* * * *

Ruskin feared that Effie's accusations — whatever they were — might have wider publicity. This was one of the reasons why he ceased to visit Winnington. He did not wish any scandal to touch the school. In addition, he had at last wearied of giving money to Margaret Bell. She had made no attempt to repay any loans, and Ruskin was paying the school's fees for at least one of its pupils. Such payments continued for a while. Ruskin had not the heart to reclaim the work by Rossetti, Burne-Jones and other artists (including himself) that he had placed at Winnington, so over the coming years such art was lost or sold. Ruskin heard of the school's decline from the Manchester artist Frederic Shields — who had married a sixteen-year-old girl and then sent her to Miss Bell to be educated — and from his god-daughter Constance Oldham, who did not leave Winnington until Christmas of 1869. He received their reports with sadness. Yet Ruskin was not exactly disillusioned. For nearly ten years he had participated in a unique and rather beautiful educational experiment. He had learnt various lessons and gained true friends. Now it was time to seek a different kind of philanthropy. Ruskin was in search of the right methods to express his social feelings and dispense his patrimony.

Only with the operations of the Guild of St George, from 1878, would Ruskin be able to feel totally content as a social benefactor. In 1868, in the months before the Guild was projected, there were uneasy occasions when he stood beside men whose political thinking was not akin to his own. In July he shared a platform with Gladstone at a meeting of the National Association for the Promotion of Social Science. The discussion concerned trade unions and strikes, and Ruskin criticised Frederick Hill's recent *Measures for Putting an End to the Abuses of Trade Unions.*[23] A fair amount of contemporary political literature was studied at Denmark Hill. Frederic Harrison, the positivist and Ruskin's former colleague at the Working Men's College, gave him his pamphlet on *The Political Function of the Working Class*, together with a request (one of many) that he should study Comte. Ruskin would not do so, but since he liked Harrison he frequently invited him to dinner and listened to his erudite conversation. Harrison, later in the century, would write interestingly about Ruskin, though often in some wonderment that this intelligent man had not joined the positivist cause.

* * * *

Though he scarcely knew how to admit it to himself, Ruskin felt some relief now that Effie had done her work. He had given up hope of a real wedding to Rose and found that there were consolations in hopeless love. Certainly he was free from the pleadings and negotiations of the last two years. His letters to Georgiana Cowper now come to a temporary halt, and his general correspondence is also sparse. Ruskin spent some time with Dora Livesey, who was visiting London with her family, and talked to her father, a Manchester industrialist, about strikes. Towards the end of August Ruskin left Denmark Hill for the continent. He did not go far, so as not to be too much separated from his mother, but settled for two months at Abbeville — as it happened, the town he had visited with Effie on the first occasion they had travelled together, in 1848, twenty years before. This stay was almost a holiday, except that Ruskin now gave more attention to his drawing than he had for some time past. For, while Ruskin never neglected his work with pencil and brush he did not often practise drawing, as he now did, to the exclusion of other activities. He never had a studio. Since his art was of description and notation, it responded to his topographical circumstances. Ruskin's art, without inherent drive, is also without 'periods', except when he made an extended effort to study a place in which he had a home for a few weeks or more. Such places were usually medieval cities. In the autumn of 1868 the Abbeville of old was recorded in some of Ruskin's most beautiful architectural drawings.

We have a further record of Ruskin's preoccupation in 1868 with the northern French Gothic he had loved since his boyhood, for in early 1869 he gave a lecture at the Royal Institution on 'The Flamboyant Architecture of the Valley of the Somme'.[24] This was written from notes he took at Abbeville. The lecture was accompanied by one of Ruskin's — alas — infrequent exhibitions. It was of drawings by himself and other artists, together with prints and photographs of architectural detail. These works were shown 'in illustration of the relations of flamboyant architecture to contemporary and subsequent art'. Some of them were by or after Titian, Mantegna, Dürer and Turner; and Ruskin also exhibited some of his drawings of Greek coins as examples of 'the flamboyant element in Greek art'. Since this exhibition was on view for only one day, it went largely unnoticed.[25] The lecture was not printed until it appeared in Volume XIX of the Library Edition in 1905.

Ruskin's diary and letters to his mother give a pleasant account of his life in Abbeville, where he 'went to work for the first time this many and many a day singing a little to myself' and entertained both his assistant William Ward and his gardener David Downs, summoned from Denmark Hill to make a study of French market gardening.[26] His correspondence with Joan Agnew reveals another aspect of this relaxation. It was now that he began to write to her in baby-talk. For the next twenty years, until his last letters to Joan in 1888, Ruskin would often write to this closest of his friends in a simulated childish language. Ruskin's first editors were not able to print any letters written in this manner and would not have mentioned the poetry from which the baby-talk derived if Ruskin had not quoted snatches of it in his autobiography. These 'pig-wiggian chaunts', as he called them, date from his summer in Keswick in 1867. Mindful that his father had chosen a boar's head when he devised the family crest, Ruskin wrote of himself as 'Little Pig', 'or', he was to explain in *Præterita*, 'royally plural, "Little Pigs"', especially when these letters (that is, to Joan) took the tone of confessions, as for instance, from Keswick, [in 1867]:

> When little pigs have muffins hot
> And take three quarters for their lot,
> Then, little pigs — had better not.[27]

These pig-wiggian rhymes seem to have dramatised overspending, wanting things he should not have, overeating, or other minor misdeeds of the nursery. Now, from Abbeville, Ruskin began to write to Joan in close domestic ways, asking her to record her dreams, demanding that she learn to cook (not a welcome suggestion to a girl with her status in the Denmark Hill household), addressing her as 'dearest wee Doanie' or 'Pussie', calling himself a 'naughty cuzzie', referring to himself in the third person as 'Donie', sending her rhymes and then writing 'Me so glad to like piggie-wig 'oetry: me tink him very pity too. — only me too coss to ite so must as he oosed — but me must, for pussy [illegible] 'ometimes'.[28] These letters, which Ruskin sometimes called 'nonsense letters' became more frequent in the next few months and introduced all sorts of nicknames, private jokes and references. They were not, however, nonsense. They reflect Ruskin's weariness with writing, his political pessimism and longing for his childhood:

> . . . And for the nonsense letters they are the only relief I have for a moment in the day, from the infinite pain of seeing — and thinking — in Italy — Oos poo wee Donie — *so* — ired — and so — tick — and so eerie — and so fightened — and so — only — dat if he hadn't his wee mamie to [illegible] him — he don't know what he oud do.
>
> For Italy is one ruined country — with idle wretches lounging about it — and Europe is coming to be little better — There was once a bonnie wee country, mamie dear — ey called it Totland — I pose because it was so nice for wee tots to play at pushing in wee

bookies . . . When I was the weeest of tots — it oosed to be so pitty, mamie . . .[29]

Here, in baby-talk, is a theme that would find more complicated and elevated expression both in *Fors Clavigera* and *Præterita*. Ruskin's mind was accustomed to making a comparison between modern Europe and an ideal Scotland that he associated both with his parents and his nurse Anne Strachan. The contrasts were simple. In the modern world there was decay and corruption. Old Scottish life — which Ruskin had glimpsed in his childhood, and whose traditions he had since learnt from John James Ruskin, Carlyle and Walter Scott, among others — was clear, truthful and vigorous. These exaggerated notions might not be defended by a careful cultural historian; but Ruskin was not such a writer. Erudition never calmed him. He took an emotional and personal view of everything he read or saw. Sometimes that view overturned mature reflection. Occasionally, it is as though he surveyed the world from the eminence of his childhood. Ruskin thought deeply about childhood at this period and at Easter had written an essay on 'Fairy Stories' (for a book of Grimm tales, illustrated by George Cruikshank: Ruskin's preface was a gift to the old artist) that no child could have understood.[30] Some of this interest may have been communicated to Ruskin's friend Charles Eliot Norton (the father of young children), who in 1868 was making another of his long visits to Europe. One of Ruskin's letters says that he had thought about 'setting down some notes of my life', but had decided against it. This remark may lie behind E. T. Cook's statement, for which there is no other evidence, that Ruskin began *Præterita* at Norton's prompting. Be that as it may, Effie's recent reappearance in Ruskin's affairs would surely have discouraged autobiography.[31]

During this summer Ruskin made a short trip from Abbeville to Paris, where he met Norton and Henry Longfellow. Ruskin had always liked Longfellow's poetry, which is occasionally discussed in *Modern Painters*, and he admired his recent translation of the *Divina Commedia*. Norton too was a Dante translator, of the *Vita Nuova*, but it does not appear that the three men talked of serious matters at a dinner they shared. Norton was anxious, however, to take Ruskin's education in hand. After a visit to the Louvre, they 'went to the Japanese shop which Whistler frequents and where there is a wonderful collection of beautiful and rare work, and where I expounded to Ruskin a little of the Japanese art, of which he knew absolutely nothing . . .'[32] Ruskin was more interested in going to a performance of *The Barber of Seville*. Reasonably enough, he thought of Paris as a place in which he would be entertained, not instructed. His real exchange of views with Norton took place in England. Ruskin returned to Denmark Hill, his mother and Joan Agnew, on 21 October 1868. Norton and his family were about ten miles away, for they had taken a house at Keston, near Bromley in Kent. From this base in the wooded hills of the North Downs the Harvard scholar surveyed the condition of England. He did so with much printed assistance. Norton was widely read in the general social literature of the day, and he knew where to find facts. The article he sent home to the *North American Review* entitled 'The Poverty of England' was based on the annual reports presented to Parliament on 'Public Health', 'The Poor Laws' and 'Agricultural Labour'.[33]

Furthermore, Norton's view of England was assisted by conversation with the intellectual clerisy. He knew a remarkable number of those people whom John James Ruskin used to call the 'leading men' of the day. In 1856, when he first met Ruskin, Norton was also introduced to Clough, Dickens, Arnold and Thackeray. During the next year he met Mrs Gaskell, Patmore, the Rossettis, the Brownings, Morris and Burne-Jones. After the break in his visits caused by the American Civil War, Norton's acquaintances were more concerned with public affairs and the more general life of the mind. In 1868–69 his neighbours at Keston were Charles Darwin, with whom Ruskin now reopened his acquaintance, and the positivist Frederic Harrison. In London, he met George Eliot, George Lewes, John Forster, Froude, John Stuart Mill, John Simon and, finally, the seventy-four-year-old Carlyle. Norton earned the respect of many of these eminent Victorians, even winning over Carlyle, and many of them had affection for him. Yet nothing in Norton's writing, whether public or personal, reveals a man of charm or kindness. He was capable of unreasoning hatred and malicious interference in other people's affairs, as will be seen.

Norton had little understanding of Ruskin. Over the years he received more than three hundred of Ruskin's most revealing letters, but his introductions to the American 'Brantwood Edition' of Ruskin's middle-period books are wretchedly obtuse. Despite their shared interests, the two men were never in real accord. Norton usually approached Ruskin through condescension. *Præterita* (at one of the points in its narrative when Ruskin was on his best autobiographical behaviour) summarises this condescension as follows. Norton, by eight years Ruskin's junior, 'saw all my weaknesses, measured all my narrownesses, and, from the first, took . . . a kind of paternal authority over me . . . he never allowed me the slightest violation of the laws, either of good writing, or social prudence, without instant blame, or warning . . .'[34] With his powers as Ruskin's literary executor Norton was able to destroy significant portions of their correspondence; so we do not have a complete record of his instruction in literary manners. *Præterita* goes on to the urbane — and unbelievable — confession that 'I was entirely conscious of his rectorial power, and affectionately submissive to it; so that he might have done anything with me, but for the unhappy difference in our innate, and unchangeable, political faiths'.[35]

CHAPTER TWENTY-FIVE

1868–1869(ii)

Among Ruskin's preoccupations at Abbeville in 1868 was a 'paper on employment', as his diary calls it.[1] Ruskin was writing on the subject because he had been invited to join a committee of public men who were concerned by current unemployment and destitution. He was also affected by the life he observed in Abbeville and its neighbourhood. By this date, Ruskin's correspondence with girls he had met at Winnington was only occasional. None the less he wrote long letters from Abbeville to Dora Livesey which tell her of his reactions to rural poverty in France:

> Abbeville is a lovely old town still lying among groves of aspen poplars beside the Somme, of which the ford was so fortunate to be English the day before Crécy; and on each side of the valley there are long swells of chalk hills, now covered with scabious & bluebells where I can get the purest air and as long walks as I care to take.
>
> I have still some remains of old sanguine plans and thoughts clinging about me — but the one thing that is borne in upon me constantly is the intense need there is for example and help in the leading of simple and useful life, with grace and pleasure. The French used to be a happy race, but the faces are much saddened in these last twenty years and the separation into unhappy poor and greedy rich is accomplishing itself fatally among us — and the absence of any joy or steady progress in life is too clearly marked by the languid & reckless air of the men — and worn, patient, resolutely stern look of the best peasant women, while the neglect and disorder about their cottages is pitiful.
>
> If only one could get a little space of ground, and establish a little colony of one's friends and get things into bright working order — and enlarge one's field of working gradually![2]

The 'paper on employment' would be published as *Notes on the General Principles of Employment for the Destitute and Criminal Classes*. This is the least Ruskinian of all Ruskin's titles, perhaps because the pamphlet had an ulterior purpose. Ruskin had it printed in November after his return from France. He was seeking to pre-empt both the agenda and the deliberations of the committee he was about to join by sending the pamphlet (marked 'for private circulation only') to his fellow committee members and other interested parties. Such a tactic had previously served Ruskin's purposes well. In 1857 he had issued pamphlets about Turner's bequest to the nation, in which he demonstrated that he alone could be trusted with its arrangement. Now Ruskin wrote a few thousand words in order to impose his views on a much wider field of public administration. He did so only in abstract terms, for his committee had no executive function. It merely debated resolutions. In general, Ruskin thought, its members were divided between 'the men who consider the poor a nuisance to be repressed, and those who consider them a material to be worked up'.[3] He disliked the former of these groups and distrusted the latter. We find Ruskin's own proposals at the end of his pamphlet. He thought that the 'idle' might be set to 'road-making', 'bringing-in of waste land', 'harbour-making', 'porterage' (the transit of heavy goods by canal), 'repair of buildings', 'dress-making' and 'works of art'. He added that 'the last two departments, and some subordinate branches of the others, would include the service of women and children'.[4]

After a fortnight of profitless talk we hear no more of Ruskin at this committee. Yet the exercise had not been totally in vain. He met two men whose characters he appreciated and who, in their turn, recognised Ruskin's unique mind and fervent belief that the modern world was not as it should be. They were Cardinal Manning, whom Ruskin would soon meet again as a fellow member of the Metaphysical Society, and William Jolly, who was one of Her Majesty's Inspectors of Schools and, within the terms of his office, a progressive thinker. Jolly now became a student of Ruskin's writings. In the years to come he made a collection of all Ruskin's opinions on education and finally published a selection from his clippings as *Ruskin on Education. Some Needed but Neglected Elements Restated and Reviewed by William Jolly* (1894).

Quite correctly, Jolly's compilation insisted on the study of natural history; always, to Ruskin's mind, the vital part of any education. In November and December of 1868 Ruskin pursued his individual researches into the wonders of nature, perhaps stimulated by his occasional meetings with Darwin at this period. In Westminster he had talks about unemployment. At home in Denmark Hill he wrote the analysis of moss which was to form the first chapter of that un-Darwinian book *Proserpina*, eventually published in 1875. The mosses beneath his pocket-lens ('of no great power', Ruskin said, for his eyesight was still that of a younger man) took his mind from the affairs of the world.[5] Yet he was determined not to ignore the condition of England. A number of letters show that he was beginning to formulate his utopian Toryism of the 1870s. When he wrote to Dora Livesey about a 'little colony of one's friends', he used the word because he was thinking of America. Charles Eliot Norton's presence in London raised the question of American democracy and American culture, a topic of occasional speculation among the Victorian intelligentsia. As we have seen, Ruskin in the 1850s had a not unfriendly curiosity about American art and thought that the young country would one day have a school of its own. He was quite well read in American literature and certainly knew the work of Emerson, Longfellow and Lowell. Ruskin's comments about America were more equivocal after the period of its civil war, and were often sardonic. None the less, he retained an interest in American utopianism and at the end of the 1860s was prepared to consider the ideas of the fraudulent Thomas Lake Harris, the founder of the Brotherhood of the New Life, and Harris's English supporter and agent, Laurence Oliphant.[6]

Ruskin heard of Harris's utopian theories through their mutual friends, William and Georgiana Cowper.[7] Here we enter an obscure part of the world of late Victorian idealism. At the end of the 1860s and the beginning of the 1870s the Cowpers developed an informal network of people who were interested in a new social and spiritual order. What that order might be, no friend of the Cowpers could precisely say. It is also difficult to establish the Cowpers' own beliefs, except to say that they were not satisfied by conventional philanthropy or orthodox religion. Georgiana, the more active of the couple, appears to modern observers to have floated in a sea of benevolent new thinking. She was at her best as a hostess. Broadlands was a large house surrounded by acres of parkland. Both partners in this marriage had inherited fortunes. The Cowpers were generous, and they welcomed utopians, Swedenborgians, artists, spiritualists and Christian Socialists to their home. Ruskin was probably the only regular guest at Broadlands who described his opinions as those of an old-fashioned Tory. Rose La Touche may have been the only visitor with obdurate evangelical views. In their separate ways they presented a challenge to the hospitable Georgiana. She delighted in 'bringing people together', to use a favourite phrase by which she implied spiritual harmony.[8] Georgiana now continued her task, which had been willingly undertaken, to bring Ruskin and Rose together and to harmonise relations between the Irish girl's suitor and the elder La Touches. It is worth trying to summarise these difficulties as they stood in the winter of 1868–69.

* * * *

So little is known about Rose, her character and health, that biographers must interpret chance pieces of information. Olive Mackenzie, whose grandparents had been servants at Harristown in the 1860s and 1870s, related that her mother had been christened Rose, after Rose La Touche, and that

> as my mother grew up, I gather that she & Rose were good friends. It was probably the interest of a young woman in an attractive child — anyway, my mother described to me how Rose was very kind to her & the highlight of each week, when she was a little girl, was when Rose drove her in a 'gig', a pony & trap into town for shopping . . .
>
> I did ask my mother about this & she told me that Rose was an unusually lovely girl — pink-cheeked and frail. My mother's opinion was that Rose probably suffered from T.B. which was prevalent and fatal in those times . . .[9]

Olive Mackenzie thus leads us to imagine Rose as a confident young woman, kind to the household servants and not altogether orthodox, for a person of her class would not usually have made such shopping trips to the local town. Perhaps she would have been more shy and reserved in London society, or among the strange people who gathered at Broadlands. It seems that Rose was well known in Naas (the market town near to Harristown) and its neighbourhood. Her mother once said of Rose's relations with the poor, 'She gets on with them better than I do. I am afraid of intruding. But Rosie runs in and out of the cabins as a breeze of wind might do and is mixed up with nearly every village bother.'[10] Rose's breezy visits were characteristically mixed with piety. She went into the cabins to distribute tracts supplied by her father.

Olive Mackenzie's speculation that Rose suffered from tuberculosis is persuasive, especially since it comes from a person who was close to the La Touche family. Yet we know that Rose had other maladies, illnesses that mystified her doctors. Ruskin heard about these afflictions and anxiously asked medical friends to help with a diagnosis. The first of these friends was John Simon. A letter exists from Simon to Ruskin. Its brusque, even coarse masculine tone cannot have soothed Ruskin's worries:

> . . . the 'fatty degeneration' is something in which I should ask you not to believe except of first-rate medical authority . . . My knowledge of your will-o'-the-wisp is neither much nor recent; but such

impression of it as I have leads me to extreme a priori scepticism as to have her having any true signs of the disease, or being likely to show any for the next 30 or 40, not to say 50 or 60 years. Fearfully and wonderfully made are the insides of hysterically-minded young women. Their 'mortal diseases' are innumerable; but the perverse sprites go living on, with their treacherous iridescent surfaces, pleading themselves to be mere plastic squash, but of an adamantinity which is of the devil.

If there is really anything beyond co-feminising twaddle to justify a *suspicion* of organic heart-disease of any kind, by all means get a conclusive medical opinion . . . But meanwhile, poet and cloud-lover, don't be sad with any forebodings as to this phantasm, except in the common and inevitable sadness that dawn-colours are not also for sunset . . . It might be anguish to see from beforehand the sweet virginal capriosities of 16 rigidifying into the staring chromo-lithographs of midlife . . .[11]

Simon's letter is not fully dated, but his 'Thursday, Mar 5' places it in 1868. In that month Ruskin had received his invitation to lecture in Dublin and imagined that he might meet Rose while he was in Ireland. The 'fatty degeneration' was probably a theory about Rose's illness because she was so alarmingly thin. We note that Simon knew (though he may have assumed) that Rose was a 'hysterically-inclined' young woman. He puts aside the possibility, evidently voiced by women who knew Rose, that she was the victim of an 'organic heart-disease' and finally hints that Rose's ailments were a part of her passage from adolescence into womanhood. Knowing Ruskin as he did, the shrewd doctor realised that his friend might be disturbed by the onset of female physical maturity. Rose was unwell during the later months of 1868 and the earlier part of 1869, the time of her twenty-first birthday on 3 January and the anniversary of Ruskin's marriage proposal on 2 February. She may have been so ill, and relations between the Ruskin and La Touche families so poor, that her suitor thought that there was no point in speaking of these sacred dates. They were not mentioned in Ruskin's correspondence and are not recorded in his diary. In December of 1868 Maria La Touche had asked Joan not to write to Rose again, perhaps not ever, though the two young women were friends. She gave her reasons to Georgiana Cowper:

After Rose had sent her first letter to Joan last Wednesday, she was seized with one of the attacks of violent pain which the slightest agitation now causes. Her doctor at once saw that she had been subjected to fresh excitement, and said it was in vain to hope for any progress as long as there was a possibility of renewed agitation . . .

I would wish you in a measure to understand how extremely painful and agitating to me, it must be to receive any letter that ever so remotely recalls the idea of Mr Ruskin and the outrage he has offered us.

I send you a copy of a legal opinion taken upon the supposed case of a man divorced on the plea of 'incurable impotency' (such are the terms of the Decree of which I possess a copy, in the Divorce case of Ruskin *v.* Ruskin), and I ask you if it is pardonable that he should have offered marriage to any woman upon earth . . .

When he came to Dublin last spring he talked familiarly of Rose in many quarters; bringing, indeed, ignominy upon himself, but much injurious notice and curiosity upon her; and of course the disgusting history of his past has been raised here, and Rose spoken of in connection with it — to the intense indignation of her family and friends. Mr Ruskin had not even the humanity, knowing as he did Rose's tendency to cerebral disease, to spare her the perplexity and misery of having to hear, over and over again, his appeals and those of his friends, against the right judgment of her natural protectors . . .[12]

Maria La Touche's anxieties are understandable, and surely Rose's illnesses made her think that Ruskin was her daughter's tormenter. This may be the correct place to print the only surviving letter from Ruskin to Rose. One sheet remains. It may have been separated from the original, no doubt much longer missive because Ruskin used clandestine methods to communicate with Rose. The writing is on Denmark Hill paper, is large, careful, and evidently addressed to an invalid. Ruskin speaks to Rose about a Victorian invention. The page is marked (2) and reads

. . . Joanna, to take her to Miss Ingelow. And I took her there; and Claribel had come there to meet us, and she sang to me, 'Take back the heart' — *so* perfectly — and my hand was on my letter the while — and my heart wondering if my darling *had* flown back to me.

Would you not have liked to have seen Claribel and Jean Ingelow together teaching Joan to sew with a sewing machine — and me kneeling between the three of them, trying to make out how the needle pulled the thread through? And all of us happy — for Joanna had more hope from the seal than I had — and had given some of her hope to me.[13]

The 'seal' mentioned in this scrap of letter probably refers to the dignities of a Harristown envelope. Rose was by nature and necessity a letter writer. By one means or another she used her correspondence to send messages to Ruskin, via Georgiana Cowper or Joan Agnew, though her messages were never clear. 'What *does* the little Beastie mean, I wonder —' Ruskin wrote to Joan after he had received one such enigmatic sign, with flowers in the slender package.

* * * *

Ruskin's intellectual work of 1869 began with a lecture, which he accompanied by a small exhibition, at the Royal Institution. In the new year he gave much effort to the composition of 'The Flamboyant Architecture of the Valley of the Somme', which is a fervent restatement of his views on Gothic and contemporary architecture. This was a personal lecture. We are reminded that French building was only a little less important to Ruskin than the architecture he celebrated and lamented in *The Stones of Venice*, and it is worth noting that in 1869 Ruskin had not visited Venice for seventeen years.

The immediate inspiration of his Royal Institution lecture (delivered on 29 January) was his work in Abbeville in the autumn of 1868. The address began with a radiant description of the town as it was seen by a traveller in former years. We may be certain that Ruskin was remembering, with diminishing pleasure, his previous visits to Abbeville in 1835, 1848 and 1858. In the lecture theatre Ruskin's tone abruptly changed after his elegiac opening. 'All that's gone — and most of Abbeville is like most of London — rows of houses, all alike, with a heap of brickbats at the end of it . . .'[14] He then (with a number of marvellous digressions) returned to the principles set down in *The Seven Lamps of Architecture*, a book much influenced by Abbeville as it existed in 1848. At that period, accompanied by his virgin bride, Ruskin had studied buildings with a passion he never showed in his married life. 'The Flamboyant Architecture of the Valley of the Somme' is also highly emotional, perhaps reflecting his longing for marriage to Rose, and at one point Ruskin claims that a true architect must be a passionate man. It seems that there were architects among his audience. Ruskin had warm words for G. E. Street, whom he respected both for his work and for his knowledge of medieval building, but other architects must have felt that they had been contemptuously dismissed. Fine building could only come about, Ruskin claimed, in a new society. 'Architecture is possible only to a people who have a Common Pride, and a Common-Wealth, — whose Pride is Civic — and is the Pride of All'.[15]

Ruskin's relations with the hierarchy of the architectural profession, never very close, were now coming to their end. He did not publish 'The Flamboyant Architecture of the Valley of the Somme' and the lecture did not see print until 1905, when it was included in Volume XIX of the Library Edition. Ruskin did however publish an interesting adjunct to his lecture, a pamphlet entitled *References to the Series of Paintings and Sketches, from Mr Ruskin's Collection, shown in Illustration of the Relations of Flamboyant Architecture to Contemporary and Subsequent Art.*[16] In this catalogue are listed fifty works which were hung in the Royal Institution to accompany Ruskin's lecture. Their relationship to 'The Flamboyant Architecture of the Somme' is not absolute. The catalogue rather calls our attention to two other matters: Ruskin's art collection as it existed in Denmark Hill at the end of the 1860s, and his own powers as an artist at that time. At Abbeville, Ruskin had made one highly finished, rather anomalous drawing, a view of the town's market place. Significantly, its style is reminiscent of English art of the late 1830s. Studies of the church of St Vulfran are more characteristic of Ruskin's drawing in his middle years. Each sheet focuses on architectural detail. There are delicate washes of watercolour, and much of the paper is left blank. The exhibition also included a number of photographs of buildings, taken by Ruskin's assistant Arthur Burgess, a former pupil from the Working Men's College, engravings and copies after Leonardo, Dürer and Mantegna, and three oil paintings. These canvases show a curious side of Ruskin's taste. He exhibited *A French Cottage Interior* by Edouard Frère, a sentimental French artist whom Ruskin admired and occasionally tried to introduce to an English audience. A portrait of Andrea Gritti, the Doge of Venice, believed by Ruskin to be by Titian, hung close to the Frère. Ruskin had bought it from the Very Revd Gilbert Elliot (Dean of Bristol) for £1,000. This was the canvas, nowadays attributed to Catena, shown in court in 1878 during the 'Whistler Trial' as an example of perfect finish. The third painting was Louis Ernest Meissonier's *Napoleon in 1814.* Ruskin had no great love for this picture but was intrigued by its technique. On an impulse, he had recently bought it from a dealer for £1,000. He was to sell the painting, at a satisfactorily high price (5,900 guineas), in 1882.[17]

Ruskin's purchases and sales were often impetuous and erratic, but he was no mere innocent in the world of dealers and sale rooms. He had, after all, been given early experience in the business side of art by two hard bargainers, Turner and his agent Thomas Griffith; he had been close to the financial fortunes of Pre-Raphaelitism; and had been collecting and commissioning art for many years. Ruskin now, in the early spring of 1869, decided to sell no fewer than forty-one of his Turners, together with minor works by William Hunt, Copley Fielding and David Cox, and also John Brett's important painting *Val d'Aosta*. He consigned the works to Christie's and wrote a catalogue for the sale, which took place on 15 April and raised 5,648 guineas.[18]

Since this was an auction, Ruskin had no control over the future ownership of works of art that had shaped his life and writing, and which included Turner's magnificent *Slavers* given by John James Ruskin to his son at the new year of 1844 in recognition of the success of *Modern Painters*. The Turners might have gone anywhere from Christie's, even to America or into the hands of gamblers. Ruskin had previously disposed of Turners — thirty-six to Oxford, twenty-five to Cambridge, both gifts in 1861 — in the knowledge that they would be preserved, studied and cherished. An auction gave no such guarantee. Ruskin never explained why he organised this sale and there are no descriptions of the occasion. E. T. Cook's 1905 introduction to Volume XIX of the Library Edition remains the best account of this depletion of Ruskin's collection of Turners.[19] Cook could not give a full list of works by Turner that belonged to Ruskin after about 1870, though in Volume XXI of the Library Edition (1906) he was able to note the drawings which were catalogued as part of the teaching collection in Ruskin's Oxford drawing schools. His résumé ends with the note that there was 'a nucleus' in Ruskin's Turner collection 'which was constant. Of the 83 drawings in the Thornbury catalogue [1862], 23 remained with him until the end.'[20]

Before Ruskin's sale (which was probably timed for the annual spring cleaning at Denmark Hill, thus helping the rehang of other pictures) some of the drawings were sent to Charles Eliot Norton at his London lodgings in Queen's Gate Terrace. Ruskin lent them for a little while because 'I thought they might amuse you . . . and that you might really wish to see some of them for the sake of your American friends . . .'[21] Ruskin's god-daughter Constance Oldham was given a special viewing of the pictures that were soon to be dispersed. This privileged experience was also given to Susan Scott and her mother Ann Scott, who were frequent visitors at Denmark Hill in the winter of 1868–69. Another guest was Dora Livesey. Lily Armstrong came to Denmark Hill from Dublin, and Agatha Tyndale may also have been a visitor. These were all 'girl friends' from Winnington. There were unhappy reasons for their reunion. All parties knew, or suspected, that Winnington was in decline. Constance Oldham, the youngest of these girls, was still at the school, but unhappy. The Winnington atmosphere had been soured by the school's unprofessional administration. Ruskin knew that Miss Bell could not manage her finances and might have to close the establishment. He had a more dreadful fear: that Winnington might die in general disgrace as his part in the school became known. In these circumstances he felt all the more tender toward Winnington girls. Now he began to involve them in a utopian scheme. As noted above, he had written to Dora Livesey in September 1868 about a possible 'colony'. In April and May of 1869 he elaborated on this dream in letters to Susan Scott, which he asked her to copy and send on to Dora. On 29 May his diary refers to 'the great plan'. The origins of the Guild of St George are many and various, but the connection with Winnington is notable.

Ruskin travelled from London to the continent on 26 April 1869, leaving behind him the manuscript of a book, *The Queen of the Air*. Although he still made much use of the editorial skills of W. H. Harrison, Ruskin asked Charles Eliot Norton to see the manuscript through press. This was an intellectual gesture. In the winter and spring of 1869 Norton had become ever more curious about Ruskin's literary and personal life. In April, he later wrote, Ruskin was troubled and 'at length he got into such a worried and nervously overstrained condition, that he broke away from home, regardless of engagements and of half-completed matters of important concern. He left me in charge of many of these matters, tossing them pall-mall into my hands, with full authority, but with scanty specific direction.'[22]

In truth Ruskin had planned his continental expedition a month before he left England. His first thought was for his mother. Margaret Ruskin was eighty-seven years old, and her sight was failing. Joan Agnew would be her companion. Ruskin also made sure that Joan and her 'Auntie' would be visited by, among others, John and Jane Simon and Ann and Susan Scott. He had arranged everything for the Christie's sale. As far as was possible, Ruskin had kept alive the Winnington circle and now perhaps had given it new life. About Rose and her family he could do nothing. Norton's account therefore seems exaggerated. Though his reminiscences were written in 1904, some thirty-five years after the time he recalled, there was one matter that rankled. A strange but powerful side of Norton's character had led him, when he had talked with Ruskin in France in 1868, to suggest that Ruskin should make his will; that he should be its executor; and that they should jointly agree its provisions. Initially, Ruskin had been interested in Norton's idea. More recently, however, his enthusiasm had cooled. This was the reason for Norton's annoyance, though he should have realised that he was being presumptuous.

Writing to Norton in April 1869, Ruskin declared that 'all my work now is posthumous'.[23] Such despairing feelings may have inclined him toward the project of the will, and perhaps he sold his Turners in the same spirit, pessimistically throwing his treasures to the winds. At the same time the 'great plan' grew in Ruskin's mind, and he continued to lecture and write. *The Queen of the Air*, the book that belongs to this period, is primarily composed of three lectures, or notes for lectures. The first was an address 'On the Greek Myths of Storm' given at University College, London, on 9 March. It became the first section of the tripartite book, 'Athena Chalinitis (Athena in the Heavens)'. The second section, 'Athena Keramitis (Athena in the Earth)', was made up from writing for a lecture that was not delivered, since Ruskin had not received an appropriate invitation. The third section, 'Athena Ergane (Athena in the Heart)', was originally an address on Greek coins, delivered at the Art School of South Lambeth on 15 March. Other passages in *The Queen of the Air* had originally been part of the lecture 'On the Flamboyant Architecture of the Somme'. Some paragraphs were reprinted from Ruskin's privately printed pamphlet *Notes on the General Principles of Employment for the Destitute and Criminal Classes*. Other paragraphs were repeated from the 1865 publication of *The Cestus of Aglaia* in the *Art Journal*.

This was the material that was given to the editorial care of Charles Eliot Norton. A contemporary description of Ruskin comes from the pen of Norton's compatriot Henry James. In Norton's company, the future novelist attended Ruskin's lecture at University College and was afterwards invited to Denmark Hill. The girl with an Irish accent in this letter was Lily Armstrong, who of course would have had the demeanour of a 'niece' rather than of an official guest. Henry James wrote to his mother:

> Ruskin himself is a very simple matter. In face, in manner, in talk, in mind, he is weakness, pure and simple. I use the word, not invidiously, but scientifically. He has the beauties of his defects; but to see him only confirms the impression given by his writing, that he has been scared back by the grim face of reality into the world of unreason and illusion, and that he wanders there without a compass or guide — or any light save the fitful flashes of his beautiful genius. The dinner was very nice and easy, owing in a great manner to Ruskin's two charming young nieces who live with him — one a lovely young Irish girl with a rich virginal brogue — a creature of

> a truly British maidenly simplicity — and the other a nice Scotch lass who keeps house for him. But I confess, cold blooded villain that I am, that what I most enjoyed was a portrait by Titian — an old doge, a work of transcendant beauty and elegance, such as to give one a new sense of the meaning of art . . .[24]

James's comments on Ruskin's 'weakness' may have derived from Norton, who often spoke and wrote of his English friend in similar terms. Although he had been at the University College lecture, James did not comprehend Ruskin's seriousness. It must be admitted that there were ways in which Ruskin's genius seemed superficial. His light voice, darting mind, his love of changing the subject, the pleasure he took in the company of young women, his eulogies of watercolours; all of these things might have been less than impressive to a young American. Ruskin knew that his mind could fly and wander. In *Fors Clavigera* and *Præterita* he lamented his 'incurably desultory character which has brought upon me the curse of Reuben, "Unstable as water, thou shalt not excel" '.[25] Yet the depths of his character, and the unusual passions of his cultured mind, were now displayed in the manuscript which Norton was to send to the printer. One convention of Ruskin's work for the press should be noted here. Beginning with *The Queen of the Air*, he numbered each paragraph (or set of short paragraphs) in each chapter. This he did until the end of his writing life. Perhaps Ruskin began this numbering to assist Norton's editorial work. Or it may have been part of a plan, as E. T. Cook surmised, to issue a 'series of my corrected works', as announced in the lecture at the Art School of South Lambeth.[26] A third possibility is that Ruskin began to number his paragraphs in an attempt, vain or not, to give order and sequence to the multifarious thoughts that flowed and rippled from his pen.

As we have seen, *The Queen of the Air* mainly consists of thoughts from Ruskin's writings and lectures between September 1868 and March 1869. Consecutive numbering of paragraphs now accompanied the rapid publication of Ruskin's views on a number of topics. His publication schedules would soon become continuous, when he began *Fors Clavigera* and realised that he could write about everything he wished, almost all at once, and distribute these views immediately. In this respect *The Queen of the Air* anticipates *Fors*. None the less the book presented a single, powerful theme to its readers: the life and influence that Greek mythology might or ought to possess in the England of 1869. As on previous occasions, Carlyle was the first and most valued of such readers. He wrote to Ruskin that

> Last week I got your 'Queen of the Air', and read it. *Euge, Euge*! No such Book have I met with for long years past. The one soul now in the world who seems to feel as I do on the highest matters, and speaks *mir aus dem Herzen* exactly what I wanted to hear! — As to the natural history of those old Myths, I remained here and there a little uncertain; but as to the meanings you put into them, never anywhere. All these things I not only 'agree' with, but would use Thor's hammer, if I had it, to enforce and put in action on this rotten world. Well done! Well done![27]

'*Mir aus dem Herzen*' ('to me from the heart') speaks of Carlyle's instinctive response to an emotional book. We do not find other positive responses to *The Queen of the Air*. The book would always sell many copies, perhaps aided by its attractive title, but was sparsely reviewed and has no critical history before 1893. In that year W. G. Collingwood, in his biography of Ruskin, attempted to place *The Queen of the Air* within the general context of Ruskin's teaching. Collingwood noted that Ruskin's interest in Greek and Egyptian mythology had increased since at least the period of the third volume of *Modern Painters*. He explained that Ruskin, impressed by the writings of the philologist Friedrich Max Müller, had taken to the new science of comparative mythology, and that *The Queen of the Air* was his contribution to that study. 'He traced with appreciation', wrote Collingwood, 'the development of the notion of Athena, as the chief power of the air, from her character of actual atmosphere to that of the breath of human life', and in the central chapter 'he worked out, as a sequel to his lecture, two groups of Animal-myths; those connected with birds, and especially the dove, as type of Spirit, and those connected with the serpent in its various significances. These two studies were continued, more or less, in *Love's Meinie* and in the lectures printed in *Deucalion*, as the third group, that of plant-myths, was carried on in *Proserpina* . . .' [28]

Collingwood gave especial and extended attention to *The Queen of the Air* because he knew that it was, among all his writings, one of Ruskin's favourites. Ruskin retained a fondness for this book despite the ways in which it reminded him of bitter struggles with the La Touche family. A copy of *The Queen of the Air* belonging to Rose La Touche has survived.[29] It is annotated, and from Rose's pencilled marginal remarks we may gauge her opposition to Ruskin's writing about myth. On the title page she wrote 'Rose La Touche August 2nd 1869'. On the last page we find 'August 7th 1869'. In the week during which she read the book, Rose evidently felt admiration, much distress and a form of complicity. For, as Ruskin confessed to Georgiana Cowper, there were messages to Rose within the text, things that only she could understand. Rose knew that the book's author was thinking of her, and that his book was also hers. That knowledge increased her pain. Above all else, Rose thought herself a Christian. Now her lover had sent her a book which was, to her, quite reprehensibly pagan. Very early in her reading, in fact on page 2 of her copy, and at the end of section I, Rose found an exhortation which surely was directed not at Ruskin's audience at University College but at the pious people of Harristown. 'I will only pray you to read, with patience and human sympathy, the thoughts of men who lived without blame in a darkness they could not dispel; and to remember that, whatever charge of folly may justly attach to the saying, — "There is no God", the folly is prouder, deeper, and less pardonable, in saying, "There is no God but for me".' Rose read on, and then at some point turned back to the title page and exclaimed 'If she could but understand it! & if it was not quite so heathenish!'[30]

Rose's pencilled comments must affect anyone who looks at her copy of *The Queen of the Air*. We confront not merely her disagreements but also the character of this unhappy young woman. Rose was now in her twenty-second year. She was intelligent but not widely read, for she preferred the scriptures to all other books. In former years a moderately convincing child poet, Rose had temporarily given up her verses, probably when she reached the age of eighteen. Illness and religious enthusiasm, perhaps also the worrying strain of Ruskin's love, had stifled her talent. Now we gather that literary ambitions were again in her mind. Next to Ruskin's classification of the *Draconidae* (foxgloves, snapdragons and their like) Rose wrote 'I have written a story about them'. She cancels and rewrites Ruskin's final sentence, then vows 'Do this for my 2nd book — to be out in November'. It is conceivable that her annotations, with their underlinings, question marks, Biblical quotations and occasional praise ('All this is delightful') were in preparation for a critique of *The Queen of the Air* which she might have sent to Ruskin, had they been on more trusting terms. But she did not write to Ruskin. She did not know or dare to guess what kind of a man he might be. In any case, how could Rose exchange views with a writer who had associated her mother with the nameless sin and guilt of all civillisation? 'Lacerta' was Ruskin's name for Maria La Touche. She appears in *The Queen of the Air* in the following sentence: 'And truly, it seems to me, as I gather in my mind the evidences of insane religion, degraded art, merciless war, sullen toil, detestable pleasure, and vain or vile hope . . . — it seems to me, I say, as if the race itself were still half-serpent, not extricated yet from its clay; a lacertine breed of bitterness'. Rose writes in the margin 'Poor green lizards! they are not bitter: Why not say serpentine?'[31]

Rose's handwriting recalls her problems and personality. The script is not quite adult. It is large, open and somehow obdurate. She has a tendency to underline, even when no added emphasis is required. Rose's copy of *The Queen of the Air*, which gives such moving testimony to the difficulties of her life, might be compared with another private work, the manuscript book in which Ruskin assembled his notes on myth.[32] Ruskin probably began to write in this large ledger in 1861. Within its pages we find the sources of *The Queen of the Air* and much other writing, for the book was in use until the early 1880s. The handwriting is fluent and expressive, both in the English and Greek script. Ruskin also employed the capitals that he reserved for indexes and catalogues. The 'Myth Book', as it is known to students of Ruskin, is arranged alphabetically, and by topic, over 152 pages. There are maps and diagrams, and Ruskin made himself an index. Within the Myth Book are two startling drawings, in pencil and wash. The first, which has the greater beauty, is a profile head in a Greek manner. It is derived from, or perhaps copies, Greek coinage. The second, larger drawing is surprising because it is a nude. A figure, which might be of either sex, appears to be making a religious offering. This is Ruskin's only known attempt to draw the naked human form. He is clearly uneasy with the nude, and especially with its sexual features. It could be said that the drawing is a failure. However, no professional Victorian artist — neither the classicising Burne-Jones, not Leighton, nor Watts — ever displayed such sympathy with the Greek spirit, for their classicism was simulated. The Myth Book is not merely a record of Ruskin's scholarship. It is the precious evidence of his intuitive understanding of a different culture. Rose La Touche persisted with her inerrant Bible and her mind remained closed. Her lover continued to explore the mysteries of both Christian and pagan life.

The Queen of the Air is at the centre of a series of mythological works which had begun with the final volume of *Modern Painters* (1860), and continued with, among other writing, *The Ethics of the Dust* (1865), *The Cestus of Aglaia* (1865–66), *Sesame and Lilies* and *The Mystery of Life and its Arts* (1865–69), and then various Oxford lectures and issues of *Fors Clavigera* in the earlier 1870s. These are the years between the onset of Rose La Touche's unnatural piety and her death in 1875. Students of Ruskin's beliefs — and Rose was one of them, though it is not known how closely she followed his publications — turn to books of this period to find a system of human and divine values expressed in myths and symbols.

Some parts of Ruskin's mythology are less obscure than others. We recognise his feelings for light and air, pure streams, great mountains, deep oceans and noble clouds. In nature he found goodness and eternal wisdom. He explains his beliefs in 'kingship' and 'queenship' in ways that were readily understood by his contemporaries. However, Ruskin's invocations of Greek and Egyptian gods were (and remain) perplexing or unintelligible. Rose must have sensed that there were symbols in Ruskin's writing that belonged to dark places of his mind. One of them was his belief in the serpent. Rose knew that Ruskin could not have rationally associated her mother with the instrument of the fall of man; for this would have been absurd and 'Lacerta' means lizard, not snake. And yet lizards are not unlike snakes, so that Ruskin must have deliberately written 'lacertine' to give a private message to Rose about some evil he found in Maria La Touche. Reading *The Queen of the Air*, Rose would in any case have been gripped by Ruskin's descriptions of snakes and serpents. 'Why that horror?' he wrote. 'We all feel it, yet how imaginative it is, how disproportioned to the real strength of the creature! There is more poison in an ill-kept drain, — in a pool of dish-washings at a cottage door, than in the deadliest asp of Nile . . .'[33]

Here is a not uncommon Ruskinian sentiment. A young woman could cope with its message. On the next page, however, Rose found the following passage:

> But that horror is of the myth, not of the creature. There are myriads lower than this, and more loathsome, in the scale of being; the links between dead matter and animation drift everywhere unseen. But it is the strength of the base element that is so dreadful in the serpent; it is the very omnipotence of the earth. That rivulet of smooth silver — how does it flow, think you? It literally rows on the earth, with every scale for an oar; it bites the dust with the ridges of its body. Watch it, when it moves slowly: — A wave, but without wind! a current, but with no fall! all the body moving at the same instant, yet some of it to one side, some to another, or some forward, and the rest of the coil backwards; but all with the same calm will and equal way — no contraction, no extension; one soundless, causeless march of sequent rings, and spectral procession of spotted dust, with dissolution in its fangs, dislocation in its coils. Startle it; — the winding stream will become a twisted arrow; —

> the wave of poisoned life will lash through the grass like a cast lance . . .[34]

Rose, who liked clear parables and definite scriptural precepts, would not have enjoyed such writing. It seemed to be aimed in her direction. Was it still Ruskin's intention to woo her? Perhaps it was his purpose to frighten a Christian person such as herself. Ruskin wrote about serpents as though he had some especial knowledge of evil. Indeed, in *The Queen of the Air* he almost says so when touching on the subject of Indian myths but not explaining them. In one passage he wrote of the serpent 'Its first meaning to the nascent eyes of men, and its continued influence over degraded races, are subjects of the most fearful mystery'.[35] For Rose, who must have had talks with her mother about her suitor, the most fearful mystery of all was Ruskin's sexual nature. Modern readers have conjectured that he associated serpents with his own sexual feelings. This cannot be verified, but a study of Ruskin's diaries reveals that he often dreamt of serpents (he does not call them snakes) and that these dreams were always loathsome. On the evidence of the diaries, they began in the early spring of 1868. Ruskin last recorded a serpent dream in the autumn of 1884. The diaries suggest that such dreams were more frequent than those he noted in any journal.

It may be significant that the serpent dreams began at the period of *The Queen of the Air* and his troubled alienation from Rose. However, the earliest dreams of this sort also include Joan Agnew, a young woman who was becoming closer to Ruskin, who slept under the same roof, was his ward, and whose future husband Ruskin did not greatly like. This is a time to mention — briefly and without speculation — a thought that may have occurred to Margaret Ruskin: that, if he were to marry again, John might find his best possible bride already looking after the Denmark Hill household. At all events, Ruskin's first serpent dreams occurred when he came to know of Arthur Severn's intentions toward Joan.

* * * *

In his four-month-long journey to Switzerland and Italy in the central months of 1869, Ruskin's goal was Verona, and the purpose of his expedition was to make a study of the monuments he had last seen in 1851–52, when he had visited the city from his base in Venice. Ruskin thought that he might produce a *Stones of Verona* to accompany his earlier architectural epic, and now re-read *The Stones of Venice*. Alas, Ruskin was never to write a book about Verona. The most tangible result of the expedition of 1869 was the lecture 'Verona, and its Rivers' and its accompanying exhibition. The lecture was not published until 1895, when it was collected, with some other addresses, by W. G. Collingwood. At the end of his writing life Ruskin was sad to think that he had not published more about Verona, so was careful to say in *Præterita* that 'She has virtually represented the fate and the beauty of Italy to me; and whatever concerning Italy I have felt, or been able with any charm or force to say, has been dealt with more deeply, and said more earnestly, for her sake'.[36]

This last phrase is familiar. Ruskin often said of Rose that all his writing was 'for her sake'. He was able to associate the reverent study of architecture with true love for a human personality. Ruskin thought of some cities, in particular Venice and Verona, as being feminine; and he linked their modern decline to the abandonment of feminine virtues or the loss of the most beautiful feminine condition, which was chastity. Metaphors of pollution and defilement were always in his mind and often in his writings. The imagery was personal. It was also used in Ruskin's denunciations of nineteenth-century industrial society. Quite intimate feelings of disgust may have contributed to the intense, even hysterical descriptions of pollution that are scattered throughout his work as a 'critic of society' or utopian reformer. There was now an outburst of this sort. On May Day of 1869, after a journey that had taken him on a familiar route from Paris to Dijon to Neuchâtel, Ruskin arrived at Vevey, in the Swiss Alps. Here was a place that had always been dear to him. He delighted in its rich and diverse ecology, the lake and the mountains. Ruskin also loved Vevey because it reminded him of happy days with his parents. His father had been 'professionally at home in the vineyards' and his mother was happy in Vevey's apple orchards and fields of narcissi.[37] While John James and Margaret Ruskin read to each other and walked in the productive countryside their son climbed to the mountain slopes, drawing and geologising, returning to the Trois Couronnes, Vevey's inn, in time for a dinner when the family would plan the next day's expedition in one of the little paddle steamers of Lake Geneva that 'called at all the places along the north shore, mostly for country folk' rather than tourists.[38] That was in former, innocent times. And now,

> This first day of May, 1869, I am writing where my work was begun thirty-five years ago, — within sight of the snows of the higher Alps. In that half of the permitted life of man, I have seen strange evil brought upon every scene that I best loved, or tried to make beloved by others. The light which once flushed those pale summits with its rose at dawn, and purple at sunset, is now umbered and

> faint; the air which once inlaid the clefts of all their golden crags with azure, is now defiled with languid coils of smoke, belched from worse than volcanic fires; their very glacier waves are ebbing, and their snows fading, as if Hell had breathed upon them; the waters that once sank at their feet into crystalline rest, are now dimmed and foul, from deep to deep, and shore to shore. These are no careless words — they are accurately — horribly — true. I know what the Swiss lakes were; no pool of Alpine fountain at its source was clearer. This morning, on the Lake of Geneva, at half a mile from the beach, I could scarcely see my oar-blade a fathom deep.[39]
>
> The light, the air, the waters, all defiled!

This agonised sentiment is from the introduction to *The Queen of the Air*, which Ruskin wrote at Vevey and dispatched to Norton in London, as though his preface were a letter. It is not possible to say whether, or by how much, he exaggerated. But it is clear that the experience of modern Swiss life as he travelled toward Italy affected Ruskin deeply: it was at this time that he wrote the letters to Susan Scott and Dora Livesey which contain the origins of the Guild of St George. At this stage the Guild was only a vague notion of a just and pure society. In other respects Ruskin was in a practical mood, for the purpose of his journey was to make an art-historical enquiry. Ruskin was not only a pioneer of this academic discipline. He is among its heroes. No other historian of Italian art has matched his ability to set up headquarters in a city, and then to spend day after day in intense study, filling notebook after notebook, using drawing much more than photography, consulting local sources and learned men, and then writing an exalted evocation of a past culture. Ruskin had already shown this ability in Pisa in 1845 and in Venice in 1851–52. In later years there would be similarly beautiful art-historical visits to Florence and Assisi.

To some minds, Ruskin's written records of such journeys are too literary and romantic. One person who thought that Ruskin was essentially a poet was Henry Liddell, Vice-Chancellor of the University of Oxford, who would soon have to deliberate the appointment of the University's first Professor of Fine Art. Ruskin was unaware that any such post was to be created. He was totally absorbed in art-historical research. As would quite shortly become apparent, Liddell could understand the principle of such research. It was the acquisition of knowledge. But he had no feeling for the spirit of Ruskin's enquiries. That spirit was more easily felt by undergraduates than by Oxford's dignitaries.

One such undergraduate was W. G. Gollingwood. Years later, Ruskin told Collingwood about his summer in Verona. 'Mr Ruskin', Collingwood reported in his biography (1893), was 'often sleepless at nights with anxiety and excitement'.[40] He felt that he had neglected Verona and that the city would be lost to him, and lost to all who might care for her. In these summer dawns he often began to draw architecture at half-past four in the morning. Ruskin was convinced that Verona's medieval buildings would shortly disappear, and that his urgent work as an historian was to commemorate their existence. Collingwood goes on: 'The restoration of Sta Anastasia and other acts of Vandalism made it evident that no time was to be lost in securing these records.'[41] Ruskin's work in Verona has never been fully evaluated, and many of his materials are missing. None the less the six weeks of work at Verona have a record, in the form of a catalogue of the exhibition that accompanied the lecture (given at the Royal Institution on 4 February 1870) on 'Verona, and its Rivers'. This exhibition, which appears to have been open for only one day, or perhaps for only a few hours, contained works by Ruskin and by two assistants. They were Arthur Burgess and the less talented John Wharlton Bunney, also a former pupil of Ruskin at the Working Men's College. Burgess and Bunney had been with Ruskin during his stay in Verona. Together with Crawley, they put up scaffolding, made lists of paintings and frescos, fashioned ground plans of buildings, drew architectural features and took photographs. Especial attention was paid to the cathedral, the Castelbanco tomb, the Scaliger palace and the churches of San Zeno and Santa Anastasia. Alas, Ruskin's Verona notebooks are lost. A number of his drawings, together with sheets by Burgess and Bunney, passed to the Oxford drawing schools. Ruskin kept other drawings for himself. Half a century later some of them were purchased from Brantwood and became part of the Ruskin collection at Bembridge.

* * * *

W. G. Collingwood's *The Life and Work of John Ruskin* pauses at this point, the summer of 1869, to give a résumé and estimate of its subject's life as an artist. The passage (found in the book's first edition of 1893, not in later editions) states that

> he soon removed to Verona, for careful studies of the Scaliger tombs and of Lombard architecture. Much of the work of this year is in pencil, or in pencil with a wash of quiet tint; but he began to paint also in realistic colour, more freely than before; sometimes with

> Chinese white, and sometimes in pure water-colour, without the pen outline; but tending to much greater completeness and elaboration. Up to 1863 his sketching had been that of a chiaroscuro draughtsman, sometimes rising into very fine broad masses of abstract colour, based upon the light and shade, and sometimes indulging in colour-experiments. Then came a period in which he drew and painted very little. Then, after 1868, he resumed his sketching in quite a new spirit, akin to the naturalistic colour of Carpaccio, in the same sense, and to the same extent, as his earlier style had been akin to the strong light-and-shade style of Tintoret: not consciously imitating either master, at either time, but reflecting in his landscape-method the feeling which had led him to sympathise with them.[42]

There are incorrect emphases in Collingwood's account. Ruskin's secretary was wrong to compare his art with that of the old masters. Ruskin's work resembles old master painting only when he is making a copy of such a painting. Otherwise he is an English watercolourist. Ruskin's personal artistic character is somewhat elusive, and we admire his drawings more fully when they are firmly related to some aspect of his studies, whether of art, architecture, landscape or natural history. His art was in the first place functional, and he scarcely ever made imaginative drawings. As we know, Ruskin was a naturally gifted draughtsman, had some lessons in his youth and, by the time that he was an Oxford undergraduate, impressed many people — including Henry Liddell — with his skill. Although he was never a professional artist in any way, Ruskin joined the expanding Victorian art world shortly after leaving Oxford. He knew Turner personally (and in 1869 there were few people living who had experienced the painter's company). Since the publication of the first volume of *Modern Painters* in 1843 Ruskin had been acquainted with most of the leading artists of his time. For many obvious reasons he belongs with the great men of nineteenth-century art. Yet Ruskin was not Olympian, nor academic, nor avant-garde. His attitude to art was formed during his Herne Hill childhood. Ruskin was most at home in the company of minor artists, especially if they were pleasant people without high pretensions. He valued modesty, correctness and devoted love of subject matter. Ruskin found such qualities in minor artists, who included his own assistants, and this was the general character of his own work.

There seem to have been no more than half a dozen attempts to paint in oils. These experiments belong to Ruskin's earliest years, before the publication of *Modern Painters I*. His few self-portrait drawings are not easy to date. Two introspective delineations of his own features, evidently unhappy in mood (Pierpont Morgan Library and the Education Trust, Bembridge School) appear to belong to the period between 1869 and 1874.[43] Three portraits of Rose La Touche are known. Alas, they do not convey her character, nor the nature of Ruskin's passion. He was not a gifted figurative artist, as he himself realised, and wisely confined himself for the most part to landscape, impressions of architecture and studies of natural history. However, one part of his artistic practice always brought Ruskin to the problems of representing the human form. He believed in the importance of copying old master paintings. Although Ruskin used photography as a professional tool he believed, with obvious justification, that a great painting would be better known if it were copied. And yet it would be impossible to copy all the paintings that he revered. Ruskin would never be able to solve this dilemma, especially since he was disinclined simply to take brief visual notes of any canvas or mural. For these reasons Ruskin came to copy paintings as though in some lengthy engagement, a period of studious homage in which he was the pupil, yet neither entirely passive nor obedient. Ruskin's copies of old masters usually show signs of uncertainty or strain. His drawings of sculpture are better, and always more relaxed, than his versions of two-dimensional art. Despite his crowded and urgent schedules, Ruskin tended to spend longer in copying than was necessary. His art was at its best when he used a fine line accompanied by thin watercolour washes. Ruskin had no instinct for touch. So, when he made a copy, he hesitated after each stroke of his brush, and lost the general rhythmic outlines of the paintings that he studied.

Ruskin now, in the summer of 1869, encountered the Venetian painter Vittore Carpaccio, whose work he would copy, with disastrous consequences, in the winter of 1875–76. From his base in Verona Ruskin made three expeditions to Venice, staying there for three or four days on each visit. His first purpose was to test his mature reactions to paintings he had loved years before. He also wanted to see his old friend, the Venetian historian Rawdon Brown. The antiquary would be able to tell him about his Venetian researches in the seventeen years since they had last met. After a cordial reunion Brown introduced Ruskin to other Venetian historians (who, by this date, were more numerous, and beginning to have an effect on the city's public affairs). He also met an engineer who was working on the construction of aqueducts and knew about the problems of the water level in the lagoon.[44] Excited, Ruskin talked with this new engineer friend about the north Italian rivers and fantasised about dams and other ways to transform the southern Alps into a vast garden of loveliness and peasant industry. As he walked around Venice, thinking of his strange life there in times gone by, Ruskin occasionally came across William Holman Hunt. As always, the painter was eager to discuss the old Pre-Raphaelite days. Ruskin and Hunt looked at paintings together, particularly those of Tintoretto, and talked about *Modern Painters*. The 'Graduate of Oxford', encouraged by Hunt, was inclined to feel that his early book had merit. On the whole its aesthetic judgements remained valid. Ruskin now changed his mind, however, about one artistic matter. He had never taken much notice of Carpaccio, though he knew of Edward Burne-Jones's enthusiasm for the late medieval master. Now Ruskin wrote to his friend, on 13 May 1869:

> My dearest Ned, —
>
> There's nothing here like Carpaccio! There's a little bit of humble pie for you! Well, the fact was, I had never once looked at him, having classed him in glance and thought with Gentile Bellini, and other men of the more or less incipient and hard schools, — and Tintoret went better with clouds and hills. I don't give up my Tintoret, but his dissolution of expression into drapery and shadow is too licentious for me now. But this Carpaccio is a new world to me; only *you* have a right to be so fond of him, for he is merely what you would have been if you had been born here, and rightly trained from the beginning — and one shouldn't like oneself so much. I've only seen the Academy ones yet, and am going this morning (cloudless light) to your St George of the Schiavoni; and I must send this word first to catch post. — Ever your loving, J. R.[45]

In other correspondence from this Italian summer we hear of a chance encounter with Longfellow in Verona. Letters to Norton and Carlyle are full of plans for river management. On his return journey Ruskin paused in Milan, had a rendezvous with Norton in Thun and visited his friend 'Marie of the Giessbach', only to find her dying from consumption. Sad at heart, Ruskin hastened back to England for a number of reasons. His mother wished him to be in Denmark Hill. If he were in London he would be nearer to Rose. He wanted to present his theories about inundations to the Alpine Club. Furthermore, he had a call to a new type of duty. In mid-August he had heard that he was to be the first Slade Professor of Fine Art at the University of Oxford.

Ruskin's Verona studies were, therefore, a sort of prelude to his professorship; and the lecture 'Verona, and its Rivers', though it was delivered in London at the Royal Institution, may be regarded as the first of his lectures as Slade Professor, especially since he made mention of his future role in the University. Ruskin spoke on Verona on 4 February 1870. Only four days later he gave his inaugural lecture at Oxford. 8 February was Ruskin's birthday, so he began a new Oxford career at the beginning of his fifty-second year of life.

CHAPTER TWENTY-SIX

1869–1870

Ruskin's professorship, together with two other chairs at Cambridge and the University of London, had been endowed by the will of Felix Slade, a wealthy lawyer and collector of antiquities. There must have been some negotiations with Ruskin before he was offered the Oxford post, but no details have survived of the way that he was first approached. We do know that he was not the only candidate. The election to the chair was organised by Henry Liddell, who in 1869 was both Dean of Christ Church and Vice-Chancellor of the University, together with Henry Acland, who served on many university committees. Acland had been trying to bring Ruskin to Oxford, in some capacity, for many years. Liddell was far less enthusiastic about Ruskin, but was obliged to vote for him because of the mediocre qualities of the other two men who were being considered. They were Tom Taylor and Francis Palgrave. Taylor was art critic of *The Times*. He was also a popular dramatist and a member of the staff of *Punch*. Palgrave, best known as the compiler of the *Golden Treasury*, also wrote for newspapers and in 1866 published his *Essays on Art*. Liddell read Palgrave's books in the summer of 1869 and was unimpressed. On the whole he preferred Taylor: but Taylor was a journalist who wrote farces. Ruskin's qualifications were of course overwhelming. Liddell still had reservations. He considered Ruskin to be 'wild',[1] so the election was made with a certain amount of caution. Ruskin knew this, and after he had accepted the post wrote to both Acland and Liddell with uncharacteristic humility. To Acland he promised 'I believe you will both be greatly surprised for one thing at the caution with which I shall avoid saying anything with the University authority which may be questionable by, or offensive to, even persons who know little of my subject, and at the generally quiet tone to which I shall reduce myself in all public duty'.

A few days later Ruskin wrote to Liddell: 'I hope that in some respects you will find that I shall be able to justify your trust in me in more that I have yet given you ground to expect, for I shall scrupulously avoid the expression of any of my own peculiar opinions when I speak by permission of the University . . .'[2]

Liddell invited Ruskin to visit Oxford and to stay at the Christ Church Deanery. They could discuss the proper nature of the professorship. Ruskin, who had returned to England at the end of August, had little wish to be at the call of the chilly Dean and his equally haughty wife. He managed to evade this proposed meeting and returned to his usual London pursuits. His first concern was for his mother, now extremely infirm. According to some notes Ruskin took of her faltering conversation, she believed that he had been elected Master of Balliol.[3] Ever a patient and thoughtful son, Ruskin sat for long hours at his mother's bedside and read to her. Returning to his study, he worked mainly on botany and geology. There is no sign in his letters or diaries that he thought of preparing any course of studies for Oxford undergraduates. Instead, Ruskin once more reverently placed himself in the position of a student of Carlyle's. In the autumn of 1869 he often drove from Denmark Hill to discuss the world in Carlyle's Chelsea home. Such occasions were far more important to him than any proposed conversation with Liddell. Carlyle thought that his disciple's summer in Verona had done him much good. He wrote to Froude on 14 September:

> One day, by express desire on both sides, I had Ruskin for some hours. Really interesting and entertaining, a much improved Ruskin since he went in May last. He is full of projects, of generous prospective activities, some of which, I opined to him, would prove chimerical. There is (in singular environment) a ray of real Heaven in poor Ruskin; — passages of that last book (Queen of the Air) went into my heart like arrows.[4]

Ruskin's diaries now tell us of his full social life. In town he met William Morris at the shop of the bookseller and publisher F. S. Ellis, and at the British Museum he talked with his old friend Charles Newton. He had a meeting with some members of the Arundel Society. They discussed frescos by Bernardino Luini. Ruskin went to a concert at Crystal Palace and often walked from Denmark Hill to the heights of Norwood, where the countryside began and one could look down on the old Croydon home of his Richardson cousins. Both William Richardson and George Richardson were visitors at Denmark Hill. Other guests included Connie Hilliard, a number of former Winnington girls — Agatha Tyndale coming more often than most — Osborne Gordon, Laurence Oliphant, John and Jane Simon, the painters Alfred Hunt, William Stillman and J. W. Inchbold, George Allen (but it is not known whether or not he ate with the servants), the young copyist Charles Fairfax Murray, Richard Litchfield from the Working Men's College and, separately, the Oxford dons Mark Pattison and Richard St John Tyrwhitt. One visitor, initially nervous about meeting the great writer, was Miss R. S. Roberts. At the suggestion of the Richmond family, she had sent Ruskin some rare Lake District mosses. Years later she set down her reminiscences of a day at Denmark Hill:

> . . . the servant was about to show me into the drawing room, when another maid came forward and said, 'If that's Miss Roberts, she is to be asked into the study'. So I followed my conductor upstairs, and found myself in John Ruskin's study — not his real *work* room, but where he evidently kept his choice sketches and pictures, books, etc. — a pleasant room with two windows looking over the garden at the back of the house, a large lawn with trees and clumps of shrubs, with a field beyond, and Sydenham in the distance. . . . the door opened, and the dream and desire of so many years was fulfilled — John Ruskin stood before me. Taking my hand in both his, and with many kind words of greeting, he at once made me feel at ease and at home. Of course, older and more worn and thin than the portrait in the *Selections*, but the same beautiful — or as my darling mother calls it, *celestial* — face, the deep blue earnest kindly eyes, light brown hair, worn rather long, and wonderfully expressive mouth . . . I had protested against staying to lunch — said I would not stay and take up his precious time; but he would not hear of my going — said lunch was ordered at two, and we had an *hour* before us. Ah me! When I heard those words, and found myself sitting in a chair he placed and drew forward for me, it seemed to be too good to be real indeed; all through I was in a dream, a beautiful dream . . .
>
> . . . he went on in a most beautiful strain to describe a kind of society he wished to form of right-minded, right-hearted people — men and women who would try and do some good in the world; girls were all for vanity, or men for avarice, getting *more, more*. He wanted people to be *content* with what they had, and to live simply, and every day to do some good. Then he gave me his ideas of a scheme for benefiting the Swiss people . . .

This description resembles many other accounts of visits to Denmark Hill (and, later, to Brantwood), except in one important respect. Miss Roberts talked to Ruskin about his views on contemporary religious life. She reported that

> he spoke of the want of faith in God shown by most of our scientific men, and the want of principle among statesmen; but spoke with admiration of Kingsley, Maurice, Stopford Brooke, and

> Tyrwhitt of Oxford . . . When did you hear the wrongs and *falsenesses* of — no, he did not use that word — people did not like to be told they were doing wrong — leading false lives — yet that was what we ought to have from the pulpit. Then he said, 'I don't go to church — I cannot'. Something was said about inspiration and the Bible, that all the good and true things said now were from God, and in their measure inspired. He said what a real *idol* many made of the Bible, calling *it* the word of God — a great mistake — but how he admired and loved the Bible, and he added 'I often think I should like to devote myself especially to try and bring out the meaning of many parts, but', he said, 'they would think me a hypocrite. I never go to church'.[5]

The remark 'I don't go to church — I cannot' is dramatic, and tantalising. It is possible to know a great deal about Ruskin's life. However, it is not at all clear when he went to church in his later years. Nor do we know if he took holy communion. That he went to church on occasion is certain, but his devotional life was private, even secret. His religious feelings were in crisis in 1869, as Miss Roberts obviously guessed. Perhaps she also had the evidence of Ruskin's last book, *The Queen of the Air*, which contained audaciously pagan meditations. It should not be thought that Ruskin was without faith. In all his life, he never ceased to believe that the Christian God was his maker and that Jesus Christ was his saviour. He loved the Bible, and a full study of his Biblical references would reveal a sensitivity to its texts without a rival in Victorian literature. Yet Ruskin had long since given up the common assumption that the Bible was inerrant. Furthermore, he was not a churchman. He disliked almost all clergymen, and indeed any educated person — except Rose La Touche — in whom he detected a thoughtless or unctuous adherence to a narrow faith. To feel doubt was to be intellectually alive. Ruskin was prone, especially at this period, to daring flights of eloquence on religious topics. He called these disquisitions 'talking naughtily', perhaps in an unconscious reference to his mother, who was lying upstairs in Denmark Hill (her son's armchair, in which he sometimes slept, beside her bed), waiting for her end. One evening in September Ruskin talked in this fashion at the dinner table, where there were guests. Joan Agnew took fright and burst into tears.[6] Ruskin was not a frightening man, but conventionally pious people could be alarmed when they had a sudden glimpse of the unusual and tortured depths of his mind.

One such person was Rose La Touche, whose parents had endeavoured to make her feel apprehensive about Ruskin. Surely two thoughts about her suitor were constantly in Rose's mind. What was the secret of his sexuality? And why did this very different, much older man so passionately wish to marry her? It did not make sense. They had little or nothing in common. Yet Rose was not a happy young woman, and Ruskin was the kindest person she had ever known. Although she did not wish to be his bride Rose never dismissed Ruskin from her life. Time and again she allowed him to know that he was in her thoughts and that she prayed for him. At the time when Rose read and reacted to *The Queen of the Air* in the summer of 1869, she and Ruskin had perhaps never been more separated, even hostile. The book contained quite obvious criticisms of her character, her religion and her mother. Now Rose acted in a characteristic manner. In early September she sent her copy of *The Queen of the Air* back to Ruskin at Denmark Hill. The package contained nothing but the book. Was this in contempt, as in returning a letter, or so that Ruskin could see her annotations of his text? There was a bit of weed and a rose leaf within the pages. Ruskin was perturbed. He knew Rose's enthusiasm (which she shared with many Victorian girls) for 'the language of flowers'. Yet in this message, if message there was, the language was opaque. As so often, Rose teased or tormented Ruskin with her contradictions. She was indeed an unpredictable young woman, especially now that she was in her early twenties. Rose was demure but possessed an Anglo-Irish wildness, like her scapegrace brother Percy, who was a gambler, a violent horseman and an *habitué* of the Kildare Street Club in Dublin, the theatre of many a misdeed. The girl who was described as resembling a 'younger sister of Jesus Christ' could fly into passions and had been known to strike her father.[7]

When Ruskin heard of Rose hitting John La Touche he — the author of *Sesame and Lilies* — felt shock and puzzlement. Here was a side of Rose's nature that he had never experienced, since their meetings had always been gentle and, in the old days, tenderly loving. Those days were long gone. In January of 1870 he had not even set eyes on Rose for four long years. Practically all their dealings came in messages borne by intermediaries. Thus it was known at Denmark Hill that Percy La Touche was about to be married to another child of the Anglo-Irish hierarchy, a daughter of the Earl of Clonmel. Joan, who had no such elevated ancestry and still harboured romantic feelings about Percy, was upset. Ruskin thought (and he was right) that there were unsatisfactory social rules at Harristown.

Then, on 7 January of 1870, always afterwards remembered as one of the most dreadful days of his life, he suddenly met the woman he loved. Ruskin was in town on some business at the Royal Academy. It happened that Rose was also in London. She walked from the La Touche family home in Curzon Street to Burlington House. At the top of the stairs, in the Academy's first gallery, Rose and Ruskin came face to face. In confusion, she walked past him without saying a word. Ruskin caught her. She broke away. But Rose did not leave the gallery. She looked at paintings. Ruskin then took from his breast pocket the silk case in which, between two sheets of gold, he kept her most precious letters. He held it out to her, saying 'I think you have dropped your pocketbook.' Rose said 'No', then again said 'No'.[8] Ruskin could speak no further and left the room, while Rose remained. In his diary for this day we find an empty page, marked only with a cross.[9]

* * * *

At the period of these heart-breaking and useless shenanigans, both Ruskin and Rose were preparing work for the press. Ruskin, who was about to send his catalogue of 'Verona, and its Rivers' to the printer, was a fluent and experienced writer who scarcely ever produced an uninteresting sentence. Rose had become crippled as a potential writer as soon as God had claimed her for his own. In early 1870, after much effort, she completed her *Clouds and Light*. It is a mixture of prose meditations and pious verse. The book would be issued by the devotional publishers Nisbet & Co. in April 1870 and its publication costs were probably met by the La Touches.[10] One looks in vain, when reading this volume, for any sign of the personality of the woman to whom Ruskin wished to dedicate his life. Ruskin himself thought that *Clouds and Light* was like its author, unapproachable and unteachable. Using a private nickname for the difficult Rose he wrote to Joan: 'Flint's book is lovely but drives me wild with pain and longing for her',[11] and then 'Flint's book is marvellous for its strange beauty',[12] and, a few days later, 'That book made me dreadfully ill again — and I've not been right at all, since . . .'[13]

Rose, for her part, did not now envisage a future life as a writer. Yet it is possible that Ruskin's social views had some effect on Rose in early 1870. For a little while she thought that she would leave Irish society and take up the modest position of a governess, in London or somewhere else in England, perhaps near to her aunt, Miss Price, in Tunbridge Wells. Maybe this plan was formed to take her away from Harristown. Governesses were well known to be impoverished young women who could never find a husband so Ruskin made derisive, hysterical remarks (using another of his nicknames) about Rose's plan to join the lower middle classes: '. . . I can't get over the notion of the

Governess! — Fancy — Tuk up in a back attic — and a party down stairs! I kept laughing all day and all the night . . .'[14]

In the late autumn of 1869, having received Rose's parcel containing her copy of *The Queen of the Air*, with the little bits of vegetation between its leaves, Ruskin had begun notes for the book we know as *Proserpina* (1875–86), his own contribution to the 'language of flowers'. This work was abandoned after the encounter at the Royal Academy, and Ruskin turned his thoughts toward Oxford. There was some contact with the wider Pre-Raphaelite circle in London, including a man who would play a significant role in Ruskin's courtship of Rose. Ruskin had known George MacDonald, vaguely, since about 1863. MacDonald had been a Congregationalist minister in his native Scotland but by that date was living in London and supporting a large family by his writing. His *Phantastes* of 1858 was his best known work before the enormously successful children's books *At the Back of the North Wind* (1871) and *The Princess and the Goblin* (1872). In early 1870 Ruskin heard that MacDonald was staying with the Cowpers (now Cowper-Temples) at Broadlands and sent him loving messages. MacDonald was friendly both with the Cowper-Temples and the La Touches. Ruskin thought that he might he able to help him with Rose; and this turned out to be so, for in 1872 MacDonald was to be the agent of their reconciliation at Broadlands.

In mid-January Ruskin had two other Pre-Raphaelites to dinner. Edward Burne-Jones brought his close friend William Morris. Ruskin had just read the third volume of Morris's lengthy poem *The Earthly Paradise*, had liked it, copied out a section for 'Isola', as he had now decided to address Georgiana Cowper-Temple, and told Joan that he was amused that a man who so energetically enjoyed his evening meal could also write 'such lovely poems about misery'.[15] Morris as a young man had been much influenced by *The Stones of Venice* and especially its chapter 'On the Nature of Gothic'. He and Ruskin had many mutual friends, among whom Burne-Jones was the first. They shared a general interest in medievalism and in the preservation of ancient buildings. Yet, in personal terms, they were not close to each other. At this period in his development Morris was not yet a Socialist but a political Liberal. He had little sympathy with Ruskin's Toryism and had not appreciated his more recent writings. Ruskin always spoke kindly about Morris. For his part, Morris was pleased to acknowledge his indebtedness to the author of *The Stones of Venice* and *The Seven Lamps of Architecture* (he had no interest in *Modern Painters*, or in any of Ruskin's writings about pictorial art) and, in 1878, volunteered to be a witness on Ruskin's behalf at the Whistler trial. During the twentieth century, Ruskin and Morris have often been described as similar people, comrades with shared beliefs. They were not. It is more reasonable to ally Ruskin with Carlyle. Ruskin thought, and often said, that it was his purpose to continue Carlyle's work. Ruskin was clearly inspired by the older man when he wrote a lecture delivered at the Royal Artillery Institution, Woolwich, on 14 December 1869, published as a pamphlet in early 1870 and then incorporated into later editions of *The Crown of Wild Olive*. The lecture was called 'The Future of England', just the sort of title that Morris might have used in his later, Socialist days. But at no time would Morris have approved of Ruskin's call to the 'soldiers of England' to help build a new society; and the soldiers themselves might have been puzzled, as they listened to Ruskin's words, to know what he expected them to do.

★ ★ ★ ★

A way of calling an audience to vast, noble and intangible tasks is also characteristic of 'Verona, and its Rivers' and Ruskin's first series of lectures at Oxford. Neither Liddell, Acland nor anyone else at the University discussed with Ruskin what his duties should be (though it is fair to add that Ruskin was not eager to talk to them on this topic). For this reason the Slade professorship had no academic programme, no thought about the way that undergraduates should be instructed. Preparing his lectures, Ruskin considered a number of themes. Although his appointment was for a period of three years, it never occurred to Ruskin that the next year's generation of undergraduates might need to learn the same lessons that had been given to their predecessors. In all the Oxford years to come, Ruskin ignored educational plans and procedures. He gave his lectures as a teacher, but in truth they are the work of an adventurous writer and should be regarded as literature rather than pedagogy. Just one advance sketch of the course of lectures is in existence. It is contained in a letter to Norton.

The twelve lectures are to be (I think I shall not now change): —

1. Introduction.
2. Relation of Art to Religion.
3. Relation of Art to Morality.
4. Relation of Art to (material) Use. (Household Furniture, Arms, Dress, Lodging, Medium of Exchange).
5. Line.
6. Light and Shade.
7. Colour.
8. Schools of Sculpture, Clay (including glass), Wood, Metal, Stone.

9. Schools of Architecture — Clay, Wood, Stone, Glass in windows.
10. Schools of Painting (Material indifferent) considered with reference to immediate study and practice —
    A. of Natural History
11. B. of Landscape.
12. C. of the Human Figure.[16]

The earlier part of this scheme was followed. Ruskin began his Oxford work in the Hilary (spring) term of 1870. After his inaugural lecture on 8 February he spoke in successive weeks on 'The Relation of Art to Religion', 'The Relation of Art to Morals', 'The Relation of Art to Use', and then on 'Line', 'Light' and 'Colour', this last lecture closing the course on 23 March. There were to be ten further courses of lectures at Oxford before Ruskin's final resignation in 1885. In 1870 he did not imagine that he would be associated with the University for so long a period, and he began his professorship with mixed feelings, determined that Oxford teaching should not divert him from the good that he might do elsewhere. Ruskin did however imagine his new public role might somehow compensate for the disappointments of his youth. His undergraduate career had been a mixture of success and failure. Ruskin mainly remembered the failure; the pain that had been given him by Adèle Domecq, his illness, the sudden departure from Oxford and the peculiar period as an invalid in Leamington Spa. To return to Oxford as a professor would help him to forget such matters. One none the less wonders why Ruskin remained at Oxford for so many years, when his interests and the deep course of his life lay elsewhere. There is a simple answer to this question. Ruskin remained at Oxford because he was so popular and successful.

The university had never known the sort of welcome that was given to Ruskin's inaugural lecture. It was to have taken place in the theatre of the University Museum. This venue was crowded out, and there were queues outside the building. Henry Acland had the solution. He announced that the lecture would now be held in the Sheldonian Theatre. There was then a procession. It was informal, but a procession none the less. Ruskin and Acland, followed by hundreds of dons and undergraduates, walked from the University Museum, which both men had helped to found, to the Sheldonian Theatre, where thirty-one years previously Ruskin had recited his prize-winning Newdigate poem. There, Ruskin spoke to a rapt audience. These scenes of general appreciation were repeated the following week, when Ruskin, looking at the front row of seats while in a flight of rhetoric, saw that Acland was in tears; '. . . he was so pleased', Ruskin told his mother, 'and relieved from the fear of my saying anything that would shock people'.[17] The attendance at Ruskin's lectures would always be large, although, in later years, his audience was increased by people who came to hear him for precisely the reasons that Acland feared. Members of the public joined with the university community in their eagerness to hear him. Sometimes he had to repeat the lectures, so great was the demand to listen to his utterances. Various ticket systems were devised to deal with the crowds. Journalists were present at the first four lectures of Ruskin's course, and his lectures were ever afterwards of interest to the press.

Although they contain sublime passages, Ruskin's first Oxford lectures do not represent his writing at its best level. When he sat down in Denmark Hill to compose his addresses (which he wrote in two large ledger volumes) he was unsure of his audience. He did not know how much, or how little, to say. Not until the fourth lecture did he introduce illustrations (in the form of drawings, pictures and photographs) which would help to give an anchor to the stormy progress of his thought. The main reason for the unease of Ruskin's first three lectures was not, however, their abstraction and fervent idealism. They were written in distress and illness in the weeks between Rose La Touche's rejection of Ruskin on 7 January and the delivery of the inaugural address on 8 February. After the end of the Oxford term Ruskin wrote to Charles Eliot Norton, 'Just as I had set myself to my Oxford work . . . on the 7th January I met with an experience which made me ill for a month, so that all I wrote was bad; and in the first days of February I had to re-write almost the whole of the inaugural lecture to be given on the 8th, being thrown full a month behind with everything, and with all my brain and stomach wrong . . . My lectures have pleased the people well enough, but they're all so far below what I thought to make them . . .'[18]

Rose's effect on Ruskin's writing can hardly be calculated or described, for her influence was both intense and elusive. Although her name never appears, there are passages in Ruskin's books in which we may be certain that Rose was personally addressed. In many places Ruskin shows his opposition to her beliefs. His second Oxford lecture, on 'The Relation of Art to Religion' is one of them, and Rose (if she read these lectures, which were issued by the University's publishers, Messrs Macmillan, in July of 1870) would have known that Ruskin's remarks about 'the Pride of Faith, which imagines that the nature of the Deity can be defined by its convictions' were intended to disturb the convictions which she herself held.[19] In the third lecture, on 'The

Relation of Art to Morals', Rose might have read Ruskin's idealised description of the labours and character of an old master painter, in which we also detect the self-portrait of a living man who offered himself as her husband:

> The movement of the hand of a great painter is at every instant governed by a direct and new intention. Then imagine that muscular firmness and subtlety, and the instantaneously selective and ordinant energy of the brain, sustained all day long, not only without fatigue, but with a visible joy in the exertion, like that which an eagle seems to take in the wave of his wings; and this all life long, and through long life, not only without failure of power, but with visible increase of it, until the actually organic changes of old age. And then consider, so far as you know anything of physiology, what sort of ethical state of body and mind that means: — ethic through ages past! what fineness of race there must be to get it, what exquisite balance and symmetry of the vital powers! And then, finally, determine for yourselves whether a manhood like that is consistent with any viciousness of soul, with any mean anxiety, any gnawing lust, any wretchedness of spite or remorse, any consciousness of rebellion against law of God or man, or any actual, though unconscious violation of even the least law to which obedience is essential for the glory of life and the pleasing of its Giver.[20]

Ruskin himself was certainly subject to 'mean anxiety', as he calls the condition. He wanted to know about Rose, to keep himself from despair; and it happened that on the very day that he gave this lecture in Oxford, 23 February, there lay on his study table in Denmark Hill a letter in which she sent him sweet love. Now it is necessary to trace the exchanges between Ruskin and Rose since the incident at the Royal Academy in early January. In this way we may understand the patterns of rejection and *rapprochement* that so agitated Ruskin and led to his breakdown in Matlock in 1871. After Rose had spurned him in Burlington House Ruskin thought of sending back to her some books that she had given him. Then he realised that the gesture would not help his courtship. For some time, however, he wished to cause Rose reciprocal suffering, perhaps by writing hotly to her, perhaps by publishing a study of flints in which she would see a symbolic denunciation of her character. This was not done, but Ruskin did write hostile comments about Rose's religious opinions. These were in the original manuscript of 'The Relation of Art to Religion'. They were wisely omitted from the spoken and published versions of the lecture.

In early February Joan Agnew met Rose in London. As a result of their conversation Rose wrote to Ruskin. This was his own account of his reaction: 'She made me more angry than I was before by this ineffably stupid & — everything that's bad — letter'.[21] Furious, Ruskin then wrote to Rose saying, among other things, that he would send her a copy of the book of his Oxford lectures with the following inscription:

To the woman
Who bade me trust in God, and her,
And taught me
The cruelty of Religion
And the vanity of Trust,
This — my life's most earnest work
Which — without her rough teaching,
Would have been done in ignorance of these things
Is justly dedicate.[22]

Ruskin concluded his letter by telling Rose that he still loved her. This was on 19 February. A few days later he returned from Oxford to find the following letter, with a drawing of a red and green and golden rose. There was no salutation, for Rose had grown shy of using her old name for Ruskin, 'St C.', and did not know what to call him. She probably never in her life addressed him as 'John'.

I will trust you.

I do love you. I have loved you, though the shadows that have come between us could not but make me fear you and turn from you —

I love you, & shall love you always, always — & you can make this mean what you will.

I have doubted your love, I have wished not to love you. I have thought you unworthy, yet — as surely as I believe God loves you, as surely as my trust is in His Love.

I love you — still, and always.

Do not doubt this any more.

I believe God meant us to love each other, yet life — and it seems God's will has divided us.

My father & mother forbid my writing to you, and I cannot continue to do so in secret. It seems to be God's will that we should be separated, and yet — 'thou art ever with me'. If my love can be any sunshine to you — take — and keep it. And now — may I say God bless you? God, who is Love — lead — guide, & bless us both.[23]

Ruskin did not reply to this letter, fearing that he might endanger a position he seemed to have gained. 'She has come back to me', he told Georgiana Cowper-Temple.[24] In the months to come he relied on Georgiana, Joan and others to relay messages. 'Isola' received letters from Ruskin which she then enclosed in her own letters to Rose at Harristown. Sometimes she sent Ruskin letters that she had received from Rose, though withholding such letters if she thought that they were likely to distress him. Thus matters proceeded, or failed to proceed, without any direct communication. Then, in August of 1870, Rose sent a photograph of herself to Georgiana Cowper-Temple at Broadlands. It was swiftly redirected to Ruskin, who now dared to write to his love. He penned a careful letter to Rose and asked his mother to address the envelope. By this subterfuge he hoped that his appeals would not meet the eyes of Rose's parents. But John and Maria La Touche knew that Ruskin was pursuing his suit, for he was writing to Lady Desart, Mrs La Touche's sister-in-law, crying 'Will you help me now — or Never?'[25]

Ruskin also sought assistance from lawyers. He wished to furnish Rose with reassurances about his marriage to Effie. Rose was now obliged to think of matters that, to her, were in a distant past. For John and Effie Ruskin were married in 1848, which was the year of Rose's birth. In September 1870, after legal consultations, Ruskin wrote a 'statement', which the Cowper-Temples then passed on to Rose. It concludes, 'I am in Law unmarried & in my conduct to my wife — I boldly say & believe — guiltless — though foolish'.[26] Rose did not respond. Her parents, however, once more appealed to Effie, Mrs Millais, asking her for assistance. They wished her to say something so privately damning that Rose would finally shudder from Ruskin's entreaties.[27]

This was in early October 1870. In March of that year, relieved by Rose's letter of 22 February, Ruskin had concluded his first course of Oxford lectures in better heart. After the elevated generalisations of the first three lectures he was more factual. He also began to look at the general provisions for the study of art within the University. Since the lectures were now illustrated, their dramatic effect was heightened. The lecturer, dressed as always in light home-spun tweed, old-fashioned frock coat and a blue stock, also wore an antique college cap which had been preserved from his days as a gentleman-commoner at Christ Church. Ruskin's long gown annoyed him and was often discarded as he pointed out various beauties in the specimens that accompanied his discourse. By modern standards, Ruskin's illustrations were awkwardly presented. Drawings and paintings were hung at the back of the lecture theatre or placed on a large table at the front of the room. Sometimes a particularly piquant illustration would be turned to the wall. At a relevant moment Ruskin's servant Crawley would lift the drawing from its place and show it to the audience. These arrangements allowed a certain amount of comedy and encouraged the lecturer to improvise.

Not all senior members of the University were as entranced as the undergraduates. The following report comes from the historian J. R. Green, who was not in fact present at the lectures but had heard of remarks by Ruskin that do not appear in the printed version. Green wrote to the historian E. A. Freeman:

> Everybody is going in 'for strong forms'. Ruskin lectures on Art at Oxford, and tells 1,000 people (Stubbs gets 20) that a chalk-stream does more for education than 100 National Schools 'with all their doctrines of Baptismal Regeneration into the bargain'. Also that cottages ought to be repaired, because 'God lives in the poor man's hovel, and it's as well He should be well housed'. To all which, Vice-Chancellor and Heads of Houses listen plaintively . . . [28]

At the end of the Oxford term in March 1870 Ruskin made his farewells to the Acland family, whose house in Broad Street had been his home in recent weeks, and at Denmark Hill wrote notes on the materials he thought he might bring to future lectures. Then he planned a summer tour to the continent, with Venice as a goal. His most recent continental expedition, when he had made his base in Verona, had been a period of hard work. The 1870 tour was more relaxed, primarily because Ruskin was giving a holiday to his companions. They were to be Joan Agnew, Mary ('Mamie') Hilliard and her daughter Constance ('Connie'). The Hilliards' maid Lucy (surname not known) was also of the party. As always, Frederick Crawley accompanied Ruskin as his valet. Significantly, Ruskin also invited his gardener, David Downs. Whenever Ruskin was bent on one of the schemes involving countryside and water that obsessed him in later life — draining Lancashire moors, purifying fountains, building a road over Oxfordshire marshland — then Downs was usually present. 'Downsie' (as Ruskin affectionately called him) helped 'the young master' (as Downs called Ruskin, for he had joined the Denmark Hill establishment in John James's day) in outdoor enterprises and was phlegmatic in all circumstances. Whether Ruskin's proposals were rational or wildly utopian, the Scottish gardener would be ready to assist. This was his first and only visit to Italy. Downs found Venice a queer sort of place but tolerated the ragamuffins who gathered around him, palms oustretched. He was happier in the Alps, where he discussed flowers with Ruskin; and from high places in the mountains he was interested to look down on the valleys that for thousands of years had been carved and excavated by rivers that the young master apparently wished to dam or divert.

In the spring and early summer of 1870 the itinerary followed by Ruskin and his party was familiar, even habitual, to its leader. They crossed the Channel to Boulogne on 27 April, were in Paris the next day, arrived at Geneva, where they paused, on 30 April; then we trace them at Vevey on 6 May and at other Swiss destinations (Martigny and Brieg) before the travellers crossed the Alps to arrive at Milan on 21 May, Verona on 25 May and Venice on the 26th. They spent three weeks in Venice before visiting Florence on 21 June, Siena on 25 June, then returning to Florence on the 28th, proceeding to Pisa on 1 July, to Padua on 4 July, Como on 5 July, Bellinzona on 7 July, Airolo on 8 July, Fluelen on 9 July; and thereafter there was a fortnight at Giessbach before the party moved to Lauterbrunnen on 20 July, Thun on the 23rd and Geneva on the 25th. Then they went via Paris to Boulogne and made the return voyage across the Channel to arrive in England on 27 July. Ruskin had therefore entertained six people for exactly three months, and with his customary generosity. They stayed in the best, though not necessarily the most luxurious, inns and hotels. There were presents and numerous excursions. Everyone ate well, and the wine merchant's son chose the vintages that would accompany their meals. Lucy, Crawley and Downs were given money in addition to their usual wages. These arrangements were not untypical of Ruskin's holidays, and here we find one of the ways by which he dispersed his father's fortune. We also remark that Ruskin spent money in the same places. Over the years, many hoteliers came to know him well, for he liked to revisit the scenes he had known in his youth and, if possible, sleep in bedrooms that he had formerly occupied. Ruskin also liked to introduce friends to his old haunts. This was a theme both of his life and of his later writing, as *Præterita* movingly demonstrates.

One chapter of *Præterita*, never written, was to have been titled 'The Rainbows of Giessbach'. Ruskin wished to describe both this expedition to Switzerland and an earlier, more poignant holiday. It will be recalled that Constance Hilliard had been with Ruskin in France and Switzerland in 1866 when her aunt, Lady Trevelyan, died at Neuchâtel. That was the summer when Ruskin met 'Marie of the Giessbach', whom he now visited for the last time. The tour of 1870 was partly devised to compensate for the unhappiness that had come to Ruskin and Connie at Neuchâtel. Their present comforts and pleasures did not, however, take Ruskin's mind away from his troubles with Rose. He was also aware that he ought to do some work for his next course of Oxford lectures. In a somewhat high-handed manner, Ruskin had obtained leave of absence from the University as soon as he had finished his first course, the addresses published this July as *Lectures on Art*. During the weeks of the Trinity (summer) term, while Oxford dons and undergraduates were at their books, Ruskin was seeking diversion in high mountains, tranquil spas and the azure lagoon of Venice. A sense of duty was allowed to disturb his relaxed mood as his party came down from the Alps. 'Now that I am the "professor",' he wrote to his mother from Milan on 21 May, 'I have so much to notice and set down every moment of my days in Italy.'[29] Ruskin imagined that in Venice he might find the subject of his next lectures. With Rawdon Brown, the Venetian friend who in 1851–52 had assisted in the gestation of *The Stones of Venice*, Ruskin re-explored, and drew, the city's palaces and churches. Perhaps, he thought, he should lecture about Carpaccio. But an Oxford audience might realise that his Carpaccio scholarship was not, as yet, extensive. Then the grandeur of Tintoretto once again gripped Ruskin's imagination. He wrote to his mother on 13 June: 'I have resolved to give my five autumn lectures at Oxford on *one* picture, Tintoret's Paradise. It will be rather too large, than too narrow, a subject. What a strange thing it is that the largest, actually in canvas, should also be the best, picture in the world . . .'[30]

This exciting plan was not followed. If Ruskin had indeed given five lectures on Tintoretto we might have been able to read his only book on a single artist. No such book exists, primarily because his mind always impelled his pen to associate one thing with another. The wandering and often unhappy course of Ruskin's life made him, and his books, 'unstable as water'.[31] The Tintoretto project (though it partly survives in the lecture 'The Relation between Michael Angelo and Tintoret') was abandoned when, in the course of his Italian journeys, Ruskin encountered the work of Filippo Lippi. He described his state of mind in a letter to Georgiana Cowper-Temple from Pisa on 1 July. 'My dearest Isola', he wrote,

> . . . I have learned much on this journey, and hope to tell things in the autumn at Oxford that will be of great use, having found a Master of the religious schools at Florence, Filippo Lippi, new to me, though often seen by me, without seeing, in old times, though I had eyes even then for some sights. But this Filippo Lippi has

> brought me into a new world, being a complete monk, yet an entirely noble painter. Luini is lovely, but not monkish. Lippi is an Angelico with Luini's strength, or perhaps more, only of earlier date, and with less knowledge. I came on to Florence from Venice feeling anxious about many of these things, and am glad that I have. I have been drawing little but thinking much, and to some good purpose. Will you send me a line to the Giessbach? I am very weary in the innermost of me, into which, you will see, there is more surrender perhaps than there used to be, and even a comparative peace; but my plans have been broken much by this work, and I am languid with unfollowed purposes . . .[32]

These 'unfollowed purposes' may be divined through Ruskin's correspondence with Charles Eliot Norton, who was also in Italy at this period. Norton was engaged in art-historical work and had rented a villa in Siena. He was one of the few people with whom Ruskin could discuss the subjects that might be covered in his future Oxford lectures. At Siena, in the early Italian summer, they spoke of, among other topics, Nicolo Pisano, Mantegna, Raphael, Lippi, Sodoma and Bernardino Luini. Yet their talks were unproductive, except that one aspect of the days and evenings at Siena is to be treasured. As night fell, they saw fireflies. Norton called them 'lightning-bugs', to the annoyance of one member of Ruskin's party, probably Constance Hilliard. Ruskin had a more poetic feeling for these darting, luminous creatures. He wrote to his mother that they 'are almost awful in the twilight, as bright as candles, flying in and out of the dark cypresses'. Nineteen years later, that impression was still vivid. The last words of *Præterita*, which are the last words from his pen that were ever published, recall those Siena evenings of the June of 1870:

> Fonte Branda I last saw with Charles Norton, under the same arches where Dante saw it. We drank of it together, and walked together that evening on the hills above, where the fireflies among the scented thickets shone fitfully in the still undarkened air. *How* they shone! moving like fine-broken starlight through the purple leaves. How they shone! through the sunset that faded into thunderous night as I entered Siena three days before, the white edges of the thunderous clouds still lighted from the west, and the openly golden sky calm behind the Gate of Siena's heart, with its still golden words, 'Cor magis tibi Sena pandit', and the fireflies everywhere in sky and cloud rising and falling, mixed with the lightning, and more intense than the stars.[33]

CHAPTER TWENTY-SEVEN

1871(i)

Ruskin and his friends returned home from Siena at speed, for the hostilities of the Franco-Prussian war had begun and they feared that roads might soon be closed. In a London August the Slade Professor of Fine Art once again confronted the problem of his forthcoming lectures. He now abandoned the idea of a course about early Italian painting. His diary tells us that he was absorbed in 'new work for Oxford on coins'. Here is the origin of the lectures given in November and December of 1870, published in 1871 as *Aratra Pentelici*. The primary theme of his lectures was to be Greek coinage. This was disputable intellectual territory. The lectures would be attended by the Vice-Chancellor, Henry Liddell, who was the most precise student of Greek culture in modern Britain. In Oxford there were many other experts in Greek civilisation. They might share Liddell's reservations about Ruskin's knowledge of Hellenic culture. But Ruskin had now decided that he could do his work in the world without troubling to evade Liddell's disapproval. Furthermore, he had the assistance of a friend who was a classicist of his old Christ Church generation, Charles Newton, the Keeper of Greek Art at the British Museum. Ruskin's diary reveals that he was often at the British Museum this summer, that he studied in its coin room and that he had many conversations with Newton. The diary for August and September of 1870 is quite full. We note the usual entertainments. Ruskin was at the Crystal Palace and in London he relished performances by the Christy Minstrels. He saw *A Midsummer Night's Dream* and a play by his erstwhile rival for the Slade professorship, Tom Taylor's *Handsome is that Handsome Does*. Guests at Denmark Hill included, as always, members of the Richmond and Richardson families; William and Georgiana Cowper-Temple; Osborne Gordon, Ned and Georgie Burne-Jones; W. H. Harrison and his wife, Henry Acland's son Harry (Ruskin's godson, whom he neglected) and Octavia Hill ('who provoked me').[1]

The most frequent guests at Denmark Hill, however, were members of the Hilliard family, Mamie and Connie, sometimes accompanied by Connie's brother, the gifted and delightful Laurence. Ruskin also spent much time at their home next to the old church at Cowley, near Uxbridge. He found that Cowley was a convenient staging post for his visits to Oxford, and enjoyed a visit to Windsor and walks by the

River Colne. Many of Ruskin's letters are dated from Cowley Rectory. This autumn he wrote from Cowley to Charles Eliot Norton with news of the progress of his Oxford lectures. The chapters of the book *Aratra Pentelici* were announced in Oxford as 'Lectures on Sculpture'. Although their initial impetus had been in Greek coins — which in essence are relief sculptures — the lectures touch on many other subjects. As if to announce that sculpture might be connected with wise agriculture, Ruskin placed a ploughshare (*aratrum*) beneath his lectern. It is probable, indeed certain, that the lectures in their printed form differ from the improvised eloquence of their delivery. It is good to have an account of the lectures from the pen of Frederic Harrison. In recent years Ruskin had lost touch with his positivist friend, though he still, in a spirit of amicable combativity, referred to his writings. For his part, Harrison was a careful follower of all Ruskin's publications, and in 1902 published a sound survey, *John Ruskin*, of a many-faceted literary achievement. There we read:

> . . . In the course of Michaelmas term 1870, he gave six lectures, now called *Aratra Pentelici*, more or less directly concerned with the relations of the arts to each other, about Idolatry and Imagination, in other words, ideals and symbols, likeness, and structure in art representation, and a comparison of the distinctive marks of the best work of Athens and of Florence in sculpture. These lectures, graceful in expression, fertile in suggestion . . . contain also some of his wittiest and some of his most eloquent sayings, and were illustrated with some admirable drawings, photographs, and diagrams . . . He is so deeply stirred by the European war (Nov. 1870) that he occupies his mind with the technique of Sculpture rather than general principles of Art. For illustration, he holds up a breakfast plate and dilates on its roundness, its rim, its ridge underneath, the one serving as continuous *handle*, the other as continuous *leg*. Then for ornament, the plate has six roses painted on its rim, and from the breakfast plate the Professor turns rapidly to the Porch of San Zenone at Verona, of which he exhibits a beautiful photograph; and thence, by a transition easy only to John Ruskin, we are taken to the lovely coin of Syracuse, the head of Arethusa by Cimon . . .[2]

Harrison, who had a good idea of the ways in which Rose La Touche influenced Ruskin's life, went on to remark how 'a man whose intensely sensitive nerves were being daily torn to shreds' could still give lectures of the highest order. 'How much of truth and charm', his book continues, 'is embodied in these fiery darts into the soul of Greek and Florentine sculpture'.

Alas, with the suggestion of 'nerves . . . daily torn to shreds' we return to Ruskin's distress. As explained above, he was in a state of high anxiety this autumn about the physical and legal nature of his marriage to Effie Gray and the possibility of a future marriage to a sickly and unstable young woman whose parents steadily opposed such a union. Despite his sometimes angry denunciations of Rose and her religious faith, Ruskin had never taken back his proposal of marriage. Neither had Rose ever said or written to Ruskin (as far as we know) that she would never be his bride. Rose still respected her parents' wishes and admonitions. In early October of 1870 her mother came to her with a further letter from Effie, Mrs Millais. On 8 October Maria La Touche had written to Effie asking for 'a contradiction of the statements Mr Ruskin is now making to Mr Cowper-Temple, who with his wife, has great influence over my daughter — and is using that influence eagerly, to justify Mr. Ruskin in all things, and persuade my unhappy child that she is bound to reward his love and constancy, by at least hearing his defence and allowing him to renew his addresses . . .'

Effie replied immediately. She wrote back to Harristown that Ruskin's mind 'is most inhuman; all that sympathy he expects and gets from the female mind it is impossible for him to return excepting upon artistic subjects which have nothing to do with domestic life'. A further subject of these exchanges of letters, and the legal opinions that Ruskin had obtained, seems to have been the question of his impotence or otherwise. At all events, Maria La Touche showed Effie's letter to Rose and by 14 October was able to report to Ruskin's former wife that her daughter was now 'quite saved', and had promised her father to have no more to do with her suitor.[3] These circumstances explain the nature of the preface to a new edition of *Sesame and Lilies* which Ruskin wrote in late 1870[4] and also help us to understand how he began the new decade with a sequence of pamphlets, *Fors Clavigera*, in which a noble mind is evidently distraught.

* * * *

The first number of *Fors Clavigera* was published on 1 January 1871. When he began the series, Ruskin did not realise that it would be the most extended labour of his life, for he wrote ninety-six issues of *Fors* before its conclusion in 1884. In 1871 he probably expected to write about a dozen of his pamphlet-like letters; or perhaps two dozen, for that was the number of letters he had addressed to the cork-cutter Thomas Dixon, published in book form in 1867 as *Time and Tide, by Weare and Tyne*. Although *Fors Clavigera* was to develop its own forms of grandeur, it did not begin with a grand design. *Fors* was initially a response to European circumstances. The immediate origins of the pamphlet series are in two letters on the subject of the Franco-Prussian war, sent by Ruskin to the *Daily Telegraph* and published on 7 and 8 October 1870. They were of interest to Carlyle, who wrote to Denmark Hill that 'I noticed on a Newsvendors Placard that there was a "Letter from Mr. Ruskin" which it would be necessary for me to see . . .'[5] Ruskin may have been pleased that his opinions on current events were advertised in the streets. The thought of winning Carlyle's good opinion, or standing beside him in battle, was more important. In mid-November the author of *Frederick the Great* wrote a long letter to *The Times* about the new European war. The earliest of the monthly numbers of *Fors* are haunted by the subject of the Franco-Prussian conflict. It may be said, therefore, that *Fors* grew from this alliance with Carlyle and that Ruskin's work was born from the contemplation of European warfare that, Carlyle believed, might spread to all capital cities if (to use Froude's words on the subject) 'their affairs were allowed to drift on under *laissez-faire* and so-called Liberty'.[6]

Ruskin owed a deeper, and more painful, debt to Carlyle. If one had to name a single precedent for *Fors Clavigera*, it would be in the older writer's *Latter-Day Pamphlets* of 1850. Ruskin had certainly not forgotten the hurt he had received from the passage on the fine arts in 'Jesuitism', the eighth and last of Carlyle's series of public letters. Instead, he had absorbed the injury, as though 'Jesuitism' had been a lesson rather than an insult. *Fors Clavigera* may be regarded as a capacious extension of Carlyle's pamphlets, sharing with them a recklessness, a display of personal torment and a dark abhorrence of the modern world. There are a number of further similarities. *Latter-Day Pamphlets* and *Fors Clavigera* were written by distinguished public figures who were willing to lose friends and risk all their influence because they wished to campaign against the superficialities of progress. Both sets of pamphlets came from men who had arrived at the crisis of late middle age. Carlyle was fifty-five when he issued *Latter-Day Pamphlets*. Ruskin began *Fors Clavigera* at the age of fifty-one. He brought *Fors* to its best expression a little later, at a time of personal strain, when his mother had died, when his relations with Rose La Touche were at their most agonised and when he had left his parents' home for uncertain abodes in Oxford and Brantwood. *Fors* could not have been written by a younger or happier Ruskin. A sense of its author's advancing age gives character to every one of its letters.

Ruskin also thought about Carlyle's old age and physical distress. When Ruskin commenced *Fors Clavigera*, Carlyle was seventy-six, and his right hand had failed him. Henceforward he wrote only by the amanuensis of his niece. Never again would Ruskin see Carlyle's distinctive and forceful handwriting when he looked through his post. In an almost literal way, therefore, Ruskin in early 1871 took up Carlyle's pen.[7]

The title page of Ruskin's pamphlet announced 'Fors Clavigera/ Letters/to the Workmen and Labourers/ of Great Britain/by John Ruskin, LL.D.' The address to a potential audience is plain enough; except that we know, as Ruskin must have known, that his letters could have only the most limited circulation among the working classes. Perhaps, having now committed himself to Oxford, Ruskin felt that he should also speak to unlettered men. As *Fors* went on, however, with its sales well below 1,000 copies a month, the appeal to 'the Workmen and Labourers of Great Britain' became an acknowledgement that his thoughts would not be welcomed or understood by anyone.[8] *Fors Clavigera* is a recondite and difficult work. It made no attempt to be otherwise. The pamphlet might have been more accessible if it were not so learned and so hostile to the spirit of its times. For instance, Ruskin was one of the few public men who was not truly interested in the expansion of the Victorian 'reading public'. Paradoxically, he was a widely read author whose unspoken wish (hinted at on occasion) was to diminish the extent of his readership. *Fors* contains many messages to its readers, but it is Ruskin's most personal book and often has the nature of soliloquy. Its riddling Latin title takes us into private ruminations. 'Fors Clavigera' means 'Fortune with the Nail'. A simple translation is not of much help in understanding the purpose of the work. It is characteristic of *Fors* that Ruskin's readers had to wait until the forty-third of his letters, that of July 1874, before they were told that

> I have no intention of explaining that purpose entirely, until it is in sufficient degree accomplished. I have a house to build; but none shall mock me by saying that I was not able to finish it, nor be vexed by not finding in it the rooms they expected. But the current and continual purpose of *Fors Clavigera* is to explain the powers of Chance, or Fortune (Fors), as she offers to men the conditions of prosperity; and as these conditions are accepted or refused, nails down and fastens their fate for ever, being thus 'Clavigera' — 'nail-bearing'. The image is one familiar in mythology: my own conception of it was first got from Horace, and developed by steady

effort to read history with impartiality, and to observe the lives of men around me with charity. 'How you may make your fortune, or mar it' is the expansion of the title.[9]

Reading this passage, an alert student of *Fors* might well have recognised an allusion to Luke 14.30, 'This man began to build, and was not able to finish.' The Horace reference is more difficult to trace. Furthermore, the image of a nail-bearing Chance or Fortune is not in fact 'familiar in mythology'. The question of the meaning of 'Fors Clavigera' was not examined in print before W. G. Collingwood published *The Life and Work of John Ruskin* in 1893. There he wrote:

> Its name, like itself, is mystic, and changes content as it goes on. The Fate or Force that bears the Club [*clava*], or Key [*clavis*], or Nail [*clavus*]: that is, in three aspects, — as Following, or Foreordaining, Deed (or courage), and Patience, and Laws (unknown or known) of nature and life; so that the 'Third Fors', that plays so large a part in this later period, is simply Fortune. The general sense of the title expresses the general drift of the work; to show that life is to be bettered by each man's honest effort, and to be borne, in many things he cannot better, by his wise resignation; but that above all, and through all, and in all, there works a Power outside of him, to will and to do, to reward and to punish, eventually, by laws which, if he choose, he may partially understand, and for the remainder, may trust.
>
> To read *Fors* is like being out in a thunderstorm . . .[10]

This last dramatic simile, often quoted in later introductions to Ruskin, is memorable. Collingwood's explanation of the purport of the title is less satisfactory. Readers might well have asked whether the 'Power' to which Collingwood refers was a Christian one, or not; and they were entitled to pose further questions, for Collingwood's interpretation seems to be that of a man who is himself puzzled. A decade after Collingwood's book appeared, E. T. Cook made his own attempt to elucidate the title. First of all he sought Ruskin's reference to Horace and found it in the *Odes*, i, 35. He then supplied a translation, which he took from a version of the Odes by Dr Philip Francis, published in 1747. It reads:

> With solemn face and firm, in awful state
> Before thee stalks inexorable Fate,
> And grasps empaling nails, and wedges dread,
> The hook tormentuous, and the melted lead.

Next, Cook considered Ruskin's study of Horace, which had begun as early as 1836, and pursued the iconography of the nail-bearing Fortune. In a notebook, which is also the diary for the years 1861–63, he read that Ruskin, while in his exile in Mornex, had considered an antique bronze mirror-case ('in some museum') whose design had apparently interpreted Horace's view of Fate. In this notebook Ruskin had written of 'the figure of the death-goddess Atropos, who is on the point of driving a nail fast home with a hammer, the symbol of unalterably determined, or fixed, fate'. Having found this visual source, Cook turned to *Fors Clavigera* itself and explained that in the series we find a first, a second and a third Fors, associated with Force, Fortitude and Fortune; and he justly associated these figures, or concepts, with the Greek Fates.[11]

All this was excellent research and wise interpretation. However, Cook omitted one important precedent for Ruskin's personal image of a nail-driving Fortune. As already noted, the Song of Deborah had a deep hold on his mind. In Judges, 4.21 we read of how 'Jael Heber's wife took a nail of the tent, and took an hammer in her hand, and went softly unto him [Sisera], and smote the nail into his temples, and fastened it into the ground: for he was fast asleep and weary. So he died.' For reasons difficult to understand, the Song of Deborah was to Ruskin 'as sacred as the Magnificat'. This we learn from the 'Grande Chartreuse' chapter of *Præterita*. It describes the public argument at the Working Men's College between Ruskin and F. D. Maurice, when Ruskin apparently praised Deborah the prophetess while Maurice mildly remarked that she 'was not a teacher of ethics'.[12]

Whether or not the debate with Maurice was the specific reason for Ruskin's abandonment of the Working Men's College, it must be true that, as *Præterita* recounts, he was irritated by 'a man neither vain nor ambitious, but instinctively and innocently trusting his own amiable feelings as the final interpreters of all the possible feelings of men and angels, all the songs of the prophets, and all the ways of God'.[13] *Fors Clavigera* might well be read in this light, and Deborah the prophetess was surely an influence on its anti-liberal *terribilità*. Although the letters of *Fors* were to convey news of the affairs of Ruskin's Guild of St George, which was in many respects a benevolent society, it was not the purpose of *Fors* to reflect philanthropic or benevolent attitudes. The title was meant to reflect a tragic and mythological attitude to human life.

A few more explanations of 'Fors' should be collected. Writing to a friend in 1875, Ruskin stated that

> The Fors is fortune, who is to the Life of men what Atropos is to their death. Unrepentant, — first represented, I believe, by the Etruscans as fastening a nail into a beam with a hammer (Jael to the Sisera of lost opportunity). My purpose is to show, in the lives of men, how their Fortune appoints things irreversibly, while yet they are accurately rewarded for effort and punished for cowardice and folly.[14]

From numerous other passages we find that Ruskin elaborated the meaning of 'Fors', and of 'Clavigera' too, when such elaboration suited his purposes. *Fors* stands for either Force, Fortitude, or Fortune. By *Clavigera* we are meant to understand that the emblematic figure might carry either a club or a key or a nail. The three 'Forses' are 'Force with the club — the wise and strong man armed; Fortitude with the key — the patience which is portress at the gate of Art and Promise; and Fortune with the nail — "the fixed power of Necessity with her iron nails"'.[15] The first Fors is associated with Hercules, or deed, the second with Ulysses, or patience; and the third with Lycurgus, or law. But these definitions are often flexible. Finally, Ruskin remarked to his readers that "By the adoption of the title "Fors" I meant (among other meanings) to indicate the desultory and accidental character of the work.'[16]

* * * *

Many pages of the first issues of *Fors Clavigera* were written from a new temporary home. In early 1871 Ruskin took up residence in the Crown and Thistle in Abingdon. The little town suited Ruskin, and so did its inn. Abingdon is in the Thames valley, only six miles from Oxford, yet has a quite separate identity. Ruskin could be close to his university obligations without actually living in Oxford. The Crown and Thistle was the sort of hermitage that he liked. It was probably of seventeenth-century origin. Like all coaching houses, it had a yard and stables. There was also a splendid kennel for Camille, a St Bernard dog that Ruskin had acquired. There were a variety of public rooms on the ground floor, including a dining room. The fireplaces were grand, staircases took odd directions and pictures of hunting scenes hung on wood panelling. Upstairs, there was a private dining room. At the top of the rambling old house Ruskin had his own properly old-fashioned quarters (with another room for Crawley), and here he set up his professorial desk, preparing the 'Lectures on Landscape',[17] three addresses given in the Hilary term of 1871, and writing letters to the press on the subject of recent Italian inundations. In the first of these letters about the flooding caused by the Tiber and the Po, Ruskin quotes Horace. At Abingdon Ruskin also wrote a paper which he was to read before the Metaphysical Society in April, 'The Range of Intellectual Conception Proportioned to the Rank in Animated Life'.[18]

Ruskin soon became so comfortable in the Crown and Thistle that he felt that he had left London for ever. This new home 'seems to put an end, abruptly, to all Denmark Hill life', he wrote to Charles Eliot Norton.[19] It was indeed the end of his Camberwell days. Joan Agnew was about to be married. In March his old nurse Anne Strachan died. Margaret Ruskin was so weak that she never left her bed. Troubled by these sad aspects of his family life, Ruskin took pleasure in the antique conviviality of the Crown and Thistle. He summoned assistants there and also entertained such friends as the Cowper-Temples and the Hilliards. A connection of the Hilliard family, the Revd E. P. Barrow, left some recollections of these Abingdon occasions:

> We were to dine with him on a particular day. 'Mamie' (Mrs Hilliard) was hostess, as often before and afterwards. I sometimes think that, but for Mamie's quiet influence, and her bright, cheery way of encouraging him to do things, the Professor would never have faced the duties of his office, perhaps could never have accepted it. He speaks in a note to me of 'serenest confidence in the stability — as far as any worldly affairs can be stable — of all her arrangements'. He certainly had a shrinking at that time from residence in Oxford, and the inn itself was a kind of half-way house, I believe, by which he reconciled himself to the change. Of the dinner I remember nothing — except that part of the dining room made an archway over the entrance — but the memory of the after-dinner ramble in the twilight, in a newly-raked meadow, where the hay was waiting to be carried, remains with me still . . .[20]

This reference to the harvest places the visit of Barrow and Mrs Hilliard in the summer of 1871. Ruskin continued to visit the Crown and Thistle as a retreat and a home until at least 1875, and he had some Abingdon friends. This is the place to recount the story of Annie Brickland, who is described in a note to Ruskin's accounts published in *Fors Clavigera* of July 1876.

> In 1871, in one of my walks at Abingdon (see *Fors*, letters 4 and 6), I saw some ragged children playing by the roadside on the bank of a ditch, and gathering what buttercups they could find. Watching them a little while, I at last asked them what they were

doing. 'This is my garden' answered a little girl about nine years old. 'Well, but gardens ought to be of use; this is only full of buttercups. Why don't you plant some strawberries in it?' 'I have none to plant'. If you had a little garden of your own, and some to plant, would you take care of them?' 'That I would.' Thereupon I told her to come and ask for me at the Crown and Thistle, and with my good landlady Mrs Wonnacott's help, rented a tiny piece of ground for her. Her father and mother have since died; and her brothers and sisters (four, in all) are in the Union, at Abingdon. I did not like this child to go there too; so I've sent her to learn shepherding at a kindly shepherd's, close to Arundel . . . this ten pounds is for her board, etc., till she can be made useful.[21]

The 'kindly shepherd' who owned an estate at Arundel was called Dawtry Drewitt. He was a jolly undergraduate-squire from Christ Church who had become friendly with Ruskin and whose good humours are celebrated in *Præterita*. After the summer of 1876 we hear no more of Annie, though her early life remains in the mind. Ruskin was her protector for about four years, the kindly saviour of a Victorian waif. Perhaps it was no coincidence that he brooded about a great contemporary while living at the Crown and Thistle and reflected, unhappily, that it might have been better for the world if there had been more of Ruskin in Dickens and more of Dickens in Ruskin. The author of *Fors Clavigera* much regretted the novelist's recent death. He had loved Dickens's books since he was a teenager, when John James Ruskin had read the *Pickwick Papers* aloud as a family entertainment. All the same, he sometimes found it his duty to scold Dickens's vulgar and secular imagination. His death, Ruskin wrote, was

> very frightful to me — among the blows struck by the fates at worthy men, while all mischievous ones have ceaseless strength. The literary loss is infinite — the political one I care less for . . . Dickens was a pure modernist — a leader of the steam-whistle party *par excellence* — and he had no understanding of any power of antiquity except a sort of jackdaw sentiment for cathedral towers. He knew nothing of the nobler power of superstition — was essentially a stage manager, and used everything for effect on the pit. His Christmas meant mistletoe and pudding — neither resurrection from dead, nor rising of new stars, nor teaching of wise men, nor shepherds . . .[22]

Ruskin's daily walks or drives from the University to the Crown and Thistle pointed to an anomaly in his professorship. He lived in a place of public resort, where there were bars and travellers. Ruskin was not a resident fellow of any Oxford college, though he held a chair and had been an honorary student of Christ Church since 1858. As its student (a word which in Christ Church denotes a fellow) it would have been natural for Ruskin to take up residence in his own college. No such accommodation was offered to him. Ruskin was however happy enough at the Crown and Thistle, where he did not have to make conversation with dons and clergymen. Then, at some point in early 1871, Ruskin was invited to Corpus Christi College. A set of rooms had been vacated by the Reverend Henry Furneaux. In a distant manner, Furneaux was related to the Ruskin family, for a few months earlier he had married Arthur Severn's twin sister Eleanor. When Furneaux and his bride moved to a college living at Lower Heyford, fifteen miles north of Oxford in the upper Cherwell valley, he may well have suggested to the President of Corpus, Dr James Norris, that Ruskin should occupy his old rooms. Such a proposal would have been supported by many of the College's fellows, especially his admirer J. W. Oddie[23] and Ruskin's friend Henry Coxe, an expert on manuscripts who was both Bodley's Librarian and Chaplain of Corpus. On 29 April 1871 Ruskin was admitted to Corpus and became an honorary fellow of its foundation. That is, he belonged to the College but had no voice in its government. In a graceful speech after his election Ruskin said that 'Mr President, I would not have left Aedes Christi for anything else than Corpus Christi'.[24] This reference to the House and the Body of Christ, his undergraduate college and his new college, appears to have puzzled the aged President; but Ruskin was perfectly sincere, and in his own way was a dedicated fellow of Corpus until his death. His one regret was the loss of Camille, who was not welcome in the college and was given away to an Oxford family.

Ruskin's rooms were on the right-hand side of the first floor of No. 2 staircase. Their windows look out on to Christ Church meadow, with the Isis in the distance. In time, as Ruskin became more confident about his place in university life, his rooms became legendary. That was because of his hospitality, and because Ruskin tended to make a museum around himself wherever he settled. By 1872 the contents of his rooms were insured for £30,000, as we learn from one of his notebooks. It is not easy to discover what was being insured. Ruskin placed various treasures at Corpus, and there they remained for years. Among them were his Titian portrait of Doge Andrea Gritti (now attributed to Catena, and in the London National Gallery) which he had bought around 1864, and mineral cases. These had a more or less permanent position. However, precious stones and pictures were often taken from one place to another; and so were manuscripts, books, and drawings by Mantegna and Turner. The museum-like nature of Ruskin's rooms was emphasised by their use when he was not in residence. The keys were entrusted to another Corpus don, who had permission to show the precious contents to interested visitors. But the main attraction of the set of rooms in Corpus was of course Ruskin himself. Many people came to call on him and listen to his enchanting, challenging conversation. On the whole, we gather, they were junior rather than senior members of the University. 'He told me one day', E. P. Barrow recalled, 'that it troubled him to think how little the senior men understood him, and how little they seemed to care to do so; he was not even sure that they cared to meet him. I did my best to assure him that sympathy and understanding were not lacking — only the opportunity for meeting, which he had never given them.'[25] A number of collegiate dinners were arranged to make Ruskin a little less distant, and with some success; but Ruskin's warmest Oxford friendships were to be with undergraduates rather than dons.

Other Oxford friends were girls or young women, in particular the daughters of two men whom Ruskin had known since his undergraduate days, Acland and Liddell. Sarah Angelina Acland, always known as 'Angie', he had known since she was a baby. Angie was a child of nineteenth-century Oxford. She was born there (in 1849) and lived in the university city all her life. Angie was crippled, and never married. She had one independent interest and occupation, which was photography. In most other ways, however, she was a prisoner of her frail body. She simply observed university life and accepted both its pieties and its peculiarities. This we gather from her long, affectionate correspondence with Ruskin (they addressed each other as 'dearest Tease' and 'dearest Cricket', i.e. critic) and her manuscript autobiography. Angie had seen more of her elders than most professors' children, because the Aclands had a policy of keeping open house and their children were not sent to the nursery when adult visitors arrived. Furthermore, Henry and Sarah Acland welcomed undergraduates to their home. They were leaders of a liberalisation of Oxford manners and of relations between dons and students. Ruskin also contributed to this unofficial reform, though he was often absent from Oxford and had no home there apart from his Corpus rooms. Undergraduates would often meet him at the Aclands' open Sunday evenings in their Broad Street house.

A more severe household was maintained by Henry and Lorina Liddell in the Deanery in Christ Church. Arrangements in Christ Church made the professor from the Crown and Thistle appear almost bohemian. Edith, Alice and Rhoda Liddell had aloof parents, their father Olympian and their mother given to disapproval. Ruskin secretly disliked both of them, as did many other Christ Church men. But he took pleasure in the company of their daughters. His favourite was Edith. Alice was too prim, Rhoda merely an amusement, but he could be himself with Edith, and flirt with her. The early death of Edith Liddell in 1883 was a heavy blow to Ruskin.

As *Præterita* confesses, Ruskin would walk round the corner from Corpus Christi to Christ Church to visit the Liddell girls when he knew that their parents would be absent. For Alice, Edith and Rhoda, Ruskin was both a grand Oxford dignitary — though nobody could be as grand as their father — and a slightly naughty uncle. Ruskin was not alone in feeling an affection for the sisters that he could not give to the Dean. It was at about this time that he came to know the Reverend Charles Dodgson, a mathematician and a student of Christ Church, who was already famous for his *Alice's Adventures in Wonderland*, published in 1865. *Through the Looking Glass, and what Alice found there*, the better book of the two, was to be published in 1872. We may therefore say that Ruskin was part of the Oxford milieu that produced the unforgettable children's story. So also was Angie Acland. Her autobiography reveals that she too went on the boating trips with Dodgson when he told his fantastic tales to the Liddell girls. Dodgson and Ruskin corresponded more than they met, though they lived in adjacent colleges. Ruskin would cut Dodgson's signature from his letters to send to girls whom he knew would like the autograph of the creator of the *Alice* books. The actual contents of the letters did not greatly interest him. They contained conventional remarks about art. At one point, irritated with Dodgson's enquiries, Ruskin brusquely referred him to a back number of *Fors Clavigera*. 'Can't afford tenpence', Dodgson replied, that being the price of *Fors*.[26] The exchange cannot have made for warm relations. Ruskin never appreciated the odd, puckish personality of Dodgson. Neither did Liddell. All three men felt animosity toward each other, though they had to discuss intellectual matters, dine together and worship together. This was in the nature of Oxford life.

The paragraph in *Fors* that Ruskin instructed Dodgson to read concerned photography. Although we are indebted to Dodgson for a fine photographic portrait of Ruskin, taken in 1874, they did not have a common view about the use or the prospects of the new art form. Oxford in the 1870s has a telling place in the history of photography. Within the two or three square miles of the university city the camera was used in significantly different ways. First, there was a relatively conventional studio photography, popular and successful because so many people wished to record their passage through the University. Secondly, in Oxford there were such amateur photographers as Dodgson and Angie Acland, who had considerable knowledge of their craft and may have believed that it produced works of art. Thirdly, there was a new tradition of scientific photography in Oxford. The use of the camera for making scientific records was pioneered by Nevil Story-Maskelyne, whom Ruskin had known since the days when they both taught at the Working Men's College. Maskelyne was a friend of Acland's and may have given Angie Acland her introduction to the camera. Fourthly, there was a use of photography for broadly art-historical investigations. Works of art, artefacts and architecture were photographed to make records, and the prints were used in teaching. In all probability, Ruskin was responsible for the increase in art-historical photography in the 1870s.

Before returning to the events of Ruskin's life in 1871 it is convenient to summarise here his attitudes to photography. As already noted, he was a pioneer of the medium and of its appreciation. *Præterita* tells us that he knew of daguerreotypes, and bought some, while still an undergraduate, probably in 1842, shortly after Daguerre had published his invention in 1839:

> It must have been during my last days in Oxford that Mr Liddell, the present Dean of Christ Church, told me of the original experiments of Daguerre. My Parisian friends obtained for me the best examples of his results; and the plates sent to me in Oxford were certainly the first examples of the sun's drawing that were ever seen in Oxford, and, I believe, the first sent to England.[27]

Daguerreotypes are warmly mentioned in the first volume of *Modern Painters*, but Ruskin did not become fully enthusiastic about their use until 1845. On his continental tour of that year he bought examples in Venice. 'Certainly Daguerrotypes taken by this vivid sunlight are glorious things', he then wrote. 'It is very nearly the same as carrying off the palace itself — every chip of stone & stain is there — and of course, there is no mistake about *proportions*.'

In 1848 Ruskin[28] acquired further daguerreotypes of Tuscan monuments and soon began to commission his own plates. It became part of George Hobbs's, then George Allen's and later Frederick Crawley's duties to take daguerreotypes and photographs under his supervision. Sometimes Ruskin drew from them; and the etchings in *The Seven Lamps of Architecture*, his first illustrated book, depend on such photographic sources. There was a possibility that *The Stones of Venice* might be illustrated with photographs. Nothing came of this plan. Perhaps Ruskin's intimate feelings for Venetian buildings demanded that he should draw them rather than use a camera. For Ruskin, photography was an invaluable aid in recording architecture, and also fresco painting; but photographs of landscape were of little interest, even if they were of Alpine valleys and glaciers. Ruskin took photographs himself, but not often. His interest was in building a collection of daguerreotypes and photographs. Many of them are beautiful, as Ruskin recognised.[29] But his photographs, whether taken by himself or by other people, were always functional. He believed that photography could never supersede art nor be an art in itself, for the simple reason that it was mechanical. Although Ruskin brought photography to his Oxford lecture rooms and studios, he always believed that a student might know more of any subject if it were drawn.

* * * *

In the spring of 1871, Ruskin had no clear policy about the illustration of *Fors Clavigera*. During the 1870s he experimented with most forms of visual display, both in the lecture hall and in his publications. *Fors*, however, rather stubbornly resisted pictorial enhancement. Pictures began to appear in *Fors*, but they were sparse. The first two were woodcuts by Arthur Burgess. He drew some Verona ironwork and made a facsimile of a woodcut from Holbein's *Dance of Death*. These were placed within the text of the second and fourth letters of *Fors*. From a professor of art, one might have expected a more generous use of pictures. A reader might also have looked forward to discussion of the reproductions. However, Ruskin scarcely offered any art history or art criticism in *Fors*. The course of the illustration in the early numbers shows how Ruskin's pamphlet could both intrigue and exasperate. In April he decided to accompany the letters with a series of photogravures of Giotto frescos in the Arena Chapel in Padua. His treatment of the pictures might have been straightforward. Instead, it was as follows. In the fifth number of *Fors* there was a frontispiece, Giotto's *Hope*. However *Hope* is not discussed in this letter. Then followed four more Giotto frontispieces. In the sixth letter (June 1871), which was written at the Crown and Thistle, the reader would have found Giotto's figure of *Envy*. Again, the picture is not mentioned in Ruskin's text. Next, in the *Fors* of July 1871, we find *Charity*. In this letter, followers of Ruskin's thought would have been surprised to learn that he called himself 'a Communist of the old school — reddest also of the red'.[30] At last, we find discussion of Giotto, who is interpreted as a communist of this type. 'His Charity tramples upon bags of gold — has no use for them. She gives only corn and flowers; and God's angel gives *her*, not even these — but a Heart.' Next, in the October *Fors*, *Injustice* is at the head of Ruskin's remarks.[31] There are comments about the image. However, this *Fors* is mainly remarkable because it contains the beginning of Ruskin's autobiography *Præterita*, with its proud statement that 'I am, and my father was before me, a violent Tory of the old school (Walter Scott's school, that is to say, and Homer's)'.[32] Finally, in the November issue of *Fors*, Ruskin writes that 'I have given you, this month, the last of the pictures I want you to see from Padua; — Giotto's Image of Justice.' There follows a passage in sardonic vein. Giotto's figure,

> you observe, differs somewhat from the Image of Justice we used to set up in England, above insurance offices, and the like. Bandaged close about the eyes, our English Justice was wont to be, with a pair of grocers' scales in her hand, wherewith, doubtless, she was accustomed to weigh out accurately their shares to the landlords, and portions to the labourers, and remunerations to the capitalists. But Giotto's Justice has no bandage about her eyes . . .[33]

From its outset, then, *Fors Clavigera* was a puzzling and contradictory work. In what ways could Giotto have presided over the thoughts of a professor writing from an Abingdon inn, or Matlock, or a south London suburb, who called himself both 'a Communist of the old school' and a 'violent Tory of the old school'? In the *Fors* of November 1871 Ruskin noted letters, presumably from workmen, in which there were complaints that he wrote above their level. 'Eventually you shall understand, if you care to understand, every word in these pages', was his unconvincing reply.[34] Much study would have been required from those who cared to understand him. The references to Giotto, for instance, would send a committed reader of *Fors* to a well-equipped library. If he or she knew how to do so, the *Fors* reader could then have read Ruskin's more elaborated views on the old master in his *Giotto and his Works in Padua*, written for the Arundel Society in 1854; and then read his discussion of the medieval conception of the cardinal and theological virtues, and Giotto's interpretation of them, in the chapter 'The Ducal Palace' in the second volume of *The Stones of Venice*, published in 1853. However, Ruskin gave no directions to these works. It is never clear whether he expected readers of *Fors Clavigera* to be familiar with his other writings. If they were, so much the better. If they were not, *Fors* was not thereby the less fascinating. Ruskin's pamphlet continually suggested a vast academic knowledge and culture that could not be summarised because it could not be grasped by minds less extraordinary than his own. If one can imagine an ideal reader of *Fors Clavigera*, that person would not be a workman but an Oxford undergraduate. Mature academic minds in Oxford found Ruskin wilfully obscure and overly dogmatic. They were distressed by his opinions and his wayward intellectual manner. Undergraduates, on the other hand, could sense that they were almost in touch with a great consciousness. Since they had recently been at school they would all have been familiar with learning by rote. In the person of Ruskin they were offered learning by inspiration.

This is why the later recollections of undergraduates so often speak of 'a spirit' being among them, as though Ruskin's lectures were uttered by no mortal being. Those who compared his addresses to preaching were not wrong, as Ruskin himself acknowledged. On the other hand it was obvious to all that he was separated from the mundane Christianity of so many Victorian pulpits. Ruskin's tone was religious, but his overriding subject was beauty. In early 1871 the notion that beautiful things might be isolated and venerated was still unusual, for Pre-Raphaelitism had not yet become Aestheticism. The idea of 'a spirit' in the lecture room was accentuated by Ruskin's delivery. This lover of the theatre became a rarified actor whenever he addressed an audience. His manner of lecturing was almost musical. Ruskin's lectures in the 1870s may be interpreted as vocal expressions of matters usually confined to print. He almost sang to the many young people who listened to his addresses.[35]

Ruskin's voice, a light tenor, could reach to all parts of a large room, however much he varied its volume. His diction was clear and crisp, an inheritance of the daily childhood reading from the Bible, when his mother had taught him in 'resolutely consistent lessons which so exercised me in the scriptures as to make every word of them familiar to my ear in habitual music'.[36] Lecturing was one of Ruskin's ways of expressing his musical feelings. At the professorial lectern he recompensed for a lost musical youth. When he was himself an undergraduate Ruskin had attended a few musical lessons, but he could not sing. Here was a sadness in his life, particularly since he felt so much emotion when listening to song. Orchestral and instrumental music meant less to him than the sound of the uplifted and lyrical voice. The elevated nature of his lectures was partly a result of Ruskin's delight in his own eloquence. His habit of introducing extempore passages, when an enthralled audience would see him put down his notes and walk a step or two closer to them, was surely operatic, at least in effect. At all events, many of his personal letters show that Ruskin regarded his lectures as having the nature of performance.

Ruskin needed his best powers of speech and persuasion when, in June of 1871, he gave his lecture in the Sheldonian Theatre on 'The Relation between Michael Angelo and Tintoret', in which the Venetian painter is preferred to the Florentine. This was the first of Ruskin's more controversial Oxford addresses. He troubled his audience in two ways. Firstly, he dared to criticise Michelangelo, for his pride and sensuality. Secondly, he implied criticism of the University itself. At Oxford there was a collection of Michelangelo drawings generally regarded as fine examples of his genius. In the previous year they had been catalogued by J. C. Robinson in his *Critical Account of the Drawings by Michael Angelo and Raffaello in the University Galleries, Oxford.* Robinson, little remembered today because he scarcely published his researches, was a significant figure in the history of nineteenth-century connoisseurship. He was Surveyor of the Queen's Pictures and a founder of the Fine Arts Club, later the Burlington Fine Arts Club. Ruskin, who did not know Robinson personally, had no fellow-feeling for his scholarship or expertise. He knew of Robinson's connection with art education at South Kensington, and therefore felt it more important to oppose his views.[37] He did so with unnecessary rudeness, claiming that Michelangelo's 'ostentatious display of strength and science has a natural attraction for comparatively weak and pedantic persons'.[38] Ruskin's lecture was not well received. He published it as a pamphlet in 1872 (and it was subsequently added to *Aratra Pentelici*), but in that same year thought it politic to write a preface to the Revd R. St John Tyrwhitt's *Christian Art and Symbolism*, in which he admitted that Tyrwhitt's interpretations 'show, throughout, the most beautiful and just reverence for Michael Angelo, and are of especial value in their account of him: while the last lecture on sculpture, which I gave at Oxford, is entirely devoted to examining the modes in which his genius itself failed, and perverted that of other men . . . Both of us see truly — both partially; the complete truth is in the witness of both.'[39]

Ruskin's views on Michelangelo were especially distressing to Edward Burne-Jones. In the earlier part of 1871, when Ruskin was dividing his time between Abingdon, Oxford and Denmark Hill, he was somewhat out of touch with his friend. Then, one evening, Ruskin read him the lecture on Michelangelo and Tintoretto. The story is told by Georgiana Burne-Jones:

> Ten years after the evening at Denmark Hill when the thing happened, Edward said of Ruskin's lecture on Michael Angelo: 'He read

> it to me just after he had written it, and as I went home I wanted to drown myself in the Surrey Canal or get drunk in a tavern — it didn't seem worth while to strive any more if he could think it and write it'.
>
> In 1871 Edward writes again about Ruskin to Mr Norton: 'You know more of him than I do, for literally I never see him nor hear from him, and when we meet we clip as of old and look as of old, but he quarrels with my pictures and I with his writing, and there is no peace between us — and you know all is up when friends don't admire each other's work'. The old world 'clip' exactly describes the greeting that usually passed between him and Ruskin in their own houses: it was an impulsive movement forward by Edward, to whom his friend's physical presence was always a joy, and a curious half-embracing action of Ruskin's in return, which clasped his arm up to the elbow and drew them quite closely together. Later still another letter to Mr Norton says: 'Ruskin is back — came one day last week, and I forgave him all his blasphemies against my Gods — he looked so good through and through. But I want you to keep the peace between us, for after a month I shall begin to quarrel again'.[40]

Georgiana Burne-Jones's account of her husband's reaction to Ruskin's lecture could not discuss a matter that has occupied the painter's later biographers. He admired Michelangelo and did not like to hear so much in his dispraise. But it is claimed that he was upset for other reasons. Burne-Jones could have felt that he was himself the subject of Ruskin's criticisms. In speaking of a 'dark carnality' in Michelangelo's art and an imagination which substitutes 'the flesh of man for the spirit' Ruskin may have been rebuking Burne-Jones for his marital infidelities.[41] It is not known whether Ruskin was aware of Burne-Jones's relationship with a woman who was not his wife. We do know, however, that Ruskin disapproved of nudity in contemporary art, and that Burne-Jones at just this period was painting a series of pictures, his interpretation of the Pygmalion myth, in which the female nude is prominent. These paintings and their associated drawings may well have disturbed Ruskin. Nervous temperaments were also tried by the nature of the two men's love affairs. Burne-Jones's passion for the Greek heiress Maria Zambaco was tumultuous and illicit. Ruskin's love for Rose La Touche was desperate and innocent. It was vital for Ruskin that he should be seen as having a stainless character. There were some people, however, who could not believe in his innocence, led by his former wife Effie Millais and the various friends who had taken her side when she had escaped from the Ruskin home in 1854. In quite different circles from those inhabited by the conventional Millais family, the society of London bohemia, there was gossip about Ruskin and a young Irish girl. One probable source of these rumours was Charles Augustus Howell. The untrustworthy Howell knew about Rose. He had left Ruskin's employment by 1870 but on occasion still managed to gain an invitation to Denmark Hill and furthermore was friendly with another raconteur, Arthur Severn. More gossip came from Ruskin himself, who often talked and corresponded about Rose, not only to friends but to anyone he thought might assist his cause. Ruskin also sought out people who might have any news of Rose's health, her activities and her attitudes to her lover. Thus was created the atmosphere of uncertainty and collusion in which gossip thrived.

Ruskin was aware of such talk, and one of the functions of *Fors Clavigera* was to demonstrate to all the world that he was a man of candour and integrity. Since he so much wrote about himself and his feelings in his pamphlet, Ruskin could not conceal his personal torments. Rose is not mentioned by name in *Fors*. She is none the less the recipient of its messages and the first influence on its anguished tone. A further emotional problem for Ruskin was Joan Agnew's engagement and marriage to Arthur Severn. In his heart Ruskin did not wish Joan to be married, to Arthur or to anyone else. This is why he had laid down strict conditions, insisting that the young man should wait for three years before asking for his ward's hand. Arthur had waited. In late September of 1870 his term of probation had ended. Arthur's memoir of Ruskin recounts that he then 'wrote to the Professor asking if I might be again on the old footing'.[42] A few days later Ruskin dined with Severn and then invited him to join a theatre party, not saying who the other guests would be. To Arthur's nervous surprise he found himself in a box with Carlyle's niece Mary Aitken, 'a pretty Irish girl' (who was Lily Armstrong) and Joan. As often before, and subsequently, Ruskin was observing the proprieties of chaperonage while also suggesting that he did not consider such conventions to be final. In the next three weeks he, Joan and Arthur were often at the theatre together, and Arthur would then dine at Denmark Hill. The engagement of Joan and Arthur was announced on 20 November 1870. Now Arthur was given another privilege: he was invited upstairs to sit with the bedridden Margaret Ruskin. 'She never lectured me, often tipped me,' Arthur's memoir tells us; 'getting her purse from under the pillow'.[43] A proud young gentleman who was affianced to the daughter of the house would never have accepted such tips. But Arthur Severn was not a proud man, as we see from this guileless account. He happily accepted gifts from Margaret Ruskin's purse as though they were his due; and this attitude was a portent of things to come.

Joan Agnew became Arthur Severn's wife on 20 April 1871 . Ruskin travelled from the Crown and Thistle to preside at the occasion. He did so with courteous assurance, though we may be certain that his thoughts strayed to the possibility of his own marriage. Severn recalled that

> I was delighted to see how au fait the Professor seemed to be. There was an old-fashioned sit-down breakfast and I shall always remember the Professor's charming and touching speech in which he alluded to my father and the death of Keats . . . the Professor looked quite the bridegroom himself, in a new bright blue stock, very light grey trousers, and almost fashionable frock-coat with a rose in the button-hole, and quite gay in manner. Old Mrs Ruskin (his mother), then in her ninetieth year, was upstairs, but quite able to see many guests . . .[44]

Thus the Severns' marriage began, with all manner of generosities from the Ruskin family. 'Just before my marriage', Severn wrote, Margaret Ruskin 'gave me a considerable sum of money. But it was only to be spent on our bedroom furniture, and that was to be mahogany'.[45] Ruskin's wedding present to the couple was a house, his own childhood home, No. 28 Herne Hill. This was the house in which the Ruskins had lived from 1823 to 1843 before removing to the nearby Denmark Hill. John James Ruskin had then retained the lease of No. 28. The lease was made out in Joan's name. It expired in 1886, when Arthur renewed it until 1907. There was a loving arrangement between Joan and Ruskin that he should have the use of his old nursery on the top floor. He would need somewhere to work and sleep when in London. Ruskin had no wish to live at Denmark Hill after his mother's death, though he had no idea where else to make his home. In this way No. 28 Herne Hill became Ruskin's London lodging. He used the house from 1872 until 1888.

Urbane though he seemed, Ruskin had been greatly disturbed by the prospect of Joan's wedding and became more agitated when the young couple left London for their honeymoon. He thought of his own honeymoon and his married life with Effie. He was also forced to think of Joan's loss of virginity. It is possible that 'The Relation between Michael Angelo and Tintoret' was affected not by Burne-Jones's situation but by Joan's marriage. Revolted by adult physical love, Ruskin could not come to terms with the fact that Joan and Arthur would henceforth share a bed. Perhaps this is why he arranged that they should spend the first week of their honeymoon under the roof of a clergyman, the Revd William Kingsley of South Kilvington in Yorkshire. Ruskin knew Kingsley because he was a Turner expert. It is not known when they first met, and Ruskin had last seen Kingsley in 1866. This North Country vicar had nothing to do with either Joan or Arthur, though they found him an amiable host. The Severns' plan was to spend a month or more touring Yorkshire and Scotland, where they would call on some of Joan's relatives. But it soon became apparent that Ruskin would not leave them alone. His daily letters to Joan grew hysterical. Five days after the wedding he wrote to her at South Kilvington '. . . Me was fitened dedful for no ettie — no ettie — no ettie — no ettie — Sat-day — Sun-day — Mon-day — Two's day — *so* fitened. At last me got wee ettie as Dr Ac's. Today — here — no ettie again — me *so* misby — misby — misby . . . Oh me miss oo — more than tongue can tell . . .'[46] A little later, when Joan had realised that her married status did not allow her to fail in a daily letter to Ruskin, her cousin recovered some equilibrium.

However, relations with Rose La Touche now drove him to a new state of frustrated despair. While Joan and Arthur were travelling he heard bad news from Ireland. There was much anxiety about Rose's health. Thus began another exchange of messages between Ruskin and his love. 'I wrote a wee line to R . . . — telling her to get well', Ruskin told Joan on 10 May.[47] Weeks later, in early June, an answer came. It was not addressed directly to Ruskin but to Mrs Cowper-Temple. Rose said in her letter that she had 'been made so happy' by hearing from Ruskin and 'would try to get well and not to die'.[48] All through May and June, Ruskin brooded on his cousin's marriage and anxiously awaited news of Rose's health. These were the circumstances in which 'The Relation between Michael Angelo and Tintoret' was written. When he delivered the lecture, on 13 June, Ruskin was close to his first mental breakdown.

Ruskin had often been ill before and there had been periods, short or long, when he had been unable to write. His illness of 1871 was more worrying — to Ruskin and to his friends — than any previous indisposition. It seems that he was close to death. The collapse may be called a mental breakdown, because Ruskin experienced hallucinations as well as physical symptoms. Therefore his disorder is akin to the illnesses, which certainly were of the mind, of 1876, 1878, 1881, 1883 and subsequent dates. The hallucinations of July 1871, which

Ruskin called 'dreams', were described in an Oxford lecture the next year, 'Design in the Florentine Schools of Engraving'.[49] Here we must record a caveat about Ruskin's own testimony. The manuscript of the lecture is lost. It was published in July 1875, just after the death of Rose La Touche, and was then gathered with other Oxford lectures into *Ariadne Florentina*. So it is quite possible that Ruskin's description of his illness and 'dreams' was written as lately as the spring or summer of 1875. In that case, his account might reflect the concerns of the period of Rose's death. At all events, the text that we have of 'Design in the Florentine Schools of Engraving' suddenly becomes autobiographical when Ruskin declares that 'In 1871, partly in chagrin at the Revolution in Paris, and partly in great personal sorrow, I was struck by acute inflammatory illness at Matlock, and reduced to a state of acute weakness; lying at one time unconscious for some hours, those about me having no hope of my life.'[50]

Ruskin's audience (if these words were spoken in 1872) might have wondered why he had been in Matlock and why he had decided to talk about his 'dreams'. There were three dreams or hallucinations, 'all distinct and impressive, and had much meaning, if I chose to take it'. The first was of a Venetian fisherman who showed Ruskin the bronze horses of St Mark's. The second was of preparations in Rome for a religious drama, the demons, priests, the people and a woman in black. The drama proved to be true, not theatrical: the fiends were real fiends. In the third dream Ruskin imagined himself to be a brother of St Francis and thought that the Cumaean Sybil had whispered a line of Virgil into his ear 'at every new trial'.[51] All these things were a regular part of Ruskin's personal symbolism, as we will see: they appear in his private writings and fancyings at times of stress or incipient madness. Ruskin was under great stress when he went to Matlock at the end of June 1871. He was in discussion with lawyers about his failure to consummate his marriage. It now had appeared that the events of 1854 had a bearing on his being able to marry again. At the same time Ruskin did not know whether Rose might not be on her deathbed. He was also neurotically anxious to be reunited with Joan. Her honeymoon had now lasted almost two months. A plan for Joan and Arthur to come to the Crown and Thistle had fallen through. Ruskin decided to travel north to meet the Severns at the Derbyshire spa he well remembered from his childhood. He arrived at the New Bath Hotel in Matlock (where he had stayed with his parents in 1829 and had pursued his childish geological interests) in strange, unseasonal weather. 'July opened with cold, dry, dark weather, dangerous for out-of-door sketching,' recorded W. G. Collingwood, Ruskin's first biographer, who had talked with him about events at Matlock. 'One morning early — for he was always an early riser — he took a chill while painting a spray of wild rose before breakfast (the drawing now in the Oxford Schools). He was already overworked, and it ended in a severe attack of internal inflammation . . .'[52] Ruskin suffered from continual violent vomiting, exhaustion, high fever and delirious dreams. He struggled to get out of bed but was too weak to stand. A local doctor was unable to cope. Joan therefore sent a telegram to Henry Acland, who immediately left his other business to be at his old friend's bedside.

CHAPTER TWENTY-EIGHT

1871 (ii)

On an express train which he knew would pass through Matlock without stopping, Henry Acland carefully judged his moment. He pulled the alarm cord, stepped on to the platform, gave his card to the guard and hurried to the New Bath Hotel. The Regius Professor of Medicine, well known as a bore in Oxford committees, could act with speed and style when occasion demanded. Acland had much personal vigour. He also had a calming influence on his patient. Having known Ruskin so well and for so long, Acland could speak to him with tender friendship as well as medical authority. Ruskin was weak, but his mind was raging wildly. Gradually, the doctor brought his patient to a condition in which Ruskin was less excited. Then Acland insisted on careful nursing, complete rest and a light diet. Arthur Severn's memoir relates that after Acland's arrival in Matlock Ruskin's symptoms 'showed improvement, but it was days before he was out of danger'. Perhaps it was at this stage of the illness that Ruskin experienced his 'dreams' or hallucinations.[1] We know that he spent hours looking intensely at mundane things at the side of his bed; a bowl of fish and some grapes. In contradiction to all wise advice Ruskin insisted on various foods and drinks. He had a craving for pepper and mustard. He drank brandy and water. Ruskin was in bed for nearly three weeks. At the end of July he was able to write to William Cowper-Temple that 'I have been up and about, these three days, and can do everything but walk — but I can't yet get any steadiness on my feet: — However, I've cut off the brandy & water stimulus and I think I stagger for want of being drunk: — but I've got back now to a couple of glasses of sherry . . .'[2]

Ruskin's Matlock illness ended on this comparatively cheerful note, as Joan remarked in one of her letters to the anxious Margaret Ruskin. On 30 July she explained that, 'strange to say', the illness

> . . . is hardly a matter of regret! since it has had the wonderful effect of making him pleased with things in general — you know he used to growl so — and now he seems so pleased — and instead of thinking that the streams and country are every-where polluted, he sees that there is still much to be admired and loved and in both his looks and conversation the old sad despondency seems to have vanished . . .[3]

The newly married Joan was too optimistic. Ruskin was aware, daily and hour by hour, of the end of life. Margaret Ruskin was near to death. Only three weeks before Joan's encouraging letter to her 'Auntie', Ruskin might have predeceased his mother. Nobody, in Ireland or in England, among friends of the La Touches or friends of Ruskin's, quite knew how grave Rose's condition might be. In May she had sent the message that she would 'try and get well and not to die'. Was she still in mortal danger? From his own recovery in August of 1871 to Rose's last days in the spring of 1875 Ruskin lived in an atmosphere of crisis, illness and imminent death. His personal agonies had an effect on his writing, particularly on *Fors Clavigera*. The Matlock illness did not interrupt the publication of *Fors*. Ruskin had written the first part of the August letter on 1 July, the day before he fell ill, and completed the pamphlet as soon as he was able to write again, on 19 July. The August letter begins as follows:

> MY FRIENDS, — I begin this letter a month before it is wanted, having several matters in my mind that I would fain put into words at once. It is the first of July, and I sit down to write by the dismallest light that ever yet I wrote by; namely, the light of this midsummer morning, in mid-England (Matlock, Derbyshire), in the year 1871.
>
> For the sky is covered with grey cloud; — not rain-cloud, but a dry black veil, which no ray of sunshine can pierce; partly diffused in mist, feeble mist, enough to make distant objects unintelligible, yet without any substance, or wreathing, or colour of its own. And everywhere the leaves of the trees are shaking fitfully, as they do before a thunderstorm; only not violently, but enough to show the passing to and fro of a strange, bitter, blighting wind. Dismal enough, had it been the first morning of its kind that summer had sent. But during all this spring, in London, and at Oxford, through meagre March, through changelessly sullen April, through despondent May, and darkened June, morning after morning has come grey-shrouded thus.
>
> And it is a new thing to me, and a very dreadful one. I am fifty years old, and more; and since I was five, have gleaned the best hours of my life in the sun of spring and summer mornings; and I never saw such as these, till now.

Ruskin then went on to consider this type of cloud:

> It looks partly as if it were made of poisonous smoke; very possibly it may be: there are at least two hundred furnace chimneys in

> a square of two miles on every side of me. But mere smoke would not blow to and fro in that wild way. It looks more to me as if it were made of dead men's souls — such of them as are not gone yet where they have to go, and may be flitting hither and thither, doubting, themselves, of the fittest place for them.
>
> You know, if there *are* such things as souls, and if any of them haunt places where they have been hurt, there must be many about us, just now, displeased enough!
>
> You may laugh, if you like. I don't believe any one of you would like to live in a room with a murdered man in the cupboard, however well preserved chemically; — even with a sunflower growing out at the top of his head.[4]

The meaning of this last paragraph remains unexplained. Much else in the letter is both mysterious and frightening. One wonders what Ruskin's readers made of *Fors Clavigera*. By now, with the eighth letter of the series, it was clear that *Fors* was more extravagant and peculiar than any of Ruskin's previous writings. It was less obvious that, month by month, he was building a unique contribution to Victorian literature. Naturally enough, most people who opened *Fors* thought that Ruskin was trying to teach them, and it is not surprising that they resisted his instruction. Ruskin also gave his readers ample reason to approach *Fors* in a pathological spirit. His descriptions of the weather were not merely exaggerated. They revealed a dangerous unease in his mind. Even if it were true — and it was true — that modern industry polluted the heavens, Ruskin's comments surely also spoke of himself. In this eighth number of *Fors Clavigera* we encounter the first description of the 'plague-wind' that would become Ruskin's obsession in the next years. He quoted the passage in his 1884 lecture 'The Storm-Cloud of the Nineteenth Century'. Ruskin then declared that 'my attention, however otherwise occupied, has never relaxed in its record of the phenomena characteristic of the plague-wind'.[5] The belief in the 'plague-wind' and 'storm-cloud' is part of Ruskin's character in his later years. We will often note his morbid preoccupation with winds and dark clouds. It was a part of his growing mental disturbance. In 1871, Ruskin's account of the weather is linked to his kind of literature. There was a sort of perverse poetry in the invocation of 'meagre March . . . changelessly sullen April . . . despondent May, and darkened June'. Dante also contributed; in his poetic vision we find winds which remained in Ruskin's mind when he wrote of the 'plague-wind'. But these matters were not appreciated by the 'workmen and labourers of Great Britain'.

Lying in bed in Matlock, Ruskin received a number of visitors. First of all there were doctors. Local practitioners called on him. Acland came to Matlock again; and then Ruskin had the welcome sight of John and Jane Simon, family friends who took reassuring messages from the New Bath Hotel to Margaret Ruskin in Denmark Hill. Lady Mount-Temple was an ineffective nurse. Charles Newton arrived. He was now not only Ruskin's old friend but also Arthur Severn's brother-in-law, for he had married his sister Mary. The artist Albert Goodwin was also at Matlock and helped with the nursing. Goodwin had recently been Ruskin's guest at Abingdon, where he painted in the surrounding countryside. Little is known about his friendship with Ruskin. It must have been warm, for in 1872 the painter was among the party that Ruskin assembled for a holiday in Venice. At Matlock, Goodwin went on sketching expeditions with Arthur Severn and brought the results to Ruskin's bedside. When Ruskin was 'well enough to sit up', Severn recorded, he

> at once made Goodwin and myself go and explore all the interesting mines and caverns in the neighbourhood. If doing so meant a long distance, he sent us with a carriage and pair, mapping out our route and giving us every information. He seemed very well up in such places for miles around and liked to hear our different accounts and to see our sketches when we came back in the evening, always telling us to spare no expense. After the anxiety and nursing we had gone through, these expeditions were very delightful and refreshing.[6]

In this way Ruskin revisited some of the geological adventures of his childhood. For at Matlock in 1829, as *Præterita* tells us, 'in the glittering white broken spar, specked with galena, by which the walks of the hotel garden were made bright, and in the shops of the pretty village, and in many a happy walk among its cliffs, I pursued my mineralogical studies on fluor, calcite, and the ores of lead, with indescribable rapture when I was allowed to go into a cave . . .'[7]

The terrible weeks in Matlock brought another change to Ruskin's life. In July and August he purchased the house with which his name will always be associated. Brantwood, at the side of Coniston Lake (Coniston Water) in Lancashire, was acquired almost in reaction to the Matlock illness; and also as a result of childhood memories, for Ruskin had been there in 1824, 1826 and 1830. *Præterita* recounts that the local scenery 'had for my father a tender charm which excited the same feeling as that with which he afterwards regarded the lakes of Italy', and Ruskin's autobiography further reveals that Coniston was a place of emotional rendezvous for his family. He and his mother would stay there at the Waterhead Inn while John James Ruskin was away 'on his business journeys to Whitehaven, Lancaster, Newcastle, and other northern towns'.[8] Then he would meet his wife and son at the Waterhead, and no doubt these were happy occasions. Ruskin bought Brantwood, which is a little more than a mile from the Waterhead Inn, partly to honour his parents' marriage and partly in sad anticipation of his mother's death. While Acland was sitting with him at a crucial moment of his illness, 'when the Professor was almost at his worst', according to Arthur Severn, he said that 'I feel I should get better if only I could lie down in Coniston Water'.[9] This was not a delirious fancy. Ruskin thought of a cool lake beneath green hills as he sought relief from his fever, and he also thought of his early life with his parents. Already we feel the impulses of *Præterita*. We also recognise the religious cast of Ruskin's mind. Why should he have wished to 'lie in' or 'lie down in' (phrases which recur in the summer of 1871) the water of the lake itself? In a literal sense, he often did so in the next ten years. When the weather was temperate Ruskin would take one of his boats, row into the lake, lie down in the boat and watch the clouds. In a religious sense, Ruskin's helpless remark to Acland reminds us of his lifelong reading of the Bible and perhaps especially of these verses: 'The needy shall lie down in safety' (Isaiah, 14.30), 'The army and the power shall lie down together' (Isaiah, 43.17), 'Thou shalt lie down and thy sleep be sweet' (Proverbs, 3.24) and 'He maketh me lie down in green pastures' (Psalms, 23.2).

Through some command of a beneficent third Fors, Ruskin was offered a Coniston home just as he began his recuperation and travelled from Matlock to London. A letter arrived from W. J. Linton (1812–98), who was a wood engraver, printer and republican. He asked whether Ruskin might wish to purchase his house, Brantwood. It would not be a large commitment. In 1871 Brantwood was little more than a cottage, with a few outhouses and some sixteen acres of rocky or wooded ground. Linton had bought the property in 1852 and had lived there only intermittently before removing to America in 1867.[10] It is not known why he approached Ruskin. It is possible that he believed that Ruskin shared his radical opinions. The author of *Fors Clavigera* was amused by the thought that he would follow a political agitator in owning a little part of the English countryside. He replied immediately and in 'a couple of letters' the two men struck their bargain. Ruskin paid Linton £1,500 for a house he had never seen. Brantwood's situation was enough. He knew nothing about the building or its state of repair; but he knew where it was and could imagine that from its windows he would look out over the lake to the Old Man of Coniston, a view he had described, many years before, in one of his childhood poems.[11] It was often said that Ruskin bought Brantwood simply for its view, since the house lacked charm. This was in part true. Although he liked domestic comforts Ruskin was not fussy about the places in which he lived. He was a rich man with no temperamental liking for grandeur. He preferred inns to hotels and was always slightly nervous in great houses. He was — or had been — a powerful architectural critic, yet never thought of designing an ideal abode for himself or anyone else. Future developments at Brantwood were done piecemeal. However much enlarged, it was always to be an inconvenient house, and some parts of it are ugly. Ruskin cared little about such matters. He was content with the thought of his cottage and decided that he would live there when his mother died.

The prospect of leaving Denmark Hill did not upset him, though the house held many dear memories. Ruskin was more grieved by the thought that he would shortly see his mother for the last time. Fortuitously, Brantwood now became part of Ruskin's vague plans for his later years. He thought that it would be better to make his home in a remote Lancashire cottage than to live in the comparative state of a south London mansion. For some time past — perhaps even from the death of his father in 1864 — Ruskin had felt that he ought to divest himself of the vanity of wealth. This is why, with his mother's death approaching, Ruskin made a startling pledge in *Fors Clavigera*. It is a classic statement of his High Tory utopianism, and begins:

> You have founded an entire Science of Political Economy, on what you have stated to be the constant instinct of man — the desire to defraud his neighbour.
>
> And you have driven your women mad, so that they ask no more for Love, nor for fellowship with you; but stand against you, and ask for 'justice'.
>
> Are there any of you who are tired of all this? Any of you, Landlords or Tenants? Employers or Workmen?
>
> Are there any landlords, — any masters, — who would like better to be served by men than by iron devils?
>
> Any tenants, any workmen, who can be true to their leaders and to each other? who can vow to work and to live faithfully, for the sake of the joy of their homes?
>
> Will any such give the tenth of what they have, and of what they earn, — not to emigrate with, but to stay in England with; and to do what is in their hands and hearts to make her a happy England?

> I am not rich (as people now estimate riches), and great part of what I have is already engaged in maintaining art-workmen, or for other objects more or less of public utility. The tenth of whatever is left to me, estimated as accurately as I can (you shall see the accounts), I will make over to you in perpetuity, with the best security that English law can give, on Christmas Day of this year, with engagement to add the tithe of whatever I earn afterwards. Who else will help, with little or much? the object of such fund being, to begin, and gradually — no matter how slowly — to increase, the buying and securing of land in England, which shall not be built upon, but cultivated by Englishmen, with their own hands, and such help of force as they can find in wind and wave . . .[12]

Here begins the complicated story of 'St George's Fund', as Ruskin called it, and the fortunes of the Guild of St George. A function of *Fors Clavigera* would now be to record the progress of the fund. In *Fors* we henceforward find details of Ruskin's personal income and expenditure. This was an unusual, probably unique, financial confession by an eminent Victorian. *Fors* declared that true men should have 'glass pockets', so that 'we must every one know each other's property to a farthing'.[13] Ruskin's frankness probably brought him more begging letters than donations, while many of his contemporaries were persuaded that he was not a man who could handle finance. As if in anticipation of such criticism, Ruskin arranged for the moneys he had made over to his fund to be administered by two trustees. In the September *Fors* he announced that they were to be Sir Thomas Dyke Acland and William Cowper-Temple. Both were themselves landowners. Cowper-Temple had inherited Broadlands. Sir Thomas Acland, Henry Acland's elder brother, and thus the successor to the Acland baronetcy, farmed the family's estates in Devon.

Cowper-Temple and his wife had visited Ruskin in Matlock, where 'Phile' had taken her part in nursing the distraught patient. Their presence in the Derbyshire spa returns us to the subject of Rose La Touche, for the Cowper-Temples had travelled to Matlock with legal documents about Ruskin's marriage. John La Touche and his wife had consulted a solicitor about Ruskin's divorce from Effie. He had advised them that Ruskin could not contract a legal marriage, and John La Touche had written to Ruskin to this effect. In late June Ruskin had therefore been forced to answer the opinion that La Touche had obtained. Hidden away in Denmark Hill were papers about his divorce. Ruskin had travelled from Abingdon to find them, then sent these old and intimate letters to Cowper-Temple while also consulting his own solicitors. A difficulty was that the decree of divorce was missing. Ruskin's and Effie's case had been heard before the Ecclesiastical Courts. These had been abolished by the Divorce Act of 1857. In June, while he was still in Abingdon and before he travelled to Matlock, Ruskin did not know whether his divorce had an eccelesiastical or a secular validity, or perhaps both, or perhaps neither.[14]

If Effie had remarried, why might not Ruskin? What fault of the marriage bed could be imputed to him? How much did Rose know? These were some of the questions that pressed on Ruskin as his physical and mental health failed. Yet the legal opinions brought to Matlock seemed to be in his favour. His cousin W. G. Richardson, who had recently taken up a second career as a lawyer, assured him that 'for all practical purposes you are free to marry again'.[15] This curiously worded assurance may reflect the quality of the advice that Ruskin received; or it might refer to the highly personal question of his virility. At all events, Ruskin now wrote to Rose on 23 July, while still confined to his bed in the New Bath Hotel, to tell her that lawyers had stated that he could marry. We know about this letter because Ruskin reported its contents to William Cowper-Temple. 'I have written straight & simply to R. herself', Ruskin said, 'telling her all is ascertained & safe . . . The rest of the letter was merely a quiet statement of what I told you I should say: that she must now correspond with me — and rationally determine if it will be advisable to marry or not.'[16]

Why might it be, or not be, 'advisable' for Rose to marry? Surely Ruskin used the word because of the state of her health. Only two months before, she had apparently been close to death. It is possible that Ruskin was too emphatic during this unpleasant phase of his courtship. If Rose was so frail that marriage could not be contemplated, then Ruskin was wrong to persist in declaring that he had any rights in the matter. The innocent, unstable Rose was so frightened and upset that she replied to Ruskin's letter in an abrupt manner. Even her close friend Joan Severn was shocked. A further letter to William Cowper-Temple, on 27 July of 1871, describes the way in which Ruskin now rejected the young woman whom, only a week before, he had been petitioning to marry:

> So many thanks for all you say about R. but I'm tired writing now & will dictate to Joanna what I've to say of her. I sent her a very civil letter to which she sent an answer which for folly, insolence and selfishness beat everything I yet have known produced by the accursed sect of religion she has been brought up in. I made Joanna

re-enclose the letter, writing only, on a scrap of paper with it — (Joanna writing, that is to say, not I) 'my cousin and I have read the enclosed — You shall have the rest of your letters as soon as he returns home — and your mother shall have hers' — so the letter went back, and the young lady shall never read written, nor hear spoken, word of mine more. I am entirely satisfied in being quit of her, for I feel convinced she would have been a hindrance to me, one way or other, in doing what I am more and more convinced that I shall be permitted to do *rightly*, only, on condition of putting all my strength into it.[17]

* * * *

In this way Cowper-Temple's services as a mediator were terminated, though only for a while. Of course Ruskin was not 'entirely satisfied in being quit' of Rose. He did not send letters to Harristown in the next months but he did write to her in another way. The tenth number of *Fors Clavigera*, dated from Denmark Hill on 7 September, contains the sad, noble paragraphs so familiar as the opening of *Præterita*, Ruskin's autobiography, which began its separate publication in 1886, and was initially composed of the passages of personal reminiscence that occur in *Fors* until Rose's death in May 1875. This was the first of them. Ruskin speaks of his father and his inherited Toryism 'of the old school', then passes to the daily Bible readings with his mother. As ever, Ruskin was concerned to demonstrate to Rose that his understanding of the Bible was greater than hers. He also wrote this autobiographical fragment in honour of Margaret Ruskin, bedridden and dying in an upper floor of his family home. It has often been claimed that *Præterita* was written in a mood of serene reminiscence. That is not so. The autobiography was begun at a deathbed in a situation of anxiety about its author's wish to marry a young woman who was hostile to his approaches and who knew about the failure of his previous marriage. The variable tone of *Præterita* is always the result of the circumstances in which each part of the book was written. In the late summer of 1871 Ruskin had no thought of setting down a coherent and consecutive account of his life. His object was to declare his filiation, to commemorate his mother and father — both of whom had known and loved Rose — and above all to show his living character. Ruskin wished to present himself as a husband in his father's mould. The endeavour may have been in vain. It is not known whether Rose read *Fors Clavigera*, though she may well have seen one or more issues, and there is no direct evidence that she knew any writing of Ruskin's after the 1869 publication of *The Queen of the Air*. Ruskin none the less wrote for Rose's attention. She might be numbered with those 'workmen and labourers of Great Britain' who were addressed by Ruskin yet gave him little or no response.

Ruskin had wished to travel to Italy in the summer of 1871, but was delayed by his illness. Now he decided that his mother was so frail that he ought not to leave the country. Instead, he travelled to the Lake District in September to look at his new home. Letters to Joan, Norton, Carlyle and others record his pleasure at finding 'my piece of ground', for Ruskin liked to think that he had bought land rather than a house. 'It's a bit of steep hillside facing West — commanding from the brow of it, all Coniston lake and the mass of hills of south Cumberland', he told Carlyle: 'The slope is half copse — half moor and rock — a pretty field beneath, less steep, a white two-storied cottage, and a bank of turf in front of it —, then a narrow mountain road — and on the other side of that — Naboth's vineyard — my neighbour's field, to the water's edge. My neighbour will lease me enough of field and shore to build a boat-house, & reach it . . .'[18] Ruskin had plans, not ambitious ones, to extend his property. 'Naboth's vineyard' (I Kings 21.1) is a piece of land coveted by a neighbour. This field belonged to the accommodating Major Benson Harrison, a descendant of the Lakeland literary 'artistocracy', for he was Dorothy Wordsworth's son. Ruskin had other invented names for parts of the surrounding land, especially the mountains he could see from his windows. The Old Man of Coniston became the 'Vecchio' and the Wetherlam he called the 'Agnello'. To reach these mountains, where he was often to walk in the years to come, Ruskin proposed to row across the lake to Coniston village. Therefore it was important to have a boathouse in 'Naboth's Vineyard'. Ruskin rowed six miles on 13 September, 'besides scrambling up the bed of a stream holding on by the heather', so his convalescence must have restored him to good health.[19] The house itself was not in good repair. 'There *is* a house, certainly, and it has rooms in it', he wrote to Joan, 'but I believe in reality nearly as much will have to be done as if it were a shell of bricks and mortar'. In an outhouse he found Linton's abandoned printing press. The slogan 'God and the People' was scratched into the whitewash. 'Well', Ruskin wrote, 'it won't be a "republican centre" now, but whether the landed men round will like my Toryism better than his Republicanism, remains to be seen'.[20] In the next years, relations with all Coniston people (except the vicar) would be excellent. Ruskin had not really lived in a local community before; but he was good at it, for the simple reasons that he was a good man and a friendly man. His life as a neighbour among other neighbours would be a theme of his later writing.

The purchase of Brantwood made Ruskin a man of the North Country, a topographical circumstance that had an effect on his books. His new home, while not impossibly remote, was far distant from the modern doings and conversations of London and Oxford. From Brantwood it was not far to the end of Hadrian's Wall at Bowness-on-Solway, to Carlisle and Scotland. A sense that he was close to Scotland was important to Ruskin in his Brantwood years; and in this September of 1871 he made a journey across the border to meet the Hilliards at Abbeythune, then travelled to Arbroath, the country of Walter Scott's *The Antiquary*. A letter describing this expedition gives a foretaste of many passages in the later numbers of *Fors Clavigera*. From Carlisle Ruskin wrote to Joan:

> I've had such an exquisite drive from Keswick over the high moorlands by the English Wigtown. The day was, most fortunately, the *clearest* I have seen this year — with the sweet *Northern* clearness I remember so well in old times — and when I got about half-way to Carlisle, to the bow of the moorland, there was all the Solway, Criffel, and the blue promontories as far as your own Wigtown on one side, and all the Liddesdale hills and the western Cheviots on the other, with the vast plain of Cumberland between. I think I never in England saw anything so *vast* and so beautiful — I saw, indeed, the Solway from Skiddaw, but that was late in the day, and from so great a height it is too much like a map — to-day it was all divided into bars of blue and gold by sunny gleams between flying clouds, rich and vast as the plain of Milan, but with a sweet wildness and simplicity of pastoral and solitary life expressed in it also; very wonderful. Then the air was as pure and bracing as air could be . . .[21]

For at least a little while, Ruskin had forgotten the 'plague-cloud', and from 'the bow of the moorland' he had seen St George's landscape. Ruskin next returned to Coniston for a few days. He organised some rebuilding of the house and, on 5 October, dated his first publication from Brantwood. This was an appendix to the first issue in book form of *Munera Pulveris* (his essays of 1862–63 in *Fraser's Magazine*), which would be published on 1 January 1872. There are six of these appendices. Four of them are over-matter from the original magazine publication. The fifth and sixth show that (as we have already noted) Ruskin had intended his *Fraser's* articles to continue more or less *ad infinitum*, for he considered the papers he had published to be merely an introduction to his subject. For this reason the appendices are a bridge between the 1862–63 articles and *Fors Clavigera*, a publication whose end could not be foreseen.

The memory of his difficulties with *Fraser's* irked Ruskin, and in his earliest days at Brantwood he began to think that he should become his own publisher. The discovery of Linton's printing press was a stimulus. From Brantwood Linton had issued his periodical *The English Republic*. Ruskin was excited to find that at the back of the house he printed 'a certain number of numbers of the *Republic* like my *Fors Clavigera*!'[22] It was now possible to envisage a publishing industry that flowed from a cottage. The books would be Ruskin's, or those that he had chosen as suitable for St George's purposes. The cottage would not be his, but that of George Allen. Ruskin's mind was moving logically, within its own lights. No normal publisher was fully qualified to keep up with the erratic flow of Ruskin's writing. It made sense to have a publisher who was a family servant. George Allen had this qualification, and many besides, for he was a meticulous craftsman who understood printing, photographic reproduction and bookbinding. Gradually, Allen became responsible for Ruskin's publishing programme. The 1872 edition of *Munera Pulveris* is the first in which his name appears on the title page. The book was 'Printed for the author by Smith, Elder & Co., 15 Waterloo Place: and sold by Mr G. Allen, Heathfield Cottage, Keston, Kent'.[23]

The next years would prove that to become his own publisher was an excellent way for Ruskin to rid himself of his father's fortune. In fifteen years he spent large amounts of money in printing many dozens of beautiful and thoughtful books which he refused to publicise and which could not be found in bookshops. These writings were highly priced and difficult to understand, especially since a reader who had managed to acquire one pamphlet from a series might not be able to find the others, even with help from Heathfield Cottage. In 1871–72 Ruskin's publishing became adventurous, self-concerned and heedless of other people's feelings. This publishing was not fully transferred to George Allen until 1873. During 1872 Ruskin found, though he was not given, a number of reasons to quarrel with Smith, Elder. It would have been kinder to break with the firm, his publishers since 1843, in a more amicable fashion. Ruskin also gave hurt to a professional colleague of even longer standing. W. H. Harrison had looked after Ruskin's manuscripts as they went through press since the days when he was the editor of *Friendship's Offering* and Ruskin was an apprentice poet. For years Harrison's position was that of a family friend. He was also a sort of retainer. Harrison was a frequent guest at Denmark Hill but the Ruskins did not call at his small, poor home in nearby

Camberwell. Now Harrison's services came to an end. He was superannuated both by reason of his age and by the enterprise of *Fors Clavigera*. It was essential to *Fors* that Ruskin should be free from wise advice. Ruskin had to be his own editor as well as his own publisher. He also wished to have a direct contact with his printer, not least because such an arrangement would make it easier for him to add thoughts, or recompose them, at proof stage. In 1873 Ruskin would finally remove all his printing to Messrs Hazell & Watson in the Buckinghamshire market town of Aylesbury. He could hardly have found a better firm, nor a more expensive one. With the head printer at Aylesbury, Henry Jowett, Ruskin soon developed a productive and affectionate working relationship. Their shared love of typography, and Ruskin's disregard of cost, enabled them to create books of much formal beauty. Considered simply as objects of art and craft, these books are an important part of the publishing history of the aesthetic movement.

Harrison was lost in these developments. His final personal contacts with Ruskin were at the time of Margaret Ruskin's death on 5 December 1871. She was then ninety. Harrison had known the Ruskins since 1837. He was one of the few people to be invited to the funeral, no doubt because of the long history of his relationship with the Ruskin family. Margaret Ruskin was buried beside her husband in Shirley churchyard, not far from her native Croydon. There is a report that Ruskin painted her coffin in a sky-blue colour. It first appears in the Revd H. D. Rawnsley's *Ruskin and the English Lakes* (1902) and was repeated in Ada Earland's *Ruskin and his Circle* (1910).[24] The story is probably true. Ruskin disliked all the dark trappings of mourning. He could well have wished to give his mother a more heavenly interment.

Margaret Ruskin's death also made her son brood about purity and defilement, cleanliness and clear running waters. These preoccupations led to Harrison's last — and inappropriate — service to Ruskin. He was enlisted in an attempt to 'keep a little bit of London perfectly clean'. That winter Ruskin had been disgusted by the filth in the streets around the British Museum. He determined to keep one crossing spotless and organised a small force of road sweepers. They included his gardener David Downs and a number of local boys, who proved mischievous. This was an unsuccessful social experiment. A more traditional memorial to his mother was Ruskin's scheme to clear a spring at Carshalton, a village about a mile to the west of Shirley. After many difficulties, water was made to flow sweetly. Ruskin then erected a tablet with the inscription

> In obedience to the Giver of Life, of the brooks and fruits that feed it, of the peace that ends it, may this Well be kept sacred for the services of men, flocks and flowers, and be by kindness called MARGARET'S WELL. This pool was beautified and endowed by John Ruskin, Esq., M.A. LL.D.[25]

The upkeep of this well was a sad and troublesome business. It is significant that the stream was the Wandle (Ruskin preferred the old spelling of Wandel), which rises near Shirley and flows past Croydon and through Carshalton on its way to the Thames. It was the stream of Ruskin's early life and his mother's life and death. The sparkling little river gave a title to one of the earliest chapters of *Præterita*, 'The Springs of Wandel'. It is the subject of the eloquent introduction to *The Crown of Wild Olive* (1866), in which Ruskin first wrote of the Wandle's pollution.[26] 'Margaret's Well' was an attempt to combat the modern progress that had made the stream dirty. As is recorded in *Fors Clavigera*, the waters soon became foul once more.[27] At some point, probably before 1880, Ruskin's tablet was lost. The Wandle was largely underground by the end of the century. In present-day Carshalton there is a Ruskin Road.

CHAPTER TWENTY-NINE

1871–1872

Ruskin's interest in the streams and rivulets of the Surrey village of Carshalton — now connected to London by the railway — coincided with his close friendship with Alfred Tylor and his family, who lived there. By strange and unhappy action of Fors, Ruskin and the Tylors saw most of each other in the four and half years between the deaths of Margaret Ruskin and of Rose La Touche. Juliet Tylor (Juliet Morse when she wrote this reminiscence) tells us that

> On the Saturday after the 5th Decr 1871, the day of Mrs Ruskin's death, just after her funeral, we drove over from Carshalton to Denmark Hill . . . Ruskin & my father were old friends, & he had sent me the King of the Golden River when I was a tiny child but I had not seen Mr Ruskin until this visit . . . I had with me several charcoal sketches, done from life at the Slade School, but he did not approve of them at all . . . Ruskin talked a great deal about Carshalton & Springs of Wandel, he was very much interested in knowing that we had quite a long stretch of the river at Shepley House; my father offered to help him about the Spring, which was polluted by being used as a washing place for various cabs and flys. I, Juliet, was to be taught to draw . . .[1]

Alfred Tylor is less well known than his younger brother Edward, whose classic of early anthropology, *Primitive Culture* (1871) had recently been published. Alfred Tylor might have made more contribution to his own academic subject, which was geology, had he not inherited their father's brass founding firm and factory. Business and commuting kept him from study. None the less he made advances in geological science. His best-known book was also his earliest, *On Changes in Sea Level* (1853), which Ruskin regarded as pioneering and in some respects analogous to his own early writing in *Modern Painters*. Tylor had four daughters and two sons. It was a liberal Quaker family. The daughter who was closest to Ruskin was Juliet. It appears that she was an early Companion of the Guild of St George, though her name appears on no list of its adherents. In the early 1870s Ruskin enjoyed testing his views on social matters against Tylor's more moderate analyses of contemporary life. Alfred Tylor was one of those people who were given copies of the early numbers of *Fors Clavigera* and found in later years that they were discussed in its pages. One part of the June 1875 number of *Fors* was written at the Tylors' Carshalton house. This letter is full of autobiography and mentions the other stream of Ruskin's youth, the Effra, which flowed beneath the little heights of Herne Hill and had been the subject of one of Ruskin's first accomplished drawings, in 1832, when he was thirteen. Ruskin had been the Tylors' guest on 23 May 1875. The next morning, looking at his manuscript as he sipped his coffee before travelling to Aylesbury to see Jowett and put this June number of *Fors* to bed, Ruskin inserted a teasing mention of the Tylor daughters, who the previous afternoon had been 'crushing and rending my heart into a mere shamrock leaf'.[2] We can imagine why Ruskin introduced a reference to shamrock. He did not know that Rose would die the next morning, at 7 a.m. on 25 May.

These matters tell us something about *Fors Clavigera*. First, *Fors* can scarcely be mastered without the help of footnotes, an index and a detailed biography of its author. Secondly, the letters of *Fors* are often obscure because they are intimate. They contain remarks that were meant to entertain, or to challenge, only two or three people. The Tylor girls would have been able to read about their afternoon's diversions with Ruskin just one week later. Nobody else who read *Fors* could have realised who they were, for their names are not given. While Ruskin's letters always have a high instructional tone, eccentric paragraphs of domestic trivia mingle with grand public statements about culture and politics. The reader surmises, but cannot know, that small matters are included because they are more important than they at first might seem. We are tempted to the thought that they are part of a pattern. In fact *Fors* has no pattern, only the stamp of its author's sensibility. In early 1872, a date to which we now return, *Fors Clavigera* was still in its first phase, when the pamphlet's derivation from Carlyle led the older writer to congratulate Ruskin with the message that 'This *Fors Clavigera*, which I have just finished reading, is incomparable; a quasi-sacred consolation to me, which almost brings tears into my eyes! . . . *Continue*, while you still have such utterances in you, to give them voice . . .'[3] *Fors* did not reach its full personal freedom until the later spring of 1872, at the time when Ruskin left Denmark Hill. However, by the time of its thirteenth letter, that of January 1872, it was evident to all concerned — Ruskin himself excepted — that this publication was so controversial that it ought not to be associated with the University of Oxford, where Ruskin was a professor.

* * * *

Ruskin was never truly happy at Oxford and might not have stayed long at the University were it not for Henry Acland's friendship and counsel. It often fell to Acland to mediate between Ruskin and Henry Liddell, who served as Vice-Chancellor of the University from 1870 to 1874. In retrospect, these years appear to be the most significant period within Ruskin's tenure of the Slade chair. Liddell had never thought that Ruskin was the right man for the post. As long ago as 1864 he had written to Acland that Ruskin 'will *never* make a Professor. He may be a great Drawing Master, or a great artistic Poet, — as he is and has been, never anything more.'[4] In January of 1871 he had again written to Acland that 'I begin greatly to regret having furthered his election'.[5] Liddell could not agree with Ruskin about aesthetic matters and was irritated by the Slade Professor's disregard of academic conventions. Part of the problem was that the Slade chair had been created with little thought about the ways in which it should function.[6] There was no course or curriculum, no tutorial teaching, no examination and no support for Ruskin's endeavours from other people within the University who had an academic interest in the history of art. Ruskin's own plans for his lectures were always subject to revision. Furthermore, he lectured only when he saw fit to do so, or when the currents of his personal life happened to mingle with the waters of the Isis and Cherwell. In Oxford the year is divided into three terms: Michaelmas (autumn), which is the first of the academic year; then Hilary (spring) and Trinity (summer). Ruskin did nor begin his tenure of office in the Michaelmas term of 1869, though he had been elected in August. His inaugural lecture and the other addresses we know as *Lectures on Art* were given in Hilary term of 1870. In Trinity term of that academic year he gave no lectures; nor was he even in residence in Oxford, for he was travelling in Italy. In the Michaelmas term of 1870 he lectured on sculpture. This is the course that was published as *Aratra Pentelici*. In the Hilary term of 1871 he walked into Oxford from the Crown and Thistle in Abingdon to give three informal talks on landscape, and in the Trinity term of that year he delivered only one lecture, his contentious views on 'The Relation between Michael Angelo and Tintoret'. In Michaelmas term he gave no lectures. By the New Year of 1872, therefore, it could well be said that Ruskin had only partially fulfilled his obligations to the University.

Ruskin had been elected to his chair for an initial term of three years. The end of this period was in sight. Ruskin now decided to be more active in Oxford. In the Hilary term of 1872 he delivered ten carefully crafted lectures under the title 'The Relation of Natural Science to Art', published later in the year as *The Eagle's Nest*. In the first of these lectures Ruskin announced a new and purposeful programme. 'To-day, and henceforward most frequently, we are to be engaged in definite, and, I trust, continuous studies; and from this time forward, I address myself wholly to my undergraduate pupils . . .' It appears that Ruskin was challenging such undergraduates to be more than usually thoughtful, for he wished to define 'the manner in which the mental tempers, ascertained by philosophy to be evil or good, retard and advance the parallel studies of science and art'.[7] The ten demanding lectures were packed into a month, for the first was delivered on 8 February and the last on 9 March, four weeks in which Ruskin was otherwise occupied in making arrangements for his removal from Denmark Hill. In some ways *The Eagle's Nest* is a repetition or a summary of the many books that Ruskin had written in his old home, and he refers to the impulses which led to *Modern Painters* in the third lecture, 'The Relation of Wise Art to Wise Science'. Ruskin told his audience that

> there is nothing that I tell you with more eager desire that you should believe — nothing with wider ground in my experience for requiring you to believe, than this, that you will never love art well, till you love what she mirrors better . . . the beginning of all my own right art work in life . . . depended not on my love of art, but of mountains and seas . . .[8]

This is the most direct passage in *The Eagle's Nest*, and was subsequently much quoted. Elsewhere in the lectures Ruskin reiterated his belief in the spiritual power of sight. Discussion of mythology takes us back to the concerns of *The Queen of the Air*. In the last two of the lectures, 'The Story of the Halcyon' (which was also given at the Royal Military Academy, Woolwich) and 'The Heraldic Ordinaries' Ruskin spoke of natural life as interpreted in fable and finally about the inherent power of heraldry in 'healthy national order'. Heraldry, it should be said, was one of Ruskin's serious intellectual hobbies. It is first discussed in the chapter 'Of Medieval Landscape' in the third volume of *Modern Painters*. In later years heraldry was to be an important component both of Ruskin's art teaching at Oxford and the literature connected with the Guild of St George, his own sketch of a perfectly 'healthy national order'.[9]

'The assertions I have made are entirely deliberate', Ruskin wrote in his preface to *The Eagle's Nest*, 'and the one which to the general reader will appear most startling, that the study of anatomy is destructive to art, is instantly necessary in explanation of the system adopted for the direction of my Oxford schools'.[10] The lectures 'On the Relation of Natural Science to Art' give a theoretical background to Ruskin's attempts to introduce drawing as a vital part of an Oxford education. In the spring of 1872 he was eager to further a project that had been in his mind since he first became Slade Professor. In his inaugural lecture of February 1870 Ruskin had announced his intention of founding a 'school' of practical art, and he shortly afterwards submitted proposals to the Curators of the University Galleries. He wished to place examples of fine or otherwise instructive drawings next to the Turners he had already presented to the University. These works on paper were to record architecture, painting and sculpture and were designed 'especially for the use of the Professor's class'. A list of such examples is found in the first of many catalogues of the Ruskin Art Collection at Oxford, issued in July 1870 as *Catalogue of Examples: Arranged for Elementary Study in the University Galleries*. The drawings became known as the 'Standard Series'. Then an 'Educational Series' was added, and finally other drawings — which often were used as visual aids in Ruskin's lectures — became the 'Reference Series'. As time went on, more and more drawings and other materials entered the collection, and its catalogues became more complicated. Nobody but Ruskin himself could understand the full significance of the accumulation of these aids to study. It is fair to say that he often failed to enlighten students who came to him for even the most elementary instruction. In any case, the 'Professor's class' was not well attended, largely because Ruskin was so often absent, or distracted by other enthusiasms.[11]

Ruskin's determination to enlarge his school enmeshed Acland and Liddell in obscure and ultimately futile controversies about the correct modes of art education. There was already an art school in Oxford, one of the provincial schools set up by the Department of Science and Art. The Oxford Art School had been established in 1865. By 1867 it had adequate premises in the University Galleries. Acland and Liddell were both Curators of the University Galleries, while Liddell was also chairman of the governing body of the Art School and Acland was chairman of the Art Branch Committee. To make matters more personal, both men had daughters who in 1869–71 attended the Art School. They were Angie Acland and Alice, Edith and Rhoda Liddell. These girls were close to Ruskin, but they would not have been taught in a way that pleased him. The South Kensington system prevailed at the Oxford Art School, where the art master was Alexander Macdonald, who varied his teaching according to his pupils' social standing. There were classes for artisans, who were taught in the evenings, and daytime classes for 'Ladies and Gentlemen'. The workmen's class was based on the needs of manufacture; the more genteel class was mainly occupied with traditional landscape. These were the arrangements that Ruskin proposed to dismantle. He conceded that an artisans' class might need to continue though hotly condemned a system 'adopted by the authorities at Kensington for the promotion of mechanical, and therefore vile, manufacture';[12] while he also managed to persuade Acland and Liddell that all other teaching of drawing should be conducted on his principles, therefore by himself, and that drawing thus taught should be pursued by members of the University and other interested people. However, since Ruskin could not guarantee to be present to take classes, there had to be a person who was able to teach on his behalf. This could only be Alexander Macdonald, who was already in position. In 1871 Ruskin offered to supply the funding that would be lost from the Department of Education and Science if the Oxford Art School were detached from its supervision, while Acland suggested that Macdonald should become overall Master of Drawing, his salary to be paid by Ruskin. Liddell was cautious. 'I hope Ruskin *will* make some permanent settlement', he told Acland, 'or we may get into a considerable scrape. We may succeed in knocking up our present school, and find ourselves left in the lurch with nothing to put in its place . . .'[13] He should have been firmer in his opposition. Ruskin's reforms were introduced, and the study of drawing within the University entered a chaos of misunderstanding from which it never wholly recovered.

The names of Ruskin's (and Macdonald's) students of drawing in 1871–72 cannot now be recovered, for no records were kept. We do know that one of them was William Gershom Collingwood, who entered Oxford as a scholar of University College in the Michaelmas term of 1871. In the years to come he would be Ruskin's disciple, his secretary, his neighbour and his first biographer. Unusually for an Oxford undergraduate, Collingwood was the son of an artist. His father was born in 1819, so was Ruskin's exact contemporary. He was the William Collingwood who is noticed in Ruskin's *Academy Notes* of 1856. This elder Collingwood had been taught, years before, by J. D. Harding, who had also been Ruskin's drawing master. Apparently at Ruskin's suggestion, Collingwood devoted himself to Swiss subjects, which he exhibited regularly at the Royal Society of Watercolourists until his death in 1903. When the younger Collingwood met Ruskin in Oxford he therefore had, through his family background, much common ground with the Slade professor. Other interests and preferences brought them together. Like his father, Collingwood was an artist. Again like his father, he did not belong to the Pre-Raphaelite, symbolist or aesthetic strain in British art. His interest was in the naturalism of recording nature. Like Ruskin, he delighted in examining all sorts of natural phenomena and was a student of geology and mineralogy.

It was a happy chance that led Collingwood to meet Ruskin at the time of his lectures on natural science and art, this being exactly his own concern. One gathers from his book *The Art Teaching of John Ruskin* (1901) that Collingwood had an especial feeling for *The Eagle's Nest*. His introduction to Ruskin's aesthetic also displays Collingwood's high analytical intelligence. He was an artist, an angler, a model-maker, a person who worked with his hands; but above all he was a person of mental strength, for whom the life of the mind was the best reason for living. Collingwood sought no fame or position in the world and was always to be content in modest, even frugal circumstances.

Ruskin's other new undergraduate friend of this time is in odd contrast to Collingwood. Prince Leopold, later Duke of Albany, was the fourth and youngest of Queen Victoria's sons. Always delicate in health, he had entered Christ Church because he was not suited to the army, because the college was associated with the Crown and because Oxford gave him the opportunity to pursue his interests in modern languages and the arts. Ruskin, who wrote so much about 'kingship' in abstract terms, had little or no interest in the contemporary monarchy. However, he was attracted by Leopold. No doubt inspired by his father, the Prince had an especial interest in the foundation of new museums. He was also concerned with social questions. For these reasons, among others, he sought Ruskin's company; and, as Collingwood delicately explains, 'The gentle Prince, with his instinct for philanthropy, was not to be deterred by the utterances of *Fors* from respecting the genius of the Professor; and the Professor, with his old-world, cavalier loyalty, readily returned the esteem and affection of his new pupil.'[14] Ruskin soon asked Leopold to be a trustee of his drawing schools, a position which the Prince accepted. Though he was quite without guile in any matter of controversy or policy, Ruskin's invitation was a political coup. If his schools and therefore his methods were endorsed by royalty, it was less likely that Liddell could interfere with Ruskin's arrangements.

Prince Leopold did not live in Christ Church but occupied Wykeham House, at the northern end of St Giles. Life at Wykeham House was organised by Sir Robert Collins, who was not a don but a courtier from Windsor. As comptroller of the Prince's household, and as his secretary, Collins was often in contact with Ruskin. They became friends and correspondents. Collins, who had a keen interest in spiritualism, was partly responsible for the recrudescence, in 1875–76, of Ruskin's attraction to such matters. In Oxford in 1872, the correct but affable courtier devised the timetable of the Prince's activities and entertainments. These were numerous. Leopold was always at Ruskin's lectures while Ruskin, we are told, 'was a frequent guest at his dinner parties, when, whatever the company might be, the Prince almost invariably seated the Professor at his side'.[15] No doubt this was because his company was more lively than that of other guests. In the spring of 1872 Ruskin was in demand in Oxford society and, now established in his rooms in Corpus Christi, was more inclined to accept invitations. An agreeable account of Oxford social life, not always accurate in its dates, is found in reminiscences by Professor Friedrich Max Müller. His account of Ruskin probably refers to this period, and allows us to gauge the mixture of charm and formality in his conversation, no doubt well suited to the table of a royal undergraduate:

> He was really the most tolerant and agreeable man in society. He could discover beauty where no one else could see it, and make allowance where others saw no excuse. I remember him as diffident as a young girl, full of questions and grateful for any information. Even on art topics I have watched him listening almost deferentially to others who laid down the law in his presence. His voice was always most winning, and his language simply perfect. He was one of the few Englishmen I knew who, instead of tumbling out their sentences like so many portmanteaux, bags, rugs and hat-boxes from an open railway van, seemed to take a real delight in building up their sentences, even in familiar conversation, so as to make each deliverance a work of art.[16]

The German-born Max Müller, who was the author of *Lectures on the Science of Language* (1861) and was the most complete linguist of his time, had an acute ear for the talk of his English contemporaries. Oxford's accents must have given him much to consider. It is probable, though one cannot prove this suggestion, that university society became much more vocal in the 1870s. A relaxation of convention allowed both women and undergraduates to display their social skills. At the Union, young men were eager to excel in debate. We note the birth of undergraduate theatrical societies at this period (opposed by Liddell, not by Ruskin), with their emphasis on entertainment and, mainly Shakespearian, verse.[17] Max Müller's memoirs suggest that dons' conversation now became self-consciously witty and competitive. It is not surprising that Ruskin's fluent and elongated sentences, with their touch of art, should soon influence the most theatrical of talkers, his undergraduate friend Oscar Wilde. Max Müller, who was Professor of Comparative Philology (and, like Ruskin, without formal pupils), also noticed Wilde and invited him to his college, All Souls, when the young Irishman was still in his first year. Ruskin was a student of Max Müller's writings and described him in *Fors Clavigera* as one of the leading scholars in Europe. There is a marked similarity, which they no doubt discussed, between Max Müller's theories of mythology and Ruskin's own mythological investigations. Ruskin regarded Max Müller as a colleague. His academic work, like Ruskin's, was puzzling to more conservative dons. Another bond between them was that they were both prolific writers who gave their writing to the world. An historian of Oxford in the 1870s hints that many a university man would 'think once and again before exposing himself to the chilling silence or the tepid appreciation of his *commilitones*, by rushing into print'.[18] It is clear that Ruskin felt no such inhibition; and although his lectures were irregular his published work was abundant.

CHAPTER THIRTY

1872

Once, years later, Ruskin confessed to Mary Gladstone that his belief in parental authority had been stressed only lightly in *Sesame and Lilies*, the book written 'to please one girl'. The reason is not far to seek. Any contact Ruskin had with Rose depended on her defiance of her parents' will. Maria La Touche may have thought that her correspondence with Effie Millais had finally put an end to Rose's relations with her lover. But she had used too crude an instrument. Effie's letters, devastating though they were, rang with ugliness. There was no sympathy for Rose in them, and even a slight odour of jealousy. And were they not unchristian? Time and again Rose's thoughts turned to what she could not understand in the letters, what she later called the 'mysterious ghastliness' of Ruskin's married life. But that reinforced her desire to live on 'higher planes' than those to which Effie was evidently bound. For all his heathenism Ruskin had still inspired her spiritual longings. She suffered greatly now from her ignorance of sexual matters and her wish to live with the 'true queenly power' of *Sesame and Lilies*. If Ruskin was a monster in the bedroom, were all his writings vile, lying, cynically disguising his true self? Surely this was not so. While his sexual nature was unimaginable, that his books were evil was simply not believable. Furthermore, his banishment seemed to have separated her from her parents, not to have reunited her with them. She heard news of Ruskin, and he of her, in messages that came seldom and faintly, often via two or three friends, making Ruskin at least a little easier in his mind, 'so thankful for that word from Ireland'.[1]

Ruskin could not be forbidden and put out of mind as Maria La Touche had wished. There were too many friends in common, and he was too famous. Rose touched on something to do with him whenever her horizons were lifted beyond the boundaries of the Harristown estate. She heard about him publicly as well as privately. She knew of his success at Oxford, of his near-fatal illness at Matlock, of the death of old Mrs Ruskin and the closing up of the Denmark Hill house. She had of course heard of the marriage of her friend Joan Agnew; and if she had never met Arthur Severn, she surely knew something of the romantic background of his family, and of his father's tender duties at Keats's deathbed. Rose might have seen Ruskin's inaugural lecture, and would have recognised in it the references to herself. What might he be saying now? Was she allowed to pray for him? What might be in *Fors Clavigera*, whose limited and awkward circulation did not reach into County Kildare? The isolation of Harristown life bore heavily upon her. Neither her intellectual ambitions nor her religious sense could be content with the neighbours' conversation, the books one might find in Dublin, the doctors who could not understand her, the new Presbyterian church at Naas, her father's new chapel at the end of the drive. She wanted to be in England. More particularly, perhaps, she wanted to be in Oxford. She asked an unidentified friend to make summaries of Ruskin's lectures for her. There still exists a black notebook of hers, ruled in feint lines, marbled on the inside covers and later embossed with her initials in gold. It contains a résumé of, and comments on, the lectures that Ruskin gave in the early spring of 1872 on the relation between science and art. These lectures, published as *The Eagle's Nest*, are not the most demanding of Ruskin's addresses, but they are far from simple and require a fair knowledge of Greek. Rose's notebook indicates, more than anything else that survives from her own hand, that she was indeed a young woman of the most competent intelligence.[2]

That intelligence, however, was at odds with the inflexible aspects of her religion, and was blighted by her frail health. This spring of 1872 she was ill once more, afflicted by that malady which gave her pain when she tried to write or think, or to pray; and as so often she responded by agitated self-assertion. Torn by thoughts of duty to her parents and a wish to cultivate her own aspirations she turned for help to a man whom she well knew to be allied with the Cowper-Temples and Ruskin, and who, like Ruskin, was no longer spoken of in Harristown society. This was George MacDonald. To him she wrote:

Dear Mr MacDonald,

I wonder if you remember me at all — Rose La Touche — it seems a long time since I sat next to you at dinner one night in London — and I have altered since then.

It seems to me you could help me, and I think you *would* help me if you could and I want help, and that is why I write to you.

Do you think God ever puts us into positions where we cannot do His will — and yet can neither alter the position we are in or get out of it? Are we always wrong in kicking against the pricks. I mean should we always consider that the circumstances in which we are placed are God's Providence for us, and should be *accepted contentedly* as such?

Or does He teach us truths and bring His own commands home to us individually while we are powerless to follow them out and obey them? And how are we to keep ourselves from being tortured with disquiet when this is so — ?

I have asked so many questions, may I explain my puzzles by telling you a little of my life. I have nothing in the world to do from day to day but what I like. All my parents want from me is that I should be well and happy. This seems a slight requirement but I cannot fulfil it — because the conditions of my life (which I cannot alter) do not make it possible for me to be well and happy — such as I am. For my daily life is simply hour after hour of spare time, bringing neither occupation, work nor amusement except what I make for myself; but any amount of leisure for thinking, pondering, wishing, praying, enduring. To drive and walk, see one or two poor people, paint, read, play, feel very tired, — this is about the most that each day offers me. And at the end of it I feel like a child tired out after a long, lonely holiday. But continual physical pain — sometimes torturing — keeps me — even if it was my nature — from being placidly content with this lethargic life. Suffering makes me realise the sufferings of others, the sufferings in the world and long vehemently, passionately, unconquerably, to help a little — to give all the help I *can* — towards lifting its weight off others. And my own needs, which are enormous have taught me to sympathise with *all* those that need — the sinful the doubting the fearful the sorrowing and the suffering. For I have learnt to *realize* not to know by hearsay but to realize how full the world is of darkness and suffering — and how impossible it is for those who are partakers of their Master's spirit to sit with folded hands saying to their own souls 'soul take thine ease' contented in believing themselves possessed of everlasting treasures (as well as this world's good) which they will not share with those that need. I go about among our poor people here and come back to mourn my own life of idle 'comfort' in despair sometimes. For it seems to me that they lead a life so much more like Christ's than mine, and I go jingling off in the carriage with my ponies and bells from their door with a sadder heartache than any of them could know. I want to be more on an equality with them, serve them, help them, learn from them. They have more child-like trust and faith in *their* suffering than I have. For I have been brought up with a paradox continually before my eyes — 'Comfort, health, quiet life and peace' being all that my parents desire, while to be pained by realising the pain of others, *to be a hundredfold more pained by being kept from doing anything towards healing it*, they cannot understand. Be happy yourself, separate yourself from the world, and preach to those you can — this is my Father's religion, and he is *very* good — but it is a religion that I cannot feel is the whole of Christianity.

We lead an entirely lonely isolated life. My Mother hates the place and does not interest herself in it at all — and cannot bear me to talk to her on the subjects I feel most strongly upon, or to wish anything to be altered. Though she has been most devoted to me when I have been very ill she is not happy with me, and only by trying to alter myself entirely and suppress everything that looks like discontent can I be with her and not pain and distress her.

And just because my Father is good and yet that his goodness leads him to such opposite conclusions and practice from mine we cannot be happy together — at least he is happy but I am not — though we love one another deeply. He thinks I am restless and discontented because though there are 'abundance of things' that I possess, my life is not happy or healthy, and he does not understand how utterly the complete loneliness of it wears out my brain and mind till I am almost in despair. Even a child cannot play alone — and life could never be a play time to me — Ought I to try and 'play' happily and think of David minding his sheep and be content. Can you give me a word of counsel? — for I believe you will understand although I have expressed myself so dimly. For the life that I now lead *is* my life, as I shall not marry (unless indeed one alters utterly and completely and miraculously during life!) and I want to live it well — and will you send me your good wishes and prayers sometimes.[3]

Rose La Touche.

To such a letter MacDonald could reply only in rather general terms. He was aware that he was *persona non grata* at Harristown. His friendship with Rose's mother had been broken.[4] He had never had her father's approval. That was not possible. To John La Touche he was a man who had abandoned his ministry, betrayed Calvinism, who lived on borrowed money in a dirty house with more children than he could afford, like a Catholic. His reply to Rose was therefore warm but circumspect. It brought him further letters from her, elaborating on her troubles.

I am unhappy and not well — *because* it seems to me, the very things my nature, spirit and soul need I have not, and have missed for years and cannot have. I can neither live the life I feel made for nor fit into my Parents lives so as to suit them happily — and I *do*

> *try* this. But you know if I was quite sure that it was God's will that I should suffer (physically) from the continual loneliness and oppression of constant thought unshared, unspoken and restrained so that it cannot spring into happy and healthful *actions* — if to alter myself (even if in so doing I paralyze or almost kill myself, and seem only a useless pain to myself and others) — is the work that, at present, God means me to do . . .[5]

Rose's letters to MacDonald contain a great deal more in this vein. She does not much speak of Ruskin. Of him and his relations with her and her parents she wrote:

> they think I have only to eat and take medicines and get quite well and then marry somebody and live after my own ideas. *I* know that what I need is not medicine and food and I shall not I believe marry. If it could have been so that I could have kept the *friend* who has brought such pain and suffering and torture and division among so many hearts — if there had never been anything but friendship between us — how much might have been spared. But now all that cannot be gone over again . . . Mrs Cowper-Temple said we should be as though living in separate worlds, and that this was best for him who is probably happy — and may — I cannot write any more about this . . .[6]

Perhaps taking his cue from this passage, MacDonald showed the correspondence to Mrs Cowper-Temple. They decided between them that if Rose understood Ruskin's love for her then her spirit would be less troubled. There appeared to them not merely the possibility of reuniting lovers but also (for they found it easy to think in such terms) a mission. They could conduct the girl-saint to the great spirit of the age. The quotidian arrangements could be quite simple. Rose was expected to visit Broadlands soon. George MacDonald and his wife could meet her there if they did not entertain her at the Retreat, MacDonald's home in Hammersmith and all would be talked over. And so Rose once more approached Ruskin, guided by his friends, hoping to find her own path, and little realising how close she was to the torrent of his passion.

* * * *

Ruskin was unaware of these movements. He had left England for the summer just as Rose's correspondence with MacDonald began. The continental tour this year, 1872, was to be an extensive one. He took with him a large party: Joan and Arthur Severn, the artist Albert

Goodwin, Constance Hilliard and her mother. They travelled rapidly across France to Geneva, where Severn and Goodwin were set to work drawing 'my well-known path, at the sunset over Bonneville', and thence posted to Lucca, Pisa and Rome, where Joan was to be introduced to her father-in-law, Joseph Severn.[7] In the three or four numbers of *Fors Clavigera* which belong to this time there may be heard a thunderous background to the journey. *Fors* moves in these months from the landscape of the English agricultural depression to European republicanism after the Commune. Addison and Sir Roger de Coverley give place to the Siege of Paris and the Franco-Prussian war. In search of the calm of early art, Ruskin conducted his party towards the late fifteenth-century masters. Not at all repentant of his harsh judgements on Michelangelo, he spent ten days in the Sistine Chapel comparing him with Botticelli, and found Botticelli superior. At Perugia he noted that Perugino had to be awarded 'a captain's place',[8] thus implying his ascendancy over his pupil Raphael; at Verona he wrote a pamphlet for the Arundel Society on the Cavalli tombs in the church of Santa Anastasia;[9] and in Venice, where the party arrived on 22 June, he once more began to study Carpaccio.

While Ruskin was thus meditating on early Italian art, Rose had left Ireland. 'I want so much that which some guide or teacher or friend could give me', she had written to MacDonald.[10] But she less wanted advice than she wished to be comforted, while all the while there was stirring in her, fitfully, a desire for some action that would break a life in which she felt trapped. From London she went on to Broadlands. She talked to both the MacDonalds and the Cowper-Temples. They were kind to her, and yet they told her that she needed Ruskin. But he was far away, and was not expected home until the autumn. Rose could hardly set off abroad to find him. She did not know what to do. She had turned to Ruskin's friends. They had soothed some of her anxieties but had once more made her feel guilt that he loved her. In some agitation she left them and went to stay with her aunt, her mother's sister, in Tunbridge Wells.

This Miss Price, a spinster who lived alone in a modest lodge house on a hill above the spa, knew more about her niece's relations with the great professor than Rose imagined. For she had kept her own correspondence with Ruskin, the letters that he had written to her at the time of his most desperate suit in 1870. Miss Price now learnt of Rose's inclination to resume relations with Ruskin. She was not sympathetic. Through loyalty to her sister, certainly with some wish to protect her niece, perhaps with some feeling for the power she wielded, she determined to stop the *rapprochement*. In Ruskin's letters, apparently, she had the means to do so. Since they have now disappeared, we do not know what these letters contained. They certainly concerned his marriage: it is possible that there was reference in them to his sexual nature. In any case, when her aunt produced the letters the effect on Rose was extreme. The nightmare of Effie Millais's accusations had arisen once again. 'They were interpreted to her, in her girlish innocence', MacDonald was later to claim. He thought that Miss Price had given 'false and devilish representation' to them.[11] That was perhaps so, but since MacDonald had not seen the letters he could not have known this. Whatever the truth of the matter, Rose, weary and distressed, far from home and with nothing gained from her initiative, now turned violently against Ruskin. 'Nothing can help me now — at least nothing can take away the burden that crushes me', she wrote to MacDonald from Tunbridge:

> I have his own account of it written two years ago — not to me. And nothing can make the darkness light to me . . . I cannot write of it. If he had been a heathen it would have been different, but he who had been brought up in Christ's religion, who had been given by God such power to know and love what was divine to sin as he did while writing as he did — it utterly overpowers me with the mysterious ghastliness of it all . . .[12]

Rose also wrote from Tunbridge to Ruskin. What she wrote she gave to MacDonald, desiring him to 'either one day give or send the enclosed to him who is your friend, and was mine'.

> After reading letters written by you in September 1870.
>
> How to call you and think of you I do not know, but you are and have been dear to me.
>
> What it has been to me to know all that I have perhaps only now, from your own writing, fully believed and known of your past life — God knows. I will not judge or condemn you. But I *must* turn away from you. Can you wonder, you who know what I have had to know, that my nature recoils from you?
>
> Your love to me, all your great perceptions of whatsoever things are good and lovely, your gifts — all that God has given you — these cannot expiate, but to my deep sorrow intensify and darken your sins against God's law . . . When I think of what you *might* have been, to Christ, to other human souls, to me! How the angels must have sorrowed over you! How some hearts are sorrowing still! I do not wonder that your faith is shipwrecked — I can use no other words — that Christ is to you only the Christ that *others*

believe in, whose belief perhaps you envy, that you cannot see beyond this life!

Better not to have known the ways of righteousness than after you had known it, and while speaking the words of a man whose 'eyes are opened', to turn aside . . .

And I who have loved you cannot alter you, could not blot out one single stain, not if I could lay down my life for you — cannot even give myself the certain hope of meeting you hereafter.

All I can do is to speak to you of Christ. At his feet we might meet; in His love our hearts might be drawn together again: in His forgiveness, redemption, renewing all that is past, even the bitter shadow of remorse, might be blotted out as a thick cloud — only teaching the infiniteness of that grace which can 'much more abound', the depth and patience and intensity of that love which passeth knowledge.

Believing as I do, the horror that your sins awake in me could only be, not removed but turned into joy by the knowledge that they had brought you to His feet, to be born again as a little child, and from henceforth *loving much* as none but one who has felt personally what Love's forgiveness is, can love.

Be Christ's and one day or other I shall find 'my piece that was lost'. For your sake, for His sake, for my sake — I who believe in a day to come when the Great White Throne shall be set and the judgement opened and our secret sins shall stand in the light of His countenance — let me look forward to a joy in store for me at that day. Hear His Voice whose love you have rejected whose promises you disbelieve — whose Laws you have trampled underfoot while speaking of them to others — hear His voice who came to save His people from their sins, to guide their feet into the ways of peace, to give them repentance and the remission of sins, the Holy Spirit, and life everlasting. Believe in Him with the faith that makes His followers life one with Him.

You may scoff at my words, but I can write no others. Is it a light thing to lose eternally what one has loved? one for whom one desires Christ's blessing and one's own?[13]

The letter, which is unsigned, here ends. To MacDonald, once of the Congregationalist ministry, the generalised and ritualistic rhetoric of Biblical Calvinism was familiar. Self-willed, accusatory, separating always the sinners from the saved, Rose's piety — if this is piety — was like her father's. From him she had inherited her stubbornness; from him she derived this insane belief in conversion experience. The letter is hysterical, beyond reason. Ruskin had received many such from her, of course, sometimes in verse. They came from that part of Rose that Ruskin could never reach, Rose whose mind he believed to be afflicted by religion, the girl for whom he had invented those hard, despairing nicknames, 'Tukup', 'But', 'Flint'. MacDonald, on the other hand, must have noticed how his own letters from Rose at this time were quieter, confessing to her own sufferings and anxieties. MacDonald thought that she had been deceived by Miss Price. He could not believe that Ruskin could have done anything to warrant such an outburst as this, and once more took it upon himself to soothe and placate her.

When Rose went to MacDonald's house in Hammersmith the following Sunday, he therefore told her that he declined to forward her letter (which he kept, never showing it to Ruskin) and sat down with her to explain as best he could what he knew of Ruskin's sexuality and spirituality. Rose had heard much of this sort of talk before, from Mrs Cowper-Temple. Its first characteristic was vagueness. MacDonald, preacher, storyteller and mystic, had an especial talent for such indistinct reassurance. In the odd surroundings in which Rose now found herself she began to relax. The Retreat, a pleasant house with an acre of garden overlooking the Thames, was famous among its many visitors for the untidiness in which the two parents and eleven children lived. There were no servants. Everywhere there was the natural detritus of charades, or improvised meals, or woodwork lessons. Rose was taken aback, but intrigued. Among the ragged but up-to-date furnishings, the Japanese plate, the paintings by Rossetti and Arthur Hughes, she felt interestingly close to that Pre-Raphaelite bohemianism she had never encountered in her Mayfair childhood and had only glimpsed on her visits to Denmark Hill. There was nothing wicked about it, as she had sometimes suspected. She decided that she liked the Retreat. There she was, not with her parents, talking to a famous author (*At the Back of the North Wind*, published in the previous year, had been an immediate success); and this George MacDonald, with whom her acquaintance was actually of the slightest, seemed, as he talked to her in that rhythmical, slightly Scottish, kindly voice, to be a man who truly lived the spiritual life. With his shoulder-length hair and red tie, he was most unlike her own father. And yet he was a good man. Rose was rapidly taken into the family. Mrs MacDonald became 'mother-bird' to her. She found them more and more convincing: convincing enough for MacDonald to be able to propose that he should write to Ruskin, indicating in his letter that Rose was in London, without her parents, and was staying at the Retreat.

* * * *

Vittore Carpaccio's series of paintings of the myth of St George are to be found in Venice in a little early Renaissance chapel, the Scuola di San Giorgio degli Schiavoni, in the Sestiere of Castello. Ruskin had not even entered this chapel when writing *The Stones of Venice*, twenty years before, but since 1869 its paintings had come to possess a wondrous significance for him. Ruskin felt that they represented the fight — 'St George's war, with a princess to save, and win' — against the basilisk of modernism, capitalism, utilitarianism.[14] He haunted the chapel in these late June days, and here he was drawing when an urgent letter from London was brought to him. MacDonald's news threw Ruskin into confusion. He did not know that Rose and MacDonald even knew each other. What was she doing? Was this marvellous news, or not? For MacDonald was unable to assure Ruskin that, given her state of mind, she would see him. After all, only a week earlier she had written of him 'with horror and loathing'. In any case, she was due to go home to Ireland; and whether she did so or not would depend on her parents, or perhaps on her aunt, or more likely on her own next change of mind. Knowing much of Rose's way of abandoning decisions, Ruskin telegraphed I WILL NOT MOVE UNLESS IN THE CERTAINTY OF SEEING HER and wrote suggesting that MacDonald and his wife should bring Rose to Geneva, where he would meet them.[15] To Rose herself he wrote 'solemnly', offering to 'do what I could to help her'.

He was perhaps right to hesitate. He had nothing from Rose herself, nothing in her hand; he was giving the Hilliards a holiday, and the Severns a kind of second honeymoon, for he and his relations with Rose had spoiled their first; and he was giving Albert Goodwin invaluable instruction in the drawing of brecciated limestone. He told MacDonald that he proposed to remain in Venice for another fortnight. In successive letters and telegrams, however, all deliberation was lost. For MacDonald had to tell Ruskin that the matter of his past sexual crimes, or inadequacies, had been raised. He did so darkly and obliquely, but Ruskin knew what he was talking about. MacDonald, of course, did not. Ruskin raged. Was there not the 'medical evidence' that he had given to William Cowper-Temple? And what had Rose been told? In vain did Ruskin demand of MacDonald to set down 'in the plainest English you know — the precise things R. says of me — or has heard said of me'.[16] For neither MacDonald nor Rose had been plain or precise in talking of such matters. 'Speak plainly and *utterly*', Ruskin once more demanded.[17] MacDonald could not. He did not know himself what was in question. He had not attempted to tell the virginal Rose the first thing about sexual character, let alone sexual perversions: it was his vagueness about such subjects that had kept Rose at the Retreat. Mrs MacDonald, calming the now distraught Rose, wrote to Ruskin too. She frankly and simply begged him to come home.

In these few days, during which Ruskin made no entries in his diary, he wrote the number of *Fors Clavigera* later entitled 'Benediction'. It is one of those times when one is tempted to say that *Fors* records his very consciousness. Paragraphs are marked with the day on which they were written, but some passages note the hour, the minute, and then the passing seconds as the pen crosses the page. It is, of course, evidence of a tortured mind. But what is most remarkable in 'Benediction' is the elevation of Ruskin's thought: his deliberate and constant will for calm, his will to live and think as a Christian should, to act and consider action as though one were blessed: for then one is blessed indeed. At one point this *Fors* letter rises dramatically to a counterpoint of peace with tumult, of grace with accursedness, that is unlike anything else in our language:

> Again, with regard to the limbs, or general powers of the body. Do you suppose that when it is promised that 'the lame man shall leap as an hart, and the tongue of the dumb man sing' — (Steam-whistle interrupts me from the *Capo d'Istria*, which is lying in front of my window with her black nose pointed at the red nose of another steamer at the next pier. There are nine large ones at this instant, — half-past six, morning, 4th July, — lying between the Church of the Redeemer and the Canal of the Arsenal; one of them an ironclad, fire smoking fiercely, and the biggest, — English and half a quarter of a mile long — blowing steam from all manner of pipes in her sides, and with such a roar through her funnel — whistle number two from the *Capo d'Istria* — that I could not make anyone hear me speak in this room without an effort), — do you suppose, I say, that such a form of benediction is just the same as saying that the lame man shall leap as a lion, and the tongue of the dumb mourn? Not so, but a special action of the members is meant in both cases: (whistle number three from *Capo d'Istria*; I am writing on, steadily, so that you will be able to form an accurate idea, from this page, of the intervals of time in modern music. The roaring from the English boat goes on all the while, for bass to the *Capo d'Istria*'s treble, and a tenth steamer comes in sight round the Armenian Monastery) — a particular kind of activity is meant, I

> repeat, in both cases. The lame man is to leap, (whistle fourth from *Capo d'Istria*, this time at high pressure, going through my head like a knife) as an innocent and joyful creature leaps, and the lips of the dumb to move melodiously: they are to be blest, so; may not be unblest even in silence; but are the absolute contrary of blest, in evil utterance. (Fifth whistle, a double one, from *Capo d'Istria*, and it is seven o'clock, nearly; and here's my coffee, and I must stop writing. Sixth whistle — the *Capo d'Istria* is off, with her crew of morning bathers. Seventh, — from I don't know which of the boats outside — and I count no more.)[18]

Meanwhile, in England, the MacDonalds were doing their best to hold on to the bewildered and desperate Rose. Ruskin was mistrustful, disinclined to leave Venice. Telegrams went astray or were misunderstood. Rose slept sometimes at Curzon Street, the La Touche family house, sometimes at The Retreat. Her parents would be pleased to know that she was visiting doctors: she made two rapid excursions to Matlock to take the waters. There was none the less a summons from Harristown. 'My father and mother want me to come home', she wrote, 'and I feel that I ought to obey them'. Ruskin still lingered in Italy. 'I am truly at my wits' end', Rose now told MacDonald. 'I shall try and wait 3 days — and yet I cannot bear the idea that you are sending for him after his apparent unwillingness'.[19] Finally Ruskin broke. Abandoning Goodwin and the Severns, dragging the Hilliards with him, he galloped at all speed across Europe. At Herne Hill there was a message that Rose would see him the next day, a Sunday. It could not be for very long. Her nervous state would not allow much excitement. She was driven by 'unconquerable restlessness' that came in 'fits', then was so much overwhelmed by 'brain-tiredness' that she could not speak.[20] Full of apprehension, 'bitter anxiety', Ruskin roamed around the Royal Academy exhibition, heedless of the pictures.

Greville MacDonald, a teenager at the time, always afterwards recalled how the Retreat was hushed, an almost reverential atmosphere prepared, for the meeting between Ruskin and Rose that Sunday afternoon.[21] They had not spoken for six and a half years. Now, as Rose turned to him, she 'put the past away as if it had not been — with the first full look of her eyes'. Ruskin was shaking with tenderness. He saw how pathetically frail she had become. She had scarcely grown up in the years of their separation: she had wasted away. For the first time Ruskin felt able to be protective. Rose's frailty had come about because of what people had done to her; she now had come to him and he would protect her. Rose, for her part, found herself able to conduct the conversation. For Ruskin could inspire in her a sweet gravity quite unlike the febrile indecisiveness of the past few weeks. She gently told him that she could not be his wife, for she would never marry. There was no question of Ruskin pleading. She was too delicate, too beautiful. And had she not returned to him? From this first interview Ruskin could take some heart. 'She still is happy to be with me, if she will let herself be happy; and she can't forbid my loving her, though she fain would; how infinitely better this is for me than if I had never found the creature. Better all the pain, than to have gone on — as I might twelve years ago — with nothing to love — through life.'[22]

There is now a gap in Ruskin's diary. A little later he wrote the entry 'To 18th August. 21 days'.[23] This was the time that he spent with Rose. However, they were not constantly together. Ruskin spoke later of only 'three days of heaven' that he had with her. It is possible that Rose was ill, or that she travelled back to Ireland to reassure her parents. But there were times at Broadlands when she made Ruskin 'as happy as it is possible for woman to make man'. On one perfect summer day they walked together from the great house down the long avenue of yews to the lake. Here an old flat-bottomed boat was used as a ferry. Ruskin stopped the boat in midstream. For a full minute they looked at each other. 'Now go on', said Rose. All that day, 'from morn to even', they were about the house and its grounds, entirely absorbed with each other, not talking to their hosts. Ruskin at least could scarcely do so, and that evening sent Georgiana Cowper-Temple a little note from his room. 'I do not believe that any creature out of heaven has been so much loved as I love that child. I am quite tired tonight — not with pain — but mere love — she was so good and so grave, and so gay, and so terribly lovely — and so merciless, and so kind — and so "ineffable".'[24] The next day he found that he could scarcely hold his pen, for joy.

Rose once more had to go back to Ireland. Ruskin went to Broadlands again and travelled up to London with her. On the train he gave her a drawing he had with him of a branch of olive. In London he made what farewells were possible in the circumstances. Neither of them knew how to say goodbye. 'She should never have gone home — except to mine',[25] he wrote to Mrs Cowper-Temple, and it was perhaps now that he wrote the letter, once glimpsed by a friend before it was burnt, in which he said how much he wanted Rose to see his home at Brantwood. Rose was bound for the Holyhead boat. A convenient place for her to break the long journey was at Toft, in Cheshire, a part of the country that Ruskin knew well, for Toft was not far from Winnington. At the manor house there lived friends of Rose's that she had met through the Cowper-Temples, whose relatives they were: Rafe Leycester and his wife, not long married, a young squire and his young family. Ruskin too had met them but knew them little. He did not wish to go back to Herne Hill. Instead, he took service rooms in Mayfair for a day or two. Waking there on the morning of 18 August, early as always, he pulled the bedclothes over him and began to pray. There he remained for hours. His petition was that 'she might not be taken from me just now — and that I might not have more change or horror of doubt'.[26] Perhaps his prayers were answered, for at ten o'clock two letters were brought to him. Both were from Rose and asked him to come up to Toft. Ruskin went immediately to Euston and by the early evening was once more with the girl he loved.

In the three weeks that had now passed since Ruskin was reunited with Rose his feelings for her had reached a pitch of exaltation. He had no thoughts for the reality of their situation. There was a religious flavour to his love but he forgot what a gulf there was between them in all religious matters. He also forgot that Rose was not a saint. 'The great good to me is finding how noble she is', he told Mrs Cowper-Temple. 'She is worth all the worship.' And after the golden day at Broadlands he felt that 'Nothing can come now that I cannot bear — nor death, nor life shall separate me from the love of God anymore. However long she is kept from me, — whatever she does to me, — I will not fear, nor grieve — but wait — and be more like her when she is given at last — and more worthy of her . . .'[27] At times Ruskin had seen that Rose's mind was disordered, that her illnesses were not now simply physical. But he was too enraptured to consider it more; and in his rapture he had forgotten the terrors that still possessed her. Ruskin felt that he gave Rose the most noble, pure adoration. But he did not know what this meant to her. She bluntly told Mrs MacDonald what Ruskin could never have guessed: 'I cannot be to him what he wishes, or return the vehement love which he gave me, which petrified and frightened me'.[28] In reality the link between them was fragile indeed, and it was Ruskin who now broke it.

The weekend at Toft was entirely social. Ruskin and Rose were not left alone together as they had been at Broadlands and the Retreat. Ruskin therefore wrote a letter to Rose and put it into her hand as they were walking to the village church next morning. Sitting next to Rose in the service, Ruskin had not thought that he had overstepped his mark. It was a letter of love, something for her to have as she went to the Holyhead boat and he returned to London. But its effect was to snap Rose's equilibrium, so precariously maintained in the weeks beforehand. Ruskin had intimated in it that some day she might become his wife. All her fears flooded back; and she expressed them, in a more complete change of mood than any Ruskin had ever known, not by silence, nor by complaint, but by bitter and furious attack. They were on the train to the junction at Crewe. She who was so demure, quiet, 'so good and so grave, and so gay, and so terribly lovely', was transformed. Hysterically, leaving him not even the opportunity to speak, Rose accused him of everything of which he might be accused. She would not stop: for mile after mile, as the little train steamed slowly along its branch line, she screamed her hatred; and at Crewe she left him.

Ruskin, stunned, got himself to London. Since he could not be more wretched he went straight from his train to the Euston Hotel, a place he loathed. Here he stayed for nearly a week, hoping for a letter from Ireland. At Euston he was visited by Joan Severn and the Burne-Joneses, whom he attempted to entertain. He went for walks through the slums at the side of the railway lines, following the Camden Road as far as the canal basin. At the British Museum he studied Mantegna and Botticelli. Two letters came from Rose. They forbade him to reply to them. In all his distress Ruskin now had practical matters to attend to. He had not written any of his lectures for the new Oxford term. There was much to arrange at Brantwood before he could move into his new home. He once more travelled north, to the old inn at Lancaster and thence to the Waterhead Hotel at Coniston. On Sunday, 18 September he was handed a packet from Harristown as he was on his way to church. In it was his own last letter, unopened. Ruskin turned back from the church porch. 'She is mad', he wrote, 'and it is an experience for me of what "possession" means . . .'[29] He himself was now possessed with fury against Rose. He wrote savagely to MacDonald demanding that he should claim back the drawing of olive that Ruskin had given her a fortnight before. 'Say I will draw her some belladonna with monk's hood: and that I could make a more delicate drawing of hemlock, but knew she would prefer Christian to Greek poisons . . .'[30]

On such a note the language of flowers ceases. So too does the correspondence both between Ruskin and MacDonald and between Rose and MacDonald, as though neither had any further use for the man who had brought them together. Ruskin was in a state of bitter religious indecision, long afterwards associated in his mind with the way that Rose's return of his letter had stopped him entering the church in Coniston. 'When the thing one is meant to pray for turns out not worth prayer — what is one to do?' To Joan he wrote, falling into baby-talk, 'Me so misby — misby — misby — I really sometimes almost wish I was a clergyman and tellin' lies all day long — it makes people so happy.'[31] To George Richardson, on the other hand, he wrote from the Euston Hotel: 'among other deadlinesses of her, she has contrived to make me religious again — (though not *quite* in her way:) and I shall miss church no more, since she has taken me there . . .' In truth Ruskin was too tormented for Christian thoughtfulness. 'I *am* very nearly mad', he told Richardson. 'But it is so much better for me to be in this pain than in ignoble peace'.[32] And to a clergyman, Tyrwhitt, he wrote a letter that gives some impression of the way that the great pain Rose caused him was entangled in cultural associations that are not at all Christian:

> I want to tell you one or two more curious things about that Irish child. She seems appointed to break me down by the vision of her always when I'm coming to a leap anywhere — and *yet* has been the root of all that I best know and ought to know — for my work. She sent me back last month from Cheshire so miserable that I couldn't speak to anyone — but went to Euston Hotel, and worked at British Museum. *In consequence of which* — I came on Sandro's engravings, just when I wanted them — and found out a lot of other things in the very nick of time for my next lectures. Well, in the next Fors as I told you, I've got to do Theseus; — and I've always hated and disbelieved the vulgar Ariadne story. Now I got at Lucca duomo the *deliciousest* medieval labyrinth — and it's to go in next Fors with the coins of Cnossos and the Minotaur and I've got all Minos and Aeacus and Radamanthus as smooth and nice as can be — but Ariadne would'nt work in, no how. Well — in thinking over her again, today, I came on the Odyssey bit; — and there it is all at once as right as right can be. My poor little Rose is dying, or like to die, at this moment, (having been to me truly Greek — Odyssey XI, v. 322 Child of the destroying Minos) — dying 'in the power of Diana', madly *pure* Greek Odyssey XI, 325 false Dionysus all the energies of her animal and passionate life becoming mortal to her. Now I knew that the labyrinth meant the entanglement of the animal nature — and Theseus is the divine law giver conquering Minos and fate — but here is Ariadne crushed in another lovely rosey — filling up the fable on this beautiful side. — and I've actually *seen* it. It makes one think one must be worth something, after all, to be plagued, in one's poor small way, like an Elgin marble —

— But did you ever hear — even in a novel — of a sensitive man's — meaning on the whole the best he can do for everybody — having two such things done to him as *that* girl has done — first — after holding fast to me against every living creature in her family for three years — and just at the end of them — suddenly believing herself deceived in me and cutting me dead when we met by chance; — that for Number one — and then, unable to bear the pain of thinking me wicked — sending for me — repenting — making me as happy as it is possible for woman to make man for three days — and then darting away again into darkness and forbidding me to write a word to her till I have ceased to hope! That for Number two — I suppose she'll die, for Number three — at the end of the seventh year since she bade me wait, and I shall go down and try to drag up Persephone. I've had the Greek Odyssey XI, 324 he married her but had no enjoyment with a vengeance. There never really was a Greek story much sadder.

I had her actually in my arms — full resting, with permitted kiss — and then suddenly she drew back — incredible in all she did — thenceforward, to all who were near us; — bright when she was with me — fixed as fate that she would not marry me — yet writing the loveliest letters — for a little while — till I was too thankful — and then she ended.

I'm not going mad, though — nor thinking myself Theseus. Still, — I have certainly now more power and purpose of defining law than any man I know among modern workers, — and surely — the pain is great enough for *anybody*.[33]

This was written from Brantwood on 29 September 1872; it is the first occasion when Ruskin reveals that Rose was now in danger of death. In the month since they had parted he had heard increasingly grave reports of her health. She had been overcome by illness as soon as she returned to Ireland and had not, apparently, made any improvement. Ruskin heard of her suffering through Joan Severn. He also found a new intermediary. This was Angie Acland. Since his election to the Slade professorship Ruskin had taken much care of Angie, and now asked for something in return. He asked her to correspond with Rose. Angie was crippled, could scarcely walk, and had been in pain for much of her young life. 'I want you to tell her about your own life and all that you have had to bear', Ruskin told her, adding, 'if you ever speak of me, mind you only do so as of her friend — she'll get into a passion directly if you imply my being or having been, anything more'.[34] Angie's exchange of letters with Rose was uncertain, but lasted some months. From her, from Joan and from the Cowper-Temples Ruskin heard frightful news: Rose was very weak, weaker than she had ever been. Yet she flung herself into violent moods when she would be physically reckless, and spoke with such vehemence and excitement that her wild words had no relation to sense. As her strength declined, her will became the more impetuous. However much her family wished to be optimistic, they were now facing the medical facts that her mind was broken and that she was likely to die.

In Ruskin's letter to Tyrwhitt he transformed his personal pain into some kind of cultural equivalent. So he did in *Fors Clavigera*: the themes of the letter are elaborated in the monthly pamphlets that autumn. Greek myths apart, it was natural in a man of Ruskin's temper that he should now turn to Dante, looking to him less for comfort than for understanding. There now begins, in *Fors*, the series of readings in Dante that explore the meaning of the lake of pitch, the divisions of hell and the circle of fraud. Ruskin's commentary is full of his deep reading of the Italian. It is also personal, for his remarks seem to be addressed to the girl in Ireland, wasted to thinness 'like the reeds of the lake of Purgatory', whose expected death would soon gather her into the transcendental world that Dante revealed to Ruskin. Poor Rose, had she read *Fors Clavigera* (and probably she did not), could have seen herself desubstantiated into iconography in these months. For at Florence in the summer Ruskin had sat in front of Botticelli's *Primavera* to draw the pattern of roses on the dress of the figure of Spring. This now became his personal colophon, a vignette stamp 'copied from the clearest bit of the pattern of the petticoat of Spring, where it is drawn tight over her thigh'.[35] It appeared not only on the title page of this October number of *Fors*, but at the front of all Ruskin's publications thereafter. Stirring in his mind were sexual metaphors that appear in *Fors* as strangely chastened by study of Dante and Botticelli. Hating, as he told Tyrwhitt, 'the vulgar Ariadne story', he seems to have set about finding a way out of the labyrinth of the 'entanglement of the animal nature'. This gave *Fors* yet another manner of being provocative, with its passing reference to Filippo Lippi, 'whose work is the finest, out and out, that ever monk did; which I attribute, myself, to what is usually considered faultful in him, — his having run away with a pretty novice out of a convent',[36] and its commendation of 'mother-naked' Theseus, 'under which primitive aspect, indeed, I would fain show you, mentally as well as bodily, every hero I give you account of'.[37]

In October and November of 1872, *Fors* obsessively returns from discussion of Alexandra Park, or F. D. Maurice, or the *Pall Mall Gazette*, to Dante, and to Dante's Minotaur rather than Theseus's. Here again, sexual and Christian motifs are excitedly clamped together. The Minotaur is 'the type or embodiment of the two essentially bestial sins of Anger and Lust; — that both these are in the human nature, interwoven inextricably with its chief virtue, Love, so that Dante makes this very ruin of the Rocks of hell, on which the Minotaur is couched, to be wrought on them at the instant when "the Universe was thrilled with love" — (that last moment of the Crucifixion) — and that the labyrinth of these passions is one not fabulous, nor only pictured on coins of Crete'.[38]

In such agitated language Ruskin seems to be sublimating all his feelings for the things that Rose was coming to represent. This imagery from *Fors* reappears in *Ariadne Florentina*, the book made out of lectures delivered at Oxford this Michaelmas term. The book is quieter than the 1872 *Fors* because it was written two years later. The lectures themselves were hardly prepared. The only notes that Ruskin had in the lecture room were materials from the current *Fors*, which was his sole writing in the months following the weekend at Toft. If Ruskin was actually reading from *Fors*, or speaking in the same vein, then he was far indeed from any plain introduction to the history of art. In place of the stately and considered inaugural lectures, and after the deliberately critical 'Michael Angelo and Tintoret' comes a change to the manner of Ruskin's dancing, desperate, pamphleteering polemic. This was not the Ruskin who had once given assurances of good behaviour to the Vice-Chancellor who had appointed him to his chair. It was now that his reputation in Oxford began to change. On the whole, his utterances had previously been regarded as authoritative. He now began to be notorious for eccentricity and wrong-headedness.

One public statement gave Oxford much to ponder. The strain of violence in the autumn numbers of *Fors Clavigera* appeared also in a letter to a periodical. After some piece of further bad news from Harristown, Ruskin went out of his way to announce to the world that Rose had become insane. His chosen vehicle was the *Pall Mall Gazette*, and the ostensible subject of his letter was a recent murder trial:

> Sir — Towards the close of the excellent article on the Taylor trial in your issue for October 31st, you say that people never will be, nor ought to be, persuaded 'to treat criminals simply as vermin which they destroy, and not as men who are to be punished.' Certainly not, sir! Who ever talked or thought of regarding criminals 'simply' as anything (or innocent people either, if there be any)? But

> regarding criminals complexly and accurately, they are partly men, partly vermin; what is human in them you must punish — what is vermicular, abolish. Anything between — if you can find it — I wish you joy of, and hope you may be able to preserve it to society. Insane persons, horses, dogs, or cats, become vermin when they become dangerous. I am sorry for darling Fido, but there is no question about what is to be done with him.
>
> Yet, I assure you, sir, insanity is a tender point with me. One of my best friends has just gone mad; and all the rest say I am mad myself. But, if ever I murder anybody — and, indeed, there are numbers of people I should like to murder — I won't say that I ought to be hanged; for I think nobody but a bishop or a bank manager can ever be rogue enough to deserve hanging; but I particularly, and with all that is left me of what I imagine to be sound mind, request that I may be immediately shot.[39]

This alarming note was Ruskin's first public letter sent from an official Oxford address. Having dispatched it, Ruskin left Corpus and went once more to stay — for no apparent reason — at the Euston Hotel. Joan Severn, understandably, was concerned about her cousin's state of mind. So were other friends. Norton was in London for the winter. Always liberal with staid counsel, he now found that Ruskin's uncertainties and desolation called for his most practical advice. The American most of all recommended that Ruskin should give up *Fors*. He told Ruskin that *Fors* dissipated his energies; but in truth he was embarrassed by it. Joan was of the same mind. Both she and Norton hoped that *Fors* would be abandoned or would peter out. This had happened to many of Ruskin's publications before. But *Fors* was not abandoned, for Ruskin had at last found the perfect medium for his sensibility, the right form for his urge to communicate. Month after month, relentlessly, it went on, and was not stopped until Ruskin's first mental breakdown in the spring of 1878: he had then published eighty-seven issues of his pamphlet. Now, as the Christmas of 1872 approached — Ruskin still not knowing what had happened to Rose — *Fors* began to mock at contemporary Christmas festivities, all Dickens and happiness; and in the next month or two continued with Dante, crimes in Mile End, Chaucer, 'Why not shoot babies instead of rabbits?', a recipe for Yorkshire goose pie, the iconography of the penny, 'Free fighting in these days: newspaper extract', the *Pall Mall Gazette* on female education, the dragon as a symbol of spiritual enmity, Goethe, drunkenness, Walter Scott, the Poor Laws, 'The Otomao Indians who live on clay and crocodile', republicanism, masters and servants, Dickens, Scott again, agricultural labourers, Theseus and Ariadne once again, 'Saints, ancient and modern'; and much more. Neither Joan nor Norton could stop this flow. One reason why they could not was that *Fors* had Carlyle's support. Ruskin saw something of the man he most revered as Christmas approached. 'Ruskin good and affectionate', Carlyle reported to John Forster. 'He has fallen into thick quiet despair again on the personal question; and means all the more to go ahead with fire and sword on the universal one.[40]

This was perhaps so. But Carlyle did not realise that Ruskin's universal fight was more and more the fight to be Rose's lover. And here there could be no certainties. As best they could, the Hilliards and the Aclands comforted him at the Christmas season. But if Angie had no letter from Harristown, then 'I don't know if she's alive or dead'; and if she was alive still, then he feared what might be in her mind.[41] 'Please be brave enough to tell me', he asked Joan, '— does she hate me now, as mad people do. Or only not speak of me. I am always thinking she hates me.'[42]

* * * *

Ruskin had no direct news of Rose La Touche all winter of 1872. In April of 1873 he asked Joan, as if casually, 'You haven't heard anything of R lately, have you?'[43] Not until October of that year, fourteen months after the events at Toft, did he resume his old pleading for contact with his beloved. He then asked Mrs Cowper-Temple 'Can't you get her to write to me again? she need never fear my having any more hope . . . but she might give me some peace — the very beauty of the heavens and earth only torments me now . . . because there is the dead wild rose always in my sight.[44] Ruskin would meet Rose again in the autumn of 1874. In the preceding months he prepared himself for her death. 'Think of me as a man whose wife is lying dead in his house — at this hour', he told F. A. Malleson, a clergyman who had ventured to address him on the subject of *Fors Clavigera*.[45] If he seldom spoke directly of Rose she was always in Ruskin's thoughts, and also his dreams. In June of 1873 he 'dreamed of R that she was still hard and cruel in heart, but that she came to me — and gave herself to me — as sweetly in body as Cressid to Troilus, in Chaucer's verse'.[46]

CHAPTER THIRTY-ONE

1873–1874

At this period of his life we should consider Ruskin as a thinker who worked side by side with his learned peers and contemporaries. If a Victorian intellectual community can be imagined, such a gathering of intelligent men and women would contain many a division. Between churchmen and free-thinkers, or radicals and conservatives, the lines of opposition are well defined. Thoughtful people were separated by other nineteenth-century developments. These were, for instance, the unequal growth of university education, the expanded horizons of learning, the interest in scientific thought and the tendency toward intellectual specialisation. No great Victorian was so little confined to one field as Ruskin. He resented the popular view that he was simply an eloquent writer on painting and architecture. The Slade Professor of Fine Art was on terms with a wide range of people of varying interests. They included scientist-doctors like Henry Acland, George Harley and Joseph Kidd; Darwin, who had listened courteously while Ruskin explained about art, in the last days at Denmark Hill; the German-born orientalist and mythologist Max Müller; the mineralogist Story-Maskelyne, with whom Ruskin discussed Homer as well as stones; Professor Daniel Oliver, Keeper of the Herbarium and Library at Kew Gardens; and numerous geologists, including his friend Alfred Tylor, the brother of E. B. Tylor, one of the founders of the science of anthropology, whose *Early History of Mankind* (1865), 'a book of rare value and research', was among the collection of frequently consulted works in the Brantwood library.[1] In this library were books by other significant friends. They included works on Comte and positivism (perhaps unread) by Frederic Harrison, on Dante by William Michael Rossetti, on etymology by F. J. Furnivall (whose Early English Text Society was supported by Ruskin), on public administration by Sir Arthur Helps and on public health by Sir John Simon.

Ruskin's position in relation to another group of intellectuals can be examined in his contributions to the Metaphysical Society, to which he was elected shortly after its foundation in 1869. This superior club had been established by Tennyson and James Knowles, the architect and editor of the *Contemporary Review*. Its purpose was to hear papers by distinguished men on philosophical issues. Among members whom Ruskin knew personally were Gladstone, Dean

Stanley, Froude, Mark Pattison, Cardinal Manning and James Hinton, the surgeon and philosopher, author of the well-known *Life in Nature* (1862), whose son Charles Hinton would soon be a 'captain' in Ruskin's road-building scheme. Ruskin read in all three papers to the Metaphysical Society. In 'The Range of Intellectual Conception Proportioned to the Rank in Animated Life', delivered in 1871, he had spoken, 'as a painter', of an approach to natural science that would be elaborated in the Oxford lectures of 1873 known as *Love's Meinie*. This talk was a reaction to the first Metaphysical Society paper he had heard, Thomas Huxley's disquisition entitled 'Has a Frog a Soul? and if so, of what Nature is that Soul?' Now, in February 1873, Ruskin presented his second paper, on 'The Nature and Authority of Miracles'. This appears from a contemporary account, a letter to his wife from Dr Magee, Bishop of Peterborough, to have attracted many churchmen to the meeting.

> . . . I went to dinner duly at the Grosvenor Hotel. The dinner was certainly a strangely interesting one. Had the dishes been as various we should have had severe dyspepsia, all of us. Archbishop Manning in the chair was flanked by two Protestant bishops left and right — Gloucester and Bristol and myself — on my right was Hutton, editor of the *Spectator* — an Arian; then came Father Dalgairns, a very able Roman Catholic priest; opposite him, Lord A. Russell, a Deist; then two Scotch metaphysical writers — Freethinkers; then Knowles, the *very* broad editor of the *Contemporary*; then, dressed as a layman and looking like a country squire, was Ward, formerly Rev. Ward, and earliest of the perverts to Rome; then Froude, the historian, once a deacon in our church, now a Deist; then Roden Noel, an actual Atheist and looking very like one! Lastly Ruskin, who read after dinner a paper on miracles! which we discussed for an hour and a half! Nothing could be calmer, fairer, or even, on the whole, more reverent than the discussion. Nothing flippant or scoffing or bitter was said on either side, and very great ability, both of speech and thought, was shown by most speakers. In my opinion we, the Christians, had much the best of it . . .[2]

It is interesting to find, in an undated scrap of a letter from Ruskin to Knowles (who acted as convenor of these meetings) that Ruskin, 'While I think I am nearly the last man in the world to stand on personalities', insisted that he should be addressed in that company as 'Professor', as Thomas Huxley was, and he apparently was not. 'On the ground of the equality of Art to Science, I am bound to stand up for it . . .[3] Ruskin now felt it his duty as artist and professor to give the lie to such fellow members of the Metaphysical Society as Herbert Spencer, the sociologist, and W. R. Greg, the authors of articles in the *Contemporary Review* that year: one, entitled 'Bias of Patriotism', in which Spencer argued that 'patriotism is to the nation what egotism is to the person', and the other, 'What is Culpable Luxury?', a piece in which the satisfied Greg endeavoured to demonstrate that consumption by the rich could not but benefit the poor. Ruskin's reply to both appeared in the *Contemporary Review* as 'Home, and its Economies'.[4]

Parts of this reply were subsequently, in December of 1875, taken into *Fors*, where Ruskin felt them to have a more appropriate setting. This was because he was also replying to the Bishop of Peterborough in *Fors*: he had been aroused by Magee's statement that the Church should remain 'neutral' in economic matters.[5] It was also in 1875 that Ruskin gave his third and last paper, on 'Social Policy'[6] It was by then clear that the author of *Fors* was an awkward member of the Metaphysical Society. Ruskin had already thought, in 1873, that he might be asked to resign. Not only had he attacked Spencer and Greg. Half of the October 1873 issue of *Fors* is devoted to the claims of another Metaphysical Society member, John Tyndall, put forward in his recent work on glaciers, *The Forms of Water* (1872).[7] Ruskin in effect accuses Tyndall of intellectual and personal dishonesty. This was because he felt that Tyndall had insufficiently acknowledged the work in that field of James Forbes, the object of Ruskin's boyhood admiration. At some point, probably in 1875, Ruskin let his membership of the Society lapse.

Surely several people (besides the painter Whistler, in 1878) could have felt that they had been libelled in Ruskin's personal publication. About Tyndall he wrote:

> The readers of *Fors* may imagine that they have nothing to do with personal questions of this kind. But they have no conception of the degree in which natural science is corrupted and retarded by these jealousies of the schools; nor how important it is to the cause of all true education that the criminal indulgence of them should be chastised . . .[8]

Ruskin was writing as a professor of the University of Oxford, with the authority he believed his chair bestowed upon him. That he was not writing about art made no difference. He could write and lecture about many matters that he had studied. His lectures at Oxford in the spring of 1873 did not concern art. They were about birds. In their published form we know them as *Love's Meinie* — the attendant company, that is, of love. The first was on the robin, the second on the swallow, the third on the chough. In the printed book a fourth 'lecture', on dabchicks, never delivered, was added; that on the chough exists only in note form. Ruskin's purpose was to study these birds through their habits, but mainly as the human eye sees them. Therefore he criticised the science that would dissect them to learn of their anatomy. The lectures are argued as Ruskin believed a painter ought to argue. His descriptions naturally led him into mythological speculation. But in the first place these acute accounts of birds are deliberately visual. Though the writing is delightful it would be mistaken to consider the book as no more than charming. Historians might consider it as a part of a gathering stream of nineteenth-century attitudes. *Love's Meinie* belongs to the vitalism that was a reaction to the supposedly mechanical and inhumane aspects of Darwinian thought.[9]

* * * *

Ruskin was in Oxford until late March of 1873, then visited Herne Hill before returning to Brantwood. In the summer he would welcome the first visitors to his new home. He now began the physical work he always enjoyed, making a demesne out of the twenty-three acres of woodland, garden and field that adjoined the house. Both Ruskin and his parents had been proud of the estate at Denmark Hill. John James Ruskin, unlike others who had made similar fortunes, had never wished to own any more land or to move into the country. His son now made modest yet individual arrangements by the shore of Coniston Water. Brantwood itself was never distinguished. Ruskin's various additions to the original building are not of architectural importance: nor were they designed to be important, only comfortable. The garden was not unlike others of the period, though there were many signs (because of diverted streams and the like) of Ruskin's pleasure in irrigation and digging holes. He liked to say that hole-digging was his favourite form of gardening. Ruskin's horticultural taste was of course his own. This connoisseur of strawberries, hater of Brussels sprouts and lifelong opponent of willow trees, who had never seen a satisfactory rockery and had been known to make 'caustic and cryptic remarks' about other people's flower borders, would make unusual dispositions of plants in the Brantwood flower beds and greenhouses.[10] That was a little later on, while he was writing *Proserpina*. In 1873 David Downs was doing the rough work in the garden, Ruskin assisting. Between them they began to rebuild the estate's neglected harbour. Soon boating would become a daily Brantwood pastime and another way of reaching Coniston, some three or four miles distant by the lakeside road. Ruskin dug and walked, and met new neighbours — one of whom, Susie Beever, of the Thwaite, Coniston, was to become a dear friend.

Inside the house the furniture was often expensive though none of it was particularly beautiful. The single attempt at principled interior decoration was a wallpaper that Ruskin ordered to be made for his study, copied from a design in a painting by Marco Marziale in the National Gallery. It was never intended that Brantwood should become a palace. None the less it was bound to contain treasures. Alexander Wedderburn's description, written in 1877, gives a good view of the house's contents. Brantwood was, he wrote,

> A moderate-sized house, half covered with creepers; its walls of a pale yellow, that looks almost white from a distance; its principal windows overlooking the Lake of Coniston, and facing the 'Old Man's' rocky peak; the rest almost shut in by the trees at either side and the hill that rises up abruptly at the back — such is the home which Mr Ruskin bought . . . wherein, amid the treasures of art he has collected and the scenery he loves, he contrives (to quote his own words) to 'get through the declining years of my aesthetic life'.
>
> A short drive, over which the shady trees almost meet, and the visitor has come from the high-road to the house, the entrance to which might seem somewhat gloomy were it not for the glimpse of blue lake he catches here and there. Pause in the hall a few minutes if you would see two figures by Burne-Jones before you pass into the cheerful drawing room. Here, since its windows look on the lake, the pleasant breakfast-table is brought in daily, and Mr Ruskin's guests enjoy the Brantwood strawberries and the cream from the farm across the hill, while their host, who has breakfasted already and been writing *Proserpina* or *Deucalion*, or whatever is in hand, almost since sunrise, reads aloud now the results of his morning's work . . . now some extracts from the letters which have just come; and now, when the meal is nearly over . . . the party are treated to no common reading of one of Scott's novels. Here, in the evening . . . all reassemble — some from the lake's shore, where a cigarette has been secretly smoked . . . and the day's last hours are spent in lively talk or at chess . . . Round them hang some good drawings by Prout; a lovely village maid from Gainsborough's easel; four Turners, which are carefully covered over when the room is unoccupied; a painting of 'Fair Rosamund' by Burne-Jones; and one or two sketches by Ruskin himself. The eye lights on two portraits by Northcote, over the sideboard, of Mr Ruskin's parents; whilst in

> the same room are two 'Annunciations', both by Tintoret, and, to omit the rest, there hangs above the chimney-piece Turner's portrait of himself in youth, and we see that the mouth which was afterwards sensual was once softly sweet. But it is in the 'Professor's Study' that those who would know Mr Ruskin at home must be most interested. The room is long and low, with two large windows opening out upon the lake. At one end is the fireplace, over which is hung Turner's 'Lake of Geneva', a water-colour remarkable for its splendour and unusual size; at the other is the occupant's writing-table. The walls are rightly covered with book-cases and cabinets rather than with pictures. Here are the original MSS of *The Fortunes of Nigel* and a volume of Scott's letters; here a 'Fielding' on large paper and an edition of Plato by a distinguished divine have honourable place; here some specimens of the binder's art and the best that printing can do; and humbly hidden here behind some other volumes are copies, kept for reference or for gift, of the Works of John Ruskin. In this corner stand three marble figures, which once helped to support a font, chiselled by Nicolo Pisano, and broken, it is said, by Dante; and lying on the table is a book of drawings in sepia, by Mantegna and Botticelli, which the British Museum thought it could not afford to buy. The cabinet contains, admirably arranged on variously coloured velvets, the half of Mr Ruskin's valuable collection of minerals, the greater part of which was once the property of the Duke of Buckingham at Stowe. These drawers are full of illuminated missals and fine old manuscripts (though the best, perhaps, lie in the Professor's rooms at Corpus); and here is a cabinet filled with drawings, not a few by Turner, which it would take long to partially enjoy . . .[11]

Wedderburn's account — the longest piece of writing about Ruskin that this reticent man and future editor of the Library Edition would ever give to the world — says little about Ruskin's library. The collection of books at Brantwood was not large and seems never to have exceeded about 4,000 volumes. This was partly because so many of them were given away, to friends or to institutions, or even to people Ruskin did not know: a young Scottish student who wrote to him for advice received by return of post the Professor's personal copy of *Past and Present.* This volume was scored, underlined and annotated. So were many of Ruskin's books, however valuable. His was essentially a working library. The treatment of the books it contained would not please a bibliophile. Ruskin happily tore out pages from missals or sawed down the covers of large books to make them fit his shelves.

From a fifteenth-century French *Books of Hours* he made a collage of twenty miniatures, to which he also pasted marginal decorations from an Italian manuscript and another miniature from the School of Bourdichon. Better care was given to books that had come from Ruskin's Herne Hill childhood, like his father's and his mother's Bibles, a Xenophon (inscribed 'John Ruskin, Herne Hill, 1834') and various sets of Mrs Edgeworth, Scott and Lockhart. Many books that are familar as influences on Ruskin's writing held an especial place in this library. Among them were Sismondi, Gibbon, Forbes, Cary's Dante and the eleven volumes of Bekker's Plato. There were numerous books on natural history and geology, but few on art. Ruskin was proud of his presentation copies from such contemporaries as Tennyson, Patmore and the Brownings. One more feature of the library should be mentioned. The chessboard (whose squares were coloured red and green) was always displayed. Ruskin was Vice-President of the British Chess Association and endowed its tournaments. Chess champions thereby received a complete set of his works. Ruskin's own style of play was adventurous and extremely rapid: he could not keep himself from impatience if an opponent took time to ponder moves. Ruskin also played many a game by post, his favourite correspondent in such contests being Alexander Macdonald, whom he could simultaneously address on matters concerning the drawing schools.

Ruskin's normally large correspondence slackened in the spring and summer of 1873, probably because he was so preoccupied with arrangements at Brantwood. Much building work was required but improvements and alterations went on piecemeal. The man who once had been a great architectural critic was not concerned with making a house whose architecture might be admired. Since Brantwood had been purchased, in part, for its view, the new dining room mentioned by Wedderburn was constructed and gave a splendid prospect of the lake and the Old Man. This was probably completed in the spring of 1877. Its seven lancet windows are said, without evidence, to have been designed to remind visitors of *The Seven Lamps of Architecture*, a book that had now disappeared from Ruskin's own memory. Brantwood did not become a large or magisterial property until the Severns took over the house in 1887–88. Ruskin often called his home 'a Lancashire cottage' and on the whole was content with its small size and the darkness of the rooms overlooked by the 'brant' or steep wooded hill at the back of the building. The gatehouse, built in 1872–73 to house Crawley and his family, is a curious feature. It seems to announce the entrance to some much larger home set at the end of a drive. In fact it is very close to the main building. Brantwood is a strange house, its character elusive. None the less, one can guess an influence. Consciously or unconsciously there may have been a feeling in Ruskin's mind that he was creating his own Abbotsford: without the absurdities of Scott's home, over which he had brooded since his teens, but with a similar feeling that Brantwood was a place in which a great squire of letters might be surrounded by family, retainers and visitors, and that the heart of such a home should be in a combined library and study.[12]

Scott's domestic arrangements had a direct relationship to his own countryside. Ruskin lacked such ties. Brantwood, Coniston and the surrounding area are not to be thought of without Ruskin. His later writings are alive with references to neighbours, the lake, the mountains, scenery and local life. Yet he is neither the poet of his neighbourhood nor its chronicler. Ruskin was genuinely a resident at Brantwood only in his last decade, when he could not write and his infirmities forbade him to go elsewhere. During the great years of his writing we find no domestic base for his expression. Always he seems on the way elsewhere, yet with no settled destination. Readers of *Fors Clavigera*, who were given the most opportunity to follow Ruskin's thoughts and emotions, found now that he addressed his letters from Brantwood; but also from Oxford, Sheffield, Cowley, Birmingham, Venice, Paris and other places. Ruskin was just as urgent a traveller in his later age as in his youth. Perhaps the idea of a fixed and settled home was forever lost to Ruskin after his parents had died. In any case Brantwood as a centre of family activities was to belong less to Ruskin than to the Severns, who had the house until they themselves died, Joan in 1924 and Arthur in 1931.

Joan and Arthur were to have been Ruskin's first Brantwood guests in the spring of 1873. They remained in London because of the birth of their first child, Lily, named after Lily Armstrong. Ruskin would have liked to show his home to this old Winnington friend, and to other girls from the school; but as he explained to Dora Livesey, 'I am obliged to be alone here by horrid etiquette.'[13] For company he had his servants, a new cat and a shepherd's dog acquired from a neighbour. Ruskin supervised work on the Crawleys' lodge and helped Downs clear paths through the woodland. Then the first visitors came. Among them were William Hunt and his daughters Venice (Ruskin's god-daughter, now aged eight) and Violet. This family later took rooms in Coniston for the summer, a common practice among later visitors to Brantwood, where there were only two spare bedrooms. Joan, Arthur and their baby arrived in the summer and stayed until November, long after Ruskin had returned to his Oxford term. Joan quite naturally took over the running of the house. Thus Brantwood was associated with the beginning of the Severns' life with their children, whether Ruskin was there or not. Arthur and Ruskin got on well together at this period. The young father, a keen boatman, was delighted to help in the reconstruction of Brantwood's little harbour. Joan's cheerful and soothing presence was of help when the Cowper-Temples called in mid-August; Rose La Touche had recently stayed with them at Broadlands.

Ruskin was sustained by work. In August of 1870 he had bought a manuscript of the *Roman de la Rose*. Ruskin believed that it dated from about 1380 and that the manuscript was in the French form known to Chaucer. He further believed that in poring over his acquisition he could be transported into the fourteenth century to translate this treasure as the father of English poetry had done.[14] In his diaries we find a pastiche Middle English written in octosyllabics. Ruskin had always enjoyed translation. In his Oxford period he often worked at the task of rendering a classic text into English. He translated medieval French (and, later, Plato) on rising. His labours were therefore the more private; but parts of his translation of the *Roman de la Rose* appear in *Love's Meinie*, in *Ariadne Florentina*, and in four separate issues of *Fors Clavigera*. In this summer of 1873 *Fors* was however mainly concerned with Sir Walter Scott. Indeed a number of its readers thought that they would enjoy a biography of Scott, month by month. Ruskin declared that he would not give them such a pleasure, stopped writing about his favourite novelist and as a further disobligation to his readers increased the cover price of *Fors* from tenpence to one shilling.

We should pursue the question of Ruskin's interest in Scott beyond that barrier. He did not really intend to write a biography. Ruskin felt that Scott's life had somehow preordained his own human existence, and that of his father John James Ruskin. The notes on Scott were for students, not casual readers. What *Fors* offered was an 'abstract' of Scott's life. Here is a word Ruskin used at this period. He meant a deep and searching gloss on the standard biographical text, which of course was Lockhart's *Life*. We surmise that he wanted to read Lockhart with undergraduates. This was certainly so with another Brantwood work of the summer, the preparation of an 'abstract' of Carlyle's *Frederick the Great*.[15] It is to be found as an appendix to a new edition of *The Crown of Wild Olive*, published on 11 December, towards the end of the Oxford Michaelmas term. During this term we also find Ruskin writing to Carlyle to say that he had been reading parts of 'Shooting Niagara' to 'my class'.[16]

What class might this be? The Slade Professor was engaged only to give lectures. In his drawing schools Ruskin could and did teach as he liked; but still the University had no understanding with Ruskin that he would conduct a tutorial group. In fact this 'class' was made up of undergraduates with whom Ruskin had become friendly and who were welcomed to his rooms in Corpus. These were the young men whom he would shortly instruct to go into the Oxfordshire countryside to build a road. First they were to read Scott and Carlyle. The new edition of *The Crown of Wild Olive* and its appendix with the 'abstract' of *Frederick* were teaching aids, designed to accompany Carlyle's text in the now readily available 'People's Edition' of his book. When he sent Carlyle his own book, Ruskin signed himself 'Ever your loving disciple — son — I have now almost a right to say — in what is best of power in me'.[17] In the following letter he addresses Carlyle for the first time as 'Papa',[18] the gesture emphasising his loneliness and emotional needs. But Ruskin was also attempting to establish a line of influence from Carlyle to his own students, with himself as the intermediary. Such an enterprise might have had only a faint interest to Carlyle himself. The elder sage had once driven through Oxford on his way to Birmingham. That had been in 1824. He had never subsequently seen any point in returning to the university city.

Ruskin, however, thought that Oxford could be a cathedral of intellectual life, a university that promoted art, love of natural beauty and the study of proper social relations; and a university that rejected and excluded such modern follies as were seen in the writings of Spencer, Greg, Huxley and other members of the Metaphysical Society. In his own way Ruskin was a progressive educationalist. His diaries show that he attended dons' discussion groups that had been set up (informally) to explore the nature and function of contemporary Oxford. He was aware that expansion and reform might be for the better. His own function as Slade Professor was none the less unclear. The absence of a curriculum in the field of the fine arts encouraged him to bring vast gifts of knowledge and experience. Alas, such gifts were scattered in ways that impeded their reception. Only the most able undergraduates, for instance, could have followed the lectures Ruskin gave in Michaelmas term of 1873. They were published in the following year as *Val d'Arno: Ten Lectures on Tuscan Art directly antecedent to the Florentine Year of Victories.*[19]

At least the first four of these addresses had been set in type before their delivery: Ruskin had probably written them at Brantwood in the summer. The comparatively relaxed Brantwood atmosphere had not encouraged a more accessible set of writings. The lectures of *Val d'Arno* are like an 'abstract' of a book that Ruskin had not in fact written. They are a gnomic distillation of his private thoughts and researches. It is possible that the very difficulty of these lectures attracted the 'disciples' who now emerged from Ruskin's more general university audience. His remarks at the lectern had to be discussed and explained. If they had the impulse (and perhaps the temerity) to call on him, Ruskin's best admirers could be delighted with his friendship and fired by his instruction. Thus by the autumn of 1873 he had gained an inner group of fervent supporters — while to the rest of the University he was a famous man, but incomprehensible.

This term Ruskin was a little disturbed that fewer people were attending his lectures. He also worried that his Italian studies might be quite solitary, unnoticed by other leaders of thought. The parts of *Val d'Arno* that had been set in type were sent to Carlyle and Froude in October. In early December Ruskin instructed George Allen to send proofs of all ten lectures to Charles Eliot Norton at Harvard. The gesture had relevance because Norton had now begun work on his *Historical Studies of Church Building in the Middle Ages: Venice, Siena, Florence*, published in New York in 1880 but based on lectures given at Harvard after Norton's return from England in 1873. Comparison of the books by Norton and Ruskin reveals more than their temperamental dissimilarities. As so many times before, from *The Stones of Venice* onwards, Ruskin's purpose was to make direct comparisons between medieval art and society and the condition of present-day England. 'I am about to ask you to read the hieroglyphs upon the architecture of a dead nation, in character greatly resembling our own . . .'[20] *Val d'Arno* is Carlylean in its tone and argument. So also was *Fors Clavigera*, read by Norton with little pleasure. Ruskin resisted the American's criticisms of his monthly publication. The December *Fors* stated that only two previous issues, 'the first, and another, I forget which' had sold more than a thousand copies.[21] Ruskin continued:

> As to these letters of mine, for instance, which all my friends beg me not to write, because no workman will understand them now; — what would have been the use of writing letters only for the men who have been produced by the instructions of Mr John Stuart Mill? I write to the labourers of England; but not of England in 1873. A day will come when we have men resolute to do good work, and capable of reading and thinking while they rest . . .[22]

This was the number of *Fors* that, while lamenting its limited circulation, also announces that its price will be increased 'and there will be no frontispieces'. Ruskin also stated that the subscriptions to St

George's Fund, to the end of 1873, came to only £263 13*s.* 0*d.* Contributors were not identified, but their names and gifts can occasionally be found in Ruskin's diaries, especially the 'Broadlands Book', as he called it, the vellum-bound volume mainly concerned with Ruskin's life in the latter part of 1876 and which also contains his translation of Plato's *Laws*.[23] Another list in this manuscript is of especial interest because it gives the names of his undergraduate followers at Oxford. It is headed 'My first list of Oxford workmen'. Here are the students who were most affected by Ruskin's presence in the university, who talked with him, attended the breakfast parties in his rooms and studied his previous works. The list reads

Anderson
Forbes
Mallock
Wilson
Stuart Wortley   Captains Hinton, McEwan
Fitzroy
Hoare
Toynbee
Wedderburn
Montefiore
Vaughan

Most of these young men can be identified. They and other road-diggers will be discussed in a later chapter. For the moment we note Ruskin's propaedeutic use of a nineteenth-century Oxford institution, the walk. Another disciple from the road-building period, Oscar Wilde, was to recall how 'my walks and talks with you' were the most vivid parts of his undergraduate life.[24] Like many friendly and earnest dons and clergy of the time, Ruskin used the shared walk as a long and informal tutorial. Beyond the city walls conventions were naturally relaxed. Here was a way for Ruskin to share experience and to elicit the character of a younger pedestrian. In Oxford this Michaelmas term Ruskin walked nearly every day, in company or alone. The diary shows him on the hills to the east, treading the lanes from Marston to Elsfield, Beckley and Shotover; while in the other direction a favoured route took him through low-lying ground around the Hinkseys. He crossed the river at Ferry Hinksey. Ruskin was interested in all this quiet, often flooded land. 'Planned survey of Oxford marsh', the diary tells us.[25]

Ruskin remained in Oxford after the end of term to work in the drawing schools. He attended splendid dinners, one in Christ Church with Prince Leopold, before going to London for a round of pantomimes and further Christmas dinners at Herne Hill. He then felt the need for fresh air and decided to visit Margate. *Fors* recounts:

> Thinking I should be better for a look at the sea, I have come down to an old watering-place, where one used to be able to get into a decent little inn, and possess one's self of a parlour with a bow window looking out on the beach, a pretty carpet, and a print or two of revenue cutters, and the Battle of the Nile. One could have a chop and some good cheese for dinner; fresh cream and cresses for breakfast, and a plate of shrimps.[26]

Such a hostelry had disappeared, so *Fors* goes on to describe Ruskin's sufferings at a new establishment, the 'Umphraville Hotel'. No letters or diary survive from this trip. Ruskin's motives for choosing Margate as a place of recuperation are not clear. He could have been following Turner, who, as *Fors* had pointed out in 1871, lived in Margate 'when he chose to be quit of London, and yet not to travel'.[27] In that *Fors* Ruskin had reported a remark of Turner's that the loveliest skies in Europe were to be seen in the Isle of Thanet. So perhaps he was keeping a promise to himself that he would follow Turner in gazing at the Kentish skies. In 1871 he had also written that 'though I never stay in Thanet, the two loveliest skies I have myself ever seen (and next to Turner, I suppose few men of fifty have kept record of so many), were, one at Boulogne, and the other at Abbeville; that is to say, in precisely the correspondent French districts of corn-bearing chalk, on the other side of the channel'.[28]

It is now right to linger on the subject of Ruskin and accommodation. Like John James Ruskin before him he was a connoisseur of inns, hotels, *auberges* and other resting places, both British and European. John James would never spend a night in another person's house, and in 1848 had declared that he had not done so for thirty years. 'I take mine ease at an inn', he had written to George Gray when John and Effie's wedding party might have demanded that he should stay under Gray's roof.[29] Ruskin often did stay at other people's homes. Some friends, among them the Cowper-Temples and (later) Susie Beever in Coniston, set aside a room for his use whenever he cared to visit. In the mid-1870s Ruskin had his own bedroom at Cowley Rectory, the Hilliards' home near Uxbridge. Then there came a rift in this arrangement. The Revd J. C. Hilliard asked Ruskin not to sign a number of *Fors Clavigera* as issuing from his address. Ruskin was offended but acquiesced.[30] Students of *Fors* will note how much of Ruskin's publication seems to come not from a pulpit or a lectern but from some old-fashioned coaching house. Here, once more, *Fors* resembles Scott's novels, with their peerless descriptions of hostelries and of the proud, combative and garrulous men to whom they gave hospitality. Nobody can tell a person what not to write from an inn. A guest there is his own master. When Ruskin chose to live at the Crown and Thistle at the beginning of his professorship he was not being eccentric. This large coaching inn, ancient in origin, timber-framed and with cobbled courtyards, suited him well. Its food, wine, service and company might have been as good as in any college. Furthermore, Ruskin could leave the dining table when he wished: by this stage in life he was the more insistent on retiring by 10 p.m., to write his diary or his daily letter to Joan, to read, pray and look forward to the morrow when, straight from bed, his mind alert, he might spend an hour on translation or on some other intellectual exercise.

From the Crown and Thistle to the centre of Oxford there was a walk of six or seven miles, depending on Ruskin's path. He liked to ramble through Bagley Wood and cross the Thames at Ferry Hinksey. Here he noted and lamented the dilapidated state of the village. It appeared picturesque but in truth was a rural slum. The pretty houses were thatched hovels. The surrounding land was often flooded and sanitation was poor. Meditating on these things — as so often in previous years, in England, Switzerland and Italy — Ruskin felt dismay that the peasantry should live in squalor amidst natural beauty. When he returned to Oxford early in 1874, after his London Christmas and the unproductive sojourn at Margate, there arose in Ruskin's mind the dawnings of a plan. The condition of Ferry Hinksey might be improved by undergraduate labour. Ruskin never gave a public explanation of his road-building enterprise: the only statement about the diggings came in a letter to the press from Henry Acland. In fact Acland may be considered the progenitor of the scheme, both practically and in terms of the road-digging's underlying symbolism. Ruskin's many thoughts about landlordism, ideal or corrupted relations between owners of land and their tenants, were behind the Hinksey enterprise. The immediate inspiration, however, was Acland's. The Regius Professor of Medicine, by inheritance a landowning Devon Tory, was interested in Ruskin's views on modern feudalism. His duty, however, had always been towards contemporary public health.

Acland had been Oxford's first doctor since the 1850s, but his work was not confined to the University. He considered that medical knowledge should benefit the whole community. Acland's first campaign as a public figure in a quite small society had been against cholera. In 1854 the disease had struck Oxford. Acland's conclusions about the afflicted areas were published in 1856 as *Memoir on the Cholera in Oxford in the year 1854, with Considerations suggested by the Epidemic.* His book shows that the water-borne disease was prevalent in the working-class areas of Oxford inhabited (characteristically) by those whose livelihood depended on the University. They supplied food or other services, were college servants or were employed by the Oxford University Press. Cholera first appeared in Jericho, the slum behind the Press's neo-classical offices. Acland's book includes a map that shows the distribution of the disease and from its key we see that Ferry Hinksey had also been affected. Ruskin knew all this. He also knew that both Jericho and Ferry Hinksey belonged to the same person or family, the Harcourts of Nuneham Courtney. Ruskin hated Jericho. One walking companion recalled how on their expeditions from Corpus the Professor could not bear to walk near this area.[31] He also disliked the Harcourts for reasons other than their negligence of their tenants' well-being. Politically, they were Liberals. In addition, Ruskin could not abide the way that the Harcourts had abandoned their Tudor manor house at Stanton Harcourt for the new pile at Nuneham, built in exactly the eighteenth-century taste that he had despised since his teens.

When Ruskin sent undergraduates to work in the neglected village of Ferry Hinksey he did so with an implicit criticism of the Harcourts' stewardship of their portion of 'the Oxford marsh'. Acland (who wrote to the Harcourts on Ruskin's behalf before students went to the village) had already given his fellow professor a precedent. The emoluments of the Regius Chair of Medicine were in part derived from estates, that included farms in the village of Marsh Gibbon, about twenty miles north-east of Oxford. Acland's biographer J. B. Atlay describes

> half-ruined cottages, a grey old Elizabethan manor-house drifting into decay, a shallow pit of brown peat-coloured water, serving as the reservoir for the inhabitants and as the common drinking-ground of the sheep and cattle . . . the character of the population was in unison with its surroundings . . . a solitary policeman would never have dared to enter the village . . . even the beauty of the warm June evening when Acland first saw Marsh Gibbon could not cast any glamour over the squalid misery . . .[32]

Among the first endeavours of Acland's professorship was his campaign to cleanse Marsh Gibbon. First he established an unpolluted water supply. Then he built new stone houses, including a 'reading room'. More to our present point, he took Oxford undergraduates and clergy to his village to give 'a practical lecture on the fundamental laws of health, on the construction of village dwellings, and on the causes of preventable disease'.[33] It is clear that the Marsh Gibbon improvements are related to Ruskin's efforts in the village of Ferry Hinksey. Many people imagined that the road-digging was a criticism of the relatively new Oxford cult of athletic sports. To an extent this was so. We may believe that the question of sanitation was more important. It is even possible that Ruskin's undergraduates were building not a road, of which the village had little need, but a sewer or a channel to distribute stagnant waters. Victorian delicacy could have inhibited public discussion of this topic. In any case Ruskin's feelings about the road include many private obsessions. We know of his fascination with pure, flowing water and of many attempts to dam and divert streams. We know that he loved to dig holes and also liked the physical activity of chopping wood. In this winter of 1873–74 he did a little axing in coppices he found on his Oxfordshire walks. We would still like to know more from Ruskin's own pen about the Hinksey diggings. He did not describe them, however; partly because he was not in Oxford when work commenced but mainly because Rose La Touche now re-entered his life.

CHAPTER THIRTY-TWO

1874

When Ruskin had returned from Margate in late January of 1874 he began a further emotional crisis. Rose La Touche was in London and was seeing Joan. As so often, Rose's thoughts and movements can be traced only through chance remarks and the few letters mentioning her that escaped Joan's later censorship. Much is obscure, but we know that in 1873–74 Rose's search for health and self-fulfilment took her from Ireland to a succession of doctors and nursing homes in England. Accompanied only by her nurse, Mary Barnes, Rose at this stage of her short life was 'wandering about the world', as Ruskin put it.[1] He exaggerated. She stayed with English relatives and friends, the Cowper-Temples at Broadlands, the Leycesters at Toft, her aunt in Tunbridge Wells, and probably also visited resorts. We hear of her, for instance, in Brighton. Rose stayed in hotels as much as in accommodation organised by her physicians. Just as old-fashioned inns appealed to Ruskin the newer types of hotel pleased Rose. The quiet, pious invalid was just as wilful as she had been in her teens, and hotels gave her more freedom to do as she wished. Ruskin was agonised both by her physical condition and her egotism. As he had done before, in 1872, he now wrote that her instabilities had led to madness. In January he spoke of 'the illness — reaching a point which her friends now think — insanity — but of which I have hoped is only a religious hysteria . . .'[2] Shortly afterwards we learn that 'my own belief is that a distinct form of insanity connected with her bodily health is on that child'.[3] Rose would not write to Ruskin nor receive his letters. At the same time she was glad of Joan's visits, and entrusted her with oblique messages for delivery to him. Usually they consisted of only a Biblical text. One of them, sent on 2 February of 1874, the anniversary of Ruskin's proposal of marriage, put him 'into a vague, despairing, last fit of goodness. But it is as the morning cloud, and as the early dew'.[4]

Powerless as lover, guide or friend, Ruskin became more agitated as Joan continued her visits to Rose. It was now Hilary term in Oxford but Ruskin was unable to attend to his university obligations. For nearly a month he sped between Herne Hill and his rooms in Corpus Christi. Three lectures on 'The Relations of Outline between Rock and Perpetual Snow in the Alps' were twice promised but not delivered. Ruskin's torment became the more acute when Rose decided to move from central London to the Queen's Hotel in Norwood. Now she was on Ruskin's home territory. There might have been medical reasons for Rose's decision to set up her camp so near to Herne Hill. Since the air was clearer than in the city the heights of Norwood were populated by doctors, and here one might choose between many nursing institutions. But Rose told Joan that she favoured the Queen's because old Margaret Ruskin had stayed there ten years before. In 1888, when Joan drove past its gates, she was to find 'all its past memories, of Auntie, & Rose, fresh in my mind!'[5] The Queen's was fashionable. Furthermore it had an air of contemporary gaiety. The Crystal Palace was within a few hundred yards. The Queen's Hotel had a ballroom and a banqueting room and was a popular rendezvous for, among other groups, army officers.

At Herne Hill Ruskin still occupied his old nursery at the top of the house. Through its barred window he could see the ridge of the hill on which stood Rose's hotel. She still would not write to him but there were moments when Ruskin thought that she had placed herself a mile from his home in order to make a *rapprochement*. Now the presents of Biblical texts, delivered by Joan's hand, became almost daily. 'As many are led by the Spirit of God, they are the Sons of God.' Or, 'Be strong and of courage, fear not; for the Lord thy God is with thee, whithersoever thou goest.' Or, in Greek, Matthew's observation: 'Narrow is the way.' With such verses to consider, Ruskin drove from Herne Hill to Norwood with his cousin. Joan went into the hotel and sat with Rose. Ruskin did not know what to do while they talked together. He found that his best diversion was to play with a chess automaton in the Crystal Palace; so the Slade Professor of Fine Art joined with other amateurs of the game in attempting to beat the machine.[6] Or he walked around the Norwood area, thinking of his father. Two places brought John James especially to his mind. The first was the hotel itself, the establishment which had prompted his 'Jonathan Oldbuck' letters. The second was the Central Hill Baptist Chapel on the corner of Gatestone Road, where the aged John James Ruskin had listened to the preaching of the Reverend S. A. Tipple, and had found it 'wretched'. It is likely that Rose worshipped under Tipple while she was living at the Queen's Hotel. This would explain *Fors Clavigera*'s violent and apparently unprovoked attack on Tipple — by no means a prominent figure in theological debate — that was written shortly after Rose's death in May 1875.[7]

We cannot know when Ruskin fully realised that Rose would die before him. It may have been while she was at Norwood. He had no access to her doctors, only to a dentist they shared in common,

Mr Woodhouse, with whom he therefore made many appointments. Ruskin was not only ignorant of the extremity of Rose's sickness: he could not estimate her 'insanity'. With only Rose's Biblical texts to guide him it was not possible to gauge the state of her mind. Once more Ruskin encouraged other young women, primarily Constance Hilliard and Angie Acland, to correspond with Rose and let him know the results. Little came of these efforts. In a state of exasperated depression Ruskin saw a doctor, who advised him to 'avoid emotion'. During February, when he was often in Oxford but unable to give his lectures, Ruskin resumed his walks through the city's flooded hinterlands. He confided in Henry Acland, talking to him about Rose's health and his own. Then he decided to go to Brantwood. Ruskin arrived at his Lancashire home on 23 February and was to stay there for a month. In early March he finally abandoned his Oxford lectures. 'There'll be rather a row', he predicted, but 'I *could* not do it this time, and it is as well Rose should know a little of the mischief she does in a definite way — I suppose she never has really got it into her stupid little head that she had done me any . . .'[8] The remark reminds us that Ruskin was a disputatious no less than a forlorn lover. His anger is found in current numbers of *Fors*. If he could not write a personal letter to Rose he could address her through his monthly publication. So, having received yet another little volume of biblical texts, Ruskin in *Fors* (in a passage dated 4 March) castigates Evangelicals in general and Rose in particular:

> One of them, for whom I still have some old liking left, sent me one of their horrible sausage-books the other day, made of chopped-up Bible; but with such a solemn and really pathetic adjuration to read a 'text' every morning, that, merely for old acquaintance' sake, I couldn't refuse. It is all one to me now, whether I read my Bible, or my Homer, at one leaf or another; only I take the liberty, pace my evangelical friend, of looking up the contexts if I happen not to know them.[9]

This mood of anger remained with Ruskin while he was at Brantwood. In more resigned moments he thought that he could escape his personal dilemma by resuming study of Italian art. Ruskin's last Italian expedition, in 1872, had been cut short by Rose's intimation that she wished to see him. This summer he could make good the intellectual loss. We surmise that Henry Acland, having seen Ruskin's distress and ill health, encouraged his friend to absent himself from Oxford until the Michaelmas term of 1874. When Ruskin resumed his lecturing in that term he would talk about Florentine art. At Brantwood in the early spring he thought more about Venice and about his father. The diary entry for 3 March contains one of the few references in his later years to his former wife:

> Evening. So my father has been dead ten years. I have not disgraced him, in them, nor misused what he left me. But what use now, to him? And still I think of those tears at the railway station, and I going away with that wretch.
>
> And yet, the Venice work was good. Let me make the best fruit of it I can, since he suffered so for it.[10]

These pages of diary suggest a grandeur in Ruskin's resentments. Four days later he climbed the Old Man of Coniston, saw the sun setting and on a grassy slope, prophet-like, 'knelt down to pray that it might not go down on my wrath'.[11] His animus was mainly directed against John La Touche. Yet Ruskin did not wish to be angry. 'Hard fight with anger all day', the diary also notes.[12] Some of his unhappiness was lifted by a Coniston friendship begun the year before. Susie Beever, now sixty-four years of age, became the best of Ruskin's women friends who was not a confidante. In the next fifteen years he was to write her some 900 letters. Unusually for Ruskin, these missives did not describe the troubles of his life and mind. Their character may be seen from the selection published as *Hortus Conclusus* in 1887. From this book we discover that Ruskin was a beloved neighbour who enchanted and enlivened Susie Beever's latter days — and those of her sister Mary, who shared a home with her, the Thwaite, at the northern end of Coniston Water. This Brantwood spring, Ruskin also became friendly, by letter, with a person at the other end of life. This was the Balliol undergraduate James Reddie Anderson. He and Ruskin were in correspondence about the plan, now clearer in Ruskin's mind, to do physical work of some sort at Ferry Hinksey. Ruskin had wished to go straight from Brantwood to Italy, but now decided to break his journey and encourage a group of undergraduates who were Anderson's friends. They were mostly from his own college. Ruskin stayed one night in Corpus. His diary records 'breakfast to Balliol men'.[13] One of them was his future friend and editor Alexander Wedderburn, who recorded the undergraduates' feelings when Ruskin asked them to commence digging.

> I remember that Ruskin on this occasion described to us his ideal state of society. The breakfast took place in the Common Room and we went to Ruskin's rooms after it. He was to go abroad at once while we started the work, and I remember saying to him,

> 'Well, we will do the rough work, and you can make it beautiful when we come back'; on which he held out both his hands and shook both of mine with pleasure. His desire for sympathy and delight at getting it were pathetic. When we came away I recall some one saying 'Well, if *he*'s mad, it's a pity there are not more lunatics in the world', and this expressed the feelings of us all.[14]

⋆ ⋆ ⋆ ⋆

Ruskin crossed to Channel on 30 March of 1874. From the Hôtel des Bains in Boulogne he wrote 'a long letter to Acland for Mr Harcourt'. Wisely, Ruskin had decided to use a distinguished intermediary between himself and the Hinksey landowner. In this way Acland became a guardian of the road-building project, though he himself took no part in the digging. Ruskin then travelled via Paris, Chambéry, Turin, Genoa and Sestri Levante and arrived in Pisa on 9 April. He consulted doctors in both Paris and Genoa but felt better in Pisa and even happy by the time he reached Assisi on 12 April. In Pisa he had 'a lovely walk outside the walls. The courtesy and dignity of the older peasants, and the essential sweetness of character of the people generally — polluted and degraded as they are, touch me more deeply every time I return to Italy . . .'[15]

Here Ruskin made two excellent watercolours of the outskirts of the city. He was further cheered by a new note in Rose La Touche's conversations with Joan. Instead of talking about Ruskin's soul, Rose had voiced the earthly fear that he might be attacked by brigands. However trivial it might seem, this was a considerable advance in their relations. For the next six months, his longest sojourn in Italy since he wrote *The Stones of Venice*, Ruskin often had the kind of contact with Rose that suited him best: he was far distant from her, in receipt of comparatively reasonable messages, and engaged in his own intellectual work in a sunny climate.

Ruskin's immediate task in Pisa was to inspect and if necessary superintend the copies of Giotto frescos that had been undertaken on behalf of the Arundel Society by the German artist Eduard Kaiser. Ruskin was still a member of the Society's Council and took an interest in its activities. A feeling of responsibility toward the Society may have moderated his individual enthusiasms. In this summer of 1874 it is possible to consider Ruskin as an art historian among others who had a more professional approach to the young but rapidly expanding discipline. His reputation as a controversialist had preceded him. On learning that he was about to arrive in Assisi the Italian connoisseur G. B. Cavalcaselle left the city, apparently fearful that he might be involved in a dispute with the English writer. Certainly Ruskin's printed references to the joint work of Cavalcaselle and Sir Joseph Crowe on the history of painting in Italy (1864) had not been admiring. In July, however, Ruskin and Cavalcaselle met and became friends. Ruskin stayed less than a week in Assisi during the spring because he was anxious to travel to Rome to meet his copyist Charles Fairfax Murray, who was engaged in work on the Botticelli frescos in the Sistine Chapel. Murray is a remarkable example of the self-educated nineteenth-century art historian. The son of a Bow draper, he had little formal schooling and much artistic talent. He became an assistant to Burne-Jones in 1866–67 and was later employed both by Rossetti and by the firm of Morris & Co. Though Murray worked as a copyist until the end of the 1870s his most significant activities were as a collector and dealer. Ruskin had little notion of Murray's commercial acumen. In 1873 he had sent him to Italy, with the Arundel Society's co-operation, to make copies of frescos in Siena and Florence. Thereafter Murray was mainly a resident in Italy, though shortly he would acquire houses in Paris and London. At one point he was considered as a candidate for the post of Director of the National Gallery. In spring 1874, when Ruskin hastened to Rome, Murray had made a good start on the copies of the Botticelli murals. These were the paintings Ruskin had first noticed in 1872 — when, to his lasting annoyance, Rose had cut short his Italian working summer — and he now wished to resume a study of their iconography and place in European Christian art.

Ruskin was not absolutely the first English intellectual to recognise Botticelli, but he is incomparably the most interesting of the painter's nineteenth-century advocates. Botticelli was to be the culminating figure in the lectures Ruskin gave in Oxford in autumn of 1874, now known as *The Aesthetic and Mathematic Schools of Art in Florence*. These lectures were the direct result of Ruskin's Italian studies this summer. They are bound up with his feelings for Rose. Ruskin would think most deeply about the spiritual meaning of Florentine painting in August. Now, in Rome for three days in mid-April, he looked at Murray's progress, spent a pleasant evening with his young assistant and then visited a quite different artist, Joseph Severn. Keats's friend, now in his eighties, brought out canvases and watercolours that dated from his first days in Italy. Ruskin politely asked if he could bring some of his own drawings for the old painter's inspection. He also gave Severn family news. Joan was now expecting her second child and Ruskin was able to report that Arthur was happy in his life as a painter and family man. Since Arthur had recently met Rose La

Touche for the first time, he had become a more interesting person to Ruskin, who wrote to him frankly about his love: 'I never thought her for a moment comparable to Dora [Livesey] or half a dozen others. But then I reverence and don't care a bit for Dora, and I don't in the least reverence — and am dying for — Rose.'[16]

Joan's daily letters to Italy now brought momentous messages. Rose's mother had come to see her ailing daughter in Tunbridge Wells. She had then talked to Joan. Despairing of doctors, Mrs La Touche had wondered whether Rose's health might improve if she resumed communication with Ruskin, perhaps even met him. This latest twist in the diplomacy between the families agitated Ruskin. But he was not to be tempted back to England. Instead he made a rather unusual journey to Sicily to visit Amy Yule, a former Winnington girl who lived with her parents in Palermo. Colonel Yule, a veteran of the Sikh wars and the Indian Public Works Department, was an expatriate who had no desire to return to England. To Ruskin's astonishment, he learnt that Amy's mother had forbidden her daughter to read the Bible; and to his pleasure he found that neither parent was interested in the dictates of chaperonage. Amy and Ruskin decided to go to sea together. They joined an overnight steamer from Palermo to Messina, went on by rail to Taormina, stayed in a hotel, then returned by the same route. Although the weather was not kind, the expedition had an agreeable smack of impropriety. As if in reaction to Rose's kind of Christianity, Ruskin wrote

> . . . I have got out of the power of the *black* wind at last; and a twilight walk, last night, when I saw the top of Etna for the first time, its smoke dark against the west, ought to be remembered by me for ever. But the overwhelming multitude of new impressions crush each other. Fancy, since yesterday morning at five o'clock, I have seen Charybdis, the rock of Scylla, the straits of Messina, Messina itself, now the second city in Italy, the whole classical range of Panormus on one side, Calabria on the other, and a line of coast unequalled in luxuriance of beauty; every crag of it crested with a Moorish or Saracenic or Norman architecture wholly new to me; a Greek theatre, the most perfect in Europe, now visible on one side of the valley below my window, and Etna on the other. And think that from the earliest dawn of Greek life that cone has been the centre of tradition and passion as relating to the gods of strength and darkness (Proserpine's city is in the mid-island, but in full sight of Etna), and you may fancy what a wild dream of incredible, labyrinthine wonder, it is to me . . .[17]

This pagan Sicilian adventure concluded the first part of Ruskin's Italian travels and studies in 1874. He was thereafter in Rome, Assisi, Florence, Perugia, Lucca and other places in Tuscany before he turned for home at the end of September. In each city he learnt more about Italian art: to be more accurate, about late medieval art. The first instrument of his study was watercolour. Pen, pencil, brush and wash were employed by Ruskin himself and by an increasing number of colleagues and assistants who examined and recorded a variety of monuments. Ruskin made use of photography, as he always had done, but watercolour was his preferred medium. The camera was indiscriminate when it recorded a building and could not take pictures of shady interiors. With watercolour and pen or pencil Ruskin could concentrate on the details he found most telling, and he could also use colour.

Ruskin was not a painter of the human figures, nor a portraitist. His occasional self-portraits are, however, memorable. He now sent two of them to Charles Eliot Norton. Of course Ruskin was often a landscapist, and he proudly told Norton how Turner himself had appreciated one of his landscapes, a drawing of Schaffhausen: 'He looked at it long, evidently with pleasure, and shook his finger at it, one evening, standing by the fire in the old Denmark Hill drawing room.'[18] But Ruskin's best work as an artist was in recording aspects of man-made artefacts, usually ancient buildings. Such drawings are generally unfinished, in the sense that the sheet is not covered from edge to edge. But their emotions and visions are complete: we realise that the drawing would not be improved by further work. Ruskin's beautiful watercolours of Italian architecture can stand as his artistic contribution to the aesthetic movement. If one were to devise an exhibition of English aesthetic art from around 1860 to the turn of the new century, a show that would display refinement, understatement, freedom from academicism and a knowledgeable love of beauty, then Ruskin's drawings of this date would equal or surpass any of the works of his contemporaries. Not for one moment did he think of them in such a way. They were made by an aesthetic mind and eye, but the purpose of Ruskin's drawings was to be instructive. They were drawn as objects of study because the things they recorded were precious and noble. Hence their reserved and often devotional air.

Back in Rome at the beginning of May, Ruskin set himself the task of understanding Botticelli's frescos in the Sistine Chapel. He did so by copying the figure of Zipporah in the fresco of *Scenes from the Life of Moses*. The copy occupied fourteen working days, which on the whole were pleasantly spent:

> I rise at six, dress quietly, looking out now and then to see the blue sky through the pines beyond the Piazza del Popolo. Coffee at seven, and then I write and correct press till nine. Breakfast, and half-an-hour of Virgil, or lives of saints, or other pathetic or improving work. General review of colour-box and apparatus, start about ten for Sistine Chapel, nice little jingling drive in open one-horse carriage. Arrive at chapel, sauntering a little about the fountains first. Public are turned out at eleven, and then I have absolute peace with two other artists — each on a separate platform — till two, when public are let in again. I strike work; pack up with dignity; get away about three; take the first little carriage at door again, drive to Capitol, saunter a little about Forum, or the like, or into the Lateran, or San Clemente, and so home to dinner at five. Dine very leisurely; read a little French novel at dessert; then out to Pincian — sit among the roses and hear band play. Saunter down Trinita steps as it gets dark; tea; and a little more French novel; a little review of day's work; plans for tomorrow; and to bed . . .[19]

Quite different letters to Joan describe Ruskin's reactions to Zipporah in ways that must have disturbed his puritanical cousin. 'Di wee ma, me's nearly driven myself quite wild today with drawing dear little Z's chemisette — you never did see such a dear little wimply-dimply, crinkly edge as it's got just across four inches under her chin — and it looks as if the least breeze would blow it loose — and di ma, me do so want to see whats inside it . . .' And again, 'I wish I could dream of seeing her with her clothes off — di ma. She would be only a "little brown girl" — for really — there's more umber than anything else — in her colour, when one comes to paint it. Quite wonderful how Botticelli makes it look like R . . .'[20]

The letters contain hints that Rose might be aroused to jealousy by Ruskin's obsessive attention to Zipporah. It is more significant, and ominous, that Ruskin had now begun to persuade himself that Zipporah actually was Rose. Botticelli's maiden was the first of a number of figures within art that became symbolic substitutes for the actual and living, or dead, young woman. More and more, Ruskin needed to see Rose within the terms of art; as lovely, distant, an icon, immortal or at least unaffected by human ills. These fantasies entered Ruskin's mind because of his apprehensions that Rose would shortly die. After her death — now only one year away — the artistic surrogates became part of Ruskin's personal religion, inseparable from his mental illnesses. In this summer of 1874, however, Botticelli's art represented the fragility of human life, its vulnerable loveliness.

★ ★ ★ ★

In Ruskin's public writing of the early 1870s we find intense mental effort, anxiety about Rose and tempestuous social criticism — beside, as always, much else. His readers may not have noticed that above all things he sought calm. If the circumstances of Ruskin's life denied him peace he could perhaps find a kind of serenity in art, especially in early Italian painting of a sort he had already described in 'The Relation between Michael Angelo and Tintoret'. There he said that 'Bellini's angels, even the youngest, sing as calmly as the Fates weave . . . this calmness is the attribute of the entirely highest class of art: the introduction of a strong or violently emotional incident is at once a confession of inferiority.'[21] So it was, Ruskin felt, in his own life. Above him were the Fates. Passions of the world were all around. But grace could be quietly worshipped, and in no more appropriate place than Assisi, where St Francis had lived and died and Giotto had celebrated his holy works.

Ruskin arrived in Assisi on 9 June and was to remain there for several weeks. We now observe him not as the Greek adventurer of his Sicilian expedition, nor as the reader of French novels who 'sauntered' through Rome: we see Ruskin as a Franciscan. It would be possible to write a long study of Ruskin's way of, as he wrote, 'holding myself a brother of the third order of St Francis'.[22] The medieval saint, a preacher but not a priest, directly in contact with the peasantry and the natural world, wedded to poverty and a lover of Christ more than the Church, was more and more appreciated in the later nineteenth century. Ruskin's writings from 1874 onwards are part of this tendency. So are many of the attitudes of the Guild of St George and its adherents. In Assisi, as his editor E. T. Cook recognised, Ruskin 'entered into a communion of spirit with St Francis which deeply coloured his later writings'.[23] An embodiment of this spirit was found in the art of the church of San Francesco and the company of two Franciscan monks who became Ruskin's friends, Fra Antonio and Fra Giovanni, 'one the sacristan who has charge of the entire church, and is responsible for its treasures; the other exercising what authority is left to the convent among the people of the town. They are both so good and innocent and sweet, one can't pity them enough'.[24]

Fra Antonio Coletti now gave Ruskin a treasured privilege, use of the sacristan's cell within the monastery of Assisi. Ruskin was sleeping in a disagreeable inn and spent as much time as possible within this sacred enclave, in perfect quiet — two little windows looking out into the deep valley which runs up into the Apennines give me light enough, and there's the lower church, with Giotto's fresco of Poverty in it, between me and any 'mortal' disturbance. St Francis in his grave a few yards away from me does not, I find, give me any interruption. I have been thinking as I walked down the hillside to the church, why you couldn't believe in Utopia; and whether you really, since you don't *see Him* either, believe in Christ. Are you quite sure, William and you, that you do as *if* you saw Him . . .[25]

These words were addressed to Georgiana Cowper-Temple; and the direct appeal to her husband was made in a kind of Christian fellowship. Ruskin sent his holy challenge from the sacristan's cell because Cowper-Temple was Trustee of the Guild of St George.

These few weeks in Assisi are the subject of one of the passages in *Fors* that describe Ruskin's personal history. In a letter written in Venice in March 1876 he noted that '*Fors* has become much more distinctly Christian in its tone, during the last two years' and ascribed his change of heart to Giotto. He had lived for sixteen years with the guidance of the 'religion of humanity', he wrote,

for rough and strong foundation of everything; but on that, building Greek and Arabian superstructure, taught me at Venice, full of sacred colour and melancholy shade. Which is the under meaning of my answer to the Capuchin (Fors, Aug. 75, §2) that I was 'more a Turk than a Christian'. The Capuchin insisted, as you see, nevertheless that I might have a bit of St Francis's cloak: which accepting thankfully, I went on to Assisi, and there, with the kindness of my good friend Padre Tini, and others, I was allowed (and believe I was the first painter who *ever was* allowed) to have scaffolding erected above the high altar, and therefore above the body of St Francis which lies in the lower chapel beneath it; and thence to draw what I could of the great fresco of Giotto, 'The Marriage of Poverty and Francis'.

And while making this drawing, I discovered the fallacy under which I had been tormented for sixteen years, — the fallacy that Religious artists were weaker than Irreligious. I found that all Giotto's 'weaknesses' (so called) were merely absences of material science. He did not know, and could not, in his day, so much of perspective as Titian, — so much of the laws of light and shade, or so much of technical composition. But I found he was in the make of him, and contents, a very much stronger and greater man than Titian; that the things I had fancied easier in his work, because they

> were so unpretending and simple, were nevertheless entirely inimitable; that the Religion in him, instead of weakening, has solemnized and developed every faculty of his heart and hand; and finally that his work, in all the innocence of it, was yet a human achievement and possession, quite above everything that Titian had ever done!
>
> 'But what is all this about Titian and Angelico to you', are you thinking? 'We belong to cotton mills — iron mills; — what is Titian to *us*! — and to all men. Heirs only of simial life, what Angelico?'[26]

This passage, like so much of the autobiography in *Fors*, is a heightened and distorted account of events. Ruskin does not mention that he began his work in Assisi by considering Cimabue rather than Giotto, and that he was vexed by ordinary and worldly art-historical problems. When he had managed to have scaffolding erected Ruskin looked at the frescos in the vault above the high altar in the Lower Church. They had suffered from damp and their original colours had faded, even disappeared. Looking at the paintings attentively, Ruskin wondered whether in truth they were not by Giotto himself but were the work of his assistants. He never published this view, which perhaps was a first impression. It was in any case so dark in the church that no attribution could be confident. So it cannot be said that these paintings struck Ruskin with the absolute force of a revelation. In fact Ruskin's renewed delight in medieval art was accompanied by perplexing questions. Like all the pioneers of the history of early painting he was beset with procedural and scholarly difficulties. Welcoming though they were, the Franciscan monks could not discuss the art in their church and had a limited knowledge of the books in their library. Ruskin was defeated by the task of copying damaged frescos. Should a copyist record exactly what he saw or attempt to interpret the original palette of a discoloured work? In Assisi Ruskin talked at length with his assistants. But he, Kaiser and James Fairfax Murray never solved the problems of making beautiful and accurate copies. In part this was because they had differing artistic talents. Their approaches could not be synthesised. The Assisi work this June was to be the last collaboration between Ruskin and the Arundel Society.

In Cimabue's painting within the Assisi church Ruskin found more certainty. Another investigator, who proved to be the 'Director of the Venetian Accademia di belle arte' (but is otherwise unnamed in Ruskin's letters) already had scaffolding and was restoring the frescos definitely painted by Cimabue. Ruskin was initially 'swearing at him' but found that this seeming rival was 'an honest and ingenious man'. Now at last meeting Cavalcaselle, who had also worked on these walls, Ruskin acknowledged that 'a long and useful talk' had made him 'sorry for what I thought against him'.[27] Ruskin was learning to respect the views of Italian experts. At the same time he looked at Cimabue's painting as though the thirteenth-century artist had a message for him alone. Here was a dangerous attitude. Three years hence, Ruskin would believe that Carpaccio's St Ursula had given him direct spiritual intelligence. In this delusion, which he wrote out and published in *Fors Clavigera*, we find not exalted knowledge but the signs of madness. In the latter part of June 1874, overworking in the sacristan's cell, Ruskin was coming near to such mental collapse. He thought that St George and St Francis together would direct his future work. 'I really ought to do something good for the world after being so tormented'. Ruskin's copy of the figure of St Francis from Cimabue's *Madonna with Angels and St Francis* now gives us a strange insight. Ruskin believed that copying should be accurate and anonymous. In the copy there is no such self-effacement. The saint's features resemble those of Ruskin himself, as sketched in the self-portraits that had been sent to Charles Eliot Norton a month earlier.[28]

In this drawing Ruskin's introspection seems to be that of a man who looks sorrowfully on the world, from afar or from a place beyond the world. He was not however detached in Assisi but busily engaged with its monuments. Simply to enumerate these investigations is to suggest the complications of Ruskin's studies and therefore of our study of Ruskin. E. T. Cook believed that he was planning a history of the city. This was not done. Instead, Ruskin wrote two numbers of *Fors*, worked on *The Laws of Fésole*, a drawing manual intended both for Oxford and St George's schools, and continued with *Deucalion* and *Proserpina*. His work on Giotto and Cimabue was to appear in *The Aesthetic and Mathematic Schools of Florence*,[29] the Oxford lectures delivered in the autumn of 1874, as well as in his later publication *Mornings in Florence* (1875–77), which was a development of the Oxford lectures. (The lectures were not themselves published before Cook and Wedderburn rescued the manuscripts and made them a part of their Library Edition in 1906.)

In addition, Ruskin had measured the upper and lower churches at Assisi for an architectural study, never separately written, and had made twelve copies of frescos or formal studies of architectural features. These drawings were intended for Oxford or St George's Museum but in the course of time were dispersed elsewhere. Some were lost, perhaps when *The Laws of Fésole* was abandoned in 1878. The study of St Francis, with its disturbing self-portraiture, is now in an American private collection. The drawing may have been given by Ruskin to Charles Eliot Norton, though it is not mentioned in their extant correspondence. The letters one may recover from Ruskin's Assisi period are copious and informative, many of them unpublished.

This intense and disparate work was done in the service of the saints and for the general good of the modern world. But neither the effort nor the spiritual yearning can have been good for Ruskin's own life. W. G. Collingwood, who by now received his letters and was beginning the study that, in time, would make him Ruskin's first biographer, judged that in Assisi he 'fell dangerously ill again, as in Matlock in 1871'. Collingwood wrote (probably with the evidence of a private letter, or perhaps with the memory of a conversation) that Ruskin 'dreamt that they had made him a brother of the third degree of the order of St Francis — a fancy that took strong hold of his mind'.[30] This was stated in 1893. E. T. Cook, who was not given access to Collingwood's Ruskin correspondence when preparing the Library Edition and his own biography, replied in 1906 that Ruskin's diary 'contains no trace of such illness; it accounts for busy work during every day which he spent at Assisi'.[31] So it does, but the contents — and the handwriting — of the diary are none the less disturbing.[32]

Ever since 21 December 1870, when he was first in Oxford as Professor of Fine Art, Ruskin's personal journal had recorded days of the 'black wind' that he would later call the 'plague wind' and describe in his 1884 lecture 'The Storm-Cloud of the Nineteenth Century'. This belief in the existence of an evil wind was not rational. The wind occurs at times of personal stress. Sometimes Ruskin gives it mythological significance. In Assisi in 1874, the diary reveals, sirocco winds are associated with the goddess Athena, either Athena of life or Athena of storm. At the same time his belief in *sortes Biblicae* gave Ruskin prophetic messages of the day when the Lord would punish those 'that leap on the threshold, which fill their masters' houses with violence and deceit'. Chancing on this passage in Jeremiah, 4. 22–7, Ruskin interpreted the prophet's verses as a description of 'The Uncreation by folly, of what had been created by wisdom . . . There is no man, but only dust; and the birds of the heaven are fled.'[33]

Ruskin's period in the sacristan's cell was by no means calm. Flashes of intuition came to him like lightning in a storm. He experienced blessed moments before art but also gave himself to un-Franciscan and apocalyptic visions such as that inspired by Jeremiah. Aware that he needed change, Ruskin travelled to Perugia on 12 July.

He stayed there for a fortnight, with frequent trips back to Assisi. Then he was in Florence on 25 July, at Lucca between 28 July and 7 August and back in Florence between 19 August and 18 September. These dates help us to clarify the flow of often contradictory thoughts and emotions in Ruskin's mind this summer, on which he enlarged in Oxford lectures, *Fors*, *Mornings in Florence* and other works. Different places in Tuscany either excited him, enraged his sensibilities as a conservationist or served to calm his weary mind. The visit to Lucca was, on the whole, a success. Here Ruskin found an Italy less affected by the progress of the nineteenth century. The little city was not too much changed from the place he had first visited in 1840 and 1845. Once settled in his inn he enjoyed 'the happiest walk in moonlight I have had, this twenty years, in this blessed place, still preserved to me' and to Joan he wrote with further detail:

> I've had the most wonderful walk tonight that I've yet found in Italy. The hills to the south are all of marble, and the ravines in them one sweet wilderness of olive, and moss, and vine, and chestnut; but I came on a little cottage among the rocks to-night, with its threshing-floor — or rather winnowing-floor — *area* of the Latins, merely a wide space of the mountain path under rocks of naked marble, while, beneath, the olives clothed all the slope of the hill-side to the plain of Lucca. I never saw anything in this world so exquisitely wild and so delicately *homely* at once — the whole level space of path covered with the golden chaff of the just winnowed corn, the quite stern, yet finishedly beautiful marble at its side, the cottage with its steps to its door cut in the rock, and an arcade of vines over the path from its roof . . .[34]

At Lucca Ruskin made a renewed study of the funerary statue of Ilaria di Carretto by Jacopo della Quercia. This is the sculpture that had first impressed him in 1845 (in 1840 he seems to have missed it) and that he had exalted in a once famous passage in the second volume of *Modern Painters*. That description is 'almost hackneyed', wrote W. G. Collingwood in 1902, reminding us that Ruskin's classic early books were once familiar to educated readers.[35] Collingwood's discussion of the early *quattrocento* tomb, to be found in his essay 'Ruskin's Ilaria', is valuable in a number of ways. He knew more than anyone about the effect of della Quercia's sculpture on Ruskin. In 1882 he drew the sculpture under Ruskin's supervision. 'Who or what the lady might have been in the flesh he hardly seems to have cared; at least he never dwelt on the story', Collingwood recalled.[36] That was so, and Ruskin's interest in della Quercia scholarship was limited. He loved the sculpture of Ilaria because it gave him a glimpse of immortality. The youthful Ruskin had written in *Modern Painters II* that 'She is lying on a simple couch with a hound at her feet . . . The hair is bound in a flat braid over the fair brow, the sweet and arched eyes are closed, the tenderness of the loving lips is set and quiet; there is that about them which forbids breath; something which is not death nor sleep, but the pure image of both.'[37] Now, three decades later, he looked at della Quercia's sculpture with a premonition of Rose La Touche's death. Perhaps this is why he had difficulty in drawing statuary that should have given him few problems. 'It's partly the paper, and the colours, and the light and the hurry, and the worry', he wrote to Joan after two weeks' work on his drawing, 'and the being like some peepies that ain't dead but are of stone'.[38]

Another work at Lucca was the composition of an issue of *Fors Clavigera* that Ruskin considered particularly important. On 30 July his diary reads 'Beginning the great central Fors I chance on and read carefully, and as an answer to much thought last night, Isaiah 6th.' Its published title is 'My Lord Delayeth His Coming. The British Squire'.[39] Ruskin referred to it privately as the 'Landlord Fors' or the 'Squire Fors'. It should be studied in conjunction with the criticisms of landlords implicit in the Hinksey road-building project. Isaiah is none the less an inspiration of the letter. Its origin may be found in notes on the prophet taken in previous continental travels in 1856, 1858 and 1859, all contained in one vellum-covered volume of Ruskin's diary that perhaps accompanied him on this 1874 tour.[40] More recent sources of this forty-fifth number of *Fors* are mentioned in a letter to Joan Severn:

> Assisi St Anthony 74
>
> . . . I've been all the morning writing in Fra Antonio's cell in the monastery — the deliciousest quiet little kitchen — looking out on the Apennines & nothing else — only the birds, outside — and cloister within I began a little study of the butter and honey bit in Isaiah — and came all at once on Isaiah's son whom I never thought of before — 'Shearjashub' — 'Causeway' — the margin says. My Hinksey men will all be called Shearjashubs, if I don't mind. but I wonder what Isaiah's wife was like, and whether she sometimes 'disappointed' him. — and whether she wouldn't give tenpence a chapter for his prophecies. And whether she had a dog, like Bruno —? and whether she called him 'the prophet' instead of 'St *C*' — (But that's my wifie's own saint.)
>
> I think on the whole the best way *is* to think of her as my wife — only mad. — and make the best of it . . .[41]

Rose had once refused to pay the cover price of tenpence for a copy of *Fors* — an old grievance, all the more so because Ruskin could never be sure whether or not Rose read any of his monthly letters. If she declined to accept his personal correspondence what guarantee was there that she would look at his extremely personal missivies addressed to the public, even though they often contained tidings for her? Alas, few records remain of Rose's familiarity with Ruskin's writings.

In Lucca he had to think once more about his literary responsibilities to Oxford, the somewhat neglected Guild of St George and his wider audience, whatever that was. Ruskin was now joined by Crawley and George Allen. Ruskin's personal publisher soon returned to England with passages of miscellaneous manuscript, scattered fruits of the labours in Assisi. It is likely that Allen then set this material in type, even though — as noted above — it had no immediate place in Ruskin's published work. This was increasingly a habit. Projected, abandoned or unfinished books became more numerous during the 1870s and early 1880s. Only one of Ruskin's publications was absolutely steady in its appearance. *Fors Clavigera*, given the erratic and often agonised nature of its contents, might have been published at irregular intervals. In fact it came out without fail on the first day of each calendar month, except when that day was a Sunday, during all these most troubled years of Ruskin's life. In this sense it was the most reliable of Ruskin's books, though there is no evidence that its regular publication either helped *Fors*'s sales or consolidated its unique character in the minds of the few subscribers who received their monthly dispatch from Sunnyside, Orpington, Kent, George Allen's home, where this unusual family retainer printed and published, did not edit, for no one did that, and struggled to keep abreast of Ruskin's writing; despaired of his master's finances and, for leisure, tended the beehives at the end of his suburban orchard.

⋆ ⋆ ⋆ ⋆

England was calling, but Ruskin felt that he should stay in Italy until the beginning of the Oxford Michaelmas term. Renewed study of Tuscan art had led him toward subjects that proved more complicated than he had imagined. He had a notion of the contents of his next course of Oxford lectures; but they had not been written, and further work in Florence was surely required. Thither he went, and on 27 July his diary records a visit to the Uffizi. 'Yesterday through the Uffizi wishing I was a boy again, and feeling myself just able to begin to learn things rightly.'[42]

In this year of 1874 he was fifty-five, not too old for dramatic new impressions nor too old to be overwhelmingly in love with a woman in her twenties. Ruskin's studies in Florence this August and September are mingled with thoughts of Rose. He now had messages from her via Joan and then letters from Rose herself, the first he had received since 1872. Her new approach had begun when he was at Lucca. A telegram arrived from Joan saying that Rose wished to write to him, just as he was composing the 'Squire's Fors' and attempting to draw the tomb of Ilaria. By the time he was in Florence Ruskin had her letters, and these (since destroyed) would always thereafter be associated in his mind with his copies of Simone Memmi, Lippi, Orcagna, Giotto and, especially, Botticelli, of whom he wrote: 'there are no words for his imagination; — solemnity of purpose, artistic rapture, in all divinely artistic things — mightier in chiaroscuro than Correggio — brighter in jewellery than Angelico — abundant, like Tintoret, and intense in contemplation like Leonardo. I never saw or thought such things possible, till I went to the Academy delli belle Arti this last time'.[43]

Ruskin's weeks in Florence established Botticelli as a saintly guide during the last days of his relations with the dying Rose La Touche. He was affected by thoughts of other people at the end of life. News of the death of W. H. Harrison, 'my first editor', was the more disturbing because this Ruskin family friend — who had looked after Ruskin's manuscripts since he first began writing for *Friendships Offering* — had been cast aside when *Fors Clavigera* began and George Allen took sole charge of Ruskin's publishing. In the same few days he learnt that Joseph Couttet was dying and had written to England to say that he wished to see Ruskin once more. His old Alpine guide, first met in 1844, whose words about Ruskin, '*pauvre enfant, il ne sait pas vivre*', had haunted him all his life, aroused particular affection and respect.[44] Ruskin as a mature man wished, very properly, to pay attention to old men who had encouraged him in his youth. Harrison, alas, was a little 'cockney', in Ruskin's use of the word. Couttet was almost an aristocrat of the Savoy peasantry. Ruskin wished to honour him both as man and as Alpinist so he decided to leave Florence and travel home via Chamonix. There he would see Couttet and find inspiration for the lectures on the Alps he had failed to deliver earlier in the year.

By the first week in October he was established in a favourite *auberge*, described in *Præterita* as 'of all my inn-homes, the most eventful, pathetic and sacred'.[45] The autobiography does not tell us why the Hôtel du Mont Blanc was so particularly 'sacred'. The chapter of

Præterita with that title is concerned with much earlier years. Had he been able to write the story of his life as he wished, Ruskin might have explained why the inn at St Martin was hallowed. The reason was that he there received a communication from Rose that amounted to a proposal of marriage. With Chamonix and Couttet within a walk, the high mountains all around him, reminiscences of the days when he wrote *Modern Painters* flooding into his mind, Ruskin imagined that some day soon he might become Rose's husband.

She was still travelling between Dublin and London, so one of her letters was written and posted at Crewe. It was penitent, apologising for the scene at the station that had ended their relations in the summer of 1872. Then came an indirect but none the less epochal message. For once, we know what Rose actually wrote. Two sentences of utter importance to Ruskin were in a letter to Joan that his cousin subsequently burnt. But Joan sent the letter to Ruskin, who copied out the message to Charles Eliot Norton. This letter from the Hôtel du Mont Blanc, Norton preserved. In it we find that Rose had written to Joan:

> Do you think that Mr and Mrs C. Temple's opinion is true — and that the Professor would really, really, really care to have me, and be happy with me — just as I am? — I can't understand it. If he could, he deserves to have the remnant, though I must say — it's only — 'suitable for a present', in Mama's sense of the expression.[46]

For months and years Ruskin had been wary of Rose's 'freaks', as he called them, sudden reversals of attitude or plans to change her life. This was not a freak. It was as though Rose, in exhaustion, had abandoned all her wayward efforts to be independent. Furthermore it appeared that Rose's parents had abandoned their opposition to Ruskin. He felt tender and even a little powerful. For a precious few days he once again felt himself to be a visionary Alpinist. He drew well, saw much of Couttet and his family and at the Hôtel du Mont Blanc wrote the forty-seventh issue of *Fors*, 'Minos Retained. The British Judge'. This is primarily about Walter Scott. Ruskin privately called his letter the 'Redgauntlet Fors'. As so often when writing about Scott, his tone became elegiac, remembering his father John James; and the diary entries from this short period in the Savoy Alps have the flavour of notes for *Præterita*, a book as yet far from Ruskin's mind. In this mood Ruskin began his final approach to Rose: each of them, 'the Professor' and 'the remnant', increasingly aware that the courtship would end not in marriage but in death.

CHAPTER THIRTY-THREE

1874–1875

In his study in Shady Hill, Charles Eliot Norton read the extract from Rose's letter with annoyance. Through his correspondence with Ruskin he had been following the Italian journey and its art-historical discoveries. These he appreciated as a worker in the same field. None the less Norton felt that it was now time to rebuke Ruskin for his wavering attitudes and unmanly English friendships:

> The extract from the letter that was not meant for your eyes or mine, and the word you cite from Joan's have both given me pain. They make me feel more keenly than ever your solitude, — a solitude partly due to misfortune of circumstances, partly to character, — and which, at this lamentable distance, I can do nothing to diminish. You, of all men, need a wise, constant friend near you. The people by whom you are surrounded are not worthy of you. Few of them can do you any good. Joan, with her 'Di pa', (abbreviated, I suppose, from Divus Pater), can at best be only a cushion; the C. Temples are weak reeds, Connie is still a child, — and, worst of all the woman to whom your heart has been given is a torment to herself & to you through her insane conceits & fluctuations. You are greatly in need of a solid man friend; one who should not be afraid of you, who should care as little for your public repute as I do; who should meet you on equal terms, & who should balance your genius by his steady sense. I wish you knew my friend Leslie Stephen, — one of the most affectionate & most honest minded & modest of men . . . a sceptic without bitterness, a thinker without pretention; muscular physically & mentally without brutality; shy, sensitive, tender, manly; looking out very strait on the world . . . I wish chance could bring you together . . . Could you know each other, & resolve to care for each other, he would be of help to you . . .[1]

Norton could have recommended a more congenial guide than Stephen, a Cambridge liberal and former don who was now engaged in random literary work. He might also have noticed that Ruskin made friends in his own way, and certainly not at anyone else's bidding. But Norton was presumably unaware that Stephen had recently published an essay on 'Mr Ruskin's Recent Writings', filled with patronising comments on *Fors Clavigera*. The article in *Fraser's Magazine* concluded:

> A sensitive nature, tortured and thrust aside by pachydermatous and apathetic persons, may well be driven to rash revolt and hasty denunciations of society in general. At worst, and granting him to be entirely wrong, he has certainly more claim on our pity than our contempt. And for a moral, if we must have a moral, we can only remark, that on the whole Mr Ruskin provides a fresh illustration of the truth, which has both a cynical and an elevating side to it, that it is among the greatest of all blessings to have a thick skin and a sound digestion.[2]

Stephen, who now remarked in a letter to Norton that Ruskin would find the world more tolerable if he took up smoking (and requested Norton to pass on this advice), was scarcely worth considering either as a friend or as an adversary. *Fors* of December 1874 deals with him in a mild fashion. None the less Ruskin was wounded by the scornful remarks about his sensitivity. For he was at a point in his life in which perfect restraint and delicacy of feeling were demanded both by Rose, mortally ill, and by an Oxford audience that would attend to his views on the aesthetics of early Italian art. Ruskin's diary shows that in November he travelled frantically between Rose in London and his Oxford colleagues and students. Yet his demeanour was not agitated. He summoned himself to calmness. This was for Rose's sake. Ruskin had crossed the Channel on 22 October and went immediately to be at her side. True to the last to her taste in hotels, Rose was spending her dying days in new establishments within the district then known as Tyburnia (in imitation of Belgravia) a modern development to the west of Marble Arch and extending toward Westbourne Park. Ruskin first ran to his beloved in Edwards' Hotel in Spring Street, quite near Paddington station on the Hyde Park side. Rose was extremely weak, but not at this stage confined to her bed. Ruskin was now to see her regularly until she returned to Ireland in mid-December. It is not known whether they discussed marriage, though it seems possible. Neither party could imagine the future. But they had a kind of domesticity. There were presents, shared books, shared days. Ruskin and Rose took short walks, generally to church. Sometimes Rose sang hymns. In November she moved to another hotel in Westbourne Terrace. There Ruskin had an 'evening with Rosie, settling many things on the hearthrug'.[3] At many other times, however, she was 'ill and restless'. One day in early December Rose was both faint and distraught. Ruskin 'had leave to nurse her — the dream of life too sorrowfully fulfilled'.[4]

★ ★ ★ ★

Now is the time to examine a peculiar consequence of this half-domesticity, Ruskin's tea shop. As he travelled back though Italy and Switzerland with Rose's letters in his pocket Ruskin had allowed himself fantasies about their possible life together. One dream was that the Cowper-Temples 'should let me build the first cottage of St George's company, for Rosie and me — in the New Forest — within — say — three or four miles of them, and sell me as much ground as we wanted to live on . . .'[5] If this could be arranged, he told Joan, Ruskin would give Brantwood to the Severns. In the same few days that he made this plan Rose, to Ruskin's delight, was teasing him by letter. One of her notes contained a peaseblossom with the message 'Sweet P stands for disagreeable Professor.'[6] In another letter she wrote to him 'Its teatime — I shd. like to pour out your tea . . .'[7] This artless remark set Ruskin's mind galloping in an unforeseen direction. Perhaps he was influenced by a characteristic Rose 'freak' of her healthier days, that she might change her life by becoming, for instance, a governess. Ruskin, in Chambery, suddenly considered her as a young grocer. He could 'take up that tea business in an exemplary — and profitable manner to show that I'm a business man!' Rose would have the shop. After Ruskin's death she would continue, 'Carrying on the business afterwards as a widow — "Mrs R. R. Tea Importer"'.[8] This scheme had its results. A retail tea shop was opened in Paddington Street, probably in late October, and on 14 November Ruskin drove Rose from Tyburnia to have tea with its manager, Lucy Tovey.

With her elder sister Harriet, Lucy Tovey had been a parlourmaid in the service of the Ruskin family since 1829. As is often explained, especially in *Fors Clavigera* and *Præterita*, it was a family tradition that no Ruskin servant was ever discarded. Therefore, with the break-up of the Denmark Hill house, some retainers went to the Severns in Herne Hill, Downs the gardener and Crawley the valet went to Brantwood and some others were given a pension and homes in Camberwell. The Toveys went to Paddington Street to one of the Ruskin properties managed by Octavia Hill. For about two years this was the tea shop. It was not commercially successful. The shop is sometimes regarded as an experiment in economics, thus a part of Ruskin's work with the Guild of St George. Expenditure on tea is indeed found in the Guild's accounts. The tea shop was none the less personal and resembled other Guild projects in the way it harked back to the utopia of Denmark Hill. Ruskin was eager for Rose to take an interest in Lucy Tovey because he wished her to become embedded, as it were, in the history and mythology of the Ruskin family. To go to Lucy's shop was part of this campaign. The old lady would talk of the old days, of the way she was sometimes taken on the Ruskins' European tours, of young John at Oxford, of Turner and his table manners. For her part, Rose had always been interested in the Denmark Hill dynasties. She had returned the affection of John James and Margaret Ruskin. Her statement that she had lived in the Queen's Hotel because it reminded her of Ruskin's mother is not quite unbelievable. Furthermore, she was now able to feel pleasure in Joan Severn's young family. So the triumph of Ruskin's reconciliation with Rose was her first ever visit to Herne Hill, on 14 December. This was the day before she returned to Ireland for Christmas. Ruskin had been elsewhere, in Oxford and giving a lecture on Botticelli and Giotto at Eton. He returned to London to find Rose shyly lingering in the back parlour of his old home — not quite confident enough to welcome him to the house that was his heritage.

Such matters have a bearing on Ruskin's autobiography. The parts of *Præterita* that were extracted from *Fors Clavigera* were primarily addressed to Rose. In the six months between the end of Ruskin's Italian journey of 1874 and Rose's death in 1875 there is a concentration of these personal fragments. In them we hear the grave, unhappy voice of a suitor who explains his character to a young woman whose earthly life was at its end. After Rose died Ruskin wrote no more autlobiography in *Fors*, apart from a couple of scraps. Nor did he much return to the subject of early Tuscan art. His feelings for Botticelli and Cimabue were too much bound up with memories of Rose's last days. A later book is *Mornings in Florence*, published in six parts between 1875 and 1877,[9] but this was taken from the material of his Oxford lectures of autumn 1874, *The Aesthetic and Mathematic Schools of Art in Florence*. Some of this writing is highly finished. It was probably composed in Italy in September and early October. Other parts of the lectures were written hurriedly, late at night in Corpus Christi or Herne Hill, or in the train between Oxford and Paddington, on the way to a sickbed in Tyburnia. Yet more passages were entrusted to extempore delivery. Ruskin's departures from prepared manuscript contributed to his reputation for an almost supernatural but also eccentric eloquence. The lectures were not easy to follow. It seems that Ruskin had no thought of their publication. We would probably not know them today had they not been recorded, week after week, by the able undergraduate Alexander Wedderburn.

He must have taken hurried notes in the lecture room, then written them up afterwards, conceivably with Ruskin's guidance. At all events, Wedderburn's first-hand knowledge of the lectures later enabled him to reconstruct their arguments from scattered pieces of manuscript and diary. This was one of his signal contributions to the editorial work of the Library Edition.[10]

Alexander Wedderburn, road-digger, 'disciple', Ruskin's friend and future editor, was born in 1854 and entered Balliol in 1873 after schooldays at Haileybury. We learn from his family compilation *The Wedderburn Book* (1898) that his forebears and close relatives were connected with India, first as merchants and then as administrators. He was the first of his family to break away from this pattern, for after Oxford he became a barrister. At Balliol Wedderburn was evidently an idealist. Eager to change the world for the better, he found inspiration in Ruskin's work and personality. Such feelings were shared by his Balliol contemporaries or near-contemporaries James Reddie Anderson, Hardwicke Rawnsley, Charles Hinton, Leonard Montefiore, Alfred Milner and Arnold Toynbee, all of whom listened carefully to Ruskin, worked on the Hinksey road and may be described as the core of his Oxford following. Other Balliol men associated with Ruskin at this period included Edward Vaughan, Charles Stuart-Wortley, Arthur Hoare and W. H. Mallock, though it is not clear that they worked on the diggings. As will be seen, many of these young men would soon have their differences with Ruskin. For the moment, we observe that the Slade Professor's disciples were predominantly Balliol men. This cannot have been wholly by chance. Balliol was an intellectual and progressive college. Therefore (one assumes) its students might have been especially interested in a new academic discipline, the history of art. And yet, as Ruskin himself so often declared, he did not represent 'progress'. Some undergraduates, first among them Mallock, appreciated Ruskin because he so differed from the modern and liberal Balliol. Others, led by Milner and Toynbee, turned from Ruskin because Balliol's modern liberalism was a rational training for their future endeavours in the world.

Such differences did not become apparent for a year or more. In early November of 1874 a distinction appears between the first band of diggers and those who were about to join them. The original labourers were those who had started work after Ruskin left for Italy at the beginning of the Trinity (summer) term. Since their professor was abroad and they were supervised by an old Scottish gardener, David Downs, it is fair to call them especially dedicated. Those who were certainly of this group were Anderson, Collingwood, Hinton,

Montefiore, Rawnsley and Wedderburn. They may have been joined by Tyrwhitt, who was the only senior member of the University (and the only clergyman) to have worked on the road. The second generation of road-builders were those young men who began their undergraduate careers in the Michaelmas (autumn) term. They are more numerous, and probably without the same commitment. Undergraduates now went to the road because the Hinksey project had become famous within and beyond the University. Some, apparently, went to Hinksey to jeer. Others came and went, or attached themselves to the enterprise because they could now work beside Ruskin himself. He was at the diggings nearly every day when he was in Oxford in the Michaelmas term. Not far from Hinksey was the station and the railroad to Rose. He must have been tempted to go to London. Ruskin none the less persevered with his digging and paving, and so he met a new intake of undergraduates and welcomed them in muddy fields as well as at his Corpus breakfast parties.

The most significant of his new adherents was Oscar Wilde, who had arrived at Magdalen College in October. With so many others, Wilde went to the University Museum to listen to the lectures that make up *The Aesthetic and Mathematic Schools of Florence*. The Hinksey road gave him the opportunity to make personal acquaintance with the renowned professor. One gathers that they now became friends. Certainly, as already noted, Wilde later wrote that 'my walks and talks with you' were the best part of his Oxford education. We cannot know the details of this friendship because Ruskin's editors and executors wished to conceal that it had existed. No doubt Collingwood and Wedderburn had observed Wilde at Oxford and formed an opinion of him. Later, in the 1880s, neither of these scholarly and possessive Ruskinians could have tolerated Wilde's fanciful accounts of the origins of the road-building, published in American journals but known on the British side of the Atlantic.[11] In any case, Wilde's disgrace in 1895 ensured that he was to find no place in the Library Edition. The biographies by Collingwood and E. T. Cook do not mention him. But one can imagine that Ruskin would have found Wilde beguiling, and of further interest because of his Dublin background. Unlike some of the 'disciples', Wilde was not pious or dour. He none the less had a serious desire for art. On their walks together Ruskin would have felt the grace of the Irishman's intelligent and creative personality. He sensed his aestheticism.

With Wilde's arrival in Oxford we are indeed at a significant moment in the development of the aesthetic movement. For Ruskin, the ethos of the Hinksey project was in the first place Carlylean. He was interested in proper and therefore elevated landlordism. There were further and unrelated themes in the diggings. The first — never publicly stated, but implicit in all Ruskin's Oxford teaching — was that undergraduates need not be bound to their college tutors and the mechanical demands of a curriculum. A second theme was opposition to the new cult of athletics. In Ruskin's own undergraduate days the recreations of his fellow-students were still those of the country gentry. By the early 1870s undergraduates had taken to codified sports. Athleticism affected both the values of university life and the social geography of the Oxford purlieus. While college servants and small tradesmen still lived in the slums of Jericho and St Ebbe's, large tracts of land just beyond the medieval colleges were made into sports fields. Cricket pavilions were erected, college barges and boathouses lined the Isis at the southern end of Christ Church meadow. Wilde led the first generation of Oxford undergraduates who mocked sporting men while proclaming themselves the initiates of art. They had a recognisable style. Affectation, mannerisms, wit, Hellenism and a strong hint of homosexuality all became associated with Aestheticism.

These things were not of Ruskin's doing and all his later comments about the aesthetic movement were hostile. Nevertheless, Aestheticism was indebted to him in numerous ways. More than any other Victorian, Ruskin had made art important. From his voluminous writings the new aesthetes took whatever they wished in proclaiming the utter importance of art to their own lives. Aesthetes probably appreciated the earlier rather than the more recent Ruskin. Certainly they were not disposed to receive the messages of *Fors Clavigera*. For some, a more attractive book than any of Ruskin's was Walter Pater's *Studies in the History of the Renaissance*, published in 1873: Wilde knew its celebrated 'Conclusion' by heart. Pater, thirty-five years old in 1874, was a don at Brasenose. Twenty years younger than Ruskin, he felt some rivalry with the senior writer. The two men never met, though in a small city like Oxford their paths must often have crossed. It is possible that they avoided each other: Pater because he wished to keep his own counsel, Ruskin because he knew of Pater's reputation. Pater's homosexuality was widely known. On one occasion his attachment to young men led to a scandal that involved a road-digger and therefore affected Ruskin closely. William Money Hardinge was said to have received loving letters from Pater. Within Balliol, Hardinge was known for impiety and for sonnets that, apparently, were of such a nature that another digger, Leonard Montefiore, thought it his duty to report him to high authority. The Master of Balliol, Benjamin Jowett, terminated Hardinge's Oxford career with as little commotion as possible.[12] Jowett then cut off his own relations with Pater. Ruskin's attitude to these events is not precisely known. But, as E. T. Cook's biography correctly states, he was not a prude.[13] Ruskin was kind to Hardinge at the time of his difficulties and talked to him frankly about his own life. It is relevant that Ruskin, at just this period, was a supporter of Oscar Browning, a schoolmaster who lost his post at Eton amid suspicions that he had corrupted boys.[14]

⋆ ⋆ ⋆ ⋆

There is a wealth of anecdote about Ruskin at Oxford because he was under scrutiny by so many intelligent young men who would later write their memoirs. Oxford itself was being examined as a result of the demands for university reform in the 1870s. Within Corpus Christi, Ruskin attended a dons' discussion group that talked about the nature of a university. Beyond Corpus and Oxford, there was concern about the purposes of higher education. London newspapers and magazines such as *Punch* began to notice Oxford and its peculiar ways. The Hinksey diggings were made amusing to *Punch* readers and criticised in *The Times*. Henry Acland, as a dignitary of the University, replied to the *Times* article in these terms:

> Mr Ruskin, a man of no narrow sympathies, has known Oxford for forty years. He is as interested in the greatness of the educated youth of England as he is in the well-being of the poor. He is loved by both. To the high-spirited youth of Oxford he has said, 'Will, then, none of you out of the abundance of your strength and of your leisure, do anything for the poor? The poor ye have always with you. Drain a single cottage; repair a single village by-way. Make good a single garden wall; make pleasant with flowers one widow's plot, and your muscles will be more strong and your hearts more light than had all your leisure hours been spent in costly games, or yet more hurtful amusements . . .[15]

Here was the Tory view of the Hinksey enterprise. A more modern attitude toward the poor is found among the diggers themselves, in particular Milner, Montefiore and Toynbee. Montefiore was to die in 1879 at the age of twenty-six. Milner became the Liberal statesman. Toynbee also died young, in 1883. His name is commemorated in Toynbee Hall in Whitechapel, for he and his Balliol friends were more interested in social problems in the East End than in country parishes. They all worked in university extension schemes while undergraduates, when the enthusiasm for digging had disappeared. Milner quite shortly dismissed his Hinksey experience as nothing more than a craze.

Toynbee felt devotion for Ruskin to the end of his days, but both his intellectual and his social career took him away from the Slade Professor.[16] He was interested in wise administration. At Balliol, he soon came to teach students who were preparing for the examinations that would admit them to the Indian Civil Service. India could hardly be ruled with Ruskin in mind. Academically, Toynbee was an economic historian. His famous book is *Lectures on the Industrial Revolution in England*, published posthumously in 1884 (with much editorial assistance from Milner). Toynbee saw that the industrial revolution, an expression he invented, had to be understood. Ruskin's writings could not assist such understanding. Thus the Hinksey labourers, whether aesthetes or social progressives, went their different ways. The only Balliol digger to join the Guild of St George was Jamie Anderson. The actual diggings continued, sporadically, until April of 1875 and were finally abandoned around the time of Rose La Touche's death at the end of May.

⋆ ⋆ ⋆ ⋆

Ruskin was never to recover from Rose's death, yet in the weeks when she lay dying his mind already began to prepare her memorial. The tributes from Ruskin to his loved one would take a number of forms. Primarily, he wrote his books with Rose in mind. We might also consider the Guild of St George as a utopia in which Rose, alive or dead, might find a spiritual home. Over Christmas of 1874, after the mortally sick young woman had returned to her family and doctors in Ireland, Ruskin elaborated his previously sketchy outlines of the Guild's constitution. How much Rose understood of the Guild we cannot know. The first 'Memorandum and Statutes of the Guild of St George', probably devised while she was in Ireland at Christmas, were not published until they appeared in *Fors* of July 1875.[17] This was the issue in which — through an enigmatic and unexplained illustration — Ruskin announced her death.[18] The Guild was a Christian enterprise, but Rose may well have thought that plain Christianity needed no modification from Ruskin. Probably the matter was not discussed. In their Tyburnia days Ruskin had ceased to criticise Evangelicalism. Their situation was too delicate for argument. Ruskin realised that Rose would go to the grave with her religious views intact, so he listened to her prayers and admonitions, however shrill, and recited with her the words of her best-loved hymns, however banal. Perhaps in reaction to such devotions Ruskin, considering the Guild of St George, began to imagine himself not only as its master but also as its bishop. Now begins a theme in Ruskin's public life that was painful to all his friends and admirers. Through *Fors Clavigera* he began to 'challenge' English bishops on theological and social matters. The *Fors* of April 1875 gives an autobiographical background to this assumption of episcopal status. Ruskin declares how his mother 'as she afterwards told me, solemnly devoted me to God before I was born: in imitation of Hannah'. He goes on to recount how a family friend, talking to his father, surmised that he might have been a clergyman if he had not turned to art criticism. '"Yet", said may father, with tears in his eyes — (true and tender tears — as ever father shed), "he would have been a Bishop"'.[19]

This story, reprinted from *Fors* in the early pages of *Præterita*, gained an undeserved authority in subsequent biographies. John James and Margaret Ruskin never thought that their son might have a career within the Church and they did not lament that he became a writer. The evidence suggests that Ruskin was gripped by the idea of a bishop's role in English life as he devised, or rather imagined, his Guild. In the New Year of 1875 his thoughts were all the more occupied with Guild matters because, once again, he found himself unequal to the task of preparing and delivering a course of Oxford lectures. Properly, he thought of resignation. Henry Acland persuaded him to take another leave of absence. As things turned out, Ruskin scarcely lectured at Oxford for years to come. In November of 1875 he talked about Sir Joshua Reynolds. In October of 1877 he gave his perfunctory 'Readings in *Modern Painters*'. Then there were no more addresses to the University before he resigned the Slade chair in 1879. In these four years, however, Oxford remained a base for Ruskin's activities and the seat of his intellectual fame. He kept his title and his rooms in Corpus Christi. Though he made no new friends among the undergraduate body, he enlarged his acquaintance in Oxford society. He had no specific role in its teaching or government but he was still one of the great men of the University.

It was the more unfortunate, therefore, that when Ruskin chose to attack or 'challenge' the English bishops he should have chosen to do so from Oxford and that the Bishop of Oxford should be specifically mentioned as one of his opponents. In the *Fors Clavigera* of January 1875, entitled (from Jeremiah) 'From the Prophet Even Unto the Priest', and written immediately after Rose had returned to Ireland and the tender Tyburnia days were terminated, we find these passages:

> The work of the Evangelist was done before they could be made Bishops; that of the Apostle cannot be done on a Bishop's throne: there remains to them, of all possible office of organisation in the

Church, only that of the Pastor, — verily and intensely their own; received by them in definite charge when they received what they call the Holy Ghost; — 'Be to the flock of Christ, a shepherd, not a wolf; — feed them, devour them not'.

Does any man, of all the men who have received this charge in England, know what it *is* to be a wolf? — recognise in himself the wolfish instinct, and the thirst for the blood of God's flock? For if he does not know what is the nature of a wolf, how should he know what it is to be a shepherd? If he never felt like a wolf himself, does he know the people who do? . . .

Dares any one of them answer me — here from my college of the Body of Christ I challenge every mitre of them: definitely, the Lord of St Peter's borough, whom I note as a pugnacious and accurately worded person, and hear of as an outspoken one, able and ready to answer for his fulfilment of the charge to Peter: How many wolves does he know in Peterborough — how many sheep? — what battle has he done — what bites can he show the scars of? — whose sins has he remitted in Peterborough — whose retained? — has he not remitted, like his brother Bishops, all the sins of the rich, and retained all those of the poor? — does he know, in Peterborough, who are fornicators, who thieves, who liars, who murderers? — and has he ever dared to tell any one of them to his face that he was so — if the man had over a hundred a year?

. . . the last character in St Paul's enumeration, which Bishops can claim, and the first which they are bound to claim, for the perfecting of the saints, and the work of the ministry, is that of the Doctor or Teacher.

In which character, to what work of their own, frank and faithful, can they appeal in the last fifty years of especial danger to the Church from false teaching? On this matter, my challenge will be most fittingly made to my own Bishop, of the University of Oxford. He inhibited, on the second Sunday of Advent of last year, another bishop of the English Church from preaching at Carfax. By what right? Which of the two Bishops am I, their innocent lamb, to listen to? It is true that the insulted Bishop was only a colonial one; — am I to understand, therefore, that the Church sends her heretical Bishops out as Apostles, while she keeps her orthodox ones at home? and that, accordingly, a stay-at-home Bishop may always silence a returned Apostle? And, touching the questions which are at issue, is there a single statement of the Bishop of Natal's, respecting the Bible text, which the Bishop of Oxford dares to contradict before Professor Max Müller or any other leading scholar of

> Europe? Does the Bishop of Oxford himself believe every statement in the Bible? If not, — which does he disbelieve, and why? . . .[20]

The Bishop of Oxford's attitude to Colenso, still Bishop of Natal, had stung Ruskin to an attack that is reminiscent of his letters to the Reverend J. Llewelyn Davies a decade earlier. However, it is obvious that Ruskin's condemnation of the whole bench of bishops had a universal rather than a personal application. It was directed toward the nature of English devotion. Ruskin called this letter his 'Clergyman's Fors' and thought it a sequel to the 'Squire's Fors' that had accompanied the Hinksey diggings. Ruskin worried that he might offend such family friends as the conservative Richmonds and Harvey Goodwin, the Bishop of Carlisle, who in later years was to be a visitor at Brantwood and close to the Severns: but he did not worry so much as to temper his writing. It was fortunate that his wild desire for theological debate existed in a vacuum. Few of the bishops or other clergymen who were regularly abused in *Fors* responded to Ruskin's goadings. If they did, they were usually relieved to let matters rest after his malevolent ripostes in the 'Notes and Correspondence' section of his monthly letter. *Fors* disturbed the Severns, Norton, the Richmonds, Acland, but not the consecrated men of God. In Oxford Ruskin was surrounded by eminent clergymen: all the heads of houses, the canons of Christ Church, college chaplains and many more. None of them expressed interest in the theological views of the Slade Professor. In August of 1875 Ruskin reissued his 1851 pamphlet *Notes on the Construction of Sheepfolds*. A new preface stated that he saw little reason to change his views on church government but that his current observations on the role of bishops were to be found in *Fors*. The republication went unnoticed.[21] Having finished his 'Clergyman's Fors' Ruskin went to Brantwood for Christmas. He stayed there a month, then left for a short driving tour in Derbyshire and Yorkshire before returning to Oxford at the end of January. In these northern counties he travelled through snowstorms that lashed the moors and industrialised valleys. Ruskin made some geological notes and prepared the lecture on glaciers he was to give at the Royal Institution on 11 March (attended by the loyal Wedderburn, who worried that he might never hear another Ruskin lecture at Oxford). The gist of this lecture became Chapters 2–4 of *Deucalion*, issued by George Allen in October 1875.

We must now describe the last months of Rose La Touche's life on earth. She would die on 25 May 1875. In this book, Rose was last seen on 14 December 1874, when she visited Ruskin's childhood home, the Severns' house on Herne Hill. More could be written about Rose's thoughts and movements if more were known. We rely on slender but sometimes important pieces of information. For instance, one letter tells us that a marriage had been contemplated, though surely not planned, in the autumn of 1874, when Ruskin and Rose talked in their Tyburnia hotel rooms. The letter was from Joan to Ruskin. It escaped her later notice. After Ruskin's death, had Joan been shown her note — which is hastily written on tissue paper — she would have burnt it or deleted the references to Rose. In the autumn of 1874 Joan told her cousin about a visit to their family dentist, Mr Woodhouse, who had a practice in Mayfair and cared for both the Ruskin family and, when she was in England, Rose. Woodhouse is a friend to biography because he was a gossip and asked direct, indiscreet, questions. Joan reported to Ruskin

> I have just returned from Mr Woodhouse where I was put to much discomfort! — he is looking forward with great joy to seeing you — he talked a little about R. who goes to him again beginning of Nov. — He thinks her very clever & charming — & is much interested! — & asked if it was to be Platonic or otherwise. I told him that was not yet certain — He fears you'll find her a *worry* if its the 'otherwise!' — but I told him that you were well prepared for all that . . .[22]

This letter was held in a packet (marked 'undated letters') that was put aside in Brantwood and remained unopened for many years. Other letters in the same packet are also from Joan to Ruskin and can be dated to the autumn of 1874. They confirm that the elder La Touches had abandoned their opposition to meetings between Ruskin and their ailing daughter. Telling Ruskin of a message from Mrs La Touche, Joan wrote to Ruskin 'she wishes very much Rosie would go & stay with a nice Dr. at Kensington — & "some people" could see her there as much as some people and other people pleased, without involving either these people or those people'.[23] We see that 'some people', Rose's evasive appelation for Ruskin, had been extended by Maria La Touche to include herself and her husband. Joan gave Ruskin further reassurances about Rose's independence. 'I hope all will now go well with you & R. for I think she has it in *her* power to do what she likes, without opposition from her father and mother . . .'[24] Another letter from this overlooked packet of correspondence tells us a little more about Rose's health: 'she's quite sure that there's no disease either in her stomach, or her breast — but gave me broad hints that it was all because she hadn't *you*, that she was ill!'[25]

The elder La Touches had often said that Ruskin's attentions contributed to Rose's fits of nervous exhaustion. This is believable. Yet Rose's difficulties with Ruskin do not explain all her illnesses, which remained mysterious. Many doctors through many years had tried to help her, and had failed. It seems that nobody knew what was wrong with Rose, nor how to treat her. No medical person (as far as is known) enquired whether her physical symptoms were connected with her desire to be ever more pious. Rose's constant changes of mood and rearranged plans had irked Ruskin and may have confused her doctors. Earlier in the year Ruskin had written to Carlyle, who knew much about Ruskin but very little about Rose, that

> — the girl whom I've been so long devoted to had to come to London, very nearly dying — at the best in great danger — half mad and half starved — (and eating nothing but everything she liked — chiefly sugar almonds I believe) — Well, she had to be forbidden food & I don't know what, and,
>
> . . . She's been physically and gravely ill; — wanted to see Joan — and not to see me . . .[26]

For years now, ever since his proposal of marriage in 1866, Ruskin had lived with such alternations. Rose wished to see him or she did not wish to see him. She loved him or did not love him, since she gave all her love to God. There had been long periods when Ruskin had not set eyes on Rose and times when he feared that she hated him. He had been continually anxious about her health. He had been exasperated, sometimes to the point of fury, by her religious enthusiasm and chilly dogma. Yet Ruskin had also allowed himself to hope. He imagined that one day he might be married to Rose. He also thought that she would mature, be less unstable, and more prepared to listen to reason or argument. Such were Ruskin's hopes, and they were in vain. All through 1874 Rose's physical and mental condition deteriorated. There had been precious moments of tenderness during their Tyburnia days. But that may have been because Rose was too weak to quarrel.

She was, however, able to travel. Almost to the end of life Rose indulged her habit of going from one place to another, one hotel to the next, one nursing home to a more attractive nursing home. On 15 December 1874 she left London for Harristown. Ruskin sensed the collapse of her mind and her death. As Rose returned to Ireland he wrote to Joan,

> I fear there is no hope of any help now, for poor Sweet-briar; — I have had much talk with her, & perceive her entire being to be undermined. The insane *cunning* is the thing that thwarts me beyond my power; her naturally keen and delicately truthful nature being turned exactly wrong side out — like a cyclamen leaf — only that curls its right side out, the moment it's long enough, — but my poor briar-rose will only drop the blighted leaves, one by one.[27]

It is not clear why Ruskin now spoke of Rose's 'insane *cunning*'. She may not have told Ruskin that she was going to Ireland the day after her visit to Herne Hill. He had hoped that she would stay there rather than live in hotels and clinics. Ruskin also feared that Rose would be upset by a return to Harristown and Irish doctors. His apprehensions were justified. Rose's health worsened as soon as she was home. She wrote to Mrs MacDonald: 'You see I am at home now — but I am sorry to say I am less well than ever'.[28] Now Rose clearly saw the approach of death and seems to have wished to die, for she added 'My only hope is for the time when I shall have "shuffled off this mortal coil" — but that may be a long way off.'[29] During the Christmas holiday John La Touche gave his daughter into the hands of an Irish physician. On 28 December Ruskin wrote to Charles Eliot Norton that he had received a letter 'in pencil from poor Rose — praying me to deliver her from her father — (who has driven her mad and is shutting her up with a Doctor in Dublin.) — I am of course helpless . . .'[30]

In these circumstances Ruskin completed his 'Clergyman's Fors', the January letter of his series. In this *Fors* he lamented, 'the woman I hoped would have been my wife is dying'.[31] It is surprising that Ruskin managed to write anything; but the enterprise of *Fors Clavigera* went on, he continued his various studies and on 31 December wrote in his diary, 'Last day of a fruitful year. I very well on the whole, thank God.'[32] Ruskin had now returned to Brantwood where, amid black and stormy Lakeland weather, he heard more bad news from Ireland. The February *Fors* describes some of his unhappy walks and local charities that gave happiness to his rural neighbours. This *Fors* also contains further plans for the Guild of St George. Ruskin worked in various ways to keep his mind from Rose, but the thought of her was always within his mind. Then, toward the end of January, Rose travelled to London for the last time. Ruskin left Brantwood to make a brief call at Oxford, no doubt to consult Henry Acland, before arriving at Herne Hill on 3 February, 'very broken in will and thought'.[33]

It is not known where in London Rose was then being treated, nor do we know how often Ruskin was able to see his beloved this early February. It may have been more than once, for only Ruskin was able to calm her. Many years later he recalled their last encounter:

> Of course she was out of her mind in the end. One evening in London she was raving violently till far into the night; they could not quiet her. At last they let me into her room. She was sitting up in bed; I got her to lie back on the pillow, and lay her head in my arms as I knelt beside it.
>
> They left us, and she asked me if she should say a hymn, and she said 'Jesus, lover of my soul' to the end, and then fell back tired and went to sleep. And I left her.[34]

Ruskin did in truth leave her and lost all hope. On 28 February he wrote to George MacDonald, 'Poor Rose is entirely broken — like her lover, and what good there may be for either of us must be where Heaven is — but I don't know that much of the Universe . . .'[35] He made no more attempts to be with Rose because her mind had failed. Many accounts of Rose tell us that her life ended in 'madness'. This cannot be verified and we do not know what the 'madness' might have been; but if Rose had still been able to hold any kind of conversation with Ruskin then surely he would not have left her side. In despair, he went from London to Oxford, then returned on 11 March to give his lecture on glaciers, later a part of *Deucalion*, at the Royal Institution. By early April Rose had been taken back to Dublin. Ruskin wrote to their mutual friend Mrs Barnard (who often appears as 'Claribel' in his correspondence)

> About my Rose — . . . She is very ill — I believed — when I wrote, 'dying' — that there was no hope for her — her mind is dead already — forms of selfish sorrow — reaching to what I cannot call less than insanity — having possessed themselves of her — except that her old self sometimes shines out in sweet hidden flashes — She has come to me — and gone from me again — now three times — this last autumn in London has taken more of my life out of me than — as far as I know — was, or is, left — but I am perhaps under physical depression from the severe winter more than I know. She is now placed by her people under some restraint with a physician in Dublin and, I hear, recovering health of body.[36]

This letter was written on 11 April. In the next month Ruskin travelled to and fro between Herne Hill and Oxford. The diary records some of his last visits to the Hinksey diggings. In Oxford he saw

Prince Leopold and briefly interrupted his University engagements to visit his young friend Dawtry Drewitt at Arundel. Among his guests at Corpus Christi were Burne-Jones and William Morris. Alexander Wedderburn, who saw Ruskin at Corpus on the same day as 'Ned' and Morris, 'made me very happy by telling me I was gaining influence with the men'.[37] Wedderburn also pleased Ruskin by reciting, by heart, the end of the second chapter of *Unto This Last*. Perhaps because they had heard of Ruskin's troubles, or sensed his distress, friends of all sorts gathered around him. In London, these tender people included Cardinal Manning, the Simons, Coventry Patmore and the poet Jean Ingelow (whom Ruskin never met very often but who has an honoured place in a list of 'old and tried friends' in *Fors Clavigera*).[38] Ruskin saw Carlyle more than once and made records of his conversation. He was at the Crystal Palace and the Royal Academy. These movements and engagements can be traced from Ruskin's diary. Then the record ceases. A page was cut from the daily journal, almost certainly by Ruskin himself. It recorded his life in the week that Rose La Touche died. Ruskin did not destroy the cut page but placed it among other papers. At some time in the 1960s the page was found in the archives at Bembridge School and was reunited with the diary.[39]

The previously missing page records 24–8 May 1875, a Monday to a black Friday. On the 24th Ruskin went from Herne Hill to Oxford. The next day he gave a breakfast party for 'nice boys', no doubt Hinksey diggers, in his rooms in Oxford.[40] This was the morning when (at 7 a.m.) Rose died in a nursing home in Dublin. On this day, 25 May, Ruskin left Oxford for Aylesbury in Buckinghamshire, a pleasant drive of some twenty miles through the Vale of Thame, and established himself at the George Inn at the top of the market square, looking down on the church. Aylesbury was a small rural town whose main employer was the printing firm of Hazell & Watson. Ruskin was staying for a week because he liked to talk with the firm's head printer, Henry Jowett. Ruskin spent some time at his works. Then a short walk took him into the countryside and 'an old English road 41 miles from London — all hawthorn and nightingales'.[41] The next day, Thursday of that week, Ruskin again visited the printing works, where he may have seen his latest *Fors Clavigera* go to press, and went for more country walks. On the morning of Friday the 28th a telegram arrived telling him of Rose's death. This was the morning when, after a funeral service at St Patrick's church in Carnalway, Rose's body was placed in the La Touche mausoleum within the Harristown grounds. Writing to Joan Severn after the news had come, Ruskin told her that he could not find the right thing to say in a telegram to Rose's parents, 'except — that it is best so . . . Of course I have been long prepared for this — but it makes me giddy in the head at first . . . don't write about it to me.'[42] Ruskin also wrote to Susie Beever that morning: 'I've just heard that my poor little Rose is gone where the hawthorn blossoms go.'[43] In Ruskin's mind the hawthorns of the Vale of Thame were ever afterwards associated with Rose's end. In the diary Ruskin drew a cross for his entry of 28 May, and a month later drew two hawthorn leaves at either side of the entry for 25 May, Rose's death-day.

CHAPTER THIRTY-FOUR

1875–1876

On Friday, 28 May Ruskin left Aylesbury and returned to Oxford. There were arrangements for him to meet royalty at the University. On Saturday the 29th he was to greet Prince Leopold and his sister Princess Alice and show them the drawing schools. They would be accompanied by the Princess's husband, the Grand Duke of Hesse. 'Giddy in the head' and almost dumb with personal misery, Ruskin spent much time with the royal visitors.[1] There was much else for them to see in Oxford, but the main purpose of the occasion was to celebrate the drawing schools and their collections, which only Ruskin could explain. This Saturday had been set aside for the execution of a deed of gift, and Leopold, Alice and the Grand Duke were to be its witnesses. The deed was important to Ruskin's relations with the University; so, as Ruskin himself did, we must attempt not to think about Rose while briefly describing the provisions of this document. Ruskin was an important benefactor of the University of Oxford. As we have seen, he made a wonderful gift of Turner drawings to the University in 1861. In the summer of 1871, at Matlock, Ruskin had given Henry Acland a cheque for £5,000 in order to endow a Master of Drawing within the University. As soon as his professorship had begun in 1870, Ruskin had accumulated specimens and examples that were used in his lectures and drawing classes. Later, in 1871, he decided to make over to the University all such materials. These gifts could not be made without being listed and described. This helps to explain the catalogues that Ruskin drew up in the early 1870s, *The Standard and Reference Series* (1870, 1872), *The Educational Series* (1871, 1874) and *The Rudimentary Series* (1872). The deed of gift that was now executed, and was set forth in the *Oxford University Gazette* of 1 June 1875, superseded his previous deeds of gift. Essentially, Ruskin was making over the whole collection in the drawing schools to the University. It was to be known as the 'Ruskin Art Collection'. The £5,000 he had given to Acland would, in perpetuity, pay the salary of a 'Ruskin Master of Drawing'. These were generous arrangements. However, since only Ruskin could understand the purpose of his collections, or the principles of his instruction in drawing, it was likely that confusions and friction would follow.[2]

Duties to royalty helped Ruskin to cope with his grief. Other matters occupied him in the first month of his bereavement. Only a few days after Rose died he completed the 'Memorandum and Statutes of the Company of St George' and presented this material to the Ruskin family solicitors, Tarrant and Mackrell, of Walbrook in the City. Its prose is uncharacteristic. Ruskin had already prepared a 'sketch' of his society for a property lawyer recommended by Tarrant and Mackrell. The lawyer then rewrote his initial proposals. The final memorandum, together with footnotes and objections from its original author, printed in the 'Notes and Correspondence' section of *Fors Clavigera* of July 1875, was the first document to define the Guild of St George. Yet it was definitive only as a brief compact between Ruskin and his solicitors. Technically, Tarrant and Mackrell sought a licence from the Board of Trade in which the Guild or 'Company' might be registered with limited liability without the world 'limited' added to its name. Further description of Ruskin's dealings with the Board of Trade would not help us to understand the Guild. For it was never a fixed entity and was not an organisation with its own history until Ruskin ceased to direct its fortunes. In the 1870s and 1880s it was an expression of its master's interests and moods. Therefore it is best to study the Guild as a part of Ruskin's biography.[3] The basic premise of Ruskin's company was not controversial. Ruskin wished to be joined by good men and women who would be its 'Companions'. Their common aim was in the first place agricultural, to show 'how much food-producing land might be recovered by well-applied labour from the barren or neglected districts of nominally cultivated countries'.[4] Labourers on such land would be employed 'under the carefullest supervision with every proper means of mental instruction'.[5] So far, this was not an extravagant aim: it might have described the situation at Brantwood. But Ruskin's instinct was always to extend and elaborate. He thought that the Guild would one day number its adherents 'in myriads'. Nor was he primarily interested in his own Lancashire moorland. In the spring of 1872 he had envisaged that, within St George's Company,

> which shall be of persons still following their own business, wherever they are, but who will give the tenth of what they have, or make, for the purchase of land in England, to be cultivated by hand, as aforesaid, in my last May number, — shall be another company, not destructive, called of 'Monte Rosa', or 'Mont Rose', because Monte Rosa is the central mountain of the range between north and south Europe, which keeps the gift of the rain of heaven. And

> the motto, or watch-word of this company is to be the old French 'Mont-joie'. And they are to be entirely devoted, according to their power, first to the manual labour of cultivating pure land, and guiding of pure streams and rain to the places where they are needed: and secondly, together with this manual labour, and much by its means, they are to carry on the thoughtful labour of true education, in themselves, and of others. And they are not to be monks nor nuns; but are to learn, and teach all fair arts, and sweet order and obedience of life; and to educate the children entrusted to their schools in such practical arts and patient obedience; but not at all, necessarily, in either arithmetic, writing, or reading . . .[6]

Who would wish to ally themselves to such an enterprise, and what might have been their motives? Usually, one can analyse voluntary social groups by reference to things shared by their members: not only ideology but class, religious affiliation, profession and so on. The first Companions of St George are not easy to describe in this way. They were usually Ruskin's personal friends or admirers with whom he had some acquaintance. The Guild might have appealed to many more thoughtful Victorians, but for a number of reasons remained a small organisation. First, there was its evident impracticality. Secondly, Ruskin's suggestion (never in fact insisted on) that members should subscribe a tithe of their income and property could never have been attractive. Thirdly, the Guild was mysterious. If one sent a sum of money to Ruskin there was no tangible return, no clear account of the destination and use of such a subscription. As Ruskin said to one interested person, 'The money is given practically to me, and if I choose to throw it into the sea and say I thought it proper first to sacrifice to Neptune, the subscribers couldn't make me refund, nor the Trustees . . .'[7] Furthermore, the Guild could only be traced through *Fors Clavigera*, especially since, in the Guild's early days, its members did not even know each other's names. If a Companion wished to know what was being done in the name of St George, he or she would be obliged to turn to Ruskin's pamphlet; and there they would read more of his disappointments, or perhaps his flower studies, or perhaps his wanderings through Europe, than of his social endeavours. In any case, *Fors* ceased publication between 1878 and 1881, and these were just the years when the Guild's membership might have expanded.

Ruskin issued in all four lists of Companions of the Guild. The two latter lists are found in *Fors Clavigera* of Christmas 1883 and in the *Trustees' Report* of 1883, which was published as an appendix to the

Master's Report of 1884. The two earlier lists are found in the 'Notes and Correspondence' section of the issues of *Fors Clavigera* for January and February of 1876. These lists are of subscribers, and so present some difficulties. The adherents to the Guild, who are identified only by their initials, sometimes gave donations without wishing to become Companions. We are on surer ground when examining a fifth list, unpublished during Ruskin's lifetime. This is the 'roll' of members that (as Ruskin often announced) was kept in his rooms in Corpus Christi. This 'roll' was in fact a sheet of paper inserted in one of Ruskin's precious manuscripts, a tenth-century Greek Book of Lessons. The sheet is headed 'Names of the companions accepted, forming St George's Company, March 1876.' There follow thirty-two names.[8] All of them are identifiable. We recognise Coniston neighbours such as Susie Beever and Robert Somervell of Kendal, well known in 1876 for his opposition to railway extension in Lakeland; then there are former Winnington girls such as Dora Livesey and Frances Colenso; Joan Severn and George Allen (whose subscription further announced his campaign not to be regarded as a servant); the cork-cutter Thomas Dixon and the manufacturer Henry Larkin. Nearly half of these companions were women, a number of whom had some position, never grand, within education. Some names are missing from the 'roll'. Susan Scott, the first person to whom Ruskin wrote at length about his plans, was certainly a Companion. Ruskin's Oxford disciple Jamie Anderson was a Companion and in one year gave a sum of money to the Guild that might have been a tithe of his income. There may well have been other unregistered Companions in 1876, including the Guild's trustees William Cowper-Temple and Sir Thomas Acland. We conclude that Ruskin was not overly concerned with an accurate register of his followers. Nor did he mount any particular campaign to recruit Companions.

It is notable that, apart from Anderson, Ruskin's Oxford pupils were disinclined to become members of the Guild. W. G. Collingwood had an amusing anecdote about his unwillingness to serve, and Ruskin's cheerful trickery when attempting to recruit his loyal secretary to the wider cause of St George:

> A dozen years ago Mr Ruskin put into my hand one of the square bits of pure gold, which at the time he was planning (I don't know if the plan was fully carried out) to present to the Companions of St George — and an 'Apocrypha'. 'I thank you', I said, 'for the present'. 'No present', said he. 'This is the enlistment shilling and now you are to serve under St George: I have caught you with

guile!' All the same, I vowed no vows, paid no tithes, fasted not, nor renounced the world . . .[9]

Collingwood wrote this in (probably) 1895 in response to an enquiry from a member of the Guild, and 'a dozen years ago' therefore places the incident around 1882–1883. We are dealing with a quite long span of time. The Guild existed in Ruskin's mind from the time of his letters to Susan Scott in 1869 to his final collapse in 1889. Thus it was an important part of his life for twenty years. Ruskin was often accused of caprice. However, the longevity of many of his enterprises is notable. He had a steady interest in various schemes, even though his writing about them was episodic.

There are a number of books whose nature resembles the interior, imaginative existence of the Guild. *Proserpina* and *Deucalion*, like the Guild, should be regarded as long poetic projects whose end could not be foreseen or necessarily desired. In this respect they are also like the lives of creative or spiritual persons, and it was appropriate that Ruskin worked on his flower and stone studies in the aftermath of Rose's death. Significant parts of *Deucalion* were written at Cowley Rectory in June 1875, and of *Proserpina* at Brantwood in the late summer of that year.

* * * *

Deucalion may claim the longer ancestry. As John James Ruskin said of his son, 'From boyhood he has been an artist, but he has been a geologist from Infancy.'[10] Ruskin was a member of both the Geological Society and the Mineralogical Society and contributed technical articles to both the *Geological Magazine* and the *Geologist*. Geology is of course much discussed in *Modern Painters*. Ruskin's geological interests were continued in Oxford lectures, and some passages from these lectures were given a place in the writing that Ruskin began at Cowley. Other parts of *Deucalion* were derived from a lecture given at the London Institute on 11 March, 'The Simple Dynamic Condition of Glacial Action among the Alps', while the chapter on 'The Valley of the Cluse', written at Cowley in June, and therefore within the Oxford term, contains remarks that were evidently directed toward undergraduates.[11] Both *Deucalion* and *Proserpina* were at one point, in July 1875, conceived as educational manuals. They might, Ruskin thought, help students to a broader knowledge not only of botany and geology, but of myth. Hence the titles of the studies that he had 'ventured to dedicate to Proserpina and Deucalion':

> Why not rather to Eve, or at least to one of the wives of Lammech, and to Noah? asks, perhaps, the pious modern reader.
>
> Because I think it well that the young student should first of all learn the myths of the betrayal and redemption, as the Spirit which moved on the face of the wide first waters, taught them to the heathen world. And because, in this power, Proserpine and Deucalion are at least as true as Eve or Noah; and all four incomparably truer than the Darwinian theory . . .[12]

This is from the introduction to *Deucalion*, whose first six chapters were issued in parts — that is, not bound together — in October of 1875, in time for the new Oxford term. At this stage, therefore, Ruskin's writing on the subject of stones was part of his Oxford campaign against materialistic science. The same is true of *Proserpina*, as Ruskin conceived it this autumn. However, Ruskin did not feel that his botanical knowledge was complete. His study of flowers was 'tentative, much to be modified by future students, and therefore quite different from that of *Deucalion*, which is authoritative'.[13] *Proserpina* is a more personal and in obvious respects a more poetic endeavour than *Deucalion*. It had the same intellectual programme, which was to oppose Darwinism and to insist on the eternal value of myth; but most readers will remember Ruskin's flower book as a meditation on life and death.

Ruskin felt that he first became a serious botanist in 1842, when he made 'a careful drawing of wood-sorrel at Chamouni'.[14] None the less, such studies were put aside. It is surprising that *Modern Painters* is little concerned with flowers. Ruskin never explained this omission. We have already placed the origins of *Proserpina* in Ruskin's Alpine botanising with Constance Hilliard and Joan Agnew in the weeks after Pauline Trevelyan's death at Neuchâtel in 1866. Some more details should be added. The first chapter of the book, 'Moss', is dated 3 November 1866, but was not published at that time. 'Moss' should probably be associated with contemporary work on *The Queen of the Air*, though it found no place in that book. A few months after the publication of *The Queen of the Air* Ruskin was thinking in definite terms of a botany book, 'to be called *Cora Nivalis*, "Snowy Proserpine": an introduction for young people to the study of Alpine and Arctic wild flowers'. This plan (without explanation of the word 'Arctic' was announced in a letter to Charles Eliot Norton dated from Denmark Hill on 17 November 1869, three months after Ruskin's appointment to the Slade chair.[15] In the same letter Ruskin announced quite distinct and parallel work for his first lectures to a male undergraduate audience. It is therefore not certain that the 'young people' who were to be given *Cora Nivalis* were the undergraduates of 1870. *Proserpina*, as *Cora Nivalis* became, was probably intended as a gift for Rose La Touche. We know that Ruskin had associated Rose with the goddess Proserpine since at least the spring of 1866 and surmise that the book we now know as *Proserpina* is, at least in part, a literary elaboration of the flower language they once had shared.

In the course of life and death between 1866 and 1875 *Proserpina* became one of Ruskin's memorials to his love. In one passage of its eighth chapter, 'The Stem', prepared for press and published in 1876 but deliberately dated 25 May 1875, which was the day of Rose's death, we find this:

> I suppose there is no question but that all nice people like hawthorn blossom.
>
> I want, if I can, to find out to-day, 25th May, 1875, what it is we like it so much for: holding these two branches in my hand, — one full out, the other in youth. This full one is a mere mass of symmetrically balanced — snow, one was going vaguely to write, in the first impulse. But it is nothing of the sort. White, — yes, in a high degree; and pure, totally; but not at all dazzling in the white nor pure in an insultingly rivalless manner, as snow would be; yet pure somehow, certainly; and white, absolutely, in spite of what might be called failure, — imperfection — nay, even distress and loss in it. For every little rose of it has a green darkness in the centre — not even a pretty green, but a faded, yellowish, glutinous, unaccomplished green; and round that, all over the surface of the blossom, whose shell-like petals are themselves deep sunk, with grey shadows in the hollows of them — all above this already subdued brightness, are strewn the dark points of the dead stamens — manifest more and more, the longer one looks, as a kind of grey sand, sprinkled without sparing over what looked at first unspotted light. And in all the ways of it the lovely thing is more like the spring frock of some prudent little maid of fourteen, than a flower; — frock with some little spotty pattern on it to keep it from showing an unintended and inadvertent spot — if Fate should ever inflict such a thing! Undeveloped, thinks Mr Darwin, — the poor shortcoming, ill-blanched thorn blossom — going to be a Rose, some day soon; and, what next? — who knows? — perhaps a Paeony![16]

Did any of Ruskin's few readers look at Maytime blossoms with this paragraph in mind? Although *Proserpina* was in print, in pamphlet and then in collected form, and was available from George Allen, there is simply no record that anyone at all had any public reaction to his botanical book.[17] And yet we are looking at literature of a high, if unusual, order. The nature of Ruskin's writing has never been much examined.[18] His gifts to English literature go unnoticed for a number of familiar reasons. He was out of step with his times; he respected no literary genre; his interests were recondite; he very seldom wrote to entertain; he had few followers, if any: and his methods of publication were so unusual as to limit the circulation of his work. A further reason is that Ruskin scarcely ever considered himself as a literary man. He had no interest in Parnassus. He thought of himself only as a teacher in this world. Considering the 'poetic' nature of *Proserpina*, its air of privacy and its evident response to a great personal loss, we are reminded of an old question. Why did Ruskin give up poetry? A conventional answer is that his poetic impulse flowed into the broader streams of *Modern Painters*. This is true. It is also likely that Ruskin feared that his talent was limited to the 'cockney' verse so despised by his hero Byron. Furthermore, however, he was impressed by Walter Scott's example. Ruskin believed that Scott had renounced poetry because he realised that the world's sterner tasks were described, or undertaken, in prose.[19] At all events, just while he was writing the prose of *Proserpina* — in which a personal poetry is always present — Ruskin simultaneously thought of his duties, and especially 'St George's work', a phrase he now increasingly used to describe his activities, whether public or private.

* * * *

St George would soon lead Ruskin to found a museum in Sheffield, far from the ethos of Oxford. In May and June of 1875 he worked in his drawing schools, not with much tangible result. At the end of June Ruskin drove with Joan and Arthur Severn from Oxford to Brantwood. He had devised a long route (whose resonances will be found in the North Country themes of *Fors Clavigera*) that took them to Warwick, thence to Lichfield, Castleton and Wakefield; and then to Bolton Bridge, Settle and Hawes. They arrived at Brantwood on 8 July and Ruskin was now to spend a quiet two months in his Lakeland home. There he completed one of the more successful parts of his Oxford teaching. At one of the open breakfasts at Corpus Christi in the spring Ruskin had said that he wished for a new translation of Xenophon's *Oeconomicus*. It had been among his favourite books since the early 1860s, he explained, and Xenophon had influenced his thinking on modern economics, firstly because of the pastoral and domestic nature of the treatise. Two Balliol undergraduates, Leonard

Montefiore and Alexander Wedderburn, volunteered for the work and began to study the Spartan philosopher. Montefiore soon decided that he was not enough of a classicist and handed over his part to W. G. Collingwood. By good fortune, Collingwood had access to a cottage on Lake Windermere (Gill Head, where he was later to live with his young family). There, during the long vacation of 1875, the two young men prepared their first draft of the translation of Xenophon's text. Then they took their copy over the fells to Brantwood and revised it under Ruskin's supervision.

Thus the enterprise resembled the 'reading parties' organised by a number of progressive Oxford dons from the 1870s onwards. As in other reading parties, the afternoons were spent in outdoor or manly exercises. Collingwood and Wedderburn laboured to build the new Brantwood harbour. This was beyond their powers, and the work was eventually completed by more professional hands. But the Xenophon was done. The two scholars thus gained a distinction that separated them from other undergraduates. Their work was published, with a preface by Ruskin, as *The Economist of Xenophon*, in July of 1876.[20] So they had made a notable contribution to classical studies by the time they took their degrees.

Collingwood and Wedderburn often stayed the night at Brantwood and would have heard Ruskin read from Walter Scott, for this was his favoured after-dinner recreation. Sometimes the readings were from Sir Walter's own manuscripts. Ruskin was making a collection of the holographs of the Waverley novels and also acquired a number of Scott's letters. They were usually bought from F. S. Ellis, another Brantwood visitor this summer, who was a partner in the publishing and bookselling business of Ellis & White. Frederick Ellis was associated both with literary Pre-Raphaelitism and with learning. He had published Swinburne and Rossetti. In 1864 Swinburne had introduced him to William Morris, who became a lifelong friend. Ruskin did not know Ellis well until the bookseller opened his New Bond Street shop in 1872. Thereafter he was especially attentive to the many drawings, prints, books and manuscripts that he knew Ellis to be selling to the British Museum. This had an influence on his own plans for a national collection. Relations between Ruskin and Ellis became closer as the dealer was enlisted in 'St George's work'. His function under this banner was to provide Ruskin with rare items that the Master of the Guild desired to place in St George's Museum, or in the projected schools of St George, or that (in the case of, for instance, Scott manuscripts) Ruskin simply wanted for himself. In the next dozen years Ruskin was to spend thousands of pounds with Ellis, expenditure that hastened his financial downfall. Joan Severn therefore distrusted Ellis. But his job was to sell, and he had a good sense of Ruskin's tastes. Ellis and Ruskin also had at least one prejudice in common. In 1872, in the back room, the 'chat-room' of Ellis's shop, they together put an edition of Goya's *Caprichos* to burn in an empty summer fireplace.[21]

At Brantwood in this summer of 1875 Joan was expecting her third child. Agnew Severn would be born in October. When Joan left for Herne Hill to prepare for her confinement Ruskin invited Arthur to accompany him on a short sketching tour in Yorkshire. Then, back at Brantwood for a few days between 19 and 22 September, he tidied books and papers and looked for a subject for his next course of Oxford lectures. He then returned to Yorkshire and gave an informal talk to workmen in Sheffield. This meeting gave impetus to the foundation of St George's Museum, to be discussed below. At the end of September Ruskin was at Lucastes. This was a country house near Haywards Heath in Sussex, the home of the physician James Oldham. His daughter Constance was a niece of Ruskin's boyhood friend Edmund Oldfield, Assistant Keeper of Antiquities at the British Museum. Constance was Ruskin's god-daughter and no doubt this is why she had been educated at Winnington. She is the 'May' of *The Ethics of the Dust*. The Hilliards were also staying at Lucastes. While his friends made a house party Ruskin retired to his room and did a little work on *Mornings in Florence*. Next he stayed briefly at Herne Hill. From his childhood home he drove to Carshalton to have lunch with the Tylor family. None of these movements, or those that were to follow in October, helped Ruskin with his grief. The diary is filled with reports of bad dreams and exaggerated descriptions of evil weather. He may have moved from house to house at this period in the hope of settling in a different location. A different home might help him to rebuild his life. Ruskin thought that he might give up Brantwood to the Severns, who so obviously wished to live there. His own Brantwood life had recently been disrupted. At the end of the summer Crawley's wife had succumbed to mental illness and Ruskin decided that his old valet should be given other work. A position was therefore created for him as a factotum in the Oxford drawing schools. Henry Acland arranged for the care of Mrs Crawley in an Oxford asylum.

Ruskin had an invitation to stay at Broadlands. He arrived there on 6 October, attended by the Swiss courier Klein, whose good nature had often been demonstrated in the previous year's tour through Italy. Once settled in the Cowper-Temples' house Ruskin sent to Brantwood for David Downs. As usual, a summons to his gardener meant that some impractical scheme was afoot. Though the details are not clear, it seems that William Cowper-Temple had offered Ruskin a couple of acres and one, or possibly two, cottages on the Broadlands estate. This may have been the same property that had been envisaged, not many years before, as a home for Ruskin and Rose after their marriage. It is possible that Cowper-Temple's gift had been offered to St George rather than to Ruskin personally. At all events, nothing came of the plan, though for a little while Ruskin thought that he might live at Broadlands. There he would be 'nursed' by the people who had witnessed so much of his painful love, in the days when his heart and mind were stronger. So far as he was able, Ruskin found enjoyment at the great house. Every day he gardened and did some drawing. In the kitchen he made models from domestic materials including napkins, sugar and flour, in illustration of his theories of Alpine glaciation. He should have been preparing his Oxford lectures, now announced in the University *Gazette* as 'Studies in the Discourses of Sir Joshua Reynolds', but they were neglected. Ruskin had always been able to work as he travelled between friends' houses, coaching inns and his own rooms in London, Oxford and Coniston. This autumn, however, he wrote much less than usual. We gather from *Fors Clavigera* that his thoughts tended more and more toward a museum in Sheffield. There is no sign that he thought about Sir Joshua.

Now he would not rest anywhere for more than a few days. Ruskin left Broadlands for another of his hospices, the rectory at Cowley. Connie Hilliard, his especial friend within the family, was away in Scotland, so Ruskin gave more attention than usual to her younger sister Ethel, often known as 'Ettie', and to their younger brother Laurence, 'Lollie', now in his twentieth year. When on holiday at Brantwood three years before, Laurence had shown that his love of boats and model-building was more important to him than his official purpose in life, which was to become an artist. He had not gone to university and was now too old to be living comfortably with his parents in the quite small rectory. It was probably during this visit to Cowley that Lollie's future was decided. He would go to Coniston, where a lodging would be found. He would paint; he could have a boat on Coniston Water: and he would also be employed as Ruskin's secretary, 'for St George's correspondence', and as a general assistant. Thus the circle of young men dependent on Ruskin was enlarged. Everyone liked Laurence Hilliard — 'a strange, bright, gifted boy', Collingwood recalled, '— admirable draughtsman, ingenious mechanician, marvellous actor; the inventor of the quaintest and drollest humours that ever entered the mind of man; devoted to boats and boating, but unselfishly ready to share all labours and to contribute to all diversions; painstaking and perfect in his work, and brilliant in his wit . . .'[22]

* * * *

Disinclined to commit himself to university life, Ruskin had no sooner arrived in Oxford in late October than he left Corpus Christi for his old and familiar lodgings at the Crown and Thistle in Abingdon. Social duties often kept him in Oxford: none the less he preferred to dine and sleep in an inn rather than a college. Though he kept his distance from university affairs Ruskin now became an even more famous Oxford figure. Alas, this was the result of his demeanour when delivering his lectures on Sir Joshua Reynolds. We may interpret these addresses from Ruskin's manuscript notes and contemporary reports. They were undignified and sometimes ludicrous. Ruskin was generally pleased with the reception of his unscripted lectures, but he did not realise that his audience had now been augmented by people who expected controversy. Serious undergraduates and many casual or curious members of his audience came to hear extravagant views and attacks on other Oxford dignitaries. One of these was George Rolleston, the Linacre Professor of Anatomy and Physiology, who a couple of years before had annoyed Ruskin when showing him a frog. The Slade Professor of Fine Art took his opportunity to criticise Rolleston and then rounded upon Huxley. 'Whatever you learn by dissecting frogs, and galvanising frogs, and so on will be false knowledge. You will come to say, as Huxley did say, "has a frog a soul?". And you will gradually think you and the nations have no soul but a frog's . . .'[23]

There were many such observations, interspersed with, for instance, readings from *The Pickwick Papers* and the Book of Revelation. Although a paragraph or two from Reynolds usually introduced each lecture, the addresses had little to do with Reynolds's thought. They were invitations to undergraduates to regard Ruskin as exceptional. 'I am, I believe, the only person here in Oxford who says he has got something entirely definite to teach'.[24] Ruskin often spoke of social matters. Political topics were treated in a manner that cannot have pleased political scientists, constitutional historians, or indeed any young person who might have looked forward to casting a vote: 'The British Constitution, of which you are so proud, — why, it is the vilest mixture of humbug, iniquity and lies that Satan ever spewed out of hell.'[25]

Ruskin was constantly advised by those who dared to advise him, principally Acland, to quieten such passages. He obeyed with the following:

> Teach no church catechism; teach only the Mosaic law and the love of God. It is a vice of mine, in the fear of not saying strong things strongly enough, to use a violence of language that takes from their strength; but this is my calm and cool conviction: I tell you, without a note of excitement in my voice or manner, in language of absolute and tamest moderation, as I stand quietly here with my arms hanging at my sides, unless you teach their children to honour their fathers and their mothers, and to love God, and to reverence their King and to treat with tenderness and take care of kindly all living creatures, to regard all things duly, even if they have only a semblance of life, and especially such as God has endowed with the power of giving us pleasure, as flowers — unless you teach your children these things you will be educating Frankensteins and demons . . .[26]

This is reported speech. Other parts of Ruskin's lectures we know to have been written before delivery:

> Or compare the roughest, cruellest Indian hunter, proud of squaw and scalp, laborious, dextrous, able with strength of his right hand at least to feed his squaw, to win his scalp; compare him with the modern youth of the civilised city — 'il ne faut que de l'argent' the one idea under his scalp — keeping his harlot from what he begs from his mother, dressing himself like a gentleman with what he filches from his employer, sodden, stupid, shameless, Godless, lifeless — a fanged but handless spider, that sucks, indeed, and swells, but cannot spin![27]

The above was delivered, according to one report, 'with an intensified sibillation that made the whole sentence a hiss'.[28] Ruskin's audience could not tell what strange thought, written or improvised, might come next. G. W. Kitchin, later Dean of Durham but in 1875 a student of Christ Church, gave this account of (probably) the second lecture in the series of twelve:

> His lectures testify to the brightness and originality of his mind in this later time. No one can appreciate their effect, unless he was so fortunate as to hear them. One saw the strange *afflatus* coming and going in his eye, his gestures, his voice. The lectures were carefully prepared; but from time to time some key was struck which took

> his attention from the page, and then came an outburst. In the decorous atmosphere of a University lecture-room the strangest things befell: and, for example, in a splendid passage on the Psalms of David (in a lecture on Birds) he was reminded of an Anthem by Mendelssohn, lately rendered in one of the College chapels, in which the solemn dignity of the Psalms was lowered by the frivolous prettiness of the music. It was 'Oh! for the wings' etc. that he had heard with disgust, and he suddenly began to dance and recite, with the strangest flappings of his M. A. gown, and the oddest look on his excited face . . . On another occasion I was present at one of his strangest utterances. It was at the Taylor Institution; a lecture on I forget what subject. Something brought up Evolution . . . and so he abandoned his subject, notes, professorial style; a new light of scorn and wrath gleamed, and he went like a terrier at the obnoxious theory. Amusement filled those who knew his ways; amazement those who did not . . .[29]

Kitchin's reminiscences were written for the sympathetic members of the Ruskin Society of Birmingham and were delivered at a meeting in 1900. A quarter of a century earlier, there were those in Oxford who felt less indulgent toward Ruskin's eccentricities. His lectures were attended by many senior members of the University. A number of them were annoyed when Ruskin's train of thought entered their own academic territory. What intellectual discipline did Ruskin himself represent? Obviously art had a history. Its history could be studied and taught. But Ruskin's teaching scarcely belonged to ordered thought and education. Therefore he lacked the primary academic virtues, however wonderful his writing and speech. It is not surprising that Ruskin gained no new followers in this new university year. Those who heard him lecture thought that he was a spectacle rather than an inspiration. Ruskin did not meet undergraduates. The open breakfasts at Corpus had ceased at about the same time as the Hinksey diggings. Students who went to the drawing schools were supervised by Macdonald rather than by Ruskin. For much of the Michaelmas term he was not in Oxford at all. Ruskin kept his distance in the Crown and Thistle, lodged in the sorrow of his bereavement.

Now he entered a more telling friendship with a man he had known vaguely for some time, a reclusive and bitter intellectual who had married a much younger woman. Mark Pattison had been the Rector of Lincoln College since 1861. In the same year Emilia Francis Strong, the daughter of an Oxford bank manager, became his bride. She was then twenty-one: Pattison was twenty-seven years her senior.

Ruskin had known Francis for some time. Since she was an Oxford girl her precocious drawings had been shown to Henry Acland, who sent them to Ruskin, who then recommended an art education. He had no part in her training, however, and Francis studied in a way of which he disapproved, at South Kensington. After her marriage, when the Pattisons were occasional visitors at Denmark Hill, Ruskin noted her independent mind. She did not at all resemble other young women whose artistic interests he had encouraged. Pattison had taught her the importance of the scholarly life. He helped her to become an art historian rather than an artist. She made a study of the art and architecture of the French Renaissance, a subject that coincided with some of her husband's interests. They both knew that she was no less capable than many a don, yet, by reason of her sex, Francis Pattison was excluded from much of university life. She called Oxford a 'hole'. By the time Ruskin took up his Slade chair she was not so much an old acquaintance as a formidable adversary. She reviewed his inaugural lectures, unfavourably, in the *Academy*, and in her criticisms allied herself with the aesthetic school: 'Art is neither religious nor irreligious, moral nor immoral, useful or useless; if she is interpreted in any one of these senses by the beholder, is she to bear the blame?'[30]

Mrs Pattison was indeed an aesthete, and was a friend of Pater's. Furthermore she spoke forcefully and sometimes in public about women's suffrage, and was attracted to Comtian positivism. All this Ruskin must have known. He was also aware that, in the summer of 1875, Mrs Pattison was living apart from her husband. In poor health, she had established herself in the south of France. It was at this point that Ruskin wrote to Pattison to offer his sympathy.

> I have just heard from Alice Owen that you are — for sorrowful cause, alone just now — and she thinks also — sorrowful in your own thoughts . . . Will you let me (for I *can*) care more for you — than I do for others, in that you have so much sympathy for me in thought — and now, which I did not before know — in sadness — and let me sometimes think that I can give you some little relief, in the assurance of my respectful affection . . .[31]

The Alice Owen mentioned here may be regarded as in many ways Mrs Pattison's opposite. She was pious, unintelligent and reverential. Another Oxford young woman, she had known Ruskin since about 1864, when he first encouraged her drawing. In 1873 she had contributed some papers on medieval art to Charlotte M. Yonge's *Monthly Packet*. 'Your editress is a very powerful and deadly form of charming bigot', Ruskin told her, evidently in a cross mood: 'her educational papers make me sick'.[32] But he was kindly disposed toward his old pupil and agreed to write a preface to a collection of Owen's articles. This explains his involvement with her *The Art Schools of Medieval Christendom*, published in 1876. Mrs Pattison, meanwhile, was in Nice, working on her first book, *The Renaissance of Art in France*, which was eventually published in 1879. By that date Mrs Pattison, later Lady Dilke, had disappeared from Ruskin's life. It is pleasant to record that in 1887 she sent him a copy of her imaginative fables *The Shrine of Death*, and in their ensuing correspondence addressed him as 'Dear Master'. Ruskin's response to the gift was that he felt

> entirely delighted — but more astonished than ever I was in my life by your pretty letter and profession of discipleship — why — I thought you always one of my terriblest, unconquerablest, antagonisticest — Philistine — Delilah powers! I thought you at Kensington the sauciest of girls — at Oxford the dangerest of Don-nas. When you sat studying Renaissance with me in the Bodleian I supposed you to intend contradicting everything I ever said about Art and History and Social Science . . . And here you come saying you have been learning of *me* . . .[33]

Ruskin was not equipped to understand the contemporary independent thought of such a person as Lady Dilke (as she had become, by the time of this letter). He believed in the certainties of past ages. Collingwood's and Wedderburn's work in preparing their version of *The Economist of Xenophon* was intended to have the first place in a series of essential books that Ruskin admired and wished to impress on other people. He thought of a 'shepherds' library', *Bibliotheca Pastorum*, 'classic books which I hope to make the chief domestic treasures of British peasants'.[34] This scheme generally belongs to 'St George's work' though, years before, in the lecture 'Of Kings' Treasuries' (1864) he had thought of 'a royal series of chosen books'.[35] A more immediate origin of *Bibliotheca Pastorum* is found in one of Ruskin's walks from Brantwood in the early spring of 1875. High above his home, beyond the 'brant' and the edge of the woods where moorland begins, lies the little stone house known as Lawson Park. Here lived the Stalker family: a shepherd, his wife, and their eleven children. As his accounts show, Ruskin helped the Stalkers with regular charity. In return, Mrs Stalker gave him cups of tea at her fireside. One day he was looking at the few little volumes read by the infant Agnes Stalker. Ruskin then, in *Fors Clavigera*, mused on the books that, in an ideal society, might be provided for 'our little Agnes of the hillside' and he thought of a uniform series of classic works to be placed in every village school. By November of 1875 the scheme was further advanced. The translation of Xenophon was to be the first of the books now projected as 'St George's Library'.[36]

The idea of a series of classics for English children and adults of all classes was more original in 1875 than it might appear today. The chosen books were also highly individual. They were to include the following: *The Economist of Xenophon*; Jeremias Gotthelf's *Ulric the Farm Servant* (the Ruskin family book that was so suggestive of Swiss journeys with his father and mother in the 1840s); a history of England after the Norman conquest, a life a Moses, a life and writing of David, a complete Hesiod; the first two *Georgics* of Virgil, together with the sixth book of the *Aeneid* and the first two books of Livy, to be published in one volume; Dante; Chaucer, including the doubtfully attributed *Chaucer's Dream* and the *Romance of the Rose*, with 'some French chivalrous literature of the same date', but excluding *The Canterbury Tales*; and St John the Divine.[37] Some notes must be added to this plan. The Xenophon was in good hands. Ruskin intended that the history of England should be written by Robert Laing, a younger Fellow of Corpus, who for reasons both aesthetic and Anglo-Saxon had taken the name Cuthbert Shields.[38] Nothing came of Shields's commission, but Ruskin invited his readers to observe that 'some of the lines of thought' that his Corpus friend might conceivably have followed were to be found in his 1884 lectures entitled 'The Pleasures of England'. A translation of *Ulric the Farm Servant* was eventually published in 1886–88. None of the other books on Ruskin's list (abstracted in the present account from *Fors Clavigera* of January 1876) saw publication.[39]

There are some other projects connected with *Bibliotheca Pastorum*. The thought of Agnes Stalker was responsible for his republication, in 1885, of *Dame Wiggins of Lee*, one of his best-loved childhood books.[40] Ruskin's editor E. T. Cook believed that his private translation of Plato's *Laws* was part of the general enterprise of *Bibliotheca Pastorum*. Ruskin had been translating Plato, at intervals, since at least 1866. A more concerted effort at translation was made between 1876 and 1880. Ruskin's version of the first two books of the *Laws* was completed and then copied out by a secretary, probably Collingwood, surely with a view to publication. Ruskin's text had to be transcribed because it is contained on the left-hand pages of the great ledger volume of his journal known as the 'Brantwood Diary'.[41]

Bibliotheca Pastorum is perhaps more to be associated with Brantwood than with Oxford, although it is certain that Ruskin's version of Plato was intended as a lesson for Benjamin Jowett, the Master of Balliol. Jowett's own translation of Plato's *Dialogues* was said to have made the ancient author into a contemporary English 'classic'. Ruskin's opinion (never published) was that Jowett's work on Plato was 'a disgrace'.[42]

Ruskin's feelings on these matters may be deduced from the May 1876 issue of *Fors Clavigera*, 'The Mount of the Amorites', which is largely concerned with the translation of Genesis, and again from the *Fors* of October 1877, the only place in which we find a public demurral from Jowett's interpretations. Ruskin held back from criticism of Jowett because so many of the Master of Balliol's most promising young men were also disciples of the Slade Professor. Jowett's pronouncement on Ruskin is well known. The Master found him 'a man of great sensibility, little sense', but he did not say this publicly.[43] The quotation comes from Walter Sichel's much later *The Sands of Time* (1923). Sichel, a Balliol undergraduate in the early 1870s, was a close friend of Alexander Wedderburn's but not a follower of Ruskin. His remarks on Jowett as a translator help us to understand Ruskin's attitude to another scholar labouring in the same field. 'His quality as a translator', Sichel wrote, 'enabled him to render Greek thoughts or records in English clear and transparent as cut crystal, and also to bring ancient philosophies and actions into an unbroken line with contemporary tendencies . . . though Plato formed the refrain of his life, there was little hellenic about him — none of the glow for beauty . . .'[44]

Ruskin probably knew that Jowett distrusted Carlyle, whom he believed to have had a bad influence on youth. This could have been embarrassing or worse; for Ruskin had given informal but probably memorable classes in Carlyle's writing, and these were attended by Balliol undergraduates. There was however no public dispute. Ruskin occasionally dined in Balliol and Jowett was a visitor at Brantwood as lately as 1884. Such relations were well-mannered. The many temperamental differences between Ruskin and Jowett were publicised in June of 1876 by W. H. Mallock, who had observed them both since he entered Balliol in 1870. Mallock was a clever, personable and flippant young man from a West of England family. The historian Froude was his uncle. Through Henry Acland (who kept up his Devon connections) Mallock had been introduced to Ruskin. 'The first thing in him which struck me', he recalled, 'was the irresistible fascination of his manner. It was a manner absolutely and almost plaintively simple, but that of no diplomat or courtier could be more polished in what was at once its weighty and its winning dignity . . .'[45]

This was probably in 1871. It is fair to say that Mallock became one of Ruskin's disciples, and for a time was close to him. He was not however the sort of follower who dug roads or volunteered to translate Xenophon. The precocious Mallock had a literary programme of his own. He wrote verse, but his main work was in a half-satirical examination of senior members of the University. This writing became the book we now know as *The New Republic*, subtitled 'Culture, Faith and Philosophy in an English Country House'.[46]

Mallock's book was long in the making, underwent many revisions and for some time was privately circulated in manuscript. It may at one stage have been more sardonic or impertinent, for Sichel recalled that he saw 'the manuscript of his *New Republic* in its unexpurgated form long before it could find a publisher'.[47] *The New Republic* may also have had a cultish following among certain undergraduates. Another contemporary, J. E. C. Bodley, records that 'there was at Balliol a gentle youth of my time, W. M. Hardinge . . . A disciple of Mallock, he used to recline on his sofa and recite to his friends pages of what he called mysteriously "Mallock's book"'.

We have already met Hardinge. He was the youth who had to leave Balliol because of, *inter alia*, his reputedly unwholesome relations with Pater. Hardinge probably was too little respectful of his tutors. Mallock certainly found a number of grander members of the University preposterous and devious, especially if they held liberal views on political and religious topics. Such dignitaries are the real targets of *The New Republic*, which is a comic but not a forgiving work. The book has three main sources, Plato's *Republic*, Petronius' *Satyricon* and Thomas Love Peacock's novels. It is in dialogue. Various identifiable figures, disguised only by invented names, discuss literature, religion, politics and art. We recognise Arnold, Pater, Jowett and Huxley, all of whom are ridiculed. There is only one person in the book of whom its author clearly approves. 'Mr Herbert' is unmistakably based on Ruskin, who is made to say,

> For, seeing how the work of the painter becomes essentially vile so soon as it becomes essentially venal, I was reminded of the like corruption of what is far more precious than the work of any painter — our own English girls, who are prepared for the modern marriage-market on precisely the same principles as our pictures for the Royal Academy . . .

And then,

> . . . how could I — who think that health is more than wealth, and who hold it a more important thing to separate right from wrong than to identify men with monkeys — how could I hope to be anything but singular in a generation that deliberately, and with its eyes open, prefers a cotton-mill to a Titian?[48]

The book first appeared in serial form. It was in the pages of the magazine *Belgravia* in the months after June 1876 — just the time when Collingwood and Wedderburn published their version of Xenophon. Not for a moment did Ruskin think that Mallock had the qualities he had elicited from his translators. But he was amused by Mallock's work. Jowett much disliked it, just as he had always disliked his nominal pupil.[49]

1. John Ruskin, *Self-Portrait*, 1861.

2. The croquet lawn, facing the Wyatt wing of Winnington Hall, *c.* 1861.

3. Undated photograph of Rose La Touche.

4. Julia Margaret Cameron, *Carlyle like a Rough Block of Michelangelo's Sculpture*, 1867.

5. Rose La Touche and her dog, Bruno, *c.* 1866.

6. John Ruskin, *Abbeville, Saint Wulfran, South Door of Western Porch*, 1868.

7. The Ruskin party in Venice, June or July, 1872. The photograph shows *(left to right)* Ruskin, Mrs J. C. Hilliard, Joan Severn, Arthur Severn, Constance Hilliard and Albert Goodwin.

8. John Ruskin, *Rose La Touche*, 1872.

9. Photograph of Ruskin seated on a bank near Brantwood, by Frank Meadow Sutcliffe, 1873.

10. Undergraduates building a road at Hinksey, Oxfordshire, 1874.

11. John Ruskin, *Self-Portrait*, 1874.

12. Lady Mount Temple, when Mrs Cowper-Temple, under the beech trees at a Broadlands conference, from a painting by Edward Clifford, *c.* 1876.

13. John Ruskin, *Study of Carpaccio's 'Dream of St Ursula'*, 1876–77.

14. Ruskin's study at Brantwood, photographed by Miss Brickhill.

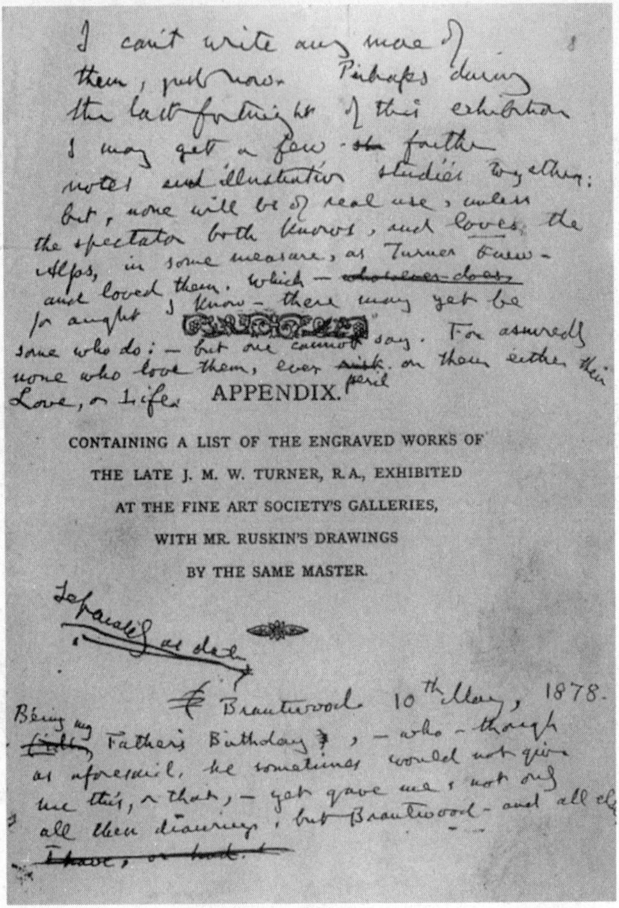
I can't write any more of them, just now. Perhaps during the last fortnight of this exhibition I may get a few further notes and illustration studies together: but, none will be of real use, unless the spectator both knows, and loves, the Alps, in some measure, as Turner knew and loved them. which — for aught I know — there may yet be some who do: — but one cannot say. For assuredly none who love them, ever peril on them either their Love, or Life.

APPENDIX.

CONTAINING A LIST OF THE ENGRAVED WORKS OF THE LATE J. M. W. TURNER, R.A., EXHIBITED AT THE FINE ART SOCIETY'S GALLERIES, WITH MR. RUSKIN'S DRAWINGS BY THE SAME MASTER.

Brantwood 10th May, 1878.

Being my Father's Birthday, — who — though as aforesaid, he sometimes would not give me this, or that, — yet gave me, not only all these drawings, but Brantwood — and all else

15. Ruskin's corrected proof of *Notes by Mr Ruskin on his Drawings of the late J. M. W. Turner*, 1878.

16. W. G. Collingwood, *John Ruskin in his Study at Brantwood*, watercolour.

17. Professor Charles Eliot Norton, probably in the 1880s.

18. John Ruskin and Henry Acland, 1893, photograph by Sara Acland.

19. Fred Hollyer, *Portrait of John Ruskin*, *c.* 1894.

20. Arthur and Joan Severn walking at Brantwood, *c.* 1920.

CHAPTER THIRTY-FIVE

1875–1876

In early December of 1875, as soon as he had delivered the last of his lectures on Sir Joshua Reynolds, Ruskin went to Herne Hill and then returned to Broadlands. For a little while his mind was calmer than it had been at Oxford. This we deduce from the large diary, begun in May of 1875, that he afterwards called the 'Broadlands book'.[1] In it we find, from 5 December, notes on the life of Moses, no doubt for his projected volume of *Bibliotheca Pastorum*, and readings of Mosaic law. Such meditations were now to be disturbed. Georgiana Cowper-Temple had invited a number of other house-guests. We hear of a Mrs Ackworth, a Miss Munro and a Mrs Wagstaff. They were spiritualists. Ruskin did not recall that this Mrs Ackworth was the Miss Andrews whom he had met when he was briefly swayed by spiritualism in the spring of 1864.[2] Mrs Ackworth knew something of Ruskin, however, and so did her friends. Mrs Wagstaff had been acquainted with Rose, no doubt through their mutual Broadlands connection. Miss Munro was the sister of the Pre-Raphaelite sculptor Alexander Munro, who had been Ruskin's friend since the 1850s. These women competed for Ruskin's interest. In years past, he had never really accepted spiritualism. It was so obviously less interesting than the Christianity on which it fed. But Ruskin always had some relish for the supernatural. We recall, for instance, his interest in ghost stories and the strange occasion when he dug a hole in search of a rumoured Swiss hobgoblin. Now Ruskin reported to Joan Severn that Mrs Ackworth 'sees all manner of ghosts about the house — and coolly told me one was standing beside me dressed in daisies the evening before last.[3]

Ruskin was credulous; and the three women, being professional spiritualists, knew how to lead him from smaller to greater revelations. He accepted that Miss Munro had seen 'little wingless angels when she was little, and now, she's exactly like St Francis, has tame butterflies! and makes them know their names!'[4] He confessed to Joan that he had become 'over-excited, over-puzzled' but assured her of the probity of his new friends. Mrs Ackworth she might have heard of through the Carter Halls, he thought: Samuel Carter Hall, the former editor of the *Art Journal*, had often visited Denmark Hill with his wife. Mrs Wagstaff was trustworthy because she was 'a doctor's wife, a noted clairvoyante — who uses her clairvoyance for illness only'. Ruskin told Joan that

> Phile had sent to say she wanted her so much to examine my cold — I said — it wasn't worth while but Phile *would* have it — so they came together . . . Well, just like a witch, as she is — Phile waved her hands for — certainly not more than twenty seconds, and sends the doctor's wife into a trance, in which she can see all through one, and out again — it seems — for she told me all about myself — with absolute accuracy; answering any questions I liked to put to her . . .[5]

Mrs Wagstaff then offered to examine Ruskin's drawings with her eyes shut, and to relate the artist's temper at the time of drawing them. Ruskin found her comments convincing. He then put one of Rose's letters into her hand. 'Presently she put it away as with great pain; on being asked to look more went on, and gave a complete analysis of the life — saying this most marked thing at last — that she had from her childhood the habit of being cruel — to those she loved best, — but that she did love intensely, that it was a form of disease belonging to one division of brain — and quite special and definite . . .'[6]

There was a week of such activities. Presumably they were tolerated, if not actually promoted, by Georgiana Cowper-Temple, who in this instance was more hospitable than wise. The spiritualists took advantage of Ruskin's bereavement. He was finally prepared to believe that Rose herself — the ghost of Rose herself — had been seen by Mrs Ackworth, of whom he recounted:

> Yesterday evening, there was some talk between her, Miss Munro, Mrs Wagstaff, the doctor's wife, and me about the relative loyalty of men and women to each other. I was maintaining that men, when good, were the truer of the two, and with some heat. Well — this afternoon — there were only Miss Munro and Mrs Ackworth — and I was holding a skein of worsted for Miss Munro in the drawing room — and I said to Mrs Ackworth — Have you seen any spirits these two last days. Oh yes, says Mrs Ackworth — there was one close to you when you were talking about men and women — last night. What kind of one, said I. 'Fair, very tall & graceful, — she was stooping down close over you, as if she were trying to say something — and there was another with her'.
>
> Why didn't you tell me — said I —
>
> 'Well said Mrs Ackworth — there were other people in the room. — I couldn't make any sign to you — I did not know that you would have liked it.'

Have you seen her before, I said —

— Yes, she came into the room with Mrs Temple all day but she has only been here for about a week'

How young? I said.

'— Oh — very young — I asked her whether she had been married, and she said "no"

— You asked her? I said

Yes — I signed to her partly — but I could not talk much to her — I think she has not been long in the spirit world — not a year perhaps, — and she can't speak yet — much

— You said she wanted to speak to me?

— Yes: she seemed to be pained by what you were saying. — to try to stop you

— As if what I said was wrong? I said

'— No — as if she was sorry for some wrong in herself

— She put her hand to her head — She does that very often'.

What was the other like, who was with her.

'I did not see her much, I think she was older'

— I was going to ask more, but people came into the room.

All this was told me just as quietly as if she had been saying the servant had been in to draw the curtains! Di wee ma — I *have* been 'hearing Moses and the prophets'. — surely I may have my little ghost?[7]

Now another visitor arrived. George MacDonald had not only known Rose; it had been through his work that Ruskin and Rose had enjoyed their magical reunion at Broadlands in 1872. Although MacDonald was of a mystical turn of mind he was not a spiritualist. He wrote to his wife: 'There is a Mrs A. here. I don't take to her much, but Ruskin is very much interested . . . She has seen and described, without ever having seen her, Rose whispering to Mr Ruskin. He is convinced.'[8] This appears to have been so. But it is not easy to state the nature of Ruskin's conviction. After all, the spiritualist was not wiser than the Master of the Guild of St George. Ruskin surely acquiesced to Mrs Ackworth's suggestions through longing, as we gather from the plaintive tone of his appeal to Joan, 'surely I may have my little ghost?'[9]

This was a turning point in his emotional life. Ruskin's grief over Rose's death became a desire for her spirit. With this desire in his heart and mind he left Broadlands for Lucastes. There he spent Christmas with Dr Oldham and his family. It was a cheerful place for Ruskin to rest, all the brighter because his god-daughter Constance Oldham invited another old Winnington girl, Isabel Marshall ('Isabel' of *The Ethics of the Dust*), to come to see him. These pleasant young women did not divert Ruskin from the thought, and indeed the pursuit, of his ghost. Lucastes was conveniently situated for Brighton, where Dr Oldham had his practice. Ruskin went to the seaside town to call on Miss Price, Rose's aunt, who now lived there. In the times of her greatest difficulties with Ruskin and her parents, Rose had occasionally stayed at Miss Price's Tunbridge Wells home. Ruskin found her 'a quiet maiden lady, now very grey and calm in age — withdrawn always from all the anger and error of the rest of her family — . . .',[10] and in her company he felt a benign spiritual grace. They talked of the power of prayer and of the way that Rose had prayed for Ruskin. It is likely that, as a result of this meeting, Miss Price assisted in the return to Ruskin of some precious items: letters that Rose had written to him from her childhood onwards, and a tress of her hair. These of course had once been in Ruskin's hands, but he had sent them back to Rose after the scene at Crewe railway station. To possess them once again was like a reconciliation after death, and henceforward they were to be among the first relics of Ruskin's private religion of Rose.

Pleased by his encounter with Miss Price, Ruskin left Lucastes for a further round of visits to friends' houses. In early January he was at Peppering, near Arundel, the home of Dawtrey Drewitt. Readers of *Præterita* will find this name in an obscure paragraph of its 'Crossmount' chapter. The passage names three young men for whom Ruskin felt especial friendship. The other two were Collingwood and Wedderburn. Drewitt is commended for being able to stand on his head and for a facility in catching vipers by their tails. This was a shared joke (as are a number of other descriptions of living people in Ruskin's autobiography). When he and Ruskin first met, probably in 1871, Drewitt kept snakes in his Christ Church rooms. He was then about to leave the University, so was not of the generation who knew Ruskin at the height of his Oxford influence. In any case Drewitt may not have been interested in the discussion of medieval art and social problems. He was a keen natural historian, a landowner and a sportsman. So, surprisingly, on 5 January 1876 Ruskin followed the hounds in Drewitt's local hunt. He remained at Peppering for a week, surrounded by country pursuits, and then for the rest of January was in London. He went to see Maskelyne and Cooke, conjurors at the Egyptian Hall in Piccadilly, and visited the Crystal Palace more than once. Ruskin did not entertain at Herne Hill because he was careful not to disturb the Severns' arrangements. Instead he made many visits in town. He saw Wedderburn, Frederick Gale (who was married to Arthur Severn's sister Claudia), Burne-Jones, Carlyle, Froude, the

Simons and Jean Ingelow. It was probably during this period that Ruskin had some of his most thoughtful conversations with another friend, Cardinal Manning. The two men had met through the Metaphysical Society. When he described the Cardinal to the Presbyterian Joan Severn, Ruskin made light-hearted remarks about Catholicism. In fact, however, he was moved by Manning's intelligence and faith. Manning, for his part, appreciated Ruskin's extraordinary gift for making literature out of his personal and intellectual turmoil. He is one of the few contemporaries we can find who appreciated *Fors Clavigera*. 'It is like the beating of one's heart in a nightmare', he wrote to Ruskin.[11] This may not have been what Ruskin wished to hear about his teaching in *Fors*, but at least the simile told him that he had touched another heart.

It is possible that Manning felt that Ruskin might become a convert to Roman Catholicism. Ruskin, who was quite happy to use the word 'catholicism' about his beliefs, wrote a quite fierce letter to the Cardinal to describe the differences between them. 'You do not separate yourselves heroically', he declared (referring to 'the Catholic Hierarchy'), 'from the rich, and powerful, and wicked of this world, but entangle yourselves in their schemes, comply with their desires, and share with them in the spoils of the poor. So I believe the existing Hierarchies of Christianity must perish — and the King Himself, in some way we dream not of, come to possess His people in peace.'[12]

Perhaps Manning had not read *Fors* attentively enough to realise that he would be thus rebuked. In its pages, however, he certainly noted the wide-ranging and cultured nature of Ruskin's spirituality. Alas, that intelligent spirituality could also be foolishly erratic, as in his relations with Mrs Ackworth. At the end of January 1876 Ruskin returned once more to Broadlands. There he was greeted by so-called messages, one from Turner, that Mrs Ackworth had intercepted on his behalf. On 2 February, the tenth anniversary of his marriage proposal, Ruskin hoped that Rose's spirit might reappear. 'But she didn't', he told Joan. None the less Mrs Ackworth was able to report to Ruskin that she had seen the ghost of Rose, 'looking quite happy'.[13]

Ruskin had suspicions, but on this visit to Broadlands he was reassured by the presence of two thoughtful men. One was the idealistic painter Edward Clifford, quite well known in later years for his book *Father Damien and Others* (1905). The other was a Cambridge don, F. W. H. Myers. He had only quite recently been introduced to Ruskin (by Prince Leopold), but Ruskin well knew his lineage, for he was the son of the once famous Frederick Myers, Vicar of Keswick. Long before, in the spring of 1848, Ruskin and Effie had spent part of their honeymoon at Keswick because the earnest young bridegroom was eager to hear the 'teachings' of Myers's sermons.[14] In this strange way Ruskin's first marriage came to haunt him as he sought a second marriage that had never taken place, except in some part of his mind.

The new friendship with Myers was useful to Ruskin. Myers helped him to believe that the spiritualists' claims were true, and this is what his heart wanted. Ruskin's desire for Rose's ghost was not easy to accommodate with his study of the Bible. From the chapters of Deuteronomy he had learnt as a child, and from the recent studies recorded in the 'Broadlands book', Ruskin well knew that spirit-raising, which is necromancy, was specifically forbidden in Mosaic law. He also knew that spiritualism had no recognition from any branch of the Christian Church. However, some individual churchmen were leniently disposed toward 'manifestations' such as had been reported to Ruskin. One of them was his old tutor Osborne Gordon. Ruskin had written him a worried letter. The learned Rector of Easthampstead wished to dispel his unease. 'I feel sure that that presence was permitted to make itself known, on purpose to cheer and comfort you', he told Ruskin. 'You think rightly that this was not designed for your evil but for your good — and you connect her visit with your prayers . . .'[15]

There were less accommodating reactions from other friends. Two of them thought that Ruskin had been cheated. Constance Oldham knew of a scandal in which Mrs Ackworth had been involved. The details were hazy, and Ruskin aloofly dismissed such mere gossip. Juliet Tylor criticised the way that spiritualists made money. 'Mrs Wagstaff's taking a fee for observations made with her eyes shut, is absolutely and in every respect as innocent as another doctor's taking a fee with *his* open', returned Ruskin.[16] This Juliet disputed. She was a more 'modern' young woman than Ruskin had imagined, and her geologist father was a rationalist. For some weeks, by letter, Ruskin argued with both father and daughter about spiritualism and its possible place in the earthly world.

Opposition from the Tylors made him eager for Myers's company. At the end of March Ruskin went to stay with him in Cambridge, at Trinity College, where he appreciated the evening service and its music but found the 'Quadrangle very dull, and rooms darker than a student's ought to be'.[17] These worldly matters were irrelevant, for Ruskin wished to talk about ghosts. As so often, his diary responds to the weather in an exaggerated manner, as though the skies were full of warning. 'Yesterday utterly pitch black all day, more miserable than I have seen often, even in this evil time . . .'[18] We do not know what

Myers said to Ruskin during the three days he spent in Cambridge, but the older man was clearly perplexed, so much did he wish for a conviction that was against reason. From Cambridge Ruskin wrote to Juliet Tylor in near desperation. The idea, Juliet's, of Mrs Ackworth's 'conspiring with Mrs Wagstaff to lie to me on the most solemn of all questions, is entirely incredible to me, signifying an amount of human depravity which my present experience does not justify me in supposing possible even in the nineteenth century'. What was credible and what was not credible to Ruskin? He now asserted to Juliet that the revelations from Mrs Ackworth and Mrs Wagstaff had given him a new hope in God. For,

> Of all things, to *my* mind, the Unlikeliest, and Unworthiest that He could possibly have done, was allowing a child like Rose to go on praying to Him every hour, from three years old to twenty seven, for guidance and help to do right, and permitting her all the while to do the things which would bring about her own death in insanity, and the destruction of an entirely faithful lover and half the usefulness of a powerful public servant.[19]

* * * *

Juliet Tylor was at the Slade School, so may count as one of the Guild of St George's two artists (the other being Alfred Hunt). Like most members of the Guild, she found that her only tasks were to correspond with the 'powerful public servant' and to puzzle over *Fors Clavigera*. In the *Fors* letters of this spring and summer of 1876 there is much that concerns the Guild. Yet we learn little about Ruskin's society apart from hearing of the legal frustrations that attended its founding. Such matters are not of major interest. To think of St George's Company as a land-holding utopian society is to understand the Guild only as the Board of Trade understood it. That was its worldly existence. Its essence was elsewhere, in Ruskin's reading of cultural history. This was so real to him that *Fors* often made social proposals that in truth were fantastic elaborations of, for instance, Ruskin's recent Biblical studies. In the February *Fors*, written at Broadlands, he returned to the view of episcopacy already treated in *Sesame and Lilies* and *Time and Tide*. Bishops within the Guild, we now learn, will follow 'the first Bishop of Israel', Moses, in appointing and overseeing 'rulers of thousands, rulers of hundreds, rulers of fifties and rulers of tens':

> and of these episcopic centurions, captains of fifty, and captains of ten, there will be required clear account of the individual persons

> they are set over; — even a baby being considered as a decimal quantity not to be left out of their account by the decimal Bishops, — in which episcopacy, however, it is not impossible that a queenly power may be associated, with Norman caps for mitres, and for symbol of authority, instead of the crozier (or crook, for disentangling lost sheep or souls from among the brambles), the broom, for sweeping diligently till they find lost silver of souls among the dust.

Here the argument breaks off, as *Fors* asks a frightening rhetorical question. 'You think I jest, still, do you? Anything but that; only if I took off the Harlequin's mask for a moment, you would say I was simply mad. Be it so, however, for this time.' With no more pause the letter goes on with the discussion of episcopacy, concluding that 'It is merely through the quite bestial ignorance of the Moral Law in which the English Bishops have contentedly allowed their flocks to be brought up, that any of the modern English conditions of trade are possible.'[20]

Of course one wonders what any bishop, or Cardinal Manning, or the Dean of Christ Church, or indeed any clergyman who respected his bishop, would have made of such a criticism. Either they did not read what Ruskin wrote, which is likely, or they ignored him, their wisest course. So Ruskin most succeeded in upsetting his own family and family friends. 'Yes, the Bishops are catching it', he wrote in answer to Joan's protests, '— the Lawyers will come next — Can't be helped, di ma: I know what I'm about.'[21] In the event Ruskin did not attack the lawyers as a class. He merely distressed Tarrant and Mackrell, his own solicitors and his father's solicitors before him, by printing in *Fors* their accounts for negotiation with the Board of Trade to ensure legal status for the Guild. Characteristically, he also printed their letter of protest and his own reply to that protest. Such disclosure of private business was unknown, he agreed: but 'You never had a client before engaged in steady and lifelong contest with the existing principles of the Law, the Church, and the Army, — had you?'[22] Exasperated at the delays in setting up his company, maddened by the possibility that he might be supervised by the Charity Commissioners, dangerously engrossed in thoughts of Rose's ghostly presence, Ruskin was little able for any rational public work.

While Ruskin was in Cambridge pursuing chimerical assurances he should have been teaching in Oxford. He had requested leave of absence from his work in October, even before he gave the lectures on Sir Joshua. In the preface to the 1887 edition of *Lectures on Art* Ruskin wrote that in 1876, 'feeling unable for Oxford duty, I obtained a year's leave of rest'.[23] Probably, as before, Henry Acland was an intermediary between Ruskin and Convocation, the University's governing body. The Slade Professor made brief visits to Oxford. 'Just a day to spend in my nest here', reads the diary entry for 11 April.[24] He needed to collect various materials from his rooms in Corpus. He emptied '*her* drawer', in which he kept mementoes of Rose. Here were photographs, letters, a drawing of 'Madonna weed' by Rose and 'the textbook we used to read together', which was probably a missal. These precious things were to be united with the letters he had retrieved through Miss Price's help. It was probably during this spring that Ruskin acquired, or had made for him, the rosewood box in which he kept such precious relics. Henceforward this box would accompany him wherever he travelled. The other things Ruskin needed from Oxford were minerals and diagrams. He was preparing two lectures to be given in London, one at Christ's Hospital and the other at Woolwich, on mineralogical topics. The gist of these lectures afterward appeared in *Deucalion*.[25]

All these tasks completed, Ruskin turned his mind — not before time — to some old-fashioned personal pleasure. Now came a happy interlude in his generally unhappy life. In March of 1876 he had decided to have a coach: one like those he had known with his mother and father in the 1830s, but perhaps even better. Fortunately, he knew a local firm of coachbuilders, Messers Tucker of Camberwell. Ruskin spent some time in their workshop assisting in plans for the new brougham. On delivery he was 'greatly delighted'. He had never chosen '*anything* that's turned out so much to my mind as that green pattern for lining. I ordered my little shield in its real colours, black white and red — and a basket for luggage on the top, and we'll have a fine time, in the spring . . .'[26]

The plan was to post from Herne Hill to Brantwood, where the coach would have its permanent home (and where it is preserved to this day). Ruskin travelled with Joan and with Arthur Severn, who later wrote some characteristically facetious memoirs of the journey. The party was on the road for nearly a month before arriving at Coniston. In 1876 it was still just possible to telegraph ahead for fresh horses and a local postilion. All the same, theirs was an antiquated method of travel, and the coach made some stir as it passed through modern England. The route was from St Albans to Hitchin, Cambridge, Huntingdon, Peterborough, Croyland, Stamford, Grantham, Southwell, Newark, Lincoln, Worksop and then to Sheffield, where they arrived on 27 April. Ruskin had business with workmen in Sheffield, but otherwise the coaching expedition was refreshingly free from worries. That is perhaps why it leaves no trace in *Fors Clavigera*. Ruskin and Arthur looked at architecture, drew, and played chess. From Sheffield they went via Pontefract, Selby, Knaresborough, Fountains Abbey, Ripon and Richmond to Greta Bridge. At this Turnerian location Ruskin wrote to Georgiana Cowper-Temple:

> . . . at last the sun has come, and the old Inn here is unchanged — and there is a window looking through blossom into the garden and up to Brignall woods — and I had a walk up the glen yesterday, wholly quiet; nothing with voice of harm — or voice any wise except the Greta, and the birds — And I found, up the glen — the little Brignall churchyard, with its ruined chapel — and low stone wall just marking its sacred ground from the rest of the violets — and the chapel untouched since Cromwell's time — the river shining and singing through the east window — scarcely larger than a cottage's — and the fallen walls scarcely higher than a sheepfold — but a little piscina and a stone or two of the altar steps left — and the window and wall so overgrown with my own Madonna herb that — One would think the little ghost had been at work planting there all the spring . . .[27]

In this frame of mind Ruskin continued his journey. The coach passed from Yorkshire to Lancashire via Brough, Appleby, Penrith, Ullswater, Kirkstone Pass and Ambleside. Ruskin and the Severns arrived at Brantwood on 6 May. It seemed appropriate to begin a new volume of diary. On the next day Ruskin started to write in a large leather-bound volume with the word LEDGER stamped in gold on its spine. This journal, inconveniently sized for Ruskin's travelling desk, was subsequently to remain at his home and is known as the 'Brantwood Diary'. Its first entry reads 'Sunday. 7, morning. Begin new diary: after seeing Helvellyn and my terrace field in divine sunshine and peace. Lake calm since morning, now breeze from north.'[28]

* * * *

Brantwood summer life soon began to take its familar form of walking, boating, study and the entertainment of visitors. As usual, the Severns were present. Joan presided as hostess while Arthur kept a little in the background, especially if there were guests of an intellectual bent. Collingwood walked over the hills to Brantwood from his cottage on Windermere. Other visitors were members of the Guild. Egbert Rydings, an enthusiast for home weaving who also oversaw the Guild's accounts, came from his home on the Isle of Man. Ruskin also saw Julia Firth, the widow of Thomas Firth of Sheffield, who had settled at Ambleside, within convenient distance of Brantwood. She was an early member of the Guild and Ruskin considered her 'one of the ablest and kindest of my women-friends'. Then came, as a house guest, Sara Anderson, known to all as 'Diddie'.[29] She was in her early twenties. Ruskin knew her because she was Jamie Anderson's cousin. Both Julia and Diddie were set to St George's work, in further developments of *Bibliotheca Pastorum*. For some time Ruskin had hoped that Carlyle's niece Mary Aitken would translate some of Jeremias Gotthelf's bucolic tales of Swiss rural life. But she had found their Swiss-German patois impossible to render into English and had relinquished her task, explaining to Ruskin that 'My uncle has goaded me on with cruel jibes; but he read the book himself, and says now that *he* could at no period of his life have translated it.'[30] Julia Firth, who knew German, was now introduced to Gotthelf's work. Eventually, in 1886–88, her translation was published as *Ulric the Farm Servant*, with an introduction by Ruskin.

Sara Anderson's work this summer was to assist with the volume of *Bibliotheca Pastorum* which Ruskin called (in an obscure reference to Psalms 81.16) *Rock Honeycomb*. It was an edition of Sir Philip Sidney's metrical version of the Psalter. The work originally dates from about 1580. Ruskin had chanced on the only printed edition, that of 1823, and had decided to make the psalms his own hymns for use in St George's schools. Sara had an abrupt and no doubt animating introduction to Ruskin's interests and methods. Though the Psalter was a comparatively gentle project, it gave Ruskin opportunity to air his views on prosody and to inveigh against evangelical hymns. The book was not in the least scholarly. Having long since abandoned his interest in the 'higher criticism' Ruskin cheerfully took all the psalms to be David's own: the idea of a king singing to his people appealed to him. The Psalmist was enlisted in many of Ruskin's own battles with modern life. The annotations have a light cantankerousness that is not very like the contemporary numbers of *Fors*. Sending *Rock Honeycomb* to press, Ruskin wrote to Allen with some satisfaction. It was 'as spicy a bit of spiteful Christianity as I've done, I think'.[31]

In June and July Ruskin was at work on his mineral collection and wrote the preface to Robert Somervell's pamphlet *A Protest against the Extension of Railways in the Lake District*.[32] Then there were more visitors. Three were American, sent with letters of introduction from their Harvard colleague Charles Eliot Norton. Professor and Mrs E. W. Gurney came from Coniston for tea, rowed in both directions by David Downs. Charles Herbert Moore, who taught drawing at Harvard and was already Ruskin's follower, was thrilled to meet the man he had admired from afar. Ruskin liked Moore, and they devised a rendezvous in Venice, for Ruskin had now decided to revisit Italy. A less congenial guest was Leslie Stephen, who was accompanied by his sister-in-law Anne Thackeray. Her reminiscences describe the high tea where

> Mrs Severn sat in her place beside a silver urn, while the master of the house, with his back to the window, was dispensing such cheer, spiritual and temporal, as those who have been his guests will best realise, — fine wheaten bread and Scotch cakes in many a crisp circlet and crescent, and trout from the lake, and strawberries such as only grow on Brantwood slopes. Were these cups of tea only, or cups of fancy, feeling, inspiration?[33]

Stephen was less charmed. On 8 August he wrote to Charles Eliot Norton in America to report on his visits to Brantwood. Stephen had 'seen the immortal author several times . . . He makes, to say the truth, a very odd impression on me. He regarded me with evident curiosity as, on the one hand, a specimen of the Alpine climbers, whom he professes to despise, and, on the other, a friend of yours . . . For my part, I could not be at ease with him . . . I was afraid of contradicting him, lest it should annoy him . . . and indeed inclined to treat him as a dangerous compound which might explode in any direction without notice . . . Nobody indeed can talk to him without seeing his genuine kindliness as well as genius, and yet it takes a more sympathetic person than I am not to be repelled by some of his crotchets . . .'[34]

Among Ruskin's 'crotchets', Stephen should have noticed, was his disposition to give courteous hospitality to the man who had recently written the unpleasant article about him in *Fraser's Magazine*. Brantwood at its social best (which was generally in midsummer) was a happy retreat, far removed from the disputes of Victorian cultural life. Ruskin was still writing *Fors*, of course, but summer issues dating from Brantwood generally have a milder tone than those written elsewhere. Ruskin was not disturbed by Stephen and was much more interested to engage with the Roman Catholic Coventry Patmore, who had recently sent him press cuttings for comment in *Fors*. Replying to the poet — an old but now distant friend — Ruskin wrote: 'You will see in next "Fors" something of Catholic Faith wider than yours'.[35] The remark echoes his recent letter to Cardinal Manning.

Ruskin was referring Patmore to his 'central Fors' of July 1876, later entitled 'Companionship'. It is a summary of the purposes of the

Guild. His mind on his Company, Ruskin was not interested in quotidian affairs as represented by Stephen. He was also preoccupied by thoughts of Venice. He had not been there since the 1872 expedition, cut short after three weeks by Rose's message that she would see him in London. Earlier in 1876 there had been discussion of a new edition of *The Stones of Venice*. The decisive encouragement, however, had probably come from Prince Leopold.[36] Ruskin took the Prince's interest in the project almost as a royal command. Therefore he had decided to go to Venice, to draw and to revise his book. He thought that he might do this work by Christmas. In the event, however, Ruskin would remain in Venice until May of 1877.

He could not leave for Italy without attending to an important piece of Guild business. This was to visit the first of its properties. In December 1874 Fanny Talbot, a wealthy widow who lived in the small coastal town of Barmouth in North Wales, had given the Guild a plot of land, including some cottages, on the steep cliffs looking out toward Anglesey and Ireland.[37] Though they had never met, the correspondence between the Master of the Guild and his generous Companion had become more and more friendly during the previous eighteen months. At the beginning of August 1876 Ruskin, on his way 'Venicewards', travelled to Barmouth 'to see the tenants on the first bit of ground, — noble crystalline rock, I am thankful to say, — possessed by St George in the island.'[38] His journey to Wales is described at some length in the September number of *Fors*. This was written from his hotel room in Dolgelly:

> I had driven from Brantwood in early morning down the valley of the Crake, and took train first at the Ulverston station, settling myself in the corner of a carriage next the sea, for better prospect thereof. In the other corner was a respectable, stolid, middle-aged man reading his paper.
>
> I had left my Coniston lake in dashing ripples under a south wind, thick with rain; but the tide lay smooth and silent along the sands; melancholy in absolute pause of motion, nor ebb nor flow distinguishable; — here and there, among the shelves of grey shore, a little ruffling of their apparent pools marked stray threadings of river-current.
>
> At Grange, talking loud, got in two young coxcombs; who reclined themselves on the opposite cushions. One had a thin stick, with which, in a kind of St Vitus's dance, partly affectation of nonchalance, partly real fever produced by the intolerable idleness of his

> mind and body, he rapped on the elbow of his seat, poked at the button-holes of the window-strap, and switched his boots, or the air, all the way from Grange to the last station before Carnforth, — he and his friend talking yacht and regatta, listlessly; — the St Vitus's, meantime, dancing one expressing his opinion that 'the most dangerous thing to do on these lakes was going before the wind'. The respectable man went on reading his paper, without notice of them. None of the three ever looked out of the windows at sea or shore. There was not much to look at, indeed, through the driving, and gradually closer-driven, rain, — except the drifting about of the seagulls, and their quiet dropping into the pools, their wings kept open for a second till their breasts felt the water well; then closing their petals of white light like suddenly shut water flowers . . .[39]

Much more follows, before Ruskin brings the reader to the point where he is sitting and writing of his day's travel. It is one of those times in *Fors* when the speed of argument or explanation is deliberately slowed, as though more completely to involve the reader in the writer's exasperations. The letter, when it resumes a few days later, says of Barmouth only that 'I find the rain coming through roofs, and the wind through walls, more than I think proper, and have ordered repairs.'[40] In fact Ruskin (accompanied on the tour of inspection by David Downs) had been shocked by the condition of the cottages. He found Mrs Talbot amiable; he immediately liked her son Quarry: but what sort of a landlord had she been? Mrs Talbot's diary tells us a little more. 'We went with him to all the cottages', she recorded, 'and introduced him to the tenants, at one of the very poorest a dark little place we found the father and mother both out of work — and a little heap of dirty children on the floor — the eldest a girl about 9 — in charge of the younger ones — it greatly distressed him and he said we must find someone to take charge of the children whilst their parents were at work — but of course that was impossible . . .'[41] Evidently Mrs Talbot's commitment to the Guild had not improved her tenants' conditions. The effect of the transfer of the little estate to St George's ownership was only that the necessary repairs would be paid for from Ruskin's own pocket. In his diary we find the names of those who would now be dependent on him. 'William Davis, wife, four children, Jane Davis, Humphrey Edwards, wife, four children, Betty Lloyd, little girl, sick baby, Margaret Davis, two children, Barbara Jones, quarryman husband, Catherine Parry, Margaret Davis, widow with three children, Peter Roberts boatman/donkey driver, Eliza Pugh, widow three children, Betty Jones . . .' Their homes were 'a weary sight for heart and eyes', and Ruskin was now 'tempted to the abandonment of St George's Company'.[42]

CHAPTER THIRTY-SIX

1876–1877

After his disappointments in Barmouth Ruskin was glad to pursue St George's work by travelling to Venice. First he visited the printer Henry Jowett in Aylesbury, and took the same sad walks that he had discovered in the week of Rose's death. He crossed the Channel on 25 August 1876, accompanied only by his new valet, a young Irishman called Peter Baxter. As a talisman or token of his spiritual intentions he carried a favourite pocket book, Cary's version of Dante. This was Ruskin's reading as he sat, sleepless, in his first-class carriage (Baxter, whose first continental expedition this was, also enjoyed a place in first class) on the night train from Paris to Geneva.

From Geneva Ruskin went on to Milan, where he spent a few days. The city is recalled with delight in *Præterita*, but briefly, for the simple reason that Ruskin seemed always to be in Milan while on his way to other destinations. Ruskin had passed through Milan in 1833, 1841, 1845, 1846, 1849, 1851, 1862, 1869, 1870 and 1872. Of course the principal city of Lombardy had treasures, and tragedies, that Ruskin had never ignored. He brooded over its political history. For years, ever since writing, at the age of fourteen, a poem about Milan's marble cathedral, he had argued with himself about the questionable merits of its Gothic architecture.[1] He well knew the church of St Ambrogio, and Leonardo's *Last Supper* is examined in many of his books. At the Brera picture gallery he studied the Bellinis, Luini, Mantegna, Raphael and Titian. On this 1876 journey he looked carefully at two paintings by Carpaccio. The doctors in *The Preaching of St Stephen*, he felt, were 'a complete assembly of highly trained Oxford men as far as expression went; but with more brains'.[2] Ruskin was never inclined to praise his own university when staying in any other European centre of learning. He was aware of cultural and historical renewal in Milan and was interested in Count Borromeo, whom he had first met in 1869. Gilberto Borromeo, a Milanese prince, had patriotic concerns and a fine collection of paintings. In 1870 Ruskin had thought that Borromeo might let him have 'a cottage' on his land, where he might live quietly, occasionally driving to libraries in Milan. In this summer of 1876 Ruskin was conscious of the work that was being done by Italian antiquaries, who were more numerous than they had been in previous years; and the prospect that he might be able to learn from other students of Italian art had a bearing on his variable plans for a new edition, or perhaps a rewriting, of *The Stones of Venice*.

At least four people had a personal interest in the possibility of a new *Stones of Venice*. The first of them was Prince Leopold, to whom Ruskin occasionally felt an obligation. The second was George Allen, who had many reasons to worry about the sales of Ruskin's books, and now sensed a commercial opportunity. The third was Carlyle, for Ruskin had hinted that he might make a new *Stones* even more Carlylean than its original version; and the fourth was Charles Eliot Norton. All were to be disappointed. A further version of *The Stones of Venice* was never written. Ruskin arrived in Venice on 8 September, at the beginning of a lovely period of Italian autumn weather. He was met at the station by his oldest Venetian friend, Rawdon Brown. Ruskin was then taken by Brown's personal gondolier Toni to the Grand Hotel, which was to be his home until mid-February, when he transferred to much cheaper accommodation on the Zattere. In September and October of 1876 Ruskin enjoyed his expensive rooms, which formed part of a Gothic palace. He read some Venetian history but wrote no history of his own. Ruskin's balcony looked out on the church of Santa Maria della Salute. From this balcony he watched, every day, the sun rise and set. He rowed on the lagoon in the afternoons and after dinner it was his pleasure to walk by moonlight in the Piazza San Marco. In Ruskin's diary, which is especially introspective in these months, while his correspondence is comparatively sparse, we find the translations of Plato's *Laws* that he made his morning task. He records work on a number of drawings of the Grand Canal, and also notes many meetings with Charles Herbert Moore, the Harvard Professor and accomplished amateur artist who had been a guest at Brantwood earlier in the year.

Moore shared Ruskin's interest in Carpaccio. They determined to study the Venetian master together, by making copies. The picture that attracted them both was Carpaccio's *The Dream of St Ursula*, one of the cycle of eight paintings in the Accademia that illustrate the saint's short and holy life. Ruskin recounted Ursula's life in the October number of *Fors Clavigera*. From this time onwards she would be a central rather than an incidental symbol in Ruskin's reading of Venetian Christianity. Curators at the Accademia may have been less interested than Ruskin in Carpaccio's teaching. *The Dream of St Ursula* was hung above the line in one of the galleries that Ruskin described as 'lighted like coalcellars'.[3] He now employed his prestige. Ruskin was an honorary member of the Accademia. Within days of arriving in Venice he had persuaded the directors of the museum to take the picture down and to place it in a private room. Undisturbed, Ruskin and Moore began their studies. Moore would shortly take up other projects. Ruskin, however, worked on his copy of the painting until March of 1877, a period of nearly six months.

The peculiar nature of this copy may be attributed to its size, overworking and roseate colour. Carpaccio's painting is large: it is nine feet high and more than eight feet wide. Ruskin dramatically reduced this size. His copy is a little less than a foot high. By thus giving Carpaccio's painting the dimensions of a miniature, Ruskin's copy suggests some of the characteristics of early Netherlandish art, or of manuscript illumination. This is not alien to the spirit of the original painting. Yet Carpaccio's picture is limpid, both in mood and execution, while Ruskin's copy is intense, fervent, and bears the marks of protracted and futile labour.[4] The copy may have been a more satisfactory work of art when it was first made, in September 1876. However, Ruskin then devised ways of overpainting his original copy. He used watercolour and body colour; that is, he added more opaque paint to his first transparent wash. He probably did so time and again, for the paint in the finished work is quite thick. Ruskin must have waited for his paint to dry before adding further touches. With such a technique, he worked for an hour or two each morning, then turned to other Venetian tasks or pleasures.

Later in the autumn and the winter of 1876–77 Ruskin went to his room in the Accademia but did not paint. He was content to be shut away with St Ursula, far from the secular world. In September of 1876, while there was still some gaiety in the early autumn, Ruskin was cheerful and even irreverent. After a session of copying work, he told Joan Severn, he read 'any vicious book I can find to amuse me — to prevent St Ursula having it all her own way'.[5] In such a mood we find Ruskin with Casanova's *Memoirs*, or with one of the French novels that he liked to read when abroad in holiday mood. His spirits were lower in the first week of October when he was alternately tired, listless, and eager to do work that seemed to have no end. '*Can't* get any writing done, and my head is so full', his diary tells us.[6] After three weeks' work in the Accademia, he had hoped to complete his copy within another week. But some idea that grew in his mind forbade him to finish his work. He thought more of St Ursula herself than of the comparatively simple task of copying a painting. Four years earlier, in 1872, when St Ursula was first considered in *Fors Clavigera*, Ruskin wrote with all the distant respect that is due to a saint of Christian tradition. In October he began to think of her more intimately, almost as though she were living, or as a person whom Ruskin had known well before her death. He began the association of St Ursula with Rose La Touche. The legend of St Ursula is of a Christian Celtic princess who is betrothed to a pagan English prince. She dies in martyrdom. Carpaccio's *The Dream of St Ursula* represents her vision, as she lies asleep, of an angel who brings her a palm. It is a sign of Ursula's future martyrdom. There are many differences between the legendary life of St Ursula and the actual life of Rose La Touche. Consciously or unconsciously, Ruskin wished to bring them together; and in doing so, in the later autumn and winter season of 1876, he lost control of his rational mind.

* * * *

For a while in this autumn, Ruskin's intellect and art-historical curiosity were stimulated by the company of Charles Moore. The American was not his only collaborator in Carpaccio studies. John Wharlton Bunney was living in Venice with his wife and children. A former clerk at Smith, Elder, Bunney had been a student at the Working Men's College in the 1850s, when he met Ruskin. He had lived in Florence and Venice since the early 1860s. Although Ruskin did not much like him, he found it useful to employ Bunney, who was often given commissions for the Guild of St George. Bunney was now set to work on his own copy of *The Dream of St Ursula*. As he considered the painting, he made suggestions about its iconography. These remarks were passed on to another of Ruskin's helpers in Venice, James Reddie Anderson. The sensitive 'Jamie', a former Hinksey digger, was in Venice to pursue his own researches. Ruskin knew his worth; and of course he was Sara Anderson's cousin. Jamie and Ruskin took long walks together. The Oxford disciple was thrilled to perambulate the city with the author of *The Stones of Venice*. He was now given the opportunity of a special task: Ruskin suggested that he should collect and harmonise the various legends of St Ursula. Anderson did so immediately. His 'The Story of St Ursula' occupies many pages of the November issue of *Fors Clavigera*, in which Ruskin also tells his readers that St Ursula might have some future close connection 'with the proposed "practice" of St George's Company'.[7]

Besides Anderson, Bunney and Moore, Rawdon Brown might be mentioned as member of Ruskin's art-historical circle. Brown was a negative influence. He disliked *Fors Clavigera* and told Ruskin that his utopian plans were merely foolish. Brown also criticised Ruskin's ideas for a new *Stones of Venice*. 'I fetched you to Venice to reprint the "Stones" & to correct their errors', he wrote to Ruskin, 'not to add to them'.[8] The friendship between Brown and Ruskin came towards its end this autumn. Yet Ruskin still had respect for Brown, whose stinging remarks may have persuaded him that he should not write a new *Stones of Venice*.

Ruskin had proposed to return to England, and to give a course of Oxford lectures, in November. But he had nothing prepared for Oxford and his Carpaccio work held him in a mysterious fealty. His diary reveals wandering thoughts and contradictory resolutions. At the end of October Ruskin decided to spend a few days in Verona. *Fors Clavigera* tells us, in the section 'Affairs of the Master':

> I am bound to state, in the first place, — now beginning a new and very important year, in which I still propose myself for the Master of the St George's Company, — that my head certainly does not serve me as it did once, in many respects. The other day, for instance, in a frosty morning at Verona, I put on my dressing-gown (which is of bright Indian shawl stuff) by mistake for my great-coat; and walked through the full market-place, and half-way down the principal street, in that costume, proceeding in perfect tranquillity until the repeated glances of unusual admiration bestowed on me by the passengers led me to investigation of the possible cause. And I begin to find it no longer in my power to keep my attention fixed on things that have little interest to me . . .[9]

Eight numbers of *Fors Clavigera* are dated from Venice between the autumn of 1876 and the spring of 1877. Ruskin issued no other publications in these months. *Fors* therefore gives us, as it were, a naked account of its author's thoughts and social proposals. It is important that these thoughts were numerous. In the Venetian issues of *Fors* — and this is characteristic of *Fors Clavigera* as a whole — different comments, ideas and sentiments come rushing and tumbling from Ruskin's pen ('this is a nice new pen, a great comfort', the diary remarks on 7 November) in such abundance that the reader can never catch their ultimate purport. If it were possible for anyone to count or compute separate thoughts, then *Fors* would be found to contain hundreds of thousands of thoughts, and perhaps does not contain everything that came to Ruskin's mind, bidden or unbidden, when he wrote such Venetian diary entries as 'how my thoughts are wasted, how my pleasures past, fruitlessly. Each day brings its own thoughts, demanding a year to write them . . .';[10] and then, a few days later, 'I have so many thoughts that I can't begin writing them, and am losing my morning . . .',[11] after which we find notes for *Deucalion* and the daily translation of Plato. Perhaps Ruskin made his version of Plato in order to subdue the various agitations of his copious and fragmented mind.[12] He realised that he needed a daily period of mental calm. For the thoughts we find in passages of the Venetian numbers of *Fors* are violent, miserable, disconnected, autobiographical and prophetic of coming madness. At breakfast time on 9 November, for instance, he wrote with his nice new steel pen, having dutifully finished his bit of Plato,

> Here is a little grey cockle-shell, lying beside me, which I gathered, the other evening, out of the dust of the Island of St Helena; and a brightly-spotted snail-shell, from the thistly sands of Lido; and I want to set myself to draw these, and describe them, in peace.
>
> 'Yes', all my friends say, 'that is my business; why can't I mind it, and be happy?'
>
> Well, good friends, I would fain please you, and myself with you; and live here in my Venetian palace, luxurious; scrutinant of dome, cloud, and cockle-shell. I could even sell my books for not inconsiderable sums of money if I chose to bribe the reviewers, pay half of all I got to the booksellers, stick bills on the lamp-posts, and say nothing but what would please the Bishop of Peterborough.
>
> I could say a great deal that would please him, and yet be very good and useful; I should like much again to be on terms with my old publisher, and hear him telling me nice stories over our walnuts, this Christmas, after dividing his year's spoil with me in Christmas charity. And little enough mind have I for any work, in this seventy-seventh year that's coming of our glorious century, wider than I could find in the compass of my cockle-shell.
>
> But alas! my prudent friends, little enough of all that I have a mind to may be permitted me. For this green tide that eddies past my threshold is full of floating corpses, and I must leave my dinner to bury them, since I cannot save; and put my cockle-shell in cap, and take my staff in hand, to seek an unencumbered shore. This green sea-tide! — yes, and if you knew it, your black and sulphurous tides also — Yarrow, and Teviot, and Clyde, and the stream, for ever now drumly and dark as it rolls on its way, at the ford of Melrose.
>
> Yes, and the fair lakes and running waters in your English park pleasure-grounds, — nay, also the great and wide sea, that gnaws your cliffs, — yes, and Death, and Hell also, more cruel than cliff or sea; and a more neutral person than even my Lord of Peterborough stands, level-barred balance in hand, — waiting (how long?) till the Sea shall give up the dead which are in it, and Death, and Hell, give up the dead which are in them . . .[13]

Far away from Venice, Joan Severn sat by the Herne Hill fireside and read her *Fors* with puzzlement and anxiety. What might people think? Her cousin's daily letters were unfailingly full of love, at least in their salutations, but otherwise were curiously moody, and filled with excited remarks about St Ursula. 'There she lies', he wrote, 'so real that when the room's quiet — I get afraid of waking her! How little one believes these things, really! Suppose there is a real St Ursula di ma, — taking care of somebody else, asleep for me?' This 'somebody else' who was 'asleep for me' must have been Rose.[14] The saint and the dead Irish girl were coming closer together. In *Fors* Ruskin discussed the nature of St Ursula's 'dream'. It might not have been a dream but a vision, he thought; and there was a possibility that a living person, not a saint of legend, might put oneself in a state that would be receptive to visions:

> You will say, perhaps — It is not a proper intellectual state to approach such a question in, to wish anything about it. No, assuredly not, — and I have told you so myself, many a time. But it is an entirely proper state to fit you for being approached by the Spirits that you wish for, if there are such. And if there are not, it can do you no harm.[15]

Ruskin wished to be visited by spirits. Here is the reason why he lingered in Venice. Joan thought that he should come home and worried that *Fors* would make him enemies. Ruskin replied that he would not change his course and that in future Joan would 'not be so much alarmed for the effect of what I say on the public, as for the effect of what I may imagine on my own mind. However . . . I'm not losing my head yet . . .'[16] Alas, Ruskin was close to the point at which he abandoned his reason. His Venetian surroundings were sympathetic to the dark unrealities that began to fill his mind. As autumn gave place to winter the city emptied. By December all the tourists had departed, shops were closed, the gondoliers unemployed. The beggars went elsewhere, Ruskin knew not where. The scampering loselry of Venetian youth was stilled. Night fell early. Sea-fogs rose from the lagoon to fill the canals and narrow passageways. Ruskin continued the night-time walks that he had begun in September. Sometimes, in blackness, he had to feel his way along the *calle* toward the next faint light in a palace or church.

Among the books that Ruskin had brought to Venice were Cary's Dante, Plato (Ruskin used Immanuel Bekker's edition of 1826), his own *Stones of Venice*, which he scarcely looked at, and one or more volumes of his old diaries. The diary he wrote at Venice this winter, which is a large volume bound in vellum, is so full of his translation of the *Laws* that Ruskin wrote PLATO on its spine. In late December, studying Plato in Bekker and his diary of the previous year, Ruskin's mind turned from the *Laws* to the entries he had made a year before, at Broadlands, when Mrs Ackworth had convinced him of the existence of Rose's ghost. Ruskin now began to pray for a sign or message from St Ursula, or Rose, or from them both, or from God. On 21 December he was made unnaturally happy, for signs and messages arrived, 'teachings' that continued, Ruskin believed, until eleven o'clock on the morning of 2 January. The answers to his prayers were not a gift from God. They came from the volitions of Ruskin's extraordinary mind. He created hallucinations that would satisfy his personal and spiritual longings. Because the messages were entirely illusory, though Ruskin believed in them absolutely, it is easy to say that he was insane between 21 December 1876 and 3 January 1877. And yet he was not ill in bed, as he had been when he experienced hallucinations at Matlock in 1871. Nor was Ruskin delirious, as he would be when he went mad in February of 1878. He was forgetful and behaved in peculiar ways, but went about his Venetian business according to routine, met people, conversed with them, kept appointments and wrote some sentences of surprising complexity and beauty.

Our knowledge of the fortunes of Ruskin's mind between 21 December and 2 January comes from three principal sources. The first is *Fors Clavigera*. The second is his diary. The third is a sequence of long letters that Ruskin wrote to Joan Severn. These he separated from his ordinary daily letters to Herne Hill. He called them 'The Christmas Story' and in later years planned to publish them in *Dilecta*, the supplementary volume of *Præterita*.[17] The sequence of events was as follows. On 21 December Ruskin brooded that it was a year since Mrs Ackworth talked to him about Rose's ghost. He began to pray for a further sign. On 24 December two letters arrived. One was from Joan, the other from Daniel Oliver, Ruskin's botanist friend who was a keeper and librarian at Kew Gardens. Joan's letter enclosed another one, a friendly communication from Maria La Touche. Oliver sent a spring of verbena (which Ruskin called vervain), no doubt at Ruskin's request, for this is the plant on the windowsill in Carpaccio's painting of St Ursula. The 'Christmas Story' diary records, retrospectively, for this entry was written on the 27 December:

> First day. Sunday the 24th began — see above — with crashing rain, intense darkness, and I utterly languid — no, *very* languid. I had been praying, but with languor inconceivable to myself, yet

> langour earnest enough in its feebleness, somehow — or at least, real and honest prayer, what little there was — for a new sign from Rose; ever since the 21st continuing so praying and hoping. On this morning of Sunday 24th, last but one of the year's Sundays, there came together by same morning post, the dried vervain from Mr Oliver, and Lacerta's letter to Joanie enclosed in hers.
>
> On which, I at last gave way and thought I would forgive poor L, not so much because Rosie wanted it as because I pitied, or couldn't refuse, poor L's baby talk with Joan, and her use of Rosie's old name St C. Also, though I don't quite know how much, I received it as a direct command from St Ursula, with her leaf: a command given by *her*, with the mythic power of her nature-origin used to make me understand that Rosie had asked her.
>
> So I forgave Lacerta, and wrote accordingly to Joan.[18]

Taking little notice of the Christmas Eve celebrations, Ruskin went to the Accademia, where he found himself in 'a dream of very right and high spirit, about St Ursula and Rosie'.[19] When he returned to his hotel he found a Christmas present. It was a pot of pinks, the dianthus that is also in the picture of St Ursula. The gift had come from Lady Castletown, an Irishwoman who was staying in Venice. Ruskin knew her slightly, and was interested to talk to her because she lived close to the La Touche estate. Delighted with the dianthus, he went to bed and slept well.

The next morning, of Christmas Day, Ruskin woke at 6.30, turned immediately to his diary and wrote, 'now, with my dianthus in the window, such a crowd of helpful and clear thoughts come to me that I cannot write'.[20] Later that morning, however, he was able to write with great boldness and skill. He decided to compose, earlier than usual, his *Fors*. The February *Fors* therefore begins

> Venice, Christmas Day, 1876.
>
> Last night, St Ursula sent me her dianthus 'out of her bedroom window, with her love', and, as I was standing beside it, this morning, — ten minutes ago only, it has just struck eight), watching the sun rise out of a low line of cloud, just midway between the domes of St George and the Madonna of Safety, there came into my mind the cause of our difficulties about the Eastern question: with considerable amazement to myself that I had not thought of it before; but, on the contrary, in what I had intended to say, been misled, hitherto, into quite vain recollection of the little I knew about either Turkey or Russia; and entirely lost sight (though

> actually at this time chiefly employed with it!) of what Little Bear has thus sent me the flower out of the dawn in her window, to put me in mind of, — the religious meanings of the matter.[21]

This is not rational, as a number of the readers of the February *Fors* observed. Later that Christmas morning, however, Ruskin's mind recovered in a remarkable fashion. Another coincidental 'sign' came to him as he was writing. It was a present from Bunney, a copy of the vessel of holy water that is on the altar of the sleeping Ursula. By good fortune, the manuscript of this Christmas morning's work on *Fors* has survived. From the holograph we see that, once the bearers of his present (Bunney's children) had departed, Ruskin took up his pen and wrote, without hesitation or revision, a sentence 204 words in length that is a marvel of his intelligence.

> I am here interrupted by a gift, from another friend, of a little painting of the 'pitcher' (Venetian water-carrier's) of holy water, with the sprinkling thing in it, — I don't know its name, — but it reminds me of the 'Tu asperges' in Lethe, in the *Purgatorio*, and of other matters useful to me: but mainly observe from it, in its bearing on our work, that the blood of Sprinkling, common to the household of the Greek, Roman, and the Jew, — and water of Sprinkling, common to all nations on earth, in the Baptism to which Christ submitted, — the one speaketh better things than that of Abel, and the other than that unto Moses in the cloud and in the sea, in so far as they give *joy* together with their purity; so that the Lamb of the Passover itself, and the Pitcher of Water borne by him who showed the place of it, alike are turned, the one, by the last Miracle, into sacramental wine which immortally in the sacred Spirit makes glad the Heart of Man, and the other, by the first Miracle, into the Marriage wine, which here, and immortally in the sacred, because purified Body, makes glad the Life of Man.[22]

Three things (at the least) may be said about this passage. First, it is intellectual. A student of *Fors* would have had to consider one reference to Canto 31 of the *Purgatorio* and no fewer than eight references to the Bible. Secondly, it is extended. Ruskin must have sensed the end of his sentence as he began to write, yet the end is a long way from its beginning. Ruskin's readers know that he became a master of the long sentence when he first embarked upon the writing of *Modern Painters*; but a sentence such as this has an intensity and architectural balance — and a spontaneity — that he could not have achieved as a young man. Thirdly, we observe that the sentence is a compressed thought, or a collection of thoughts. It was remarked a few pages above how many individual thoughts issued from Ruskin's pen, and that, in Venice this winter, he had more thoughts than he could possibly write down, however rapidly he covered his manuscript paper. In the Venetian diary, the word we most often discover is 'thoughts'. In the period of the 'teachings' from Rose and St Ursula this Christmas, thoughts were spurred by letters, or plants, or Bunney's watercolour, or works of art in galleries, or by Dante, or by *sortes Biblicae*, or by encounters in Venice; as, for instance, when deep in the night Ruskin met a gondolier with bloodshot eyes whom he thought might be the devil; or, in daylight, he was smiled upon by a simple Venetian girl whom he thought might be a saint. During a period of some ten days, Ruskin roamed around Venice and found strange inspiration wherever he went. Meaning was everywhere, as though the past, present and future worlds were joined together by a system of symbols that were occasionally revealed in brilliant light when the clouds of mundane knowledge parted. Ruskin mostly felt exalted, sometimes contrite; but in either mood he knew that he was learning mysteries that would help him to be a better man and would further the work of St George's Company.

Ruskin believed that the 'teachings' ended at mid-morning on 2 January, though his diary is disturbed for some days after that date. To judge from some dark, scribbled, strangely expressionistic drawings, one of which dates from his excursion to Verona, there must have been times on either side of the Christmas period when his artistic hand, as well as his mind, was out of control.[23] In later years Ruskin often looked at old diaries in the hope of discovering reasons for his repeated fits of madness. But he never thought that his Venetian winter had any bearing on his later periods of insanity. Ruskin never regretted or denied the Christmas 'teachings' and proposed to make them a part of his autobiography. This was proper. His Christmas experiences changed the cast of his mind. A fervent, disordered belief in the afterlife now becomes characteristic of many of Ruskin's writings, both public and private. Such books begin with *St Mark's Rest*, which is the detritus of Ruskin's work toward a new *Stones of Venice*, and is discussed in the next chapter. Here is the moment to mention Ruskin's short *Guide to the Principal Pictures of the Academy of Fine Arts at Venice*, which was issued in March 1877. This unsatisfactory pamphlet reflects various annoyances given to Ruskin as he returned to a mental normality in January of that year. After his mystical experiences, it seems that paintings in Venice pleased him less often, and he was irritated both by the arrangements of the Accademia's galleries and by supposed expectations of visitors to whom he proposed to act as *cicerone*. Reading the pamphlet, we find him bullying them, hurrying them from one room to the next.[24]

Ruskin did some calmer work in the New Year in the company of Venetian historians and artists. Venice still did not have a university at this date, but there was a strong and growing patriotic tradition of research into the city's past. Ruskin joined these efforts, though he worked sporadically and without a programme. He also encouraged artists to make copies and to take casts of significant monuments. Prominent among these collaborators or assistants were Raffaele Carloforti, Alvise Zorzi and Angelo Alessandri, whose watercolours and drawings were to find their way into the collections of the Oxford drawing schools and the Guild of St George.[25] Zorzi was the organiser of a vigorous campaign to oppose aspects of the restoration of St Mark's. Ruskin helped him, and at one point was sufficiently moved by their joint efforts to cry 'I am yours! I am yours! I am at last a Venetian!' Antiquarian potterings, and much further copying of Carpaccio, occupied Ruskin for the next months.

He made one significant new girl friend. She was a Scottish teenager, Lilias Trotter, a person of remarkable charm, some artistic talent and strong religious convictions. In later life she would become a missionary. Lilias (Ruskin would have noted that she was named after the heroine of *Redgauntlet*, a paragon of pure, sisterly love) was in Venice with her parents. She was to be a welcome guest at Brantwood before her missionary zeal took her elsewhere. Ruskin was now missing his Lakeland home. Many other matters called him to England, in particular the organisation of the Guild of St George. He left Venice in May and travelled, not too rapidly, through Switzerland. Ruskin was at Boulogne on 16 June. The next day he was back in Herne Hill. The diary vows: 'My old nursery feeling like true home. May I value and use rightly what hours remain to me in it!'[26]

CHAPTER THIRTY-SEVEN

1877–1878

After Ruskin returned from Venice in June 1877 his mind turned to the contributions St George might make to contemporary English culture. The result was the foundation of a museum in a perhaps unexpected place, Sheffield. In the Venetian issues of *Fors Clavigera* Ruskin had written many an exhortation to 'my good Sheffield friends', 'my Sheffield ironworkers', 'working men of Sheffield', and he made many a contrast between the Venice of the middle ages and the modern English town. Partly because his hopes for influence at Oxford had been disappointed, Ruskin looked increasingly toward Sheffield as a centre for St George's work. But he had no intention of spending much time in south Yorkshire. He had an assistant there. Henry Swan, his former student at the Working Men's College, had settled in Sheffield to pursue his trade as an engraver. In the spring and summer of 1875 Swan had been in correspondence with Ruskin, and we gather that the Slade Professor was already thinking of transferring his attention from the University to the 'workmen and labourers of England' whom *Fors* addressed. He had in mind 'a working man's Bodleian Library'[1] that would supplement the volumes constituting *Bibliotheca Pastorum*. This project was abandoned when Ruskin realised that he could easily found a museum.

The idea came to him in the period just after the death of Rose La Touche. In July of 1875 he had told Swan that

> it is very wonderful to me the coming of your letters just at this time. The chief point in my own mind of material of education is getting a museum, however small, well explained and clearly and easily seen. Can you get with any Sheffield help, a room with good light, anywhere accessible to the men who would be likely to come to it? If so, I will send you books and begin with minerals of considerable variety and interest, with short notes on each specimen and others of less value, of the same kinds which the men may examine and handle at their ease.[2]

Thus was founded the Museum of St George, 'a manifestation of what is lovely in the life of nature and heroic in the life of man'.[3] Henry Swan's own life was from this point devoted to the museum, of which he soon became the curator and guide. In many ways he exemplifies

Ruskin's influence over his working-class, rather than his Oxford, followers. Although Swan (born in 1825) had become a Quaker in the 1850s, he had renounced none of his interest in art and music. He was a shorthand expert, a keen photographer, the inventor of a system of phonetic spelling, a sandal-wearer. George Allen considered him 'a crank'. Ruskin described him as 'an honest, though somewhat dreamy person'. He teased Swan about his vegetarianism but had respect for another of his enthusiasms, which was spiritualism. As we have already noted, Ruskin had travelled to Sheffield on 26 September of 1875. This was the turning point of Swan's career. He had convened a number of working men to meet Ruskin. Their discussions were inconclusive. None the less Ruskin was encouraged to proceed with his museum. Its home might have been anywhere, but it became a Sheffield foundation because of Swan's personal enthusiasm. Ruskin wrote to his solicitors instructing them to buy a small cottage and a parcel of land at Walkley, on a hill just outside the town. There, with a salary of £40 a year, Swan was to curate (with his living quarters on the top floor) the Museum of the Guild of St George, whose multifarious treasures, some from Brantwood, some from Oxford, continually augmented by Ruskin's impetuous collecting, were to become the Master's 'national store'[4] of precious and beautiful objects: drawings, manuscripts, gems, shells, minerals, photographs, birds' feathers, sculptures, books and paintings, whose classification and arrangement have bemused successive curators from Swan's day to our own.

St George's Museum may have been assembled in a wayward manner, but this is not a criticism. All museums are in some degree the product of circumstance. The museum in Sheffield had, and retains, the benefit of the circumstances of Ruskin's life, his knowledge, imagination and taste. Nobody but Ruskin could have devised such a 'national store', and it should be regarded as one of his achievements. As would soon become clear, the Guild of St George was well suited to making collections of precious objects. However, the Guild was a failure in its principal purpose of land-holding. In April of 1876 Ruskin had again visited Sheffield to meet working men whom Swan knew. They were, according to W. G. Collingwood, 'Secularists, Unitarians, and Quakers, who professed Communism'.[5] None of them wished to be members of the Guild. Ruskin none the less bought thirteen acres of land at Totley, just across the Derbyshire border, for their use. Swan provided Ruskin with a list of potential tenants for this 'Abbeydale Farm'. In time some of them came to farm the land in smallholdings. But the poor soil did not encourage their cooperation: there were disputes; and we find Ruskin commenting in

Fors Clavigera of November 1877 that 'the root of all mischief is of course that the Master is out of the way, and the men, in his absence, tried at first to get on by a vote of the majority; — it is at any rate to be counted as no small success that they have entirely convinced themselves of the impossibility of getting on in that popular manner.'[6]

Relations were not improved by Ruskin's choice of a manager for the farm. This was William Harrison Riley, a Lancashire man who had spent periods in the United States, knew Walt Whitman (Riley gave *Leaves of Grass* to Ruskin, who thought the poems 'quite glorious things'), and was in 1877 editing the Sheffield monthly *Socialist*.[7] The presence of Riley and his family at Abbeydale, apparently representing Ruskin's authority, led to further problems. Most of the tenants departed. So did Riley. The property was eventually managed by David Downs, and there the Scottish gardener was to end his days.

* * * *

Difficulties of the sort presented by Riley, inevitable in the Guild's public affairs, are frankly chronicled in *Fors Clavigera*. The issues of *Fors* dated from Venice are both distant and frantic when discussing business, while the 'Notes and Correspondence' sections of the letters are filled with legal and financial problems. There was one great improvement in this area: the Guild's accounts were now being professionally checked by Egbert Rydings, one of the original Companions of St George. But nobody had any influence over Ruskin's personal spending, which was patently uncontrolled. While in Venice he had decided to make his finances public. In the *Fors* of April 1877, within the paragraphs entitled 'Affairs of the Master', Ruskin tried to explain to the world, in an attempt to rid himself 'not only of dishonesty, but of avarice and pride', all that he had done with the fortune left to him by his father.[8] The letter shows that a large part of his patrimony had disappeared. Ruskin's confession shows generosity at every turn confounded with self-indulgence. When this April *Fors* was circulated it was clear to all that Ruskin had guarded his inheritance unwisely.

This publication of matters normally kept private caused some public stir. People close to Ruskin were worried. The Severns saw how particularly they were affected. Joan, Arthur and their children depended entirely on Ruskin. As the Venetian letters of *Fors Clavigera* arrived at Herne Hill it became more clear to the Severns that the Guild of St George was not a passing enthusiasm, but a gathering one, and that more and more of the Ruskin family money would pass to the Guild's properties and be used for purchasing its treasures.

Joan Severn, increasingly bound to Victorian proprieties as she grew older, cannot have been glad to read how 'my Herne Hill leases and little properties that bother me' had been made over to 'my pet cousin — whose children, and their donkey, need good supplies of bread and butter, and hay; she always promising to keep my old nursery for a lodging to me, when I come to town'. Joan was also forced to wonder what would become of the man who declared that

> Of my ready cash, I mean to spend to the close of this year, another three thousand pounds, in amusing myself — with such amusement as is yet possible to me — at Venice, and on the Alps, or elsewhere; and as, at the true beginning of St George's work, I must quit myself of usury and the Bank of England, I shall (at some loss you will find, on estimate) then buy for myself twelve thousand of Consols stock, which, if the nation holds its word, will provide me with three hundred and sixty pounds a year — the proper degrees of the annual circle, according to my estimate, of a bachelor gentleman's proper income, on which, if he cannot live, he deserves speedily to die. And this, with Brantwood strawberries and cream, I will for my own poor part, undertake to live upon, uncomplainingly, as Master of St George's Company, *or* die. But, for my dependents, and customary charities, further provision must be made; or such dependencies and charities must end. Virtually, I should then be giving away the lives of these people to St George, and not my own . . .[9]

This April *Fors* had consequences which Ruskin could not have foreseen. Disclosure of his finances probably distressed his contemporaries more than any of his attacks on the English bishops. In the 1870s personal wealth was all the more serious because it was undiscussed. Not only did Ruskin make such private matters public. He also devalued middle-class notions of riches and property. It was as though, by the account of *Fors Clavigera*, large sums of money belonging to individuals were of no importance whatsoever, unless they could be scattered in the general direction of art, or the countryside. The painter James Whistler, another person unwise with money, may have noted Ruskin's attitudes. Whistler may also have heard strange stories of Ruskin's expenditures from the brothers Arthur and Walter Severn, whom he knew on bohemian social terms.

All in all, Ruskin's honesty about his fortune caused him much trouble. The Guild of St George's two trustees, Sir Thomas Acland and William Cowper-Temple, decided to resign their positions. They did so together, and abruptly. Ruskin had heard of their abandonment of his cause while he was still in Venice. 'This important and difficult business, coming on me just as I was in the midst of twelfth-century divinity in the mosaics of St Mark's' was not immediately worrying.[10] The Guild was Ruskin's creation, he managed it by himself and he had never taken any notice of his trustees. Still, he realised that he would have to do something concrete about his affairs, and this was one of the reasons why he returned to England in June of 1877.

Ruskin now spent a month at Herne Hill. An unavoidable task was to arrange for new trustees of the Guild. His invitations went to a person with whom he had only a slight acquaintance, Quarry Talbot, 'virtually the donor, together with his mother, who has so zealously helped us in all ways, of our little rock-estate at Barmouth', and to George Baker, whom he had never met. Baker was the mayor of Birmingham.[11] A landowner, Baker had decided to give the Guild twenty acres of woodland at Bewdley in Worcestershire, a pleasant place quite near to Birmingham in the rich soil of the upper Severn valley. The grateful Ruskin arranged to stay with Baker in Birmingham on his way from Herne Hill back to Brantwood. Together they could make an expedition to Bewdley to view the Guild's new property. First, however, Ruskin made some visits in London. He looked in at a recently opened private art gallery in Mayfair before having dinner with the Burne-Joneses. The Grosvenor Gallery was owned by Sir Coutts Lindsay, a wealthy man who was also a painter. At this inaugural exhibition, whose general design was in the aesthetic taste of the day, Lindsay had hung canvases by Burne-Jones, Millais, Spencer Stanhope, J. M. Strudwick and others. There were seven paintings by Whistler. The larger part of the next month's *Fors* (the July letter, dated 'Herne Hill, 18 June, 1877') had already been written. But Ruskin now added comment on the Grosvenor Gallery at the end of his letter. Most of his review is in praise of Burne-Jones and in faint appreciation of Millais's new paintings. Ruskin concluded, however, with a comparison of faults: those to be found in Burne-Jones and those, far more apparent, that made Whistler's paintings unacceptable:

> Lastly, the mannerisms and errors of Burne-Jones' pictures, whatever may be their extent, are never affected or indolent. The work is natural to the painter, however strange to us; and it is wrought with utmost conscience of care, however far, to his own or our desire, the result may yet be incomplete. Scarcely so much can be said for any other pictures of the modern schools: their eccentricities are always in some degree forced; and their imperfections gratuitously, if not impertinently, indulged. For Mr Whistler's own sake, no less than for the protection of the purchaser, Sir Coutts Lindsay

> ought not to have admitted works into the gallery in which the ill-educated conceit of the artist so nearly approached the aspect of wilful imposture. I have seen, and heard, much of Cockney impudence before now; but never expected to hear a coxcomb ask two hundred guineas for flinging a pot of paint in the public's face.[12]

Fors then passes to other matters, the 'Affairs of the Master' and Baker's benefaction. In general terms, Ruskin was thinking about the good use of wealth and modern ways of demanding money. Specifically, however, he had maligned a famous artist who was always in financial difficulty. In the 650,000 words of *Fors Clavigera* lawyers could doubtless find graver libels than this on Whistler. But Ruskin's hostile comments on the Grosvenor Gallery exhibition led to the only legal problem that *Fors* encountered. In July of 1877 Whistler announced his intention to sue. Ruskin was unperturbed. He was even eager for the courtroom, perhaps not realising the nature of legal proceedings. 'It's mere nuts and nectar to me', he told Burne-Jones, 'the notion of having to answer for myself in court, and the whole thing will enable me to assert some principles of art economy which I've never got into the public's head, by writing, but may get sent all over the world vividly in a newspaper report or two'.[13]

The trial did not take place until the following year, when Ruskin was too ill to attend court. In the summer of 1877 the business of Whistler's legislation did not detain a man who had communed with St Ursula. Ruskin was mainly concerned with the limitless future of the Guild of St George. In August he travelled to Birmingham. For a couple of nights he stayed with George Baker at his home, Bellefield, and met local people. Baker had called a small convention, as Swan had done in Sheffield, of men who might wish to discuss Ruskin's political ideas. There was a difference. Baker's guests were not operatives. They were the fathers of the city. On matters of housing, drainage, elementary schooling, libraries and other civic amenities they had practical experience far beyond Ruskin's. He was not ignorant of such things, and for years had discussed them with such friends as John Simon and Henry Acland. But civic government was not part of his vision of the Guild, and Ruskin was lost. This Birmingham meeting was the only occasion when Ruskin was obliged to listen to reasoned opposition to his utopian plans. It was an unsettling experience. Ruskin confessed in the number of *Fors* he wrote under Baker's roof that Birmingham's leaders were 'very kind to me, and have taught me much'. None the less 'I never yet sate down to write my *Fors*, or indeed to write anything, in so broken and puzzled a state of mind . . .'[14]

Perhaps this was true. Yet there is not one of the ninety-two issues of *Fors* which may be called entirely despondent: Ruskin's writing always triumphs over unhappy circumstance. The Birmingham *Fors* now continues with a memorable passage describing Ruskin's and Baker's expedition to see the Bewdley land:

> Do you think that the Maker of the world intended all but one in a thousand of His creatures to live in those dark streets; and the one, triumphant over the rest, to go forth alone into the green fields?
>
> This is what I was thinking, and more than ever thinking, all the while my good host was driving me by Shenstone's home, the Leasowes, into the Vale of Severn; and telling me how happily far away St George's ground was, from all that is our present England's life and — pretended — glory. As we drove down the hill a little further towards Bewdley (Worcestershire for 'Beaulieu', I find; — Fors undertakes for pretty names to us, it seems, — Abbey-dale, Beau-lieu, and if I remember, or translate, rightly, the House by the Fountain — our three Saxon, Norman, and Celtic beginnings of abode), my host asked me if I would like to see 'nailing'. 'Yes, truly'. So he took me into a little cottage where there were two women at work, — one about seventeen or eighteen, the other perhaps four or five and thirty; this last intelligent of feature as well could be; and both, gentle and kind, each with hammer in right hand, pincers in left (heavier hammer poised over her anvil, and let fall at need by the touch of her foot on a treadle like that of a common grindstone). Between them, a small forge, fed to constant brightness by the draught through the cottage, above whose roof the chimney rose: — in front of it, on a little ledge, the glowing lengths of cut iron rod, to be dealt with at speed. Within easy reach of this, looking up at us in quietly silent question, — stood, each in my sight an ominous Fors, the two Clavigerae.
>
> At a word, they laboured, with ancient Vulcanian skill. Foot and hand in perfect time: no dance of Muses in Parnassian mead in truer measure; — no sea fairies upon yellow sands more featly footed. Four strokes with the hammer in the hand: one ponderous and momentary blow ordered of the balanced mass by the touch of the foot; and the forged nail fell aside, finished, on its proper heap; level-headed, wedge-pointed, a thousand lives soon to depend daily on its driven grip of the iron way.
>
> So wrought they, — the English matron and maid; — so was it their darg to labour from morning to evening, — seven to seven

> by the furnace side, — the winds of summer fanning the blasts of it. The wages of the matron Fors, I found, were eight shillings a week; her husband, otherwise and variously employed, could make sixteen. Three shillings a week for rent and taxes, left, as I count, for the guerdon of their united labour, if constant, and its product providently saved, fifty-five pounds a year, on which they had to feed and clothe themselves and their six children; eight souls in their little Worcestershire ark.[15]

In this way a cultivated and compassionate mind met a poor family at the very heart of the English industrial revolution. Baker and the worried Ruskin then drove on to look at the Bewdley woodland. It was pretty country, perhaps best left alone. Neither Ruskin nor his new trustee made plans for its future. They then returned to Birmingham. Ruskin retired to his room to write about the women who made nails for the railway permanent way and the next day travelled, by rail, to Coniston.[16]

⋆ ⋆ ⋆ ⋆

After nearly eleven months of absence from his home, Ruskin returned to Brantwood on 21 July 1877 and was to remain there until 5 November, when he left Lancashire for Oxford. We trace his activities through the 'Brantwood Diary', whose entries record a sociable and productive summer and early autumn. Four numbers of *Fors Clavigera* were written during this period. They are letters 81–4 of the series, and in letter 84, that of December 1877, dated from Brantwood on 29 October, Ruskin noted that he had been writing *Fors* for seven years. This Christmas number is one of the pamphlets that most resembles Ruskin's 'Sunday letters' to the girls of Winnington School. It concludes with a beautiful commentary on Revelation II and III. The preceding November letter had been relaxed. Under the section 'Affairs of the Master' Ruskin wrote that 'I have nothing interesting to communicate under this head, except that I have been very busy clearing my wood, and chopping up its rotten sticks into faggots . . .'[17] This *Fors* had been about Sir Walter Scott, whose life and work was almost always described by Ruskin in good-humoured rather than challenging terms; and in the September *Fors*, after some remarks about usury, Ruskin had written 'With this passage, and some farther and final pushing home of my challenge to the Bishops of England, which must be done, assuredly, in no unseemly temper or haste, — it seems probable to me that the accusing work of *Fors* may close . . .'[18] All in all, then, this small subsection of *Fors* letters presents Ruskin as a prophet who was comparatively at ease with his life. His diary and correspondence are similarly genial. There was however one grief at Brantwood. In early October Joan Severn had a miscarriage. Ruskin, who in general shied away from such matters, was swift and tender during the crisis.

Apart from his continual work on *Fors*, Ruskin's other intellectual labours at Brantwood in 1877 were in the further progress of *St Mark's Rest*, his Venetian book; the composition of the first part of *The Laws of Fésole*, which is a drawing manual; the writing of a lecture on 'Yewdale and its Streamlets', which was delivered in Kendal on 1 October and later became a chapter of *Deucalion*; together with four public letters (to the *Birmingham Post* and other papers); a catalogue of siliceous minerals for the Sheffield museum: and a preface to the second edition of *The Ethics of the Dust*.

* * * *

The publication of *St Mark's Rest* had come to a halt after Ruskin issued the first three numbers of the book on St Mark's Day, 25 April of 1877. Ruskin brought many notes and half-finished chapters back to Brantwood. With their help he was able to write Chapters 4–7. These form Part II of the book and were published on October. There followed, in December 1877, the 'First Supplement', a pamphlet subtitled *The Shrine of the Slaves, Being a Guide to the Principal Pictures by Victor Carpaccio in Venice*, named here in italics because it should be regarded as a separate publication. Part III of *St Mark's Rest* was published rather later, after Ruskin's mental breakdown in 1878. It contains Chapter 8. There followed a 'Second Supplement', *The Place of Dragons*, published in 1879. This chapter, which should also be considered as a substantial separate publication, was written not by Ruskin but by James Reddie Anderson. Finally, an 'Appendix' appeared in 1884, which was also the year of the first publication of *St Mark's Rest* in volume form. This is Chapter 9 of the final work. It is an account of the mosaics in the baptistery of St Mark's and was written in 1882 by Alexander Wedderburn, who also compiled the index to *St Mark's Rest* for its completed, or rather abandoned, book form.[19]

This abbreviated account of the complex bibliography of *St Mark's Rest* is given for three reasons. Firstly, Ruskin's more recent Venetian researches here led to a fluent and changeable book which could incorporate the writing of his Oxford disciples. Secondly, these fruitful studies were to cease after Ruskin's illness of 1878, a terrible watershed in his academic life. Thirdly, it is proper to give credit to Wedderburn and Anderson, even at this late date, for their work.

Nobody did so at the time. Wedderburn had long been occupied by his career as a lawyer when, in 1882, he first visited Venice. Yet he did not approach the St Mark's mosaics in the spirit of a hobbyist. We recognise his work as that of a scrupulous classical scholar. Anderson's pamphlet is even more remarkable. It was written when he was in his twenty-sixth year. Carpaccio scholarship was still in its infancy in the mid-1870s. Perhaps Anderson's own youth contributed to the spirit in which he wrote his pioneering, confident account of the frescos of the chapel of San Giorgio de' Schiavoni.

Alas, Anderson was not to be productive in his further years of life. Promised further instalments of his contribution to *St Mark's Rest* did not appear. Anderson had no guidance or inspiration after Ruskin's 1878 breakdown. Furthermore, he was self-effacing. Like Collingwood, Wedderburn and other Ruskinians he thought it right to work quietly and modestly, not seeking fame or public position. Jamie Anderson lived at Crosthwaite Green, above Lake Windermere, so was one of a number of Ruskin's followers who made their homes in the Lake District. At Crosthwaite, according to a memorial sonnet by his Oxford contemporary H. D. Rawnsley, published after Anderson's early death in 1907, this disciple of 'him who bade/Us toil at Hinksey with the pick and spade' was always a scholar who 'Lived out your student life, and plied your trade/of seeking Thought, Art, History, Faith to aid/the quest for Truth that grew with quest more keen . . .'[20]

One or two passages from Ruskin's manuscript of *St Mark's Rest* were reserved for another project that he followed in the Brantwood summer of 1877. Ruskin had begun *The Laws of Fésole* (he liked to use Milton's version of the Italian Fiesole) in 1874 or 1875. Once more he had decided to address the intractable problem of writing an elementary drawing manual. Just as *The Elements of Drawing* related to Ruskin's teaching at the Working Men's College in the 1850s, so *The Laws of Fésole* belongs to his work in his drawing schools at Oxford. An inappropriate, even ludicrous intermediary between the two books is found in the person and writings of the Revd R. St John Tyrwhitt. *The Elements of Drawing* had been out of print for many years. Ruskin had allowed Tyrwhitt to use its woodcuts, and much of the text, in his book *Our Sketching Club*, published in 1875. He was probabaly disappointed with the results of his generosity, for Tyrwhitt's volume has a frontispiece, by its author, of a hunting scene, and throughout its narrative equates 'sketching' with manly and sporting activities, some of them promoted by Tyrwhitt's fictional hunting vicar of 'St Vitus's' in Holywell.

The publication of *Our Sketching Club* gave an opportunity to William Bell Scott, Ruskin's old enemy, to write a hostile review in which he repeated many of his earlier criticisms of *The Elements of Drawing*.[21] Ruskin had no interest in Scott's views about art but was inclined to make *The Laws of Fésole* a noble book that could not be denigrated. Its first chapter, 'All Great Art is Praise', opens with the statement that 'The art of man is the expression of his rational and disciplined delight in the forms and laws of the Creation of which he forms a part.'[22] Further chapters are more practical, though a tone of high endeavour persists through all Ruskin's miscellaneous comment on drawing practice.

The Laws of Fésole was intended not only for undergraduates but for those who might attend 'St George's Schools'. More of Ruskin's work this summer of 1877 was directed toward such schools, imaginary though they were. His *Catalogue of Siliceous Minerals permanently arranged in St George's Museum, Sheffield* may count as a fine example of *The Laws of Fésole's* 'rational and disciplined delight in the forms and laws of Creation', especially since so many of its descriptions, instinctively or not, seem to give advice to a watercolourist. The title of this work (printed in 1877, but never formally published) is a little misleading. Although the minerals catalogued by Ruskin were destined for Sheffield they were in fact at Brantwood. The catalogue is therefore the result of happy hours Ruskin spent in his study in his own home, sorting through his collection of some 3,000 minerals while deciding which ones he would give away. Some idea of the meticulous personal attention Ruskin gave to his minerals may be found by reading such notes as these: 'Questions. (a) What angle may sheaves of plumose oxide reach when involved in quartz? I have never seen them reach a quadrant, still less becoming stellate. (b) Where the plumes emerge, I think they will be found running into plates, and connecting themselves with the forms of micaceous iron. I want larger examples of this intermediate structure . . .'[23] While working on his catalogue Ruskin also wrote a preface for a new edition of *The Ethics of the Dust*, another mineralogical work, though in a different vein. The reissue was at the suggestion of his friend Henry Willett, of Brighton, a self-taught scientist and geologist, who was an occasional benefactor of the Sheffield Museum and of the Guild of St George, though not a member of the Guild.

Turning from his study to the countryside, Ruskin made more general enquiries into the geology of the neighbourhood of Coniston. In his part of the Lake District Ruskin would have found a number of people with whom to discuss this interest. One of them was W. G. Collingwood, who at about this time was starting to construct ingenious models of the Lancashire and Cumberland mountains. Another was the Revd James Clifton Ward of Keswick, who in 1876 had published his *Geology of the Lake District*. Ward was one of the numerous Victorian clergymen with a keen and expert interest in natural science. Geology was not his profession, but that did not mean that he was merely an amateur. The same could be said of Ruskin, whose many geological writings — doubtless with Ward's agreement — had all proclaimed that a love of the natural world was a way to understanding the love of God. Ruskin appreciated Ward's drawings and watercolours, some of which appeared in *Deucalion*. Ward may have suggested that Ruskin be invited to lecture on a geological topic at the Literary and Scientific Institute in Kendal. At all events, these local geological enthusiasms give us the background to Ruskin's talk about the fast-flowing little rivers that fed Coniston Water, 'Yewdale and its Streamlets'.[24] As one would expect, Ruskin did not limit his comments to description of the scenery that lay around the homes of his audience. His address was in opposition to all materialistic 'modern science'. Intriguingly, he also made some questioning comments about the possible reasons for his own, or anyone else's existence. This part of the lecture reflects his thoughts when he visited a dark mountain tarn formed by the Yewdale Beck, on a walk when he was accompanied by the pregnant Joan. Ruskin felt nervous about 'Yewdale and its Streamlets', but the lecture was a success and he repeated it at Eton College later in the year.

⋆ ⋆ ⋆ ⋆

A list of Brantwood visitors in the summer of 1877 helps us to observe the Ruskin 'circle' as it existed in this period of relative calm. It consisted of the closer family friends; then Oxford disciples; then neighbours; and, finally, people who made their way to Coniston because they were members of the Guild of St George or were otherwise concerned with social and political problems.

Such 'pilgrims' to Brantwood were often met at the door by Joan Severn, for she and Arthur — and of course their children — had been encouraged by Ruskin to think of the lakeside house as their second home. They had often stayed there while Ruskin had been abroad in the previous year. Joan's nieces Martha and Marion Gale were at Brantwood for weeks this summer. So was Sara Anderson, now becoming Joan's close friend. Sara's cousin Jamie Anderson came with his Balliol contemporary W. H. Mallock in September. They were followed by another Balliol disciple of that generation, Alexander

Wedderburn, who arrived with his sister Marion. They probably stayed at the Waterhead Hotel in Coniston, for Brantwood was already a crowded small house.

Ruskin was often in Coniston, usually to have tea with Susie Beever. He also made a courtesy call on Leslie Stephen and had a brief, disappointing conversation with Matthew Arnold. In Coniston there were warmer welcomes for Lazarus Fletcher and the Catholic poet Aubrey de Vere. Lakeland was a popular holiday destination for such men as these, and Ruskin met them as an affable local resident. More serious hours were spent with Guild members. Henry Swan had many important plans for the Museum of St George, and proposed a portrait bust of Ruskin by a Sheffield grinder, Benjamin Creswick. With Egbert Rydings Ruskin discussed the Guild's accounts, and with Robert Somervell its legal affairs. He also gave a day to the thoughtful Manchester industrialist Thomas Horsfall.

However, all this varied social life came to an end after Joan's miscarriage on 8 October. There were no more visitors. Ruskin's mind turned to graver subjects. He made notes on a proposed *Life of Moses*, yet another of his unwritten books. He also worried about his next course of Oxford lectures, for term would shortly begin. Ruskin had not been in Oxford since the autumn of 1875. His year's leave of absence from the University had brought him many adventures of the mind, but he decided that his recent investigations were not suitable for Oxford. The material which entered *St Mark's Rest* could have provided a thrilling set of lectures, but Ruskin preferred book publication, so Oxford heard little of Carpaccio and St Ursula.

At one point Ruskin thought that he would lecture on Turner. While he was still in Venice some Turner drawings had come up for sale at Christie's. Four of them, Ruskin defiantly wrote to William Walker (who helped Rydings with the Guild's accounts) 'I've been looking after for thirty years — and I would have bought them with my last guinea, as Goldsmith his bottle of claret . . .'[25] Part of the significance of these Turners was that they had come from the collection of Munro of Novar, John James Ruskin's rival in the matter of Turner acquisitions. After Munro's death, it was easy for Ruskin to feel that he had an ancient right to these watercolours. He had therefore sent Arthur Severn to the sale to bid on his account. Arthur had bought (probably among other items) *Caernarvon Castle*, *The Bridge of Narni* and *Leicester Abbey*. They were waiting for Ruskin in Herne Hill when he returned from Venice in June. Quite apart from the pleasure they gave him, Ruskin also felt a new conviction in the rightness of his lifelong love of Turner. The cost of his purchases did not matter (the *Caernarvon Castle* was knocked down to Severn at £798, a considerable sum). But perhaps the expense of buying Turners made Ruskin the more irritated at Whistler's far more modest, yet also self-assured prices. At all events, Ruskin had declared to Joan Severn that 'I think the getting these new Turners will be of great importance to me. It will set me *on* Turner again, and I think I shall now give a course of lectures on him at Oxford, incorporating all I've said and would say of him, and add some sufficient account of his life, and so publish . . .'[26]

Sadly, this plan was abandoned. Ruskin never told all that Turner meant to him, and could not have done so, for his estimate of the painter was so much confused with his own sorrows and disappointments. Instead, he devised the series of lectures known as 'Readings in *Modern Painters*'. There were twelve of these addresses, packed into three weeks in November of the Michaelmas term. Ruskin read passages from his famous book and improvised some comments, which were often autobiographical. In one lecture he did the same with *Unto This Last.* A further lecture included descriptions of Carpaccio. In thus addressing a new undergraduate generation Ruskin once again became the most prominent lecturer in the University. The Slade Professor's social life was spent with the Acland family and other senior members of the University. He showed his drawing schools to distinguished visitors, but did not teach in his own little academy of art. This term the most significant of his new devotees was Edward Tyas Cook of New College, who in later years would be Ruskin's editor, his biographer, and the foremost authority on his life and writings. No doubt to Cook's disappointment, he did not meet Ruskin at this time. But Cook had his first taste of direct Ruskin scholarship. He had studied Ruskin during his Winchester schooldays. Now he was eager to record his personality and the dazzling *obiter dicta* of his lectures. The 'Readings in *Modern Painters*' were to be reconstructed in 1906 for the Library Edition not only from scraps of Ruskin's manuscripts, found at Brantwood, but also from notes that Cook had made in the lecture room and had carefully preserved.[27] Only one of Ruskin's 1877 addresses was fully written out and published, as 'An Oxford Lecture', in the *Nineteenth Century* of January 1878. Ruskin was pleased to see this discourse in print, for he had been delighted by the success of the series as a whole. He wrote to Susie Beever in Coniston that

> I gave yesterday the twelfth and last of my course of lectures this term, to a room crowded by six hundred people, two-thirds members of the University, and with its door wedged open by those

> who could not get in; this interest of theirs being granted to me, I doubt not, because for the first time in Oxford I have been able to speak to them boldly of immortal life. I intended when I began the course to read only Modern Painters to them; but when I began, some of your favourite bits interested the men so much, and brought so much larger a proportion of undergraduates than usual, that I took pains to reinforce and press them home; and people say I have never given so useful a course yet . . .[28]

From Cook's reconstruction of the lectures we gather that Ruskin's new confidence in speaking 'boldly of immortal life' came to him while he was describing Carpaccio. The course of lectures ended on 1 December. Ruskin now began a dangerous personal experiment. As the anniversary of St Ursula's mystical teaching approached he hoped that it might be repeated. He therefore decided to spend Christmas at Oxford, where he might be alone. In London after the end of term he indulged the Severns, dined with Stacy Marks, went to the circus, saw his old pupil and employee George Butterworth, attended to his charities and thus completed the secular part of the festive season before returning to Corpus Christi late on 23 December. On Christmas Eve he went to a service in Christ Church cathedral, then closed himself away in his rooms. As often before, he took Rose's 'star-letter' to his desk and copied it out. His diary on Christmas morning reads 'My star-letter was sent to me again last night, for which I am thankful; but very lifeless compared with this time last year.'[29] That is, no ghost or spirit returned to him, despite his prayers and other preparations. Ruskin then remained quietly in Oxford until the New Year. He did little work, for *Fors Clavigera* was well ahead of its publication schedule. Ruskin did however use *Fors* to settle a score. Its February 1878 issue contains his contemptuous denunciation of his former assistant Octavia Hill, who had unwisely criticised the organisation and the efficacy of the Guild of St George.[30] Ruskin had also come to loathe her sanctimonious manner and style of social management, and much preferred such an errant bohemian as George Butterfield to the woman who dared to call herself his follower.

Disappointed by St Ursula, furious with Octavia Hill, Ruskin was in a wavering frame of mind when, at the New Year of 1878, he travelled to Windsor Castle to stay there as the guest of Prince Leopold. Once again he tried to find a mystic significance in this short visit. From the royal home he wrote to Joan about St Ursula. 'On Christmas day last year', he declared, 'she took me — without any intent of mine to St George's Chapel in Venice. This afternoon, she took me to St George's chapel, Windsor — and made me sit in Prince Leopold's own stall . . .'[31] Ruskin had genuine affection for the Prince, but could not feel comfortable in the Castle. A letter to Susie Beever told her that 'I'm horribly sulky this morning, for I expected to have a room with a view, if the room was ever so little, and I've got a great big one looking into the Castle yard, and I feel exactly as if I was in a big modern county gaol . . .'[32] Leopold's serious mind was the more fixed on eternal matters because he suffered from extremely poor health. 'Certain colloquies of Mr Ruskin's at the bedside of Prince Leopold — as he lay recovering from perilous illness, and still in danger of a relapse — will dwell in the mind of him who heard them . . .',[33] F. W. H. Myers recorded.

Leopold was not ill while Ruskin was at Windsor, but the two men talked of the ultimate truths of life after death. The 3rd of January was the anniversary of Rose La Touche's birth, so Ruskin decided to tell Prince Leopold of his love for her and of her influence on the Guild of St George. He also sent some instructions from the Castle to George Allen. *Fors Clavigera* was to be regularly dispatched to Windsor; so we should now count Prince Leopold among the small number of people who received, even if they did not study, Ruskin's letters to working men.

From Windsor Ruskin went to London, where he called on Carlyle and spent an evening with his friend Jean Ingelow, the poet. Then he worked at Oxford before travelling, with a heavy heart, to Gladstone's home at Hawarden in Cheshire, where he expected to be even more out of place than at Windsor Castle. There were two reasons for this unlikely expedition. First, Gladstone had recently read and admired the Oxford lecture that Ruskin had contributed to the January number of *The Nineteenth Century*. Secondly, Mary Drew, Gladstone's daughter (married to the Revd Harry Drew), who had known Ruskin for some years through the Burne-Joneses, had asked her father to invite him to the family seat and had persuaded Ruskin to accept the invitation. She imagined, rightly, that the two men would be interested in each other. The politician was Ruskin's senior by ten years, but he too had been a Christ Church undergraduate and shared the Slade Professor's antique concern for Oxford and its institutions. Ruskin and Gladstone were renowned public speakers, one a lecturer and the other an orator, and both were conversationalists. They were two exceptional men who, from their different points of view, held passionate views about the well-being of their nation. Yet the prospects for a friendship cannot have been good. The Guild of St George was at all points opposed to Gladstonian liberalism, and *Fors Clavigera*, which was roughly contemporary with the first two Gladstone governments of 1868–74 and 1880–85, was the constant critic of those administrations. In the *Fors* of September 1875 Ruskin had attacked Gladstone personally, denouncing not only his concept of 'Liberty', which in Ruskin's teaching 'whether in the body, soul or political estate of man, is only another word for Death . . . the body, spirit and political estate being alike healthy only by their bonds and laws; and by Liberty being instantly disengaged into mephitic vapour'; but also his role — so important to Gladstone — as a churchman. He was, this *Fors* continued, 'nothing less than a negative system, hundred-unction in the manner of pomade, to the scald and moribund English pates that still wear their religion decoratively . . .', a Carlylean metaphor that may have been designed to please Ruskin's 'earthly master'.[34]

There are interestingly different accounts of that first Hawarden weekend. E. T. Cook, a political Liberal and always anxious to play down the divisions between Ruskin and Gladstone, suggests that peace was signed and that Ruskin, after two days of the politician's company, 'left Hawarden almost persuaded to be a Gladstonian'. A letter from Ruskin to Joan Severn gives a more personal account of the visit and its formalities. He reported

> a horrid big fashionable dinner — and Miss Gladstone (whom I took in as hostess — her mother not appearing) — though a nice girl (and she had gathered some primroses and put in my room) yet oppressed me terribly by that macadamised manner which girls get who see everybody in the world every day; and a daughter-in-law whom Mr Gladstone took in was worse — a trained London beauty — very beautiful, and dressed like a figure in the Paris costume books — but with a face that froze me hard like the east wind, and broke one to bits afterwards, and there was a brown thin-faced man who came with me from Chester — and knows me at Oxford and I don't know him and can't make him out — and Mr Gladstone talked — and is nice — but a mere shallow stream with deep pools in it that are good for nothing: and I'm fitened and bovyed and misby . . .[35]

Henry Scott Holland, this 'brown thin-faced man', wrote a reminiscence of the occasion in 1898. He recalled that 'Mr Ruskin threw off every touch of suspicion with which he had arrived, and showed with all the frankness and charm of a child his new sense of the greatness and nobility of the character of his host . . .'[36] Another guest, probably George Wyndham, though he wrote anonymously, was more sensitive. He recorded that although Ruskin's 'talk at dinner was altogether delightful' there was also 'an utter hopelessness; a real, pure despair beneath the sunlight of his smile, and ringing through all he said. Why it does not wholly paralyse him I cannot make out.'[37]

After leaving Hawarden Ruskin cancelled the passage in the September *Fors* that likened Gladstone to a barber.[38] But he was to resume his public scorn in 1880, when he referred to Gladstone and Disraeli as 'two old bagpipes with the drone going by steam'. A further (undated) reminiscence is valuable. According to the Pre-Raphaelite painter Henry Holiday, Gladstone said this of Ruskin:

> We had a conversation once about quakers, and I remarked how feeble was their theology and how great their social influence. 'As theologians, they have merely insisted on one or two points of Christian doctrine; but what good work they have achieved socially! — Why, they have reformed prisons, they have abolished slavery, and denounced war'. To which Ruskin answered, 'I am really sorry, but I am afraid I don't think that prisons ought to be reformed, I don't think slavery ought to have been abolished, and I don't think war ought to be denounced'.[39]

Ruskin was exaggerating in order to give a more pronounced opposition to Gladstone's liberal view of the world. Here was a trait he inherited from John James Ruskin and the ultra-Tories who were his father's friends. Such illiberal belligerence often arose from personal irritation, dislike of reformers themselves rather than their causes. John James had found the prison reformer John Howard insupportable and thought anti-slavery campaigners pietistic; and his son was inclined to quarrel with Christian Socialists, all missionaries, and such forward-thinking women as Octavia Hill and Harriet Beecher Stowe. Ruskin admired George Eliot; but at a distance, and grudgingly. As he continually reminded his readers, his old Tory feelings had been perfectly preserved. His humanitarian impulses and his prejudices belonged alike to the 1830s.

Ruskin's early life was much pondered in the first weeks of 1878, for 'being asked by the wife of a dear old friend, W. H. Harrison, to say a few words of our old relations together, I feel like a boy again . . .'. He was composing the memorial essay 'My First Editor', in which he recalled the days when he contributed to Harrison's (who was an ultra-Tory) *Friendship's Offering* — the days when Turner came to dinner in Herne Hill, when his father and mother and nurse were all at home, and no one had heard of Darwin or disestablishment. In this delightful piece may be found many barbs against the radicals both of the 1830s and of the 1870s. 'My First Editor' resembles some of the best of the earlier parts of *Præterita*, and could easily have become a part of Ruskin's autobiography.[40]

* * * *

When Ruskin talked to Gladstone about war he was thinking about conflict in abstract, perhaps Homeric terms; and he was also influenced by the Ruskin family's long acquaintance with soldiers. The most treasured of their army friends was Major-General Sir Herbert Edwardes, Ruskin's exact contemporary and a guest at Herne Hill and Denmark Hill since the 1840s. He would be the subject of Ruskin's book *A Knight's Faith*, published in 1880. During the 1860s Ruskin had made a number of visits to the Royal Military Academy at Woolwich. When he lectured there on 'The Future of England' in 1869 he had become friendly with the gifted teenager Flora Shaw, the daughter of a high-ranking officer. Flora's mother had died in that year, her father was often absent, and she was glad to have an open invitation to Denmark Hill, and then to Joan and Arthur's house at Herne Hill. In 1874 Flora began to write the children's book (though it is best read by adolescents) *Castle Blair*, about a young governess in rural Ireland. Ruskin received its chapters and discussed them with their author. Thus he became the godfather to a best-selling novel for young people which was strikingly 'modern' and quite free of piety. In 1878 — to which date we now return — Ruskin rejoiced in the publication and success of *Castle Blair.* Flora was to have visited Brantwood to celebrate her book, but Ruskin's mental illness delayed her visit.

In the first days of their friendship Flora Shaw had been one of the younger people whom Ruskin had taken to Cheyne Walk to meet Carlyle. He knew that this could be an unnerving experience. 'Now, dear Mr Carlyle', Ruskin had said on the occasion of Flora's visit, 'I have brought this little girl to see you and she will remember it all her life. I want you to say something nice to her.' Carlyle responded quite kindly to this request. He said 'Well, remember this, little girl; I have seen and talked with Goethe. When you are as old as I am, you can say that you knew a man who knew Goethe.'[41] Carlyle was far less interested in young people than was Ruskin, who still insisted on introducing him to people in their twenties. After his visit to Hawarden Ruskin decided to take Gladstone's nephew, Alfred Lyttelton, whom he had met there, for an audience at Chelsea. Lyttelton's account of this meeting records one of the last two or three occasions when Ruskin and Carlyle met:

> Mr Ruskin had prepared me to expect a very old man, not very smooth in temper, nor did he lead me to hope that I should hear much in the way of dialogue between them, for, when less infirm, Carlyle had rarely taken a successful part in dialogue, seizing the bit of conversation between his teeth, and either sustaining it alone, or else remaining silent . . . We were shown into a pretty room, pictures of some of his heroes hung around — Frederick the Great beating a drum (the only sign of militarism which seemed very antipathetic to him in his youth), Cromwell, Luther, and others, with several of himself. A few minutes after, Carlyle came down; he looked very infirm and his hand trembled excessively, while at first he groaned and sighed a good deal, receiving kindly enough however Ruskin's kiss, most tenderly given. He greeted me civilly . . . for the first five or ten minutes Mr Ruskin anxiously humoured his feeble querulous talk of the heat, and the wretched fatigue of a drive to the East End, and the effects of a 'great drench of champagne' which Mary Aitken his niece had given him. But soon he led him to the much-loved topic of Burns, 'one of whose odes is worth an eternity of these poets', including our Patmore, who had been mentioned rather contemptuously as 'one who wrote poems on Cathedrals and cathedral closes'. It was very delightful to see the brilliant smile and to hear the rough loud laugh with which he greeted a Burns quotation which Ruskin made . . .[42]

Lyttelton further recorded of this visit, 'The old man never addressed a word to me until we were leaving, when he suddenly said: "Does the rising generation read me?" — a question which I found it difficult to answer, although it represented obviously his chief interest in the rising generation'. This question of readership was not of much concern to Ruskin. His more popular books were still widely read by young people. As for *Fors Clavigera*, Ruskin had long since conceded that it would have only a minuscule circulation. He might not have minded if *Fors* were read by Carlyle alone. In mid-January of 1878 Ruskin left London for Brantwood. Soon he wrote to Carlyle, thanking him for seeing Alfred Lyttelton and adding ('for this is my chief business') that he wished Carlyle to 'tell me a little of what you would have me say in next *Fors* — of *anything*'. This plan could not be followed. Ruskin, at Brantwood in February, had completed his eighty-seventh number of *Fors*, 'The Snow Manger'. This was to be the last letter of the series before his mental breakdown. *Fors Clavigera* was not resumed before March of 1880.[43]

CHAPTER THIRTY-EIGHT

1878

Ruskin travelled from London to Coniston in mid-February of 1878, taking with him Laurence Hilliard, who was to undertake various secretarial duties while Ruskin prepared *The Laws of Fésole* for press and wrote his preface to James Reddie Anderson's *The Place of Dragons* chapter in *St Mark's Rest*. There are few signs of ill temper in Ruskin's diary, and he occasionally notes that he is happy in his work. At Brantwood, Laurence Hilliard's main task was to help in the preparations for an exhibition. This was to be a show of Turners belonging to Ruskin, organised by the Fine Art Society in Bond Street. The Fine Art Society was one of the new art galleries that opened in London in the later 1870s. Despite its name, it was a commercial enterprise. Unlike the more avant-garde Grosvenor Gallery, the Fine Art Society was interested in mounting historical loan exhibitions of nineteenth-century British art. One of its directors was Marcus Huish. Ruskin looked on Huish with favour because he had offered to lend material to the Guild of St George Museum in Sheffield. He was also amenable to the dealer's proposal of a Turner exhibition. Huish had a simple, excellent idea. In his Bond Street rooms he would show all of Ruskin's Turners from Brantwood and elsewhere, and Ruskin would write an explanatory catalogue. No doubt there would be some difficulties, especially since many Turner drawings that had affected Ruskin were no longer in his possession. None the less an exhibition was feasible, and Ruskin set about arrangements for the show in good spirits. Its opening was scheduled for March of 1878, and by the beginning of February Ruskin was writing entries for its catalogue.

This catalogue, issued as *Notes by Mr Ruskin on his Drawings by the late J. M. W. Turner, RA*, is distressingly incomplete. Its writing was curtailed by Ruskin's illness, and may indeed have contributed to his breakdown. For, as the *Notes* reveal, Ruskin could scarcely contemplate Turner without much sorrowful brooding about his own emotional past. He thought about his youth, his indebtedness to his father, his own early writings; also about his quarrel with Turner and his conviction that the painter's mind and character had deteriorated in his later years. 'Scott's mind failed slowly, by almost imperceptible degrees', Ruskin now wrote, 'Turner's suddenly with snap of some vital chord in 1845.'[1] So it was to be, very soon, with the mind of Turner's greatest interpreter. On 12 February 1878, seated before dawn at his writing table in the Brantwood downstairs study, Ruskin was thinking of Turner's early (1798) painting *Morning among the Coniston Fells* and then concluded his introduction to the *Notes* with two short, poetic and desolate paragraphs:

> Morning breaks as I write, along those Coniston Fells, and the level mists, motionless, and grey beneath the rose of the moorlands, veil the lower woods, and the sleeping village, and the long lawns by the lake-shore.
>
> Oh, that some one had but told me, in my youth, when all my heart seemed to be set on these colours and clouds, that appear for a little while and then vanish away, how little my love for them would serve me, when the silence of the lawn and wood should be completed; and all my thoughts should be of those whom, by neither, I was to meet more!
>
> Brantwood 12th February 1878.[2]

The manuscript of this introduction shows that Ruskin rewrote the second of these paragraphs. As always, he had the shape of any long sentence in his mind before his pen flew to complete its composition, so the only significant change is in using the word 'silence' (of lawn and wood) for the earlier and cancelled 'appearing'. Perhaps Ruskin was thinking of the noises he would hear when the Brantwood household began its daily tasks. At all events, he had been writing while it was still night — though he was by nature a daytime writer — and this circumstance increased his feelings of loneliness. He also, compiling notes on his Turner drawings, once more thought that there was some foredoomed way in which his own life resembled that of the painter. 'Howsoever it came to pass', he recorded of Turner in this February week, 'a strange, and in many respects grievous metamorphosis takes place upon him, about the year 1825. Thenceforward he shows clearly the sense of a terrific wrongness and sadness, mingled in the beautiful order of the earth; his work becomes partly satirical, partly reckless, partly — and in its greatest and noblest features — tragic'.[3] This might be a description not only of Turner but also of the author of *Fors Clavigera*. One naturally turns to *Fors* for evidence of Ruskin's concerns in this February, when snow lay on the fells and the weather was dark. At the same time as his work on the Turner catalogue Ruskin was writing 'The Snow Manger', his March *Fors*. This issue of the monthly letter begins with criticism of Harriet Martineau, continues with praise of Flora Shaw's *Castle Blair*, which had just been published, and then apologises for some hostile comments in a previous *Fors* about Gladstone. These few opening pages are quite normal, by Ruskin's standards. Soon, however, the letter becomes agitated, and we find the following passage, written three days after Ruskin's conclusion of his preface to the Turner catalogue:

> . . . It can't be the end of this *Fors*, however, I find (15th February, half-seven morning), for I have forgotten twenty things I meant to say; and this instant, in my morning's reading, opened and read, being in a dream state, and not knowing well what I was doing, — of all things to find a new message! — in the first chapter of Proverbs.
>
> I was in a dreamy state, because I had got a letter about the Thirlmere debate, which was to me, in my purposed quietness, like one of the voices on the hill behind the Princess Parazide. And *she* could not hold, without cotton in her ears, dear wise sweet thing. But luckily for me, I have just had help from the Beata Vigri at Venice, who sent me her own picture and St Catherine's, yesterday, for a Valentine; and so I *can* hold on: — only just read this first of Proverbs with me, please . . .[4]

These paragraphs demand annotation; and notes will now be given to many of Ruskin's letters and diary entries in the week to come. Looking at the 'Snow Manger' *Fors*, we understand that he had been reading Proverbs and thought to make a commentary, probably in the same way that he had concluded his *Fors* of December 1877 with a discussion of Revelation. The 'Thirlmere debate' refers to the proposals by the Corporation of Manchester to supply the city with water from Thirlmere. Other comments on the matter are in the *Notes* on Turner, still being written in this week. The Princess Periezadeh will be found in the *Arabian Nights*. Her adventures were an influence on Ruskin's book for children, *The King of the Golden River*, written in 1841, now so long ago. For an explanation of Ruskin's 'Valentine' we turn to his diary. On 14 February he records that 'I've had the Madonna for a Valentine! — Fors gave me her from the Beata Vigri — the first thing I set eyes on — and all her beauty in the moon dawned on me as I looked . . .'[5] This 'valentine' may be identified. It was a watercolour copy by Mrs Henry Goodwin, an associate though not a member of the Guild of St George, of Caterina Vigri's painting of St Ursula, later described by Ruskin as 'St Ursula with four saints; the nun, Caterina Vigri, who painted the picture, at her feet'.[6]

By mid-February, then, Ruskin's writing had fallen into 'free association', both in *Fors Clavigera* and in his diary. The 'twenty things I meant to say', the rush of thoughts, memories, plans for writing and personal talismans that came into his mind are to be found in the lengthening and, at first sight, incomprehensible diary entries. His correspondence was also strange. Letters to Joan Severn at this period are missing, though there is in existence an empty packet marked 'The Morning Letters 22nd February 1878'.[7] This suggests that Ruskin then wrote to Joan in the same extended and confessional vein he used in the 'Christmas Story' letters of December 1876. 'Teachings' and 'messages' entered Ruskin's mind from (probably) the night of 13–14 February, when he lay awake after he 'overate and drank myself and had one of the old horrible bilious serpent dreams', then got up to write some of the 'Snow Manger' *Fors.*[8] By 20 February Ruskin's correspondence is deranged. He wrote to Georgiana Cowper-Temple on that date:

> Darling Isola
>
> I couldn't understand till last night, why I had put the 'Beautiful Island' in my Oxford school series in the cabinet illustrating the 'Sentiment of Landscape'. Now wasn't it odd I didn't think of *that.* And isn't it odd you didn't think who came into the room? Well look here the last message but one I got, last night — was 'They of Italy salute you'. Nero — you just write to that little Duchess, and tell her, she's to pick up sticks in *Italy* for *Polly*'s put the kettle on, and we'll all have tea.
>
> Polly's a vulgar word — very — but Duchesses picking up sticks must learn low English And look here ask that little beauty from Cheshire if she remembers my one nearly 'boiling over' at breakfast. And see Punch for boiling over generally — and good-bye for to-day Ever your lovingest St C.[9]

Some of these references can be explained. One would expect the 'Beautiful Island' to be a Turner. However, only his *Boats on a Beach* was both in the Fine Art Society exhibition and in one of the cabinets of landscapes in the 'Rudimentary Series' at the Oxford drawing schools. It was one of three that Ruskin borrowed from Oxford for the exhibition. Who was it that 'came into the room'? Probably Rose La Touche, when she and Ruskin were guests at Broadlands in 1872. 'Look here' a phrase Ruskin uses twice in the letter, was one of his nicknames for Rose, an allusion to the argumentative side of her nature. 'Nero' was the name of the Carlyles' dog. The 'little Duchess' may also be Rose, now instructed to be less haughty. The 'little beauty from Cheshire' is Mary Gladstone: Ruskin is remembering an incident during his recent visit to Hawarden, her father's Cheshire home.

On 16 February 1878 the magazine *Punch* had a cartoon of a kettle whose steam is drawn to resemble the heads of politicians.

In the week before Ruskin's delirium began, he wrote more letters of this sort while also leading a normal country life. His neighbour Susie Beever records, for instance, that on Sunday, 17 February Ruskin called on her and '*Never* did I see him so happy or so cheerful . . . Never did I so enjoy his conversation . . . Almost his last words as he went away were "I'm coming again very soon".'[10] But by Thursday of this week of 17–23 February Ruskin had retreated into private fantasies. He dreamt or imagined that he and Rose had at last married. He was a bridegroom waiting at the altar. All around was a sea of faces, in which he recognised William Cowper-Temple. Rose, wearing a white dress, approached him. An organ played and Bruno, Rose's dog, barked in happy excitement.[11] Now (on Thursday, 21 February) Ruskin wrote to George MacDonald — addressing him for the first time since the reunion with Rose at Broadlands in 1872 —

> Dear George, we've got married — after all after all — but such a surprise! — Tell the Brown Mother, and Lily. Bruno's out of his wits with joy up at the Chartreuse Grande — and so am I, for that matter — I meant — but I'm in an awful hurry, such a lot of things to do — Just got this done before breakfast — the fourth letter. Ever your lovingest, John Ruskin. Oh Willie — Willie — he's pleased too, Georgie dear.[12]

Hoping to explain this letter, one surmises that the 'Brown Mother' was MacDonald's wife Louisa. 'Lily' would be their daughter Lila. 'Willie' is probably Ruskin's cousin William Richardson, who had helped Ruskin's attempts to become Rose's husband seven years before, at Matlock in 1871. One of the chapters in *Præterita* was to be 'La Grande Chartreuse', in which Ruskin discusses the life of monks in its Carthusian monastery. The founder of the Carthusian order was of course St Bruno.

In these letters to Georgiana Cowper-Temple and George MacDonald we may, therefore, find relatively transparent references to Ruskin's concerns. His correspondents may not have understood all that he was talking about; but some of them were accustomed to a teasing, confidential manner. Sara Anderson was one of these people. In the week of the 17–23 she indulged Ruskin, when it would have been wiser to talk to Joan (who was in Herne Hill) about the need for a doctor. Sara was to receive one of the last of Ruskin's letters before his insanity. Dated 22 February (the Friday of that week) it reads

Darling Secretary,

Jamie has just left me — after doing — (he knows not what,) with me, since lunch — and teaching me such lots about Leuchothea's veil that saved Ulysses, that I don't know how to be grateful enough to him. — But what he taught me was summed up in a little piece of information he gave me ten minutes ago — which I take to mean permission to tell my darling secretary — How old are you — Diddie? — I wonder how old you are! and if you *can* keep a secret? — or keep — your countenance — when people touch near it?

I was showing him my new prosody — and saying I *couldn't* think why it was so hindered that it was now a year and half or so since begun at Verona — all ready for the press — and see — copied all fair by somebody — 'Diddie', said he, I hadn't looked close and didn't recognise the hand at once.

— Well, in the page he had opened were my favourite lines,

> If she love me, this believe
> *I* will die, ere *she* shall grieve

And the thing I may tell you — perhaps — I don't know — I may not be allowed yet — is that Rosie has told me. — she knows it, and that she will never grieve anymore so that I needn't die — unless I like!

Ever your lovingest Task-master.[13]

As with the two previous letters, some explanation is called for. It will be recalled that Sara Anderson was James Reddie Anderson's cousin. Leucothea, and her iconography, is the subject of a couple of paragraphs in the April 1876 number of *Fors Clavigera*. Jamie obviously had more to add about the goddess. Ruskin's 'new prosody' was a work that had occasionally occupied him since his visit to Verona in the autumn of 1876. Its theories would be published as *Elements of English Prosody* in 1880. The lines of poetry are from the song beginning 'Shall I, wasting in despair' by George Wither (1588–1667). Thoughts of Wither and then of Rose led Ruskin to make excited comments about the nature of death, grief, and life after death. Are these the thoughts of a man who was insane? It is not easy to say that Ruskin's musings were rational. On the other hand he collected his thoughts, wrote them out and put them in letters to correspondents whose names and addresses he could remember. No one can read these three letters, to Georgiana Cowper-Temple, George MacDonald and Sara Anderson without feeling that Ruskin's mind had strayed far beyond normality; and yet, if we know that mind, they make a certain sense. We recognise the themes of Ruskin's writing and the main tragedy of his personal life. The same might be said of Ruskin's diary during this week of 17–23 February. The 'Brantwood Diary' is a precious and unique document. Nothing else in literature resembles this record of a great intellect falling into madness. Viewed casually, the entries in the diary after 14 February 1878 appear to be random and inexplicable. They may none the less be annotated, if not fully understood. The next pages of the present biography reproduce the diary of the hours (Friday–Saturday, 22–23 February) before Ruskin's delirium began. The diary text is in the left-hand column, with explanatory notes on the right.[14]

22 February

Fors text kept open by Pallmall, — no — I kept it open — (the Bible) all night long at II Timothy 3, with the Pallmall Gazette in it and on my dressing table — with it, my box-bible with the Cardinal binding; my present from Jamie, and Susie's Shakespeare.	Presumably writing for the April number of *Fors Clavigera*, never issued. There are in all fifteen references to the *Pall Mall Gazette* in *Fors*. The most recent had been in the issue of March 1878, written on 15 February. See XXIX, 374. 'For men shall be lovers of their own selves, covetous boasters, proud blasphemers disobedient to parents . . . But continue thou in the things which thou has learned and hast been assured of, knowing of whom thou has learned them. And that from a child thou hast known the holy scriptures . . .' The 'box-bible' is not identified. Ruskin's collection of Bibles is partially described in W. G. Collingwood, *Ruskin Relics*, 1903, 195–211. Mr Dearden suggested to Viljoen that the volume had probably belonged to a cardinal, had an accompanying box and had been a present to Ruskin from James Reddie Anderson. Susie Beever's compilation *Remarkable Passages in Shakespeare* (1870).
On my little dressing table — by my head, Richter's Love is Stronger than Death.	Not identified, but probably the fourteenth drawing in *Fürs Haus*, by Ludwig Richter: *Liebe ist stärker als Tod*, which shows a girl crowned with roses while Death, a skeleton, is about to cut down a rose bush.

— With all I've left there.	
— And on my chimney piece, Turners Jerusalem — and Blake's Ruth. Left there also	Turner's watercolour *Jerusalem: the Pool of Bethesda* belonged to Ruskin and would shortly be exhibited at the Fine Art Society. If the drawing had already been packed for transfer to London Ruskin would have looked at its engraving in his copy of *Illustrations of the Bible from Original Sketches Taken on the Spot* (1836). William Blake's *Ruth Parting from Naomi* is in his *Illustrations of the Bible.*
Now — opening by Fors, I get John III. 3 and read on, to — wrought in God, but hastily, knowing it by heart	That is, practising *sortes Biblicae.*
Leaning a little selfishly on 'How can a man be born when he is old'?	'Verily, verily, I say unto thee: Except a man be born again, he cannot see the kingdom of God. Nicodemus saith unto him, How can a man be born when he is old? can he enter the second time into his mother's womb, and be born . . . ?'
— Too much to write. — I don't think I shall forget — the chief message to myself as a painter, coming after a Sculptor.	In Ruskin's 1870 lecture 'Of the Division of Arts', subsequently part of *Aratra Pentelici,* he had stated: 'Whenever and however we bring a shapeless thing into shape, we do so under the laws of the one great art of sculpture'. See XX, 201. The sense is that sculpture as an art preceded the invention of painting.
Delphi first. Then Aegina. Behind Carpaccio.	The triangular arrangement was perhaps meant to be symbolic of Ruskin's teaching since about 1869. For Ruskin's Delphic symbolism see *The Queen of the Air,* XIX, 363, and *Aratra Pentelici,* XX, 269. In the undelivered lecture 'The Tortoise of Aegina', XX, 382, we find a discussion of human and divine justice. Ruskin had most recently written about Carpaccio in the chapter 'The Shrine of Slaves', published separately in 1877 and later a part of *St Mark's Rest.* See XXIV, 191–400.

February 22. *Good* Friday

Recollected all about message from Rosie to me as was drawing on the scaffolding in St Georges Chapel — My saying I would serve her to the death —

A conflated recollection of Ruskin's work in copying Carpaccio in San Giorgio degli Schiavoni in Venice in 1870 and his mystical experiences there in 1876–77.

Tonight — (last night) — lying awake — came — Ada with the Golden Hair.

Perhaps Ada Hartnell. But note also 'Ada! sole daughter of my house and heart . . .' 11, Byron, *Childe Harold*, III, i.

1. — Can the Devil *speak truth* — confer letter to Francie about her little feet).

Banquo in *Macbeth*, I, ii.
Francie is Frances Graham.

And 2. If that thou beest a devil &c. connected with, (Made wanton — &c. the night with her)

Iago in *Othello* II, iii.

To Burne-Jones. — Oh my Black Prince — and they take you for one of the firm of Brown — &c. — See Brown, &c. away on Lago Maggiore —

Burne-Jones shared his Christian name with the 'Black Prince' Edward, son of Edward III, the 'typical knight or squire' who took St George for his master. See XXVII, 384–45.

Ruskin means that Burne-Jones had been wrongly associated with the coarser art of Ford Madox Brown.

The Lago Maggiore was for Ruskin the 'divine' lake on the last stage of his journeys to Venice. See XII, 210 and XXXV, 320.

Tintoret — (Sempre si fa il Mare Maggiore)

The last words of the second lecture of *The Two Paths* come from Tintoretto's remark '*E faticoso lo studio della pittura e sempre si fa il mare maggiore*' (The study of painting is fatiguing work, and the sea is always growing larger). See IV, 27 and XVI, 318.

To Connie — oh Connie — didn't we quarrel among the Alpine Roses, and make it up again by the moonlight.

Constance Hilliard. Ruskin recalls two incidents from their summer together in Switzerland in 1866 and their visit to Verona in 1872.

— And wasn't I naughty sometimes! — and do you recollect bidding me go before you at Verona? Ask Rosie to make your back better She knows something about backs.

— To Madge. Oh, Madge — so do *you* don't you, but why do you ever play with darling old vulgar Baxter — see opposite —

Madge remains unidentified. Perhaps a servant or a Coniston neighbour. Peter Baxter had become Ruskin's valet in 1876.

Here Ruskin continues his entry on the left-hand page of the diary.

darling old vulgar Baxter — (and our American cousin —): Baxter did so spoil that loveliest part of yours — Madge, — when you made somebody so jealous, and had to go away again — you naughty lamb of a Madge.

Unidentified, unless Charles Eliot Norton.

To Joseph Severn — Keats — Endymion — quenched in the chaste beams — yes — oh yes — Proserpina mine. I have not looked back nor took my hand from the Jason plough.

Keats's friend and Arthur Severn's father, whom Ruskin had first met in Rome in 1840.

Keats' opening line of *Endymion*, 'A thing of beauty is a joy for ever' was often quoted by Ruskin. In 1880 it would provide the title for the reprinted version of *The Political Economy of Art*, then published as *A Joy for Ever* (*And its Price in the Market*).

'. . . But I might see young Cupid's fiery shaft / Quench'd in the chaste beams of the watery moon, / And the imperial votaress passed on, / In maiden meditation, fancy-free.' *A Midsummer Night's Dream*, II, i.

Viljoen comments, 'Within the region of Proserpina, the man who memorably "looked back" was Orpheus at his Eurydice, having lost his patience. Contrastingly, Ruskin believed that he himself had patiently pressed forward . . .' BD, 125–6.

	Ruskin had described the ploughing of Jason in *Aratra Pentelici* as 'this great mythical expression of the conquest of the earth-clay and brute-force by vital human energy'. See XX, 328–30.
And when gold and gems adorn the plough. Oh — you dear Blake — and so mad too —	'When Gold & Gems adorn the Plow / To Peaceful Arts shall Envy Bow.' William Blake, *Auguries of Innocence*, III, 101–2.
Do you know what Titians good for *now* you stupid thing?	Blake had criticised Titian's work, as Ruskin knew from Alexander Gilchrist's *Life of Blake* (1863).
I didn't know where to go on — but don't think I should stop. — And Andrea Gritti — then? quite unholy, is he, you stupid? And Dandolo then, I suppose? and the Blind Guide that had celestial light? Yes — and you barefoot Scotch lassies — Diddie and all of you dears — — if only you would go barefoot a bit, in the streets So pretty — so pretty.	Ruskin's handwriting awkwardly strays from one page of the diary to the next. Ruskin owned a portrait of Doge Andrea Gritti (now attributed to Catena), which he believed to be by Titian, and which hung in the Brantwood dining room. Doge Enrico Dandolo, who is discussed in *The Queen of the Air* (XIX, 391–92). Milton, 'So much the rather thou Celestial light / Shine inward, and the mind through all her powers / Irradiate, there plant eyes . . . / that I may see and tell / Of things invisible to mortal sight.' *Paradise Lost*, III, 51–55). Sara Anderson, Frances Graham and Joan Severn, all Scottish.
Naked foot. That shines like snow — and falls on earth — or gold — as mute.	As Ruskin would write in *Præterita*, 'Joanie could always dance everything *rightly*, having not only the brightest light and warmth of heart, but a faultless foot . . . in its swiftest steps rising and falling with the gentleness which only Byron had found words for — . . . Naked foot, That shines like snow — and falls on earth as mute.' See XXV, 559. The quotation is from *The Corsair*, II, 13–14.
Oh — dear Doge Selvo, I want to know the shape	Doge Domenico Selvo appears in *St Mark's Rest*. Ruskin wished to know about the

of your cap, terribly. I don't know which is best — yours — or Gritti's. — Tell me all about it — Raphael dear — from the angle then and please angel of the lagoons from the Paradise, — tell me what my own sweet Tintoret meant by those —	shape of his cap to help him date some mosaics in St Mark's cathedral. See XXIX, 268–69 and 295. The angel Raphael. In the lecture 'The Relation between Michael Angelo and Tintoret', given at Oxford in 1872, Ruskin had described Tintoretto's *Paradise,* in which 'In front, nearer, flies Raphael; and under him is the four-square group of the Evangelists . . . Far down, under these . . . rises the Angel of the Sea, praying for Venice . . .' See XX, 106.
Yes	
'Send for the lady to the Sagittary'.	*Othello*, I, iii.
(And praise be to thee — oh God. We praise thee Oh God, we acknowledge thee to be the Lord)	From the *Te Deum*. See XXV, xxv.
Finished, and my letter from 'Piero' my Venetian gondolier put in, here, and all. I am going to lock up with the Horses of St Marks. $^1/_4$ to one (20 minutes) by my Father's watch — 22nd February 1878*	Piero had been Ruskin's gondolier in 1876–77.
*I couldn't find the key and then remembered I had not thanked the dear Greek Princess — nor Athena of the Dew — and Athena	The Greek maid who, in legend, became the wife of Doge Selvo before he became a monk. See XXIV, 274. Athena of the Dew and Athena in the Earth are discussed in *The Queen of the Air*. See XIX. 334–5.

Here the diary breaks off, but after writing these words Ruskin did not go to his rest. The events of this terrible Friday night and Saturday morning of 22–3 February are recorded in an article by 'H' published in the *British Medical Journal* shortly after Ruskin's death in 1900. 'H' is almost certainly Dr George Harley, a friend of Ruskin's last active years. They had mineralogical interests in common, and Harley was a Brantwood visitor in 1887. In his article 'H' reports that Ruskin told him that during that night he became 'powerfully impressed by the idea that the Devil was about to seize me'. Ruskin then thought, 'H' continues, that

> the only way to meet him was to remain awake waiting for him all through the night, and combat him in a naked condition. I therefore threw off all my clothing, although it was a bitterly cold February night, and there awaited the Evil One . . . I walked up and down my room, to which I had retired about eleven o'clock, in a state of great agitation, entirely resolute as to the approaching struggle. Thus I marched about my little room, growing every moment into a state of greater exaltation; and so it went on until the dawn began to break, which, at that time of year, was rather late, about half-past seven o'clock . . .

Ruskin then, according to 'H', went to the window to watch the dawn.

> As I put forth my hand toward the window a large black cat sprang at me from behind the mirror! Persuaded that the foul fiend was here at last in his own person, though in so insignificant a form . . . I grappled with it in both my hands, and gathering all the strength that was in me, I flung it with all my might and main against the floor . . . Then, worn out with bodily fatigue, with walking and waiting and watching, my mind racked with ecstasy and anguish, my body benumbed with the bitter cold of a freezing February night, I threw myself upon the bed, all unconscious, and there I was found later in the morning in a state of prostration and bereft of my senses.[15]

Although this does not reproduce the tone of Ruskin's conversation, 'H's article appears to give an authentic account of the breakdown. Of far greater value, of course, are the diary entries. They possess their own eloquence and are not a report. The diary brings us to the abyss of Saturday morning. We know that Ruskin's mind is about to break, yet are continually reminded of the nobility of that mind. These diary jottings are filled with meaning. The annotation given above could often be augmented, especially when diary entries prompt us to reach deeply into Ruskin's personal biography. Here are two examples. The quarrel with 'Connie', Constance Hilliard, took place during the sad, beautiful holiday in the Swiss Alps in 1866 after the death of Connie's aunt Pauline Trevelyan. Those weeks in Neuchâtel, Interlaken and Lucerne were to have been the subject of a *Præterita* chapter, 'The Rainbows of Giessbach', projected but never written. Ruskin's autobiography does however mention his long-standing knowledge of Turner's *Jerusalem: the Pool of Bethesda.* He first studied this drawing in his copy of *Illustrations of the Bible from Original Sketches taken on the Spot,* engraved by W. and E. Finden, with descriptions by the Revd T. H. Horne, BD (2 vols, 1836), which contains landscapes by Turner, Augustus Callcott and Clarkson Stanfield. The book had been lent to him at some point in the late 1830s by Eliza Fall, the sister of his childhood friend Richard Fall.[16] Although he had little need to refer to its illustrations, still less to its text, Ruskin kept the Findens' volume by his side. In fact he had two sets of 'Finden' at Brantwood, one for the library and the other kept in the bedroom.

The book was an emblem of his past life. It is possible to read the diary entries preceding Ruskin's madness as a collection of such emblems. They might be actual objects within the small private museum of his bedroom, such as books, drawings, his father's watch, or the box containing the Cardinal's bible; or the emblems could be quotations from Tintoretto, or from letters from Rose, or an arrangement (as in the entry 'Delphi first. Then Aegina. Behind Carpaccio') of some of the leading principles of his thought.

This is only one of a number of possible approaches to the diary. Ruskin could not remember writing the entries during the days before his madness, and thought they were notes for a future number of *Fors Clavigera.* The monthly letter had now arrived at its eighty-seventh issue, and its delivery had been unfailing. *Fors* made personal demands on Ruskin for many reasons, one of which was its unremitting campaign for good. During the night of 22 February Ruskin was gathering tokens of his best thoughts to keep his mind from evil. We may imagine him in the winter darkness, looking at his Bible and other treasures by candlelight, his fire low, thinking of the devil and allowing all sorts of the devil's thoughts to disturb him. 'Can the Devil *speak truth*', he asked himself in the diary. Perhaps the black midnight of 22 February had stirred memories of *Macbeth,* for this is Banquo's horrified exclamation after hearing the prophecies of the three witches. A few lines later Banquo says '. . . But 'tis strange;/ And oftentimes, to win us to our harm,/The instruments of darkness tell us truths;/Win us with honest trifles, to betray us/In deepest consequence — '. Did Ruskin fear that he might be tempted in this way? The idea of the devil's untruthfulness then sent him to *Othello,* which rivals *Macbeth* as Shakespeare's most satanic play. Quoting Iago's lying speculation about Desdemona's love-making, Ruskin makes one of his rare references to sexual matters. The diary mentions the devil and sex elsewhere in the course of the week of Ruskin's mental decline. On 17 February he quoted Ophelia's mad song about a girl losing her virginity.[17] Later that day he imagined that the devil had put him in mind of the scene in *Cymbeline* (II.2) in which Iachimo pores over the naked, sleeping Imogen.[18]

These scraps of Shakespearian verse — so unlike the passages that Susie Beever had collected for her anthology — had probably disturbed Ruskin through all his adulthood. Not for the first time in his life, he was agonised by the thought of his sexual nature. As he approached madness, Ruskin thought of physical desire and virginity, but did so through the remote hand of Shakespeare. He looked for explanations of lust in the work of a supreme poet of life. This is characteristic of the diary in February. It is a markedly cultured document which ranges over wide areas of Ruskin's scholarship, his Christianity and his responses to art. Studying the diary, we find autobiographical icons and historical patterns that point us to the themes of Ruskin's books.

The actual 'Brantwood Diary' (which was not published until 1971) was for some years in the collection of its editor Helen Gill Viljoen, who treasured the manuscript volume. Its contents had been known to E. T. Cook, the editor of the Library Edition, but he made little use of his transcripts of the original and avoided all comment on the entries of 17–23 February. Perhaps it needed a child of the age of psychoanalysis to look at the diary with a different attitude. Professor Viljoen (1900–74) was such a person. She offered no clinical analysis, for her expertise was not in that area. But her view of the entries of 17–23 February should now be cited. 'It is also revelatory', she wrote, 'that, as the subconscious gains ascendance, we should be companioned not by the ugly and the gross but, rather, by the beauty and the purity evoked by almost every reference he makes'.[19]

None of that beauty of mind would have been apparent to those who found Ruskin, naked and deranged, on the morning of Saturday, 23 February. The first person to have entered Ruskin's bedroom would have been his valet Peter Baxter, who sought help from other servants and from Laurence Hilliard. Telegrams were sent to the Severns at Herne Hill and to Henry Acland and John Simon, old friends of Ruskin who were medical men. The first doctor to see Ruskin was George Parsons, who had a practice at Hawkshead, some five miles from Brantwood on the other side of the Monk Coniston moor. Dr Parsons had first treated Ruskin in 1873 and is noted in *Fors*

Clavigera of March 1876 as 'my good doctor'.[20] In future years he would often be in attendance on Ruskin, who came to depend upon him. In the *Fors* of March 1880, the first public letter that Ruskin was able to write after his breakdown, Parsons is described as 'the one who really carried me through, and who never lost hope'.[21]

John Simon sped to Brantwood on hearing of Ruskin's collapse and thereafter took overall charge of his treatment. One account of the earlier stages of Ruskin's illness is found in Simon's letter to Henry Acland, sent on the Friday after the Saturday of his friend's breakdown:

Brantwood
Mar 1 1878

Dear Acland,

If I had written to you twelve hours ago I must have made an almost hopeless report of the state in which our poor friend then was, but since that time the improvement which has taken place (and which if I had not seen it I would scarcely have believed possible) has been so great, and seems so fixed and progressive, that we are now, comparatively, with bright outlook.

You have heard the nature of the attack. The acute mania which on Saturday became unmistakeable had apparently been felt by himself to be coming on for some previous days. The excitement on Saturday was great and on Sunday and Monday greater, and it was not till late on Tuesday that narcotics got the upper hand. When I arrived on Wednesday morning, he was under their influence, and remained so until late in the afternoon, when he emerged, not free from delirium, but with less excitement than before. As night approached, it became evident that he must again have the narcotic, and with this he remained quiet till midday yesterday: when his waking was with apparently still less tendency to relapse into excitement, and we were hoping that the worst had passed. But at about 8 p.m., he began to show such signs of exhaustion as alarmed us. These increased, till it became impossible to rouse him even to swallow, and for three or four hours I thought he would hardly live till morning. Gradually we caught sight of opportunities again of getting a little stimulus and food into him, and step by step he rallied. At the present time he is quiet, ready to take all nourishment which is offered him, recognising all who are about him, puzzled and bewildered as to his state and circumstances, but with no flagrant signs of insanity, though probably, if he were let talk, he would show disorder.

I have made arrangements to remain here as long as it may seem that I can be of real use or comfort; and I hope to see him fairly advanced in convalescence before I leave.

The attack throws a strong explanatory light on the past, and must be an imperative warning for the future.

Yours faithfully
John Simon.[22]

From Simon's firm but optimistic letter it is clear that Ruskin knew, probably by the Friday morning of the week of 23 February–1 March, that he had been insane; and, further, that he was able to tell Simon that he could remember premonitions of the 'acute mania' in the days before he was struck down. This self-knowledge was not to last. Soon Ruskin was shouting senselessly, or in his quieter moments would repeat 'Rosie-Posie' to himself, or reiterate the phrases 'Everything white! Everything black!' Male nurses were brought to the house. They restrained Ruskin when he was violent and administered the forcible feeding. Henry Acland arrived from Oxford, anxious to see his old friend. He had a cold reception from Simon and from Joan Severn, who both disliked him. So demanding was Brantwood's patient that the routines of the house broke down, and so did the proprieties of hospitality. Acland was sent to join the servants at lodgings in Coniston; their rooms were now occupied by the burly nurses.

Joan was distraught. Then another crisis occurred. She found that she had no money for the household expenses. She had none of her own. Neither had her husband. Arthur Severn was dispatched to London to appeal to Ruskin's solicitors and his bank while Joan looked at the awful prospects of her family's financial future. If Ruskin died, or were committed to an asylum for the rest of his life, how would his fortune be administered? At this time, in mid-March, money problems became the more distressing to Joan because Ruskin's ravings so often returned to that very subject. About a month after his breakdown he could recognise Joan and spoke to her in terms she reported to John Simon.

While I write I am down in the depths after a good cry. It is so difficult *not to mind* when he speaks in a calm deliberate voice, accusing me of the most dreadful things — saying he *knows* I am the cause of all this — and *through me* he has been poisoned; or that he is lying dead in his coffin, as he holds my hand, and that I only *think* he is living, and that I have set everybody against him, and that I have killed him to get his house and property — it breaks my heart!'[23]

At times, even Dr Parsons came close to despair. At the end of March, a month and more after Ruskin's mind had broken, he despondently thought that other doctors would be consulted and that they would recommend that Ruskin should be placed in an asylum, 'if the worst comes to the worst'. That is, he feared that his patient's condition might be permanent.

Ruskin was insane for a month before Joan's bulletins to the Simons could report any signs of hope or recovery. Even when he returned to a more gentle self, reality and fantasy were intermingled in Ruskin's mind. By 27 March, when he could sit in a chair in his bedroom and would take food if Joan gave it to him, he said: 'I wonder which is the dream. *You* standing there feeding me — or Jackson [a nurse] holding me down so cruelly in bed?'[24]

Gradually, as his health improved, Ruskin had more sense of the world around him. He was glad to see flowers in his room and the whiteness of snow outside his window. He understood favourite old books when they were read aloud. On 4 April he read one by himself, choosing Maria Edgeworth's *Moral Tales*, a volume he had known since childhood. We observe here, not at all parenthetically, that Ruskin had always liked the passage in Maria Edgeworth's *Helen* in which Lady Davenant scorns the adage that 'no man is a hero to his valet de chambre'.[25] Ruskin thought, as a matter of principle, that fine men should appear heroic to their servants. So it was with Ruskin's personal attendant Peter Baxter. He is himself a relatively unsung hero of the 1878 illness and of others that were to follow. In the eighteen months since he had joined Ruskin's service this young Irishman (still in his mid-twenties in 1878) had developed a genuine admiration for his employer. Baxter had known Ruskin odd, even crazy, in Venice, and had now helped to nurse him in extreme and degrading circumstances. Baxter never thought of a different life. He left the side of his 'beloved master' only once, at Folkestone in 1887, when ordered to do so by Joan. Baxter was at the bedside when Ruskin died in 1900 and remained in service at Brantwood, living with his wife and children in the lodge, until his own death in 1918.

The loyal Peter Baxter helped to re-establish normal Brantwood life in early April, when the nurses left, the servants returned, and all parties considered what to do next. On 7 April Ruskin was able to go downstairs to his study. For once in his life, he scarcely knew how to occupy himself at his writing table, but looked in his diary and sorrowfully considered its mid-February entries. Not only was Ruskin too feeble to write. All his friends and doctors were telling him that his illness had been the result of overwork. He now told Joan that he would give up his public activities, by which he meant *Fors Clavigera* and the Guild of St George; that he would not return to Oxford; that he would give all his Turners to her and to Arthur; and that, in the part of life that remained to him, he would quietly study birds. Ruskin maintained this mood of resignation through most of the spring. He sent short notes to Susie Beever and other undemanding friends. Laurence Hilliard had charge of most of his public correspondence. There were many anxious enquiries about Ruskin's health, for this had not been entirely a private illness. The breakdown had been reported in the newspapers. Announcements about the patient's progress were made by the Fine Art Society. This was because the exhibition of Ruskin's Turners, which ran from March until the summer of 1878, was visited by thousands. The exhibition has been somewhat overlooked by Turner scholarship. It was none the less important, and its popularity may be gauged from the catalogue, which had reached its thirteenth edition by the end of the show.

Inside the front cover of the first edition of the catalogue was a slip reading 'In consequence of Mr Ruskin's sudden and dangerous illness the latter portion of these Notes is presented in an incomplete state, and the Epilogue remains unwritten. February 27, 1878.' The seventh edition of the catalogue, issued at the end of May, contains the first intellectual work of Ruskin's convalescence. He now wrote the Epilogue and dated it 'Brantwood, 10th May 1878. Being my father's birthday, — who — though as aforesaid, he sometimes would not give me this, or that, — yet gave me not only all these drawings, but Brantwood — and all else.'[26] Ruskin thought of the Fine Art Society exhibition as a memorial to his father as well as to Turner himself. The epilogue mentions one or two drawings that Ruskin had coveted in the 1840s, while Turner was still alive, yet had not managed to acquire because John James Ruskin's generosity had reached its limits. Among them was the *Pass of the Splügen* (1842), which had been bought by Munro of Novar and then passed to the collection of Munro's nephew. Now Marcus Huish of the Fine Art Society showed his own generosity and imagination. While Ruskin was ill the *Splügen* came up at a Novar sale. The Fine Art Society bought the drawing for Ruskin, then invited subscriptions to cover the cost. The intention was to present the picture to Ruskin on his recovery. The money (1,000 guineas) was quickly raised. Ruskin therefore found himself with a present that took him back to the days when he was first writing *Modern Painters*. Both the success of the exhibition and the immediate response of Huish's subscribers gave heart to Ruskin. He reflected that he was not so solitary as he often imagined himself to be. One wonders whether Whistler observed the mood at the Fine Art Society. If so, he must have seen that public opinion within the Victorian cultivated classes had much sympathy for Ruskin, and for his love of Turner.

Gladdened by the gift of the *Splügen*, Ruskin expanded and augmented the Fine Art Society's exhibition. Turning now to the ninth edition of its catalogue, we find that he sent to London many of his own drawings, together with engravings, photographs and other materials. He chose them not only to help his explication of Turner but as a partial record of his own work as an artist. Ruskin was neither modest nor immodest about his artistic life. He simply attempted to show that he had always done his work in reverent and loving admiration of God's nature and the most beautiful works of man. Although Ruskin had no thought of Whistler, some people who saw his exhibition would have realised that his attitude was quite opposed to 'cockney impudence'. Yet Ruskin was still affected by the more heated side of his mind. He may have been once more close to madness as he prepared new comments. The ninth edition of the catalogue includes 'Notes on Mr Ruskin's own Handiwork illustrative of Turner'. This extended piece of writing was in progress in late May and its preface was signed on 5 June. Less than two months after he went back to his study, therefore, Ruskin had undertaken writing work that was more than usually public, since it accompanied an exhibition, and furthermore concerned one of the passions of his life. 'The doctors still say I must not write of anything that much excites me', Ruskin told his old family friend George Richmond on 31 May.[27] The catalogue was surely of that sort. As always, we learn from Ruskin's prose that something is amiss. The tone is mostly even, but some passages resemble the precipitous extremes of *Fors Clavigera*. For instance, at one point Ruskin was suddenly reminded of Thomas Hood's ballad 'Miss Kilmansegg and her Precious Leg: A Golden Legend' and then wrote

> Well, if it be not our fault, is it poor Peggy's fault, who hates the smell of roses! or is it — you will think I am going crazy again, if I tell you it is — in any wise the fault of Mephistopheles and his company, who detest it more than Peggy, and have introduced the preferable perfumes of tobacco, sulphur, and gunpowder, for European delectation . . .[28]

Devotees of *Fors Clavigera* would not have been surprised by such an outburst. Ordinary visitors to the Fine Art Society may have been puzzled by the contrast between the author of this passage and the genial collector of Turner drawings. Ruskin sensed this, which is why his 'Notes' claim that *Fors* in the last seven years had taught the same essential truths as *Modern Painters*, begun so long ago. In some ways the catalogue prefigures *Præterita*, which is a book about youth whose author was a broken man. The 'autobiography of drawings' was put together from works that were kept at Brantwood, but with such haste or inconsistency that the editors of the Library Edition, even with the help of Ruskin's catalogue, were unable to make a firm list of the exhibits. We know that Ruskin opened his display with his father's drawing of Conway Castle, later to be so lovingly recalled in the second chapter of *Præterita*. Then Ruskin showed some old Swiss prints, and in the catalogue he copied out (in French) a long extract from Jeremias Gotthelf, whose work had so often been read during the Ruskin family's travels in the 1840s. There followed photographs of Turner drawings at Farnley Hall; an engraving of a Turner of the Grand Canal; then a drawing by Ruskin himself of the Ducal Palace in 1874. But he had not been in Venice in 1874, so this may have been a study he made in Oxford as a teaching aid in the drawing schools. Ruskin's visitor would then have found maps of France and Africa that he had drawn in his childhood: this juvenile skill in cartography was a source of pride, and would be mentioned in *Præterita*. There were a number of Ruskin's studies of rocks and flowers, one of them dating from the fateful holiday with Millais at Glenfinlas in 1853, and finally some studies after Giotto, made in 1874, and after Carpaccio, by both Ruskin and Charles Fairfax Murray: these dated from the winter of 1876–77.

A number of passages in Ruskin's catalogue refer to his Oxford teaching and to *The Laws of Fésole*. Such references imply that these were his current work. Everyone had told him to rest, but he could not take this advice. Quite shortly, Ruskin returned to the extended intellectual projects that had been interrupted by his illness. The first of them was his private translation of Plato, now once more found in the diary after 18 June. Then he looked again at *Proserpina*. Happily for Joan, studies for the botanical book could be combined with quiet Brantwood gardening. At the same time, however, there were ominous signs that Ruskin wished to enter the world of public controversy. He wrote to Carlyle announcing a critique of Gibbon. In July he devised a plan for the removal of some 250 Turner drawings from the National Gallery's safe keeping. Ruskin was still Slade Professor. He wished the drawings to be lent to Oxford, and would himself make the selection within the next fortnight. The success of this exigent proposal — the drawings did go to Oxford, and were there from 1879 to 1906 — was owed to Prince Leopold, whom Ruskin had invited to negotiate with the National Gallery's trustees. At the end of July and the beginning of August Ruskin himself talked to curators at Trafalgar Square. Then he was shown to the National Gallery's storage basement, where he reopened the tin boxes in which he had placed Turner's work when first arranging the artist's bequest to the nation in 1857. Thus he once more encountered Turner's past, and his own. A checklist of the loan, which gives titles but no dates and contains no writing by Ruskin, was issued in 1878 as *Catalogue of the Sketches by Turner Lent by the Trustees of the National Gallery to the University of Oxford.*[29]

John Simon was worried by this activity at the National Gallery, especially since he had been given to believe that his convalescent friend was in London only to see his dentist. He prevailed on the Severns and other interested parties to take Ruskin away from his Turner studies and his too numerous London engagements with friends who included George Richmond, F. S. Ellis (who was eager to sell him books), James Knowles (who asked him if he would contribute to the *Nineteenth Century*) and Mary Gladstone (who invited him to visit Hawarden once more). The Severns agreed with Simon; but they thought it unwise for Ruskin to go straight from the boxes of Turners to his Brantwood study. They looked for a place in some remote area of England where he could do little work apart from drawing. Ruskin and Arthur Severn therefore went by rail to Malham in North Yorkshire for a 'sketching holiday'. Malham was the village they had previously visited together in September of 1875, as Ruskin recovered from the shock of the death of Rose La Touche. Perhaps there were landscape subjects at Malham that Ruskin the artist wished to revisit. He would also have been interested in the geology of the area, which is of limestone. The Buck Inn was home to Ruskin, Arthur Severn and Baxter for a fortnight. Then Ruskin drove home over the Yorkshire moors. He paused at Settle. At Ingleborough he walked to the summit of the hill, with its extensive view over the northern counties he had once, in *Fors* of May 1873, called 'Sir Walter's Land'. Ruskin entered the Lake District at Kendal and reached Brantwood on 22 August.

CHAPTER THIRTY-NINE

1878–1880

In January of 1878, before his breakdown, Ruskin had written to Sara Anderson about a recently discovered girl friend. 'The new pet is Frances Graham of Glasgow! She must be known to some of your friends (and she is a great pet of Edward Jones's) . . .'[1] Well-connected and sociable, a friend of the Gladstones, the Lytteltons and other leading families, 'Francie' was pleased to have charmed the old professor and had been helpful in collecting money for the purchase of the *Splügen*. In September Ruskin went to stay at Dunira, Crieff, Perthshire, the summer home of Frances's father, William Graham. He was a rich Presbyterian merchant and the Member of Parliament for Glasgow. It was unusual for Ruskin to sleep at the house of a person he did not know, especially if that person was a Liberal politician. But Graham had especial qualifications. Ruskin told Burne-Jones that 'Rosie wrote to me of the first time they met at dinner and I've always associated him with her . . .'[2] What was more, Frances had written out for Ruskin a hymn which Rose had once sent to her father. Frances's autobiography, written as Frances Horner, *Time Remembered* (1933), gives a story of Ruskin that is repeated, with variations, in a number of accounts of his character:

> He used to stop when he came to a heap of stones for road-mending, and get out and look them over and pick up one, and then begin a sort of ethics of the dust to us. He asked the old man who was breaking stones whether he would like to have one of his books about stones and crystals, and when the old man said that he could not read, Ruskin was so pleased that, much to our surprise, he put his arms round him and kissed him.[3]

Frances Graham had met the Burne-Joneses because her father bought contemporary art. His collection was to be the subject of the papers Ruskin now sent to the *Nineteenth Century*, 'The Three Colours of Pre-Raphaelitism', published in November and December of 1878.[4] When he had arrived at Dunira Ruskin found a number of works by Burne-Jones, together with two early Pre-Raphaelite paintings he may not have seen before, Millais's *The Blind Girl* (1856) and Rossetti's annunciation picture, *Ecce Ancilla Domini* (1848–49). In his bedroom there was an Arundel Society photograph of the tomb of Ilaria di

Caretta at Lucca, the sculpture that had so moved him on his 1845 expedition to Italy, and had always subsequently been his ideal of late medieval art.

These three works are the main subject of Ruskin's two articles, which he gave to James Knowles at the *Nineteenth Century* because he wished to state truths about Pre-Raphaelitism in the same journal that had carried a clever but superficial article about modern art in the previous month. It was by W. H. Mallock. Only a little while before, Ruskin had written to Jamie Anderson, 'Give my love to Mallock when you write. I am more and more impressed with his wonderful power.'[5] Now Mallock had transgressed. Ruskin loathed all his article but was most angered by the imputation of a sexual flavour in Burne-Jones's paintings. Mallock had said of his women that 'the only sorrow they know is the languor of exhausted animalism'. Ruskin wrote to Knowles that 'Your insertion of Mallock's article at all was a violent insult to every soul interested in the Arts at all — That you should allow a dilettante puppy to heave up his leg & piss over the things I have been spending my soul on all my life!'[6]

Some other unpublished material, in wild handwriting, suggests that Ruskin was thinking of a revival of *Fors Clavigera* so that he could chastise his errant disciple. But this did not come about, and in the event Ruskin's poised and generous papers made no mention of Mallock. His anger had passed; and he was thinking more of the della Quercia marble, and of Rose, when he made his contribution to Knowles's magazine:

> And through and in the marble we may see that the damsel is not dead, but sleepeth: yet as visibly a sleep that shall know no ending until the last day break, and the last shadow flee away; until then, she 'shall not return'. Her hands are laid on her breast — not praying — she has no need to pray now. She wears her dress of every day, clasped at her throat, girdled at her waist, the hem of it drooping over her feet. No disturbance of its folds by pain of sickness, no binding, no shrouding of her sweet form, in death more than in life. As a soft, low wave of summer sea, her breast rises; no more: the rippled gathering of its close mantle droops to the belt, then sweeps to her feet, straight as drifting snow. And at her feet her dog lies watching her; the mystery of his mortal life joined, by love, to her immortal one . . .[7]

'The Three Colours of Pre-Raphaelitism' was Ruskin's most prominent appearance in print since his breakdown. It happened that the two articles were published at just the time of the 'Whistler trial'. Such was the publicity surrounding the case, however, that the papers went largely unnoticed. They none the less provide interesting material about his aesthetic, and are the more remarkable for some generous praise of Millais. The articles are probably so temperate because Ruskin sent them to a journal conducted by a man whom he respected as an editor. In what tone, one wonders, might Ruskin have written had he *Fors Clavigera* at his disposal, not only to reply to Mallock but also to comment on Whistler's action? The absence of *Fors* had a dampening effect on both Ruskin's public and personal life. It may have been good for his mental health not to write the monthly letter; but still he was unhappily frustrated that he could not write as he wished. For the tremendous licence of *Fors* could not be transferred to other publications, especially if they were edited by so judicious a man as Knowles. Furthermore, St George's cause could not be advanced without *Fors*. The Guild was at last legally constituted in October of 1878, but a new status with the Board of Trade did not mean that it was more active. In this late autumn Ruskin's convalescence was unproductive, yet restless. He refused to stay quietly at Brantwood. After the expedition to Scotland to see the Grahams, Ruskin visited Liverpool with Alexander Wedderburn and then was once again a guest at Hawarden, where he arrived on 12 October of 1878. Gladstone's diary records that 'Mr Ruskin developed his political opinions. They aim at the restoration of the Judaic system, and exhibit a mixture of virtuous absolutism and Christian Socialism. All in his charming and modest manner.'[8]

⋆ ⋆ ⋆ ⋆

Ruskin was at Brantwood when Whistler's libel action was tried before Baron Huddleston in November 1878. All his doctors had forbidden him to attend court. Ruskin had imagined, characteristically and wrongly, that he might promote correct principles of art by appearing in confrontation with the plaintiff. He had written some notes about his criticism of Whistler in anticipation of cross-examination. These were passed to his counsel, who were Sir John Holker, the Attorney-General, and Mr (afterwards Lord) Bowen, but were not used. The lawyers no doubt preferred to take a more professionally legal approach than was suggested by Ruskin's comments. Certainly the trial itself did little to elucidate Ruskin's position as a critic, or Whistler's as an artist. It began with an address by Serjeant Parry, for Whistler, who spoke of the way that (in the words of *The Times* report) his client

> occupied a somewhat independent position in art, and it might be that his theory of painting was, in the estimation of some, eccentric; but his great object was to produce the utmost effect which colour would enable him to do, and to bring about a harmony in colour and arrangement in his pictures. Although a man adopted such a theory and followed it out with earnestness, industry, and almost enthusiasm, yet it was no reason why he should be denounced or libelled . . .[9]

Whistler's own defence was more memorable, especially since he seemed to regard the court as a theatre in which he was the principal actor. When cross-examined by Holker he produced a riposte that subsequently became famous. The Attorney-General asked him '"Can you tell me how long it took to knock off that Nocturne?" "Two days." "The labour of two days, then, is that for which you ask two hundred guineas?" "No; I ask it for the knowledge of a lifetime".'[10]

Whistler came out of the trial with an even sharper public personality than he had hitherto enjoyed. Nobody else said anything of interest. Expert witnesses from both sides gave prejudiced or foolish evidence. Whistler called Albert Moore, William Michael Rossetti and W. G. Wills. Ruskin's witnesses were the popular academician William Powell Frith, the journalist Tom Taylor and Burne-Jones. Frith and Taylor, prominent men but not Ruskin's friends, were surely chosen by his lawyers. The only aesthetic issue of the trial soon emerged. It concerned the degree of finish which a painting ought to possess. Whistler's 'Nocturnes' were produced and compared with the Titian from Ruskin's own collection (now attributed to Catena) that Arthur Severn brought into court from Herne Hill. Burne-Jones now gave his evidence. He was delicately placed, for he had exhibited alongside Whistler at the Grosvenor Gallery exhibition and had hitherto been on reasonable, if not exactly friendly, terms with him. None the less Burne-Jones was prepared to criticise his fellow-artist. *The Times* reported him thus:

> Mr Edward Burne-Jones said that he had been a painter for twenty years, and during the last two or three years his works had become known to the public. Complete finish ought to be the standard of painting, and artists ought not to fall short of what for ages had been acknowledged as essential to a perfect work. The 'Nocturne' in blue and silver representing Battersea reach was a work of art, but very incomplete . . . Its merits lay only in colour. Neither in composition, nor in detail, nor in form had it any quality whatever . . .[11]

This evidence from Burne-Jones was the longest of the trial. But it was not enough to persuade the jury. They retired for little more than an hour, returned to give a verdict for Whistler and proposed the derisory damages of one farthing. The judge did not award costs, so both Ruskin and Whistler were out of pocket at the end of their unpleasant and wasteful encounter.[12]

Ruskin's costs amounted to some £400. He did not pay this sum himself. Marcus Huish of the Fine Art Society, the dealer who had organised Ruskin's Turner exhibition in February, opened a subscription on his behalf. Perhaps Huish was eager to purchase Ruskin's good will and to take his side against the rival Grosvenor Gallery. He was certainly eager to purchase any of Ruskin's Turners, and the two men had corresponded about possible sales in 1875. Huish's subscribers, 118 of them in all, sent Ruskin a message saying that 'your lifelong, honest, endeavours to further the cause of art should not be crowned by your being cast in the costs arising out of that action'.[13] Whistler had no comparable group of supporters. He claimed his farthing from the court and wore it at the end of his watch-chain.

This cockney gesture may be said to symbolise the outcome of the trial. Whistler had failed to make money out of Ruskin's libel, but in another way he had succeeded. For he had brought Ruskin down. The Slade Professor now decided that he must resign his chair. It was not at all an obligation, but Ruskin had always felt that his writing in *Fors Clavigera* had the especial authority of his position at Oxford. In the New Year of 1879 the resignation was effected, and Ruskin explained to Liddell that 'although my health has lately been much broken, I hesitated in giving in my resignation of my Art-Professorship in the hope that I might still in some imperfect way have been useful at Oxford. But the result of the Whistler trial leaves me no further option. I cannot hold a chair from which I have no power of expressing judgement without being taxed for it by British Law.'[14]

Ruskin's resignation left the University with a number of problems. He was still capable of causing Oxford much embarrassment. No successor to the Slade professorship could be as interesting as its first incumbent, and it was a puzzle what to do with the drawing schools. In these circumstances the University, or more precisely Liddell, made a sensible appointment. William Blake Richmond was the son of George Richmond, and had known Ruskin as a family friend since he was a boy: Ruskin (Liddell reasoned) would therefore look kindly on his stewardship of a position he probably still regarded as his own. Richmond had begun his career in the 1850s as a follower of Pre-Raphaelitism. In latter years he had regularly shown serious and uncontentious work at the Royal Academy. He had spent four years in Italy and had a good knowledge of classic European art. Liddell had known him since 1858, when he painted a group portrait of the Liddell daughters. All in all, Richmond was qualified for the professorship.

Reporting always to Liddell, Richmond began a cautious examination of the drawing schools. 'I cannot help feeling very great delicacy', he told the Vice-Chancellor, in developing art education in a way 'which Mr Ruskin would wholly dislike, in a school set on foot by him, endowed by him, and over which he has expended not only a very great deal of money but time and energy'. On the other hand Richmond knew that what was needed was 'a drawing school . . . which would be a creditable beginning in the direction of figure drawing painting and modelling'. The problem was that 'Mr MacDonald told me that anything but water colour painting was forbidden and that Mr Ruskin would not allow oil colour in the room — Now as I want to have a class in oil painting, and to paint in fresco and tempera and to model in clay, I must have room to meet these wants, and where I can make a *mess* without fear of calling down wrath, in fact a workshop is what I want . . .'[15] In this request, however, Richmond had gone too far. It sounded as if he wanted to train undergraduates to become artists. This the University could not countenance. No workshop was ever set up and no coherent system of studio work ever devised.

Ruskin kept silent about these developments, even when Richmond, greatly daring, gave an inaugural lecture on Michelangelo that flatly contradicted his predecessor's survey of the Florentine master's faults.[16] He was not to set foot in Oxford again until his re-election to the Slade chair in March of 1883. In this winter and spring of 1878–79 he remained at Brantwood, still trying to understand his breakdown, wondering whether he would ever recover the strength for his tasks on earth. Quietly despondent about his future as a writer, he told Rawdon Brown that 'though I think I can draw and write nearly as well as ever on subjects that do not excite me, I fear I am past all emotional and historical work'.[17] Brantwood guests had the impression that Ruskin had passed many years of life in the weeks of his delirium. Constance Hilliard, who spent much of December at Brantwood, lamented that 'he is aged by this illness, more irritable, poor dear, and more sad; though he draws and works hard every morning, chops for an hour in the wood till dinner, rests a good deal in the afternoon, and reads " Sir Charles Grandison" or listens to music until bedtime.'[18]

We none the less begin to find hopeful notes in Ruskin's diary, as his sixtieth birthday approached. On 6 February, 'Thawing storm all night — after lovely snow all day . . . Let me see that I don't thaw away into waste myself, now the Spring's come again for me, once more! Snowdrops on my table . . . with my room in fairly good order, and mind and body fairly in tune . . .'[19] A few days later, on the 14th, the diary includes some plans for the resumption of *Fors Clavigera*.[20] Ruskin's letter would not in fact appear again until March of 1880, but other literary projects now began to move forward. In March 1879 Ruskin issued the fourth part of *The Laws of Fésole*, the drawing manual begun in 1874. He completed the first volumes of both *Proserpina* and *Deucalion*, and prepared their indexes; and with the help of Jamie Anderson he finished the description of the mosaics of the Baptistery of St Mark's that appears in Part III of *St Mark's Rest*, published in July, as well as a new 'Traveller's Edition' of *The Stones of Venice*, in which Ruskin added some notes to a selection from the book's original three volumes.

If, as Connie reports, Ruskin was sometimes irritable, that might have been because he was engaged with some irritating people. *Fors Clavigera* had often presented an invitation to correspondence: in Ruskin's mail there were many requests for advice, dissensions from his views and begging letters. From about this period, that of Ruskin's convalescence, Collingwood, Hilliard, Sara and Jamie Anderson would often take charge of such correspondence as part of their secretarial duties. But Ruskin often preferred to answer letters himself and, if the opportunity arose, could not resist the temptation to spar with a clergyman. He now became involved with the Reverend F. A. Malleson, the vicar of the small lakeland town of Broughton-in-Furness. Their exchanges were to produce the book *Letters to the Clergy on the Lord's Prayer and the Church* (1880), published not by George Allen but in London by Strahan and Company. The tiresome Malleson had first approached Ruskin in 1872. He then indicated to him that he knew something of his unhappy marriage and suggested that they should take walks together to discuss church restoration and other topics. Ruskin's replies to these invitations were not exactly temperate: rather they were challenging; and so they were not so final as to deter his admirer. At length, in September of 1877, after some years in which Ruskin had sent him copies of *Fors* in answer to his letters, the clergyman had his wish. He accompanied Ruskin in a 'most interesting ramble' up the Old Man of Coniston. Now, in the late summer of 1879, Ruskin agreed to write some letters to Malleson which would then be discussed by the members of the Northern Clerical

Society, of which body Malleson was the secretary. These letters, each treating one of the clauses of the Lord's Prayer, were privately printed by a local firm at the expense of the Reverend Hardwicke Rawnsley, one of Ruskin's original road-diggers, who by now had entered orders, had married and was the young vicar of Wray, on Windermere. Rawnsley's pamphlet was not under Ruskin's supervision. Malleson then sent the letters to the *Contemporary Review*, asking for comments from its 'thoughtful readers'. Such comments he promised to publish in book form, with an introduction by himself and an epilogue by Ruskin. When this book appeared in its 1880 London edition, Ruskin seemed robbed of his individuality. The volume did not give everything he wished to say. For of course his original correspondence with Malleson had ranged over topics other than the Lord's Prayer. His missives had returned once more to usury, the Bishop of Manchester and the social duties of the clergy. None of this matter appeared in the published version. Malleson had managed to rid Ruskin's contribution of its *Fors*-like quality.[21]

One of Ruskin's letters suggested that Malleson, who proposed to write a life of Christ, would be better occupied in a biography of any one of his poor parishioners (a thought Ruskin derived from Carlyle). As so often, he had lost his manners when he detected self-esteem in a man who followed a pastoral profession. Ruskin found it hard to remain friendly with local schoolmasters and clergymen. He was never on good terms with the Vicar of Coniston. They were especially liable to be in dispute over the village school. Despite his plans for *Bibliotheca Pastorum*, Ruskin was not convinced that literacy would make the children of the peasantry happy or good, so his interest in their education was unorthodox as well as benevolent. Spying a child in the lanes, he might keep her from classes with an improvised lesson in elementary geology, or wood-chopping, or — as *Fors* recounts — the habits of the four most common British bees. His numerous neighbourhood charities were often placed because he knew the children of a family before the parents. Many of his gifts were anonymous, for he used the local Baptist minister as an almoner. He was not at all anonymous himself: during his convalescence Ruskin became much more familiar to his Coniston neighbours. Most content when taking tea in Susie Beever's garden, walking on the hills or botanising for the continuation of *Proserpina*, Ruskin might have appeared, this autumn of 1879, as though he were a retired, slightly unorthodox gentleman of letters. But he was not such a person. He wanted *Fors*; and even in his hobbies there appears some wish to tease, to provoke, or to proclaim some difficult loyalty. His interests in natural history he matched against the orthodox Darwin, who was a visitor to Coniston in August. Alas, there is no record of their conversations. His daily translation of Plato was undertaken for private edification, but he still intended to use this study for an attack on Benjamin Jowett. When he took delivery of a new boat he had designed, for splashing across to Coniston village, or for drifting in the lake while he lay on his back to study cloud formations, he christened it *Jumping Jenny*. Why? It was to honour the craft owned by the alcoholic smuggler, Nanty Ewart, in *Redgauntlet*.

★ ★ ★ ★

Three portraits of Ruskin were executed in 1879, two of them sculptures. The busts were made by Benjamin Creswick, a Sheffield artisan who later became a master at Birmingham School of Art, and by Sir Jacob Boehm: this latter was given to Oxford University by a group of subscribers in 1880. Herbert von Herkomer's portrait of Ruskin is a rather beautiful likeness. The expression is sad, thoughtful; but one also senses the vivacity of mind, and the thoughts of a man who has much to do in the world. By September Ruskin had returned to his business with the Guild of St George. The first 'Master's Report', issued earlier in the year, had not been able to report much expansion. 'The St George's Guild may be able to advance but slowly', he there conceded, 'but its every step will be absolute gain, and the eternal principles of right, on which it is founded, make its failure impossible'.[22] Alas, one of Ruskin's present obligations was an unhappy one for the Guild. He had to attend court in London to give evidence against James Burden, one of the original Companions, who had forged his signature on two cheques. Burden was jailed for a year. ('No sooner was the prisoner released', Collingwood reported, than Ruskin 'took him kindly by the hand and gave the help needed to start him again on a better career'.)[23] There was more pleasant Guild business in Sheffield. Ruskin spent ten days there at the end of September. He wrote to Joan Severn, from 158 Fulton Road, Walkley, that

> It was lucky I came — for Mrs S[wan] had put things in which 'she thought pretty' and a lot of weeds in glasses . . . and the minerals had all been turned topsy-turvy by a mineralogist whom I let Mr Willett send to *move* them — but I never meant him to *arrange* them!
>
> And I'm in such funny wee lodgings di ma, with a nice carpenter and his wife (only I never see the carpenter) and was rather taken aback when his wife sate down at the fireside while I had

> my dinner. — she was by way of waiting — but sate down quietly like an old-fashioned landlady — in her own house and talked as serenely as if she'd been the Princess Louise — without the least impudence.
>
> Everything beautifully clean — but too much *china* di ma — and things on tables — and everywhere — a little Swiss cottage as good as can be, and — pics and photos . . .[24]

Princess Louise was in Ruskin's mind because he had just had the pleasure of welcoming her brother, Leopold, to his Sheffield museum. In this way the working-class museum was quickly blessed with royal favour. Ruskin proudly showed Leopold the collections, then stood aside in embarrassment and surprise as the visitor was presented with Creswick's bust. Not all of Ruskin's conversation with Leopold that day concerned the museum. They also talked about spiritualism. After his duties at Sheffield Ruskin was bound for Herne Hill and then Broadlands, where seances were planned. Later, he wrote in reply to Leopold's enquiry 'the only *definite* thing I felt this time was a quiet natural guidance (in all ways) in right directions.'

It was said above, describing Ruskin's life at Brantwood, that he might have seemed an unusual man to his neighbours. A number of his Oxford colleagues, we may be sure, considered that he often had a peculiar turn of mind. Yet Ruskin was not an eccentric, even when he was mad. All his writings, activities and errant thoughts have their place in his generous character and keen experience of the world. We may even find within Ruskin's biography the origins of a hobby, or interest, or relaxation, whatever it was, that seemed aberrant even to his closest friends. Ruskin had always been a lover of the theatre. It was a taste inherited from his father, who in his first days in London had gone from the counting house to see the romantic tragedians and ever afterwards had defended them, and all other actors, from Margaret Ruskin's Evangelical strictures. It is sad that Ruskin did not meet young actresses before he was an old man. This was no doubt because of his mother's sway over the Denmark Hill household. John James Ruskin had better theatrical taste than his son, who rarely stayed to the end of any tragedy and whose delight was in the atmosphere of performance rather than in the work performed. Ruskin was enchanted by the *divertissement* of any French farce, or any pantomime. At Christmas he might go to *Cinderella* or *Jack-in-the-Box* five or six times. His correspondence is littered with catch-phrases taken from the entertainments of the day, and the popular drama occasionally enters his books. Ruskin's friends learnt to dread a night in town at one of his favoured theatres. W. G. Collingwood, who often had to accompany him, records his enthusiasm for the Christy Minstrels. 'I remember Sir Edward Burne-Jones's account of a visit to them; how the Professor dragged him there, to a front seat, and those burnt-corked people anticked and shouted, and Burne-Jones wanted to go, and Ruskin wouldn't, but sat laughing throughout the whole performance as though he loved it. An afternoon to him of oblivion to the cares of life . . .'[25] Other acquaintances, like C. E. Hallé, remark on Ruskin's 'hopelessly bad taste' in music.[26] Alice Helps tells of his preference for sentimental songs like 'The lark now leaves her watery nest': '"The sweetest song ever written", said the great Professor'. At Cowley Rectory with Alice Helps, Ruskin had shown this surprising side to his character. 'Later came the charades. One of them, improvised with some fear and trembling as being rather advanced, represented a smart young bachelor who falls desperately in love with a lady doctor . . . how the Professor laughed! He laughed till he cried, and clapped his hands till he nearly fell off his chair . . .'[27]

Visits to the theatre were not a part of Coniston life but there were many diversions at Brantwood and Ruskin found a further 'oblivion to the cares of life' by indulging in family reminiscence. In the autumn of 1879 we may even find the first stirrings of the impulse behind *Præterita*. Once again, Marcus Huish and the Fine Art Society had devised an exhibition that required Ruskin's help. The idea was to show Samuel Prout and William Hunt. Here were two unfashionable artists. Prout had died in 1852, Hunt in 1864, and their art belonged to the 1830s. But Huish could hardly have invented a project nearer to Ruskin's heart. The exhibition took him back to his early days and the catalogue introduction, published in 1879–80 as *Notes by Mr Ruskin on Samuel Prout and William Hunt*, contains some of Ruskin's most gentle, yet also playful, use of memoir.[28] Prout had been a frequent guest at John James Ruskin's table; and watercolours by Hunt were among the first works of art that the wine merchant and his son had purchased together. Ruskin's notes dwell on the anti-aristocratic, modest, suburban (yet not cockney) taste that the Ruskins shared with other visitors, and contributors, to the annual events of the Old Water-Colour Society, where Prout and Hunt had regularly shown their work.

He had a further, autobiographical purpose. Since Prout's most characteristic subject matter had been north European, and since the artist had guided Ruskin's first tours in France, 'I meant, when this exhibition was planned, to have made it completely illustrative of the French flamboyant architecture, which Prout had chiefly studied'.[29] Ruskin had made such a study himself, in years long past, so he introduced some of his own drawings into the exhibition, together with a photograph he had taken in 1858 of a courtyard in Abbeville.

In this way Ruskin returned to the French inspiration of *The Seven Lamps of Architecture*, written thirty years before. In 1879 the book was on Ruskin's mind because George Allen hoped to issue a new edition. Ruskin's personal publisher was curious about the commercial prospects offered by the Fine Art Society. He had regular dealings with Huish, for the gallery in New Bond Street was the only place in which an interested person might find all of Ruskin's books and pamphlets on sale (as we discover from the advertisements in one edition of the *Notes on Prout and Hunt* published by the Society). This dispensation must have been engineered by Allen, who was also shrewd enough to know that much more money could be made from reissues of his master's earlier works than from the pamphlet publication of his recent writings. Thinking of the *Seven Lamps*, written in the early days of his marriage, Ruskin felt impatient with the 'utterly useless twaddle of it — the shallow piety and sonorous talk'.[30] None the less he still loved the church architecture that the *Seven Lamps* had described and wished some day to re-examine its principles. Furthermore, Allen had impressed Ruskin, and no doubt Joan Severn, with an estimate that sales of a new edition might bring its author as much as £1,500. Such a large sum would help to offset Ruskin's (and St George's) expenses. Allen made the further point that there were many pirated American editions of the book, all with unsatisfactory plates. Ruskin was finally persuaded. He wrote a new introduction and fifty-five mordant notes to the original text and was happy enough when the new edition was finally published in May of 1880, especially since he had excised various passages of evangelical opinion.[31]

Ruskin and Huish did not collaborate on any more exhibitions, though they were in correspondence until 1886. Huish is, however, the unnamed addressee of a series of letters published in the *Art Journal* of June and August 1880, for he was interested in the founding of the municipal gallery in Leicester. These papers, in 1885 reprinted in *On the Old Road*, are there titled *A Museum or Picture Gallery: its Functions and its Formation*.[32] At the same period Ruskin was making a more extended contribution to the *Nineteenth Century*. We know his five papers, published between June 1880 and October 1881, and again reprinted in *On the Old Road*, as *Fiction, Fair and Foul*. Because he was pleased with a further extension of his usual readership Ruskin's writing now has the air of performance. *Fiction, Fair and Foul* is also extremely amusing. It mocks Ruskin's younger self, and his older self too. Both Ruskin's darker thoughts about the world and his sense of humour lead him to compare his personal temper with the characters of Rousseau, Shelley, Byron and Turner, all of whom, he remarks, had a 'love of impending mountains, coiled thunder-clouds, and dangerous sea, being joined in us with a sulky, almost ferine, love of retreat in valleys of Charmettes, gulphs of Spezia, ravines of Olympus, low lodgings in Chelsea and close brushwood at Coniston'.[33] Both the tone and the weird content of such remarks represent a triumph of the late Ruskinian manner. In *Fiction, Fair and Foul* a great, serious writer allowed himself a holiday in which he could say whatever he wished. There is commentary on Walter Scott, a surprising knowledge of fashionable French fiction and unorthodox discussion of poetry. Ruskin was glad to say how much more he liked Byron than Wordsworth (a preference that his public, familiar with the quotation from *The Excursion* on the title-page of each volume of *Modern Painters*, might not have guessed), and he now confessed his dislike of George Eliot's writings (he had preferred not to do so while she lived, for 'I had some personal regard for her').[34] The essays are not particularly interested in more contemporary fiction or verse. Indeed they mockingly boast of their antique sensibility. But their vivid and, some might say, wayward judgements are not merely old-fashioned. They are the frank comments of a fellow-writer, not a professional literary critic.

Ruskin had now been a writer for some forty years. In *Fiction, Fair and Foul* we often detect his pride in literary craftsmanship. Ruskin seldom printed an imperfect sentence, but his prose could be flawed by its manner, for he was simultaneously a reflective and a combative writer, and his taste for combat too often led his pen. This was the shortcoming of the work called 'Usury: A Reply and a Rejoinder', which appeared in the *Contemporary Review* in February 1880. E. T. Cook considered that this piece of polemical writing was 'somewhat stilted and overweighted'.[35] That is so, but the piece fails because Ruskin had not recaptured the pitch and rhythm of *Fors Clavigera*, the natural home for this skirmish with the Bishop of Manchester, James Fraser. The background of the dispute is as follows. Ruskin had recently mentioned, in an aside comment in *Letters to the Clergy on the Lord's Prayer and the Church*, that the Bishop had never replied to his 'challenges' in *Fors* about usury. Ruskin had also written a private challenge to Fraser, who was chosen for this goading because his bishopric was known as Britain's most mercantile area. The Bishop had not received this letter because Ruskin's helper, the Reverend R. St

John Tyrwhitt, had not dared to deliver it (nor had he dared to tell Ruskin of his failure as a messenger). The Bishop did not read *Fors* as a general rule, he told Ruskin, but he did read the *Contemporary Review*, and there he had read of Ruskin's desire for a Christian statement on usury. Fraser accordingly wrote a long letter to Ruskin setting out his views. Ruskin sent this letter to the *Contemporary Review*, together with his own much longer 'rejoinder', which occupied twelve of the magazine's pages. Thomas Hughes, Fraser's biographer, tells us that 'the bitter tone of the rejoinder, sprinkled over profusely as it was with "my Lord" and "your Lordship", after the manner of Junius, made any prolongation of the argument impossible so far as the Bishop was concerned. He had no notion of quarrelling with Mr Ruskin under any provocation, and so, with a shrug of the shoulders, went his way about his work.'[36]

Fraser also wrote to a fellow-clergyman that Ruskin's comments 'seem to me more like the ravings of a lunatic than anything else'. And the Bishop of Carlisle, Harvey Goodwin, whom Ruskin had also attempted to embroil in his challenges, wrote to Malleson that 'I have a great reverence for Mr Ruskin's genius & what he has written in the past, and on this account I would rather not say a single word in comment about these letters'.[37] For years and decades, since he began to write about political economy, it had been said that Ruskin's views were not authoritative. He was now often dismissed as a madman. This is hardly surprising. Ruskin's illness had been reported and was well known to have been a mental breakdown. Furthermore, he had decided to write about his affliction in a new series of *Fors Clavigera*. Since at least 14 February of 1879, as we discover from his diary, Ruskin had been planning a resumption of *Fors*. A year later strength had been added to this determination. He began a new *Fors* on New Year's Day, 1880, wrote it 'twice over' at the beginning of February, and was able to date the new letter 'Brantwood, 8th February, 1880'. It was his sixty-first birthday, and this was the eighty-eighth number of *Fors*, in which he immediately turned to the question of his illness and the consequent absence of *Fors*, stating that

> for a physician's estimate of it, indeed, I can only refer his friends and readers to my physicians. But there were some conditions of it which I knew better than they could: namely, first, the precise and sharp distinction between the state of morbid inflammation of brain which gave rise to false visions (whether in sleep, or trance, or waking, in broad daylight, with perfect knowledge of the real things in the room, while yet I saw others that were not there), and the

> not morbid, however dangerous, states of more or less excited temper, and too much quickened thought, which gradually led up to the illness, accelerating in action during the eight or ten days preceding the actual giving way of the brain (as may be enough seen in the fragmentary writing of the first edition of my notes on the Turner exhibition); and yet, up to the transitional moment of the first hallucination, entirely healthy, and in the full sense of the word 'sane'; just as the natural inflammation about a healing wound in flesh is sane, up to the transitional edge where it may pass at a crisis into morbific, or even mortified, substance. And this more or less inflamed, yet still perfectly healthy, condition of mental power, may be traced by any watchful reader, in *Fors*, nearly from its beginning, — that manner of mental ignition or irritation being for the time a great additional force, enabling me to discern more clearly, and say more vividly, what for long years it had been in my heart to say . . .[38]

An unsympathetic reader could easily conclude that Ruskin himself had admitted that there was a taint of insanity in all his writing since about 1871. He had never been careful to improve his public image. Now Ruskin made himself look ridiculous. For reasons hard to imagine, he had allowed his name to be put forward as a candidate for the position of Lord Rector of Glasgow University, standing against John Bright. He unwisely wrote to a student body which had asked him to define his political views *vis-à-vis* the parties of the day:

> What in the devil's name have *you* to do with either Mr D'Israeli or Mr Gladstone? You are students at the University, and have no more business with politics than you have with rat-catching. Had you ever read ten words of mine with understanding you would have known that I care no more either for Mr D'Israeli or Mr Gladstone than for two old bagpipes with the drone going by steam, but that I hate all Liberalism as I do Beelzebub, and that, with Carlyle, I stand, we two alone now in England, for God and the Queen.[39]

This letter was forwarded to the press, where it caused a commotion: Ruskin was decisively beaten by Bright; and he had much trouble in explaining himself to Mary Gladstone, who was hurt on her father's behalf. Joan Severn was shocked by this episode and was worried by the new series of *Fors Clavigera*. She thought that the pamphlets publicised all the things that she found embarrassing in her cousin. Joan had long since given up thinking of Ruskin as a great man. He was too familiar. Of course she was content that he should be on friendly terms with Gladstone and Prince Leopold, but she also knew that Ruskin could spoil everything with his opinions. His real place in the world was beyond Joan's comprehension, for her horizons hardly extended beyond her family life. Consciously or unconsciously, Joan began to contract the circles of Ruskin's acquaintance and influence. She had little control over the guests at Brantwood; but at Herne Hill, on her own territory, she firmly repulsed the admirers, assistants or members of the Guild who sought Ruskin's company. The Hilliards counted as family, so Laurence and Connie were frequent visitors to the London house. Sara Anderson was similarly favoured. Joan and 'Diddie' now became much closer friends. In two years' time, around 1882, Sara was employed full-time as Ruskin's secretary, a position she held until 1891. In effect, this came to mean that she was working for Joan.

One of Joan's family problems was that Ruskin could not always get on with her husband. Arthur Severn had an official position in life. He was an artist. Occasionally he had some minor successes in this field. At the beginning of 1880, for instance, he was included in a group show at the Dudley Gallery. But Arthur's talent was meagre, and it was clear that he would never be successful, since he was also indolent and unintelligent. He was best employed in copying, or in such tasks as the preparation of diagrams for Ruskin's lectures, such as the one now given, at the London Institution on 17 March 1880, entitled 'A Caution to Snakes'[40] (a virtuoso description of the reptiles that had long fascinated Ruskin, subsequently a chapter of *Deucalion*, though better suited to *Love's Meinie*). It cannot have been easy for Arthur to live as closely to Ruskin as he did. On the other hand he made great demands on Ruskin's tolerance. The irritating nature of Arthur's character may be examined in the memoir he wrote about Ruskin. It is childish and lacking in any respect or affection for the man who supported him financially throughout his adult life. Ruskin's and Arthur's only real common interest was in the theatre, and so it helped good family relations that Ruskin took pleasure in light entertainment. The two men often went together on expeditions to some spectacle or show. Thus Ruskin became acquainted with slightly bohemian artists he might not otherwise have met, like Hercules Brabazon (a landscapist, musician and traveller with private means)[41] and was friendly with the Gale family. Arthur's elder sister Claudia had married Frederick Gale, a barrister and well-known cricketer who wrote about the game under the pseudonym 'The Old Duffer'. He and Ruskin were fond of each other, and for this reason the art critic is the dedicatee of Gale's *Modern British Sports* (1882). It was in such company — undemanding, close enough to his Herne Hill family to be familiar — that Ruskin now spent a holiday. He had not been abroad since his return from Venice in the spring of 1877. Various recent writings, and the reissue of *The Seven Lamps of Architecture*, made Ruskin wish to see France again. In the late summer and autumn of 1880 he was in the French northern provinces for several weeks. He was accompanied in the first part of this tour by Laurence Hilliard and his younger sister Ethel. Then, after a short return to England when he stayed at the Gales' house in Canterbury, Ruskin returned to France in the company of Severn and Brabazon.

* * * *

'*Les parties de rallye-paper sont plus que jamais en vogue*', Ruskin read in a copy of *La Revue des Jeux des Arts et du Sport* which he found in his hotel in Chartres on 12 September.[42] Idly, he marked the news with a question mark. There follow an increasing number of his exclamation marks as he read on to learn of one *rallye-paper* (a paperchase), for women only, in which *les costumes écossais étaient en grand nombre*, read of Mme de Verselles in her *costume de sportsman anglais* and of (many exclamation marks) the *fête vénitienne* which had *dignement couronné cette journée.* Ruskin's ink splatters the margins of the newspaper, but he was not ireful. In his relaxed mood he found amusement in observing modern folly, and this continental tour, officially devoted to the study of French cathedrals, contained much lighthearted entertainment. Ruskin, Laurence and Ethel enjoyed a visit to the Paris International Exhibition and wasted many an hour at the *Cirque d'été*, the *Folies dramatiques* and the *Opéra comique*. Ruskin took the best rooms at the Hôtel Meurice (as his father had never done) and spent freely on his young companions, for 'when one is out for a lark — one mustn't lose the fun for love of a sixpence'.[43] His letters to Joan from this tour are shorter than usual, and on the whole are cheerful. Much had changed in the towns that had delighted the Ruskin family forty years before, but at Rouen there was 'far more left than I expected'. At Beauvais, thinking of his mother, he had 'a sweet evening walk in old places which she knew well' and at Abbeville 'the old square is still beautiful'.[44]

The book we now know as *The Bible of Amiens* was the result of this tour. Later, Ruskin decided that it should be the opening of a larger design, a history to be entitled *Our Fathers Have Told Us*. The subtitle of this undertaking explains its purpose. It was to give 'Sketches of the History of Christendom for Boys and Girls who have been held at its Fonts'. This was never completed, though certain writings of the next two or three years, *Ara Coeli*, *Candida Casa* and the beautiful lecture on Cistercian architecture, 'Mending the Sieve', belong to its design. *The Bible of Amiens* may be considered separately. It was begun because of a promise Ruskin had made to lecture at Eton College on Amiens cathedral. The book was given further impetus by a disciple, Janet Leete, a governess and reader of *Fors Clavigera*. She had made bold to request Ruskin to write 'some pieces of history which her pupils could gather good out of'. His response had been immediate and characteristic. He renamed her 'Jessie', wrote to her with egotistical charm — 'My poor Jessie, you are an orphan then — like me' — and although she had 'begged him not to picture me as a pretty girl but as a plain woman of 28' addressed her as though it were proper of him to display ardour. Although Ruskin agreed to write something for Janet, it was not what she had asked for: a letter to her from Herne Hill in the autumn of 1880 announces that 'I've begun with a bit of French instead of English history.'[45]

The Bible of Amiens is, with *The Seven Lamps of Architecture*, the most French of Ruskin's books. It has an additional French interest, for this is the book translated by Marcel Proust.[46] To read Proust's version is an un-Ruskinian experience: and this reminds us how singular, how peculiar to Ruskin's own writings, that experience is. Proust's dissimilar literary skills even out the wandering tone of the English original, with its almost obligatory attacks on railways, its sorrowful reveries, sudden revivals of interest, half-hearted or exasperated references to sources and occasional imitations of a schoolmaster. This is one of the occasions when Ruskin's writing is affected by variable notions of his audience. Another letter to Janet Leete told her that 'I should like to address it to girls, only there are a great many naughty things one has to tell — and one doesn't quite like to look girls in the eye as one's telling them — and one can't skip them in a real history as one could in a school lecture — so I suppose I must write it for the workmen.'[47] But *The Bible of Amiens* has not the vigour of *Fors*, the writing for workmen. Nor has it the ease and seeming simplicity which, years before, we might have found in a book of Ruskin's written for schoolgirls. Its value as historical writing is limited. The story of the Franks, the Burgundians, of Clovis and his conversion, is confusingly intermingled with the legend of St Martin. Ruskin is tempted into parody: one passage recounts the story of King Lear in the manner of a nineteenth-century girl's-school textbook (a bizarre translation problem for Proust); he lingers over St Geneviève and Joan of Arc, in consideration not so much of their saintly lives as of fancied similarities with Rose; and there are many omissions and loose ends. Yet, in isolated sentences and paragraphs, and finally in the analysis of the cathedral of Amiens itself, both the fervour and the gentleness of Ruskin's late Christianity is apparent. It is not to the foremost when he writes as an ecclesiastical historian, for that leads him into querulousness: but it is luminous in his love of Christian art that he had first seen with those who were now long dead, and it is there always, mysteriously, in his faith that the communion of saints is a great reality. As Ruskin says in his fourth chapter,

> This conception of the company of Christ with His saints . . . was at the root of the entire disposition of the apse with its supporting and dividing buttresses and piers; and the architectural form can never be well delighted in, unless in some sympathy with the spiritual imagination out of which it rose. We talk foolishly and feebly of symbols and types: in old Christian architecture, every part is *literal*: the cathedral *is* for its builders, the House of God . . .[48]

* * * *

Ruskin spent six weeks in France with Laurence and Ethel, rather less time in the subsequent trip with Arthur and Brabazon. 'I got very fond of Brabazon', Ruskin told Joan, 'and he is delicious in his way with Arthur. They left me feeling very happy in feeling they were all friends.'[49] Yet his diary entries this autumn show that Ruskin grew tired. His high spirits left him. It was time to be home; and when he reached England, on 5 November of 1880, he was agitated and worn out. The Eton lecture on Amiens was to be given the next evening. Ruskin was nervous, for despite the success of 'A Caution to Snakes' he had not been happy about speaking in public since his breakdown. But the lecture appears to have had much effect on his young audience. A vivid account was written by A. C. Benson, deputed to meet the distinguished guest:

> There were at that time some quaint survivals at Eton, but the figure before me seemed to have come from a different century. As I remember, his tight-waisted dress-coat had a velvet collar, the sleeves were long, and the delicate hands that emerged were enveloped in long, somewhat crumpled cuffs; and he showed a soft and pleated shirt-front over a double-breasted waistcoat. I think he wore a long gold watchguard.
>
> His hair was thick and grizzled and grew very full especially over the forehead; he had large side-whiskers and bushy eyebrows; the face was extraordinarily lined, and the big mouth, with a full

> underlip, gave him a tenacious and, I thought, a rather formidable air. He was standing in silence, and the matron was much too awed to speak. However, she called me by name, and said faintly, 'Benson, this is Mr Ruskin'. Ruskin extended his delicate hand and shook mine very warmly and cordially. And as he did so, he gave me a delightful smile from his pale blue eyes, and set me at my ease at once . . . he talked a little of the future, and asked me what I thought of doing in the world, all kindly and confidingly, in a way that won my regard, it was so modest and courteous: but there was a sense of strain and weariness in the background. Then he said that he must rest a little and be quiet and that I might fetch him just before eight. He smiled and nodded, and then sate, leaning his brow upon his hand . . .

Later in the evening, Benson continues, Ruskin faced his audience and

> began in his thin high voice, very clearly and audibly, but with formal and monotonous cadence and intonation, what I afterwards recognised in *The Bible of Amiens*, the beautiful and scornful description of the railway-station and the tall warehouses and smoking chimneys, and the slender, lovely minaret of the cathedral rising behind all . . . there is little of it that I remember; there was much that I did not understand, for the whole was lacking in coherence and logical connection; but it was an inspiring, appealing, intensely moving performance. I felt that he was a great man, with great and beautiful beliefs passionately held, yet both oppressed and obviously unhappy. He was contending with something, perhaps a vulture gnawing at his heart, like Prometheus. There was never a sign of placid or easy mastery; no appearance of enjoyment, even of interest: it was a duty he had to perform, a service he might do; and at the end he looked old and weary. Then he was thanked and cheered to the echo. He listened patiently enough — but with no satisfaction . . .[50]

* * * *

At Herne Hill a few days later Ruskin was surprised by a hoax. On 12 November the newspapers carried a letter purportedly written by him refusing an invitation to visit the Chesterfield Art School. In extravagant language, it extolled Venice and denounced the blockheads who had dared to invite him to a town where there was a railway. Through Alexander Wedderburn, Ruskin immediately announced that the letter was a forgery. Privately, he was amused by the affair and even saw it as fine publicity for the appearance that month of *Arrows of the*

Chace, the first of his publications since 1871 to be sent to the press for review. *Arrows of the Chace* is a compilation of all Ruskin's public letters to newspapers and journals. The idea had been suggested to Alexander Wedderburn, the book's editor, by the publication in 1878 of R. H. Shepherd's *A Bibliography of Ruskin*. Alec Wedderburn was now well advanced in his chosen career in the law. He combined his public profession with his private interest in Ruskin, which led him to amass notes, manuscript material and other Ruskiniana, in particular rare pamphlets. At this point in Wedderburn's life we can say that he had become a Ruskin scholar rather than a disciple. Like his future co-editor E. T. Cook, his first desire was to assemble and preserve information, and in years to come Wedderburn's legal mind would complement the approach of Cook, a journalist-scholar.

When he had found Ruskin's public letters — 152 of them written over a period of forty years — Wedderburn decided to arrange them topically rather than chronologically. There was some sense in this approach, which Ruskin probably encouraged. But much was thereby lost, especially since so many of the missives had to be classified as 'miscellaneous'. The letters reached far back into Ruskin's career, for the first of them belong to the 1840s, the period of his first battles over Turner. Their number increased in the next decades, just as Ruskin himself became more interested in journalism. Cook, less happy than Wedderburn about this aspect of Ruskin's public life, later lamented that in his Brantwood years Ruskin was 'prone to write *de omnibus rebus et quibusdam aliis*'. Ruskin himself would not have admitted that his wide reference was a fault, and no doubt considered that a critic of society must be able to criticise all aspects of that society. Furthermore, such a critic must engage with all the other organs of opinion. One of the functions of *Fors Clavigera* was to comment on the contemporary press, with the result that editors came to solicit letters from Ruskin to enliven their columns. And it was Ruskin's practice in later life to suggest to his private correspondents that they should publish his replies to their queries. *Arrows of the Chace*, for these reasons, provides yet another example of the indistinction between the private and the public Ruskin. Its epigraph is appropriate: it is the pronouncement in *Fors* in 1875 that 'I never wrote a letter in my life which all the world are not welcome to read if they will'.[51]

The book was widely reviewed, on the whole unfavourably. Mark Pattison's careful piece in *The Academy* is the most interesting response. He remarked on what he took to be Ruskin's assumption of omniscience, wondering at the variety of topics 'from foreign politics to domestic servants, from war to silk-worms'. Pattison was more disturbed by Ruskin's deliberately provocative avowal that in all the 152 letters 'there is not a word I wish to change, not a statement I have to retract'. How, Pattison wondered, could there be such constancy of opinion in a great contemporary, a great Victorian? The age in which they had lived had been one of intellectual exploration, had it not? This observation once again raised the question of discipleship. For Pattison was dismayed that Ruskin's stubborn and antiquated opinions had been gathered by one who signed himself 'An Oxford Pupil'.[52] The Rector of Lincoln, a scholar who had known the deep intellectual currents of his time, could not see how the twenty-six-year-old Wedderburn could have wished to toil over this eccentric, cantankerous volume and given it such respectful editing and annotation. The reason is not difficult to find. As Ruskin became more and more detached from his age, more that figure which the young Etonian Benson thought of as belonging to 'a previous century', so his appeal became the more personal. He did not have influence: he had followers, disciples, Ruskinians. Perhaps Pattison (like his wife) had never understood Ruskin. He had certainly lost him now. But Wedderburn, Collingwood, Jamie Anderson and Laurie Hilliard, though they would dissent from his views in many ways, treasured Ruskin. Their personal loyalty in the madnesses that were now to follow, year after year, did much to sustain Ruskin's active life.

CHAPTER FORTY

1880–1881

There now begins, from the late autumn of 1880, a deterioration in Ruskin's mental condition that would end in his second breakdown. Hardly recovered from the weariness that had settled on him in France, Ruskin was none the less busy about London. He was writing *The Bible of Amiens* and was at work on the last, and the least profitable, of his Turner projects. In large part this was an imaginary endeavour, for Ruskin had devised an arrangement of Turner's drawings in the National Gallery that the Gallery itself had no intention of adopting. Hence the futility of the description of his proposals, issued by George Allen in 1881 as *Catalogue of the Drawings and Sketches by J. M. W. Turner, R. A., at present exhibited in the National Gallery. Revised and Cast into Progressive Groups, with Explanatory Notes.*[1] Alas, this exercise in Turnerian study led Ruskin to think with excited sorrow of his own past.

Once again, the diary reveals, diabolical modern weather was contrasted with the happier skies of his childhood. He was at Herne Hill, sleeping as usual in his old nursery. Up early one day, 'a scarlet dawn, in my old room, made me feel how much I had forgotten of the dawns I once saw so often'. But the weather usually oppressed him. Ruskin felt that it was evil. All was 'pitch black; ragged fiend-cloud flying steadily from south-west. I, with crying and choking cold, waking with it in my throat . . .' The next day '. . . black and wild again. I again, good for nothing, with choking cold. Wind howling and the devil getting his own way variously, but we'll see who's best man, yet.' A few days later, 'Sky clouds over of course as soon as the breakfast bell rings; this fast clouding being a chief sign of the diabolic time.' Ruskin was still delighted by one or two mornings, and he thought of 'Amiens work' and of another inscription for his mother's memorial at Carshalton. Careless days were none the less few. He was spent. In the diary he wrote: 'Much beaten and tired, and must positively take to the rocks and grass again for a while'.[2] With the Severns, he returned to Brantwood for Christmas.

In his Brantwood bedroom Ruskin began a rearrangement of his own especially beloved Turners. The motive was autobiographical. In the centre of the main wall of Turner watercolours he now hung John James Ruskin's watercolour of Conway Castle, the picture around which, fifty years before, the father who 'gave me Brantwood — and all else' had improvised stories for his son. Below, Ruskin put the first Turner he had ever known, *Vesuvius in Eruption*, familiar to him since its appearance in *Friendship's Offering* in 1830. In that publication it was the engraving on which 'I used to feast . . . every evening for months'. Between these two pictures he hung 'like a brooch' a still life by William Henry Hunt, whose works were among the most sweetly remembered of all the paintings of his Herne Hill childhood.[3] Now there was a change of mood. Desolately aware of all that he had lost, counting the sixth Christmas since Rose had died, working a little on his thoughts of St Genevieve — 'A shepherd maid she was — a tiny thing, barefooted, bareheaded — such as you may see running wild and innocent'[4] — Ruskin was suddenly aroused to anger by the friendly bookseller F. S. Ellis. Ruskin had asked him to purchase Scott manuscripts at an auction, as his agent. Ellis judged that the holograph of *Guy Mannering* had been bidden up beyond its market value, and declined to over-bid. So the manuscript was lost to Ruskin, who raged, and then sent this letter:

> Dear 'Papa' Ellis,
>
> I've a particular reason for writing to you today — especially because I am *really* angry with you for being so much of a Papa; and I have seen that you were quite right, and I'm entirely and deeply grateful to you. And yet I'm going to be as extravagant as ever at heart, but can't tell you now.
>
> Ever your affectionate J. Ruskin.[5]

At about the same time, asking Ellis to acquire for him, at whatever cost, the manuscript of *St Ronan's Well*, he signed his letter 'ever your loving SON GEORGE'.[6] These signatures and salutations may easily be interpreted. For Ruskin to call himself George is surely to adopt a Christian name from his position as Master of the Guild. He called Ellis 'Papa' because, like John James Ruskin, the bookseller wished to restrain him from spending money on anything he coveted. Once more, the old resentment at his father's management had returned: once more, on the same sheet of paper, Ruskin immediately realises that 'Papa' is 'quite right'. Only as Master of the Guild of St George could he have his way. And a secret determination remains, to be 'as extravagant as ever at heart'.

A deeper grief than the loss of a Scott manuscript now visited Ruskin. On 5 February 1881 Carlyle, whom Ruskin had latterly addressed as 'Papa', and who was indeed the father of so much of the younger man's attitudes, died in London. Ruskin marked the death in his diary with a drawing of a crucifix, probably the Byzantine cross 'now always somewhere on my table — meaning love of St Mark's' that he had bought while writing *The Stones of Venice.* In losing Carlyle he was now all the more solitary: 'There were only Carlyle and me . . . now there's only me.'[7] By a coincidence of Fors he heard too of the death of a well-remembered figure of his childhood, George Richmond's wife Julia. It was Richmond, he now recalled, who had first put a book of Carlyle's into his hands. Walking alone in early moonlight Ruskin was 'woefully ill and despondent' and, he confessed in a letter to Georgiana, 'lost in a wildrness of thoughts again'. What those thoughts were we do not quite know, for nothing is recorded in Ruskin's diary for a week after Carlyle's death. These were the days that preceded his mental collapse. One letter gives a sign of what was to come. To Burne-Jones, two days before the delirium began, he was writing: 'I've found out why Georgie [Burne-Jones] was of so boundless importance to me in that old dream — this time three years', and announced to the artist that he had sent his 'little sketch given me long ago, of Cupid with the roses under his feet . . . this sketch I say I sent on St Valentine's day to the Sheffield Museum, to be the Captain of its Modern Art . . .'[8] Much of his correspondence, however, was reasonable. Joan Severn, in Herne Hill, had her usual daily letter. She had no inkling that madness was to seize him again, as it did, fiercely, on 20 February.

Laurence Hilliard was at Brantwood when Ruskin's mind collapsed. He immediately called for Dr Parsons and sent a telegram to Joan at Herne Hill. 'It must be *very sudden*', Joan wrote to Mrs Simon that day, 'as I had an excellent report of him yesterday.'[9] Weeks later, on his recovery, Ruskin looked back on his life in early February and decided that the illness had not been sudden at all. There exists a remarkable document in which he describes the approach of insanity. It is contained in two long letters to Sara Anderson and includes the 'story of Rosie's cup' mentioned in a diary entry of 1885 as essential to his plans for *Præterita.* These letters so embarrassed Ruskin's editors that they decided not to print them. The first was written on Good Friday of 1881. Ruskin told Sara:

> The whole thing began with my resolving to have family worship from New Year's day this year. I only read about ten verses of Testament — said — in five minutes what I could to make them felt — in so much as I understood: and then read one Psalm or bit of Psalm — and two short collects, which I wrote every morning, one on the Gospel and one on the Psalm.

This went on for fifty days — and I've kept the written services, because in the strangest way, the Gospel and Psalm seemed always to play into each other's hands — and light each other up, though I read straight forward in the Gospel (St Luke) and missed only the lugubrious or revengeful Psalms — which are of no use to housemaids or housewives — or house-men — or beasts. By the way we always had the cat at prayers — and she behaved like an abbess — except sometimes she used to get on my shoulders while I was reading (which I soon taught the servants not to object to — or think profane, even if she looked over the book) Well: this naturally brought me back into a great deal of old thought — and you know I'm none the better for being 'a new man' whatever the Evangelicals may be. — So — he saith — or I say — the Old is better — of the wine of life. Well, I got into really what I thought a very promising sort of way! — and saw into a lot of things as it seemed to me — but of course, all living Gospel teaching depends on the one question whether the dead are raised — and after reading the passage about the Seventy — (the Lord appointed other Seventy also, etc) and explaining to the servants how much wider a thing the Christianity of Christ's time was than any of us ever thought — I got thinking too much about dead of my own — and what I told you — do you recollect — in the wood once, which you said was so beautiful.

So I got — quietly every night — completing my morning service, with a try for myself — if I could get that ghost back, visible or invisible. Now — there was *nothing* insane in all this! at least I was never more sane in my life! and all the work I did in those days was as good and strong as I ever did. But the insanity came in the strangest way, by the mixing of thought with reality — as if it *were* reality.

When Joan was away in town I took the two little boys up to see Mrs Stalker. I have always thought they were not allowed scrambling enough — and insisted on their being under my charge only — and took them into the difficultest places, watching them all the while — and meaning afterwards to give them a lesson about — Shepherds of which I'll tell you more afterwards. But I got a good deal excited in the climb, and I suppose the blood too much into my head.

Well — when we got to Mrs Stalker's — I had some earnest talk to do with her (for we've been taking away our milk custom and giving it to the Mellys) and, I took it in my head too — being as

I say over-excited, that she was not well — dangerously not well and that made me more serious still, of course.

Well — Isabel was there, and very glad to see us — and she made tea for us, and I was sitting at the round table with the two children and trying to be cheerful — and really enjoying my tea, for I was very hot and thirsty — when — all of a sudden — Isabel (as it *seemed* to me) held out an empty cup across the table to me and said — aloud 'Rosie's cup'. Now — that was just as real to ME as the cottage — or the Table — or as any thing that Isabel had said. I had not the smallest doubt at the time of its being absolutely real — and yet — gesture and saying must alike have been imagined by me! . . .

Ten days later Ruskin wrote again to Sara:

After that dream at the cottage a day or two went on quietly enough — but then what with Amiens work, and old thoughts — (three years ago, you know the dream began by my fancying Rose had brought Joan of Arc with her for her bridesmaid) — I got too much on Joan of Arc, and thinking how one could bear being burnt oneself, till, one afternoon, I put my hand three times into the fire to try. I took it out fast enough — each time — but — though it was a completely rational experiment — it frightened the parlourmaid (I didn't know she was in the room) who was laying the cloth! — Then she told other people — and they were grave at dinner — and frightened *me*, and so — played into the dream's hands: — so that, the same evening, I put everything in order in the study in a quite tremulous way, as if I was going to die: — but I don't remember now, *why* I did so — only I perfectly recollect doing it, and when I came down again, weeks afterwards, I found things upside down and downside up, as if the devil had done it! Well — that night I knew no more after I went to bed — but the continuous dream began by my fancying I walked in the dark night away bare-footed — like one of the 'other 70' — with nothing in my purse! — to go to Scotland and raise Rosie, practically — but when I had gone a mile or two — I began thinking first whether people really *would* feed me on the way — and secondly, however I was to get across in the steamer! and then somehow I was turned back, with understanding that I had done enough in fairly starting — and that Rosie would now come herself without being gone for. Then I had a time of fancying her crossing the sea, — and then, I was lying awake in my own room in the night, — with the

> consciousness that she and her mother were in the next room (the one I was ill in before) and that Rose was writing a little note, quite wild with joy — for fear of doing me harm by coming in too suddenly — and then — all at once — close to the window seemingly, there came an owl's cry. (And *that* was *real* — and throughout this dream, the real and the visionary mixed in the same extraordinary way) and then, I *felt*, that Rosie stopped writing with a start, and then! — Now really, I won't begin another sheet — for this really is a point to finish a chapter at — like Walter Scott — isn't it now . . . ?[10]

However, Ruskin sent no further chapter of his story to Sara, or nothing that has survived.

On 21 February Joan summoned Arthur from one of his holidays and travelled alone to Coniston. When she arrived at Brantwood in the winter darkness of late afternoon she found her cousin 'ill again as he was before, with a breakdown of brain — it is in every way similar to the last attack — but as yet, without such violence and malice'.[11] Laurence Hilliard took charge of all the secretarial work and Joan began to nurse. If there was not, so far, any sign of the aggressive behaviour that Joan feared, yet the dissociation from the real world was extreme. Ruskin seemed not to recognise anyone, was silent for long periods and then talked nonsense. All the routines of the busy house were changed. Callers were forbidden. Children were kept out of the way, embarrassing arrangements made with the servants. As much as possible of the ordinary Brantwood life was transferred to the lodge, while the house itself became enclosed. There, in frightful parody of Ruskin's normal relations with those who were close to him, the delirious Master, attended only by Joan, Arthur, Hilliard and Baxter — the family, the disciple and the servant — began a month of life together. Ruskin could not be kept in bed, and when he was downstairs the difficulty of managing him was increased. He had to be followed as he went from room to room. Joan, who had fallen and sprained her ankle, limped after him wherever he went, afraid that he might put his hand in the fire again, or break things, or run away to some imagined rendezvous with Rose. Ruskin's energy and constant need to be busy were as much evident in madness as ever: more so, even, for he neither read nor wrote. He exhausted his attendants. 'He sleeps scarcely at all', Hilliard lamented. Through the long nights Baxter and Arthur Severn, in turn, waited outside his door, listening.

On 3 March Laurence Hilliard was 'very much afraid of his settling down into a hopeless condition as regards his mind'[12] though Joan, the day before, had noted 'more frequent intervals of consciousness' when he seemed to listen if Scott or Maria Edgeworth were read aloud. Hilliard worried chiefly about 'certain fixed delusions from which nothing will shake him'. Many of these concerned Rose and important persons of state. On 5 March, for instance, rather more than a fortnight after the delirium had begun, Ruskin sat quietly in his study. He was perhaps in a docile temper. But then he stamped upstairs, quite carefully broke a pane of glass in his bedroom window, swore at everyone and ordered them to leave the house. Returning via the back door they found him kneeling in the front hall 'to receive Cardinal Manning'. Ruskin was convinced that Rose was coming to dinner. She would arrive with 'another lady' and would be escorted by the Duke of Argyll. Best clothes should therefore be worn. Enraged when his guests failed to appear, Ruskin flung accusations at his household then, also carefully, broke another pane of glass next to the first. As in 1878, the question of being 'master in my own house' was dominant. He gave absurd and contradictory orders. Ruskin was not to be humoured and there could be little consistency in the way that Joan and her fellow-sufferers treated their charge. They lived in constant squabbling about food, and mess. One day Joan found 'he *would not* take food — so I got up — & hobbled in & tho' he was very angry he promised if I'd carry his dinner with my own lame foot he'd take it — I did, and he dashed it all at me, swearing, and ordered me out of the room. Later on, he rang & ordered soup — sherry — mince collops — bread — & ate all up heartily.'[13]

In time, there came the blessed relief of a quiet, exhausted Ruskin. His reversion to the childlike was then a delight to Joan. 'He became *almost* himself — & said he was tired — so Arthur with my persuasion got him to lie down on the sofa beside me (I being in bed) & wrapt him up — & he fell fast asleep — how I thanked God for that! — he woke much refreshed in about half an hour — wandering a *very* little — calling me 'mama' — & himself 'a little donkey boy' — but quite calm and sweet . . .' None the less the grandiose fantasies returned. As before, they often concerned royalty. The second broken window, Ruskin told Joan, was 'a signal to be given at Windsor Castle — of breaking a spell of witchcraft'. The Brantwood cook he at one point believed to be the Queen. He contrived to lock her in his bedroom while, Joan reported to Mrs Simon, 'he screamed out to me "don't move another step or I can't be answerable for your safety — but I'll do what I can, with the Queen's help".' Such dramas became less frequent after about three weeks. But in the quieter times, when Ruskin spoke as he normally did, with the beautifully turned phrases and sustained cadences that were natural to him, the nonsense was all the more heart-rending. Joan wrote to the Simons that 'He looks well — & speaks in his own firm natural voice — which makes it all the more distressing . . . It almost breaks my heart — I'd rather hear him jabbering nonsense — than *seeming* so much himself, & yet so insane.'[14]

Yet Ruskin's health was mending. Towards the end of March he was able to hold conversations, though he remained capricious and ill-tempered. 'The Coz has continued so rapidly to improve that I think we need not fear any further relapse at present', Joan could now tell John Simon.[15] Gradually she brought life at Brantwood back to normal. On 7 April Ruskin was able to write a diary entry: 'The first primrose out . . . And the first soft sunshine of the year — lasting into far twilight.'[16] The storm was over. Work might begin again. But Joan was now annoyed. For Ruskin seemed to have only a slight interest in how ill he had been and how she had suffered on his behalf. 'He little knows the intense anxiety & sorrow for him we have had this past month!' she complained.[17] Though recrimination was later to be a versatile weapon in her armoury, it was not now in Joan's mind. She was too relieved that her beloved cousin had been restored to something like his former self. But she had to tell him how he had behaved and how she had borne with it, if only to impress on him that his recuperation would be slow and that his convalescence must be careful. Ruskin would listen to her as he would listen to no one else, and she made it clear to him that she had managed the whole illness. This was little less than the truth. There had been little medical attendance. It had been a family affair. Dr Parsons's occasional interventions in the tempests of the delirium had been ineffectual. Joan had kept in touch with the Simons by letter, but had not asked for advice and had usually addressed herself to Jane Simon rather than her doctor husband. Henry Acland — Regius Professor of Medicine — had wished to come to Brantwood, but Joan's hostility to Ruskin's oldest friend had prevailed. 'Dr Acland has of course offered to come if we wish it', she wrote to Jane Simon, 'and we particularly do *not* wish it'.[18] For as long as possible Joan had resisted the idea of a trained medical attendant in the house. When one finally arrived from London she kept him away from her patient. In short, the treatment of Ruskin's illness had been by Joan's love and patience. It was from this time that her role in Ruskin's life began to change. She who had undergone so much for him was the only one who could arrange for his comfort and mental safety. Once his ward, Joan now became Ruskin's keeper.

As she brought him to realise what he had done, Ruskin was

contrite. He agreed that he should avoid 'excitement'. To Joan's great pleasure, he offered to relinquish the mastership of the Guild of St George. She therefore hoped that he would give up tiring activities and avoid the subjects that inflamed his mind. But this could not be, for Ruskin sought an internal coherence in his madness which he did not explain to his cousin. As we have seen, he wrote long letters to Sara Anderson which described the onset of the illness. Turning to the diary, we discover analysis of the illness itself in notes from early February of 1883. It is notable that Ruskin thought of it in religious terms:

> The first part of it was my setting out to walk to [Rose's] grave — the second part, her coming with her mother, and the interruption by the owl's cry . . . the Madeleine part was . . . I suppose, the period of highest exaltation, showing the exact connection of pride with insanity — I thought I had a kind of crucifixion to go through — and to found a farther phase of Christianity and that Rose was the Magdalen to me . . . [19]

This interpretation had dangers, for Ruskin was inclined to believe that something had been achieved at the end of an ordeal. He also, alas, wished to believe that his experience had given him a graver understanding of the world. Thus he under-emphasised the seriousness of his illness while exalting the significance of the 'dream'. He told George Allen, 'These so-called insanities are really only prolonged dreams, passing into states of trance and sleep-walking or talking. They are very slightly connected with my actual *work*; but depend on states of sorrow — conscience — and religious study — of which nobody knows anything but myself — on the whole, both the illnesses have been *lessons* . . . of the most solemn value and import.'[20] To another dependant, Alexander Macdonald, he claimed that 'the doctors know really nothing about the conditions of insanity which attack men like Blake or Turner or me . . . The Doctors enrage me more and more the longer I live. More was taken out of me by the preparation of one lecture at Oxford — (and you know I sometimes gave three a week) than by three weeks of delirium.'[21]

Joan understood little of this, for she could not enter the labyrinth of Ruskin's imagination. She concentrated on keeping him away from business. Hilliard attempted to close down all correspondence — no simple matter, for Ruskin often wrote a dozen letters a day, and received more. A circular requested that (and this must have been Ruskin's jest) 'His friends are to consider him in California'. Joan had in fact taken him to the Cumberland coast, to Seascale ('a railway station on a beach — with three attached lodging houses and seven shops: in a row').[22] It was a brief and not a cheerful holiday. Ruskin felt older and also looked older, for he had grown his beard and moustache. Despite his fatigue he was determined to return to his study. Hilliard felt, rightly, that 'he is in a critical state and might easily be knocked off balance again'.[23] But the resumption of 'St George's work', at first tentative, soon acquired a momentum that neither Hilliard nor Joan could control. Once again he took up *The Bible of Amiens*; he issued a set of photographs, entitled *The Shepherd's Tower*, to complement *Mornings in Florence*; in June and July he was writing *Proserpina*, *Love's Meinie* and *The Bible of Amiens* at the same time. He projected another number of *Fiction, Fair and Foul*, rearranged the greenhouse on *Proserpina* principles and began a system of experimental drainage on the moors above the house. Against Joan's wishes he insisted on entertaining visitors. Not only, on some occasions, were they people she did not know: he did not know them either. Janet Leete, the governess who had asked for the English history that became *The Bible of Amiens*, came to Brantwood and was bewildered, not knowing what to do or say. Some of her embarrassment may have been occasioned by Ruskin's excitement over little girls. She had been teased with 'that terrible weakness in me about sylphs . . . Do you really understand . . . That I'm — more of a Turk than a christian?'[24] Prepared to ask Ruskin earnest questions, she heard much talk of the 'sylphs' who were coming to stay next, Rosalind and Peggy Webling. They were girls from a theatrical family who specialised in recitations: Ruskin had met them in London through Marcus Huish. Joan disapproved of Ruskin's enthusiasm for Rosalind and Peggy. None the less they had a delightful holiday. They were perhaps too young to notice what tension there was at Brantwood.[25]

* * * *

It is worth observing how Scottish the Brantwood household was. Ruskin felt himself to be Scottish; to be Scottish was Joan's pride; Alexander Wedderburn was a Scot; so were the cousins Sara and Jamie Anderson. Sir Walter's novels, of which there were now five original manuscripts in the house ('not bad for a Lancashire cottage') were the staple evening entertainment and a guide to all domestic loyalties. After his breakdown, writing to John Brown in Edinburgh about 'the ways of the modern world' Ruskin used a near-obsolete Scottish word meaning 'loyal', 'faithful'. '*I* go back to live with my Father and my Mother and my Nurse — and one more — all waiting for me in the land of the Leal'.[26] Here is a familiarly wistful note, but it is not quite a note of elegy. When Ruskin talked of his family background, or of

Scott, or Carlyle, he did so with a wish to declare that he shared their culture. Ruskin was stimulated this summer of 1881 by the controversy over Froude's publication of Carlyle's *Reminiscences*, a book widely considered too frank and disagreeable. Not only did Ruskin support Froude's decision to publish this material. The public dispute led him to say that 'I think I shall have to write *my* reminiscences'.[27] To Allen, lamenting the loss of *Fors Clavigera* — a publication in Carlyle's spirit, in which Ruskin had written some of his own biography as well as Scott's — he announced 'I'm hungering to write some more autobiography of a boastful nature'.[28] We may find *Præterita* in this remark. However, Ruskin envisaged an autobiography vastly different from the one he was later to write. It was to be a trumpet-call, not a lament: not an apology but a challenge. The disciple who had produced *Arrows of the Chace* would understand. Alexander Wedderburn was coming to stay at Brantwood. As soon as he arrived, toward the middle of September, Ruskin sat down with him and brought out all the volumes of the diaries which recorded his life since the 1840s. But this autobiographical project was dangerous. Ruskin once more came near to the brink, the renewed madness that Laurence Hilliard feared. The diary he was using at the time now falls once more into free association.[29]

Later, on the opposite page to this part of the diary, Ruskin commented: 'Here begins writing for 22nd September. This 22nd September begins the time of excitement following arrangement of diaries with Alic: and it goes on virtually to 20th October, when I collapse'. The diary entries resemble those which preceded the mental breakdown of 1878, except that they are a little less personal. We note a comparison between Byron and Shelley; some sexual ruminations occasioned by looking at Ophelia's 'dead men's fingers' in Susie Beever's garden; a wandering train of thought initiated by *sortes Virgilianae*; recollections of Henry Melvill in the Camden Chapel; some scattered references to imperialism, probably suggested by the thought of Sir Herbert Edwardes; Socrates and Xanthippe; Alexander Pope; owls and witches; *Macbeth*, and the ghost story he had heard from Mrs Wingfield in Venice in 1876; Saussure; chivalry; Christ Church in his undergraduate days; and old numbers of *Fors Clavigera*. Such a mixture of topics is, of course, reminiscent of the heterogeneous material to be found in *Fors* itself. It is intelligible in the letters of *Fors,* but frighteningly disordered in the diary. However, the 'collapse' Ruskin mentions was physical rather than mental. He was in bed for a week in October, and his mind survived.[30]

Joan was in London at the time. She had left Brantwood after her first important quarrel with her cousin. They were not opposed on any specific issue, though Ruskin later indicates that they had been in dispute 'whether the house should go on, or not'. We hear of a disagreement, probably trivial, over some flowers Ruskin wished to uproot to send to Maria La Touche. The main cause of the trouble was certainly that Ruskin refused to be managed. He did not resign the mastership of the Guild, as he had said he would. Instead he floundered among secretaries, assistants, helpers and the Guild's companions. Ruskin wrote to Allen that '1. you, 2. Ward, 3. Bunney, 4. Swan, 5. Downs, 6. Butterworth, 7. Crawley are all it seems to me as much at cross purposes with each other as if you were the Seven Mortal Sins or seven devils — gone out of me into Dry places . . .'[31] These were not all. There were also the rest of Allen's family, helping in the publishing business in various ways; Alexander Macdonald in Oxford, still treated by Ruskin as his employee; there were a number of people employed in Sheffield; and there were also Mr Rusch (who cut and polished minerals, and with whom Ruskin was now in continual correspondence), and the copyists Randal, Burgess, Goodwin, Fairfax Murray, Hackstoun and the Italians Boni and Alessandri. Nominally, most of these men were in the service of the Guild of St George. Practically, they were working directly for Ruskin. As had always been the case with Ruskin family servants, no one was ever dismissed (when Ruskin was sane). An occupation was found for them, or invented. Thus Ruskin himself became increasingly occupied, and so did his secretarial helpers at Brantwood, who were Sara and Jamie Anderson, Laurie Hilliard, Collingwood and Wedderburn.

Joan was growing more worried about the thousands of pounds that flowed from Ruskin into wages, gifts, manuscripts, missals, gems, books, pictures, building projects, museums, psalters, continental trips and miscellaneous charities. It seemed to her that the work of St George's Guild was fulfilled only by more and more acquisitions and the employment of yet more people. 'My money is running away like cinders through a shovel', Ruskin absent-mindedly noted. Joan, who had been taught housekeeping by Margaret Ruskin, believed that most of this was waste. Furthermore, she disliked or distrusted a number of assistants (like Hackstoun) and Guild members (like Albert Fleming, who lived nearby at Ambleside, and enthusiastically accepted Ruskin's support for his linen-weaving experiments). While Ruskin scattered his money and his personal energy Joan tried to caution him. But then he was off to unpack another consignment of minerals, or write the daily letter that taught Greek to little Rosalind Webling, or supervise the large workforce from Coniston that he was employing to irrigate the moor: and if he was crossed he flew into a rage. Finally Joan could bear Brantwood life no longer and left for Herne Hill. Not all of the letters that then passed between the cousins have survived. But Joan must have been particularly exasperated if many of them were like this:

> My dear Joanie,
>
> Your yesterdays letter was the first since you went to London, that has said a word about any of my books, or anything that people were saying of them. If you were a little more interested in either the Scott papers, or the history of Amiens, and of — several other places, — which are at present my true work, — you would not immediately think me out of my wits because I tell you simple truths either about Lacerta or yourself — which are not subjects of my usual talk to you. I usually treat you only as a loving child or loving pet. But you are now on the point of forgetting that I cannot always be amused by the ballet, or the Rogue's march or the Christy minstrels.
>
> Try to recover some of the feeling you used to have when I taught you your drawing — and let me see that *even* as the mother of a family, you can be interested in my present work — and can trust me to choose the instruments of it — whether Hackstoun — Burgess — or Randal . . . It is at least, one little comfort to me, in this time of extraordinary — health — to see how much better *you* get on without *me*, than I without you.
>
> Ever your lovingest Di Pa.[32]

Joan could be reassured by knowing that at Brantwood that autumn were Sara Anderson, calm, efficient and discreet, and the secretary-disciples Collingwood and Hilliard. No doubt she corresponded with them about Ruskin's health. Slowly, by letter, the rift between Joan and Ruskin was mended. He wrote in early November that 'as long as we are both well enough — you to enjoy your children and take care of them — and I to write my promised books — we should "let well alone". When we cannot talk without you getting neuralgia and my getting cross, we should hold our tongues . . .'[33] And so there was a reconciliation. Neither cousin knew that worse, much worse, was to follow.

CHAPTER FORTY-ONE

1881–1882

Joan would not return to Brantwood until Christmas of 1881. For nearly three months this autumn, Ruskin presided over a saddened and apprehensive household. He was helped by Collingwood and Hilliard, who encouraged his more hobby-like interests. These included boating, improvements to the house, mineralogy and the drainage of the moor above the Brantwood estate. Ruskin also experimented with music and wrote songs. It is hard to say, as with other of his enthusiasms, whether music was a hobby or a more elevated part of Ruskin's general philosophy. The latter view was taken by Augusta Wakefield, a celebrated contralto who lived at Kendal and had been an occasional Brantwood visitor since 1875. She was to publish *Ruskin on Music* in 1894. While researching the book she corresponded with Collingwood, who directed her to some obvious sources and also to the rare *Elements of Prosody* of 1880, which contains interesting comparisons between musical and poetic rhythm. Collingwood added some reminiscences of his collaboration with Ruskin in setting words to music. Ruskin had probably begun his essays in composition in 1879, when he wrote some music for two of the *Odes* of Horace. Perhaps his gift as a composer was suited to more simple and modern poetry. Two of his own compositions and poems may be dated to this autumn of 1881. One is about Joan, the other probably about Rose. Ruskin wrote the songs and airs and asked Collingwood to devise their accompaniment. Joan's song, 'A Note of Welcome', later titled 'Joanna's Care', reads

> What shall we say to her,
> Now she is here? —
> Don't go away again,
> Joanie, my dear!

The other song is familiar because it was included in 1900 in A.T. Quiller-Couch's *Oxford Book of English Verse*.

> Trust thou thy Love: if she be proud, is she not sweet?
> Trust thou thy Love: if she be mute, is she not pure?
> Lay thou thy soul full in her hands, low at her feet; —
> Fail, Sun and Breath! — yet, for thy peace, *she* shall endure.[1]

As Collingwood pointed out in an article he later contributed to *Good Words*, this quatrain might be the motto of the 'Queens' Gardens' section of *Sesame and Lilies*.[2] The thought of music often returned Ruskin to Winnington and his old ideas of girls' education. Eager to moderate Ruskin in enterprises that might madden him, Hilliard and Collingwood joined his interest in the local school. They also observed classes for girls in which he taught some kind of elementary singing and dancing. The local Coniston school had reason to be grateful to Ruskin. The previous Christmas he had donated a splendid dinner for all its pupils and many other children from the district. Illness did not prevent his frequent visits. 'His interest in the school and schoolchildren was unabated', Collingwood relates, 'and he was always planning new treats for them, or new helps to their lessons'.[3] However, such treats could interfere with the school's normal routines. After a time, Ruskin's assistance at the school became less welcome. Collingwood's biography of his old friend and master diplomatically explains that

> About this time he was anxious to get the village children taught music with more accuracy of tune and time than the ordinary singing-lessons enforced. He made many experiments with different simple instruments, and fixed at last upon a set of bells, which he wanted to introduce into the school. But it was difficult to interfere with the routine of studies prescribed by the Code. Considering that he scorned 'the three R's', a school after his own heart would have been a very different place from any that earns the Government grant; and he very strongly believed that if a village child learnt the rudiments of religion and morality, sound rules of health and manners, and a habit of using its eyes and ears in the practice of some good handicraft or art and simple music, and in natural philosophy, taught by object lessons — then book-learning would either come of itself, or be passed aside as unnecessary or superfluous . . .[4]

The progress of Ruskin's own contribution to 'book-learning' may be gauged from his diary entry of 1 December 1881.

> I begin the last twelfth of the year, in which I proceed, D.V., to finish IInd Amiens and 7th Proserpina; and in the year, I shall have done, in spite of illness, 3 Amiens, I Proserpina and the Scott paper for Nineteenth Century, besides a good deal of trouble with last edition of Stones of Venice. But alas, what a wretched year's work it is, and even that not finished yet! But there was some good drawing in spring.[5]

All in all, he had little reason to find his endeavours 'wretched', and in truth he was pleased with his current writing. There was a pleasant Christmas with the Severns. Joan was happy because she had begun to persuade Ruskin that he should buy no further works of art and that he should sell some of his own collection. Ruskin was happy because Joan had returned to his side. Yet there was always a threat that he might once more lose his reason. In January of 1882 Ruskin wrote to his old servant Crawley that 'I'm quite well — I believe — if I don't worry or work — which I always do. But I'm not afraid of any attack this spring, like the last.'[6] The problem was that the sorrows and excitements of his mental life could not easily be quietened, as we see from a letter to Maria La Touche. Rose's mother had evidently written to him in terms not unlike those of many missives and instructions from Joan. So Ruskin now complained 'I wonder what you and Joanie call "being good": *I* call being good to think of the past and hope for the future, and then I go mad. Joanie calls it good to amuse myself as well as I can, and then I fall lower and lower till nothing will amuse me but the Theatre des Folies.'[7]

One amusement for Ruskin was to take the chair at Frederick Gale's lecture on 'Modern British Sports'; an occasion which served him as a reason to leave Brantwood for Herne Hill, Coniston pursuits having at length failed to hold his attention. Life in his old London home led him to sorrowful reflections on past life. On Shrove Tuesday and Ash Wednesday he was thinking both of Adèle and of Rose. Somewhere, Adèle was still alive. 'I must not play with any symptoms of breaking down', he told Mary Gladstone.[8] This was not merely because of a cold that was troubling him. It was the time of her father's Irish Land Bill, which Ruskin hated. He thought that political matters might dangerously over-excite his mind. For a fortnight in March Ruskin stayed indoors, his cold not improving, his temper worsening, his work among the saints of *Ara Coeli* (the intended third part of *Our Fathers Have Told Us*) becoming more confused. Then we hear of a sudden, furious disagreement with the cook, whom he dismissed: and the next day he wrote to a friend to whom he had not much appealed in recent years, Lady Mount-Temple.

Darling Phile

Please come and look after me here tomorrow or any day, as soon as you can. I'm afraid I'm going off the rails again — and it looks to me more like a terminus than the other two times. Joan's not well neither, and we all together want a good look and a word in season.

Ever your loving St C.

> I've been working hard on Ara Coeli and find the first Popes people whom one would gladly climb the steps after. Also I've been very wildly forgetting Ara Coeli and everything and perhaps am only getting another flogging — but this is a very nasty one — Love to Philos — P; S; Monday I am better — and have no good time to spare you *today*, but please answer this fixing your own time, to come, tomorrow, or Wednesday — no telegrams to be sent, or asked for.[9]

Then the delirium began. This time Joan, perhaps encouraged by Lady Mount-Temple, called for professional medical help almost immediately. 'You know when people are insane they always turn against those whom they love most when they're well', Ruskin had recently remarked to her.[10] She knew it only too well, and was not minded to bear the abuse alone. So she appealed to Sir William Gull. He was both a prominent physician and almost a family connection, for he had a partnership with James Oldham, the father of Ruskin's god-daughter Constance. Gull was able to keep Ruskin in bed, perhaps by sedating him with laudanum. He also introduced a nurse. This was Ruth Mercier, who became a friend and in years to come was often at Brantwood for both personal and professional reasons. In the delirium itself, as far as we are able to understand it, there are now familiar themes. First, there is an obsession with royalty and messages. Ruskin fancied that Ada Dundas[11] had come down from heaven to him, sent on a mission by Princess Alice of Hesse. There were fantastic visions. Ruskin later told Cardinal Manning that he could remember them but could find no words to write them down. There was always Rose, Rose who could return to him from the dead. 'I got better faster this time', Ruskin was later to tell Charles Eliot Norton, 'because Sir William Gull got me a pretty nurse, whom I at first took for Death (which shows how stupid it is for nurses to wear black) and then for my own general Fate and Spirit of Destiny, and then for a real nurse who had nursed Rose and kept *her* alive and got her hidden from me . . .'[12]

In his diary, at Candlemas the following year (2 February 1883), seeking the meaning of his madnesses, he observed 'the sad part of the third vision, and the terrible, was all in its beginning and crisis, but, as soon as I began to get better, I had the delightful notion that Ruth had been Rosie's nurse, and that she had hidden Rosie away and was going to bring her back to me, and I was expecting Rose every evening to come to tea — and watched the different doors of the nursery — and then when Ruth or Martha came in, instead — bore it as best I could, waiting always for tomorrow . . .'[13]

The 'Martha' here may have been the maid Martha Ray, but more probably was Martha Gale. Joan, after a fortnight of the delirium, could bear Herne Hill no longer and had left for the shelter and rest of the rectory at Upper Heyford, the home of Arthur's sister Eleanor and her husband, the Reverend Henry Furneaux. In Joan's absence Sara Anderson and Martha Gale had been asked to help with the nursing. Martha (who is the 'Mattie' sometimes mentioned in the diary and correspondence) was the prettiest of Frederick Gale's daughters, had been a visitor at Brantwood and was one of Ruskin's favoured 'pets'. He was glad to have her attentions when his rational mind began to return at the end of March.

His first letter after the illness shows that he had pleasure in Sara and Mattie but was worried by the separation from Joan. This pathetic note, written in a shaking hand, reads:

> Darling Doanie,
>
> I did not try to answer your sweet little letter myself, because I really didn't know how it would be good for you to be home — or indeed, how far I was myself recovered. I have been out several times — today I walked from my pond at Carshalton to near Croydon — but of course Arfie & the doctors & the girls only can tell you if you should come back — without being fitened! — I can't make anything out about this illness, but it's very nice being nursed by the girlies . . . Arfie says you've had pains in the back — di wee ma — if oo'll come back, me'll take the pains on my shoulders or be thumped anywhere Pease come back — if you don't mind my looking a little pale and weak yet . . .[14]

The recovery was gradual, and Ruskin's return to the world the more delayed because correspondence was discouraged. During the convalescence callers were still turned away from Herne Hill. There was one significant exception. Ruskin insisted on Froude's company. The historian often walked out from his home in Onslow Gardens to sit at Ruskin's bedside. They were dissimilar people, but bound together by their strong affection for Carlyle. Froude was still troubled by the controversy over his publication of Carlyle's *Reminiscences*, and was pained by the attacks on his character that had been launched by Ruskin's friend Charles Eliot Norton. Since Ruskin took Froude's part in the quarrel he found it difficult to write to Norton in his usual familiar way.[15] Correspondence between the two men ceased for a year. When Ruskin again began to send letters to Shady Hill he firmly pointed out that 'I am very fond of Froude, and am with him in all that he has done and said, about C, if it *had* to be said or done at all and I never saw anyone more deeply earnest & affectionate in trying to do right . . .'[16] Despite a manner that many people found forbidding, Froude was gentle at Herne Hill, 'as tender as a sister',[17] Ruskin thought; and he knew about Rose, had even met her: that had been fifteen years before, at the first height of Ruskin's passion. Now, in the spring of 1882, Ruskin and Froude were closer than at any other time in their lives. Upstairs in the tiny nursery, with its view over the Surrey hills through a window that had been barred since Ruskin's childhood, among the detritus of the illness — 'the chimney-piece with its bottles, spoons, lozenge boxes, matches, candle-sticks and letters jammed behind them' — Carlyle's and Ruskin's friend was gravely shown Rose La Touche's photograph. What was the right thing to say? 'More French than Irish', ventured Froude.[18]

That was characteristic. He could not enter the depths of Ruskin's ineradicable attachment to Rose. But there was a sane and worldly way in which he could listen to Ruskin and encourage him. He talked about the Land Bill rather than about saints. This was useful, but it did not reach to Ruskin's heart. Nobody could fully understand his sorrows. Now he wrote to Mrs La Touche in optimistic terms, but also with the implication that Rose was involved in his episodes of insanity. 'These fits of illness are all *accidents* (what an accident is — God knows — not I) not in the least consequences of my general work; and I rather fancy the three of them are all I'm meant to have. They were all of a piece, and Ireland and her "Rest" has much more to do with them than my English work.'[19] He had much darker thoughts, as we may find by looking again at his diary entry for Candlemas of 1883. There he returned to his conviction that there had been 'lessons of my three illnesses, of contention between good and evil'. Thus, he could feel a contrast between the great visions, the thought of Rose alive again, and the recurrent smallness of daily life. If there had been 'phrenzy — yet how much nobler than most of my sanity'.[20] Was it not ordained that he should believe in the Resurrection more fully when mad than when sane? Most private now was a guidance that he sought in the later part of his convalescence. He turned to Cardinal Manning, admitting that his recovery had left him 'very cowardly and faithless and sad'. To no one did he mention that he had asked the Cardinal to hear his confession.

As happened quite often in the last years of his active life, Ruskin now revived Joan's spirits by offering to sell works of art from his collection. Joan, who was once again pregnant, felt that Brantwood should be enlarged. This would help to accommodate her growing family. Furthermore, it was possible that her cousin might need a permanent nurse, who would have to live in the house. The simplest way to raise the necessary money was to put pictures on sale. Ruskin suggested that he should part with ten or more of his Turners. He also sent for auction a canvas that had never had a natural place in his collection, Meissonier's picture of Napoleon at the head of the French army. Ruskin had bought it in 1870. He admired its technique and finish but had no emotional tie to the painting and was content to let it go. To everyone's surprise, it fetched 6,000 guineas at Christie's. 'Hallelujah' said old Mr Tarrant when Ruskin took him Christie's cheque and announced to his father's solicitor that he was there to buy stock rather than to sell.[21]

This successful piece of business was only one of the diversions of the early summer of 1882. Ruskin was often at the British Museum and spent a weeked in Wiltshire at the home of Professor Maskelyne, the Museum's Keeper of Mineralogy. With Arthur Severn and Frederick Gale he watched a cricket match against the Australians at the Oval. Thus he became (probably) the only great Victorian writer to witness the English defeat commemorated in the Ashes. He continued his musical experiments. With Frances Graham he attended the first English performance of a Wagner opera. This night out at *The Meistersingers* was not a success. 'In the interval he stood up very tall, stretched himself and said "Oh, that someone would sing 'Annie Laurie' to me!".'[22] Georgiana Burne-Jones, with better sense than Francie, took him the next evening to *Don Giovanni*. He stayed the night at the Grange and the next morning breakfasted with William Morris. Ruskin had one amiable meeting with Gladstone and saw something of Cardinal Manning.

Joan and her children were at Brantwood, During the spring and early summer Ruskin's letters to his cousin often occupy, as does the following, a full four sides of his script.

Thursday 11 May 82.

Darlingest Doanie

I had a very sweet day for my Father's birthday yesterday. Drove in open Hansom, enjoying fresh air all the way in to T. and Mackrells — and was at the entrance to Broad Court by 10.55 A.M! where I met good Mr Baker! we went in together, found both partners and chatted till 12 — usefully. Then Mr Baker came with me to Fishmongers' Hall where we met Arfie to see exhibition of model ships (and I drew the Norman Sea King's of ninth century, found in opening tumulus, in 1880) — then Arfie went to sketch Thames, in lovely day, and I, with David (whom I had left to bring Arthur in, not wanting David at Walbrook) drove to Epitot to lunch, and then to British Museum, where the head of Minerals, Mr Fletcher — showed me a unique diamond with a six-rayed star, *dark* seen through every side [drawing] (Show Collie) Then I recommended purple instead of white cotton! — and mean to send Mat to buy some to show. Then I left my card on Froude: and *walked* from Onslow Gardens through Knightsbridge to Duke's Statue where I went into the park and observed — various objects — of scientific interest. Then I walked down end of Grosvenor Place — where I had told David to wait — drove home — had tea (with an egg, from Lucastes — my own boiling — and I buttered other 16, myself.) then into garden where I walked for an hour before dinner — Evening closed with Arfie's beating me at chess — but he had a fight for it! I slept perfectly well and have done a nice piece of geometry for Collie well before breakfast. As I walked through Knightsbridge I saw rather a pittier phot of Princess Helen and bought it to send oo, as enclosed: but, please di Ma, there's an article in the Morning Post of today (sent also), which makes me velly anxious about people's healths — particularly Lockie's — It says — Di Ma, that girls are never poppily in health unless their waists are 30 inches round. Now Di Ma, could oo be so velly good as to take a little measure of satin riband and send me the *exact* measure round Lockie's waist, — when she has'nt got anything on, oo know, di Ma — so that oo can run it quite fine. — its velly important for me to know before I write anything more for young ladies — And me's so obliged for nice Chart of the rooms Di Ma and for nice news of Miss Beever and me's velly well for my tea, this afternoon, and it promises to be fine, and me's oos poo wee deserted Donie.[23]

Could Joan be reassured by such a letter? Ruskin's spirits seem high. He is not spending money. George Baker appears to be looking after the Guild's affairs. There is nothing wrong with her cousin's appetite. He is sleeping well and getting on well with Arthur. There is, however, the question of his attraction to little girls, the 'objects — of scientific interest' he often watched in Hyde Park. While Joan and Lockie (she was a nursery governess to the Severn children) humoured Ruskin's wish to know about waist measurements — discussion of them fills the letters for a week — Joan, ever attentive to her cousin's moods, and increasingly expert at reading them, viewed with alarm the now constant talk of 'sylphs' and 'tookts' in his letters. Excitement over girls comes and goes in Ruskin. It does not necessarily presage a breakdown, but both Joan and Sara Anderson, who was her first confidante in such matters, began to suspect that there was something unhealthy in it. A twentieth-century mind might have entertained the thought earlier on. To many people who knew Ruskin personally, however, it was one more sign of his sweetness and amiability, his love of children; and he was, after all, the author of *Sesame and Lilies*, in whose pages were to be found — all agreed — the most noble passages addressed to girlhood in the English language. Only to Joan did he write fully about girls, so his predilections were not widely known. Joan, however, knew a great deal. A day after the letter given above he was lamenting that the bloom had gone off the Tylor daughters; the next day, he is thinking of painting a naked Lockie; that Sunday, he 'took a drive to Lewisham . . . I saw some little beauties going to church out of the villas at Sydenham Rise . . .'; and when he was at Maskelyne's for the weekend he rejoiced in 'seven young ladies who were down to dinner as girlies should be — and not kept up in nurseries'. At the Mount-Temples' in Stanhope Street he met a lady who 'has a pretty daughter Sophy whom she's promised to let me see'. At another social occasion there were 'some very pretty ones — (and one with pitty eggie pegs in brown tights!–) — and — that sort of thing . . .' A few days later, 'I had a lovely time with Mary Gladstone yesterday, and am to have another on Monday — but she gave me such a tebby tebby tebby twite *tilling* account of a girlie of 15 — going out to play cricket with blue eyes and the most golden hair that ever was, and the rosiest cheeks — and a schoolboy's cap on — and me's been utterly misby ever since!'[24]

'Misby.' How real are these infatuations? Do they belong to some less than serious realm that is appropriately described in baby talk: that is, that Ruskin was 'misby' but not miserable when thinking of the girl in the schoolboy's cap? One imagines so, and there is evidently much that is playful in these reports. Soon enough, however, Ruskin will declare himself to girls such as these, will attempt to adopt them or propose marriage to them. In the summer of 1882 Joan had no idea that there might be such developments. The question of girls, in her mind, was put in a general category of matters likely to cause the dreaded 'excitement', a category which also included art, *Fors Clavigera* and the study of early church history, among other things. Furthermore, some of her distrust was probably social. She had a stiff attitude toward the semi-theatrical world in which Ruskin had first encountered the Webling sisters, and which now provided him with a new 'pet', the child actress Tiny White. Of her, Ruskin reported, 'Tiny has nice large soft eyes and flaxen hair, and — rather pretty eggie pegs, but one may see prettier — in the Park. Still, she's a find.'[25] At a tea party *chez* White, where Lady Wilde was also a guest, and told Ruskin, to his pleasure, that 'Oscar was still the faithfullest of my disciples', Tiny played up to the Professor. 'Di wi ma, I nevy — no — nevy got such a lot of long, soft — hard kisses as Tiny White gave me yesterday — before all the company too!'

This was at the end of a period of some three weeks in which practically every letter to Joan had included similar passages. She now wrote back in rebuke. Ruskin then assured her that he was '*writing* absolutely nothing, except necessary letters — so that all book excitement is withdrawn' and that he was 'keeping off all subjects of sad thought'. As far as girls were concerned, 'I *am* very naughty about Tinys & Rosalinds — and I've less and less hope of mending'.[26] There the matter rested.

* * * *

As we have seen, Ruskin could believe that his illnesses represented and dramatised the struggle between good and evil. The Guild of St George was his instrument in this fight, and yet it was no instrument. The transformation of England that had once been promised remained a part of Ruskin's mind. The Guild was a vast, ghostly cathedral that existed in Ruskin's learning and imagination, and it is often a private thought of his, in a letter or a diary entry, that records for us an accretion to its structure. Sometimes we may feel that we know the Guild best, as we may know Ruskin best, when he is insane or near to insane. On the other hand the onset of madness, or the fear of it, could forbid Ruskin's involvement in his own creation. 'I must not let my thoughts at present be carried in that too exciting direction', he wrote in answer to an enquiry from his follower Thomas Horsfall about Guild policy.[27]

It was of course more difficult to know where the Guild stood on any subject because Ruskin was not issuing any numbers of *Fors Clavigera*. Even without *Fors*, however, the Guild was gaining new members, and by 1884 there would be some seventy Companions. There are also borderline members. What was the status of those who, like Janet Leete, addressed Ruskin as 'Master', wished to do his work, yet were at no time enrolled? Or of those whom, as in the case of Collingwood, Ruskin tried to entrap with gold? The Reverend John Faunthorpe, at the time of Ruskin's excited mental state in the autumn of 1881, found gold sent to him through the post. A fortnight later came an explanation. The 'square bit of gold means that you are an accepted adherent, or outside worker, of St George's company, looked upon by us as our friend, and invited to further cooperation —. I am now for the first time thus distinguishing our elect candidates . . .'[28]

No more is heard of this type of election, or of any proposed candidature of Faunthorpe's. In the next year or two Ruskin had to speak optimistically of his society while its real, that is to say mundane, fortunes were in abeyance. When he wrote his official report as Master in 1884 he stated that 'Several have left us, whose secession grieved me; one or two, with my full consent. Others, on the contrary, have been working with their whole hearts and minds, while the Master was too ill to take notice of their labour . . .'[29] By 1883, as a letter to Horsfall indicates, any strict attitude to Guild membership — at least in Horsfall's case — had disappeared. Ruskin wrote to him that

> Really the only obstacle *I* can see to your being a member of the Guild is that — I can't always read your letters, and can't in this one make out 'what you are going to tell me'. But anyhow I shall be very glad if you'd be a member in your own way. I want now to give force and weight to the Guild, never minding whether it gets mixed up with what it wants to be eventually quit of — as steam and the like. I've thought of asking you to be our new trustee — but don't know what the other one, Mr Baker, is doing about it yet.[30]

This is far from the Guild at the time of its inception. Are we to think of this new attitude as a wavering of purpose, as a victory of the world over Ruskin's spirit; or as an accommodation of the best sort, in thus accepting the general help of a man so energetic and sensible as Horsfall?

This Mancunian philanthropist brought that problem in a new, disconcertingly concrete fashion. For he wrote to Ruskin about the foundation of the Ruskin societies. Such bodies were inaugurated at just this period. The first was in Manchester, the next in Liverpool, two more following in Glasgow and Birmingham. Their membership hardly at all overlapped with the membership of the Guild. They had no creed. They were open to all, and their constitutions were voluntary and democratic. Ruskin was both flattered and taken aback when first approached by the secretary of the embryonic Manchester society: 'No, indeed, I don't want to discourage the plan you have so kindly and earnestly formed, but I could not easily and decrously promote it myself, could I? . . . I can at once assure you that the taking of the name of St George *would* give me endless trouble, and cause all manner of mistakes, and perhaps even legal difficulties. We must not have that, please.'[31]

Ruskin suggested to his correspondent that the new association should be called 'The Society of the Rose' and that its object should be 'to promote such English learning and life as can abide where it grows'. His interest was polite but always distant. It could not be otherwise. For in the Ruskin societies he surrendered his essence to his 'influence'. And in the last years of his life Ruskin's 'influence' might mean anything, and in the end meant next to nothing at all. The Ruskin societies show this process almost as soon at they were founded. Examination of their prospectuses and reports suggest that they were initially reading and discussion groups. Often, there was an emphasis on the lending out and exchange of Ruskin's rare and expensive books. Only a little later — and this coincides with George Allen's new practice of issuing cheap editions, available through bookshops — the Ruskin societies became lecturing societies, and had no other point.[32] In Glasgow in 1885, four years after its formation, the Society of the Rose had no programme other than a series of talks. They were on the topics of, for instance, vegetarianism, George Eliot, Matthew Arnold and 'A Sketch of the Human Spirit as a Contribution towards Individual Cultivation'. This was not Ruskinism. The Society had come adrift from its nominal inspiration. Nobody in the Glasgow Society knew Ruskin personally. Horsfall, who did, may have wished to pull the Ruskin societies toward a purpose of the Guild that now seemed quiescent, if not totally forgotten, or so we might infer from Ruskin's reply to a lost letter from Manchester: '. . . your idea of using the Ruskin societies to make the Church Christian! Alas! I am far downhill beyond any much hope . . .'[33]

Although he had first encountered the Revd John Faunthorpe in 1877, Ruskin took little notice of his admirer before 1880. Faunthorpe then quoted some of Ruskin's opinions about money in his *Household Science: Readings in Necessary Knowledge for Girls and Young Women (1881)*, and a correspondence ensued. Ruskin could not think highly of this book, but toyed with the idea of making Faunthorpe 'chaplain' of the Guild of St George. Two things about Faunthorpe now interested Ruskin. The first was that he was a self-professed expert in *Fors Clavigera* and, believing the series to be finished, offered to make an index of its contents. 'When, some day or other, you find out quite what Fors *does* mean, you won't let me inside your doors any more!'[34] Ruskin noted. Secondly, Faunthorpe enjoyed more genial relations with Ruskin because of his professional relationship with girls. He and

Ruskin instituted the May Day festivities at Whitelands College in Chelsea. This was an institute for training women teachers, and Faunthorpe was its Principal. Ruskin proposed an annual award to a 'May Queen', thus reviving an idea from Winnington days. 'In the quieter and yet more dignified conditions in which this experiment will be tried at Whitelands', he told Faunthorpe,

> it has better chance of success. And for my own part of the business, I will give you the entire series of my *constant* publications, every year, from the first to the last. This does not include the *Seven Lamps*, of which the supply is limited, or *Fors*, which is not meant for girls — but all the blue-backed ones, with *Frondes*, the new *Stones of Venice*, the *Bible of Amiens* etc; and the Queen shall, by necessary rule, keep for herself either *Sesame and Lilies* or *The Queen of the Air*, whichever she likes best; and the rest she shall give, one book to each of the girls *whom she shall choose for it* . . .[35]

Thus was initiated a practice which continued at Whitelands for some years. Ruskin presented to the college books, drawings, a 'May Queen cross' wrought in gold after designs by Burne-Jones and Arthur Severn, and paid for a number of stained-glass windows designed by Burne-Jones and executed by William Morris's company. Although he was often at the college, Ruskin never attended the May Queen ceremonials. But reports of the annual presentation gave him pleasure for years after his final collapse: especially, no doubt, when it had been arranged that people associated with Rose (like Mrs Bishop or Mrs Rafe Leycester) should preside over the occasion.[36]

The Whitelands May Queen festivities belong to the category of symbolic public events occasionally devised by Ruskin — the road-building at Hinksey, and crossing-sweeping outside the British Museum are others — that have a definite place within the Ruskinian scheme of things but were not fully comprehended by other people. The picturesque aspects of the Whitelands ceremony spoke of Merrie England to the participants. But this enterprise was also a covert memorial to Rose La Touche. One member of the College's staff, a Miss Martin, on being appointed to a school in Cork, winningly remarked to Ruskin that Irish girls were no less deserving of his affection than English ones. 'This remark touched Ruskin's heart more nearly than she knew', comments E. T. Cook, and so there came to be May Queen festivities in Ireland.[37]

Faunthorpe was so delighted by Ruskin's interest in his college that he exaggerated his patron's position in the mental history of the world.

In an article in the *Pall Mall Gazette*, probably written by Cook, we find a report of his address to Whiteland girls after the presentation of 1885. 'They were taught to regard [Ruskin] as one of the major prophets, as doing for this age what Plato, Aristotle and Bacon have done for others. A hundred years hence, Mr Faunthorpe told them, the nineteenth century will be remembered only or chiefly because Ruskin lived and wrote in it . . .[38] Not even the most impassioned admirer of Ruskin, then or now, will concur with this view of Faunthorpe's. More relevant is the extent to which we can agree with the *Pall Mall Gazette*'s reporter that 'very pretty it is to see the fresh young faces of the girls, one hundred and fifty, perhaps, or more, gathered thus together in the chapel, "not taken out of the world in monastic sorrow, but kept from its evil in shepherded peace"'.[39]

This seems an outdated attitude. But it would be an unfeeling historian of the nineteenth century who could not see that such remarks have their validity. For some girls did indeed live in such 'shepherded peace'. Many of them received some sweetness or beautiful ambition by reading Ruskin's words or listening to his talk. It has to be said that — to take only a few girls, already mentioned in this book — Angie Acland, Blanche Atkinson, Mary Gladstone, Constance Hilliard, Dora Livesey, Constance Oldham, Rose La Touche, Mattie Gale, Aggie Marks, Ada Maskelyne, Henrietta Cary, Maud and Alice Bateman, Frances Graham, Edith Irvine, Rosalind and Peggy Webling, Ada Dundas, Alice Owen, Flora Shaw, took from Ruskin a precious part of their young lives.[40]

Or, to reintroduce Lilias Trotter, whom, it will be recalled, Ruskin had met in Venice in October of 1876, one finds a life and personality not much applauded in modern times; and not, for that matter, much applauded by Ruskin. Beautiful Lilias, tall, thin, with brown hair and bright brown eyes, had an odd connection with Rose La Touche's milieu. Lilias, with her mother, had been at the first of the Broadlands conferences in 1874 and the next year had attended Moody's revivalist meetings in London. Like Rose, she was a child of revivalism and her mind was claimed by the Evangelical spirit. Her biographer wrote that 'when Ruskin wished her to devote herself to the service of Art, he found that Another had laid his hand upon her life.' But this is too simple. Ruskin's personal influence had always encouraged an intermingling of religious and artistic impulses. Lilias's strength of purpose was derived from Ruskin as much as from Moody. She worked hard, bringing the gospel to London prostitutes; she was active in the Young Women's Christian Association and helped to set up hostels for working girls. These projects often kept her from Herne Hill. Ruskin missed her, especially when he decided that she was 'still human — not wholly Evangelicalized' and grumbled if she did not call. 'Am I not bad enough . . . to be looked after a little when I'm ill, as well as those blessed Magdalenes?' In later years Lilias was often at Brantwood. After breakfast she would open Ruskin's letters and read them to him, and he would read her what he had written of *Præterita*. Uncommemorated now, Lilias led the life she chose, as a missionary in Algiers, where she died in 1942.[41]

★ ★ ★ ★

In May of 1882, after Ruskin had recovered from the illness in which he was attended by Sir William Gull, there was a plan that he should take a continental tour, accompanied by Arthur Severn. But this tour was much postponed by London activities and a visit to Sheffield (where 'there are only little boys') on Guild business. Not until mid-August did he set off on his thirty-fourth, and penultimate, visit to the continent. 'I should like to take a girl's school abroad with me!' he remarked to Joan.[42] In fact his companion was W. G. Collingwood, whose character and interests were to have considerable effect on the last years of Ruskin's life. After taking his degree Collingwood had left Oxford to study art at the Slade School. Then he had a studio in Chelsea and exhibited one painting at the Royal Academy in 1880. Collingwood, as his self-portrait demonstrates, was a talented painter, but he had no particular wish to become a professional artist. Perhaps the Slade under Alfred Legros brought a conflict of loyalties to the young man who had been a student in Ruskin's drawing schools. At all events, London and London art meant nothing to a man singularly free of personal and social ambition. Collingwood cared little for politics or religion. In other respects, however, his interests were taken from Ruskin or shared with the older man. Collingwood liked measuring and fashioning things. His daily hours were spent in geologising, drawing, studying the classics and local history. Collingwood was clever and patient. He had known Ruskin now for eight years and had been a visitor at Brantwood as disciple, friend and secretary for much of this time. In 1881 he had moved from London to his family cottage on Windermere in order to be within reach of Brantwood. This was in the aftermath of Ruskin's second mental breakdown. He had then found Ruskin 'dreadfully altered'.[43]

In Collingwood there was pity, devotion and watchfulness. He was a far better companion for a long tour than Arthur Severn. He was not irritating and, unlike Arthur, could converse with Ruskin on intellectual and cultural topics. But he was not a disciple who believed what Ruskin told him. Wary of things he considered monkish, Collingwood had little time for the kind of work that went into *The Bible of Amiens* and its related writings. Years later, he wrote an account of this 1882 tour. In its sorrowful pages Collingwood stated his conviction that 'to the few who cared more for himself than his mission, St George and St Benedict were the enemies'. As they went through northern France, following the old road to 'the old places', from Calais to Laon, Rheims, Troyes, Sens, heading towards Dijon and Champagnole, he none the less heard as much about saints as about geology or art.[44] A letter from Ruskin to his friend Lazarus Fletcher, of the Natural History Museum, gives the flavour of the early part of the tour. It was written from Laon:

> This place is very odd in its geology — hard limestone on the top of sands — an outlier — and with lovely springs at the top of it! The surface is not more than three square miles, at most, so the springs can't be supplied by any superficial rain. It's the oddest thing to me that ever was and I'm going to look for some Laonnais Moses in the Cathedral legends. Mr Collingwood worked out the facts for me; he doesn't approve of legends, and rubs my hair the wrong way — but he does lovely models and drawings for me, and gets forgiven every morning . . .[45]

Collingwood now found that the holiday was not as convalescent for Ruskin as he would wish. He had not realised how much work was accomplished on Ruskin's continental journeys. 'It was always rather wonderful how he would make use of every moment, even when ill-health and the fatigue of travelling might seem a good reason for idling. At once on arriving anywhere he was ready to sketch, and up to the minute of departure he went on with his drawing . . .[46] Collingwood learnt much more of Ruskin this summer: of his delight in terrain, in the geology of *coteaux*, in French food and wine. He saw the way that Viollet-le-Duc's restoration at Vézelay gripped him, as though Ruskin had been present during the rebuilding; and he witnessed his nervous sensibility — as they drove past a ruined country homestead Ruskin 'shrank back in the carriage, as if some one had thrown a stone at him'.

At Avallon, where, Collingwood believed, they lingered because of 'one of those obscure associations which so often ran in his mind . . . Avalon he called it always, dominated by the idea of the island-valley of repose where King Arthur found the immortality of fairyland', Ruskin wrote the preface to a new edition of *Sesame and Lilies*.[47] There, in its account of 'college education for women — out-of-college education for men; positivism with its religion of humanity, and negativism with its religion of Chaos, — and the like, from the entanglement of which no young people can now escape', one may perhaps overhear the conversations between Ruskin and Collingwood as Ruskin learnt more about Collingwood's generation.[48] To be sure, that would not have altered Ruskin's wish to be, like his own *Sesame and Lilies*, 'wholly of the old school'. But he now felt that he had not done with talking to young men. In only a few weeks' time he would ask to resume the Oxford Slade professorship.

A return to Oxford, however, was not presently in Ruskin's thoughts, At Cîteaux, the birthplace of St Bernard, in a little grassy garden on a hill among vineyards, with Dijon beneath them, Mont Blanc and the hills of Burgundy beyond, Ruskin fell to his knees and spent long in fervent prayer. Collingwood was taken aback. As they approached the Alps he had been worried by the fits of depression which overtook Ruskin, when the old man would not rest but would draw that which seemed little worth drawing, would walk far in the afternoon and dine alone, writing. Now Collingwood began to be alarmed by Ruskin's exaggerated sensitivity to the weather. As they climbed into the mountains, thunder, cold east winds and 'a dark haze' oppressed his spirits. The Alpine air was unpleasantly strange. It was the weather of 'The Storm-Cloud of the Nineteenth Century'. Collingwood was to be little convinced by that famous lecture. Yet he too records how the very atmosphere in the high mountains seemed blighted.

> All the way up from Mornex [Ruskin] wanted me to come into the carriage and shut the window because of a treacherous east wind, and in my sketch you can see a certain smoky, not only thundery, look in the clouds. At Saint Cergues this east wind haze was still more pronounced, the lake of Geneva ruffled and white, with patterns of shadow from small 'sailor-boy' clouds, while the whole range opposite was not exactly shrouded but veiled in a persistent thickness of air. Above, the sky was bright, with blue and streaky cirrus, and between the showers the sun glittered on the trees. That fitful wind with the brownish-grey haze he called the plague-wind, and in all his lecture there is no very definite explanation of it, but much declamation against it as the ruin of landscape, and some vague hints of portent, almost as if he had been a prophet of old, seeing the burden of modern Babylon in the darkened sun.[49]

Of this latter aspect of 'The Storm-Cloud of the Nineteenth Century' more will be said in its place. Meanwhile, this odd couple, two Englishmen with their watercolour boxes and sketchbooks, one forty years older than the other, look up from the heights of the Swiss mountains into the skies. At the Col de la Faucille, where, Collingwood knew, Ruskin 'always used to get his first full view of the "Mount Beloved"', there was no sign of the great mountain. 'For a moment, too short for a sketch, Mont Blanc loomed through the dull haze, red in the sunset, brick red, not Alpine rose; and then all was grey. We found our carriage and drove off.'[50] Ruskin, peering out from the little inn at St Cergues at a quarter to six on the morning of 7 September, saw 'all the Alps covered and the lake wholly concealed by what seemed a mass of London smoke, silvered at the top only. Plague wind below the turn of the valley, sharp from the south, and cold.' He wrote this diary entry at half-past six that morning. Later that day, going on to Geneva, he found 'the sky and air exactly like Sheffield . . . Bitter cold, with hot sun as we climbed the Dole, only to see from it the entire chain of Alps smothered entirely down and snuffed out by one mass of foul, brown gray, natural — or supernatural — smoke of the Devil's best patent make, reaching nearly across the lake so that we could not see Geneva, much less the Salève . . .'[51] On 11 September, at Sallenches, Ruskin was up at half-past five. 'In a quarter of an hour, the plague cloud formed, from the west, coming from Mont Joli, brown, and in heavy flakes, covering all as low as the aiguille de Boissay. By half past six one could only see a black point or two of the aiguilles; the valley was half filled with cloud, thin and streaky but dirty, and all in a state of flux, flight, change and diseased motion and make.'[52]

Collingwood knew Ruskin, and furthermore he was a student of Ruskin's writings. He must now have had to think about the extent to which Ruskin believed that such phenomena were supernatural. Collingwood knew what the plague-cloud was. It was smoke. He also knew that the notion of defilement was deeply in Ruskin's mind, in his character, in his books: most pertinently now, in *The Queen of the Air*, and its preface written at the other end of the lake, at Vevey, in 1869, when Ruskin had found that the light, the snow, the air, were 'as if Hell had breathed on them'.[53] There was no direct way in which Collingwood could reason with Ruskin about the weather. His mind wandered beyond discussion. In any case, it would have been impossible to put to Ruskin the suspicion that his notes on the natural world were determined by a metaphor, that of purity stained and befouled. Collingwood confined himself to the facts, and did not argue.

> At Annecy, in the pleasant Hotel Verdun, he confessed himself already stronger, and fit for anything except proofs and business letters; but the 'plague-cloud' still hung over the view. He noted that

> the smoke from the factory chimneys could not be told from the clouds except by its density, and mixed with the mist so as to throw a pall over the lake from the town to La Tournette — the great mountain of the neighbourhood above Talloires. But still he did not see that the black, ragged, dirty weather was caused by the smoke, though he compared it with a London November.[54]

Collingwood, his future biographer, came to know so much of Ruskin's past life during this tour that by some transference he afterwards had the impression that his host was working on *Præterita* when alone in the evenings. It is true that, as so often before, Ruskin's aim in travelling was to summon past experiences and to pay homage to his parents. At one point he had hurried, therefore, to reach Champagnole for 2 September 'on the morning instead of the evening of my mother's birthday — she & my father loved it so much'.[55] The privileged Collingwood was conducted along the same paths to the same views that, years before, Ruskin had shown Charles Eliot Norton. On a visit to Mornex they went to see the house where Ruskin had written much of *Munera Pulveris*. Collingwood was fascinated, for from the vantage point of the 1880s the Mornex sojourn was an obscure period in Ruskin's life. Mornex, where he was remembered by the villagers, pleased Ruskin; but once he and Collingwood were on the Italian side of the Alps there were renewed signs of restlessness and worry. Business letters had to be answered. More taxing were instructions about copying art, for he was obliged to deal with a number of assistants who were working for the Guild of St George. Ruskin also had a lecture to prepare. Months before, he had engaged himself to talk about crystallography at the London Institution. However, since Christian traditions were now uppermost in his mind, he determined to change his subject. Collingwood was nervous because 'I did not quite see why he should lecture on either; but he declared himself quite well, and as we had dropped crystallography — the chief subject before the tour — for cathedrals and abbeys in Italy, he shut himself up at Pisa, cold and all, to write his lecture'. Collingwood's fears were of a relapse. He considered 'the monks and myths chasing one another through his brain' a danger.[56] So they were; but 'Mending the Sieve', the lecture Ruskin now wrote, turned out to be a triumph.

* * * *

When the plague-wind did not blow, Ruskin found in Italy that his feelings of delight in nature had scarcely diminished and that he could be 'almost as happy as a child again'. He and Collingwood were in Turin on 22 September, whence they drove to Genoa and arrived at Pisa on the 26th. The whole of October was spent between Lucca and Florence. Now they were often accompanied by other artists and assistants such as Angelo Alessandri and Giacomo Boni, who were set to make drawings of architectural details for the Guild of St George. A more independent artist was the American expatriate Henry Newman. He also undertook commissions for St George, and had done since 1877, but cannot be described as one of Ruskin's employees. His villa in Florence was a social centre, especially for American visitors to Italy. Ruskin's own drawing this October was often not as firm as it could have been, and perhaps the same was so of his opinions. After a walk through the Uffizi he reported to Joan that 'I used to think Botticelli's little Venus the nicest thing to see in the world, but when I saw her again yesterday I only thought that to see a *real* pitty girl without any clothes but roses would have been ever so much nicer!'[57] Once more he fell into depression and there seemed to be nothing in Florence that could lift his spirits. 'I'm very miserable here', he explained to Joan, 'and shall get away the moment I've shown Collingwood the things he ought to see'.[58] However, later on the day he wrote this letter, Ruskin saw some art, new to him, which moved him deeply and occupied him for the rest of his working life. It was in the manuscript and drawing books of Francesca Alexander. She was another American expatriate, and was introduced to Ruskin by Henry Newman. Francesca and her mother Lucia because dear friends of Ruskin's and, though they never met, of Joan. They had good reason to be grateful for Ruskin's friendship. Francesca became famous through his enthusiasm for *The Story of Ida*, *Roadside Songs of Tuscany* and *Christ's Folk in the Apennine*, which he bought, edited, published and announced as great art in lectures in Oxford and London the following year.

In these lectures Ruskin conveyed the impression that Francesca was a young artist, a 'lassie'. She was in reality forty-five years old when they met and had been a professional artist for twenty years. She was the daughter of Francis Alexander, a Boston portrait painter who had settled in Florence in 1853. He had died in 1880, eighteen months before Ruskin entered Francesca's life. She and her mother lived in apartments in Florence, with no lack of style. In their salon hung two reputed Giottos and a Ghirlandaio, neatly and cheaply acquired from churches at the time of the Italian war with Austria. The Alexanders also had a summer house in the district above Florence known as the Abetone. There they spent the hot months of the year. Recently the

Abetone had become an inland resort: there were a few hotels there, catering for wealthy Florentines, Americans and English. The Alexanders, however, were interested in the local peasantry. Members of the Italian Evangelical Church themselves, they none the less found some pure and simple piety in the faith of the country folk. They also looked for other kinds of indigenous folk culture. The district was noted for an especially 'pure' Italian spoken thereabouts, and there survived many interesting *rispetti*, both sacred and secular folk ballads. In 1862 the Alexanders had sought out the most celebrated singer of such ballads, the *improvrosatrice* Beatrice degli Otani, and had formed a friendship with her. By the next year Francesca was writing down *ottave* from her dictation. Such songs Francesca further collected from other first-hand sources and then from old Florentine song-books.[59] Her first thought was to publish them. Then she realised that they could be made into a form of contemporary art. She translated the songs into simple literary English, wrote them out in delicate script into expensive manuscript books and illustrated them in pen and ink. Thus each book was a unique object. These she sold. The very high prices she charged were fixed by her father. Before Ruskin arrived, her clientele was also inherited from her father, who specialised in portraits of American visitors to Italy.

This was the background to the manuscript books that Ruskin saw. The day after his first visit to the Alexanders Ruskin wrote to Francesca's mother and declared his 'happy and reverent admiration' for the illustrations,

> reverent not only of a quite heavenly gift of genius in a kind I had never before seen, but also of the entirely sweet and loving spirit which animated and sanctified the work . . . In absolute skill of drawing, and perception of all that is loveliest in human creatures, and in the flowers that live for them, I think these works are in their kind unrivalled . . . I came to the conclusion that I might, for the service of the English peasantry, be mean enough to take Miss Alexander at her frank word as to the price of the book . . .[60]

Here, for once, Ruskin was being financially prudent. The price of *The Story of Ida* was £600. In the excesses of appreciation the previous afternoon Ruskin had offered £1,000. We can understand why he was so enthusiastic about this particular book. Ida could well fit into his growing martyrology of girl saints. Hers is the tale of a seventeen-year-old of great piety who fades away and dies in religious exaltation. Its frontispiece shows Ida in bed, in her last sleep before death. In this drawing, as in the illustrations to *Roadside Songs of Tuscany* (whose purchase Ruskin also arranged) one may rapidly perceive some things that Ruskin's heart willed him to ignore. Francesca was not possessed of any 'absolute skill of drawing'. As one would expect, her art has a mingling of naivety and calculation. Its first models are in the late medieval old masters; but the pervasive influence is that of commercial religious illustration from the previous thirty or forty years. Ruskin now, in mid-October, spent two days at Lucca drawing architecture with Edward Robson,[61] the designer of the proposed Guild museum at Bewdley, then returned to Florence and the 'loving and generous Alexanders'.[62] Taking from them *The Story of Ida* and a present they gave him, 'the marble *pelican* that used to be over the altar at Orvieto . . . Giovanni Pisano's I suppose — anyhow — a master's work', he set off for the North and home, and slept in his old nursery at Herne Hill after 'three months and twenty days without a single serious misadventure', as the diary puts it, on 2 December.[63]

This had been Collingwood's first visit to Italy. In nearly four months he had amassed considerable knowledge of art, architecture and of course of his guide. In conditions of much strain, he studied the person who set him to study. Eleven years later, in 1893, he would publish the first official biography of Ruskin, and the seeds of that book were in this tour. However, there were many things that Ruskin kept to himself, perhaps because his young companion was in some sense his keeper. He was meditating a return to Oxford. Ruskin never mentioned this to Collingwood, though it is possible that the quickness and interest of this artist-cum-intellectual, a pupil from his early Oxford period, might have contributed to his wish to become Slade Professor once more. From Lucca Ruskin wrote to Alexander Macdonald: 'It is curious I can't think it's only three years since Richmond took the Professorship. I believe I'm quite able now to take it again myself, if they'd like me to. I shouldn't give exciting lectures any more — but sufficient ones on practical matters, and I should like to finish the arrangements of the schools as I meant them to be. You might say this to Acland when you see him . . .'[64] Writing to Maria La Touche on the same day, telling her that 'I've been quite amazingly rational lately', Ruskin remarked that 'having occasion to write to Oxford today, I sent word if they liked to have me for Professor again for a while they might'.[65] The reasons why Ruskin should have wished to return to Oxford remain mysterious. It seems that he hoped to continue with his rearrangements of the drawing schools more than to give lectures. But a personal optimism lay behind his message to the University. He hoped and believed that his attacks of 'brain-fever' were all in the past. As Collingwood's biography mistakenly says, they had 'passed over him like passing storms, leaving a clear sky'.[66]

In December of 1882, however, the many doubts in the minds of

Ruskin's friends about his fitness to do anything, let alone return to Oxford, were dispelled by the lecture he had written while on tour and which he delivered at the London Institute just two days after he had disembarked at Folkestone. Collingwood quite frankly admitted to Joan that he was glad to have got Ruskin home without another breakdown. But to everyone else he seemed marvellously well. The confusion over the title and the subject of his talk he immediately turned to good account. The lecture was not to be on crystallography, he said, nor precisely on Cistercian architecture. His audience would have wondered why his address was called 'Mending the Sieve'. As perhaps few of them would have remembered, the mending of a sieve was a miracle attributed to St Bernard. As this became clear, it became clear also that the lecture was a performance, and that Ruskin had summoned the urbanity to beguile his audience into an expectation of eccentricity, and yet to demonstrate to them, with many a deft change of direction, that to follow the seeming divagations of his mind was to learn something and to be stirred by that learning. Collingwood must have held his breath many times. But the lecture was totally a success. Edward Burne-Jones was present, and could report in a letter to Charles Eliot Norton that 'Ruskin flourishes — gave a lecture on Cistercian architecture the other day that was like most ancient times and of his very best, and looks well — really stronger than for many a year past'.[67]

CHAPTER FORTY-TWO

1883

In this comparatively vigorous mood Ruskin spent Christmas at Herne Hill. With the New Year of 1883 he went to Brantwood. Ruskin had not seen his Coniston home for thirteen months and looked forward to a spell of quiet Lakeland life. He was also rather pleased to be alone. Joan remained at Herne Hill, and Collingwood had other things to attend to, for he was to marry later this year. Ruskin was 'Down to work in good health', as he noted in his diary on 7 January, 'among more treasures than I could use in fifty years'.[1] He was thinking of his mineral collection, a constant pleasure of his life. Mineralogy was far more than a hobby, as *Deucalion* and other writings attest. Ruskin could find worlds of meaning in stones, yet his researches into their significance did not trouble his mind. He was perhaps at his happiest when geologising or sorting through his mineral cabinets. At Brantwood Ruskin had about 3,000 specimens, collected on all his tours and expeditions since teenage years and also acquired from dealers. Now he selected and catalogued 100 of his minerals for St David's School at Reigate. The school belonged to the Revd W. H. Churchill, who had recently married Connie Hilliard. This benefaction should be noted among a number of other gifts of sets of minerals. Ruskin presented minerals, and wrote explanatory catalogues for them, chiefly to St George's Museum, Sheffield, from 1877 to 1886; and also to Whitelands College (1883), the British Museum (1884), the Museum of Kirkcudbright (1884), the Coniston Institute (1884) and the Cork High School for Girls (1889). Other uncatalogued gifts of minerals had been made to Winnington School throughout the 1860s and there is record of similar gifts to Harrow School (1866) and to Balliol College, Oxford (probably in 1883 or 1884).[2] While this generosity was mostly directed toward institutions there were also numerous presents of minerals to individuals, and surely Ruskin gave many an agate, flint or jasper to W. G. Collingwood. He and Ruskin were successful colleagues in geological investigation.

An interesting product of their shared European tour the previous year was Collingwood's second book, *The Limestone Alps of Savoy: a Study in Physical Geology*, published by George Allen in 1884. Ruskin wrote its introduction at some point in 1883. This essay is valuable for its autobiographical account of Ruskin's geological interests and hints that Collingwood's account of Savoyard limestone is a completion of work that Ruskin had begun in the summer of 1854 and had published in the fourth volume of *Modern Painters*.

The impulses that would produce *Præterita* were now beginning to form in Ruskin's mind. Three more publications from this period have autobiographical significance and are connected with the 1882 tour with Collingwood, three months when the contrast between youth and age was often discussed. They are a 're-arranged' edition of *Sesame and Lilies*, a new edition of the second volume of *Modern Painters* and the chapter 'Revision', which ended Ruskin's work on his geological book *Deucalion*. The edition of *Sesame and Lilies* was issued in late autumn of 1882: Ruskin's new preface is dated from Avallon on 27 August of that year. *Sesame and Lilies* was a Victorian classic in permanent demand, but the revival of the second volume of *Modern Painters* was unexpected. Of all Ruskin's works, one might have thought this book the least likely to quality for a new publication. In 1882–83, its author's feelings were mixed. The notes he added to the text, most of them written on the Collingwood tour, are often sardonic. But Ruskin now found that the piety with which the book had been composed, back in 1845, was neither narrow nor dated. Much of his future character was to be found in its pages. 'I had no memory, myself, when I began the revision of the text, that it was anywise so pregnant with the design of subsequent works.' The text is not in fact revised so much as annotated. The religious tone could not be taken out, though Ruskin had long since discarded the Evangelical faith that gave the book its passion. Ruskin in 1882 found that the attitude of his former writing 'becomes pardonable to me, when I see the general fervour of belief in God's goodness and man's possible happiness, which runs through all the theology in this volume'.[3] Ruskin's new satisfaction with *Modern Painters II* is also mentioned in 'Revision'. Both were given to the public in the spring of 1883, and it was intended that the *Deucalion* chapter should be read with the earlier book in mind.

In 'Revision' Ruskin mentions *Fors Clavigera* as one of his unfinished works, and in April of 1883 he once more attempted to resume his series of letters. There had been two issues of *Fors* since Ruskin's breakdown in 1878. They were published in May and September of 1880. Now he began again. The *Fors* of May 1883 was his ninetieth letter. There would be ninety-six in all, and the final six, written after three spells of mental illness, inevitably have a different character. Ruskin's great undertaking had previously been disputatious and valiant. The final letters, however, are quieter and resigned. 'I am putting my house in order', Ruskin wrote from Brantwood in opening his ninetieth letter, 'and would fain put my past work in order too, if I could'.[4] This was typical of Ruskin's mood in the spring of 1883. He wished to make a fresh start. At the same time his studies always seemed to be retrospective, and the reappointment to the Slade chair was bound to return him to past sorrows and unfinished business. Ruskin's messages to Oxford about a return to his old position had been well received, and on 17 January a telegram had arrived at Brantwood from Henry Acland. It was a confirmation of a decision reached by Convocation and read 'Dear friend may all good attend you and your work in this new condition, once again welcome to Alma Mater.'[5] A few days later Ruskin took down his 'Myth Book', the large manuscript volume in which, years before, he had made his analysis of Greek thought while meditating such books as *The Queen of the Air*. On its end pages he now began notes for his new Oxford lectures. They adumbrate a discussion of both Greek and Christian art in an expansion of his old dictum that 'All great art is praise.'[6] These notes, however, were not used.

The return to Oxford was the major mistake of Ruskin's public life, as he perhaps knew before he took up his old responsibilities. He felt that his post was one of awesome duty: on the other hand he was more than a little wary of mental effort, and so his attitude to the University often appeared lackadaisical. He told Faunthorpe, 'I have only taken the Professorship again in order to keep my hand on the helm, not to talk. They will be quite content to hear me read *Proserpina* or anything else I am doing.'[7] In the event his first set of lectures, which we know in their published form as *The Art of England*, were prepared in a desultory fashion. With innocent disregard for the Richmond family feelings, he told George Richmond that he was not thinking of giving an inaugural lecture, 'for I am really only going back to finish what I left ineffective in the system of the schools; but may perhaps in the first or second lectures, which I hope to give after Easter, glance at the present state of English art, so far as I can feel it to be happy'.[8] The health of English art was also the concern of William Blake Richmond, who had graciously resigned the Slade chair to make way for Ruskin's return, but Ruskin seems to have been heedless of 'Willie's' professorial efforts. Relations with the Richmonds were not impaired, because they were prepared to make allowances for Ruskin. That was so with many old friends. Acland had simply ignored Ruskin's furies during the time that Richmond had been Slade Professor. In 1880 Ruskin had told him that

> Oxford has *no* future to look to, or think of. God only knows what will happen to her, and He will tell her, in his own time, — In the meantime, She is no more a University — but a mere shop of adulterate knowledge — poisoned to the customers taste — which is principally for skulls patched with venereal disease — and new shops and streets — such as have been opened since I came in 1870 . . .[9]

Acland knew that such storms would pass; and indeed, by the time that Ruskin was thinking of his new lectures he was writing to his friend in a quite different spirit. 'I well know the changes in the place — nor shall I weary myself in contention with them —: but speaking no more of any religious or emotional art, limit myself to fixing the methods of elementary practice . . .'[10]

* * * *

Ruskin travelled from Brantwood to Oxford at the beginning of March 1883. He had decided to lecture on the English art he had known during his own time. This was a pleasant task, the composition of his addresses was well forward and he felt confident that he would be well received. His old rooms in Corpus Christi were 'in excellent order', and from Corpus he made a round of visits. On his walks he was sometimes accompanied by Benjamin Jowett, who in his position as Vice-Chancellor of the University felt responsible for the Slade Professor's good humour. Thus Ruskin encountered a new atmosphere within the University. Since 1877, the last time he had been in Oxford, there had arisen a different ethos, in taste, learning and social commitment. Ruskin's reactions are contained in a letter to Maria La Touche:

> Things are so changed, and I am changed not a little also, chiefly with having more sympathy with modern life not quasi-steam but in its activities and hopes for larger and more levelled multitudes. There are such nice people now if one looks for them, and assuredly some great reaction must take place against what is brutal and cruel in Socialism, and new codes of dealing with the poor . . .[11]

He had felt the presence of the pragmatic liberalism that took sane public service as its watchword. E. T. Cook, ever afterwards grateful that he had been an undergraduate during this period, wrote of a 'new Oxford movement', and such an optimistic attitude was common to his generation. The idea that a modern Oxford had been born in the early 1880s helps to account for the large number of memoirs of university life that were published some four decades later. Ruskin often appears in these books. He is sometimes described as an inspiration and sometimes as an anachronism. Sir Arthur Quiller-Couch's account is representative.

> In this autumn of 1882 the 'aesthetic movement' had — in Oxford at any rate — almost run itself out of breath . . . poetry and the arts for a while gave place in discussion to philosophy (notably that of T. H. Green) and social philanthropy — *The Bitter Cry of Outcast London*, Toynbee Hall, the crusades of W. T. Stead, etc., — a backwash from the prophetic teachings of Carlyle and Ruskin. Ruskin himself came back to us; to walk the street in velvet 'square' and blue double-breasted frock-coat; to revive veneration rather than the ardours of an earlier time; to lecture once or twice and finally to collapse in face of a sorrowful audience. But we undergraduates held meetings and started missions in dire tracts of London — in such places as Bethnal Green and Stratford. We gathered to listen to C. T. Studd and his cricketer missionaries from Cambridge. Some few, even of the rowdies, left our company to join the Salvation Army, renouncing all.[12]

Ruskin had returned to an Oxford in which women's colleges had been founded.[13] To Elizabeth Haldane, a student at this date, who in working for Octavia Hill had come across what she took to be Ruskinism in the 'Maypole dances in Paradise Court', to her matter-of-fact Scottish mind 'rather out-of-date and foolish', Oxford's new alignments

> signified a time of wonderful cheerfulness and hope. On the intellectual side there was the movement dominated by Professor T. H. Green and Arnold Toynbee of Oxford, which made for an outlook on the universe which was not only satisfying to reason but also encouraging to those who wished to work for their fellows. This movement, which was founded on the idealistic philosophy dominated by Hegel, influenced us all greatly. Green's Lay Sermons and his *Prolegomena to Ethics* and Bradley's Ethics were books we read . . . on the practical side, one tried hard to see how to bring one's theories into practice, as Green did in the City of Oxford; while Toynbee's influence went to the founding of Toynbee Hall and many other settlements and clubs for working men and women . . .[14]

Examples of such thinking could be multiplied. It was a common attitude among serious undergraduates and the tutors they admired. Ruskin could hardly respond. The personal opposition he would instinctively bring to such modernisms — as, most recently, in the

Sesame and Lilies preface and the notes to *Modern Painters II* — he had promised to abjure. He had given assurances of quiet behaviour to Acland, for the sake of general good relations, and to Joan Severn, on account of his mental health. The more, therefore, he felt himself attracted to his drawing schools. The collections there had been inert without him, unused, never properly framed, arranged or catalogued. Nobody could comprehend the correct order: nobody, not even Macdonald, could use the collection for teaching or study. But Ruskin could busy himself in the schools for months. And in the mere act of drawing, or so he imagined, there might be an antidote to aestheticism and Whistlerism. 'I shall keep the students down at Oxford in the Ruskin schools to Duck's feather for a while to cure them of aesthetics and peacocks . . .'

To many, Ruskin was a superannuated figure; yet he was probably the most famous person in the University. His lectures (which had been announced in the *Oxford University Gazette* as on 'Recent English Art') were even more popular than those he had given in the 1870s. Their larger audience may be attributed to an increase in the student population. None the less, his following was remarkable. Around 200 people had to be turned away from the first lecture of the series and thereafter Ruskin repeated each lecture on the following day. Admission was by ticket, and newspaper reporters were present. No doubt many people were attracted to the lectures — the first ever given in Oxford on living artists — because their subject was novel and because it was well known that Ruskin had been closely associated with the painters of whom he spoke. An undergraduate might expect to hear an account of Ruskin's association with Pre-Raphaelitism. However, this was not quite the subject of 'Recent English Art', for Ruskin had scarcely changed his old conviction that the history of Pre-Raphaelitism was also a history of moral failure, and this was not an appropriate topic for a lecture course. Once again, some of the evidence was omitted by Ruskin's editors E. T. Cook and Alexander Wedderburn. In 1872 Ruskin had explained in a letter to Froude that he, with Pre-Raphaelitism in general, had been part of the 'Reaction for Veracity in Art'. Then the Library Edition excludes this crucial passage from the original letter:

> *Rossetti*, who began the entire figure art movement, fell away from it involuntarily, unconsciously by his servitude to his own fancies. *Millais* with infinitely versatile capacity but essentially vulgar nature, only brought discredit on it by his carpenters shop etc, and then left the whole service for money — the Judas of his day. *Hunt* with

> far inferior intellect to Rossetti, and still more inferior art capacity to Millais, has been intensely, fiercely, patiently and in purity of life faithful to his conviction and his power . . .[15]

In 1882, a year before the lectures on 'Recent English Art', Ruskin's views had hardly changed, as may be seen from a letter to Cardinal Manning, which Cook and Wedderburn also decided not to print. Ruskin had seen the Cardinal's portrait by Watts at the Grosvenor Gallery:

> I have been at the Grosvenor and looked hard at the portrait, but it is one of my chief subjects of mental depression that all my friends are failing around me, as well as myself. My main battle in early life was for the school composed of Rossetti, Millais, Holman Hunt, and one or two minor men (of whom Brett has recently obtained some public attention) — while from Watts I expected the collateral development of a real historical school founded on Greek art. Rossetti is dead — Millais my worst enemy — Holman Hunt utterly gone to caricature of himself — Brett a mere colour photographer — and Watts is sick to death in striving for inconsistent ends with broken health and more feeling for art than genius . . .[16]

These opinions are so discordant with the lectures that Ruskin was about to give on the same artists that we ask whether the Oxford addresses were merely a matter of form. The answer is quite simple. Ruskin made contradictory comments about the artists of his time because he had no thorough knowledge of their work. He made a reappraisal of Holman Hunt just before going on his tour with Collingwood. Apart from their chance meeting in Venice in 1869, Ruskin had then hardly seen Hunt for twenty years. During this time the Pre-Raphaelite painter had been nurturing his grievances to the point at which they became mature and unchangeable characteristics of his mind. On the two occasions when Ruskin called at Draycott Lodge in the summer of 1882, both Hunt and his wife ('a little hard — considering herself & her husband as martyrs', says a letter to Joan) told him much about the probity of his art.[17] The Pre-Raphaelite's main complaint about the world concerned his religious position. He was the most avowedly Christian painter of the age. Yet (as he explained to Tyrwhitt, looking back over his career), 'I was 24 when I began, and — from my poverty — 26 when I finished "The Light of the World" and then in the whole 35 since I have never had an honour, and never a commission offered by the church . . .'[18] Ruskin made an effort to be sympathetic, and to Hunt it must now have seemed that he was about to receive a major public tribute. For Ruskin had lavishly praised the painting that was then on his easel, *The Triumph of the Innocents*, and on his re-election to the Slade chair told Hunt that he wished to speak especially of him in his opening lecture, for 'You have a strange and great part to take now in England — as the only representative she has of her old faith, so far as her works of hand can show it . . .'[19]

Fortunately, Hunt did not attend this lecture. If he had, he would have felt himself publicly insulted. Rising once more to speak in the lecture room of the University Museum, a place that many must have felt hallowed by his former utterances, Ruskin gravely referred to his predecessor, Richmond, and to Rossetti's death in the previous year. He then turned to Holman Hunt, but called him Rossetti's 'disciple'. Had he sought to do so, Ruskin could not have found a surer way of infuriating Hunt. For over the years Hunt had come to hate his former Pre-Raphaelite brother, and had insisted that the origin and leadership of the movement were his alone. Quite unconscious of his solecism (and furthermore his plain historical mistake), Ruskin passed to praise of *The Triumph of the Innocents*. But in fewer than five minutes the subject of Hunt's painting was suddenly dropped. Two artists were introduced of whom the audience had not previously heard. The first was Lilias Trotter, by this date not an artist but a committed evangelist. The second was Francesca Alexander, who scarcely counted as a representative of 'Recent English Art' since she was an American who lived in Italy and had never been to England. Ruskin then went on to describe the book illustrations of the German wood engraver Ludwig Richter. The lecture concluded with an account of two of Ruskin's assistants in Italy, Angelo Alessandri and Giacomo Boni, whom Ruskin compared to Michelangelo. Jowett then said a few words and, a contemporary account tells us, 'his graceful remarks were received with a storm of applause'.[20]

After this lecture Ruskin returned to Brantwood, where for nearly a month he entertained another artist of whom he was shortly to speak in Oxford. This was Kate Greenaway. Like Francesca Alexander, another middle-aged spinster, Kate was a comfort to both Ruskin and Joan in the years to come. This most successful of illustrators of children's books, small volumes peopled by little girls in Queen Anne costumes, long dresses, large bows, mob-caps and pretty frills, was herself the daughter of a popular artist who worked for such magazines as *Punch* and the *Illustrated London News*. Her childhood was spent in Hoxton. She was trained at local art schools and at South Kensington, where she was a fellow-pupil of two other women artists known to Ruskin, Lady Butler and the Helen Patterson who married William Allingham. Greenaway exhibited one or two watercolours at the Dudley Gallery but had no pretensions to fine art. She understood that illustration was her forte and would provide her livelihood. By the late 1870s she was celebrated for her book designs, Christmas cards and almanacs. Ruskin first noticed her work in 1879. For a year or two afterwards they exchanged greetings, by letter (or Christmas card), or through their mutual friend Stacy Marks. Kate was delighted, though not a little frightened, to have come to Ruskin's attention. For his part, Ruskin was pleased to hear from her that she was an admirer of *Fors Clavigera*. She was then in her mid-thirties.

She had praise from Ruskin, of a type with which we are familiar. Her Christmas card 'Luck go with you, pretty lass' was to him 'a greater thing than Raphael's St Cecilia'. He assigned her large spiritual tasks, to be completed in watercolour. Just as Holbein had left the world his *Dance of Death*, a 'bitter legacy to the Eternities,' so, Ruskin instructed Kate, 'Leave you yours — the Dance of Life'. While she could not believe in such comparisons the invitation to friendship was irresistible. Ruskin wrote: 'you are fast becoming — I believe you are already, except only Edward B. Jones — the helpfullest in showing me that there are yet living souls on earth who can see beauty and peace and goodwill among men — and rejoice in them'. When at length he met the small, dark Kate, Joan noticed Ruskin's 'rapturous delight' in her. Joan too liked Kate and thought her 'one of the sweetest, kindest and most gifted of women'.[21] She was accordingly invited to Brantwood and arrived there at Easter of 1883, in the midst of the best daffodil season for years. Joan accompanied her to Coniston and the necessary chaperonage was thereafter provided by Lily Kevill-Davis — Lily Armstrong, a friend since Ruskin had first met her. in 1864, when she was a twelve-year-old child at Winnington School. Lily's little daughter 'Scrappy' was a lucky girl on this holiday: she coloured the famous Miss Greenaway's designs. Kate, though often bemused by drawing exercises that Ruskin thrust upon her, enjoyed her stay. 'After breakfast', she told a friend, 'I am allowed (which is a great favour) to go into the study and see all sorts of beautiful things, with little talks and remarks by Mr Ruskin as he writes; then we go on drives, walks, or on the lake till tea-time. Then it is dinner-time; then he reads to us something nice, or talks in the most beautiful manner. Words can hardly say the sort of man he is — perfect — simply . . .'[22] Ruskin too was in good spirits. One day, Baxter ill, he dressed himself and practised a music-hall dance to celebrate the unusualness of his toilet. He scrambled up the Old Man with ease. He teased Kate 'quite awfully', and in the mornings he tinkered with his Oxford lectures.

Choosing his date, Ruskin returned to Oxford on his father's birthday, 10 May. There he remained until June while he gave six more lectures in the series 'Recent English Art'. Probably because he did not now live, as formerly, at the Crown and Thistle in Abingdon, Ruskin had some social life within the University. He saw more of young girls than of undergraduates. Angie Acland's autobiography tells the following story. At the Aclands' house in Broad Street, where there still hung the portrait Millais had painted of Ruskin at Glenfinlas, Ruskin met Julia Margaret Cameron and was shown her portfolio of portrait photographs of great Victorians. She probably hoped to add Ruskin's likeness to this collection. Angie recounts:

> During the time that Mr Ruskin was with us Mrs Cameron, a very well-known artistic portrait photographer of those days was also with us on a visit and the two had frequent skirmishes about photography. I was lying on my couch in the drawing room one day when Mrs Cameron insisted on showing Mr Ruskin some of the wonderful heads of well-known people which she had taken. He got more and more impatient until they came to one of Sir John Herschel in which his hair all stood up like a halo of fireworks. Mr Ruskin banged to the portfolio upon which Mrs Cameron thumped his poor frail back exclaiming 'John Ruskin you are not worthy of photographs!' They then left the room. Mrs Cameron wore a red bonnet with strings & when she got very excited she pushed it back & it hung down her back by the strings. Apparently they went out but arrived back to luncheon with bonnet on & peace signed.[23]

It is through the observant Angie (who as a child had held Rossetti's palette while he painted in the Union, had laid the final stone of the University Museum with a silver trowel, and had listened to Lewis Carroll's stories as they floated down the Isis from Godstow) that we often glimpse the eccentric side of nineteenth-century Oxford life. There Ruskin seems to fit, as it were, naturally; playing hide-and-seek in Christ Church cathedral, humming chords to himself as he stared at the ceiling in Taphouse's music shop, dancing a Highland reel, dining with Dodgson, instructing young ladies from Lady Margaret Hall how to carry coal scuttles, riding on the roof of his carriage, black gown fluttering in the wind. Oxford's wide tolerance of eccentricity was not stretched to its limits this Trinity term, but it is plain that Ruskin had to be allowed much oddness. 'A man of much sensibility, little sense', Jowett had once said of him. Perhaps, from Ruskin's point of view, Jowett was a more congenial Vice-Chancellor of the University than Liddell had been. At all events they were often together, and Ruskin dined in Balliol. It fell to Jowett to introduce the Slade Professor to official Oxford visitors; and apparently he developed an expertise in steering Ruskin away from 'dangerous' subjects. Ruskin was delightful: but eccentricity could all too suddenly become something else.

Ruskin was most at home in his drawing schools, among prints, specimens, daguerreotypes, casts and other materials. Students were few, but the official nature of their instruction gave Ruskin much trouble. William Blake Richmond had attempted to introduce a modern curriculum, but this had not been a success. Ruskin now inherited life-drawing classes instituted by Richmond. He did not approve of such tuition but did not close the classes down. Part of the problem was that they were taught by Alexander Macdonald. He was officially Ruskin's instrument in Oxford art education, and his salary came from Ruskin rather than from the University. But he could not maintain his family nor afford his large house, 84 Woodstock Road, without extra funds. Macdonald therefore took any pupils who came to him for instruction and did not necessarily teach them on Ruskinian principles. He also taught at the Oxford School of Art and had a part-time post at Radley College.

On his return to Oxford in 1883 Ruskin made an attempt to impose disciplined artistic study. He announced that 'Certificates of Merit' would be given to students who had regularly attended the schools and made progress. A few months later, we find in the *Pall Mall Gazette*, through E. T. Cook's conscientious monitoring of the lectures, that he had been obliged to announce a change of plan. 'This "modest ordinance" having had the effect of emptying the school of its former pupils, and not having tempted new scholars, is now to be withdrawn, and the young ladies of Oxford are once more to be admitted to "copy Turner in their own way".' Ruskin went on, as Cook reports, 'As for the undergraduates, it will make no difference, for I never succeeded in getting more than two or three of them into my school, even in its palmiest days.' The result was that students had no planned tuition and had more attention if they were attractive. 'There was *such* a pretty girlie in the schools for the first time this afternoon — I'm thinking it an awful shame to leave her after only a first lesson!'[24] And again, 'I shall have to turn out two or three old women, explaining to them that I do not anticipate further improvement. I've a lot of regulation to do at the schools — Macdonald lets anyone in — and lets them do what they like.' This 'regulation', however, was never attempted.[25]

In May of 1883 Ruskin completed his series of lectures on English art. He spoke of Watts, Leighton, Alma-Tadema, as well as of Kate Greenaway, Mrs Allingham and the *Punch* cartoonists Tenniel and Leech. In only one lecture does one feel the Ruskin of old, of the 'Myth Book'. It is that on Burne-Jones. Ruskin had made a studio visit to Burne-Jones, as he had to Hunt, at the time when he was planning his lectures. 'I want to come and see all the pictures you've got and to have a list of all you've done! The next lecture at Oxford is to be about you — and I want to reckon you up, and it's like counting clouds.' After this visit, however, we find a sad diary entry. 'At National Gallery and Ned's, but vexed with his new pale colours and linear design.'[26] Had he paid more real attention to Burne-Jones's art over the years Ruskin might have been less disappointed in what he now saw, and would have been better placed to write a lecture about his friend. He knew that he was not going to be able to do justice to 'Brother Ned' and wrote a note apologising in advance for the thinness of his material and promising that it was 'merely the sketched ground of what I hope at length to say in the future'.[27] On the other hand, Swinburne wrote to Burne-Jones to say

> I never did till now read anything in praise of your work that seemed to me really and perfectly apt and adequate. I do envy Ruskin the authority and the eloquence which give such weight and effect to his praise. It is just what I 'see in a glass darkly' that he brings out and lights up with the very best words possible; while we others (who cannot draw), like Shakespeare, have eyes for wonder but lack tongues to praise.[28]

A few months earlier, both Burne-Jones and William Morris had been honoured by Oxford. They had been elected honorary members of Exeter College, where forty years before they had first met and read *The Stones of Venice* together. If there was a single starting point of the later stages of Pre-Raphaelitism, then surely it was in this undergraduate comradeship. Ruskin did not quite grasp how the course of English art had brought his first two disciples to their present eminence. He quite liked Morris, appreciated his *Earthly Paradise* as a stimulus for Burne-Jones's designs, and was pleased that he had formed the Society for the Protection of Ancient Buildings. Ruskin loved Burne-Jones, yet had always suspected that Ned's art was not all that it should be. In 1883 this was especially so, for it appeared that Burne-Jones was close to being a modern aesthete. Ruskin's new notes to the second volume of *Modern Painters*, written in 1882–83, are full of hostile references to Aestheticism. He referred to the movement as making art into 'at once the corruption, and the jest, of the vulgar world'. The word 'jest' is used because Ruskin's knowledge of the new social tendency was derived from his reading of *Punch*, in whose cartoons of drawing rooms one discerns schematised paintings of a late Pre-Raphaelite sort. Their languid ladies are obviously drawn in mockery of Burne-Jones's paintings. Here was a difficulty for Ruskin. With Whistler in mind, one might easily describe Aestheticism as a modern Parisian fad, imported by an impudent American. With Burne-Jones in mind, one would have to consider whether Aestheticism was Pre-Raphaelitism in enervated collapse. Ruskin could not address himself to such questions. He wished, rather, to accommodate Burne-Jones into that period when the artist's friendship had been most valued. That had been around 1869, the time of the 'Myth Book'. There are many echoes of the mythological Ruskin in his Burne-Jones lecture, so numerous that they obscure the nominal subject. When reading of the command 'over the entire range both of Northern and Greek Mythology' and the 'tenderness at once, and largeness, of sympathy which have enabled him to harmonize these with the loveliest traditions of Christian legend' one feels that Ruskin is describing his own sensibility rather than that of his friend.[29]

So little is recorded of Ruskin's feelings about Morris, and even less of Morris's equivocal feelings about Ruskin, that it is good to record an occasion when the older man came to the assistance of the younger. In November of 1883 Ruskin was among the audience when Morris spoke on 'Art and Plutocracy' at University College. Several dignitaries made objections to Morris's political views. Then Ruskin spoke. The report in the *Pall Mall Gazette* states that

> Mr Ruskin, whose appearance was the signal for immense enthusiasm, speaking of the lecturer as 'the great conceiver and doer, the man at once a poet, an artist and a workman, and his old and dear friend' said that he agreed with him in 'imploring the young men who were being educated here to seek in true unity and love one for another the best direction for the great forces which, like an evil aurora, were lighting the world, and thus to bring about the peace which passeth all understanding'.[30]

These emollient but meaningless remarks had the desired effect, and the episode was closed, except that in one of his own lectures, delivered three days later, Ruskin returned to the subject, saying that the changes in Oxford 'which he so deeply deplored, and so grandly resented, in this once loveliest city, are due wholly to the deadly fact that her power is now dependent on the Plutocracy of Knowledge, instead of its Divinity . . .'[31] He meant that undergraduates should not study in the expectation of advancement in the material world once they had graduated. This had not been Morris's point. He and Ruskin were mostly allied in their dislike of new buildings in the city they remembered from days long past.

The *Pall Mall Gazette's* reporter at these Oxford lectures was Edward Tyas Cook, whose long career as both a journalist and a Ruskinian had much effect on Ruskin's reputation. Cook was born in 1857. While at Winchester in the 1870s he edited the *Wykehamist* and refused to play games in order to give more time to his study of Ruskin. He insisted, says a schoolfellow, 'on my reading *Fors Clavigera*, a pursuit which was thoroughly uncongenial to me'. Cook also began an index to help him in his reading of *Modern Painters*. So full and methodical was this work that its cards were still of use in the compilation of the great index of the Library Edition thirty years later.[32] Unlike Wedderburn or Collingwood, Cook had become a Ruskinian without the advantage of the personal friendship of the man whose work he studied. It is interesting that he found Ruskin at just the same time that he came to question the values of his school. In this he was not quite unique. Another schoolboy, just about Cook's contemporary, was Rudyard Kipling. In *Stalky & Co*, which is autobiographical — and also a more literary book than at first appears — one of Stalky's companions in the struggle against good manners, discipline and authority in the United Services College is 'Beetle', young Kipling himself; and peculiar to Beetle, part of his rebellion and part of his cleverness, something which accompanies forbidden drinking and smoking and yet is connected with his own literary ambitions, is his treasured collection of old numbers of *Fors Clavigera*. Here is what Stalky's other close comrade, 'M'Turk', in later life the soldier G. C. Beresford, had to recall of the matter:

> Various movements, crazes and fads winged their way at this time over the world and us . . . Gigger [this is the bespectacled schoolboy Kipling] flung Ruskin into it — the kind of thing he would do. Ruskin made a most horrid mess. The time spirit of the 'seventies or even 'eighties was just the medium in which Ruskin could do his damnedest. In suitable minds, he produced a disaffection for almost the whole fabric of life in the nineteenth century; for the material fabric especially. Ruskin's view of every kind of ethics and the spiritual fabric, widely seen, was rather mixed pickles.[33]

That is the old soldier speaking, but Beresford's opinions demand respect. He reminds us that Ruskin might have had much sway over 'suitable minds' if only such minds had studied his later writing. Kipling, who came from a Pre-Raphaelite family, had a good sense of Ruskin; but for the very many who knew only something of him he was a resounding puzzle. Those who could see him for what he was, the real and coherent Ruskin, were few. Of intellectuals, they were Froude, Collingwood, Wedderburn, perhaps Acland, perhaps Hilliard, Mallock and Cook. His circle was of course much wider. From the evidence of correspondence and Ruskin's diary we may reckon that it numbered about 100 people. A social selection from this number were at the 'drawing-room lecture' entitled 'Francesca's Book' that Ruskin gave in London in the summer of 1883, after the end of the Oxford Trinity term. This conflation of his recent lectures on Francesca Alexander and Kate Greenaway was held at Mrs Bishop's house in Prince of Wales Terrace. Admission was by invitation. The guest list was controlled by Joan Severn. Francesca Alexander, who no doubt was told of the occasion, could scarcely have hoped for a more distinguished audience. For apart from friends of Ruskin such as Lilias Trotter, the Bateman sisters, the Severns and the Richmonds, cards were sent to Tennyson, Leighton, Cardinal Manning, *et al.*: it was even thought that royalty might attend.

The most complete of the accounts of this occasion, unfortunately written some years later, is found in an obituary reminiscence of Mrs Bishop. Its author, who evidently recalled this as one of Ruskin's first appearances in public since his illness of 1881, felt that 'his coming into the world again was something in the nature of a resurrection. Such at least, it seemed to some; and there was about the whole man a spiritual presence belonging only to those who, in one way or the other, are dead to this world. During his illness he had grown his brown beard, and his thick brown hair was brushed close to his head, which is abnormally flat at the top; so that, at a little distance he looked like the picture of a Capuchin friar.' This correspondent recalled that among the audience were Lowell, Matthew Arnold, Burne-Jones, Jean Ingelow, Mary Gladstone, Hallam Tennyson ('a little bored by talk of "Francesca's book" and took notes of the blue tie of the lecturer') while 'Mr Hutton, of the *Spectator*, sat beside Mr Knowles of the *Nineteenth Century*, a contrast in editors'. Ruskin showed twenty pages of drawings by Francesca Alexander and praised them in the same terms he had used in Oxford. Of the rest of the lecture, we hear that he 'spoke of children's books — their needed grace, their imagination, their sweet mission in dealing with peace, dutifulness and innocence. Kate Greenaway, he said, he adored . . . it was only when Christianity was fully interpreted to the nations that the Woman and Child became the centre of all that was beautiful in Nature and Art . . .' Then Ruskin 'paid homage to Dickens' but 'no word had he for George Eliot, an author he scorned'. This miscellaneous talk 'was gaily interspersed with denunciations of railway bridges, steam printing-presses, mowing machines, and *The Times* newspaper. Mrs Bishop was a happy hostess that afternoon, or should have been; but when you congratulated her she only said "What a pity that Mr Browning could not come".'[34]

* * * *

A number of Ruskin's friendships were begun or maintained, or both, by correspondence. One thinks of John Brown of Edinburgh; of Patmore, Tyrwhitt, Faunthorpe and Horsfall; recently, of Susie Beever, Kate Greenaway and the Alexanders; and most of all one thinks of Rose La Touche. In such cases, when the correspondents rarely met, we feel that their letters are not merely the evidence of a friendship but actually the friendship itself. One of the longest sequences of letters in Ruskin's life was addressed to Charles Eliot Norton. As we know it today, this correspondence is incomplete. Norton burnt many letters. Sometimes he was embarrassed by Ruskin's confessions of his love for Rose. Letters also disappeared because Ruskin expressed views which Norton did not share, especially about the American civil war, liberalism, and mutual acquaintances in England. The first reason why Norton censored letters was to strengthen the impression of fellowship between Ruskin and himself, and in general he succeeded in this aim.

The profusion of Ruskin's letters conceals the fact that the two men scarcely knew each other. In thirty years they spent scarcely thirty days in each other's company. They had met in the mid-1850s, met again in Abbeville and Paris in 1868, were in Siena, Florence and Pisa together in 1870, both lived in London in the winter of 1872–73, and were now to meet once more. On 27 June 1883 Ruskin left Flora Shaw, who was a guest at Brantwood at the time, and drove round the lake to Coniston station to meet the American, lately arrived at Liverpool from the transatlantic steamer. Norton's introduction to his edition of the correspondence recalls finding Ruskin 'an old man, with look even older than his years, with bent form, with the beard of a patriarch, with habitual expression of weariness, with the general air and gait of old age'.[35] He exaggerated. Nearer the truth was the letter he wrote to his children the day after his arrival. As he looked at Ruskin he found

> his heart unchanged, his welcome as living as a welcome could be, and in an instant the ten years had gone . . . Ruskin has aged a good deal in these late years. He looks as old as he is, — sixty four. He stoops a good deal, but he seems physically well enough, and his mind is as active and perhaps as vigorous as ever. He has always been perverse and irrational, and does not grow less so, but his heart has all its own sweetness, and Miss Shaw and I differ from him and laugh at his extravagances of expression, and at his follies of sentiment, without ruffling the smoothness of his temper . . .[36]

In speaking of Ruskin's ageing, Norton did not mention that he would have found much more change in Joan Severn. When he last saw her in 1873 she was still a young wife, pregnant with Lily, her first child. She had now borne five children in ten years and had suffered one miscarriage. Her sprightliness had long since disappeared. For her, the path from girl to matron had been short indeed. She who had once loved dancing had now become settled, and wished to become more settled. She was the leader of the Severn family. Arthur made no decisions. Joan managed everything, for the good reason that the Severns depended on Ruskin. The money that Arthur earned as an artist never exceeded a couple of hundred pounds a year. But the Severns and their children wanted for nothing. They lived in effect as members of the professional upper middle classes. There were two dangers to the structure of the Severns' comfort. The first was that Ruskin might succeed in a purpose he had publicly announced: give away his fortune and die with nothing. Suppose he took it into his head to give all his treasures to the Guild and all his money to the poor? Joan was also fearful of Ruskin's periods of mental illness. Only then did he mention the unmentionable: that the Severns lived off him and controlled his life. While mad, he might turn against them and cast them off. This is why it was important to Joan that Ruskin should make a simple and complete will. She wanted the position of the Severns to be clear in case 'anything happened': that is, if Ruskin died, or was certified insane and had to be locked away in an asylum. While Norton was at Brantwood these matters were settled. Ruskin was not averse to making his will, and it is a straightforward document. His executors were to be William Mount-Temple, John Simon and Alexander Wedderburn. To the Severns, who already had the house at Herne Hill, he promised much more. They were willed his fortune,

Brantwood and all it contained, apart from certain books, minerals and pictures which were destined for the Bodleian Library. These arrangements reassured the Severns. There was, however, the question of Ruskin's literary remains. The executors of the will were not to be the literary executors, for now, at Brantwood, talking to Ruskin and Joan Severn, Norton asserted himself.

In making Norton a literary executor (or, which is more likely, in agreeing to Joan's suggestion that the American should act as such) Ruskin could hardly have thought of the implications. The other executors were to be Joan and Alexander Wedderburn. This was reasonable, since Joan was to be the beneficiary from Ruskin's copyrights and Wedderburn was both a lawyer and a Ruskinian. But Norton was not a Ruskinian, in the scholarly sense, and privately considered that much of Ruskin's writing had been a mere waste of its author's efforts. Ruskin gave Norton no introduction to the mass of literary material that was at Brantwood. He issued no instructions, laid down no guidelines, considered no principles. Surely Ruskin had no thought of the damage that would be caused. The man who had always stated that 'I never wrote a letter in my life that all the world is not free to read if they will' should have remembered a missive he had received from Norton some years before. Ironically, it is one of the few that survived when Norton destroyed his side of their correspondence.

35 Cleveland Square, W.
April 2nd 1873.

My dearest Ruskin,

I have to give you a disappointment, which makes me sorry, and to tell you a story of my doing to explain it. — it is an old custom of mine when a heap of letters has collected on my table, to look them over, and to burn two sorts among them, — one, the mere trivial notes; the other, those that are like intimate talks, when confidences are given to which no third party should be privy. I hold these last letters sacred, & often make a holocaust of what it pains me to sacrifice, and of what I would keep among my treasures if I could be sure that they would be buried with me. I have burned some of the sweetest love letters ever penned, because I would make sure that no eye but mine should ever see them. I have burned letters with the tears blinding me, — but I keep the memory of them safe in my heart. Some times I have burned letters from you, — those in which you told me of sorrowful experiences in love, for they were secrets between you & me. No man or woman shall have to reproach me with violating the trust they have given me.

> And, only yesterday afternoon, I read & re-read your letter about Connie, and questioned with myself, & wanted to keep it, and then thought, *no*, I alone can interpret it perfectly, it is a little *scène de la vie intime* for me, I shall not forget it, I will not leave it to chance, & to cold eyes, — and so I cut the first pages off to keep, & put the rest in the flames and it sparkled & shone for a moment — like a symbol of itself, — and then turned gray & fell to ashes, like a symbol of so much else. And now, this morning, you ask me for a copy of it, and I can only send Astolfo to look for it, with little chance of his ever finding it.
>
> So, hereafter, when you write me intimate letters, be sure you say, if you think you may like them again, — be sure you say upon them *Burn not* —Your letter went to immortality in good company. I never burn all in a heap. The mass of common trifles flames up together; but the letters I care for go to the fire, one by one, and I watch the sparks fly upwards to add to the brightness of the Ariadne's Crown that shines for me alone in the night . . .[37]

There is something unbalanced about Norton's confession, or rather boast. Ruskin must have noticed the curious attitudes in the letter, but made no response (or not in any surviving correspondence). His attitudes to Norton remain unexplained. There was no temperamental common ground between the open, generous Ruskin and the cautious and suspicious American. Perhaps the presumption of Norton's letter gives a clue to their relationship. Norton had such self-esteem that with all his acquaintances he habitually assumed the manner of the older and wiser man. He did so even with Carlyle. Norton's dealings with Victorian intellectuals were never, in any instance, of value to them. But he sailed home with a feeling of distinction, saying that he enjoyed their trust. This notion of trust he time and again invoked, not thinking that trust is given more than it is claimed. At Brantwood in 1883 he asked for a great deal, always in his new alliance with Joan. Ruskin's cousin attempted to make Ruskin surrender his diaries to Norton, for him to take back to America. This was not done, or the diaries might not be in existence today. Ruskin explained to Joan that he preferred to retain them because they might be of use in writing future books. His mood seems to have been unusually and puzzlingly quiescent. He said that he would like Norton to have the diaries in time. He also said to Joan, who told Norton, that he hoped that the American would write his life.

Ruskin gave little further thought to the disposal of his papers, or even their location, even when the question was raised in acute form by the writing of *Præterita*. E. T. Cook has a story which is now relevant. Telling Cook of his fear that he would not be able to write as much of his life as he wished, Ruskin replied to his future editor's question about the missing chapters of *Dilecta*, the autobiography's accompanying volume of documents, 'Any kind friend or editor can do them for me when I am dead. The material is all at Brantwood.'[38] So it was, at that time. But after Norton had burnt all the evidence that bore on the deepest experience of Ruskin's life, and the letters that were 'perhaps the most beautiful things he ever wrote', and Joan Severn and Sara Anderson had burnt yet more, there were still quantities of papers that were not made available after Ruskin's death to any biographer or editor: not even to Wedderburn, who was both Ruskin's literary executor and the executor of his will.

CHAPTER FORTY-THREE

1883–1884

In June of 1900 Norton, Joan Severn and Wedderburn walked into the Brantwood garden to burn the correspondence between Ruskin and Rose La Touche, together with such memorials as photographs, drawings and locks of the girl's hair. Wedderburn, running across the lawn to retrieve a letter that had fluttered from the bonfire that Norton was feeding, had sight of a sentence or two, Ruskin's hope that one day Rose would be able to visit Brantwood. She never did: but in 1883, after Norton's fateful visit, her father and mother came to Ruskin's home. It was late high summer, hay-time. Maria La Touche had been to Brantwood once before, very briefly, in 1881. This meeting and reconciliation had been arranged by Joan, who had always kept up some contact between the two families. The shock of Percy's abandonment, the dreadful alliance between Maria La Touche and Effie Millais, Rose's death, Ruskin's grief and madness: none of these things had prevented Joan (or not for any great length of time) from corresponding with her 'dear v.m.', 'dear vice-mother'. Joan had now all but forgotten the episode with Percy. Her friendship with Rose had been part of her youth, a girlhood that had now long disappeared. The letters she exchanged with Mrs La Touche chatted about the children and the Harristown garden. They never touched on the past. However, Ruskin's relations with his former opponent could never be so relaxed. He maintained and glorified the memory of Maria La Touche's daughter. He looked for Rose's spiritual influence. Each morning a precious missal, 'Rosie's book', gave him the texts with which he sought to give meaning to his work for the day. Rose's mother was also a part of Ruskin's cultural imagination, and had been so from the late 1860s. At that period she was associated with the lacertine imagery of *The Queen of the Air* and related works. More recently, Maria La Touche had been present in Ruskin's Venetian visions at Christmas of 1876 and had appeared in the delirium of his mental illness of 1881.

Thus, when Mrs La Touche had first come to Brantwood for a day in 1881, after Ruskin's illness, he had been able to interpret her real appearance in terms of his insane spiritual life. In his madness Ruskin believed that she had brought Rose to him, though in real life she had done quite the opposite. A few weeks after the end of the 1881 delirium Ruskin attempted to understand what had happened to his mind. 'The visionary part of it was *half* fulfilled — as soon as I was well enough to make it safe for me, by Lacerta's coming to see me', he wrote.[1] Now, in 1883, with his mental health in some sort of equilibrium, Ruskin could greet the La Touches simply as a person who had known them for many years. It seems, though, that there was much spiritual conversation and that the talk, through 'The Story of Ida', must have touched nearly on Rose. Maria La Touche recounts:

> We had a reception worthy of the Prodigal Son. The Professor was delightful, carried off the Master, & showed him enchanting things, all Francesca's wonderful drawings, & his garden & his wood & his drawing, building etc etc & Joan showed me all the children and the new rooms . . . Kate Greenaway is much loved at Brantwood but Francesca more. I quite believe in Francesca, she must be a wonder & a real love & the master is entirely fetched (after reading The Story of Ida), by seeing her drawings. I really do 20 times a day bless Mr Spurgeon (though of course I had far rather it had been the Archbishop of Canterbury or even Cardinal Manning), for rescuing the Master out of the blighting narrowness of Boeotianism, & enabling him to see the beauty of things he never gave a thought to when he was young . . .[2]

John La Touche, 'The Master', soon went back to Ireland to see to his harvest while his wife remained at Brantwood. Much time was spent quietly in botanising, the interest that Ruskin and Maria La Touche had in common. It will be recalled that *Proserpina*, Ruskin's study of flowers, had much of Rose in it, and that there were parts of the book that he had written to contain messages for her, 'bits that only she could understand'. Maria La Touche, too, may be found in the book's arcane references and symbolism. While she was at Brantwood Ruskin's interest in *Proserpina* revived, and he once more took up the chapter 'Monacha' that had been abandoned some years before.

* * * *

This was the period when Ruskin brought *Fors Clavigera* to a close and began to think of writing his autobiography as a separate book. In a chapter of *Proserpina*, 'Giulietta' (which is concerned with the plant known to us as milkwort), Ruskin had given a long description of early tours to the Alps with his parents. A footnote explained this diversion from the subject of wild flowers. 'I deliberately, not garrulously, allow more autobiography in *Proserpina* than is becoming, because I do not know how far I may be permitted to carry on that which was begun in *Fors*.'[3] This remark is explained by the circumstances in which it was written. 'Giulietta' belongs to April of 1882. Ruskin had just recovered from the illness in which he was attended by Sir William Gull and his Alpine reminiscences were written in anticipation of the continental tour that had been planned for his convalescence. The companionship of W. G. Collingwood on this expedition to France, Switzerland and Italy stirred further autobiographical impulses in Ruskin. It is possible that the subject of autobiography was discussed with Froude, who was a frequent visitor at Herne Hill after the illness of 1882. The historian appears in 'Giulietta', and in years to come he had a keen, occasionally proprietorial interest in *Præterita*. Ruskin's hankering in 1882 to write the story of his life is neither quoted nor indexed by Cook and Wedderburn in their account of the origins of *Præterita*. Cook wrote that *Præterita* was begun at the suggestion of Charles Eliot Norton. There is no independent evidence for this story, which one might expect to have heard from Norton himself. All in all, it is more likely that Ruskin began his autobiography for a number of reasons. He was fatigued. He feared another mental breakdown, perhaps a final one. He was by nature a confessional writer. Recently he had made his will. His reconciliation with the La Touches had brought him a spirit of forgiveness, and without such spirit *Præterita* could not have been imagined. Furthermore, Ruskin had the feeling for friendly explanation that comes to a number of writers in old age. He knew that his many younger friends understood little of, for instance, Turner as a man, or Oxford in the late 1830s, or of the pure skies and streams he had loved as a boy. Ruskin wished to please older friends, especially the women whom he had known since they were girls at Winnington; and surely he wanted to write about John James Ruskin, whom Joan Severn had never known, and to whom he knew he owed 'Brantwood, and all else'. The preface to *Præterita* is carefully dated 10 May, John James's birthday.

Among all these influences on the enterprise of *Præterita*, some no doubt more potent than others, we may even mention an expedition to Scotland in the autumn of 1883. Ruskin had never been a frequent visitor to Scotland, 'North Britain' (the envelopes of Ruskin's letters to Scotland are always addressed 'N.B.'), but the country was hallowed to him because it was his father's, and Walter Scott's, and Carlyle's. Ruskin associated Scotland with his childhood, and in September he went there to revive memories and to look once more at the landscape which (in his view) formed the character of his favourite novelist. An immediate result of this visit was the November issue of *Fors Clavigera*, 'Ashestiel', which is dated from Abbotsford and opens

> I can never hear the whispering and sighing of the Tweed among his pebbles, but it brings back to me the song of my nurse, as we used to cross by Coldstream Bridge, from the south, in our happy days.
>
> 'For Scotland, my darling, lies full in my view,
> With her barefooted lassies, and mountains so blue'.
>
> These two possessions, you perceive, my poor Euryclea felt to be the chief wealth of Scotland, and meant the epithet 'barefooted' to be one of praise.
>
> In the two days that have passed since I this time crossed the Border, I have seen but one barefooted lassie, and she not willingly so, — but many high-heeled ones: — who willingly, if they might, would have been heeled yet higher. And perhaps few, even of better minded Scots maidens, remember, with due admiration, that the greater part of Jeanie Deans' walk to London was done barefoot, the days of such pilgrimage being now, in the hope of Scotland, for ever past; and she, by help of the high chimneys built beside Holyrood and Melrose, will henceforward obtain the beatitude of Antichrist, — Blessed be ye Rich.[4]

The first paragraph of this *Fors* is in the manner of reminiscence typical of *Præterita*. Then the letter becomes combative in the old manner of Ruskin's addresses to workmen. His thoughts were prompted by annoyance with a number of people he had met at dinner in Scottish grand houses. To Mrs La Touche he wrote 'Your letter comes to cheer me among worse Philistines than yours. The beasts in Nineveh were nothing to the people here. I've had no recourse but doing accounts.'[5] Alone in his bedroom, Ruskin made a 'mudpie' of St George's income and expenditure while looking forward to the next day's drive through border country. Staying at Laidlawstiel with Lord Reay he was a little more content. 'This house is delightful', he told Joan, '— and so is Lord Reay — but not everybody else — and they *will* make me talk and I get nothing to eat and am always in fear and misery'.[6]

Another guest, a Mr Rutson, gives us this story:

> Mr Ruskin . . . came to Laidlawstiel . . . I was delighted with his courtesy and charming manner and his eloquence. We went to Ashestiel. You should have seen the reverent way in which he

> approached, with his hat off, an old man who had worked for Scott, and how expressed his sense of the honour of seeing a man who had known Scott, and how the sense of having known Scott must make the man himself very happy. All this, said in a low and rich tone of Ruskin's beautiful voice, while he stood slightly bowed, made a memorable little picture, the man standing in his doorway, with Ruskin just outside the cottage . . . In the afternoon we partly drove and partly walked to Traqhuair, getting our first view of it from outside the great gates, looking down the avenue guarded by the stone bears. From nearer at hand, Ruskin made a sketch of the house, which he declares (we not dissenting) to be a true work of art, faithful to the genius of the place, towers, height and pitch of roof, size and mutual relation of windows, and strength of material — all harmonising with each other and suited to the needs of its inhabitants and to its situation among Scottish hills . . .[7]

After ten days north of the border Ruskin returned to Brantwood on 4 October. Two days later he welcomed Wedderburn and the sisters Alice and Maud Bateman as house guests. Maud Bateman, who had become a Companion of the Guild, was occupied with an important task. With Grace Allen, George Allen's daughter, and probably with Wedderburn's advice, she was compiling *The Ruskin Birthday Book: a Selection of Thoughts, Mottoes and Aphorisms, for Every Day of the Year, from the Works of John Ruskin, LL.D.*, which would be published in time for Christmas. Without a doubt, this gift book was the product of George Allen's commercial intuition. Unlike *Frondes Agrestes* (and the only other previous book of selections, published by Smith, Elder at John James Ruskin's urging in 1861, and in copyright until 1907), Maud and Alice's anthology did not serve as an introduction to a more substantial body of writing. It was unashamedly a collection of jewels. Thus the book reinforced the public impression that Ruskin was a writer of detached sentiments rather than of sustained and logical argument. This was often remarked of his conversation, especially by people who met him for the first time. As Mr Rutson remarked, his kindly manner and attentiveness immediately won him friends. When Ruskin spoke, he used long, fully formed sentences which conveyed unusual and often challenging thoughts on a variety of topics. Despite the annoyances of his Scottish expedition, Ruskin now began another round of visits to houses where he would be expected to talk for his supper. At High Elms, Hayes, Kent, the home of the natural scientist and Liberal politician Sir John Lubbock, he 'had lovely times with Sir James Paget — and have said explosive things at every meal, to the consternation and edification of society'.[8] While in Kent Ruskin also visited the Allen family, then travelled to London to stay at the British Hotel in Cockspur Street. This was his base for a week or two while he visited Oxford, went to the theatre, dined with Stacy Marks, called on Marcus Huish and then set off for Claremont, near Esher, which was a royal residence, the home of Prince Leopold and his wife, the Duke and Duchess of Albany.

Ruskin had now known Queen Victoria's gentle son for the best part of a decade and they had a number of mutual acquaintances, in Oxford and beyond. One of these acquaintances now reminded Ruskin of a part of his life that he would have preferred to forget. Francis Hawkesworth Fawkes of Farnley Hall in Yorkshire, a friend of Turner's and the dedicatee of Ruskin's 1851 pamphlet *Pre-Raphaelitism*, had sided with Effie Ruskin at the time of her divorce. He had then refused even to acknowledge Ruskin's letter giving his side of the case. The two men had been estranged ever since. Just before Ruskin's visit to Claremont Prince Leopold had been staying at Farnley. He wrote to Ruskin from this well-remembered house to say how much he had appreciated the Slade Professor's help in his growing knowledge of Turner's art.

Both Ruskin and Leopold looked forward to future aesthetic discussions. On arrival at Claremont, Ruskin found the royal etiquette rather inhibiting. However, courtly manners must soon have been abandoned, as we gather from a letter to Maria La Touche:

> I was at Claremont for a couple of days, where the baby, to see whom I was chiefly invited, is really a pleasant sight, made up of round lines and surfaces. They've got a lovely grinding piano organ in the hall, and the first afternoon after tea, the Duchess sate on the lowest step of the hall stairs with the baby, her husband ground the organ, and *I* danced extempore dances of a fantastic character . . .[9]

Alas, these dances, or some other exertion, brought on a rupture. Ruskin left Claremont in extreme discomfort. He was intermittently visited by pain and inconvenience from this 'groin strain', as he called it, until the end of his active life. The rupture was bravely suffered, as we gather from Ruskin's diary, but none the less had its effect on his habits and temperament. His walks were shorter and less vigorous. He was no longer able to enjoy clambering over the rocks of his Lakeland mountains. Ruskin now realised that he had entered physical old age. He had often pretended to be older than his years, at least since Winnington days, when he had so often danced with the girls and called himself 'Old Lecturer (of incalculable age)'; but he had always been proud that on walks, his principal physical activity, he could lead much younger men over moors and upland trails. This aspect of his life was now in the past, and we surmise that a new frailty of body contributed to the decision to end *Fors Clavigera* and begin his autobiography.

Sometimes Ruskin found pages of manuscript on his desk that seemed to belong to *Fors*, and yet he could not recall whether they had been set in type or published. Young Grace Allen (she and Ruskin called each other 'Valentine') received letters from Brantwood that asked, for instance, 'My dear, useful, venerable Valentine — *can* you tell me if this stuff has been used in Fors — if it has, please send to Jowett to break up — if it hasn't — keep it, and I'll get some more bits together to patch with it. Ever your loving V.'[10] At his Aylesbury works, the craftsmanlike Henry Jowett printed whatever he was sent, to his usual high and expensive standards. With George Allen and his family, he gave Ruskin high standards of publication. Inevitably, though, confusions arose as copy and proofs went from Brantwood or Oxford or Herne Hill to Orpington or Aylesbury and then back again. Ruskin could lose his temper with Allen; but when he was irascible about publishing matters it was always a sign that his spirits in general were over-excited, and perhaps that another spell of mania was to be feared.

George Allen and Joan Severn therefore became closer because of their mutual worries and interests. They both wanted a sane and contented Ruskin. They also wanted him to write intelligible, popular books with a wide appeal. The audience of *Fors Clavigera* was so small that the sale of the monthly letters could not hope to recover the cost of their printing and publication. Allen was eager to issue new editions of Ruskin's books that now, in 1883, were regarded as classics and would surely sell to a new generation. Such plans were welcome to Joan. Ruskin himself, however, was still the master of his own publishing programme and was still inclined to make books from whatever he liked, and to send his writing to George Allen from wherever he might happen to be, without consultation with Joan or anyone else.

Fors Clavigera, Ruskin's most personal and wilful publication, gave him difficulties which he could scarcely discuss with any other party. For this reason we do not find remarks about his public letters within his private letters. It is not clear why Ruskin decided to bring *Fors* to an end. Some clues may be found if we return to the time of 'Giulietta'. This was the period of retrospection between his 1882 illness and the continental tour with Collingwood. Just as Ruskin then looked back within his diaries for warning signs of mental affliction he also looked into *Fors*, and perhaps with the same motive. What he saw there was both familiar and remote: writing that belonged to a time of strength. Ruskin then set himself to give titles to the ninety numbers of his letter so far issued. Perhaps it is surprising that this had never been done at the time of their composition. Ruskin had always had a relish for titles and devised ways to make them gnomic and redolent. The new names for *Fors* letters were not of quite the same sort as his book titles. Those had aimed to give the essence of his treatises. The *Fors* titles are allusive or coincidental. The sound of them, so much less familiar than the book titles, seems to echo that strangeness in *Fors*, its remoteness, which is often at odds with the urgency of its declarations. Here are some, at random. 'The Snow-Manger', 'The Great Picnic', 'The Baron's Gate', 'Dogs of the Lord', 'Property to whom Proper', 'The Message of Jael-Atropos', 'Looking Down from Ingleborough', 'Lost Jewels', 'Companionship', 'The Cart goes better, so', 'Minos Retained: the British Judge', 'Father-law', 'Star-law', 'The Squirrel Cage: English Servitude', 'Bernard the Happy', 'Children, have ye here any Meat?', 'The Four Funerals', 'Gold Growing', 'Rain on the Rock', 'Aunt Jessie'. Perhaps in this naming (and Ruskin must have composed his abstracts of the letters at the same time) there was a sense of recapitulation, a feeling that the time had come for *Fors* to be terminated. Certainly the short discussion with Faunthorpe about indexing the work had raised the question of its end. For it is obvious that such a labour as *Fors Clavigera* would conclude with an index rather than a peroration. Faunthorpe's index to *Fors* was eventually published in 1887. Privately, Ruskin had been working on his own indices since 1873. Much of this work remained in manuscript. It was not seen in print until incorporated by Cook and Wedderburn in Volume XXXIX of the Library Edition, published in 1907. There we may read of, for instance, 'Bright, Mr John, his speech on the adulteration of food, as illustrating blockheadism', 'Whistler, Mr, impudence of', 'Impudence, taught in England as the chief duty of man' and 'Dying, as poor as possible, one of the objects proposed to be skilfully attained by the course of the author's life'.[11]

This last entry reminds us of Joan Severn and her financial anxieties. To this subject we must often return. Meanwhile, it is worth noting the publishing history of the last numbers of *Fors*. After 'Ashestiel' came 'Invocation', a letter for Christmas of 1883. Then Ruskin published 'Retrospect' in March of 1884, 'Fors Infantiae' in October and finally 'Letter 96 (Terminal): Rosy Vale' for Christmas of 1884. The publication of *Præterita* was begun in July 1885. Its first issues reprinted parts of *Fors* that had been written many years before. The autobiography's opening words, 'I am, and my father was before me, a violent Tory of the old school', belong to the tenth letter of *Fors*, that of October 1871. These dates indicate that *Fors Clavigera* was not abruptly ended, nor *Præterita* suddenly begun. During this period Ruskin began different working habits. For instance, he was often spurred to composition by looking at his old diaries and letters. He began to send his writing to Maria La Touche before publication, and it is certain that *Præterita*, if it had been fully written, would have attempted an account of Rose to please or console her mother. In short, Ruskin's attitude to his own writing became less imperious in the months between the late autumn of 1883 and the spring of 1885. By the latter date, Ruskin's composition had become domestic. When he began to write original material for *Præterita* he would read his day's work to Joan and Arthur after dinner, and they would say how much they liked the reminiscences of his early life. In such ways we may trace a slackening of Ruskin's writing and a change of its mood. In the autumn, winter and spring of 1883–84, however, few of his friends noticed a diminution of his activities, and some of them thought that his criticism of modern life had reached a climax. For in these months Ruskin gave more lectures in Oxford, was variously busy at Brantwood and Herne Hill and then delivered his famous address 'The Storm-Cloud of the Nineteenth Century'.

Ruskin's two lectures in Oxford concluded the series announced as 'Recent English Art'. They were 'The Fireside', on John Leech and John Tenniel, and 'The Hillside', on George Robson and Copley Fielding. Mostly genial comments on recent popular art are interspersed with passages that feel like an adieu to the University. It would have been well if Ruskin had left Oxford at this time, but still he felt that he had work to do in his *alma mater*. Furthermore, he seemed to be no less popular. Each of his addresses had to be repeated, since the lecture room in the University Museum held only 500 people. For a fortnight in November, traditionally a hospitable season in Oxford, he went out to dinners. One was in Christ Church hall, where he dined for the 'first time this thirty years!'[12] Brief visits from Oxford to Herne Hill allowed Ruskin to see Kate Greenaway, Stacy Marks and Lilias Trotter. Then he travelled via Sheffield to Coniston to join Susie Beever for her birthday on 27 November.

Now began a quite individual period of Lakeland life, the more companionable yet also introspective because the Severns remained at Herne Hill. Susie's home, 'The Thwaite', in whose sitting room and garden Ruskin spent many hours of his late life, was in a village that had almost become a small town. In Coniston there was a tourist industry, served mainly by the Waterhead Hotel and also by other hostelries. Local people now worked not only in agriculture but in domestic service given to the retired middle classes; and others were employed in boatbuilding, quarrying, or the copper works. In the neighbourhood were a significant number of residents, including young Collingwood, old Major Benson Harrison, his mother Dorothy Harrison, née Wordsworth, Laurence Hilliard, Augusta Wakefield and Albert Fleming, who all had some relationship with culture. Maria La Touche, who visited Brantwood from an intellectual desert, County Kildare, thought that the district around Coniston was filled with people devoted to art and poetry. She might also have noted its inter-demoninational character. The mixed community supported an Anglican church, a Roman Catholic church and a Baptist chapel. Coniston had a railway station and a Mechanics Institute, where on 22 December Ruskin talked on 'The Battle of Kinyree'.

This was a tribute to the Ruskin family friend Sir Herbert Edwardes.[13] In 1885 the lecture became part of *A Knight's Faith*, a book which belongs to *Bibliotheca Pastorum*. Though he need not have been, Ruskin was nervous before talking about a man who had known Denmark Hill in the old days. The evening was a success. Ruskin's more definite problem this Christmastide was his groin strain. One reason why he was at Brantwood was to see how far he could walk. In a month of generally stormy weather he managed some expeditions, but he was in pain. At the end of December his rupture was treated by mechanical means. On 19 December we read in the diary: 'Yesterday much put out with steel and leather, learning what penance means; no doubt sent because I wanted that knowledge. D.G! Beginning of a new phase of decline of life, for me.'[14] Saddened by this decline, and facing a lonely Christmas, Ruskin wrote on Christmas Eve to his friend Collingwood, who had been married for just six weeks:

> Of course I needn't wish you a *happy* Christmas. I'll wish you — what it seems to me most of us more need, and particularly my poor self — a *wise* one! When are you coming — in search of wisdom of course — to see *me*? I ought to call first, oughtn't I? but I don't feel able for long days out just now. Could you lock up house for a couple of days over there, and come and stay with me over here? It seems to me as if it would be rather nice. The house is — as quiet as you please. I'd lock you both out of my study, and you might really play hide-and-seek in the passages about the nursery all day long. Will you come?[15]

Collingwood knew that this was a summons from an unhappy man. He and his bride Dorrie (née Edith Mary Isaac) went to Brantwood for the New Year. Dorrie, who was a musician, accompanied singing as they saw in the young 1884. The next day the party was joined by Laurence, Ethel and Frederick Hilliard. Ruskin missed the Severns and their children, but he appreciated this household of clever and individual disciples. They were merry too, for Ruskin produced fine old bottles from his father's cellar. After the Professor's bedtime Collingwood and Hilliard were able to smoke. 'Laurie' would treat the company to his renowned impressions of Ruskin's voice, mimicking the explanations of some piece of mineralogy. Upstairs, Ruskin slept badly. He was troubled by toothache, the pain in his groin and many private thoughts. He woke before dawn on the morning of 3 January, Rose La Touche's birthday. The diary reads: 'Rosie sent me good peace and active thought, from ½ past 4, when I woke, and I hope to get out to-day with Santa Zita. Pouring rain — not a ray of sunshine these ten days!'[16] Santa Zita appears in *Roadside Songs of Tuscany*, which began publication in April of 1884. We do not hear elsewhere of Rose's message. In general, the diary appears obsessed with dark and violent winter weather. Day after day, Ruskin writes that he had been tormented by the black heavens. On 4 January, 'fog and rain, with no break, no beauty, no anything to see — dead nothings — for weeks together . . .' On 5 January, 'Rain all day yesterday. Now breaking up of plague-cloud, wholly dismal . . .' On the 6th, 'The plague wind an hour ago simply a London fog gone crazy: frantic yellow desolation flying from the South . . .' On 7 January, 'Such wrathful, sulphurous, black smoke cloud as the plague wind, wild and strong from S. W., drove on Helvellyn, I've scarcely yet seen . . .' On the next day, 'Pouring rain with total fog — as this month past . . .' On the 9th, 'To-day, plague wind from south.' On 10 January, 'Plague wind, but with less rain. Sky grey all over, wind rough from south.' On the 11th, 'Plague wind and rain all day yesterday. To-day wilder, but giving gleams of clearing.'[17]

During the weeks of such diary entries Ruskin was composing a public statement about the weather. On 4 and 11 February of 1884 he gave two lectures at the London Institution, the second repeating and adding notes to the first. This material was published in May as *The Storm-Cloud of the Nineteenth Century*.[18] The lectures themselves caused much comment, not all of it respectful. Ruskin's audience felt that they had been at a special occasion, but few of them could concur with his analysis of modern storms and their cause. The drama of

Ruskin's delivery was heightened, and to some made risible, by his visual aids. Collingwood and Arthur Severn had been set to make coloured enlargements of Ruskin's drawings and watercolours of skies. In the darkened lecture hall these were thrown on to a screen by limelight. The illustrations were to some extent autobiographical. The first of them dated from 'an autumn twilight of 1845 — sketched while I was changing horses between Verona and Brescia'.[19] Another was of a July thunder cloud, sketched in the Val d'Aosta in 1858. Consciously or not, Ruskin had chosen drawings made on two of his most significant, and solitary, early foreign tours. The impression given by the lecture is of an utterly lonely man who had seen things that nobody else had seen, and whose thoughts had never been expressed by any other person. It is not surprising that 'The Storm-Cloud' is often interpreted as Ruskin's most 'prophetic' utterance, especially as it attributes recent weather to the devil and ends with warnings to the nation. Other views of the lecture stress its mythological aspects and connect it with Ruskin's religious and cultural theories since at least the time of the fifth volume of *Modern Painters*. E. T. Cook was always at pains to insist that the prophetic nature of Ruskin's thought was balanced by his sober and accurate observations. The weather was indeed more malign, Cook argued, because of smoke. This was just. There is no need today to describe the pollution of the air in London and provincial manufacturing cities. The presence of industrial smoke in the Lake District is less well known. But Brantwood was, as one neighbour put it, 'ringed' by mineral works and blast furnaces, at Harrington and Cleator and nearby at Barrow and Millom. Soot from these furnaces could dim the sun and alter the colour of the hills around Coniston Water. Reference to his diaries shows that Ruskin had noted such phenomena since at least 1879.

The 'Storm-Cloud' lecture may have been the first occasion when E. T. Cook met Collingwood and also his future co-editor of the Library Edition of Ruskin's works, Alexander Wedderburn. Cook was present as a reporter for the *Pall Mall Gazette*. Wedderburn too was preparing a report, to be completed at a slower pace, for the *Art Journal*'s April issue. Other notices of the lecture were numerous, perhaps because of an approach to newspapers from the London Institution. Some papers ridiculed Ruskin's views. He replied to comment in the *Daily News* during the second of his lectures but otherwise was not troubled to continue the controversy he had begun. As Collingwood noted, 'his prophetic function was not all sackcloth and ashes'. In London this early spring of 1884 Ruskin wished to be entertained and wrote 'What *is* the world coming to? *I wish I could stay to see*!'[20]

His intellectual work was mainly with Lazarus Fletcher and the minerals at the British Museum, which were Fletcher's curatorial responsibility, but Ruskin often drove from Herne Hill to pantomimes and the theatre. Sometimes he was at Kate Greenaway's house in Holloway. Ruskin had made friends with one of her child models, a cabman's daughter, and was happy in buying toys for her: a kaleidoscope, a magnetic fish and a skipping rope. They played with them together while Greenaway vainly attempted to sketch the prophet's portrait. Ruskin dined with the Burne-Joneses, Stacy Marks, Sir William Gull and the Gale family. He was at Frederick Gale's lecture, so unlike his own comments on the modern plague-wind, which in 1885 was preserved as *Modern English Sports: Their Use and Abuse. Dedicated by Special Permission to Professor Ruskin.* By Frederick Gale (The Old Duffer). The dedicatee of this pleasant pamphlet wrote in thanks to Gale that 'You always do me good, whether in talking or writing, by showing me the brightest side of what I may have seen mostly on the opposite one, by your memorials of the frank hearts and cheerful ways of the country people of half a century since . . .'[21]

Mindful of his own 'country people', Ruskin had also been buying equipment for the school in Coniston. His gifts included bells, which could be rung in consort with his musical theories, mariners' compasses and maps of the world. Ruskin was missing his Brantwood study but also wanted to stay at Herne Hill to be near to Joan. His cousin liked the way that he relied on her, and with Ruskin close at hand it was easier to take note of his moods, which were uneven and generally worrying.

All through the earlier part of 1884 he alternated between irritability, over-excitement and depression. Inevitably this had an effect on others. His fondness for, as he called it, 'teasing' women and girls often annoyed and indeed distressed them. Joan sometimes had to comfort people like the attractive 'Clennie', Miss McClelland, who had come from the Isle of Skye to be the Severn children's governess. From about this time quarrels were not infrequent in the extended Ruskin–Severn family. For evidence of disputes, we have letters between Ruskin and Joan, and between Joan and other friends of the household. Arthur Severn's fragmentary memoir reveals that he had no particular liking for Ruskin, little sympathy with his benefactor's aims in life, no knowledge of his writing and no feeling for his sufferings. The memoir was begun, probably, in the 1890s and was eventually published as *The Professor* in 1967. The book is a series of anecdotes, written not to celebrate but to mock the man to whom Severn owed all his comforts. From the general tone of Severn's stories one may gather how much Ruskin must have been tried by his idle and foolish dependant; and certain passages indicate that there were hostilities between the two men. Severn was twenty-three years Ruskin's junior, so a generation separated them. But Ruskin had many friends who were young men and with whom he was never in dispute. Severn explains matters as follows:

> Ruskin had many curious characteristics, and it was by no means a bed of roses, living with him. Although extremely kind and generous to a fault in some ways, he could be just the opposite. No one dared contradict him on any subject without his flying into a passion. What he liked was absolute obedience and in return he would pet and flatter. His ideal was a 'kind feudal system', everyone round him willing to help, to obey and to love him. To all such he would be kind and helpful, but woe betide the man or woman who ventured to differ or put him right. Of course a pretty girl could do it a little and it amused him, but hardly any other kind of human being. I did more than any other man in sticking well up to him now and then, but it required courage, and I think he took it from me better than he would from other people. Of course I was very careful to be on the right side and this is not very difficult when dealing with an over-wrought and excited brain, as his often was.[22]

Ruskin returned to Brantwood at the end of March. Soon after arriving at his home he was hurt to hear of the death of Prince Leopold. During a short visit to London in April he travelled to Claremont to give his condolences to the Prince's young widow. Otherwise he was at Brantwood until October. Ruskin was now sixty-five, and in a delightful spring and a warm summer we observe the last comparatively untroubled seasons of his active life. There were the usual Brantwood pursuits and many welcome guests. Ruskin's work was not onerous, nor likely to inflame his marvellous, fragile mind. He was preparing *Roadside Songs of Tuscany* and the *Catalogue of a Series of Specimens in the British Museum (Natural History), Illustrative of the more common Forms of Native Silica*, which was published in September.[23] This catalogue was the result both of long years of geological study and recent conversations with Lazarus Fletcher. A paper entitled 'Of the Distinctions of Form in Silica' was read to a meeting of the Mineralogical Society in July,[24] but not by its author, for Ruskin remained at Brantwood. Characteristically, he complained in this lecture that his geological observations were as completely ignored by learned societies, 'as my remarks on political economy by the Directors of the

Bank of England'. This was a rueful joke at his own expense. Always happy with minerals, Ruskin was also generally content when exchanging views with mineralogists. His British Museum catalogue should be regarded as a collaboration with Lazarus Fletcher, who modestly declined to take credit for the work. Ruskin's friendship with Fletcher would result (in 1887) in gifts to the British Museum. They were not his first donations. In 1850 he had presented some rare pink fluor crystals. With old age, Ruskin wished to commemorate people who had influenced his early life. Therefore he proposed more gifts, but with the condition that inscriptions should be attached. The first is

The Couttet Rose-Fluors
Presented in 1850 by John Ruskin
'In Honour of his Friend, Joseph Couttet,
The last Captain of Mont Blanc,
By whom they were found'.[25]

The second was:

The Edwardes Ruby
Presented in 1887 by John Ruskin
'In Honour of the
Invincible Soldiership
And loving Equity
Of Sir Herbert Edwardes' Rule
By the Shores of Indus'.[26]

Perhaps the most valuable of these stones is

The Colenso Diamond,
Presented in 1887 by John Ruskin
'In honour of his Friend, the loyal
And patiently adamantine
First Bishop of Natal'.[27]

In 1884, to which date we now return, this diamond was already loaned to the British Museum. Joan Severn correctly suspected that the loan would become a gift. She also knew that Ruskin had paid a dealer £1,000 for the diamond. This was money that could have been well used in, for instance, extensions to the Herne Hill house, so obviously too small for the Severns, Clennie and numerous other servants. Ruskin's old nursery at Herne Hill was still kept as his alone. But energetic professors cannot always live in their nurseries. Increasingly cramped conditions at Herne Hill certainly caused family quarrels. Ruskin felt less free to use his family house. When in London, he often dined at the homes of friends. It is possible that Joan and Arthur Severn now thought of selling up in Herne Hill and moving to Brantwood: but this could not easily be done while Ruskin lived.

At Brantwood in the early summer of 1884 the lonely Ruskin often thought of books that would be collaborations with other people. His work on silica had been shared with Lazarus Fletcher. His neighbour W. G. Collingwood was a natural partner for many enterprises, and they had planned a *Grammar of Crystallography* together. Ruskin wished to give some of the writing of *Proserpina* to his fellow botanist Maria La Touche. Nothing came of this scheme. Ruskin's work as an editor was more productive, for the simple reason that he could send any material that interested him to Henry Jowett and George Allen and have it published, if not distributed, within about a fortnight. His main editorial work was now with material provided by Francesca Alexander, pretty verses and tales that she had culled from the Italian peasantry. It is convenient to notice Alexander's books here and furthermore appropriate, since Ruskin's beautiful thoughts about Santa Zita, which are at the heart of *Roadside Songs of Tuscany*, were written at Brantwood in May, by which time the storm-cloud and plague-wind had largely disappeared from his diary. Ruskin's editorial programme, inevitably a little erratic, was eventually given shape by E. T. Cook, who devised a volume of the Library Edition under the title 'Studies of Peasant Life'. It comprises Alexander's *The Story of Ida* (1883), her *Roadside Songs of Tuscany*, with preface, notes and essays by Ruskin (1885) and her *Christ's Folk in the Apennine* (1887), which has a preface by Ruskin. To these publications Cook added Ruskin's 1883 lecture 'Francesca's Book'. As we have seen, this was an expansion of an Oxford lecture, given in a private home but reliably reported in the *Spectator*. Then Cook added Julia Firth's translation of Jeremias Gotthelf's *Ulric the Farm Servant*. Ruskin's interest in this book was described above. Firth's translation, again with a preface and notes by Ruskin, was first published in 1886–68. In this way Ruskin's edition of Gotthelf celebrated the author whose curious, pastoral work he had known since the 1850s, when John James Ruskin read the Ulric stories to his wife and son in their favourite Fribourg inn. Once more, we find an inspiration of *Præterita*.

CHAPTER FORTY-FOUR

1884

On 7 May 1884 Ruskin's diary notes, 'loveliest day I've ever seen Lancaster Bay in — all clear and golden! And I today with cold virtually gone and wonderfully cheerful in beginning summer's work. D. G.'[1] In fact Ruskin did not work hard this summer, at least not by his standards. Instead he was constantly occupied by friends, visitors and the Severns. The diary notes many of these visitors, not all of whom can now be identified. Brantwood was not quite a place of pilgrimage, since it was a private home; but the house was also rather like a private museum, and museums attract a miscellany of guests. Ruskin's friends often brought their own friends or relatives. So Ada Dundas arrived with her sister and mother. Ruskin welcomed a number of connections of the Hilliard family. Alexander Wedderburn came with a friend known only as Dave. Mrs Sly of the Waterhead Hotel was accompanied by her sisters. A child who was often in the house, and was set little tasks, was Jane Anne Wilkinson, whose family had recently moved into Lawson Park, formerly the home of the Stalkers. Jane Anne was sometimes in the company of children from the local school, who preferred Ruskin's high teas to his lessons. Also at Brantwood this summer were artists who worked for Ruskin, such as T. M. Rooke and the sculptor Conrad Dressler, who was preparing a bust of the Professor, and members of the Guild of St George such as Julia Firth and Grace Allen. Grace was on her way to see George Baker of Birmingham, probably on Guild business connected with the proposed museum at Bewdley. E. R. Robson, the designer of this museum, was a Brantwood guest. As usual, we find Collingwood at Ruskin's home, now with his wife Dorrie. Ruth Mercier, who had nursed Ruskin in his 1881 illness, came not as a nurse but as a friend. Ruskin was visited by thoughtful Northern men of business, such as George Melly of Liverpool, and also by Charles Eliot Norton and Lazarus Fletcher.

By Brantwood tradition, all such visitors to the lakeside house were entertained with conversation, the display and discussion of the house's treasures, walking, boating, music and readings from Scott, Maria Edgeworth and other authors of an antique nature. Reading was perhaps somewhat imposed on house parties, and writers chosen with decision. As Ruskin wrote to his girl friend Lizzie Watson, later Mrs L. Allen Harker, '[I] don't read any more George Eliot or Thackeray —

but Scott *continually*, and more old-fashioned poetry — George Herbert's "Church Porch" to begin with, and Spenser's minor poems . . .'[2] To Margaret Ferrier Young, who had been a governess to Rose Ward, Emily La Touche's daughter, Ruskin declared: 'I should like all girls whatever to bathe in Scott daily, as a sort of ever-rolling, ever-freshening sea; and indeed I would let Jane Anne read anything (except George Eliot), but for girls in general I should say very broadly anything they like — written before 1800.'[3]

When Ruskin was fatigued, Baxter sometimes read to him; and tiredness was now the old writer's constant companion. In this summer of 1884 he might have been healthier if he had written more and entertained less often. In the long months of hot weather there were no dramas in Ruskin's life, and on the whole he was content with his rural and domestic routines. However, three more Brantwood guests troubled his mind, and Ruskin's thoughts about them contributed to the further deterioration of his mental health. They were Ernest Chesneau, Maria La Touche and Benjamin Jowett. Each of them came to Coniston or Brantwood for a few days, and Ruskin was gladdened or excited by their company. Chesneau was a French writer on English art who had been in correspondence with Ruskin since 1867. His *La Peinture Anglaise*, issued in London (by Cassell) as *The English School of Painting* (1885) has a friendly preface by Ruskin written in December of 1884. In this year Chesneau hoped to write a life of Turner, and he had travelled to Brantwood to secure Ruskin's encouragement of this ambition. Perhaps surprisingly, Ruskin did not have a proprietorial attitude toward Turner studies. Thirty years earlier he had indulged Walter Thornbury, whose book he knew would be unsatisfactory. Now Ruskin even thought of working together with Chesneau and formed a scheme to take him over to Yorkshire to see the pictures at Farnley. But it was dangerous for Ruskin to brood on Turner, who reminded him of the sorrows of the world. His last substantial work on Turner had precipitated his collapse of 1878. The plan for a shared Turner book was soon abandoned.

It was also dangerous for Ruskin to have the company of Maria La Touche, who arrived in late July, this time without her husband but with Margaret Ferrier Young. We know Miss Young not only as a dependant of the La Touche family but also as its historian, for in 1908 she would publish *Letters of a Noble Woman*, a book devoted to Maria's correspondence. She never met Rose La Touche, who had died before her service began, but Margaret Ferrier Young realised that there were terrible secrets about her relations with Ruskin. Taking her into the Coniston church (a place he seldom visited) with Maria La Touche, or sitting with Maria all evening on his garden terrace, Ruskin inevitably thought deeply of Rose. He now, talking in the warm nights of this splendid August, elaborated his theory that Francesca Alexander's tales from the Italian peasantry gave a magical illumination to the character of the girl that he and Maria had lost.[4]

A more intellectual visitor to Brantwood was Benjamin Jowett. He and Ruskin differed in many ways, but Jowett liked his Slade Professor. 'I should never wish to lose the impression of the kind welcome which I received from him', the Master of Balliol recorded. 'He is the gentlest and most innocent of mankind, of great genius but inconsecutive; and he has never rubbed his mind against others, so that he is ignorant of very obvious things.'[5] What manner of things might Jowett have been thinking of? Ruskin was as well informed on a wide range of subjects as any thinker of his time. His intellect was wider and more piercing than Jowett's. On the other hand, he could not easily belong to any educational institution and was in constant danger of losing his sanity. Jowett should have considered such matters, for he was the Vice-Chancellor of the University and in many respects its governor. Ruskin's connection with Oxford might not have ended in so grievous a fashion if Jowett had realised, in this September of 1884, how precariously the Slade Professor's mind was balanced. He should have seen how close Ruskin was to another breakdown. Vice-Chancellors have a duty to review the mental condition of their professoriat. But this was not done. Perhaps Ruskin simply gave Jowett too successful a dinner party. Lazarus Fletcher was there, with the Balliol man Alexander Wedderburn, whom of course Jowett already knew, while the ladies were Ethel Hilliard, Sara Anderson and 'Clennie' (for Ruskin would not expect governesses to dine separately, especially if they were as pretty as Miss McClennan). Reflecting on the party the next morning, Ruskin thought that the girls had all been at their best. He of course was a polished host who preserved the congenial traditions of John James Ruskin's table. So Jowett may have considered that Ruskin was still suited to Oxford life.

As Jowett knew, Ruskin was currently at odds with the University. In his will of October 1883 he had been generous to Oxford. He bequeathed his books to the Bodleian, together with a number of Turner watercolours and a significant painting, the portrait of Doge Andrea Gritti. This was the painting produced in court, and praised there by Burne-Jones, as a fine example of the painterly finish that Whistler should have emulated. It was therefore a thoughtful as well as an expensive promised gift. Ruskin, who admittedly understood little of university government, thought that Oxford should respond to the gesture in his will by purchasing two Turners that had recently come on the market, so that they might be studied in his drawing schools. The University declined his request. Then Ruskin proposed an extension of the drawing schools at the back of the University galleries, offering to pay for the building if the land were made available. This offer was refused. Angered, Ruskin revoked his bequests to the University in June of 1884 (a stroke of good fortune for Arthur Severn, who sold the portrait of the Doge, as a Titian, after Ruskin's death). It is possible that Jowett's visit to Brantwood in September was intended to repair relations with his munificent and capricious colleague. He would also have been interested in Ruskin's plans for future lectures. Ruskin had not spoken to an Oxford audience for two terms, and he had decided not to ask for a further leave of absence. He proposed to give lectures on 'The Pleasures of England' during the Michaelmas term. Some of the material in these lectures, but by no means all, was already written at the time that Jowett paid his visit. Nor was the writing completed when Ruskin went to Oxford for the new university year. He trusted that his gift for verbal improvisation would carry him through. He was mistaken. That gift had disappeared, and with it his power of winning over an audience.

* * * *

Joan Severn knew better than Jowett how unsettled Ruskin was, and she now began to ask Peter Baxter for daily reports of his master's activities and temper. Often this information was supplied by telegrams to Herne Hill. Some have survived, and the following is typical:

> MADAM YOUR FEARS WERE CORRECT BUT HAPPY TO SAY ENTIRELY GROUNDLESS TONIGHT QUITE WELL GONE OUT TO DINE WITH THE MASTER WILL WRITE AND EXPLAIN PETER BAXTER BALIOL [SIC] COL OXFORD[6]

Baxter had this address because Ruskin often stayed the night in the Master's lodgings after dining in hall, or perhaps in the old common room. These dinners included a 'ladies' night', an Oxford custom which may have been invented in Balliol this term, and which was the sole Oxford innovation to have Ruskin's approval. The date when Ruskin gave up his rooms in Corpus Christi is not known, but it was probably now, in the autumn of 1884. We may say that Jowett and Balliol gave Ruskin his last Oxford home. As Jowett's biographer writes, 'when Ruskin's health was beginning to fail, he entertained him in his house with a watchful and almost tender courtesy, which left on me an indelible impression'.[7]

Jowett was right to be watchful. If Ruskin was not in Balliol it was hard to know where he might be. He slept under Henry Acland's roof, or Alexander Macdonald's, but most often we find him in hotels in London. They were the Euston Hotel — so full of memories of his worst times with Rose, when he stayed there in 1872 — the British Hotel in Cockspur Street and perhaps Morley's Hotel in Trafalgar Square, which was later to be something of a home when Ruskin had no home of his own. The continual agitation of movement from one bedroom and hotel to the next cannot have been good for his health or his writing. When Rose was dying, ten years before, Ruskin had been able to hurry from an Oxford lecture room to her hotel bedside, transported by the railway service he officially deplored. In 1884 Ruskin went by train from Oxford to London just as frequently as in 1874. But now he had no spiritual mission in Tyburnia. He saw Frederic Leighton, who was interested in discussing Turner, dined with both Froude and Sir William Gull, busied himself at the British Museum and was often at Kate Greenaway's house. He did not 'keep' the Oxford term in the usual sense that he was part of the University and its functions while undergraduates were in residence. As the term went on he was more like a visitor to Oxford, displeased with all he saw, sometimes silent, sometimes querulous and sometimes thunderous.

The improved train services, whose timetables are often jotted in Ruskin's diary, also brought journalists to and from London and Oxford. Ruskin's professorial pronouncements had been a matter of casual interest to newspaper editors since at least the time of the Hinksey road-building. Now his lectures were more attentively covered. There were two reasons for this development. Ruskin's warnings about 'The Storm-Cloud of the Nineteenth Century' provided editors with dramatic and diverting copy. Secondly, the talented young E. T. Cook of the *Pall Mall Gazette* made a point of attending and summarising all Ruskin's lectures. The *Pall Mall Gazette* was by far the most innovative of contemporary journals. Other publications would follow where it led. Thus it was that London reporters using shorthand sat with Oxford undergraduates to listen to musings on early Christian art and related matters. Ruskin was forced to abandon his series on 'The Pleasures of England' partly because of criticism in the London press. This was often vehement and appeared in leader columns as well as in reports. Our best guide to the furore, and to the lectures themselves, is E. T. Cook, though we should recall that Cook's instinct was to present Ruskin as a more temperate man than he appeared to others. The first two lectures of 'The Pleasures of England' were restrained. However, there is something uncertain in their tone. It is as though Ruskin had attempted to exceed any of his previous utterances, not so much in wisdom or eloquence as in professorial gravity. Then the manner of the lectures declined, because of weariness, improvisation, anger and a use of allusion that was hard to follow for members of the audience who were not versed in Carlyle or who had never heard of, for instance, Jeremias Gotthelf.

To many, it seemed that Ruskin was talking nonsense. The one person who fully grasped what was being said was Cook, for he was a Ruskinian. His account of the lectures in the *Pall Mall Gazette* was an editorial achievement as well as a report. This was Ruskin's own opinion. In a letter to Cook's superior W. T. Stead, the paper's editor, Ruskin wrote 'Sir — I have seldom had occasion to pay either compliments or thanks to the British reporter; but I must very seriously acknowledge the help now afforded me by the digested plans of my Oxford lectures drawn up for the *Pall Mall Gazette* — very wonderful pieces of work, it seems to me, not only in summarising, *without any help from me whatever*, a line of thought not always by me enough expressed; but in completing and illustrating it from other parts of my books — often more fully than, against time, I could do myself . . .'[8] Ruskin went on to correct some details in Cook's reports, but this was obviously a friendly letter about work in which the journalist could take pride. Cook reprinted his summaries in his *Studies in Ruskin* (1890), with the mild prefatory remark that 'the course had not been so carefully prepared, nor was the lecturer's line of thought so closely reasoned, as in "The Art of England"'. In truth the new 'line of thought' was erratic, though Cook proved that it could be reconstructed and made to seem reasonable. Only five of the proposed seven lectures were delivered and of these Ruskin printed only the first four. Cook pointed out that 'Lectures I–IV, as thus reported [by Cook], often differ from the text as afterwards printed by Ruskin'. In *Studies in Ruskin* and in his final and definitive account in the Library Edition Cook harmonised the lectures he had heard with Ruskin's printed versions; and in the Library Edition 'additional passages are now quoted from the reports in footnotes'.[9]

In summarising 'The Pleasures of England' in 1884 and 1890 Cook announced his qualifications as Ruskin's future editor and biographer. He did so in a way that was later to become characteristic. Cook must have been disturbed by the sentiments he heard and transcribed. He could see that Ruskin's educative pronouncements were in crazy disarray. But when he wrote about the lectures his instinct was to give an account of them that would be consonant with his own good sense.

As all later critics have found, it is possible to stress either the aberrations of Ruskin's mind or its native sweetness, gravity, intelligence and knowledge. Cook always preferred the latter approach, as no doubt was proper in an editor. He may also have been correct in his respectful view of 'The Pleasures of England'. He thought it was 'nothing less than a sketch of the tendencies of national life and character'. This description implies that Ruskin had a grand plan; as was later claimed by W. G. Collingwood, who believed that the lectures were 'intended as a sketch of the main stream of history from his own religious standpoint . . . a noble theme . . .'[10] However, other people at Ruskin's last lectures quite reasonably thought that the Slade Professor was saying anything that came into his head.

The fifth and final lecture of the aborted series, announced in the *University Gazette* as 'Protestantism. The Pleasures of Truth', was given on 15 November of 1884. The flavour of the occasion was described by Cook as follows:

> The popularity of the lectures, the applause, the excitement, were in no way diminished — perhaps, as an undergraduate audience is not the most judicious in the world, they were rather increased — by the great man's vagaries. This encouraged Ruskin to discard the work of preparation, and to trust more and more to improvisation. 'Lecture fluent', he notes in his diary (November 18), 'but very forgetful'. At the same time the topics were becoming more and more disturbing to his equanimity. The lecture on 'Protestantism' had not been much prepared, but the delivery of it — as might be expected from the subject — caused great stir in his audience; there was a strong contingent of Catholics present, and they cheered loudly the winged words of their fiery ally. Ruskin had always been fond of spicing his lectures with surprise-packets in the matter of illustrations. The little jest in this kind with which he ended the lecture on 'Protestantism' created, if much amusement among the undergraduates, yet amazement and scandal among their grave and reverend seniors. Carpaccio's St Ursula had been shown as 'a type of Catholic witness'. What, he went on to ask, shall be the types and emblems to represent the spirit of Protestantism? Amidst breathless excitement the Professor proceeded to untie two pictures lying on the table before him. There are two aspects, he went on to say, of the Protestant spirit — the spirit when it is earnest, and the spirit when it is hypocritical. 'This', he explained, 'is the earnest spirit'; and he showed to an audience, which held its sides, an enlargement of a pig by Bewick. 'It is a good little pig', he remarked patronisingly:

> 'a pig which is alert and knows its own limited business. It has a clever snout, eminently adapted to dig up and worry things, and it stands erect and keen, with a knowing curl in its tail, on its own native dunghill'. The hypocritical type was Mr Stiggins, with his shappy gloves, and a concertina. The jest might have passed in the privacy of a classroom; but the lectures were reported in the London papers, and in leading articles a call was made for some kindly and benevolent veto to be placed upon 'an academic farce'.[11]

This 'academic farce' was the headline of a leader in *The World* of 19 November. Ruskin's next lecture was to be given on the 22nd, and the last of his series was scheduled for the 29th. They had been announced as 'Atheism. The Pleasures of Sense' and 'Mechanism. The Pleasures of Nonsense'. It was known that Ruskin intended to return to an old theme (first heard in Oxford in the 'Love's Meinie' lectures of the spring of 1873): the difference between natural history as perceived by scientists and as more truly studied by artists. Senior members of the University also gathered that Ruskin was preparing to criticise other professors, especially those who held scientific chairs. Now Acland and Jowett, followed by Alexander Macdonald, hastened to avert the possible scandal. Jowett, as Vice-Chancellor, begged Ruskin to lecture on other topics. Acland, as a friend and a medical man, told Ruskin that his health would be endangered if he spoke on the emotional subject of 'mechanism', by which Acland meant a modern, non-spiritual attitude to medical research. The deputation must have been persuasive, for Ruskin immediately agreed to cancel his proposed lectures and to substitute less controversial, and taxing, addresses on 'Patience', 'Birds and how to Paint Them' and 'Landscape'.

We learn a little more about these embarrassing university affairs from a letter to Susie Beever. 'I have been thrown a week out in all my plans', Ruskin told her, 'by having to write two new lectures, instead of those the University was frightened at. The scientists slink out of my way now, as if I was a mad dog, for I let them have it hot and heavy whenever I've a chance at them.'[12] Ruskin was combative, but his new lectures were in general subdued. That on 'Patience' consisted mainly of readings from *The Cestus of Aglaia* and *St Mark's Rest*. As before, E. T. Cook's summaries in the *Pall Mall Gazette* gave the impression of a wise, genial professor looking back over his long career. However, at least one other member of the audience could only grieve over Ruskin's demeanour. This was Herbert von Herkomer, who in the next year would succeed him in the Slade chair. In Herkomer's memoirs we read: 'How shall I describe that painful performance? And painful it was to his friends who so loved and revered him, who so plainly saw how he played to the gallery, how, in the perversity of spirit that sometimes overtook that brilliant mind, he seemed only to wish to arouse hilarity among the undergraduates . . .'[13]

Although Ruskin did not know it, the talk on 'Landscape' was to be his last Oxford lecture. After December of 1884 he never returned to the university he had first known as an undergraduate in 1837. In 1884, however, he did expect to be present for the Hilary term of spring 1885, and regarded the lectures on atheism and mechanism as being postponed rather than cancelled. Indeed, the *University Gazette* dated 10 March 1885 announced that they would be his only lectures that term, and therefore it is likely that Ruskin wished to insist on their importance. In the winter and spring of 1884–85 he still thought of Oxford as a centre of his activities. He even asked the members of the Guild of St George to an Oxford meeting. This was the only occasion when Ruskin presided over a gathering of the Guild's adherents. It must have been in some sense a public occasion, for E. T. Cook was present as a journalist when the Companions of St George assembled in the Randolph Hotel on 4 December.

From Cook's report in the next evening's *Pall Mall Gazette* we learn that Ruskin presented the Guild's accounts for 1881–83; explained that the Guild's books, pictures and minerals were at present distributed between Sheffield, Oxford, Whitelands College 'and other places'; and finally described the plans for a Guild museum at Bewdley, which was to be built from marble quarried in the Greek island of Paros.[14] As Ruskin spoke, there must have been Companions of St George who wondered what treasures might be the property of their association. But this was never fully explained. Ruskin's collections were always in flux. It is not easy to follow the locations and provenances even of his most prized and famous possessions, the Turner watercolours held at Herne Hill, Sheffield, Oxford and Brantwood. These matters are the more difficult to reconstruct because of disputes with Arthur and Joan Severn. One letter to Joan helps us to understand how Ruskin's art collection was increasingly a problem rather than a delight. Undated and unsigned, it is addressed from Balliol College, so must belong to the Michaelmas term of 1884.

> . . . I am so very sorry I can't [illeg.] — as you call it the pics. I want them all immediately here, and you're only to send word to Williams when he may come — I'll tell him to bring the horse fair Turner with him — which Arthur can keep or sell as he likes. — but he must not sell it under 350. I will send him from Brantwood

> his copy of St Gothard. — which he may sell for what I gave him for it, 100; but *not under.* — or use for decoration — with any other study he might care to make from Nat.Gall. But in any case I'll send you some choice of other things . . . Your letter just come. I had noticed lately that Arthur was beginning to 'think' — and sometimes also to hint in saying — that I had given the Lewis's — I had been giving easily and too much. I meant only at first to give *you* the Schaffhausen — then I gave, farther, the Scarborough — then merely because he copied it well the Buckfastleigh — and that is enough. You have your own old Linlithgow and those three others — Schaffhausen yours, — the other two his. You have my two drawings. In Highlands — and [damage] on Lake Lucerne, and one at Chamouni and one at Thun, and three Venices all of great value still, at least to me. You have also a portrait of me by myself, which I am going to ask for as a gift — for you don't care about it, and I do: — of shells — feathers, and whatnot else, I take no account. You need have no fear of future claims for restitution. And observe finally. This, that I watched all the time patiently to see if having the pictures — so much admired! beside him, would do Arfie any good. He has never learned a single thing, nor even attempted to learn, from *one* of them.[15]

Here the letter breaks off. Ruskin's agitation was caused not only by Arthur Severn's failings. He was also excited and disturbed by Frederic Leighton's plans for an exhibition of Turner watercolours at the Royal Academy. Sir Frederic had been President of the Academy since 1878. He had recently shown himself to be adept in the politics of the London art world. Probably to the surprise of such an institution, the Academy had felt the rivalry of, for instance, the Fine Art Society and the Grosvenor Gallery. In 1883 Leighton had responded to the Grosvenor's expertise in late Pre-Raphaelitism with a Rossetti memorial exhibition. This was an unusual tribute to a man who had never been an Academician. He was now interested in mounting a better Turner exhibition than the Fine Art Society could hope to accomplish. Ruskin and Leighton were not close; but they appreciated each other, and had done so ever since Ruskin praised the younger man's *Cimabue* in 1855, the year in which they were introduced by Browning. There were at least two sheets by Leighton in the Oxford drawing schools, chosen as examples of fine draughtsmanship; and Leighton knew that any Turner exhibition would benefit from Ruskin's interest. He could not have realised that Turner projects set Ruskin's mind to race toward sorrowful autobiography and mythological speculation.

He would certainly have found an expert interest in Turner drawings that were currently on the art market. Ruskin was still acquiring Turners from time to time. He was invited to buy more often than he bought, for dealers offered Turners to him before they approached any other collector. In a businesslike way, Leighton often had Ruskin to breakfast in November of 1884. However, the proposed exhibition did not take place, perhaps because of Ruskin's breakdown in the summer of 1885.

The prospect of a Turner exhibition encouraged Ruskin to visit his fellow collector Walter Fawkes at Farnley Hall in mid-December of 1884. Before leaving London he saw Froude. The third and fourth volumes of the historian's great biography had been published earlier in the year as *Thomas Carlyle: A History of his Life in London 1834–1881*, and Ruskin wished Froude to know that the controversial book had his support. Next, Ruskin went from London to spend a day in Oxford and attend a meeting of an anti-vivisection society. He spoke briefly, sharing the platform with the Bishop of Oxford, the same bishop whom he had 'challenged' in *Fors Clavigera* of January 1875. This (9 December 1884) was Ruskin's last visit to Oxford. He was glad to leave the modernising city for another part of England that reminded him of his youthful days. As his father would have done, Ruskin proposed that he should stay in the local inn while visiting Farnley. But the hospitality of the Fawkes family prevailed, and so we have a pleasant account of his conversation after dinner. Edith Mary Fawkes recalled that

> he talked a great deal about Sir Walter Scott . . . Of Carlyle he spoke with the utmost love and veneration. He said he had been more than a father to him, that there was nothing in literature, so far as history went, like his *French Revolution* and *Frederick*, and that he had done immortal work. I said how sad it seemed that with his great aspirations he should have led such a miserable life. Mr Ruskin said he was not really as unhappy as the life by Froude made him out to be; that he had a wretched digestion and a way of talking about his miseries, but that his life was not really as unhappy as Turner's.
>
> The next morning Mr Ruskin went away. I drove with him to the station, and as we got near the little town, he said, 'Look! look! a Turner drawing!' — and engraved on my memory is the familiar view of Otley bridge, the river Wharfe gleaming in veiled sunshine, a soft mist half hiding the town, and the great hill rising slate-coloured above the mist into a luminous sky.[16]

Ruskin now wrote to Joan '. . . I had no idea Farnley was so grand . . . I am very thankful also to find the Turners in good state — spotted a little, some, but not faded . . . It is a little pleasant to me to hear the talk of a real Tory squire. I leave on Tuesday for home, *D.V.*'[17] By 'home' he meant Brantwood, where, as a more recent type of Tory squire, he was to remain from Christmastime of 1884 until August of 1887.

CHAPTER FORTY-FIVE

1885

Only a couple of years earlier, Ruskin's miscellaneous publications would have been numerous. Now he had lost vigour, and for weeks at the beginning of 1885 he wrote little beside letters, though his lecture on Sir Herbert Edwardes was prepared for press. Ruskin had arrived at Brantwood from Farnley and despondently looked forward to a solitary Christmas. Troubled by colds and fits of shivering he appealed to Dr Parsons of Hawkshead, and it may have been during this season that his local doctor first gave him chloral. 'I feel entirely unable now to engage in or for anything', Ruskin wrote to Joan, '— I am writing out the Sir H lecture in a form for publication but do not think I can come up to town or do more than vegetate this spring. I am so seriously frightened at the feeling of collapse, and the sense of despondency is so terrible . . .'[1]

Thus the year began. Jane Anne Wilkinson was often at Brantwood, pleasing but also saddening Ruskin with her childish, country ways. Her parents had caught an owl, she said. She would bring it to Ruskin as a present, and the owl would catch his mice. Ruskin thanked her, but said that he did not want his Brantwood mice to be eaten. When his cold was better and the weather had improved Ruskin ventured outside the house. For companionship he had his dog Bramble. On fine days Baxter sometimes rowed master and dog to the other side of the lake, Ruskin in wideawake hat and greatcoat, eager Bramble standing at the prow of the *Jumping Jennie.*

A study of Ruskin would not be complete without an account of his dogs. As Collingwood wrote in the first biography of Ruskin, he was 'a devoted lover and keen observer of animals. It would take long to tell the story of all his dogs, from the Spaniel Dash, commemorated in his early poems, and Wisie, whose sagacity is related in *Præterita*, down through a long line of bulldogs, St Bernards, and collies, to Bramble, the reigning favourite . . .'[2] This was written in 1893. Bramble first appears in Ruskin's diary in 1884 and probably replaced an earlier Brantwood dog, Maude, often mentioned in letters of the mid-1870s. One suspects that Ruskin's relations with dogs might repay more study, though evidence about particular dogs is scanty. He celebrated St Bernards in a very early piece of writing (1835–36), never published in his lifetime, 'The Chronicle of St Bernard', in which they are described as 'the most efficient humane society in the world'.[3] Perhaps he owned one when living at Mornex in 1862–63; he told Collingwood about the dog or dogs when they visited his old house together in 1882. We know from *Fors* of December 1874 that bulldogs are 'the gentlest and faithfullest of living creatures if you use them well. And the best dog I ever had was a bull-terrier . . .'[4] The name of this bull-terrier is not known. Among other significant dogs should be mentioned Lion, the Newfoundland terrier who bit the five-year-old Ruskin's lip, leaving a scar for life. 'Not the slightest diminution of my love for dogs, nor the slightest nervousness in managing them, was induced by the accident', we read in *Præterita*.[5] Another dog mentioned in the early part of *Præterita* was Towzer, who belonged to Ruskin's aunt Bridget Richardson and guarded her baker's shop and bakehouse in Market Street, Croydon. Ruskin also took an interest in other people's dogs: Rose La Touche's enormous Bruno (said by Maria La Touche to be her daughter's husband), Lady Trevelyan's Peter, the Acland family's Bustle, and many more, for Ruskin would make friends with the dog of the household wherever he went.

A dog's master 'is his best possession', Ruskin wrote in *Fors*.[6] Bramble might have sensed this truth, though his master was too often absent from home. Bramble's life in January and February of 1885, when he had Ruskin to himself, is important for two reasons. Firstly, his master was brooding over the monstrous 'scientific' practice of vivisection, and therefore considered the proper bonds between animals and men. Secondly, private notes suggest that he had the idea of describing dogs in illustration of his Herne Hill childhood for his autobiography.[7] And this would not have been an unreasonable approach, if it had served to elicit an especial kind of memory. Ruskin did not wish to write an autobiography in which he would state the titles of his books with their years of publication, relate his other achievements, speak of his relations with his fellow great Victorians. He hoped for more unorthodox and subtle ways of describing the past. The appearance of Lion and Towzer in the early pages of *Præterita*, written at Brantwood this spring, helps to give an unusual flavour to the evocation of a child's world. In general, *Præterita* is evocative rather than consequential. Therefore its narrative lines are blurred, minor events are often given more prominence than great occasions, and the impetus for any chapter might come from the memory of a pet, or the rediscovery of an old drawing, or the changed look of a once familiar landscape.

In his penultimate *Fors*, dated October 1884, Ruskin had announced his intention of terminating his periodical letter in order to write 'some brief autobiography'.[8] At Brantwood in January of 1885 he tentatively began to make plans for the book. The tangled story of *Præterita*'s composition can be reconstructed from its various manuscripts, proof sheets, Ruskin's diaries and private memoranda, and his correspondence with George Allen, Henry Jowett, and many other people who were interested in the book and occasionally made suggestions about its contents. As already noted, the first sentences of *Præterita* are taken from the tenth letter of *Fors Clavigera*, published as long ago as 1871. A date is given at the end of *Præterita*'s last chapter, a sign that Ruskin would write no more, 'Brantwood, June 19th, 1889'. This is therefore a book written over a number of years, though the more definite work on *Præterita* as an autobiography began now, in January of 1885. This moving and puzzling book was the result of varying moods. It had different audiences in its author's mind and was often written when that mind was not at its full strength. There were crises as the narrative progressed and long intervals between the issue of separate chapters. These gaps in publication were caused by Ruskin's mental illnesses. Fatigue, loss of memory and the old habit of exaggeration mar the accuracy of Ruskin's account of his life. Facts were rarely checked, mistakes were never corrected. *Præterita* is furthermore obscure. Sometimes Ruskin seems to be talking to himself, or sharing reminiscences not with a readership but with a single friend. The passage on Dawtry Drewitt and the vipers, explained above, is one of a number of such mysterious paragraphs. Friendship is important to *Præterita*. Whole sections of the book were designed as gifts. John and Jane Simon, for instance, who loved Swiss holidays, found the manuscript of *Præterita*'s Alpine descriptions in their post. The story of Ruskin's Venetian dog Wisie was written in honour of John Brown of Edinburgh, the author of the famous dog story *Rab and his Friends*.

Many more parts of *Præterita* were affected by some local circumstance. The major influences on the autobiography, as one would expect, came from the people who had been most important in Ruskin's life. Prominent among them are John James Ruskin, whose old-fashioned Toryism is invoked in the book's first sentence, like a motto or a text; then Rose La Touche, for whom Ruskin wrote so much of the history of his life in *Fors Clavigera* of the early 1870s. Now, after their reconciliation, Maria La Touche was an influence too, for Ruskin wished to comfort her and share sweet thoughts of Rose. He proposed to send Maria the first revise of the text 'so that you can give me advice and help before printing', and she was grateful for this offer.[9] We may think of other, perhaps less obvious, influences. One of them was Turner. More than three-quarters of the twenty-eight chapters of *Præterita* (and also of the unwritten chapters) have landscape titles. Like Turner, Ruskin proposed to meditate on history within the magical confines of a vista. Such titles as 'The Col de la Faucille', 'Christ Church Choir', 'Roslyn Chapel', 'Fontainebleau', 'The Simplon', 'The Campo Santo' and 'Macagnuna' were conceived before Ruskin wrote words to illustrate them. The writing in chapters without landscape titles, like 'The State of Denmark' and 'The Feasts of the Vandals' may strike the reader as more agitated, less reflective and forgiving. This is a matter of opinion, and it is never easy to assess the effect of Turner on Ruskin's spirit. But we may be certain about another influence on *Præterita*: Joan Severn. She was not herself an inspiring woman. The point is that, on the contrary, she was receptive. As he knew, Joan had a large capacity for being pleased or displeased by Ruskin. She showed her worries, and she showed when they were relieved. Joan had always told Ruskin how much she was alarmed by his polemical writings, however little she read of them. Although she was a Companion of St George, Joan had no wish that the Guild's activities should be extended. She wanted Ruskin to leave Oxford, believing (rightly) that lecturing was bad for his health. For all these reasons, Joan was anxious that her cousin should now write a book without the slightest hint of controversy. She visited Brantwood in late January, when these two very old friends and distant relatives discussed the autobiography. Ruskin agreed that no dispute should enter its pages, and letter after letter to Joan in the next four years told her that the object of *Præterita* was to please her.

Joan seldom looked in Ruskin's diaries or personal papers. Had she done so, she might have foreseen that the later parts of *Præterita* could be embarrassing. Both plans for *Præterita* and extended sections of its manuscript are contained in Ruskin's diaries, while other drafts of the book were written on his usual lined foolscap. Three small manuscript volumes contain a number of chronological entries beginning on 15 January of 1885, but otherwise are so filled with autobiographical writing that they were subsequently considered as manuscripts for *Præterita* rather than diaries. They were sold as such in the Brantwood dispersal sales, so became separated from the main sequence of the diaries, the twenty-seven volumes purchased by J. H. Whitehouse in the 1930 sale.[10] Additionally, in the diaries saved by Whitehouse there are numerous and significant plans for *Præterita*. In Volume XXV we find notes and suggestions about the very earliest years of Ruskin's life:

HUNTER ST. The Lozenge
The frowning window

HERNE HILL Nanny Clowsley
Journeys on Green Horse
The Coat of Arms
The Dancing school and butcher's boy

Four pages later in this volume:

Love of Stars
In speaking of my constant love of stars — give contrary modern slang — of southern Cross[11]

The proposed passage on stars was never written. *Præterita* records a Nanny Clowsley living in Chelsea and described her as 'a poor relative', but no blood relationship with the Ruskins can be established. The 'Coat of Arms' probably refers to John James Ruskin's bearings, arranged with the College of Arms in 1836: or the reference might be to a remark in 'The Springs of Wandel', *Præterita*'s first chapter, in which we read about 'my maternal grandmother', who 'was the landlady of the old King's Head in Market Street, Croydon; and I wish she were alive again, and I could paint her Simone Memmi's King's Head, for a sign'.[12]

The revelation that Ruskin's grandmother ran a public house was not welcome to Joan Severn,[13] and soon she would be uneasy about a projected chapter entitled 'Joanna's Care', for this might have related how she came to the Denmark Hill household on a largely charitable basis. As we will see, 'Joanna's Care' was transferred to a later part of *Præterita*, and is the concluding chapter of the abandoned book. Ruskin there describes Joan's care of him, in his old age; but the chapter originally had to do with Joan's attendance on his mother. This may be seen from a sketch of future *Præterita* chapters found among Ruskin's papers. The middle years of his life were to be described as follows:

The Grande Chartreuse
Mont Velan
L'Esterelle
Joanna's Care
The Source of the Arveron
Konigstein
The Rainbows of Giessbach

Regina Montium
The Hunter's Rock
Fairies' Hollow
Shakespeare's Cliff
Calais Pier[14]

The first three of these chapter titles survive in the book as it was published. The other titles, because they are deliberately resonant, enable us to guess at the probable contents of unwritten chapters. 'The Source of the Arveron' was to be about Ruskin's expeditions from Chamonix in 1849 and Turner's illustration of the site in his *Liber Studiorum.* In 'Konigstein' he would write about 'my last happy walk with my father', when he and John James were there in 1859. 'The Rainbows of Giessbach' was to describe the sad days after Lady Trevelyan's death in 1866.[15] 'Regina Montium' would recall Ruskin's studies in Verona in 1869. A piece of manuscript tells us that 'The Hunter's Rock' was 'the rock of marble between Lucca and Pisa, where Ugolino dreamed he was hunting'.[16] Ruskin was in both cities in 1872 and 1874. Scraps of this chapter were preserved, and they show that Ruskin would have discussed his love of Dante. A further manuscript note explains 'Fairies' Hollow'. It says 'At Chamouni, my last happy days there with old Couttet and Rose's last letters'.[17] Some of these letters Ruskin set in type, but they were not published in *Præterita.* Yet another piece of manuscript indicates that 'Shakespeare's Cliff' was to be about England, 'in a last review', while 'Calais Pier' was to be 'a last review of France'. These proposals appear to echo Ruskin's first intentions when asked to write the book which became *The Bible of Amiens.*

The above is just one of many plans. One that sketches out a description of Ruskin's later life was written in an earlier diary, Volume VII of the Whitehouse sequence:

The Bridge of St Martin's
Chamouni
Vevay
Monte Viso
Konigstein
First sight of R. spring 1859 —? Her journey to Riviera — 59 — 60. — But how did I get back to England before she went?
Marie of the Giesbach
Matlock
The Sacristan's cell
The Vale of Thame

The Vision
The Field under the Wood[18]

As before, some of the subjects of these chapters may be identified from their titles. 'Matlock' refers to Ruskin's illness in the Derbyshire spa in 1871. 'The Sacristan's Cell' (the forty-sixth letter of *Fors Clavigera* had been titled 'The Sacristan') refers to his life in Florence in 1874. Ruskin drove through 'The Vale of Thame', the country around Aylesbury and south of Oxford, in May and June of 1875, after Rose La Touche's death. 'The Vision' was to be an account of Ruskin's mental breakdown in 1878. 'The Field under the Wood' is unexplained, but may have introduced the reader to the quiet countryside around Brantwood, an appropriate place for Ruskin to conclude both his life and the story of his life.

There were many such plans. Notably, some topics were never considered. The chapter schemes do not mention, for instance, Effie, Ruskin's wife;[19] nor the author's friendship with the members of the Pre-Raphaelite Brotherhood; nor Carlyle; nor *Fors Clavigera* and the Guild of St George. Ruskin had participated in great nineteenth-century debates, but in January of 1885 it appeared that his autobiography would be uncontroversial, domestic in nature and mainly concerned with his foreign travels. Joan was glad that this should be so. However, the more Ruskin thought about his book the more convinced he was that it should recount his love for Rose. He also proposed to describe his periods of insanity. The 'story of Rosie's cup', for instance, which he knew to have been a sign of his impending madness, was to be a part of *Præterita* (and is published for the first time in the present biography), and in 'The Vision' all the world might be able to read of his hallucinated fantasies during the mental illness of 1878. Descriptions of Ruskin's madness and of his passion for Rose could never have pleased Joan Severn, but for the moment she was content; for Ruskin at Brantwood, writing her loving letters and roaming through the woods with Bramble, had apparently given up controversy. Only in the silence of his notebooks did Ruskin contemplate a final daring in his career as a writer. Had not his books always been unusual? He had always written as he wished and through the long years of *Fors Clavigera* he had ignored proprieties. Ruskin was further encouraged to exceed the conventional bounds of Victorian biography by the example of Carlyle's *Reminiscences* and Froude's recent and ill-received account of Carlyle's life and character.[20] Froude had appealed to Ruskin for support, and this was freely given. Now Ruskin himself had the opportunity to write some innovative autobiography.

If *Præterita* had been completed in the ways that Ruskin devised in 1885 we would have an even stranger addition to Victorian literature than the book we know today.

Plans for *Præterita* can seldom be securely dated. Examination of the diaries suggests that Ruskin was revising his schemes as late as May of 1887. This was appropriate to an elusive and poetic book written in the early height of the symbolist movement. The more numerous and elastic its plans, the more *Præterita* was likely to achieve its instinctive goal, which we find in the last paragraph of the book, beginning 'How things bind and blend themselves together!' The chapter schemes were changeable.[21] They are repeated, dropped, then restored. The plans melt into the diary, as though memory and fact were both in flux. At first they are on pages opposite the chronological entries, and then they are written on the same page. At one point, when Ruskin was searching through old diaries for mentions of Rose, he wrote a poem about her:

> Here we go up, and here we go down
> And the sea's like me in a green-backed gown.
> Sure, it's me that's myself — says Mary Jane.
> — Herrs from Germany, Dons from Spain.
> His complexion was dark, with a tingling of tan,
> And his name was so dainty in I-ta-li-an,
> That she never remembered that Bruno meant Brown
> Till she'd been and got married in Camden Town.[22]

As he began the autobiography, Ruskin was content to write for no more than half an hour each day, while he looked through Brantwood cupboards and bookshelves for materials that might bring back the distant past: a batch of letters from Thomas Pringle, for instance, or Saussure's *Voyages dans les Alpes*. Soon he decided to make more haste. On 1 February 1885 the diary reads 'Lying awake, this morning, it seemed to me desirable not to let this writing run on hither and thither as it will, but to resolve that if I keep well, in every month of this spring I will bring it up to another ten years of life, so that by the turn of the sun, I may have given some account of myself up to my 60th year — and to perhaps by Christmas, if all is well, have it ended and retouched supplementarily.' This programme was not followed, for he did not 'keep well', but it shows that he was optimistic about his new book.[23] There are numerous signs that, after his wandering and enfeebled performances in Oxford three months before, Ruskin's writing had regained its individual vigour. An essay 'Notes Upon Gipsy Character' (which unfortunately has eluded the many chroniclers of Romany literature) was added to Francesca Alexander's *Roadside Songs of Tuscany*, now being issued at quite regular intervals by George Allen; and in this spirited defence of a generally maligned race Ruskin shows his old relish for controversial attitudes:

> Honestest, harmlessest of the human race — under whose roof *but* a Gipsy's may a wandering Madonna rest in peace?
>
> Nor in less strange and admirable distinction from the herd of unthinking men, does the Gipsy stand to me, in his acute, perseverant, uncontentious extrication of himself from the fetter, or the snare, of every physical and moral despotism, justly so called: and in his love and true attainment of liberty of soul and body in all the meanings and privileges of liberty that are rational and guiltless. He is imprisoned neither in mansion, nor in money-chest. His paternal acres are by every roadside; he owes neither duty to tenant, nor rent to lord; he is enslaved by no creed — attached to no party — weakened by no dissent — disgraced by no bribe. Disdainful of forms of law, he is neither at pains for their abolition, nor under penalties by their observance; he is untaxed for their support, and unentangled by their practice . . .[24]

The essay goes on to contrast the sympathy felt for gipsies by the Italian and Scottish peasantry with the distrust felt by 'the prosperous middle classes of our own island' and 'the vulgar British citizen'. Ruskin was happy with his piece of anarchism, all the more so because its sentiments derive from knowledge of his beloved Walter Scott. A part of Ruskin wished to be more like Scott than Carlyle, and *Præterita* gave him the opportunity to relinquish social prophecy in favour of legend and romance. Many parts of the autobiography might have been written by a novelist rather than by a critic of society. With *Præterita*, Ruskin sensed that he need not be a sage and could be more purely a writer. He could take leave from his duties as a teacher. The book allowed him to escape from his roles as the wise Master of the Guild of St George and the grave Oxford Professor of Fine Art. Perhaps that is why it so often insists on his foolishness and callow ignorance.

By fortunate chance, Ruskin was now given a perfect opportunity to leave Oxford. There was not, as is sometimes stated, a major public dispute between the Slade Professor and the University. All was quickly and on the whole amicably arranged in private letters between Ruskin and Benjamin Jowett. At issue was the question of a grant of £500 per year, to be given by the University for work in the new physiological laboratories. Research there was to be supervised by Professor

Sir John Burdon-Sanderson. A problem, Henry Acland's memoir relates, 'was the practical recognition of vivisection, in which Professor Sanderson was a famous expert, and author of an important manual'. Acland further recalled how 'a violent concerted opposition was organised: non residents were brought up from all parts of the country, and a scene ensued in the Sheldonian theatre . . .'[25] Ruskin hated the idea of vivisection, but he was not engaged in this meeting, nor in its preparations. He did not join any public discussion of vivisection, but simply sent a letter of resignation to Jowett and had the Vice-Chancellor's letter of acceptance by return of post. The resignation letter was written on 12 March. The next day Ruskin began to write an account of his undergraduate life in Oxford, the chapter 'Christ Church Choir'. Here, then, was the first test of *Præterita*'s equanimity. Ruskin might have used the chapter to criticise the University. He did not do so, but wrote an idealistic hymn to his old college. It seemed, therefore, that *Præterita* was set on a fair course. Not even a matter such as vivisection could disturb Ruskin's determination to write his memoirs (as the preface puts it) 'frankly, garrulously, and at ease; speaking, of what gives me joy to remember, at any length I like . . . and passing in total silence things which I have no pleasure in reviewing . . .'[26]

The first two chapters of *Præterita* (whose subtitle is 'Outlines of/Scenes and Thoughts/perhaps/Worthy of Memory in my Past Life') were to be published in July of 1885, with the following 'Advice' to the reader. 'The first two numbers of *Præterita* are little more than reprints from *Fors Clavigera*; but the collected passages are here placed in better order, and in some cases retouched or further expanded . . .'[27] This was so. With quite an amount of editorial skill, and the assistance of George Allen and his daughter Grace, Ruskin had begun his book with paragraphs taken from eleven issues of *Fors*, from its tenth (October 1871) to its sixty-fifth (May 1876) number. Ruskin had hoped to begin publication on his father's birthday, but in the event had to content himself with signing his preface on 10 May. Although the composition of *Præterita*'s new matter had begun cautiously Ruskin was well ahead of schedule by mid-April, as is shown in a letter to Allen. '. . . I've sent orders to Jowett today to set up this title page . . . with rose vignette as for Fors — I want to publish the first two numbers punctually on 10th May, and continue monthly. I've got good twelve numbers written ahead — but it's to begin with the bits out of Fors, put together — will you please look them out and send to Jowett to print next week . . .'[28]

We gather, then, that Ruskin had been writing confidently in the month after his resignation from Oxford. It is almost certain that the manuscript was not written in a consecutive fashion, with one event following another. It is more likely that Ruskin composed different parts separately, and then returned to his manuscripts to fill in gaps, adjust the chronology or add afterthoughts. However that may be, he had enjoyed a profitable writing period. Furthermore, Ruskin had continued editorial work on *Roadside Songs of Tuscany* and was compiling a little anthology made from his studies of clouds in *Modern Painters*. This was *Coeli Enarrant*, whose first and only part was published this year as a companion to *In Montibus Sanctis* (1884), a study of mountains, whose separated paragraphs had also been taken from *Modern Painters*. Allen thought that these would be popular gift books. In his retrospective mood, Ruskin felt a little proud when he looked again at *Modern Painters*. In early May, pleased with his recent labours, he felt energetic enough to leave Brantwood for a while and make a trip to London.

* * * *

Ruskin went to Herne Hill because he was a sociable man and wished to see friends old and new. Kate Greenaway was probably the first of them; but he also caught up with, among others, the Simons, Froude, the Burne-Joneses, his Croydon cousin William Richardson and Alexander Wedderburn, with his fiancée. Another reason to be in London was that Ruskin was worried about money. He needed to discuss family finances with Joan and also with George Allen. His personal publisher brought income, but Ruskin himself maintained the Herne Hill and Brantwood houses. He paid Allen's own salary, the costs of printing at Hazell & Watson in Aylesbury and school fees for Arthur and Agnew Severn, who had now joined Mr Churchill's (Connie Hilliard's husband's) school at Reigate. Beyond these duties and the usual charities there was the burden of the cost of the continuing, though faltering, good works of the Guild of St George: expenditure which included payment to numerous assistants who had been sent to study and copy early Italian art and architecture.

Ruskin went from Herne Hill to stay with the Allens at Orpington. They discussed financial and other matters, but it is doubtful whether they found more effective ways to sell Ruskin's books. For instance, Ruskin had always been opposed to translation of his works, and would not abandon this principle. He now instructed that *Præterita* should not be sent to the press for review. E. T. Cook's devoted

Ruskinian work for the *Pall Mall Gazette* gave him the reward of review copies, but otherwise there was no publicity for the saleable autobiography. Cook wrote abstracts of each chapter in the *PMG* until 10 July 1889, when *Præterita* finally collapsed. He subsequently commented that 'No other notices of the book appeared in any of the daily or literary journals'.[29]

As Ruskin approached the end of his capital, one might have expected him to take a keener interest in the promotion of his books. He did not. In the years since he had broken with Smith, Elder, Ruskin had developed a method of publishing that suited his writing and his character. Here was yet another domestic arrangement he was disinclined to change. There is something almost aristocratic in Ruskin's disdain for booksellers and their trade. At the same time his publishing was perversely suburban. The warehouse which held stock of his extremely various and beautifully printed books was a shed in the garden of Sunnyside, George Allen's Orpington home. If an order was received for any book or pamphlet, Grace Allen would go to this shed and make up a neat parcel. Her father continually chafed against the restrictions keeping him from modern commerce. He must have looked at Kate Greenaway's popularity and the huge sales that this year had allowed her to move from Holloway to a new mansion (designed by Norman Shaw) in Hampstead. It is curious to note that, if George Allen had published Kate Greenaway, the Ruskin family fortunes might not have fallen into such disrepair. But Ruskin did not wish Allen to become a businessman. He was Ruskin's servant, and Ruskin's word was law. In his advanced age, the author of the gentle *Præterita* was too often autocratic with the Herne Hill servants. When he scolded an old family retainer or one of Joan's new maids, it was usually a sign that he had 'brains on the over-boil'. Madness was not far distant, though on most days Ruskin wrote an enchanting piece of autobiography, to be read to Joan and Arthur by the fireside he had known for fifty years. In these days of May and June he was always occupied with *Præterita*. He also enjoyed shrimp teas with some new girl friends. They were 'Shrimper' and 'Diamond Eyes', who with Miss Katie Macdonald had formed an association called 'The Friends of Living Creatures'.[30] They had been so bold as to ask Ruskin to be its President. He was of course pleased to accept such a new post.

Letters to Katie Macdonald show Ruskin in a playful and genial mood but, as everyone around him feared, the patron of the Friends of Living Creatures was close to another breakdown. Ruskin had been well when he left Brantwood a month before. Now he was often depressed and agitated. The Severns imagined that Ruskin's mind was soothed by work on *Præterita*. Soon they would find that this was not always so. There was a forewarning in a letter to Kate Greenaway:

Whit-Black Monday, 85
(May 26)

. . . I was down to very low tide today, and am still, but partly rested, still my head not serving me, — the driving about town continually tires me fearfully, — then I get vexed to be tired — then I can't eat because I'm vexed — then I can't sleep and so it goes on . . .

I'm at the saddest part of my autobiography — and think extremely little of myself — then and now — I was sulky and quarrelled with all life — just because I couldn't get the one thing I chose to fancy. — *Now* — I can get nothing I fancy — all the world ebbing away, and the only question for me now — What next?[31]

E. T. Cook, comparing the chronological diary with the notes for *Præterita*, established that this 'saddest part' of the book was the account of Ruskin's infatuation with Adèle Domecq. Writing in the house in which he had been flung into the tortures of adolescence, and then humiliated, Ruskin changed the tone of his reminiscences. They are not so much 'sad' as written in bitter resentment. The futility of his desires appears both in the letter to Kate Greenaway and in the contemporary passage of *Præterita*.[32] In this mood, tired and even disgusted, Ruskin left Herne Hill for a Brantwood summer.

CHAPTER FORTY-SIX

1885–1887

Ruskin was at odds with himself and the world when he left London but then enjoyed an untroubled fortnight at Brantwood in the latter part of June 1885. These two weeks of precarious calm were the gift of Lilias Trotter, who had come to stay with her brother Alec and sister Minnie. It was now thirteen years since Lilias had been claimed by evangelical Christianity at the Broadlands conference of 1872. Ruskin saw in her the kind of young woman who might have been a friend of the largely friendless Rose La Touche. For this reason Lilias had a special place in his heart, though he would always dissent from her missionary attitudes and was still determined that she should study art rather than seek conversions among fallen women. Perhaps Lilias was herself glad to have a holiday from 'rescue work', as she called it. Every day, Ruskin wrote a little part of *Præterita* before breakfast; then Lilias read his letters to him before they settled down to a morning class. Minnie reported that

> . . . it seemed a differently shaped lesson at every hour of the day. One time [Lilias] admitted a dislike for the colour purple, which called forth stern reproof. Cupboards full of lovely minerals were opened, rock crystals and amethysts of every shade were spread forth, flowers were picked, water-colours of birds by William Hunt, mountain scenes by Turner, were all called into contribution by her master to persuade her of the greatness of the heresy. She never dared to object to purple again![1]

These were some of the last practical art lessons that Ruskin ever gave, perhaps the very last. They followed a pattern laid down many years before, in the late 1840s and early 1850s. While the teaching was improvised within each class, its principal guides were constant. Although Turner was always invoked, landscape in the larger sense was never considered. Strangely, Ruskin seldom taught drawing out of doors. Instead, materials were brought in from outside. Stones, leaves and flowers were to be represented with meticulous realism. Painting in oil was vehemently discouraged, as was drawing from the figure. All in all, little had changed in Ruskin's teaching practice since the classes at the Working Men's College at the first height of Pre-Raphaelitism. In 1885 as in 1854, his personal comments were essential. Ruskin's art teaching was barren without his conversation. For this reason it was now impossible for Alexander Macdonald, still in Oxford and supervising the drawing schools, to pretend that he was teaching on Ruskin's principles or in a Ruskinian tradition. At Brantwood, Oxford problems had been forgotten. In Oxford, nobody wished to re-entangle themselves with the former Slade Professor's theories of elementary art. Therefore the question of the future of the drawing schools was put aside. Meanwhile, Ruskin had pleasure when he sat next to Lilias and showed her ways in which watercolour might reproduce the pungency, or the vaporous evanescence, of the colour purple as it existed in nature; for purple is to be found in mountains and skies and also (as Ruskin had already explained, while discussing Homer in his 'Addresses on Colour and Illumination' of 1854) in the sea. Lilias would not have known the 'Addresses': they were not published until E. T. Cook rescued their gist and edited them for Volume XII of the Library Edition in 1904. We may imagine, however, that Lilias Trotter heard of Homer and purple while she was at Brantwood in this summer of 1885.[2]

Now that Ruskin had left Oxford it appeared that his work as an art teacher had been concluded. Only one person, W. G. Collingwood, thought of summarising his aesthetic. In the summer of 1885 he began his attempt to codify Ruskin's system of art education. The results were published in 1891 as *The Art Teaching of John Ruskin*, a volume which ranges over a great deal of Ruskin's more formal writing, beginning with the very earliest defence of Turner after the artist had been attacked in *Blackwood's Magazine*. 'This essay, long supposed to have been lost, I have had the good fortune to find among the author's early papers', Collingwood explained.[3] We are reminded of his qualifications for writing about Ruskin and art. He may not have had so acute a mind as his former collaborator Alexander Wedderburn, and he lacked E. T. Cook's historical and bibliographical expertise. But Collingwood was Ruskin's neighbour and associate; while acting as Ruskin's secretary he had access to his manuscripts; he was himself an artist: and his instinct was to describe human experience in philosophical terms. Collingwood's thoughtful book reflects these aspects of his discipleship. It scarcely notices the practicalities of work in sketchbook or studio, for it is designed as a tribute to Ruskin's literary teachings about art. The sort of class that Lilias Trotter enjoyed was not Collingwood's concern, though over the years he himself had known many such lessons.

Like so many of Ruskin's girl pupils, Lilias was a gifted amateur from a prosperous middle-class background. Another group of artists was instructed in rather different ways. They were people who worked for Ruskin and the Guild of St George, principally in recording early Italian art. A third category of artists might be mentioned here. Ruskin made sporadic attempts to teach or influence independent professionals. Burne-Jones, still a treasured friend, Watts, Leighton, Holman Hunt and other prominent artists he met only occasionally. While they felt his criticisms, or his praise, Ruskin cannot be said to have taught them. He did attempt to instruct his friend Stacy Marks in the proper way of painting birds, but without really expecting to be heeded; for 'Marco', as Ruskin and all the other guests at his St John's Wood house called him, was famous in the world and knew very well what he was about. Marks had earned his living, and bought his home, as an entirely dependable artist with a set repertoire. The genial, sensible and contentedly professional Marks had known Kate Greenaway since she was a girl. Marks recognised that she had a special talent, one which would bring her even greater rewards than those she had so far enjoyed (which of course included her new house in Frognal), and he advised her not to change her style in an attempt to please Ruskin. Kate was aware that she could delight the old critic with her drawings of pretty girls, but she was never sure how to proceed when he asked her to do something else, and on occasion she was upset by his instructions. For a number of reasons it was well that proposed collaborations between Ruskin and Kate Greenaway came to little. She had already provided a drawing, of a girl in a bonnet, for 'Rosie Vale', the last letter of *Fors Clavigera*, and hinted to Ruskin that she might illustrate *Præterita*. Wisely, Ruskin did not encourage this plan. Kate designed frocks for the May Queen festivities at Whitelands College; but her only published collaboration with Ruskin was to add four illustrations to his new edition of *Dame Wiggins of Lee*, issued by George Allen in October of 1885.

As we learn from *Præterita*, the tale of Dame Wiggins had been among the volumes which made up 'my calf milk of books' and she had been part of a puppet show devised at Herne Hill by the ten-year-old Ruskin in 1829.[4] At Brantwood the retired professor had the manuscript of his juvenile 'The Puppet Show: or Amusing Characters for Children'. It is of 30 leaves, contains 57 drawings and at some point was bound in leather.[5] Ruskin must have looked out his early puppet show writings when preparing the early chapters of his autobiography. Memories of his early days might intermingle with Kate Greenaway's visions of girlhood, or so he imagined when inviting her to Brantwood for the summer. In fact this conjunction helped to break his rational mind for the fourth time. Other summer visitors had disturbed Ruskin's mental equilibrium. First came Joan Severn and Sara Anderson, accompanied by Clennie and the younger Severn children. For nearly a fortnight Ruskin was happy in their company, only seldom irritated. Then came Maria La Touche, for whom a summer visit to Brantwood was now a regular pleasure of her older life. In this year she brought her granddaughter, Rose's niece, who had been baptised Florence Rose but was always known as Rose. Here was a bright girl who reminded Ruskin of the grave, and of much else. Emily, Rose La Touche's elder sister, had died in 1867. She had left her husband Bernard Ward desolated by his loss and not quite capable of bringing up a daughter. Rose Ward had therefore spent most of her childhood at Harristown, amid the griefs and tensions of that peculiar Anglo-Irish estate. We can imagine her, as Ruskin must have done, observing her grandfather at his stern prayers; or worrying about her uncle Percy, a drunkard and a sportsman, waiting to inherit; or talking to her helpless, vague grandmother, who was only happy in her gardens, and therefore could not be happy in wintertime. As Maria La Touche had already told Joan Severn, this Rose was 'a delightful child — but I don't find that she has any talent for anything, tho' full of intelligence & a wonderful natural tact & discretion — & such a perfect temper — & she takes no sort of interest in *herself* — whether her clothes, or her "inner consciousness". This is, I think, a singular blessing — . . .'[6]

Maria was hinting that Rose Ward did not resemble her aunt Rose La Touche. Ruskin, of course, looked for similarities between the dead girl whom had wished to marry and the girl he now met, at Coniston station, on 15 July. The arrival of 'Lacerta' was troubling enough. That she should have been accompanied by an Irish girl called Rose threw Ruskin into a fit of mournful excitement. The few days before he broke down may be traced in his diary. The journal shows that he had already been looking for 'signs' from Rose as he worked on the part of *Præterita* that described *Dame Wiggins of Lee* and other childhood reading and writing. On 16 July Ruskin and Rose Ward 'gathered the first of my wild strawberry bank together'. On 18 July Ruskin encountered one of his 'teaching days',[7] by which the diary means that mystic messages came to his mind. That night he was sleepless. The next day George Baker and his wife came to Brantwood, so Ruskin was reminded of his duties to St George. Another guest was Kate Greenaway, who was set to illustrate the story of Dame Wiggins. Just after Kate had settled into her work Ruskin's mind collapsed. Joan explained to Charles Eliot Norton what had happened. 'He evidently got rather excited in the autobiography', she wrote, 'and I think puzzled what to say, and what not! — then he got off his sleep, more and more, and new ideas poured into his poor brain, and less and less could *he* realise the danger. New projects were daily developed — people asked to come — and daily a sort of bell ringing all out of tune with Kate Greenaway and Mrs La Touche here — both contrary, and exciting elements.'[8]

As before, the onset of madness was signalled by imperious commands, most but not all directed toward the servants, and furious reactions if the orders were not immediately obeyed. Joan, terrified, asked the guests to leave. Ruskin ordered them not to go. Maria La Touche and Rose Ward went back to Ireland. Kate Greenaway stayed for a little while. Then Arthur Severn and the elder Severn children arrived at Brantwood to find Ruskin mad. Kind neighbours, the Marshalls of Monk Coniston, took in the Severns and Clennie. Nurses were brought for the demented Ruskin. Sara Anderson comforted Joan and looked after the correspondence; and for some three months Brantwood was sealed from the world.

Little is recorded of this illness, though it was afterwards remembered as more frightful than any of the three previous breakdowns. Joan was helped by the thought that Ruskin's state might not be permanent. There seemed to be a pattern in the approach of madness, the high delirium, the periods of total silence, then a gradual return to human understanding. From notes kept by Kate Greenaway, to whom Joan wrote with daily news, we gather that Ruskin first came downstairs on 19 August, therefore about a month after his breakdown, that he was first taken for a drive on 26 August and on 28 August was well enough to be 'out in garden alone'.[9] Ruskin was able to write some little notes by the beginning of September, to such a person as Katie Macdonald; but most of his correspondence was now dictated to his amanuenses Joan Severn and Sara Anderson. This explains the first sentence of this pathetic letter to the founder of the Friends of Living Creatures:

> My very darling Katie, —
>
> I must thank you for all your sweetness with my own hand. I wish I could tell you I was better — the chief sorrow of this suddenly overwhelming illness is in the sorrow of those who loved me and had begun to find help in me.
>
> I send you back your rosebud with the most grateful and tender kiss that can be. You may at least remember with gladness and throughout your life how kind you were to your old and sick friend.
>
> Yours most deeply grateful J. Ruskin.[10]

Only a few more scraps of correspondence are preserved from this convalescence. Ruskin wrote to Charles Eliot Norton and resumed his exchange of opinions with Professor Oliver Lodge, a scientist with an interest in spiritualism. These letters are all sad. Not until the approach of Christmas did Ruskin's informal writing recover any verve. On 27 November he sent a delightful letter to Susie Beever for her birthday, imagining 'celestial teas'[11] together in a future life. To Mary Gladstone, recently wed, he wrote, 'don't you know I hate girls marrying curates? You must come directly and play me some lovely tunes — it's the last chance you'll have of doing anything to please me, for I don't like married women; I like sibyls and children and vestals and so on. Not that I mean to quarrel with you, if you'll come now and make it up . . .'[12] Behind this banter we note how Ruskin's mind continually returned to the themes of death, marriage and his quarrels with orthodox religion. He felt that he was near to death, yet still had a longing for 'sibyls and children and vestals and so on', a subject he hoped to treat in a future number of *Præterita*. This would of course have decribed Winnington School.

During the months of Ruskin's incapacity, between July of 1885 and January of 1886, *Præterita* had continued to appear. Thus the world at large was given an impression of its author's good health and benign disposition. However, these chapters had been written long before. When Ruskin began to write again, around October of 1885, he was far from sure that he would ever be able to finish his autobiography, and despondently concluded that his work in the world was over.

★ ★ ★ ★

This work included Ruskin's activities on behalf of St George. With his illness of 1885 the Guild of St George did not come to a complete halt. We may trust that it was maintained by individual members in their separate ways. Egbert Rydings continued to encourage hand spinning on the Isle of Man, Albert Fleming interested himself in spinning and other rural industries in the Lake District, Julia Firth could look with satisfaction on her translation of *Ulric the Farm Servant*, published in 1885, George Thompson of Huddersfield ran his woollen business on co-operative lines, Fanny Talbot thought of opening a school, to be conducted on Guild principles, in Barmouth; Blanche Atkinson attempted to become a writer, and moved from her parental home in Cheshire to Barmouth, where she discussed new forms of philanthropy with Mrs Talbot. Furthermore, the museum at Sheffield was by now an accepted part of the didactic culture of south Yorkshire, while George Baker actively (though vainly) sought subscriptions for the proposed museum at Bewdley. These endeavours, and no doubt a number more by other members of the Guild, may not have had much impact on early modern Britain; but they show that the Guild's spirit had not been extinguished by its Master's collapse.[13] In another respect, however, Guild work came to an end. A number of its servants were cast off or forgotten. These were the artists who had been set to work by Ruskin and were paid from his own purse. Almost always, they had made copies or studies for St George's purposes: that is to say, for the Guild's museum or for use in education, whether in 'St George's schools', or occasionally at Oxford, or for Ruskin's books. Few of these artists have found a firm place in biographical studies, for they were assistants, often lived abroad, saw Ruskin rarely and played only a minor role in his life. They none the less were part of the fiefdom of his imagination. Many of them have been briefly mentioned in the present biography. Now that Ruskin's personal direction of his Guild had ended, their lives and works may be briefly (and alphabetically) summarised.[14]

Angelo Alessandri, whose dates are not known but who was a young man in the 1870s and probably died in the 1930s, met Ruskin in Venice in the winter of 1876–77. He was instructed to copy Carpaccio, and this work occupied him between 1877 and 1879. At the same time Ruskin asked Alessandri to give his attention to Turner. Until 1885 he was regularly employed by Ruskin, who commissioned copies of Tintoretto in 1880–81, and subsequently sent him from his native Venice to copy Botticelli and Perugino in Rome.

John Wharlton Bunney (1827–82) belonged to the first generation of Ruskin's students and assistants, for he attended the Working Men's College between 1854 and 1858, then worked for a short while at Smith, Elder. In the late 1850s he occasionally showed studies from nature at the Royal Academy. Ruskin sent Bunney to the Alps in 1859 and to Italy in the early 1860s. He settled permanently in Italy after about 1865, living in Florence and after 1871 in Venice. Although Bunney had an independent career as an artist, he was first and foremost Ruskin's assistant. His master appreciated Bunney's gift for watercolours recording medieval architecture. Ruskin commissioned his large study of the façade of St Mark's cathedral. This work (unusual among Ruskin's commissions, for it is an oil painting) occupied at least 600 sittings between 1877 and 1882. Whistler is said to have attached a note to Bunney's back as he sat at his easel. It read 'I am blind'. Relations between Bunney and Ruskin were not always easy. Bunney maintained a wide correspondence with other Ruskin dependants, and with others who knew Ruskin but were not his dependants.

Arthur Burgess (d. 1887), dismissed by Bunney, perhaps with some professional jealousy, as 'a most dreary fellow without the least energy', was much appreciated by Ruskin, as we learn from the tribute published in *The Century Guild Hobby Horse* after Burgess's death. One of Ruskin's last pieces of published writing, this account may be compared both with *Præterita* and with other long, peculiar obituaries which assessed the painter Frederick Walker (1876) and his editor W. H. Harrison (1878). True to St George's principles, Ruskin was inclined to describe the lives of the humble more than those of the great. This preference had its effect on *Præterita*, a book which seldom shows interest in the mighty figures of Ruskin's times; and the Burgess obituary, which resembles *Præterita* in tone, is also a self-portrait of its writer. Burgess's character — in Ruskin's estimation — resembled his own, at least in the 'modes of overstrain which afflicted alike Arthur Burgess and myself in our later days . . . in writing so much as this implies of my own epitaph with my friend's, I am thankful to say, securely for both of us, that we did what we could thoroughly, and that all we did together will remain trustworthy and useful — uncontradicted, and unbettered — till it is forgotten'. Burgess, a wood engraver by training, first met Ruskin in 1860. In 1869 Ruskin took him to Verona to study the Scala tombs. There he made a clay model of the Castelbarco tomb, a project which suggests that he was by nature a sculptor rather than a watercolourist. While Ruskin taught at Oxford in the 1870s he paid Burgess a salary for preparing lecture diagrams and materials for the drawing schools. His woodcuts and wood engravings for Ruskin and the Guild may be found in *Proserpina*, *Love's Meinie*, *Ariadne Florentina* and *Aratra Pentilici*. He visited Ruskin at Brantwood 'several times . . . the last happy walk we had together was to the top of the crags of the south-west side of the village of Coniston'. In 1880 Burgess directed photography of the west front of Rouen cathedral and he sometimes drew, to Ruskin's satisfaction, in black and white chalk, taking his motifs from such photographs.

Raffaele Carloforti (d. ?1904) is mentioned in *Fors Clavigera* of April 1876 as 'a youth whom I am maintaining in art study at Venice'. Carloforti knew the Venetian citizens who were most concerned with its ancient buildings, Giacomo Boni and Count Zorzi. His work for Ruskin was mainly in the study of sculpture. Each of his surviving sheets is inscribed to Ruskin as by 'Il suo Discipulo Ubidiente, Raffaello Carloforti'. He was in touch with Ruskin as lately as 1888.

William Hackstoun (d. 1925). The name is Scottish. Hackstoun sent examples of his work to Ruskin in 1878, and thereafter received some instruction by letter. In the 'Master's Report' of 1881 Ruskin announced that Hackstoun was to work for the Guild 'in carrying out some of the projected works on Swiss and French landscape . . .' He was in northern France, paid for by Ruskin, in 1883. Joan Severn disliked Hackstoun, and this may be the reason why he was not employed after that date.

Alexander Macdonald (1847–1921). His functions in the Oxford drawing schools have been described above. Only one of his drawings, a mineralogical study, is recorded in the Guild's Sheffield collection. Ruskin obviously thought that Macdonald's work should be confined to Oxford.

Charles Fairfax Murray (1849–1919). Murray first encountered Ruskin in 1872, mainly through the good offices of Edward Burne-Jones. Ruskin paid for Murray's visit to Italy in 1873, when he made copies of frescos in Siena and Rome. Since he worked as a copyist for Ruskin all through the 1870s Murray must be counted as an assistant. However, he was also an independent artist, a connoisseur and a shrewd collector. Differences about financial matters led to an end of his relations with Ruskin in 1883. His most telling work for the Guild of St George was a purchase. As reported in *Fors Clavigera* of July 1877, 'for £100 of the £150 last paid to Mr Murray, I have also secured, with his assistance, a picture of extreme value that has been hitherto overlooked in the Manfrini gallery; and clearly kept for us by Fors, as the exactly right picture on the possession of which to found our Sheffield school of art. It is a Madonna by Verrocchio, the master of Leonardo da Vinci, of Lorenzo di Credi, and of Perugino, and the grandest metal-worker of Italy.' This painting, the Guild's most valuable asset, was sold in 1975 and is now in the National Gallery of Scotland, Edinburgh. A secretive man, Murray left no record of his acquaintance with Ruskin, nor indeed of his many dealings with other art experts in Italy, France and England.

Henry Roderick Newman (1843–1917) was a successful independent artist but in some measure Ruskin's assistant because he carried out so many commissions for the Guild. He was brought up in New York, exhibited there and taught art before moving to Europe in 1870. He lived in Florence and then in Venice. Another American artist, Charles Moore, showed Ruskin Newman's work in 1877 and the two men met in England in 1879. By 1882 Newman had settled permanently in Florence, and in this year he introduced Ruskin to Francesca Alexander. Newman's Florentine home is said to have had the nature of a salon.

Frank Randal (*c.* 1858–?). No fewer than 137 works by Randal are recorded in the collection of the Guild of St George, but he remains an obscure figure. Randal probably first worked for Ruskin in 1881. He was sent to France and then to Italy, with instructions to put himself under the tuition of Angelo Alessandri. Ruskin employed him until at least the spring of 1887. Randal subsequently worked for S. C. Cockerell and the Society for the Preservation of Memorials of Ancient Buildings. He wrote the introduction to T. J. Wise's edition of *Ruskin's Letters to Ernest Chesneau* (1894).

Thomas Matthews Rooke (1842–1942). Like Fairfax Murray, Rooke came to Ruskin from the firm of Morris and Co., and with the encouragement of Edward Burne-Jones, who was an influence on his small, jewelled watercolours and paintings. Rooke exhibited at the Royal Academy, the Grosvenor Gallery and the New Gallery and might have had an independent career had he not entered Ruskin's employ in 1879. Rooke was then sent to record aspects of St Mark's in Venice, and in 1884 made copies of mosaics there before going on to record mosaics at Ravenna. Until 1886 Rooke worked in Switzerland and France, notably at Chartres, with return visits to Florence, and was still receiving a monthly wage from St George in 1887. Like Randal, he subsequently worked for S. C. Cockerell and the Society for the Preservation of Memorials of Ancient Buildings. He was Burne-Jones's studio assistant from 1869 to 1898 and recorded his conversation.

William Ward (1829–1908). Another veteran of the drawing classes at the Working Men's College, Ward showed enough ability to take classes, and for some years Ruskin sent him pupils whom he did not wish to teach himself. Ward specialised in copying Turner. In the late 1870s and early 1880s he helped his old friend George Allen with the publication of photographs illustrating *The Bible of Amiens*. In 1878, on the occasion of the exhibition of Ruskin's Turners at the Fine Art Society, Ruskin commented as follows on Turner originals and Ward's copies-cum-facsimiles: '. . . precious drawings, which can only be represented at all in engraving by entire alteration of their treatment and abandonment of their finest purposes. I feel this so strongly that I have given my best attention, during upwards of ten years, to training a copyist to perfect fidelity in rendering the work of Turner; and have now succeeded in enabling him to produce facsimiles so close as to look like replicas — fascimiles which I must sign with my own name and his . . . to prevent their being sold for real Turner vignettes.'[15]

* * * *

Many other artists did occasional work for Ruskin, who also made use of the services of etchers, engravers, secretaries, model-makers, bookbinders, framers, carpenters, masons, craftsmen skilled in polishing gems, caretakers, general labourers, gardeners and photographers. Joan Severn wished to reduce the number of such employees, so was glad that a number of them disappeared as a result of Ruskin's illness of 1885. To her relief, the number of drawings and watercolours acquired by Ruskin and the Guild had almost come to a halt by the end of that year. However, Ruskin now began to buy more and more books and manuscripts. Some of the first letters from his convalescence of 1885 are to booksellers. We have noticed Ruskin's relations with F. S. Ellis. His business with Bernard Quaritch was more substantial and lasted for longer, indeed for some twenty years. Letters are recorded between the two men from 1867 to 1888. Latterly, they illustrate the grievous decline of Ruskin's mind and his reckless desire to possess books that he could not afford. In the earlier years of their friendship Ruskin had looked at Quaritch's catalogues with more discrimination and restraint. In the late 1860s and early 1870s we find him buying books about Irish manuscripts, old botany books, Bibles, a twelfth-century psalter, an Ovid, an unidentified Holbein book: all quite carefully chosen and sometimes sent back to Quaritch after inspection. Ruskin occasionally sold books from his own library to Quaritch and in 1873 briefly thought of selling him the copyright 'of all my books published before 1870', a proposal which must have alarmed George Allen, if he ever heard about it. Ruskin's dealings with Quaritch were private, even secret, for Joan did not understand what he was buying and Ruskin had no reason to tell her how much he was spending. All Joan knew was that parcels of old books often arrived at Brantwood and that chats with Bernard Quaritch were a happy diversion when Ruskin was in London.

Like F. S. Ellis, Quaritch was often asked to bid for Ruskin at auctions. Therefore Quaritch sent him notices of sales as well as his own firm's catalogues. Ruskin, never an enemy of the telegram and usually happy when in the *Jumping Jenny*, would write out his bids and dispatch them by telegraph after rowing across the lake to the Coniston post office. In this agreeable fashion his collection was further augmented, though when buying at auction he did not have the opportunity to inspect books before bidding. This scarcely mattered, for he could trust his agent. Quaritch was the only bookseller who fully matched Ruskin's antiquarian concerns. Not only was he a learned man and a linguist. He also held an immense stock. It is estimated that, at the end of the 1870s, he had some 200,000 books for sale. Quaritch sent Ruskin his catalogues with marked personal suggestions. For instance, he knew that Ruskin would always be attracted by illustrated antique volumes on birds and plants. Some of his wares appear in *Love's Meinie* and *Proserpina*, as well as in other of Ruskin's publications, for it is possible that the receipt of a parcel of books from Quaritch's Piccadilly office had set off some train of thought in *Fors Clavigera* or *Bibliotheca Pastorum*. Now that Ruskin, by Christmas of 1885, was writing only his autobiography, he bought rare books as a substitute for writing learned ones. As he did so, he could feel that he was still building the museum of St George. So he was. However, many precious volumes disappeared; or never found their way to Sheffield and were sold from Brantwood after Ruskin's death; or were sold back to Quaritch during the period 1886–89, when Ruskin's personal finances had crashed to the ground.

★ ★ ★ ★

Ruskin's diary had fallen silent on 20 July of 1885 and was not resumed until 21 December, although there are a few notes for *Præterita* dated 18 October. By the last week of October he had once again taken up his autobiography. On 8 November he was able to tell George Allen that 'I have sent 6th Praet today, passed for press, and will send copy for 7th as soon as this is out . . .'[15] Because Ruskin had written so much of the book before he collapsed in July, the publication of *Præterita* was more or less continuous.

However, it is clear that the illness of 1885 changed the nature of his autobiography. There are eccentric divagations in its tone. Factual mistakes are even more frequent. Little is remembered with pleasure and the overall mood is more desolate than ever before. *Præterita*'s publishing programme enables us to match successive chapters of the book with Ruskin's emotions and mental health as he wrote about the past. The chapters completed before the 1885 illness are those which precede Chapter V of Volume II, 'The Simplon', published on 28 October. The new chapters Ruskin announced to Allen at the beginning of November were 'The Campo Santo', published on 17 November, and 'Macugnaga', published on 4 December. These numbers were written quickly enough and Ruskin wished to 'get on', a phrase he often used about his composition of *Præterita*. However, the mood of the chapters is despairing rather than purposeful. In 'The Campo Santo', led on by memories of the tomb of Ilaria di Caretto and the Pisan frescos of 'The Triumph of Death, as Homer, Virgil, and Horace thought of Death', Ruskin's manner is almost posthumous, as though he were meditating not on the past but on a previous existence:

> And the days that began in the cloister of the Campo Santo usually ended by my getting upon the roof of Santa Maria della Spina, and sitting in the sunlight that transfused the warm marble of its pinnacles, till the unabated brightness went down beyond the arches of the Pont-a-Mare, — the few footsteps and voices of the twilight fell silent in the streets, and the city and her mountain stood mute as a dream, beyond the soft eddying of Arno.[16]

In 'The Campo Santo' Ruskin invoked his Italian travels in 1845. 'Macugnaga' is about the same continental summer. In December of 1885 *Præterita* was already quite a long book, but it had not taken the history of its author's life beyond his carlier days. Indeed, *Præterita* as a whole is about Ruskin's life before his father died. It will be recalled that the 1845 tour was the first that Ruskin had taken without his parents' company. Now Ruskin set himself to recall John James and Margaret Ruskin as they had been forty years before, and his memories were confused, bitter and contrite. The result was the next chapter of *Præterita*, 'The State of Denmark'. In this number Ruskin does not 'get on'. On the contrary, he halts or reverses his narrative. He regards himself as a child and is scornful of his own achievements. As in other parts of the book, one is scarcely given the impression that Ruskin had ever had a public career, though in his Denmark Hill days he had become one of the prominent writers and thinkers of his time. Instead, 'The State of Denmark' concludes with childish rhymes, the 'Pig-Wiggian chaunts' which (as we have seen) led to Ruskin's use of baby-talk when writing to Joan, a private language also used in speech when she comforted him as his mind returned to the world from bouts of delirium.

'The State of Denmark' was completed and sent to Henry Jowett on 23 December 1885. Ruskin's uneasy feelings about his writing may be gauged from a letter to Jane Simon three days earlier:

> . . . It will be of invaluable service to me that you tell me, as you find time and power — anything that comes into your head or heart about my Father and Mother — of whom I knew scarcely

anything but the foibles; and never valued the affection. My own cruelty to them is now altogether frightful to me in looking back.

Very little of the deeper calamities of all that chanced and mischanced to us, will be shown in *Præterita*. It will not the least be 'Confessions' — nor even, in pleasant things — far analysed — it will be what the public may be modestly told to their own benefit — no more. But it is quite *vital* to my doing even so much as this rightly — that *you* should tell me what you knew and felt about them both.

I shall not alter a word in the already written chap VIII that occurs about my mother, and there is a good deal, but in Chapter IX, *with your leave*, I shall give your letter nearly entire, only mind, that write with the certainty of my never using anything or words you do not wish . . .[17]

John and Jane Simon had of course been dear friends of the elder Ruskins, and it is unfortunate that we have no reminiscence from Jane of their life at Denmark Hill. She did, however, send some other material to Ruskin, and this was published in the collection of documents he called *Dilecta*. By the beginning of 1886 Ruskin had decided that his autobiography needed a companion volume. *Dilecta*'s subtitle is therefore 'Correspondence, Diary Notes, and Extracts from Books, illustrating *Præterita*'. Jane Simon's contribution is her dramatic and well known account of meeting Turner on a train in 1843. They travelled through a storm, and she believed that this was the origin of his painting *Rain, Steam and Speed.*[18] *Dilecta* as first issued, in September of 1886, contained much other Turner material. This was supplied by Robert Leslie, the son of the Royal Academician C. R. Leslie, who had been a friend of Turner's and had also known John James Ruskin. For a while, *Dilecta* appeared to be a useful medium for the publication of documents bearing on Ruskin's family history, and elaborate plans were made for its separate issues. Alas, its publishing history is a short one. Three parts were published, the first in 1886, the second in 1887 and the third in 1900, after Ruskin's death. Ruskin had in fact prepared this third chapter for press in 1886, but the material was mislaid after his mental breakdown that summer. Its publication is owed to Alexander Wedderburn, one of his first acts as Ruskin's literary executor. The invention of *Dilecta* had solved one of Ruskin's problems in writing *Præterita*, which was to describe Turner without allowing the painter to dominate the book. Description of his parents raised other difficulties. In January of 1886 Ruskin was struggling with the next chapter of *Præterita*, 'The Feasts of the Vandals', by which title he perversely referred to dinner parties at Denmark Hill in the early 1840s. Ruskin's hesitations over this chapter might have been resolved if he had looked at his parents' correspondence. At Brantwood were more than 200 letters exchanged between John James and Margaret Ruskin in the early days of their marriage and the time of their son's youth. Ruskin did not consult them, though he knew where they were kept. He wanted to describe his parents; and yet the evidence seems to have been untouchable, as though a part of him wished not to approach the happy days of forty years before.

This family correspondence was known to W. G. Collingwood, who drew on it in *The Life and Work of John Ruskin*, published in 1893.[19] Collingwood began this book after 1889, when it was clear that *Præterita* would never be completed or even continued. But Ruskin's former secretary had been collecting materials for a biography, consciously or unconsciously, for many years. He therefore looked at the successive chapters with a special and critical interest, while other members of the Brantwood circle merely told the stricken old man how charmingly he was writing. Each number told Collingwood things that were not in Ruskin's published works and that he might not have heard in conversation. At the least, new chapters of the autobiography indicated some of the emphases that Ruskin placed on people and events. Yet it had always been in the nature of *Præterita* that emphases slip away from the reader, and are therefore less emphatic than one might have supposed.

Ruskin's ways of changing the subject had given exciting character to his mature major writing. In the later stages of *Præterita*, however, he appears to have abandoned his topics as a result of lassitude, forgetfulness or some deeper mental inability. Collingwood cannot have failed to see what was happening. From early 1886 Ruskin lost control over his autobiography as he lost control over his mind and life. 'The Feasts of the Vandals' may be said to mark the beginning of the decline of *Præterita*. In the circumstances, it is remarkable that Ruskin managed to issue a further seven chapters of the book. In each of these chapters there are passages that he alone could have written, sentences and paragraphs that clearly come from the pen of a master. At the same time, however, much of Ruskin's subject matter is trivial or inconsequential; he approaches subjects only to evade them, copies out entries from old volumes of diary, fails to explain who people are, and often seems to have lost all sense of a narrative. The reminiscences are beautiful. They are also disordered.

Entries in the journal for the earlier part of the year 1886 show that Ruskin was worried, short-tempered, sleepless, 'very sad and sulky and ill'.[20] On the other hand he was gladdened by spring weather and took pleasure in the correspondence generated by *Præterita*, especially when the mail brought him letters from Burne-Jones, Froude, Kate Greenaway, Robert Leslie and Maria La Touche, all enthusiasts of the book. Contacts with such friends helped Ruskin to write his autobiography, and he always felt relieved and thankful when each 'bit' of the book had been composed, as happened quite often, for the memoirs were written every day. Other work during the first half of 1886 was more agitating. Between 5 January and 28 June Ruskin sent nineteen letters to the press. Some were spontaneous. Others were elicited by editors and a number were in reply to critics of Ruskin's views. The first of this sequence of public letters was a temperate note on 'The Irish Question', sent without any particular purpose (apart from recommending Maria Edgeworth) to W. T. Stead, the editor of the *Pall Mall Gazette*. It happened that the *PMG*, in this month of January, had begun a public debate on the question 'Which Are the Hundred Best Books?' The idea had been picked up by the editorial desk after a lecture on this subject by Sir John Lubbock at the Working Men's College. Ruskin knew Lubbock, though not well. He had visited his home in 1883, when he was 'greatly pleased by finding Sir John Lubbock's library here as gay as a painted window with beautiful bindings'.[21] Lubbock's selection of books for the public was far less pleasing. Ruskin — the instigator and editor of *Bibliotheca Pastorum* — took his pen and inked out 'the rubbish and poison of Sir John's list'. The *PMG* printed these vigorous emendations in facsimile, and in subsequent numbers published three characteristic letters from Ruskin on the proper choice of books.[22]

Next there was a brief skirmish with the *Daily Telegraph*[23] before Ruskin returned to the pages of the *Pall Mall Gazette* with letters on the subjects of, *inter alia*, 'Modern Education', 'The Life of St Patrick', 'The Bible', 'The Crime of Debt' and 'Darwinism'. The series of letters ends with one headed 'Unobjectionable Theft':

> Sir, — You would wonder how many people have written to me from the neighbourhood of Sherwood Forest, and that of the Clachan of Aberfoil, to express their surprise that I don't object to thieving! Well, I *do* object to some sorts of it, but one can't speak all one's mind to Mr Spurgeon in ten minutes. I don't object to Orlando's coming in with his sword drawn and telling the Duke he shan't have any of his own dinner till Adam is served. But I do extremely object to Mr Forster's breaking into my own Irish servant's house, robbing him of thirteen pence weekly out of his

poor wages, and, besides, carrying off his four children for slaves half the day to play tunes on Wandering Willie's fiddle, instead of being about their father's business.

I am, Sir, your faithful servant, John Ruskin.[24]

The letter is dated 27 June. Two or perhaps three days later this Irish servant, Peter Baxter, had to telegraph the Severns at Herne Hill with the news that Ruskin's mind had failed yet again.

'I was quite unprepared for it,' Joan wrote to Charles Eliot Norton, 'which makes the shock and distress of it all the greater. I was at H. H. and came off at a moment's notice — and have now got everything into good working order — and a trained man nurse. The present phase is *most trying*, and consists in the vile abuse of Arthur and me — every crime we are accused of, including plots to murder him . . .'[25] Ruskin was often violent, and sprained his wrist while struggling with his nurse. For week after week he spoke nothing but nonsense. Joan was under great stress, but she had a team of helpers. They were doctors, nurses and intimates of the Brantwood circle. Sir William Gull advised her by letter, and he curbed Dr Parsons's tendency to give Ruskin chloral. Sara Anderson performed secretarial duties. Collingwood and Laurence Hilliard came to Brantwood every day and took it in turns to sit with Ruskin: during these attacks he was never left alone. For Collingwood the spectacle of a mind in complete disarray must have been doubly painful. He had formed a purpose in life: to understand and explain Ruskin's philosophy. Now he sat with the man whose writings he so admired and listened to his demented ravings.

Joan's personal distress was compounded by social embarrassment. Ever since Ruskin's first breakdown in 1878 Brantwood had been the subject of much local gossip and was popularly known as 'the madhouse'. Joan, a less neighbourly person than her cousin, had fewer friends in Coniston and its vicinity. She felt uneasy about village talk. Joan was also upset that Ruskin's illness had been reported in newspapers and that journalists had found their way to Brantwood. These newspaper reports brought extra correspondence to the Ruskin household, most of which was answered by Sara Anderson. When he had recovered, in mid-August, Ruskin himself replied to some of the enquiring letters. We find him writing to one concerned person:

The actual illnesses of which accounts, to my great regret and inconvenience, go to the papers, are fits of, sometimes trance, sometimes waking delirium, which last their time, like a fit of the gout, and then leave me, weaker in limb and nervous energy, of course, but quite as 'well' in the proper sense of the word, as I was before — only, with each fit, more cautious of plaguing, or even interesting, myself about things in general, and more grateful for letters expressing, as yours does, a sense of good in my past work . . .[26]

This letter to an admirer was typical. Ruskin was becoming used to the idea that he had 'fits', and wrote almost carelessly about the horror of his attacks. 'My poor old Rose', he told Norton,

. . . came alive again to lecture me, and came over from Ireland and woke me suddenly in the night with a candle! — Then she took command in the house — but I thought everyone was frightened of her — because she sometimes wore a death's head instead of her own! — Then I got up to heaven with her — but was presently sent down again, and lost in more confused horrors of earthly Death than I ever dreamed yet. As I came back to myself I became more violent than usual! — fought all my gardeners and broke windows and tumblers enough for Alnaschar himself. My wrist is sprained — and my ribs sore — but for the rest I'm pretty well myself again (the gardeners rather dilapidated!) — and I'm going on with *Præterita* rather prettily . . .[27]

So *Præterita* went on, but Ruskin now decided to abandon *Proserpina*, a book he had begun in 1879. In its last paragraph we find

Life is really quite disgustingly too short; one has only got one's materials together by the time one can no more use them. But let me say, once for all, in closing this fragment of work old and new, that I beg my friends very earnestly never to mind paragraphs about me in the public papers. My illnesses, so called, are only brought on by vexation or worry (for which said friends are often themselves in no small degree answerable), and leave me, after a few weeks of wandering thoughts, much the same as I was before, — only a little sadder and wiser! — probably, if I am spared till I am seventy, I shall be as sad and wise as I ever wish to be, and will try to keep so, to the end.

Brantwood,
10th August 1886.[28]

Joan was understandably vexed by such a casual attitude to the breakdowns, and was soon to be much more disturbed when Ruskin reverted to an autocratic attitude to his household. Previously, tantrums about being 'master in my own house' had belonged to periods of delirium. Now, while relatively sane, Ruskin wrote to Joan in Herne Hill that

> . . . things are *not* to be on their old footing here — ever again. If you come here, you must come to do whatever is in your power to please *me* and not only yourselves. I mean to be master henceforward in this house, while I live in it — and to have the things done that I wish to be done — whether of play or lessons — by every one whom I ask to stay in it.
>
> — By you — your husband — and your children — most certainly & chiefly — And if you do not choose to please me, — you had better all of you stay in London. I am not yet so paralytic as to need more looking after than my servants are capable of. — Ever your — Di Pa.[29]

Rather than send a mild reply, Joan thought it best to return to Brantwood immediately. She once again took control of the household and brought her cousin to order. First she took him on a short holiday to the nearby seaside town of Heysham, a place Ruskin loathed. Next, Joan attempted to regulate and diminish the number of visitors to Brantwood. A contest of wills was bound to develop. Ruskin thought that he could invite anyone to his home. Joan was certain that he should be kept quiet and that some visitors were a danger to his mind. In this category she placed all young women, anyone from Oxford and such a person as the controversial James Froude. She knew Carlyle's biographer to be disliked by Charles Eliot Norton; and since she trusted Norton and his advice she felt suspicious of this honest friend. Froude and his wife had been given *carte blanche* to stay at Brantwood 'whenever they like', as Ruskin had firmly written to Joan, and he had recently renewed his invitation. The Froudes arrived at Coniston just after Ruskin's visit to Heysham and stayed for four days. Carlyle's two best disciples now met for the last time, and Froude saw how lamentably his comrade's intellect and charm had declined. When they had 'Carlyle talk', the two men were in accord, as so often before. However, as Joan told Norton, Ruskin 'certainly didn't enjoy Froude's visit, and was always either disagreeing with him or put out with him . . . But of course the poor Coz gets less and less able for society and exertion of either brain or body . . .'[30] It is true that Ruskin was often cross with the people around him. On the day the Froudes left, to 'go to the — deuce, or wherever they have arranged to go', as the diary uncharacteristically puts it, Ruskin had an unpleasant dispute with Arthur Severn.[31] Perhaps trivial in itself, the episode shows how Brantwood was passing to the Severns, while the aged and cantankerous

Professor spoilt their enjoyments. Among Arthur's innovations was the Brantwood tennis court. Thus Ruskin lost one of his lawns to a modern and fashionable game. Walking past Arthur, Clennie and another girl who was a friend of the Severns, Agnes Greig, Ruskin watched their play and made sardonic comments. The girls were confused. Arthur asked Ruskin to go away. Ruskin was furious but obeyed. Later, the matter was smoothed over, but never quite forgotten. Hostilities between the two men became ever more common. On 9 January 1887 the diary reads: 'Fierce quarrel with Arfie — final in many respects.'[32]

* * * *

By this New Year of 1887 Ruskin had published twenty-one parts of *Præterita*. The autobiography had become his only occupation apart from a little editorial work on *Christ's Folk in the Apennines*.[33] On New Year's Day he recorded 'I've done ten numbers this past year, and nearly an eleventh, but little else'.[34] However, he continued to entertain guests and rearranged things in the house as though to emphasise that Brantwood remained within his ownership.

Ruskin's correspondence also increased. Sometimes he wrote two dozen letters a day. Most of them were pleasant notes to friends, members of the Guild or other admirers. One sequence of letters, however, was entirely negative in its tone and ultimate effect. From January of 1886 to late May of 1887 Ruskin taunted and berated his former friends and colleagues in Oxford. His drawing schools were still in nominal operation, though they were scarcely attended, and Ruskin bore their costs. Principally, he paid Alexander Macdonald's salary. In October of 1886 Ruskin attempted to dismiss Macdonald and to replace him with T. M. Rooke. This was opposed by Acland and Liddell, who were trustees of the drawing schools. At the same time, in another campaign directed at the University, Ruskin claimed that various drawings belonging to Oxford, or lodged at Oxford, had not been properly conserved. In October of 1886 he wrote to his solicitor Henry Mackrell:

> Will you please go down to Oxford now, at your earliest convenience and put yourself in communication with the Dean of Ch.Ch. and Sir H. Acland respecting the drawings by Turner in the Taylor buildings — I am at issue about the mode of their preservation, with the Trustees, and think this a right and now necessary time for taking what action I may . . . I want if possible to get all back that I gave myself and to obtain a University decree for the

better preservation of that which the University before possessed of its own . . .[35]

This appeal to a legal mind had some benefits. Acland and Liddell preferred to deal with the sane, polite Mackrell rather than with Ruskin. But there were long delays in the negotiations and Ruskin sent increasingly heated letters to Liddell. Some of them, clearly written in a half-crazed state of mind, were held back by Joan. There was a further problem. Ruskin wished to repossess as many drawings as possible, but his possessions or gifts had been confusingly catalogued. In order to determine what belonged to Ruskin, or perhaps to the Guild of St George, or had already been accepted as a gift by the University, or was a promised gift, or a gift renominated as a loan, it would have been necessary to compile a completely new catalogue of all materials which had come under Ruskin's hand during his connection with the University in the two previous decades. Nobody could have made such a catalogue but Ruskin himself; yet no party wished Ruskin to return to Oxford to undertake such a work. At the end of the day 111 examples were returned to Ruskin — or rather to the Severns — including 55 of his own drawings and sketches and others by Burne-Jones, Arthur Burgess, Albert Goodwin, Kate Greenaway, Leighton, Prout and Turner, among other artists. The cataloguing and indeed the location of all these works remains to be established.[36]

While this campaign of annoyance to his former university was in progress, Ruskin wrote the later chapters of the second volume of *Præterita*. 'Crossmount' was finished toward the end of January, while Ruskin had two house guests at Brantwood, the cousins Lizzie and Marion Watson. Marion appears as 'Tenzo', her nickname, in Ruskin's diary and correspondence. The girls' visit was opposed by Joan Severn, for she feared that Ruskin would be over-excited. Yet he was cheered by their company and was a delightful host, as we gather from Lizzie's later reminiscences, published in a number of magazines under her married name L. Allen Harker.[37] Ruskin's moods had become totally unpredictable. They are also difficult to reconstruct, for on one and the same day he might give different reports of his feelings.

Sombre but probably thrilling accounts of Ruskin's opinions were given to a new young friend. Sydney Carlyle Cockerell, in later life the Director of the Fitzwilliam Museum in Cambridge, was twenty years old in 1887. He was a clerk in his grandfather's business, but held idealistic views that extended far beyond the counting house. Cockerell's hobby was conchology, and he began his acquaintance with Ruskin by sending him shells. He already knew William Morris, and on 26 March 1886 had ventured to write to Ruskin to ask whether his and Morris's political views were in accord. Ruskin had then replied: 'Of course I am a socialist — of the most stern sort — but I am also a Tory of the sternest sort. I am silent at present because no one could understand a word I said. But see *Fors Clavigera* . . . Morris is perfectly right in all he says — only he shouldn't *say* it. But do all he can in his own art'.[38]

Now, in early spring of 1887, Cockerell arrived at Brantwood and heard more of Ruskin's opinions, which he noted and later published. Much of this record is worth repeating:

> We were soon talking of men that I admired. Morris was 'beaten gold', he said, 'a great rock with a little moss on it perhaps'. His 'love of Turner, primroses and little girls' had prevented his ever being Morris's close friend, but he had a great reverence for him and his views . . . He was 'sorry to be so nearly done for'. He was 'Christian in ethics, like all true men, but he could not but believe that death was the end of all things'.
>
> . . . I asked about his autobiography *Præterita*. He was at work on the last two chapters of the second volume. There were sad things, his father's death and so on, to be told of in the third volume. The thought of these pained him and brought on his brain attacks — he feared that they might 'end in palsy'.[39]

Cockerell was acquainted with Octavia Hill, who had worked with his father in philanthropic projects. Therefore,

> Towards the end of this second day's visit I felt so much at home with him that I was emboldened to allude to his lamentable quarrel with Octavia Hill . . . Miss Hill had felt the onslaught keenly, disastrously. My father's death and other troubles coming at the same time, her health broke down and it took her many months to recover. 'Will you not now forgive Miss Hill' I urged, though in my heart I felt that forgiveness was at least as much due from her as from him. 'I never forgive', he answered firmly; 'it was too great an injury — And yet I *can* forgive', he added after a pause, 'I forgave the parents who denied me the girl I loved and invited them to Brantwood . . .'[40]

Cockerell was a happy young man when he left, conscious that Ruskin had liked his frank and enthusiastic manner. He also had an invitation to return the next month with his sister Olive, and to stay in Brantwood itself rather than in lodgings. So Sydney and Olive came back together, but did not see Ruskin, who was confined to his bedroom, dumb with grief. On the 13 March terrible news had come to Ruskin's home. Laurence Hilliard had died of pleurisy while on a yachting holiday in the Aegean. Ruskin was able to receive 'Lollie's' sisters Connie and Ethel on 15 March, but then collapsed. There was an autobiographical element in his sorrow. The loss of Hilliard, grievous in itself, took Ruskin's mind back to the summer of 1866. In that year, it will be recalled, Pauline Trevelyan, who was Laurence's aunt, had died while travelling with Ruskin, Joan and Connie. Pauline Trevelyan's death at Neuchâtel, then Ruskin's encounter with Marie of the Giessbach are found in most of the plans for *Præterita*, for there in Switzerland was one of the pools of sad memory that were so important to the autobiography. Laurence's death stirred memories of the 1866 summer. At the same time, the shocking message from Greece silenced Ruskin's ability to converse and halted his pen. When he was once more able to work, three weeks after Hilliard's death, there are a few pathetic notes in the diary that suggest how little able Ruskin now was for the intellectual effort of the composition of *Præterita*. 'Then out to anemones — clear sun and stream. This must begin Marie of the Giessbach — peace of it so great that I lost myself under my own crabtree between it and the holly. Losing oneself in love. St Bernard &c. Only true love forgets like that. Coming in tired. No: first the law given at lunch about lambs (i.e. that sheep and lambs are always to be let all over the place except the garden). Tell it [illegible] on. Up with Jane Anne to see owl . . .'[41] The chapter about Pauline Trevelyan and Marie of the Giessbach was never written.

Laurence Hilliard had been a much-loved secretary, friend and neighbour, and with his death a happy part of the old Brantwood life came to an end. The future of the household was uncertain. Joan feared that her cousin would soon become either a helpless invalid or permanently insane. Sara Anderson realised that Ruskin's active life was over and wished to resign her secretarial duties. Much to his surprise, she offered the position to Cockerell, 'the pros and cons of which she explained' when he and Olive came to tea. Upstairs in his bedroom, Ruskin had no idea of this proposal. Cockerell made the right decision. 'This was a tempting offer', he recalled, 'though the drawbacks she alluded to, connected with Ruskin's health, were formidable; but circumstances at home and in the business made a change of plans impossible for me'.[42] The episode had one pleasant consequence. Sara and Sydney Cockerell became lifelong friends. His obituary notice of Sara, published at the time of her death in 1942, mentions the qualities that made her such a valuable secretary to Ruskin, to Joan, and then to such eminent Victorians as Kipling, Lady Ritchie, George Moore and Meredith. 'Being on terms of intimacy with her employers', he then wrote, 'she . . . was possessed of many secrets which, however valuable as "copy", were very safe in her hands. Her lively understanding was happily lit up by a sense of humour, and she had an appreciation of their foibles, as well as of their genius, their strivings and their achievements. But after the great ones had departed, Sara Anderson never came into the open, never wrote down what she knew, never lectured or broadcast . . .'[43]

All Sara's tact and discretion were needed in the next three months. Between May and July of 1887 Ruskin's reign at Brantwood came to its end, amid much local scandal. Ruskin's downfall had predictable causes. They were his attraction to little girls, his wild spending on books and manuscripts, crazed and imperious behaviour in the household and the breakdown of his loving relations with Joan Severn. As has been seen, Ruskin had unorthodox attitudes toward girls' education. His relations with the local Coniston school, officially warm, were in fact strained. Ruskin was wont to upset normal classroom routines. It was noticed that he had no interest in the pupils if they were boys. His gifts to the girls were over-generous. None the less, many Coniston parents had cause to know that Ruskin was a good and kindly man and had no objections when he began his 'Saturday girls' class in Botany'. Originally, in the summer of 1886, these lessons were an emotional substitute for the abandoned *Proserpina*. By the spring of 1887 they had a different tone. As many as a dozen children would present themselves at Brantwood for instruction, play and tea. Ruskin liked to watch the girls dancing, sometimes to tunes he had himself composed. The dances encouraged unbecoming behaviour. Ruskin confessed to Kate Greenaway: 'I thought at first they would be prim and orderly in class time, as they are at school. Not they! They set each other laughing, and look at anything they like in the room, and get tired, and are not the least a credit to me!'[44] Innocent in themselves, such romps too often excited Ruskin's mind, especially when he was tense about other matters. At such times he could behave foolishly. It is known that he proposed to adopt at least one of the girls who came to the botany class. But we do not know more about such matters, partly because Sara Anderson efficiently removed the evidence of Ruskin's more embarrassing behaviour.

By May of 1887 Joan had put an end to the girls' classes. She was also obliged to intercept hostile letters that Ruskin addressed to Liddell. Peter Baxter added his own notes to letters Ruskin sent to other servants. He wrote to Frank Randal, for instance, 'I hope you will take no notice of his scolding, no one can do anything right for him now, he has not been well lately and he is irritable a little . . .'[45] This was a mild way of describing Ruskin's rages. His outbursts of anger became ever more frequent. Sometimes he was quietly writing *Præterita*, however, and on 2 May a letter to Kate Greenaway allows us to estimate progress on the autobiography. 'I am still at work on the XIth and XIIth of Vol II and 1st and II of Vol III. The most gloomy and difficult chapter of all *Præterita* will be the 1st of III Vol. The Grande Chartreuse — I am at work on it, and can think of little else — write of nothing else — except those Stones of Johnnies.'[46] The chapters in question, 'L'Hôtel du Mont Blanc', 'Otterburn' and 'The Grande Chartreuse', show Ruskin's fitful wanderings between old diaries, his memories, and comments on favourite books and drawings.

Meanwhile he continued to spend absurd sums of money, doubled all the Brantwood servants' wages and picked quarrels with George Allen and Bernard Quaritch. When Joan remonstrated with him Ruskin returned to his old refrain of being 'master in his own house'. Then there was a disaster. After a particularly heated dispute Joan ran upstairs and locked herself into her bedroom. Ruskin went to his own bedroom, took some of his favourite Turners from the walls and then had himself driven to the Waterhead Hotel, where he demanded a room.

The Waterhead Hotel was situated at the northern end of Coniston Water, a little way from the village. Many Brantwood visitors stayed there and the landlady, Mrs Sly, knew Ruskin well. She was also familiar with Arthur Severn, who soon arrived to find out what was going on. Ruskin was not suffering from delusions but was full of fury, now mostly directed against Arthur. He wanted the Severns to leave Brantwood for ever. Until they left he would not set foot in his own home. Arthur returned to Joan with this message. Now Ruskin enlisted help from a neighbour, Albert Fleming, who was a Companion of the Guild. Fleming was a successful London Solicitor who owned property in Ambleside and interested himself in the revival of a linen-weaving industry. He came to the Waterhead and listened to Ruskin's complaints. Then he offered to assist, perhaps with legal advice. Soon afterwards Ruskin wrote to him:

> I knew you would do all you could for me, but there is nothing whatever to be done — except to get the Severns out of my house — which Joan being ill — of her own rage and shame mostly I believe — I can't yet effect by police force. I am perfectly 'com-

> fortable' in my rooms here — having lived in inns all my life and am really more at home in them than at home! I have long borne the misery of seeing Joan spoiled into folly and ingratitude by her ——— of a husband — but have been accustomed to bear everything of evil from men or clouds — as the nature of them. The Severns *must* go back to their own affairs — in a week or so — and D.V. I shall go back to mine.[47]

After less than a week at the Waterhead Ruskin decided to leave the inn and asked his former servant, Kate Raven, to accommodate him at her quite humble home in Coniston village, Hollywath Cottage. As we learn from *Fors Clavigera*, she had been the 'indoor stewardess' at Brantwood in the earlier 1870s, one of the servants whom Ruskin 'wouldn't change for anyone else's servants in the world'.[48] Kate had helped during Ruskin's first mental breakdown in 1878 but had left his employment when she married later that year. Thereafter, 'tea at Kate's' is a frequent entry in Ruskin's diary. Now he wanted shelter until Joan and Arthur returned to Herne Hill. As before, we note the tact and loyalty of Ruskin's servants in all these grievous times. Joan Severn, ill with worry, knew that she could rely on Kate. It was better that Ruskin should be at Hollywath Cottage than in such a public place as the Waterhead. Joan also calculated that Kate could return Ruskin to Brantwood and look after the household as she had done in previous years. After a few days, therefore, she and Arthur set off for London. They were apprehensive, yet confident that Kate, Peter Baxter and other servants would give Ruskin the attentions he needed. Certainly his servants were of more use to Ruskin than were the local Companions of St George. Albert Fleming, proud of his new position as Ruskin's champion, suggested that Brantwood should be cared for by another companion, Julia Firth. He felt that she had the qualifications to become the Master's housekeeper. She was the translator of *Ulric the Farm Servant*, lived nearby at Ambleside and was a widow. Bewildered, Julia Firth arrived at the house where she had often been a guest and awaited Ruskin's return. Kate Raven then brought Ruskin back to his home. The anger had left him. He was hardly able to speak, so great was his melancholy and guilt.

Ruskin's only wish was that Joan would return, and Julia Firth's blundering attempts to please him made the loss of his cousin all the harder to bear. Soon he was writing to Herne Hill: 'I could have wept tears of blood for you, in seeing the beauty of the place, yesterday evening and today, all lost to Doanie and me . . . Your room shall stay as you left it . . . Perhaps later in the year you might like to come down with Baby and Violet . . . Send me word how you are as soon as you can,'[49] All June he wrote with miserable protestations. 'You have never really known how I have loved you, and the desolation of all sweetness to me in garden or wood, for want of you, has been the saddest thing I have ever known in all this life . . .'[50] Still Joan remained in London. By the end of the month Ruskin was desperate, and declared that 'the love you send me at the end of your letter is worth more than worlds to me, and believe me in anything I'm trying to get done about Brantwood I am only thinking now of how to quit you of trouble about it and have you mistress of it'.[51] Joan had known for years that she would become the 'mistress' of the house and its contents, so long as Ruskin did not change his will. If, in some fit of madness, he decided to do so, Albert Fleming might be present. Joan feared Fleming's legal mind. Once again she took the train to Coniston, this time accompanied by Sara Anderson. They arrived to find that Ruskin was suffering from delusions. After a week in bed he returned to some kind of normality. A few years later, Sara Anderson recalled how she had found him one day 'sitting at his study table with his head between his hands and groaning, "Oh, why didn't Albert see that I was mad?"'[52]

CHAPTER FORTY-SEVEN

1887–1888

Ruskin was so depressed by the events at the Waterhead Hotel that the return to his home had meant nothing to him. Joan's concern made him feel guilty rather than grateful. He could not work for any length of time and was scarcely able for his walks. He kept no diary and wrote few letters. There were none of the usual summer visitors, the Guild of St George was forgotten and *Præterita* came to a halt. Ruskin's consolation was in the little tales sent to him by Francesca Alexander. He began his sad, beautiful introduction to her 'The Nuns' School in Florence', the fourth part of *Christ's Folk in the Apennine*, which George Allen would issue in the autumn. This preface is Ruskin's adieu to his village school and educational experiments on the shores of Coniston Lake: he knew that he would never again be allowed to teach his neighbours' children. Thinking of the restorative holiday he had taken with Collingwood after his illness of 1882, Ruskin decided to go to France. The Severns had no desire to accompany him but assumed that he would be cared for by Peter Baxter. By slow stages, Baxter, Joan and Arthur took Ruskin to the Channel port of Folkestone, where they arrived on 24 August 1887. Joan gave her cousin money in return for his chequebook, which ever afterwards remained in her hands. The Severns then returned to Brantwood. But Ruskin did not proceed to the continent. For the next year he lived in and near Folkestone, at first in a hotel and then in a lodging house in the neighbouring resort of Sandgate. The Severns told friends that Ruskin was by the sea for the sake of his health.

Ruskin's first three weeks at Folkestone were spent in the Paris Hotel, recently enlarged yet still the kind of inn that he had known from the earliest of his family coaching expeditions. In this way it was characteristic of 1880s Folkestone. The town was modern in appearance but was built around its ancient foundation as one of the Cinque Ports. Ruskin went for drives, visited the circus and spent much time on the beach, where there were boats, fishing tackle, lobster pots, nets, dogs — the Turnerian foreshore litter that reminded him of *The Harbours of England*, written so long before. He had with him the architectural tape he had used to survey the buildings of Venice, forty years in the past, now 'thank God, in service once again, when I never expected to unroll it more'. With this tape, some notes reveal, he spent hours measuring an old barge on the mud-flats of the harbour.[1] Thinking of Turner reminded him of childhood games with boats, and, mindful of an old fantasy that his mother's father had been a 'master mariner', Ruskin's imagination became almost infantile. 'Me got a French peach and a French pear', he wrote to Joan, but 'wanted my di ma to put them into my mouth'.[2] He was pleased to make the acquaintance of some seamen and occasional ferry workers. They seemed rough and grown-up. He pressed sovereigns on them.

Peter Baxter was happier when his master was on the shore than when he was in the Paris Hotel. He had created disturbances at the White Hart in St Albans, on the way down to Folkestone. Now, at the Paris Hotel, Ruskin sent gifts of sherry and champagne to his chambermaids. One of them was made to tie his wideawake hat into the form of an 'episcopal bonnet'. Another, he decided, should serve only his personal needs. He would pay her wages and provide her with a less funereal uniform. This girl, to her bewilderment, was then sent north to Brantwood with instructions to telegraph Joan if she were to lose her way. Ruskin's worried cousin had already been alerted of her arrival, for she had almost daily letters from Baxter, which told her of the strains of his position. He also begged to be allowed home to his wife and child, Mary and Johnny, and their comfortable rooms in the Brantwood lodge:

> *Please to burn*
> Mrs Arthur Severn
> Madam I thank you very much for your note enclosed with Marys. I should certainly not advise you to come here at present I am sure the Master would make your life not worth living. I was in great hopes all day yesterday that he would cool down, but this morning he is up to his games again — and his face like scarlet he swore at one of the porters like a goodfellow. then after lunch he wanted to see the labels on the champagne bottles . . . everyone takes notice of him and then he goes out and gets into such tempers at things and people which he has nothing at all to do with. the House maid has just gone and he has given her a sovereign he has given her since he came here about three pounds he is having champagne for dinner he says he wont give me any in case I should meet some of my Irish friends afterwards . . .

The next day,

> I have just got my Master dressed he is very bad this morning. he struck me for the first and his face was awful red. But he has cooled

> down since a little. wanted to know when I wanted to go home. I told him I was in no hurry and at least I would wait until he was suited . . .

A week later,

> I am sorry to say that I feel very unwell myself I have not any strength & can't sleep. I am thoroughly crushed — I fear that I'll be ill next — so I have been thinking that Mr Severn ought to suggest that he will come to London and get a Proper Man for him he declares he will stay here till Xmas . . . of couse he is Mad half his time he is really not fit to be at large . . . *Madam* I implore of you & Mr Severn to get him another man at once for I feel I can't hold out any longer. the cruel insults I never can forget . . .

The next day,

> I can't tell you how grieved I am at everything it is quite time that you & Mr Severn his appointed guardians ought to adopt stringent measures for my dear Masters own sake & reputation for he is simply the laughing stock of the people about . . . Mr Severn ought to come at once and bring a keeper for him and take him from here at once . . .[3]

Joan and Arthur now made a decision. They told Baxter to come home to Brantwood and to leave Ruskin to his own devices in the Paris Hotel. They would not commit Ruskin to an asylum, nor find a 'keeper for him', but they did not wish him to return to Brantwood or the other family home in Herne Hill. The French expedition had not been entirely abandoned. The Severns knew that it would be dangerous for Ruskin to go abroad without an experienced servant or a close friend. But since Joan had impounded his chequebook, and he had spent so many of his sovereigns, there was little likelihood that he would leave the country, even though Ruskin knew — and now sometimes remarked — that he could step on to the ferry and be in France in two hours. At all events, he was now abandoned.

Then, quite suddenly after Baxter's departure, Ruskin had an accident. One of his occupations at Folkestone was in walking along the very edge of the waves, looking in pools and scrambling over shingle and seaweedy rocks. He fell, and in attempting to get to his feet disturbed his rupture. Bewildered by Joan's treatment of him, incapacitated and in great pain, Ruskin was now doubly and trebly helpless. His misadventure had occurred at the first time in his adult life when he was without a manservant, and he was now in his sixty-eighth year. Rescue and help came from the new friends he had made on the beach. Among these natives of Folkestone was Edwin Trice, 'a slightly horsey man' as Ruskin explained him to Joan, who now took charge of the crippled and incoherent Professor. Ruskin had much reason to be grateful to Edwin. Lacking any social grace, he was as gentle to Ruskin as Couttet had been in Ruskin's youth. He carried him, dressed him, then took him away from the Paris Hotel. Edwin knew a boarding-house in Sandgate, a small resort two miles along the coast, not quite yet a suburb of Folkestone. No. 2 Devonshire Terrace was one of a row of small, newly built houses let by their owners in the summer months. Now, in autumn, Mr and Mrs Foulds were persuaded by Edwin to give up their front two rooms to Ruskin. It was not an attractive lodging. Ruskin's first impressions were of 'broken palings and ragged garden, and vulgar people'.[4] But there was a sea view, there were no difficult stairs to climb and none of the bustle of a hotel. Furthermore, Edwin found it convenient: so Devonshire Terrace became Ruskin's new home.

* * * *

Ruskin was in touch with a local medical man, Dr Bowles of Folkestone, and corresponded with Dr Parsons back in Hawkshead. But Parsons's letters, as usual, only recommended rest and Dr Bowles, who had no expertise with ruptures, wanted Ruskin to see another doctor. As soon as he was able to walk, therefore, in late October of 1887, Ruskin travelled from Devonshire Terrace to London and the help of John Simon. His old friend introduced him to Thomas Pebardy of the Truss Society, who in turn found a medical attendant to fit Ruskin with 'torturing hoops of steel'.[5] These attentions took place in a small room in Morley's Hotel on the south side of Trafalgar Square, with Edwin looking on and learning. Anxious that he would not be able to pay its bill, Ruskin lived quietly in Morley's. He went to the National Gallery, though 'the idea of going out is quite dreadful to me — and the crossings are dangerous . . .'[6] His only guest was John Simon. Many other people knew that he was in London and he had to warn Joan that they 'are beginning to find out' his true circumstances. Although the Severns had continued to say that he was living at the seaside for the sake of his health, Ruskin could hardly walk, was intermittently deranged, was without money and alone; and he was too shy, frightened or embarrassed to go in a coach to Herne Hill, to his own old home and the family servants who were paid from his family's fortunes. It was as though he shared some shameful secret with Joan. He did not wish to return to the Kentish coast 'but where to go I know not'. One invitation came to him. Edward Lees, the husband of his old Winnington pupil Dora Livesey, happened to be staying in Morley's and was distressed to learn of Ruskin's position. In a note he pushed under Ruskin's door, Lees offered him a home at Thurland Castle, near Kirkby Lonsdale, a property he and Dora had recently bought for themselves. There was some correspondence about this proposal. Joan Severn quite liked the idea. But Ruskin's abject letters of gratitude to Dora and her husband explain that he thought it best to look for 'some hermitage where, under direction from my friends, I might be taken care of without alarming or encumbering their own households'.[7] He then left London and returned to his rooms in Sandgate.

* * * *

While he was in London, this October of 1887, Ruskin had made a new friend. She was a girl to whom he would soon propose marriage. Kathleen Olander was in her late teens and was a student at the art school in Bedford Park. She lived with her Quaker parents in Acton. Kathleen was copying a Turner picture in the National Gallery when Ruskin hobbled by. Sixty years later she recalled how

> Seeing my oil palette he asked me, rather gruffly, 'How is it you are painting in oils?' but he consented none the less to come and look at my work.
>
> As we walked back together he grumbled quite audibly about much of the students' work, and declared, as he passed some Constables, that he did not like them and hoped I did not either. I was relieved when he came to my copy, which was about half the scale of the original and nearly finished. He commended it and said I had great feeling for Turner. I knew enough about Ruskin to know that this was praise worth having, and it was particularly gratifying as my enthusiasm about Ruskin at that time was unbounded.
>
> I told him that I had begun to read his books. 'Do you like them because of the way I write?' he asked. 'No', I replied at once, 'it is what you write that I like.' After some further discussion he offered to make me his pupil, provided I left the Art School, which it was evident he detested.
>
> After he had left I felt indescribably happy. I packed up my gear, gave the attendant a shilling, and wandered into the empty church of St-Martins-in-the-Fields, where I sat in a pew and cried for joy . . .[8]

On a further medical visit to London some ten days after this encounter, Ruskin met Kathleen again, set her to copying a water-colour by Turner and wrote to her father in formal terms to enquire whether he might have the privilege of taking 'some part with you in your daughter's training'.[9] Edmund Olander was an engineer with the Great Western Railway, and one gathers from his daughter's reminiscences that he did not share her interest in the arts. He declined an invitation to visit Sandgate to talk about Kathleen and her education. But, at Ruskin's request, he did not ask to read his daughter's correspondence with her new tutor. Very soon she came to write to Sandgate 'with complete unreserve'.

This was a little before Christmas of 1887, for Ruskin a quiet and unhappy festival. Joan and Arthur had paid a brief visit to Devonshire Terrace on 22 December but they did not take him back to Brantwood. Ruskin therefore spent Christmas alone, looking at the sea. After the holiday he wrote to Joan to say that 'I am very thankful to hear of you all being so happy at Brantwood', told her that he was gladdened to hear her report of the traditional servants' party and assured her that 'I am very thankful to have you for Vice-reine at Brantwood.'[10] Letter after letter expresses pleasure that home life is continuing its course without him: for himself, Ruskin usually says, he wishes nothing 'but the peaceful continuance of what powers of sight & thought still remain with me'.[11] In this pathetic correspondence, in which Ruskin's fortitude seldom manages to conceal his despair, he is always eager to know of Joan's happiness and careful to relieve her of anxiety.

His own loneliness was none the less difficult to disguise. The New Year was the anniversary that the Ruskin family had always preferred to Christmas. On the night of 31 December, as the year turned, he was awake, 'sitting up — to hear the chimes — the sea meanwhile falling full and soft at the end of the garden in high tide . . .'[12] At times such as this he needed religious comfort. On 3 January it would be Rose's birthday. He asked Joan to send him 'Rosie's box', the personal feretory in which he kept all her letters, various drawings and photographs, Bibles, missals and prayer books. Ruskin was not sure that Joan would allow him to have these memorials: 'I was afraid you would think it would be bad for me', he told her. But she sent the box, and not until the night of Rose's birthday did Ruskin find that he could not celebrate her life as he wished to do. 'Send me the *Key* of R's box *safe here*', reads his scrawled, irritated letter of the next morning.[13]

In this final stage of Ruskin's writing career, Joan's attitudes to her cousin have much bearing on the unfinished *Præterita* and the 'Bible of Amiens work — which I find now thoroughly interesting, and not painful or exciting like my own biography — though that also is progressing slowly'.[14] He had more to contribute to literature, yet his will to publish was entangled with the unspoken bargaining that occupies so many of his letters. Joan would write to Sandgate with news of her family and would tell Ruskin of her apprehensions about her finances. Ruskin replied with half-promises, or promises, that he would sell books and pictures. He asked her to look into his study to find various pieces of gold he had collected over the years. These were to be distributed among her children. He gave Joan some Turner watercolours, among his most precious possessions. He wrote that his personal diaries belonged henceforward to Joan, for her to dispose of as she wished. This offer proved to be at the heart of the bargaining problem. Ruskin would have given Joan his life, which in some ways these diaries represented: yet he needed them in Sandgate for the writing of *Præterita*. Now, in the first months of 1888, he especially wanted those volumes of his journal which record his life when Rose was alive. He wanted to write about her. Rose La Touche had been an influence on him for a quarter of a century past, yet in all his books she had scarcely been mentioned. It was time to describe her directly. Ruskin had already sent a drawing of Rose to the engravers Stodart to make an illustration for the chapter in which she would first appear. With her box and his diaries at his side in Sandgate he could explain his love. Readers of *Præterita* will note that 'The Grande Chartreuse', which is the chapter Ruskin wrote at Sandgate, suddenly gallops through the ten years between 1850 and 1860 in only three pages of text. The purpose of the acceleration was not only to travel past the period of his marriage but to clear the ground for the entrance of Rose.

'The Grande Chartreuse' takes its title from a visit Ruskin had made, with his parents, to a Carthusian monastery during their Swiss tour of 1849, but it reflects his religious attitudes of the later 1880s. The chapter dismisses both fashionable Evangelicalism and Christian Socialism, the 'Puritanism of Belgravia' and the 'Liberalism of Red Lion Square', and contains the heated account, evidently hostile to F. D. Maurice, of their differences over the Song of Deborah. The purpose of these reminiscences was not merely to describe the quarrels of thirty years before. It was to prepare for a confession of Ruskin's 'early Catholicism', as he called it; that is, his mystical personal religion, sometimes also referred to as his 'Bible of Amiens work', in which Rose was a saint and Ruskin her priest. Joan, reading manuscript or galleys of *Præterita* as Ruskin or George Allen sent them to

Brantwood, became increasingly troubled. It appeared that Ruskin was likely to become as controversial in *Præterita* as he had been in *Fors*. In reply to Joan, Ruskin argued that the issue of further numbers of the autobiography would let the world know that he was in good health and in possession of his faculties. He also promised that there would be a chapter or chapters devoted to her care for him. But Joan feared for the time when *Præterita*'s narrative would reach the point when Ruskin fell in love. The plans for the book were there for her to see in his diaries. They show that he also proposed to describe Rose's death, the visitations from her ghost and her place in his deliriums. Joan realised that the effort and excitement of writing such chapters might turn Ruskin's mind yet again. There was too much risk of embarrassment. Furthermore, a mental disaster for Ruskin could lead to financial disaster for all who depended on him. Her interest was not to have *Præterita* advanced. The book that was written to please could please no longer.

Ruskin was still enquiring after his diaries four months later but Joan would not send them to him. He also asked for books. At the beginning of 1888 he wanted Gibbon's *Decline and Fall of the Roman Empire* and Dean Milman's *History of Latin Christianity*. Milman's is a graceless book, and he had been an enemy of Ruskin's since their meeting in Venice in 1851. Nor was Gibbon a favourite author, though Ruskin read him carefully and always acknowledged his power. The usefulness of these volumes would not be in charm. Gibbon's epic history and Milman's compilation of Christian legends were to be used as a starting point for Ruskin's own exploration of his 'early Catholic opinions'. In Sandgate, as Ruskin's intellectual powers declined, his religious thought was scarcely theological. It ruminates over Rose, rehearses stories of the saints and occasionally — dangerously — flashes into exaltation. Gibbon and Milman could not provide Ruskin with these ecstatic glimpses of Christian myth. They came from Rose's box and also from manuscripts he ordered, without Joan's knowledge, from the bookseller Bernard Quaritch. At the same time, Ruskin was now prone to religious depressions. These dark fits troubled the Quaker Kathleen Olander, to whom Ruskin sent 'The Grande Chartreuse' in proof, and who now learnt, 'shocked but not dismayed', that Ruskin's illnesses had been mental.[15] Kathleen copied out hymns for Ruskin, so that she could 'show him the falsity of his position'.[16] In return, Ruskin wrote her the last of those 'Sunday letters' he had once sent to the girls at Winnington. It might well have frightened its recipient.

. . . What I can tell you of myself is that you must never read my books as if they were the least an expression of my personal character, except only *Fors*, and *Præterita*. The others are *meant*, at all events to define laws of art and work for everybody, — Christian or Jew, Cretan or Arabian; and if I appeal continually to the text of the Bible, it is simply because it is the religious code of England — just as I should appeal to the Koran in writing for Turks.

What I myself believe or feel about it, I hold to be no manner of consequence: what I allow myself to say of the fulfilment of such and such prophecies I say only as Carlyle would — recognising the bearing of such passages on the present state of the world.

But you will be perplexed, as you read more of me, (— if you do. —) — by the undertone of constant melancholy arising from my own doubt of the immortality of any Soul, (— except in pain) — which has not '*worked out its salvation*' in the Fear of God.

— For our God is a *consuming* fire

— and shall burn up the Chaff with unquenchable — (not *eternal*) Fire: — for you cannot make an enduring fire of Chaff, — but *unquenchable* in that (— as *I* read the Bible) no oblation nor blood of sprinkling can redeem the souls of the idle — proud — selfish — and good for nothing.

— I put this darkness of my creed before you at once — briefly — in the terror and wide range of it. — but remember that I hold also that millions are saved — (whatever Salvation may mean to each of them) — who have simply suffered innocently in this world, like Lazarus; not because Christ's blood was shed for them — but because their own blood also has been poured on the earth like water.

And it is in this part of my belief that I am chiefly separate from all your joy in the Communion. If I believed it as you do, and felt as you feel — I should be a Roman Catholic at once. It is *only* their doctrine of the Mass that separates me from them — and *that* is certainly my own fault. But the extreme forms of religious distress into which I continually fall, are manifestly diseased; possibly diabolic, temptations and it is only in having more or less conquered — or passed through — one of them that I am able to write you this letter at all. — or that I can dare to sign myself, dearest Kathleen
Your faithful Servant J Ruskin.[17]

This was comparatively energetic writing. During his later months in Sandgate, however, there is seldom much vigour in Ruskin's letters.

His physical capacities declined rapidly after the lonely Christmas and New Year of 1887–88. The short, cold days and long evenings seemed endless, as though spring would never come. Ruskin began to think that he would be in this lodging house until he died. To open and peruse his daily letters from a period of around three weeks in that January and February is indeed to have the impression of a man near to death, so halting and feeble is Ruskin's hand. Infirmity and lassitude now became the permanent conditions of his life. He had 'no power of doing more than the cat does, all day'.[18] His eyesight was hazy and he saw spots when he tried to concentrate. Near the end of his life as a writer, he was now also concluding his life as an artist. He had pens, brushes and colours but could not draw. Instead, Ruskin returned to a childhood game of sixty years before: he cut up maps of England and France into their counties and provinces, then coloured the different pieces before fitting them together again. Mrs Foulds brought in his meals, which often he ate on his lap.

With the failure of his health came a loss of intellectual pride. In the previous autumn, only four months since, there had still been a spirit of defiance in him as he surveyed his position and thought of his writing: 'I never intended to live in penitence opposite Folkestone harbour.'[19] Yet that was now Ruskin's fate. Apology was now his daily task. Every morning brought Joan's letter with worries and complaints. Ruskin promised his obedience. 'My Di Ma has me under her hand and can order what she will' is the theme of dozens of his replies.[20] Then, in mid-January, quite unexpectedly, Sydney Cockerell arrived at Sandgate with his sister Olive. Ruskin was taken aback, especially since he associated his visitor with the final disasters at Brantwood. But he managed to take the young people to supper at a hotel and afterwards read them some pages from *Præterita*. After this reading Cockerell came to the purpose of his visit. He repeated his demand that Ruskin should make some sort of apology or reparation to Octavia Hill, Sydney's father's friend and, as now transpired, Olive's godmother. Ruskin gave in. He was 'quite vanquished', the triumphant Cockerell subsequently wrote. 'He owned that he had misjudged her, promised to do what we asked of him . . . kissed us both, joined our hands, and bade us farewell, we being touched to the heart and in tears.'[21] Ruskin reported to Joan that 'I've been obliged to make it up with Octavia Hill and am choked with humble pie.'[22]

Young Cockerell had not really effected a reconciliation, as was sometimes claimed. But he had inflicted a humiliation on Ruskin's writing. He had brought with him to Sandgate the original issues of *Fors Clavigera* in which the dispute with Octavia Hill had been conducted. Producing the pamphlets, he rebuked Ruskin and asked that they should be suppressed or in some way struck from the record. After the Cockerells' departure Ruskin looked at these old numbers of his monthly letter and fell even further into dejected contrition, 'not for that error merely', he wrote to Cockerell, 'but for total wrongness in all one's thoughts, in all one's angers, all one's prides . . .'[23] A letter to George Allen shows that he now thought of a revision of the whole of the first series of *Fors*, cancelling the wilder and more contentious passages. But this was too complicated a task to pursue, and in the event *Fors* remained intact.

However, Cockerell's juvenile gallantry had reinforced what people had been saying to Ruskin for years: that they much preferred his autobiography to his opinions. *Præterita*'s story was still full of problems. Ruskin was usually too weak and depressed to sit at his small table and continue the story of his life. Even if he managed to do so, there would be further troubles with Joan. For there was a central readership of the autobiography, consisting of Ruskin's friends and followers: his old disciples and helpers, his large acquaintanceship, the members of the Guild of St George. Ruskin again pointed out to Joan that new mumbers of *Præterita* would reassure such people that he was well and happy. In truth, of course, he was unhappy and ill; and Joan feared the arrival of disciples at Sandgate. She scolded Ruskin for receiving visitors, even if they had appeared without warning. His pathetic reply was this: 'Me's quite crushed and broken hearted with my Doanie's 'ettie to day: me did'nt ask Miss T. or dream of seeing her till she came in at the door — but oh — di ma — you know peepies will want to come and see for themselves how oos own Di Pa is; and it is better that they hear from my own lips that I want Doanie to take care of me, and that all I want now is to please her . . .'[24]

Joan realised that it was only a matter of time before a close friend went to see Ruskin. What might Dora Lees, or some other friend from Winnington days, make of the circumstances in which he was now living? Suppose he were visited by John Simon or Henry Acland, who were doctors? Or by Alexander Wedderburn, who was now a qualified lawyer? Hoping to forestall investigations, Joan asked her cousin for a public statement of his well-being. This she could circulate to those who felt concern about him. 'Indeed I will write anything you wish me to, — to assure people of the relations of trust and affection between us', Ruskin replied.[25] He repeated yet again, however, that 'the only thing to do real good would be the steady issuing of *nice* new *Præteritas*'. In this exchange we may detect the origin of the famous final chapter of the autobiography, 'Joanna's Care'. And in fact the period of Joan's neglect of her cousin was now coming to an end, as Ruskin once more emerged from depression into a state of violent excitement.

After the Cockerells' visit, only one thought had given him comfort: he expected that Joan would come to see him on his birthday. Joan and Arthur (who had been in the Herne Hill house, where they often stayed in the winter months) arrived for the occasion on 8 February, when Ruskin became sixty-nine years old, but there were few celebrations. Arthur wanted to please his daughter Lily Severn, whom he now took on a trip to France, while Joan talked only about business arrangements. Ruskin longed for the company of someone who cared about him for independent reasons. As soon as Joan was back in Herne Hill he begged her to bring Kate Greenaway on a visit. This was arranged but when the two women returned to Sandgate at the beginning of March Ruskin was uncontrollable. They had to listen to his fantasies about girls. He gave absurd orders and insulted Kate. He cried out excitedly about medieval manuscripts he had ordered from Quaritch and insisted that he was in communication with Rose, in heaven. In these moods Ruskin found spasmodic physical strength and would strike out at those who displeased him. The events of the following days are not clear. But Joan went to London to engage two male nurses and brought them back to Sandgate with instructions to guard over Ruskin at all times. Grotesque and violent scenes ensued. Some of them can be imagined from a letter of Ruskin's which by chance escaped Joan's later destruction of their most embarrassing correspondence.

> Darling di wee ma,
> Your letter this afternoon is entirely satisfactory to me — though you leaving as you did without warning, caused me to be dragged by violence from the Hotel via this house, with every possible suggestion of lunacy and imbecility — and afterwards stopped on my way to Dr Bowles's on Sunday — as if I had been an escaped convict — and the use of the Sandgate banker's paper by Mr Watts was his own intrusion of it, — refusing my usual written signature on Prescotts. As the deuce would have it, the Dr [Bowles] intercepted, and gave to you, — two letters to Mr Bond Prof. Colvin of the highest importance advising them of my attempt to get the Psalter of Boulogne — the best M.S. in Europe of Charlemagne's time, for the British Museum.

But what made me most of all angry, was your not attending to what I told you of my having at last obtained direct & happy spiritual communication with Rosie — (as Phile had at Broadlands) Your face changed to the old hard expression — just as a vulgar infidel's would. And Rosie will not condescend to speak to you any more than for these long years to me, until you are ready to do as she bids you. It was Kathleen Olander who forced me to pray for help — and Rosie answered instantly — giving the unmistakeable sign of that Greek m.s.s. with St John instead of St Matthew.

And — absolutely under her orders, I have asked Tenny Watson to marry me and come abroad with her father, if she likes to have him see how we get on, — as far as Paris — if he can spare time Chamouni. Where Tennie and I would wait to receive you and Arthur and Lily.

And I think — Jennie will come — (as Harry said of Constance) But if not — Kathleen will; for I'm resolved to have Kathleen or Tennie for a nurse instead of the hospital hacks I've had these last years. But I don't think Kathleen's quaker Papa and mama would like it. She's most likely at the Nat gallery this afternoon. If you liked to drive in and ask Oldham to find her, you would see how you liked her — She's not the least in face like R but is almost the same in spirit, — and has complete power over *me*.

Enough news for tonight

I am entirely well, and greatly enjoying my work.

Ever your lovingest seepy
Poo Di Pa.[26]

Ruskin's 'mad-nurses', as he called them, were named Bowles and Baker. They were soon joined by a Mr and Mrs Watts. Ruskin was still served by the raffish but devoted Edwin, so a body of people followed him as he went about his daily business. Their procession was of course noticed in the small seaside town though 'the rumour of my being a violent lunatic being spread all over Folkestone' did not trouble Ruskin overmuch. Such things had often been said in the larger world. There were certain incidents, as when 'that blackguard Baker' attempted to give orders to Edwin, and the occasional struggle, in banks or the post office, for Ruskin wished both to spend money and dispatch letters to loved ones and public figures. In these letters, which might be addressed to Cardinal Manning or the Director of the British Museum, Ruskin would describe how Rose was sending him messages, or would propose changes in the British

Museum's arrangements under the guidance of St George. Joan and the mad-nurses were never able to terminate Ruskin's correspondence. However, Joan controlled his orders to Quaritch and suspended his account with Prescott's, his London bank.

Ruskin's condition was no doubt extreme. His mental illness often incapacitated him for normal thought or conversation. Yet matters could have been worse. He was not mad every day, or all through the day. He did not hear voices. If he fell he could get to his feet again. Edwin was fairly near. Perhaps Ruskin's state of mind was preferable to that of the dismal surrender after Christmas. In March and April he once more became the active Ruskin. When he asked for books from Brantwood he could remember their positions on his shelves. He began to draw again and resumed work on *Præterita*. He took music lessons with a Folkestone medical man, Dr Forbes, whom he thought to employ both as physician and personal pianist if he should decide to travel abroad in the springtime.

CHAPTER FORTY-EIGHT

1888

In April of 1888 there was a further improvement in Ruskin's health, and the 'keepers of lunatics' were called off, perhaps after his most grieving complaint to his cousin: 'my Doanie, how could you? how could you?'[1] He then went to London. He had to see his dentist, Mr Woodhouse, but Ruskin was also considering an escape from his life in Devonshire Terrace. The 'ten months misery of Sandgate' — ten months in which he might have finished *Præterita*, had he been living comfortably elsewhere — had to come to an end. He had no idea where to go, but since he wanted company he travelled to London. Half-decisive, Ruskin installed himself with Edwin in Morley's Hotel. He ordered his carriage from Herne Hill, a simple request he had not dared to make on his previous visits. Now he felt able to visit museums and the opening of the annual exhibition of the Institute of Painters in Watercolours. Ruskin was gratified that so many people wished to come to shake his hand, and at Morley's he received a few visitors. Two of them were to be important in the fashioning of his life's story. The first was Froude. There is no account of their conversation, but it can hardly not have included the question of Froude's biography of Carlyle and the attacks that were still being made on Froude's integrity, especially by Charles Eliot Norton. Both Ruskin and Froude were aware that 'of all literary sins Carlyle himself most detested a false biography.' These followers of Carlyle knew that Froude had done his work honourably. But was Ruskin writing a false autobiography, and who would be his biographer? Quite soon Norton, with typical sly arrogance, would propose that he should be the author of a part of *Præterita*. On receiving the chapter 'The Grande Chartreuse' he wrote to Ruskin: 'I should like to write one of the next numbers of the book. I could say something of your Past which you do not know, and if you knew would not tell; and I should omit some things which you will tell . . .'[2]

Froude liked to talk to Ruskin about Oxford and its place within the national culture. Oxford was dead to Ruskin now, but it happened that another visitor to Morley's was also preoccupied with the university city. E. T. Cook, a comparatively recent graduate, felt that he was a part of 'that practical interest in social questions which was . . . the next Oxford movement'; a development which had begun, in his view, with the road-digging of 1874 and had spread, via Toynbee Hall, to the younger wing of the Liberal Party. Cook was too young to have been one of Ruskin's road-building disciples: he had been at New College in the period between Ruskin's two tenures of the Slade chair. On leaving the University he might have had a parliamentary career, especially since he was then offered the Liberal nomination for the Oxford City seat. Instead, he had become a journalist. Encouraged by Alfred Milner, a road-digger now far advanced in Liberal circles, Cook free-lanced for the *Pall Mall Gazette*, then joined its staff under W. T. Stead. A scholarly person, he continued the detailed private study of Ruskin that he had begun as a schoolboy. Cook returned from London to Oxford to hear the lectures that Ruskin gave in 1883–84 and his admirable résumés of these addresses, with some other short articles, prompted Ruskin to write to Stead that 'you have a man on your staff who knows more about my works than I do myself'.[3] By the later 1880s Cook had become just as expert a Ruskinian as Collingwood or Wedderburn — except that he knew only Ruskin's books, and not their author.

* * * *

The *Pall Mall Gazette* had become a Liberal journal in 1880 when sold by Smith, Elder. Its new editor, John Morley, was not of interest to Ruskin. But his successor, W. T. Stead, reckless, flamboyant and a crusader, caught Ruskin's attention. There was a similar newspaperman within Ruskin's own personality. On one occasion he had remade the front page of the *PMG*, scrawling and spreading ink to shorten some columns and lengthen others. Liberal or not, he liked the vivid daring of the paper. Cook's own account of the changes at the *PMG* under Stead hints at his alarm when he found that journalism was not as he had previously imagined. The *Pall Mall Gazette*, he wrote, 'delighted us at Oxford with its grave, philosophical radicalism, its deliberate and weighty views and its subdued style . . . between the concept of journalism which I had thus formed and the reality as I found it when I joined the regular staff under Mr Morley's successor, what a change! I found myself suddenly thrust into what Matthew Arnold called "the new Journalism" with its "novelty, variety", sensation, sympathy and generous instincts . . .'[4] Cook's own instincts, in all departments of journalism and life, were closer to Morley's than to Stead's. But he relished his position, became indispensable to the paper, and was no longer a junior member of the staff when, on 19 April 1888, he presented himself to Ruskin.

In an uncritical way, Cook was a lover of art. His home contained a studio, for in 1884 he had married Emily Baird, a young painter whose charm and intelligence may be found in her book *Our Sketching Tour.*[5] In 1887, probably with her help, Cook compiled his *Popular Handbook to the National Gallery*. This guide lists the Trafalgar Square pictures and reproduces comments on their beauties. Since he had culled most of these criticisms from Ruskin's writings, Cook asked him to contribute a preface. Ruskin had found himself unable to oblige when at Sandgate but wrote the piece with ease at Morley's. It is humorous, assured, and kindly towards his old aesthetic opponents. When Cook called at Morley's to collect his copy he and Ruskin had a lengthy conversation. Ruskin revealed that he had not been able to read the parts of the book that dealt with Turner because of the memories of the artist that were aroused in him. He also confessed to Cook that, like Turner, he was often 'crazy' and that, despite the love that he and Joan had for each other, they could not live together. Cook was surprised by the radicalism of some of Ruskin's views. When Ruskin had been at Morley's the previous November, he had observed the workers' demonstrations that culminated in 'Bloody Sunday'. Reporting Ruskin, Cook's journal tells how 'he had gone about the Square and talked to some of the Black Flag people — very nice fellows they were, and quite right, too, in demanding bread'.[6] Ruskin then talked about prostitution, apparently without inhibition. Cook did not press Ruskin on any topic. One reflects that it was just at this period that the 'new journalism' had invented the personal interview. But Cook was not of the breed of new journalists, though he was of their generation; and so his conversation with Ruskin — the only one he would ever have — remained buried in his private journal.[7]

Cook was self-effacing, courteous and methodical. He hated disputes and any form of scandal. His extraordinary memory for detail was accompanied by a way of ignoring or forgetting matters that did not accord with his own view of the world. He received his knighthood for his work in censoring newspapers in the First World War. He also acted as a censor in his duties as Ruskin's editor. When Kathleen Olander showed him her bundle of letters from Ruskin, probably in the early 1900s, he persuaded her to burn three of them that were critical of Joan Severn and offered to include her name in his biography of Ruskin if she would destroy the rest of her collection. Since she refused to do so, her name was subsequently omitted from the Ruskin literature. It was Kathleen whom Ruskin now met, in the National Gallery, on the day after he had talked to Cook. Kathleen was dismayed because Ruskin told her that he had given up praying. The meeting was not a success and they decided to have a rendezvous elsewhere.

> I was copying in water-colour a picture by Faed, 'What the poor do for the poor', when next we met at the South Kensington Museum. It was not the kind of picture of which Ruskin approved, but it was a commission, for which I was paid nearly three pounds, and I excused myself by calling it a 'necessary evil.'
>
> The day we spent at South Kensington was the happiest I ever had with him. I did not paint, but walked around the gallery talking. We went to the restaurant in the Museum for lunch, though we ate little. Rosie, he said, had sent me to him.
>
> After I left him I went home rejoicing, loving him with all my heart and soul; for we seemed to find peace in our complete sympathy and understanding of each other. Before we parted he had led me to Turner's 'Hornby Castle' and asked me to paint it for him. I gladly accepted the commission, and was proud to tell my parents about it when I reached home. Their attitude quickly dampened my enthusiasm. The sum of twenty guineas that Ruskin wanted to give me for the painting seemed to them preposterous, and they immediately became suspicious. I was to have met him again two days later at South Kensington, but I was forbidden to go and it was arranged that my mother should take my place.[8]

Kathleen was forbidden to write to Ruskin, and when they met at the museum Mrs Olander told him to stop troubling her daughter. The rebuff contributed to his depression of spirits, as he sat in Morley's and wondered what to do next. The slight from the Olander parents was bearable. But for how long could he stay in Morley's? Where would he go next?

In Acton, Kathleen began to wonder whether Ruskin would adopt her, so that he would be her father. She was mistaken, however, if she believed that she was his only 'girl-friend', in Ruskin's phrase. Emily Warren and Tenzo Watson, to name only two of his recent enthusiasms, may have received the kind of ardent letters that E. T. Cook and Joan Severn later sought to destroy. Joan was anxious for Ruskin to find somewhere to live and someone to look after him. There were a number of possible shelters. Edward and Dora Lees's offer was still open. Joan wanted Ruskin to go to Broadlands and asked Georgiana Mount-Temple if she would take him in. But Ruskin declined even to visit this palatial home of Christian revivalism, once so dear to him and to Rose, 'my whole mind being at present in a spiritual despair which would be torture to them'.[9] George Allen and his wife Hannah offered Ruskin a home at Sunnyside. Of course there was sense in this proposal. The whole Allen family had always been dependent on Ruskin and his books. Hannah had been a maid at Denmark Hill forty years before, long before Joan had ever entered the house. Grace Allen, the daughter of Sunnyside, loved Ruskin and wished to make his old age happy. So when Ruskin left Morley's Hotel he travelled to Orpington. Almost as soon as he arrived at the Allens', however, he realised that he could not live there. He caught a train back to Folkestone and returned to his little bed-sitting-room in Devonshire Terrace. A couple of days later Grace Allen asked if she could visit him. Ruskin asked her not to come: he said it would be too upsetting.

Ruskin now began the last month of his Sandgate life. His surviving letters are to Joan and they are about financial arrangements. This was the period when George Allen was engaged in new editions of Ruskin's earlier and more famous books. The various projects were undertaken at Joan's urging: she anticipated, correctly, that much money could be made from a reissue of *Modern Painters*. 'The trouble I have given you about money', as Ruskin now put it to Joan, was that he had spent too much on himself and the Guild and had not set aside enough for the Severns. It is not believable, however, that Ruskin kept Joan poor. Through his solicitor Mackrell he had given her £1,000 a year for the upkeep of Brantwood. All the servants there were paid from his funds, and so were the older servants, 'the pensioners', at Herne Hill. Ruskin also gave a personal allowance to Arthur and Joan. The sum involved has never been known, but the Severns found it inadequate. Arthur Severn only occasionally sold a painting. He did not really try to earn his living as an artist. But he and Joan were used to living well, and now they found that they were not as comfortable as they had been ten years earlier. Arthur never asked Ruskin for money and the subject was never raised between them, except when Ruskin was mad. All financial matters were handled by Joan. This May of 1888, angered by Ruskin's repeated attempts to buy rare books from Quaritch, she began a new campaign to make Ruskin sell objects from Brantwood to help her family budget. Quaritch was therefore offered the manuscripts of novels by Walter Scott that Ruskin possessed, for of what use were these to Ruskin?

Some items could not be sold as easily as others. For instance, Ruskin had often bought more costly objects on behalf of St George. They therefore belonged to the Guild, though they might be housed in Brantwood rather than at the museum in Sheffield. Perhaps the

Severns were not especially careful of the distinction between Ruskin's property and the Guild's. They were certainly not careful of Ruskin's feelings. In mid-May Joan asked Ruskin to sell his *Leicester Abbey*, one of the Turners that were so close to his life and feelings. This picture had once belonged to Munro of Novar. Ruskin had bought it in 1877, and flaunted the acquisition in *Fors Clavigera*. But the purchase had not been impetuous. Hugh Munro was the young Scottish laird who in 1836 had travelled to the Val d'Aosta with Turner, and had painted with him. He was the collector of the great Swiss watercolours that John James Ruskin had failed to purchase. It was Munro who had received, from the artist himself, the manuscript of the first defence of Turner that Ruskin ever wrote, for he was also the owner of *Juliet and her Nurse*. Ruskin had never been friendly with Munro, which was a loss to them both. But when he bought the *Leicester* and three other works from his collection 'which I've been looking after for thirty years', he then said, '— and I would have bought them with my last guinea' matters were somehow mended. Furthermore, in Ruskin's imagination the fact that he had come to own these pictures reunited him both with his beloved father and with the wonderful promise of his youth. John James Ruskin would have wept to see his son in the circumstances of Devonshire Terrace. John Ruskin now hid the personal hurt that was being done to him. He was pierced by Joan's request. But, even in the course of writing his letter of reply, he overcame his injury and surrendered to Joan what she wanted. The note is scrawled and difficult to read.

> Dearest Doanie,
> The post was late this morning — your letter lovely like all, had the terrible thought of parting with Leicester — and I couldn't answer at once — nor can I now but I send this line by 2 o clock post — in hope it may still reach you tomorrow morning — so that you may'nt think I was displeased — So vilely written too — as if I *was*! — Oh my Doanie — if I could give you back your old Di Pa — and your [illegible] — and your peace of heart — *all* the Turners might go to heaven — and truly, — you may do what you can with them for *I* shall have no peace of heart in them . . .[10]

It is possible that Joan and Arthur preserved this letter, with a number of similar ones, in case their right to sell Ruskin's Turners might be questioned. Much other material they burnt. It is not now an easy task to trace the dispersal of Ruskin's art collection and library, and at no time is the work edifying. For when Ruskin gave his collections to Joan he also abandoned to her care the taste and knowledge with which he had assembled them. The Severns could not recover this knowledge, for they had never studied Ruskin's mind. They did not catalogue the objects they sold, partly out of ignorance and partly because their sales were often covert. In such ways as this, works of art — and rich knowledge about art — simply disappeared.

On 30 May Joan arrived at Sandgate, where she stayed for two nights. She pointed out to Ruskin that she had travelled from Brantwood to London in a third-class railway carriage, thus throwing him into a fit of remorse. This was a business trip for Joan, but she was pleased to see that Ruskin's health was, on the whole, pretty evenly balanced. He had his hobbies and his occupations. Pottering about the streets, the pier and the foreshore with Edwin, he found interest in pleasing or displeasing discoveries. He had got 'entirely clear views into the rascality of the railway S. E. company', for instance, and had 'done some lovely smuggling work in the old Folkestone back town'.[11] Joan distrusted Edwin, with his aura of betting and billiards, and now ended his period of service. Baxter, Ruskin's valet who had abandoned him in the Paris Hotel the previous September, would return to his post. He and Arthur Severn would accompany Ruskin on a recuperative continental holiday. This seemed very like the aborted trip that had brought him to the Kent coast ten months before; and since Joan also talked about a possible return to Brantwood Ruskin had the impression that his life might be returning to normal after a period of banishment. Ten days later Arthur Severn reappeared with Baxter, and the three men took the ferry from Folkestone to Boulogne. On his honour not to behave extravagantly, Ruskin kept notes for Joan of every franc and centime he spent, so she soon knew the price of French apricots, pencils, and of three photographs of Beauvais cathedral. He was generally depressed and silent. Arthur found him less trouble when 'low' than he was 'when he rides his high horse', but it was a tedious holiday for him. Joan asked him not to leave Ruskin and he replied as follows: 'I am keeping abroad as long as I can stand it — to be of service to you — besides I feel we had such a nice time at Brantwood. But between ourselves I am dreadfully bored sometimes . . . Just read through your long letter! All right — I will stay on for the present, I only thought of going if he seemed much better . . .'[12]

Then, a chance encounter raised both Ruskin's and Arthur's spirits. A day after they had arrived at the old Tête de Boeuf inn at Abbeville they went down to breakfast to find that Sydney Cockerell and a friend were also staying there. Cockerell's companion was Detmar Blow, a nineteen-year-old architectural student. They had with them a copy of *The Bible of Amiens* and were on holiday to study French

Gothic with Ruskin's book as their guide. The difficulties between Cockerell and Ruskin over *Fors Clavigera* were forgotten, or not mentioned, and Cockerell was later to say that the week he now spent with Ruskin was the happiest of his life. Ruskin was enlivened by the young people and led them in sketching expeditions. His kindness to his students was matched by their respect, desire to know his opinions and ask his advice. This was not Arthur's attitude to Ruskin, but he was pleased that the young men thought that he too was a rather senior person. Though a charming host, Ruskin was not a happy man. In private moments he spelt out his pain to another young admirer. Kathleen Olander had persuaded her parents that to cut her off from Ruskin was to damage her artistic career. They agreed that the correspondence might resume, provided it contained no 'sentiment'. Kathleen, however, 'anxious to get him to think differently on religious matters and efface his terrible gloom and despair', drew tenebrous and violent thoughts from her teacher. She told him to think of God's grace, for instance; and he replied: 'I have grieved and quenched the Spirit — and when I think of what I might have been, and see — as I draw nearer Death — what God meant to me, and would have helped me to be — there seems to me no word of condemnation in all the Bible too dark for my disobedience . . .'[13]

Ruskin told Cockerell that he was so conscious of having misspent his life that he had abandoned the Christian hope that he might one day be reunited with Rose. By this he might have meant that there was no afterlife, or that he would go to hell when he died. Here was something for Cockerell to think about as he took his leave of Ruskin and returned to London. Shortly afterwards Arthur Severn also travelled back to England, having persuaded himself that it was safe to leave Ruskin. This was not wise. Ruskin was sixty-nine, was suffering from delusions, often talked uncontrollably, was sunk in gloom or transported by rage, was physically frail, could not be trusted not to spend all his money, had no clear idea where he was going or whether he would ever return to his native land. He should have had a doctor with him. Instead he was cared for by a boy who was still in his teens, whom he had known for one week. Detmar Blow accepted Ruskin's invitation to go on with him to Paris, and perhaps beyond, if he should take his 'old road' to the Alps and Italy. As things turned out, Blow stayed at Ruskin's side for the next five months, shepherding him from place to place until his final collapse. It must have been a terrible experience for him, and that perhaps is why he never afterwards gave any account of their life together. A young man whose mind was just opening, he was immediately plunged into the disarray of Ruskin's intellect. At the Hôtel Meurice in Paris Ruskin read out condemnations of George Allen and talked at too great length about 'Gussie, Jane Anne and Maggie Borns', Coniston schoolgirls. None the less, there were rewards for Blow. In the Louvre and at Notre Dame he heard comments, especially on architecture, that were more vital than any talk he had heard before. Ruskin now began to write with some confidence and even optimism. He thought of going down to Venice to see Francesca Alexander and then returning to Paris for the winter months. He wrote to Francesca that 'It seems as if my life had been given back to me as it was in 1878, before any of the delirious illness. I am drawing and writing with my old decision and pleasure, doing what delights Joan in *Præterita*, and giving the French copyists in the Louvre something to think about . . .'[14]

Joan was not necessarily delighted by *Præterita*, especially now that Ruskin had reached the point in his book at which Rose was to appear. The whole story might soon be in print. *Præterita* could easily cease to be an autobiography and might devote chapter after chapter to a celebration of Rose. Her letters from the rosewood box would fill the pages of *Dilecta*. Joan felt apprehension. How would Ruskin deal with the hostility of the La Touche parents? What might he say about Percy La Touche, Joan's suitor, who had so cruelly abandoned her? And what embarrassing revelations would there be about Rose's ghost (who, very recently, had sent Ruskin a message at Beauvais), her holiness and Ruskin's 'catholicism', his worship at her rosewood shrine? Not least among Joan's worries was the probable reaction of the La Touche family. They too wanted nothing said. Certainly the Baptist John La Touche would not like to find his daughter talked of as a Catholic saint. But 'L'Esterelle', the chapter which introduces Rose, was now under way. Ruskin was writing it, Detmar Blow making a fair copy. Successive pages were being sent from France to Aylesbury for Jowett to put into type. 'Some wise, and prettily mannered, people have told me that I shouldn't say anything about Rosie at all', Ruskin writes in this chapter, 'but I am too old now to take advice . . .'[15] He therefore describes the first time he saw Rose and the early days of his friendship with the La Touche family in the late 1850s. The chapter then reproduces, in its entirety, the long letter addressed to 'Dearest St Crumpet' that the twelve-year-old Rose had sent him from Nice in 1860. Here the chapter suddenly stops. 'L'Esterelle' is a more slender pamphlet, by several pages, than was the usual issue of *Præterita*. Ruskin had in fact written more of the chapter, and his continuation of the story, in which he confesses that 'Rose, in heart, was with me always, and all I did was for her sake' reached the state of galley proof, one copy of which survives.[16] It seems likely therefore that Joan or some other 'wise, and prettily mannered' person had intervened at Aylesbury and simply cut off the narrative of Ruskin's life — which indeed was never taken any further, for the last *Præterita* chapter of all, 'Joanna's Care', deals with other topics.

'L'Esterelle' was written in Paris, Sallanches, Chamonix and Brig, on the Simplon Pass, as Ruskin and Detmar Blow went slowly and haltingly towards Venice. It contains a number of factual errors, as do so many chapters of *Præterita*. Ruskin had even forgotten how old Rose was when he met her. Perhaps this does not much matter. 'L'Esterelle' is a delicate and moving piece of writing. Ruskin's other literary production on this journey was the 'Epilogue' to the new edition of *Modern Painters* that Allen was preparing. The final 'clause', in Ruskin's word, of this 'Epilogue', written on 16 September at Chamonix, is grave, sane and conspicuously intelligent. The diary is also firmly expressed. But other writing is wild. It is surprising that Kathleen Olander was not more conscious that Ruskin's letters were near to madness. She ought to have realised, when in March he had asked her to forward his secret messages to Cardinal Manning, that he was deluded. But still she did not understand. His peculiar letters from the Alps seem to have delighted her. Only five days after Ruskin completed his *Præterita* chapter about Rose, he wrote as follows:

> My own Kathleen,
> That little postscript to the second letter, the 22nd, sent me quite wild with joy — for now, because you can be to me all I need, — so can I be to you — If you had held back, I would have tried all I could to be what you would have had me — but you know — it could only have been — torment as well as joy — not health and peace, as with God's blessing, it will be now — The Sainte Chapelle was built by St Louis. I wanted you at Paris, — to give yourself to me there — I want you *now* in St Mark's, quicker, if I can get you anyhow — but now my sorella and I will settle things and meantime I'll write you *such* love letters! — I never had a chance of writing a love-letter to Rosie — she was always furious with me for loving *her* better than God, — (and I didn't — but I loved God better for the gift of her, — as of you — whom, the moment I saw, I thought He had sent me, literally to save me when nothing else could, but Love.) I've been in such pain thinking you were displeased — or that people were coming between us, — I shall not any more now — but I had written the Paris plan in a

> mysterious way which you might have thought was mere dream. I was getting ill again — the two letters this morning are new life.
> — And you *will* be happy with me, while yet I live — for it was only love that I wanted to keep me sane — in all things — I am as pure — except in thought — as you are — but it is *terrible* for any creature of my temper to have no wife — one cannot but go mad — And if I am spared to stay with you — suppose — it were but seven years like the seven wreaths of that chain — you would have many to love you and honour you — when I left you. — I'm not going on to speak of that — to day, — but only to rejoice in you and over you . . .[17]

This meeting between Kathleen's naivety and Ruskin's craziness led to storms of incomprehension between west London and north Italy. Kathleen showed Ruskin's letter to her mother. There were further family disputes. What letters might she have been writing to him, to receive a reply such as this? Kathleen, defiantly, went to a local clergyman to ask about the legality of the marriage that had apparently been proposed. To her disgust, he suggested that she might live with Ruskin as his housekeeper. It happened that this was also a plan of Ruskin's. He thought that he might find a home in Acton, at the Olanders' house: on the other hand, he also wondered whether Kathleen might not come out to live with him in Venice. When he was not excited by this prospect, however, Ruskin once more fell into depression: 'I find myself so miserable in Italy — and so much feebler, my ancles swelling — and a languor on me . . .'[18] Furthermore, he had exhausted his present funds. For the only time in his life Ruskin borrowed money. He requested Joan to ask Edward Lees to lend him £500. Lees immediately agreed to the loan, so Ruskin was relieved of the anxiety he felt about hotel bills. He could go wherever he wished, if he did not like Italy: Detmar Blow, who had taken over a number of secretarial duties, would accompany him and copy out his further reminiscences of Rose. This could be done in the high Alps. It seemed proper, however, even inevitable, that the goal of their journey should be Venice. It was one of the homes of his lifetime's work, and the city in which Rose and St Ursula had first sent messages to him. Francesca Alexander and her mother had been begging Ruskin to come to stay with them at their summer villa in Bassano, 'the sister of Venice'. Now he decided to accept. Ruskin and Blow arrived in Bassano at the end of September, 1888.

Bassano had no particular significance for Ruskin, though he had printed Francesca's descriptions of its customs in the last number of

Fors Clavigera, 'Rosy Vale'. When he got to the Alexanders' villa he was bewildered by the strange company. There was no real familiarity between Ruskin, his 'Sorella' and her 'Mammina'. This was only the second time that he had met them. Their friendship was a matter of correspondence. The interest they shared was in Francesca's tales of peasant life. But there were no simple peasants in the company Ruskin now joined. His fellow guests were a Count and Countess Pasolini and their children. Much of the conversation was in German. More and ever more important people kept calling and asking Ruskin his opinions. He now began to ask openly for his Brantwood home. He told Joan: 'I am so sick at heart to be so far from you . . . It is impossible to say how kind these people are to me, but they take me to see gardens and picture galleries, when the ladies of the gardens and the directors of the gallery come out to do me honour . . . My own Brantwood-Strawberry-hill is worth any quantity of Italian gardens and the pictures above my bed worth any quantity of Italian galleries and I don't know what to say or how to answer and am in misery . . .'[19]

After a week in Bassano he left for Venice. His departure was so abrupt and led to such illness that Joan and the Alexanders later tried to reconstruct what had happened. 'His change of feeling was great and sudden after he had received some letters', Francesca wrote to Brantwood. These had come from Kathleen Olander and her parents. Kathleen sent her love and, effectively, her *adieux*, while her father and mother once again forbade Ruskin to write to her, no doubt reiterating the comments they had already made to their daughter: that he had 'acted a most dishonourable part . . . completely broken faith with us', since he had introduced 'sentiment, and of a most objectionable kind to a young girl'.[20]

Some part of Ruskin's mind now entirely collapsed. He could scarcely look at the Venetian architecture around him. Blow had never been to the city but Ruskin, its great historian, could not explain what the buildings were. Nor could he manage to introduce the young man to Italian friends who approached him. Alone, he had halting conversations with Boni and Alessandri, but for long periods he would remain quite silent. Then, when he spoke, it was to rue the follies and crimes of his life. After ten days of this mute depression, Blow and Baxter decided that it would be best to go back to the fresher air of the Alps. Ruskin had ceased to take interest in their itinerary. He still sometimes said that he would never return to England. But Baxter had his wife and family at Brantwood, and Blow had to return to England to his architectural studies and his own life. They decided to leave Venice and take Ruskin some part of the way towards England. They hoped that one of the Severns would then come to relieve them and bring a doctor. Thus they began a journey in the direction of home, though Ruskin had no home to go to. It was to be six weeks before they reached Paris and Joan finally joined them to take Ruskin into medical care. During this period Ruskin became progressively less able to speak. At first, however, he was still able to write. We now reach the end of the sequence of some 3,000 letters he had addressed to Joan since she had first come to Denmark Hill to join the Ruskin family. The handwriting is weak and has begun to shrink in size, towards the microscopic script of his very last written words. He is very weak, obviously; but the letters have their occasional moments of eloquence as he repeats, over and over again, that he loves Joan, wants to make her happy, wants to be with her, yet knows that he should be punished for all that he had done, the things that were 'ruinously and unpardonably wrong'.

> Oh my Doanie my Doanie — if only I can see your sweet face again — and be yet the source of some happiness to you. I hate sending this, but I *am* in one of my low fits — that's a fact — and its no use trying to hide it . . . There's nothing to answer to such a letter as this. I know with what loving comfy you would answer, if you could . . .
>
> I can't bear leaving the mountains yet it seems doing me no good to stay . . . They are so lovely in the autumn colour and light — but I do want my Doanie more than all the lights and colours in the world — only I should make her misby if I came to her . . .
>
> You are to me all — and a thousand times more than all you ever were — & if there has come (by my fault always) division between us — I have had no rest night nor day — and oh my precious one, I would give all the round world, if I had it — to have you beside me this instant — but I can't travel — symptoms of physical illness struck me at Lucerne, on the way to Berne, such as I have not had before . . .[21]

This letter was dated from Merlingen on 14 November. The final letter of all was written from Berne on 27 November. Here Ruskin became so ill that his companions decided to speed towards England as quickly as possible. Two days later they were in Paris and sought the shelter of Ruskin's old friends at the Hôtel Meurice. Blow now telegraphed Joan, imploring her assistance or at least her attendance, for it seemed that Ruskin was dying. When at length Joan arrived in Paris she found her cousin prostrate and weeping, imagining that he was in hell, trembling violently and uncontrollably. He remained in this state for five days and nights. Joan then decided to get him to medical attention in London. This she effected; and by 8 December he was back in his old nursery in Herne Hill. There was no substantial change in his condition. Joan wrote to Charles Eliot Norton to say that she feared the illness would not now leave him and that the end had come.

CHAPTER FORTY-NINE

1888–1900

Among the visitors at the inn at Sallanches where Ruskin and Blow had stayed in the summer of 1888 was H. W. Nevinson, whose suggestive memoirs must now be added to the story of Ruskin's final decline. Henry Woodd Nevinson's second name was taken from his connection with the family of Charles Woodd, the wine merchant of Belsize, near Hampstead, who had been friendly with John James Ruskin. Nevinson knew Ruskin only in a distant way. When an undergraduate he had felt no need to attend his lectures. Nevinson's hero was Carlyle. As a young man he had waited outside his Chelsea house for a glimpse of 'that demonic man of genius'.

> A few biggish trees grew on the further side of the street to 'Number 5', and having hidden myself carefully behind the largest, I waited. The brougham was standing ready there, and presently the door opened. Supported by Froude, a small and slightly bent old figure came down the steps. A loose cloak, a large, broad-rimmed hat, a fringe of white beard and white hair, a grave and worn face, deeply wrinkled and reddish brown, aged grey eyes turned for a moment to the racing clouds — that was all . . .[1]

Nevinson's autobiography claims that Carlyle influenced his generation. This is doubtful. Even Ruskin, who was much older than Nevinson, thought that only he and Froude remained, of those who once had been nourished by Carlyle's power. Loyalty to Carlyle would soon bring Ruskin to a final explosion of pride and grief. At Sallanches, Nevinson did not encounter the Carlylean Ruskin, only the old and pathetic survivor of a former age. 'In the old Belle Vue Inn', he recorded,

> I was horribly disturbed every morning by someone in the next room creaking about with noisy feet. As there was an attendant or valet who dined with us in the evening, I took my plaguey neighbour for a lord, perhaps insane, and cursed him at random. One day I was talking to 'the keeper' at dinner when the conversation turned on Carlyle's country. Whereupon 'the keeper' told me he had held Carlyle's cup while he drank tea, so feeble had the old man become, and then I said 'I'm afraid Ruskin will be the next to go'. 'I never

knew him so well for years', the amazing 'keeper' replied. 'Haven't you seen him?' 'Very often in the old days', I said. 'I mean here — now', he answered; 'I am with him here' . So my crazy lord was Ruskin himself, and in the morning when awakened by those creaking boots, I did not say one single damn. Next day that trusty servant, Baxter, brought an invitation for Margaret Nevinson and myself, and I wrote that evening:

'He came to meet us with words of thanks, a little bit *empressés*; I mean there was something almost religiously solemn in his thanks (for a lot of cyclamen), as though we were in church or at a deathbed — eyes turned down and voice subdued . . . He looked much older than in Oxford ten years ago . . . We were looking across the fertile valley to the red precipices of Varens, which rose sheer opposite the window, and he said there was no place like Sallanches for beauty and sublimity combined. "And yet", I said, "hardly a soul comes here to stay". "Very few people have souls", he answered, "and those that have are generally ambitious and want to climb heights. Hardly anyone cares about beauty. If people did they wouldn't build London or pull down Paris".

'He paused, and as though to correct exaggeration, then went on: "There are, of course, good people still, but they spend all their time in undoing the harm that the others have done. They go nursing, or reforming the East End, or teaching *crétins*, while the healthy and hopeful are neglected. The other day there was a woman singing here about the street with a lovely voice. But her only song was about 'Liberté, Liberté', and that sort of thing. I asked her what she knew of Liberty and tried to get her to sing some of the other songs in the book she was selling, such as 'La Rosiere', but I found she did not know any, and could not read".

'I said something about the melancholy of the mountain people. "Yes", he answered, "the people are gloomy and no wonder. They are neglected and left to themselves, and not allowed to see or hear anything. There are no gentry in the country; they have all swarmed into the towns to make money. The peasants have a very hard time, especially in such seasons as this, and now there is so much disease among the vines . . ."'[2]

Nevinson's diary thus recorded a moving and surely authentic account of Ruskin's conversation and demeanour. He is old, tired, perhaps a little querulous. But he is not mad; and Baxter, so used to Ruskin's moods, assures Nevinson that 'I never knew him so well for years'. Of course Baxter would not have told Nevinson the full story of his master's health. Perhaps he spoke with delibrate confidence because Nevinson had revealed his guess that Baxter was the 'keeper' of an insane peer of the realm. At all events, the encounter at the inn at Sallanches reminds us how delicate was the balance between Ruskin's anger and his sadness, and how quickly his moderately good health and charming talk could change to excited rantings or despondent silence. Like Baxter, Joan Severn was inclined to give positive accounts of Ruskin's condition. In the years to come she would often let it be known that he was cheerful, able to read and to play board games with the younger members of the Severn family. One hopes that this was so. Yet there were probably many months of crazed talk, incapability and mute unhappiness in the years to come.

* * * *

The years of Ruskin's disabled life began rather well. Five weeks after Joan had rescued him from Paris the trembling stopped and he began to speak rationally. He had 'recovered wonderfully', Joan wrote. 'We have quite long intervals . . . when he is apparently his sweet self again.'[3] As Ruskin returned to consciousness he became aware that he was back at Brantwood, his own home. From his bed he could see paintings he had known since childhood. Soon he learnt that he was seventy years old, for his birthday had passed. After the snows, when the first spring flowers were seen, he was able to get dressed. Then he could leave his bedroom and be assisted downstairs. A few days later he could take some steps in the garden. He had to explore carefully and was always attended. Brantwood was not as he had left it. David Downs, the old foreman of all Herne Hill, Oxford and Brantwood works, had died.[4] New young servants emerged from the dark corridors that led to the back of the house. Their work was to look after the Severn children. The house had been enlarged for the sake of the younger Severns. A second storey had been built. It contained a schoolroom, three rooms for the boys and a large, light studio for Arthur. Brantwood's grounds had also been extended. Joan had been purchasing land, and would continue to do so until about 1895, when the estate comprised 500 acres of woodland and farmland. Ruskin himself never legally owned more than the original 16 acres he had bought from Linton in 1871. But during his lifetime the Severns acquired the neighbouring house 'Thurston', then Lawson Park Farm — once the sheep farm of the monks of Furness Abbey — then Low Bank Ground, whose house and gardens reach down to the lake, and finally Fir Island, in the lake itself. While he was in Sandgate and France, the harbour Ruskin had built in 1875 with Downs,

Collingwood and Wedderburn had been enlarged by local labour to accommodate Arthur Severn's boats.

All this was a wonderful domain for children, in which Ruskin became only a frightening and unwelcome presence. The younger Severns, like everyone else in the household, always knew where he was. Ruskin was not able to walk to any of the higher parts of the estate and he probably never climbed the stairs to the new second storey. On fine days there were expeditions to 'the Professor's garden' behind the lodge. Here was a stone seat. He could look at the tumbling of the beck as it ran down from the fells to Coniston Water. In good weather he would always be taken out in a wheelchair to watch the sunset. As Ruskin recovered strength, towards the end of April of 1889, he tried to find the threads of his former mental life. The rosewood box was safe. It was in his bedroom, and he often looked inside it. Probably much else was safe, but he did not know where his possessions might be. Since he could not concentrate he could not even ask what had been lost, sold or left behind, in Sheffield, Oxford, Sandgate, Paris. He spent a whole day looking through the drawer where his Kate Greenaway drawings were kept, and was able to write her a little letter about them. Some other letters of this time were dictated. They are in Joan's hand and Ruskin's signature is at the bottom of the sheet. Other sheets of Brantwood writing paper are blank except for his signature at the lower margin. This stock of signed paper was used by Joan when she wished to give instructions on Ruskin's behalf. The relation between Ruskin's dictation and Joan's desires has a bearing on his last piece of published writing. This was 'Joanna's Care', the chapter at the very end of *Præterita*. It is popularly supposed — even by those who have read it — to describe Joan's solicitude and tender nursing. But this was not the real purpose of the chapter, and its composition led to yet more disputes between the loving cousins.

Ruskin had been writing his thoughts on the world for sixty years or so, and for fifty of those years had published what he had written. He was a writer. It is not surprising that, in May of 1889, he resumed an activity that was natural to him. It is remarkable, however, that after the fearful battering of recent months he attempted to raise his mind to the proud level of years before. For 'Joanna's Care' and the public letters that were to accompany the chapter in *Dilecta* are more like *Fors Clavigera* than *Præterita*. Joan sensed that the old troubles of Ruskin's authorship were to be renewed. 'He has been writing again', she complained to Norton, '. . . *Præterita* . . . *My* life is now full of increasing anxiety about *him* — and one might as well prevent the sea coming in . . . as keep him from *working*. In defiance of all entreaties, he drowns one's reasoning with his own, and anger at any thwarting of his wishes is worse than anything.'[5] In this atmosphere of tension Ruskin pressed on with his chapter. It does not continue the story of his life. The real subject of 'Joanna's Care' is the Scottish background of Ruskin's personal culture. His feeling for his father's native 'land of the leal' had been lost while he was at Sandgate. In Brantwood he could feel the proximity of the border country. He was also stimulated by meeting W. G. Collingwood again, for his old secretary was still living 'within call' at Gillhead. The shrewd remarks on Ruskin's Scottishness which open Collingwood's biography probably have their origin in their conversations at this time. The opening of 'Joanna's Care' explains that a further description of Rose has to be postponed. There is then an account of how Joan left her native Galloway to come to live at Denmark Hill. This is not written by Ruskin but by Joan herself. When Ruskin resumes the narrative it is with a sentence that would have read strangely to anyone who had known his life in Sandgate: 'Thus far Joanie; nor virtually have she and I ever parted since.'[6] No more is related of Joan, for Ruskin now introduces memories of Carlyle before writing at length about Walter Scott. He then discusses music and dancing, and 'gods', a subject illustrated in a long footnote reproduced from *Fors*. This material was written in the middle of May and perhaps beyond. Then there is a break in the composition of 'Joanna's Care' before the final paragraphs, which were not written but dictated and were signed on 19 June.

In the hiatus of the earlier part of June Ruskin had written a final homage to Carlyle, in the manner of *Fors Clavigera*. It took the form of three letters addressed to Charles Eliot Norton. These letters proclaim that the American liberal had no understanding of the honour that was due to Carlyle's writing and personality. The immediate cause of Ruskin's letters was annoyance that Norton proposed to take a hand in the writing of *Præterita* and, mostly, the pirated re-edition of Carlyle's *Reminiscences* that Norton had published in America in 1887. The copyright of the *Reminiscences* belonged to Froude, but the absence of a copyright agreement between England and America had allowed Norton to pirate Froude's property. Norton's introduction to the book continued his denigration of the man he had robbed. But Ruskin's letters are not merely a defence of Froude's integrity. They combat Norton's habitual assumption that he knew best, while the writing goes back to Ruskin's own autobiography, to his father, to Swift and as well as to Carlyle:

My dearest Charles,

I use Joan's hand today, for mine would begin to shake badly as I went on to say — what I've got to say; namely, that it is my ill luck, helpless fate — or perhaps, appointed duty, to give Professor Charles Eliot Norton, editor of Carlyle's early letters, as thorough a literary dressing, pickling, and conserving, as ever one living man got from another, — if only my rod-hand does not fail me before I can get the lash laid on, and my capsicum pickle does not run short before I get it rubbed in. And, being minded at present that the form of tub in which this 'Tale of a Tub' shall be told, shall be, by no means Greek, but Spanish, in the form of my father's butts (wherein to prepare the quality of Malmsey required,) that is to say, of direct correspondence, dealing mainly in plain question, and plain answer, on both sides, — will you kindly tell me, in as swift answer to this letter as may be, whether, at page 268 of your second volume, and the tenth line, 'Calv*a*nistic' is Carlyle's mistake, or *your* mistake? in the fourteenth line, whether you suppose 'wan coll' to represent indeed the Scottish, pronunciation of 'one coal'? whether, in page 269, line twelfth . . .[7]

This and more, was dictated on 11 June. Ruskin is pointing out, in his own way, that Norton's criticisms of Froude's editorial errors could be levelled also at his own edition. There was a much larger issue. Ruskin's distaste for Norton's 'niggling-naggling' pedantry was far exceeded by his antipathy to Norton's complacent feeling that he could be wise about Carlyle's personal life.

My dearest Charles,

I could not 'continue in my next' yesterday, for another of my vexatiously erratic friends, Master Gershom Collingwood (who won't wash out his glacier basins, to my mind), came innocently in, to be lectured on that subject; but, to-day, I am in better trim for my farther talk to you, having had a quiet morning's thought over past time, and being thus able more firmly to assure you, that in affection I hold you as closely, and tenderly, as ever; and that all your late vagaries, and rejections of every counsel or petition of mine, to your own estreme damage, have only changed my former reverent affection into the even deeper, and more pathetic, sentiment of Betty to her idiot boy, — nay, in some respects into the enduring and comforting strength of love, which Michael feels to Luke, driven at last 'To seek a hiding place beyond the seas.' Nor this without the better hope, that I may finish my own sheepfold in Greenhead Ghyll before I die, and that my apostolic Luke — my Charlie over the water: may yet return, repentant, some happy day, for companionship with me in the Brantwood cottage named the 'Evening Star.'

This much said in all seriousness, I proceed to my four questions for to-day. The first (fifth in consecutive order, from my last letter), whether you yourself consider that the first letter that Carlyle ever writes to Miss Welsh — addressing her, then six years younger than himself, as 'My dear Madam', and advising her with magisterial authority immediately to commence authorship — is, either in substance, temper, or language, characteristic of Carlyle — worthy of him, or, in the concealed feeling which dictates it, worthy of any honourable lover, or wise tutor?

Question second (and sixth): As you re-read it in print, does the page of your own writing, in which at the close of your second volume of letters you summarize your opinion of Carlyle's married life, strike you, *now*, either as a graceful specimen of English writing, or worthy of your own elegant and acute literary manner? I ask you this very earnestly, because, though I always knew that manner to be merely epistolary, therefore more or less feminine, and not implying any capacity of writing a good book, I yet never thought it possible that in any state of temporary obfuscation, fog in the head, or cramp in the stomach, *my* Charles Eliot Norton could ever have written anything so flat, stale and unprofitable.

Question third, and a short one: What ever put it into your head that *you* could understand Carlyle better than Froude and I could?

Question fourth, and shortest of all: What demon of insolence, and cowardice, provoked you (the era of duelling past) to write of one of the most deliberate, learned, and religious of European historians, in terms which, when the era of duelling was *not* past, you could not have used to the poorest parliamentary hanger on to his party's petticoats, without being thrashed, or shot, on the following morning?[8]

Having said this on behalf of Froude, Ruskin's next letter goes to the main point at issue, which was that Norton had never been a true admirer of Carlyle, and was therefore not qualified to have opinions of him.

Dearest Charles,

I think four more questions will pretty nearly cover our questionable ground; and it is as well to get them as quickly as possible *off my* mind, and *on yours*; that you may contemplate them in peace, and arrange their answers in harmoniously consecutive form. We had got to number eight. Number nine is to me, personally, the most interesting of all. At what date, my dear Charles, of your own indefatigable student-ship may I place there (?) the even on which you have not yet accepted my congratulations your conversion to Carlyle? I am interested: on ne peut plus in knowing which of his works you have studied with most benefit; and with how many of them you feel yourself thoroughly acquainted?

Question tenth: In your lectures at Cambridge, on what subjects do you now commend the teaching of Carlyle to your young Americans? On Slavery, Kinghood, Stump Oratory, Hudson's Statuary? — or the Navigation of Niagara?

Question eleventh: What advantage of personal intercourse had you with the living Carlyle himself, after becoming his disciple?

And question twelfth: As yourself a man of extreme refinement, and acquainted, in America, with what are supposed to be manners, how came you to indulge Mrs Alexander Carlyle in her singular wish to illustrate the 'sanctities of private life' by supplementing Mr Froude's account of her uncles literary consumption of the oil of midnight with his own journal of the sanitary effects of the castor oil of morning?

Ever, my dear Charles, your affectionately anxious friend.[9]

Norton burnt these splendid letters, dismissing them as 'sad, insane outbursts of unbridled resentment at my exposure of Froude's violation of the trust reposed in him by Carlyle.' He refused to enter any discussion with Ruskin about the questions that had been raised. Instead, he and Joan wrote to each other with many a reassurance that Ruskin was 'not himself'. But this was not quite the end of the dispute. Ruskin had written the letters for publication. He had managed to have them copied — perhaps by Collingwood — and had sent them to Jowett in Aylesbury to be put into type. They were to be part of *Dilecta*. Ruskin had realised that he could make new use of this supplementary collection of documents and letters. In *Dilecta* he could say what he wished. Ruskin would be free from the obligatory pleasantness of *Præterita*. Ruskin therefore wrote an introduction in which he announced that *Dilecta* would henceforward serve an old purpose: 'it will be needful sometimes to let it supply the place of my ceased Fors.'[10] The third chapter of *Dilecta* was therefore to contain letters on 'the position held by my great grandfather among the persecuted Scottish puritans'; a family tree of the Ruskins and their Scottish forebears; interesting documents relating to Turner, including a letter from Jane Simon about the origin of 'Rain, Steam and Speed'; and finally the three letters to Norton, which — at the least — would have made an interesting contribution to the debate about Froude's work as biographer and editor. But Joan sided with Norton against Froude. For this reason, and many others, she did not want the letters to become public. Once again there was an intervention at Aylesbury. The proposed number of *Dilecta* never appeared. We know of it only because the galley proofs were preserved, and were used to issue the chapter — but without the Norton letters — in 1900, after Ruskin's death.[11]

In Ruskin's third letter to Norton, the list of possible Harvard lecture titles — 'Slavery, Kinghood, Stump Oratory' and so on — refer to the titles of the separate numbers of Carlyle's *Latter-Day Pamphlets*. We note that Ruskin still could not bring himself to mention 'Jesuitism', the pamphlet in which he himself had been attacked, nearly forty years before. In his lifelong advocacy of Carlyle there is not one single overt reference to 'Jesuitism', though a memory of its language may occasionally be detected in Ruskin's later writing, Strangely, perhaps, one of these memories occurred now, at the very end of Ruskin's literary career. The last paragraphs of 'Jesuitism' begin with the explanation 'How all things hang together!' The final paragraphs of *Præterita* begin 'How all things bind and blend themselves together!'[12] — a valedictory reminder, to those who would read him attentively, that Ruskin's more perfectly cadenced prose, and his more humane social analyses, were the result of a creative attitude to his discipleship. Ruskin had become very weak after his three letters to Norton, so much so that he could not write or dictate. While she looked after him, Joan managed to make him feel proper remorse for his work on *Dilecta*. Perhaps that is why Norton is reintroduced at the end of 'Joanna's Care', in the paragraphs which Ruskin dictated to Joan. It is possible to hear the very tones of Ruskin's voice, an old man's voice, quavering, repetitious, getting his tenses wrong, as one reads the end of *Præterita*; and perhaps the full sadness of this farewell to writing can only be appreciated by reading it aloud:

> I draw back to my own home, twenty years ago, permitted to thank Heaven once more for the peace, and hope, and loveliness of it, and the Elysian walks with Joanie, and Paradisiacal with Rosie, under the peach-blossom branches by the little glittering stream which I had paved with crystal for them . . . It wasn't the Liffey, nor the Nith, nor the Wandel; but the two girls were surely a little cruel to call it 'The Gutter!' Happiest times, for all of us, that ever were to be; not but that Joanie and her Arthur are giddy enough, both of them yet, with their five little ones, but they have been sorely

anxious about me, and I have been sorrowful enough for myself, since ever I lost sight of that peach-blossom avenue. 'Eden-land' Rosie calls it sometimes in her letters. Whether its tiny river were of the waters of Abana, or Euphrates, or Thamesis, I know not, but they were sweeter to my thirst than the fountains of Trevi or Branda.

How things bind and blend themselves together! The last time I saw the Fountain of Trevi, it was from Arthur's father's room — Joseph Severn's, where we both took Joanie to see him in 1872, and the old man made a sweet drawing of his pretty daughter-in-law, now in her schoolroom; he himself then eager in finishing his last picture of the Marriage in Cana, which he had caused to take place under a vine trellis, and delighted himself by painting the crystal and ruby glittering of the changing rivulet of water out of the Greek vase, glowing into wine. Fonte Branda I last saw with Charles Norton, under the same arches where Dante saw it. We drank of it together, and walked together that evening on the hills above, where the fireflies among the scented thickets shone fitfully in the still undarkened air. *How* they shone! moving like fine-broken starlight through the purple leaves. How they shone! through the sunset that faded into thunderous night as I entered Siena three days before, the white edges of the mountainous clouds still lighted from the west, and the openly golden sky calm behind the gate of Siena's heart, with its still golden words, 'Cor magis tibi Sena pandit' and the fireflies everywhere in sky and cloud rising and falling, mixed with the lightning, and more intense than the stars.

Brantwood,
June 19th, 1889.[13]

★ ★ ★ ★

Ruskin was not to know that this was the end of all his writing. He knew only that there was much more that he had to say, however tired he felt. Perhaps more of *Præterita* could have been produced. Ruskin's hand often shook too much to hold a pen. But he had always spoken in a manner that produced complete sentences; and, as these last dictated paragraphs show, he could still be an author if someone else wrote down what he said. There would of course be difficulties. The scribe would have to attend Ruskin when he was in the right mood. He should not be too despondent, and therefore silent: nor should he be excited and therefore declamatory. And there would be many other awkwardnesses. Joan could have coaxed more of *Præterita* out of

Ruskin, but she wanted it to end. There was one other person who could have helped Ruskin to write. William Gershom Collingwood had known Ruskin for a quarter of a century. He was a devoted disciple and a learned student of Ruskin's writings. He had been his travelling companion and nurse: he had been Ruskin's secretary and had taken his dictation. Collingwood and his wife had settled at Gillhead in order to be close to Brantwood, so they were neighbours. However, personal loyalty to Ruskin had led to a reserve between Collingwood and the Severns. Nor were the Severns particularly forthcoming with Collingwood. While Ruskin was at Sandgate, Collingwood had no idea where he was, though he was helping with the new edition of *Modern Painters*. He communicated with him only by sending brief, embarrassed notes to be forwarded by Sara Anderson. Collingwood was highly conscious that Sara was not Ruskin's secretary at all, but Joan's. Therefore there was a coolness. None the less Collingwood was invited to accompany Joan and Ruskin on a trip. For some reason, perhaps to separate him from his books, Joan had decided that Ruskin should have a holiday. They were to go to Seascale. Ruskin disliked the place, and indeed had too much recent knowledge of seaside boarding houses. He was unhappy, bewildered, and now incapable of writing. Four years later Collingwood wrote this description of the holiday.

> In the summer of 1889, at Seascale, on the Cumberland coast, Mr Ruskin was still working at *Præterita* . . . In his bedroom at Seascale, morning after morning, he still worked, or tried to work, as he had been used to do on journeys farther afield in brighter days. But now he seemed lost among the papers scattered on his table; he could not fix his mind upon them, and turned from one subject to another in despair; and yet patient, and kindly to those with him whose help he could no longer use, and who dared not to show — though he could not but guess — how heart-breaking it was.
>
> They put the best face upon it, of course: drove in the afternoons about the country — to Muncaster Castle, to Calder Abbey, where he tried to sketch once more; and when the proofs of 'Joanna's Care' were finally revised, to Wastwater for the night — but travelling was no longer restorative . . .[14]

The short, unsuccessful holiday at Seascale was Ruskin's final expedition from the reassuring surroundings of Coniston. A glimpse of his departure and return is provided by Edward Woolgar, who was at that period the Coniston stationmaster:

> The last railway journey taken by Professor Ruskin was from Seascale to Coniston in June 1889.
>
> On travelling to Seascale shortly before this, after expressing pleasure at seeing me, he said he was going to the seaside for a change and hoped good would result. However, he did not stay long at Seascale.
>
> On arriving back here, where I opened the carriage door, he said 'I've returned earlier than I anticipated, but I wanted to be at home again. There's no place like Coniston'.
>
> He leaned on my shoulder on getting out of the train and I assisted him to his own carriage. When passing through the Waiting Room he said 'Now, don't go away and leave us. We have got to know and like you. I don't want to see a strange face when I next come'.
>
> On reaching his carriage door he shook hands with me, and as I helped him in, repeated as with an effort 'I'm glad to be back. There's no place like Coniston — no place like Coniston' and his head sank wearily forward as the carriage drove off.[15]

In this simple anecdote there are a number of matters of interest. Woolgar could see that the holiday had not raised Ruskin's spirits and he realised that the great man who was his neighbour was not only old and ill, but exhausted. The stationmaster correctly emphasised that Ruskin 'wanted to be at home again'. In the decade of life that remained to him, Ruskin would scarcely stir from his house and the Brantwood grounds. His days of travelling were over. In the years since he had bought the property in 1871 Brantwood had often been a headquarters or a resting place rather than a home. Ruskin, who often liked to say that half of his life had been spent in inns, had been absent from Brantwood for long periods, had other centres at Oxford and Herne Hill and had been obliged to live at Sandgate while the Severns made his house their own. Yet it was appropriate that Ruskin should end his days in this corner of Lancashire and that he should wish to be buried in Coniston churchyard. He had said to Joan Severn, apparently more than once, that 'if I die at Herne Hill I wish to rest with my parents in Shirley churchyard, but if at Brantwood, then I would prefer to rest at Coniston'.[16] When Ruskin left the Seascale train and returned to Brantwood with his head sunk 'wearily forward' it was as though he acknowledged that Coniston, not Herne Hill and Shirley, would receive his mortal remains.

In Ruskin's mind there was a connection between the place of his home and the great cycles of nature, life and death. During his near-fatal illness at Matlock in 1871, as we have seen, he felt a longing to 'lie down in Coniston Water'. In 1874, writing a preface to *Frondes Agrestes*, the selections from *Modern Painters* compiled by Susie Beever, Ruskin imagined his friend 'under her quiet woods at Coniston — the Unter-Walden of England', thus making reference not only to the ancient Swiss canton but also to a late chapter in the fifth volume of Modern Painters, 'The Leaf Shadows', which describes Underwalden with strange intimations of death and celebrates quiet lives pursued and completed in lakeside valleys beneath precipices and forests of pine. Brantwood was a dark house, overshadowed by trees. Some visitors — especially toward the end of the nineteenth century, the time of the Queen Anne revival in domestic architecture — found it gloomy. Yet the view of the mountains across the lake was unchanged in its beauty, and Brantwood was still a place of pilgrimage. To Joan's occasional irritation, there were numbers of people who wished to call and pay homage to a man whose writings had inspired their best thoughts. Among such visitors may be named the Coniston station-master. Edward Woolgar had been a railway worker all his life, and was in charge of Coniston station between 1888 and 1902. He had artistic interests and built a collection of watercolours by Ruskin, Arthur Severn, W. G. Collingwood and others. He also collected books by Ruskin and, in later years, possessed a number of volumes from Ruskin's own library. Perhaps Woolgar should be described as a student and admirer of Ruskin rather than as a disciple. He would have been uneasy, for instance, in the Guild of St George, for he was devoted to the principles and practical aims of local government. For many years he represented Coniston on the Ulverston Rural District Council. Woolgar was also a member of the Lancashire County Council, a county alderman and a magistrate.

In May of 1889 Ruskin had hoped that he might entertain old friends during the summer. He wrote to Lily Armstrong (Mrs Kevill-Davies, we recall, since 1875) urging her to come to Brantwood and to bring her daughter Violet. His letters to Lily are charming and firmly written. So are other letters to R. C. Leslie, one of his sources for *Dilecta*, and to women friends such as Francesca Alexander, Kate Greenaway and Susie Beever. But Ruskin could not sustain his optimistic and genial mood after the Seascale holiday. By mid-June, when he had managed to write both the last pages of 'Joanna's Care' and his furious letters to Norton, he had lost interest in welcoming visitors. Now he scarcely ever put pen to paper and did not read. Joan, who kept up a steady correspondence with Norton, sent word to Boston about the aftermath of Ruskin's combative challenges:

> I am sure he feels the remorse and pain the matter merits, only we must bear and forgive, knowing that he was *not himself* when we wrote those letters . . . just as when he nearly breaks *my* heart with torture and reproaches . . . Yes, I thank you gratefully for grasping in some measure what I have continually to endure . . . in these terrible attacks and yet, just now, he is as sweet and tender and dear as ever at his best time . . .[17]

This was written on 11 July. Joan would not be able to enjoy Ruskin's 'sweet and tender' mood for more than another three or four weeks. In August his mental illness entered a new phase. Ruskin fell silent, as though struck dumb by despair. Joan did not have to tolerate the raging denunciations that had previously accompanied his spells of madness. Instead, she had to yearn for any kind of communication. Ruskin was put to bed and remained upstairs in his room for several months, probably until the spring of 1890. He did not know where he was, did not recognise Joan or anyone else and seldom spoke. However, he ate quite normally, slept at nights, and did not seem to be in distress. A male nurse was in attendance for only the first part of this long illness. Thereafter, Baxter and Joan attended to Ruskin's simple needs. Baxter could have managed by himself, but Joan would not leave Brantwood for more than a couple of days. Her hope was always that her cousin might one day know who she was; and then, she felt sure, he would be able to speak to her, perhaps in their familiar and loving baby-talk.

Ruskin did eventually recover, knew Joan to be his own Joan and could also think of friends: on occasion, probably until as late as 1895, he attempted to write notes to them. The ebb, flow and failure of his mental capacities in the last decade of Ruskin's life cannot be described because it was not recorded. Joan's policy, always, was to say that her cousin was in good spirits, but old and tired and unable to receive visitors. There was much bravery in 'Joanna's care', to use Ruskin's chapter title. She insisted that Ruskin would never be removed to an asylum or nursed in any kind of hospital. Brantwood was his home. There he would stay, and she would stay with him. This was her unalterable position, maintained through all the stages of Ruskin's final decline. After the long months when he was in bed in 1889–90 Joan never again thought that her cousin would fully recover. She hoped only that he would recognise her, smile, say a few words; and this was eventually her reward.

The grandees of Victorian medicine who had previously been Ruskin's doctors, all now honoured and in retirement — Sir Henry Acland, Sir William Gull, Sir John Simon — left their patient to the care of the much younger George Parsons of Hawkshead. Parsons had at least two of the primary virtues of a country physician. He was competent in many areas of simple medicine, and was familiar. Parsons could treat his patients as a trusted friend, whatever their problems or social station. It is true that (like everyone else) he had not been able to cope with Ruskin's great mental illnesses in the years after 1878, and at that period Parsons may have been too inclined to prescribe chloral for the fractious master of Brantwood. Now, in the 1890s, the doctor had an easier task. In a sense, Ruskin was out of danger, for he had no will of his own. His illnesses were much the same as those suffered by most elderly or bedridden people. So Dr Parsons was asked to visit, and he came and went. He looked after Ruskin's colds and rheumatism. Sometimes there were other people at Brantwood who were glad of his help. On occasion he cared for Joan or one of the servants before continuing his rounds in Coniston and Ambleside. In this way the invalid Ruskin became just one more of Parson's occasional patients in his little corner of rural Lancashire.

Arthur Severn, who had always preferred London to Brantwood during the winter months, was now often alone at Herne Hill. He found many metropolitan diversions and enjoyed boating and sketching holidays in England, Scotland and on the continent. Joan took no holidays until Ruskin died. Because she was permanently at Brantwood, Joan had more contact with Coniston life than in previous years. Yet she still could not make easy friendships with her neighbours and seldom received casual guests. Many pilgrims were turned away from Ruskin's door. A friend of days gone by, or an old correspondent, or a member of the Guild of St George, might occasionally arrive at Brantwood. They were told that Ruskin was not well enough to see visitors. This was often, but not always, true. In any case, Ruskin had lost interest in the wider world. He took no notice of letters unless they were from such people as Kate Greenaway or Francesca Alexander. Joan read their loving, gossipping letters out loud, not knowing how much Ruskin comprehended. Other letters were ignored, returned or curtly acknowledged. An unhappy reminiscence from Kathleen Olander tells us of the reception always given to Ruskin's 'girl friends', who, Joan suspected, were likely to disturb her cousin's rest and equilibrium. It will be recalled that Kathleen had been forbidden by her parents to write to Ruskin in the autumn of 1888.

> Afterwards [she wrote in 1953], despite my parents' prohibition, I often wrote to Ruskin at Brantwood, but I believe that all my letters were intercepted by Mrs Severn.

Some years later my mother, sister and I went to Keswick and Ambleside for a holiday. One day, to my surprise, my mother herself suggested that we should take a carriage and go to Coniston. On arrival she did not get out, but my sister and I walked round the lake. Half-way Mary stopped and waited for me, while I went on to Brantwood.

I was exceedingly nervous of meeting Mrs Severn, and went round to the back door where I handed my card to a butler, asking him to give it to Mr Ruskin, and requesting that he should see me. I do not believe the card reached Ruskin, for the butler returned with the answer 'not today'.

I then went round to the other side of the house and saw Ruskin at the first French window, sitting alone. But I was too alarmed to stay, for I was in full view of the next French window, where people were evidently dining.

I kissed my hand to him, but he never saw me. Nor did we ever meet again.

The newspapers told me of his death, and it saddened me to think that I should never more see him in this world. I grieved particularly lest I might have added to his sorrows by failing to act as he would have wished, and dashing his hopes and plans for our happiness together. My greatest consolation was to learn from the report of Canon Scott Holland, who was at Ruskin's bedside near the end, that he had asked for the hymn, 'Peace, perfect peace', that I had copied out and sent him twelve years before.

I hope and believe he found such peace in a renewed awareness of the love of God, during his last quiet years.[18]

No exact date can be given for this poignant episode in Kathleen's life. In this long period of the end of Ruskin's life, dates and occurences came to have little significance, since he did so little and hardly reacted to company. For perhaps a year after the long illness of 1889–1890 a visitor to Brantwood might notice that the Professor (as he was still called) still went about his normal daily activities. Such a visitor would see, for instance, Ruskin's wide-awake hat on a table next to the front door, together with the small hatchet that he used for one of his favourite activities, chopping wood. But these were merely tokens, like the books on his study table. Although Ruskin's physical strength had lasted well into his old age and his hair showed only a few flecks of grey among the brown, he was scarcely able for physical exertions. Ruskin was mobile, to some extent. He could walk into his garden quite easily, and perhaps happily, and ventured with

Joan or Baxter (always with Joan on Sundays) along the lane that led from Brantwood to Coniston. If he was taken to sit in Susie Beever's garden, Ruskin climbed, with assistance, into his carriage. He could manage the familiar steps to his bedroom. None the less there were parts of the house and the Brantwood grounds that Ruskin did not enter, either because of awkward stairs or because some rooms were the domain of the servants or the Severn family. He was no longer the master of his house. The painter Henry Holiday, who was a friend of the Severns', paid a visit in the summer of 1890 and was struck by Ruskin's 'peculiarly gentle' manner after his illness. They talked together before Arthur came into the room to suggest that Holiday might like to come into his studio to smoke a cigarette. Such a thing could never have been countenanced in the Brantwood of old. Ruskin now merely smiled and said something to the effect that his old prejudices had been abandoned.

In December of 1890 Joan was able to tell Charles Eliot Norton that 'The Coz shuns pen and ink and paper as a child the fire who has been burnt and a good thing too'.[19] There was none the less much literary work to be done at Brantwood, for the only income that supported the house and its occupants came from the sale of Ruskin's books. This was George Allen's responsibility. He was intermittently busy, with help from his family, in the rustic warehouse in the garden of Sunnyside. At Brantwood, decisions about publishing matters were in Joan's hands. She consulted Norton by letter. Sara Anderson gave secretarial assistance. Neither Joan nor Sara knew Ruskin's writings well, and they were often confused by his books. They therefore turned to W. G. Collingwood for advice. Ruskin's road-digging disciple was nearby. Collingwood moved from Windermere to Lanehead, Consiton, a short walk from Brantwood, in 1891. He and his wife Edith now had four children. Collingwood supported his family, who grew up to expect frugal rations, by his writing. He produced, among other general works, a guide to the Lake District and a book about fishing. Perhaps he gave too much time to the composition of his well-researched historical novels. Collingwood was a regular visitor at Brantwood, increasingly a strange and unwelcoming house, for a number of reasons. He explained Ruskin's publication history to Joan, and Ruskin was always glad to see him. They played chess together, for the part of Ruskin's mind that understood chess moves was largely intact. By 1891 Collingwood's book *The Life and Work of John Ruskin* was almost complete. It would be published by Methuen, not by George Allen, in 1893. The book was commissioned, Collingwood later explained, 'with the intention of contributing a volume to a series of University Extension Manuals. A purpose of the book was therefore to provide a straightforward introduction for a 'common reader' who might not have received much formal secondary education. This class would have included Joan Severn.[20]

Collingwood also wished to issue more specialised studies of Ruskin but could not easily find an audience for his scholarship. As George Allen well knew, there was a public demand for Ruskin's books only if his writing was not presented as being difficult, or abstruse, or long. In 1891 Allen and Collingwood had a notable success with a handsome edition of *The Poems of John Ruskin*. In this book Collingwood collected many obscure and unpublished verses and added them to the poems that John James Ruskin, against his son's inclinations, had privately printed in 1850. Even more popular was the *Selections from the Writings of John Ruskin*, edited by Collingwood in two volumes and issued in 1893. No fewer than 29,500 copies of this book were printed between its first publication date and 1907, when a further 'Popular Edition' bore the words 'Thirty-fifth thousand' on its title page. In such ways Collingwood helped the Severns' finances, though he himself received little reward for his expertise. His last volume of literary selections was *The Ruskin Reader* of 1895, which contained passages from *Modern Painters*, *The Seven Lamps of Architecture* and *The Stones of Venice*. In the same year Collingwood was responsible for *Studies in Both Arts*, a carefully prepared album of ten drawings by Ruskin with short letterpress taken from various sources, none of them recondite. Collingwood's preface to this volume, which was made all the more attractive by a cover designed by Burne-Jones, states that its production was 'under Mr Ruskin's personal direction and superintendance', though it is likely that Ruskin simply acquiesced in Collingwood's choice of drawings from those that were preserved in the Brantwood study.[21]

While Ruskin wrote no more, everyone in his immediate circle was concerned to put more of his writings on the market. Much of the last chapter of Collingwood's 1893 biography concerns publishing. He first of all described the nature of American pirated editions, a source of great annoyance to Ruskin for many years:

> Towards the end of the 'Fifties' Mr Riley of New York had begun to print cheap Ruskins; not, indeed, illegally, but without any acknowledgement to the author, and without any reference to the author's wishes as to form and style of production . . .
>
> Not only that, but it was a common practice to smuggle these editions, recommended by their cheapness, into other countries. Mr Riley sent, on an average, five hundred sets of *Modern Painters* to

Europe every year, the greater number to England. His example was followed by other American publishers, so that in New York alone there are now half a dozen houses advertising Ruskin's works, and many more throughout the cities of the States. Mr Riley, the first in the field, proposed to pay up a royalty upon all the copies he had sold if Mr Ruskin would recognise him as accredited publisher in America. The offer of so large a sum would have been tempting, had it not meant that Mr Ruskin must condone what he had for years denounced . . .

Though the sales of Mr Ruskin's books in America has never, until so recently, brought him any profit, his own business in England, started in 1872 at such disadvantages, had singularly prospered. It is impossible to reckon the total number of copies of Ruskin's works throughout the world; but a rough estimate gives the number of bound volumes published by Messrs. Smith & Elder and Mr George Allen, exclusive of parts and pamphlets, as about 300,000. For the first few years there was a loss upon the Orpington business; then the scale turned, as the new system of publishing became better known . . . In spite of occasional difficulties, such as the bringing out of works in parts, appearing irregularly or stopping outright at the author's illnesses, there has been a steady increase of profit, bringing in an income of two to three thousand pounds a year.

Fortunate it was for Mr Ruskin that his bold attempt succeeded. The £200,000 he inherited from his parents have gone, — chiefly in gifts and in attempts to do good. The interest he used to spend on himself; the capital he gave away until it totally disappeared, except what is represented by the house he lives in and its contents. The sale of his books is his only income, and a great part of that goes to an army of pensioners to whom in the days of his wealth he pledged himself, needy relatives and friends, discharged servants, institutions in which he took an interest at one time or other. But he has sufficient for his wants, and need not now fear poverty in his old age . . .[22]

In the 1890s and at the turn of the century there were many publications by and about Ruskin. Classic works such as *The Seven Lamps of Architecture*, *Sesame and Lilies* and *The Ethics of the Dust* were reprinted many times. We may imagine that they became presentation copies or school prizes, not only because of their messages but because they were printed and bound with exemplary care. Some books, principally *The Stones of Venice*, were taken abroad by cultured travellers. Ruskin 'gift books', usually containing aphorisms or well-turned sentiments, were common. Many were piracies. After 1907, when copyright expired in many of Ruskin's works, there were numerous unauthorised English selections of this sort. Some of the better, authorised selections of the 1890s have already been mentioned in the present book. They include A. M. Wakefield's *Ruskin on Music* and William Jolly's *Ruskin on Education*, both published in 1894. *Ruskin's Thoughts About Women* (1892) were collected by Kate Stanley, who was Head Governess at Whitelands College. In 1898 Mary and Ellen Gibbs published *The Bible References of John Ruskin*. This is not in itself a work of reference, although it contains an appendix of 'The Books of the Bible as quoted or referred to in this volume'. The Gibbs sisters did not attempt to be comprehensive, for that would have been a near impossible task; but they chose well, and were not shy of quoting from *Fors Clavigera*. Their enterprise has scarcely ever been acknowledged. Yet, in reprinting Ruskin's words, they produced a book of high literary quality and searching piety. It is a moving tribute to a religious mind. A reference work that originated in America and — alas — was never available in Britain is *Comments of John Ruskin on the Divina Commedia*, compiled by George P. Huntington (Cambridge, Mass., 1903), whose preface remarks that 'the selections form an extensive commentary on the poem. Of the *Inferno* all but two, and of the *Purgatorio* all but three of the cantos are referred to; and of the *Paradiso* more than one half'. Charles Eliot Norton's introduction to Huntington's work states, justly, that 'No other great English writer has shown such familiarity with the Divine Comedy as Mr Ruskin. The references to it scattered throughout his writings . . . form a comment on the poem, partial and irregular indeed, but of peculiar interest'.[23]

Perhaps only the atmosphere of Boston and Harvard could have produced such a book as Huntington's. In this New England academic society (which, in the early century, helped to form another great writer who was absorbed by the *Divina Commedia*, T. S. Eliot) there was a self-conscious appreciation of Dante.[24] It was part of an aspiration toward high European culture. In Harvard, Ruskin may have been regarded as an oracle, or at least as a great interpreter. That was not the case in Oxford. Memories of his vagaries were still fresh in Ruskin's own university, and his contributions to knowledge were forgotten. Nobody in Oxford knew what to do with the drawing schools and their school and its collections. The history of European art was not studied, although Ruskin had been an energetic pioneer of the new academic discipline. His reputation stood higher elsewhere in

Britain, particularly in the northern industrial cities, where his 'message' appeared most relevant.

During the 1890s, the period of Ruskin's silence, his work became public property in ways he had not foreseen. He had always hoped that people would study his writings. But he had not imagined that his teachings would be disseminated through the work of intermediaries. From the 1890s until the First World War large numbers of people gained their knowledge of Ruskin from secondary sources. Such people often attended lecture courses in municipal libraries, institutions or similar venues. The nature of such courses (which often stressed Ruskin's social thought) may be gathered from John W. Graham's *The Harvest of Ruskin* (1920) which, the author states, began 'as lectures in the past years under the Manchester and Liverpool University Extension Committees, at Summer Schools, and elsewhere'. One of Ruskin's most significant followers, John Howard Whitehouse, was affected by such lectures. While still a young clerk in his native city, the future owner of Brantwood helped to organise the Ruskin Society of Birmingham. Whitehouse (born 1873) both attended and delivered lectures to this society in the late 1890s. Thus he taught Ruskin, and learnt about Ruskin, at one and the same time.

Whitehouse owned Collingwood's recent *The Life and Work of John Ruskin*, his only guide, apart from *Præterita*, to the outlines of Ruskin's literary career. Collingwood's book was the only expert critical-cum-biographical study before Frederic Harrison's *John Ruskin*, which appeared in Macmillan's 'English Men of Letters' series in 1902. Harrison could claim a longer, though more distant, relationship with Ruskin than had been Collingwood's privilege. He had first known Ruskin in the 1850s and had been a frequent visitor at Denmark Hill when the house still belonged to John James Ruskin. Harrison therefore knew Joan of old. He remembered her from the days when she was still Joan Agnew. While not exactly a family friend, Harrison had so long been an acquaintance of the Ruskins that, in about 1898, he was not only allowed to visit Brantwood but to sit with the helpless master of the lakeland house; where, Harrison wrote (having recognised some pieces of old furniture), 'you would not immediately perceive that you were in anything but the ordinary comfortable home of a professional gentleman'.

Harrison continued:

> but a year or two before his death, I found him in his quiet Brantwood home — to look at just like Lear in the last scene, but perfectly reposeful, gentle, and happy, taking the air of the fells with

> delight, joining in games or reading with the family at intervals., but for the most part sitting in his library and softly turning over the pages of a poem, a tale of Walter Scott, or Dickens, or some illustrated volume of views, himself in a bower of roses and gay flowers; silently and for long intervals together gazing with a far-off look of yearning, but no longer of eagerness, at the blue hills of the Coniston Old Man, across the rippling lake, as if — half child again, half wayworn pilgrim — he saw there the Delectable Mountains where the wicked cease from troubling and the weary are at rest . . .[25]

From Harrison's account, which is a little too pious in tone, one imagines that Ruskin, in his extreme old age, had lost the faculty by which we notice the passage of time. He probably lost his memory at the same period when, in 1895 or 1896, he no longer spoke in connected sentences. If he was well enough, he saw dawns and sunsets but could not remember how recent days, or months, or years, had passed. He continued to have attacks of 'brain fever' and perhaps also suffered from strokes. During the 1890s, as a result of such illnesses, there were periods when he was bereft of any kind of speech. Then he recovered a little, though never completely, and was able to communicate with Baxter or Joan. There were occasions when he attempted to write a letter. Joan Severn opened the doors of Brantwood to Ruskin's visitors only when her cousin was relatively alert, and such guests were in any case rare. In all the decade of the 1890s we hear of only about a couple of dozen people who came to Brantwood and saw Ruskin. Harrison was one. Walter Crane was another: he was a guest at Brantwood because he was a friend of Arthur Severn's. Sydney Cockerell was a third. Harvey Goodwin, the Bishop of Carlisle, visited the Severns. He went to Ruskin's room and blessed him. Ruskin's oldest friend, Henry Acland, was at Brantwood in 1893. He was accompanied by his daughter Angie, who took some memorable photographs of Ruskin and her father.

There was no pattern or purpose in these occasional visits. If Ruskin had shown signs of enjoying company, then Joan no doubt would have been more welcoming. One quite significant visit can be recorded. John Howard Whitehouse wished to celebrate Ruskin's 80th birthday on February 8 1899. Whitehouse was now the most prominent member of the Ruskin Society of Birmingham (a successful organisation, for we know that in 1903 it had 567 members) and was also the editor of its interesting publication *St George*. In January of 1899 Whitehouse approached the Guild of St George and the Ruskin

Societies of Glasgow and Liverpool. He proposed a national address of congratulation. The address was prepared, illuminated and expensively bound. Together with William Wardle, the secretary of the Liverpool Ruskin Society, Whitehouse travelled to Coniston on February 7. The next day, his diary tells us:

> The morning was fairly bright and clear and at 11 o'clock we started for Brantwood. It is a glorious road, going for some distance by the margin of the lake and commanding exquisite views. At Brantwood we were very politely received by Mr & Mrs Arthur Severn. They explained that the Master felt equal to seeing us and had expressed a wish to do so. Mr Severn said that he was really wonderfully well and that although we should find him in his bedroom, we were not to conclude from that, that he was ill. They did not want him to come down stairs as the staircase was rather narrow, &c. &c. We were then conducted to Mr Ruskin's presence. He was dressed and sitting in an armchair before a little table. As we entered he attempted to rise, but was evidently too feeble to do so. We shook hands and I told him I was glad to hear he was so well. I then explained that we had brought him a national address, and I read it to him. As I was doing so, I occasionally heard him give a low exclamation — half sob it seemed to be. When I had finished he tried to reply but could only utter a few broken words. He was evidently deeply moved and quite overcome with emotion. After he had looked at the address we withdrew . . . What most impressed me when I saw the Master were his wonderful eyes. They are blue and very clear and bright. When, during the reading of the address, I looked up at him, I found them fixed upon me as though he were searching me through and through. No one who meets his eyes can doubt that his mind is perfectly clear . . .[26]

In less than a year's time Whitehouse was again at Coniston, on this occasion to attend Ruskin's funeral. The end came quickly and peacefully, even with a minor winter celebration, for Ruskin's last meal was sole, pheasant and champagne, his supper on Thursday 18 January 1900. A number of Brantwood servants had influenza. The illness passed to Ruskin. He died, in his sleep, at 3.30 p.m. on Saturday 20 January 1900. Joan was holding his hand. Baxter and Dr Parsons were in attendance. *The Times* tells us (from a statement prepared by Joan) that

> a little later, when the first shock was over, Mrs Severn's daughter prevailed upon her to look from his little turret window at the

> sunset, as Ruskin was wont to look for it from day to day. The brilliant, gorgeous light illumined the hills with splendour; and the spectators felt as if Heaven's gate itself had been flung open to receive the teacher into everlasting peace.[27]

Joan now had to attend to the details of the funeral. As we have seen, Ruskin had told her that he wished to be buried in Coniston churchyard. With some presumption, and presumably because he was a national newspaperman, E. T. Cook prepared a 'memorial', as he called it, stating that Ruskin should be buried in Westminster Abbey. He obtained the signatures of many eminent men and presented their view to the Dean and Chapter of Westminster. In the event, Ruskin's wishes were followed, and he was given a parochial rather than a national funeral. He was indeed a glory of the nation's literature, and an important part of its social conscience, but in many ways preferred to consider himself as a man who strove to do a little good and who lived in an English village. There was a simple service at Coniston. The mourners, who were mainly local people, saw Ruskin buried next to his friend Susie Beever. It was raining, so few people lingered by the grave. 'There was no black about his burying', Collingwood recorded, 'except what we wore for our own sorrow; it was remembered how much he hated black, so much that he would even have his mother's coffin painted blue'.[28] Ruskin's own coffin was covered with a pall of bright crimson silk. For, as he had once written to Susie Beever, 'Why should we wear black for the guests of God?'[29]

POSTSCRIPT

Later developments among Ruskin's friends and disciples are not within the scope of this biography. The following notes merely summarise the fortunes of his papers and collections in the years after his death. Ruskin's will, dated October 23, 1883, says

> I leave all my estate of Brantwood aforesaid and all other real estate of which I may die possessed to Joseph Arthur Palliser Severn, and Joanna Ruskin Severn, his wife, and to the survivor of them and their heirs for their very own, earnestly praying them never to sell the estate of Brantwood or any part thereof, but to maintain the said estate and the buildings thereon in decent order and in good repair in like manner as I have done, and praying them further to accord during thirty consecutive days in every year such permission to strangers to see the house and pictures as I have done in my lifetime.[1]

Ruskin envisaged a home for the Severns that would also be a museum. Arthur, Joan and their children continued to live at Brantwood and made extensions to the building. However, the house was seldom if ever opened to the public. The Severns were not by nature the museum curators. Although they were eager to preserve Ruskin's memory, they preferred that his reputation should thrive by the sale of his books. The most elementary curatorial duty was neglected. Nobody made a full catalogue of the contents of the house. It is therefore difficult to know which items left the Brantwood collection, though it is certain that the Severns sold paintings, rare books such as illuminated missals, and other materials. Joan died in 1924. Arthur, who preferred to live in London, allowed the house to decay. He died in 1931. In 1932 Brantwood was bought by John Howard Whitehouse, who re-opened it as a national memorial to Ruskin.

Whitehouse had been the Liberal MP for Mid-Lanark from 1910–18. In 1919 he established Bembridge School, which has a pleasant and sunny position on the south coast of the Isle of Wight. The school became the home for Whitehouse's remarkable collection of Ruskin books, manuscripts, drawings and associated items. He acquired this material from many sources. The major purchases were made from the 'Dispersal Sales' held at Brantwood in 1930 and 1931.

Whitehouse had an especial love for Ruskin's drawings. He was less interested in the manuscripts he had bought, which included most of Ruskin's diaries and more than 3,000 letters from Ruskin to Joan Severn. Years before, probably around 1902, these letters had been carefully packed into parcels by Sara Anderson. Whitehouse opened some but not all of them. Ruskin's most informative and often heartfelt letters were therefore occluded for many years.[2]

Sara Anderson had a privileged knowledge of the books and papers that were preserved at Brantwood. With much expertise, and firm tact, she assembled the materials that were given to E. T. Cook and Alexander Wedderburn for the preparation of their 'Library Edition' of Ruskin's works. The 39 volumes of this edition, published between 1903–12, are the basis of all subsequent Ruskin scholarship and interpretation. Joan Severn and George Allen were confident that the enterprise would bring a financial reward. In this hope they were mistaken. Instead, they presided over a colossal feat of publishing and of editorial devotion. Some idea of the labours involved may be gained by looking at Volume 39, the index. It contains around 25,000 separate titles and more than 150,000 references. Most of the editorial work was Cook's. His introductions to the successive volumes were the basis of his *The Life of John Ruskin* (1912).

Ruskin's influence is always difficult to define. It was probably at its height — though the influence was a diffused, not a specific, part of the ethos of the age — during the great period of self-education. Very broadly, this period may be said to have extended from the 1880s to the First World War. At Oxford, Ruskin College was founded by two of his American admirers in 1899. The college had little to do with the teaching of the author of *Fors Clavigera*; but its very existence seemed to be a link between Ruskin himself, the trade union movement and the cause of working-class education. In British universities generally, Ruskin was ignored for many years. The Library Edition found none of the respect and fame that it deserved. Ruskin studies were confined to a small number of collectors and devotees, none of whom was attached to universities and who scarcely knew of each other's existence.

In 1929, thus before the Dispersal Sales at Brantwood, a young American research student arrived at Coniston. Helen Gill, later Helen Gill Viljoen, saw Brantwood in its dilapidated, almost ruinous condition. Searching through the library she chanced on Rose La Touche's diary, which had been hidden behind a bookcase. Gill transcribed this pathetic document. The discovery probably made her protective of the neglected Ruskin heritage. So did her friendship with W. G. Collingwood, who still lived within a mile or two of Brantwood. He welcomed and encouraged Gill's interest in Ruskin. Collingwood had long been disenchanted with the Severns. Ruskin's former secretary also had reservations about Cook and Wedderburn's work on the Library Edition. He thought that their work was done entirely at the behest of the Severn family. Collingwood's criticisms reappear in Helen Gill Viljoen's *Ruskin's Scottish Heritage* (1956), which was dedicated to Collingwood's memory and to his daughter Barbara Gnosspelius, who assisted Viljoen when she edited *The Brantwood Diary of John Ruskin*, eventually published in 1971.[3]

Viljoen had been given this volume of Ruskin's diaries, often mentioned in the above pages, by the collector F. W. Sharp, who had died in 1957. Sharp was a self-educated man from Barrow-in-Furness, which is not far from Coniston. He had acquired the diary at about the time of the Brantwood Dispersal Sales. It is not surprising that Sharp, and then Viljoen, felt that this precious document should not be given a rough or premature entry to the world. Sharp withheld the volume from Joan Evans, whose inadequate edition of the complete diaries (which appeared in 1956–9: Whitehouse is credited as co-editor of these manuscripts, though he was merely their owner) gave rise to her brief, hostile biography *John Ruskin*, published in 1954. It seemed to claim that the diaries themselves, which recorded Ruskin's daily life in his own hand, had no bearing on Evans's opinions.

The publication of Joan Evans's book was the darkest moment of Ruskin's posthumous reputation. Fortunately, from 1957, the Bembridge archive had been entrusted to James S. Dearden. A former pupil who taught printing at the school, Dearden is a native of Barrow-in-Furness who, with his parents, had known F. W. Sharp. Dearden began to sort and catalogue Whitehouse's collection. This work took many years. At Bembridge, Dearden was the host and guide of another significant American scholar, Van Akin Burd, the editor of *The Winnington Letters of John Ruskin* (1969) and *The Ruskin Family Letters* (1973). He was later the author of *John Ruskin and Rose La Touche* (1979). This book printed the transcripts of Rose's diaries, which Viljoen had willed to Burd after her death in 1974.

The general inheritance of Ruskin scholarship and research has been, on the whole, private and confined to specialists. Some of them clung obsessively to the material they had uncovered. A growing spirit of co-operation was noticeable after the 'Ruskin Conference' organised by Dearden and Burd at Brantwood in 1969. In the subsequent decade a number of enthusiasts and researchers brought more Ruskin letters and diaries to light. The Guild of St George was reorganised.

The Ruskin Museum in Sheffield was revivified. In 1997 the Bembridge collections were transferred to the University of Lancaster, and were thus re-united (by a short journey) with the various books, paintings and memorabilia that remain at Ruskin's Brantwood home.

NOTES

Quotations from Ruskin's published works are taken from the Library Edition, *The Works of John Ruskin*, ed. E. T. Cook and Alexander Wedderburn, 39 vols., London, 1903–12. References are given by volume and page number thus: XVI, 432. Place of publication of titles referred to in the Notes is London unless otherwise stated.

Material once at Bembridge is now at the Ruskin Foundation (Ruskin Library, University of Lancaster).

Abbreviations

BD. *The Brantwood Diary of John Ruskin*, ed. Helen Gill Viljoen, New Haven and London, 1971.

Diaries. *The Diaries of John Ruskin*, ed. Joan Evans and John Howard Whitehouse, 3 vols., Oxford, 1956–9.

EV. Mary Lutyens, *Effie in Venice*, 1965

IMT. *The Letters of John Ruskin to Lord and Lady Mount-Temple*, ed. John Lewis Bradley, Ohio, 1964.

MR. Mary Lutyens, *Millais and the Ruskins*, 1968.

RFL. *The Ruskin Family Letters. The Correspondence of John James Ruskin, his Wife, and their Son John, 1801–1843*, ed. Van Akin Burd, Ithaca and London, 1973.

RG. Mary Lutyens, *The Ruskins and the Grays*, 1972.

RI. *Ruskin in Italy. Letters to his Parents 1845*, ed. Harold I. Shapiro, Oxford, 1972.

RLT. *John Ruskin and Rose La Touche: Her Unpublished Diaries of 1861 and 1867*, ed. Van Akin Burd, 1979.

RSH. Helen Gill Viljoen, *Ruskin's Scottish Heritage*, Urbana, Illinois, 1956.

TC. *The Correspondence of Thomas Carlyle and John Ruskin*, ed. George Allan Cate, Stanford, California, 1982.

WL. *The Winnington Lettters. John Ruskin's Correspondence with Margaret Alexis Bell and the Children at Winnington Hall*, ed. Van Akin Burd, 1969.

Chapter One

1. On all these matters see RSH and RFL. Both Professor Viljoen and Professor Burd provide information about Ruskin's ancestry. RSH has an appendix covering 'The Edinburgh Ruskins and their descendants and relatives of Croydon'. RFL contains a family tree.
2. XXXV, 62.
3. XXXV, 62.
4. XXXV, 18.
5. Ms *Præterita* Beinecke Library, Yale University.
6. From Sir Albert Gray's papers concerning his family and the Ruskins. Bodley Ms Eng Letts c 228.
7. JJR-Catherine Ruskin, 5 Oct 1812, RFL 54.
8. RSL, 116. See also RFL, 64n-65n.
9. JJR-Georg Gray, 31 Aug 1848, RG 150.
10. JJR-Catherine Ruskin, 13 Apr 1815, RFL 76.
11. JJR-Catherine Ruskin, 30 Jun 1815, RFL 79.
12. XXXV, 15-16.
13. XXXV, 34.
14. JJR-MR, 23 Jun 1819, RFL 95.
15. JJR-MR, 6 Dec 1829, RFL 211-12.
16. See RFL, 374-413 for this journey.
17. MR-JJR, 10 Apr 1820, RFL 98.
18. XXVIII, 345-6.
19. MR-JJR, 30 Jan 1822, RFL 109.
20. These favourite chapters are discussed by Viljoen in RSH 162.
21. The Bibles are described and illustrated in W. G. Collingwood, *Ruskin Relics*, 1903, 193-213.
22. XXXV, 40.
23. XXXV, 39-40.
24. JR-JJR, 15 Mar 1823, RFL 127-8.
25. XXXV, 88.
26. XXXV, 131.
27. Ms Bembridge 28.
28. JJR-JR, 6 Nov 1829, RFL 209-10.
29. JR-JJR, 10 May 1829, RFL 199-200.
30. To Jane Simon, for instance. Bembridge Ms L 12.
31. XXVI, 294n.
32. XXXV, 75.
33. XXXV, 63.
34. JJR-R. Gray, 17 Jan 1833, RFL 276.
35. XXXV, 16.
36. II, 286-97.
37. XXXV, 25.
38. Howels is identified in a letter from Ruskin to Joan Severn which includes both a letter from Howels and this contemporary comment; JR-JRS, 3 Jan 1876, Ms Bembridge L 41. The *Præterita* passage was taken from *Fors*, but Ruskin evidently did not correct the mistaken name when the autobiography was issued. For Howels see also Edward Morgan, *A Memoir of the Life of William Howels*, 1854.
39. XXVIII, 297-8.
40. For Andrews (and other clergy in the area) see E. G. Cleal, *The Story of Congregationalism in Surrey*, 1908, 105.
41. XXXV, 132.
42. MR-JJR, 10 Mar 1831, RFL 242.
43. MR-JJR, 10 Mar 1831, RFL 243.
44. JR-JJR, 19 Jan 1829, RFL 173.
45. See Van Akin Burd, *The Winnington Letters*, 1969, 60n.
46. XXXV, 25.
47. XXXV, 143.
48. XXXV, 73.
49. XXXV, 142.
50. XXXV, 143.
51. JJR-Mary Russell Mitford, 17 Dec 1853, Ms Bembridge L 11.
52. JR-JJR, 27 Feb 1832, RFL 267-8.
53. XXXV, 115.
54. Ms Bembridge 33.
55. II, 387. See also 359-68.
56. The description of the tour is at II, 340-87.
57. See XXXVIII, 3 *et seqq.* for Ruskin's publications. His first appearance in print was with 'On Skiddaw and Derwent Water', a poem in the *Spiritual Times*, Feb 1830, II, 265-6.
58. XXXIV, 365.
59. XXXV, 395.
60. XXXV, 83.
61. XXXV, 139-40.
62. See J. Garden, *Memorials of the Ettrick Shepherd*, 1894, 273-7.
63. I, xxviii.
64. XXXV, 102-3.
65. JJR-W. H. Harrison, 6 Jan 1839, Ms Bembridge L 5.

66. See George Croly, *Historical Sketches, Speeches and Characters*, 1842, 45 *seqq*., and 310 *seqq*.
67. *Don Juan*, XI, Cantos 57-8.
68. XXXIV, 95.
69. The majority of Ruskin's diaries are preserved at Bembridge. References are given in this book to the published version (ed. Joan Evans and John Howard Whitehouse, Oxford, 1956-9), but also to the Bodleian Library transcripts, which contain the full text, and to the original volumes, in which there are diagrams and drawings.
70. VI, 476.
71. 3 Jun 1835, Diaries 2.
72. XXXV, 152.
73. XIV, 389-91.
74. XXXV, 179.
75. XXXV, 179.
76. XXXV, 180.
77. XXXV, 180.
78. JJR-George Gray, 28 Apr 1847, RG 27.
79. JR-JJR, 25 Mar 1836, RFL 350.
80. The *Iris*, 1834.
81. The essay is printed at I, 357-75.
82. XXXV, 217.
83. Extracts from Eagles's review are at III, xviii.
84. Ruskin's defence was found among his papers after his death. It is printed at III, 635-40.
85. XXXV, 218.

Chapter Two

1. XXXV, 191-2.
2. XXXV, 193.
3. XXXV, 610.
4. G. W. Kitchin, *Ruskin in Oxford and Other Papers*, 1904, 27-8.
5. JR-JJR, 12 Aug 1862, *The Winnington Letters*, ed. Van Akin Burd, 1969, 369-70.
6. XXXV, 196.
7. For Gordon see G. Marshall, *Osborne Gordon*, 1885.
8. XXXV, 252.
9. XXXV, 198.
10. H. L. Thompson, *Henry George Liddell*, 1899, 215n.
11. A. J. C. Hare, *The Story of my Life, 1896-1900*, V, 358.
12. Liddell-Acland (1854). Bodley Ms Acland d. 69.
13. XXXV, 205.
14. The manuscript of *Præterita* is preserved in the Beinecke Library, Yale University. Some plans, notes and passages are in Ruskin's diaries. For these extracts see S. E. Brown, 'The Unpublished Passages in the Manuscript of Ruskin's Autobiography', *Victorian Newsletter*, 16, Fall 1959, 10-18.
15. XXXV, 229.
16. JJR-MR, 13 Mar 1840, RFL 667.
17. 28 Dec 1839, Diaries 73.
18. 12 Mar 1841, Diaries 165.
19. I, xliii.
20. JJR-W. H. Harrison, 9 Jun 1839. Ms Bembridge L 5.
21. XXXV, 255-6.
22. XXXV, 259.

Chapter Three

1. 22 Jun 1840, Diaries 82.
2. XXXV, 305.
3. JJR-JR, 20 Apr 1842, RFL 734.
4. II, 343.
5. W. G. Collingwood, *The Life and Work of John Ruskin*, 1900, 75.
6. 31 Mar 1840, Diaries 74.
7. 15 Nov 1840, Diaries 110.
8. I, 380.
9. I, 381-2.
10. Mary Richardson's diary, 30 May 1840, Ms Bembridge T 49.
11. JJR-W. H. Harrison, n.d., Bodley Ms Eng Letts c 32 fol 55.
12. Mary Richardson's diary, 7 Feb 1840, Ms Bembridge T 49.
13. Mary Richardson's diary, 3 Apr 1840, Ms Bembridge T 49.
14. XXXV, 274-5.
15. XXXV, 275.
16. For George Richmond and his family, see A. M. W. Stirling, *The Richmond Papers*, 1926, and Raymond Lister, *George Richmond*, 1981.
17. JJR-W. H. Harrison, 25 Dec 1840, Bodley Ms Eng Letts c 32 fol 54.
18. For Ruskin's relations with Zorzi, see Jeanne Clegg, *Ruskin and Venice*, 1981, 183-7.
19. XXXV, 297.

Chapter Four

1. XXXV, 299.
2. XXXV, 304, *The King of the Golden River* was perhaps too long for *Friendship's Offering*, or Ruskin was perhaps unwilling to publish it there. John James wrote to W. H. Harrison that 'I expect in a week to receive manuscript of a Fairy Tale but which I must to follow orders dispatch to Scotland directly. I should like when it comes for you to cast your eye over it . . . if it would do for any monthly

. . .', 27 Sep 1841, Bodley Ms Eng Letts c 32 fol 78.

3. JJR-JR, 25 Aug 1841, RFL 680.

4. XXXV, 306.

5. See, for instance, the similarities between MPI and Harding's *The Principles and Practice of Art*, 1845. There are a number of stories of Harding's later opposition to *Modern Painters*. Ruskin claimed that Harding was jealous of the position given to Turner (XXXV, 401). Henry Holiday describes a Harding drawing class in 1858. Holiday had been drawing a large landscape from nature. '"What", [Harding] said, "are you a Pre-Raphaelite?" "I am." The diplomatic sky darkened and his face was itself a declaration of war. He at once attacked what he assumed to be my main body, viz., Mr Ruskin, and opened fire with two charges. 1st, that the writings of his renegade pupil were a mass of pernicious heresies; and 2nd, that they were merely a re-cook of his (Mr Harding's) own works on art . . .' Henry Holiday, *Reminiscences of my Life*, 1914, 49.

6. Ruskin thought Prout a little staid but always remembered him kindly, perhaps because the artist died after the party John James held for his son's birthday, while Ruskin was in Venice in 1852. W. H. Harrison recalled him 'at dinner at Mr Ruskin's . . . in wonderful spirits, and I remember his challenging me in a glass of champagne, and my rallying him on some circumstance . . . He was stepping into his carriage at the door at night, and shook hands very heartily, adding, "Why don't you come and see me?" This was eleven o'clock, and before twelve he was dead.' Harrison, 'Notes and Reminiscences', *University Magazine*, May 1878, 545.

7. 6 Jul 1841, Diaries 209.

8. XIII, 478.

9. XXXV, 309-10.

10. XXXV, 311.

11. XXXV, 314.

12. XXXV, 316.

13. Ruskin's correspondence with Clayton was published in 1894 as *Letters Addressed to a College Friend 1840-1845*. Some additional letters are at Bembridge. See I, 407-502.

14. Ruskin's degree has puzzled historians. The most reasonable explanation is Collingwood's. 'He could not now go in for honours, for the lost year had superannuated him. So in April he went up for a pass. In those times, when a pass-man showed unusual powers, they could give him an honorary class; not a high class, because the range of the examinations was less than in the honour-school. This candidate wrote a poor Latin prose, it seems; but his divinity, philosophy, and mathematics were so good that they gave him the best they could — an honorary double fourth.' W. G. Collingwood, *Life*, revised ed., 1911, 69.

15. III, 665-6. The letter is dated 10 Mar 1844.

16. XXXV, 381.

17. A. M. W. Stirling, *The Richmond Papers*, 1926, 138.

18. 8 Feb 1843, Diaries 242.

19. 24 Feb 1843, Diaries 245.

20. 1 May 1843, Diaries 245.

21. The circumstances are explained at III, xxxii. A number of John James's letters to Harrison are concerned with the shortcomings of magazines and their publishers. It is the father of *Fors Clavigera* who writes 'I have *used my endeavours* to peruse Blackwood from old associations but in vain . . . you are right in a good monthly being wanted, but to start a new one would require a devotion to the Cause of more than one amateur of large fortune, for *publishers* are the smallest souled merchants in London — hard ignorant blockheads iron hearted pawnbrokers — receiving brains in pawn, doling out the merest pittance . . .' JJR-W. H. Harrison, 16 Dec 1843, Ms Bembridge L 5.

22. See William Knight's *Life of William Wordsworth*, 1889, II, 334, III, 243.

23. *Alfred, Lord Tennyson*, A Memoir by his Son, 1897, I, 223.

24. *The Letters of Elizabeth Barrett Browning*, ed. F. G. Kenyon, 1897, I, 384.

25. *Macmillan's Magazine*, Aug 1891, lxiv, 280.

26. J. W. Cross, *The Life of George Eliot*, 1885, II, 7.

27. John James Ruskin's press cuttings books are preserved in the library of the Ashmolean Museum, Oxford.

28. XXXV, 401.

29. III, 668. The letter is dated 12 Oct 1844.

30. 27 May 1843, Diaries 248.

31. 21 Nov 1843, Diaries 249.

32. 12 Dec 1843, Diaries 254.

33. III, 571-3.

34. 24 Nov 1843, Diaries 250.

35. III, 571-3.

36. *Macbeth*, II, 2, 64.

37. XXXVI, 81. The letter is dated 28 Sept 1847.

38. XXVI, 219-20.

39. XXXV, 329.

40. XXXV, 325.

41. XXVI, 222.

42. XXXVI, 38-9. The letter is dated 12 Aug 1844. The Hotel Meurice, in the rue de Rivoli, was used by Ruskin until his last visit to Paris

in 1881.
43. 20 Oct 1844, Diaries 318.

Chapter Five

1. XXXVI, 406.
2. XX, 25, and see also VII, 453 and XVIII, 148.
3. JR-Thomas Carlyle, 12 Jun 1867, in *The Correspondence of Thomas Carlyle and John Ruskin*, ed. G. A. Cate, Stanford, California, 1982, 136.
4. XXXV, 341-2.
5. JR-Acland, 27 Dec 1844, Bodley Ms Acland 4 b-c.
6. JR-JJR, 10 Apr 1845, RI 13.
7. XXXV, 346.
8. JR-JJR, 3 May 1845, RI 51.
9. IV, 347.
10. JR-JJR, 6 May 1845, RI 55.
11. XXXV, 346.
12. 8 Nov 1840, Diaries 106.
13. 18 Nov 1840, Diaries 108.
14. JR-JJR, 18 May 1845, RI 67.
15. JR-JJR, 18 May 1845, RI 68.
16. Ibid.
17. JR-JJR, postmarked 21 Jun 1845, RI 123.
18. JR-JJR, 22 Jun 1845, RI 124.
19. JR-JJR, 16 Jul 1845, RI 148. This was in Milan.
20. JR-JJR, 27 Jul 1845, RI 163. In fact Turner would never leave England again.
21. XXXV, 369.
22. JR-JJR, 6 Aug 1845, RI 168.
23. JR-JJR, 10 Aug 1845, RI 170.
24. JR-JJR, 15 Aug 1845, RI 172.
25. JR-JJR, 10 Sept 1845, RI 198.
26. JR-JJR, 11 Sept 1845, RI 200.
27. JR-JJR, 14 Sept 1845, RI 202.
28. JR-JJR, 4 Sept 1845, RI 211-12.
29. JR-JJR, 28 Sept 1845, RI 216.
30. 4 Jan 1846, Diaries 321-2.
31. 19 Jan 1847, Diaries 322. The entry is a long gloss on that of 4 Jan 1846.
32. IV, 60.
33. See the 'Epilogue' to the 1883 edition, IV, 343-57, which describes the 1845 tour and 'the temper in which, on my return to England, I wrote the second volume of *Modern Painters*'.
34. W. G. Collingwood, *The Art Teaching of John Ruskin*, 1891, 117.
35. XXXV, 413.
36. A. J. Finberg, *Life of J. M. W. Turner*, 1939, 418.
37. On the other hand, it is clear from his writings that Ruskin had amassed a great deal of Turner lore in the early years of his involvement with the artist. No doubt this came from other artists, other collectors, and from Griffith. Some of these matters are dealt with in vol. XIII of the Library Edition, but there is no modern book on Ruskin's knowledge of Turner, except for the necessarily partial (but excellent) volume by Luke Herrmann, *Ruskin and Turner: A Study of Ruskin as a Collector of Turner, Based on his Gifts to the University of Oxford*, (1968).
38. XIII, 167.
39. JR-Griffith, 31 Nov 1854, Ms Bembridge T 73.
40. Famous for his *Horæ Subsecivæ* (1858-61 and 1882), which includes the celebrated dog story 'Rab and his Friends'. See *Letters of Dr John Brown*, ed. by his son and D. W. Forrest, with biographical introductions by Elizabeth T. M'Laren, 1907.

Chapter Six

1. *Church of England Quarterly Review*, July 1846, 205.
2. VIII, 95n.
3. XXXV, 418-19.
4. JJR-W. H. Harrison, Venice, 25 May 1846, Bodley Ms Eng Letts c 32 fol 243.
5. XXXVI, 64. The letter is dated 30 Aug (1846).
6. XXXV, 422.
7. XXXV, 249.
8. XXXV, 422.
9. XXXV, 249.
10. XXXV, 422.
11. JR-JJR, postmarked 21 Jun 1845, RI 123.
12. Ibid.
13. Quoted in RI, 123n.
14. XXXV, 422.
15. XXXV, 423.
16. XXXV, 249.
17. XXXV, 422.
18. VIII, xxv. The letter is dated 18 Mar 1847.
19. Ibid.
20. JJR-George Gray, 28 Apr 1847, RG 32-3.
21. ECG to her mother, 28 Apr 1847, RG 32-3.
22. ECG to her mother, 4 May 1847, RG 35.
23. ECG to her mother, 5 May 1847, RG 35.
24. ECG to her mother, 5 May 1847, RG 35-6.
25. XXXV, 423.
26. XXXVI, 71.
27. JJR to his parents, 27 Jun 1847, VIII, xxv-xxvi.
28. 30 Jul 1847, Diaries 351.
29. 21 Aug 1847, Diaries 362.
30. 25 Aug 1847, Diaries 364.

Chapter Seven

1. See XVII, 417-22, 'Of Improvidence in Marriage in the Middle Classes; and of the Advisable Restrictions of it', a letter from *Time and Tide*.
2. JR-ECG, 2 Nov (1847), Ms, Private Collection. This and other letters of the period are discussed in Mary Lutyens, 'From Ruskin to Effie Gray', *Times Literary Supplement*, 3 March 1978.
3. JR-ECG, 6 Mar (1847). Ms, Private Collection.
4. By a coincidence which must later have struck Margaret Ruskin as ominous, the Gray family had moved into Bowerswell in 1829.
5. JJR-George Gray, 23 Feb 1848, RG 90-1.
6. The evidence about Ruskin's wedding night has been collected by Mary Lutyens. See MR, 154-7.
7. MR 188-92.
8. ECG-George Gray, 25 Mar 1854, MR 156.
9. MR 188-92.
10. MR 219.
11. ECG-George Gray, 10 Jun 1848, RG 120.
12. ECG to her mother, 12 Nov 1848, RG 168.
13. He was Frederick Myers, a Cambridge Evangelical. Ruskin wrote to his brother-in-law, Dr Whewell, Master of Trinity College, Cambridge, of 'a day or two I am enjoying here — happy in the neighbourhood of St Johns church — and in the teaching of Mr Myers — an advantage which was indeed the chief motive of my choosing Keswick for our place of sojourn . . . I am especially gladdened by the return of the services and teaching of my own church — after some weeks experimentalising among the Scotch Free churchmen . . .' Keswick, 17 Apr 1848. Trinity Coll Cambridge Add Ms c 90/83.
14. JJR-George Gray, 28 Apr 1848, RG III.
15. ECG to her mother, 28 Apr 1848, RG III.
16. JJR-George Gray, 24 May 1848, RG 116.
17. Quoted and discussed at VIII, xxiii and 278.
18. See IV, 37-41.
19. JR-JJR, Florence, 30 May 1845, RV 89.
20. VIII, 3n.
21. J. G. Links, *The Ruskins in Normandy*, 1968, 14.
22. Ibid., 19.
23. XXXV, 156.
24. XII, 314-15.
25. Links, op. cit., 26-7.
26. Ibid., 41.
27. The letter was to W. H. Harrison. Links, op. cit., 83-4.

Chapter Eight

1. *Prospectus of the Arundel Society*, 1849, 8.
2. JJR-George Gray, 4 Mar 1849, RG 180.
3. JR-ECR, 24 Apr 1849, RG 185.
4. JR-ECR, 29 Apr 1849, RG 187.
5. 30 Apr 1849, Diaries 374.
6. 3 Jun 1849, Diaries 381.
7. Ruskin had a lifelong interest in this poem: he wished to know how far his own experience resembled Wordsworth's. See V, 364, 368, and XXXV, 233.
8. 3 June 1849, Diaries 381.
9. 3 Jun 1849, Diaries 382.
10. V, 289.
11. 4 May 1849, Diaries 375.
12. 22 Aug 1849, Diaries 431.
13. II Jul 1849, Diaries 408.
14. XXXV, 437.
15. JR-ECR, 3 May 1849, RG 195.
16. JJR-George Gray, Chamonix, 13 Jun 1849, RG 213.
17. George Gray-JJR, 22 Jun 1849, RG 218.
18. JR-George Gray, 5 Jul 1849, RG 231-2.
19. JR-ECR, Champagnole, 2 Sept 1849, RG 249.
20. ECR-George Gray, 9 Oct 1849, EV 45-6.
21. ECR-George Gray, 28 Oct 1849, EV 53.
22. ECR-George Gray, 28 Oct 1849, EV 53-4.
23. JR-W. L. Brown, 11 Dec 1849, XXXVI, 104.
24. ECR to her mother, 15 Dec 1849, EV 89.
25. ECR to her mother, 18 Jan 1849, EV 133.
26. ECR to her mother, 24 Dec 1849, EV 99.
27. ECR to her mother, 3 Feb 1849, EV 131.
28. ECR to her mother, 28 Dec 1849, EV 99.
29. See EV, 146.
30. Ruskin did not visit Venice between 1852 and 1869. On 10 May 1862 he told Rawdon Brown of his fear of sadness at returning there. See XXXVI, 408.
31. Effie told her mother that 'The gentlemen here are very goodnatured, I think, for when they come to see me they leave their cards for John and say all manner of Civil things too of him and he cuts them all on the street unless I am with him and make him, and he never calls on anybody.' 14 Dec 1851, EV 229.
32. ECG to her mother, 24 Feb 1850, EV 149.
33. See Robert Hewison, *Ruskin and Venice*, 1978, 54-5.

Chapter Nine

1. IX, xxxi. Queen Pomare of Otaheite (Society Islands) had appealed some years before for British protection.

2. See *Journals and Correspondence of Lady Eastlake*, 1895, 192.
3. ECG-Rawdon Brown, n.d., but written at Bowerswell, EV 170.
4. See IX, xlv. The Ruskins made little attempt to promote John Ruskin's books and were more eager that they should be widely read than that they should be well reviewed, though John James was nervous of his son's reputation. In his diary is an interesting list of the recipients of presentation copies of the first volume of *The Stones of Venice*. They practically all went to family friends and the engravers who had worked on the book. They were sent to 'Rogers, Acland, Brown W. L., Richmond, O. Gordon, Dale, Rev. D. Moore, Telford, Croly, Melvill, Harrison, Richardson, Inglis, Lockhart, Murray, Mitford, Edwardes (the soldier Herbert Edwardes, whose career Ruskin would examine in *A Knight's Faith,* 1885), Prof. Owen (probably the geologist Sir Richard Owen), Lady Trevelyan, Cheney, Eastlake, Mr George (a family friend who was possibly also a geologist), Runciman, Carlyle, Lady Davy, Dickens, Lupton, Armitage (the engraver J. C. Armytage), Boys (another engraver), R. Fall. Ms Bembridge 33.
5. Croly's alliance of political and religious prejudice, and his great interest in the press, were much remarked. See, for instance, James Grant, *The Newspaper Press*, 1871-3, vol. III, 24, on John James's favourite reading, the *Britannia*: 'Its principles were Conservative, but its chief feature was its thorough Protestantism. This will be readily believed when I mention that it was at first under the editorship of the late Rev. Dr Croly . . .' This was so of all the Ruskins's admired clergymen. Grant also reports, in *Travels in Town*, 1839, II, 103, that 'nearly all the clergy of the Church of England, in London, are decided Tories in their political views . . . The Rev. Mr Melville of Camden Chapel, Camberwell . . . is one of the most furious Tory partizans I ever knew, in the pulpit as well as out of it . . . the Rev. Mr Dale, of St Bride's Church, Fleet St; and the Rev. Dr Croly, of St Stephens, Walbrook, do severally now and then indicate their political views in their pulpit ministrations . . .' In *The Metropolitan Pulpit*, 1839, II, 15, Grant claimed of Melville that 'I have heard him deliver sermons in which there were passages of so ultra-political a character, that had a stranger been conducted blindfolded into the place in which he was preaching . . . he would have been in danger of mistaking the sermon of the reverend gentleman, for a speech of the Earl of Winchilsea in the Lords, or of Sir Robert Inglis in the Commons . . .'.
6. For the 'Papal Aggression', see E. R. Norman, *Anti-Catholicism in Victorian England*, 1968. For the background of the Ruskins's political views see D. G. S. Simes's valuable *Ultra-Tories in British Politics, 1824-34,* Bodley Ms. D Phil c 1442.
7. See Thomas Carlyle, *Latter-Day Pamphlets*, No. VI, 'Parliaments', June 1850.
8. F. J. Furnivall, in his foreword to *Two Letters Concerning 'Notes on the Construction of Sheepfolds' by John Ruskin*, 1890, 8.
9. ECR-Rawdon Brown, 9 May 1854, MR 207.
10. William Holman Hunt, *Pre-Raphaelitism and the Pre-Raphaelite Brotherhood*, 1905, I, 50-1.
11. XXXVII, 427.
12. XIV, III.
13. XII, 319.
14. XII, 320.
15. XII, 322.
16. XII, 327.
17. Quoted at XII, 1n.
18. J. G. Millais, *Life and Letters of Sir John Everett Millais*, 1899, I, 116.
19. III, 624.
20. Hunt, op. cit.
21. 1 May 1851, Diaries 468.
22. ECG-George Gray, 24 Aug 1851, EV 183.
23. See also the letter to W. L. Brown given in Jeanne Clegg, *Ruskin and Venice*, 1981, 81-3. *Centesemi* were coins, the smallest part of the lira.
24. XVIII, 539.
25. ECG to her mother, 24 Feb 1852, EV 283.
26. JR-JJR, 16 Nov 1851, EV 184.
27. JR-JJR, 6 Mar 1852, J. L. Bradley ed., *Ruskin's Letters from Venice*, 1955, 212.
28. For these letters see XII, lxxviii-lxxxv. Some of the letters themselves are given at XII, 591-603.
29. See XI, 258-63.
30. See XII, lxxxiv.
31. See XII, l-lii.
32. JR-JJR, 28 Sept 1851, Bradley, op. cit., 23.
33. JR-JJR, 28 Dec 1851, Bradley, op. cit., 112. Ruskin recorded 'Turner buried' on 30 December 1851, and then abandoned diary entries until 20 July 1853, when he arrived at Glenfinlas.
34. Eastlake, op. cit., I, 273.
35. Collingwood, *Life*, 1900, 136.
36. XIII, xxvi-xxvii.
37. Eastlake, op. cit., I, 273.
38. ECR to her mother, 4 Jan 1852, RV 242.

39. JR-JJR, 1 Jan 1852, Bradley, op. cit., 119-20.
40. See XIII, xxx.
41. JR-JJR, 22 Feb 52, Bradley, op. cit., 191-20.
42. JR-JJR, 5 Feb 1852, Bradley, op. cit., 164.
43. JR-JJR, 8 Feb 1852, Bradley, op. cit., 171. Written on his birthday, this letter is a very extensive discussion of Ruskin's health in recent years.
44. 3 March 1874, Diaries 777.
45. See XVIII, 32 and XXV, 122.
46. XXXVI, 115.
47. JR-JJR, 25 Jan 1852, Bradley, op. cit., 149. This letter was written on a Sunday: Ruskin always gave more space to religious matters when he wrote on the sabbath.
48. JR-JJR, 22 Feb 1852, Bradley, op. cit., 192.
49. ECR to her mother, 8 Feb 1852, EV 263.
50. Ibid., 265.
51. Ibid., 265-6.
52. JR-JJR, 27 Dec 1851, EV 261.
53. ECR to her father, 19 Jan 1852, EV 249.
54. ECR to her mother, 20 Feb 1852, EV 271.

Chapter Ten

1. XXXVI, 142.
2. ECR to her mother, 3 Aug 1852, MR 17.
3. See MR, 15.
4. JR-Mrs Gray, 28 Aug 1852, MR 19-22.
5. Betty Miller, *Robert Browning*, 1952, 172.
6. Cate, op. cit., 1-2.
7. XXXV, 539-41.
8. See Cate, op. cit., 15. Jane Welsh Carlyle was never sympathetic to Effie. On 23 Feb 1856 she wrote to William Allingham '. . . what can be expected from a man who goes to sleep with, every night, a different Turner's picture on a chair opposite his bed "that he may have something beautiful to look at on first opening his eyes of a morning". (so his mother told me) . . . I never saw a man so improved by the loss of his wife! He is amiable and gay, and full of hope and faith in — one doesn't know exactly *what* — but of course *he* does . . .'. National Library of Scotland, Ms 3283 foll 123-4.
9. ECR to her mother, Feb 1853, MR 29.
10. Millais, op. cit., 92.
11. ECR to her mother, 27 Mar 1853, MR 39.
12. JR-W. L. Brown, 31 Mar 1853, Bodley Ms Eng Letts c 33 fol 110.
13. JJR-MR, 15 Dec 1854, Ms Bembridge L 2.
14. ECR to her mother, 15 Apr 1853, MR 42-3.
15. ECR to her mother, 3 May 1854, RG 45.
16. XI, 53.
17. XI, 53n.
18. ECR-Rawdon Brown, 20 Jun 1853, MR 50.
19. JR-W. L. Brown, Jun 1853, Bodley Ms Eng Letts c 33 fol 46.
20. A. J. C. Hare, *The Story of My Life, 1896-1900*, II, 348-51.
21. *Letters of Dr John Brown*, 88.
22. Pauline Trevelyan's review was to appear in *The Scotsman*. See Virginia Surtees ed., *Reflections of a Friendship: John Ruskin's Letters to Pauline Trevelyan 1848-1866*, 1979, for her connections with Ruskin and Millais.
23. XII, xix.
24. Millais-Holman Hunt, 28 Jun 1853, MR 55.
25. JR-JJR, 3 Jul 1853, MR 59-60.
26. XII, xxiv.
27. See RI, 166.
28. V, 122.
29. ECR to her mother, 10 Jul 53, MR 65-6.
30. XII, xxiii.
31. Acland to his wife, 27 Jul 1853, Bodley Ms Acland d 9 foll.134-5.
32. Acland to his wife, n.d., Bodley Ms Acland d 9 fol 136.
33. JR-JJR, 28 Jul 1853, MR 75.
34. Diaries 479.
35. Millais-C. A. Collins, n.d., MR 81.
36. Deposition by William Millais dated 9 March 1898, Bodley Ms Eng Letts c 228, fol 62.
37. JR-MR, 16 Oct 1853, MR 97.
38. JR-Hunt, 20 Oct 1853, MR 101.
39. JR-JJR, 6 Nov 1853, MR 107-8.
40. JJR-JR, 8 Dec 1853, Ms Bembridge L 4.
41. Millais-Mrs Gray, 19 Dec 1853, MR 114.
42. JJR-George Gray, 16 Feb 1854, MR 135.
43. ECR to her father, 7 Mar 1854, MR 154-7.

Chapter Eleven

1. For a description of this book, see Diaries 487.
2. XXXV, 415.
3. Bodley Ms Eng Letts c 33 fol 152.
4. A correspondence conducted through Griffith which Fawkes cut off. The two men were estranged for many years afterwards.
5. See MR 230.
6. 2 July 1854, Diaries 497.
7. 27 Sept 1854, Diaries 511.
8. Surtees, op. cit., 88.
9. Charles P. Lucas, 'Llewelyn Davies and the Working Men's College, *Cornhill*

Magazine, Oct 1916, 421 ff.
10. A successful painter at this period would decline to give lessons: this proved that he was more than a drawing master. Philip Gilbert Hamerton records Ruskin's opinion of drawing masters in the year before he began teaching at the Working Men's College. In 1853 Hamerton had asked him to recommend a master. Ruskin replied 'There is no artist in London capable of teaching you and at the same time willing to give lessons. All those who teach, teach mere tricks with the brush, not true art, far less true nature.' *An Autobiography, 1834-1858*, 1897, 128-30.
11. JR-Sarah Acland, 19 Oct 1854, Bodley Ms Acland d 72 fol 39.
12. XIII, 539.
13. V, xl.
14. Virginia Surtees ed., *The Diary of Ford Madox Brown*, 1981, 196, 16 March 1857.
15. See J. P. Emslie, 'Recollections of Ruskin', *Working Men's College Journal*, vol. 7, 180; and, generally, J. F. L. Harrison, *A History of the Working Men's College*, 1954, 16-85.
16. JJR-JR, 1 Dec 1853, MS Bembridge L 4.
17. Sarah Angelina Acland, 'Memories in my 81st Year', Ms notebook, Bodley Ms Eng Misc d 214.
18. *Letters of James Smetham*, 1891, 54-5.
19. XXXVI, 143-4.
20. XII, 55.
21. *Letters of Dante Gabriel Rossetti*, ed. Oswald Doughty and J. R. Wahl, Oxford, 1965-7, 134.
22. XXXVI, 32.
23. Rossetti was writing to his aunt, Charlotte Polidori. *Letters*, 250.
24. See V, 24-34.
25. See James S. Dearden, 'The Production and Distribution of Ruskin's *Poems*, 1850', *Book Collector*, Summer 1968.
26. Basil Champneys, *Memoirs and Correspondence of Coventry Patmore*, 1900, II, 277.
27. Ibid., II, 278-9.
28. *The Critic*, 27 Oct 1860.
29. Champneys, op. cit., I, 130n.
30. See David J. DeLaura, 'Ruskin and the Brownings: Twenty-Five Unpublished Letters', *Bulletin of the John Rylands Library*, 54, Spring 1972.
31. Ibid. Shenstone is commended for his love of nature at V, 360.
32. Ruskin's relations with Stillman are described in his *Autobiography of a Journalist*, 1901.
33. See R. B. Stein, *Ruskin and Aesthetic Thought in America, 1840-1900*, Cambridge, Mass., 1967.
34. VII, 451.
35. XXXV, 520.
36. *Letters of Matthew Arnold*, 1848-88, ed. G. W. E. Russell, 1895, I, 38-9.
37. J. B. Atlay, *Sir Henry Wentworth Acland*, 1903, 140-53.
38. Ruskin-Acland, n.d., Bodley Ms Acland d 72 fol. 37 a-b.
39. Ruskin-Sarah Acland, 19 Oct 1854, Bodley Ms Acland d 72 fol 39.
40. XVI, xliii.
41. XVI, xliv.
42. Ruskin-Acland, n.d., Bodley Ms Acland d 72 fol 43.
43. XVI, xlv.
44. XII, 430.
45. For whom, see Royston Lambert, *Sir John Simon 1816-1904 and English Social Administration*, 1963.
46. See Atlay, op. cit., 192-3.
47. XVI, 221.
48. Atlay, op. cit., 227.
49. Rossetti to his mother, 1 Jul 1855, *Letters*, 262.
50. Atlay, op. cit., 225-8.
51. Bodley Ms Acland d 72 fol 58.
52. Quoted in XVI, xlix.
53. See XVI, 207-40.
54. Ms Bembridge L 17.
55. JJR-Acland 25 Jun 1855, Bodley Ms Acland d 72 fol 54.
56. XVI, 436.

Chapter Twelve

1. Louisa, Marchioness of Waterford, was a rich amateur and patroness. She had mixed in Pre-Raphaelite circles since at least 1853. Ruskin's letters to her are collected in Virginia Surtees ed., *Sublime and Instructive*, 1972.
2. XVI, 213-14.
3. XIV, 152.
4. The letters are given at XII, 328-55.
5. Ibid.
6. IV, 333.
7. See XIII, xxi.
8. XIV, 5.
9. XIV, 9-10.
10. XIV, 13-14.
11. XIV, 18.
12. XIV, 19.
13. XIV, 20.
14. See A. M. W. Stirling, *The Richmond Papers*, 1926, 163 *seqq.*
15. Dante Gabriel Rossetti-William Allingham, 11 May 1855, *Letters*, 252.
16. XIV, 27.

17. XIV, 35.
18. Virginia Surtees ed., *The Diary of Ford Madox Brown*, 1981, 144, for 13 July 1855.
19. XIV, 43-6.
20. See XIII, 41 and 168.
21. *Athenæum*, July 26, 1856.
22. *Oxford and Cambridge Magazine*, June 1856.
23. XXXV, 519.
24. For Ruskin's early acquaintance with Norton, see *Letters of Charles Eliot Norton*, eds. Sara Norton and Mark A. DeWolfe Howe, Boston, 1913; and Kermit Vanderbilt, *Charles Eliot Norton, Apostle of Culture in a Democracy*, Cambridge, Mass., 1959.
25. 7 Sept 1856, Diaries 519.
26. See XXVIII, 517.
27. 21 Oct 1856, Diaries 524.
28. See XXXVI, liii.
29. 16 Oct 1856, Diaries 524.
30. 28 Nov 1856, Diaries 525.
31. See Dore Ashton, *Rosa Bonheur*, 1981, 111.
32. See William Bell Scott, *Autobiographical Notes*, 1892, II, 9-10.
33. A favourite phrase of Ruskin's. The first sentence of *Præterita* begins, 'I am, and my father was before me, a violent Tory of the old school.' XXXV, 13.

Chapter Thirteen

1. From George Butterworth's diary, Ms Bembridge 35.
2. Ibid.
3. XXXV, 488.
4. See XXXVI, 186-7 and 278-9.
5. Butterworth, op. cit.
6. See Brian Maidment, *John Ruskin and George Allen*, D. Phil. thesis, University of Leicester, 1973, 48.
7. See XXX, lv-vi and XXXVI, 186.
8. See XIV, 349-56.
9. Surtees, *Sublime and Instructive*, 8.
10. Ibid., 93.
11. V, 4.
12. See XIII, 161-2.
13. See XIII, 173-81.
14. See XIII, 186-226.
15. XIV, 106-11.
16. XIV, xxxvi and 464-70.
17. XXXVI, 263.
18. Ibid.
19. Ibid.
20. XXXVI, 273.
21. JJR-Jane Simon, 19 Feb 1858, Ms Bembridge L 12.
22. XXXVI, 319n.
23. XXIX, 593. John James's accounts show that he was a regular contributor to Guthrie's charities.
24. VII, 4.
25. XII, xxxvi-xxxvii.
26. H. Stacy Marks, *Pen and Pencil Sketches*, 1894, II, 165.
27. Surtees, *Sublime and Instructive*, 215.
28. Ibid.
29. JR-JJR, 20 Jun 1858, *Letters from the Continent 1858*, ed. John Hayman, Toronto, 1982, 51-2.
30. XIII, 119.
31. XII, 99.
32. This is a problem that underlay Ruskin's writing for the 1878 exhibition at the Fine Art Society. The catalogue was written at a time when his own mind failed. See XIII, 409-10 and 520-1.
33. See *The Brantwood Diary of John Ruskin*, ed. H. G. Viljoen, 1971, 98.
34. V, 5.
35. XIV, 151.
36. XIV, 161-2.
37. JR-JJR, 5 Jun 1858, Hayman, *Letters from the Continent*, 28-9.
38. See *Letters from the Continent*, 14-80, for Ruskin's letters home from Switzerland. Very many of them discuss Swiss character and institutions.
39. XIV, 172.
40. JR-JJR, 26 Aug 1858, *Letters from the Continent*, 147.
41. See Allen Staley, *The Pre-Raphaelite Landscape*, 1969.
42. JR-JJR, Sept 1858, *Letters from the Continent*, 171.
43. XIX, 83.
44. XXIX, 89.
45. XXXV, 496.
46. XXXV, 493.
47. JR-Lady Trevelyan, 27 Sept 1858, *Reflections of a Friendship*, 132.
48. 23 May 1858. Diaries 535. Ruskin wrote beneath the sketch, 'This drawing of orchises was the first I ever made on Sunday: and marks, henceforward, the beginning of total change in habits of mind. 24th Feb. 1868.'
49. A. J. C. Hare, *The Story of My Life, 1896-1900*, II, 107-9.
50. VII, xli. Although Ruskin sent these views to his father they were not exactly in a letter, but in one of the 'Notes on the Turin Gallery' he was composing with a view to *Modern Painters* V.
51. See *Letters from the Continent*, 141-4.

Chapter Fourteen

1. XVI, 171.
2. See XVI, 259-92n. The whole lecture is a fine statement of Ruskin's views in the latter days of his Pre-Raphaelitism.
3. XVI, lxv.
4. XVI, 336n.
5. XVI, 336-7.
6. XVI, 340.
7. JR-JJR, 12 Sep 1858, *Letters from the Continent*, 170.
8. In 1880 Ruskin looked back on his experience of sermons. 'I am now sixty years old, and for forty-five of them was in church at least once on the Sunday, — say once a month also in afternoons, — and you have about three thousand church services. When I am abroad I am often in half-a-dozen churches in the course of a single day, and never lose a chance of listening . . . add the conversations pursued, not unearnestly, with every sort of reverend person . . .' XXXIV, 217n.
9. W. J. Fullerton, *C. H. Spurgeon*, 1920, 39.
10. Joseph Johnson, *Popular Preachers of our Time*, 1864, I, 613.
11. Quoted in Fullerton, op. cit., 39.
12. XXXVI, 275.
13. XXXIV, 659-61.
14. Ibid.
15. See XV, 189.
16. For this background, see Van Akin Burd, *John Ruskin and Rose La Touche*, 1979, 23–49.
17. XXXV, 525. Ruskin mistook her age in this passage: she was ten years old. But factual mistakes in *Præterita* were seldom corrected.
18. Bodley Ms Eng Letts c 34 fol 3.
19. XXXV, 526.
20. See Waldo Hilary Dunn, *James Anthony Froude*, 1961-3, I, 64-7.
21. XXXV, 533.
22. JR-Jane Simon, 20 Jun 1858, *Letters from the Continent*, 187.
23. JR-Jane Simon, 9 Nov 1858, Bodley Ms Eng Letts c 34 fol 88.
24. JR-JJR, 26 Jun 1858, *Letters from the Continent*, 59.
25. JR-Anna Blunden, 20 Oct 1858, *Sublime and Instructive*, 98-100.
26. XXXV, 503.
27. Logan Pearsall Smith, *Unforgotten Years*, 1938, 39–40.

Chapter Fifteen

1. Ms Bembridge 33.
2. XXXVI, 338–9.
3. XIV, 234–8.
4. Ruskin would have been the more displeased in noticing that the painting depicts the back garden at Bowerswell.
5. JR-Margaret Bell, 3-4 Apr 1859, *Winnington Letters*, 149-50.
6. XIV, 240-3.
7. XIII, 539.
8. XXII, 511-12.
9. For this background, see Van Akin Burd, *The Winnington Letters*, 1969, 19-54.
10. XXXVI, 324.
11. XXXVI, 331.

Chapter Sixteen

1. XXXV, 485.
2. Bembridge MS 11.
3. JR–Margaret Bell, Denmark Hill, 26 March 1859, WL, 125.
4. See WL, 19–89.
5. JR–Margaret Bell, Denmark Hill, 18 March 1859, WL, 112.
6. For Shields's relations with Ruskin see *The Life and Letters of Frederic Shields*, ed. Ernestine Mills, 1912.
7. WL, 95.
8. 1, 224–34.
9. Olive Wilson (ed.), *My Dearest Dora*, Kendal, n.d. but 1984, 12.
10. JJR Account Books, Bembridge MS 29.
11. JJR Diary, Bembridge, MS 33.
12. WL, 640.
13. JR–Margaret Bell, Denmark Hill, 21 March 1859, WL, 115. Ruskin wrote to Simon 'Please find and get for me the nicest piano setting of "il suono dell' arp'angelica" — from Donizetti . . . I want to study the peculiar form of vulgarity which there is in that air as attached to such words. — and to find a bit of Handel or Mozart to set against it . . .' 17 October 1858, Bodley MS Eng Letts c 34 fol. 90.
14. VII, 419–20.
15. Bembridge MS 33.
16. JR–Margaret Bell, Denmark Hill, 22 March 1859, WL, 121.
17. JR–Winnington children, Denmark Hill, 19 February 1860, WL, 226–7.
18. E. T. Cook, *The Life of Ruskin*, 1911, II, 26–7. Cook probably heard this story, which is not mentioned in the Library Edition, when he talked to Allen at Ruskin's funeral in 1900.

Chapter Seventeen

1. JR–Lady Trevelyan, early January 1860?, *Reflections of a Friendship*, 1979, 140.
2. See VII, 479–85.
3. A. J. Scott-Carlyle, Manchester, 2 August

1859, National Library of Scotland MS 1767, fols. 221–4.

4. See XXXVI, xxxiii–ix.

5. XXXIV, 659–61, quoting *C.H. Spurgeon: a Biography*, by his Wife, 1898, II, 287–8.

6. Dickens, and especially his *Hard Times*, may also have been an influence. Dickens is discussed in *Unto This Last* at XVII, 31, n.

7. JR–Walter Brown, n.d. but October 1859, Bodley MS Eng Letts c 34 fols. 167–9.

8. XXXV, 485.

9. See XVII, 25, 85, 485.

10. For modern discussions of Ruskin's attitude to Mill see J. Sherburne, *John Ruskin or the Ambiguities of Abundance*, Cambridge, Mass., 1972, and Alan Lee, 'Ruskin and Political Economy' in R. Hewison, ed, *New Approaches to Ruskin*, 1981.

11. XVII, 143.

12. Quoted at XVII, xxviii.

13. JJR–Jane Simon, Billiter Street, 21 July 1860, Bembridge MS L 12.

14. JJR–Jane Simon, Denmark Hill, 25 October 1860, Bembridge MS L 12.

15. W. J. Stillman, *The Autobiography of a Journalist*, 1901, I, 260–7.

16. JR–Harriet Beecher Stowe, Geneva, 18 June 1860, XXXVI, 337.

17. JR–Charles Eliot Norton, Neuchâtel, 12 July 1860, CEN, 57–8.

18. JR–Lady Trevelyan, 1 Jan 1861, *Reflections of a Friendship*, 1979, 163.

19. JJR–Lady Trevelyan, 27 March 1861, *Reflections of a Friendship*, 1979, 165.

20. JR–Winnington children, Denmark Hill, 15 April 1861, WL, 297–8.

21. Carlyle to his brother John, 23 April 1861, quoted at VII, lix.

22. JR–Winnington children, Denmark Hill, 22 April 1861, WL, 298.

23. JR–JJR, Winnington (March 1861), XXX XXXVI, 359–60.

24. Bembridge MS 33.

25. Sir Richard Owen (1804–92) was Superintendant of the Museum's Natural History collections between 1856–83.

26. XXXV, 529. In RLT, 49, Van Akin Burd comments 'Ruskin made this graceful explanation in *Præterita*, where he chose to forget the painful years when he had tasted the venom of Mrs La Touche's revenge.'

27. Quoted in *Præterita* at XXXV, 529–33. In a passage not published as part of the original book Ruskin adds '. . . the quite singular character of the letter is its sympathy. There is not a sentence in which the child is thinking of herself. She knows exactly what *I* am feeling, and thinks only of that, without a shadow of vanity, or of impulsive egoism . . . her subsequent knowledge of me being deeper than a child's only in its religious anxiety . . . And in the year 1860 the 'new epoch of life' . . . began for me in this wise, that my father and mother could travel with me no more, but Rose, in heart, was with me always, and all I did was for her sake.' (XXXV, 533).

28. JR–Sir John Murray Naesmyth, 28 April 1861, WL, 309.

29. JR–Winnington children, 6 May 1861, WL, 312.

30. XXXV, 533, and see XVII, xxxvii.

31. XXXV, 533.

32. See the letter at XXXVI, 368–72, preserved because Ruskin made a copy for his parents.

33. See JR–Georgiana Burne-Jones, XXXVI, 373–4.

34. JR–JJR, Harristown, 2 September 1861, RLT, 59.

Chapter Eighteen

1. JJR–Jane Simon, Queen's Hotel, Norwood, 19 August 1861, Bembridge MS LI2.

2. JJR sent cuttings of these letters to Jane Simon. Bembridge MS LI2.

3. JJR–Jane Simon, Norwood, 7/9 September 1861, Bembridge, MS LI2.

4. Bembridge MS33.

5. JR–JJR, 4 October 1861, RLT 61.

6. JR–JJR, 13 October 1861, RLT 63–4.

7. JR–JJR, 22 October 1861, RLT, 64.

8. Maria La Touche–JR, RLT, 64.

9. XXXV, lxvii.

10. XXXV, lxviii.

11. JR–JJR, 25 October 1861, RLT, 65.

12. Ibid.

13. XXXV, lxviii.

14. Cited in JR–JJR, Lucerne, 22 December 1861, RLT, 70.

15. Cited in JR–JJR, Lucerne, 21 December 1861, RLT, 70.

16. Preserved at Bembridge.

17. RLT–JR, 26 December 1861, RLT, 71–3.

18. JR–JJR, Lucerne, 25 December 1861, RLT, 73–4.

19. *Brantwood Diary*, 91.

20. JR–Charles Eliot Norton, Denmark Hill, 6 January 1862, CEN, 68.

21. JR-John Brown, Denmark Hill, 16 January 1862, XXXVI, 403–4.

22. 'The General Principles of Colour' at the Architectural Museum. See XII, 507.

23. J. A. Froude, *Thomas Carlyle, A History of his Life in London*, 1884, II, 244.

24. JR–Carlyle, 23 January 1855, TC, 62–3.
25. VII, 310–12.
26. In the *Letters of James Smetham*, 94, is recorded a visit 'to Gilchrist's on Saturday. Found him living next door to Carlyle, and to be an intimate friend of his. The day before he had gone with C. to hear Ruskin lecture at the Royal Institution. (Carlyle kept enquiring the time every ten minutes, and at last said, "I think he ought to give over now"). Ruskin is a favourite of his, or he would not have gone at all, for he hates art in reality; but R. sent him a ticket . . .' See VII, lix.
27. Carlyle–JR, 29 October 1860, TC, 89–90.
28. For an explanation, see Cook's introduction, XVII, lxv.
29. XVII, 162–3.
30. XVII, 208–16.
31. XVII, 229–30.
32. XVII, 290.
33. Frederic Harrison, *John Ruskin*, 1903, 103.
34. JJR–Jane Simon, Denmark Hill, 24 April 1862, Bembridge MS 12.
35. JR–John Simon, early February 1862, Bodley MS Eng. Letts c 35, fol 8.
36. JR–Lady Trevelyan, Milan, 20 July 1862, *Reflections of a Friendship*, 188.
37. JR–John Simon, February 1862, Bodley MS Eng. Letts c 35, fol. 8.
38. JR–Lady Naesmyth, 4 March 1862, Bodley MS Eng. Letts c 35, fol. 115.
39. JR–Rawdon Brown, 10 May 1862, XXXVI, 407–8.
40. Georgiana Burne-Jones, *Memorials of Edward Burne-Jones*, 1904, XXX, I, 147.
41. JR–JJR, Geneva, 12 August 1862, WL, 369–71.
42. *Memorials*, ibid, I, 243.

Chapter Nineteen

1. JR–Lady Trevelyan, Milan, 20 July 1862, XXXVI, 414.
2. Bembridge MS 12.
3. Diaries, 566.
4. JR–JJR, Mornex, 17 September 1862, XXII, lvii.
5. *Letters of Dr John Brown*, 1907, 297–8.
6. XXXVI, 417, and XVII, lxxxii.
7. XXXVI, 417–8.
8. Rose's personal writings have disappeared. Helen Gill Viljoen's transcripts, made in 1929, were eventually published by Van Akin Burd in RLT, 1979, 146–81.
9. RLT, 156.
10. RLT, 158.
11. RLT, 159.
12. RLT, 159.
13. RLT, 160.
14. Cited in JR–JJR, 28 December 1862, RLT, 83.
15. Cited in JR–Charles Eliot Norton, Mornex, 10 March 1863, CEN, 77.
16. Bayne's views on Carlyle, Tennyson and Ruskin are in his *Lessons from my Masters*, 1879. On p. 376, discussing Ruskin, he remarks 'What is art? A good many years ago I had occasion to consider this question very carefully, and I stated the result in an essay on the Elementary Principles of Criticism.'
17. WL, 377, n. The background of the Colenso dispute is described at WL, 70–5.
18. The book led to Colenso's deposition on 16 December 1863 and his subsequent excommunication by the Bishop of Cape Town.
19. JR–Margaret Bell, Mornex, 26 October 1862, WL, 383.
20. JR–Margaret Bell, Mornex, 16 October 1862, WL, 380–2.
21. JR–Margaret Bell, Mornex, 11 March 1863, WL, 403–4.
22. Mornex, 20 December, 1862, *From a Victorian Post-Bag: Letters Addressed to the Rev. J. Llewelyn Davies by Thomas Carlyle and Others*, 1926, 16.
23. XXXV, 486–8.
24. JR–Miss Corlass. Mornex, 20 February 1863, Bembridge MS LI8.
25. Given at the Royal Institution, 5 June 1863. See XXVI, 3–27.
26. *Le Gaulois*, 18 September 1904, quoted at XVII, lix.
27. JR–(?) JJR, n.d., quoted XVII, lxxii.
28. Conceivably a *verbatim* report. Ruskin's evidence is given at XIV, 476–89.
29. Quoted at XIV, xxxvii.
30. Quoted at XXXVI, xlvi.
31. For a summary of Ruskin's relations with Rossetti, see XXXVI, xliii–lii.
32. XXXVI, 454 and Plate 18.
33. Mary Bradford–Margaret Bell, 30 June 1863, WL 406–8.
34. JR–JJR, Winnington, 25 August 1863, WL 415–16. From Chamonix on 3 October 1863 Ruskin wrote of the 'difficulty I feel in understanding the general temper of persons belonging to your class: — The strange mixture of modesty and pride . . . the kind feelings — harmonized with a consistent and conscientious selfishness — above all the terrible *polish* . . . you have been content to have it said in every English drawing room — over the coffee — "How clever Lady Waterford is!"' *Studies in English Literature 1500–1900*

(Rice University), Vol 1, no. 4. Autumn 1961, 117–19.
35. JR–Lady Trevelyan, 7 April 1863, *Reflections of a Friendship*, 212–13.
36. Quoted in *Reflections of a Friendship*, 217, n.
37. See Virginia Surtees, ed., *Sublime and Instructive*, 1972, 51–2.
38. Georgiana Burne-Jones, *Memorials of Edward Burne-Jones*, 1904, 263–4.

Chapter Twenty

1. See RLT, 88–9.
2. Rose's autobiography, at RLT, 169.
3. See RLT, 89.
4. Maria La Touche–George Macdonald, 19 November 1863, in Derrick Leon, *Ruskin, the Great Victorian*, 1949, 359–60.
5. *Ibid*, 360.
6. JR–Miss Corlass, n.d. but mourning paper, Bembridge MS L 18.
7. See I, xi.
8. XVII, lxxv.
9. JR–JJR, Winnington, 16 December 1863, XXXVI, 460–1.
10. W. G. Collingwood made an especial study of Ruskin's interest in music. See his *The Life and Works of John Ruskin*, 1893, I, 74 *seqq*. and II, 193.
11. See XXIX, 234 and 261–2.
12. See Georgiana Burne-Jones, *Memorials of Edward Burne-Jones*, 1904, 1, 300–1, and Ada Earland, *Ruskin and his Circle*, n.d. but probably 1910, 20.
13. See XVIII, xxix–xxx.
14. XXXV, 537–9.
15. XVII, lxxvii.
16. For these antecedents, see Helen Gill Viljoen, *Ruskin's Scottish Heritage*, Urbana, 1956, *passim*.
17. The Cowpers' interest in spiritualism is summarised in Van Akin Burd, *Christmas Story*, Newark, 1990, 69–134. See also Alex Owen, *The Darkened Room: Women, Power and Spiritualism in Late Victorian England*. Ohio, 1964.
18. See Burd, *op.cit.*, and John Lewis Bradley (ed.), *Thee Letters of John Ruskin to Lord and Lady Mount-Temple*, 1989, henceforward cited as LMT.
19. LMT, 31–2, 34.
20. See XXXV, 342 and *Christmas Story*, 58.
21. See William Raeper, *George MacDonald*, Tring, 1987. Ruskin felt sympathetically toward MacDonald, and at this period gave him financial help.
22. G. MacDonald, *Reminiscences of a Specialist*, 107.
23. XXXV, 486–8.
24. John Ludlow, *The Autobiography of a Christian Socialist*, ed. A. D. Murray, 1981, 141–4.
25. For Mansfield, see Charles Kingsley's tribute in his *Letters and Memories*, 1878, I, 441–4. 'He was more like an antelope than a man. He had a gymnastic pole in his room on which he used to do strange feats . . . He was a good shot, and captain of his boat at Cambridge . . . during the last war, he has said to me that he wished he was at Sebastopol, handling a rifle . . .' Mansfield was not a clergyman but a chemist, and died young during an experiment with naphtha.
26. Ludlow, *op.cit.*, 144.
27. XXVIII, 696.
28. See the discussion of the origins of *Fors Clavigera* at XXVII, xxi–ii.
29. This correspondence is collected by Jay Wood Claiborne (ed.), *Two Secretaries: the Letters of John Ruskin to Charles Augustus Howell and the Rev Richard St. John Tyrwhitt*, University of Texas at Austin Ph.D., 1969.
30. JR–Tyrwhitt, Basle, 16 August 1860. The letter also mentions the chapter 'Peace' at the end of the fifth volume of Modern Painters (VII, 441–60): 'The obscurity in the end of that last volume does not come of puzzlement but of my not choosing to tell people what I know — until I think they are ready to accept or try it — I put them on the scent. They can follow it as far as they have noses. Of course in some matters the mystery is not of *my* making. I assure you — the Sphinx is as alive as ever she was; and makes short work — ultimately with all demons. You will have to face her, some day — in spite of Church Catechism . . .'
31. January 1866, p. 176.
32. See XVIII, lxxv–vi.
33. XVIII, 453.
34. XVIII, 457–8.
35. XVIII, 459.
36. A wish only partly fulfilled by *A Knight's Faith* (1885). Among many references to military history see especially XXXI, 477–8, XXVII, 74 and XXXIV, 522–5.
37. For whom, see Vanda Morton, *Oxford Rebels: the Life and Friends of Nevil Story Maskelyne*, Gloucester, 1987.
38. The Ruskins met Joseph Severn, Keats's friend, in Rome in 1840. Joseph was the father of the twins Arthur, who married Joan Agnew, and Eleanor, who married the Revd Henry Furneaux. Their siblings were Mary, who married Charles Newton, and Walter, who became an artist.

39. JR–Henry Acland, n.d. but 1864, Bodley MS Acland d. 170.
40. JR–Georgiana Burne-Jones, 13 September 1864, XXXVI, 475.

Chapter Twenty-One

1. XXXV, 539–40.
2. XVII, 518–27.
3. See XVII, 491, n.
4. See J.W. Robertson Scott, *The Story of the Pall Mall Gazette*, 1950, and Stephen Koss, *The Rise and Fall of the Political Press in Britain*, 1981.
5. JR–Editor of the *Daily Telegraph*, printed 6 August 1868, XVII, 530–1.
6. XIX, 60–1.
7. See XIX, lxiii.
8. XIX, 87–8.
9. XIX, 87, n.
10. XIX, 82–3.
11. Hilton, *John Ruskin: The Early Years*, 1985, 253–4.
12. Maria La Touche–Mrs MacDonald, Harristown, 14 March 1865, cited in RLT, 93–4.
13. XVIII, lxxii.
14. XVIII, 201.
15. XVIII, 224–5. The reference is to an account of the building of the pyramids in C. J. Bunsen's *Egypt's Place in Universal History*, translated from the German by Charles H. Cottrell, 1848, II, 164 *seqq.*
16. Quoted at XVIII, 195.
17. Carlyle–JR, Chelsea, 20 December 1865, *The Correspondence of Thomas Carlyle and John Ruskin*, ed. George Allan Cate, Stanford, 1982, 113–14. Hereafter cited as TC.
18. Jane Carlyle–JR, Thornhill, Dumphriesshire, 15 July (1865), TC, 111–12.
19. XVIII, 54.
20. A chronological list is given at XXXVIII, 40–7.
21. XVIII, 83.
22. XVIII, 84–90.
23. XVIII, 84–105.
24. XVIII, 113.
25. J. A. Froude, *My Relations with Carlyle*, 1903, 7–8.
26. XXVIII, 123.
27. XVIII, 47. The dedicatee of the book was Lady Mount-Temple.
28. Yale.
29. July 15, 1865.
30. October 1865. Wise was a family friend and a writer on Shakespeare, and is acknowledged by Ruskin at XVII, 258, n.

Chapter Twenty-Two

1. Quoted at XXXVI, xlviii.
2. JR–Charles Eliot Norton, 28 January 1866, CEN, 96–7.
3. See XVI, xlviii.
4. 'On 21st December 1865 R comes to me. Walk in garden; "some people look better dressed". The Saturday before, the 16th. At British Museum. The Sunday before, the 10th, I saw her first after three years.' *Diaries* 585.
5. Bembridge MS 51.
6. JR–Sarah Angelina Acland, 5 January 1873, Bodley MS Acland d 170.
7. XXXV, 560–1.
8. JR–Edward Burne-Jones, Denmark Hill, 3 February 1866, Fitzwilliam Museum, Cambridge.
9. It is not however certain that Ruskin proposed on February 2nd, only that Rose on that day asked him to wait for three years.
10. JR–Henry Acland, Denmark Hill, 10 October 1866, Bodley MS Acland d 72.
11. JR–Georgiana Cowper, 19 February 1866, LMT, 52–3.
12. JR–Georgiana Cowper, 22 March 1866, LMT 68–9.
13. *Ibid.*
14. Rose's reading did not exclude fiction and her mother was the author of two novels, *The Clintons* (1853) and *Lady Willoughby* (1855).
15. W. G. Collingwood, *The Life and Work of John Ruskin*, 1893, 11, 61–2.
16. JR–Rawdon Brown, Interlachen, 11 June 1866, XXXVI, 509–10.
17. JR–Margaret Ruskin, Vevey, 2 July 1866, Bembridge MS B VI.
18. For Gotthelf (the pseudonym of Albert Bitzius, 1797–1854) see XXXII, xxxii–xxxv.
19. See VII, 429–30.
20. See XXVIII, 131, 285.
21. Bembridge MS B VI.
22. JR–Georgiana Cowper, Hotel of the Giessbach, 10 June 1866, MLT, 72–4.
23. W. G. Collingwood, *The Life and Work of John Ruskin*, 1903, II, 114–5. When Ruskin took a 'party into town' to go to the theatre he sometimes included Denmark Hill servants. See Diaries, 608.
24. See Lord Olivier, *The Myth of Governor Eyre*, 1933.
25. JR–Thomas Carlyle, Denmark Hill, 1 October 1866, TC 122.
26. JR–Georgiana Cowper, Denmark Hill, 28 September 1866, MLT, 87–8.
27. As quoted in JR–Georgiana Cowper, Denmark Hill, 18 October 1866, LMT, 97–8.

28. Rose La Touche–Georgiana Cowper, 18 October 1866, cited in Derrick Leon, *Ruskin the Great Victorian*, 1949, 370–1.
29. JR–Georgiana Cowper, Denmark Hill late October 1866, LMT 99–100.
30. Sarah A. Tooley, *Daily Chronicle*, 24 July 1905.
31. See XIX, xxxiv–v.

Chapter Twenty-Three

1. Diaries, XXX II, 608.
2. XXXV, 529.
3. The revivalism of 1859 was particularly dramatic in Ireland. John La Touche would have been aware of, and perhaps affected by, the new contacts between pastors from the Waldensian church in Piedmont and the Presbyterian General Assembly in Dublin. For a history of the Irish revival see W. Gibson, *The Year of Grace*, 1860, W. D. Killen's *The Ecclesiastical History of Ireland*, 1875, II, 528–9, and his *Reminiscences of a Long Life*, 1902.
4. See, for instance, *Some Records of the Life of Stevenson Arthur Blackwood*, 1896, 236–7, which records that it 'was on the . . . 11 May, 1861, that Mr Blackwood first spoke at these meetings for the Upper Classes in Willis's Rooms, St James, so familiar to the class whom it was desired to reach . . . The Room was filled . . . I remember hearing at the time how the line of carriages stretched all down St James' Street . . . Now, in the very height of the London season . . . an assembly is held in these rooms, which is nothing less than a Revival meeting . . . Outside, the empty carriages were drawn up in rows . . . From these meetings arose many other smaller gatherings which were held in various Drawing Rooms during the London Season . . .'
5. XXXV, 489.
6. Logan Pearsall Smith *Unforgotten Years*, 1938, 26–7.
7. JR–A. Froude *The Fronde–Ruskin Friendship*, ed. H. G. Viljoen, 1966, 48.
8. JR–Margaret Ruskin, Keswick, 28 July 1967, Bembridge MS L VI.
9. Rose La Touche–Georgiana Cowper, 18 October 1866, cited in Derrick Leon, *Ruskin the Great Victorian*, 1949, 370–1.
10. Cited in JR–Margaret Ruskin, Keswick, 28 July 1867, Bembridge, MS L VI.
11. JR–Georgiana Cowper, Denmark Hill, February 27 1867, LMT, 109–10.
12. *Ibid.*
13. XVII, 326.
14. Diaries, II, 610.
15. JR–Joan Agnew (henceforward 'JRS') Denmark Hill, 17 June 1867, Bembridge MS L 33.
16. XVII, 347–51.
17. See XVIII, xliv.
18. XVII, 421–2.
19. At the Royal Institution, on July 7 1867.
20. JR–Edward Burne-Jones, 27 December 1864, Fitzwilliam Museum, Cambridge.
21. JR–Charles Woodd, Bodley MS Eng. Letts c 35, n.d. Woodd, of Belsize, Hampstead, was an evangelical and a wine merchant.
22. JR–Edward Burne-Jones, 14 March 1867, Fitzwilliam Museum, Cambridge.
23. JR–Thomas Carlyle, 30 May 1867, TC, 131.
24. JR–Thomas Carlyle, 12 June 1867, TC, 135–6.
25. See XIX, xxvii. The Public Orator particularly commended (in Latin) *The Crown of Wild Olive*.
26. JR–Georgiana Cowper, Denmark Hill, 26 March 1867, LMT, 114–5.
27. Jowett reported that 'As an illustration of his religious belief he told me this story. "Once I had been very much excited by a letter which I had received from a friend, and so great was my passion that my nerves were shaken for a fortnight. On a dark and stormy day I walked up the hill out of Keswick, and as I walked a sign came to me from heaven. I was praying to be delivered from my burden, when suddenly a streak of light appeared in the heavens. I walked on, and the clouds gathered, and the old frame of mind returned. Again I prayed, and again I saw the light . . ."' *The Life and Letters of Benjamin Jowett*, 1897, II, 257.
28. JR–Margaret Ruskin, Keswick, 20 July 1867, Bodley, MS Eng. Letts c 36, fol. 173.
29. JR–JRS, Keswick, July 9 1867, Bembridge MS L 33.
30. JR–JRS, Keswick 15 August 1867, Bembridge MS L 33.
31. JR–George Richardson, Keswick, 24 July 1867, Ms, Bembridge.

Chapter Twenty-Four

1. Diaries, II, 628.
2. Diaries, II, 642.
3. Diaries, II, 644.
4. Arthur Severn, *The Professor*, ed. J. S. Dearden, 1967, 27.
5. Whistler's *The Last of Old Westminster* (1862) had been painted at lodgings that

Arthur Severn shared with his older brother Walter.
6. JR–Georgiana Cowper, Denmark Hill, 4 March 1868, LMT, 128–9.
7. JR–JRS, Denmark Hill, January 1868, Bembridge MS L 34.
8. XXVI, 35–84.
9. JR–George Richardson.
10. See RLT, 112–13.
11. JR–Georgiana Cowper, Denmark Hill, n.d., 29 and 30 March 1868, LMT 130–147.
12. JR–Georgiana Cowper, Denmark Hill, 4 May 1868, LMT 150.
13. JR–Georgiana Cowper, Winnington, 6 May 1868, LMT 153–4.
14. JR–Georgiana Cowper, Denmark Hill, 4 May 1868, LMT 150.
15. JRS–Margaret Ruskin, Winnington, 11 May 1868, WL, 620–1.
16. XVIII, 185–6.
17. XVIII, 186.
18. JR–Georgiana Cowper, Dublin, 13 May 1868, LMT, 155.
19. JR–Georgiana Cowper, Dublin, 14 May 1868, LMT, 156–7.
20. 'The children's farewell to me was most delicious', he wrote to Miss Bell, recalling their parting gift of wild flowers. JR–Margaret Bell, Denmark Hill, 2 June 1868, WL, 648.
21. JR–Georgiana Cowper, Denmark Hill, 2 June 1868, LMT, 167–8.
22. JR–Lily Armstrong, Denmark Hill, 29 January 1868, WL, 611.
23. XVII, 563–9.
24. XIX, xx.
25. XIX, 243–69.
26. 18 September 1868. Diaries, II, 655.
27. XXXV, 393–4, and JR–JRS, Keswick, 2 July 1867, Bembridge MS L 33.
28. JR–JRS 'Abbeville — 15th 'Eptember — 'ixty-ate', Bembridge MS L 33.
29. JR–JRS, Verona, 13 July 1869. Bembridge MS L 34. The baby-talk grammar and vocabulary were firmly established by the time of Ruskin's letters to Joan from Italy in June of 1869. Joan only occasionally responded in this mode, but in later years used baby-talk when nursing Ruskin after illnesses.
30. XIX, 233–9.
31. XXXV, l. Although an autobiography was not mentioned, Norton continually prompted Ruskin at Abbeville to make his will and talked of inheriting some of his papers. See CEN, 126 *et seqq.*
32. Norton to his wife, Paris, 7 October 1868, *Letters of Charles Eliot Norton*, 1913, I, 311–2.
33. Norton had been the editor (with James Russell Lowell) of the *North American Review* since 1863. See Kermit Vanderbilt, *Charles Eliot Norton: Apostle of Culture in a Democracy*, Cambridge, Mass., 1959, 86–96.
34. For these estimates of Norton see XXXV, 519–20 and 524.
35. XXXV, 520.

Chapter Twenty-Five

1. September 28 1868, Diaries, II, 656.
2. JR–Dora Lees, Abbeville, 25 September 1868, *My Dearest Dora*, n.d., 57–8.
3. JR–Mrs Norton, October 1868, XXXVI, 558.
4. XVII, 541–6.
5. XXV, 208.
6. For whom, see Anne Taylor, *Laurence Oliphant*, 1982.
7. For Oliphant's relations with the Cowpers, see Taylor, *op.cit.*, 115–19 and 130–2.
8. For a description of the Broadlands 'conferences' and lists of guests, see Edward Clifford, *Broadlands as it Was*, 1890 (issued anonymously and privately circulated). On page 9 Clifford writes of Ruskin, 'I met him there and listened breathlessly to his talk, which was the most exquisite talk I ever heard. They called him St Chrysostom, the golden-mouthed, and he called them Lily and William, and was very much their comrade . . .' On p. 14 Clifford relates that 'A humble east-end worker, a working-man socialist, and a budding theosophist came dressed in their best to behave nicely with lords and bishops, and lo and behold there was Mrs Girling, the shakeress, being rescued from starvation, or Rowena Cassidy, the ex-slave, being taken in to dinner by the host, while a countess brought up the rear. Dante Gabriel Rossetti, George MacDonald, and Mr Timmins, of the Universal Mercy Band, might get on happily together . . .' See also Mrs Rundle Charles, *Our Seven Homes*, 1896, 205 *seqq.*, and *The Pilot*, 26 October 1901.
9. MS, Bembridge.
10. Greville MacDonald, *Reminiscences of a Specialist*, 1932, 106.
11. MS, Bembridge.
12. Maria La Touche–Georgiana Cowper, Dublin, 11 December 1868, in Derrick Leon, *Ruskin, the Great Victorian*, 1949, 415.
13. Mr Dearden comments on this page of letter that JR called on Jean Ingelow on 1 November 1867 and the 23 December 1868; that 'Claribel' was Mrs Barnard, a singer, who died on 30 January 1869; that the

writing paper suggests that the letter was not written after 1868; and that the last three lines of the MS may refer to Joan's engagement to Percy La Touche, broken off on 4 March 1868.
14. XIX, 244–5.
15. XIX, 264.
16. XIX, 269–77.
17. Many of these exhibits would shortly be transferred to Oxford and used for Ruskin's university teaching.
18. XIII, 569.
19. XIX, xlvi.
20. XIX, xvii–lii.
21. JR–Charles Eliot Norton, 29 March 1869, CEN, 129.
22. Cited in CEN, 89.
23. JR–Charles Eliot Norton, 26 April 1869, CEN, 132–3.
24. See Leon Edel, *The Life of Henry James*, 1977, I, 239–40.
25. See XXVIII, 275.
26. XIX, 410–20. The lecture was entitled 'The Hercules of Camarina' (a Greek coin in the British Museum).
27. Thomas Carlyle–JR, 17 August 1869, TC, 146–7.
28. W. G. Collingwood, *The Life and Work of John Ruskin*, 1893, II, 88–90.
29. Bembridge.
30. XIX, 296.
31. XIX, 365.
32. Bembridge MS 45.
33. XIX, 362.
34. XIX, 362–3.
35. XIX, 361.
36. XXXV, 371.
37. XXXV, 518.
38. *Ibid.*
39. XIX, 293.
40. W. G. Collingwood, *The Life and Work of John Ruskin*, 1893, II, 95.
41. *Ibid.*
42. W. G. Collingwood, *op.cit.*, 1893, II, 94–5.
43. For portraits of Ruskin, see James S. Dearden, *John Ruskin: a Life in Pictures*, Sheffield, 2000. For portraits of Rose, see RLT, xiii–xiv.
44. This visit is summarised in Jeanne Clegg, *Ruskin and Venice*, 1981, 133–41.
45. IV, 356, n.

Chapter Twenty-Six

1. Henry Liddell–Henry Acland, 19 July 1869, Bodley MS Acland d 69.
2. JR–Acland, Hotel Giessbach, Lac de Brienz, 19 August 1869, XX, xix–xx, and JR–Liddell, Denmark Hill, 2 September 1969, XX, xx–xxi.
3. Bembridge, MS 9I.
4. J. A. Froude, *Carlyle's Life in London*, 1884, II, 383.
5. XVIII, 1–liii.
6. September 28 1869, Diaries, II, 680.
7. A glimpse of Percy La Touche and his milieu is provided in Lord Rossmore, *Things I Can Tell*, 1912. Of Rose, Ruskin reported 'I got such a lovely description of somebody today from Mrs Henry King. She says — "some one who had seen her, told me, she looked like a young sister of Jesus Christ."' JR–JRS, n.d. but Corpus Christi paper, Bembridge MS L 53. Henry King was a partner in Messrs. Smith Elder.
8. JR–Georgiana Cowper-Temple, 8 January 1870, LMT, 247.
9. Diaries, II, 693.
10. *Clouds and Light* received one review. It reads, in its entirety, 'A little book comprising an allegory in which truth, hope, pleasure, etc., are personified; with other short papers on such themes as sorrow, pain, faith, etc. It is thoughtful, devout, and deeply spiritual.' *Evangelical Magazine*, May 1871, 284.
11. JR–JRS, n.d. but April 1970, Bembridge MS L 35.
12. JR–JRS, 12 April 1870, Bembridge MS L 35.
13. JR–JRS, 16 April 1870, Bembridge MS L 35.
14. JR–JRS, n.d. but March 1870, Bembridge Ms L 35.
15. JR–JRS, Denmark Hill, 21 January 1870, Bembridge MS L 35.
16. JR–Charles Eliot Norton, 1 January 1870, CEN, 182–3.
17. JR–Margaret Ruskin, n.d. Bembridge MS B VI.
18. JR–Charles Eliot Norton, 26 March 1870, CEN, 185–6.
19. XX, 5I.
20. XX, 79.
21. JR–Georgiana Cowper-Temple, 6 February 1870, MLT, 259.
22. JR–Georgiana Mount-Temple, Denmark Hill, 20 March 1870, MLT 272–4.
23. JR–Georgiana Mount-Temple, 20 March 1870, LMT, 273–4.
24. JR–Georgiana Mount-Temple, Denmark Hill, 23 February 1870, LMT, 268.
25. JR–Lady Desart, Denmark Hill, 15 September 1870, cited in RLT, 121.
26. Cited in RLT, 122.
27. The letters are printed by Mary Lutyens in 'The Millais-La Touche Correspondence', *Cornhill Magazine*, Spring 1967, 1–18.

28. XX, xxxviii. For a hostile view stressing Ruskin's appeal to a female audience see Green's paper in *Macmillan's Magazine*, 1871, reprinted in his *Oxford Studies*, 1901: 'What more entrancing than the new Art-Professor, and the wonderful fireworks which throw their magical light on every subject on earth but the subject of his chair? Quiet art-students there have been in Oxford for a long time; its art-circle is one of the most real and worthy results of the life of young Oxford; but the Vestal of the Parks votes their talk a bore, and hurries off to the Taylor to see a great genius crown itself with foolscap and burn the Church Catechism in effigy before the nose of the Vice-Chancellor . . .'
29. JR–Margaret Ruskin, 21 May 1870, Bembridge MS B VI.
30. JR–Margaret Ruskin, n.d., Bembridge MS B VI.
31. 'The incurably desultory character which has brought on me the curse of Reuben, "Unstable as water, thou shalt not excel"' was a frequent lament. See XXVIII, 275.
32. JR–Georgiana Cowper-Temple, Pisa, 1 July 1870, XX, lii–liii.
33. XXXV, 561–2.

Chapter Twenty-Seven

1. 1 August 1870. Diaries, II, 699.
2. Frederic Harrison, *John Ruskin*, 1902, 124–5.
3. See 'The Millais–La Touche Correspondence', *Cornhill Magazine*, Spring 1967, 1–18.
4. XVIII, 47–8.
5. Thomas Carlyle–JR, 10 October 1870, TC, 155.
6. J. A. Froude, *Carlyle's Life in London*, 1884, II, 406.
7. For some other antecedents, see Oscar Maurer, '"My Squeamish Public": Some Problems of Victorian Magazine Publishers and Editors' in *Studies in Bibliography*, Charlotteville, 12, 1959, 21–41.
8. George Allen supplied Ruskin with a list of copies of *Fors* sold before 31 December 1871. They were: January, 821; February, 732; March 615; April, 603; May, 605; June, 570; July, 569; August, 541; September, 537; October, 546; November, 513; December, 446. In addition, 325 copies were 'supplied to Author's orders'. Bembridge MS 91.
9. XXVIII, 106–7.
10. W. G. Collingwood, *The Life and Work of John Ruskin*, 1893 II, 117.
11. XXVII, xix–xxiii.
12. This was the occasion recalled, with a different emphasis, by J. M. Ludlow. See above p. 71.
13. XXXV, 486–8.
14. The correspondent was Walter Severn. See Walter Sharp, *The Life and Letters of Joseph Severn*, 1892, 219.
15. XXXVII, 28.
16. XXVII, xix–xx, summarises these symbolic meanings.
17. See XXII, xxiii.
18. XXXIV, 107–11.
19. JR–Charles Eliot Norton, 23 February 1871, CEN, 218–9. For a description of the Crown and Thistle in the 1930s, see Richard Cobb, *The End of the Line*, 1997, 65–7.
20. See 'Peter' (the Revd E. P. Barrow) in *St George*, Vol. VI, 1903, 103–115.
21. XXVIII, 661.
22. JR–Charles Eliot Norton, Venice, 19 June 1870, CEN, 194–5.
23. Whose acquaintance with Ruskin is recorded in his 'Ruskin in Oxford' in the *Pelican Record*, Vol. II, No. 4, June 1894, 101–7.
24. Oddie, *op.cit.*
25. 'Peter', *op.cit.*, 108.
26. XXXIII, 202.
27. XXXV, 372
28. JR–JJR, Venice, 7 October 1845, Harold Shapiro (ed), *Ruskin in Italy*, 1972, 220.
29. See Paolo Constantini and Italo Zaunier, *I dagherrotipi della collezione Ruskin*, Venice, 1986.
30. XXVII, 116.
31. XXVII, 130.
32. XXVII, 167.
33. XXVII, 191–2.
34. XXVII, 181.
35. See W. G. Collingwood, *The Life and Work of John Ruskin*, 1893, II, 102.
36. See XXXV, 13 and 40–3, passages in *Præterita* taken from early issues of *Fors Clavigera*.
37. For Robinson, see Anthony Burton, *Vision and Accident*, 1999, 37–8, 68–71 and 131–2.
38. XXII, 100.
39. XXII, 110.
40. Georgiana Burne-Jones, *Memorials of Edward Burne-Jones*, 1906, II, 18–19.
41. Penelope Fitzgerald, *Edward Burne-Jones*, 1975, 131.
42. Arthur Severn, *The Professor*, ed. James S. Dearden, 1967, 34.
43. Severn, *ibid.*, 35.
44. Severn, *ibid.*, 36.
45. Severn, *ibid.*, 36.
46. JR–JRS, Abingdon, 25 April 1871, Bembridge MS L 36.
47. JR–JRS, Abingdon, 10 May 1871, Bembridge MS L 36.

48. JR–JRS, Denmark Hill, Bembridge MS L 36.
49. XX, 301–90.
50. XXII, 442–5.
51. XXII, 445–7.
52. W. G. Collingwood, *The Life and Work of John Ruskin*, 1893, II, III.

Chapter Twenty-Eight

1. Arthur Severn, *The Professor*, ed. James S. Dearden, 1967, 40.
2. JR–William Cowper-Temple, 27 July 1871, LMT 309.
3. JRS–Margaret Ruskin, 'Sunday', July 1871, Bembridge MS B VI.
4. XXVII, 132.
5. XXXIV, 32–3.
6. Severn, *op.cit.*, 44–5. For Goodwin see *Albert Goodwin RWS, 1845–1932*, Chris Beetles Gallery, 1996.
7. XXXV, 75–6.
8. XXXV, 95.
9. Severn, *op.cit.*, 47.
10. See W. J. Linton, *Memories*, 1895, 97.
11. 'Song' of 1833, quoted at 11, 3, includes the stanzas

> I weary for the woodland brook
> That wanders through the vale;
> I weary for the heights that look
> Adown upon the dale.
>
> The crags are lone on Coniston,
> And Loweswater's dell;
> And dreary on the mighty one,
> The cloud-enwreathed Scawfell.

12. XXVII, 95.
13. XXXVII, 139.
14. See Mary Lutyens, 'The Millais–La Touche Correspondence', *Cornhill Magazine*, Spring 1967, 1–18, and Sheila Birkenhead, *Illustrious Friends*, 1965, 196–202.
15. W. Richardson–JR, 21 July 1871, cited in RLT, 123.
16. JR–William Cowper-Temple, 23 July 1871, LMT 298.
17. JR–William Cowper-Temple, 27 July 1871, LMT 310.
18. JR–Thomas Carlyle, 23 October 1871, TC 162–3.
19. JR–JRS, 13 September 1871, Bembridge MS L 36.
20. XXII, xxii.
21. XXII, xxii.
22. JR–JRS, 14 September 1871, XXII, xxi and see J. S. Dearden, *Printing at Coniston*, Bembridge, 1958.
23. Allen's home address until he moved to Orpington in 1874.
24. Ada Earland's book contains one or two pieces of information not found elsewhere, notably her report that Carlyle 'did not sympathise' with Ruskin's plans for the Guild of St George. 'He flatly refused to contribute to the funds, and denounced the scheme as absurd . . .' Ada Earland, *Ruskin and his Circle*, 1910, 111–12.
25. XXII, xxiv.
26. XVIII, 385–6.
27. See XXVII, 622, and XXVIII, 177, 204.

Chapter Twenty-Nine

1. Bodley MS Eng Letts c 38 fols 213–14.
2. XXVIII, 352–3.
3. Thomas Carlyle–JR, 28 April 1871, TC, 159.
4. Henry Liddell–Henry Acland, 10 October 1864, Bodley MS Acland d 69 fol. 54.
5. Henry Liddell–Henry Acland, 15 January 1871, Bodley MS Acland d 69 fol. 94.
6. Liddell had long been aware of the need for an enlightened professoriat. In 1854 he had written to Acland 'What we want is something at once permanent and intelligent. The Heads of Houses are permanent but not intelligent . . . Real Professors, qualis sentis tantum, would afford the double qualification required in one. They would be permanent & intelligent — a true Aristocracy — . . .' Henry Liddell–Henry Acland, 23 February 1854, Bodley MS Acland d 69 fol. 32.
7. XXII, 123–4.
8. XX, 152–3.
9. See XXVIII, 285, and n.
10. XXII, 121.
11. See Robert Hewison, *Ruskin and Oxford*, 1999.
12. JR–Acland, 14 March 1871, XXI, xix–xxi.
13. Henry Liddell–Henry Acland, 1 April 1871, Bodley MS Acland d 69 fol. 96.
14. W. G. Collingwood, *The Life and Work of John Ruskin*, 1893, II, 147.
15. XX, xxxv.
16. Friedrich Max-Müller, *Auld Lang Syne*, 1878, 127–8.
17. See Alan Mackinnon, *The Oxford Amateurs*, 1910.
18. R. W. Macan, 'Oxford in the "Senties"', in *The Eighteen-Seventies: Essays by Fellows of the Royal Society of Literature*, ed. Harley Granville Barker, Cambridge, 1929.

Chapter Thirty

1. JR–JRS, June 27 1873, Bembridge MS L 38.
2. Bembridge.
3. Rose La Touche–George MacDonald (late April) 1872, MS Yale, partially cited in RLT, 124.
4. See Leon, *Ruskin the Great Victorian*, 1949, 412.
5. Rose La Touche–George MacDonald, 15 May 1872, MS Yale, partially cited in Leon, *op.cit.*, 486.
6. Rose La Touche–George MacDonald, n.d., cited in Greville MacDonald, *Reminiscences of a Specialist*, 1932, 111–13.
7. See Diaries, II, 723 and n.
8. XXII, 346–490, and notes from Diary given at XXII, xxvii–iii.
9. *Monuments of the Cavalli Family in the Church of Santa Anastasia, Verona*, XXIV, 127–38.
10. Rose La Touche–George MacDonald, 15 May 1872, MS Yale.
11. See Leon, *op.cit.*, 490–1.
12. Rose La Touche–George MacDonald, Tunbridge Wells, 18 June 1872, cited in Leon, *op.cit.*, 489.
13. Rose La Touche–JR, 16 June 1872, MS Yale, partially cited in Leon, *op.cit.*, 488–9.
14. XXVII, 293.
15. Venice, 30 June. Telegram, Yale.
16. JR–George MacDonald, Venice, 5 July 1872, Leon, *op.cit.*, 490.
17. Another letter written on 5 July 1872, Leon, *op.cit.*, 491.
18. XXVII, 341–2.
19. Leon, *op.cit.*, 491–2.
20. Leon, *op.cit.*, 494.
21. He later wrote 'I remember the frail Rose, so amazingly thin yet with such high colour and her great eyes, with the tenderest of smiles possessing so readily her exquisite lips. I was astonished at her being alive, seeing that, I well remember, her dinner once consisted of three green peas, and, the very next day, one strawberry and half an Osborne biscuit! She was too frail to sit at table, of course. But Ruskin would be left alone with her either in the drawing room or in the study . . .' Greville MacDonald, *Reminiscences of a Specialist*, 1932, 120.
22. MacDonald, *op.cit.*, 120–1.
23. 26 July 1872, Diaries, II, 728.
24. See LMT, 339.
25. JR–Georgiana Cowper-Temple, 13 August 1872, LMT, 328.
26. JR–Georgiana Cowper-Temple, 18 August 1872, LMT, 330.
27. JR–Georgiana Cowper-Temple, 15 August 1872, LMT, 329.
28. MacDonald, *op.cit.*, 121.
29. Leon, *op.cit.*, 497.
30. Leon, *op.cit.*, 497.
31. JR–JRS, 6 November 1872, Bembridge MS L 37.
32. JR–William Richardson, 21 August 1872, Bodley MS Eng Misc E 182, fol. 78.
33. JR–Tyrwhitt, Brantwood, 29 September 1872, Jay Wood Claiborne (ed.), *Two Secretaries*, University of Texas at Austin Ph.D., 1969.
34. JR–Sarah Angelina Acland, Brantwood, 1 September 1872, Bodley MS Acland d 170 fol. 139.
35. XXVII, 371.
36. XXVII, 373.
37. XXVII, 397.
38. XXVII, 413–4. The quotation is from Cary's version of the *Inferno*, xii. 40.
39. *Pall Mall Gazette*, 4 November 1872. Ruskin reprinted this letter in *Fors Clavigera*, December 1874. See XXVIII, 219.
40. Leon, *op.cit.*, 498.
41. JR–Sarah Angelina Acland, 5 January 1873. Bodley MS Acland d 170 fol. 143.
42. JR–JRS, n.d., Bembridge MS L 53.
43. JR–JRS, Brantwood, 15 April 1873, Bembridge MS L 38.
44. JR–Georgiana Cowper-Temple, Brantwood, n.d. but spring 1873, Bodley MS Eng Letts c 51 fol. 202.
45. JR–Malleson, Corpus, 28 November 1872, MS Bembridge.
46. 15 June 1873, in a page torn from the diary and printed at BD, 353.

Chapter Thirty-One

1. XXVIII, 613.
2. XXXIV, xxix–xxx.
3. JR–James Knowles, 'Arthur Severn's, Herne Hill', n.d. but 1873.
4. XVIII, 466.
5. XXVIII, 757–8 and 770.
6. XVI, 161.
7. XXVII, 636–47. Ruskin's criticisms of Tyndall continued for some years. Collingwood comments 'Mr Ruskin did not make the most of his position in the eyes of the public by inserting his remarks on Professor Tyndall, — insufficiently supported with argument and illustration, — among very different kinds of matter in *Fors*, and by allowing himself to write at moments when

the ill-health of three years left him — "the greatest gladiator of the age", as he has been called — hardly a match for the cool fence of his opponent.'

8. XXVII, 642.

9. This vitalism, which extends from the middle of the century to a dispersed influence in the vegetarian, ecological and 'Nature Study' concerns of the 1890s, may have had its origin in the 'Law of Help' set forward in the fifth volume of *Modern Painters*, in which we learn that 'the power which causes the several portions of the plant to help each other, we call life . . . Thus, intensity of life is also intensity of helpfulness — completeness of depending of each part on all the rest.' See David Elliston Allen, *The Naturalist in Britain*, 1976.

10. See Dorothy McCall, *When That I Was*, 1952, 26, 41, 51, 168.

11. XXIII, xxvii–xxx. The complete version of Wedderburn's essay is in *Celebrities at Home*, reprinted from 'The World', 1878, 291–301.

12. See VIII, 8–9 and the exquisite description of Ruskin's 1883 visit to Ashestiel and Abbotsford at XXXIX, 460–4.

13. JR–Dora Livesey, Brantwood, 8 February 1873, Olive Wilson, ed., *My Dearest Dora*, n.d., 87. One of Ruskin's numerous complaints about chaperonage.

14. August 18 1873, Diaries, II, 754. This was the anniversary of Rose's rejection of Ruskin at Toft. His poem begins

> Love, it is a wrathful peace,
> A free acquittance, without release,
> And truth fret-full of false head,
> And Security, set all in dread.
> In heart it is despairing hope
> And full of hope, it is wanhope,
> Wise madness, and void reasonne
> And sweet danger, wherein to drown.

15. XVIII, 515–33.

16. JR–Thomas Carlyle, October 1873, TC 173–4.

17. JR–Thomas Carlyle, 3 December 1873, TC 176.

18. JR–Thomas Carlyle, December 1873, TC 177.

19. XXIII, 9–177.

20. XXIII, 4.

21. XXVII, 668.

22. XXVII, 669.

23. Bembridge MS 20.

24. Oscar Wilde–JR, May 1888, Rupert Hart-Davies, ed., *The Letters of Oscar Wilde*, 1962, 217–8. The note accompanied a gift of *The Happy Prince, and other Tales*.

25. 31 October. Diaries, II, 765.

26. XXXVIII, 39.

27. XXVII, 161–4.

28. XXVII, 161.

29. XX. JJR–George Gray, 23 February 1848, RG 90–1.

30. XXXVIII, 483.

31. J. W. Oddie, 'Ruskin at Corpus', *Pelican Record*, Vol. 11, No. 4, July 1894, 101–7.

32. J. B. Atlay, *Henry Acland*, 1903, 252–4.

33. Atlay, ibid., 294.

Chapter Thirty-Two

1. Identified by Catherine Williams in her *Ruskin's Late Works*, Ph.D. thesis, London University, 1967.

2. JR–Sir Robert Collins, 8 January 1874, Bodley MS Eng Letts c 39 fol. 400.

3. JR–Georgiana Cowper-Temple, 22 January 1874, Bodley MS Eng Letts c 51 fol. 39.

4. 4 February 1874. Diaries, III, 772.

5. JRS–JR, Herne Hill, n.d. but 1888, Bembridge MS L 56.

6. Diaries, III, 773.

7. XXVIII, 363.

8. JR–JRS, Brantwood, March 1874, Bembridge MS C 39.

9. XXVIII, 70.

10. Diaries, III, 777.

11. Diaries, III, 777.

12. Diaries, III, 777.

13. 28 March. Diaries, III, 781.

14. XX, xliii.

15. JR–JRS, 9 April 1874, Bembridge MS L 39.

16. Cited in Sheila Birkenhead, *Illustrious Friends*, 1965, 236.

17. See Jeanne Clegg, 'Circe and Proserpina: John Ruskin to Joan Severn. Ten Days in Sicily, 1874' in *Quaderni de Dipartimento di Linguistica*, Universita della Calabria, 1986.

18. JR–Charles Eliot Norton, 11 April 1874, CEN, 313–4.

19. JR–JRS, 4 June 1874, Bembridge MS L 39.

20. JR–JRS, Florence 29 May 1874, Bembridge MS L 39.

21. XX, 84.

22. See Van Akin Burd, *Christmas Story*, 1990, 92–7.

23. XXI, xxxviii.

24. JR–Susie Beever, Assisi, 14 April 1874, XXXVII, 93.

25. JR–Georgiana Cowper-Temple, Assisi, 14 June 1874, LMT, 355.
26. XXIX, 90–1.
27. XXIII, xl.
28. See Van Akin Burd, *Christmas Story*, 82, 102, 105.
29. XXIII, 285–91.
30. W. G. Collingwood, *The Life and Work of John Ruskin*, 1893, II, 144.
31. XXIII, xlvii, n. 5.
32. Bembridge MS 16.
33. June 17, 1874. Diaries, III, 795.
34. JR–JRS, Lucca, 18 August 1874, XXIII, xlviii.
35. W. G. Collingwood, *Ruskin Relics*, 1903, 90.
36. *Ibid.*
37. IV, 123.
38. JR–JRS, Lucca, 27 September 1874, Bembridge MS L 39.
39. Diaries, III, 802.
40. Bembridge MS XI.
41. JR–JRS, Bembridge MS L 39.
42. Diaries, III, 801.
43. JR–Charles Eliot Norton, Lucca, 26 August 1874, CEN 329–30.
44. XXVII, 61, 85.
45. XXXV, 433.
46. JR–Charles Eliot Norton, Hotel du Mont Blanc, St Martin's, 12 October 1874, CEN, 340–2.

Chapter Thirty-Three

1. Charles Eliot Norton–JR, Shady Hill, 30 October 1874, CEN, 344–7.
2. *Fraser's Magazine*, 1 January 1874.
3. 6 December 1874. Diaries, III, 829.
4. 6 December 1874. Diaries, III, 830.
5. JR–JRS, 13 October 1874, Bembridge MS L 39.
6. Cited in JR–JRS, Chamonix, 15 October 1874, XXX Bembridge MS L 39.
7. Cited in JR–JRS, Lucca, 27 September 1874. Bembridge MS L 39.
8. JR–JRS, Chambery, 4 October 1874. Bembridge MS L 39.
9. See XXIII, lx and 179–279.
10. See XXIII, 10.
11. Richard Ellmann, *Oscar Wilde*, 1988, 46–50.
12. See Ellmann, *op.cit.*, and Billie Andrew Inman, 'Estrangement and Connection' in Laurel Brake and Ian Small, eds., *Pater in the 1990s*, Greensboro, NC, 1991.
13. E. T. Cook (writing of the Rossetti circle), *The Life of Ruskin*, 1911, I, 500.
14. See H. E. Wortham, *Oscar Browning*, 1927, 99–112.
15. XX, xliii–xliv.
16. See Terence H. O'Brien, *Milner*, 1979, 33–45, and Alon Kadish, *Apostle Arnold: the Life and Death of Arnold Toynbee 1852–1883*, Duke University Press, 1986, 33–9.
17. XXVIII, 376–82.
18. See XXXVIII, 375. The illustration, a woodcut of roses growing from a tomb, was probably by Arthur Burgess and is now identified as a copy after Filippo Lippi. See introduction to this volume.
19. XXXIII, 296.
20. XXVIII, 242–5.
21. XII, 521.
22,23,24,25. JRS–JR, Herne Hill, all undated but autumn 1874. Bembridge MS L 62. One large envelope in this box is marked (in Joan's hand) 'These to be destroyed in this parcel about Sandgate'.
26. JR–Thomas Carlyle, February 1874, TC 178–9.
27. JR–JRS, 15 December 1874, Bodley MS Eng Letts c 51.
28. Rose La Touche–Mrs MacDonald, 17 December 1874, MS Yale, cited RLT, 130.
29. Rose La Touche–Mrs MacDonald, 17 December 1874, MS Yale, cited in Leon, *op.cit.*, 499.
30. JR–Charles Eliot Norton, Brantwood, 28 December 1874, CEN, 349–50.
31. XXVIII, 246.
32. Diaries, III, 832.
33. Diaries, III, 837.
34. JR–Francesca Alexander, in Lucia Gray Swett, *John Ruskin's Letters to Francesca and Memoirs of the Alexanders*, 1931, 118.
35. JR–George MacDonald, 28 February 1875, cited in Leon, *op.cit.*, 500.
36. JR–Mrs Barnard, 11 April 1875, Bembridge MS B V.
37. 18 May 1875. Diaries, III, 845.
38. XXXIX, 184.
39. Bembridge MS XIX.
40. Bembridge MS XIX.
41. Bembridge MS XIX.
42. JR–JRS, 28 May 1875, Bembridge MS L 40.
43. JR–Susie Beever, 28 May 1875, cited in RLT, 133.

Chapter Thirty-Four

1. 1 June 1875. Diaries, III, 847.
2. See XXI, xiv. This volume of the Library

Edition is devoted to 'The Ruskin Art Collection at Oxford: Catalogue, Notes and Instructions'.

3. The other official and published documents that directly pertain to the Guild's constitution and affairs are as follows. They are the *Abstract of the Objects and Constitution of St George's Guild* (1877) and the *Memorandum of Association* (1878); the *Master's Report* (1879) and the *Master's Report* (1881); the *General Statement Explaining the Nature and Purposes of St George's Guild* (1882), the *Master's Report* (1884) and the *Master's Report* (1885). In addition, Ruskin published the Guild's accounts. They are to be found in the pamphlets *Accounts of the St George's Guild*, 1871–82 (1884), *Accounts of St George's Guild*, 1881–3 (1884) and *Accounts of St George's Guild*, 1884 (1885). All these pamphlets are published in XXX. This volume of the Library Edition is devoted to 'The Guild and Museum of St George: Reports, Catalogues and other Papers'. There are in all 30 short articles generally headed 'Affairs of the Guild' in the 'Notes and Correspondence', section of *Fors Clavigera*. The first of them was published in February 1875 and the last in February 1878.

4. XXX, 45.

5. XXX, 17.

6. XXVII, 296.

7. XXIX, 589.

8. The names are printed in the section 'Ruskin's Library and Marginalia' at XXXIV, 703.

9. In Edith Hope Scott, *Ruskin's Guild of St George*, 1931, 83. See also Collingwood's *Ruskin Relics*, 1903, 210. Collingwood adds 'He had more respect for the Apocrypha than most Protestant Bible-readers'.

10. XXVI, xxvi.

11. See XXVI, 89.

12. XXVI, 98–9.

13. XXV, 413.

14. XXV, 204.

15. JR–Charles Eliot Norton, 17 November 1869, CEN 180–1.

16. XXV, 300–1.

17. Private reactions are also lacking. No doubt because of its connection with Rose, Ruskin himself said little about *Proserpina* and was modest in his claims for the book. The first chapter contains his well-known statement 'Some one said of me once, very shrewdly, When he wants to work out a subject, he writes a book on it.' Ruskin continues '. . . this book will be nothing but process. I don't mean to assert anything positively in it from the first page to the last.' XXV, 216.

18. See the disappointing *Ruskin: the Critical Heritage*, ed. J. L. Bradley, 1984.

19. See XXVII, 586.

20. See XXXI, 37–98, and note the excellent index. The translators' preface is dated 'Easter Term'. Early copies of the book were available in the last weeks of June. For a modern edition see Xenophon, *Oeconomicus*, ed. Sarah B. Pomeroy, 1994.

21. XXXVII, 53, n. For this friendship, see Ellis's private publication *Stray Letters from Professor Ruskin to a London Bibliopole*, 1892.

22. W. G. Collingwood, *The Life and Work of John Ruskin*, 1893, II, 489, n.

23. XXII, 504.

24. XXII, 507.

25. XXII, 507.

26. XXII, 507. The words are taken from a report by James Manning Bruce in the *Century Magazine*, February 1898. See XXII, 492.

27. XXII, 506.

28. Bruce, *op.cit.*, cited at XXII, 506, n.

29. G. W. Kitchin, *Ruskin in Oxford and other Studies*, 1903, 40–1.

30. See Betty Askwith, *Lady Dilke*, 1969, 38.

31. JR–Mark Pattison, Brantwood, 17 July 1875, Bodley MS Pattison 57.

32. JR–Alice Owen, 26 January (?) 1875, Bodley MS Eng Letts e 85.

33. XXXVII, 588.

34. XXXI, 7.

35. XVIII, 104.

36. See XXVIII, 276 and XVIII, xiii–xv.

37. XXVIII, 500–1.

38. R. C. Robertson-Glasgow records of his Corpus days 'Anyone of a moderately romantic and sociable turn would have welcomed a short chat with the ghost of Cuthbert Shields. He it was who had told his friends "When I am dead, I shall return as a bad smell in the corner of my room." He was a history tutor, of vast but disorderly learning, and of a habit of mind so discursive that, in a series of lectures on the French Revolution, he had only reached the Flood by the end of term.' *46 Not Out*, 1948, 79. See also Claude R. Blagden, *Well Remembered*, 1953.

39. XXVIII, 499–501.

40. See XXXV, 41.

41. More than 100 left-hand pages of this diary contain the translation, which is also to be found in the 'Venetian diary' used in 1876–7. It remains unpublished. See BD, 142–3.

42. JR–Charles Eliot Norton, Brantwood, 9 July 1879, CEN, 431.

43. Walter Sichel, *The Sands of Time*, 1923, 114.
44. Sichel, *op.cit.*, 119.
45. W. H. Mallock, *Memoirs of Life and Literature*, 1920, 59.
46. The sub-title may be significant. See chapter VIII of his *Memoirs*, 'Society in Country Houses'.
47. Sichel, *op.cit.*, 106.
48. See *The New Republic*, chapter III.
49. Mallock was to recall 'the only human being at that time who held and expressed views similar to my own, so far as I knew, was Ruskin . . . he confessed himself a victim of a tragic and desolating doubt, but he did boldly proclaim that until some solution was found, the men of the modern world were of all men the most miserable . . . here . . . was the true voice of reason and challenging passion combined — a voice which would not say "peace when there was no peace", and which I missed altogether in Jowett and the Oxford liberals generally . . .' See Mallock, *op.cit.*, 64.

Chapter Thirty-Five

1. Bembridge MS XX.
2. See Van Akin Burd, *Christmas Story*, 1990, 22–35.
3. JR–JRS, Broadlands, 10 December 1875, Bembridge MS L 40.
4. JR–JRS, Broadlands, 17 December 1875, Bembridge MS L 40.
5. JR–JRS, Broadlands, 19 December 1875, Bembridge MS L 40.
6. JR–JRS, Broadlands, 20 December 1875, Bembridge MS L 40.
7. JR–JRS, Broadlands, 20 December 1875, Bembridge MS L 40.
8. George MacDonald–Mrs MacDonald, Broadlands, 21 December 1875, Greville MacDonald, *George MacDonald and his Wife*, 1924, 472.
9. JR–JRS, Broadlands, 21 December 1875, Bembridge MS L 40.
10. JR–JRS, 1 January 1876, Bembridge MS L 41.
11. XXXVI, lxxxvi.
12. JR–Cardinal Manning, 25 January 1878, XXXVII, 240–1.
13. JR–JRS, 2 February 1876, Bembridge MS L 41.
14. See Hilton, *John Ruskin: The Early Years*, 1985, 285.
15. Osborne Gordon–JR, 14 January 1876, Bembridge MS L 7.
16. JR–Juliet Tylor, Cambridge, 3 April 1876, MS Guild of St George, Sheffield.
17. 1 April 1876. Diaries, III, 891.
18. 2 April 1876. Diaries, III, 891.
19. JR–Juliet Morse, Cambridge, 3 April 1876, MS Guild of St George, Sheffield.
20. XXXIII, 628–9.
21. JR–JRS, Corpus Christi, ?10 March 1876, Bembridge MS L 41.
22. XXVIII, 628–9.
23. XXI, 13.
24. 11 April 1876. Diaries, III, 892.
25. See XXVI, 563 and 591, n.
26. JR–JRS, 6 October 1875, Bembridge MS L 40. For the Ruskin family arms, see XXXV, 389–91.
27. JR–Georgiana Cowper-Temple, 3 May 1876, LMT 370.
28. Around the time of the Brantwood Dispersal Sale of 1930 this diary was bought by a Grasmere antique dealer, who sold it to F. J. Sharp of Barrow-in-Furness. Sharp would not lend this document to Evans and Whitehouse for their edition of the diaries. In 1957 he bequeathed it to Helen Gill Viljoen, who published it as *The Brantwood Diary of John Ruskin* in 1971. See BD vii–xiii and James S. Dearden, *Ruskin, Bembridge and Brantwood*, Keele, 1994, 49.
29. XXXIII, 343, n.
30. XXXII, xxxiii.
31. JR–George Allen, 3 July 1877, XXXI, xxviii.
32. XXXIV, 137–43.
33. Anne Thackeray Ritchie, *Records of Tennyson, Ruskin, Browning*, 1892, 68–77.
34. F. W. Maitland, *Life and Letters of Leslie Stephen*, 1906, 298.
35. XXVIII, 633 and 634, n.
36. See XXIV, xxxiv–v.
37. See Margaret Spence (ed.), *Dearest Mama Talbot: a Selection of Letters from John Ruskin to Mrs Fanny Talbot*, 1966, 9–29.
38. XXVIII, 687.
39. XXVIII, 690–1.
40. Bembridge MS XXI.
41. Bembridge MS XXI.
42. Spence, *op.cit.*, 54, n.

Chapter Thirty-Six

1. 'Milan Cathedral', II, 376–7.
2. 6 September 1876. Diaries, III, 905. Ruskin quotes this description, in a politer form, in *St Mark's Rest*. See XXIV, 360–1.
3. 13 September 1876. Diaries, III, 907.

4. The copy is in the Ashmolean Museum. A copy of St Ursula's head, studied from the same painting, is at Somerville College. Remarks in Ruskin's diary may refer to either of these studies. See *Ruskin and Venice* (exhibition catalogue, ed. Robert Hewison), J. B. Speed Art Museum, Louisville, Kentucky, 1978, 92–3.
5. JR–Charles Eliot Norton, Venice, 5 October 1876, CEN, 385–7.
6. 3 October 1876. Diaries, III, 909.
7. XXVIII, 740–6.
8. See Van Akin Burd, *Christmas Story*, 1992, 145.
9. XIX, 50.
10. 22 October 1876. Diaries, III, 912.
11. 29 October 1876. Diaries, III, 912.
12. See BD, 142–3.
13. XXVIII, 757–8.
14. JR–JRS, Venice, 19 September 1876, Bembridge MS L 41.
15. XXVIII, 736.
16. JR–JRS, Venice, 9 December 1876, Bembridge MS L 41.
17. The letters of the 'Christmas Story' were acquired by F. J. Sharp, probably in the 1930s. In 1957 he bequeathed them to Helen Gill Viljoen. After her death in 1974 they passed to the Pierpont Morgan Library. They were eventually published by Van Akin Burd in *Christmas Story*, 1990, 253–79.
18. JR–JRS, 'Christmas Story' letters, Venice, 27 December 1876, in Burd, *op.cit.*, 253–8.
19. 24 December 1876. Diaries, III, 922.
20. 25 December 1876. Diaries, III, 920.
21. XXIX, 30.
22. XXIX, 32, and see Burd, *op.cit.*, 259–60. The MS of the first pages of this *Fors* is in the Yale University Library.
23. Eight of these drawings are reproduced in the introductory pages of XXIV, as Plates A–D.
24. XXIV, 149–90.
25. The work of these assistants and colleagues is summarised in Jeanne Clegg, *Ruskin and Venice*, 1981, 180–7.
26. 17 June 1877. Diaries, III, 962.

Chapter Thirty-Seven

1. XXIX, 397.
2. BD, 42, n.
3. XXX, li.
4. See XXVIII, 428–9.
5. W. G. Collingwood, *The Life and Work of John Ruskin*, 1893, II, 160.
6. XIX, 273.
7. For Riley, see BD, 601.
8. XXIX, 99–104.
9. XXIX, 103.
10. XXIX, 137.
11. XXIX, 164.
12. XXIX, 160.
13. Georgiana Burne-Jones, *Memorials of Edward Burne-Jones*, 1906, II, 86.
14. XXIX, 170, and see Edith Hope Scott, *Ruskin's Guild of* St George, 1931, 32 and illus.
15. XXIX, 173–4.
16. The later history of the Guild's stewardship of land at Bewdley is described in Peter Wardle and Cedric Quayle, *Ruskin and Bewdley*, 1989.
17. XIX, 273.
18. XIX, 200.
19. Many of Ruskin's notes for the continuation of *St Mark's Rest*, found after his death, are printed at XXIV, 425–57.
20. Quoted in BD, 560. Anderson's lectures to the Keswick Literary and Scientific Society were posthumously published as *The House of Bondage* (1908).
21. See XV, xx and 491–2.
22. XV, 351.
23. XXVI, 452.
24. XXVI, 243–66.
25. JR–William Walker, Simplon, June 9 1877, XXXVII, 223.
26. JR–JRS, Simplon, 10 June, quoted at XXV, xix.
27. See XXII, 492–528.
28. JR–Susie Beever, 2 December 1877, XXXVII, 231.
29. 25 December 1877. Diaries, III, 970.
30. See XXIX, 354–60.
31. JR–JRS. Windsor Castle, 2 January 1878, Bembridge MS L 43.
32. JR–Susie Beever, Windsor Castle, 2 January 1878, XXXVII, 236.
33. Frederick W. H. Myers, *Fragments of Prose and Poetry*, 1904, 90–1.
34. XXVIII, 403, n. The passage was cancelled in January 1878, after Ruskin's visit to Hawarden. See XXIX, 364.
35. JR–JRS, Hawarden, 13 January 1878, Bembridge MS L 43.
36. Henry Scott Holland, 'Gladstone and Ruskin' in *The Commonwealth*, July 1896.
37. Quoted in *Letters to MG and HG*, 1903, 4.
38. XXXIV, 548–9.
39. Henry Holiday, *Reminiscences of my Life*, 1914, 177.
40. See XXXIV, 91–104.
41. E. Moberly Bell, *Flora Shaw* (*Lady Lugard*), 1947, 21.

42. Edith Lyttelton, *Alfred Lyttelton*, 1917, 71–3.
43. JR–Thomas Carlyle, Brantwood, 17 February 1878, TC, 240.

Chapter Thirty-Eight

1. XIII, 409.
2. XIII, 409–10.
3. XIII, 343.
4. XXIX, 374.
5. 14 February 1878. BD, 91.
6. See XXX, 356.
7. Bembridge MS L 48.
8. 14 February 1878. BD, 90–1.
9. JR–Georgiana Cowper-Temple, 20 February 1878, Bodley MS Eng Letts c 42, fol. 68, and see BD, 500–1.
10. BD, 64.
11. See Leon, *Ruskin the Great Victorian*, 1949, 509–10.
12. JR–George MacDonald, 21 February 1878, cited in Leon, *op.cit.*, 510.
13. JR–Sara Anderson, Brantwood, 22 February 1878, Bodley MS Eng Letts c 42, fol. 71.
14. The following notes are in large part derived from suggestions made by Helen Gill Viljoen in BD, 114–32.
15. *British Medical Journal*, 1900, and see XXXVIII, 172.
16. See XXXV, 152.
17. See BD, 107. Ophelia's song is again found in Ruskin's diaries when he became mad in 1881. See 22 September 1881, Diaries, III, 1000.
18. See BD, 94.
19. BD, 79.
20. XXVIII, 559.
21. XIX, 382.
22. Bodley, MS Acland d 116 fols 103–4.
23. JRS–John Simon, Brantwood, 27 March 1878, in *Dearest Mama Talbot*, ed. Margaret Spence, 1966, 85–7.
24. *Ibid*.
25. XXVII, 397.
26. XIII, 485.
27. JR–George Richmond, Brantwood, 31 May 1878, XXXVII, 246–7.
28. XIII, 520.
29. Printed at XIII, 560–8.

Chapter Thirty-Nine

1. JR–Sara Anderson, Oxford, 5 January 1878, Bodley MS Eng Letts c 42, fol. 12.
2. JR–Edward Burne-Jones, Oxford, 10 February (1878?), Bodley MS Eng Letts c 42 fol. 48.
3. Frances Horner, *Time Remembered*, 1933, 55–6.
4. XXXIV, 147–174.
5. JR–James Reddie Anderson, 8 February 1878, Bodley MS Eng Letts c 42, fol. 46.
6. JR–James Knowles, Brantwood, 21 August 1878, Bembridge MS 21. See also sheets of unpublished matter, marked in Alexander Wedderburn's hand 'Part of an intended answer to an article by W. H. Mallock' at Bembridge MS 51/1 and John Hayman, 'Ruskin, Mallock and the Pre-Raphaelites' in *English Language Notes*, XIV, 4 (June 1977), 283–9.
7. XXXIV, 171.
8. See *Letters to MG and HG*, 1903, v–vi and XXXVI, lxxix.
9. See XXIX, xxiii.
10. See XXIX, xxiv.
11. After giving this evidence Burne-Jones wrote to a frind 'I wish all that trial-thing hadn't been; so much I wish it, and I wish Whistler knew that it made me sorry — but he would not believe . . .' Georgiana Burne-Jones, *Memorials of Edward Burne-Jones*, 1904, II, 88.
12. The trial is examined in detail by Linda Merrill, *A Pot of Paint: Aesthetics on Trial in Whistler v Ruskin*, 1992.
13. XXX, 95 and see XXIX, xxv.
14. JR–Henry Liddell, Brantwood, 28 November 1878, quoted at XXIX, xxv.
15. XXII, xxxi.
16. XXII, xxxi.
17. BD, 139.
18. Constance Hilliard–Charles Eliot Norton, 1 December 1878, BD 139.
19. February 6 1879. BD, 154.
20. It was to be a 'Museum Fors'. See BD, 157.
21. See XXXIV, 179–90, a section preceded by Cook's remark that 'The letters to the Rev. F. A. Malleson form one of the most complicated and tiresome chapters in the Bibliography of Ruskin.
22. XXX, 15.
23. W. G. Collingwood, *The Life and Work of John Ruskin*, 1893, II, 208.
24. JR–JRS, Sheffield, n.d. but October 1879, Bembridge MS L 42.
25. W. G. Collingwood, *Ruskin Relics*, 1903, 156.
26. C. E. Halle, *Notes from a Painter's Life*, 1909, 66.
27. See XXX, xxx.

28. XIV, 365–454.
29. XIV, 373–448.
30. JR–George Allen, 15 August 1879, Bodley MS Eng Letts c 43 fol. 31.
31. See VIII, 17.
32. Part of a compilation, edited by Alexander Wedderburn, of essays and articles from 1871–88 on the subject of museums. See XXXIV, 85–90 and 245–62.
33. XXXIV, 343.
34. See Ruskin's comments at XXXIV, 559.
35. XXXIV, xxxvi.
36. Thomas Hughes, *Life of Bishop Fraser*, 1887, 305.
37. 'H. Carlisle'–F. A. Malleson, Rose Castle, Carlisle, 1 November 1879. MS, Bembridge.
38. XXIX, 381–2.
39. XXXIV, 547.
40. Where it is the first chapter of the second volume, and retitled 'Living Waves'. See XXVI, 295–332.
41. For whom, see Al Weil, *Hercules Brabazon* (exhibition catalogue), Chris Beetles Gallery, 1989.
42. *Revue des Jeux, des Arts et du Sport*, 28 août, 1880.
43. JR–JRS, n.d. Bembridge MS L 42.
44. JR–JRS, Abbeville, 26 August 1880, Bembridge MS L 42.
45. Janet Leete submitted her correspondence to Cook and Wedderburn, who preserved the letters at Bodley MS Eng Letts c 44.
46. See Richard Macksey, *et al.*, *On Reading Ruskin: Prefaces to 'La Bible d' Amiens', and 'Sesame et les Lys' by Marcel Proust*, New Haven, 1987.
47. JR–Janet Leete, n.d., Bodley MS Eng Letts c 44.
48. XXXIII, 124.
49. JR–JRS, Amiens (October 1880), Bembridge MS L 42.
50. A. C. Benson, *Memories and Friends*, 1924, 27–31.
51. XXVIII, 449.
52. See XXXIV, xli.

Chapter Forty

1. Printed at XIII, 355–88.
2. 9 November–10 December 1880. Diaries, III, 993–6.
3. See BD, 250–1 and 259.
4. XXXIII,55–6.
5. JR–F. S. Ellis, 16 February 1881, XXXVII, 342.
6. JR–F. S. Ellis, February 1881, XXXVII, 342–3.
7. JR–Sara Anderson, 16 February 1881, Bodley MS Eng Letts c 44 fol. 123.
8. JR–Edward Burne-Jones, 18 February 1881, Bodley MS Eng Letts c 44 fol. 125.
9. JRS–Jane Simon, Herne Hill, 20 February 1881, BD, 255.
10. JR–Sara Anderson, Brantwood, 'Good Friday' 1881, Bodley MS Eng Letts c 44, fols 151 *et seqq.*
11. JRS–Jane Simon, Brantwood, 21 February 1881, BD 544–5.
12. Laurence Hilliard–Alexander Macdonald, Brantwood, 3 March 1881, Bodley MS Eng Letts c 44, fol. 129.
13. JRS–John Simon, 9 March 1881, BD 547.
14. Details from letters from JRS–John and Jane Simon, 20 February–21 March 1881, BD 544–51.
15. JRS–John Simon, 21 March 1881, BD 551.
16. 7 April 1881, BD 268.
17. JRS–John Simon, 21 March 1881, BD 551–2.
18. JRS–Jane Simon, 15 March 1881, BD 551.
19. 3 February 1883, BD 297.
20. JR–George Allen, 31 March 1881, Bodley MS Eng Letts c 44, fol. 142.
21. JR–Alexander Macdonald, 27 March 1881, Bodley MS Eng Letts c 44 fol. 138.
22. JR–John Simon, 20 July 1881, Bodley MS Eng Letts c 44 fol. 234.
23. Laurence Hilliard–Alexander Macdonald, 14 June 1881, Bodley MS Eng Letts c 44 fol. 197.
24. JR–Janet Leete, Brantwood 10 July 1881, Bodley MS Eng Letts c 44 fol. 227.
25. For the Webling sisters and Brantwood, see Peggy Webling, *Peggy: the Story of One Score Years and Ten*, n.d. (1929?), 45–66. Of the sisters' public recitations, Peggy records, pp. 70–1, 'The two Wilde brothers, Oscar and Willie, often came to hear us . . . Oscar Wilde expressed his opinion in a really charming sentence, spoken to Ruskin: "Is not Peggy Webling a wave of delight from God?" On another occasion, at a dinner-party, when the Professor happened to speak about us, Oscar Wilde turned to him and exclaimed: "Great Master! Is not Peggy Webling *too* precious!"'
26. JR–John Brown, Brantwood, 29 March 1881, XXXVII, 347–8.
27. JR–George Richmond. 20 May 1881, XXXVII, 360–1.
28. JR–George Allen.

29. 22 September 1881. Diaries, III, 999.
30. Although he was at Brantwood, Ruskin chose to keep his diary from 15 September in Bembridge MS XXI. Writing in BD resumed on January 4 1883.
31. JR–George Allen.
32. JR–JRS, 'Sunday' (October 1881), Bembridge MS L 42.
33. JR–JRS, Brantwood, 9 November 1881, Bembridge MS L 42.

Chapter Forty-One

1. See II, 250 and 527.
2. Reprinted in his *Ruskin Relics*, 1903, 149–65.
3. W. G. Collingwood, *The Life and Work of John Ruskin*, 1893, II, 225.
4. *Ibid.*, 226.
5. 1 December 1881. Diaries, III, 1008.
6. JR–Frederick Crawley, Brantwood, January 1882, Bodley MS Eng Letts c 45 fol. 31.
7. JR–Maria La Touche, 5 December 1881, BD, 262.
8. JR–Mary Gladstone, *Letters to MG and HG*, 1903, 72.
9. JR–Lady Mount-Temple, 5 March 1882, BD, 502–3.
10. JR–JRS, (March 1882?), Sheila Birkenhead, *Illustrious Friends*. 1965, 290.
11. Ada Dundas (incorrectly identified in the Library Edition and BD) was from St Andrews, Fife. She began corresponding with Ruskin in 1879, when she was 14, and visited Brantwood with her mother in September 1881. Her letters from Ruskin are gathered at Bodley MS Eng Letts d 138.
12. JR–Charles Eliot Norton, Avallon, 30 August 1882, CEN 447–8.
13. 3 February 1883, BD, 297.
14. JR–JRS, n.d., Bembridge MS L 43.
15. See Helen Gill Viljoen (ed.), *The Froude–Ruskin Friendship as Represented through Letters*, New York, 1966.
16. JR–Charles Eliot Norton, Avallon, 30 August 1882, CEN, 447–8.
17. JR–Charles Eliot Norton, Lucca 3 October 1882, CEN, 449–50.
18. JR–Maria La Touche, Herne Hill, 23 June 1882, BD 485.
19. JR–Maria La Touche, 5 April 1882, BD 268.
20. 2 February 1883, BD 296.
21. JR–JRS, Herne Hill, July 1882, XXXVII, 403.
22. See XXXVII. 402 and 452.
23. JR–JRS, Herne Hill, II May 1882, Bembridge MS L 43. 'David' is the coachman David Fudge. 'Epitot' is unidentified.
24. JR–JRS, Herne Hill, in letters from late June and early July 1882. Bembridge MS L 43.
25. JR–JRS, Herne Hill, 6 July 1882, Bembridge MS L 43.
26. JR–JRS, Herne Hill, 8 July 1882, Bembridge MS L 43.
27. JR–Thomas Horsfall, 25 November 1882, Bembridge MS T 34.
28. Thomas J. Wise (ed.), *Letters from John Ruskin to the Rev. J. P. Faunthorpe*, 1895, and see XXXVII, 641–8.
29. XXX, 69–84.
30. JR–Thomas Horsfall, n.d. but 1883, Bembridge MS T 34.
31. JR–Thomas Horsfall, n.d. but 1883, Bembridge MS T 34.
32. A file on the Ruskin societies is preserved at Bembridge. It contains information about the availability of books by Ruskin in public free libraries, evidently a matter of concern. In 1880 the first report of the Manchester Society of the Rose analysed the holdings of books by Ruskin in 74 such libraries. Manchester had 42 titles, followed by Liverpool (38), Leeds, Newcastle and Birmingham (32), Sheffield (29), Southport (28), and Cardiff and Walsall (21). Of these titles, the most popular was *The Stones of Venice* (in 42 libraries), followed by *Modern Painters* and *The Queen of the Air* (36), *The Two Paths* and *The Ethics of the Dust* (34), *Lectures on Art*, (33), *Lectures on Architecture and Painting* (31), *The Crown of Wild Olive* and *Sesame and Lilies* (27), *The Seven Lamps of Architecture* (26) and the *Selections* (25). *Fors Clavigera* was represented in 17 libraries. Books issued in pamphlet form were generally rare. Often, Ruskin's books were reserved for reference and were not for borrowing, no doubt because of their expensive formats.
33. JR–Thomas Horsfall, Brantwood, 22 June 1883, Bembridge MS T 34.
34. See XXIX, 553.
35. JR–Rev. J. P. Faunthorpe, Brantwood, 28 January 1881, XXXVII, 338–9.
36. See XXX, xxxix and 336–9.
37. XXX, xxxix.
38. XXX, 336–8.
39. XXX, 337–8.
40. Although Ruskin called all these young women 'girls' they might be of any age below about 40.
41. See Blanche A. F. Pigott, *I. Lilias Trotter*, n.d., and especially pp. 17–27.

42. JR–JRS, Herne Hill, Calais, 11 August 1882, Bembridge MS L 43.
43. See W. G. Collingwood, *The Life and Work of John Ruskin*, 1893, II, 213–5.
44. 'Ruskin's Old Road' in W. G. Collingwood, *Ruskin Relics*, 1903, 45–63.
45. XXVI, li.
46. Collingwood, *op.cit.*
47. Collingwood, *op.cit.*
48. XVIII, 50–1.
49. Collingwood, *op.cit.*
50. Collingwood, *op.cit.*
51. 7 September 1882. Diaries, III, 1022.
52. 11 September 1882. Diaries, III, 1024.
53. XIX 293.
54. Collingwood, *op.cit.*
55. JR–JRS, Avallon, 28 August 1882, Bembridge MS L 43.
56. Collingwood, *op.cit.*
57. JR–JRS, Florence (6 October) 1882, Bembridge MS L 43.
58. JR–JRS, Florence 7 October 1882, Bembridge MS L 43.
59. See E. T. Cook's account at XXXII, xviii–xxxv, (which was written while Francesca was still alive) and Lucia Gray Swett, *John Ruskin's Letters to Francesca*, Boston, 1931. There is only one letter to Francesca in the Library Edition. Swett reports, p. 21, 'A great number of Mr Ruskin's letters were destroyed in Florence'.
60. XXXII, xxi–ii.
61. For whom, see Peter Wardle and Cedric Quayle, *Ruskin and Bewdley*, 1989.
62. JR–JRS, Florence, n.d., Bembridge MS L 43.
63. 2 December 1882, Diaries, III, 1043.
64. The message brought an immediate response from both Acland and Liddell. See XXXVII, 402–1.
65. JR–Maria La Touche, Lucca, 22 October 1882, BD, 485–6.
66. W. G. Collingwood, *The Life and Work of John Ruskin*, 1893, II, 219.
67. XXXIII, xlv.

Chapter Forty-Two

1. 7 January 1883, BD, 287.
2. See XXVI, 396–532.
3. IV, 3–9.
4. XIX, 423.
5. XXXIII, xlv–vi.
6. Bembridge MS 45.
7. JR–Faunthorpe, 24 January 1883, XXXVII, 434.
8. JR–George Richmond, 27 February 1883, XXXVII, 439.
9. JR–Henry Acland, n.d. but marked 1880, Bodley Ms Acland d 73, fols. 149–50.
10. XXX, xlv–vi.
11. JR–Maria La Touche, Brantwood, 19 March 1883, BD 486–7.
12. See XXXIII, xlv–xlvi.
13. See Vera Brittain, *The Women at Oxford*, 1960.
14. Elizabeth Haldane, *From One Century to Another*, 1937, 107.
15. JR–J. A. Froude, XXXVI, 52.
16. JR–Cardinal Manning, 25 May 1882, Bodley MS Eng Letts c 51.
17. JR–JRS, Herne Hill, Bembridge MS L 43.
18. Holman Hunt–Tyrwhitt, 18 November 1889, Bodley MS Eng Letts e 116, 193–4.
19. JR–Holman Hunt, 18 February 1883, XXXVII, 438–9.
20. See XXXIII, 259.
21. XXXVII, 332.
22. XXXVI, civ.
23. Sarah Angelina Acland, 'Memories in my 81st Year', Bodley Eng Misc d 214, fol 46.
24. See XXXIII, xlvii–iii.
25. JR–JRS, Oxford, n.d., Bembridge MS L 45.
26. March 16 1883. Diaries, III, 1048.
27. JR–Edward Burne-Jones, Brantwood, May Day 1883, XXXVII, 449–50.
28. A. C. Swinburne–Edward Burne-Jones, 15 May 1883, Georgiana Burne-Jones *Memorials of Edward Burne Jones II*, 1904, 132.
29. XXXIII, 296–7.
30. XXXIII, 390, n.
31. XXXIII, 390.
32. See J. Saxon Mills, *Sir Edward Cook*, 1921, 4–37.
33. See Major-General L. C. Dunsterville, *Stalky's Reminiscences*, 1928, 43–59. His *Stalky's Adventures*, 1933, is the same book.
34. See XXXII, xxiii and 535.
35. See BD, 279.
36. *Letters of Charles Eliot Norton*, 1913, II, 150.
37. Charles Eliot Norton–JR, 2 April 1873, CEN 285–8. The holograph is preserved at Bembridge.
38. E. T. Cook, The Life of Ruskin, 1911, II, 500–1.

Chapter Forty-Three

1. JR–Lady Mount-Temple, 2 August 1881, LMT 379.

2. See M. F. Young, *Letters of a Noble Woman*, 1908, 92–4.
3. See XXV, 451–65.
4. XIX, 449.
5. JR–Maria La Touche, Abbotsford, 17 September 1883, Bodley MS Eng Letts c 46 fol. 108.
6. JR–JRS, Laidlawstiel (September 1883), Bodley MS Eng Letts c 46 fol. 98.
7. See XIX, xxvi.
8. JR–JRS, High Elms, (October 1883), XXXVII, 469–70.
9. JR–Maria La Touche, Old Nursery, Herne Hill, 12 November 1883, Bodley MS Eng Letts c 46 fol. 151.
10. JR–Grace Allen, 16 January 1884, Bodley MS Eng Letts c 46 fol. 266.
11. Ruskin's index is at XXIX, 609–76.
12. November 19 1883. Diaries, III, 1051.
13. XXXI, 375–510.
14. 19 December 1883, BD 341.
15. W. G. Collingwood, *The Life and Work of John Ruskin*, 1900, 374.
16. 3 January 1884. Diaries, III, 1053. On the previous day Ruskin had begun a new diary, Bembridge MS XXIV.
17. January 4–11 1884, Diaries, III, 1053–4.
18. XXXIV, 7–80.
19. A number of the illustrations are reproduced in XXXIV.
20. W. G. Collingwood, *The Life and Work of John Ruskin*, 1893, II, 231, n.
21. See XXXIV, 581.
22. Arthur Severn, *The Professor*, ed. James S. Dearden, 1967, 94.
23. XXVI, 372–88.
24. See XXVI, liii.
25. XXVI, lv.
26. XXVI, lv.
27. XXVI, lv.

Chapter Forty-Four

1. 7 May 1884. Diaries, III, 1065. On this day Ruskin returned to Brantwood from Herne Hill.
2. JR–Lizzie Watson, Brantwood, Good Friday 1884, XXXVII, 481.
3. XXXVII, 493.
4. This was the time when Ruskin wrote the final letter of *Fors Clavigera*, 'Rosy Vale'.
5. See XX, xxx.
6. Bembridge MS L 44.
7. Evelyn Abbott and Lewis Campbell, *The Life and Letters of Benjamin Jowett*, 1897, II, 75.
8. XXX, 414.
9. See XXXIII, 413–7.
10. W. G. Collingwood, *The Life and Work of John Ruskin*, 1893, II, 232.
11. XXXIII, liii–iv.
12. JR–Susie Beever, Oxford, 1 December 1884, XXXIII, liv.
13. See XXXVIII, 210.
14. XXX, 87–9.
15. JR–JRS, Oxford, (Autumn 1884) Bembridge MS L 44.
16. XXXIV, 670–1.
17. JR–JRS, Farnley Hall, 13 December 1884, XXXVII, 501–2.

Chapter Forty-Five

1. JR–JRS, 27 December 1884, Bodley MS Eng Letts c 47.
2. W. G. Collingwood, *The Life and Work of John Ruskin*, 1893, II, 205.
3. I, 522–51.
4. XXVIII, 213.
5. XXXV, 67.
6. XXVIII, 715.
7. XXXV, 633–4.
8. XIX, 512.
9. JR–Maria La Touche, 19 May 1885, Bodley MS Eng Letts c 48 fol. 49.
10. See James S. Dearden, *Ruskin, Bembridge and Brantwood*, Keele, 1994, 49–50 and 103.
11. Bembridge MS XXV.
12. XXXV, 17.
13. Cook and Wedderburn tactfully omitted the passage from the Library Edition index.
14. XXXV, 633.
15. XXXV, 485.
16. XXXV, 637–8.
17. XXXV, lxix.
18. Bembridge MS VII.
19. There was a plan, however, to mention Effie in *Dilecta*, with material relating to *The King of the Golden River*. She is mentioned, though not by name, at XXXV, 304.
20. For this dispute, see Hyder E. Rollins, 'Charles Eliot Norton and Froude' in *Journal of English and Germanic Philology*, 1958, 651–64.
21. XXXV, 561.
22. Diaries, III, 1136.
23. Diaries, III, 1096.
24. XXXII, 163–4.
25. J. B. Atlay, *Henry Acland, a Memoir*, 1903, 420 *et seqq.*
26. XXXV, II.
27. XXXV, lxxxiii.
28. JR–George Allen, 18 April 1885, Bodley MS Eng Letts c 48 fol. 37.
29. XXV, lxxxix.

30. See 'Friends of Living Creatures and John Ruskin', *Fortnightly Review*, October 1907.
31. JR–Kate Greenaway, 26 May 1885, XXXVII, 535.
32. See XXXVII, 535, n.

Chapter Forty-Six

1. Blanche A. F. Pigott, *I. Lilias Trotter*, n.d., 13.
2. The 'Addresses on Colour and Illumination', which Cook found in reports in the *Morning Chronicle* and the Builder of November 1854, had been delivered at the Architectural Museum but were directed toward artists rather than architects. See XII, 504–5.
3. W. G. Collingwood, *The Life and Work of John Ruskin*, 1900, 46–8.
4. XXXV, 51.
5. II, 530.
6. Maria La Touche–JRS, (1880), BD, 469.
7. Diaries, III, 1116.
8. JRS–Charles Eliot Norton, quoted in Sheila Birkenhead, *Illustrious Friends*, 1965, 308.
9. See *Illustrious Friends*, 309.
10. JR–Katie Macdonald, 8 September 1885, XXXVII, 539.
11. JR–Susie Beever, 27 November 1885, XXXVII, 545.
12. JR–Mary (Gladstone) Drew, 29 December 1885, XXXVII, 545.
13. For the individual work of such Companions, see Edith Hope Scott, *Ruskin's Guild of St George*, 1931.
14. Other biographical notes on Ruskin's assistants are in Robert Hewison, *Ruskin and Venice*, J. B. Speed Art Museum, Louisville, 1978 (exhibition catalogue) and Jeanne Clegg and Paul Tucker, *Ruskin and Tuscany*, Sheffield, 1992 (exhibition catalogue).
15. JR–George Allen, 8 November 1885, Bodley MS Eng Letts c 48, fol. 181.
16. XXXV, 358.
17. JR–Jane Simon, 20 December 1885, XXXV, 541.
18. XXXV, 598–601, and see John Gage, *Turner: Rain, Steam and Speed*, 1972.
19. The letters were eventually published in Van Akin Burd, *The Ruskin Family Letters, 1801–1943*, Ithaca, 1973.
20. 12 April 1886. Diaries, III, 1123.
21. JR–May Bateman, 21 October 1883, XXXVII, 469.
22. XXXIV, 583–4.
23. 18 January 1886. Ruskin there claimed that his political philosophy was Homer's. See XXXIV, 589.
24. XXXIV, 597.
25. See *Illustrious Friends*, 1965, 310.
26. Bembridge MS BT 37.
27. JR–Charles Eliot Norton, Brantwood, 18 August 1886, CEN 493–4.
28. XXV, 536.
29. JR–JRS, 17 August 1886, Bembridge MS L 47.
30. JRS–Charles Eliot Norton, 7 October 1886, *Illustrious Friends*, 1965, 311.
31. 4 October 1886. Diaries, III, 1135.
32. 9 January 1887. Diaries, III, 1239.
33. *Christ's Folk in the Apennines* was published by Ruskin in March 1887 as 'by Francesca Alexander'. The sub-title is 'Reminiscences of her Friends among the Tuscan Peasantry'. The book reprints, with his comments, sections of letters sent by Alexander to Ruskin.
34. 1 January 1887, Diaries, III, 1139.
35. JR–Henry Mackrell, Brantwood, 17 October 1886, Bodley MS Eng Letts c 49 fol. 66.
36. The cataloguing of the collections as they stood in 1906 is found in Vol XXI of the Library Edition, *The Ruskin Art Collection at Oxford*.
37. See XXXIII, li, liii, lv and XXXV, xxv.vii.
38. Viola Meynell (ed.), *Friends of a Lifetime: Letters to Sydney Carlyle Cockerell*, 1940, 26.
39. Cockerell, *ibid.*, 31.
40. Cockerell, *ibid.*, 33–4.
41. Bembridge MS 25. This passage is not included in the published version of the Diaries.
42. Cockerell, *ibid.*, 38.
43. *The Times*, 30 November 1932, and see BD, 561.
44. See JR–Kate Greenaway, 9 November 1886–5 April 1887, Bodley MS Eng Letts, c 49, fols 86–271 for numerous letters concerning the village school.
45. MS, Bembridge.
46. JR–Kate Greenaway, 2 May 1887, Bodley Ms Eng Letts, c 49 fol 293.
47. JR–Albert Fleming, 20 May 1887, in *Illustrious Friends*, 1965, 315.
48. XXVIII, 520.
49. JR–JRS, 8 June 1887, Bembridge MS L 48.
50. JR–JRS, 19 June 1887, Bembridge MS L 48.
51. JR–JRS, 26 June 1887, Bembridge MS L 48.
52. Sara Anderson–JRS, 13 December 1891, BD, 379–80.

Chapter Forty-Seven

1. BD, 356.
2. JR–JRS, Folkestone, 24 August 1887. Bembridge MS L 48.
3. MSS, Bembridge.
4. JR–JRS, Sandgate, October 1887, Bembridge MS L 48.
5. JR–JRS, 14 October 1887, Bembridge MS L 49.
6. JR–JRS, 21 October 1887, Bembridge MS L 49.
7. For these letters, see Olive Wilson (ed.), My Dearest Dora, n.d., Kendal, 113–5.
8. Rayner Unwin (ed.) *The Gulf of Years. Letters of John Ruskin to Kathleen Olander*, 1953, 15–16.
9. *Ibid.*, 19.
10. JR–JRS, 27 December 1887, Bembridge MS L 49.
11. JR–JRS, 30 December 1887, Bembridge MS L 49.
12. JR–JRS, 31 December 1887, Bembridge MS L 49.
13. JR–JRS, 4 January 1888, Bembridge MS L 50.
14. JR–JRS, 28 December 1887, Bembridge MS L 49.
15. *The Gulf of Years*, 1953, 29.
16. *Ibid.*, 29.
17. JR–Kathleen Olander, 26 February 1888, *ibid.*, 32–3.
18. JR–JRS, 22 January 1888, Bembridge MS L 50.
19. JR–JRS, Folkestone, (October) 1887, Bembridge MS L 49.
20. JR–JRS (January) 1888, Bembridge MS L 50.
21. Cockerell, *op.cit.*, 43–4.
22. JR–JRS, 16 January 1888, Bembridge MS L 50.
23. Cockerell, *op.cit.*, 45.
24. JR–JRS, 1 February 1888, Bembridge MS L 50.
25. JR–JRS, 3 February 1888, Bembridge MS L 50.
26. JR–JRS, (March) 1888, Bembridge MS L 49.

Chapter Forty-Eight

1. JR–JRS, 18 April 1888, Bembridge MS L 50.
2. Charles Eliot Norton–JR, 4 June 1888, CEN, 500.
3. See XXI, xlv, and J. Saxon Mills, *Sir Edward Cook*, 1921, 37–84. Ruskin's letter to Stead (14 March 1886) is at Bembridge MS L 24.
4. Saxon Mills, *op.cit.*, 58–9.
5. n.d., and published anonymously.
6. Saxon Mills, *op.cit.*, 77–81.
7. Cook offered Ruskin accommodation after seeing him in Morley's Hotel. The reply was 'I have the entirest confidence in Mrs Cook's kindness, as in yours, — but I do not think either of you would be happy in having me — So I am going to stay at Allen's — where I can see the blossoms opening and run up for what including teethwork is to be done . . .' 30 April 1888, Bembridge MS L 24.
8. *The Gulf of Years*, 1953, 47.
9. JR–JRS, (April?) 1888, Bembridge MS L 50.
10. JR–JRS, 15 May 1888, Bembridge MS L 50.
11. JR–JRS, (April?) 1888, Bembridge MS L 50.
12. See *Illustrious Friends*, 1965, 334–5.
13. *The Gulf of Years*, 1953, 49.
14. See *Illustrious Friends*, 1965, 338.
15. XXXV, 529.
16. XXXV, 533, The proof (preserved at Bembridge) contains the conclusion of 'L'Esterelle' printed at XXXV, 532–4.
17. *The Gulf of Years*, 1953, 77–8.
18. JR–JRS, Milan, 23 September 1888, *Illustrious Friends*, 1965, 339.
19. JR–JRS, 2–3 October 1888, *Illustrious Friends*, 1965, 340.
20. See *The Gulf of Years*, 1953, 86–8.
21. JR–JRS, Merlingen, 14 November 1888, *Illustrious Friends*, 1965, 341.

Chapter Forty-Nine

1. Henry W. Nevinson, *Fire of Life*, 1935, 27–8.
2. *Ibid.*, 41–3.
3. JRS–Charles Eliot Norton, *Illustrious Friends*, 1965, 342.
4. '. . . I hear of poor Downs' death, as you may think — with sadness enough for the embittering of his last years . . .' JR–JRS, June 25 1888, Bodley MS Eng Letts c 50 fol. 304.
5. JRS–Charles Eliot Norton, 14 May 1889, *Illustrious Friends*, 1865, 343.
6. XXXV, 539.
7. JR–Charles Eliot Norton, Brantwood, 11 June 1889, CEN, 505.
8. JR–Charles Eliot Norton, Brantwood, 23 June 1889, CEN, 506–7.
9. JR–Charles Eliot Norton, (June 1889), CEN, 507–8.

10. XXXV, 593.
11. See XXXV, lxxxvi–ii.
12. XXXV, 561.
13. XXXV, 560–2.
14. W. G. Collingwood, *The Life and Work of John Ruskin*, 1893, II, 242–3.
15. Edward Woolgar, *No Place Like Coniston*, Bembridge 1977.
16. See XXXV, xlv.
17. JRS–Charles Eliot Norton, 11 July 1889, *Illustrious Friends*, 1965, 344.
18. *The Gulf of Years*, 1953, 88–9.
19. JRS–Charles Eliot Norton, 27 December 1890, *Illustrious Friends*, 1965, 346.
20. See Collingwood's 'Preface to the Seventh Edition' of his book, 1911.
21. See XXXVIII, 33.
22. W. G. Collingwood, *The Life and Work of John Ruskin*, 1893, II, 249–50.
23. See XXXVIII, 35.
24. See Van Wyck Brooks, *New England: Indian Summer 1865–1915*, Cleveland, Ohio, 1946, 25–7.
25. Frederic Harrison, *John Ruskin*, 1902, 162–3.
26. James S. Dearden, *Ruskin, Bembridge and Brantwood*, Keele, 1994, 20–1.
27. XXXV, xlv.
28. W. G. Collingwood, *The Life and Work of John Ruskin*, 1900, 308.
29. JR–Susie Beever, 26 October 1874, quoted at XXXV, xlvi.

Postscript

1. See XXXV, xlvii.
2. See James S. Dearden, *Ruskin, Bembridge and Brantwood*, Keele, 1994.
3. See BD, 1971, vii–xii, and the introductions by Van Akin Burd to his *John Ruskin and Rose La Touche*, 1979, and *Christmas Story*, 1990.

INDEX

NOTE: Works (including lectures) by Ruskin appear directly under title; works by others under authors' names.

Abbeville, 420–2, 425, 431–2, 546, 688, 843
Abbeydale Farm, Derbyshire, 635–6
Abbeythune, 500
Abbotsford (Scott's house), 541, 758
Abingdon: Crown and Thistle inn, 473–6, 480, 506, 547, 598
Academy (journal), 697
Academy Notes (JR), 210, 226–30, 237, 239, 243–4, 251, 253, 273, 276, 288, 509
Ackworth, Annie Elizabeth (*née* Andrews), 350, 607–9, 611–13, 629
Acland family, 784
Acland, Angie *see* Acland, Sarah Angelina
Acland, Harry, 206, 359, 466
Acland, Sir Henry: at Oxford, 47; and Liddell, 48; gives JR letter of introduction to Severn, 59; not told of JR's *Modern Painters*, 71; and JR's religious views, 83–4, 167; JR discusses university reading with, 100; absent from JR's wedding, 117; JR's aversion to baby, 120, 122; JR and Effie visit, 122; and Millais at Glenfinlas, 189–90; Millais portrait of, 191; and JR's Edinburgh lectures, 194; JR writes to on marriage to Effie, 198; promotes study of sciences and art at Oxford, 216–20; *Remarks on the Extension of Education at the University of Oxford*, 217; *Memoirs on the Cholera at Oxford*, 219; and building of Oxford Museum, 220, 222; examines Lizzie Siddall, 220–1; *The Oxford Museum* (with JR), 220, 225–6; and proposed Working Men's College for Oxford, 223; and JR's road-mending project, 225, 554; JR teaches drawing by letter, 236; elected honorary student of Christ Church, 246; JR discusses *Political Economy of Art* with, 246; friendship with JR, 472, 533, 647; JR stands godfather to son, 340; writes on JR's father's death, 348; letter from JR on work at British Museum, 359; and JR's proposal to Rose La Touche, 381; and JR's appointment to Slade Professorship, 449, 456–7, 615; and JR's lectures, 457–8, 778; JR stays with in Oxford, 462, 775; family life, 477; journeys to JR in Matlock, 489-90, 493–4; supports JR in Oxford, 506; and art education at Oxford, 508–9; and public health, 547–8; JR confides in over Rose La Touche's health, 552; defends JR's Hinksey project in *Times*, 576; persuades JR to take further leave of absence from Oxford, 578; and JR's attacks on bishops, 580; JR visits in Oxford, 583; JR gives money to endow Master of Drawing at Oxford, 587; finds asylum for Mrs Crawley, 596; advises JR to tone down lectures, 599; and Emilia Francis Strong's drawings, 601; introduces Mallock to JR, 604; JR discusses public affairs with, 639; and JR's Brantwood breakdown, 669–71; Joan Severn dislikes, 671, 706; offers to visit JR during 1880 mental collapse, 706; and JR's reappointment to Slade professorship, 733, 737–8, 740; understanding of JR, 749; and Oxford opposition to vivisection, 792; and JR's complaints of Oxford neglect of Turner works, 815-16; and JR's condition in Sandgate, 833; retirement and honours, 864; visits JR in old age, 872
Acland, Sarah (Henry's wife), 214, 217, 221, 477
Acland, Sarah Angelina (Henry's daughter; 'Angie'): Lewis Carroll tells stories to, 49; visits Denmark Hill, 206; JR gives drawings of Oxford Museum windows to, 224; crippled, 477; photography, 477, 479, 872; relations with JR, 477, 725; attends Oxford Art School, 508; corresponds with Rose La Touche, 529–30, 533, 552; on JR and Julia Margaret Cameron, 744; visits JR at Brantwood, 872
Acland, Sir Thomas Dyke, 496, 590, 637
Adam, Dr Alexander, 1, 28
'Addresses on Colour and Illumination' (JR), 797
Aeschylus, 375
Aesthetic and Mathematical Schools of Art in Florence, The (JR), 555, 562, 572, 574
Agassiz, Louis, 62, 80
Agnew, George, 348
Agnew, Joan *see* Severn, Joan
Aitken, Mary, 485, 617, 653
Albany, Helene Friederike Auguste, Duchess of (Leopold's wife), 760, 768
Alessandri, Angelo, 633, 710, 731, 742, 802, 805, 848
Aletheme, 263
Aletsch torrent, 81
Alexander, Francesca, 731–3, 742, 749, 756, 770, 773, 805, 845, 847–8, 863, 865; *Christ's Folk in the Apennine*, 731, 770, 815, 823; *Roadside*

Songs of Tuscany, 731–2, 765, 768, 770, 791, 793; *The Story of Ida*, 731–3, 756, 770
Alexander, Francis, 731
Alice Maud Mary, Princess, Grand Duchess of Hesse-Darmstadt, 587, 715
Allen family, 760
Allen, George: marriage, 70, 240; at Working Men's College, 240; assists JR with Turner bequest, 243, 248; learns line engraving, 262; boating expeditions with JR, 291; with JR in Alps, 325–7, 335; resists JR's scheme to live in Alps, 345; moves from Denmark Hill, 363; engravings of agates for JR, 413; visits Denmark Hill, 450; takes Daguerrotypes, 479; and publication of JR's later works, 501, 593, 699, 770, 798; sends proofs of *Val d'Arno* to Norton, 544; joins JR in Lucca, 566; publishes *Fors Clavigera*, 566–7, 649, 709; membership of Guild of St George, 590; and printing of *Rock Honeycomb*, 617; and new edition of *Stones of Venice*, 623; considers Swan a crank, 635; publishes new edition of *The Seven Lamps of Architecture*, 688; and JR's mental collapse, 707; and JR's autobiographical writing, 709; and Guild of St George, 710; issues cheap editions, 723; publishes Collingwood, 735; publishes *The Ruskin Birthday Book*, 759; and Jowett's printing, 761; relations with Joan Severn, 761; and JR's *Præterita*, 785, 792, 807, 829; publishes Francesca Alexander, 791, 823; and JR's finances, 793; and sale of JR's books, 794, 867, 869; publishes *The Bible of Amiens*, 805; and JR's copyright, 806; JR quarrels with, 820; and JR's proposed revision of *Fors Clavigera*, 833; offers home to JR, 841; prepares new editions of JR's earlier works, 841, 846
Allen, Grace, 759, 761, 771, 792, 794, 841
Allen, Hannah (*née* Hobbs; George's wife), 71, 240, 325, 841
Allingham, Helen (*née* Paterson), 743, 746
Allingham, William, 210, 215, 218, 229, 743
Alma-Tadema, Sir Lawrence, 746
Alpine Club, 447
Alps: JR's study of, 26, 33–4, 79, 93, 132, 134, 233, 255, 335–6; JR visits and stays in, 61, 79–80, 92, 133–4, 136, 139, 306, 311, 324, 325, 336, 344, 442–3, 728–9; JR writes on, 96, 200; condition of peasantry in, 139, 158; Turner and, 168, 366–7; JR's attachment to, 171; JR composes *Unto This Last* in, 296; in *Præterita*, 319; JR dreams of transforming, 447; Downs in, 463; JR's sensitivity to weather in, 728–30; JR's reminiscences of in *Proserpina*, 756–7; *see also* individual places
Amaranth (journal), 30
Ambleside, 108–9
American Civil War, 423, 427
Amiens, 200, 233
Anderson, James Reddie: in JR's road-building team, 545, 573; friendship and discipleship with JR, 553, 573, 698; membership of Guild of St George, 577, 590; and cousin Sara, 617, 625; in Venice, 625; *The Place of Dragons*, 642–3, 655; at Brantwood, 645, 710–11; JR mentions in letter and diary during Brantwood breakdown, 660–1, 665; and Mallock, 678; helps answer JR's *Fors Clavigera* correspondence, 683; helps JR with *St Mark's Rest*, 683; Scots background, 708
Anderson, Sara ('Diddie'): helps JR with Guild work, 617, 660; in JR circle, 645, 692, 773; JR writes to, 659–60, 677, 701, 703–4, 707; and JR's attachment to Frances Graham, 677; performs secretarial duties for JR, 683, 692, 710–11, 800, 812, 819; and JR's illness, 701, 703–4, 707, 800, 820; helps nurse JR, 716; suspects JR's paedophilia, 720; burns JR letters, 754; visits JR at Brantwood, 799–800; relations with Cockerell, 818; resigns position with JR, 818; assists Joan Severn, 822, 861, 867; assembles JR papers, 876
Andrews, Annie Elizabeth *see* Ackworth, Annie Elizabeth
Andrews, Revd Edward, 19–22, 152
Andrews, Emily, 22, 28
Anerley Woods, 204
Angelico, Fra, 92, 100, 124, 257, 567
Antonio, Fra, 559
Aosta, 158
Apollo, 289
Ara Coeli (JR), 694, 714–15
Aratra Pentelici (JR), 466, 467, 483, 506, 662, 803
Architectural Association, 242
Architectural Magazine, 286
Ariadne Florentina (JR), 488, 531, 542, 803
Aristophanes: *Plutus*, 383
Armitage, Sir Elkanah, 258–9, 284
Armstrong, Lily (*later* Kevill-Davis), 340, 371, 386, 415, 417–18, 433, 435, 485, 743, 863
Armstrong, Richard, 415
Arnold, Matthew, 216, 261, 405, 423, 605, 646, 723, 749, 838
Arnold, Thomas, 341
Arrows of the Chace (JR), 696–7, 709
Art of England, The (JR), 737, 776
Art Journal, 162, 318, 364–5, 367–8, 435, 688, 766
Art School of south Lambeth, 435
Arundel, Sussex, 585
Arundel Society, 108, 129–30, 163, 207, 242, 323, 450, 481, 518, 554–5, 561, 677
Assisi, 554–5, 557, 559–63, 565–6
'Atheism. The Pleasures of Sense' (JR; lecture), 778
Athenaeum, 74, 100, 149, 162, 232
Athenaeum club, London, 152
Atkinson, Blanche, 725, 801
Atlantic Monthly, 215
Atropos (death-goddess), 353–4, 472–3
Austria, 122, 124; *see also* individual towns
Austrians, 137, 140, 141, 159, 160, 171, 258
Auxerre, France, 69
Avallon, France, 727

Avranches, France, 127
Aylesbury, Buckinghamshire, 585

Baker, George, 638–41, 718–19, 722, 771, 799, 801
Baker (JR's nurse), 835
Balliol College, Oxford, 42, 216, 603–5, 735, 774–5
'Banded and Brecciated Concretions' (JR; paper), 413
Bar-le-Duc, 30
Barmouth, Wales, 619–20, 622, 801
Barnard, Mrs ('Claribel'), 584
Barnes, Mary, 550
Barrow, Revd E. P., 474, 477
Barry, Sir Charles, 203
Bartolommeo, Fra, 87, 88
Basle, 233, 251
Bassano, 847–8
Bateman, Maud and Alice, 725, 749, 759
Baudelaire, Charles, 238
Baveno, 93
Baxter, Johnny (Peter B's son), 824
Baxter, Mary (Peter B's wife), 824
Baxter, Peter: accompanies JR to Venice, 622; as JR's valet, 622, 664; in JR's 'Brantwood Diary', 664; and JR's mental illness, 669, 672, 821, 864, 872; at Malham with JR, 676; and JR's isolation at Brantwood, 704; falls ill, 743; reads to JR, 772; Joan Severn asks for reports on JR, 774, 812; rows JR on lake, 783; adds notes to JR's letters to servants, 819; with JR in Folkestone, 823–5, 843; with JR on 1888 trip abroad, 848; assures Nevinson of JR's good health, 852–3; at JR's death, 873
Bayeux, 127
Bayne, Peter, 330
Bedborough, Mrs, 287
Beever, Mary, 553
Beever, Susie: JR's friendship and correspondence with, 538, 553, 646, 673, 684, 709, 719, 750, 763; JR stays at home of, 546; JR informs of Rose's death, 586; membership of Guild of St George, 590; JR writes to about Oxford lectures, 647, 778; and JR's delirium, 659; *Remarkable Passages in Shakespeare*, 661, 669; JR visits and writes to on birthday, 763, 801; compiles selection (*Frondes Agrestes*) from *Modern Painters*, 863; JR buried near, 874
Bekker, Immanuel, 628–9
Bell, Margaret Alexis, 278, 284–5, 287, 289, 301, 307, 322, 332, 341, 386, 415, 419, 434
Bellini family, 94
Bellini, Gentile, 447
Bellini, Giovanni, 195
Bellini, Vincenzo, 27
Bellinzoa, 249
Bembridge School, 585
Benson, Arthur Christopher, 695–6
Beresford, G. C. ('M'Turk'), 748–9
Bergamo, 93
Berlin, 277
Berne, 849
Bernese range, 80, 233
Bewdley, Worcestershire: Guild of St George acquires land at, 638, 640–1; proposed museum, 771, 779, 802
Bewick, Thomas, 778
Bezzi, Aubrey, 129
Bible: JR's knowledge of and attitude to, 13–14, 184, 261, 285, 297–8, 331, 399, 408, 452, 494, 498, 831; belief in inerrant prophecies, 331; Colenso on, 332; Maurice expounds, 351–2; JR doubts literal truth of, 352, 399–400, 406–7, 452; JR's references to, 870
Bible of Amiens, The (JR), 693–6, 699, 708, 727, 788, 805, 828–9, 843
Bibliotheca Pastorum (JR's classics series), 374, 602–3, 607, 617, 634, 684, 764, 807
Bicknell, E., 64
birds: JR writes on, 536–7, 778
'Birds and how to Paint Them' (JR; lecture), 778
Birmingham, 12, 639–41, 871; Ruskin Society, 500, 871–2
Bishop, Mrs, 724, 749–50
Blackwell, Miss, 268
Blackwood's Edinburgh Magazine, 15, 23, 30, 31, 39, 40, 56, 74, 75, 797
Blair Atholl, 117
Blake, William, 60, 209, 232, 662, 665, 707
Blonay, 133
Blow, Detmar, 843–8, 851
Blunden, Anna, 269, 270, 273
Bodley, J. E. C., 604
Boehm, Sir Jacob, 685
Bolding, Parker, 112
Bolton Bridge, 299
Bonheur, Rosa, 190, 235, 237
Boni, Giacomo, 710, 731, 742, 803, 848
Bonneville, French Alps, 306, 308, 345
Booth, Mrs (Turner's housekeeper), 291
Bordeaux, Duc de, 143
Borns, Maggie, 845
Borromeo, Gilberto, Count, 622
Botticelli, Sandro, 518, 527–8, 530, 555, 557, 567, 572, 731, 802
Boulogne, 124, 303–4, 306, 386, 391, 546, 843
Bourbons, 122
Bowen, Charles Synge Christopher (*later* Baron), 679
Bowerswell: JR's parents rent, 4; Margaret Ruskin dislikes, 8, 117; JR invites Grays to, 114–15; JR marries at, 117; Effie returns to, 130–1, 148, 178–9, 195
Bowles, Dr (of Folkestone), 826, 834
Bowles (JR's nurse), 835
Boxall, William, 96, 101
Brabazon, Hercules, 692–3
Bradford, 12, 258, 259, 260, 356, 370
Bradford, Mary Frances, 284–5, 287, 338
Bradley, Francis Herbert, 739
Brantwood, Lancashire: Joan Agnew (Severn) at, 363, 596; visitors to, 451, 595, 617–18,

645–6, 708, 712, 743, 765, 771–3, 799, 814, 816, 863, 872; JR purchases, 493–5, 499–500; JR develops and improves, 499, 537–41; JR moves to, 505, 537, 552; library, 539–40; JR's life at, 553, 583, 594, 596, 615–17, 641–2, 653–5, 682–3, 687, 699, 712, 735, 771–2, 782, 795–6; JR's coach at, 615; *Fors* numbers written from, 641–2; JR's 1878 mental breakdown at, 656–72; JR rearranges Turner collection, 699–700; JR's second breakdown at (1880–1), 699, 701–4; industrial pollution at, 766; art teaching at, 796–7; JR's 1885 breakdown at, 799–800; Severns take over and extend, 814, 853; and JR's quarrel with Severns, 820–2; JR loses control of, 822; JR gives money to Joan Severn for upkeep, 841; JR's last years in, 853–4, 862, 867, 872; character, 863; JR bequeaths to Severns, 875; Whitehouse purchases, 875; 'Ruskin Conference' (1969), 877

Brett, John: JR praises, 251–2; works with JR, 252–3, 255; *Val d'Aosta*, 253, 264, 273, 433; JR discusses notion of vulgarity with, 288; JR teaches, 298; JR criticises, 323; and Pre-Raphaelites, 741

Breven, 139

Brezon, the (mountain), 344–5

Brickland, Annie, 474–5

Bright, John, 388, 691, 762

Brighton, 610

Britannia (journal), 74, 159

British Association, 112

British Chess Association, 540

British Hotel, Cockspur Street, London, 760, 775

British Medical Journal, 666

British Museum: Newton's post at, 48, 76; JR works at, 76, 107, 358–9, 527, 718, 775; JR and Rose at, 301–2; Egyptian antiquities at, 359–60, 372; JR gives mineral specimens to, 735, 769

Broad Church movement, 331

Broadlands (house), Hampshire, 271, 301, 396, 427, 455, 518, 525, 542, 550, 596–7, 607–9, 611, 686, 796, 840

'Broken Chain, The' (JR), 56

Brontë, Charlotte, 73, 149

Brooke, Stopford, 451

Brotherhood of the New Life, 427

Brown, Ford Madox, 205, 230, 244, 663

Brown, Dr John: friendship and correspondence with JR, 103, 199, 708, 750; admires JR's *Pre-Raphaelitism*, 183, 327; differences with JR over political economy, 297, 326–7, 339; JR writes to of personal anxieties, 313, 320; *Rab and his Friends*, 327, 785; admires JR's Turner drawings, 340; recommends Downs to JR, 363

Brown, Rawdon: JR meets in Venice, 141, 446, 464, 623, 625–6; gives brooch to Effie, 146; Effie writes to on unhappy marriage, 148; parents plot Effie's flight with, 197; and new edition of *Stones of Venice*, 619, 625; friendship with JR ends, 626; JR confesses mental exhaustion to, 682

Brown, Dr Thomas, 6

Brown, Revd Walter Lucas, 46, 47, 54, 62, 78, 181, 230, 295–7

Browning, Elizabeth Barrett, 697; Margaret Ruskin reads, 23; and JR's *Modern Painters*, 73, 273; influence on JR, 175–6; JR's friendship with, 210, 212–14, 270, 338, 561; and Spurgeon's preaching, 261; Thackeray declines poem for *Cornhill*, 294; *Aurora Leigh*, 294; 'Lord Walter's Wife', 294; relates mesmeric experiences, 349; Norton meets, 423

Browning, Oscar, 576

Browning, Robert: and JR's *Modern Painters*, 73, 273; influence on JR, 175–6; friendship with JR, 210, 212–13, 279; JR puzzled by poems, 213–14; and Spurgeon's preaching, 261; and JR's knowledge of literature, 377; Norton meets, 423; introduces JR and Leighton, 780

Brunnen, 251, 252

Brussels, 25, 277

Buckland, William, 49, 113

Builder (journal), 162

Bulwer-Lytton, Edward *see* Lytton, 1st Baron

Bunnett, Miss (Rose La Touche's governess), 302

Bunney, John Wharlton, 240, 444, 531, 625, 710, 803

Bunsen, C. C. J.: *Egypt's Place in Universal History*, 359

Bunyan, John, 22, 83, 261

Burd, Van Akin, 877

Burden, James, 685

Burdon-Sanderson, Sir John, 792

Burgess, Arthur, 240, 432, 444, 480, 710–11, 803

Burke, John, 15

Burlington House, London, 230

Burne-Jones, (Sir) Edward: friendship with JR, 209, 275–6; JR praises, 209, 275–6; praises *Modern Painters*, 232; JR visits, 235, 610, 638, 793; JR never criticises, 236; teaches at Working Men's College, 236; travels on continent with JR, 321–2; JR's regard for, 323; JR takes to Winnington, 341; begs JR not to build home in Alps, 345; JR commissions illustrations from, 346; JR urges to draw Egyptian antiquities, 361; JR discusses fine books with, 374; Swinburne and, 377–8; and JR's attachment to Rose La Touche, 379, 381; depicts chivalry, 402; paintings at Winnington, 419; Norton meets, 423; and classical spirit, 439; enthusiasm for Carpaccio, 447; JR entertains, 455, 466; and JR's poor view of Michelangelo, 483–4; female nudes, 484; love affairs, 484; visits JR on return from Italy (1872), 527; employs Fairfax Murray as assistant, 555; visits JR in Oxford, 585; exhibits at Grosvenor Gallery, 638; and Whistler's libel action against JR, 639, 680, 773; associated with Ford Madox Brown, 663; and Frances Graham, 677;

Mallock on sexual flavour in, 678; sees Christy Minstrels, 687; letter from JR on Georgiana, 701; designs May Queen cross, 724; attends JR's 'Mending the Sieve' lecture, 734; JR compares with Kate Greenaway, 743; honoured at Oxford, 746; JR lectures on, 746–7; caricatured in *Punch*, 747; attends JR's 'drawing-room lecture', 749; JR dines with, 767; and JR's art teaching, 798; introduces J. F. Murray to JR, 804; employs T. M. Rooke as studio assistant, 805; corresponds with JR, 811; designs cover for *Studies in Both Arts*, 868

Burne-Jones, Georgiana, Lady: accompanies JR on 1862 continental trip, 321, 323; with JR at Winnington, 341; and JR's Egyptian interests, 361; JR wishes to introduce Rose La Touche to, 379; visits Denmark Hill, 411, 466; on Edward's reaction to JR's view of Michelangelo, 483–4; visits JR on return from Italy (1872), 527; JR visits, 638, 793; JR writes to on desolation, 701; takes JR to *Don Giovanni*, 718; JR dines with, 767

Burne-Jones, Philip, 321

Burnley, 259

Burns, Robert, 653

Butler, Elizabeth Southerden, Lady, 743

Butterworth, George, 239–40, 262, 291, 648, 710

'Byron Gallery', 29

Byron, George Gordon, 6th Baron: JR's father reads, 12, 15, 22; *Childe Harold*, 25; in Switzerland, 26; Alexander Elder delivers proofs to, 29; Hogg on JR's reliance on, 30; and Mary Duff, 31; *Don Juan*, 32; JR praises, 38, 51, 57, 333, 689; Todd condemns, 38; and JR's *Stones of Venice*, 150; 'Address to the Ocean', 232; JR quotes, 663, 665; JR compares with Shelley, 709

Caen, 127

Caesar, Julius, 14

Calais, 25, 69, 199, 200, 233

Callcott, Sir Augustus Wall, 55, 668

Calvin, John, 261

Camberwell: Working Men's Institute, 358

Cambridge, Adolphus Frederick, Duke of, 110

Cambridge School of Art, 258

Cambridge University: JR gives Turner collection to, 300, 433; awards honorary degree to JR, 383, 405; JR delivers Rede Lecture at, 404–5

Cameron, Julia Margaret, 744

Camille (St Bernard dog), 473, 476

Candida Casa (JR), 694

Capheaton, 184

Carloforti, Raffaele, 633, 803–4

Carlyle, Mrs Alexander, 858

Carlyle, Jane Welsh: meets Effie, 176; JR sends *Sesame and Lilies* to, 373, 375; death, 384, 388; Carlyle first writes to, 857

Carlyle, Thomas: and Edward Irving, 20; and Turner's slight on JR's integrity, 82, 102; disputes and reconciliation with JR, 101–2, 403, 405, 859; influence on JR, 150, 175, 279, 314–19, 353, 373, 403, 450, 456, 469, 543, 781, 831, 851; JR meets and visits, 151, 176; JR dedicates *Munera Pulveris* to, 247, 316; and JR's interest in political economy, 247; Spurgeon's antipathy to, 261; friendship with A. J. Scott, 285, 293; and *Cornhill*, 293–4; relations with Mill, 297, 314; JR's mother warns against, 298; dines with JR, 301; praises JR lecture, 301, 315; indifference to art, 314; *Latter-Day Pamphlets*, 314, 316–17, 469, 859; *On Heroes and Hero-Worship*, 314; *Past and Present*, 314; 'Model Prisons', 315; social/intellectual circle, 318–19, 375; death, 319, 700–1; Bayne criticises, 330; differences with Spurgeon, 330; relations with JR, 346, 383, 388, 543, 585, 610, 649, 675; fondness for Joan Agnew, 362; marriage relations, 375; JR introduces Gotthelf to, 385; JR introduces Rose La Touche to, 388; supports Eyre's actions in Jamaica, 388; 'Shooting Niagara: And After?', 389, 542; in JR's dreams, 410; and Scottish ethos, 422; Norton meets, 423; praises JR's *Queen of the Air*, 437, 450; and JR's plans for river management, 447; on Franco-Prussian War, 469; and JR's *Fors Clavigera*, 469–70, 505, 533, 653–5; ageing, 470; JR writes to on purchase of Brantwood, 499; *Frederick the Great*, 542–3; JR sends *Val d'Arno* lectures to, 544; JR writes to on Rose's illness, 582; Jowett distrusts, 604; and Gotthelf's language, 617; and new edition of *Stones of Venice*, 623; JR introduces young people to, 652–3; political stance, 691; Scottishness, 708–9; *Reminiscences*, 709, 716, 789, 855; Norton's attitude to, 753; JR alludes to in lectures, 776; Froude's biography of, 781, 789, 837; in *Præterita*, 789, 855; Nevinson idolises, 851; JR's three letters to Norton on understanding, 855–9; 'Jesuitism', 859

Carpaccio, Vittore, 67, 446–7, 518, 522, 562, 622–6, 629, 633, 642–3, 646, 648, 662–3, 675, 777, 802

Carretto, Ilaria de, 564–5, 567, 677–8, 808

Carroll, Lewis *see* Dodgson, Charles Lutwidge

Carshalton, Surrey, 502–5, 596, 699

Cary, Henrietta, 725

Casanova, Giovanni Jacopo de Seingalt: *Memoirs*, 624

Castletown, Augusta Mary, Lady, 630

Catalogue of the Drawings and Sketches by J. M. W. Turner . . . in the National Gallery (JR), 699

Catalogue of a Series of Specimens in the British Museum (Natural History) of the more common forms of Silica (JR), 768

Catalogue of Siliceous Minerals . . . in St George's Museum, Sheffield (JR), 642, 644

Catena, Vincenzo, 432, 476, 665, 773

Catherine of Bologna, St, 312

Catholicism *see* Roman Catholicism

Cattermole, George, 35

'Caution to Snakes, A' (JR; lecture), 692, 695
Cavalcaselle, G. B., 554–5, 562
Century Guild Hobby Horse, The, 803
Cestus of Aglaia, The (JR), 253, 317, 364–7, 369, 373, 383, 435, 778
Chambéry, 134, 137
Chamonix, 26, 33, 34, 69, 79, 81, 122, 133, 136, 139–40, 202, 234, 277, 296, 788, 846
Champagnole, 84
Charity Organisation Society, 392
Charles Albert, King of Sardinia, 122, 136
Charles Street, London, 178
Chartists, 122
Chartres, 200
Chateaubriand, F. R. de, 15
Chaucer, Geoffrey, 37, 368, 402
Cheney, Edward, 141, 143, 148, 166, 172
Chesneau, Ernest, 772
chess: JR's interest in, 540
Chester, 12
Chesterfield Art School, 696
Cheyne Row, Chelsea, 318
Cheyne Walk, London, 176, 338, 404
Chillon, castle, 26
chivalry, 374–5, 401–2
cholera: in Oxford, 219, 547–8
Christ Church, Oxford: JR attends, 20, 41–9, 52, 63, 237, 262; religious outlook, 20, 43; old master drawings collection, 48; Buckland at, 49; JR entertains old friends from, 128; William Russell at, 169; and cholera outbreak, 219; workers' cottages on college land, 224; Liddell appointed Dean, 246; JR's honorary studentship, 476; JR dines with Prince Leopold at, 545; *see also* Oxford
Christian Socialism, 151, 203, 224, 240, 262, 352–3, 829
Christie's (auctioneers), 433
Christ's Hospital (school), London, 278, 615
Christy Minstrels, 687
'Chronicle of St Bernard, The' (JR), 783
Churchill, Revd W. H., 735, 793
Cicero, 15
Cimabue, 561–2, 572
Clancarty, Richard Somerset Le Poer Trench, 1st Earl of, 263
Claremont, near Esher, Surrey, 760, 768
Clarkson, Thomas, 277
Claude Lorrain, 64, 164, 203
Clayton, Edward, 57, 63, 68, 83, 84
Clifford, Edward, 611
Cloncurry, 263
Clough, Arthur Hugh, 51, 215, 423
Clowsley, Nanny, 787
Cock, Bridget, 14
Cock, Mary, 2, 7
Cock, William, 2
Cockburn, Robert and Mary (*née* Duff), 31, 101, 107
Cockerell, Charles Robert, 258, 277
Cockerell, Olive, 817–18, 832, 834
Cockerell, Sydney Carlyle, 805, 816–18, 832–4, 843–4, 872
Coeli Enarrant (JR), 793
'Colenso diamond', 332, 769
Colenso, Frances, 285, 332, 590
Colenso, John William, Bishop of Natal, 285, 331–4, 579–80, 769
Colenso, Sarah Frances (*née* Bunyon), 338
Coleridge, Samuel Taylor, 56, 72, 78, 100
Coletti, Fra Antonio, 559
Collingwood, Edith Mary (*née* Isaac; WGC's wife), 765, 771, 867
Collingwood, William Gershom: issues JR's *The Poetry of Architecture*, 52; travels with JR in France, 56; on *Modern Painters*, 100; and JR's compositions for Winnington pupils, 346; on JR's mother, 387; on JR's *Queen of the Air*, 437; collects and edits JR's writings, 442, 867–8; and JR's visit to Verona, 444; *The Life and Work of John Ruskin*, 444, 471, 810, 855, 867, 871, 876; on JR's drawing style, 445; on meaning of *Fors Clavigera*, 471; on JR's 1871 visit to Matlock, 488; studies drawing at Oxford, 509–10; meets JR, 510; *The Art Teaching of John Ruskin*, 510, 797; in *Præterita*, 520; on JR's illness in Assisi, 563; on JR's description of della Quercia sculpture, 564; makes no mention of Wilde at Oxford, 574; resists membership of Guild of St George, 590–1, 721; helps translate Xenophon, 595, 602, 606; praises Laurence Hilliard, 597; as JR's secretary, 603; at Brantwood, 616, 710, 712, 726, 771; on Swan and Sheffield working men, 635; interest in geology of Lake District, 645; *Ruskin Relics*, 661; helps answer JR's *Fors Clavigera* correspondence, 683; on JR's charity to Burden, 685; and JR's theatre-going, 687; devotion to JR, 698, 726; and JR's songs, 712–13; and JR's interest in local school, 713; accompanies JR on 1882 tour, 726–31, 733–4, 736, 741, 757, 823; interests, 726; and JR's mental condition, 733–4; publishes biography of JR, 733; JR gives minerals to, 735; marriage and children, 735, 764, 867; *The Limestone Alps of Savoy*, 735–6; understanding of JR, 749; at Coniston, 764; JR invites to call, 764–5; Cook meets, 766; helps JR with lectures, 766; collaborates with JR, 770; believes in JR's grand plan, 776; on JR's dogs, 783–4; on JR's aesthetic, 797; knows of JR's parents' correspondence, 810; visits JR in later years, 855–6, 867; copies JR's letters to Norton, 858; as potential amanuensis for JR in old age, 861; writings, 867–8; at JR's funeral, 874; friendship with Helen Gill Viljoen, 876–7; disenchantment with Severns, 877
Collingwood, William (WGC's father), 509
Collins, Charles, 183, 190
Collins, Sir Robert, 510–11
colour, 288–9

Colquhoun, Mrs, 101
Combe, Thomas, 156
Como, Lake, 92–3
Comte, Auguste, 318, 419, 534
Coniston: geology of, 17, 644–5; JR's family at, 493–4; JR builds house at, 499–500, 537; JR's social life in, 541, 684–5, 764; school at, 713, 767, 819, 823; tourism, 763–4; JR's attachment to, 862–3; JR buried at, 874; *see also* Brantwood
Coniston Institute, 735
Coniston Water, 493–4, 537
Contemporary Review, 356, 534, 536, 684, 689–90
Conway Castle, 675, 699
Cook, (Sir) Edward Tyas: edits vol. XVII of Library Edition of JR's works, 363–7, 371; on *Sesame and Lilies*, 373; on genesis of *Præterita*, 422, 757; on JR's sale of Turners, 433; on JR's numbering paragraphs, 436; on meaning of *Fors Clavigera*, 471–2; on JR and St Francis of Assisi, 559, 562; denies JR's illness in Assisi, 563; makes no mention of Wilde, 574; on JR's non-prudishness, 574; reconstructs JR's 'Readings in *Modern Painters*', 647; on JR's visit to Gladstone, 650; knows of JR's 'Brantwood Diary', 669; criticises JR's prose in 'Usury', 689; assembles and collects JR material, 697, 797, 876; and Irish May Queen festivities, 724; on new liberalism at Oxford, 738; and JR's views on Pre-Raphaelites, 740–1; and JR's art teaching at Oxford, 745; discipleship of JR, 748, 838; reports JR's lectures and writings for *Pall Mall Gazette*, 748, 775–7, 778, 793–4, 838; understanding of JR, 749; and disposal of JR's private papers, 754; publishes index to *Fors Clavigera*, 762; on JR's prophetic thought, 766; meets Collingwood and Wedderburn, 766; prepares JR's works for publication,770; *Studies in Ruskin*, 776; reports JR's presentation of Guild of St George accounts, 779; involvement with Oxford, 837–8; background and career, 838–9; meets JR, 838–9; censorship in editing JR's works, 839–40; *Popular Handbook to the National Gallery*, 839; proposes JR's burial at Westminster Abbey, 874
Cook, Emily (*née* Baird; ETC's wife), 839
Cooke (conjurer), 610
Cooke, Revd Samuel Hay, 284, 306
Cork High School for Girls, 735
Corlass, Miss (of Hull), 334
Cornhill Magazine, 292–4, 296–8, 317
Cornwall, 53
Corpus Christi College, Oxford, 476–7, 576, 738, 774
Correggio, 38, 567
Couttet, Joseph: Ruskins hire as guide, 80; JR travels and climbs with, 83, 85, 88, 90, 92–3, 134, 136, 139, 233, 251, 253; warns JR of overwork, 96; meets Effie, 139; and JR's lodgings in Mornex, 325–6; JR visits in decline, 567–8; JR memorialises with gift to British Museum, 769
Coventry, 12
Cowley Rectory, near Uxbridge, 340, 346, 383, 386, 411, 466–7, 546, 591, 597, 687
Cowper, George Augustus Frederick, 6th Earl, and Countess, 271
Cowper, Georgiana *see* Mount-Temple, Georgiana, Lady
Cowper, William (*later* Cowper-Temple) *see* Mount-Temple, William Cowper-Temple, 1st Baron
Cowper-Temple, Edward, 163, 271
Cox, David, 433
Coxe, Henry, 476
Crane, Walter, 872
Crawley, Frederick: accompanies JR to Wallington, 182; JR helps educate, 223; in Alps with JR, 326; owns manuscript of JR's 'Gold', 363; on 1866 tour, 384; accompanies JR to Keswick, 405; helps JR in Verona, 444; accompanies JR on 1870 Venice tour, 462–3; assists at JR's lectures, 462; with JR at Abingdon, 473; takes Daguerrotypes, 479; at Brantwood, 541, 571; joins JR in Lucca, 566; appointed factotum in Oxford drawing schools, 596; and Guild of St George, 710; and JR's anxieties about mental state, 714
Crawley, Mrs Frederick, 596
Creswick, Benjamin, 646
Crimean War (1854–6), 214, 273
Cristall, Joshua, 35, 101
Croly, Revd George, 31–2, 58–9, 74, 107, 149–50, 210, 340
Crossmount, 114
Crowe, Sir Joseph, 555
Crown of Wild Olive, The (JR; lectures), 355–6, 358, 382–3, 456, 503, 542–3
Cruikshank, George, 391, 422
Crystal Palace, 157, 159, 259, 585, 610
Cumming, Revd John, 330–1

Daguerre, Louis Jacques Mande, 479
Daily News, 162, 766
Daily Telegraph, 362, 364, 469, 811
Dale, Dr Thomas, 28, 29, 37–8, 39, 49, 51, 58, 107, 129, 330
Dallas, Eneas Sweetland, 247, 346; *The Gay Science*, 346
Dame Wiggins of Lee (JR), 798–9
Dandolo, Enrico, Doge of Venice, 665
Dante Alighieri: JR reads, 88, 214, 327, 622, 628; JR's references to, 92, 133, 377; on womanhood, 375; JR compares Homer with, 416; Longfellow and Norton translate, 422; influence on JR's 'Storm-Clouds' lecture, 492; discussed in *Fors Clavigera*, 530–1; JR reads W. M. Rossetti on, 534; JR comments on *Divine Comedy*, 870
Dart, J. H., 29, 51

Darwin, Charles, 49, 388, 423, 426, 534, 593, 685
Darwinism: JR opposes, 592
Davies, Revd J. Llewellyn, 203, 334, 580
Davy, Sir Humphry, 107
Davy, Lady (*formerly* Apreece), 107, 110, 121, 128, 141
De Wint, Peter, 74
Deal, 206, 231
Deane, Woodward and Deane (architects), 218
Dearden, James S., 877
Deborah (Biblical figure), 352–3, 472, 829
Denmark Hill, London: Ruskins move to, 70–1; Turner paintings and drawings at, 76–7, 152, 299–300; JR's life with family at, 83, 115, 129, 152; JR writes to parents at, 96, 161, 170; entertaining and visitors at, 101, 121, 129, 152, 174, 206–7, 213–15; Effie at, 109–12; JR and Effie live at, 120–1, 123, 127, 181, 197; JR keeps books and effects at, 128; JR writes at, 147, 175; Furnivall visits, 151, 223; Millais visits, 155, 195–6; Hobbs sends copy of *Stones of Venice* to, 167; Carlyle visits, 176, 362, 404; Butterworth at, 239–40; La Touches visit, 264, 267, 289, 301, 313, 572; JR leaves for Winnington Hall, 278; Margaret Bell visits, 287; Smith and Williams visit, 293; Simons visit, 303; JR stays at, 306, 346, 386; Harrison visits, 318, 501; religious arguments at, 330; at JR's father's death, 348; Joan Agnew (Severn) lives at, 348–9, 356, 362–3, 369, 384; JR's mother inherits, 348; JR attends to after father's death, 362; servants, 362–3; JR entertains at, 370, 450–51, 466; Rose La Touche revisits, 379; Constance Hilliard at, 383–4; Winnington girls visit, 387; JR's art collection at, 432; Henry James visits, 435; JR leaves, 495, 505, 513
Derbyshire, 53
Derwentwater, 18, 24
Desart, Catherine, Countess of (*later* Price), 262–3, 461
Desart, John Otway Cuffe, 2nd Earl of, 262
Desart, John Otway Cuffe, 3rd Earl of, 262
'Design in the Florentine School of Engraving' (JR; lecture), 488
Deucalion (JR), 17, 79–80, 437, 562, 584, 591–2, 626, 642, 645, 683, 692, 735–6
de Vere, Aubrey, 646
'Diamond Eyes' (girl friend of JR), 794
Dickens, Charles, 22, 62, 151, 251, 357, 388, 423, 475, 750
Dijon, 131
Dilecta (JR; supplement to *Præterita*), 629, 809, 845, 858–9
Dilke, Emilia Francis, Lady (*née* Strong; *then* Pattison), 600–2
Disraeli, Benjamin (Earl of Beaconsfield), 161, 397, 691
Dixon, Thomas, 206, 398, 403, 468, 590
Dobell, Sydney, 212, 213
Dodgson, Charles Lutwidge (Lewis Carroll), 49, 478–9, 744
Domecq, Adèle-Clotilde (*later* Baroness Duquesne): JR meets and falls in love with, 27, 35–6, 50–1, 53, 109, 112; in JR's *Marcolino*, 37; JR mentions aristocratic connections, 43; at school in England, 51; engagement and marriage to Duquesne, 52, 54, 146; daughter, 146; Effie meets in Paris, 146; effect on JR, 270, 457; JR thinks of in later life, 714, 795
Domecq, Caroline, 35
Domecq, Cécile, 35
Domecq, Diana *see* Maison, Comtesse
Domecq, Elise, 35
Domecq, Pedro, 6, 11, 26, 35, 36, 51, 52
Domenichino, 73
Dover, 24, 33, 122, 199
Downey, William, 338
Downs, David, 70, 295, 362, 405, 420, 462–3, 502, 537, 541, 571, 573, 596, 617, 620, 636, 710; death, 853
Drayton, Capt. Alfred, 350
Dresden, 277
Dressler, Conrad, 771
Drew, Mary (*née* Gladstone), 513, 649, 658, 676, 691, 714, 720, 725, 749, 801
Drewitt, Dawtry, 475, 585, 610, 785
Drogheda, Mary Caroline, Marchioness of, 263
Dublin: JR lectures in, 411, 413–17, 429
Ducie, Henry John Reynolds-Moreton, 3rd Earl of (1860s), 395
Dulwich College picture gallery, 72
Dundas, Ada, 715, 725, 771
Dunira, Crieff, Perthshire, 677
Duquesne, Baron, 52, 146
Dürer, Albrecht, 202, 204, 315, 322
Dyce, William, 150, 153, 229

Eagle's Nest, The (JR), 507, 510, 514
Eagles, Revd John, 39
Earland, Ada: *Ruskin and his Circle*, 502
Early English Text Society, 534
Eastlake, Sir Charles: at Denmark Hill, 101; JR reviews in *Quarterly*, 108, 113–14, 116; *Materials for a History of Oil Painting*, 113, 116, 228; co-founds Arundel Society, 129; JR meets, 147–8; cleaning and restoration policy at National Gallery, 162–3; JR requests to buy Venetian paintings, 163; believes JR hypocritical, 198; JR reviews paintings, 228; ignores JR's *Times* letter on Turner bequest, 242; JR's relations with, 243
Eastlake, Elizabeth, Lady (*née* Rigby): affection for Effie, 148, 178, 197; JR meets, 148; on Turner bequest, 163, 242; on Turner's life, 165; on Ruskin family's kindness to Effie, 174; connives at Effie's flight, 197; and JR's criticism of husband's paintings, 228; attacks JR, 230–2, 244
Eastnor, Charles Somers Cocks, Viscount (*later* 3rd Earl Somers), 44, 128

Edgeworth, Maria, 15, 65–6, 194, 195, 705, 771, 811; *Moral Tales*, 672
Edinburgh, 1, 184, 189, 193, 196, 198
Edinburgh Philosophical Institution, 181, 194
Edward, Prince (*later* King Edward VII), 304
Edwardes, Major-General Sir Herbert, 652, 709, 764, 769, 783
Effra, river, 10, 505
Egypt: JR on art and antiquities of, 359–61, 371–2
Elder, Alexander, 29–30
Elements of Drawing, The (JR), 236–7, 241, 244, 286, 643–4
Elements of English Prosody (JR), 660, 712
Elements of Perspective, The (JR), 237, 286
Eliot, George, 74, 423, 651, 689, 723, 750, 771
Eliot, T. S., 870
Elliot, Gilbert, Dean of Bristol, 432
Elliott, Lady Charlotte, 147
Ellis & White (booksellers), 595
Ellis, Frederick S., 450, 595–6, 676, 700, 806
Emerson, Ralph Waldo, 214, 427
Emma (Denmark Hill servant), 384
English Republic, The (journal), 501
Essays and Reviews (collection; 1861), 331
Ethics of the Dust, The (JR), 284, 360, 370–3, 439, 596, 610, 642, 644, 869
Etna, Mount, 556
Eton College, 645, 695–6
Euclid, 52, 195, 235, 286
Evangelicalism, 19, 31, 42, 167, 254–5, 266–7, 276, 395–6, 427, 552, 577, 725, 736, 829
Evans, Joan: edits JR's diaries, 877; *John Ruskin*, 877
Exeter College, Oxford, 746
Eyre, Edward John, 387–9, 397

Faido (St Gothard), 93
Falaise, 127
Fall, Eliza, 668
Fall, Richard, 29, 62, 72, 117, 134, 668
Falmouth, 231
Farnley Hall (Yorkshire), 156, 181, 675, 760, 772, 781–2
Faunthorpe, Revd John, 721–5, 737, 750, 762
Fawkes, Edith Mary, 781
Fawkes, Francis Hawkesworth, 156, 760, 781
Fawkes, Walter, 156, 199
Feilding, Louise, Viscountess, 175
Feilding, Rudolph William Feilding, Viscount (*later* 8th Earl of Denbigh), 169
Ferry Hinksey, Oxfordshire, 547–9, 554, 565, 573–4, 576–7, 580, 584, 724
Fiction, Fair and Foul (JR), 28, 688–9, 708
Fielding, Copley, 34–5, 64, 74, 121, 433, 763
Fiesole, 92
Finberg, A. J., 101
Finden, W. & E. (engravers), 668
Fine Art Society, Bond Street, London: Turner exhibition, 655, 658, 662, 673–4, 805; buys Turner's *Pass of the Splügen* for JR, 673; exhibition of Prout and Hunt, 687–8; rivalry with Royal Academy, 780
'Fireside, The' (JR; lecture), 763
Firth, Julia, 616–17, 770–1, 801, 821–2
Firth, Thomas, 616
Fitzgerald, Edward: *Rubáiyát of Omar Khayyám*, 346
Fitzroy (Oxford undergraduate), 545
Fleming, Albert, 710, 764, 801, 820–2
Fletcher, Lazarus, 646, 719, 727, 767, 769–71, 773
Florence, 57, 91–2, 108, 557, 566–7, 731–3
Folkestone, 116, 823–6, 841
Fontainebleau, 33, 68–9
Forbes, Dr (of Folkestone), 836
Forbes, James, 80, 113, 536
Forbes (Oxford undergraduate), 545
Ford, Northumberland, 338–9
Forman, H. Buxton, 363
Fors Clavigera (JR): themes, 150; addressed to workmen of England, 206, 634; attacks Evangelicals, 254, 552; and JR's Winnington letters, 286, 296; writing and meaning, 299, 468–73, 481–2, 491–2, 564–5, 626, 641; criticises Tipple, 301, 551; influenced by Carlyle, 314; affected by *Munera Pulveris*, 318; on story of Jael and Deborah, 353; intimacy and confession in, 355; contents and complexity, 366, 505, 532–3, 536, 619–20, 631, 709, 720; commemorates Marie of the Giessbach, 386; and Carlyle's 'Shooting Niagara', 389; and JR's intemperance, 404, 436; on fate, 410; idealises Scotland, 422; and *Queen of the Air*, 436, 498; and JR's distraught mind, 468, 562, 626–7, 629–31, 656–64, 668, 674, 690–1; Carlyle and, 469–70, 505, 533, 653; and Rose La Touche, 469, 485, 498, 514, 530, 565–6; and Guild of St George, 472, 496, 588–9, 613, 721; on Annie Brickland, 474–5; JR and Dodgson, 478; illustrations, 480–1; and JR's Matlock illness, 491; High Tory utopianism, 495, 498; JR edits and publishes personally, 502, 505; on river Wandle, 503; Alfred Tylor given copy, 505; on Max Müller, 512; on European republicanism, 518; 'Benediction' section, 523; Norton dislikes, 532, 544; and Brantwood, 541; Scott in, 542, 547, 568, 641; translations of *Roman de la Rose* in, 542; addresses from which written, 546–7; on Margate, 546; on Assisi, 560–1; George Allen publishes, 566–7, 649, 709; regular publication, 566; JR abandons autobiographical writing after Rose's death, 572; lacks appeal to Oxford aesthetes, 575; challenges bishops on theological and social matters, 578–9, 613–4, 641, 689–90, 781; on dying Rose, 583; lists JR's friends, 585; and JR's classics series, 603–4; Manning appreciates, 611; on Roman Catholicism, 618; on Guild of St George, 619, 636; on St Ursula, 624–5; JR discloses personal finances in, 636–7; on non-cooperation of working

men, 636; prints JR's attack on Whistler, 638–9; and Birmingham meeting, 639–40; denounces Octavia Hill, 648, 832–3; sent to Prince Leopold, 649; criticises Gladstone, 650–1, 657; publication interrupted, 654, 679; describes Dr Parsons, 669–70; on Turner, 674–5; JR considers reviving, 678, 683, 690, 736; provokes correspondence, 683; resumes (1880), 690; comments on contemporary press, 697; Faunthorpe compiles index to, 723, 762; JR continues writing (1883), 736; JR ends, 756, 761–3; on Scotland, 758; JR numbers and titles, 762; JR's index to, 762; on pet dogs, 783–4; and *Præterita*, 792; and Quaritch catalogue, 807; on Bassano, 848

Forster, John, 423, 533

Fortnightly Review, 376, 392

Foster (aide-de-camp of Radetsky), 172

Foulds, Mr and Mrs (of Folkestone), 826, 832

Foxe, John, 22

'Fragments from a Metrical Journal' (JR), 34

France: JR visits, 57, 124–7, 233, 345, 425, 693, 695, 727–8, 823, 843–4; JR on rural poverty in, 425; *see also* individual places

France, Phoebe, 286

Franceline (of Mornex), 326

'Francesca's Book' (JR; lecture), 749, 770

Francis of Assisi, St, 261, 559–60, 562–3

Francis, Philip, 471

Franco-Prussian War (1870–1), 466–7, 469, 518

Fraser, James, Bishop of Manchester, 689–90

Fraser's Magazine, 32, 315–17, 321, 323, 326–7, 346, 500, 570, 618

Freeman, Edward Augustus, 462

Frère, Edouard, 238; *A French Cottage Interior*, 432

Fribourg, 34, 385

Friends of Living Creatures, The (association), 794, 800

Friendship's Offering (journal), 30, 32–5, 37, 105, 501, 567, 651

Frith, William Powell, 251, 680

Frondes Agrestes (selection of JR), 759, 863

Froude, James Anthony: on La Touche family of Delgany, 267; on Carlyle's acquaintance with JR, 314; requests political contributions from JR for *Fraser's*, 315–16; JR's friendship with, 318, 331, 535, 610, 716–17, 719, 775, 781, 814, 837; and JR's religious ideas, 331; Dallas discusses *Fraser's* with, 346; on Jane Welsh Carlyle, 375; supports Governor Eyre, 388; JR describes efficacy of Rose's prayer to, 396; effects reconciliation between JR and Carlyle, 404; Norton meets, 423; JR sends *Val d'Arno* lectures to, 544; and Mallock, 604; publishes Carlyle's *Reminiscences*, 709, 716, 855; Norton attacks, 716–17; on Rose La Touche, 717; estimate of JR, 749; JR speaks of autobiography to, 757; publishes biography of Carlyle, 781, 789, 837; corresponds with JR, 811; Joan Severn restricts visits to Brantwood, 814; influenced by Carlyle, 851; JR defends in letters to Norton, 855–9

Fudge, David, 363

Furneaux, Eleanor (*née* Severn), 476

Furneaux, Revd Henry, 476

Furnivall, Frederick James: devotion to JR, 151; as intermediary between JR and Maurice, 151, 203; JR writes to on marriage, 199; invites JR to join Working Men's College, 203; and JR's claims to be shy, 207; and plans for Oxford Museum, 222; gives books to Denmark Hill servants, 223; JR visits, 235; introduces JR and Elizabeth Gaskell, 259; JR sees at Working Men's College, 262; Ruskins' response to, 318; writings, 534

'Future of England, The' (JR; lecture), 456, 652

Gainsford, Thomas, 46, 48

Gale family, 767

Gale, Claudia (*née* Severin), 610, 692

Gale, Frederick, 610, 692, 714, 718, 767; *Modern British Sports*, 693

Gale, Marion, 645

Gale, Martha ('Mattie'), 645, 716, 725

Galignani's Messenger (newspaper), 255

Gambart, Ernest, 190, 231, 235, 237–8, 258, 291

Gaskell, Elizabeth, 73, 259, 423

Gaulois, Le (journal), 336

Genesis, Book of, 301, 332

Geneva, 33, 69, 83, 123, 200, 234–5, 277

Geneva, Lake, 234, 442–3

Genoa, 261, 554

Geological Magazine, 413, 591

Geological Society, 17, 49, 53, 72, 591

Geologist (magazine), 591

geology: JR's interest in, 16–17, 33–4, 49–50, 102, 112, 302, 335, 493, 591, 644–5, 735–6

George, St: significance for JR, 522, 562, 594–5; *see also* Guild of St George

Germ (journal), 215

Germany, 70, 277; *see also* individual places

Ghirlandaio chapel (Florence), 92

Ghirlandaio, Domenico, 130

Gibbon, Edward, 77, 393, 548

Gibbs, Mary and Ellen: *The Bible References of John Ruskin*, 870

Giffard, Stanley, 32

Gilchrist, Alexander: *Life of Blake*, 665

Gill Head (cottage), Lake Windermere, 595

Gill, Helen *see* Viljoen, Helen Gill

Giorgione, 94

Giotto, 90, 92, 130, 230, 480–1, 554, 560–2, 567, 572, 675

Giotto and his Works in Padua (JR), 130, 481

Giovanelli, Prince Joseph, 143

Giovanni, Fra, 559

gipsies: JR defends, 790–1

Gladstone, Mary *see* Drew, Mary

Gladstone, William Ewart: made honorary student of Christ Church, 246; oratory, 357, 649; and 1867 Reform Bill, 397; at meeting of

National Association for the Promotion of Social Science, 419; in Metaphysical Society, 534; JR visits at Hawarden, 649–51, 658, 679, 692; JR's disagreements with, 651–2; JR attacks in *Fors Clavigera*, 657; JR criticises Glasgow students for interest in, 691; and Irish Land Bill, 714; JR meets in London, 718
Glasgow: Society of the Rose, 723
Glasgow University: JR stands for Lord Rectorship, 691
Glenfinlas, 184–90, 192–3, 208, 675
Globe (newspaper), 230
Gnosspelius, Barbara, 877
'Gold: a Dialogue' (JR), 363–4
Goodwin, Albert, 493, 518, 522, 524, 710
Goodwin, Harvey, Bishop of Carlisle, 580, 690, 872
Goodwin, Mrs Henry, 657
Gordon, George: hanged by Eyre, 388
Gordon, Murphy & Co (wine importers), 6
Gordon, Revd Osborne: friendship with JR, 46–7; visits JR at Leamington, 62; enters Church, 63; not told of JR's *Modern Painters*, 70–1; with Ruskin family in Alps, 80; JR avoids in Italy, 91; recommends Hooker to JR, 99; discusses university reading with JR, 100; JR entertains at Park Street, 128; protests at restoration of Catholic hierarchy, 150; JR meets sister (Mrs Daniel Moore), 157; advises JR against building house in Alps, 345; visits Denmark Hill, 387, 450, 466; JR visits at Easthampton, 405; on spiritualism, 612
Gothic, 420, 431, 455, 622
Gothic Revival, 104–5, 149, 222, 226
Gotthelf, Jeremias, 385, 617, 675, 776; *Ulric the Farm Servant*, 603, 617, 770, 801
Gower, Sir John, 37
Gozzoli, Benozzo, 90, 130
Graham, Frances, 663, 665, 677, 679, 718, 725
Graham, John W.: *The Harvest of Ruskin*, 871
Graham, William, 677, 679
Graphic Society, 104
Gras du Barry, Baroness, 144
Gray, Euphemia (*later* Ruskin; 'Effie'; 1828–97): meets JR, 62; visits Windus with JR, 76; as guest at Denmark Hill, 109–10; on JR, 110–12; courtship, engagement and marriage, 112–17; marriage unconsummated, 117–20, 178, 192, 197–8, 488; honeymoon, 120, 612; relations with JR's parents, 120, 123, 129, 131–2, 157; social life in London, 121, 147, 151, 176, 204; tour of southern England, 122–3; trip to France, 124–7; in Park Street house, 128; at Bowerswell, 130–1, 148; letters from JR, 131–2; sees doctor, 137; travels to Venice, 139; politics, 140, 160–1; and Venetian society, 140–1, 143–6, 158–9, 171; desire for children, 148; Lady Eastlake supports, 148, 230; visits Millais with JR, 155; in Switzerland, 158–9; opposes Turner biography, 165; exclusion from Ruskin family, 167; complains of Ruskins, 170–1; Austrian officers fight duel over, 171; and challenge to JR, 172; as ally of Mrs Ruskin, 174; on JR's pride, 174; meets Brownings, 176; informs parents of marriage difficulties, 178, 197; involvement with Pre-Raphaelitism, 178–81; last London season, 178–9; unhappiness at Herne Hill, 178; and Millais' *The Order of Release*, 179–81; looks after household of artists, 181–2; Scottish tour, 181; painted by Millais, 184–90; JR's oblivion to love for Millais, 192; travels to Edinburgh, 193–4; relations with JR, 194–6; Millais writes to Mrs Gray on, 196; flight, 198; marriage ends, 200; departure causes London scandal, 226; and Millais's *The Rescue*, 229; children by Millais, 135; correspondence with Maria La Touche on JR, 417, 419, 434, 513, 519, 755; JR's anxiety over, 468; disbelieves JR's sexual innocence, 484–5; divorce and JR's ineligibility to remarry, 496–7, 760; omitted from *Præterita*, 789
Gray, George (Effie's father): administers Richardson trust, 62; stays at Denmark Hill, 76; and JR's courtship and engagement to Effie, 109, 114; financial difficulties, 116, 118, 125, 127; Effie writes to about non-consummation, 117, 197; JR's father writes to, 117, 120–1, 131; suggests JR's parents leave JR and Effie in peace, 137–8; asked to find house in Highlands for JR to rent, 181–2; and Effie's separation from JR, 197–8; and JR's father's staying at inn, 546
Gray, Mrs George (Effie's mother): stays at Denmark Hill, 76, 129–30; describes JR-Effie wedding to Margaret Ruskin, 117; Effie writes to on welcome at Denmark Hill, 120; Effie returns to Bowerswell with, 130; and Effie's unhappiness, 137–8; concern over Effie in Venice, 143–5; and Newton's advice to Effie, 170; JR defends interest in Catholicism to, 174; Millais writes to, 196; and Effie's separation from JR, 197–8
Gray, Mr & Mrs Richard, 14
Gray, Robert, 131
Gray, Sophie, 196, 198
Gray's Inn, London, 8
Great Cumberland Street, London, 264
Great Exhibition (London, 1851), 157, 259
Greek culture, 274, 336, 466, 865
Greek language, 304, 308–9, 336
Green, John Richard, 462
Green, Thomas Hill, 739
Greenaway, Kate: background, 742–3; friendship with JR, 742–4, 756, 763, 767, 775, 793, 811, 863; JR lectures on, 746, 749–50; success and popularity, 794; and JR's autobiography, 795, 820; drawings for JR,

798–9, 854; Stacy Marks advises, 798; and JR's illness, 799–800, 820; and JR's lessons for Coniston schoolchildren, 819; visits JR at Sandgate, 834
Greenwood, Frederick, 363
Greg, William Rathbone, 536, 543
Gregory, Mrs William, 350–1
Greig, Agnes, 815
Griffith, Thomas, 55–6, 65, 72, 77, 81, 101–2, 164, 387, 433
Grimm brothers, 62, 422
Grimston, Robert, 44
Gritti, Andrea, Doge of Venice, 432, 476, 665–6, 773–4
Grosvenor Gallery, London, 638–9, 655, 780
Grote, George, 359
Guide to the Principal Pictures of the Academy of Fine Arts at Venice (JR), 632
Guild of St George: inspired by agricultural conditions in Alps, 136, 158, 252; JR's father's reaction to, 162; Cowper and, 219; Companions and subscribers, 287, 332, 589–90, 616–17, 721–2; Winnington girls join, 341; and Gotthelf's novels, 385; Paul Huret's gifts to, 391; and chivalry, 402; JR supports, 419; founding and constitution, 434, 443, 496, 577, 588–9, 591, 614; and JR's *Fors Clavigera*, 472, 496, 588–9, 613, 619, 636, 721; and heraldry, 507; values, 559–60; and JR's Paddington tea shop, 571; as utopia for Rose La Touche, 577, 649; aims and ethos, 588–9, 613, 619; given land at Barmouth, 619–20; and Museum of St George, 635; funded by JR, 636–8, 710, 793; trustees changed, 637–9; given land at Bewdley, 638; Birmingham civic leaders discuss, 639; Octavia Hill criticises, 648; JR's 'Master's Reports', 685, 722, 804; JR retains mastership, 710; and JR's mental illnesses, 721, 801–2; Italian copyists make architectural drawings for, 731; JR presides at Oxford meeting of, 779; omitted from *Præterita*, 789; activities, 801–2; artists and servants, 802–4; JR purchases objects for, 841; recognised after JR's death, 877
Gull, Sir William, 715, 726, 757, 767, 775, 812, 864
Gurney, Professor and Mrs E. W., 617
Guthrie, Dr Thomas, 247

Hackstoun, William, 710–11, 804
Haldane, Elizabeth, 739
Hall, Samuel Carter, 365, 517
Hallam, Henry, 121, 128
Hallé, Sir Charles, 284, 687
Hammersley, John, 240
Hannah (biblical figure), 50
Hapsburgs, 160
Harbours of England, The (JR), 206, 231–3
Harcourt family (of Nuneham Courtney), 548, 554
Harding, James Duffield, 32, 34, 55, 63, 72, 74, 92, 94, 96, 509
Hardinge, William Money, 575–6, 605
Hare, Augustus, 182–3, 255
Harker, Lizzie (*née* Watson), 771, 816
Harley, Dr George, 534, 666–7
Harper's New Monthly Magazine, 298
Harris, Thomas Lake, 427
Harrison, Major Benson, 499, 764
Harrison, Dorothy (*née* Wordsworth), 499, 764
Harrison, Frederic: friendship with JR, 318, 419; on Jamaica Committee, 388; *The Political Function of the Working Class*, 419; friendship with Norton, 423; *John Ruskin*, 467, 871–2; writes on positivism, 534
Harrison, W. H.: edits *Friendship's Offering*, 32, 105; JR's memorial of, 35; and JR's poetry, 51; told of JR's Newdigate presentation, 53; JR's father decries St Peter's ceremony to, 58–9; not told of JR's *Modern Painters*, 71–2; JR entrusts publication of *Modern Painters* II to, 100; as guest of Ruskins, 101; requests contributions from JR in Venice, 105; JR sends *Seven Lamps of Architecture* to, 131; JR's friendship with, 210; helps JR with inheritance, 348; visits Denmark Hill, 387, 466; edits JR's works, 434; JR ends connection with, 501–2; death, 567; JR writes on, 651–2; JR's obituary of, 803
Harristown, Co. Kildare, 263, 303–5, 308–10, 315, 324, 328–9, 344, 386, 389, 416, 428, 582
Harrow School, 735
Hartnell, Ada, 663
Hawarden, Cheshire, 649–51, 658, 679
Hazell & Watson (printers), 502, 585, 793
Hazlitt, William, 15
Heaton, Ellen, 249
Heenan (prize-fighter), 291
Helps, Alice, 687
Helps, Sir Arthur, 218, 247, 319, 534; *Some Thoughts for Next Summer*, 219
Helps, Mary, 687
Henry VIII, King, 43
'Heraldic Ordinaries, The' (JR; lecture), 507
heraldry, 507
Herbert, George, 84–5, 214, 351, 771
Herbert, John Rogers, 229
Herkomer, Herbert von, 685, 778
Herne Hill (London): Ruskins purchase and occupy, 8, 10–12; described, 10; garden, 13; social and family life at, 15–16, 27, 31, 53; Mary Richardson at, 17–18; JR educated at, 19; Andrews composes sermons at, 22; books and library, 25, 43; Adèle stays at, 35–7; JR convalesces at, 55; Effie visits, 62; Prout visits, 64; JR returns to after Oxford exams, 69; JR and Effie move to (no.30), 173, 197; Millais at, 179; JR gives no.28 to Severns as wedding present, 204, 596; Joan Agnew manages, 363; ex-Winnington girls visit, 433; Hilliards visit, 466; JR occupies old nursery, 551, 633, 699, 714, 769; Rose La Touche at,

572, 581; Joan Severn protects JR at, 692; necessary extensions not made, 769
Herschel, Sir John Frederick William, 49, 744
Hesse-Darmstadt, Frederick, Grand Duke of, 587
Hessler, Baroness, 143
Heysham, Lancashire, 814
High Elms (house), Hayes, Kent, 759
Highlands of Scotland, 120, 181, 184
Hill, Frederick: *Measures for Putting an End to the Abuses of Trade Unions*, 419
Hill, Octavia: relations with JR, 391–3, 466, 651, 817, 832; housing scheme, 392; manages properties, 571; JR denounces in *Fors*, 648; Cockerell and, 817
Hilliard family, 474, 500, 546, 692
Hilliard, Constance (*later* Churchill): JR first meets, 340, 383; JR's regard for, 346, 466; accompanies JR on trips abroad, 383–4, 462–5, 518, 522, 524, 592, 663; friendship with Joan Agnew, 411, 692; in JR's dreams, 411; visits JR, 450, 692; correspondence with Rose La Touche, 552; Norton on, 569; in Scotland, 597; quarrel and reconciliation with JR, 663, 667; on effect of JR's Brantwood illness, 682–3; effect of JR on, 725; marries Churchill, 735, 793; and brother Laurence's death, 818
Hilliard, Ethel ('Ettie'), 383, 597, 693, 695, 765, 773, 818
Hilliard, Frederick, 383, 765
Hilliard, Revd J. C., 340, 383, 546, 683
Hilliard, Laurence ('Laurie'; 'Lolly'): JR meets, 346; as JR's secretary at Brantwood, 383, 597, 655, 673, 711–12, 765, 812; visits Herne Hill, 466, 692; and JR's mental breakdowns, 669, 701, 704–5, 707–8, 812; accompanies JR on 1888 visit to France, 693, 695; loyalty to JR, 698; and JR's interest in local school, 713; understanding of JR, 749; at Coniston, 764; death, 818
Hilliard, Mary ('Mamie'), 340, 383, 462, 466, 474, 518, 522, 524
'Hillside, The' (JR; lecture), 763
Hinksey *see* Ferry Hinksey
Hinton, Charles, 535, 545, 573
Hinton, James, 535
Hitchin, 480
Hoare, Arthur, 545, 573
Hobbs, Hannah *see* Allen, Hannah
Hobbs, John (George): as family servant, 62, 71; travels with JR, 62, 83–5, 90, 93, 98, 108, 124, 132, 134, 139–40; Bible reading with JR, 84; copies JR's writings in Venice, 167; takes Daguerrotypes, 479
Hogg, James, 30
Holbein, Hans: *Dance of Death*, 480
Holiday, Henry, 651, 867
Holker, Sir John, 679–80
Holland, Henry Scott, 650, 866
Holzammer (Austrian officer), 144
Home, Daniel Dunglas, 350–1
'Home, and its Economies' (JR; article), 536
Homer, 15, 375, 416, 481, 797
Honfleur, 127
Hood, Thomas, 214, 674
Hook, Walter, 121
Hooker, Richard, 99
Horace, 316, 326, 354, 470–2, 712
Horne, Revd T. H.: *Illustrations of the Bible from Original Sketches taken on the Spot [by Turner]*, 668
Horner, Frances: *Time Remembered*, 677
Horsfall, Thomas, 646, 721–3, 750
Hortus Conclusus, 553
Houghton, Richard Monckton Milnes, 1st Baron, 75, 100, 261
Howard, John, 651
Howell, Charles Augustus, 378, 387, 391, 485
Howels, Revd William, 20
Huddleston, Sir John Walter, Baron of the Exchequer, 679
Hughes, Thomas, 203, 353, 388, 690
Huish, Marcus, 655, 673, 681, 687–8, 708, 760
Hungary, 122
Hunt, Alfred, 450, 613
Hunt, Venice (William Henry's daughter), 541
Hunt, Violet (William Henry's daughter), 541
Hunt, William Henry, 286, 433, 541, 687, 700, 796
Hunt, William Holman: JR's friendship with, 152; and Pre-Raphaelite Brotherhood, 155, 162–3; artistic principles, 156–7; on neglect of Turner, 156; Effie introduces to Monckton Milnes, 180; invited on JR's Scottish tour, 181; visits Holy Land, 182, 193–4; letter from Millais, 184; letter from JR on Millais, 193; JR writes on in *Times*, 198, 227; JR commissions paintings for Working Men's College, 205; Rossetti and, 209; and Leighton's *Cimabue*, 229; at Simons party, 338; in Venice, 447; and Pre-Raphaelitism, 741–2; religious convictions, 741; JR lectures on, 742; and JR's art teaching, 798
Hunter Street, London, 8, 20, 395
Huntingdon, 12
Huntington, George P. (compiler): *Comments of John Ruskin on the Divina Commedia*, 870
Huret family (of Boulogne), 304, 391
Huret, Paul, 391
Hutton, Richard Holt, 749
Huxley, Thomas Henry, 388, 535, 543, 598, 605

In Montibus Sanctis (JR), 793
Inchbold, John William, 252–3, 255, 298, 323, 450
Ingelow, Jean, 405, 430, 585, 611, 649, 749
Inglis, Sir Robert Harry, 32, 75, 128, 228
Innsbruck, 33
Institute of Painters in Watercolours, 837
Interlaken, 26
Ipswich, 12
Ireland: JR visits, 304, 306; *see also* Dublin; Harristown
Iris (annual), 37

Irvine, Edith, 725
Irving, Edward, 20, 285
Italy, 25–7, 33, 57–8, 82–96, 123–5, 176, 463, 517–18, 552–67, 730–2; floods in, 473–4; *see also* individual places

Jael (Biblical figure), 352–3, 472–3
Jamaica: 1865 insurrection, 387–8
James, Henry, 435
Jameson, Anne, 95–6
Jarves, J. J., 214–15
Jephson, Dr (of Leamington), 62, 113–14
Jeremiah, Book of, 380, 563
Jericho (Oxford), 219, 548
Job, Book of, 168
John, St: Gospel of, 235
Johnson, Samuel, 12, 15, 53
Jolly, William: JR meets, 426; *Ruskin on Education*, 426, 870
Jones, George, 65
Journal of the Royal Society of Arts, 245
Jowett, Benjamin: JR meets, 331; on rigorous study of Bible, 331; JR recounts religious revelation to, 405; acts against Hardinge and Pater for homosexuality, 575; JR dislikes translation of Plato, 603–4, 685; on JR's 'great sensibility, little sense', 604; depicted in Mallock's *New Republic*, 605–6; relations with JR at Oxford, 738, 745; and JR's Oxford lectures, 742, 778; visits Brantwood, 772–4; hospitality to JR, 774–5; and JR's resignation from Slade Professorship, 791–2
Jowett, Henry (printer), 501, 505, 585, 761, 770, 785, 792, 808, 845, 858
Jungfrau (mountain), 34
Jura, 33–4

Kaiser, Eduard Chaples, 554, 561
Kean, Edmund, 23
Keats, John, 59–60, 214, 246, 333, 412, 555, 664
Keble, John, 216
Keepsake (journal), 30
Kemble, Charles, 23
Kendal, 12, 18, 315, 642, 645
Ker, Charlotte, 139–41, 143, 145–6
Kerr, C. H. Bellenden, 129, 151, 207
Keston, near Bromley, 423
Keswick, 19, 120, 405, 408–10, 421, 611–12
Kevill-Davis, Lily *see* Armstrong, Lily
Kevill-Davis, Violet ('Scrappy'; Lily's daughter), 743, 863
Kidd, Joseph, 534
Kildare, Charles William Fitzgerald, Marquess of (*later* 5th Duke of Leinster), 44
King of the Golden River, The (JR), 61, 110, 113, 264, 369, 657
King's College London, 37, 42, 58
King's Lynn, 12
Kingsley, Charles, 203, 331, 388, 451
Kingsley, Revd William, 339, 387, 487
Kipling, Rudyard, 819; *Stalky and Co*, 748–9
Kirkcudbright: Museum of, 735
Kitchin, G. W. (*later* Dean of Durham), 43–4, 599–600
Klein (Swiss courier), 596
Knaresborough, 259
Knight, Henry Gally, 108
Knight's Fate, A (JR), 652, 764
Knowles, James, 534–5, 676, 678–9, 749
Knox, John, 261
Königstein, 283

Laing, J. J., 240, 279
Laing, Robert *see* Shields, Cuthbert
Lake District, 17–18, 53, 109, 499; JR's attachment to, 17–19, 53, 499; JR's depression in, 109; railways extension in, 617; geology, 644–5; visitors to, 645–6; *see also* individual places
'Landscape' (JR; lecture), 778–9
Landseer, Sir Edwin, 121
Lansdowne, Henry Petty-Fitzmaurice, 4th Marquess of, 121, 130, 163, 180
Larkin, Henry, 590
La Touche family (of Dalgeny), 267
La Touche family (of Harristown), 267, 289, 301–4, 308, 313, 321, 324, 327, 399–400, 416
La Touche, Emily (Rose's sister): JR meets in London, 264, 267; JR nicknames 'Wisie', 302; relations with father, 329; marriage, 369; death, 418, 799; daughter, 772
La Touche, John (Rose's father): business, 263–4; religious convictions, 266–7, 290, 301, 305; disapproves of JR's activities, 291; baptised by Spurgeon, 296, 330; JR opposes economic views, 296; JR gives no pet-name to, 302; property at Harristown, 305; conflict with Rose, 308; objects to JR's teaching Rose Greek, 309–10; and Rose's religious piety, 328–9; accompanies Rose to communion, 342 shock at and objections to JR's marriage proposal to Rose, 381–2, 390; and JR's *Crown of Wild Olives*, 383; forbids Rose to see JR, 394, 397; Rose strikes, 453; knows of JR's correspondence with Rose, 461; takes legal advice on JR's marrying, 496; disapproves of George MacDonald, 516; JR's anger for, 553; abandons objections to Rose's marriage to JR, 568, 581; blames JR for Rose's nervous exhaustion, 582; and Rose's final illness, 583; visits Brantwood, 755–6; apprehensions over JR's *Præterita*, 845
La Touche, Maria (*née* Price; Rose's mother): background, 262–3; JR meets, 262, 264, 266–8; JR refers to as Lacerta, 302, 411, 438, 440, 630, 755; JR confesses religious doubts to, 305, 330; relations with Rose, 308, 329; tells JR of Rose's illness, 309, 343–4; and JR's relations with Rose, 310–11; accompanies JR to Owen lecture, 313; religious tolerance, 328; opposes Rose's communion, 342; and George MacDonald, 351, 516; and Emily's marriage, 369; shock at and objections to JR's marriage proposal to

Rose, 381, 390; forbids Rose to see JR, 394, 397; inability to cope with JR, 395; corresponds with Effie, 417, 468, 513, 755; asks Joan Agnew not to write again to Rose, 429; knows of JR's correspondence with Rose, 461; suggests Rose resume communication with JR, 556; abandons objections to Rose's marriage to JR, 568, 581; blames JR for Rose's nervous exhaustion, 582; JR wishes to send flowers to, 710; correspondence with JR, 714, 717, 733, 738, 758, 760, 811; visits Brantwood, 755–6, 764, 772–3, 799–800; JR sends writings to before publication, 763; JR considers collaboration with on *Proserpina*, 770; on Rose's dog, 784; and JR's *Præterita*, 785, 845

La Touche, Percy (Rose's brother): wild character, 329, 453; returns from tour abroad, 383; requests permission to marry Joan Agnew, 401–2; Joan breaks off engagement, 409, 411, 755, 845; JR criticises, 416; relations with sister, 418; engagement to Clonmell's daughter, 453; and Rose Ward, 799

La Touche, Rose: and image of dead wife, 87; JR wishes marriage with, 115; JR proposes marriage to, 200, 376, 381–3, 390–1, 429–30, 468; JR first meets, 210, 264; JR writes *Sesame and Lilies* for, 212, 313, 376, 513; mother asks JR's advice on art education for, 262; JR tutors and influences, 267–8, 301–2, 308–9, 329–30; JR's relations with, 267–8, 279, 283, 290–1, 296, 301–4, 309–13, 320–1, 333–4, 405, 513–14, 517–20, 725; Georgiana Cowper acts as JR's intermediary with, 271, 386, 389–90, 414, 427, 431, 461; character, 289–90, 312–13, 379, 396, 428, 438–9, 453, 550; JR speaks of to Margaret Bell, 289; exchanges pet names with JR, 302, 320, 390; letters to JR, 302, 310–12, 323–4, 386, 394, 405, 410, 414, 415, 459–61, 519–21, 567–8, 571, 845; travels, 302–3; and JR's visit to Ireland, 305; illnesses, 307–9, 328, 342–4, 418, 428–30, 487, 491, 529–30, 550–1, 581–3; JR's father's fondness for, 307; differences with parents, 308; piety and religious faith, 312–13, 324, 328–30, 396, 405, 407–8, 438, 452, 514–17, 519–21, 550–1, 577; gifts from JR, 313; poetry and writings, 320–1, 438, 454; JR separated from, 321, 342, 453; JR's obsession with, 321, 334–5, 349, 376, 389–91, 394, 397, 399, 402, 407, 410, 413–14, 419, 453, 458–60, 487, 526, 531, 533, 556, 582; death, 328, 488, 505, 551, 565, 577, 580–1, 585–6, 588; diary and autobiography, 328, 342, 344, 394, 876–7; relations with father, 328–9; breakdown, 342, 394; first communion, 342, 344, 394; spirituality, 343–4; appearance, 344, 381, 418, 524; medium claims to have seen ghost of, 350; attends MacDonald's lectures, 351; recovers strength, 369, 379; friendship with Joan Agnew (Severn), 379, 381–3, 386, 389–90, 395, 399–400, 550, 554; JR reunited with (1865), 379; JR's poem to, 379–80; forbidden to write to or see JR, 382, 394, 396; Howell relays stories of, 387; JR introduces to Carlyle, 388; virginal nature, 394–5; Evangelicalism, 395–6, 427; impersonal references to JR, 395; fears JR's loss of faith, 407; changeable nature, 413; sends flowers to JR in Dublin, 416; letter from JR, 430; owns and reads JR's *Queen of the Air*, 437–41, 453; and JR's beliefs, 440–1; portraits by JR, 446; JR encounters at Royal Academy (1870), 453–4, 458–9; and JR's sexuality, 453, 513, 522–3; returns *Queen of the Air* to JR, 453; plans to become governess, 454–5; *Clouds and Light*, 454; effect on JR's writing, 458–9; declares love for JR, 460; Frederic Harrison understands, 467; and JR's writing of *Fors Clavigera*, 469, 498–9, 565–6; public gossip about, 484–5; and JR's eligibility to remarry, 497; and parental authority, 513, 514–15; letters and visits to George MacDonald, 514–18, 520–4; makes resumés of JR's Oxford lectures, 514; visits London and Broadlands (1872), 518, 775; JR seeks ghost of, 519–21, 629–30; JR returns from Venice to meet (1872), 524–6, 555; abuses JR on parting, 527–8; JR claims to be insane, 531, 550; stays at Broadlands, 542; serious manner, 548; returns to England (1874), 549; concern for JR's safety, 554; JR sees as art icon, 558; revives marriage proposal, 568–9, 581; JR visits while dying, 570–1, 584; JR plans tea shop for, 571–2; visits Denmark Hill, 572; and Guild of St George, 577, 649; JR's *Proserpina* memorialises, 593; spiritualists claim to see, 608–9, 611; JR keeps memorabilia ('Rosie's box'), 615, 828, 845; JR associates with St Ursula, 625, 630, 632; JR re-reads 'star-letter', 648; JR alludes to and fantasises about during breakdowns, 658–60, 663, 668, 703–5, 707, 715, 813, 834–5; JR associates with Ilaria de Carretta, 678; alluded to in *The Bible of Amiens*, 695; JR thinks of in later life, 714; JR suggests as cause of own insanity, 717; and Whitelands May Queen, 724; JR maintains friendship by correspondence, 750; correspondence with JR burned, 755; and JR's *Præterita*, 763, 785, 788–90, 829–30, 845–6; posthumous mentions in JR's diary, 765; pet dog (Bruno), 784

La Touche, William (Rose's uncle): death, 394

Laws of Fésole, The (JR), 562, 642–4, 655, 675, 683

Leadbetter, Mary Anne, 284, 286, 371

Leamington Spa, 62, 65, 113

Lear, Edward, 59

Lecture on Architecture and Painting (JR), 194, 217

Lectures on Art (JR), 506, 614

'Lectures on Landscape' (JR), 473

'Lectures on Sculpture' (JR), 467
Leech, John, 251, 746, 763
Leeds, 12
Leeds Mercury, 398
Lees, Dora (*née* Livesey): friendship and correspondence with JR, 287, 340, 386, 425, 427, 541, 725; on Le Vengeur, 287; gives list of Winnington girls to Cook, 371; revisits Winnington, 415; and JR's view of rural poverty in France, 425; and JR's utopianism, 427, 434; visits Denmark Hill, 433; and Guild of St George, 443, 590; JR contrasts with Rose, 556; offers home to JR, 556, 840; and JR's decline, 833
Lees, Edward, 827, 840, 847
Leete, Janet, 694, 708, 721
Legros, Alfred, 726
Leicester, 12; Municipal gallery, 688
Leighton, Frederic, Baron: *Cimabue's Madonna*, 213, 229–30; JR corresponds with, 338; and classical spirit, 439; JR lectures on, 746; invited to JR's lecture on Francesca Alexander, 749; JR visits, 775, 781; plans Turner exhibition at Royal Academy, 780–1; and JR's art teaching, 798
Le Keux, John Henry, 240, 262
Leonardo da Vinci, 622
Leoni: a Legend of Italy (JR), 36
Leopold, Prince (*later* Duke of Albany): JR's relations with, 510–11, 546, 585, 587, 619, 623, 648–9, 676, 686, 692, 760; death, 768
Leslie, Charles Robert, 101, 809, 863
Leslie, Robert, 809, 811
Letters to the Clergy on the Lord's Prayer and the Church (JR and Malleson), 683, 689
Le Vengeur, Mr (mathematics master at Winnington), 287
Lewes, George Henry, 423
Lewis, John Frederick, 228–9, 235
Lewis, Matthew Gregory, 23
Leycester, Rafe, 526, 724
Liddell, Alice (Henry's daughter), 46, 478, 508
Liddell, Edith (Henry's daughter), 478, 508
Liddell, Henry George, Dean of Christ Church: tutors JR at Oxford, 47; and JR's drawing skill, 48, 445; JR describes *Modern Painters* to, 75; introduces JR to Rio's *Poetry of Christian Art*, 76; Acland writes to on bringing JR back to Oxford, 100; marriage, 112; visits JR at Denmark Hill, 112; proposes model houses for Christ Church workers, 224; restores and rebuilds at Christ Church, 246; believes JR essentially a poet, 443; and JR's appointment to Slade Professorship, 443, 449–50, 456, 506; attends JR's Oxford lectures, 456, 466; home life, 477–8 relations with JR, 478, 745; and Daguerre's photography, 479; and art education at Oxford, 508–10; conservatism, 511; nominates Richmond as JR's successor for Slade Professorship, 681–2; JR's hostile letters to, 816, 819
Liddell, Lorina (Henry's wife), 112, 477–8
Liddell, Rhoda (Henry's daughter), 478, 508
Lincoln, 12
Lincoln's Inn Fields, London, 37
Lind, Jenny, 112
Lindsay, Alexander William Crawford, 33rd Lord (*afterwards* 25th Earl of Crawford), 108, 130
Lindsay, Sir Coutts, 638
Linnell, John, 227
Linton, William James, 494, 501
Lippi, Fra Filippo, 92, 464–5, 530, 567
Litchfield, Richard, 450
Liverpool, 12, 120, 679; Ruskin Society, 873
Livesey, Dora *see* Lees, Dora
Livy, 15
Lockhart, Charlotte, 107–10, 112, 114, 121
Lockhart, James, 30, 107–8, 121
Lockhart, John Gibson, 542
Lockie (nursery governess), 719–20
Lodge, (Sir) Oliver, 801
Lombardo-Veneto, the, 122, 140
London Association for the Prevention of Pauperisation and Crime, 392
London Institution, 692, 730, 734, 765–6
London, University of, 28; *see also* King's College London
Longfellow, Henry Wadsworth, 214, 346, 422, 427, 447
Longley, Charles, Archbishop of Canterbury, 316
Loudon, John Claudius, 34, 153
Loudon's Magazine of Natural History, 28
Louis-Philippe, King of France, 122
Louise, Princess, 686
Louvre museum, the (Paris), 81–2, 96, 202, 235, 238, 257
Love's Meinie (JR), 437, 535–7, 542, 692, 708, 778, 803, 807
Lowell, James Russell, 215, 272, 298, 427, 749
Lubbock, Sir John, 759, 811
Lucastes (house), near Haywards Heath, Sussex, 596, 609–10
Lucca, 85, 88, 91, 518, 557, 564–6, 731, 733
Lucerne, 106, 200, 252, 306, 309, 323
Lucy (Hilliards' maid), 462–3
Ludlow, John, 353
Luini, Bernardino, 323, 359, 450, 465
Lupton, Thomas, 231, 240, 262
Luther, Martin: JR compared to, 227, 232
Lyell, Sir Charles, 17, 388
Lyttelton, Alfred, 653
Lytton, Edward George Earle Lytton Bulwer-, 1st Baron, 15, 38

Macaulay, Thomas Babington, Baron, 128
McClelland, Miss ('Clennie'), 767, 769, 773, 800, 815
McCracken, Thomas, 208
Macdonald, Alexander: teaches drawing at Oxford, 509, 600, 745, 797, 804; JR plays chess by correspondence with, 540; tells Richmond of JR's ban on oil painting at Oxford, 682; and JR's mental illness, 707; as JR's paid employee, 710, 745, 815; and JR's resumption

of Slade Professorship, 733; and disorder of JR's Oxford collections, 740; JR stays with, 775; and JR's controversial Oxford lectures, 778; drawing in Guild collection, 804
MacDonald, George: background and writings, 351, 455; La Touches' friendship with, 351, 455; at Broadlands, 455, 609; JR cultivates friendship with, 455; letters from Rose La Touche, 516–19; Rose visits, 517, 521–4; on Rose's confusion over JR, 519–21; writes about Rose to JR in Venice, 522; and JR's rupture with Rose, 527; JR writes to about dying Rose, 584; JR writes to on fantasy marriage with Rose, 659–60
MacDonald, Greville, 524
Macdonald, Katie, 794, 800
MacDonald, Louisa (Mrs George McD), 521, 523, 526, 593, 659
MacDonald, Maurice, 351
Macdonald, William, 101, 112, 114, 117
McEwan (Oxford undergraduate), 545
Mackail, J. W., 240
Mackenzie, Olive, 428
Mackrell, Henry, 815–16, 841
Maclise, Daniel, 228–9
Macmillan, Messrs (publishers), 458
Macugnaga, 92–3
Magee, William, Bishop of Peterborough (*later* Archbishop of York), 535–6
Maginn, William, 32
Magoon, Daniel, 214
Maison, Comte and Comtesse of (*née* Diana Domecq), 26, 251
Malham, Yorkshire, 676
Malleson, Revd F. A., 533, 683–4, 690
Mallock, William Hurrell, 545, 573, 604–5, 645, 678–9; *The New Republic*, 605–6
Manchester: JR visits, 12, 18; JR lectures in, 245, 258–9, 370, 373; Assize Courts, 356; plans water supply from Thirlmere, 657; Ruskin Society, 722–3
Manchester Daily Examiner and Times, 398
Mandeville, Sir John, 37
Manin, Daniele, 122, 139, 141
Manning, Cardinal Henry Edward: converts to Catholicism, 174; JR's friendship with, 174; influence on JR, 175; JR meets, 426, 535, 611, 718; comforts JR, ii.585, 717; and *Fors Clavigera*, 618; JR describes visions to, 715; confesses JR, 717; and JR's views on Pre-Raphaelites, 741; invited to JR's lecture on Francesca Alexander, 749; JR asks Kathleen Olander to forward secret letters to, 846
Mansfield, Charles, 353
Mantanvert, 136
Mantegna, Andrea, 477, 527
March, Charles Henry Gordon-Lennox, Earl of (*later* 6th Duke of Richmond), 44, 322
Marcolino (JR), 37
Margate, Kent, 546–7
Marie of the Giessbach, 386, 389, 402, 447, 463, 818
Mariolatry, 169
Marks, Aggie, 725
Marks, Stacy, 248–9, 648, 743, 760, 763, 767, 798
Marsh Gibbon, Oxfordshire, 548
Marshall family (of Monk Coniston), 800
Marshall, Isabel, 371, 609–10
Marshall, Mary, 350
Martigny, 202
Martin, Miss (teacher at Whitelands College), 724
Martineau, Harriet, 656
Marylebone: JR's property in, 362, 392
Masaccio, 92
Maskelyne (conjurer), 610
Maskelyne, Ada, 725
Maskelyne, Nevil *see* Story-Maskelyne, Mervyn Herbert Nevil
Matlock, Derbyshire, 17, 459, 488–91, 493, 629, 963
Matson, Edward, 29
Matterhorn, 136, 158
Maurice, Frederick Denison: JR corresponds with, 150; Christian Socialism, 152, 203; as Principal of Working Men's College, 203, 224, 262; portrait at Winnington Hall, 278; friendship with A. J. Scott, 285; religious ideas, 331, 351–2, 451; abandons Colenso, 332, 334; JR's disagreement with, 351–3, 472, 829
Max Müller, Friedrich, 437, 511–12, 534, 579
May Queen festivities, 723–4
'Mechanical Art' (JR), 370
'Mechanism. The Pleasures of Nonsense' (JR; lecture), 778
Meissonier, Louis Ernest, 226; *Napoleon in 1814*, 432, 718
Melly, George, 771
Melvill, Revd Henry, 72, 99, 101, 330, 709
Memling, Hans, 322
Memmi, Simone, 90, 567
Mendelssohn-Bartholdy, Felix, 195
'Mending the Sieve' (JR), 694, 730, 734
Mercier, Ruth, 715, 771
Meredith, George, 819
Merlingen, 849
Metaphysical Society, 426, 534–6, 543, 611
Methuen (publishers), 867
Michelangelo Buonarroti, 94, 483–4, 518, 682
Milan, 26, 92, 140, 323–4, 622
Mill, John Stuart, 297, 314, 388, 423
Millais, Sir John Everett: marriage and children with Effie, 119, 198, 417; friendship with JR, 152, 155–7; and Patmore, 152; and Pre-Raphaelite Brotherhood, 152–3, 155; appearance, 155; at Denmark Hill, 155, 195–6; career, 155–6; artistic principles, 156–7; declines JR's invitation to Switzerland, 156–7; paints and draws Effie, 179–80, 184–7, 190; success and popularity, 179–80; *The Order of Release*, 179–81, 229; on Scottish tour with JR and Effie, 181–90; at Glenfinlas, 184–6; portrait of JR, 184–6, 188, 194, 198, 744; growing intimacy with

Effie, 187, 189–90, 192–6; designs architectural ornaments, 190, 217–18; relations with Gambart, 190; behaviour, 192–4; elected ARA, 195; writes to Mrs Gray, 196; JR's relations with, 207–8; declines to contribute to Oxford Museum, 222; JR praises, 229–30, 273, 679; and Leighton, 229–30; *Christ in the House of his Parents*, 229; *The Rescue*, 229; *Sir Isumbras at the Ford*, 244; *Apple Blossoms*, 273; *The Vale of Rest*, 273–4; illustrates Trollope, 294; exhibits at Grosvenor Gallery, 638; holiday at Gelnfinlas with JR, 675; *The Blind Girl*, 677; and Pre-Raphaelitism, 740–1

Millais, William, 181–2, 187, 190–1

Milman, Henry Hart, Dean of St Paul's, 128, 159, 277; *History of Latin Christianity*, 830

Milner, Alfred (*later* Viscount), 573, 576–7, 838

Milnes, Richard Monckton *see* Houghton, 1st Baron

Milton, John, 42, 150, 256, 665

Mineralogical Society, 591, 768

Minischalchi, Count and Countess, 143

Minotaur (mythological figure), 531

'Mirror, The' (JR), 37

Mitford, Mary Russell, 73, 112, 122, 210

Mocenigo, Countess, 143

'Modern Manufacture and Design' (JR; lecture), 259

Modern Painters (JR): origins, 40, 68, 235, 507; and JR's liberal education, 42; on superiority of Christian art, 47; and JR's Newdigate poem, 51; Dutch art in, 64, 72; exalts Protestantism, 64; tone, 67, 96, 229, 251; writing, 67, 70–1, 100, 102, 140, 199, 202, 214, 234, 241; spirituality, 68, 168, 200, 242; and Alps, 69–70, 81, 136, 200; published anonymously, 69, 75, 107; publication and reception, 73–9, 101, 131, 159, 162, 292; title, 73; prefaces, 75, 124, 257; sequence of volumes, 75–6, 90–1, 100, 102–3, 106, 110, 123, 131; on Turner's *Slave Ship*, 77–9; Turner disapproves of strictures in, 82; and JR's copying of Pisa frescoes, 90–1; and JR's reading, 99–100; written for JR's father, 99, 167, 234, 255, 257, 272, 277, 279; on Turner, 101–2, 164–5, 232, 339; and Lindsay's *Sketches*, 108; and JR's feeling for nature, 116, 156; on destruction of old buildings, 123; and Arundel Society, 130; on aesthetic emotion, 133, 202; Holman Hunt reads and discusses with JR, 152, 447; and Rossetti, 209; on Crimean War, 214; Acland cites on education, 217; reprints *Academy Notes* as addenda to 2nd ed. of vol. II, 227; and Turner's *Harbours of England*, 231–2; on condition of Turner drawings at National Gallery, 248; on history of Switzerland, 252; Allen illustrates 5th vol., 262; completion, 272; notes for, 283; and definition of 'vulgarity', 288; obscurity of final section, 292, 296, 306, 316, 354; debt to Carlyle, 315; and Greek culture, 336, 439; prose style, 338, 369, 594; on Gotthelf, 385; on Longfellow, 422; on Daguerrotypes, 479; on sculpture of Ilaria de Carretto, 564–5; on geology, 591; JR's 'Readings' from, 647; new edition of vol. II (1882), 736; earnings from, 841; JR writes epilogue for new edition, 846; Susie Beever's selections from, 863; pirated US editions, 868–9

Monk, Henry Wentworth, 330–1

Mont Blanc, 69, 98–9, 199, 728–9

Mont St Michel, 127

Mont Velan, 144

Montefiore, Leonard, 545, 573–6, 594–5

Monthly Packet (Charlotte M. Yonge's magazine), 601

Montzig (Austrian officer), 144

Monuments of the Cavalli Family in the Church of Santa Anastasia, Verona (JR), 130

Moody, William Vaughan, 725

Moore, Albert, 680

Moore, Charles Herbert, 617–18, 623–5, 805

Moore, Revd Daniel, 101, 157

Moore, George, 819

Moore, William Morris, 162

Morley, John (*later* Viscount), 838–9

Morley's Hotel, Trafalgar Square, London, 826–7, 837, 841

Mornex, Switzerland: JR rents lodgings in, 325–7, 330, 332, 334, 336, 354, 472; JR bids to buy land in, 343, 345; JR revisits with Collingwood, 728

Morning Post (newspaper), 306

Mornings in Florence (JR), 562, 564, 574, 596

Morris & Co., 555

Morris, William: praises *Modern Painters*, 232; JR visits, 235; and George Allen, 240; works on Oxford Union, 246; Norton meets, 423; JR meets, 450; relations with JR, 455–6, 718, 747–8; JR lacks interest in, 558; visits JR in Oxford, 585; friendship with Ellis, 595; manufactures May Queen crosses, 724; elected honorary member of Exeter College, Oxford, 746; Cockerell and, 816–17; JR's view of, 817

Moses, 607, 646

Mount-Temple, Georgiana, Lady (*née* Tollemache; *then* Cowper): JR meets in Rome, 59, 270; JR's fondness for, 268, 270, 349; marriage, 271, 321; JR stays with, 301, 546, 596; and JR's passion for Rose, 321, 389–90, 405, 413; interest in spiritualism, 349–50, 607–8; as intermediary for JR with Rose La Touche, 386, 390–1, 414, 417, 419, 427, 431, 461, 468, 487, 517, 530, 533; and Rose La Touche's impersonal references to JR, 395; interest in utopianism, 427; and Maria La Touche's request to Joan Agnew not to write to Rose, 429–30; JR tells of references to Rose in *Queen of the Air*, 438; MacDonald stays with, 455; and Rose's return to JR, 461; at Denmark Hill, 466; JR entertains at Abingdon, 474; nurses JR at Matlock, 493,

496; Rose visits at Broadlands, 518, 550; and JR's reunion with Rose at Broadlands and Toft, 525–6 visits Brantwood, 542; letter from JR in Assisi, 560; and Rose La Touche's late hopes of marriage to JR, 568; Norton on, 569; and JR's dream of cottage for life with Rose, 571; letter from JR in Greta Bridge, 616; letters from JR during Brantwood breakdown, 659–60; JR appeals to to come to Brantwood, 714–15; JR declines to revisit, 840

Mount-Temple, William Cowper-Temple, 1st Baron (*earlier* Cowper): John Simon works with, 219; background, name and titles, 271; marriage, 271; JR stays with, 301, 546, 596; friendship with JR, 349; interest in spiritualism, 349–50; and Rose La Touche's references to JR, 395; interest in utopianism, 427; MacDonald stays with, 455; at Denmark Hill, 466; and JR's attachment to Rose La Touche, 468; JR entertains at Abingdon, 474; JR writes to from Matlock, 490; and JR's divorce and eligibility to remarry, 496–8, 522; as trustee of St George's Fund, 496; visits JR at Matlock, 496; visits Brantwood, 542; JR challenges lack of faith in, 560; and Guild of St George, 590; offers land on Broadlands estate to JR, 597; resigns trusteeship of Guild of St George, 637; in JR's breakdown dream, 659; as JR's executor, 751

Moxon, Edward, 73

Müller, Friedrich Max *see* Max Müller, Friedrich

Mulready, William, 227

Munera Pulveris (JR): dedicated to Carlyle, 247; and JR's articles for *Cornhill*, 297; socio-political content, 314, 317, 339, 355; publication and printing, 316, 501; foreshadows *Fors Clavigera*, 318; part-written at Mornex, 336; Burne-Jones invited to illustrate, 347; on railways, 364; style, 366; appendix, 500

Munich, 277

Munro, Alexander, 607–8

Munro, Hugh (of Novar), 646, 673, 842

Munro, Miss (spiritualist), 607

Murano, 163

Murchison, Sir Roderick, 113

Murray, John, 29, 72, 95, 108, 141, 237

Murray, John Fairfax, 450, 555, 561, 675, 710, 804

Murray, Lindley, 15

Museum or Picture Gallery, A: its Function and its Formation (JR; letters), 688

Museum of St George *see* Sheffield: St George's Museum

'My First Editor' (JR), 651–2

Myers, Revd Frederick, 611–12

Myers, Frederick William Henry, 611–13, 649

'Mystery of Life and its Arts, The' (JR; lecture), 374, 411, 415

Mystery of Life and its Arts, The (JR; 1865–9), 439

mythology, 289, 354, 356–7, 411, 435, 437–40, 747

Naas, Co. Kildare, 428, 514

Naesmith, Lady, 320, 323

Naples, 58

Napoleon I (Bonaparte), Emperor of France, 26

Napoleonic Wars, 6, 24, 80, 122

Nasmyth, Alexander, 1

National Association for the Promotion of Social Science, 419

National Covenant of Scottish Presbyterians, 19

National Gallery, London, 107, 162–3, 210, 279, 404, 675–6, 699; Cook compiles guide to, 839

'Nature and Authority of Miracles, The' (JR; lecture), 535

'Nature Untenanted' (JR), 37

Nazarenes (school of painters), 72, 237, 277

Nebuchadnezzar, 209

Nesfield, William, 65

Neuchâtel, 385, 463, 667

Nevinson, Henry Woodd, 851–3

Nevinson, Margaret, 852

Newark, 12

Newdigate prize, 41, 50–1, 53

Newman, Cardinal John Henry, 50, 216

Newman, Henry Roderick, 731, 804–5

Newton, Charles: JR's friendship with, 48–9, 71, 101; marriage to Mary, 60, 412, 493; JR discusses university reading with, 100; entertains Effie, 112; and Arundel Society, 130; appointed vice-consul at Mitylene, 157; travels in Switzerland with JR, 157–8; Effie confides in, 170; works as Keeper at British Museum, 358, 450, 466; dines with JR, 411; classical knowledge, 466; visits JR at Matlock, 493

Newton, Mary (*née* Severn), 60, 358, 412, 493

Nineteenth Century (magazine), 647, 649, 676, 677–8, 688

Norfolk Street, London, 264, 266–7, 310, 329

Normandy, 125

Norris, James, 476

North American Review, 423

North, Christopher (pseud., i. e. John Wilson), 23

Northampton, Charles Douglas-Compton, 4th Marquess of, 113

Northern Clerical Society, 683–4

Norton, Andrews, 215

Norton, Charles Eliot: JR gives diary to, 68; background, 215; JR first meets, 215; JR's friendship with on continent, 233–4; and JR's *Political Economy of Art*, 246; JR writes to on Stillman, 298; and JR's withdrawn state, 313; JR recommends Swinburne to, 378; discussions with JR, 422–3; JR meets in Paris, 422; and JR's writing on fairy stories, 422; observations and writings on England, 423; writes introductions to Brantwood Edition of JR's work, 423; as JR's literary executor, 424, 752–3; and American culture, 427; JR lends pictures to, 433; attempts to persuade JR to make will, 434–5; and printing of JR's *Queen of the Air*, 434–6, 443;

describes JR, 436; and JR's plans for river management, 447; and JR's Oxford lectures, 456, 458, 467; JR's correspondence and relations with, 465, 750–1; letters from JR in Abingdon, 474; Burne-Jones writes to, 484, 734; JR writes to on purchase of Brantwood, 499; concern for JR's mental state, 532–3; pleads for abandonment of *Fors Clavigera*, 532–3; JR's *Val d'Arno* proofs sent to, 544; *Historical Studies of Church Building in the Middle Ages*, 544; JR sends self-portraits to, 557, 562–3; and Rose La Touche's late hopes of marriage to JR, 568–9; letter from JR on Rose's final illness, 583; and JR's proposed botany book, 592; sends visitors to JR at Brantwood, 617–18; Leslie Stephen writes to, 618; supports new edition of *Stones of Venice*, 619, 623; possible allusion to in 'Brantwood Diary', 664; and JR's mental breakdowns, 715, 799, 801, 812–13, 850; dislikes and attacks Froude, 716–17, 814, 837; with JR on Alpine travels, 730; burns JR papers, 752–5; suggests JR write *Præterita*, 757; visits JR at Brantwood, 771; proposes writing part of *Præterita*, 837, 855; Joan Severn reports JR's writing of *Præterita* to, 854; JR's three letters to on understanding Carlyle, 855–9; Joan Severn writes to in JR's later years, 863–4, 867; writes introduction to Huntington's *Comments*, 870

Norwich, 12
Norwood, 306, 409, 450, 551
Notes by Mr Ruskin on his Drawings by the late J. M. W. Turner, RA (JR; catalogue), 655–7, 673–4
Notes by Mr Ruskin on Samuel Prout and William Hunt (JR; catalogue), 687
Notes on the Construction of Sheepfolds (JR), 149–50, 153, 167, 169, 256, 315, 580
Notes on the General Principles of Employment for the Destitute and Criminal Classes (JR), 425–6, 435
Notes on the Turner Gallery at Marlborough House (JR), 243–4, 251, 339
'Notes Upon Gipsy Character' (JR), 790
Notre Dame de Paris, 127
Noyes, Sibyl Evelyn Herbert, 371
Nuremberg, 277

Oddie, J. W., 476
'Of the Division of Arts' (JR; lecture), 662
'Of King's Treasuries' (JR; lecture), 370, 373–4, 602
'Of Queens Gardens' (JR; lecture), 370, 374–6, 380
Olander, Edmund, 828, 848
Olander, Mrs Edmund, 840, 848
Olander, Kathleen, 827–8, 830, 835, 839–40, 844, 846–7, 848, 865
Old Water-Colour Society *see* Society of Painters in Water-colour
Oldfield, Edmund, 29, 79, 129, 340, 596
Oldham, Constance, 340, 386, 419, 433–4, 596, 609, 612, 725
Oldham, Sir Henry, 340
Oldham, Dr James, 596, 609–10, 715
Oliphant, Laurence, 427, 450
Oliver, Daniel, 534, 629–30
'On the Causes of the Colour of the Rhine' (JR), 28, 34
'On the Flamboyant Architecture of the Valley of the Somme' (JR; lecture), 420, 431–2, 435
'On the Forms of the Stratified Alps of Savoy' (JR; lecture), 336
'On the Greek Myths of Storm' (JR; lecture), 435
'On the Nature of Gothic' (JR), 169, 203
On the Old Road (*A Museum or Picture Gallery*; JR letters), 688
On the Opening of the Crystal Palace, The (JR), 202, 217–18
'On the Present State of Modern Art' (JR; lecture), 402, 404
'On the Relation of Natural Science to Art' (JR; lectures), 507
Orcagna, Andrea, 90, 130, 567
Oriel College, Oxford, 42
O'Shea, James, 222, 226
Otani, Beatrice degli, 732
Otterburn, Northumberland, 340
Our Fathers Have Told Us (JR; projected), 693, 714
Owen, Alice, 601–2, 725
Owen, Sir Richard, 301, 313, 358
Oxford Art School, 508–9
Oxford Book of English Verse (ed. Sir Arthur Quiller-Couch), 712
Oxford (City): JR visits, 18; JR's parents stay in, 44–6; JR and Effie visit, 122; cholera in, 219; public health in, 547–8
Oxford Movement, 50, 149, 169, 216, 279
Oxford Museum of Natural History, 104, 210, 216–18, 221, 233, 246
Oxford Museum, The (JR and Acland), 220, 225–6
Oxford University: JR matriculates at and attends, 40, 42–9, 54–5, 62, 69, 76; JR attends British Association meeting in (1847), 112–13; JR on education at, 161; natural science studies resisted, 216–17; Museum, 217–18, 220, 224, 233, 279; Union, 222, 224, 246; JR gives Turner collection to, 300, 433, 508, 587, 815; JR declines Professorship of Poetry, 401, 405; Galleries, 405, 508; appoints JR first Slade Professor of History of Art, 443, 447–50, 456, 506–8; JR's status and life in, 476–8, 506–12, 531, 545, 576, 578, 598–600, 647, 744–5, 774–5; art education at, 508–9, 543, 647, 733, 740, 745–6, 774, 815, 870–1; Ruskin art collections and catalogues, 508, 587; social life, 511; JR 'class' and disciples in, 542–5, 573, 604–5; aestheticism at, 575, 601, 739; JR endows Master of Drawing post, 587; Turner drawings sent from National Gallery to, 675–6; JR resigns Slade Professorship, 681; Richmond succeeds Ruskin at, 681–2; JR resumes Slade Professorship, 728, 733, 737–8; new liberalism at, 738; and JR's will, 773–4;

JR finally leaves (1884), 779, 791–2; JR complains of neglect of Turner works at, 815–16; returns art works to JR, 816; JR's diminished reputation in, 870
Oxford University Gazette, 470, 777, 779

Padua, 96, 146
Paget, Sir James, 759
Palgrave, Sir Francis, 95, 449
Pall Mall Gazette, 363, 367, 530, 531, 661, 724–5, 745, 747–8, 766, 775–6, 778, 794, 811, 838
Palmer, Samuel, 60, 101, 209
Palmerston, Henry John Temple, 3rd Viscount, 160, 163, 242, 271, 301
Panizzi, Sir Anthony, 129
'Papal Aggression', 149
Paris: JR visits, 25, 81, 96, 251, 306, 384–5, 422, 554, 693, 844–5; JR visits with Effie (1848), 127; Effie visits Adèle in, 146; JR never visits *Salons* in, 238; 1871 Revolution and Siege, 488, 518; Joan Severn meets JR in (1888), 849–50; *see also* Louvre museum
Paris International Exhibition, 693
Park Street, London, 128, 147, 151–2, 155, 157, 170
Parker, Son & Brown (publishers), 316–17
Parry, John Humffreys, 679
Parry, Sir Thomas Gambier, 159
Parsons, Dr George, 669–70, 672, 701, 706, 783, 812, 826, 865, 873
Pasolini, Count and Countess, 848
Pater, Walter: at Oxford, 575–6, 601, 605; *Studies in the History of the Renaissance*, 575
Paterson, Helen *see* Allingham, Helen
'Patience' (JR; lecture), 778
Patmore, Coventry, 22, 152–3, 176, 210–13, 423, 585, 618, 653, 750
Patmore, Emily, 152, 211
Pattison, Emilia Francis *see* Dilke, Lady
Pattison, Mark: visits Denmark Hill, 450; friendship with JR, 535, 600–1; reviews JR's *Arrows of the Chace*, 697–8
Paulizza, Charles, 145–6, 158, 160
Paxton, Sir Joseph, 157
Peacock, Thomas Love, 605
Pebardy, Thomas, 826
Peel, Sir Robert, 110
Pembroke College, Oxford, 219
Peppering (house), near Arundel, Sussex, 610
Perth (Scotland), 109, 114, 117, 138, 180–1
Perugia, 557, 563–4
Perugino, 204, 802
Petronius: *Satyricon*, 605
photography, 144, 478–80
Piedmont, 122, 136
Pignatel, Lucy and Emily, 284, 287
Pisa, 57, 88–91, 105, 123–4, 260, 443, 518, 554, 730–1, 808
Pisano, Giovanni, 733
Pius IX, Pope, 149
Plato, 43, 315, 337, 346, 355, 410, 626–8, 675, 685; *Republic*, 336, 605; *Laws*, 545, 603, 629
'Pleasures of England, The' (JR; lectures), 603, 774–7
Poems of John Ruskin, The (ed. Allen and Collingwood), 868
Poetry of Architecture, The (JR), 34, 43, 52–3, 88, 104, 325
Political Economy of Art, The (JR), 224, 246, 258
Pontgibaud, 57
Pope, Alexander, 376, 709
Port Meadow, 219
Ports of England, The (JR), 231
positivism, 419, 601; *see also* Comte, Auguste
Poussin, Nicholas, 38
Præterita (JR): on JR's family and forebears, 1–2; on JR's boyhood in London, 8, 13, 15, 31; on JR's early reading, 14; on Howels's preaching, 20; on family churchgoing, 22; on Byron and Margaret Ruskin, 23; on JR's schooling, 28; on Croly, 32; on Adèle Domecq, 37, 51; on Oxford life, 42, 47, 60; and JR's 1885 attack of madness, 60; on Venice, 60, 62; on Turner, 64, 74, 809; on drawing from nature, 67–8; on Couttet, 80; on Lucca, 85; on Shakespeare, 93; on Anna Jameson, 96; on purpose of *Modern Painters*, 100; on Charlotte Lockhart, 108–9; allusion to William Macdonald's mother, 112; on agricultural conditions in Alps, 136; on Carlyle's devotion to JR's parents, 176; reproduces drawing of jib of Dover-Calais packet, 199; on JR's first meeting with Norton, 215; on Butterworth, 239; on Liddell's ignoring JR when restoring Christ Church buildings, 246; and JR's religious thoughts, 254, 332; describes JR's first meeting with Rose and La Touche family, 264, 266; on Georgiana Tollemache/Cowper ('Egeria'), 270, 349; writing, 283, 730, 736, 796, 801, 813, 815–17, 820, 828–9, 836, 845, 854–5; on Alps, 296, 319, 366, 785; on *Unto This Last*, 296; quotes letter from Rose La Touche, 302; final chapters, 303, 315; and Huret family, 304; JR plans, 324, 422, 709, 757, 770, 784–5, 789–90, 818; scorns Maurice, 334; on Otterburn, 340; on JR's mother in widowhood, 347; on Joan Agnew (Severn), 348–62, 846, 854–5, 859; on F. D. Maurice, 352, 472; Rose La Touche in, 380, 572, 829–30, 845–6; projected chapter on 1866 trip to Venice, 384; JR refers to little pigs in, 421; Norton instigates, 422; on Norton, 423–4; on JR's character, 436; on Verona, 442; and JR's revisiting old sites, 463; on fireflies, 465; on Drewitt, 475, 610, 785; on Liddell girls, 478; on photography, 479; on JR's politics, 481; on Coniston, 493; and JR's geological excursions at Matlock, 493; beginning, 498, 762–3; on Wandle river, 503; on Alpine hotel, 567; on Milan, 622; on Carthusians, 659; on Joan Severn's dancing, 665; and death of Pauline Trevelyan, 668, 788; and JR's Turner exhibition catalogue,

675; JR reads to Lilias Trotter, 726; and Giulietta in *Proserpina*, 757; reminiscent style, 758; publication begins, 762; on JR's pet dogs, 784–5; character and composition of, 785–792, 795, 807–8; describes Guild artists, 803; and JR's decline, 810–11; readership, 833; final writing, 859–60
Pre-Raphaelitism: JR introduced to, 22; fidelity to nature, 67, 114, 156, 273; Brotherhood admire Patmore, 152–3; JR's association with, 152–7, 244, 246; JR's letters to *Times* on, 153, 155–7, 226–7; JR believes Turnerian, 155–7, 186; criticised, 162; Effie's involvement with, 178–82; and JR's Scottish tour, 182; interests and aesthetic, 183; Acland and, 189, 216; Brotherhood dissolved, 193; JR lectures on, 194; friendships and camaraderies in, 207–8; Rossetti and, 208–10; success, 209, 251; Stillman appreciates, 214; Lizzie Siddall and, 220–1; and Oxford Museum, 222, 224; social power, 224, 226; in JR's *Academy Notes*, 227–8; JR's view of, 229, 251, 740–1; Fitzroy Square exhibition (1857), 244; Laing praises, 279; JR's father's suspicion of, 322; influences JR's remarks to Royal Academy, 337; and ancient Egyptian art, 360; Carlyles unmoved by, 375; poetry, 377–8; and chivalry, 402; financial position, 433; Frederick Ellis and, 595; JR writes on, 677–8; beginnings at Oxford, 746; omitted from *Præterita*, 789
Pre-Raphaelitism (JR), 156, 158, 162, 256, 760
Prescott's bank, London, 836
Price, Miss (Rose La Touche's aunt), 454, 518–19, 521, 610, 615
Price, Rose Lambert, 262
Pringle, Thomas, 30, 32–3, 790
Prinseps, Mr & Mrs H., 235, 275
Pritchard, John & Mrs (*née* Gordon), 157
Proserpina (JR): genesis, 385; Rose's flowers in, 416; on moss, 426; Collingwood on, 437; writing, 455, 537, 562, 591–4, 675, 683, 684, 708, 756; as memorial to Rose, 593; Burgess's illustrations in, 803; advertises Quaritch's books, 807; JR abandons, 813
Protestantism, 83–4, 149–50, 161, 175, 305, 777
'Protestantism. The Pleasures of Truth' (JR; lecture), 777
Proust, Marcel: translates JR's *Bible of Amiens*, 694
Prout, Samuel: *Sketches in Flanders and Germany*, 24–5; view of Rhine, 34; JR writes on, 35, 64, 74; JR imitates, 49; admires Turner's *Slave Ship*, 77; Effie meets, 121; JR associates with Rouen, 125; Effie and JR examine sketches, 147; joint exhibition with William Hunt (1879), 322–8
Psalms, 617
Pugin, Augustus Welby Northmore, 149
Punch (magazine), 576, 659, 747
'Puppet Show, The: or Amusing Characters for Children' (JR), 798
Pusey, Edward Bouverie, 221, 216
Pyne, James Baker, 55
Python (Greek mythology), 289, 411

Quaritch, Bernard (bookseller), 806–7, 820, 830, 836, 841
Quarles, Francis, 22
Quarterly Review, 108, 113, 148, 230, 244
Queen of the Air, The (JR), 411, 434–441, 443, 450, 452–3, 455, 498, 507, 592, 662, 665–6, 729, 737, 755
Queen Anne Street, London, 101, 121, 163–5, 232, 235, 248
Queen's Hotel, Norwood, 306
Quercia, Jacopo della, 67, 87–8, 564–5, 678
Quiller-Couch, Sir Arthur, 712, 739

Radetzky, Field Marshal Josef, Count of Radetz, 140, 146, 159–60, 171–2
railways: JR writes on, 364–5; in Lake District, 617
'Railways and the State' (JR; papers), 364
Randal, Frank, 710–11, 805, 819
'Range of Intellectual Conception Proportioned to the Rank of Animated Life, The' (JR; paper), 474, 535
Raphael Sanzio, 57, 154–5, 237
Raven, Kate, 821
Rawnsley, Revd Hardwicke D., 573–4, 643, 684; *Ruskin and the English Lakes*, 502
Ray, Martha, 715–16
'Readings in *Modern Painters*' (JR; lectures), 647
Reay, Donald James Mackay, 1st Baron, 758
'Recent English Art' (JR; lectures), 740–2, 744, 746
'Recent Progress of Design as Applied to Manufacture, The' (JR; lecture), 233
Red Lion Square, London, 204–5, 235, 241
Rede Lecture: JR delivers, 404–5
References to the Series of Paintings and Sketches . . . of Illustration of the Relations of Flamboyant Architecture to Contemporary and Subsequent Art (JR), 432
Reform Bill (1832), 150, 162
Reform Bill (1867), 389, 397–8
'Reform' (JR; address), 336
'Relation between Michael Angelo and Tintoret, The' (JR; lecture), 464, 483, 486–7, 506, 531, 559, 666
'Relation of National Ethics to National Art, The' (JR; Rede Lecture), 404
'Relation of Wise Art to Wise Science, The' (JR; lecture), 507
'Relations of Outline between Rock and Perpetual Snow in the Alps, The' (JR; lecture), 550
'Remarks on the Convergence of Perpendiculars' (JR), 286
'Remembrance' (JR), 37
republicanism: JR's dislike of, 122, 124, 140
Revelation, Book of, 124, 168, 200
revolutions of 1848, 116, 121–2, 124–5, 136–7, 140

Revue des Jeux des Arts et du Sport, La, 693
Reynolds, Sir Joshua, 578, 597, 598, 607, 614
Rhadamanthus, 315
Rheims, 233
Rheinfelden, 251
Ricardo, David, 297
Richardson family, 14–15, 96, 98, 348, 387, 466
Richardson, Bridget, 784
Richardson, Charles, 29
Richardson, George, 258, 413, 450, 528
Richardson, Mary (*later* Bolding): lives with Ruskins, 17–18; collaborates with JR on journal of Lakes tour, 18–19; liberal upbringing, 21; drawing lessons, 24; on 1833 tour of Switzerland and Italy, 25; proficiency in French, 27; and JR's infatuation with Adèle, 36; in Oxford, 44; diary on Ruskins in Naples, 58–9; and JR's writing of *Modern Painters*, 71; marriage to Bolding, 112; and JR's knowledge of women, 119
Richardson, Patrick and Jessie, 2, 6, 17, 62
Richardson, Samuel, 194–5
Richardson, W. G., 497
Richardson, William, 206, 450, 659, 793
Richmond family, 387, 466, 580
Richmond, George: JR meets, 60; friendship with JR, 64; JR discusses art with, 72; portrait of JR, 72; and JR's writing of *Modern Painters*, 74, 273–4; JR writes of Alps to, 81; attempts to influence JR, 82; Turner dines with at Denmark Hill, 101; JR writes to on interest in architecture, 106; JR enquires about Lindsay's *Sketches*, 108; JR entertains at Park Street, 128; gives Carlyle's *Past and Present* to JR, 150; portrait of Effie, 179; and JR's purchase of Blake works, 209; JR commends portrait of Inglis by, 228; drawings of JR, 298–9; dines with JR, 301; friendship with Arthur Severn, 412; JR writes to on convalescence, 674; JR's meetings with, 676; death of wife, 701
Richmond, Julia, 701
Richmond, Thomas, 128, 411
Richmond, (Sir) William Blake ('Willie'): on JR's appearance, 72; praises Leighton's *Cimabue*, 229; exhibits at Royal Academy, 338; succeeds JR as Slade Professor, 681–2, 733; resigns Slade chair, 737, 745; introduces new curriculum at Oxford, 745; attends JR's 'drawing-room lecture', 749
Richter, Ludwig, 661, 742
Riffenberg, 80
Riley (New York publisher), 868
Riley, William Harrison, 636
Rio, Alexis Francis: *De La Poésie Chrétienne*, 76, 93
Ritchie, Anne Isabella, Lady (*née* Thackeray), 618, 819
Ritchie, Henry, 330
Riviera, French, 57
Roberts, David, 34, 36, 121, 159, 230
Roberts, Miss R. S., 451–2
Robinson, J. C.: *Critical Account of the Drawings by Michael Angelo and Raffaello in the University Galleries, Oxford*, 483
Robson, Edward, 733
Robson, E. R., 771
Robson, George, 763
Rochdale, 12, 259
Rock Honeycomb (version of Psalter), 617
Rogers, Samuel: *Italy*, 24–6, 30, 38, 75, 91; JR visits, 30; JR meets in Rome, 60; promotes JR's *Modern Painters*, 73; JR socialises with, 75, 151, 210; Effie and JR visit, 121; on council of Arundel Society, 130; resigns executorship of Turner bequest, 165; criticises JR for reading E. B. Browning, 176; Tennyson borrows *Modern Painters* from, 213
Rolleston, George, 598
Roman Catholicism, 19, 50, 149–50, 168–9, 174–5, 298, 611, 618, 777, 829–31
Roman de la Rose: JR translates, 542
Rome, 58, 518, 555, 557–8
Rooke, Thomas Matthews, 771, 805, 815
Rossetti, Christina, 377
Rossetti, Dante Gabriel: buys Patmore's first poems, 152; friendship with JR, 152, 208–10, 236, 291, 338; and Working Men's College, 205, 236, 240; early lack of success, 208–10; and Pre-Raphaelitism, 208–10, 273, 740–1; reads Browning with JR, 213; JR introduces Norton to, 215; and design of Oxford Museum, 218, 221–2; in Oxford with Lizzie Siddall, 220–1; and decoration of Oxford Union, 224; JR describes as genius, 224; on Leighton's *Cimabue*, 229; recommends Royal Academy pictures to JR, 230; and JR's visit to Morris and Burne-Jones, 235; and Watts, 275; protects Burne-Jones, 276; drawings at Winnington, 286; financial help from JR, 292, 322; marries Lizzie Siddall, 292; 'Jenny' (poem), 294; JR offers to share house with, 325; admires style of JR's *Modern Painters*, 338; portrait of JR, 338; praises JR's testimony to Royal Academy, 338; JR commissions decorations from, 345; 'Burden of Nineveh' (poem), 360; and knowledge of poetry and literature, 377; friendship with Howell, 378; paintings at Winnington, 419; Norton meets, 423; employs Fairfax Murray, 555; published by Ellis, 595; *Ecce Ancilla Domini* (painting), 677; death, 742; Grosvenor Gallery memorial exhibition of, 780
Rossetti, William Michael: buys Patmore poems, 152; writes on art, 154; writes for *Crayon* magazine, 215; relays stories of JR and Rose La Touche, 387; Norton meets, 423; writes on Dante, 534; testifies for Whistler at libel trial, 680
Rouen, 69, 123, 125–7
Rousseau, Jean-Jacques, 333, 417
Rowbotham, John, 19
Royal Academy, London: Turner exhibits at, 25, 38–9, 69, 74, 226; excludes water-colour

artists, 34; association with National Gallery, 107; Effie at, 121; Eastlake's presidency of, 148; Pre-Raphaelites exhibit at, 153, 156–7, 227; Turner leaves money for professorship at, 164; private views, 179; Millais elected Associate of, 195; JR attends with father, 198; Rossetti and, 209; and JR's *Academy Notes*, 226–7, 230; JR's difficulties with, 279; JR gives view of to Commission (1863), 337–8; JR encounters Rose at, 454–5, 478–9; JR visits during Rose's final illness, 585; Leighton plans Turner exhibition at, 780
Royal Artillery Institution, Woolwich, 456
Royal Institution, London: JR lectures at, 276, 300, 336, 404, 420, 431–2, 444, 448, 580, 584, 591
Royal Literary Fund, 348
Royal Military Academy, Woolwich, 358, 370, 456, 615, 652
Royal Scottish Academy, Edinburgh, 184
Rugby school, 341
Rugg, Revd Mr (of English colony, Rome), 59
Runciman, Charles, 24, 34
Rusch, Mr (mineral polisher), 710
Ruskin Birthday Book, The: a Selection . . . from the Works of John Ruskin, 759
Ruskin, Catherine (*née* Tweddale; JR's grandmother), 1–2, 4, 8, 19
Ruskin, Euphemia ('Effie') *see* Gray, Euphemia
Ruskin, Jessie (JR's aunt), 1–2
Ruskin, John (1819–1900)
HEALTH: pleurisy, 28; first breakdown, 54–5; 1885 attack of madness, 60; illness, 60; Leamington rest-cure, 62; preoccupation with health, 91, 112–13, 116–17, 166, 170, 320, 324; depressions and introspection, 112–15, 298–9, 311, 313–14, 319, 345–6, 413; feverish attack (1856), 235; breaks down during Royal Institution lecture, 300, 315; exhaustion, 303; attacks of madness, 312, 366, 394, 399; breakdown in Matlock (1871), 459, 487–91, 493, 629, 863; mental breakdown (1878), 532; loses mind in Venice (1876), 625–33; breakdown and convalescence at Brantwood (1878), 656–76, 690–1; mental deterioration and second breakdown (1880–1), 699, 701–7, 709, 715–16, 755–6; suffers rupture and groin strain, 760, 764, 825–6; breakdowns (1885–6), 781, 794–5, 799–801, 809, 812–13; mental disorder in Folkestone, 834–6; mental collapse and illness in Venice (1888), 848; disabled last years, 853–4, 864–7, 871–2; bouts of dumbness, 864, 872
PERSONAL LIFE: ancestry, 1–8; birth, 8; early memories, 8, 10; upbringing, 12–16, 22–3; importance of Bible to, 13–14, 84, 331; toys, 13; reading and books, 14–16, 22–4, 52, 76, 233, 326–7, 346, 539–40, 624, 628, 771; at Herne Hill, 15, 173; early education, 15–16, 19–22; interest in geology, 16–17, 33–4, 49–50, 102, 112, 302, 335, 493, 591, 644–5, 735–6; religious background, 19–22, 50; baptism, 20; Sunday activities, 22; love of theatre, 23; theatre-going, 23, 686–7, 692; early drawing lessons, 24, 34; schooling, 28–9; diaries, 33, 57, 68–9, 82, 96, 123, 133–4, 233–4, 279, 283, 324, 387, 405, 411, 420, 454, 466, 525, 543, 545, 563, 585, 629, 632, 699, 707, 709, 715, 753, 770–1, 786, 807, 829, 877; attends King's College London, 37–8, 42; university studies, 40–56; appearance and manner, 41, 72, 151, 298–9, 338, 341, 451, 461, 695–6, 708, 749, 750–1, 871; classical education, 42–3, 46, 336; parents stay in Oxford, 44–5; drawing at Oxford, 49; wins Newdigate prize, 50–1, 53; return to Oxford, 62, 69, 76; religious vocation, 63; Oxford degree, 69; in Denmark Hill, 70–1, 298; visits British Museum, 76, 107, 301–2, 358–9, 527, 708, 775; oil painting, 79, 445–6; haymaking, 92; family letters, 96, 98; overwork, 96; spirituality, 99, 611; reputation and social life, 107, 110, 121, 128, 178–81; and Effie at Denmark Hill, 110–12; courtship and engagement, 112–16; return to Leamington Spa, 113–14; marriage, 117; marriage not consummated, 117–20, 178, 192, 198, 488; social life with Effie, 121; marriage relations, 122, 195–7; in Park Street, 128–9; and friction between family and in-laws, 137–8; and Effie's 'incipient insanity', 138; interest in ghost story, 140; marriage ends, 151, 193, 197–200; relations with Effie deteriorate, 170–2; challenged to duel, 172; Millais portrait of, 185–6, 188, 194, 198; and relations between Effie and Millais, 192–7; shyness, 207; and Patmore's *Angel in the House*, 211–12; and cholera in Oxford, 218–19; attacked by Lady Eastlake, 230–1; 'paedophilia' and interest in young girls, 253–4, 340–1, 368, 708, 719–21, 819, 834; 'unconversion', 254–7; relationships with women, 268–71; visits Winnington school, 278–9, 321, 338, 340, 345, 415–17; 'Sunday letters' to Winnington girls, 285–6, 288–90, 295, 300, 303, 308, 331, 830; financial support for Winnington, 287–8; moonlight boating expeditions, 291; writes for *Cornhill*, 293–4, 297; Richmond portrays, 298–9; eloquence and speaking, 302, 482, 511–12, 759; studies Greek, 304, 308; godchildren, 321, 340; social manner, 325–6; studies Plato's *Republic*, 336; Rossetti portrait of, 338; understanding of children, 340; bids to buy land in Alps, 343, 345; and father's death, 347–8, 362; generosity and extravagance, 348, 463, 636, 700, 711, 819–20, 869; inheritance, 348; uses nicknames and pet names for friends, 349, 390; intellectual problems, 354–5; nightmares, 355; buys and lets Marylebone property, 362; and servants, 362–3, 571, 710, 794; changed literary style after father's death, 370; love of fine

illustrated books, 374; knowledge of poetry, 377; poem to Rose, 379–80; awarded honorary Cambridge degree, 383; charitable gifts and philanthropy, 387, 391–2, 419; interest in mineralogy, 391, 735, 768–9; and Octavia Hill's housing charities, 392–3; Percy La Touche requests permission to marry Joan Agnew, 401; records dreams, 410–11, 441; sense of destiny, 410; and Effie's correspondence with Maria La Touche, 417; supposed masturbation, 417–18; ceases to visit Winnington, 418–19; employs baby-talk in letters to Joan Agnew, 420–2, 487, 528, 558, 716, 719–20, 808, 824, 833; Norton assumes literary executorship, 424, 752; art and book collection, 432–3, 476–7, 806–7, 819; sells Turners, 432–3, 435; Henry James describes, 435–6; resists Norton's suggestion to make will, 435; resumes sketching, 445; sexual nature, 453, 513, 519, 521, 669; pet dogs, 473, 476, 783–4; stays in Abingdon, 473–6; Dodgson portrait photograph of, 478; and Joan Agnew's marriage to Arthur Severn, 485–7; shrinks from adult love-making, 486–7; hallucinations (dreams), 487–8, 490, 629, 667, 705; on 'plague-wind', 492, 556, 563, 729–30, 767, 770; buys Brantwood, 493–5, 499–500; divorce and ineligibility to remarry, 496–8; financial position, 496, 636–8, 793–4; life in Oxford, 506–12, 543, 576, 578; intellectual range and interests, 534–7; garden improvements at Brantwood, 537; home life at Brantwood, 539–41; treatment of books, 539–40; 'Broadlands Book' (diary), 545, 607, 612; use of inns and accommodation, 546–7, 567–8; chess-playing, 550; self-portraits, 557, 562–3; Leslie Stephen criticises for over-sensitivity, 570; and Paddington tea shop, 571–2; fantasies of being bishop, 577–8; collects Scott manuscripts, 595–6; reads from Scott, 595; 'Brantwood Diary', 603, 616, 641, 661–9; depicted in Mallock's *New Republic*, 605–6; acquires coach, 615–16; preserves mementoes of Rose, 615; supports Barmouth tenants, 620–1; sued by Whistler for libel on painting, 638–9, 678–81; buys Turner drawings of Venice, 646; at Windsor Castle, 648–9; acquires boat (*Jumping Jenny*) for Coniston Water, 685; portraits and busts of, 685, 744, 771; interest in local Coniston school, 713, 767, 819, 823; offers to sell works of art, 717; eccentricities, 744–5; makes will, 751, 773, 875; and disposal of private papers, 753–4, 875–8; correspondence burned, 755; and 'Rosie's book', 755; prophetic utterances, 766; and disposal of art collection, 779, 842–3, 875–6; rages and abuse, 819–20, 824, 834; loses control of Brantwood, 822; stays in Folkestone and Sandgate (1887–8), 823–37, 841, 843; accident in Folkestone, 825–6; seeks home in declining years, 840–1; borrows money, 847; Nevinson describes in old age, 851–2; death and funeral, 866, 873–4; 80th birthday national address to, 872–3

PROFESSIONAL ACTIVITIES: early prose and poetry, 27–8, 38; poetic vocation and writing, 29–34, 63, 211, 594; defends and expounds on Turner, 39–40, 339–40; made Fellow of Geological Society, 53; and genesis of *Modern Painters*, 68–72; adopts writing career, 74–5; traces and copies paintings and sculptures, 85, 87–91, 95, 97–8; admires and paints Tomb of Ilaria di Caretto, 87–8; and Tintoretto, 94–5; beginning of architectural studies, 104–6; exhibits work, 104, 420; lectures, 104, 190, 194, 205–6, 233, 242, 246, 258, 258–60, 268, 276, 300, 337, 339, 355–8, 370–1, 374, 402, 404, 411, 413–16, 420, 431, 435–6, 442, 444, 447–8, 456–8, 460–2, 464–7, 473, 482–3, 487–8, 492, 506–8, 531, 535–6, 543–4, 550, 555, 562, 572, 584, 591, 597–600, 615, 642, 645, 647–8, 692, 695, 730, 734, 737–8, 740–2, 744, 746, 749, 763, 764–6, 775–9; reviewing, 108–9; absorption in architecture, 123–7; joins council of Arundel Society, 129–30; and photography, 144, 478–80, 557; literary style, 149, 292, 443, 594, 631, 689; champions Pre-Raphaelites, 153–7; and Turner bequest, 163–5, 236, 242–4, 248–51, 426; Edinburgh lectures, 194, 207; drawing class and lessons, 203–5, 236–7, 241; and Working Men's College, 203; requests University Museum at Oxford, 216–18, 222; alienation from Working Men's College, 224, 262; relationship with press, 232–3; teaches by letter, 241–2; Manchester lectures, 246–7; and Turner drawings, 248–51; teaches at Winnington school, 283–5; drawings from figure, 298; gives away collection of Turners, 299–300; copies Luini's *St Catherine*, 323, 359; testifies to Royal Academy Commission (1863), 337; composes music and verses for Winnington school, 346; architectural interests, 356, 420, 431–2; journalistic writings, 363–5; botanical studies, 391, 591–2; offered Oxford Professorship of Poetry, 401, 405; practises drawing, 420; numbers paragraphs, 436; appointed first Slade Professor of History of Art at Oxford, 443, 447–50, 506; as pioneer of art history, 443; artistic style, 445–6; copies of old masters, 445–6, 557–8, 560, 567, 624; on river and water management, 446–8, 462–3; admitted honorary fellow of Corpus Christie, Oxford, 476–7; private publishing and printing, 501–2; moves printing to Hazell & Watson, 502; road-digging scheme, 535, 545, 547–9, 553–4, 565, 573–6; 'class' and disciples at Oxford, 542–5, 573; copies ancient buildings, 557; quality of drawings, 557; gives art collecion to Oxford, 587;

founds Guild of St George, 588–91; founds Museum of St George, Sheffield, 594–7, 634; and 'St George's work', 594–5; plans series of classics for children and adults, 602–3; resigns Slade chair, 681, 791–2; stands for Lord Rectorship of Glasgow University, 691; musical composing and experiments, 712, 718; applies for and resumes Slade Professorship, 728, 733, 737–8; art teaching at Oxford, 745; drawing-room lecture on Francesca Alexander, 749–50; collaborative writings, 770; art teaching methods and principles, 796–8; letters to press, 811–12; contributes preface to Cook's *Popular Handbook to the National Gallery*, 839; selections and unauthorised editions of works, 868–71; total books sales, 869; critical studies of, 871; posthumous influence and reputation, 876–7

RELATIONSHIPS: childhood friends, 14, 28–9; devotion to father, 14; and Mary Richardson, 18; importance of Samuel Rogers to, 24–5; meets Adèle, 26–7; and George Croly, 31–2; second meeting with Adèle, 35–7; and Henry Acland, 46–9; and Osborne Gordon, 46–7; and Charles Newton, 48–9; love for Adèle, 51–4; meets Turner, 55–6; letters to Dale published, 57–8; meets Effie, 62, 76–7; relations with father, 65–7, 91, 99, 105, 167, 301, 320–3, 325, 339, 345; and Turner, 72, 76–7; farewell to Turner, 82–8; meets Mrs Jameson, 95–6; disputes and reconciliation with Carlyle, 101–2, 403–5, 469; and Turner's health, 102, 232, 249–51; meets Charlotte Lockhart, 107–9; effect of Adèle on, 109; disregard of Effie, 127; letters to Effie, 131–2; meets Eastlakes, 148; influenced by and loyalty to Carlyle, 150, 176, 185–6, 314–16, 353, 373, 388, 403, 450, 456, 469, 543, 649, 781, 851; friendship with Patmore, 152–3; friendship with Millais, 155–7; and Trevelyans, 182–3; and arrival of Acland, 189–90; concern for Millais, 193; closeness to family, 206–7; meets Rossetti, 208–10; acquaintance with poets, 210–14; friendship with Brownings, 213; meets Norton, 215; and Lizzie Siddall, 220; and Turner's private life, 232; relations with Butterworth, 239–40; relations with Pre-Raphaelites, 244, 246; and Turner's 'insanity', 249–51; friendship with Spurgeon, 260–1; meets La Touche family, 262–6, 572; relations with and effect on Rose La Touche, 267–8, 279, 283, 290–1, 301–4, 308–13, 320–1, 333–5, 513, 517–21; tutors and influences Rose La Touche, 267–8, 301, 329; and Burne-Jones, 275–6; relationship with Watts, 275–7; anxiety over Rose's illness, 308; relations with Burne-Joneses, 321; passion for Rose La Touche, 335, 349, 376, 387, 389–91, 394, 397, 399, 402, 410, 413–14, 453, 458–9, 467, 487, 526, 531, 533, 556, 582, 845; proposes marriage to Rose La Touche, 376, 381–3, 429–30, 468; reunited with Rose La Touche (1865), 379; Rose forbidden to see, 394, 396; dispute with Turner, 404; and Arthur Severn's courtship of Joan Agnew, 412–13; letter to Rose La Touche, 430; encounters Rose at Royal Academy (1870), 453–5, 458–9; relations with Morris, 455–6; resumes correspondence with Rose, 461; friendships with Oxford girls, 477–8; and gossip about Rose, 484–5; letter from MacDonald about Rose La Touche, 522; returns from Venice to see Rose (1872), 524–6; Rose abuses on parting, 527–8; claims Rose to be insane, 531–2, 550; friendship and correspondence with Susie Beever, 538, 546, 553, 646, 673, 684, 709, 450, 763; and Rose's return to England (1874), 549–52; and Rose's late suggestion of marriage, 568, 581; concern for dying Rose, 570; visits dying Rose, 571, 584; effect of Rose's death on, 577, 584–6, 591, 597–600, 615, 642, 645, 647–8, 692, 695, 730, 734, 737–8, 740–2, 744, 746, 749, 763–6, 775–9; seeks ghost of Rose, 609–11, 629–30; visits Gladstone at Hawarden, 649–52, 679; quarrel with Joan Severn, 709–11; effect on young girls and women, 725–6; entertains La Touche parents at Brantwood, 755–6; breakdown of relations with Joan Severn, 819–22; proposal to Kathleen Olander, 846–7

TRAVELS: annual family tours, 18, 53, 69; in Lake District, 18–19; 1833 tour to Switzerland and Italy, 25–7; at Schaffhausen, 25–7; 1835 tour to Switzerland and Venice, 33–4; 1848 visit to France and Italy, 57, 124–7; in Venice, 60–1, 139–46; 1842 tour to Switzerland, 69–70; 1844 Alpine tour, 79–81; 1845 tour to Italy, 82, 83–99, 808; in Lucca, 85–8; in Pisa, 88, 90–1; in Florence, 91–2; 1846 visit to Venice, 106; English summer tour, 122–3; 1849 tour to Switzerland, 131–6; 1851 tour to Switzerland, 157; at Venetian carnival, 171; Scottish tour, 181–2; at Glenfinlas, 184–7; 1854 tour to Switzerland, 199–200; 1856 tour to France and Switzerland, 233–5; 1858 tour to Italy, 251; in Turin, 255; visits Bradford, 259–60; 1859 tour to Germany, 277; visits La Touches in Ireland, 304–6, 315; 1861 trip to Alps, 306; 1862 trip to Italy and Alps, 323–4; stays in Mornex, 325–7, 330, 332, 334, 336, 354; 1863 visit to Switzerland, 342; 1866 tour to Switzerland and Italian lakes, 383–5; 1867 stay in Keswick, 405–10; 1868 visit to Abbeville, 420–2, 431; 1869 visit to Verona, 441–2, 444–7, 450, 462; 1870 tour to Venice, 462–3; 1872 tour to Italy, 517–18; 1874 tour to Italy and Sicily, 552–67; experiences in Assisi, 559–63, 565–6; 1876–7 visit to Venice, 618–19, 622–33; 1882 continental tour with Collingwood, 726–32, 736; 1883 visit to

Scotland, 757–9; final holiday (to Seascale, 1889), 761–2; 1888 trip to France and Venice, 843–9
VIEWS & OPINIONS: on Scott, 14; interest in political economy, 50, 93, 247, 296–7, 326–7; on Florence, Rome and Turin, 57–8; on naturalism, 68; on Effie, 77; and Turner's *Slave Ship*, 77–9; and Protestantism, 83–4, 777; religious thinking and observance, 83–4, 99, 149–50, 161, 167–9, 173–5, 183, 235, 254–6, 261–2, 285, 290, 294–5, 297–8, 305–6, 327, 329–34, 350–4, 396, 399–400, 406–7, 416, 438–9, 451–2, 556, 558, 829–31; on Shakespeare, 92–3; on spoliation of Venice, 93–4; formal aesthetic, 100, 133; dislikes babies, 118–20, 122, 395; hatred of republicanism, 122, 124, 140; on desecration in Italy, 123–4; nature and aesthetics, 132–6; dislikes London social life, 147, 151–2; political views, 150, 160–1, 203, 245–6, 317–18, 336, 388–9, 397–8, 419, 427, 455, 480–1, 495, 499, 651, 691, 763, 817, 839; on Venice, 158–72; on Catholicism, 169, 174–5, 611, 829–31; on Gothic, 169; on friendship, 207; interest in American literature, 214–15; interest in democratic art, 226; on Holman Hunt, 227; lacks interest in modern foreign art, 237–8; attitude to France, 238; on Switzerland, 252; on loss of spirituality in art, 276; on meaning of 'vulgarity', 288; and mythology, 289, 354, 356–7, 411, 435, 437–40, 507, 528–31, 591–2, 737, 747; social convictions and interests, 294–5, 316–17, 363, 419, 425–7, 839; theories on girls' education, 346; belief in immortal soul, 350; interest in spiritualism, 350–1, 365, 511, 607–9, 611–13, 686, 801; on war, 358, 651–2; on ancient art, 359–61; and ancient Egypt, 359–61, 372–3; on railways, 364–5; on art, 365–6, 456–7; on admirable women, 374–5; on chivalry, 374–5, 401–2; supports Carlyle in defence of Governor Eyre, 388; idealises virginal state, 394–5; on prayer, 396; on popular franchise, 397–8; and serpents, 410–11, 440–1; denounces pollution, 442; idealism, 451, 495; on heraldry, 507; musical tastes, 687, 718; educational theories, 713, 819, 823; disbelieves in afterlife, 844

Ruskin, John James (1785–1864; JR's father): birth, 1; education, 1; life in London, 2; and establishment of Ruskin, Telford & Domecq, 6; travels, 6, 10–12; works for Gordon, Murphy & Co., 6; breakdown, 7–8; father objects to marriage, 7; engagement and marriage, 8, 14; letters to wife Margaret, 10–12; reading and library, 12, 15; family Bibles, 13; entertains at Herne Hill, 15, 31, 290, 330; wish for self-improvement, 15; hopes for JR's future, 16–17; relations with sister's family, 17–18; religious belief, 19–20; passion for Byron, 23; theatrical interests, 23; 1833 tour to Switzerland and Venice, 25–7; in Paris and Brussels, 25; and JR's poetic vocation, 29–30, 591; 1835 tour to Switzerland and Venice, 33; Domecq girls stay with, 35, 50; and JR's attraction to Adèle, 36–7, 109; Scottish accent, 41; purchases place for JR at Oxford, 43; in Oxford, 44, 46–7; 1840 tour of France and Italy, 56, 58, 59; criticises St Peters service, 58; visits JR at Leamington, 62; mistrust of religious ardour, 63; on Harding, 64; dislikes Griffith, 65; and Turner's 'Splügen', 65–7; 1842 tour to Switzerland, 69; and JR's Oxford exam results, 69; toryism, 70, 651, 763; as JR's literary agent, 72; portrait of JR, 72; and reviews of JR's *Modern Painters*, 74; purchases Turner paintings, 76–7; and JR's absences, 83, 105, 159, 161; and JR's health on travels, 91; desire for JR's return from Italy, 98; and JR's writing of *Modern Painters*, 99, 167, 234, 255, 257, 272, 277, 279; relations with Turner, 101; and JR's involvement in architecture, 105; on JR's attachment to Adèle, 109; correspondence with Gray family, 114; and JR's prospective marriage to Effie, 115; refuses to attend JR's wedding, 117; seeks accommodation for JR, 120; on younger Ruskins' social success, 121; tour of southern England, 122–3, 785; accompanies JR and Effie to Boulogne, 124; and Gray family's difficulties, 127; finds Park Street house for JR and Effie, 128; worsening relations with Effie, 129; letter from wife on JR's marriage, 130; 1849 tour to Switzerland, 133; grievances and remarks about Effie, 137–8, 180; pays for JR-Effie trip to Venice, 139; influences JR's political ideas, 150; welcomes Furnivall to Denmark Hill, 151; buys Effie's ticket for Great Exhibition, 157; fears for JR's reputation, 162; JR writes to on Turner's death, 163; and Turner bequest, 164, 166; relations with JR, 167, 301, 320–3, 325, 339, 345; religious doubts, 167–9; buys Herne Hill, 173; concern over JR's challenge to duel, 173; Carlyle appreciates, 176; on Millais, 195; writes to Gray complaining of Effie's behaviour, 197; and Effie's leaving JR, 198, 200, 207; birthday, 199; concern over JR's lectures, 205, 245; has JR's early poems printed, 211; on Working Men's College, 223; keeps press-cuttings book, 232; 1856 tour to France and Switzerland, 233–4; on JR's study of Political Economy, 247, 297; letters to Jane Simon, 247, 297, 319; and Turner drawings, 249; and JR's religious observances, 256, 260; and JR's friendship with Miss Blackwell, 268; 1859 visit to Germany, 277; and Christ's Hospital, 278; and JR's devotion to Winnington school, 283; financial support for Miss Bell, 287, 322; on Rose La Touche, 289, 572; interest in periodical press, 293; sees JR's *Unto This Last* through press, 296; and JR's giving away Turners, 299–300; character, 301; diary, 301; retains lease on 28 Herne Hill, 302; and La Touche family, 304; baffled by JR's spiritual invocations, 306; complains of hotels, 306–7; stays in Norwood, 306–7, 551; death and burial, 307, 347–8, 362, 502; letters to JR, 307; anxiety over Rose's illness, 308; and JR's relations with Rose, 310, 312; and JR's depression, 319, 345–6; suffers from gravel, 320; withholds support for JR, 321–2; opposes JR's plan to build house in Alps, 345; will, 348; working routine, 358; opposes printing of JR's 'Gold', 363; dislike of railways, 364; reads Gotthelf, 385; charitable gifts, 391; chooses boar's head as crest, 421; and Scottish ethos, 422; gives Turner paintings to JR, 433, 673, 842; at Vevey, 442; reads *Pickwick Papers*, 475; business trips in north, 494; and writing of *Præterita*, 498; pride in Denmark Hill property, 537; Scott's influence on, 542; stays in inns, 546; JR's memory of, 553; and founding of Guild of St George, 577–8; and JR's prospective Church career, 578; and JR's interest in geology, 591; watercolour of Conway Castle, 675, 699; visits theatre, 686; restrains JR's extravagance, 700; and genesis of JR's *Præterita*, 757; in *Præterita*, 785, 787, 808–10; correspondence with wife, 810; poems published by Collingwood, 868

Ruskin, John Thomas (1761–1817; JR's grandfather), 1–2, 4, 7–8

Ruskin, Margaret (1781–1871; *née* Cock; JR's mother): birth and education, 2; love for John James, 2–4; religion and piety, 2, 19–22, 50, 167, 331; Bible reading, 6, 13, 36; father-in-law objects to marriage, 7; and Rose La Touche, 7, 264, 266, 379, 397, 572; marriage, 8; correspondence with husband, 10, 810; gardening, 10; on young JR, 12–13; ambitions for JR's ecclesiastical career, 16, 20, 50, 63, 578; relations with Richardsons, 17; literary tastes, 23; tour to Switzerland and Italy (1832), 25–7; in Oxford, 44, 50; fears of Catholicism, 50; in Denmark Hill, 70; preparations for JR's 1845 Italian tour, 83; relations with Effie, 120–3, 129–31; poem to JR, 170–1; fear of JR's conversion, 172–4, 257; visit to Germany (1859), 277; hurt in falls, 298, 306; sends gift of scarves to La Touches, 304; puzzled by Monk, 331; widowhood, 347–8, 362; has Joan Agnew as companion, 348–9, 387, 434; inheritance and will, 348; letters from JR on 1866 tour, 384; visitors in old age, 387; JR on virginal nature of, 395; JR writes to, 405, 420; pride in JR's public honours, 405; fears JR's loss of faith, 407; stays in Norwood with JR, 409, 551; recounts stories to friends, 411; decline and old age, 434, 450, 452, 474, 495; at Vevey, 442; Arthur Severn accepts gifts from, 485–6; and JR's illness at Matlock, 493; and writing of *Præterita*, 498; death and burial, 502; memorial well, 502–3, 699; dislike of theatre, 686; memorialised in *Præterita*, 808–10

Ruskin College, Oxford, 223, 876

Ruskin Reader, The (ed. Collingwood), 868

Ruskin societies, 600, 722–3, 871–3

Ruskin, Telford & Domecq (company), 348

Russell, William, 169

Rutson, Mr (guest at Laidlawstiel), 758–9

Ryan, Miss (model), 180

Rydal Mount, 73

Rydings, Egbert, 616, 636, 646, 801

Sabbatarianism, 297–8

St Aldate's, Oxford, 54

St David's School, Reigate, 735

St Ebbe's, Oxford, 219

St George (journal of Ruskin Society of Birmingham), 872

St George, Museum of *see* Sheffield: St George's Museum

St George's Fund, 496, 544–5

St George's Library (series), 603

St Gothard pass, 323

St James's Place, London, 30, 121

St Laurent du Pont, 134

St Mark's Rest (JR), 632, 642–3, 646, 655, 662, 665, 778

St Martin's School of Art, London, 242

Saint-Pierre, Bernardin de: *Paul et Virginie*, 16

Salisbury, 122, 124

Sallanches, 202, 846, 851–3

Salvador (JR's courier), 25–6

Salzburg, 33

'Salzburg' (JR), 34

Sand, George, 234

Sandgate, Kent: JR stays in (1887–8), 823, 827–37, 841, 843

Sandwich, Kent, 231

Saturday Review, 227, 297, 372

Saussure, Henri-Bénédict de: *Voyages dans les Alpes*, 33, 80, 709, 790

Savoy, 122, 136

Sayers, Tom (prize-fighter), 291

Schaffhausen, 25, 277, 557

Scotland: JR visits with Effie and Millais, 181–95; JR idealises, 421–2, 708, 757; accessibility from Brantwood, 500; JR revisits (1883), 757–8; in *Præterita*, 854; *see also* individual places

Scott, Alexander John, 285, 293

Scott, Ann, 434

Scott, Sir Gilbert, 159

Scott, Susan, 285, 293, 340, 415, 433–4, 443, 590–1

Scott, Sir Walter: JR's father reads, 12, 15; JR reads and admires, 14, 38, 62; poems imitated by JR, 27; Pringle and, 30; Todd condemns, 38; JR meets granddaughter, 107; Lockhart and, 107–8; JR compares Burne-Jones with, 322; and JR's idealisation of Scotland, 422; toryism, 481; *The Antiquary*, 500; Abbotsford house,

541; JR writes on in *Fors Clavigera*, 542, 547, 568, 641; JR buys manuscripts, 595, 700, 708; JR reads to Brantwood visitors, 595, 771–2; JR on mental collapse, 655; *Redgauntlet*, 685; in JR's *Fiction, Fair and Foul*, 689; read aloud to JR, 705, 708; and JR's 1883 visit to Scotland, 757–9; JR talks of, 781; and gipsies, 791; Joan Severn offers manuscripts to Quaritch, 841; in *Præterita*, 855
Scott, William Bell, 237, 338, 340, 398, 644
Seascale, Cumberland, 707, 861–3
Seddon, Thomas, 242, 244–5
Sedgwick, Adam, 113
Selections from the Writings of John Ruskin (ed. Collingwood), 868
Selvatico, Marquis, 144
Selvo, Domenico, Doge of Venice, 665–6
Senlis, 232
Sens, 69
serpents: significance for JR, 410–11, 440–1
'Servants and Houses' (JR; letters), 363–4
Sesame and Lilies (JR): written for Rose La Touche, 212, 313, 376, 513; composition, 370, 374; reception, 373, 375–6; myth in, 439; JR writes new prefaces, 468, 727; on parental authority, 513; on episcopacy, 613; and JR's songs, 713; addressed to young girls, 720; 're-arranged' edition (1882), 736; reprints, 869
Sestri, 85
Seven Lamps of Architecture, The (JR): foreshadowed by *The Poetry of Architecture*, 53; writing, 104, 106, 122, 124, 127, 129, 131; new editions and reprints, 105, 688, 693, 869; influence on *Modern Painters*, 123; on Abbeville, 431; Morris praises, 455; photographic sources for, 479; and Brantwood dining room, 540
Severn, Agnew (Joan/Arthur's son), 596, 793
Severn, Arthur: courtship and marriage to Joan, 60, 412–13, 441, 485–8, 513; friendship with Howell, 485; takes gifts from Margaret Ruskin, 485–6; on JR's breakdown and treatment in Matlock, 490, 493–4; on 1872 Italy tour with JR, 517–18, 522, 524; improves and occupies Brantwood, 540–2, 815; children, 541, 555; death, 541, 875; relations with JR, 542, 556, 692–3, 726, 767–8, 814–15, 820–1; meets Rose La Touche, 555; accompanies JR to Brantwood, 594, 615–16; on Yorkshire sketching tour with JR, 596; financial dependence on JR, 636–7, 751, 841; buys Turner works for JR at Christie sale, 646–7; seeks money in London during JR's 1878 breakdown, 671; accompanies JR on drawing trip to Malham, 676; slight artistic talent, 692; and JR's 1880–1 mental collapses, 704–5, 707–8, 715; at cricket match with JR, 718; in London with JR, 718–19; designs May Queen cross, 724; on 1882 tour with JR, 726; in JR's will, 751–875; role in family, 751; JR reads *Præterita* to, 763, 794; helps JR with lectures, 766; *The Professor*, 767; considers selling Herne Hill home, 770; sells JR's Gritti portrait, 774; and disposal of JR's art collection, 779–80, 842–3; and JR's 1885–6 breakdowns, 800, 812; visits JR in Sandgate, 834; accompanies JR on 1888 trip to France, 843–4; at extended Brantwood, 853–4; spends time in London, 865; friendship with Walter Crane, 872
Severn, Arthur (son), 793
Severn, Joan (*née* Agnew): marriage, 60, 362, 412–413, 474, 485–8, 513, 541; appears in *Præterita*, 348–62, 665, 854–5, 859; lives at and manages Denmark Hill, 348–9, 356, 362–3, 369, 384; as Margaret R's companion, 348–9, 386, 434; becomes JR's ward, 362; JR's attachment to, 376, 383; friendship with Rose La Touche, 379, 381–3, 386, 395, 397, 399–400, 431, 461, 513, 533, 550–1, 554, 567; visits Harristown, 382, 386, 389–90, 409; on 1866 tour with JR, 383–6, 592; accompanies Octavia Hill on rent-collecting, 392; Percy La Touche requests permission to marry, 401, 409; and JR's plans for little country house, 402; letters from JR, 405–6, 408–9, 420, 547, 558, 564–5, 607, 624, 629, 648–9, 650, 658, 685, 693, 701, 711, 716, 718, 731, 782, 783, 828, 833, 834–5, 841, 842, 849, 876; breaks off engagement to Percy, 409; friendship with Constance Hilliard, 411; hears Margaret Ruskin's family stories, 411; in JR's dreams, 411, 441; edits *Præterita*, 412, 846; visits Winnington with JR, 415; JR writes to in baby-talk, 420–2, 487, 528, 558, 716, 719, 720, 808, 824, 833; Maria La Touche asks not to write to Rose again, 429–30; JR describes in letter to Rose, 430; as prospective wife for JR, 441; and JR's religious doubts, 452; upset at Percy La Touche's engagement, 453; JR writes to on Rose's book, 454; meets Rose in London (1870), 460; Venice holiday with JR (1870), 462; and JR's breakdown in Matlock, 488–9, 491; and JR's insistence on marriage with Rose, 497; and JR's purchase of Brantwood, 499–500; on 1872 Italy tour with JR, 517, 522, 524; visits JR on return from Italy, 527; on Rose's illness, 529–30; concern for JR's mental state, 532–3; improves and occupies Brantwood, 540–2; children, 541, 555, 596, 717–18; death, 541, 875; Maria La Touche visits, 556; and Rose La Touche's late hopes of marriage to JR, 568, 581; Norton on, 569; JR considers giving up Brantwood to, 571, 596; and JR's Brantwood breakdown, 571, 659, 665, 669, 671–3, 675; and JR's attacks on bishops, 580, 614; JR predicts Rose's death to, 582–3; JR writes to on Rose's death, 585–6; as Companion of St George, 590; accompanies JR to Brantwood, 594. 615–16; distrusts Frederick Ellis, 596; and JR's interest in spiritualism, 607–9; JR describes Manning to, 611; entertains at

Brantwood, 618, 645; puzzles over *Fors Clavigera*, 628; and JR's mental disorder, 629; financial dependence on JR, 636–7, 751; suffers miscarriage, 642, 646; and JR's acquisition of Turner works, 647; and JR's visit to Gladstones, 650; dislikes Acland, 671, 706; financial anxieties, 671, 762, 793, 829, 841; and Allen's proposed new edition of *Seven Lamps*, 688; shocked at JR's views given to Glasgow University students, 691–2; restricts JR's social contacts and visitors, 692, 816, 863, 865–6; and JR's 1880 mental collapse, 701. 704–6; adopts role of keeper to JR, 706–7, 714, 767, 814, 836; pride in Scottishness, 708, 872; quarrels with JR, 709–11, 819–22; and JR's extravagance, 710, 714; JR's song to ('Joanna's Care'), 712; and JR's selling works of art, 714, 717; and JR's interest in young girls, 720–1; and JR's 1882 tour in Italy, 731; and Collingwood's accompanying JR on 1882 Italy tour, 734; stays at Herne Hill, 735; JR assures of quiet behaviour at Oxford, 740; affection for Kate Greenaway, 742–3; controls admission to JR's 'drawing-room lecture', 749; ageing, 751; in JR's will, 751; shares JR's literary executorship, 752; burns JR papers, 754–5, 834, 840; arranges La Touche parents' visit to Brantwood, 755–6; relations with George Allen, 761; JR reads *Præterita* to, 763, 794; and JR's gift of Colenso Diamond to British Museum, 769; considers selling Herne Hill home, 770; anxiety over JR's unsettled state, 774; and disposal of JR's art collection, 779, 842–3; and writing of JR's *Præterita*, 786, 787, 789, 855; at Brantwood, 799; on JR's 1885–6 breakdowns, 799–800, 812–13; dislikes Hackstoun, 804; hopes to reduce number of artists working for JR, 806; and JR's book collecting, 806, 841; breakdown of relations with JR, 819–22; and JR's stay in Folkestone and Sandgate, 823–6, 828–9, 833–4; JR gives Turner watercolours to, 829; JR sends sections of *Præterita* to, 829–30; apprehensions over *Præterita*, 833–4, 845–6, 861; seeks refuge for JR, 840–1; visits JR at Sandgate, 843; JR asks to borrow money from Lees, 847; and JR's wish to return to Brantwood from Bassano, 848; meets ill JR in Paris (1888), 849–50; acquires and extends Brantwood lands, 853; positive reports on JR's condition, 853; JR dictates late letters to, 854; sides with Norton against Froude, 859; JR expresses wish to be buried in Shirley, 862; writes to Norton in JR's later years, 863–4, 867; nurses and attends JR in last disabled years, 864–5, 867; Frederic Harrison's long acquaintance with, 871; at JR's death and funeral, 873–4; lives in Brantwood after JR's death, 875

Severn, Joseph (Arthur's father), 59, 101, 129, 412, 518, 555, 664, 860

Severn, Lily (Joan/Arthur's daughter), 541, 834

Severn, Mary *see* Newton, Mary

Severn, Walter (Arthur's brother), 637

Shakespeare, William: JR's father reads aloud, 12; JR praises, 38; JR alludes to and quotes, 78, 92, 96, 113, 663–4; Anna Jameson on, 96; women in, 374–5, 725; JR's knowledge of, 377

Shar, F.W., 877

Shaw, Flora: friendship with JR, 652. 750–1; *Castle Blair*, 652, 656

Shaw, Norman, 794

Shaw-Lefevre, Charles, 147

Shee, Sir Martin Arthur, 155

Sheerness, 231

Sheffield: St George's Museum, 594–7, 634–5, 642, 644, 646, 655, 686, 735; JR visits, 685

Sheldonian Theatre, Oxford, 457

Shelley, Percy Bysshe, 231, 333, 709

Shenstone, William, 214

Shepherd, R.H.: *A Bibliography of Ruskin*, 697

Shephers's Tower, The (JR; photographs), 708

Sheppard, Elizabeth: *Charles Auchester*, 382

Sherwood, Mary Martha (*née* Butt): *Lady of the Manor*, 22

Shields, Cuthbert (Robert Laing), 603

Shields, Frederic, 284, 419

Shirley, near Croydon, 307, 348, 502, 862

'Shrimper' (girl friend of JR), 794

Shrine of the Slaves, The (JR), 642, 662

Sichel, Walter: *The Sands of Time*, 604–5

Sicily, 556–7

Siddall, Elizabeth, 120, 209, 220–1, 226, 292, 322

Siddons, Sarah, 23

Sidney, Sir Philip: metrical version of Psalter, 617

Siena, 57, 465–6

Simon, 'Boo' (John and Jane's adopted daughter), 319

Simon, Jane: and Pre-Raphaelites, 246; JR's father writes to, 247, 297, 306; friendship with JR, 268, 338; visits Denmark Hill, 303, 411, 434, 450; JR gives sections of *Præterita* to, 319, 785, 808; JR invites to Mornex, 325; advises JR against buying Alpine chalet, 345; calls on Margaret Ruskin, 387; dissuades JR from writing to Rose, 397; visits JR at Matlock, 493; comforts JR, 585; JR visits, 610, 793; and JR's mental collapse, 701, 705–6; contributes material for *Præterita*, 809; on origin of Turner's 'Rain, Steam and Speed', 858

Simon, Sir John: JR meets, 219; and JR's father's objections to JR's writings on political economy, 246–7; and JR's enquiry about meaning of 'vulgar', 288; orders JR to rest, 303; visits Denmark Hill, 303, 434, 450; JR gives section of *Præterita* to, 319, 785; JR invites to Mornex, 325; friendship with JR, 338; advises JR against buying Alpine chalet, 345; calls on Margaret Ruskin, 387; dissuades JR from writing to Rose, 397; Norton meets, 423; on Rose La Touche's health,

428–9; visits JR at Matlock, 493; writings, 534; comforts JR, 585; JR visits, 611, 793; JR discusses public affairs with, 639; and JR's 1878 Brantwood breakdown, 669–72, 676; and JR's 1880 mental collapse, 706; as JR's executor, 751; and JR's rupture, 826; and JR's condition in Sandgate, 833; retirement, 864
'Simple Dynamic Condition of Glacial Action among the Alps, The' (JR; lecture), 591
Simplon, 79–80
Simpson, Dr James, 137, 139, 148, 184
Sion, 202
Sismondi, Jean-Charles-Léonard Simond de, 93, 233
Skiddaw, 24, 408
Slade Professorship of History of Art, Oxford: JR's occupancy of, 447–50, 456, 506, 508, 543; JR first resigns, 578, 681–2; Richmond succeeds JR in, 681–2; JR re-elected to (1883), 682; JR resumes, 728, 733, 737–8; JR resigns (1884), 791–2
Sly, Mrs Joseph, 771, 820
Smetham, James, 206–7, 209
Smith, Adam, 297
Smith, Elder (publishers), 29–31, 40, 72, 130, 197, 210, 230, 241, 292–3, 297, 298, 363, 501, 794, 869
Smith, George, 29, 73, 293, 297
Smith, Logan Pearsall, 271, 396
Smith, Robert, 396
'Social Policy' (JR; lecture), 536
Society for Diffusion of Useful Knowledge, 129
Society of Painters in Water-colour (Old Water-Colour Society), 34, 64, 69, 121, 198, 687
Society for the Protection of Ancient Buildings, 746
Society of the Rose, 723
Socrates, 709
Somers, 3rd Earl *see* Eastnor, Viscount
Somervell, Robert, 590, 646; *A Protest against the Extension of the Railways in the Lake District*, 617
Sophocles, 29, 42
Southey, Robert, 37
Spain, Infanta of, 159
Spectator (journal), 749, 770
Spencer, Herbert, 318, 388, 536, 543
Spenser, Edmund, 214, 772
spiritualism, 349–50, 365, 511, 607–9, 611–12, 635, 686, 801
Spurgeon, Charles Haddon, 260–2, 266–7, 279, 294, 296, 301, 316, 329–30, 356, 756
Stalker family, 602, 702, 771
Stalker, Agnes, 602–3
Stamford, 12
Stanfield, Clarkson, 20, 32, 55, 64, 74, 121, 227, 277, 668
Stanhope, Spencer, 638
Stanley, Arthur Penrhyn, Dean of Westminster, 51, 331, 534–5
Stanley, Kate (compiler): *Ruskin's Thoughts about Women*, 870
Stead, William Thomas, 739, 776, 811, 838
Stephen, (Sir) Leslie: on Jamaica Committee, 388; Norton proposes as friend for JR, 569; patronising article on JR's *Fors Clavigera*, 569–70; visits JR at Brantwood, 618–19; JR calls on in Coniston, 646
Stephens, Frederic George, 154, 215
Stevenson, Asenath, 371
Stillman, William J., 214–15, 297–8, 450
Stirling, 184–5
Stodart, Messrs (engravers), 829
Stones of Venice, The (JR): and JR's Newdigate poem, 51; origins, 59, 88, 106; opening, 94; writing, 104, 122, 145–6, 175; Rawdon Brown and, 141; publication and reception, 149, 153; and JR's political views, 150, 160; appendix on education, 161, 169, 217; and *Modern Painters*, 165–6; and JR's father's suffering, 167; changed tone of vol. II, 169; religious quality, 169, 200; Acland reads, 217; inspires library of Trinity College, Dublin, 218; Carlyle praises, 314–15; influenced by Carlyle, 314; on Venetian architecture, 431; JR re-reads, 441; influence on Morris, 455; illustrations, 479–80; Giotto in, 481; new edition proposed and rejected, 619, 623, 625–6; 'Travellers Edition' published, 683; popularity with travellers, 869
'Storm-Cloud of the Nineteenth Century, The' (JR; lecture), 492, 563, 728, 763, 766, 775
Storm-Cloud of the Nineteenth Century, The (JR; publication), 765
'Story of the Halcyon, The' (JR; lecture), 507
Story-Maskelyne, Mervyn Herbert Nevil, 358, 479, 534, 718, 720
Stothard, Thomas, 24
Stowe, Harriet Beecher, 234, 236, 298, 651
Strachan, Anne, 12, 18–19, 25, 36, 140, 206, 234, 351, 362, 422; death, 474
Strahan & Co. (publishers), 683
Strasbourg, 25, 33
Stratford-on-Avon, 62, 113
Street, George Edmund, 431
Strudwick, J.M., 638
Stuart Wortley, Charles, 545, 573
Studd, C.T., 739
Studies in Both Arts (JR drawings; ed. Collingwood), 868
Sulman, Thomas, 204–5
Sunderland Art School, 398
Swan, Henry, 634–5, 639, 646, 710
Swan, Mrs Henry, 685
Swinburne, Algernon Charles, 184, 238, 246, 377–9, 412, 595, 746
Swinburne, Sir Charles, 184
Switzerland: JR visits, 25–7, 69, 92, 131–6, 199, 233, 251–2, 264, 297, 311, 312, 323, 342, 384–6, 389, 442–3; JR's study of, 33, 233, 252; and 1848 revolutions, 122; peasant life in, 136; Norton in, 215; *see also* individual places

Tacitus, 15, 42
Taglione, Marie, 139, 144

Talbot, Fanny, 619–20, 801
Talbot, Quarry, 620, 638
Tarrant and Mackrell (solicitors), 588, 614, 718
Tay, river, 17–18
Taylor, Isaac, 47
Taylor, Jeremy, 205, 261
Taylor, Tom, 449, 466, 680
Telford, Henry, 6, 11, 18, 24–5, 75, 128
Tenniel, Sir John, 746, 763
Tennyson, Alfred, 1st Baron: wishes to read JR's *Modern Painters*, 73; writes *In Memoriam* for Hallam, 121; acquaintance with JR, 210, 213–14; JR compares with Patmore, 211; 'The Princess', 220; influence on JR, 273; and JR's views on Titian, 274–5; JR writes of to Miss Bell, 278; writes for *Cornhill*, 293–4; and JR's *Cestus*, 367; supports Eyre, 388; and chivalry, 402; founds Metaphysical Society, 534; invited to JR's lecture on Francesca Alexander, 749
Tennyson, Hallam, 749
Terence, 43
Thackeray, Anne Isabella *see* Ritchie, Lady
Thackeray, William Makepeace, 151, 194, 230, 293–4, 297, 423, 771
Theseus, 529–31
Thirlmere: as water source, 657
Thompson, George, 801
Thomson, James, 78
Thornbury, Walter: *Life of Turner*, 300, 772
'Three Colours of Pre-Raphaelitism, The' (JR; article), 677–8
Thun, Count, 172
Time and Tide, by Weare and Tyne (JR), 389, 398–401, 403, 469, 613
Times, The (newspaper): praises JR's *Poetry and Architecture*, 53; letters from JR on Pre-Raphaelites, 153, 155–7, 208, 226–7; and JR's writings on socio-political subjects, 161–2; and JR's duel challenge in Venice, 172; and JR on Holman Hunt paintings, 198; on Turner bequest, 242; criticises JR's lecture on political economy, 247; Dallas works on, 346; on JR's dispute with Carlyle, 403; letter from Carlyle on Franco-Prussian War, 469; criticises Hinksey diggings, 576; on Whistler libel trial, 679–81; JR attacks, 750; on JR's death, 873
Tintoretto: JR esteems and writes on, 94–6, 100, 105–6, 123, 130, 279; JR requests Eastlake purchase paintings for National Gallery, 163; and JR's teaching of workmen, 204; JR proposes to lecture on *Paradise*, 464; JR compares with Michelangelo, 483, 666; and Botticelli, 567; on painting as fatiguing work, 663; in JR's 'Brantwood Diary', 666, 668; Alessandri copies, 802
Tipple, Revd S.A., 307, 551
Titian: JR's interest in and writing on, 94–5, 106, 277, 279; and Venice, 140; Watts's knowledge of, 274; and Gritti portrait, 432, 476, 665, 773–4; Henry James admires painting by, 436; JR compares with Giotto, 560; Blake criticises, 665
Todd, Revd John, 38
Toft, Cheshire, 525–6
Tollemache, Georgiana *see* Mount-Temple, Georgiana, Lady
Tours, 123
Tovey, Harriet, 70, 571
Tovey, Lucy, 70, 571–2
Toynbee, Arnold, 545, 573, 576–7, 739
Toynbee Hall, 739, 838
Tractarians, 50, 183
'Traffic' (JR; lecture), 356, 370, 382
'Tree Twigs' (JR; lecture), 300, 315
Trevelyan, Pauline, Lady: JR visits at Wallington, 181–4, 339–40; letters from JR, 202, 233, 292, 300, 320; JR's friendship with, 268; keeps photograph of JR, 298; JR speaks of *Munera Pulveris* to, 339; death on 1866 tour with JR, 384–5, 389, 463, 588, 592, 667, 818; pet dog, 784
Trevelyan, Sir Walter, 181–4, 199, 339, 384–5
Trice, Edwin, 826, 835, 837, 843
Trinity College, Dublin, 218
Trollope, Anthony, 294, 376
Trotter, Alec, 796
Trotter, Lilias, 633, 725–6, 742, 749, 763, 796–7
Trotter, Minnie, 796
Troubetzkoi, Prince, 144
Tucker, Messrs (Camberwell coachbuilders), 615
Tuckwell, Revd W., 222
Tuileries, Paris, 127
Tunbridge Wells, 454, 518
Turin, 26, 58, 253, 255–6
Turner, Joseph Mallord William: illustrates Rogers's *Italy*, 24, 26, 30; exhibits at Royal Academy, 25, 38–9, 69, 74, 77, 110; *Childe Harold's Pilgrimage*, 25; JR's drawings imitate, 28, 186; JR defends and expounds, 38–40, 69, 71–4, 101, 797, 842; JR given *Winchelsea*, 53; JR meets, 55–7, 65, 72; qualities and manner, 55–6; Harding and, 63–4; and Griffith, 65, 77; Swiss drawings, 65–7, 69; *Pass of the Splügen*, 65–7, 673–4; John Murray dismisses, 72; JR's father collects works by, 76–7, 207, 264, 266; JR's relations with, 76–7, 81, 101, 129, 300, 445, 772; *The Slave Ship*, 77–9; 'The Fallacies of Hope', 78; slight on JR's integrity, 82, 102; *Liber Studiorum*, 82, 178, 202; JR invites to Val Anzasca, 92; in Alps, 93, 168, 186; decline and death, 101–2; estrangement from JR, 101–2; visits Denmark Hill, 101; JR claims suffering mental disease, 102; architecture in, 104; Effie on, 110; JR visits with Effie, 121; *The Fighting Temeraire*, 121, 232, 243; restricted by Napoleonic Wars, 122; *The Rivers of France*, 125; in old age, 154; and Pre-Raphaelites, 155–7, 186, 229; Farnley collection of, 156, 675, 772, 781–2; Millais disclaims, 156; death and bequest, 163–5, 210, 235–6, 242–4, 248–51, 313, 426; JR considers biography of, 164–5, 203; and

Millais's painting, 186; JR lectures on, 194, 339; and JR's teaching of workmen, 204, 279; influence on Stillman, 214; Magoon buys works by, 215; JR describes as genius, 221; importance to JR, 229, 244, 253, 273–4; and publication of *The Harbours of England*, 231–3; National Gallery exhibition of oils, 235; copied by craftsmen, 240–1; collection in National Gallery, 242–4, 248–50; 'obscene' drawings burned, 250; in north of England, 259; Lupton works for, 262; art works at Winnington Hall, 278; drawings at Winnington, 286; JR ruminates on, 288–9; and Alps, 298, 366–7; JR gives away collections of, 299–300, 433, 508, 587, 773; influence on JR's *Præterita*, 309, 785–6, 788; JR determines to purchase watercolours, 324; JR attempts to print tracings from, 327; JR catalogues collection, 339; Kingsley and, 339, 387; lashed to mast at sea, 339; in Scottish Borders, 339; dispute with JR, 404, 677; JR sells part of collection, 432–3, 435; bargaining, 433; in Margate, 546; praises JR landscape, 557; sends spirit message to JR, 611; JR buys drawings of Venice at Christie's, 646–7; JR describes mental collapse, 655, 707, 839; JR organises Fine Art Society exhibition (1878), 655–8, 662, 673–5, 805; *Jerusalem: the Pool of Bethesda*, 668; Fine Arts Society buys *Pass of the Splügen*, for JR, 673–4; drawings removed from National Gallery to Oxford, 675; JR devises arrangement of drawings for National Gallery, 699; JR rearranges Brantwood collection, 699–70; Chesneau's interest in, 772; JR expects Oxford to purchase works by, 774; JR's collections diposed of and dispersed, 779–80; Leighton plans Royal Academy exhibition of, 780–1; Alessandri copies, 802; Ward copies, 805–6; Jane Simon's account of meeting, 809; JR complains of Oxford neglect of works, 815–16; Kathleen Olander copies, 827–8. 840; JR gives watercolours to Joan Severn, 829; JR offers personal diaries to, 829; Joan Severn asks JR to sell *Leicester Abbey*, 842; in JR's *Dilecta*, 858
Tweddale family, 387
Tweddale, John Ruskin, 348
Two Paths, The (JR), 258, 663
Tylor, Alfred, 504–5, 534
Tylor, Edward, 504
Tylor, Juliet (*later* Morse), 504, 612–13, 720
Tyndale, Agatha, 433, 450
Tyndall, John, 388, 536
Tyrwhitt, Revd Richard St John, 298, 354–5, 452, 528, 530, 690, 750; *Christian Art and Symbolism*, 483; *Our Sketching Club*, 643–4

Ullswater, 24
United States of America: democracy and culture in, 427
'Unity of Art, The' (JR; lecture), 259
University College London, 297, 435–6, 438
Unterseen, 34
Unto This Last (JR), 12, 262, 292, 294–7, 304, 315–16, 321, 338, 355, 366, 647
Urmenyi, Baron, 14
Ursula, St, 312, 623–5, 628–32, 646, 648, 657, 777

Val d'Aosta, 253
Val d'Arno: Ten Lectures on Tuscan Art (JR), 543
Van Dyck, Sir Anthony, 105
Vaughan, Edward, 545, 573
Veneziano, Antonio, 90
Venice: JR visits and explores, 33, 60–1, 104; JR deplores spoliation of, 93–4; JR's knowledge of architecture of, 106; republic declared (1848), 122; JR visits with Effie, 125, 139–46, 157–72, 178, 186, 200; besieged, 140–1; festivals suppressed, 141; society and life in, 141, 143–5, 159; JR writes on, 159–60, 431; JR's commitment to, 165; Carnival, 171; and JR's *Modern Painters*, 257; JR discusses purchasing pictures from, 258; Burne-Jones visits, 323; JR fails to reach on 1866 trip, 384; JR believes feminine, 442; JR's art-historical visits to, 443; Rawdon Brown on, 446; Holman Hunt in, 447; JR's 1870 tour to, 462–4; JR's 1872 tour to, 493, 518, 522–4; Carpaccio paintings in, 518, 522; JR's 1876–7 visit to, 618–19, 622–33; JR's rendezvous with Moore in, 618; JR writes guide to Academy pictures, 632–3; Turner drawings of, 646; JR visits with Blow (1888), 846–9
Verona, 93, 146, 171, 292, 323, 441–2, 444–7, 450, 518, 626
'Verona and its Rivers' (JR; lecture and exhibition), 442, 444, 447, 454, 456
Veronese, Paolo, 140, 254–6, 351
Verrocchio: *Madonna*, 804
Vevey, Switzerland, 26, 133, 442, 729
Vézelay, France, 727
Vicenza, 146
Victor Emmanuel II, King of Piedmont-Sardinia (*later* of Italy), 137
Victoria, Queen, 150, 159, 304
Vieusseux, André, 252
Vigri, Caterina, 657
Viljoen, Helen Gill, 661, 664, 669, 876–7; (ed.) *The Brantwood Diary of John Ruskin*, 877; *Ruskin's Scottish Heritage*, 877
Viollet-le-Duc, Eugene Emmanuel, 727
Virgil, 42
Visp, 80
Voltaire, François Marie Arouet de, 333
vulgarity: JR ponders meaning of, 288

Waagen, G.F., 76
Wagner, Richard, 718
Wagstaff, Mrs (spiritualist), 607–8, 612–13
Wakefield, Augusta, 764; *Ruskin on Music*, 712, 870
Waldensians, 58, 255–6, 260
Wales, 62

Walker, Frederick, 803
Walker, William, 646
Wallington, 182–4, 237, 339–40
Wandle, river, 10, 503
'War' (JR; lecture), 358, 370, 382
Ward, (Florence) Rose (Maria La Touche's niece), 772, 799–800
Ward, Revd James Clifton, 645
Ward, Lord, 322
Ward, William, 240, 243, 262, 420, 805–6
Wardle, William, 873
Warren, Emily, 840
Warwick, 12, 62, 113
Waterford, Louisa, Marchioness of, 226, 241, 262–3, 338–9
Waterhouse, Alfred, 356
Watson, Lizzie *see* Harker, Lizzie
Watson, Marion, 816
Watson, Tenzo, 840
Watts, George Frederic: JR's acquaintance with, 151, 798; JR describes as genius, 221; Prinseps speak of, 235; and writing of *Modern Painters*, 273; and Greek themes, 274, 439; JR on art of, 275; JR writes of to Miss Bell, 278; JR lectures on, 746
Watts, Mr and Mrs (JR's nurses), 834–5
Webling, Rosalind and Peggy, 708, 710, 720, 725
Wedderburn, Alexander: on Brantwood, 538; helps JR as road-digger, 545, 553, 574; rescues JR manuscripts, 562; records JR's lectures, 572–3; background and career, 573; praises JR's influence, 585; helps with Xenophon translation, 595, 602, 606; friendship with Sichel, 604; in *Præterita*, 610; works on JR's *St Mark's Rest*, 642–3; at Brantwood, 645–6, 709–10, 759, 771, 773; and hoax Chesterfield letter, 696; edits JR's *Arrows of the Chace*, 697–8, 709; Scots background, 708; and JR's views on Pre-Raphaelites, 740–1; understanding of JR, 749, 797; as JR's executor, 751–2, 754; JR papers not made available to, 754; burns JR correspondence with Rose, 755; on origins of *Præterita*, 757; publishes index to *Fors Clavigera*, 762; Cook meets, 766; JR visits in London, 793; and publication of JR's *Dilecta*, 809; and JR's condition in Sandgate, 833; prepares 'Library Edition' of JR's works, 876
Wedderburn, Marion, 646
Weekly Review, 330
Welsh, John, 176
West, Benjamin, 38
Westall (model), 180
Westminster Review, 376
Westminster, Richard Grosvenor, 2nd Marquess of, 128
Whewell, William, 148, 150
Whistler, James Abbot McNeill: JR lacks understanding of, 238; Swinburne inscribes poem to, 377–8; Arthur Severn associates with, 412; and Japanese art, 422; Morris appears as witness in trial, 455; sues JR for libel on painting, 536, 638–9, 678–70; and JR's attitude to money, 637; Burne-Jones on, 639, 773; price of paintings, 647; and public sympathy for JR, 674; and aestheticism, 747; in JR's *Fors Clavigera* index, 762
White, Tiny, 762
Whitehouse, John Howard, 786, 871–3, 875–7
Whitelands College, Chelsea, 679, 723–5, 735, 798
Whitman, Walt, 636
Wigtown, 294
Wilde, Jane Francesca, Lady (*née* Elgee), 721
Wilde, Oscar: at Oxford, 512, 545, 574–5, 721
Wilkie, Sir David, 69, 251
Wilkinson, Jane Anne, 771–2, 783, 818, 845
Willett, Henry, 644
William III (of Orange), King of England, 263
Williams, W. Smith, 73, 293
Willis, Robert, 104–5
Willis's Rooms, London, 395
Wills, William Gorman, 680
Wilson (Oxford undergraduate), 545
Wilson, Richard, 164
Wimpffen, Count, 143
Windermere, 19, 24
Windsor Castle, 648–9
Windus, B. Godfrey, 55–6, 64, 72, 76, 81
Wingfield, Mrs, 709
Winnington Hall, Cheshire: art works at, 278, 419; JR visits and teaches at, 278–9, 283–5, 287, 301, 321, 338, 340, 345, 415–17; JR's 'Sunday letters' to, 285–6, 288, 290, 306, 308; JR writes to on breakdown at Royal Institution lecture, 300; JR writes to about Rose, 303; and JR's dispute over Colenso, 331; Colenso stays at, 332; character, 341–2, 415; JR composes music and verses for, 346; JR's dialogues at, 360; and JR's *Ethics of the Dust*, 370–1; JR's extempore addresses at, 370–1; JR's attachment to girls, 376, 415, 425, 433; JR's correspondence with former pupils, 386; JR ceases to visit, 418–19; decline, 419, 434; and origins of Guild of St George, 434; JR's interest in, 713, 801; JR gives minerals to, 735
Wise, John de Capel, 376
Wise, Thomas James: *Ruskin's Letters to Ernest Chesneau*, 805
Wiseman, Cardinal Nicholas Patrick Stephen, Archbishop of Westminster, 43
Wither, George, 660
Wolsey, Cardinal Thomas, 4
Wonnacott, Mrs (of Abingdon), 475
Woodd, Charles H., 199, 330, 348, 402, 851
Woodhouse (dentist), 552, 581, 837
Woodward, Benjamin, 218, 221–2, 224
Woolgar, Edward, 861–3
Woolner, Thomas, 152, 208, 214
Woolwich *see* Royal Military Academy
Worcester College, Oxford, 219
Wordsworth, Dorothy *see* Harrison, Dorothy
Wordsworth, William, 19, 53, 73, 96, 132, 214, 221, 689

'Work' (JR; lecture), 370
'Work and Wages' (JR; papers), 364
Working Men's College: Funivall invites JR to join, 151; founding, 203, 334; JR teaches at, 203–4, 210, 218, 226, 235–6, 286, 291, 370, 796; Furnivall teaches at, 222; and teaching of working men, 223; JR's attitude to, 224, 240, 278–9; JR gives addresses to, 233, 238, 258, 336; Burne-Jones and Rossetti teach at, 236; Butterworth attends, 239–40; JR's religious arguments at, 262, 330; pupil photographs JR, 298; JR meets Harrison at, 318
World (journal), 778
Wornum, Ralph, 243–4, 250
Wouverman, Philips, 257
Wyndham, George, 651

Xanthippe, 709
Xenophon, 315, 326; *Oeconomicus* (translation), 594–5, 602–3, 606

'Yewdale and its Streamlets' (JR; lecture), 642, 645
Yonge, Charlotte M., 601; *Heartsease*, 415
Yorkshire, 53
Young, Edward, 214
Young, Margaret Ferrier, 772–3
Yule, Amy, 556
Yule, Colonel (Sir) Henry, 556

Zambaco, Maria, 484
Zermatt, 133, 136
Zipporah (angelic figure), 557–8
Zorzi, Count Alvise, 61, 633, 803
Zwingli, Huldreich, 252